# THE PACIFIC ISLANDS
## *Environment & Society*

Edited by Moshe Rapaport

3565 Harding Ave. Honolulu, Hawai'i 96816 (808) 734-7159 www.besspress.com

Library of Congress Cataloging-in-Publication Data

    The Pacific islands : environment and society / Moshe Rapaport, editor.
        p.  cm.
    Includes illustrations, bibliography, index.
    ISBN 1-57306-083-6 (hardcover)
    ISBN 1-57306-042-9 (paperback)
    1. Islands of the Pacific – Social life and customs. 2. Islands of the Pacific – History. 3. Islands of the Pacific – Geography. I. Rapaport, Moshe, ed. II. Title.
DU23.P36  1999    919–dc20

Copyright © 1999 by The Bess Press, Inc.

ALL RIGHTS RESERVED

No part of this book may be reproduced or transmitted in any form by any means, electronic or mechanical, including photocopying and recording, or by any information storage or retrieval system, without permission in writing from the copyright holder.

Printed in Hong Kong

For Mom, Dad, Lorraine, Leilani, and Kainui

# Preface

## The Study of Regions

The study of regions is one of the oldest and most fundamental themes of scholarly inquiry and has long engaged academic interest alongside systematic approaches to scientific understanding. While populations and land areas of the Pacific Islands are relatively small, this vast archipelagic world is in many ways unique and offers special opportunities for regional study. Courses focusing on the Pacific Islands are offered at many universities, and Pacific Island Studies programs have been established. There is currently a vital need for a basic reference on Pacific Islands environment and society, which this book aims to fill.

The revaluation of place in the social sciences and humanities offers a contemporary rationale for the study of regions. As political boundaries have become permeable to economic, demographic, and cultural flows, distant places and regions come increasingly into view. Yet local institutions and cultures endure, providing the reassurances of stability, tradition, authenticity, and care. Modernization, long seen as transcending place and region, is conditioned by locale (Daniels 1992). Even in Hawai'i and New Zealand (sometimes considered part of the Pacific Rim) there is keen awareness of the historical and current linkages with other parts of the Pacific Islands region.

Regions, of course, are at best models of the real world. This is particularly so for the Pacific Islands, which range from far-flung coral atolls to large islands with fast-flowing rivers and high mountain ranges; from cultures where traditional chiefs still rule to those where indigenous languages have become endangered. The boundaries of regions are notoriously difficult to define. Yet like all models, regions allow useful generalizations. Like other forms of education, regional awareness is an essential mode of dispelling ignorance, misunderstanding, mistrust, and conflict (Johnston 1990).

Other rationales for Pacific Island regional study have been

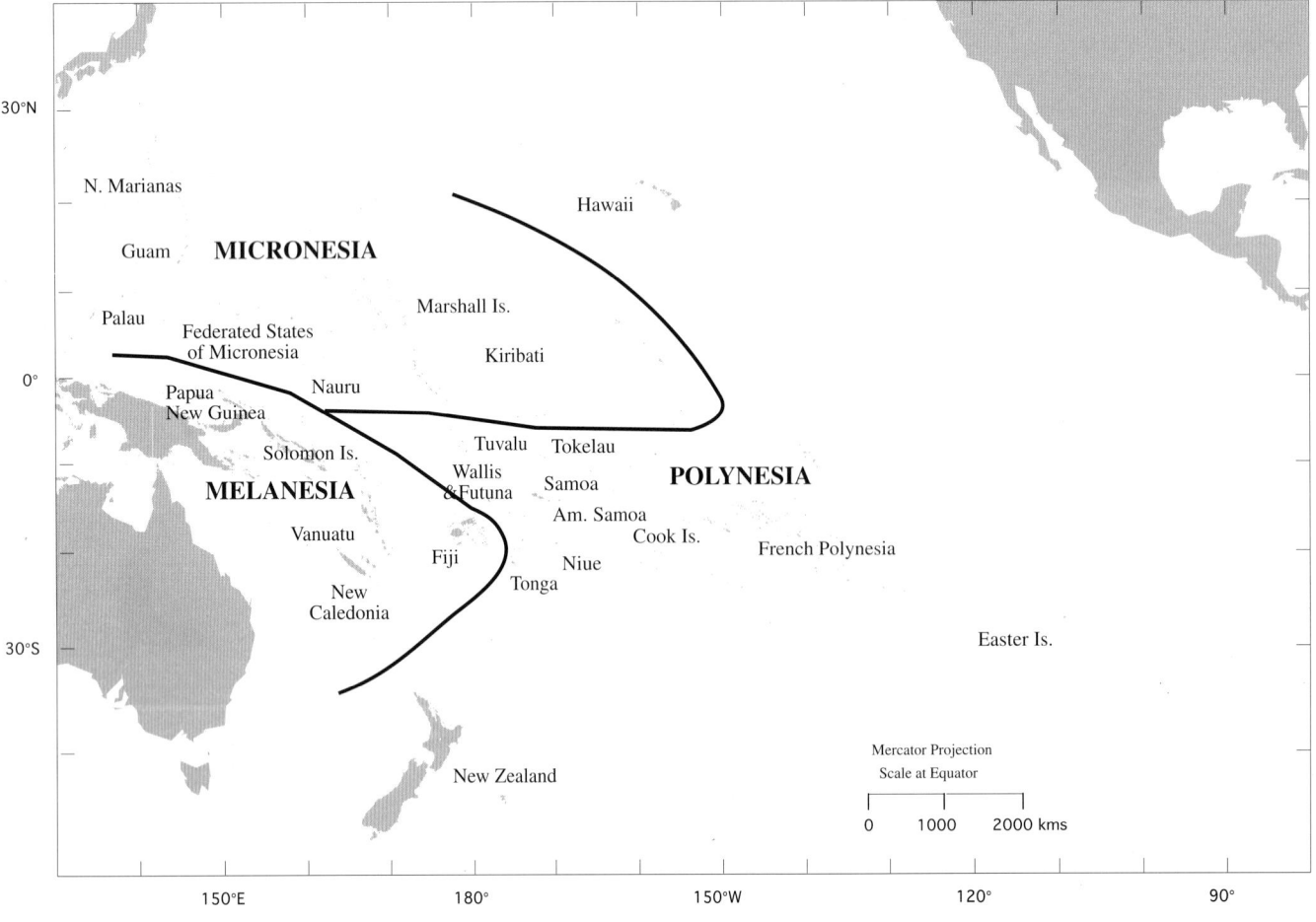

discussed by Wesley-Smith (1995). The diversity, isolation, and small-scale dimensions of islands and island populations present laboratory-like opportunities for research on general questions about nature and society. Information from the Pacific has sparked debate and rethinking on topics ranging from evolution to philosophy and culture. National interest has been an important factor in launching and funding regional studies programs. Regional study can also provide a venue for reorienting education to become more attuned to local needs.

## Organization and Scope

To address the above need for a regional study, overviews of key topics in Pacific environment and society have been newly written for this volume. While no rigid style was imposed, authors were requested to address issues of theory, historical change, and regional variability. In order to give priority to explanation, the chapters are organized topically, covering both the natural environment and human society. References to particular locations are made where necessary for explanation and example and to illustrate intraregional variation, as deemed appropriate for the respective topics.

The book opens with the Physical Environment (Section 1), which provides the foundation for the Living Environment (Section 2). Coverage of society begins with History (Section 3), followed by selected aspects of Culture (Section 4). This sequence provides a broad basis for subsequent focus on Population and Economy (Sections 5 and 6). Interdisciplinary connections are present throughout, and a certain degree of overlap was unavoidable (thus the chapters on politics, race, and literature are placed in accordance with their strong historical emphasis, but could alternatively have been grouped elsewhere).

Within the book's geographic scope are the island groups of Melanesia, Micronesia, and Polynesia.[1] While there are cultural affinities between the Pacific Islands and Southeast Asia, the latter region has experienced two millennia of powerful influences from Asian civilizations. In the Pacific, distance and other factors (such as disease in lowland New Guinea) permitted society to develop in relative isolation from Asia, fostering a largely independent historical trajectory. Within the region, environmental and cultural differences are considerable; yet the Pacific Islands have long had much in common, joined, rather than divided, by the world's largest ocean (Hau'ofa 1993).

The study of the Pacific Islands region draws on the work of many academic disciplines, and selection of authors has not been constrained within a narrow disciplinary or ideological framework. Authors include natural scientists, social scientists, and humanists who have devoted their research and careers to the Pacific Islands region, with experience including fieldwork and knowledge of the relevant literature. Several authors are of indigenous descent or affiliation. Most are faculty members at Pacific Island universities and long-term residents of the region. All chapters were reviewed by competent scholars in the appropriate fields.

## Themes

Among the chapters, emphases differ considerably depending on the subject and the interests and areas of expertise of the authors. Nonetheless, it is possible to briefly present four key themes tying together the diverse chapters in this volume. These include environmental process (Chapters 1–9), social change (Chapters 10–20), population-resource relations (Chapters 21–33), and the Pacific Islands as region (a theme implicit in this project as a whole).

*Environmental process.* Island groups as diverse as New Guinea, Hawai'i, Niue, and Tokelau are all products of plate tectonic activity. Prevailing pressure and wind systems influence ocean currents and rainfall, which in turn affect landforms, biota, and the feasibility of human settlement. Having evolved in isolation, island ecosytems were severely affected by the arrival and proliferation of human settlers. This disturbance is exacerbated today by increasing overexploitation, soil erosion, exotic introductions, species extinctions, and pollution.

*Social change.* Factors of size and distance left island societies vulnerable to colonial intervention. Traditional systems of resource use, leadership, social organization, and beliefs have changed significantly since contact. Island societies have adapted, and have been able to benefit from modern technologies and cultural offerings. Concurrently, there is a desire to maintain and revive indigenous identity—raising important questions in polyethnic and multicultural societies. Systems of tenure, law, education, and governance introduced during the colonial period are being reevaluated today.

*Population-resource relations.* Relative to continents, the Pacific Islands are remote, fragmented, and resource poor. Population growth remains high, straining the capacity of governments to provide jobs and services. Subsistence horticulture and fisheries are losing ground. Sources of economic output include agriculture, fisheries and aquaculture, mining, tourism, and offshore fisheries licensing and other schemes. The emerging communications industry holds promise. Yet island communities remain dependent on foreign aid and migrate in large numbers to Pacific Rim countries.

*The Pacific Islands as region.* The Pacific Island region is the world's largest grouping of islands, spanning a third of the Earth's surface. Both physical environments and ecosystems have striking similarities across the region. Island societies have common roots and historical experiences, and they share many cultural features. Regionalism persists today through transnational networks of kin; a plethora of regional organizations; a literary and artistic renaissance; a close-knit academic community; and related identities, cultures, and destinies.

---

[1] For the origins and limitations of this regional subdivision, see Thomas 1989.

## Acknowledgments

Sincere thanks are due to the numerous reviewers: Tim Adams, Chuck Birkeland, David Chappell, Bill Clarke, John Connell, John Culliney, Bryce Decker, Derrick Depledge, Sitaleki Finau, Michael Hamnett, Alison Kay, Kimberlee Kihleng, Robert Kiste, Stephen Levine, Nancy Lewis, Jim Mak, Harley Manner, Michael McCarthy, Steve Montgomery, John Morrison, Patrick Nunn, Wali Osman, Jim Parrish, Andrew Pawley, Karen Peacock, Jean-Louis Rallu, Rick Scaglion, Mary Spencer, Matthew Spriggs, Dick Stroup, Frank Thomas, Garry Trompf, and Terence Wesley-Smith.

For photos, thanks are due to Wendy Arbeit, Glenn Banks, John Barker, Freeport Mining Company, Gerard Fryer, Honolulu Academy of Arts, E. Alison Kay, Lamont Lindstrom, Harley Manner, Len Mason, Glenda Mather, Father Bernie Miller, John Morrison, Dieter Mueller-Dombois, Patrick Nunn, Michael Ogden, Ok Tedi Mining Company, Andrew Oliphant, Jean-Louis Rallu, Rick Scaglion, South Pacific Commission, Andrew Sturman, University of Guam Marine Laboratory, U.S. Navy, Deborah Waite, Paul Williams, Jeff Witter, Don and Carolyn Yacoe.

For referrals, thanks to Charles Birkeland, Jenny Bryant, Linley Chapman, Pierre Flament, Nicholas Thomas, R. G. Ward, Everett Wingert, and many of the contributors to this book; for Internet communications help to Naomi Okinaga; for reference help to Karen Peacock and Hamilton Library Specials Collection staff; for abbreviation sleuthing to Eileen Herring; for style consulting to Linley Chapman; and for publishing, editorial, and graphics support to Ben Bess, Revé Shapard, and Carol Colbath. Support from the University of Hawai'i at Mānoa Geography Department and from the Social Sciences Division of Kapi'olani Community College is also acknowledged.

## References

Daniels, S. 1992. Place and the geographical imagination. *Geography* 77(4):310–22.

Hau'ofa, E. 1993. A new Oceania: rediscovering our sea of islands. In *A new Oceania: rediscovering our sea of islands*, ed. E. Waddell, V. Naidu, and E. Hau'ofa, 2–16. Suva: School of Social and Economic Development, University of the South Pacific.

Johnston, R. J. 1990. The challenge of regional geography: some proposals for research frontiers. In *Regional geography: current developments and future prospects*, ed. R. J. Johnston, J. Hauer, and G. A. Hoekveld, 122–139. London: Routledge.

Thomas, N. 1989. The force of ethnology: origins and significance of the Melanesia/Polynesia division. *Current Anthropology* 30:27–34.

Wesley-Smith, T. 1995. Rethinking Pacific Islands studies. *Pacific Studies* 18(2):115–136.

# Contents

Preface ..................................iv

## The Physical Environment

1. Climate
   *Andrew P. Sturman and Hamish A. McGowan* .......3

2. Oceanography
   *Lynne D. Talley, Gerard J. Fryer, and Rick Lumpkin* ....19

3. Geology *Gerard J. Fryer and Patricia Fryer* .......33

4. Geomorphology *Patrick D. Nunn* ...........43

5. Soil *R. John Morrison* ....................56

6. Water *Derrick Depledge* ...................66

## The Living Environment

7. Biogeography *E. Alison Kay* .................76

8. Terrestrial Ecosystems *Harley I. Manner, Dieter Mueller-Dombois and Moshe Rapaport* .......93

9. Aquatic Ecosystems *Stephen G. Nelson* .........109

## History

10. The Precontact Period *Frank R. Thomas* .......121

11. The Postcontact Period *David A. Chappell* ......134

12. Changing Patterns of Power
    *Terence Wesley-Smith* ....................144

13. "Race," Identity and Representation
    *RDK Herman* ...........................156

14. Here Our Words *Selina Tusitala Marsh* .......166

## Culture

15. Language *Andrew Pawley* ..................181

16. Social Relations *Lamont Lindstrom* ..........195

17. Tenure *Ron Crocombe* ....................208

18. Law *Richard Scaglion* ...................221

19. Religion *John Barker* ...................234

20. Art *Deborah Waite* .....................246

## Population

21. Demography
    *Jean-Louis Rallu and Dennis A. Ahlburg* .........258

22. Mobility *Moshe Rapaport* ..................270

23. Health *Nancy J. Pollock and Sitaleki A. Finau* .....282

24. Education *Glenda Mather* ..................296

25. Women *Camilla Cockerton* .................305

26. Urbanization *Jean-Pierre Doumenge* ..........315

27. Urban Dilemmas
    *John Connell and John P. Lea* ...............326

## Economy

28. Economy *Geoffrey Bertram* .................337

29. Agriculture and Forestry *William C. Clarke, Harley I. Manner, and Randolph R. Thaman* .......353

30. Ocean Resources
    *Tim Adams, Paul Dalzell, and Esaroma Ledua* .....366

31. Mining *Glenn Banks and Frank McShane* .......382

32. Tourism *Michael Fagence* ..................394

33. Communications
    *Michael R. Ogden and Suzanna Layton* .........405

Abbreviations ..............................419
Island Gazetteer ...........................421
Color Plates and Sectional Maps
Contributors ..............................427
Subject Index .............................431
Place-Name Index .........................438

# SECTION 1

# THE PHYSICAL ENVIRONMENT

The Pacific Islands were created through the cumulative action of volcanism, tectonism, and reef growth over millions of years. At the same time, many of the dramatic landscapes visible today—steep cliffs, deeply dissected valleys, sprawling coastal plains, and even reef *motus*—owe their existence in large extent to erosion induced by climatic and oceanographic forces. Section 1 describes the physical environment of the Pacific Islands, with chapters on climate, oceanography, geology, geomorphology, soils, and water. Contributors include Andrew P. Sturman, Hamish A. McGowan, Lynne D. Talley, Rick Lumpkin, Gerard J. Fryer, Patricia Fryer, Patrick D. Nunn, R. John Morrison, and Derrick Depledge.

# Climate

*Andrew P. Sturman and Hamish A. McGowan*

## Introduction

The islands of the Pacific Ocean experience a diverse variety of weather and climate (aggregate weather) due to their wide-ranging geographic locations, which encompass both midlatitude and tropical settings. Because Pacific islands are surrounded by vast areas of ocean, their climates are strongly influenced by maritime processes. However, atmospheric circulation systems, terrain, and surface vegetation cover frequently modify the maritime air masses that pass over islands. This results in distinct microclimates.

The main climate-related concerns for many Pacific Island nations are providing adequate water supplies and minimizing exposure to atmospheric hazards. The nature of atmospheric circulation in the Pacific region is such that there is considerable temporal and spatial variability. Some regions experience drought at the same time that others are flooded. The sustainability of many island societies is marginal, so that such problems can place significant pressure on community viability.

Because of the immense diversity of atmospheric processes observed in the Pacific Basin, this chapter focuses only on some of the principal atmospheric phenomena relevant to the region. Local examples of these features are provided and their significance discussed. Observed and predicted climate change and variability are also reviewed. The major impacts of weather and climate on natural and human environments are also summarized. For additional information, the reader is referred to the list of references at the end of the chapter.

## Global Atmospheric Circulation and the Pacific Islands

### The Importance of the Global Energy Balance

The driving force for weather and climate processes originates with incoming solar radiation. It is the uneven distribution of this energy across the globe that results in the Earth's atmospheric circulation (Sturman and Tapper 1996). The central part of the Pacific region receives a net radiation surplus of more than 80 W/m² (watts per square meter), while areas north and south of about 40° experience a net deficit of energy (Figure 1.1). The surplus in the tropics results in high air and sea surface temperatures, causing rapid evaporation of water into the atmosphere.

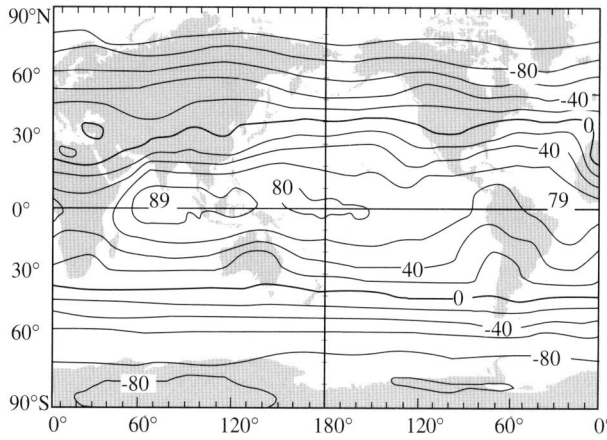

*Figure 1.1.* Global distribution of net all-wave radiation, measured at the top of the atmosphere (W/m²) (modified after Peixoto and Oort 1992).

### Global and Regional Circulation Systems

The atmospheric circulation (assisted by the oceanic circulation) serves to transport surplus energy from the tropics toward the high-latitude region of deficit (Sturman and Tapper 1996). The broad features of the global atmospheric circulation are represented schematically in Figure 1.2. Strong rising motion (convection) is characteristic of the intertropical convergence zone (ITCZ), where the northeast and southeast trade winds meet. Subtropical anticyclones (high-pressure zones of descending air) are located poleward of the trade wind belt. This completes the Hadley cell, linking the tropics with the midlatitudes (Figure 1.3).

The westerly wind belt lies farther poleward, where outflow from the anticyclones meets cold air from the poles, turning toward the east as they meet. For both the westerlies and the trade winds, east-west movement is due to the Coriolis effect (deflection caused by the Earth's rotation). The Southern Hemisphere westerlies are much stronger and more enduring than those to the north, where the major continental landmasses disrupt the westerly airflow (Figure 1.4).

Seasonal changes in pressure distribution are considerably greater over the North than the South Pacific (Figure 1.4). During January an area of low pressure dominates the northern section of the North Pacific, while the subtropical high is reduced in intensity. In contrast, the pressure pattern over the South Pacific retains a more zonal structure throughout the year, though the climate zones shift northward and southward with the seasons.

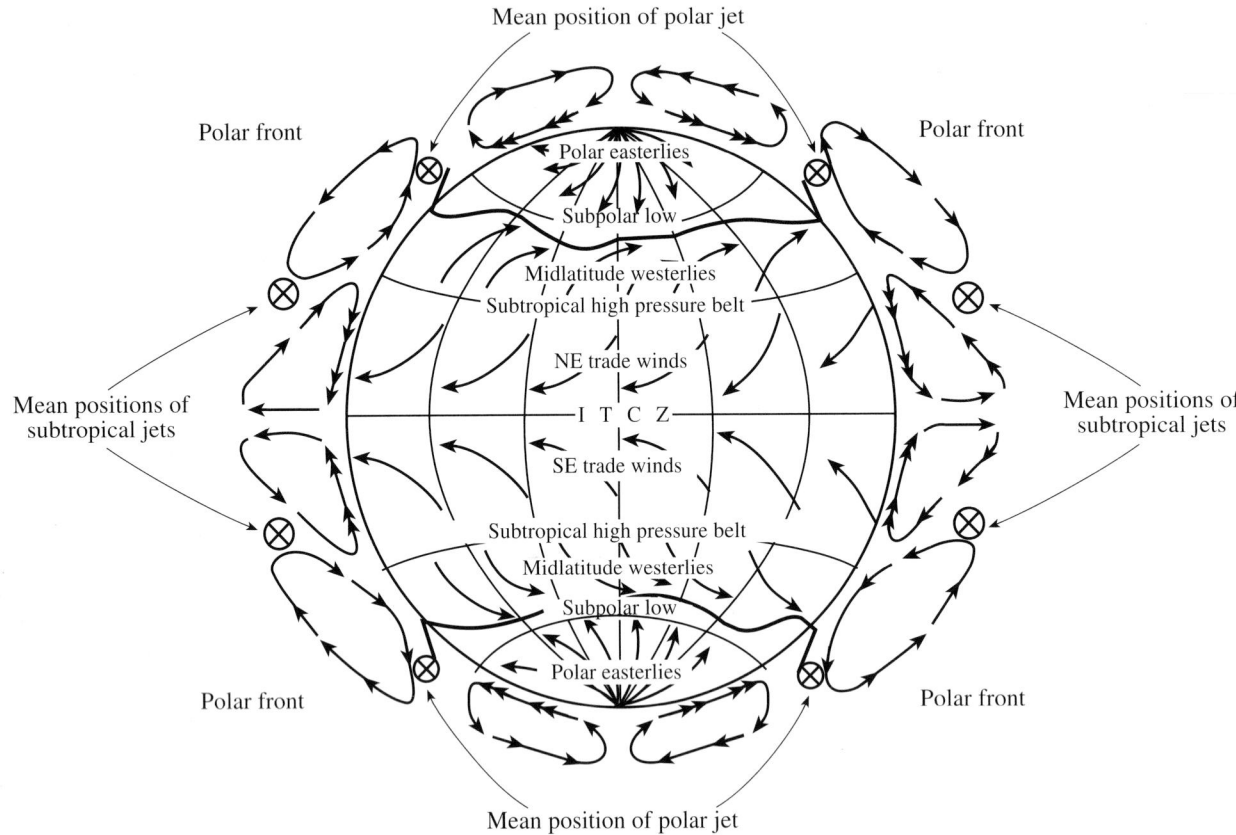

*Figure 1.2. Schematic representation of the global atmospheric circulation (modified after Miller and Anthes 1985).*

Another extensive feature driving Pacific pressure and wind systems is the Walker circulation. This is a primarily west-east oriented cell, with rising motion over the Indonesia region (known as the maritime continent) and subsidence over the southeast Pacific (Figure 1.3). This circulation cell provides the easterly component of the trade winds and is closely linked to oceanic circulation. Fluctuations in the intensity of the Walker Cell contribute to the El Niño–Southern Oscillation (ENSO) effect discussed later (Sturman and Tapper 1996).

The ITCZ dominates atmospheric circulation of the central Pacific, but moves north and south seasonally, particularly over the western Pacific (Figure 1.5). The intensity of convection along the ITCZ varies, with major activity occurring over Indonesia. A smaller center of action occurs over equatorial South America. In the narrow intermediate zone, there is a lessening of convective activity from December to February. This general pattern of convective activity results in cloudiness and precipitation over the western section of the ITCZ, where it merges with the South Pacific convergence zone (SPCZ) (Figure 1.5).

The SPCZ is a zone of cloudiness and precipitation occurring where southeast trade winds meet southerly flow from the New Zealand region (Vincent 1994). This is also a region where tropical cyclones frequently originate. Sea-surface temperature patterns are thought to play a part in its development, although the mechanisms are not fully understood. The SPCZ shows an increase in strength when it moves southward in the southern summer (December–March). At this time, cross-equatorial flow appears to increase low-level convergence.

Monsoons have traditionally been defined as reversals of wind resulting from seasonal heating and cooling of major continental areas. However, there is sometimes confusion in the literature, as the movement of convergence zones across the Pacific during the year generally produces seasonal variations in the influence of different wind regimes. For example, movement

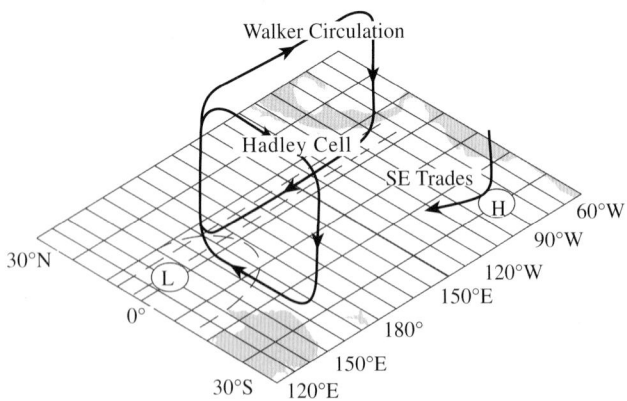

*Figure 1.3. Circulation cells over the central and South Pacific (from Sturman and Tapper 1996).*

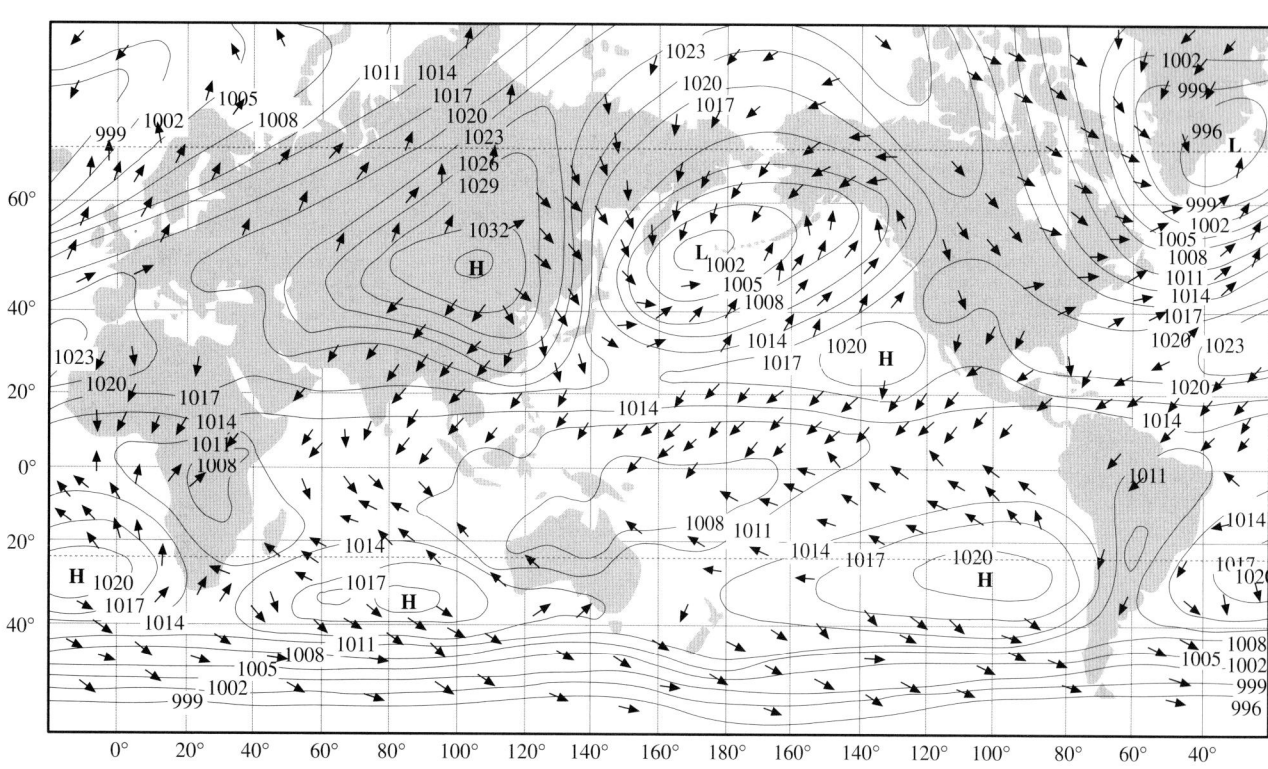

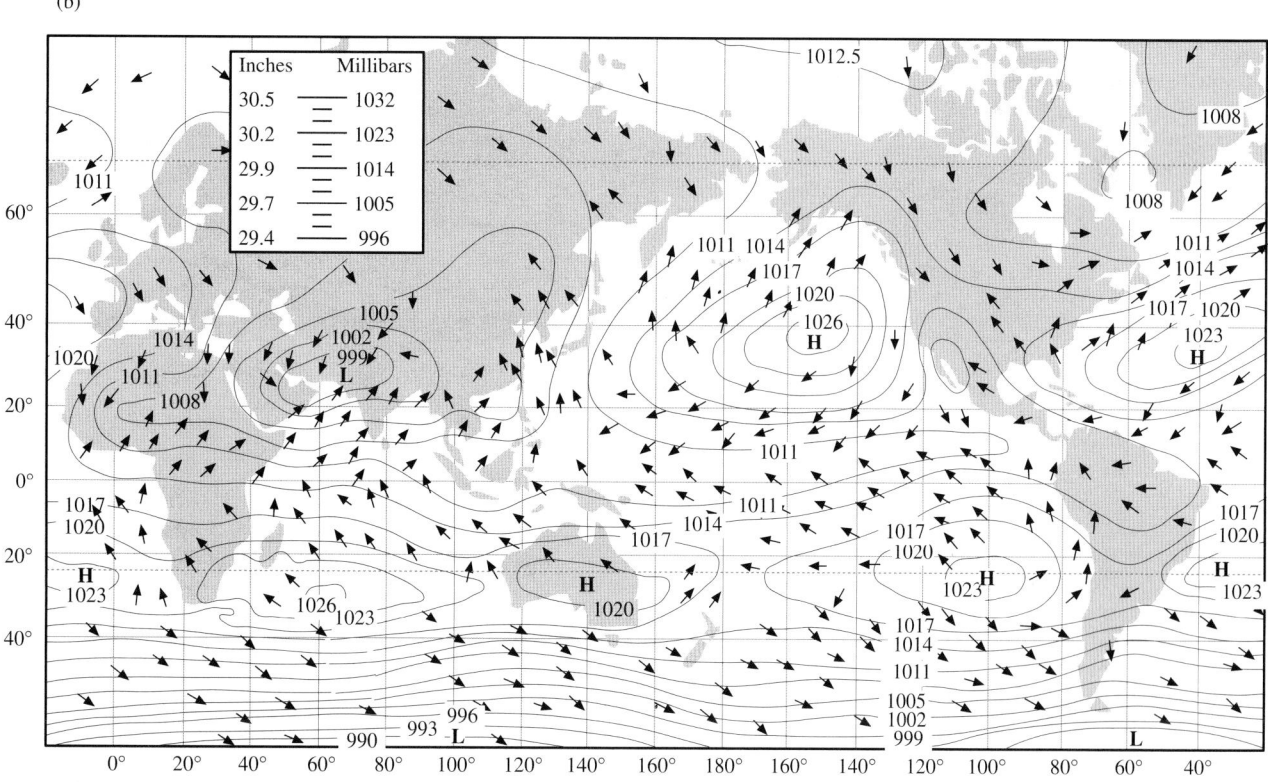

*Figure 1.4.* Mean sea-level pressure distribution (mb) and simplified wind field for the globe in a) January and b) July (Strahler and Strahler 1978).

of the SPCZ results in seasonal variations in the airflow and precipitation regime of the islands of Samoa, but this is not considered a true monsoonal regime.

Monsoons (see Ramage 1971) occur along the margins of the Asian continent, over the western central Pacific, and over northern Australia. The development of heat lows over Australia during the southern summer encourages a southward movement of the ITCZ. As a result, the northeast trade winds are drawn southward across the equator. South of the equator, the winds are deflected by the Earth's rotation, resulting in a northwest monsoonal flow (Figure 1.5).

Similarly, in the northern summer (June–August), the southeast trade winds are drawn northward across the equator by the powerful heat low in central Asia. Deflected to the right by the Earth's rotation, the winds shift to carry air northeastward across Southeast Asia and the Southern Marianas. The resulting monsoon winds then encounter the northeasterly trade-wind flow from the central North Pacific along a section of the ITCZ (Figure 1.5). This convergence of wind streams causes a high frequency of tropical cyclones in the Guam region (Ding Yihui 1994).

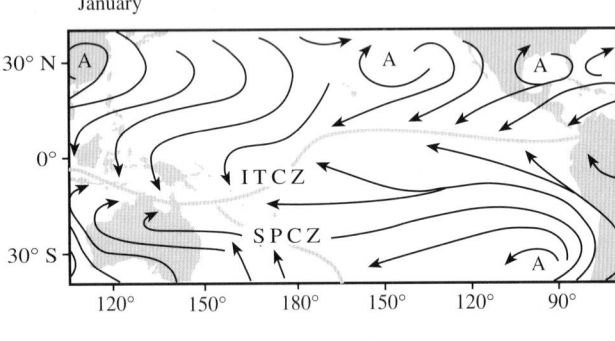

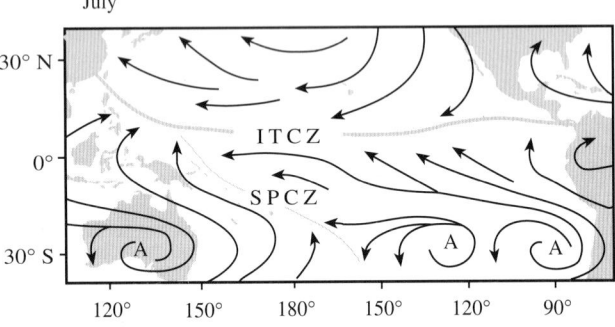

*Figure 1.5.* Mean position of the intertropical convergence zone (ITCZ) and South Pacific convergence zone (SPCZ) during January and July, showing the near-surface airflow. A represents an anticyclonic center (modified after Hastenrath 1988 and Thompson 1987).

## Synoptic-Scale Weather Systems

Synoptic (large-scale) weather systems include anticyclones, midlatitude depressions, and tropical cyclones. These phenomena range in size from approximately $10^4$ to $10^7$ km$^2$ and generally prevail for several days to a week or more; they largely determine the observed daily weather (Sturman and Tapper 1996). Smaller-scale structures such as ridges of high pressure, troughs of low pressure, and fronts are frequently associated with these systems. In this section we discuss the synoptic-scale weather systems that most commonly affect the Pacific Islands.

### Subtropical and Blocking Anticyclones

Subtropical anticyclones are regions of high pressure with descending, diverging, and revolving air (counterclockwise in the Southern Hemisphere and clockwise in the Northern Hemisphere), and are the driving force of the trade winds. They generally occur around 30° over the North and South Pacific and are characterized by clear weather. Subsidence produces warming due to compression, which acts as a lid on the lower atmosphere (preventing rising, condensation, and precipitation) called a temperature inversion. This can be seen in Color Plate 1A, showing fair-weather cumulus with flattened tops where they reach the inversion layer.

The anticyclone over the North Pacific shows a strong annual variation in intensity, with a maximum in July (Figure 1.4). The strongest anticyclones are at the eastern side of the Pacific. Thus, the temperature inversion tends to be stronger and at a lower elevation over the eastern subtropical Pacific, declining in strength and lifting toward the western equatorial region (Figure 1.6). The trade wind belts equatorward of these anticyclones have steady winds, with little variation in temperature and humidity. However, daily variations do occur in convective cloud and rainfall.

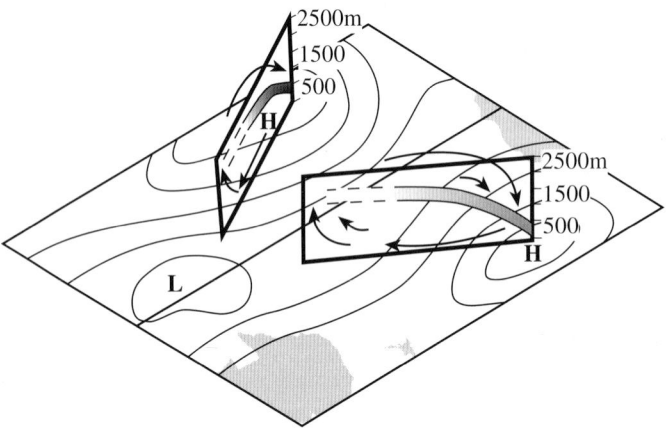

*Figure 1.6.* Schematic representation of the link between subsidence in the subtropical anticyclones and the development of temperature inversions in the trade wind belts north and south of the equator. The two cross sections illustrate the circulation of air across the northern and southern Pacific (using arrows), and the changing strength and height of the subsidence inversions (the shaded bands).

In the New Zealand region to the south, high-pressure ridges separate low-pressure troughs (often containing fronts) in the westerly wind belt (Figure 1.7). Following the passage of a frontal trough, subsiding air associated with the following ridge suppresses convective activity, resulting in fair weather cumulus (Color Plate 1B). Several days of fine settled weather are then usually experienced. In certain locations, local circulations, such

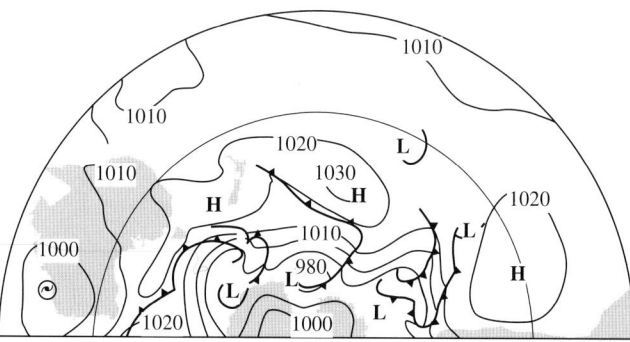

*Figure 1.7. Typical pattern of alternating high-pressure ridges extending from the subtropical anticyclones and low-pressure disturbances embedded in the Southern Hemisphere westerlies (after Streten and Zillman 1984).*

as sea/land breezes and valley/mountain winds, may then ensue (discussed later).

Anticyclones can develop poleward of the subtropical high-pressure regions and become almost stationary. These blocking anticyclones cause a temporary halt to the normal eastward progression of weather systems in midlatitudes (Sturman and Tapper 1996). Two favored locations for anticyclonic blocking are east of New Zealand and in the northwestern Pacific. Blocking anticyclones to the east of New Zealand typically bring northeasterly winds and widespread stratiform cloud cover (called anticyclonic gloom) over east coastal regions.

### Tropical Low-Pressure Systems

The most severe weather experienced in the tropical Pacific is associated with tropical cyclones (also called hurricanes or typhoons). These are intense, nonfrontal low-pressure systems occurring over tropical or subtropical waters (Holland 1993). Intense solar radiation over the oceans causes warm, humid air to converge and rise. Air rushing into the cyclone's core is deflected by the Earth's rotation, resulting in a spiral shape (Figure 1.8). A well-defined eye (10–50 km diameter) may be seen near the center, characterized by gentle descent of air, clear skies, and light winds at the surface.

At maturity, these weather systems can produce wind speeds in excess of 300 km/hr, torrential rain, storm surges, and large sea swells. The extreme wind speeds cause havoc on atolls and low-lying coastal areas. The powerful winds destroy crops and homes and often combine with heavy rainfall and high seas to produce severe flooding. Tropical cyclones occur primarily during summer, but they may occur at other times under favorable meteorological and oceanic conditions. Pielke (1990) outlined five conditions favorable or necessary for tropical cyclone formation. These are listed in Table 1.1.

In the southern summer, tropical cyclones typically originate in a region extending from the northeastern coast of Australia into the SPCZ (5°S and 20°S) and generally track westward (Sturman and Tapper 1996). They often veer toward the midlatitudes, becoming subtropical depressions, with their motion influenced by strong westerly flow (as shown in Figure 1.9a). As they move poleward, they become progressively weaker and

*Figure 1.8. Satellite image of tropical cyclones Justin, off the coast of northeastern Australia, and Gavin, between Fiji and New Zealand, on 9 March 1997 (image received from the Japanese GMS-5 satellite).*

### TABLE 1.1

**Conditions Favorable or Necessary for Tropical Cyclone Genesis (modified from Pielke 1990)**

1. Sea-surface temperatures higher than 26°C.
2. Little change of wind speed and direction with height through the troposphere, so that heat energy remains concentrated.
3. An existing tropical disturbance of some sort at the surface (e.g. an easterly wave or large convective complex).
4. Unstable thermal structure, enhancing deep vertical development (i.e. no trade wind inversion).
5. Location poleward of about 4°-5° from the equator, where the Coriolis force equals zero.

develop cold cores in response to colder sea-surface temperatures.

Table 1.2 presents the monthly and seasonal occurrence of tropical cyclones in the South Pacific region from October 1979 to May 1989, over which period 107 tropical cyclones were identified. The main season between January and March is evident, although there is some variability between years.

In the northern summer the most active region for tropical cyclone formation is the northwestern Pacific (Figure 1.9b), where monsoonal southwesterlies encounter easterly trade winds. In this region, tropical cyclones are usually referred to as typhoons, or supertyphoons when sustained wind speeds exceed 240 km/hr. For example, on the island of Guam the Joint Typhoon Warning Center names on average 28 tropical cyclones annually, of which 4 typically reach supertyphoon status (Joint Typhoon Warning Center 1993).

## Table 1.2

**Monthly and Seasonal Numbers of Tropical Cyclones South of the Equator from 145°E to 125°W Occurring from October 1979 through May 1989**
(after Thompson et al. 1992)

| Season | Oct-Nov | Dec | Jan | Feb | Mar | Apr-May | Total |
|---|---|---|---|---|---|---|---|
| 1979/80 |  | 1 | 2 | 3 | 4 | 1 | 10 |
| 1980/81 | 1 |  | 2 | 7 | 6 |  | 13 |
| 1981/82 |  | 1 | 2 | 3 | 1 | 3 | 7 |
| 1982/83 | 2 | 1 | 3 | 4 | 6 | 4 | 16 |
| 1983/84 |  | 2 | 1 | 4 | 2 | 1 | 10 |
| 1984/85 |  | 2 | 6 |  | 2 |  | 9 |
| 1985/86 |  |  | 2 | 4 | 2 | 3 | 10 |
| 1986/87 | 1 | 3 | 3 | 4 | 3 | 2 | 12 |
| 1987/88 |  |  | 2 | 3 | 3 | 1 | 6 |
| 1988/89 |  | 2 | 3 | 5 | 2 | 5 | 14 |
| Total | 4 | 12 | 26 | 37 | 31 | 20 | 107 |

Tropical cyclones may also form off the west coast of Mexico from May to November, and typically move westward and sometimes northward toward Baja California (Figure 1.9b). Cyclones are much rarer in the vicinity of the Hawaiian Islands, with 1 to 2 cyclones every ten years (Martyn 1992).

Other low-pressure systems in the central part of the region include tropical and subtropical depressions. These features are much less intense than tropical cyclones, but still are important features of the region. Tropical depressions have reduced wind rotation, due to close proximity to the equator, and are relatively weak. As they move away from the equator they may intensify to become tropical cyclones. Subtropical depressions can develop farther poleward in such areas as the north Tasman Sea, affecting New Zealand weather as they drift downwind to the east.

Over the North Pacific, the major region for the development of such low-pressure systems is over and southeast of Japan. Explosive development of subtropical depressions sometimes occurs north of Hawai'i at around 35° to 45° N (Gyakum et al. 1989), bringing intense rainfall known as Kona storms (Carlquist 1980), particularly during the winter season. A small number of such depressions may also form along the coast of California and Mexico. There is some suggestion that upper tropospheric disturbances control the development of these weather systems (Schroeder 1993).

### Mid-latitude Low-Pressure Systems

Midlatitude weather systems affect only the New Zealand section of the Pacific Islands, and so will be dealt with only briefly. More details can be found in Sturman and Tapper (1996). The most significant feature of this region is the strong westerly wind belt, which produces rapid west to east movement of alternating lows and highs and their associated troughs and ridges. This region is one of rapid weather changes due to strong air mass interaction and the development of fronts. Low-pressure systems develop poleward of the subtropical anticyclones, and the frontal extensions periodically affect weather in New Zealand and (less frequently) Hawai'i.

## Local Island Weather

On individual islands and parts of islands, synoptic-scale weather and climate is modified by local geographic factors. Specifically, the levels of temperature, wind, precipitation, and cloud cover of particular places are determined by the interaction of maritime air masses with local topography. Readers are also referred to Schroeder (1993), who provides a more detailed case study of the weather and climate of the islands of Hawai'i.

### Local Winds

Islands have both dynamic and thermal effects on airflow. For example, interaction between thermally induced local winds, easterly trade winds, and local topography causes flow splitting of the easterly trades as they pass around the island of Hawai'i (Figure 1.10). Downslope (katabatic) winds develop just prior to sunset on leeward slopes as a result of surface cooling and spread to other slopes during the night. Cessation of the nocturnal wind regime starts approximately 1 to 2 hours after sunrise with the onset of upslope (anabatic) winds (Schroeder 1993).

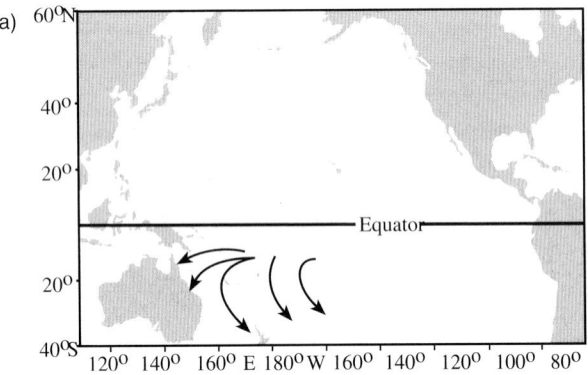

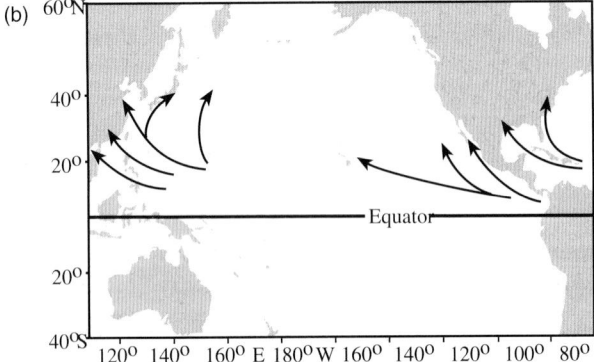

*Figure 1.9.* Schematic representation of tropical cyclone tracks over the Pacific in a) February and b) August (adapted from Gray 1975).

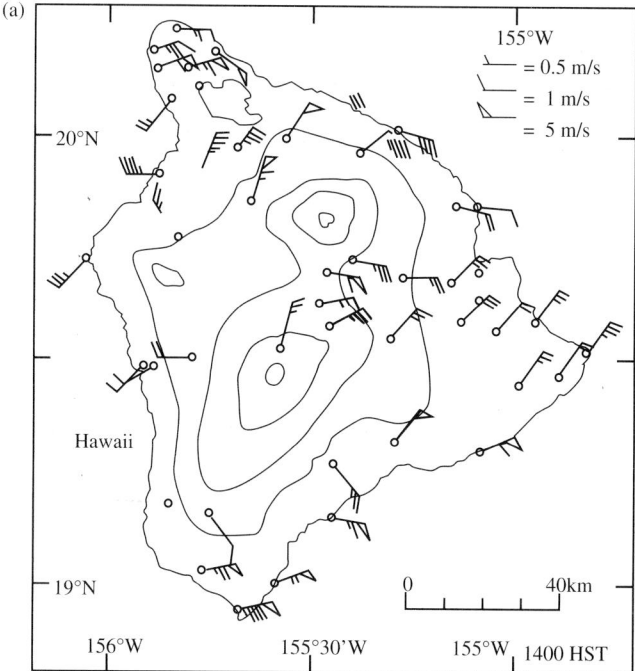

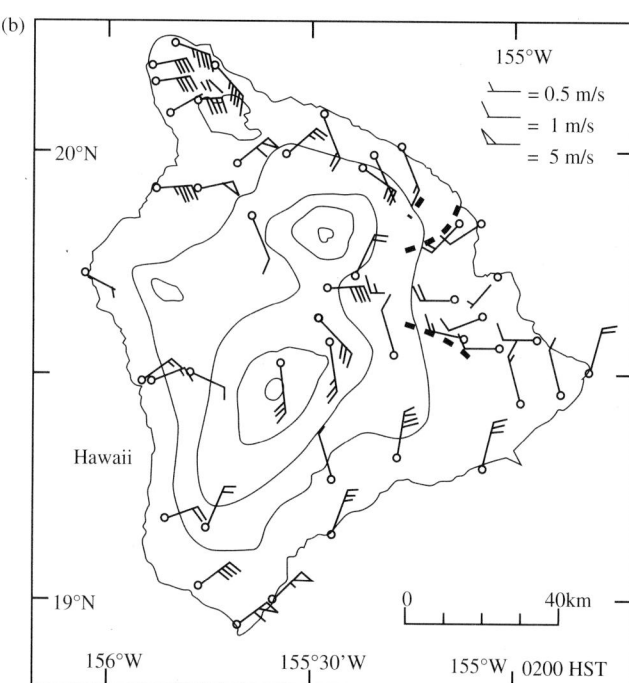

*Figure 1.10.* Interaction of the prevailing northeast trades with thermally developed a) daytime sea breeze and anabatic flow and b) nocturnal land breeze and katabatic flow over the island of Hawai'i (after Chen and Nash 1994).

Observations from Papua New Guinea indicate that local sea breezes may travel as far as 150 km inland across coastal plains and may continue well after sunset at inland sites. The sea breeze front can bring showers and thunderstorms at inland sites later in the afternoon and early evening. Sea breezes also contribute to thunderstorm development over tropical islands. Sea breeze convergence is a common phenomenon leading to

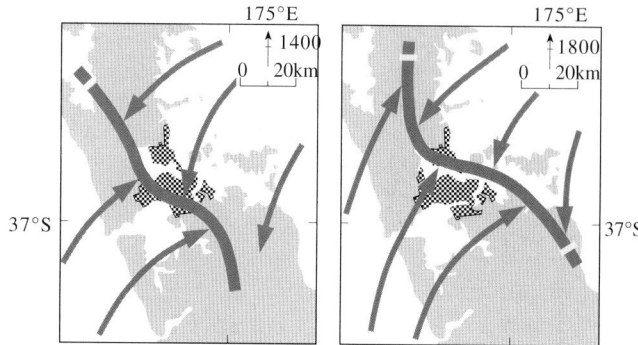

*Figure 1.11.* The convergence of sea breezes from opposing coasts over Auckland, New Zealand, at 1200 and 1800 hr (after McKendry 1989, with kind permission from Kluwer Academic Publishers).

convective development over Auckland, New Zealand, as illustrated in Figure 1.11.

## Orographic Effects

Orographic (mountain) induced precipitation is especially important in the larger Pacific Islands, such as Hawai'i and New Zealand. However, even relatively small hills only 50 m or so above the surrounding terrain height have been observed to increase precipitation by 25% to 50% (Holgate 1973, Browning et al. 1975). Moist air meeting an obstacle is forced to rise, creating a feeder cloud (Figure 1.12a). Continued arrival of warm, moisture-laden air on windward slopes quickly leads to coalescence of condensed droplets and intense precipitation.

If a seeder cloud is present at higher levels as a result of large-scale vertical motion, precipitation falling from this cloud will coalesce with droplets in the feeder cloud, thereby enhancing rainfall (Figure 1.12b). Such orographic enhancement of cyclonic precipitation occurs in South Island, New Zealand, producing a pronounced west to east precipitation gradient. Immediately upwind of the Southern Alps, annual rainfall of more than 10,000 mm can occur, while to the east of the

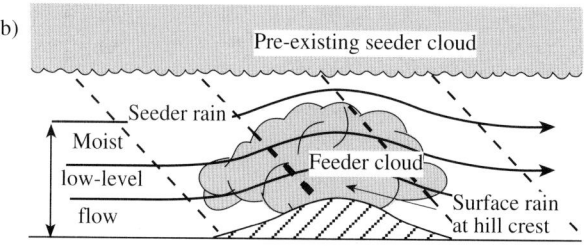

*Figure 1.12.* Effects of a hill or island obstacle on precipitation development. **a)**. the development of a feeder cloud and **b)**. the seeder-feeder mechanism (after Browning 1979).

The Pacific Islands

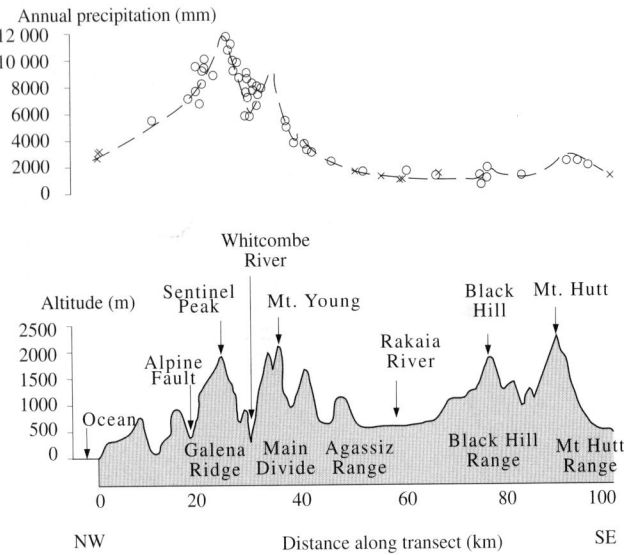

*Figure 1.13. Precipitation transect over the Southern Alps of New Zealand (after Griffiths and McSaveney 1983).*

mountains values drop to less than 600 mm (Figure 1.13).

In the Hawaiian Islands, maximum rainfall (up to 7,000 mm) corresponds to areas of persistent orographic lifting of the northeast trade winds on windward slopes. Lowest annual rainfall totals on the island of Hawai'i are recorded over leeward slopes in an area of rain shadow (as low as 500 mm), and high above the trade wind inversion (as low as 250 mm) (Chen and Nash 1994, Juvik and Nullet 1994). These patterns are complicated by the diurnal fluctuations discussed above (upslope/downslope and onshore/offshore breezes).

On the islands of Savai'i and 'Upolu (Samoa), orographic enhancement of precipitation occurs in response to the seasonal oscillation in the region's wind regime. During the southern summer the SPCZ is situated poleward of the islands, and moist equatorial northeasterlies dominate (Figure 1.14a). During southern winter the SPCZ moves equatorward of the islands. The islands are then affected by drier southeasterlies in close proximity to subtropical anticyclones (Figure 1.14b).

### Thunderstorm Development

Thunderstorms are characterized by the development of cumulus and then cumulonimbus clouds, heavy rain, and strong winds (Figure 1.15 and Color Plate 1C). In the tropics, these storms are usually triggered by intense surface heating during daytime, initiating convection over land. Sea breezes may subsequently converge over the island, generally from midafternoon to late evening. In midlatitudes, thunderstorms may also be associated with frontal disturbances and orographic forcing,

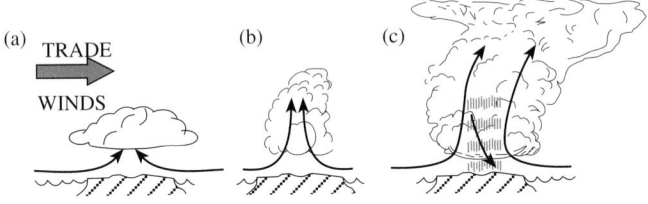

*Figure 1.15. Schematic illustration of island thunderstorm development. Convergence of sea breezes produces initial cumulus development during late morning (a) which is followed soon after by cumulus congestus (b) and a fully developed cumulonimbus by early afternoon (c).*

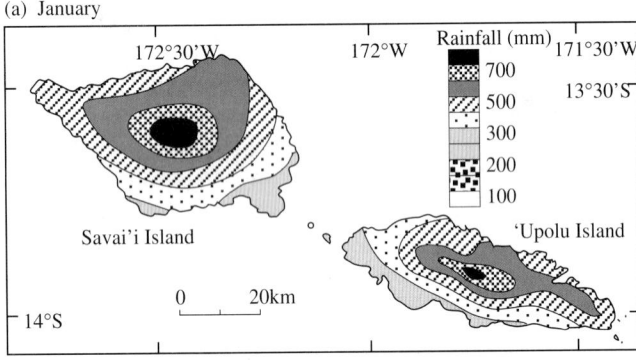

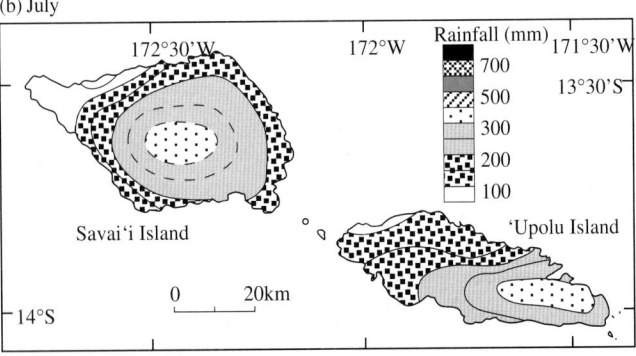

*Figure 1.14. Monthly mean precipitation (mm) over Western Samoa for a). January and b). July, showing both seasonal and orographic influences (after Tualevao 1991).*

for example over the Southern Alps of New Zealand.

Precipitation during thunderstorms is linked to downdrafts, which may exhibit mean velocities between 5 to 8 m/s, with gusts exceeding 20 m/s (Cotton and Anthes 1989). Such gusts can cause damage to crops and homes and present a hazard to aircraft operations at and near airports. Thunderstorms are also often associated with tornadoes and lightning. On average at least twenty tornadoes are reported in New Zealand each year (Tomlinson and Nicol 1976). Tornadoes are much less common in other Pacific islands (Omolayo 1991).

Where local winds converge with the trade winds, as on the east coast of Hawai'i Island, complex rainfall patterns ensue (Chen and Nash 1994). During nighttime, katabatic winds converge with the northeast trade winds, resulting in a nocturnal rainfall peak. During the day, anabatic winds contribute to rainfall over the ridgetops. In Papua New Guinea, offshore convergence of katabatic drainage flows with southeasterly trade winds (May to October) or equatorial westerlies (December to March) results in heavy rainfall (McAlpine et al. 1983).

## Snowfall

Snowfall is frequently recorded in the Southern Alps, where annual snow accumulation may exceed 4,000 mm water equivalent. Snowfall may reach sea level in other parts of South Island, although in general the transient winter snow line averages 1,000 m in southern New Zealand and 1,500 m on North Island mountains (Fitzharris et al. 1992). Snow also falls on the high mountains of New Guinea, even near the equator. In this region, the snowline is above approximately 4,500 m. In the Star Mountains of Irian Jaya, extensive snowfields and glaciers exist.

## Regional Climate Patterns

The distribution of Köppen-Geiger climate types provides a general overview of climate in the Pacific Island region (Figure 1.16).

The dominant climatic influence is the latitudinal difference in solar radiation and air temperature, with maximum air temperatures of greater than 28°C over the equatorial region. Seasonal variation in temperature becomes significant only with distance from the equator. The latitudinal gradient is disturbed by the ocean circulation, particularly along the eastern edge of the Pacific, due to cool ocean currents. Westward ocean currents and trade winds result in the accumulation of warmer air over the western central Pacific (Figure 1.17).

The spatial pattern of precipitation is more complex than that of air temperature, as a result of the dependence on rising motion within the atmosphere. Island rainfall is strongly affected by the location of convergence zones such as the ITCZ and SPCZ, sea-surface temperatures, the passage of midlatitude troughs, depressions, and their associated frontal systems, and the interaction of maritime air masses with island topography.

Figure 1.18 shows a region of maximum precipitation of over 3,000 mm annually slightly north of the equator. The shape of this region reflects the merging of the ITCZ and SPCZ over the western central Pacific. The areas of least precipitation occur over the high-pressure, eastern side of the North and South Pacific, with minimum values below 200 mm annually. The remainder of the Pacific Ocean receives between about 500 and 2,000 mm annually.

Some tropical islands, such as Fiji and the Cook Islands, experience distinct wet and dry seasons as a result of changes in the location and intensity of convection associated with the convergence zones. Seasonal variability is particularly evident

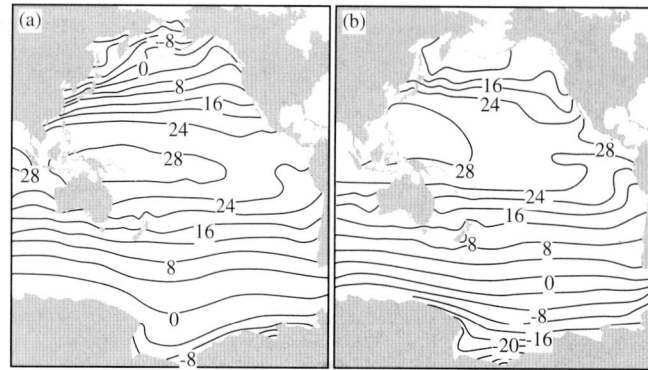

*Figure 1.17.* Distribution of mean air temperature (°C) over the Pacific Ocean during a) February and b) August (after Martyn 1992).

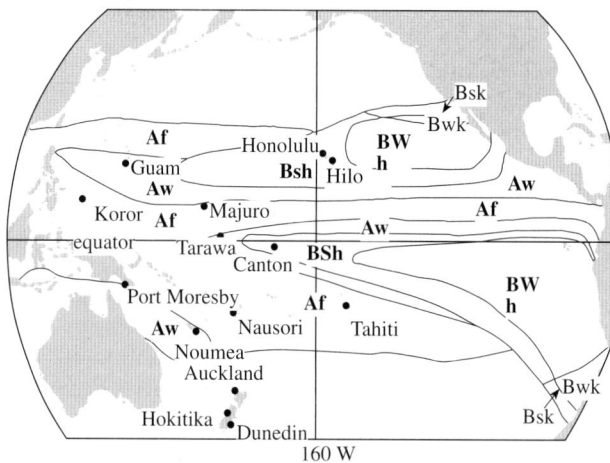

*Figure 1.16.* Classification of climate types across the Pacific (after Thomas 1963). The types are defined using the Köppen-Geiger method, which is based on temperature and rainfall. Minor topographically induced variations are not included. The classification codes are: A = tropical (hot) and wet enough for tall trees; Af = rain all year; Aw = dry season in winter; B = dry (hot or cold); BS = steppe-like climate; BSh = hot; BSk = cold; BW = desert; BWh = hot; BWk = cold.. New Zealand would be classified as type Cfb (mild humid, warm summers).

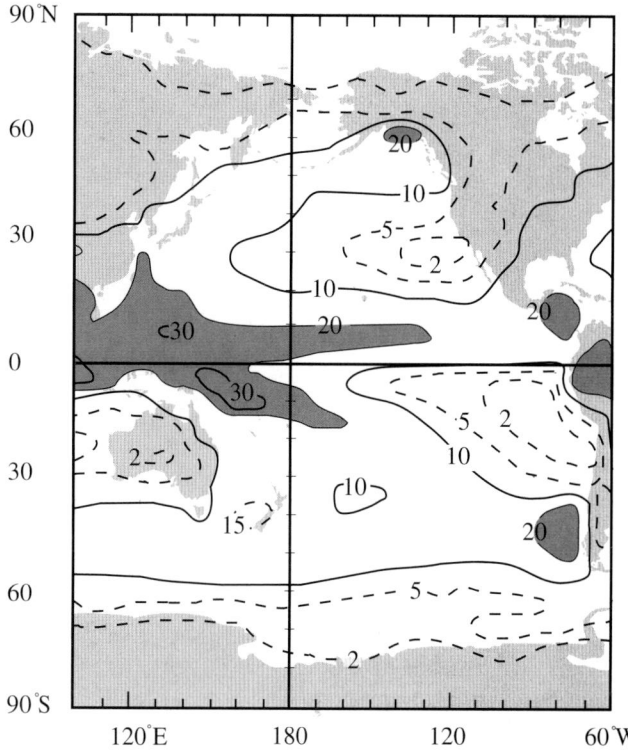

*Figure 1.18.* Distribution of annual mean precipitation (X 100 mm) over the Pacific Ocean (after Peixoto and Oort 1992).

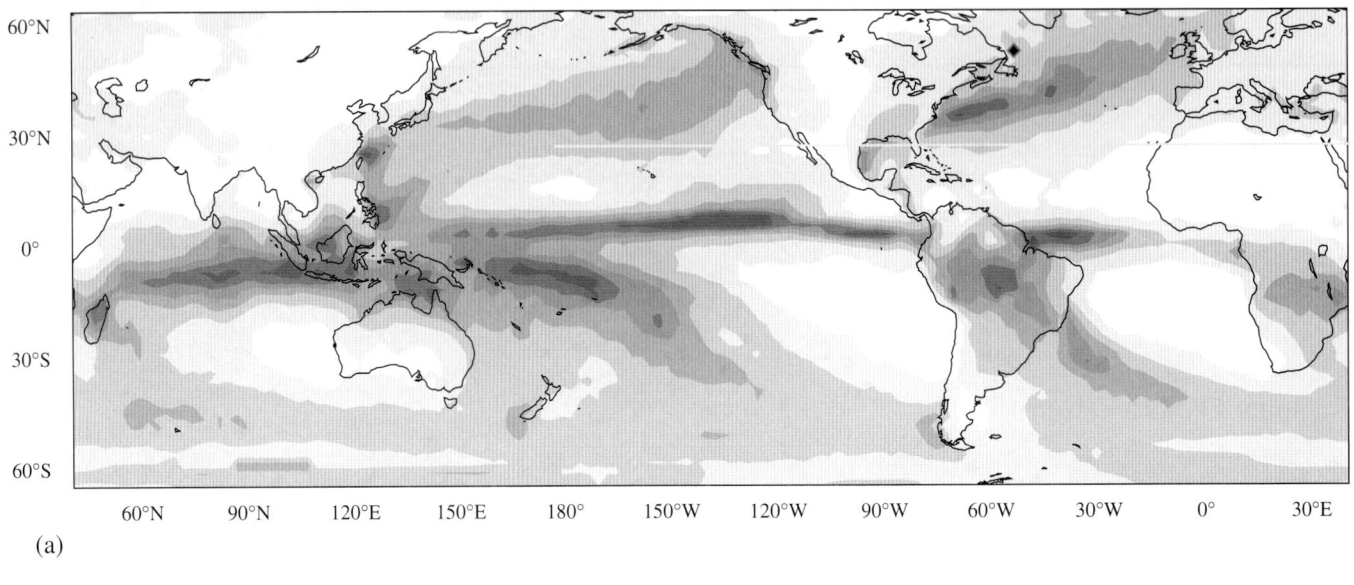

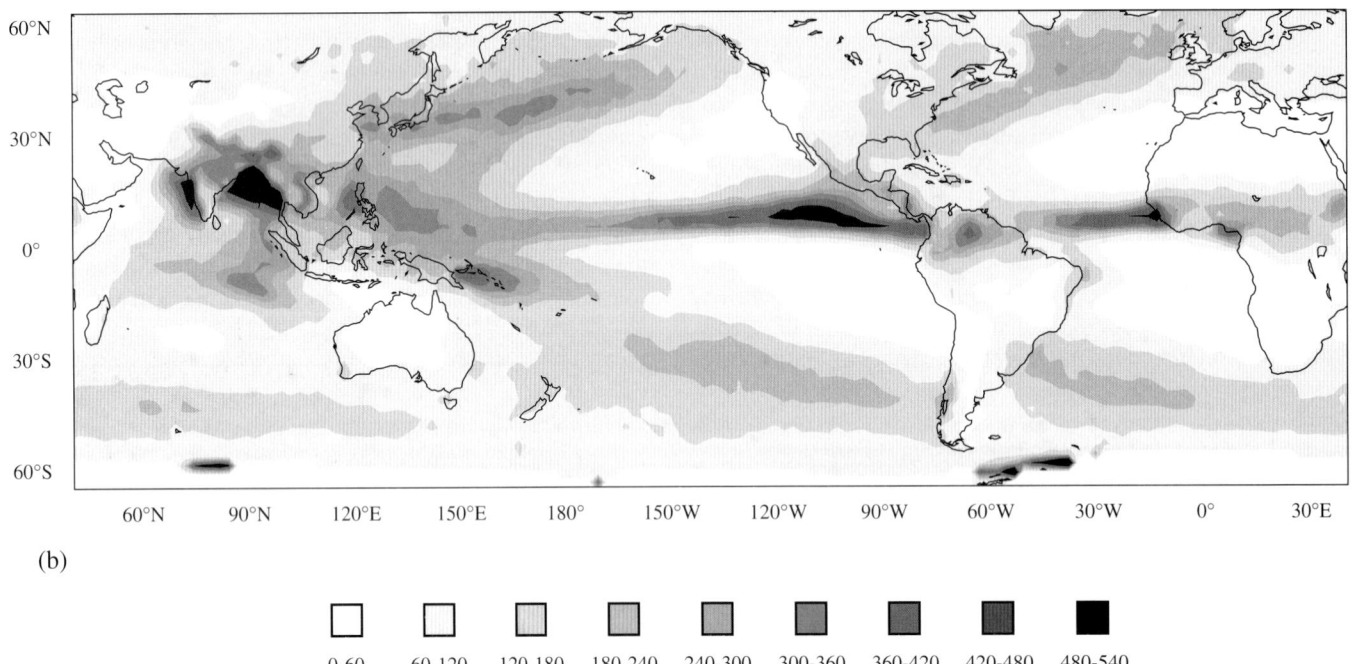

*Figure 1.19.* Mean monthly precipitation (mm) over the western South Pacific in a) January and b) July (after Wallace, Mitchell, and Lau 1995).

over the islands of the central South Pacific (Figure 1.19), where a relatively strong SPCZ results in heavy summer rainfall. A similar increase in rainfall occurs over the western North Pacific during summertime, when the ITCZ moves poleward. Some islands, such as Tuvalu and Kiribati, have two wet seasons as convergence zones migrate back and forth over them. At higher latitudes, fronts are responsible for the majority of annual precipitation totals.

Climate graphs (Figure 1.20) provide further illustration of the main climate regimes. Temperature follows obvious latitudinal effects, with warm, almost constant monthly averages observed at sites located close to the equator. The most extreme annual temperature variations are observed in New Zealand, while other sites lie somewhere in between. There is a clear seasonal cycle in rainfall. In the tropical South Pacific, peak rainfall occurs between January and April; north of the equator, peak values occur between July and October.

Island topography plays an important part in the nature of these rainfall variations, as illustrated by the two stations on Hawai'i. Similar differences in rainfall are illustrated between stations on either side of the Southern Alps of New Zealand (Hokitika and Dunedin). The pattern is made a little complicated by time lag differences between some sites. Canton Island provides an example of a hot, dry site dominated by the stable

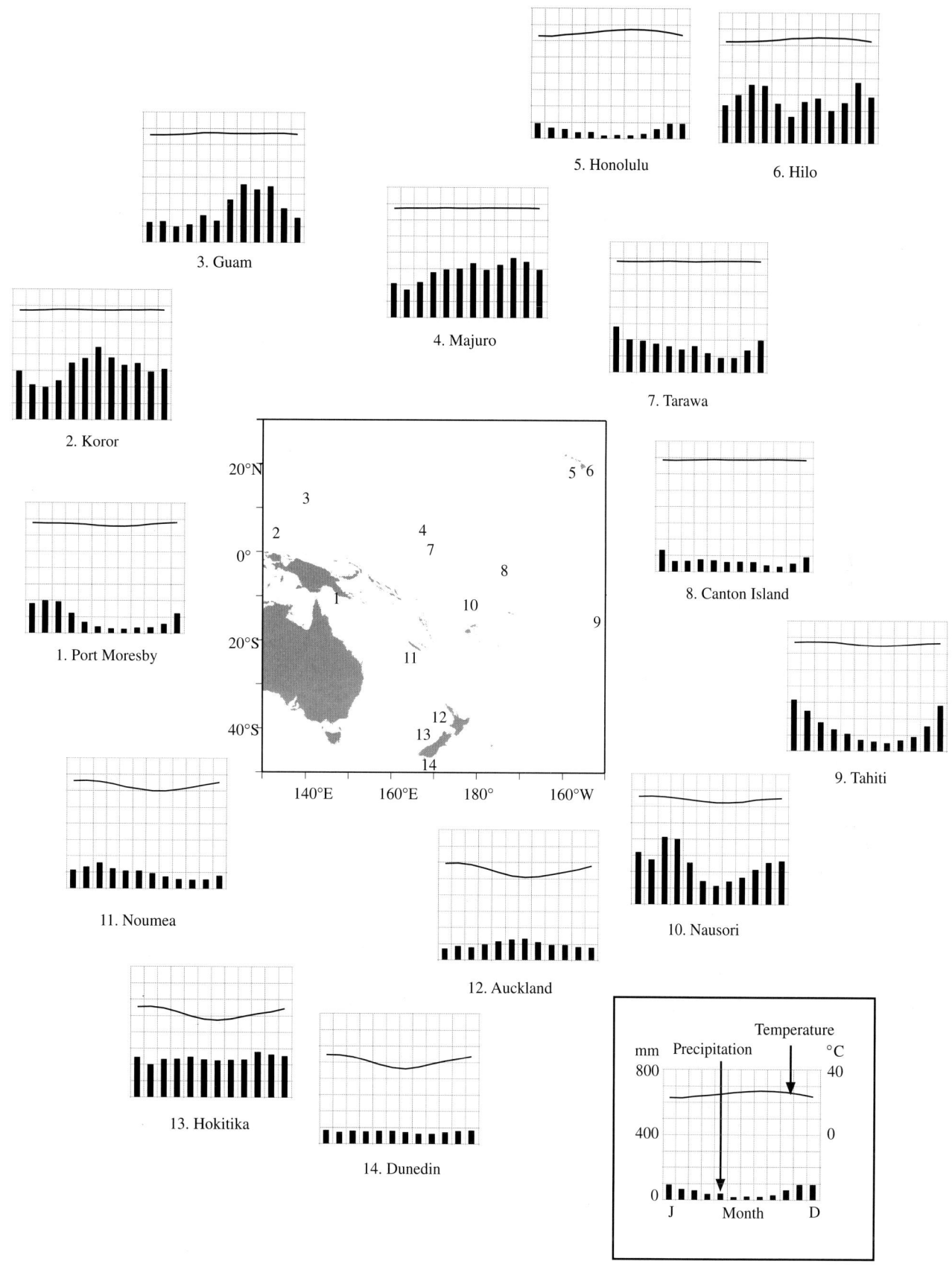

*Figure 1.20.* Graphs of temperature and rainfall for representative climate stations across the Pacific (data from Hoare 1996-1998).

The Pacific Islands

13

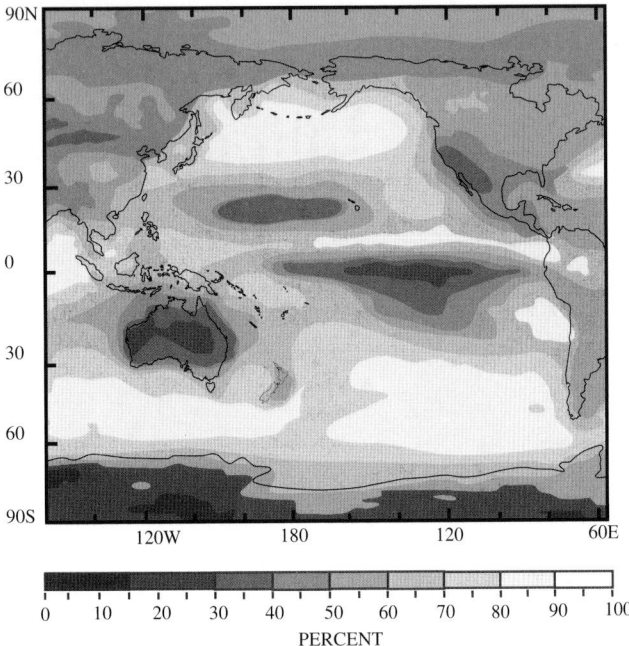

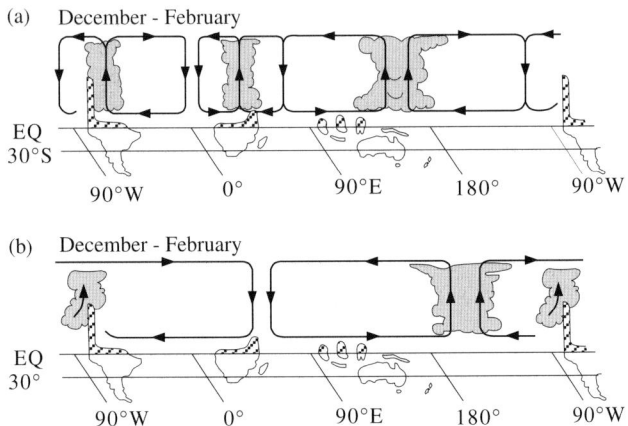

*Figure 1.22.* a) Typical Walker circulation and b) its breakdown during El Niño events (after World Meteorological Organization 1984).

*Figure 1.21.* Mean satellite-derived cloud amount over the Pacific Ocean, based on two years of data (after Rossow 1993).

trade wind regime.

The pattern of precipitation is related to that of cloud cover, with satellite imagery showing a relationship with the ITCZ and SPCZ (Figure 1.21). However, this relationship is not always clear, as some relatively dry areas may be dominated by cloud as well, such as the cold current regions over the eastern Pacific.

## Climate Change and Variability

Earlier sections have already identified some sources of climate variability experienced across this sector of the globe. This section will focus on long-term climate change and variability.

### El Niño–Southern Oscillation (ENSO)

The El Niño–Southern Oscillation phenomenon refers to periodic alterations in ocean-atmosphere circulation of the Pacific. It has significant effects on the weather and climate of this region, as well as on many other parts of the globe. The Southern Oscillation is represented by fluctuations in the intensity of the Walker circulation (Figures 1.3 and 1.22). When the La Niña predominates, strong trade winds drag warm surface water across the ocean toward the western central Pacific. At the same time, cooler water upwells along the coast of South America (Figure 1.23).

During El Niño events, ocean and atmospheric circulations slow down. Trade wind effects on ocean surface temperatures are reduced, affecting regional sea level (Figure 1.24) as well as water temperatures (Figure 1.25). The latter determine the productivity of the fisheries of areas such as the Peruvian coast (where the term El Niño originated). El Niño is also of global significance, with parts of the world as distant as Europe experiencing a recognizable ENSO influence.

The pressure difference measured between Tahiti and Darwin is used to monitor the strength of the Walker circulation and indicate La Niña (positive pressure anomaly) and El Niño events (negative pressure anomaly). The Southern Oscillation Index (SOI) is derived from this pressure difference (Sturman and Tapper 1996). Variations in this phenomenon have a periodicity of between two and ten years, although since the

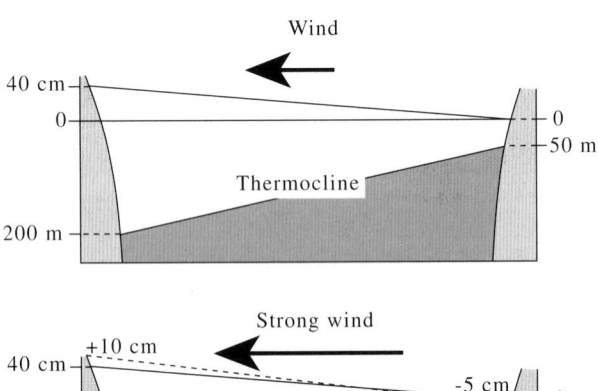

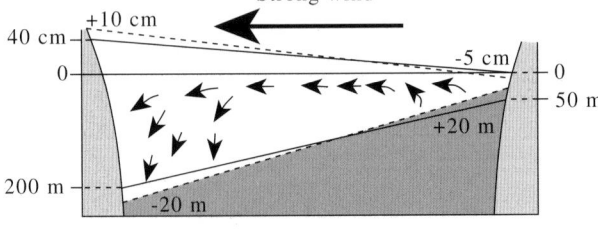

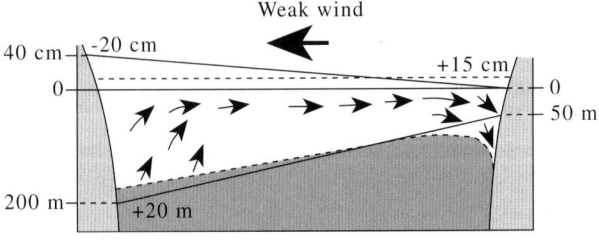

*Figure 1.23.* Link between surface wind and ocean circulation during changes in phase of the Walker circulation (after World Meteorological Organization 1984).

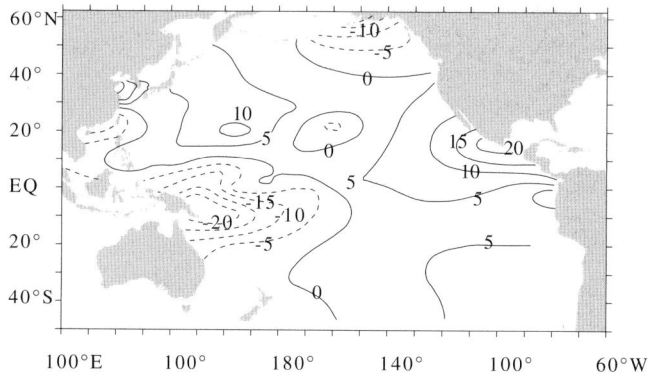

*Figure 1.24.* Height anomalies (cm) of the ocean surface over the Pacific Ocean during the 1986/7 El Niño (after World Meteorological Organization 1987).

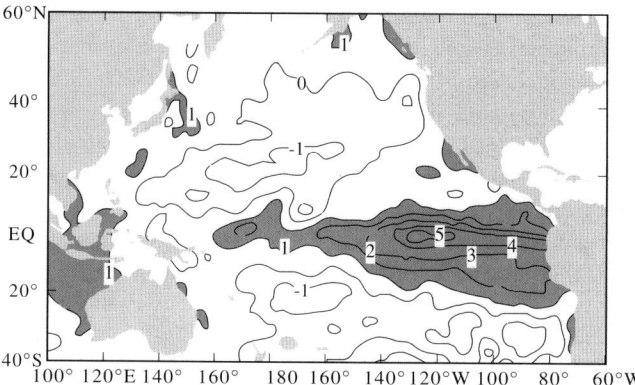

*Figure 1.25.* Sea-surface temperature anomalies (°C) over the central Pacific Ocean during the 1982/3 El Niño event (after World Meteorological Organization 1984). Warming greater than one degree is indicated by shading.

late 1970s there has been a tendency for more frequent El Niño events (Trenberth and Hoar 1996) (Figure 1.26).

Several climate features of the Pacific are affected by these ENSO events (Ropelewski and Halpert 1987). During El Niño, the normally wet western Pacific experiences drought conditions, a consequence of relatively higher pressures. Conversely, in the eastern Pacific the normal anticyclone is weakened, displacing the SPCZ to the north and east. Islands directly under the SPCZ during normal years will experience less rainfall during El Niño events; the reverse is true for islands lying at the margins of the SPCZ (Mullan 1992).

Farther from the equator, the Hawaiian Islands experience below-normal rainfall in the winter and spring of the year following an El Niño (Schroeder 1993, Chu 1995). In the New Zealand region, the El Niño situation results in an increase in southwesterly flow. This interacts with orography to produce enhanced precipitation over the south and west of the country, with a decrease to the north and east (Gordon 1985, 1986).

During El Niño years, the SPCZ migrates north and east of its normal position, in parallel with a pool of warm water (that otherwise accumulates over the western central Pacific). As a result, a much larger region of the South Pacific is susceptible to tropical cyclone hazards (Figure 1.27). In the North Pacific, no relationship has been identified between the number of tropical cyclones and the ENSO phenomenon. However, it has been found that cyclones originate farther east when the SOI is negative and farther west when it is positive (Lander 1994).

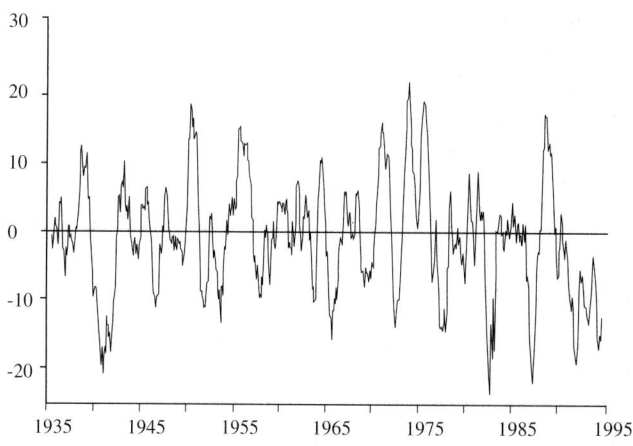

*Figure 1.26.* Variations in the Southern Oscillation Index 1935 to 1995 (after Sturman and Tapper 1996).

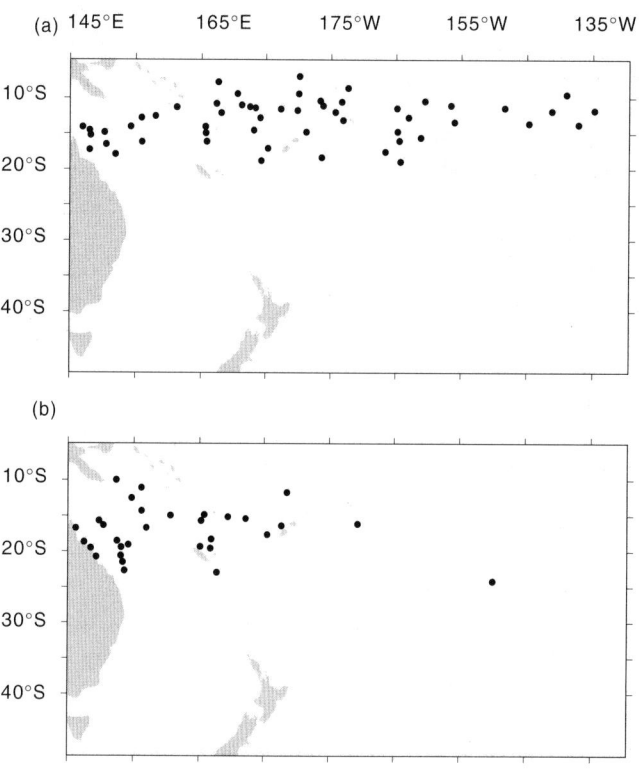

*Figure 1.27.* Points of origin of southwest Pacific tropical cyclones during a). El Niño and b) La Niña situations (after Hastings 1990).

The Pacific Islands

## Volcanic Eruptions

Volcanic eruptions can eject huge quantities of ash and gaseous sulphur into the atmosphere. Suspended particulates from such eruptions reduce radiation receipts. They may also act as condensation nuclei for rainfall. The most recent volcanic eruption to affect climate in the Pacific region (and globally) was the eruption of Mt. Pinatubo. The June 1991 eruptions lowered mean global temperatures following the eruption by several tenths of a degree (Parker et al. 1996) due to increased atmospheric turbidity.

Similar observations have been made following the eruptions of El Chichón (April 1982) and Krakatau (August 1883). Recent evidence suggests that these and similar large volcanic eruptions may trigger temperature fluctuations in the stratosphere that in turn may affect stratospheric circulation patterns (Parker et al. 1996). These may manifest themselves in tropospheric weather and climate anomalies, such as below- or above-average surface temperatures.

## The Enhanced Greenhouse Effect and Global Warming

Greenhouse gas emissions could have a profound impact on Pacific Island nations. Of particular concern are emissions of $CO_2$ from the combustion of carbon-based fuels and the continued destruction of tropical rain forests. Global warming due to enhancement of the greenhouse effect is predicted to result in a sea-level rise of between 13 and 94 cm by 2100 (Warrick et al. 1996). A sea-level rise at the top end of this range could accelerate coastal erosion and inundation of coastal lowlands and would have a dramatic impact on coral atolls.

Other possible impacts include an increase in the frequency of droughts and floods. The potential impact of climate change on the occurrence of tropical cyclones is uncertain (Pittock et al. 1995). One possible effect is an alteration of present tropical cyclone paths due to modification of large-scale circulation patterns. For example, a greater expanse of warm sea-surface temperatures, particularly in subtropical regions, may result in tropical cyclones' reaching midlatitude areas more frequently.

There is some suggestion that the enhanced greenhouse effect could produce a regional increase in precipitation (Pittock et al. 1995). Recently, analysis indicates a trend toward increasing precipitation over a large area of the tropical Pacific, extending from near the dateline on the equator to near 20°S and 140°W. However, two regions of decreasing precipitation on either side of the wetter region were also identified, including the Caroline Islands, Tonga, and the Cook Islands (Morrissey and Graham 1996).

The Amazon, the Congo, and the maritime continent centered on Indonesia are the three main regions of convection on the globe. There is concern that deforestation in these areas may cause serious climate change, resulting from impacts on the large-scale global circulation. Global circulation models (GCM's) have been used to predict future climatic conditions in these regions, suggesting that deforestation will increase local air temperature by approximately 2°C and reduce rainfall and evaporation by 20% to 30% (Eltahir 1996).

In general, large areas of tropical rain forest, as occur in Irian Jaya and Papua New Guinea, contribute strongly to large-scale atmospheric circulation, as they trigger and enhance vertical air motion. Their removal may not only significantly modify local weather and climate as already outlined, but potentially weaken these circulations, thereby possibly affecting the weather and climate of the Pacific Basin.

## Summary

The weather and climate of the Pacific Island region have a significant impact on the lives of the people living there. As discussed in this chapter, the atmosphere provides a number of hazards, due to such extreme events as localized thunderstorms, tropical cyclones, floods, and droughts. Through development of knowledge about this region, it is possible to improve the accuracy of forecasts of these phenomena and therefore to reduce possible impacts on human activity.

In the long term, there is concern about possible impacts of global warming, in regard to the frequency and intensity of atmospheric hazards, as well as sea-level rise. Decadal-scale climate fluctuations also create problems for the local inhabitants, as seen with the Southern Oscillation. In this case, the complex interaction of atmospheric and oceanic circulation can lead to floods, drought, and reduction in the viability of fisheries.

Although the island peoples have traditionally operated a subsistence economy based on a plentiful supply of the basic necessities of life, it is apparent from contemporary knowledge of weather and climate that they have always had to respond to fluctuations and trends in atmospheric conditions. If the predicted effects of global warming come about, many island communities may well be unable to adapt. The response to changing conditions should be based on knowledge, in conjunction with careful planning and environmental management to ensure sustainability into the future.

However, the very extensive nature of the region and the fact that it is sparsely inhabited and mostly ocean has meant that knowledge of weather and climate processes in the Pacific Island region is far from complete. A good understanding has been obtained of the general circulation, but more knowledge is required of local and regional variability and its causes.

# Bibliography

Browning, K. A., C. W. Pardoe, and F. F. Hill. 1975. The nature of orographic rain at wintertime cold fronts. *Quarterly Journal of the Royal Meteorological Society* 101:435–452.

Browning, K. A. 1979. Structure, mechanism and prediction of orographically enhanced rain in Britain. *Global Atmospheric Research Programme Series*, No. 23, 88–114. Geneva: World Meteorological Organization.

Carlquist, S. 1980. *Hawaii, a natural history*. Hawaii: The Pacific Tropical Botanical Garden.

Chen, Y., and A. J. Nash. 1994. Diurnal variation of surface airflow and rainfall frequencies on the island of Hawaii. *Monthly Weather Review* 122:34–56.

Chu, P. S. 1995. Hawaii rainfall anomalies and El Niño. *Journal of Climate* 8:1697–1703.

Cotton, W. R., and R. A. Anthes. 1989. *Storm and cloud dynamics*. San Diego: Academic Press.

Ding Yihui. 1994. *Monsoons over China*. Dordrecht: Kluwer Academic.

Eltahir, E. A. B. 1996. Role of vegetation in sustaining large-scale atmospheric circulations in the tropics. *Journal of Geophysical Research* 101:4255–4268.

Fitzharris, B., I. Owens, and T. Chinn. 1992. Snow and glacier hydrology. Chapter 5 in *Waters of New Zealand*, ed. M.P. Mosley, 75–94. Christchurch, New Zealand: The Caxton Press.

Gordon, N. D. 1985. The Southern Oscillation: a New Zealand perspective. *Journal of the Royal Society of New Zealand* 15:137–155.

Gordon, N. D. 1986. The Southern Oscillation and New Zealand weather. *Monthly Weather Review* 114:371–387.

Gray, W. M. 1975. *Tropical cyclone genesis*. Atmospheric Science Paper 234. Fort Collins, Colorado: Colorado State University.

Griffiths, G. A., and M. J. McSaveney. 1983. Distribution of mean annual precipitation across some steepland regions of New Zealand. *New Zealand Journal of Science* 26:197–209.

Gyakum, J. R., J. R. Anderson, R. H. Grumm, and E. L. Gruner. 1989. North Pacific cold season surface cyclone activity: 1975–1983. *Monthly Weather Review* 117:1141–1155.

Hastenrath, S. 1988. *Climate and circulation of the tropics*. Dordrecht: Reidel.

Hastings, P. A. 1990. Southern Oscillation influences on tropical cyclone activity in the Australian/southwest Pacific region. *International Journal of Climatology* 10:291–8.

Hoare, R. 1996-98. World climate, weather and rainfall data. http://worldclimate.com.

Holgate, H. T. D. 1973. Rainfall forecasting for river authorities. *Meteorological Magazine* 102:33–38.

Holland, G. J. 1993. "Ready Reckoner." Chapter 9 in Global guide to tropical cyclone forecasting, WMO/TC–No. 560, Report No. TCP–31. Geneva: World Meteorological Organization.

Joint Typhoon Warning Center. 1993. *Distribution of western North Pacific tropical cyclones*. 1993 Annual Tropical Cyclone Report, NTIS AD A235097, JTWC.

Juvik, J. O., and D. Nullet. 1994. A climate transect through tropical montane rain forest in Hawaii. *Journal of Applied Meteorology* 33:1304–1312.

Lander, M. A. 1994. An exploratory analysis of the relationship between tropical storm formation in the western North Pacific and ENSO. *Monthly Weather Review* 122: 636–651.

Martyn, D. 1992. *Climates of the world*. Developments in Atmospheric Science 18. Amsterdam and New York: Elsevier.

McAlpine, J. R., G. Keig, and R. Falls. 1983. *Climate of Papua New Guinea*. Canberra, Australia: Australian National University Press.

McKendry, I. G. 1989. Numerical simulation of sea breezes over the Auckland region, New Zealand—air quality implications. *Boundary-layer Meteorology* 9:7–22.

Miller, A., and R. A. Anthes. 1985. *Meteorology*. Columbus, Ohio: Merrill.

Morrissey, M. L., and N. E. Graham. 1996. Recent trends in rain gauge precipitation measurements from the Tropical Pacific: evidence for an enhanced hydrologic cycle. *Bulletin of the American Meteorological Society* 77:1207–1219.

Mullan, A. B. 1992. Atmospheric circulation processes and features in the tropical Southwest Pacific. *Weather and Climate* 12:59–72.

Omolayo, A. S. 1991. Forecasting freak winds in Fiji. *Proceedings of the conference: South Pacific environments; interactions wth weather and climate, 2–7 September 1991*, ed. John E. Hay, 143–144. Auckland, New Zealand: University of Auckland.

Parker, D. E., H. Wilson, P. D. Jones, J. R. Christy, and C. K. Folland. 1996. The impact of Mount Pinatubo on world-wide temperatures. *International Journal of Climatology* 16:487–497.

Peixoto, J. P., and A. H. Oort. 1992. *Physics of climate*. New York: American Institute of Physics.

Pielke, R. A. 1990. *The hurricane*. London: Routledge.

Pittock, A. B., M. R. Dix, K. J. Hennessy, J. J. Katzfey, K. L. McInnes, S. P. O'Farrell, I. N. Smith, R. Suppiah, K. J. Walsh, P. H. Whetton, S. G. Wilson, D. R. Jackett, and T. J. McDougall. 1995. Progress toward climate change scenarios for the Southwest Pacific. *Weather and Climate* 15:21–46.

Ramage, C. S. 1971. *Monsoon meteorology*. New York and London: Academic Press.

Revell, C. G. 1981. *Tropical cyclones in the southwest Pacific, November 1969 to April 1979*. Miscellaneous Publication 170, Wellington: New Zealand Meteorological Service.

Ropelewski, C. F., and M. S. Halpert, 1987. Global and regional scale precipitation patterns associated with the El Niño/Southern Oscillation. *Monthly Weather Review* 115:1606–1626.

Rossow, W. B. 1993. Clouds. In *Atlas of satellite observations related to global change*, ed. R. J. Gurney, J. L. Foster, and C. L. Parkinson, 141–163. Cambridge: Cambridge University Press.

Schroeder, T. 1993. Climate controls. In *Prevailing trade winds: climate and weather in Hawaii*, ed. M. Sanderson, 12–72. Honolulu: University of Hawai'i Press.

Strahler, A. N., and A. H. Strahler. 1978. *Modern physical geography*. John Wiley: New York.

Streten, N. A., and J. W. Zillman. 1984. Climate of the South Pacific Ocean. In *Climates of the oceans*, ed. H. van Loon, World Survey of Climatology, Amsterdam: Elsevier.

Sturman, A. P., and N. J. Tapper. 1996. *The weather and climate of Australia and New Zealand*. Melbourne: Oxford University Press.

Taylor, R. C. 1973. *An atlas of Pacific Islands rainfall data*. Hawai'i Institute of Geophysics. 25 HIG-73-9, Honolulu: University of Hawai'i.

Thomas, W. L. 1963. The variety of physical environments among Pacific Islands. In *Man's place in the island ecosystem: a symposium*, ed. F. R Fosberg, 7–37. Honolulu: Bishop Museum Press.

Thompson, C. S. 1987. *The climate and weather of Tuvalu*. Miscellaneous Publication 188(6), Wellington: New Zealand Meteorological Service.

Thompson, C., S. Ready, and X. Zheng. 1992. *Tropical cyclones in the Southwest Pacific: November 1979 to May 1989*. Wellington: New Zealand Meteorological Service.

Tomlinson, A. I., and B. Nicol. 1976. *Tornado reports in New Zealand: 1961–1975*. Technical Note 229, Wellington: New Zealand Meteorological Service.

Trenberth, K. E. 1991. General characteristics of El Niño–Southern Oscillation. In *Teleconnections linking worldwide climate anomalies,* ed M.H. Glantz, R.W. Katz, and N. Nicholls, Cambridge: Cambridge University Press.

Trenberth, K. E., and T. J. Hoar. 1996. The 1990–1995 El Niño–Southern Oscillation event: longest on record. *Geophysical Research Letters* 23:57–60.

Tualevao, P. N. 1991. The climate and weather system of W. Samoa. *Proceedings of the conference: South Pacific environments; interactions with weather and climate, 2–7 September 1991,* ed. John E. Hay, 166–175. Auckland, New Zealand: University of Auckland.

Vincent, D. G. 1994. The South Pacific convergence zone (SPCZ): a review. *Monthly Weather Review* 122:1949–1970.

Wallace, J. M., T. P. Mitchell, and A.R.-H. Lau. 1995. Legates/MSU precipitation climatology. http://tao.atmos.washington.edu/legates_msu.

Warrick, R. A., C. Le Provost, M. F. Meier, J. Oerlemans, and P. L. Woodworth. 1996. Changes in sea level. In *Climate Change 1995: the science of climate change,* ed. J. T. Houghton, L. G. Meira Filho, B. A. Callander, N. Harris, A. Kattenberg, and K. Maskell, 363–405. Cambridge: Cambridge University Press.

World Meteorological Organization. 1984. *The global climate system— a critical review of the climate system during 1982–84.* Geneva: World Climate Data Program.

World Meteorological Organization. 1987. *Climate system monitoring.* Monthly Bulletin, No. 1987–8, August, World Geneva: Climate Program.

# Oceanography

*Lynne D. Talley, Gerard J. Fryer, and Rick Lumpkin*

## Introduction

This is a brief introduction to the physical oceanography of the Pacific Island region: the circulation, tsunamis, waves, temperature and salinity distributions, and the forces that create these. Since the tropical Pacific contains most of the island groups, and since the dynamics and properties of the tropical oceans differ somewhat from those at higher latitudes, this chapter primarily concerns tropical oceanography, but New Zealand is also briefly discussed.

The tropical Pacific is usually considered to lie between the astronomically defined tropics: the Tropic of Cancer (23.5°N) and the Tropic of Capricorn (23.5°S). There are other useful definitions of the tropics, based on how far the effect of the equator extends to the north and south in the atmosphere—approximately 20°. Within the ocean itself, the currents within 15° to 20° of the equator are oriented much more east-west than the currents at higher latitudes.

The tropics are a region of excess heating from the sun and towering cloud convection and rainfall in narrow latitudinal bands. Compared with areas at higher latitudes, the frequency of storms and the average strength of the winds are low. Because these conditions affect the average height of surface waves, the wave climate of the tropics is relatively mild. However, tsunamis can pose an important danger, particularly in certain locations.

The tropical Pacific is the center of the global climate cycle known as El Niño, which occurs every three to seven years. When the easterly trade winds weaken in the tropical Pacific, warm water builds up across the equatorial Pacific. This further changes the weather patterns in the atmosphere above, and the changes are propagated enormous distances around the globe.

## Surface Waves, Tides and Tsunamis

The ocean is constantly moving. Surface waves are what catch our eyes; they are created by wind blowing over the sea surface either nearby (small or choppy waves) or far away (long ocean swell). We are also usually aware of the daily or twice daily cycle of tides, as beaches and reefs are successively covered and exposed. At times of the year when tides are very high and storms create large surface waves, storm surges can become a problem in low-lying coastal areas. Once in a long while, residents of coastal areas may be affected by a large and long-period wave called a tsunami, generated by an earthquake either nearby or very far away. These three types of waves, which have periods of minutes to hours, are described in this section.

### Surface Waves

The wave climate of the Pacific Island region is dominated by long-period swell reaching the area from distant storms, by relatively low amplitude, short-period waves generated by more local winds, and the occasional bursts of energy associated with intense local storms.

Waves are characterized by their wavelength (distance between crests or troughs), their period (time between successive passage of a crest past a fixed point), and their height (crest to trough). Each type of wave can also be characterized by its restoring force. For surface waves, the restoring force to perturbations in sea-surface height is gravity, and so the waves are sometimes referred to as surface gravity waves. (For the very small "capillary" waves, the restoring force is the surface tension.)

Surface waves are mostly created by wind blowing across the sea surface. (The exceptions are the tides and tsunamis, which are described in the following sections.) If the wind persists, longer and longer waves are generated. The wave heights build proportionally to the strength and duration of the wind. Local waves forced by the wind travel in the direction of the wind. The period of a wave is the time between the passing of successive crests. For wind-generated waves, periods are on the order of seconds to many minutes for the shortest to the longest waves, respectively.

A large storm generates surface waves moving in all different directions under the storm. These travel away from the storm location, so if the storm is localized, waves will radiate outward from the storm area. The longer the waves, the faster they travel. Short waves are damped out much more rapidly by friction than are long waves. Long waves generated by storms at high latitudes, such as in the Gulf of Alaska, or far south in the Antarctic (or generated by earthquakes) can travel clear across the Pacific without much attenuation.

Typically the sea state (field of waves) is a jumble of waves of many different wavelengths, moving in many directions since the wind forcing can be in many different directions. In the tropical Pacific, the wave field can be thought of as a superposition of waves forced by the local trade winds—the trade wind sea—and waves forced by distant storms. The trade wind sea is of small amplitude, and choppy since it is produced locally by winds that shift. The long-period swell from faraway storms is of relatively low amplitude in the open ocean, and much more unidirectional than the trade wind sea.

The height of waves is now determined by various satellite sensors. A measure commonly used is significant wave height, which is the average height of the highest one-third of the waves, where the height is measured from trough to crest. NASA routinely produces maps of significant wave height from satellite altimetry information. The altimeter measures the height of the sea surface, although the significant wave height is actually constructed from the properties of the radar pulse. Maps and information are available online, both for previous years and also in near real-time. Monthly analyses for the globe show that the average wave height in the tropical Pacific is typically less than 3 m, regardless of season, whereas wave height at high latitudes in the winter hemisphere typically reaches 3-6 m due to large storms (Color Plate 2A).

As waves reach the shallow waters of a reef and island, they increase in amplitude, and eventually break. The short-period, trade wind sea produces relatively small surf height because of the short wavelengths. Large surf is produced by the long-period swell from distant storms associated with the correspondingly longer wavelength. The north shores of the Pacific Islands receive this long-period swell in the northern hemisphere winter, and the south shores in the southern hemisphere winter. Wave heights of 6 m in the surf zone are not uncommon. Surf from the winter swell on the north shore of O'ahu occasionally reaches over 15 m (Flament et al. 1997).

Because most Pacific islands are small and rise steeply from the sea floor, there is little shelf area that can affect the progress of the long waves. (Continental shelves typically refract waves.) Thus the waves impinge directly on the shore or reef and do not wrap around the islands.

Breaking waves contain a lot of energy, some of which goes into production of local currents—first into longshore currents and then into rip currents that carry water back out to sea. Most of the circulation in the surf zone, and in lagoons inside reefs, is produced by breaking waves.

## Tides

Tides are produced by the gravitational attraction between the Earth and the moon and sun, and the centrifugal force on the Earth pulling in the opposite direction. Since the orbits of these bodies are regular, tides are regular, and are in fact the only part of the ocean's motion that can be exactly predicted. A full description of the tidal potential is beyond the scope of this text; the reader is referred to texts such as those of Knauss (1997) or Neshyba (1987).

The complete tide is a composite of the moon (lunar) and sun (solar) tides. The gravitational attraction between the Earth and moon (and to a lesser degree the sun) creates bulges of water on opposite sides of the Earth. The water bulge nearest the moon is due to domination of gravitational attraction over centrifugal force; the water bulge opposite the moon is due to domination of centrifugal force. Since the Earth rotates daily, a point on the Earth passes through these bulges twice a day, resulting in semidiurnal (twice daily) components to the tide at each location. Because the moon does not generally lie over the equator, one of the bulges at a given point on the Earth is larger than the other, which lends a diurnal (daily) component to the tide.

A modulation of the tidal range results from the relative positions of the moon and the sun: when the moon is new or full, the moon and the sun act together to produce larger spring tides; when the moon is in its first or last quarter, smaller neap tides occur. The cycle of spring to neap tides and back is half the 27-day period of the moon's revolution around the Earth and is known as the fortnightly cycle. The combination of diurnal, semidiurnal, and fortnightly cycles dominates variations in sea level throughout the islands.

The geometry of the oceans—the basin shape, local coastline, bays, and even harbor geometry—has a major effect on the local behavior of the tides. On scales of oceanic basins, tides exist as very long waves propagating in patterns determined by their period and the geometry of the basin. Color Plate 2B shows the response of the Pacific to the tidal period of 23 h 56 min, the largest diurnal (once daily) component. The tidal amplitude is very low in the central Pacific, but is higher in the tropical region of Australia, New Guinea, and Indonesia, as well as far to the north in the Gulf of Alaska and subpolar region.

Lines along which high tide occurs at the same time (called phase lines, contours of constant color in Color Plate 2C) converge to several points where the tidal range is zero. There are four of these points, called amphidromes, in the Pacific: one in the North Pacific near the dateline, one near the equator in the

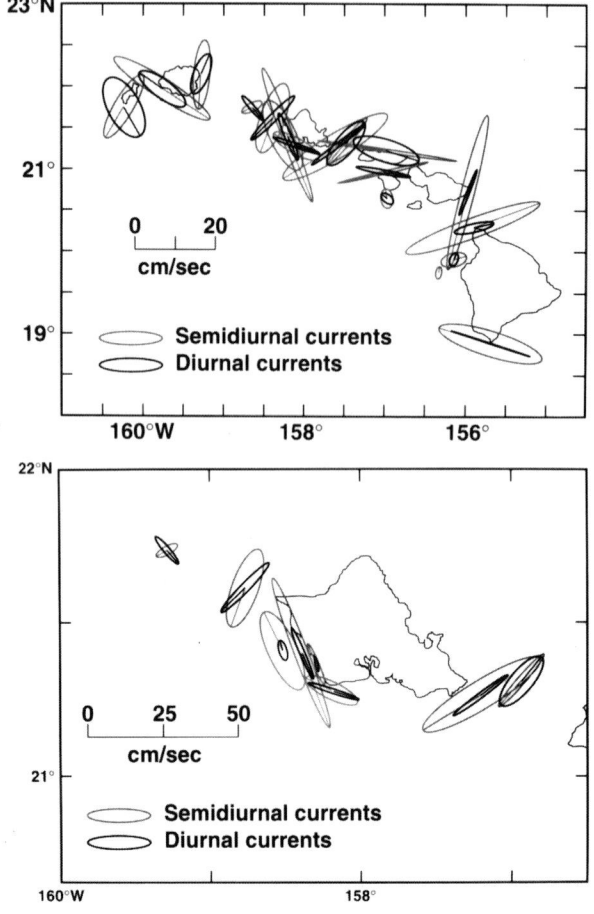

*Figure 2.1.* Tidal currents (cm/sec) at semi-diurnal (gray) and diurnal (black) periods for the Hawaiian Islands. The major axes of the ellipses show the most probable orientation and strength of tidal currents. Data were taken variously from 1960 to 1995 and were provided by the University of Hawai'i, Hawai'i Institute of Geophysics; National Ocean Data Center, NOAA, and Science Applications International Corporation (after Flament et al. 1997).

eastern North Pacific, one in the central South Pacific near Tahiti, and one east of New Zealand. Phase lines rotate counterclockwise around the amphidromes in the North Pacific and clockwise around the ones in the South Pacific. For example, at the Hawaiian Islands, the offshore diurnal tide reaches the island of Hawai'i first, then sweeps across Maui, O'ahu and finally Kaua'i. Local bathymetry affects the ranges and phases of the tides along the shore, as the tidal waves wrap around the islands. For example, high tide at Hale'iwa on the north shore of O'ahu occurs over an hour before high tide at Honolulu Harbor.

Tidal currents are associated with tidal variations of sea level, and near the shore are often stronger than the large-scale circulation. Complete mapping of tidal currents requires direct measurements. As an example, in Hawai'i (Figure 2.1) the semidiurnal and diurnal tidal currents tend to be aligned with the shoreline. Due to high variability of tidal currents around the islands, however, this statistical picture may not correspond to the flow at a particular time: tidal currents cannot be predicted as precisely as sea level. Strong swirls often result from tidal currents flowing around points and headlands and present hazards to divers.

## Tsunamis

When the seafloor is raised (or lowered) suddenly during a shallow earthquake, water is raised with it, producing a mound of excess water at the sea surface. Gravity collapses the mound, producing a series of waves: a tsunami. Tsunamis are gravity waves, just like those generated by the wind, but their period is much longer, on the order of 10 to 60 minutes. While earthquakes are the most common cause of tsunamis, the waves are generated by any phenomenon that rapidly changes the shape of the sea surface over a large area: volcanic eruption, landslide, even meteorite impact. Since the largest shallow earthquakes occur in the subduction zones that ring the Pacific, and since these same subduction zones are dotted with volcanoes, the tsunami hazard throughout the tropical Pacific is high.

On the open ocean, the wavelength of a tsunami may be as much as two hundred kilometers, many times greater than the ocean depth, which is on the order of several kilometers. This huge wavelength means that the entire water column, from surface to bottom, is set into motion. For typical ocean depths of 5 km, a tsunami will advance at 800 km/hr, about the speed of jet aircraft. A tsunami can therefore travel from one side of the Pacific to the other in less than a day. The speed decreases rapidly as the water shoals: in 15 m of water the speed of a tsunami (or of any wave with long enough wavelength to feel the ocean bottom) will be only 45 km/hr.

As the tsunami slows in shoaling water its wavelength is shortened. Just as with ordinary surf, the energy of the waves must be contained in a smaller volume of water, so the waves grow in height. Even though the wavelength has shortened, a tsunami will typically have a wavelength in excess of ten kilometers when it comes ashore. Each wave therefore floods the land (Figure 2.2) as a rapidly rising tide (hence the common English term tidal wave) lasting for several minutes, posing serious danger to some areas. The individual waves are typically

*Figure 2.2.* Third wave of a tsunami from the Aleutian Islands running ashore on the island of O'ahu, Hawai'i, in 1957. Runup here is about 2 m (NOAA photo).

from ten to thirty minutes apart, so the danger period can last for hours.

Runup (maximum height the tsunami reaches on shore) can vary dramatically depending on seafloor topography. Small islands with steep slopes experience little runup; wave heights there are only slightly greater than on the open ocean (around 1 m). For this reason the smaller Polynesian islands with steep-sided fringing or barrier reefs are only at moderate hazard from tsunamis. Such is not the case for the Hawaiian Islands or the Marquesas, however. Both of these island chains are almost devoid of barrier reefs and have broad bays exposed to the open ocean. Hilo Bay at the island of Hawai'i and Tahauku Bay at Hiva Oa are especially vulnerable. During a tsunami from the Eastern Aleutians in 1946, runup exceeded 8 m at Hilo and 10 m at Tahauku; 59 people were killed in Hilo, two in Tahauku (Shepard et al. 1950, Talandier 1993). Similarly, any gap in a reef puts the adjacent shoreline at risk. The tsunami from the Suva earthquake of 1953 did little damage because of Fiji's extensive offshore reefs. Two villages on Viti Levu located opposite gaps in the reef, however, were extensively damaged and five people were drowned (Singh 1991).

Tsunamis are generated by shallow earthquakes all around the Pacific, but those from earthquakes in the tropical Pacific tend to be modest in size. While such tsunamis may be devastating locally, they decay rapidly with distance and are usually not observed more than a few hundred kilometers from their sources. That is not the case with tsunamis generated by great earthquakes in the North Pacific or along the Pacific coast of South America. About half-a-dozen times a century a tsunami from one of these locations sweeps across the entire Pacific, is reflected from distant shores, and sets the entire ocean oscillating for days. The tsunami from the magnitude 9.5 Chile earthquake of 1960 (Figure 2.3) caused death and destruction throughout the Pacific: Hawai'i, Samoa, and Easter Island all recorded runups exceeding 4 m; 61 people were killed in Hawai'i, 200 in Japan. A similar tsunami in 1868 from northern Chile caused extensive damage in the Austral Islands, Hawai'i, Samoa, and New Zealand. There were several deaths in the Chatham Islands (Iida et al. 1967).

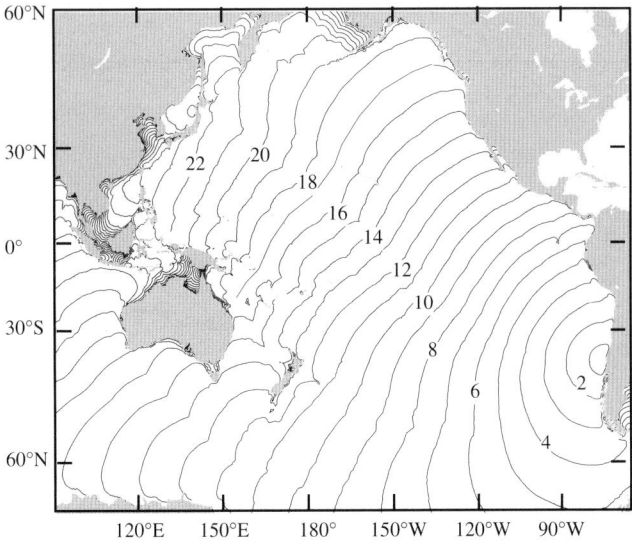

*Figure 2.3.* Travel times (hours) for the tsunami resulting from the magnitude 9.5 Chile earthquake of 1960.

The tsunami from a local earthquake may reach a nearby shore in less than ten minutes, making warning a difficult task (though in this case the shaking of the ground provides its own warning). For tsunamis from more distant sources, however, accurate warnings of a tsunami's arrival time are possible because tsunamis travel at a known speed. The current international tsunami warning system has twenty-six member nations that coordinate their warning activities through the Pacific Tsunami Warning Center in Hawai'i. The Hawai'i center uses seismic data from the global seismic network to identify and characterize potential tsunamigenic earthquakes, then verifies if a tsunami has been generated by querying tide gauge stations near the source. While the system is far from perfect (about half of the warnings are false alarms), performance is constantly improving and there have been no missed warnings.

## Temperature and Salinity Distribution in the Tropical Pacific

The temperature of the sea has a large effect on local climate (and what can grow in the water and on nearby land), fog and precipitation, production of hurricanes, and so on. The salt in seawater is what most obviously distinguishes it from fresh water and affects the ecology of coastal lagoons, tidal flats, and river mouths. The salt has less overt influence than temperature on climate, but it does affect how deeply the surface layer of the ocean can mix and hence affects the temperature of the surface layer; it thus has a subtle effect on climate.

### *Temperature*

Ocean surface temperature globally is dominated by excess heating in the tropics compared with higher latitudes, resulting mainly from higher radiation from the sun in the tropics. This leads to a sea-surface temperature difference from equator to pole of about 30°C (Figure 2.4). In the tropics, including the

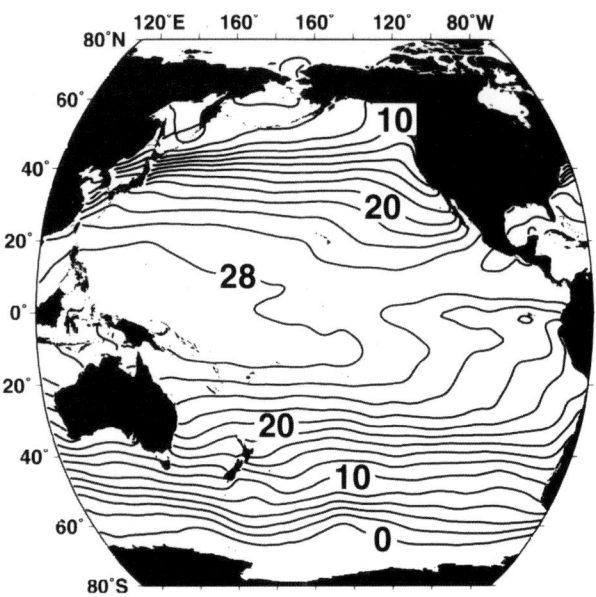

*Figure 2.4.* Surface temperature (annual mean) (°C). The gridded data are freely available from the National Oceanic and Atmospheric Administration atlas (Levitus et al. 1994a).

tropical Pacific, the maximum sea-surface temperature is around 28°C and can rise to at most 30°C. This is considerably cooler than the maximum temperatures of about 50°C regularly found over land. It is currently hypothesized that the main regulation on the maximum ocean temperature is through cloud formation. Cloud formation increases dramatically when the sea-surface temperature is greater than about 27.5°C (Graham and Barnett 1987). The increased cloudiness increases the albedo (reflectivity of the Earth/atmosphere to space), which reduces the solar radiation reaching the sea surface (Ramanathan and Collins 1993); and thus keeps the surface temperature from rising much more.

The sea-surface temperature is not uniformly high in the tropical Pacific. A large warm pool is found in the central and western Pacific (Figure 2.4), and also extends into the eastern Indian Ocean. Surface water in the eastern equatorial Pacific is

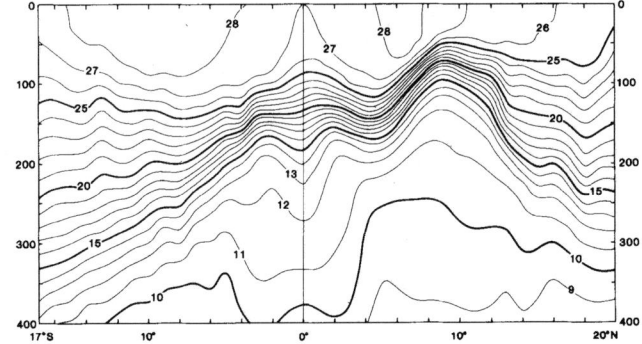

*Figure 2.5.* Mean subsurface temperature computed from 43 separate cross sections at 150° to 158°W, collected over a period of 17 months in 1979–1980 (Wyrtki and Kilonsky 1984.)

several degrees cooler than in the west. The vertical thermal structure of the upper ocean is responsible for these differences. In the western Pacific, the surface layer, which is fairly well mixed, is approximately 100 m thick and warmer than about 28°C. Just below this surface layer, the temperature changes rapidly downward; this is called the thermocline.

In the central and eastern Pacific, the surface layer is shallower, and so colder water and the thermocline are found closer to the surface. Upwelling in the eastern Pacific (caused by offshore current flows) draws this cooler water to the surface, creating the equatorial cold tongue at the sea surface. Upwelling of cold water at the equator is apparent in sections crossing the equator (Figure 2.5). Upwelling in the western Pacific is somewhat weaker than in the east and draws up only warm water, and so an equivalent cold tongue along the equator is absent.

Upwelling is common along the west coast of South America, off Ecuador and Peru, and along the west coast of Central and North America. As a result of both the upwelling and the eastern boundary currents that flow toward the equator in these regions, sea-surface temperatures are relatively low along these coasts. The winds that create upwelling are strongest in the area just west of Costa Rica. Here the thermocline is lifted to within 10 m of the sea surface and is called the Costa Rica Dome (Hofmann et al. 1981).

Below the sea-surface, temperature decreases to the ocean bottom (Figure 2.6). The most rapid change is in the upper 500 m, in the thermocline. Changes are more gradual below this. Temperature reaches about 1.2°C in the abyssal tropical Pacific. The initial temperature and salinity of all ocean water is set at the sea surface. The sea-surface temperature distribution (Figure 2.4) shows that water colder than about 18°C comes from latitudes higher than about 30°, hence outside the tropics. Waters of about 4°–6°C come from latitudes of about 40°–45° (northern and southern hemisphere). The coldest waters flow northward from the Antarctic region. These southern hemisphere waters, which fill the Pacific below 1,000 to 1,500 meters, are part of a circulation that extends through all of the oceans.

The deepest waters come from the Weddell and Ross Seas of the Antarctic and the Greenland Sea just north of the North Atlantic. The North Pacific does not produce any of this deep water, and so its deep waters have traveled a long distance from their sea-surface origin. These deep waters have spent about 500 years making the journey to the deep North Pacific (and slightly less time to the deep tropical Pacific). Waters that have been far from sea-surface forcing (heating/cooling and evaporation/precipitation) for a long time are fairly uniform because they mix with each other. Thus the deep Pacific contains a large amount of water in a very narrow range of temperature and salinity.

## Salinity

Sea water density depends on temperature (warm water is less dense), and also on the amount of material dissolved in the water. The latter is mostly what is referred to as sea salt, and is a combination of various salts. The total amount of salt in the world ocean is constant on all but the longest geological time scales. However, the total amount of fresh water in the ocean is not constant; it is affected by evaporation, precipitation, and runoff. Hence salinity, which is more or less the grams of salts dissolved in a kilogram of seawater, varies as a result of surface freshwater inputs and exports.

The total range of salinity in most areas of the ocean is small enough that temperature actually contributes more to sea water density differences, but salinity differences are significant. For instance, if saltier water lies above fresher water, then the temperature difference between the two must be large enough to ensure stability (light water over dense water).

Surface salinity in the Pacific (Figure 2.7) shows clearly the net result of the atmospheric circulation described in the Climate chapter. Cloud formation and high precipitation occur in regions of rising, humid air, which are associated with low atmospheric pressure at the sea surface, such as in the intertropical convergence zone (ITCZ) at 5°–10°N and subpolar regions poleward of 40°. Surface salinity is low where precipitation is high. Evaporation and hence surface salinity are high where the air is dry—regions of atmospheric divergence (high-pressure zones at the surface).

Because temperature dominates the vertical density differences in the ocean, it decreases downward almost everywhere. The salinity distribution can be more complex, with regions of salty water lying over fresher water and vice versa (Figure 2.8). Such salinity inversions are common. The high salinity in surface evaporation cells extends down to the thermocline. Below the high-salinity surface water is a layer of low-salinity intermediate water that extends from the rainy subpolar latitudes in the south and north toward the equator. Below this, the deep Pacific is filled with relatively more saline waters originating

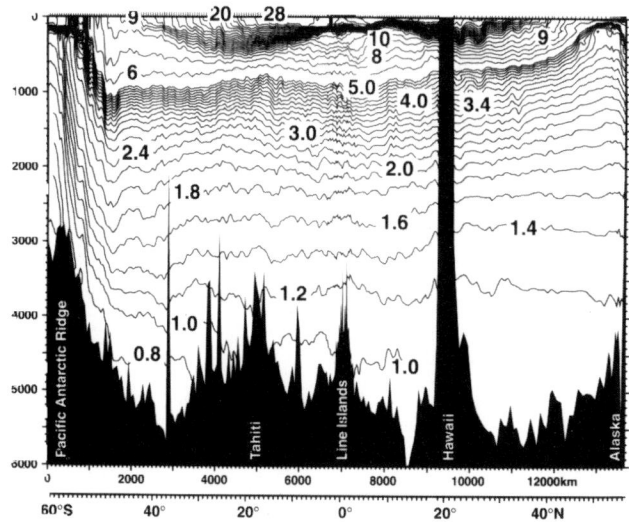

*Figure 2.6.* Vertical section of potential temperature (°C) along 150°W from data collected in 1991–1993 as part of the World Ocean Circulation Experiment. Data north of Hawai'i were collected in 1984 (Talley et al. 1991). Potential temperature is the temperature a parcel of water would have if moved to the sea surface with no change in heat content, and is lower than measured temperature since temperature increases when water is compressed due to the high pressure in the ocean.

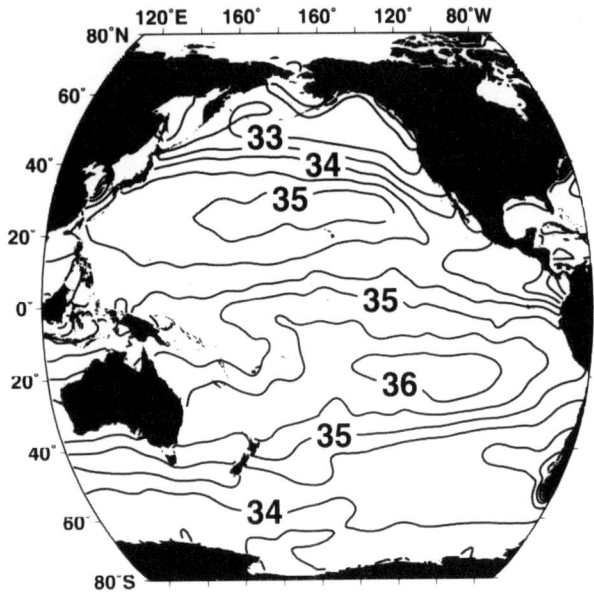

*Figure 2.7.* Surface salinity (annual mean). Data sources as in Figure 2.4 (Levitus et al. 1994b). Note: Salinity units are equivalent to parts per thousand.

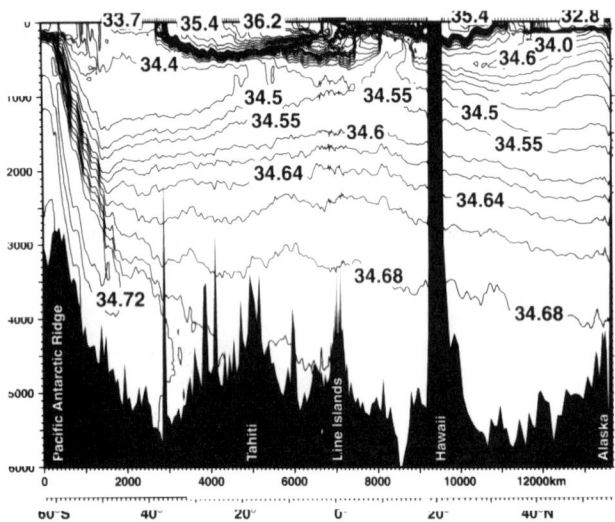

*Figure 2.8.* Vertical section of salinity along 150°W. Data sources are the same as for Figure 2.6.

from the deep waters around Antarctica and from the Atlantic.

Along the equator, surface salinity is lowest in the western Pacific, where normally there is much more rainfall than in the central and eastern equatorial Pacific. The freshest surface water in the western equatorial Pacific actually extends only partway down into the vertically uniform, warm surface layer, with salinity increasing strongly downward midway within this uniform temperature layer. A relatively sharp front separates the fresh western equatorial surface water from the more saline central Pacific surface water. During periods such as El Niño, when the trade winds slacken (see page 31), the western low-salinity, warm water floods eastward toward the central Pacific along the equator (Roemmich et al. 1994).

Biological productivity in the sunlit surface layer of the ocean (euphotic zone, about 100 m depth) relies on a continual supply of nitrate, phosphate, dissolved silica, and other nutrients. These are regenerated at depth as the decaying plants and animals and fecal pellets fall through the water column, with some portion, especially of the silica-bearing hard parts, reaching the ocean bottom. Thus nutrients are severely depleted in the surface layer, where they are used almost as quickly as they appear there. Nutrients are found in abundance below the surface layer, especially where waters have been separated from the sea surface for a long time.

Nutrients reach the euphotic zone through upwelling, and so upwelling regions have slightly higher nutrient content and much higher biological productivity than downwelling regions (see below). The most productive regions occur where upwelling is vigorous and where the nutrient-rich thermocline is near the sea surface. Near-surface nutrients in the Pacific are high in the equatorial and eastern tropical Pacific, where upwelling is high, and low in the subtropical downwelling regions poleward of about 20°.

## Ocean Circulation in the Tropical Pacific

Aside from the waves, tides, and tsunamis discussed thus far, the ocean also has large-scale current movements that vary slowly over weeks to months, years, and many decades. These affect navigation. Currents are also important in moving water from one place to another, which redistributes heat, salt, and nutrients.

### Surface Circulation

The Pacific sea-surface circulation (Figure 2.9) consists of two large subtropical gyres centered at 30°N and 30°S, which rotate clockwise in the northern hemisphere and counterclockwise in the southern hemisphere, a subpolar gyre centered at about 50°N and rotating counterclockwise, a major eastward flow that circles Antarctica called the Antarctic Circumpolar Current, and complicated but predominantly zonal (east-west or west-east) currents in the tropics between the gyres. Surface flow is westward between 30°S and 5°N (the South Equatorial Current). Between 5°N and 10°N lies a strong eastward flow (the North Equatorial Countercurrent), corresponding to the climatic intertropical convergence zone (ITCZ). The westward flow between 10°N and 30°N is called the North Equatorial Current. The South Pacific convergence zone, fluctuating in strength in the southern hemisphere, creates an occasional appearance of a South Equatorial Countercurrent.

In the western tropical Pacific, the circulation is dominated by strong currents that abut the western ocean boundary (Figure 2.10), but complicated by the many islands and deep ridges. Australia forms the largest single part of the boundary. In the North Pacific, the North Equatorial Current reaches the western boundary at Mindanao in the Philippines and then splits northward (Kuroshio Current) and southward (Mindanao Current). The Kuroshio is one of the strongest currents in the world, similar to the Gulf Stream in speed and transport. It

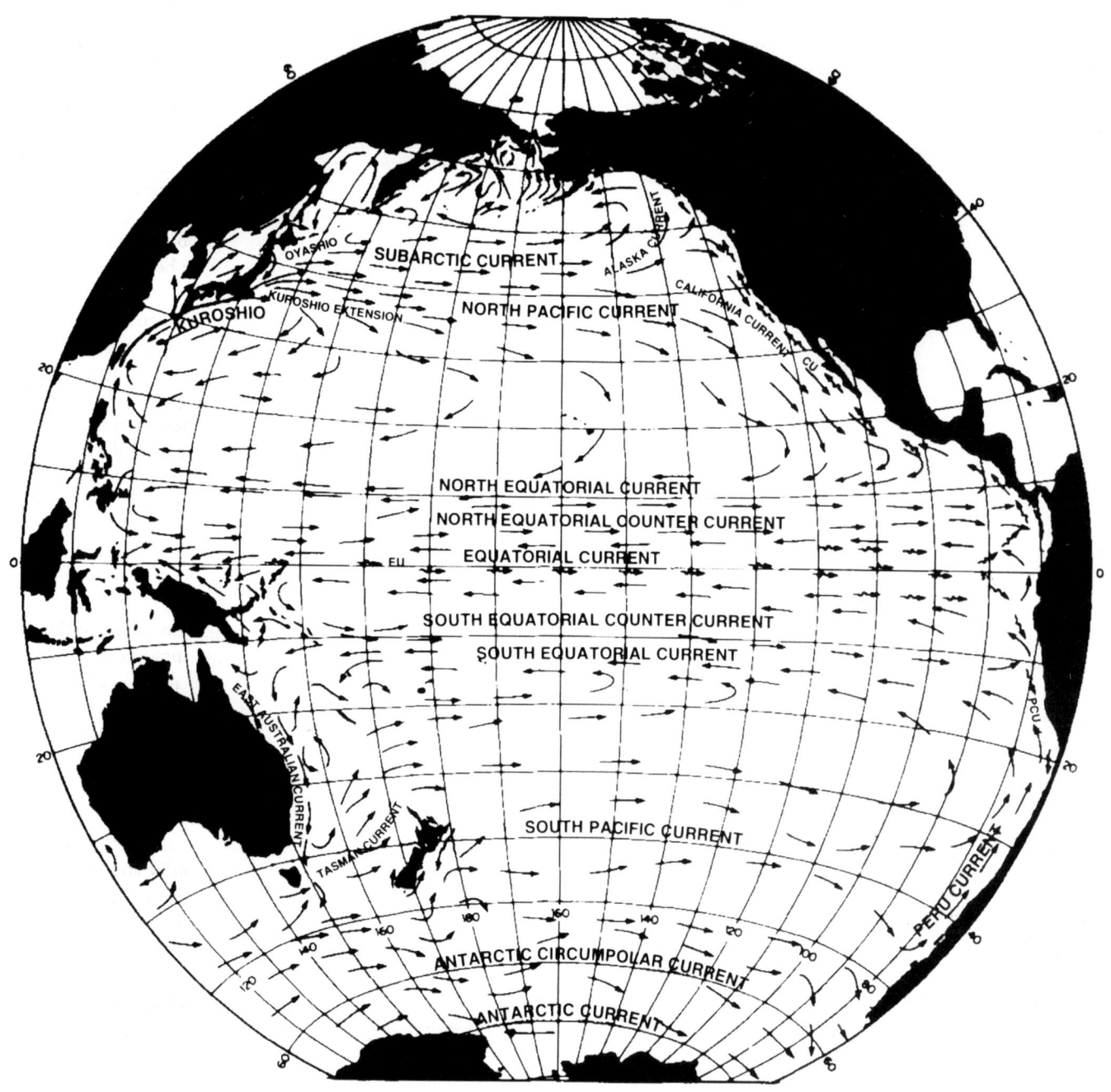

*Figure 2.9. Schematic of the surface circulation of the Pacific during the northern summer (after Tabata 1975). Undercurrent abbreviations: EU (equatorial undercurrent), PCU (Peru-Chile undercurrent).*

affects climate in Japan through its warmth and fisheries off Japan through both its warmth and relative lack of nutrients. The Mindanao Current separates from the coast of Mindanao around 5°N, flowing eastward into the North Equatorial Countercurrent and westward into the Celebes Sea. Eddies (circulations of about 50-200 km size that are often variable over a period of weeks to months) are usually found east of Mindanao and east of Halmahera. The water entering the Celebes Sea forms the beginning of flow westward through the complex of Indonesian islands, threading through to Java and thence into the Indian Ocean.

In the South Pacific, the very broad, westward-flowing South Equatorial Current reaches the western boundary through a complex of islands. The northern portion forms a northward-flowing western boundary current along New Guinea, called the New Guinea Coastal Current (Lindstrom et al. 1987, Tsuchiya et al. 1989). This flows northward to the equator. A portion of it turns eastward along the equator and apparently forms part of the eastward-flowing subsurface Equatorial Undercurrent. A portion may continue slightly northward, joined by the westward flow just north of the equator, and then turns eastward, joining the separated

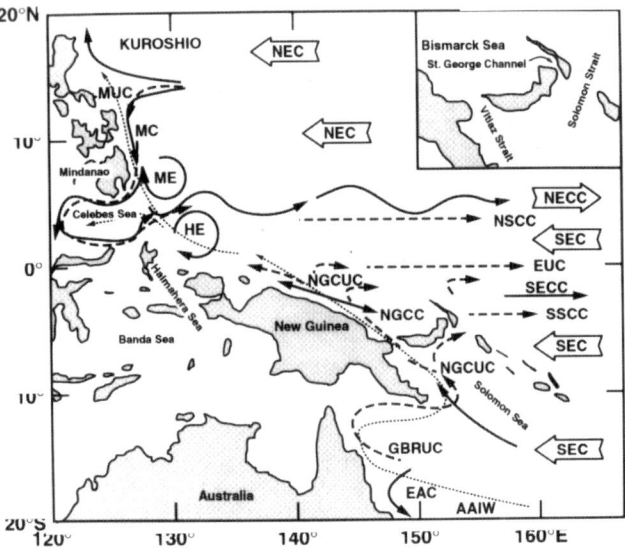

*Figure 2.10. Schematic of the surface circulation of the western tropical Pacific (Fine et al. 1994). Surface current abbreviations (solid arrows): NEC (North Equatorial Current), NECC (North Equatorial Countercurrent), SEC (South Equatorial Current), MC (Mindanao Current), NGCC (New Guinea Coastal Current), EAC (East Australia Current), ME (Mindanao Eddy), HE (Halmahera Eddy). Subsurface current abbreviations (dashed arrows): MUC (Mindanao Undercurrent), NGCUC (New Guinea Coastal Undercurrent), NSCC (North Subsurface Countercurrent), EUC (Equatorial Undercurrent), SSC (South Subsurface Countercurrent). The light dashed boundary shows the limit of the AAIW (Antarctic Intermediate Water), which is the low-salinity subsurface layer seen at about 700–800-m depth in Figure 2.8.*

Mindanao Current, into the North Equatorial Countercurrent.

The remainder of the westward-flowing South Equatorial Current flows north of Fiji into the Coral Sea and reaches the western boundary at Australia. Here it turns southward into the East Australian Current, which is the western boundary current, and then flows southward to the northern tip of New Zealand. At this point, the current meanders a great deal and some portion of it separates and flows eastward just north of New Zealand as the North Cape Current. The broad flow between New Zealand and Fiji is also eastward.

The large-scale surface flow is affected only by the larger land masses, and not much by the small islands dotting the tropical and South Pacific. Intermediate and abyssal flow however are strongly affected by the ridges in which the small islands are embedded, as described next.

## Subsurface Equatorial Circulation

The currents below the sea surface seem of less immediate importance to humans, as they do not affect sailing or have an obvious effect on local sea-surface conditions such as temperature. However, the surface and deeper flows are strongly coupled to each other. It has become clear in recent years that successful computer models of the ocean circulation must include the flow below the surface, all the way down to the ocean bottom, where undersea rises and mountains strongly steer the bottom currents.

In most places of the world ocean, the currents vary gradually from surface to bottom. They are usually strongest at the surface, where they are closest to the wind forcing, and gradually blend into the circulation of the abyss. However, within 2° or 3° latitude of the equator, the subsurface currents are much more complicated (Figure 2.11). Between 50 m and 250 m depth lies the strong eastward-flowing Equatorial Undercurrent. The undercurrent was originally discovered by Townsend Cromwell during a research expedition in the 1950s when the drogues deployed at that depth moved strongly eastward while the surface current was westward (Cromwell et al. 1954). In speed, the Equatorial Undercurrent matches the strongest currents in the world (> 100 cm/sec or 1 km/day). However, the undercurrent is vertically very thin (about 200 m thick), in contrast with the other major currents such as the Kuroshio, Gulf Stream, and Antarctic Circumpolar Current, which reach to the ocean bottom.

Below the undercurrent, and flanking it on either side of the equator, lie the North and South Subsurface countercurrents, flowing eastward (centered at around 4° on either side of the equator and from around 200 m depth downward). Directly beneath the Equatorial Undercurrent lies a somewhat weaker westward flow, which extends to about 1,000 m depth. Below this there is a regime of the so-called stacked jets, with many reversals in current direction, extending to the ocean bottom, and with vertical extent increasing toward the bottom (Firing 1989). Between 2° and 5° latitude, the vertical structure may show only a reversal or two. Farther away from the equator, the surface circulation extends to depths of 1,000 to 2,500 m, with much weaker flow below dominated by bottom topography.

The most general characteristic of circulation in the tropical Pacific is the exaggerated east-west nature compared with flow poleward of 20° latitude in both hemispheres, where gyres that also include more north-south flow are the norm. This zonality is characteristic of the tropical circulation in the Atlantic and Indian oceans as well as the Pacific.

## Deep Circulation

With increasing depth, the surface circulation weakens and shifts latitude. In the tropics, the surface circulation signatures disappear by about 500–1,000 m depth. Flow beneath this is predominantly zonal (east-west), with very slight north-south movement. Various analyses show counterclockwise circulation north of the equator and clockwise circulation south of the equator, in very elongated cells between the equator and about 10° latitude. (See Reid 1997 for an analysis of the whole of the deep circulation.) The deepest circulation is affected by the topography of the ridges and basins. Overall, there is net northward flow in a deep western boundary current, which enters the Pacific from the Antarctic east of New Zealand and passes through a deep gap near Samoa called the Samoan Passage. It moves on northward to the equator, crossing it in the western Pacific. North of the equator, a portion branches eastward to pass south of the Hawaiian Islands, and the other portion continues northward. The northward flow appears to move westward under the Kuroshio and then northward along the

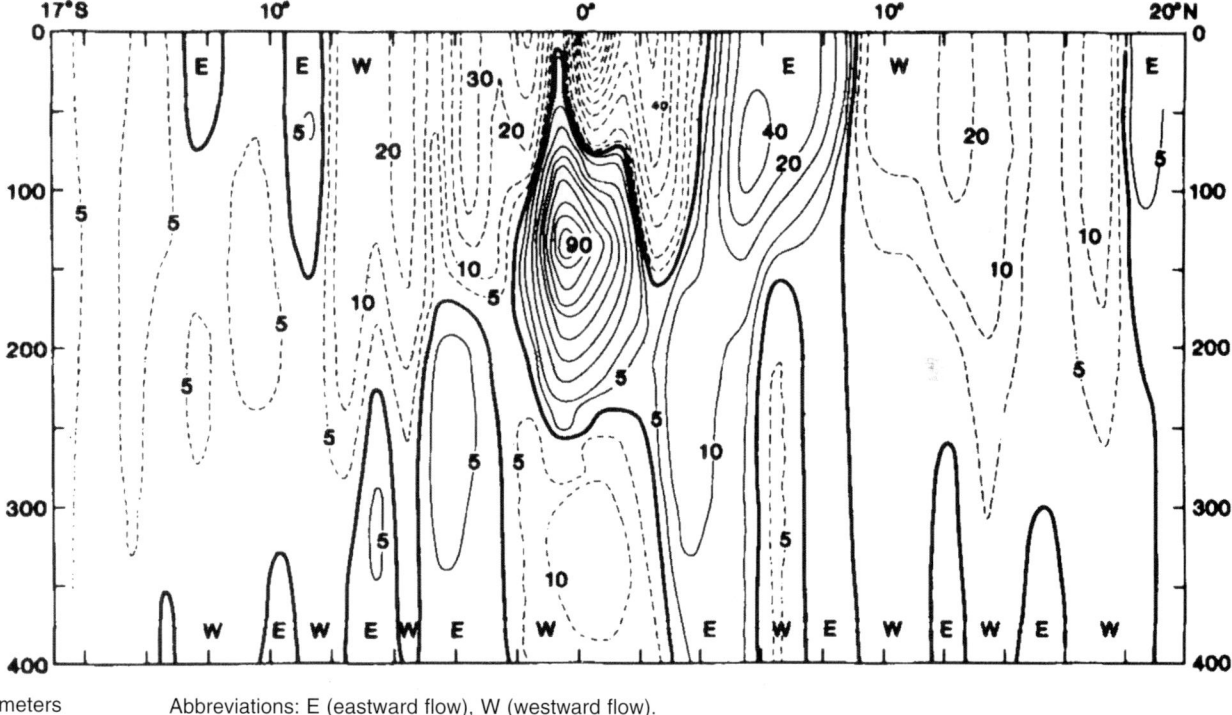

*Figure 2.11. East-west currents in the central Pacific. Numbers are flows in cm/sec. These velocities were computed from the same locations as Figure 2.5 (Wyrtki and Kilonsky 1984).*

western boundary to the subpolar Pacific. Return flow to the south probably occurs along the East Pacific Rise in the eastern Pacific and then westward along the equator (Johnson and Toole 1993, Firing 1989).

### Circulation Near Islands and Island Groups

Local circulation near islands and island chains can be affected by eddies generated by the ocean currents moving past the islands. Large island groups and especially the ridges upon which they sit also affect the large-scale ocean circulation. An example is flow near the Hawaiian Islands, which form a ridge for deep flow. On the north side of the Hawaiian Islands, large-scale currents or large eddies (time-dependent currents of possibly smaller spatial extent) are sometimes found along the ridge (Price et al. 1994, Roden 1991, Talley and deSzoeke 1986). An eddy is often generated at the passage between the islands of Maui and Hawai'i. Southwest of the ridge, in the lee of the flow of ocean currents toward the west, eddy activity is reduced.

## Forcing of the Circulation

All movement of ocean water must be generated by some force. Surface waves are created by the wind's blowing over the sea surface and catching on smaller waves to make larger ones. Tides are created by the gravitational pull between the Earth and the moon and sun. Tsunamis are created by undersea earthquakes. Ocean currents and large eddies are created by the wind's acting much more indirectly than for surface waves, and also by cooling and evaporation, which can cause the water to overturn.

The upper ocean circulation in the tropical Pacific is driven mostly by the stress from the wind. The prevailing winds in the tropical Pacific are the trades or easterlies, which blow from east to west. Together with the westerlies of higher latitudes, these force the large subtropical gyres. The dominant influence of these gyres on the tropics is the broad-scale westward flow mentioned above, called the North Equatorial Current (north of 10°N) and the South Equatorial Current (from 5°N southward). We divide the wind forcing of the tropics into two regimes: off the equator and on the equator. The difference between these is due to the Coriolis effect (deflection by the Earth's rotation), which is significant only off the equator.

### Forcing of Nonequatorial Flow

Winds push on the very top of the ocean and move the water through frictional stress. Due to the Coriolis effect the resulting effect is a flow to the right of the wind in the northern hemisphere and to the left in the southern hemisphere. This very thin water layer (around 1 m thick) then pushes on a thin water layer below it through friction, and so on, slightly more to the right (in the northern hemisphere), and the frictional stress dies out at about 20 to 100 m below the sea surface. The overall effect of the wind on this total layer is to drive a net flow of water exactly to the right of the wind in the northern hemisphere and exactly to the left in the southern hemisphere; this effect is known as Ekman transport (Figure 2.12). This 20–100-meter-deep frictional layer is referred to as the Ekman layer.

At all depths, from the very surface to the bottom, there is

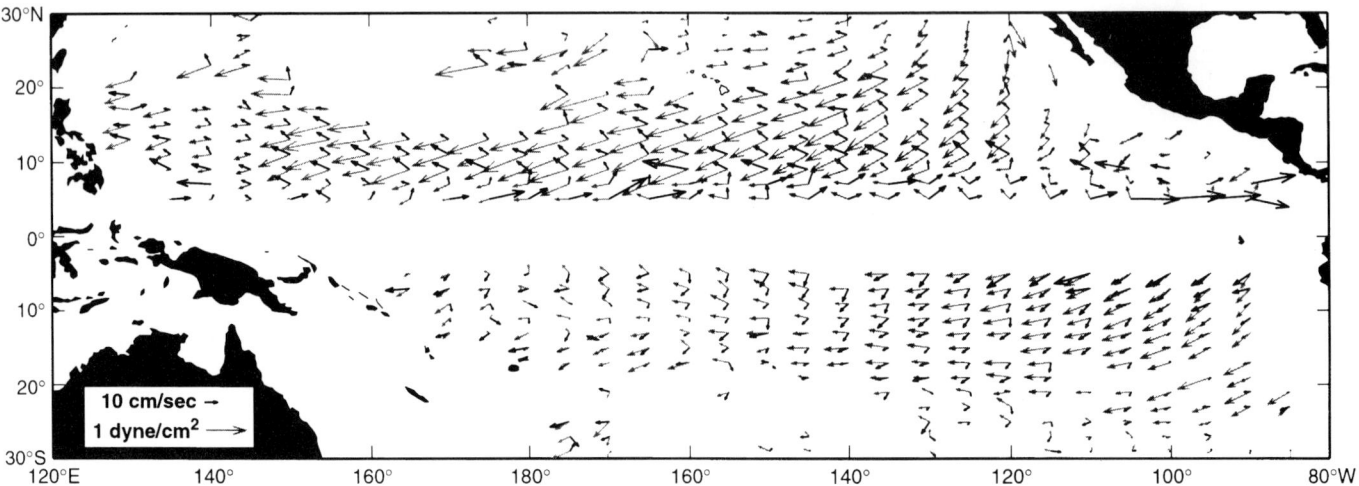

*Figure 2.12.* Annual average surface wind stress (gray arrows in stress/unit area) and the average near-surface flow (black arrows in cm/sec), which arises directly in response to the winds. The surface wind stress acts on just the very surface of the ocean. This force is transmitted through friction into the surface layer, and the direction of the stress turns with depth due to the rotation of the Earth. The direct stress disappears at a depth of only about 50 m. The resulting flow in the top 50 m or so of the ocean is to the right of the surface wind in the northern hemisphere and to the left in the southern hemisphere and is called Ekman transport. The black arrows in the figure are the average velocity based on thousands of satellite-tracked surface drifters after the average flow resulting from the ocean's pressure field (geostrophic flow) is subtracted out (Figure from E. Ralph). (Arrows do not appear near the equator because the Ekman effect is very weak there, as discussed in the text.)

also geostrophic flow, which is driven by horizontal pressure differences and deflected by the Coriolis force. The resulting geostrophic flow is always at exactly right angles to the pressure difference—to the right in the northern hemisphere and to the left in the southern hemisphere. The geostrophic flow at the sea surface is due to small, but large-scale and long-lasting, differences in sea-surface height, generally less than a meter, which create a horizontal difference in pressure. The largest height differentials, stable for long periods of time, drive the fastest currents, such as the Kuroshio in the Pacific and the Gulf Stream in the Atlantic. Where these flows are most vigorous, they can extend to great depth and even to the ocean bottom.

Net surface layer transport (Figure 2.13) is the sum of the geostrophic and Ekman components. In general, the geostrophic component is steadier than the Ekman component and so the flow averaged over months is dominated by geostrophic flow. Below the sea-surface Ekman layer, flow is solely geostrophic except in a frictional layer within 100 m of the ocean bottom.

The pressure gradient that creates geostrophic flow can be created in two ways: (1) through heating/cooling and evaporation/precipitation (buoyancy forcing) and (2) indirectly by the winds via the Ekman layer. However, buoyancy forcing is weak compared with indirect winds forcing. How do the winds produce the pressure difference that drives geostrophic flow? Where Ekman transport converges, downwelling occurs. The ocean responds with slow equatorward geostrophic flow between the sea surface and about 2,000-m depth, creating heightened pressure in the western Pacific. Where Ekman transport diverges, upwelling occurs. The result is a slow poleward flow, with a reverse pressure differential.

As an example, at subtropical latitudes, westerly winds occur north of 30°N, and trade winds occur south of 30°N. The resulting Ekman layer is convergent, resulting in downwelling all the way across the subtropical Pacific between about 15°N and 40°N. The ocean then flows slowly southward in this whole region, with fast northward return flow in the Kuroshio. The Kuroshio connects to the interior (central Pacific) flow through eastward flow (North Pacific Current), and the interior flow connects back to the Kuroshio through westward flow (the North Equatorial Current). This creates the familiar large clockwise "gyre" in the midlatitude North Pacific.

The variation in trade wind strength due to the intertropical convergence zone between 5° and 10°N leads to a permanent Ekman divergence and upwelling there. This off-equatorial upwelling results in slow northward flow in this narrow latitude range, which is returned southward by the Mindanao Current. This creates a counterclockwise circulation that is very narrow

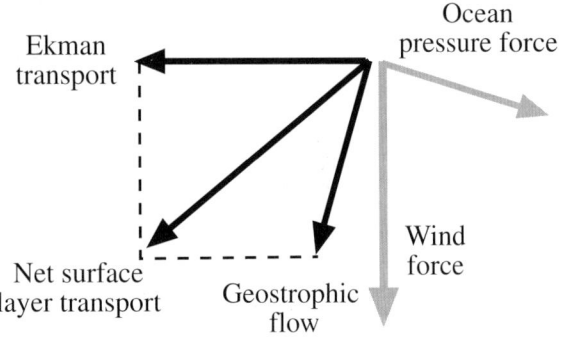

*Figure 2.13.* Forces and flow in the ocean's surface layer, after Tomczak and Godfrey (1994), illustrated for the northern hemisphere. Transport is the total flow within the surface layer, which is about 50 m thick. Ekman transport is exactly to the right of the wind. Geostrophic flow is exactly to the right of the pressure difference force. Net transport is the sum of the two.

from north to south but extends all the way across the Pacific in the east-west direction. The southern part of the westward-flowing North Equatorial Current is part of this gyre. The swift eastward flow of the North Equatorial Countercurrent is also part of this gyre.

*Forcing at the Equator*

Directly on the equator, the effect of rotation on the circulation vanishes, and so these concepts of geostrophic and Ekman flow do not apply. At the equator, the easterly trade winds push the surface water directly from east to west. This water piles up gently in the western Pacific (0.5 meters higher there than in the eastern Pacific). Because it is higher in the west than in the east, there is a pressure difference that causes the flow just beneath the surface layer to be eastward. This strong eastward flow is the Equatorial Undercurrent. The alternating eastward and westward jets found below the Equatorial Undercurrent on the equator die out about 2° from the equator; the cause has not been clearly identified.

Upwelling occurs at the equator due to poleward Ekman transport on either side of the equator, in turn a consequence of the easterly trade winds, which are strongest and steadiest in the eastern Pacific. Along the equator just below the surface, waters in the east are colder than in the west, partly a result of the rising of the Equatorial Undercurrent from west to east. Upwelling in the eastern Pacific thus accesses much cooler water than in the western Pacific, and as a result the surface waters in the east are colder than in the west. However, even in the eastern Pacific, trade winds respond to seasonal changes. Equatorial upwelling is weaker in the northern winter and spring, giving rise to mini-El Niño conditions each year in the eastern equatorial Pacific.

*Response to Changing Winds in the Tropics*

When the trade winds weaken or even reverse, the flow of water westward at the equator weakens or reverses and upwelling weakens or stops. Surface waters in the eastern Pacific warm significantly since upwelling is no longer bringing the cool waters to the surface. The deep warm pool in the western Pacific thins as its water "sloshes" eastward along the equator in the absence of the trade winds that maintain it.

*Heating/Cooling and Evaporation/Precipitation*

Ocean water density is a function of temperature and salinity, and so can be changed through heating/cooling and evaporation/precipitation. The resulting density changes can drive circulation. However, the effects of temperature and salinity on density and circulation are much smaller than the effect of the wind. Temperature and salinity-driven density changes, caused mainly by fluxes at the sea surface, are the only means of forcing

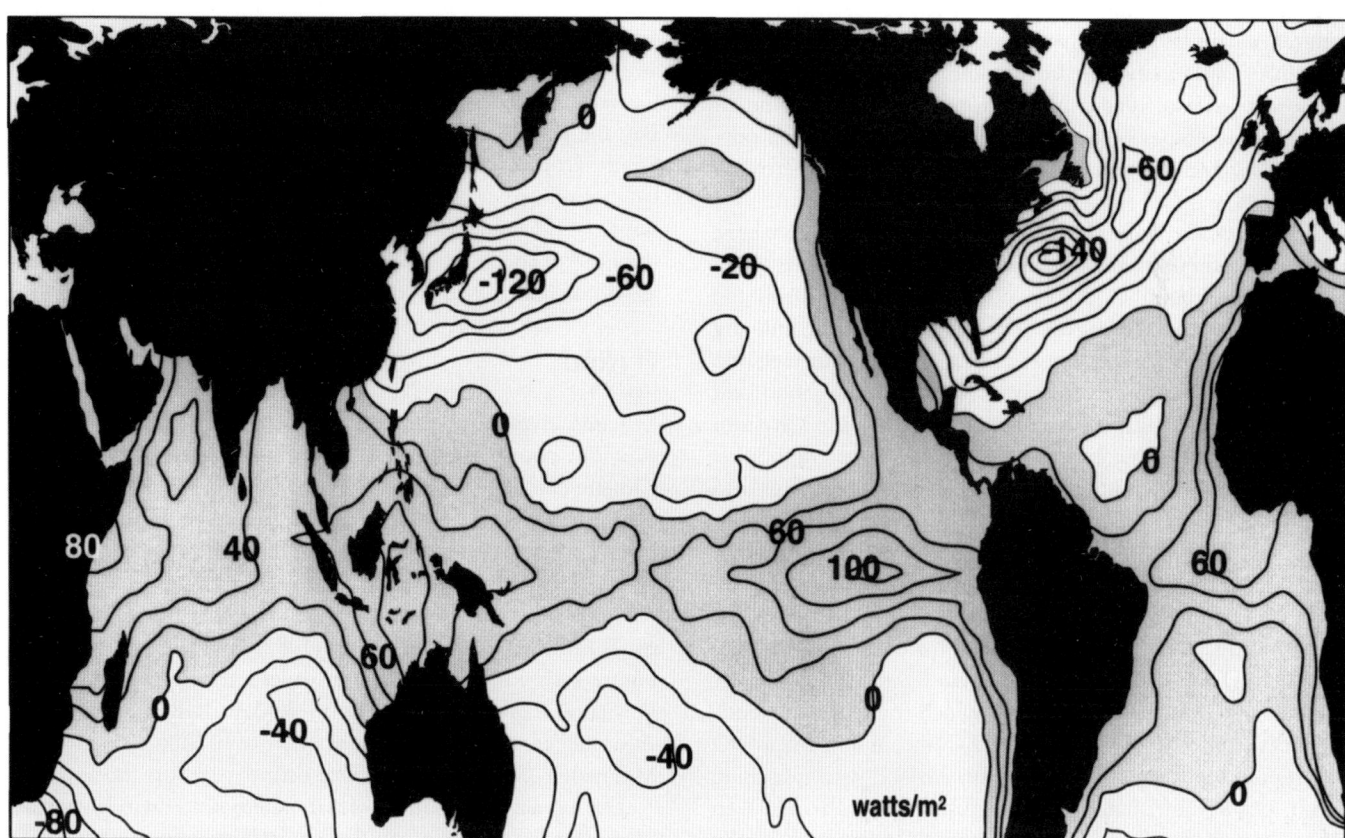

*Figure 2.14.* Annual mean heat flux from the atmosphere to the ocean, based on Hsiung (1985). Units are Watts/m2, which is an energy-per-unit area. Positive numbers indicate that the ocean is being heated. Contributing to the heat flux, in order of relative importance, are the incoming radiation from the sun, loss of heat due to energy used in evaporation, loss of heat due to blackbody radiation, and loss of heat due to the difference in temperature at the surface between the water and overlying air.

The Pacific Islands

circulation where the indirect effect of wind forcing vanishes, as in the ocean deeper than about 2,000 m. In the upper ocean, even though density fluxes do not greatly change the flow, they do have a major effect on ocean properties and on the overlying atmosphere, which is heated from below by the ocean.

The total surface heat flux into the ocean averaged over all years of data (Figure 2.14) shows the greatest heating along the equator and in the western warm pool region around Indonesia. The units of heating are Watts/m$^2$, or energy per unit area. In the subtropics, where the western boundary currents bring warm water to midlatitudes, there is strong cooling. In order to maintain a fairly steady distribution of temperature, the ocean must transport heat from the areas where it gains heat to the areas where it loses it.

In the western warm pool region and all along the ITCZ there is major convection in the atmosphere, creating towering clouds. Precipitation in these regions creates pools of freshened surface waters. In subtropical and midlatitude dry regions, excess evaporation under the atmospheric high-pressure cells creates high-salinity surface water. These waters can be traced by their salinity as they move to below the sea surface and are carried far by the ocean currents.

## Oceanography of New Zealand

New Zealand extends over some 15 degrees of latitude, into subtropical and midlatitude waters. Its islands are large and have extensive embayments. Its surrounding oceans differ substantively from that of islands in the tropical Pacific in terms of current flow, temperature, and salinity, and will be briefly outlined below. For additional information, readers are referred to Heath (1985).

Bottom depths around New Zealand are relatively shallow, interrupting the eastward-flowing East Australia current, which bifurcates at around 45°S. The northward branch forms the Westland Current, feeding the D'Urville, East Auckland, and East Cape currents. The eastward branch flows through the Foveaux Strait, turning northward to form the Southland Current. The East Cape Current is blocked by the Chatham Rise and veers northeastward, resulting in a large eddy. Spin-offs from this eddy often raise southerly temperatures and salinities above the seasonal mean in some coastal areas (Figure 2.15).

Surface temperature and salinity vary with latitude, ranging from 25°C and 35.8 in the north to 10°C and 34.5 in the south. Seasonal ranges of 6.7°C and .3-.4 occur for temperature and salinity respectively. Subtropical and Subantarctic waters occur at the surface. The line along which the two water bodies meet, south and east of New Zealand, is known as the Subtropical Convergence. Beneath the surface, with increasing depth, occur the Antarctic Intermediate Water, Pacific Deep Water, and Bottom Water. Temperatures decline continually with depth; salinity is lowest in the Antarctic Intermediate Water, but rises slightly in deeper waters.

Localized circulations occur in the many embayments of New Zealand, reflecting the input of different currents, as well

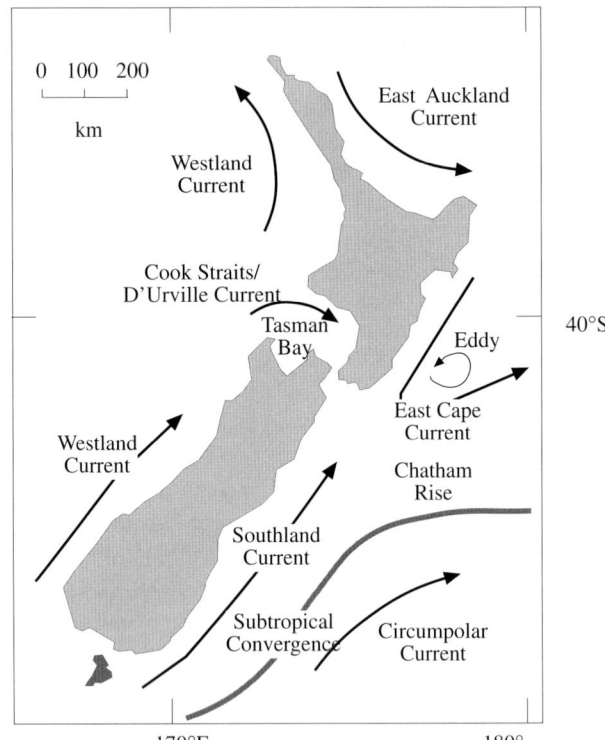

*Figure 2.15. Ocean currents surrounding New Zealand (after Heath (1985).*

as freshwater runoff. For example, input from the D'Urville Current results in counterclockwise flow within the Tasman Bay and an output on the eastern side of the bay into the Cook Straits. Considerable variability in surface circulation is caused by prevailing winds. Between October and March, northerly winds are dominant, and surface circulation is mainly toward the head of the bay. Between April and August, southerly winds are dominant, and surface circulation is out of the bay.

## El Niño

Large changes in the climate occur in the tropical Pacific over the course of three to seven years, as described in the Climate chapter. This phenomenon, known as El Niño, is a coupled interaction between the atmosphere and ocean. Its effects reach far beyond the tropical Pacific through connections in the far-ranging atmospheric circulation.

The events that form a typical El Niño have been described by Rasmussen and Carpenter (1982) and are illustrated in Figure 2.16. Philander (1990) provides a textbook summary of El Niño. A Report to the Nation (NOAA OGP 1994) provides an excellent summary, as do a number of El Niño web sites (see McPhaden 1997 in the reference list).

During an El Niño, the normal easterly trade winds slacken, as indicated by a decrease in the atmospheric pressure difference between the central and western Pacific. Weakened trade winds result in reduced westward flow at the equator, which leads to a draining of the western warm pool toward the east. Equatorial ocean upwelling is reduced, which results in warmer sea-surface

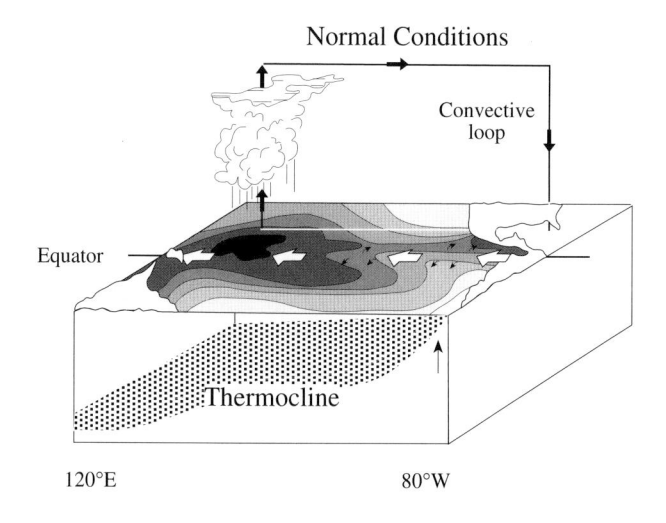

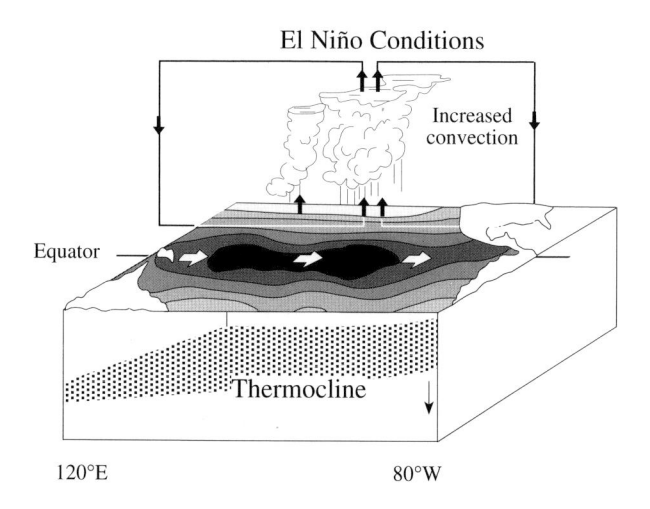

*Figure 2.16. Schematic of the relations between the ocean's temperature structure, surface winds (broad open arrows), ocean upwelling (small black arrows), atmospheric convection (up and down black arrows and dashed cells) and cloud patterns in the tropical Pacific during normal conditions and during an El Niño. (This figure is from the TAO Project office, Dr. Michael J. McPhaden, Director, and is available on the El Niño theme page of the NOAA/Pacific Marine Environmental Laboratory - http://www.pmel.noaa.gov/toga-tao/el-nino, where one can find much more information about El Niño as well as current conditions and forecasts. (Note: Horizontal scale in thousands of km; vertical scale in hundreds of m.)*

temperatures in the eastern Pacific. As the western warm pool cools slightly and the central and the eastern equatorial Pacific warm, the strength of the trade winds is further reduced. The large atmospheric convection cell over Indonesia moves eastward. This results in drought in the western Pacific (including Indonesia and Australia) and increased rainfall in the central and eastern Pacific (notably at Christmas Island, the Galapagos, and Ecuador).

The warm water in the eastern Pacific spreads to the eastern boundary and splits to flow north and south there. Upwelling off northern Peru might weaken, or just draw on the warm, nutrient-poor equatorial water. The result is a decline in production in this important fisheries area. If the El Niño is particularly strong, its effect in the ocean can reach as far north as the California coast. The opposite phase of the El Niño is called La Niña, characterized by especially strong trade winds, a well-developed warm pool in the western Pacific, and cold water at the equator in the central and eastern Pacific, with strong rainfall in the western Pacific, little rainfall in the eastern Pacific, and major fisheries production in the eastern boundary regions.

El Niño affects midlatitudes through teleconnections in the atmosphere. Changes in the western tropical Pacific reach far to the northeast and southeast through the atmosphere and directly affect climate in the coastal regions of the United States and South America.

El Niño occurs irregularly, but generally every three to seven years. Major progress has been made in predicting an El Niño about one year in advance because the sequence of events in an El Niño is often the same. Thus detection of early signs of El Niño, such as the appearance of warm water in the eastern tropical Pacific or a change in the strength of the trade winds, often allows prediction of changes in rainfall and air temperature later in the year throughout the Pacific region. A major observing network and computer modeling effort is in place to assist in observing and forecasting El Niño occurrences (see the web site in the reference list under McPhaden 1997).

The strength of El Niño varies greatly over an even more irregular time scale of about ten to thirty years. For instance, El Niño in the 1940s were strong, followed by several decades of weak events, and were then followed by very strong El Niños again in the 1980s and 1990s. Long records of El Niños have been extracted from the reasonably long pressure records at Tahiti and Darwin and from growth and properties of the annual accretion in coral heads in the tropical Pacific. This so-called decadal modulation of El Niño is much less well understood than El Niño itself. Major research on these ocean-atmosphere feedbacks, which affect much longer time scales, is being planned for the next decade.

## Acknowledgment

We are grateful for the extensive review of this chapter by Dick Stroup, respected colleague and friend who died shortly before this book went to press. Dick's professional and personal contributions to ocean science were wide-ranging, and he will be missed.

## Bibliography

Conkright, M. E., S. Levitus, and T. P. Boyer. 1994. *World ocean atlas*. Vol. 1, *Nutrients, NOAA Atlas* NESDIS 162 pp. [Available from NODC/NOAA, E/OC5 1315 East-West Highway, Silver Spring, MD 20910.]

Cromwell, T., R. B. Montgomery, and E. D. Stroup. 1954. Equatorial Undercurrent in the Pacific Ocean revealed by new methods. *Science* 119:648–649.

Fine, R. A., R. Lukas, F. M. Bingham, M. J. Warner, and R. H. Gammon. 1994. The western equatorial Pacific: a water mass crossroads. *Journal of Geophysical Research* 99:25,063–25,080.

Firing, E. 1989. Mean zonal currents below 1500 m near the equator 159W. *Journal of Geophysical Research* 94:2,023–2,028.

Flament, P., S. Kennan, R. Lumpkin, M. Sawyer, and E. D. Stroup. 1997. The ocean atlas of Hawaii. 24"x 36" poster and copyrighted website: http:/satftp.soest.hawaii.edu/atlas.

Graham, N. E., and T. P. Barnett. 1987. Sea surface temperature, surface wind divergence, and convection over tropical oceans. *Science* 238:657–659.

Heath, R. A. 1985. A review of the physical oceanography of the seas around New Zealand—1982. *New Zealand Journal of Marine and Freshwater Research* 19:79–124.

Hofmann, E. E., A. J. Busalacchi, and J. J. O'Brien. 1981. Wind generation of the Costa Rica dome. *Science* 214:552–554.

Hsiung, J. 1985. Estimates of global oceanic meridional heat transport. *Journal of Physical Oceanography* 15:1405–1413.

Iida, K., D. C. Cox, and G. Pararas-Carayannis. 1967. Preliminary catalog of tsunamis occurring in the Pacific Ocean. *Hawaii Institute of Geophysics* Pub. HIG-67-10, Honolulu: University of Hawai'i.

Johnson, G. C., and J. M. Toole. 1993. Flow of deep and bottom waters in the Pacific at 10°N. *Deep-Sea Research* 40:371–394.

Knauss, J. A. 1960. Measurements of the Cromwell Current. *Deep-Sea Research* 6:265–286.

Knauss, J. A. 1997. *Introduction to physical oceanography*. Second Edition. New Jersey: Prentice-Hall.

Lander, J. F., and P. A. Lockridge. 1989. *United States tsunamis (including U.S. possessions) 1690-1988*, Publication 41-2. Boulder, CO.: National Geophysical Data Center.

Levitus, S., and T. P. Boyer. 1994a. World ocean atlas. Vol. 4, *Temperature, NOAA Atlas NESDIS* 129 pp. [Available from NODC/NOAA, E/OC5 1315 East-West Highway, Silver Spring, MD 20910.]

Levitus, S., and T. P. Boyer. 1994b. World ocean atlas. Vol. 3, *Salinity, NOAA Atlas NESDIS* 111 pp. [Available from NODC/NOAA, E/OC5 1315 East-West Highway, Silver Spring, MD 20910.]

Levitus, S., M. E. Conkright, J. L. Reid, R. G. Najjar, and A. Mantyla. 1993. Distribution of nitrate, phosphate and silicate in the world oceans. *Progress in Oceanography* 31:245–273.

Lindstrom, E., R. Lukas, R. Fine, E. Firing, S. Godfrey, G. Meyers, G. and M. Tsuchiya. 1987. The western equatorial Pacific Ocean circulation study. *Nature* 330:533–537.

Lukas, R., and E. Lindstrom. 1991. The mixed layer of the western equatorial Pacific Ocean. *Journal of Geophysical Research* 96:3,343–3,357.

McPhaden, M. J. 1997. NOAA/PMEL TAO Project Office: El Niño theme page. Website: http://www.pmel.noaa.gov/toga-tao/el-nino.

National Oceanographic and Atmospheric Administration (NOAA) Office of Global Programs. 1994. El Niño and climate prediction. *Reports to the Nation on our Changing Planet.*

Neshyba, S. 1987. *Oceanography: perspectives on a fluid Earth*. New York: John Wiley and Sons.

Philander, S. G. 1990. *El Niño, La Niña*, and the Southern Oscillation. San Diego, California: Academic Press.

Pickard, G. L., and W. J. Emery. 1990. *Descriptive physical oceanography: an introduction*. Oxford, England: Pergamon Press,

Price, J. M., M. L. Vanwoert, and M. Vitousek. 1994. On the possibility of a ridge current along the Hawaiian Islands. *Journal of Geophysical Research* 99:14,101–14,111.

Ralph, E. A., and P. P. Niiler. 1998. Wind-driven currents in the tropical Pacific. *Journal of Physical Oceanography*, in press.

Ramanathan, V., and W. Collins. 1993. A thermostat in the tropics. *Nature* 36 11:410–411.

Rasmusson, E. M., and T. H. Carpenter. 1982. Variations in tropical sea surface temperature and surface wind fields associated with the Southern Oscillation/El Niño. *Monthly Weather Review* 110:354–384.

Reid, J. L. 1997. On the total geostrophic circulation of the Pacific Ocean: flow patterns, tracers and transports. *Progress in Oceanography* 39:263-352.

Reverdin, G., A. Morliere, and E. Gerard. 1991. *Compagne oceanographique trans-pacifique*. Paris, France.

Roden, G. I. 1991. Effects of the Hawaiian Ridge upon oceanic flow and thermohaline structure. *Deep-Sea Research* 38:623–654.

Roemmich, D., M. Y. Morris, and W. R. Young. 1994. Equatorial fresh jets. *Journal of Physical Oceanography* 24:540–558.

Shepard, F. P., G. A. Macdonald, and D. C. Cox. 1950. The tsunami of April 1, 1946, *Bulletin of the Scripps Institution of Oceanography of the University of California*, 5:391–470.

Singh, R. 1991. Tsunamis in Fiji and their effects, in *Workshop on coastal processes in the South Pacific Island Nations, SOPAC (U.N. South Pacific Applied Geoscience Commission)*, Technical Bulletin 7:107–120.

Tabata, S. 1975. The general circulation of the Pacific Ocean and a brief account of the oceanographic structure of the North Pacific Ocean. Part I - circulation and volume transports. *Atmosphere* 13:133–168.

Talandier, J. 1993. Le volcanisme et la sismicit. In *Atlas de la Polynesie Française*, ORSTOM (Inst. français de recherche scientifique pour le developpement en cooperation, Dept. en Territoires d'Outre-Mer), Paris, maps 26–27.

Talley, L. D., and R. A. deSzoeke. 1986. Spatial fluctuations north of the Hawaiian Ridge. *Journal of Physical Oceanography* 16:981–984.

Talley, L. D., T. M. Joyce, and R. A. deSzoeke. 1991. Transpacific sections at 47N and 152W: distribution of properties. *Deep-Sea Research* 38:S63–S82.

Tomczak, M., and J. S. Godfrey. 1994. *Regional oceanography: an introduction*. England: Pergamon Press, England.

Tsuchiya, M. 1968. *Upper waters of the intertropical Pacific Ocean*. Baltimore: The Johns Hopkins Press.

Tsuchiya, M., R. Lukas, R. A. Fine, E. Firing, and E. Lindstrom. 1989. Source waters of the Pacific Equatorial Undercurrent. *Progress in Oceanography* 23:101–147.

Worthington, L. V. 1981. The water masses of the world ocean: some results of a fine-scale census. *Evolution of physical oceanography: scientific surveys in honor of Henry Stommel*, ed. B. A. Warren and C. Wunsch. Cambridge: The MIT Press.

Wyrtki, K., and B. Kilonsky. 1984. Mean water and current structure during the Hawaii-to-Tahiti shuttle experiment. *Journal of Physical Oceanography* 14:242–254.

Zhang, Y., J. M. Wallace, and D. S. Battisti. 1997. ENSO-like interdecadal variability: *1900-93. Journal of Climate* 10: 1004–1020.

# Geology

*Gerard J. Fryer and Patricia Fryer*

## Introduction

The islands of the Pacific and the landmasses around it have been crafted by plate tectonics and volcanism. The Pacific Plate, part of the brittle outer layer of the Earth, is in constant northwestward motion. Where it passes over stationary sources of molten rock (hot spots) volcanoes grow. Dozens of linear island chains are scattered across the Pacific, marking the passage of the plate over such hot spots. Along the western margins of the ocean are islands very different in character. These islands are generally in arcuate chains bordered by deep ocean trenches, the greatest ocean depths on Earth. They are home to explosive volcanoes, and are wracked by earthquakes. Such violent processes are characteristic of locales where plates converge. When fragments of continents get caught up in the midst of such processes, changes occur in the geometry of convergence zones. The fragments themselves are deformed and may be sundered or uplifted along great faults. As we shall see, the Pacific and its western margins exhibit all of these geologic processes.

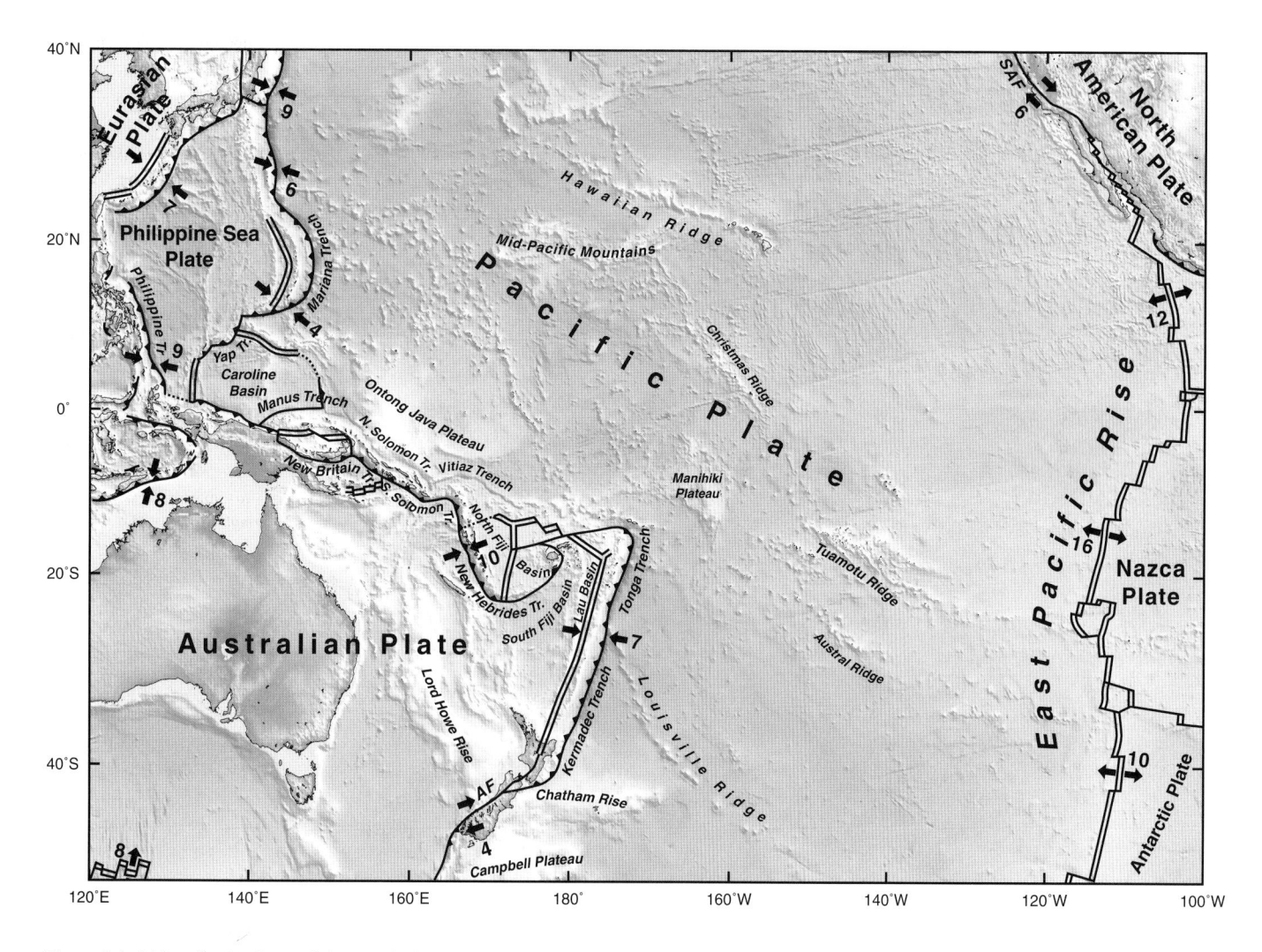

**Figure 3.1.** *Lithospheric plates of the Pacific basin. Subduction zones are marked by triangles on the overriding plate. Arrows show relative plate motions across plate boundaries. Relative plate speeds are given in centimeters per year. SAF is the San Andreas Fault; AF is the Alpine Fault. Western Pacific plate margins are taken from Scheibner, et al. (1991).*

## Plate Tectonics

Many Pacific Island chains show a clear age progression: young, volcanically active islands at the southerly end of the chain and old, extinct, and eroded islands to the north. J. Tuzo Wilson (1963) first showed that the age progressions mean that the sea floor is moving over stationary, episodically erupting hot spots. The idea of a horizontally moving sea floor, together with the much older observation that the continents themselves move (Wegener 1929), led to the realization that continents and sea floor together are carried along passively as part of the brittle outer layer of the Earth.

The brittle outer layer of the Earth is the lithosphere. The idea that the lithosphere moves is the basis of the theory of plate tectonics. According to this theory, the lithosphere is organized into eight major plates and several smaller ones that together cover the Earth. Motion of the plates relative to each other explains earthquakes, volcanoes, mountain building, and the origins of islands and continents. The lithospheric plates themselves are the surface expression of giant convection cells in the mantle of the Earth—the slow circulation of rock by which the Earth rids itself of internal heat.

The sea floor is created by volcanism at midocean ridges. These ridges stretch for thousands of kilometers, defining the diverging edges of the lithospheric plates. Here hot, upwelling rock from deep in the mantle begins to melt. The melt, called magma, inflates the ridges, stretching the lithosphere until it breaks in a long, narrow fissure. Lava erupts at the sea floor and forms vertical dikes (thin sheets of solidified magma) beneath the surface. As the sea floor is rafted away to either side, the underlying magma chamber is cut off, to be replaced by a new magma chamber. The surface lavas, the dikes, and the old, frozen magma chambers together form the oceanic crust, which is about 5 km thick.

Beneath the crust, the mantle is hot and deformable. As the sea floor spreads and cools, the underlying upper mantle also cools and becomes stiffer. Together with the overlying oceanic crust, this rigid part of the upper mantle comprises the lithosphere. Because of the cooling, the lithosphere thickens with age; it grows from a thickness of only a few kilometers at the ridge to about 70 km beneath old sea floor. The lithosphere of most of the Pacific was formed, and continues to form, at the East Pacific Rise (Figure 3.1).

Lithospheric spreading at one location requires convergence elsewhere. Where plates converge, lithosphere either sinks beneath an overriding plate or is compressed and uplifted to form mountain ranges (Figure 3.2). The plate-to-plate interactions in convergence zones cause earthquakes and feed the volcanoes that make up island arcs. Subduction, the sinking of cold lithosphere into the mantle, draws down the sea floor to form deep ocean trenches. The sinking lithosphere forms the downwelling limb of a mantle convection cell; the upwelling limbs provide the source material for sea-floor spreading.

Where plates neither converge nor diverge, but simply slide past each other, the boundary between the two plates is a transform fault, which may stretch for hundreds of kilometers. California's San Andreas Fault is the best-known example, though the Alpine Fault of New Zealand is of comparable size.

## Hot Spots and Linear Island Chains

Mantle rock rising beneath a midocean ridge does so as a vertical sheet, but the source rock for hot spots rises in confined plumes. The plumes are thought to form over topographic irregularities at the core-mantle boundary. These irregularities concentrate heat, making the overlying mantle rock hotter than adjacent rock. The hot rock rises buoyantly through the entire mantle, forming a path, the plume, along which more material can rise. As rock in the plume rises to depths shallower than 70 km it begins to melt, because the reduction of pressure near the surface lowers the melting point. Less than 5% of the upwelling rock is melted, but this is enough to provide the source magma from which to build island chains (Figure 3.3) such as the Hawaiian Islands.

The composition of the magmas formed depends on the composition and degree of melting of the source rock. When mantle rock is partially melted, the resulting magma is basaltic.

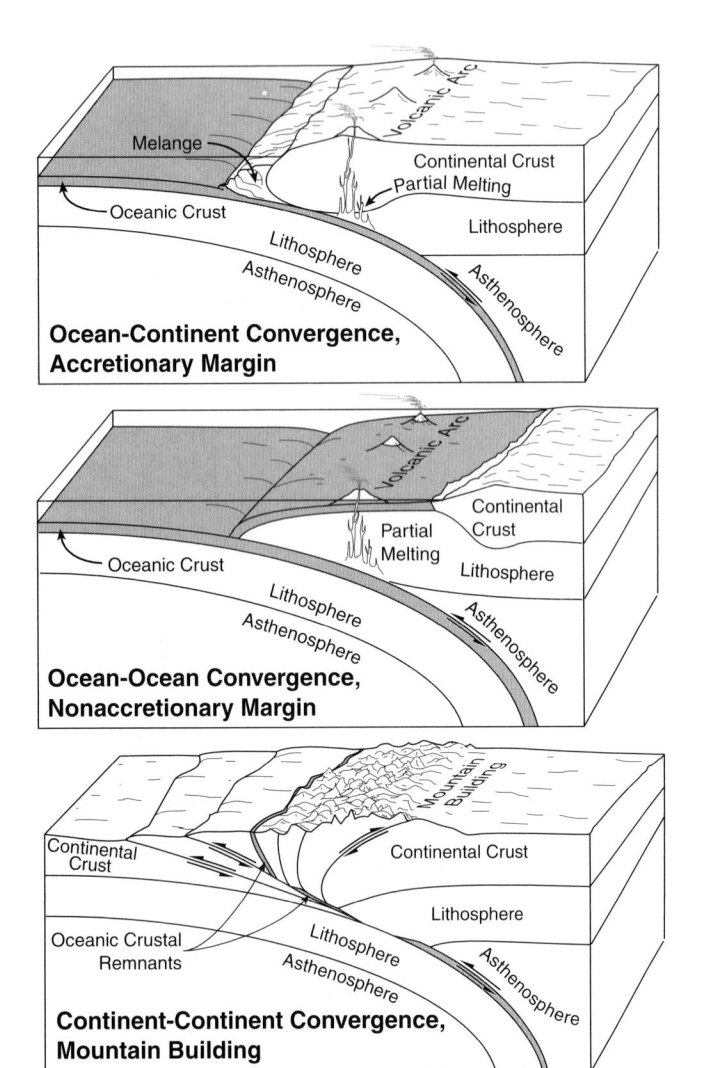

*Figure 3.2. Sketch of three different types of convergent plate boundaries: ocean-continent, ocean-ocean and continent-continent.*

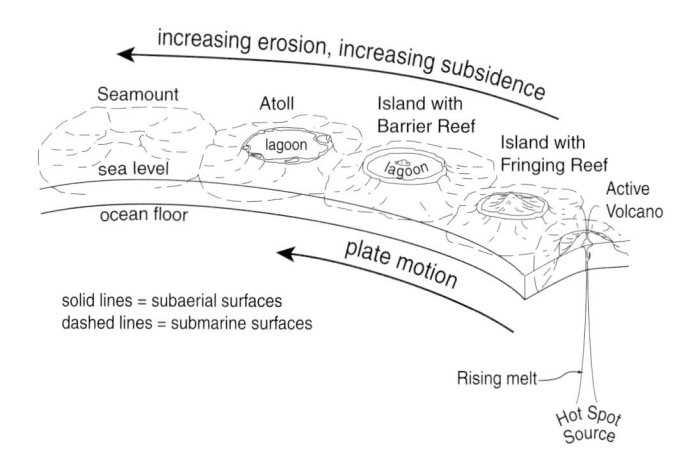

*Figure 3.3.* A schematic cross section of an oceanic lithospheric plate showing how plumes of rising melt feed hot spots. Volcanoes formed above the hot spot are rafted away in the direction of plate movement and thus increase in age with distance from the hot spot.

Basalt is the most common rock type in the Pacific basin. It is a dark gray to black rock (Color Plate 3A) with a low silica ($SiO_2$) content and a low content of volatile (low melting point) compounds such as water and carbon dioxide. Basalt erupts at high temperatures, more than 1100°C (Macdonald et al 1983).

The first lavas from a hot spot will be erupted on the sea floor. The surface of lavas erupted underwater is rapidly chilled to form a glassy skin. The skin swells and splits to release more lava, which in turn chills over. This repetitive process forms round extrusions of lava and discrete blobs that break off and tumble downslope. When exposed in cross section, these underwater lava forms look like a stack of pillows, so they are called pillow lavas.

The pile of pillow lavas is weak, so gravity begins to pull the growing volcano apart. Tension produces radial cracks, called rifts. Once rifts form, much magma is diverted from summit eruptions and instead injected through rifts to feed flank eruptions. The magma left in a rift solidifies to form a dike.

Rift zones expand and are filled repeatedly as new pulses of magma rise into the volcano. Eventually, the rift becomes a zone several kilometers wide underlain by solid dike rock. The dike complexes are more competent than the intervening rubbly flanks of pillow lava and thus act as buttresses, imparting localized internal strength to the seamount. Many seamounts on the Pacific Ocean floor are star-shaped, with arms extending along the rift zones. Collapsed flanks, composed of piles of talus (mainly pillow lava fragments), lie between the arms.

As the seamount approaches sea level, pressure is reduced, and steam boiling off the hot lava expands explosively. Sea water becomes involved in the eruption, and explosions shoot volcanic ash (fine, solidified magma particles) into the atmosphere. Falling ash is swept away by waves and currents, but eventually the volcano breaches the surface. Once a solid surface has formed above sea level, fluid lava flows predominate, commonly from rift zone eruptions. The freely flowing lava forms broad sheets, characterized by a smooth, ropy surface (*pāhoehoe*), or a jagged, clinkery one (*'a'ā*) (Macdonald et al. 1983).

The low silica, low gas content and high temperature of basaltic lavas gives them low viscosity, which results in relatively gentle eruptions with very little ash. The low viscosity also produces thin flows, often less than a meter thick. Repeated gentle eruptions and thin lava flows form broad, convex shield volcanoes (Color Plate 3B). From initial eruption at the sea floor to formation of an island shield volcano, the process takes at least a million years.

Between the rift zones, the unbuttressed flanks of an island (built on weak, rubbly pillow lava) may collapse if shaken loose by an earthquake or if oversteepened as the volcano inflates with magma. Fault scarps (cliffs) oriented approximately parallel to the shoreline indicate that the flank has failed; the cliffs are headwalls of large slump blocks. Slump blocks may fail catastrophically as giant landslides (Figure 3.4). Sonar mapping of the sea floor around the Hawaiian Islands shows slide deposits extending two hundred kilometers from the islands (Moore et al 1989). Similar evidence for large-scale slope failure is found around most volcanic islands.

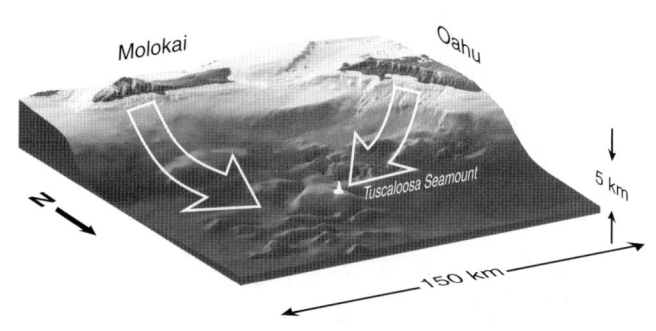

*Figure 3.4.* Landslide paths in the Hawaiian Islands. The hummocky terrain of the sea bottom north of Moloka'i is characteristic of a landslide deposit. The entire north flank of Moloka'i has collapsed into the sea, as has the northwest flank of the Ko'olau Volcano of O'ahu. Tuscaloosa Seamount is a piece of the Ko'olau Volcano that slid over 70 km from its original location. These landslides are the largest known landslides on Earth.

Such landslides, together with the slow, continuous erosion by surf, rain, and wind, whittle away at the island. As long as the island is fed by the hot spot, volcanism will counter the erosion. Inevitably, however, sea-floor spreading carries the island away from its source. Volcanism declines, then stops, and erosion reduces the island to sea level. Thus, in a midocean chain of islands, the degree of erosion correlates with distance from the active hot spot (Figure 3.3).

As islands age, there is also an increase in the size of coral reefs (Darwin 1860). Because reef communities require sunlight, they must initially form in the shallow waters near shore to form fringing reefs. More severely eroded volcanoes are surrounded by a ring of shallow coralline shoals, a barrier reef, separated from the remnant of the volcano by a lagoon. In still older islands (atolls) the central volcanic remnants are missing altogether, and only a ring of coral and coralline islands remains around a shallow lagoon.

The progressive aging continues. With the advent of acoustic profiling in the 1940s many seamounts with flat tops (called guyots) were discovered. Some, though not all, have coralline caps that thicken and increase in depth below sea level with distance from the hot spot. Erosion can explain the flattening of the tops of the volcanoes as the land surface is worn down to sea level, but it cannot explain the increasing depths.

What is happening is that the sea floor itself is sinking. Ocean lithosphere migrates away from midocean ridges at rates of a few centimeters per year. As the plate ages it cools, increases in density, and subsides relative to the ridge crest. As it subsides, overlying islands and guyots subside with it. Ocean floor subsidence, if slow enough, will allow continued growth of coral, but subsidence faster than coral can grow (or transport of an atoll beyond the tropical belt of warm water) will result in a guyot.

As the volcanoes grow, they become an increasing burden on the lithosphere beneath, which sags under the load (Wessel 1993). This sagging creates a moat ("deep") around the volcano on the sea floor, forming a broad arch in the surrounding lithosphere (Figure 3.5). Because the currently active volcanoes are least eroded, they form the most concentrated load. As each island in turn is rafted away from the hot spot, it rises over the arch formed by the new volcanic center before settling back into a slow subsidence. Rising over the arch puts the island in tension, which may trigger a posterosional rejuvenation of volcanism. Posterosional features are scattered small cones of cinder and ash or small shield volcanoes. Diamond Head on the Hawaiian island of Oʻahu is a typical example.

Gradual subsidence of guyots is the normal aging process, but there are variations. A guyot may be transported over the arch around another hot spot and so be exposed again. Flexure (bending) of the lithosphere prior to its subduction into a trench forms similar arches or upwarps. A guyot carried up onto such an arch may reemerge as an island. The Loyalty Islands (see Figure 3.6) have been uplifted by upwarping of the North Loyalty Basin prior to its subduction into the New Hebrides Trench (Nunn 1994). Niue Island, an uplifted atoll east of the Tonga Trench, was created in similar fashion. The lagoon was elevated well above sea level and is now dry.

An apparent vertical motion is also imparted by variations in sea level. During the last maximum in glaciation, about 21 thousand years ago, sea level was at least 110 m below its present level (Peltier 1996). Sea level variations from glaciation over the last two million years are thought to have oscillated between -130 m and +10 m. Glacial variations in sea level coupled with continuous uplift has produced elevated erosional benches on many Pacific islands (as on Tongatapu Island, Tonga). Similarly, sea level variations coupled with continuous subsidence will produce a succession of submarine terraces. All Hawaiian islands display such terraces; those on the northwest slope of the island of Hawaiʻi descend to 4 km depth.

Some intraplate island groups (notably the Cook Islands) appear not to show a clear age progression, and thus have cast doubt on the hot-spot hypothesis. Wessel and Kroenke (1997), however, have demonstrated that confusing age progressions result from changes over geological time in Pacific plate motion (so that the islands trail off from the hot spot in varying

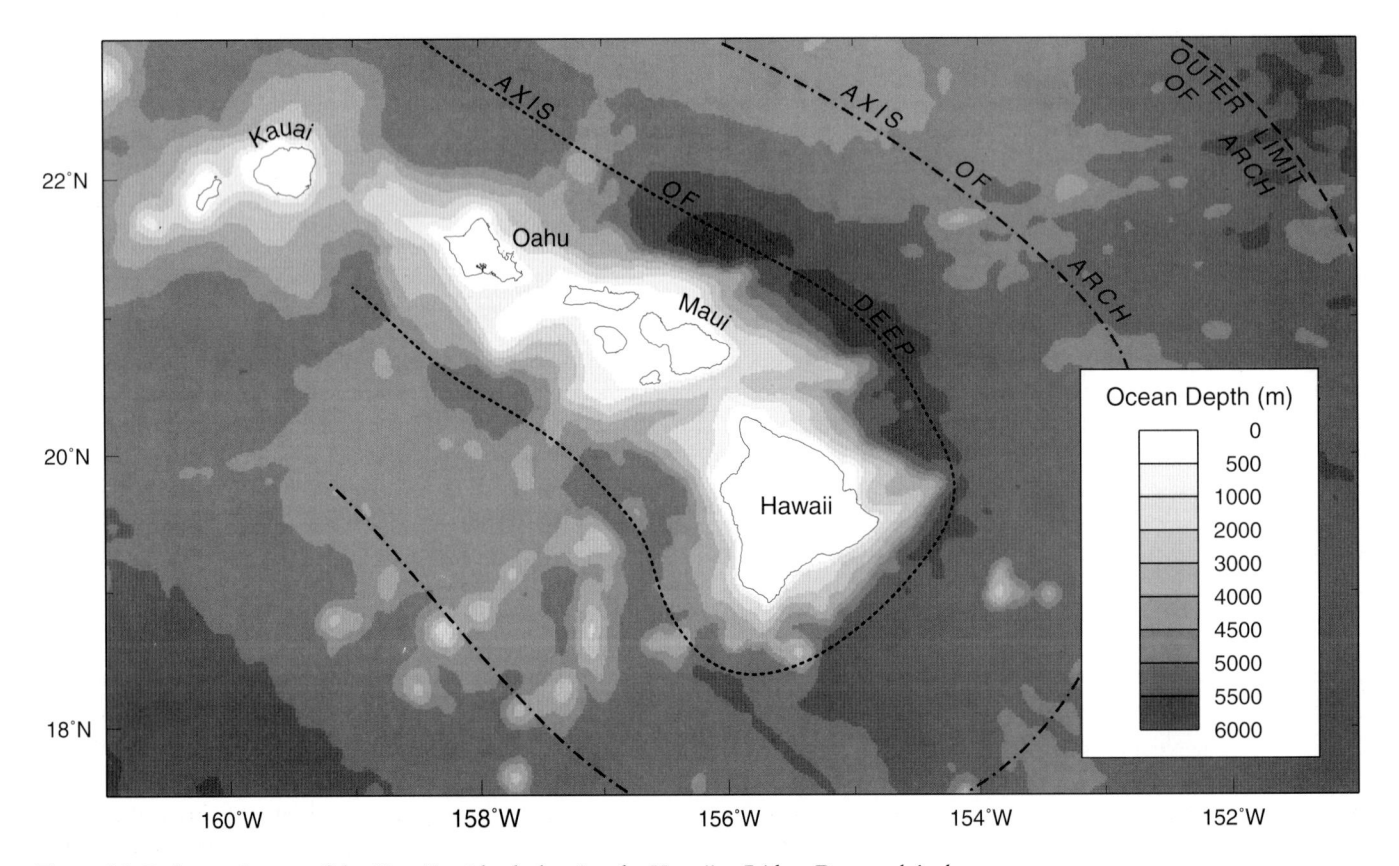

*Figure 3.5.* Bathymetric map of the Hawaiian Islands showing the Hawaiian Ridge, Deep and Arch.

directions). Moreover, episodic rejuvenation of volcanism can result as islands rise over adjacent hot-spot arches. Thus, superficial lava flows on the more distant, older islands may yield younger geological dates than islands closer to the hot spot.

## Islands at Spreading Centers

Young sea floor is hot, buoyant, and shallower than the surrounding sea floor. That is why divergent plate boundaries (also called spreading centers) form ridges. Sometimes a spreading center, or a volcano that first grew at a spreading center, breaches the sea surface to form an island. This can happen either because a nearby hot spot has fed additional magma to the spreading center, or because the spreading center itself is in shallower than normal water. In the Pacific, only Easter Island is associated with a true midocean ridge spreading center, the East Pacific Rise (Figure 3.1).

Not all divergent plate boundaries occur in the middle of large ocean basins, however. There is also spreading going on in several of the shallower seas around the western margin of the Pacific (we shall consider the formation of these marginal seas in a later section). Islands formed in such an environment include the Niua Group (Tonga), Tikopia (Solomon Islands), and the Witu Islands (Papua New Guinea).

Volcanism at spreading centers is responsible for rich ore deposits. Circulation of heated sea water into fissures in hot rock leaches out metals (e.g., copper, zinc, and lead), which are deposited at hot springs on the sea floor. Most such deposits lie at water depths greater than 2 km and cannot be mined economically. Sometimes, however, a spreading center is carried into a subduction zone and caught up in a collision between a subducting landmass and the island arc. Fragments of the spreading center may then be scraped off and upthrust onto land, taking the ore deposits with them. The metal deposits of New Britain (Papua New Guinea) and Malaita (Solomon Islands) were formed in this way.

## Island Arcs

The Pacific Plate is being subducted all along its western boundary. Subduction zones tend to establish themselves in broad, sweeping curves, so island chains formed along subduction zones are called island arcs. Island arc volcanism is driven by magma generation related to the subduction, as we shall discuss. But in a subduction environment, islands can also form for other reasons. Flexing of the downgoing plate may upwarp the sea floor, lifting guyots to become islands, as we have already seen.

If the subducting lithospheric plate has abundant sediment, that sediment my be scraped off onto the overriding plate. The scraped-off sediment builds up into a wedge called a melange (see Figure 3.2). The wedge may build up so much that it produces a ridge that dominates the forearc, the region between the island arc and the trench axis. If the forearc is uplifted by tectonic forces, the ridge may be lifted above the surface to form islands. Examples of such islands include Guam, Yap, and 'Eua (Tonga).

To explain how the island arc itself forms, it is necesssary to consider the origin of island arc magmas. Earthquake studies and seismic imaging show that the subducting plate penetrates to depths of 700 km or more. As the lithosphere subducts into the mantle, increases in pressure and temperature drive off water and carbon dioxide (this is essentially distillation of the plate). The presence of these distillates lowers the melting point of overlying mantle rock so much that magma is produced. The magma then rises, because it is less dense than the surrounding solid mantle. Resultant volcanism at the sea floor builds a volcanic arc above the subduction zone. The islands that make up the Mariana arc, for example, are the summits of active volcanoes that formed on the sea floor about 100 km above the top of the subducting Pacific Plate.

Along a volcanic arc, volcanoes are spaced roughly every 50 km. This characteristic spacing seems to be controlled by how much melt it takes to sustain a conduit from the melt zone. Melting begins where the subducting slab reaches a depth of 100 km, so, as already pointed out for the Marianas, volcanoes grow above that point. Since volcanoes grow directly above the melt zone, the distance of the volcanic arc from the trench axis depends on the dip of the subducting plate (Gill 1981). If the plate dips steeply, as it does beneath the Bismarck Archipelago, the arc is close to the trench—in the Bismarcks the arc-trench distance is only 50 km. More typical are the Marianas, where the volcanic arc is 200 km from the trench axis (corresponding to a dip on the subducting plate of 30°). The shallowest dips of all occur below Western South America; in Chile, the arc-trench distance is 500 km.

Magma formed above subducting plates is most commonly of basaltic composition, at least initially. The magmas of island arcs can also be andesitic. Andesite is a medium gray to green rock often containing visible white to light gray crystals (e.g., Macdonald et al. 1983). Andesite has higher silica and more volatile content than basalt. Andesite can form either by incorporation of crustal materials into basaltic magma or by the cooling and partial crystallization of basaltic magmas in a magma chamber. In partial crystallization the early-formed crystals settle out from the magma, leaving a melt with a different composition (more andesitic) than the parent basaltic magma.

Andesitic lavas are chiefly found landward of the trenches that mark the circum-Pacific subduction zones. For this reason, the ring of volcanoes that encircles the Pacific is sometimes called the "Andesite Line." Volumetrically, andesites make up only a small proportion of island arcs, but that proportion is commonly exposed at the summits of the volcanoes. Subduction zones sometimes generate magmas with silica and volatile contents even higher than andesite. The resulting lava is rhyolite. Rhyolites are pink or light gray and often have visible quartz crystals.

Magma formation in island arcs is another process that concentrates metal-bearing minerals to potential ore status. Metals are concentrated in fluids associated with the late stages of crystallization of magmas, especially andesitic and rhyolitic magmas. If these late-stage magmas crystallize underground and subsequently undergo partial melting, the new magmas may have an even greater concentration of ore minerals and metals. Repeated episodes of magma generation in arc environments can produce exceptionally rich ore-bearing deposits, such as the copper ores of Bougainville Island.

Island arc volcanoes are composed of lava flows interlayered between deposits of ash or coarser volcaniclastic material (tephra). Alternating lavas and volcanic debris layers permit the volcano to build up steep slopes (around 35°), forming a stratovolcano or composite cone (Color Plate 3C). Eruptions are often explosive, a characteristic of andesitic and rhyolitic volcanoes. These eruptive explosions occur because the magma is highly charged with gases (derived from the subducting plate) and because the higher silica content of andesitic and rhyolitic magmas results in higher viscosity. Gases dissolved in a magma come out of solution as the magma rises and pressure decreases. Higher viscosity makes the rising magma more resistant to the expansion of gas bubbles. If the amount of expanding gas is great enough, it can blow the magma apart very near the surface, hurling gas and fragmented rock debris high into the atmosphere. The result is a voluminous ash deposit (Color Plate 3D).

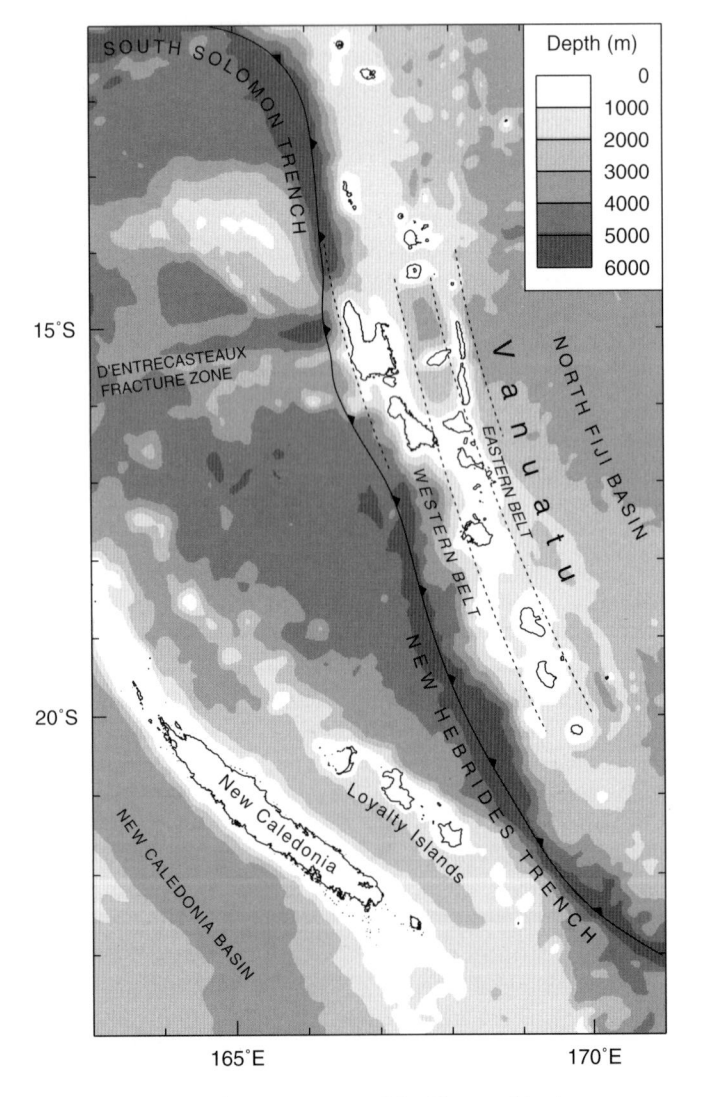

*Figure 3.6.* Regional structure map of the Vanuatu island arc.

If subduction occurs at a constant rate and in a constant direction, volcanoes tend to form a single arc above the magma source. Such simple geometry is easily disrupted. When a large, buoyant object, such as a continental fragment or an ancient island arc (both less dense than oceanic lithosphere), is rafted into the subduction zone, subduction may be blocked. If convergence between the plates continues, a new subduction zone must form away from the obstruction. Further, any change in motion at one margin of plate will affect all other margins. Such changes influence the location and nature of volcanism above the subduction zone.

The Vanuatu (New Hebrides) island arc, for example, has experienced a complex sequence of volcanic successions and structural disturbances in response to changes in the direction of subduction. Vanuatu consists of three separate volcanic arcs that lie parallel to one another (Figure 3.6). The western volcanic belt is the oldest (Kroenke 1984, Nunn 1994). Volcanic centers on these islands were active from about 15 to 11 Ma (millions of years ago), during a period in which the oceanic plate to the east of the chain was being subducted toward the west (Figure 3.7). At the end of this period subduction stopped, cutting off the magma supply to the volcanoes. A new subduction zone formed to accommodate continued convergence between the plates, but the new subduction was in the opposite direction.

The plate to the west of the islands began subducting eastward beneath the Western Belt. This subduction uplifted and deformed the Western Belt and induced extension of sea floor east of it. By about 8 Ma, the eastward subduction had generated enough magma to form a new volcanic chain: the Eastern Belt. About 5 Ma the eastward-dipping, downgoing plate adopted a steeper angle of subduction. The locus of active volcanism, following its magma source, migrated westward to its present position and formed yet another chain of volcanoes, the currently active Central Chain.

Such complex evolution of subduction zones may concentrate minerals to produce ore bodies. For example, in New Caledonia, ultramafic rock (dark rock rich in iron and magnesium) is exposed at the surface. This is now recognized as deep oceanic crustal material upthrust on land when it was squeezed between an island arc and a continent. Subsequent erosion and leaching of silica from the ultramafic rock enriched the residual surface layers in nickel and other metals. The nickel now supplies a thriving mining industry. Similar ultramafics are exposed in New Guinea and New Zealand, although there metal concentration is not to ore grade. New Caledonia, New Guinea, and New Zealand are all continental fragments; we discuss such landmasses in a later section.

## Marginal Seas and Backarc Basins

Around its western margin, the Pacific proper is separated from adjacent continents by marginal basins (seas). Marginal basins separate islands made of continental rocks from their parent continents; backarc basins form on the overriding-plate side of island arcs.

Marginal basins, such as the Tasman Sea, which separates

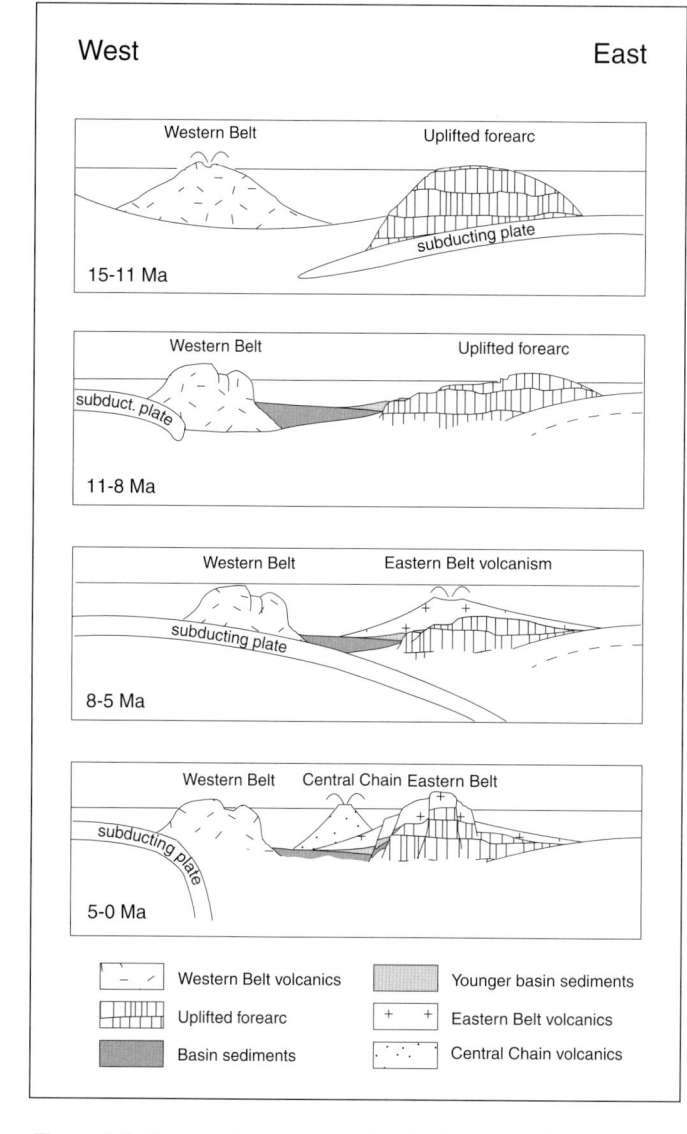

*Figure 3.7. Cross sections showing the development of the Vanuatu arc as a consequence of reversals in direction of subduction (redrawn after Nunn 1994).*

New Zealand from Australia, are the result of rifting and breakup of a continent. Roughly 150 Ma the southern supercontinent Gondwana started to break up to form present-day Australia, South America, Africa, India, and Antarctica. The rifts between these continent-sized pieces became centers for sea-floor spreading, creating the Indian, South Atlantic, and Southern oceans. But smaller fragments were rifted off too, to produce marginal seas.

Continental rifting and the formation of oceans may be triggered by the continent's drifting over a hot spot (Morgan 1981). The formation of marginal basins seems to have a similar origin: the Tasman Sea and the Coral Sea opened after Gondwana drifted over the Lord Howe hot spot (Yan and Kroenke 1993). Continental rifting, and the formation of ocean basins and marginal seas, are part of the same process that forms and sustains midocean ridges. That process is thought to be driven by deep convection of the mantle.

Backarc basins also owe their origins to sea-floor spreading, but they involve processes operating at shallower depths. Backarc basins form from rifting and spreading behind island arcs, phenomena that are driven by subduction and which do not appear to have any direct link to deep convection.

The origin of the driving forces that initiate and sustain backarc basins is a matter of some debate. Karig (1971) suggested that rising diapirs (plumes) of mantle material behind subducting plates provide the extensional forces necessary for the formation of backarc basins. Moberly (1972) suggested that subducting plates "roll back" toward the ocean basins from which they come and in so doing drag the subduction systems oceanward. Such trench rollback and the associated migration of the outer edge of the overriding plate produce tension forces sufficient to cause backarc extension.

Backarc basins follow a two-stage evolution of rifting and spreading (Fryer 1995). Along the island arc, volcanic eruptions and intrusions (magma solidified at depth) build up a thick, brittle crust. The brittle crust is weak, so any tension in the overriding plate will cause it to rift (i.e., to split) along the line of active volcanoes. Magma rises up to seal the rifts and build new lithosphere, which again rifts, because it is the weakest region of the overriding plate. With repeated rifting and sealing, the new lithosphere grows, separating the still-active line of arc volcanoes from the remnant arc, the ridge that was cleaved off from the volcanic arc by the initial rifting.

During the initial stage of extension, lavas erupted in the rifts may be of virtually any composition from basaltic through rhyolitic (Fryer et al 1990). In the initial stages, volcanism occurs over a broad region of the backarc basin. Eventually the extension in the backarc region widens the basin sufficiently, so that sea-floor spreading, like that at midocean ridges, becomes the mechanism by which the backarc basin grows. These processes may occur repeatedly, producing a series of island arcs, backarc basins, and remnant arcs.

The Mariana convergent margin (Figure 3.8) provides an example (Fryer 1996). The Mariana system was an established convergent margin prior to 50 Ma. A rifting event split the volcanic arc between about 31–15 Ma, isolating the Palau-Kyushu Ridge as a remnant arc and producing the central Parece Vela Basin until spreading ceased at 17–15 Ma. A second phase of rifting began about 10 Ma, separating an active volcanic arc from what was to become another remnant arc, the West Mariana Ridge. Extension of the Mariana Trough over the last 6–8 m.y. contributed to the increasingly bow-like shape of the arc as the rifting and sea-floor spreading continued to separate the active Mariana Ridge from the extinct West Mariana Ridge.

Ore formation often occurs in backarc basins. In part, this is because the periodicity of volcanism in arc environments provides opportunities for repeated enrichment episodes. As in midocean ridge complexes, metals are concentrated by hydrothermal circulation (temperature-driven circulation of sea water through the crust). Moreover, large volumes of ash from the nearby volcanoes creates a thick blanket of volcaniclastic sediment, significantly slowing heat loss and making ore production more efficient.

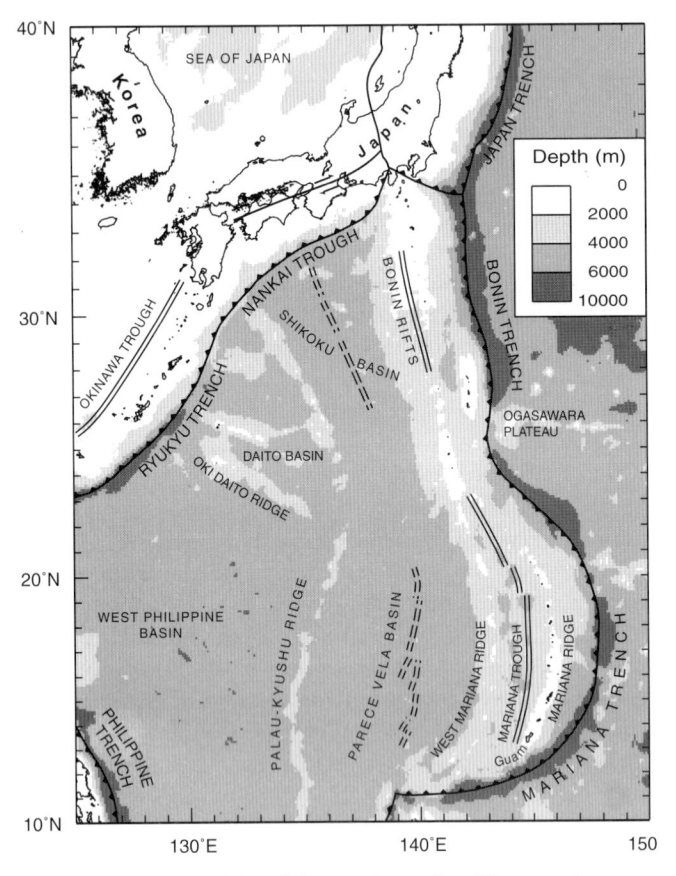

*Figure 3.8. Features of the Philippine Sea region. Plate margins are denoted as in Figure 1. Dashed double lines are relict spreading centers.*

## Continental Islands

The large islands of the southwest Pacific (New Guinea, New Caledonia, Fiji, and New Zealand) are fragments of the ancient southern continent Gondwana, together with island arc accretions. The geology of these islands is complicated by extensive faulting, metamorphism, and magmatic intrusion. Much of the old geology has been further obscured by more recent volcanism. Nevertheless, guided by plate tectonics, a coherent story of how these islands evolved is beginning to emerge (Coleman 1997). The discussion here will focus on New Zealand, and will necessarily be brief.

Since 300 Ma, the New Zealand area was the site of a succession of subduction systems, with associated trenches and island arcs, lying some distance off the east coast of Gondwana (Grindley and Davey 1982). Sediments from the continent accumulated in the intervening sea to form thick sequences of greywacke (sandstone) and argillite (siltstone), which were interlayered with volcanics. At 125 Ma subduction was blocked by the accumulated buoyant material, resulting in a major change in plate motions.

The growing mass of sediment and volcanic accretions off Gondwana was compressed, uplifted, and intruded by granite (granite is mineralogically identical to rhyolite, but has larger crystals due to slower cooling). Slivers of underlying mantle—ultramafic rock—were also thrust up into these structures. Much rock was metamorphosed by being buried and subjected to higher pressure and temperature (which changes the minerals). This resulted in the metamorphic rocks greenschist and blueschist. Through such complex processes the margin of Gondwana was extended, forming the ancestral New Caledonia and New Zealand. The present Lord Howe Rise and Campbell Plateau were also part of this landmass (Figure 3.9).

The final breakup of Gondwana occurred about 90 Ma when spreading began between Australia and Antarctica. At about 80 Ma, additional spreading rifted New Zealand away from Australia and Antarctica to create the Tasman Basin and the Southwestern Pacific Basin. The Tasman spreading ended around 60 Ma, but the Southwestern Pacific Basin spreading continued, carrying New Zealand northward (Figure 3.10). During this time, the mountains of New Zealand were eroded away to form a large area of subdued relief, which was repeatedly inundated by the sea. Organic matter deposited in coastal swamps formed coal deposits, while the shells of shallow-water marine organisms accumulated as limestone (Gage 1980).

Since the separation from Gondwana, New Zealand has been carried north, rotated counterclockwise, and stretched out along the Alpine Fault. Today New Zealand straddles the boundary between the Pacific and Australian Plates (Figure 3.9). To the north the Pacific Plate is being subducted along the Kermadec and Hikurangi trenches. To the south, the Australian Plate is being subducted beneath the Pacific Plate along the

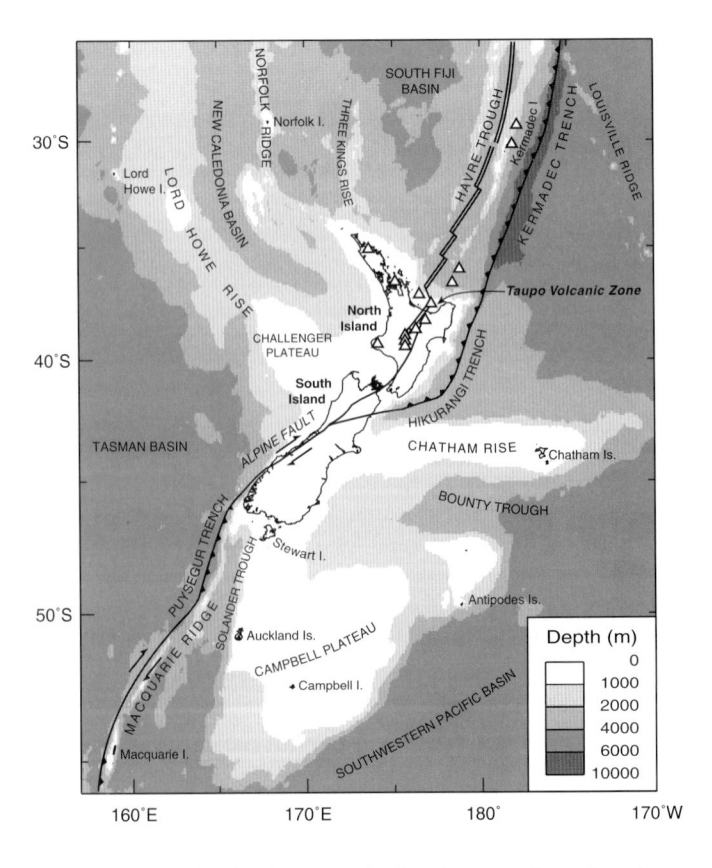

*Figure 3.9 The islands of New Zealand and surrounding submarine features. Volcanoes active within the last 1,000 years are marked by white triangles.*

40      The Pacific Islands

Puysegur Trench. New Zealand is thus caught between two subduction systems with opposite polarity. Between these subduction systems, motion between the Australian and Pacific Plates is taken up along the Alpine Fault, which extends the length of South Island.

The Alpine Fault has predominantly transform motion (horizontal slip parallel to the trace of the fault), with a total displacement of 450 km in the last 27 million years. But it also has a small component of convergence, which causes uplift. Uplift on the fault has raised the Southern Alps. These mountains, among the highest in the Pacific Islands region, have reached 3,700 m and continue to rise today.

Volcanism has occurred episodically on both islands throughout New Zealand's geological history. The modern volcanics of North Island are driven by subduction of the Pacific Plate into the Hikurangi Trench. Other volcanoes have also been active in the recent past: Mt. Egmont in the west and the Auckland and Bay of Islands volcanic zones on the northern peninsula of North Island. The Taranaki Plain (around Mt. Egmont) and the city and suburbs of Auckland remain regions of significant volcanic hazard. Subduction is also causing volcanism in the Kermadec Islands. Backarc spreading is active in the Havre Trough and extends onshore into the Taupo Volcano Zone.

## Concluding Remarks

The Pacific region displays each of the major processes of plate tectonics: hot-spot volcanism, divergent and convergent plate margin processes, and transform fault motion. All of the plate boundaries throughout the Pacific shift through time, adjusting to changes in plate motion. Such changes will continue. The modern southwest Pacific is a clutter of rifted continental fragments, abandoned island arcs, and shallow oceanic plateaus. This material is so resistant to subduction that a future adjustment in plate motions is inevitable. That adjustment may already be happening. A diffuse band of earthquakes has developed on the Pacific plate between Yap and Samoa, far north of the current subduction zones that stretch from New Guinea to Tonga (Kroenke and Walker 1986). Nearby, a bathymetric deep has developed on the sea floor. This may mark the birthplace of the Pacific's newest subduction zone, the Micronesian Trench.

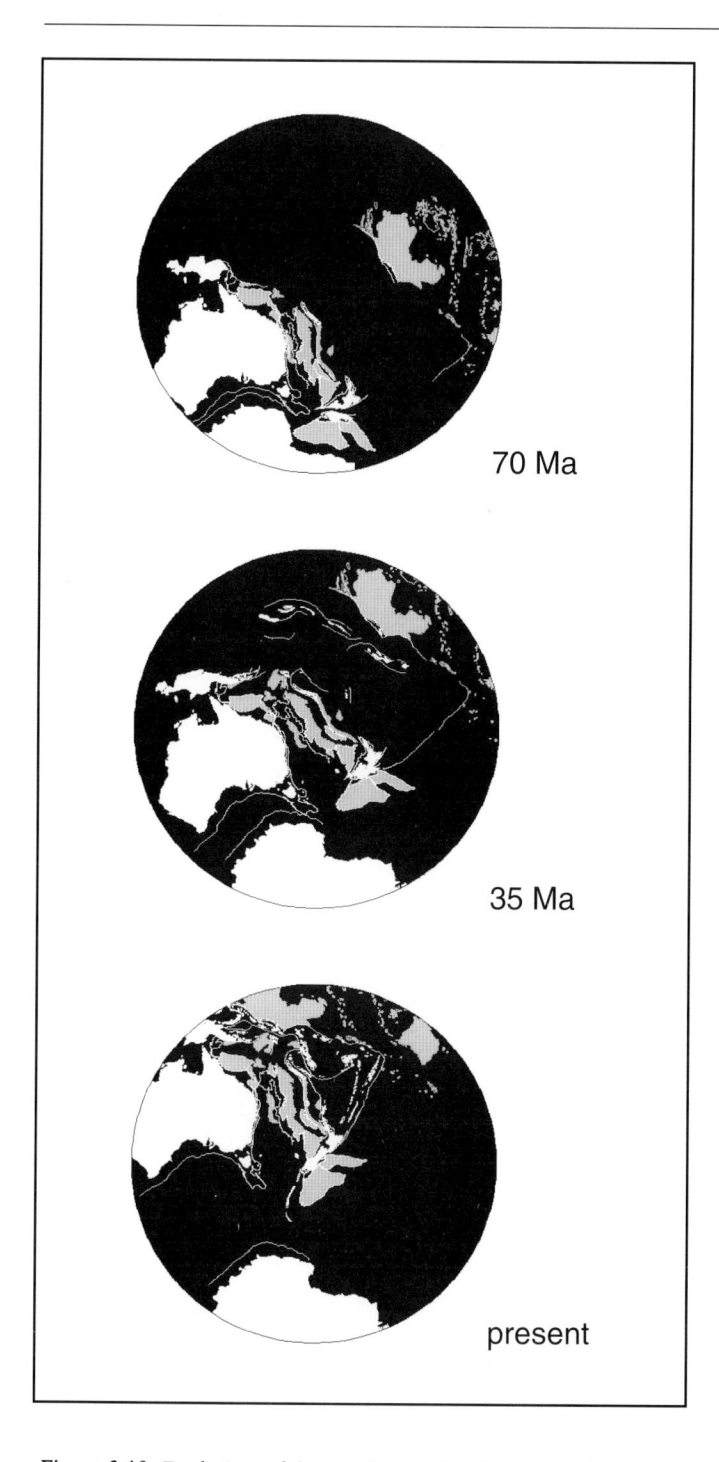

*Figure 3.10. Evolution of the Southwest Pacific over the last 70 million years. Continents are black; oceanic plateaus and submerged continental fragments are gray. Continental margins and subduction zones are represented as dark lines. At 70 Ma, spreading between Australia and Antarctica has been going on for 20 million years, but the spreading was slow so the continents are still close to each other. Spreading is going on in the Tasman Basin, separating New Zealand from Australia. Spreading has just split South Island and the Campbell Plateau from Antarctica. At 35 Ma, Tasman spreading has ended, but more rapid spreading is going on between Australia and Antarctica and between Antarctica and New Zealand. New Zealand is being carried north. The Kermadec Trench is about to become active. In the present, New Zealand has been carried farther north, while South Island has been stretched along the Alpine Fault. (Simplified from Yan and Kroenke 1993).*

# Bibliography

Coleman, P. J. 1997. Australia and the Melanesian arcs: a review of tectonic settings. *Journal of Australian Geology and Geophysics* 17:113–125.

Darwin, C. R. 1860. *A naturalist's voyage (Journal of research into the natural history and geology of the countries visited during the voyage of HMS 'Beagle' round the world)*. London: Henry Colburn, final revised edition. Reprinted in 1906 as *The voyage of the Beagle*, London: J.M. Dent.

Fryer, P., B. Taylor, C. Langmuir, and A. Hochstaedter. 1990. Petrology and geochemistry of lavas from the Sumisu and Torishima backarc rifts. *Earth and Planetary Science Letters* 100:161–178.

Fryer, P. 1995. Geology of the Mariana Trough. In *Backarc basins; tectonics and magmatism*, ed. B. Taylor. New York: Plenum Press, 237–279.

Fryer, P. 1996. Tectonic evolution of the Mariana convergent margin. *Reviews of Geophysics* 34:89–125.

Gage, M. 1980. *Legends in the rocks: an outline of New Zealand geology*. New Zealand: Whitcoulls Publishers.

Gill, J. B. 1981. *Orogenic andesites*. Berlin-Heidelberg: Springer-Verlag.

Grindley, G.W., and F.J. Davey. 1982. The reconstruction of New Zealand, Australia, and Antarctica. In *Antarctic Geoscience*, ed. C. Craddock. Madison, Wisconsin: University of Wisconsin Press.

Karig, D. E. 1971. Origin and development of marginal basins in the western Pacific. *Journal of Geophysical Research* 76:2452–2561.

Kroenke, L. W. 1984. Cenozoic tectonic development of the Southwest Pacific, U.N. ESCAP, CCOP/SOPAC Technical Bulletin 6.

Kroenke L. W. 1996. Plate tectonic development of the western and south-western Pacific: mesozoic to the present. In *The origin and evolution of Pacific Island biotas, New Guinea to eastern Polynesia: patterns and processes*, eds. A. Keast and S. E. Miller. Amsterdam: SPB Academic Publishing, 19–34.

Kroenke, L. W., and D. A. Walker. 1986. Evidence for the formation of a new trench in the western Pacific. *Eos, Transactions of the American Geophysical Union* 67:145–146.

Moberly, R. 1972. Origin of lithosphere behind island arcs, with reference to the western Pacific. In *Studies in Earth and space sciences*, eds. R. Shagam, et al. Geological Society of America Memoir 132. Boulder, Colorado: Geological Society of America, 35–55.

Moore, J. G., D. A. Clague, R. T. Holcomb, P. W. Lipman, W. R. Normark, and M. E. Torresan. 1989. Prodigious submarine landslides on the Hawaiian Ridge. *Journal of Geophysical Research* 94:17,465–17,484.

Morgan, W. J. 1981. Hotspot tracks and the opening of the Atlantic and Indian Oceans. In *The sea*, Vol. 7: *The oceanic lithosphere*, ed. C. Emiliani. New York: J. Wiley, 443–487.

Macdonald, G. A., A. T. Abbott, and F. L. Peterson 1983. *Volcanoes in the sea: the geology of Hawaii*, Second Edition. Honolulu: University of Hawai'i Press.

Nunn, P.D. 1994. *Oceanic islands*. Oxford: Blackwell Publishers.

Peltier, R. W. 1996. Mantle viscosity and ice-age ice sheet topography. *Science* 273:1359–1364.

Scheibner, E., T. Sato, and C. Craddock. 1991. Tectonic map of the Circum-Pacific region, Southwest Quadrant, Circum Pacific Map Series, Map CP-37. Denver, Colorado: US Geological Survey.

Wessel, P. 1993. Observational constraints on models of the Hawaiian hot spot swell. *Journal of Geophysical Research* 98:16,095–16,104.

Wessel, P. and L. W. Kroenke. 1997. A geometric technique for relocating hotspots and refining absolute plate motions. *Nature* 387:365–369.

Wegener, A. 1929. *Die Entstehung der Kontinente und Ozeane*, 4th edition (revised), translated by J. Biram 1967, *The Origin of continents and oceans*. London: Methuen.

Wilson, J. T. 1963. Evidence from islands on the spreading of ocean floors. *Nature* 197:536–538.

Yan, C.Y., and L.W. Kroenke. 1993. A plate tectonic reconstruction of the Southwest Pacific, 0–100 Ma. Proceedings of the Ocean Drilling Program, Scientific Results, 130:697–709.

HIGP Publication 1011.

SOEST Publication 4667.

# Chapter 4

# Geomorphology

*Patrick D. Nunn*

## Introduction

The Pacific Islands region extends over 130° of longitude and 70° of latitude. Some islands are more than 100,000 km² in size; others are miniscule in size. Some islands are pieces of ancient continent, hundreds of millions of years old; other islands are still forming, and periodic volcanic eruptions give subaerial landforms little chance to develop. Some tropical islands are so high they have ice caps; others are so low they can barely be seen on approach by sea. Some islands are rain-soaked; others sometimes go for years without rain.

Prevailing climatic and geological controls produce seemingly infinite permutations and militate against sweeping generalizations. Yet generalize we must to get some appreciation of Pacific Island landscapes. This chapter begins by looking in detail at the principal causes of landscape diversity in the Pacific Islands, along with some pertinent examples. This is followed by a systematic account of landscapes on distinct island types. The chapter concludes with a discussion of rates of change and two key issues in Pacific Island landscape study.

## Controls on Landform Development

Climate, oceanography, and geology are the principal controls on global landform development. Climatic and oceanographic controls, particularly precipitation, are important causes of landform variation throughout the Pacific Islands. Geological controls are also important, but less so relative to continents, owing to the more restricted range of geologic structures and histories on islands (Nunn 1987). Many Pacific islands are seismically and volcanically active. In these cases, vertical tectonics (land-level movements) may overwhelm the influence of other factors in landscape evolution.

Long-term changes of climate and sea level (Figure 4.1) have also brought about changes in landforms on certain Pacific islands. Some landforms are relict in character, formed in the past when conditions were significantly different. On some islands, people have been the principal agents of landscape change, often blithely unaware of the long-term effects of their actions.

### Climatic and Oceanographic Controls

Climate in the Pacific varies mostly with latitude. Islands nearest the equator are generally hotter and wetter and experience more tropical cyclones (hurricanes, typhoons) than those farther from the equator. Changing amounts of solar radiation in the course of a year are responsible for significant seasonal

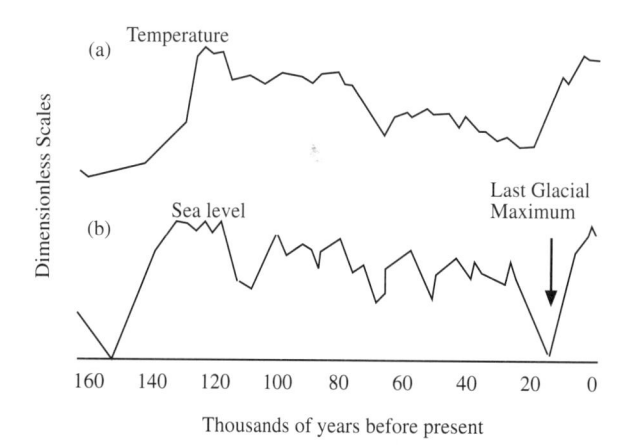

*Figure 4.1. Changes in temperature and sea level during the past 150,000 years (after Nunn 1997). Temperature changes are derived from oxygen-isotope analyses of marine microorganisms; sea-level changes from studies of emerged reefs on the Huon Peninsula, Papua New Guinea.*

variations of temperature and rainfall. On Tarawa, Kiribati, twice-yearly crossings by the intertropical convergence zone produce two peaks in precipitation. Geomorphic processes on such islands are affected by periodic changes in rainfall and water-table level. For example, it is possible that seasonal shifts in the relative amounts of fresh and saline groundwater in the intertidal zone are important in beachrock formation (Schmalz 1971).

Various aspects of climate also act as limiting factors in the development of particular landforms. Amphitheater-headed valleys, for example, can develop only on those high parts of volcanic islands where annual precipitation exceeds 2,000 mm (Nunn 1994a). The development of phosphate rock on many Pacific reef islands is one reason why they have survived so long. Phosphate rock of this kind requires deposition of guano and low annual precipitation levels to prevent its decomposition and leaching (Stoddart and Scoffin 1983).

In some of the westernmost Pacific islands, the reversal of winds associated with the Asian and Austral monsoons brings large amounts of orographic moisture to opposing sides of islands during summer and winter. Landform development on both sides may be similar, though during any season a different set of climatic processes predominates. The aridity of Easter Island is associated with the stationary high-pressure cell in the eastern Pacific. This has given rise to a set of semiarid landforms quite different from those of the nearest islands in French Polynesia, 2,400 km to the west.

The ocean circulation of the Pacific is dominated by two large gyres. The gyre in the North Pacific involves clockwise movement of water; that in the South Pacific involves a counterclockwise movement. The impact of ocean currents on landform development is well represented by the presence of coral at unusually high latitudes in the western Pacific, where warm equatorial water is driven poleward.

A final consideration involves the gross distribution of islands within the Pacific. Most islands are within or just outside the tropics; there is a conspicuous paucity of islands in temperate and high latitudes. One reason for this is that the ocean water in these areas is too cool for coral growth. When an island drifts into these areas and sinks, it disappears. Yet an island that sinks within the coral seas will often develop a capping of coral reef and thus retain expression at the ocean surface.

An example is provided by the northern volcanoes in the Hawai'i–Emperor Island seamount chain. When the islands initially subsided beneath sea level, they were in warmer waters and developed a reef capping. However, the northwest drift of the Pacific Plate has moved these islands into cooler waters. Subsequently, the islands along with the reef caps disappeared beneath the ocean surface, forming a chain of guyots.

The Lau Islands of eastern Fiji lie centrally within the coral seas. When the original volcanic islands (on which the modern islands are founded) sank, they developed either a reef cap or a reef fringe. Subject to uplift some two million years ago, these islands now appear as raised limestone islands. Where reefs have risen along with a center volcanic core, a *makatea* island has been created.

## Topographic and Geologic Controls

On account of their small sizes and locations within a persistent wind belt, many Pacific islands have well-defined windward and leeward sides, with marked differences in mean annual precipitation, vegetation, landforms, and landforming processes. Examples abound in the trade wind belts, particularly in the South Pacific.

The large island Viti Levu in Fiji lies in the path of the southeast trade winds all year (although cyclonic precipitation, generally in short bursts, commonly affects the entire island during the southern summer). Typical annual precipitation inland from the coast varies from 4,000 mm on the southeast side to 1,500 mm on the northwest side (see Table 5.1).

The southeast (windward) side of Viti Levu (Color Plate 4A) has a thick covering of regolith, or weathered rock (a consequence of high rainfall and chemical weathering). Much of the terrain is still forested, with sinuous streams following narrow valleys. The northwest (leeward) side of Viti Levu (Color Plate 4B) is covered largely by grasslands probably established during the aridity associated with the Last Glacial Maximum 17 Ka (thousands of years ago). There is little regolith, and soil has accumulated mainly in valley bottoms.

Farther south, the influence of topography on climate and landform development is illustrated by South Island, New Zealand. The Southern Alps, which fringe the island's west coast, lie in the paths of the prevailing westerlies all year. The western slopes are wet, forested, and characterized by short, swift rivers and a narrow, discontinuous coastal plain. The eastern slopes are much drier, generally lacking in forest cover, with plains built largely from glaciofluvial (glacial melt) outwash, and crossed by long, wide rivers.

## Volcanic and Tectonic Controls

Many Pacific islands are volcanically active, ranging from the large shield volcanoes on the island of Hawai'i to the many stratovolcanoes along the Pacific Rim such as Anatahan (Marianas) or the underwater Fonuafo'ou (Tonga). Particularly in the case of volcanoes that have become dormant or extinct in the last few hundred thousand years, much of the original volcanic shape may remain (Figure 4.2). In recently active volcanoes, cinder cones and other eruptive features may also be preserved.

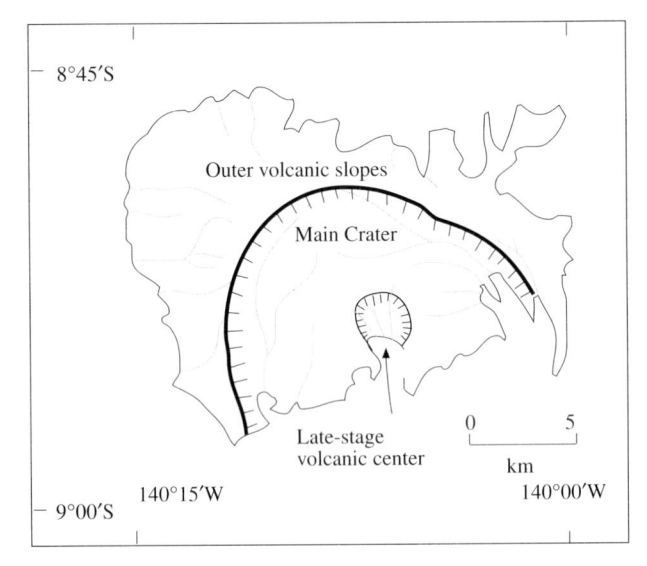

*Figure 4.2.* Influence of volcanic structure on landscape. The island Nuku Hiva in the Marquesas group (after Brousse et al. 1978, and Thomas 1990). Most of the island is formed from the slopes of the original volcano. The south-central part is a caldera in which a late-stage volcano formed.

Most young volcanoes are radially drained. Slopes soon become deeply dissected, particularly where volcanic (rather than sedimentary) material makes up a large part of the surface. Amphitheater-headed valleys develop in the wetter, usually higher, parts. Where the walls of these valleys intersect, sharp, serrate ridges may form (Color Plate 4C). Isolated, triangular-shaped parts of the original volcanic slopes, known as planezes, may remain. Volcanic sediments transported from upland ranges are important components of lowland landscapes, and have been so for much of the Neogene (Table 4.1).

### TABLE 4.1

**Geologic Time Scale Since the Cretaceous, Showing the Neogene Subperiod**

| Period | Subperiod | Epoch | Millions of years ago |
|---|---|---|---|
| Quaternary | Neogene | Holocene | .01-present |
| | | Pleistocene | 1.8-.01 |
| Tertiary | | | 24-1.8 |
| | Paleogene | | 66.4-24 |
| Cretaceous | | | 144-66.4 |

Such processes and landscapes cannot occur without significant precipitation. The need for moisture to produce alluvial sediments on volcanic islands is exemplified by arid Pinzon Island in the Galapagos group, where there has been a lack of significant erosion or soil development in the past several hundred thousand years (Baitis and Lindstrom 1980).

Islands in the western Pacific (where the oldest and largest island groups are located) are subject to plate boundary tectonic processes, resulting in uplift and subsidence. Uplift and subsidence also occur near midplate islands, where volcanic loading causes a moat-and-arch formation. Several examples of raised reefs occur in the Southern Cook Islands as a consequence of loading by the high island, Rarotonga.

Most inhabited islands in Tonga are emerged limestone islands, marking the rising edge of the Australian Plate (Figure 4.3). Linear ridges mark old reef barriers, and residual hills mark old patch reefs. Successive uplifts during the Holocene (10 Ka–present) elevated the *Porolithon onkodes* algal ridge on Tongatapu (Nunn 1993).

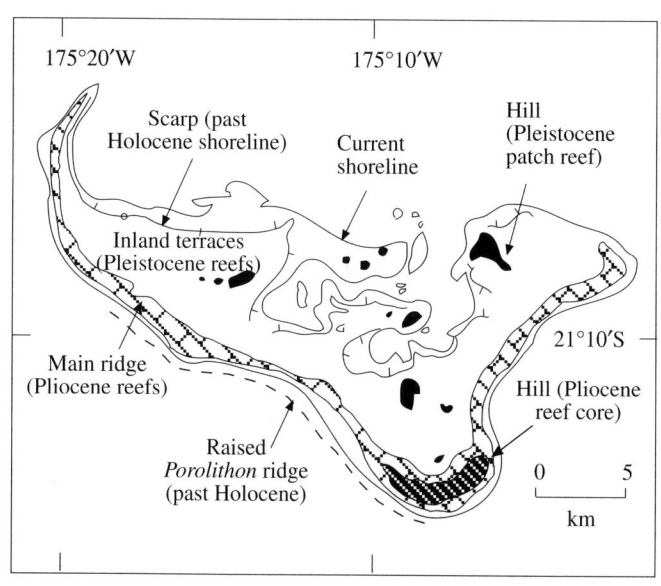

*Figure 4.3.* Geomorphology of the island of Tongatapu in Tonga. (Nunn and Finau 1995). Most landforms are from Roy (1990).

Karst (eroded limestone) landscapes form when emerged reef is subjected to solution processes, characterized by dolines (depressions), with conical hills and steep pinnacles. The types of karst landscapes that develop on emerged reef surfaces of various ages were described for parts of Vanuatu by Strecker et al. (1987). Raised limestone islands are often rich in phosphate (valued for fertilizer), and decades of mining activities have resulted in dramatic alterations to the landscape.

Uplift outside the coral seas often also produces staircases of emerged shoreline indicators, but these are commonly less easy to interpret than their counterparts within the coral seas, as residual deposits are often absent. Good examples are provided in various parts of New Zealand, where most landforms manifest the effects of emergence (Pillans 1986).

Subsidence may occur as a consequence of midplate volcanic loading, Pacific Plate drift, and tectonic instability at plate margins. Landforms produced by subsidence, such as embayments, may be visible along the coasts of Pacific islands. Embayments along the south coast of Vava'u, Tonga, provide a good example (Figure 4.4). Subsidence occurs on many Hawaiian islands, but the coast lacks embayment except where the shoreline is sufficiently dissected.

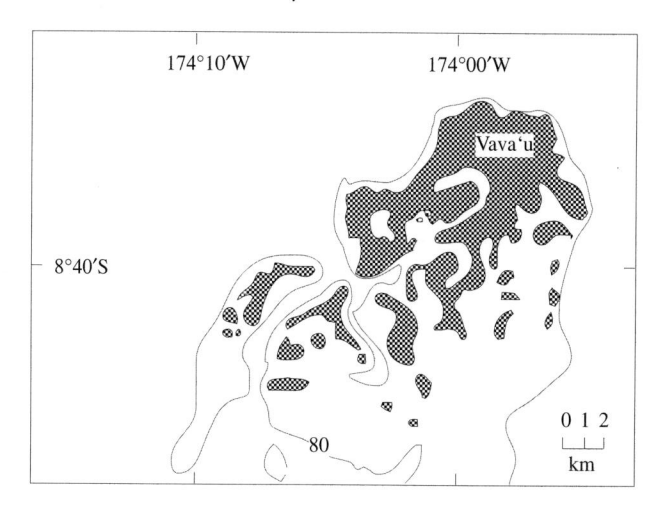

*Figure 4.4.* Map of the Vava'u island group on the Tonga frontal arc (Nunn 1994a). The insular shelf is delimited by the 80-m isobath. The form of the island group suggests increasing submergence from north to south.

## Environmental Change

Explaining Pacific island geomorphology requires some understanding of the environmental conditions that prevailed at the time island landforms first began evolving.

The tropical Pacific is known to have been drier around the Last Glacial Maximum. Yet islands in Hawai'i received heavy rainfall, at least on their windward sides, creating a degree of dissection that is anomalous under present climate conditions (Gavenda 1992). In other parts of the Pacific, lowland sediment bodies began accumulating around the end of the Last Glacial, when precipitation exceeded present levels.

Vegetation is one of the most sensitive indicators of environmental change and also affects the types and rates of geomorphic processes. An example is provided by the past 30,000 years of vegetation change in the New Guinea highlands (Flenley 1979). A site 3,000 m above sea level would have lain above the forest limit until (about) 28 Ka; below it until 26 Ka; above it during the Last Glacial Maximum; and below it again following deglaciation (15–10 Ka).

The caldera Rano Kao on Easter Island is filled with erosional sediment, but it is uncertain whether this sediment accumulated under the present short-grass vegetation or under forest (long since removed). Pollen analyses suggest the latter option. The grassland is probably a recent phenomenon on Easter Island (with dry forest dominant previously), occurring some time after human settlement (Flenley and King 1984).

Sea-level changes have left a profound imprint on many Pacific coasts. Sea level rose from a low of −130 m at 17 Ka during the Last Glacial Maximum to a high of +1.5 m 4 Ka (Color Plate 4D) (Pirazzoli and Montaggioni 1988; Jones 1992;

*Figure 4.5. Part of the north coast of the island Tahiti, French Polynesia (Davis 1928).*

Kayanne et al. 1993; Nunn 1995). Early Holocene sea-level rise inundated the lower parts of valleys that had existed during the Last Glacial. Subsequently, falling sea levels led to the emergence of coastal plains that were ideal for human settlement (Figure 4.5).

## Human Impacts

Humans have profoundly influenced the landscapes of most Pacific islands, but the precise extent of this influence, particularly with regard to pre-European populations, is the subject of debate at present (Nunn 1992, 1994b).

Undoubted effects include the deliberate reshaping of the landscape, ranging from the reclamation of nearshore areas for coastal development to the removal of hills for roadways. Over 1,000 years ago, artificial islands were being constructed in the Langa Langa lagoon off Malaita in Solomon Islands for habitation sites. Reclaimed lands form the basis of much of downtown Honolulu and Waikīkī Beach, on Oʻahu, Hawaiʻi.

Mining has also been a major cause of landscape change. Extreme examples come from the island arcs of the western Pacific, rich in mineral ores. The effects of indiscriminate extraction of ore and mining waste disposal on Bougainville, Papua New Guinea (closed since 1989 after protests from local people), were detailed by Brown (1974). The effects of mining waste on estuaries and as a cause of recent shoreline progradation (extension) in New Caledonia were described by Bird et al. (1984).

Deforestation is a major contributor to landscape change in many parts of the Pacific. A tripling in volume of log exports from Papua New Guinea between 1979 and 1988 indicates the extent of the contemporary problem. Demand for hardwoods has led to rapidly increasing pressure on governments and landowners to sell this valuable resource. A recent estimate suggested that, if deforestation in Solomon Islands continued at its present rate, there would be no forest remaining by 2010.

Deforestation exposes the ground to direct impact by rain, which, in the tropical Pacific, is often torrential. The result, particularly on steep slopes, is soil erosion by sheet wash, rilling, and eventually gullying. Many Pacific Island gullies are cut in regolith; the soil was lost long ago (Figure 4.6). On temperate Pacific islands, the effects of deforestation are also severe. In the Wairarapa area of North Island, New Zealand, as many as 90 soil slips per $km^2$ have been recorded on areas cleared of forest for sheep grazing (Glasby 1986).

*Figure 4.6. Roadcut in regolith, Nuku-Lutu road, central Viti Levu Island, Fiji. Regolith forms in the humid tropics under rain forest and is rapidly eroded when exposed. Rilling and gullying are already affecting this outcrop, which is liable to failure as long as it remains exposed (photo PDN).*

Forest clearance and other types of land-use changes have profoundly altered Pacific Island landscapes. Many river channels have become filled with sediment, and channel capacity has been reduced. Such rivers thus flood frequently and intensely (compare Figures 4.7 and 4.8). Many river terraces, favored for planting crops, have become flood-prone and can be used no

*Figure 4.7. The former bridge at Matainasau, central Viti Levu Island, Fiji, was built to ensure that the transinsular road would remain open even when the river flooded. This view is from downstream (photo PDN).*

*Figure 4.8. Flooding associated with Tropical Cyclone KINA in 1993 washed the Matainasau bridge away (see Figure 4.7) and moved most of the boulders on the floodplain several kilometers downstream. The remains of the bridge are viewed from upstream (photo PDN).*

*Figure 4.9. Prices much higher than those that could be obtained on the open market are presently guaranteed for Fiji sugar under the Lomé Convention. This has encouraged farmers to plant cane on steep slopes where such practices cannot be sustained for long and will lead to land degradation if continued. This view is of cane fields near Talekosovi, northern Viti Levu island (photo PDN).*

longer. This has forced farmers onto steeper slopes, exacerbating the problems associated with lowland flooding (Figure 4.9).

Other human impacts are impossible to catalogue meaningfully in a short space. Many modern human impacts are plainly evident, but controversy often attends the cause(s) of longer-term landscape changes following human settlement. The debate has become polarized between those who attribute the majority of landscape changes within this period to human actions and those who regard these changes as primarily the consequence of natural fluctuations in climate, sea level, and geomorphic processes.

## Pacific Island Landscapes

Given the principal controls on landform development discussed above, the potential for landscape variability within the Pacific region is considerable. Pacific islands a thousand kilometers apart may have similar assemblages of landforms because of similarity in climate and geotectonic character. Conversely, on large, complex islands such as New Guinea and others in the western Pacific, landform type may exhibit considerable variability over a short distance.

To accommodate these variations within a rational framework, several categories are defined in Table 4.2 and used as a basis for landscape description in the remainder of this section. There is clearly scope for overlap, but this need not be a problem, as the categorization is intended only as an arbitrary device to facilitate landscape description.

### Volcanic Midplate Islands

Most small, remote islands in the Pacific are volcanic in origin. They may be products of intraplate island-forming processes, such as are taking place at the southeast ends of many hot-spot chains. Examples include the Hawaiian, Samoan and Society island chains (Duncan and Clague 1985).

Many of these islands formed from single volcanoes, so,

**TABLE 4.2**

**Classification of Pacific Islands Used As a Basis for Systematic Landscape Description**

Volcanic midplate islands
Volcanic plate margin islands
Continental islands
Limestone islands
Atolls
Islands of mixed lithology

depending on the time elapsed since the last major eruption, their landscapes exhibit a set of landforms that vary only slightly with latitude and altitude. Young islands of this kind commonly develop radial drainage, sometimes manifested as parasol ribbing in its initial stages, progressing to gullied slopes (Figure 4.10). Capture of adjacent streams by headward erosion of others leads to a less regular drainage pattern, often characterized by isolation of planezes.

Amphitheater-headed valleys are characteristic of midocean

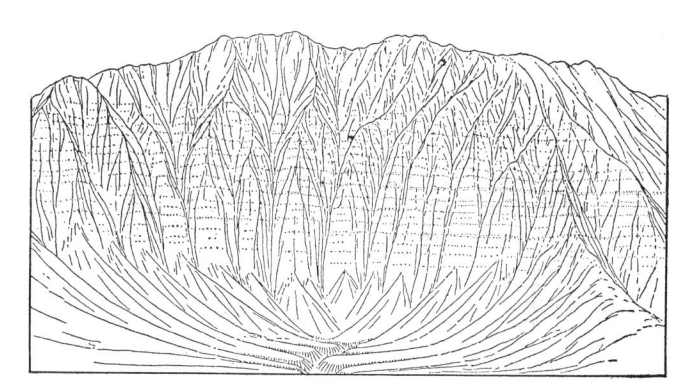

*Figure 4.10. Sketch of the Pali, northeast O'ahu, Hawai'i (Davis 1928). Note the steep gullied slopes with the fans at their foot. The river channel is cut into sediments derived from the cliffs.*

volcanic islands of the Pacific, though they are also found in islands at convergent margins. These occur mostly on igneous rocks where annual rainfall exceeds 2,000 mm, and where elevation exceeds 500 m. Such valleys are typically narrow in their middle sections but open upstream into large amphitheaters surrounded by near-vertical slopes.

Early studies of such valleys demonstrated that they developed by parallel retreat of the surrounding walls (Figure 4.11). Scott and Street (1976) showed that this was accomplished by periodic soil avalanching during heavy rain. Recent work has shown that seepage of water from the base of these slopes carries sediment away, resulting in steep valley sides (Onda 1994). Resistant dike rock remains near vertical at valley heads, as in the Pali (Cliffs), on O'ahu, Hawai'i (see Figure 4.10).

An important control on islands that owe their origin to hot-spot volcanism is the progressive subsidence of the islands

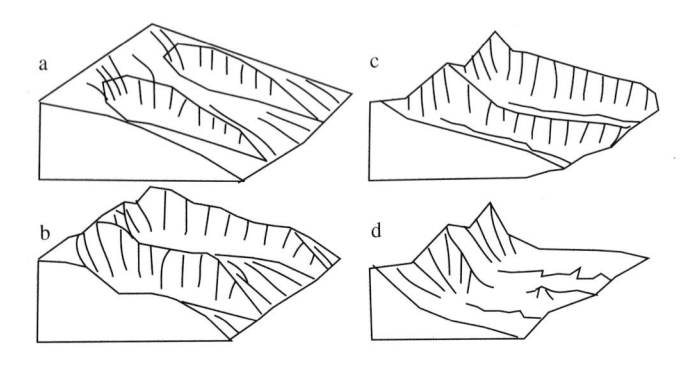

*Figure 4.11. Stages in the formation of amphitheater-headed valleys in Hawai'i (after Nunn 1994a and sources therein): a. Orographic precipitation carves deep valleys. b. Valleys widen. c. Valley sides are lowered and breached. d. Only the steep headwall remains.*

as they move away from the fixed hot spot. Subsidence affects gross form in a regular manner. This was realized by some of the earliest scientists to work in the Pacific (Dana 1890) and has been quantified for the Society Islands (Morhange 1992).

## Volcanic Plate Margin Islands

Island arcs of the western Pacific, such as those in Solomon Islands and the Bismarck Archipelago, have been influenced by their geographic location near continents (altering climate patterns) and along plate boundaries (intensifying tectonic activity).

Monsoon winds, related to summer heating on continental land masses, bring heavy rainfall in some areas. Erosion of sediment from uplands has created extensive lowlands, especially along the coast. Lowland sediment bodies are moved in floods, often as mudflows or debris flows. Upland slopes are also prone to fail when their sediment cover becomes saturated.

Intense seismic and tectonic activity is present in island arcs. Earthquakes often trigger landslides and are a significant geomorphic agent in such settings (Peart 1991). Uplift is common, signaled by raised reefs surrounding many islands (Figure 4.12).

Some islands in the western Pacific are being uplifted so rapidly that the land surface is unable to reach an equilibrium condition with respect to landforming processes. Upland erosion is thereby catalyzed, and catastrophic processes tend to be significant agents of denudation. Thus, the denudation rate of the island Taiwan is among the highest in the world (Li 1976).

## Continental Islands

Fragments of Gondwana exist in New Guinea, New Zealand, and New Caledonia. The landforms of such continental islands are old and highly diverse, in comparison to those on other Pacific islands. Even in tectonically active New Zealand, erosion surfaces of late Cretaceous age are found (Pillans et al. 1992).

New Zealand has been much modified by glaciation. Substantial shifts in geomorphic process regime (alternating between glaciation and stream erosion) have thus occurred over past geological history. Conversely, in tropical New Guinea, which was affected to a lesser extent by Neogene climate changes, glaciation has been limited to a narrow band of high-altitude landscapes.

Sediment yields from some rivers in Papua New Guinea (Table 4.3) are among the highest in the world, reflecting the high rainfall (which can reach 10,000 mm annually in the headwaters of the Fly River) (Pickup et al. 1980), its intensity, the structure and lithology of the bedrock being eroded, and uplift.

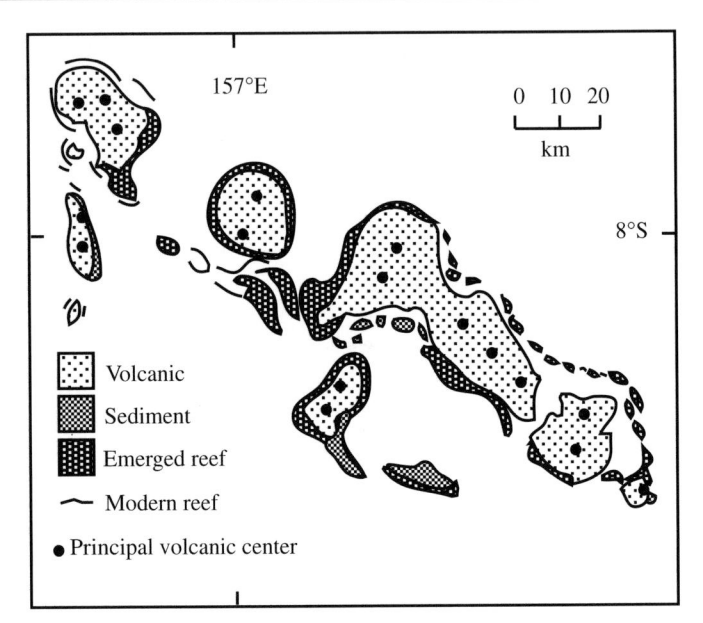

*Figure 4.12. Emerged coral reefs in Solomon Islands (after Nunn 1994a).*

### TABLE 4.3

**Sediment Yields of Rivers in Papua New Guinea**
(from Douglas and Spencer 1985, and sources therein)

| Station | Catchment area (km²) | Runoff (mm/year) | Vegetation cover (%) | Suspended sediment yield (m³/km²/year) |
|---|---|---|---|---|
| Ok Ningi | 4.56 | 7208 | 95 | 2980-4050 |
| Ok Tedi | 420 | 5695 | 95 | 1720-2960 |
| Ok Menga | 240 | 6660 | 95 | 370-460 |
| Alice | 3900 | 5870 | 95 | 300-560 |
| Fly at Kiunga | 6300 | 5360 | 95 | 260-350 |
| Aure | 4360 | 2220 | 95 | 4190 |
| Purari at Wabo | 26300 | 2830 | 95 | 790 |
| Ei Creek | 16.25 | 2625 | 85 | 36.3 |

On both New Guinea and New Zealand, a great range of karst landforms is found (Figures 4.13 and Color Plate 4E). When karst geomorphologists first began working in Papua New Guinea, they found such an extraordinary array of landforms that existing terminology proved inadequate to describe them (Williams 1972). It is the older, often larger-scale

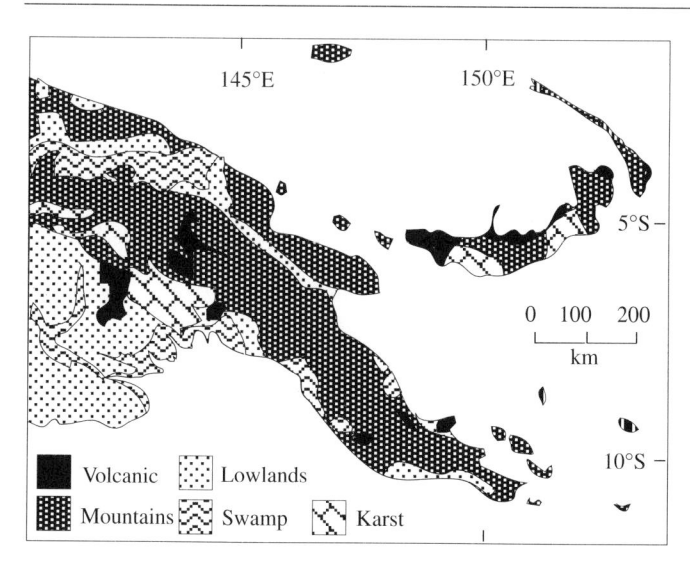

*Figure 4.13. Landforms of Papua New Guinea (after Löffler 1982).*

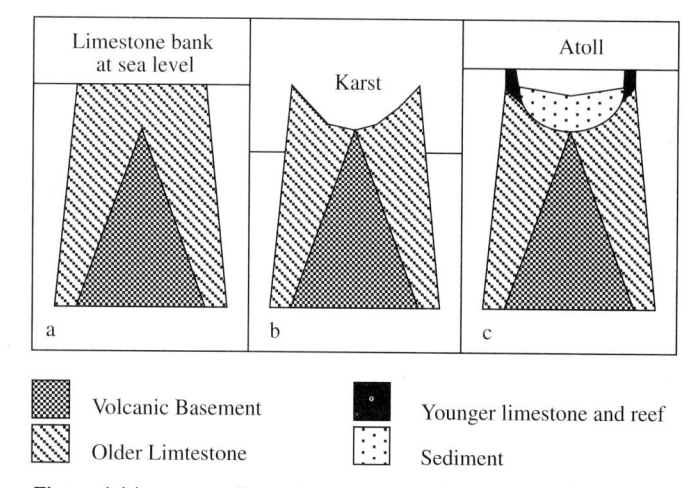

*Figure 4.14. How atolls might form from a limestone bank (after Nunn 1994a). a. Limestone bank exists at sea level. b. Sea level falls and a saucer shape develops through rainwater solution. c. Sea level rises. Reef grows along rim, but is stifled by sediment in the center of the lagoon.*

features that are distinctive relative to other Pacific Island karst landscapes.

By virtue of their plate-boundary locations, such continental islands are sites of considerable tectonic activity, which tends to obscure the effects of other landscape processes.

## Limestone Islands

Limestone islands are formed when reefs or other carbonate bodies emerge above sea level. They most commonly occur in the tropical Pacific. For an island to have emerged more than a few meters since the late Neogene, that island must have been uplifted. Many such places are close to convergent plate boundaries. Limestone islands also occur away from plate boundaries, as when lithospheric loading (at a growing hot-spot volcano) causes compensatory uplift of a surrounding arch (Nunn 1994a).

Most karst on uplifted Pacific islands has formed on Neogene reef limestones and consequently does not display many landforms associated with older limestones. Such landforms range from shallow solution dolines to more extensively hollowed karren forms. Karren karst is exposed on Niue (Schofield 1959) and Henderson (Paulay and Spencer 1988) and may become filled with phosphate, as on Nauru and Banaba, Kiribati (Hill and Jacobson 1989).

There has been much debate over the origins of high limestone islands, such as in Tonga and Lau (eastern Fiji). Based on the characteristic rim-and-basin morphology, Davis (1928) regarded these islands as emerged atolls. Later investigators (Hoffmeister and Ladd 1935, Ladd and Hoffmeister 1945, Nunn 1996), found that *in situ* corals were absent from their rims, suggesting that rim-and-basin morphology could be due to subaerial solution of an emerged limestone bank (Figure 4.14).

Other islands in the Pacific are undoubted emerged atolls. Makatea, in the Tuamotu group, provides an example of a raised atoll, related to lithospheric loading by the nearby Mehetia-Tahiti complex. Dating of exposed reefs indicates that emergence began in the late Tertiary, followed by the accumulation of phosphates. Uplift has continued subsequently, though there is some debate about the details of the geological history (Montaggioni 1985, Nunn 1994a).

## Atolls

Within the coral seas, islands that subside beneath the ocean surface commonly retain terrestrial expression on account of coral reef growing upward from the flanks of sinking islands. A ring reef (or an atoll reef) is so formed. A late Holocene fall of sea level in the Pacific of around 1–2 m caused emergence and lateral outgrowth of many such reefs (Nunn 1994a 1995). Carbonate sediments derived from surrounding reef slopes were washed onto reef surfaces, particularly during storms, forming islets around the cores of emerged reef. These islets are where most people live today in Kiribati and other atoll groups (Figure 4.15).

Reef islets of this kind have been classified as cays and *motu* (Nunn 1994a). Cays are superficial and ephemeral, often forming or disappearing during large storms. *Motu* are formed in part of more consolidated materials (beachrock or phosphate rock), which protect their windward coasts from wave attack and ensure that their unconsolidated sediment cores endure longer than those of cays, which lack such protection.

Reef islet landforms in Tuvalu were found to differ depending on whether the islet had formed on an atoll reef or a table reef (lacking a central lagoon). The difference is manifested by the proportion of reef platform occupied by *motu*. *Motu* are many and occupy 8%–23% of the atoll reefs. Conversely, there is usually only a single *motu* on a table reef, occupying 77% of the available space in the case of Niutao (McLean and Hosking 1991).

Along most ocean-facing coasts, sediment ridges are found. Those on the windward sides are generally coarser and more abrupt in form than those to leeward. Lagoon-facing shorelines also have ridges, but these tend to be more subdued because of lower wave energy. On the lagoon side, inlets known as *barachois* are often present (Nunn 1994a). These represent

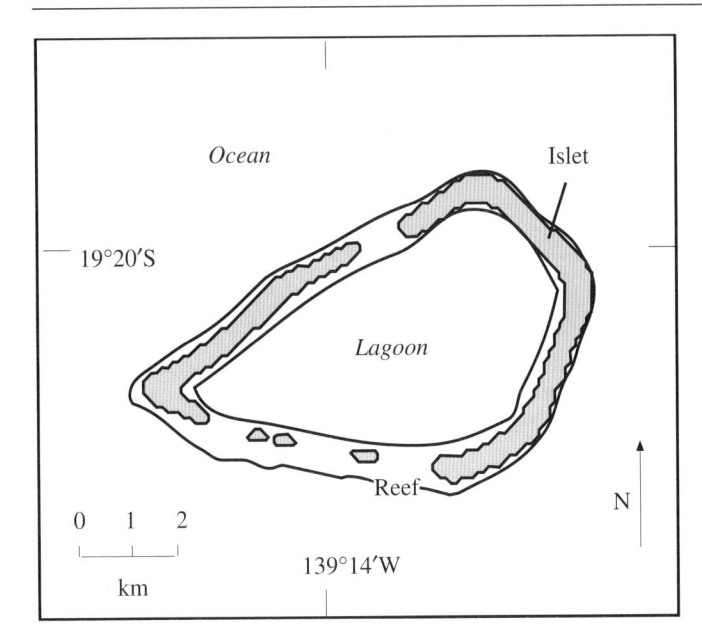

*Figure 4.15.* Vairaatea, one of the smaller atolls in the Tuamotus, French Polynesia.

stages in the lagoonward extension of an atoll islet (Figure 4.16). Subsequent solution produces depressions in which ponds may form.

*Figure 4.16.* Lagoonward extension of islets in the Tuamotus, French Polynesia (photo MR).

## Islands of Mixed Lithology

The most distinctive Pacific islands with a mixed lithology are of the *makatea* type, characterized by a volcanic interior fringed by uplifted reef limestone (Figure 4.17 and 4.18). The best examples of such islands occur in the Southern Cook group, raised by lithospheric loading of the nearby high island, Rarotonga. Makatea Island in the Tuamotus differs from the islands in the Southern Cooks in that it lacks an emerged central volcanic core.

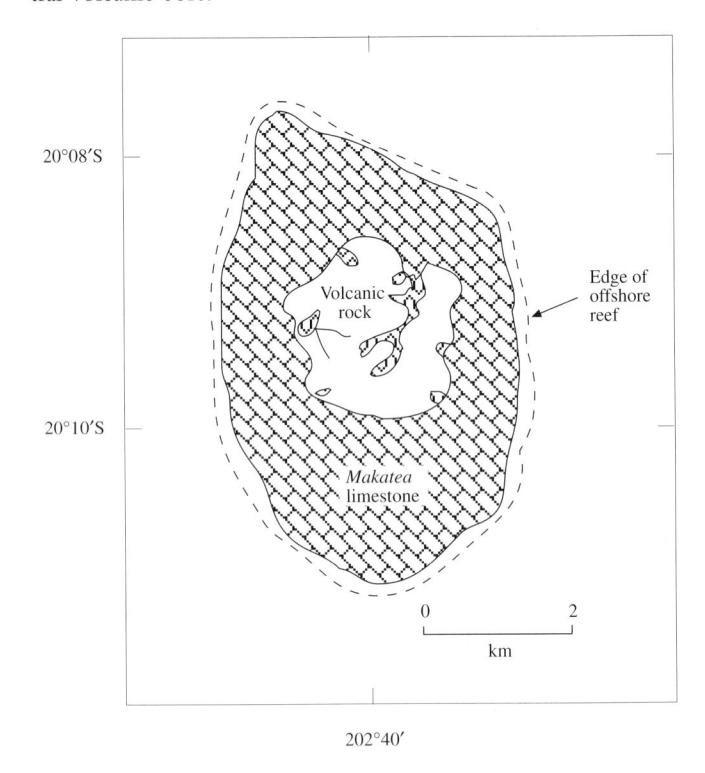

*Figure 4.17.* Mauke, a makatea *island in the Southern Cook Group.*

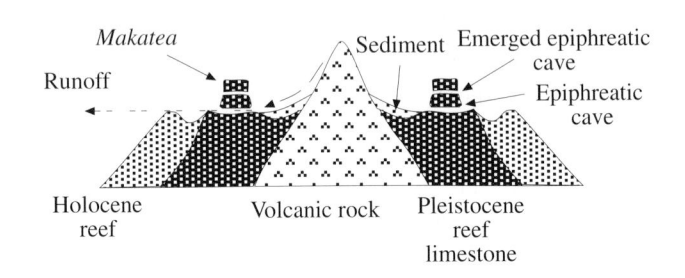

*Figure 4.18. Diagrammatic section across a* makatea *island.*

Typical *makatea* islands have a beveled volcanic core dissected by steep-sided, radial valleys. Transported regolith and soil fills the valley floors and the swampy depressions just landward of the contact between volcanics and limestone. Such depressions are prized for growing root crops, commonly taro (Figure 4.19). The elevated limestone walls are marked by basal epiphreatic (water-table) caves. Abandoned epiphreatic caves higher up mark relative stillstands in the emergence process

Other Pacific islands with a mixed lithology are usually comparatively large and formed by a variety of processes,

50         The Pacific Islands

*Figure 4.19. Swamp depression with taro and other crops growing at the edge of the volcanics, Atiu, Cook Islands (photo MR).*

commonly associated with convergent plate boundaries. Good examples are found in Fiji, as in parts of the island of Viti Levu. Variations in landform type attributable to lithology, while recognizable, are largely obscured by differences associated with climate (Wright 1973, Nunn 1998).

## Rates of Change

Comparatively little work has been done on the rates of landform change in the Pacific Islands. This is largely because most researchers have been based outside the region and have been unable to visit it regularly, and also because such measurements have not been a common priority. Yet knowledge of the rates at which landforms evolve is an essential prerequisite to understanding the relationship between process and form on Pacific islands.

Three examples of the types of rates available are given in the following sections.

### Coastal Change

Few Pacific Island coasts can be considered stable on a scale of hundreds of years. Within the last century, many coasts have either receded, prograded, or alternated between the two. Selected rates of recession and progradation are listed in Table 4.4.

In those parts of the Pacific Islands where systematic observations have not been made for very long, the best record of coastal change comes from oral evidence from elderly, long-term residents of long-established coastal settlements. Using such data, rates of lateral inundation (encroachment of the sea on the land) were recorded for selected island countries (Table 4.5).

The existence of coral reefs off many Pacific coasts reduces the potential for their mechanical erosion by wave attack. On such coasts, most of the erosion is achieved by corrosion (chemical action), particularly along limestone coasts. In such places, groundwater often reaches nearshore waters through underwater springs, marking the seaward edge of a freshwater lens.

The ferocity of wave attack along many reefless coasts in the Pacific Islands is manifest. For example, in Kaua'i (Hawai'i) and many of the islands in the Marquesas (French Polynesia), offshore

### TABLE 4.4

**Selected Rates of Recession and Progradation on Pacific Island Coasts**

| Site, island | Rate (cm/year) | Source |
|---|---|---|
| **RECESSION** | | |
| Easter Island (cliffs) | 10.0 | Paskoff 1978 |
| Hawai'i - Waimea Bay, O'ahu (beach) | 125.0 | Campbell and Hwang 1982 |
| New Zealand - Ngapotiki | 346.0 | Gibb 1978 |
| **PROGRADATION** | | |
| New Zealand - Tauranga Harbour | 500.0 | Healy 1977 |

### TABLE 4.5

**Rates of Lateral Inundation for Selected Island Groups in the South Pacific (from Nunn 1990)**

| Island group | Number of stable sites studied | Rate of lateral inundation(cm/year) |
|---|---|---|
| Cook Islands | 2 | 8.4 |
| Fiji | 16 | 15.0 |
| Hawai'i[1] | 1 | 125.0 |
| Samoa | 4 | 51.4[2] |
| Solomon Islands | 20 | 10.8 |
| Tonga | 4 | 10.0 |
| Tuvalu | 1 | 18.0 |
| Vanuatu | 1 | 7.8 |

1  data from Waimea Bay on O'ahu (Campbell and Hwang 1982), regarded as the only stable island in the group (Moore 1970)
2  this figure is greatly influenced by the high rate for Satalo on 'Upolu Island

reef development is often poor or absent. This is testimony to the rapidity of lateral cutback of cliffs and the consequent impotence of subaerial denudation to reduce cliff-slope angle.

### Denudation

Selected denudation rates are given below. This is one aspect of geomorphology which has received little attention in the Pacific Islands, so no coherent synthesis can yet be made.

Rates of surface lowering for various Hawaiian islands range from 0.04–0.19 mm/year (Li 1988). Contrast these values with those for the Ok Ningi in the New Guinea highlands, where the ground surface is being lowered at 3–4 mm/year (Pickup et al 1980). The difference is explicable not only by climate but by process. In New Guinea mass wasting is a dominant agent of erosion. In Hawai'i, erosion is related mainly to chemical weathering.

A study of monzonite (a form of granite) cliff retreat in the high interior of Viti Levu Island, Fiji, was made by Nunn (1998). The area is subject to significant wet-dry seasonal conditions that drive processes of water erosion, such as sheet wash and basal undermining at springs. Combined with the effects of gravity, this causes scarp retreat. The maximum rate of scarp retreat was 2.46 mm/year.

On some Philippine islands under primary forest, around 3 tons/ha/year are lost through erosion; loss from open grasslands is 84 t/ha/year; and overgrazed areas lose 250 t/ha/year (Myers 1988). Commercial agriculture elsewhere has produced similar rates. Sugarcane planted on 18°–22° slopes in Fiji were associated with a soil loss equivalent to 90 t/ha/year (Clarke and Morrison 1987). Such rates greatly exceed the tropical soil-loss tolerance level of 13.5 t/ha/year (Hudson 1971) and will inevitably lead to land degradation if unchecked.

### Tectonic Change

Tectonic changes in the Pacific Islands include uplift and subsidence. These processes may operate aseismically (nonseismically), usually as long-term unidirectional movements upward or downward. They may also operate coseismically (earthquake-induced) as abrupt movements in one direction, followed by a slower movement in the opposing direction (Nunn 1994a). Both types of movement are common on islands close to convergent plate boundaries in the Pacific (Berryman et al. 1992).

Representative rates of these movements from Pacific islands are listed in Table 4.6. The potential influence of these for landform evolution is clearly very great.

## Critical Issues in Landscape Study

Two major issues affecting the study of geomorphology in the Pacific Islands at present are, first, whether landscape change is primarily catastrophic or gradual in nature and, second, whether or not humans have played the principal role in post-settlement landscape change on Pacific islands. These issues are discussed below.

### Catastrophic Versus Gradual Change

For more than 150 years, geomorphologists have argued about whether the landscape change that occurs during high-magnitude, low-frequency (catastrophic) events is more significant in landform evolution compared with the gradual change that occurs at most other times. The prevailing wisdom at present appears to favor the gradualist view, but this perhaps reflects the fact that few geomorphologists work and reside in the tropics, where floods, hurricanes, earthquakes, and volcanic activity are especially common.

An area of focus in this debate concerns the role of periodic storms in the long-term growth of atoll islets. From work in Ontong Java, Bayliss-Smith (1988) suggested that catastrophic storms, although often causing much erosion, have generally maintained atoll islets by simultaneously supplying coral debris to atoll reefs. According to Bayliss-Smith, the high frequency of mid-Holocene tropical cyclones allowed reef islets to maintain a steady state, but a recent decline in tropical cyclone frequency was causing the destruction of islets (Figure 4.20).

### TABLE 4.6

**Selected Rates of Uplift and Subsidence for Pacific Islands** (after Nunn 1994a, and sources therein)

| Island | Rate (mm/yr) |
|---|---|
| **1. Aseismic uplift** | |
| Anaa Atoll, Tuamotus | 0.1 |
| Hateruma, Ryukyu Is. | 0.1-0.3 |
| Huon Peninsula, Papua New Guinea | 3.3 |
| Maré, Loyalty Islands, New Caledonia | 1.6-1.9 |
| North Island (axial ranges), New Zealand | 4.0 |
| **2. Aseismic subsidence** | |
| Enewetak, Marshall Islands | 0.1-0.2 |
| Hawai'i Island, Hawai'i | 4.4 |
| Moruroa, Tuamotus | 0.12 |
| North Island, New Zealand | 0.1 |
| **3. Coseismic uplift** | |
| Guadalcanal, Solomon Islands (1961) | 1.5 |
| Malakula, Vanuatu (1965) | 1.2 |
| Montague Island, Alaska (1964) | 11.3 |
| New Zealand (1929) | 4.5 |
| Vatulele Island, Fiji (Quaternary) | 1.79 |
| **4. Coseismic subsidence** | |
| Kodiak Island, Alaska (1964) | 2.3 |

Other work has distinguished storms that either largely remove material from atoll reefs or cause it to accumulate (Blumenstock 1961; Bourrouilh-Le Jan and Talandier 1985). It is unclear precisely what causes particular effects to occur. An example of a landform constructed by hurricanes is provided in Figure 4.21.

Some catastrophic events occur so infrequently that they can hardly be thought to interfere with long-term landform evolution. Tsunami waves, which could have been caused by giant landslides or meteor impact, may have reached several hundred meters in height. The Hulopo'e Gravel on Lāna'i, Hawai'i, 326 m above sea level, is believed to have been deposited by such a wave 105 Ka (Moore and Moore 1984). Waves generated by that event may also have deposited gravels in Samoa, Fiji, and along the New South Wales coast of Australia (Nunn 1998; Young and Bryant 1992).

### Human or Nonhuman Impacts

The debate over human versus natural environmental changes in Pacific island postsettlement history has been outlined above. Further development of this debate will require considerably more data concerning early human-environment interactions in the region. The presence of charcoal in heavily

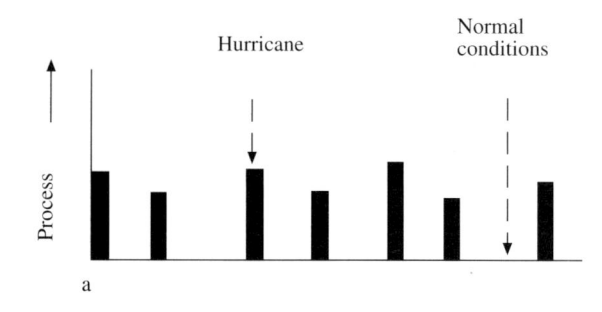

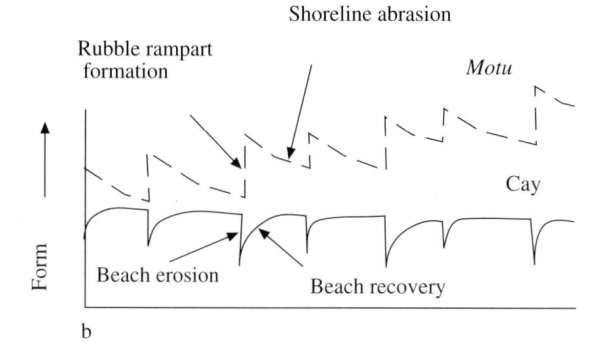

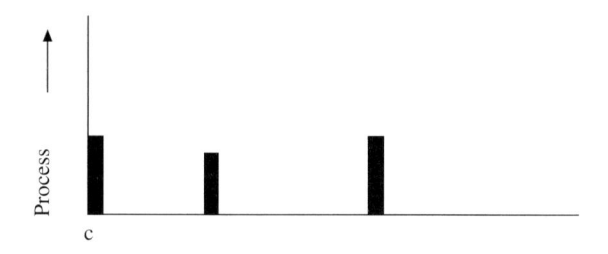

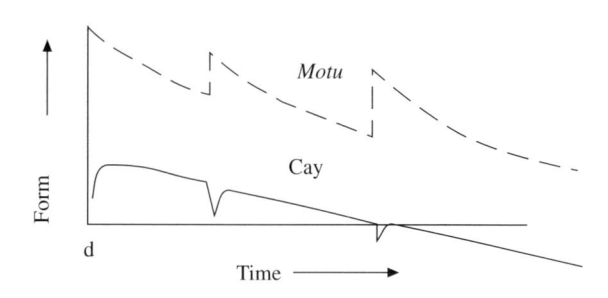

*Figure 4.20. Possible role of tropical cyclones in reef-island geomorphology at two times during the Holocene on Ontong Java, Solomon Islands (after Bayliss-Smith 1988). a. Mid-Holocene conditions with frequent storms, high wave energy and reef productivity. b. Mid-Holocene landforms: cays are in a steady state; motu are growing. c. Late Holocene conditions with less-frequent storms, lower wave energy and reef productivity. d. Late Holocene landforms: cays are intermittent or disappearing; motu are being eroded.*

impacted areas is often used as evidence of human causation.

On some islands, there is a proven coincidence between early human settlement and the first appearance of charcoal (Stevenson and Dodson 1995); but on other islands, there is not (Pillans et al. 1992). Yet a causal association has rarely been questioned (Nunn 1994b). Some studies have suggested that the earliest Holocene charcoal is an indicator of the earliest

*Figure 4.21. Rubble rampart on Fakaofo Atoll, Tokelau, built through hurricane action (photo MR).*

human presence (Kirch and Ellison 1994), even though archaeological evidence places this much later (Spriggs and Anderson 1993).

An important question is whether the earliest settlers sought to conserve or to radically modify the new island environments they settled. Support for the conservation argument comes from studies of traditional horticulture (Zan and Hunter-Anderson 1987) and reevaluations of the role of people in landscape change (Athens and Ward 1993).

The importance of these debates for geomorphology is evident. According to one scenario, the landscape was rapidly and abruptly altered only when the first people arrived, but would otherwise have been more resilient. Conversely, if the landscape was already changing due to falling temperatures, falling sea levels and changing rainfall levels, humans may have only marginally altered the rates of prexisting processes.

## Conclusions

The landforms of Pacific islands pose exciting new challenges for the next generation of geomorphologists. Many existing explanations of landform evolution in the Pacific have been uncritically transferred from continental areas, where different conditions prevail. In the next few decades, recognition of the unique character of Pacific Island landforms will lead to critical reevaluation of these explanations and to the development of more effective environmental management in the region.

# Bibliography

Athens, J. S., and J. V. Ward. 1993. Environmental change and prehistoric Polynesian settlement in Hawai'i. *Asian Perspectives* 32:205–223.

Baitis, H. W., and M. M. Lindstrom. 1980. Geology, petrography, and petrology of Pinzón Island, Galápagos archipelago. *Contributions to Mineralogy and Petrology* 72:367–386.

Bayliss-Smith, T. 1988. The role of hurricanes in the development of reef islands, Ontong Java atoll, Solomon Islands. *The Geographical Journal* 54:377–391.

Berryman, K. R., Y. Ota, and A. G. Hull. 1992. Holocene coastal evolution under the influence of episodic tectonic uplift: examples from New Zealand and Japan. *Quaternary International* 15/16:31–45.

Bird, E. C. F., J. P. Dubois, and J. A. Iltis. 1984. *The impacts of open-cast mining on the rivers and coasts of New Caledonia.* Tokyo: United Nations University.

Blumenstock, D. I. 1961. A report on typhoon effects upon Jaluit Atoll. *Atoll Research Bulletin* 75:1–105.

Bourrouilh-Le Jan, F. G., and J. Talandier. 1985. Sédimentation et fracturation de haute énergie en milieu récifal: tsunamis, ouragans et cyclones et leurs effets sur la sédimentologie et la géomorphologie d'un atoll: motu et hoa, á Rangiroa, Tuamotu, Paçifique SE. *Marine Geology* 67:263–333.

Brousse, R., J-P Chevalier, M. Denizot, and B. Salvat. 1978. Etude géomorphologique des Iles Marquises. *Cahiers du Pacifique* 21:9–74.

Brown, M. J. F. 1974. A development consequence: disposal of mining waste on Bougainville, Papua New Guinea. *Geoforum* 8:19–27.

Campbell, J. F., and D. J. Hwang. 1982. Beach erosion at Waimea Bay, O'ahu, Hawai'i. *Pacific Science* 36:35–43.

Clarke, W. C., and J. Morrison. 1987. Land mismanagement and the development imperative in Fiji. In *Land degradation and society,* ed. P. Blaikie and H. Brookfield, 76–85. New York: Methuen.

Dana, J. D. 1890. *Characteristics of volcanoes.* New York: Dodd, Mead.

Davis, W. M. 1928. *The coral reef problem.* Washington: American Geographical Society (Special Publication 9).

Douglas, I., and T. Spencer. 1985. Present-day processes as a key to the effects of environmental change. In *Environmental change and tropical geomorphology,* ed. I. Douglas and T. Spencer, 39–73. London: George, Allen and Unwin.

Duncan, R. A., and D. A. Clague. 1985. Pacific plate motions recorded by linear volcanic chains. In *The Ocean Basins and Margins,* Vol. 7A, *The Pacific,* ed. A. E. M. Nairn, F.G. Stehli, and S. Uyeda, 89–121. New York: Plenum Press.

Fairbridge, R. W., and H. B. Stewart. 1960. Alexa Bank, a drowned atoll on the Melanesian border plateau. *Deep-Sea Research* 7:100–116.

Flenley, J. R. 1979. *The equatorial rain forest: a geological history.* London: Butterworths.

Flenley, J. R., and S. M. King. 1984. Late Quaternary pollen records from Easter Island. *Nature* 307:47–50.

Gavenda, R. T. 1992. Hawaiian Quaternary paleoenvironments: a review of the geological, pedological, and botanical evidence. *Pacific Science* 46:295–307.

Gibb, J. G. 1978. Rates of coastal erosion and accretion in New Zealand. *New Zealand Journal of Marine and Freshwater Research* 12:429–450.

Glasby, G. P. 1986. Modification of the environment in New Zealand. *Ambio* 5:267–271.

Healy, T. R. 1977. Progradation at the entrance to Tauranga Harbour, Bay of Plenty. *New Zealand Geographer* 33:90–91.

Hill, P. J., and G. Jacobson. 1989. Structure and evolution of Nauru Island, central Pacific Ocean. *Australian Journal of Earth Science* 36:365–381.

Hoffmeister, J. E., and H. S. Ladd. 1935. Foundations of atolls: a discussion. *Journal of Geology* 43:653–665.

Hudson, N. W. 1971. *Soil conservation.* London: Batsford.

Jones, A. T. 1992. Holocene coral reef on Kauai, Hawaii: evidence for a sea-level highstand in the central Pacific. *Society for Sedimentary Geology, Special Publication* 48:267–271.

Kayanne, H., T. Ishii, E. Matsumoto, and N. Yonekura. 1993. Late Holocene sea-level change on Rota and Guam, Mariana Islands, and its constraint on geophysical predictions. *Quaternary Research* 40:189–200.

Kirch, P.V., and J. Ellison. 1994. Palaeoenvironmental evidence for human colonization of remote Oceanic islands. *Antiquity* 68:310–321.

Ladd, H. S., and J. E. Hoffmeister. 1945. *Geology of Lau, Fiji.* B.P. Bishop Museum, Bulletin 181.

Li, Y. H. 1976. Denudation of Taiwan Island since the Pliocene epoch. *Geology* 4:105–107.

Li, Y. H. 1988. Denudation rates of the Hawaiian Islands by rivers and groundwaters. *Pacific Science* 42:253–66.

Löffler, E. 1977. *Geomorphology of Papua New Guinea.* Canberra: Australian National University.

Löffler, E. 1982. Landforms. In *Papua New Guinea atlas: a nation in transition,* ed. D. King and S. Ranck, 82–83. Port Moresby: University of Papua New Guinea.

McLean, R. F., and P. L. Hosking. 1991. Geomorphology of reef islands and atoll motu in Tuvalu. *South Pacific Journal of Natural Science* 11:167–89.

Montaggioni, L. F. 1985. Makatea island, Tuamotu archipelago. *Proceedings of the 5th International Coral Reef Congress* 1:103–158.

Moore, J. G. 1970. Relationship between subsidence and volcanic load, Hawaii. *Bulletin Volcanologique* 34:562–575.

Moore, J. G., and G. W. Moore. 1984. Deposit from a giant wave on the island of Lanai, Hawaii. *Science* 226:1312–1315.

Morhange, C. 1992. Essai de quantification de l'évolution géomorphologique d'un archipel volcanique tropical né d'un point chaud: le cas des îles de la Société en Polynésie française. *Zeitschrift für Geomorphologie* 36:307–324.

Myers, N. 1988. Environmental degradation and some economic consequences in the Philippines. *Environmental Conservation* 15:205–214.

Nunn, P. D. 1987. Small islands and geomorphology: review and prospect in the context of historical geomorphology. *Transactions of the Institute of British Geographers,* New Series 12:227–239.

Nunn, P. D. 1990. Recent coastline changes and their implications for future changes in the Cook Islands, Fiji, Kiribati, the Solomon Islands, Tonga, Tuvalu, Vanuatu and Western Samoa. In *Implications of expected climate changes in the South Pacific region: an overview,* ed. J. C. Pernetta and P. J. Hughes, 149–160. UNEP Regional Seas Reports and Studies 128.

Nunn, P. D. 1992. *Keimami sa vakila na liga ni Kalou* (Feeling the hand of God): human and nonhuman impacts on Pacific Island environments. East-West Center, Occasional Paper (2nd revised edition).

Nunn, P. D. 1993. The role of *Porolithon* algal-ridge growth in the development of the windward coast of Tongatapu island, Tonga, South Pacific. *Earth-Surface Processes and Landforms* 18:427–439.

Nunn, P. D. 1994a. *Oceanic islands.* Oxford: Blackwell.

Nunn, P. D. 1994b. Beyond the naive lands: human history and environmental change in the Pacific Basin. In *The margin fades: geographical itineraries in a world of islands,* ed. E. Waddell and P. D. Nunn, 5–27. Suva, Fiji: Institute of Pacific Studies, The University of the South Pacific.

Nunn, P. D. 1995. Holocene sea-level changes in the south and west Pacific. *Journal of Coastal Research,* Special Issue 17:311–319.

Nunn, P. D. 1996. *Emerged shorelines of the Lau Islands.* Fiji Mineral Resources Department, Memoir.

Nunn, P. D. 1997. *Keimami sa vakila na liga ni kalou* (Feeling the hand of God): human and nonhuman impacts on Pacific Island environments, 3d.ed. Suva: University of the South Pacific, School of Social and Economic Development.

Nunn, P. D. 1998. *Pacific Island landscapes*. Suva: Institute of Pacific Studies, The University of the South Pacific.

Nunn, P. D., and F. T. Finau. 1995. Late Holocene emergence history of Tongatapu Island, South Pacific. *Zeitschrift für Geomorphologie* NF 39:69–95.

Ollier, C. D., and C. F. Pain. 1978. Geomorphology and tectonics of Woodlark Island, Papua New Guinea. *Zeitschrift für Geomorphologie* NF 22:22–20.

Onda, Y. 1994. Seepage erosion and its implication to the formation of amphitheatre valley heads: a case study at Obara, Japan. *Earth Surface Processes and Landforms* 19:627–640.

Paskoff, R. 1978. Aspects géomorphologiques de l'île de Pacques. *Bulletin de l'Association Géographique du France* 452:142–157.

Paulay, G., and T. Spencer. 1988. Geomorphology, palaeoenvironments and faunal turnover, Henderson Island, S.E. Polynesia. *Proceedings of the 6th International Coral Reef Symposium* 3:461–466.

Peart, M. 1991. The Kaiapit landslide: events and mechanisms. *Quarterly Journal of Engineering Geology* 24:399–411.

Pickup, G., R. J. Higgins, and R. F. Warner. 1980. Erosion and sediment yield in the Fly River drainage basins, Papua New Guinea. *Publications of the International Association of Hydrological Sciences* 132:438–456.

Pillans, B. 1986. A late Quaternary uplift map for North Island, New Zealand. *Royal Society of New Zealand, Bulletin* 24:409–417.

Pillans, B., W. A. Pullar, M. J. Selby, and J. M. Soons. 1992. The age and development of the New Zealand landscape. In *Landforms of New Zealand*, ed. J. M. Soon and M. J. Selby. Auckland: Longman Paul, 2nd edition.

Pirazzoli, P. A., and L. F. Montaggioni. 1988. Holocene sea-level changes in French Polynesia. *Palaeogeography, Palaeoclimatology, Palaeoecology* 68:153–175.

Roy, P. S. 1990. The morphology and surface geology of the islands of Tongatapu and Vava'u, Kingdom of Tonga. *United Nations ESCAP, CCOP/SOPAC Technical Report* 62.

Schmalz, R. F. 1971. Beachrock formation on Eniwetok Atoll. In *Carbonate Cement*, ed. O.P. Bricker, 19:17–24. Johns Hopkins University, Studies in Geology.

Schofield, J. C. 1959. *The geology and hydrology of Niue Island, South Pacific*. Wellington: New Zealand Geological Survey (Bulletin 62).

Scott, G. A. J., and J. M. Street. 1976. The role of chemical weathering in the formation of Hawaiian amphitheatre-headed valleys. *Zeitschrift für Geomorphologie*, NF 20:171–189.

Spriggs, M., and A. Anderson. 1993. Late colonization of East Polynesia. *Antiquity* 67:200–217.

Stevenson, J., and J. R. Dodson. 1995. Palaeoenvironmental evidence for human settlement of New Caledonia. *Archaeology in Oceania* 30:36–41.

Stoddart, D. R., and T. P. Scoffin. 1983. Phosphate rock on coral reef islands. In *Chemical sediments and geomorphology*, ed. A.S. Goudie and K. Pye, 369–400. London: Academic Press.

Stoddart, D. R., C. D. Woodroffe, and T. Spencer. 1990. Mauke, Mitiaro and Atiu: geomorphology of *makatea* islands in the southern Cooks. *Atoll Research Bulletin* 341.

Strecker, M., A. L. Bloom, and J. Lecolle. 1987. Time span for karst development on Quaternary coral limestones: Santo island, Vanuatu. In *Processus et mesure de l'érosion*, ed. A. Godard and A. Rapp, 369–86. Paris: Editions du Centre National de la Recherche Scientifique.

Thomas, N. 1990. *Marquesan Societies*. New York: Oxford University Press.

Williams, P. W. 1972. Morphometric analysis of polygonal karst in New Guinea. *Geological Society of America, Bulletin* 83:761–796.

Wright, L. W. 1973. Landforms of the Yavuna granite area, Viti Levu, Fiji: a morphometric study. *Journal of Tropical Geography* 37:74–80.

Young, R. W., and E. A. Bryant. 1992. Catastrophic wave erosion on the south-eastern coast of Australia: impact of the Lanai tsunamis ca. 105 ka? *Geology* 20:199–202.

Zan, Y., and R. L. Hunter-Anderson. 1988. On the origins of the Micronesian "savannahs": an anthropological perspective. In *Proceedings of the Third international Soil Management Workshop for the Management and Utilization of Acid Soils in Micronesia*, February 2–6, 1987, Republic of Palau, ed. J. L. Demeterio and B. DeGuzman, 18–27. Agricultural Experiment Station, College of Agriculture and Life Sciences, University of Guam.

# CHAPTER 5

# Soils

R. John Morrison

## Introduction

Soils are one of the major resources of Pacific Islanders. Despite the islanders' dependence on the marine environment, soils are the source of a major proportion of the food, building materials, clothing, and medicines. The islands vary enormously in size, geomorphology, and geology, with a resultant diversity in soils. From the small atolls to the large continental islands, traditional technologies have been developed to effectively utilize this invaluable resource (Morrison et al. 1994). Many Pacific Island groups earn significant portions of their foreign exchange earnings through the export of agricultural and forest products (Fairbairn 1985).

The Pacific Islands region covers a vast area extending from the Northern Marianas and Hawai'i in the north to French Polynesia and New Zealand in the south. This encompasses at least twenty-five countries and territories. Given the space limitations on this chapter, it is impossible to adequately discuss separately the soils of each of these island groups. The emphasis will, therefore, be on the factors and processes controlling the soil patterns in the region and issues relating to soil management, notably including erosion.

One of the difficulties encountered when discussing Pacific Island soils is classification, as important changes have taken place over the last fifty years. In the last twenty years or so, the system of soil classification most widely used in the Pacific Islands has been Soil Taxonomy (Soil Survey Staff 1975; 1996). This system is commonly used throughout the world and is continually being modified as new information or better criteria for grouping soils become available. In this chapter all soils are classified in accordance with the criteria of Soil Taxonomy.

### Soil Distribution - Some General Comments

A review of the information available on Pacific Island soils (Morrison and Leslie 1982, Leslie 1984a; Asghar et al. 1988) shows that Inceptisols are the most abundant soils. There are also significant areas of Mollisols, Alfisols, Ultisols, Oxisols, Andisols, and Entisols, and smaller areas of other soils (Color Plates 5A-G).

Inceptisols ("young soils") have discernible signs of genesis, but without major diagnostic features. These soils occur in a wide range of landform situations and parent materials, including highly resistant parent material and recent volcanic ash deposits. Their characteristics vary significantly, from shallow to deep profiles, and from very sandy to clay-rich soils.

Mollisols ("soft soils") have a thick, dark, organic-rich, base-rich A horizon (the "topsoil"). These exceptionally fertile "prairie" soils develop through extension of grass roots into the ground and reworking of the soil by earthworms, ants, rodents, and other subsurface animal life. These soils are more common in the region than would be expected from a purely climatic and topographic basis.

Alfisols are base-rich, with an argillic (clay-enriched) B horizon. These soils are highly fertile, with adequate supplies of necessary minerals, clays, and nutrients. They are found in humid conditions, in areas where base-rich materials have weathered in a relatively stable landform position. They are found in small areas in several island groups and more widely in New Zealand.

Ultisols ("ultimate soils") are base-poor, with an argillic B horizon. These highly weathered soils, usually dominated by red and yellow colors, are found mainly in stable landscapes in the older parts of large islands. The bulk of the nutrients is often in the surface layer, and productivity diminishes with use. The problem can be alleviated by the application of fertilizers, but these soils must be protected from erosion if fertility is to be maintained.

Oxisols ("oxide soils") are deep, highly weathered oxide-rich, red, base-poor soils. These soils have undergone desilication and ferritization (accumulation of iron oxides), and are found in stable landform positions on older islands. They are usually free-draining and have good structural characteristics. Here too, fertility declines rapidly after a few seasons of use, when nutrients become exhausted.

Andisols ("dark soils") are relatively young, derived mainly from volcanic ash, with a high content of allophane (an amorphous clay mineral). These soils are found in Fiji, Hawai'i, New Zealand, Papua New Guinea, Samoa, Solomon Islands, and Vanuatu, derived from basaltic or andesitic ash. The areal extent is not great, but where they do occur, they are important agricultural soils.

Entisols are very young and lack well-developed horizons. These are dominant in atolls, on a base of coral sand, rubble, or reef limestone; and in coastal and riverine areas on larger islands. These soils, occurring in relatively flat terrain, are important for agriculture, even if they do have limitations due to their youth (e.g., sandiness, low water retention, flood hazard).

Vertisols ("inverted soils") are self-churning soils, usually dominated by expanding clays (montmorillonites). These soils are found in limited areas on the larger islands where a significant dry season occurs.

Histosols ("organic soils") are dominated by organic materials. They are found where hydrological conditions allow the build-up of organic matter, as in swampy coastal alluvial plains, upland depressions, and calderas. Where they have been drained they have considerable agricultural significance.

Other soils uncommonly found include Spodosols and

Aridisols. Spodosols ("ashy soils") are characterized by leaching of organic matter, iron, and aluminium. These soils are present in Hawai'i, New Caledonia, and Fiji, but are generally rare. Aridisols ("arid soils") are found in areas with dry climates. In the Pacific Islands they occur in very limited areas, such as rain shadow locations in Hawai'i.

Color Plates 5H and 5I show the major patterns of soil distributions in the Cook Islands (as a profile diagram) and Hawai'i (as a simplified map). At the scale shown, these are necessarily very generalized classifications and obscure much of the detail at the local level. Much of the terrain is mountainous and can be characterized as Inceptisols. However, as mentioned, significant patches of other soils exist within these zones, as well as areas where little soil cover exists. Oxisols and Ultisols are present in areas of lower relief. Mollisols are found where grasslands are present; Andisols reflect geologically recent volcanic activity. Entisols are present in swamplands and beach ridges.

The Pacific Islands region is generally wet, with few very dry zones. Soils are either udic (dry less than 90 days in any year), perudic (moist continually), or ustic (dry for 90 or more days in most years, but moist for more than half the year). Soils on windward coasts of the larger islands usually have udic or perudic moisture regimes; ustic soils are found in leeward rain shadow areas. On atolls, rainfall is often irregular, and the classic definition of soil moisture regimes holds little meaning.

Temperature regimes are generally either isohyperthermic (average soil temperature greater than 22°C) or isothermic (average temperature of 15° to 22°C, in both cases with minimal seasonal variation). At the highest elevations, over 3,000 m (or at lower elevations in New Zealand), cooler temperatures are found. The isohyperthermic/isothermic elevational boundary varies with latitude, but for most of the region the boundary lies at around 500–700 m above sea level.

Mineral components of Pacific soils commonly include clay silicates (kaolinite, halloysite, and smectite), aluminum and iron oxyhydroxides (gibbsite and goethite), and carbonates (calcite). On Niue and Nauru, soils may be dominated by phosphate minerals. There are significant areas of young volcanic ash soils dominated by the short-range-order (transient) minerals allophane, imogolite, or ferrihydrite; for example, in northern Vanuatu, in Taveuni, Fiji, in the Santa Cruz group in Solomon Islands, and in Savai'i, Samoa.

The soil profile observed at any given location is the result of all the pedogenetic processes operating. The nature and extent of the processes occurring are determined by a number of soil-forming factors, which are discussed below.

## Factors in Soil Formation

### Climate

Climate is perhaps the most important factor in soil formation (providing sufficient time is available), as it determines, to a marked degree, the extent of weathering, the vegetation cover, and hydrological patterns.

Climate includes rainfall and temperature components and has varied over geological time. For the Pacific Islands, formation of most soils has taken place during the Quaternary (the last 2 million years), although older soils are found. While world climate has varied during the Quaternary (Dodson 1992), the Pacific Islands have generally been relatively wet and warm throughout this period.

Factors influencing soil temperature in the Pacific Islands include elevation and aspect. The drop in temperature with elevation varies with distance from the equator, but averages about 1°C for each 100-m rise in elevation. Most locations in the Pacific Islands have a relatively high mean annual temperature, with minimal seasonal variation. Consequently, the water percolating the soil is always warm (around 25°C), leading to relatively rapid weathering, vegetation growth, and microbiological activity.

Two rainfall parameters are important: mean annual rainfall and temporal distribution. Definition of the dry season is a problem, but it usually includes the months in which the soil has a water deficit (in which evapotranspiration exceeds rainfall). The principal effects of rainfall relate to leaching, determined by the volume of water passing through the profile. In the large Pacific islands, there is often a marked difference in rainfall between windward and leeward sides (see Table 5.1),

### Table 5.1

**Average Rainfall Data (mm) for Suva (Windward Side) and Nadi (Leeward Side), Fiji Islands***

| | J | F | M | A | M | J | J | A | S | O | N | D | Year |
|---|---|---|---|---|---|---|---|---|---|---|---|---|---|
| Suva | 324 | 315 | 383 | 385 | 254 | 172 | 147 | 140 | 209 | 220 | 266 | 272 | 3087 |
| Nadi | 293 | 293 | 358 | 185 | 84 | 71 | 48 | 61 | 87 | 95 | 142 | 175 | 1892 |

*Source: Fiji Meteorological Service, Information Sheets 21, 53, 71

leading to significant soil differences.

Climate affects organic matter content, base saturation, profile depth, texture, and clay mineral synthesis (Young 1976, Buol et al. 1980). Topsoil organic matter (and associated nitrogen content) increases with increasing rainfall and with a fall in temperature (which retards decomposition). Increased rainfall tends to decrease pH, base saturation, and the silt:clay ratio. High temperature and rainfall cause leaching, and result in desilication and ferratization. Gibbsite is found where temperature and leaching are high throughout the year; smectites (expanding clays), where the profile dries out seasonally.

### Parent Material

The parent material of soils may consist of solid rock, regolith, volcanic ash, alluvial deposits, beach sands, or a previous soil profile. Three main attributes of parent materials influencing pedogenesis are the degree of consolidation, grain size, and mineral composition.

Pedogenesis can usually be evaluated once the initial state can be identified. This is one of the most important problems in soil development studies, as the parent material can be identified only by inference. It is not sufficient to dig through the soil to reach rock unaltered by weathering and assume this is the patent material. Such an assumption would be incorrect when the soil is derived from a thin superficial drift deposit, or from rocks higher up the slope, or when the underlying rock is non-homogeneous.

The common parent materials in the Pacific Islands are volcanic basalts (as in Samoa) or andesites (Chioseul, Solomon Islands); volcanic ash and scoria (a porus volcanic rock, heavier than pumice) (Taveuni, Fiji); weathered uplifted mantle material (New Caledonia); carbonates (Funafuti, Tuvalu); sediments derived from volcanics (north Guadalcanal, Solomon Islands); sediments of mixed origin (Muri series, Rarotonga, Cook Islands); uplifted marine sediments (south east Viti Levu, Fiji); phosphates (Nauru); or decomposed organic matter (Kuk, Papua New Guinea).

The highly active tectonic nature of the region has led to interesting situations. In Tongatapu (Tonga), the island is covered with soils derived from andesitic tephra (Cowie 1980). These soils overlie a raised coral platform. The tephra varies in depth from about 5 m in the west to just over 1 m in the east, suggesting an origin in the volcanic islands to the west of Tongatapu. Two distinct tephra deposits have been recognized, the older (approximately 20,000 years old) giving rise to yellowish brown clays and the younger (< 5000 years old) giving rise to reddish brown clays and clay loams (soils of balanced texture).

The influence of volcanic ash on Pacific Islands soils cannot be overemphasized. Even in islands where ash is not a major soil parent material, ash additions from the numerous active volcanoes in the region have occurred in many locations. Even on atolls, the influence of pumice and scoria transported by sea has been recognized as important, with atoll residents collecting the washed-up material and adding it to their most productive garden soils.

Interesting parent material investigations have been conducted on Niue. Initially, interest was aroused by the radioactivity in the soils, detected by Fieldes in 1955 (Marsden et al. 1958). The exact source of the radiation has been the subject of considerable debate for over forty years. The problem relates not to identifying the isotopes responsible, but to determining how they got there. For example, $^{230}$Th and $^{231}$Pa are present in relatively large amounts, but the parent isotopes $^{235}$U, $^{238}$U, and $^{240}$U occur in only very small quantities.

The favored explanation at present (Whitehead et al. 1992) is that after the formation of weathered soils on the volcanic surface of the island, it was submerged for a period during a high–sea level event. During the submergence, gibbsite- and goethite-rich soils adsorbed elements from seawater, including uranium. Upon reemergence, the uranium daughter products accumulated, followed by leaching. The soils of Niue represent one of the most unique geochemical situations encountered in Pacific Island soils.

## Relief and Landform

The major influence here is that of slope. Slope effects can be observed in the depth of the profile; the wetness, color, thickness and organic matter content of the surface horizon; the base saturation; and the presence and nature of pans (highly compacted layers). Relief has a direct effect on climate: precipitation through orographic uplift, and temperature through aspect (slope in relation to the sun). Relief also affects hydrology and vegetation.

Two very different classes of islands are present: atolls and other limestone islands with low relief (although raised coral islands have small areas of very steep slopes resulting from uplift), and volcanic and continental islands with steep, mountainous country deeply incised by rivers and streams. In Fiji, steepland (slopes > 18°) covers 68% of the land surface, and rolling country (slopes 3°-18°) 21%, with areas of low relief (< 3°) representing only 11%. A similar picture is found in Samoa and many other high-island groups.

Relatively dry, oxidized (redder) soils are found in low-relief upper slope positions; wetter, grayer soils, in toeslopes. In steep positions, soils are generally shallow, but there is significant variability in the region. In younger islands dominated by volcanic flows (e.g., 'Upolu, Samoa), soils are generally very shallow and stony, often occurring in patches on the slope where eroded material accumulates. In older islands (New Caledonia), or where volcanic ash is dominant (Taveuni, Fiji), weathering has proceeded to much greater depth, and the profiles on slopes > 20° can often be > 1 m deep.

## Hydrology

In some cases, soil materials are saturated long enough for all the oxygen in the profile to be removed and for reducing (deoxygenated or anaerobic) conditions to prevail. The consequences include soils that are characterized by gray colors (due to $Fe^{2+}$ species) or (when the soils are saturated for long periods but dry out long enough to allow some oxidation of iron to occur) extensive mottling (multiple colors) occurs. If the soils are saturated almost all of the time ("gley soils"), organic matter decomposition is severely inhibited due to lack of oxygen.

The main cause of wetness is impeded drainage. This is often caused by the presence of groundwater near the surface, but can be related to other landscape features. A typical situation is found at the bottom of slopes, where downward water slows and moves into the soil surface. If the profile at this point contains a layer that impedes drainage, the surface layers can become saturated for quite long periods, leading to reducing conditions. Decay is then inhibited and organic material accumulates. This is most prominent in the upper layers of the profile, giving rise to a surface water gley or pseudogley. A classic example occurs at Koronovia in Fiji (Leslie 1984b).

Soils showing a marked influence of wetness occur in coasts, lowlands, and poorly drained uplands. Reducing conditions often occur in mangrove areas, as the soils are subject to water immersion and major surface additions of organic matter. These areas have often been cleared, particularly in backswamp locations, in order to facilitate intensive agriculture. This has resulted in acid sulphate soils (Dreketi and Bua, on Vanua Levu, Fiji), and subsequent agricultural developments have proved either technically or economically unviable (Lal 1990).

## Vegetation

As the main contributor of organic material, vegetation is one of the most important formative agents of soil. Vegetation is in turn dependent largely on climate.

Apart from the atolls, forests were probably the dominant vegetation on most islands prior to human contact. Palynological (pollen) studies (see Southern 1986) indicate that in some islands grasslands developed during drier climates in the late Quaternary. In some locations, grassland establishment coincided with the arrival of the first human settlers. Most grasslands are found where a marked dry season occurs and where fire may have a significant effect (such as North Guadalcanal, Solomon Islands, and Southern Highlands, Papua New Guinea).

Even after grasslands have become established, the effects of burning can be a significant factor in soil transformation. In the Guadalcanal Plains, for example, regular burning, with the loss of organic matter, has contributed to soils deficient in sulphur (Chase and Widdowson 1983). On other islands, the soils of areas that have burned regularly have been found to be lower in organic matter and nitrogen than comparable soils with lower frequency of burning (Morrison et al. 1987a).

On atolls, soils with undisturbed vegetation cover often have a well-developed, organic-rich A horizon. Disturbance of the native vegetation leads to a rapid reduction in the organic matter content and thinning of the A horizon (Morrison and Seru 1986). A special situation of vegetation influence on atolls is the Jemo series, identified by Fosberg (1954, 1957) in the Marshall Islands. This unique soil, with layered phosphatic material in the B horizon, appears to form under exclusively *Pisonia* vegetation, with the acidic decomposing organic matter combining with guano and coral limestone to produce the phosphate layers.

## Time

Most Pacific islands are relatively young in geological terms, with the period of soil formation restricted to the Quaternary. Some very young parent materials are known. These include volcanic ash in Savai'i, Samoa, and Taveuni, Fiji, that is less than 1,000 years old; recent alluvium deposits in the deltas of some of the major rivers; and coral sand deposited in coastal areas. Older soils and parent materials have been identified in Fiji, New Caledonia, and Solomon Islands; and Tertiary limestone has been identified on numerous raised islands (Guam, Niue, and Vatu Vara in Fiji).

Given the climate of the region, the rates of weathering and soil formation are relatively fast, with significant profile development occurring in 1,000 years or less in some locations. Identification of chronosequences to facilitate studies on soil formation rates has proved difficult in the Pacific Islands, but attempts have been made to examine age sequences in a few locations. One of the best has been in Samoa, where the parent materials are dominantly basaltic lava flows.

The work of Wright (1963) and Schroth (1971) has shown that recent (< 300 years b.p.) flows have very weakly developed stony soils, while flows dating from 150 Ka have profiles of up to 60 cm deep with significant clay contents and base saturation. Flows dating from the Tertiary (2–2.5 Ma) have deep, oxidic profiles and are base-poor. This picture is somewhat clouded by the influence of ash additions to the soil surface during each period of volcanic activity.

An unusual chronosequence has been provided by the phosphate rock mining activities on Nauru. Mining left behind phosphate materials in which soil formation occurred. As the dates of mining were accurately known, it was possible to examine the rate of soil development through the accumulation of carbon and nitrogen (Figure 5.1, Manner and Morrison 1991).

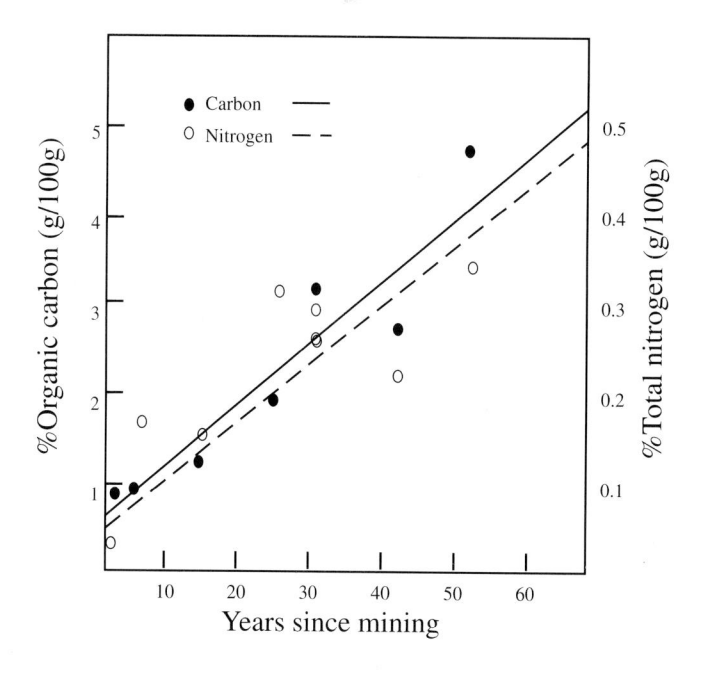

*Figure 5.1. The rate of soil development on Nauru as shown by the accumulation of carbon and nitrogen (Manner and Morrison 1991).*

On older stable landforms, where the processes of weathering and pedogenesis have been operating for long periods, Oxisols and other oxic soils tend to dominate. This has been observed in Fiji (Morrison et al. 1987b), Guam (Young 1988), New Caledonia (Latham et al. 1978), Palau (Smith 1983), and Solomon Islands (Wall and Hansell 1976).

## Human Beings

The role of human beings in soil genesis has been recognized in many locations. In the Pacific Islands, these effects manifest themselves through the impacts caused by slope modification, as in terraces for yam and taro production (Kuhlken 1994; Roe 1989) and vegetation change associated with fire and erosion. Other human-related effects that have been observed are the effects of drainage (discussed above) and intensive grazing, particularly of goats on very small islands. The extent of such impacts varies enormously in the region, from small terraces to major areas of vegetation change on some islands.

## Processes in Soil Formation

The processes of soil formation are summarized in Figure 5.2 (modified from Simonson 1959). The processes are not unique to the Pacific Islands, but some processes are of greater importance due to the prevailing environmental conditions.

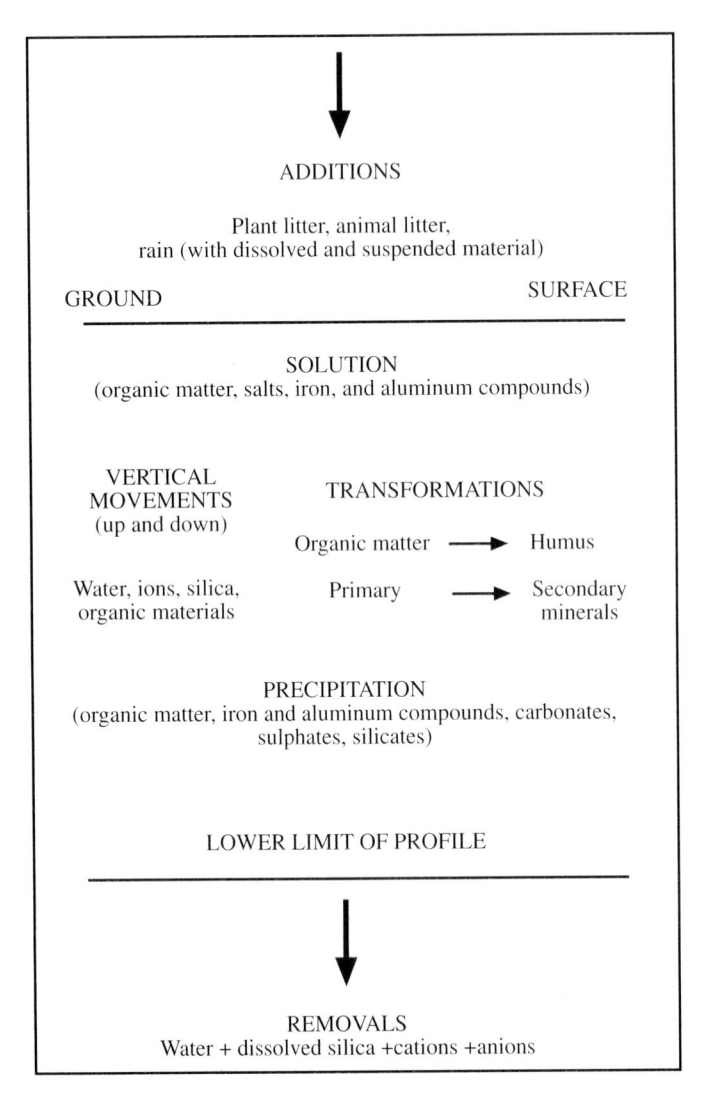

```
                    ↓
                ADDITIONS
           Plant litter, animal litter,
      rain (with dissolved and suspended material)
GROUND                                      SURFACE
─────────────────────────────────────────────────────
                    SOLUTION
       (organic matter, salts, iron, and aluminum compounds)

  VERTICAL          TRANSFORMATIONS
  MOVEMENTS
  (up and down)     Organic matter  →  Humus

  Water, ions, silica,  Primary  →  Secondary
  organic materials                   minerals

                  PRECIPITATION
  (organic matter, iron and aluminum compounds, carbonates,
                  sulphates, silicates)

              LOWER LIMIT OF PROFILE
─────────────────────────────────────────────────────
                    ↓
                 REMOVALS
       Water + dissolved silica + cations + anions
```

*Figure 5.2. Diagrammatic representation of soil-forming processes.*

The dominant climatic conditions in the region (high temperatures and rainfall) are especially conducive to high weathering rates. The generally wet conditions mean that chemical weathering is dominant, with primary minerals being rapidly attacked. In addition, the relatively high temperatures contribute to the high weathering rates because

(a) ionization of water increases with temperature, making it more corrosive;
(b) the solubility of most substances in water increases with temperature;
(c) reactions (such as solution) proceed more rapidly with increasing temperature;
(d) water viscosity decreases with increasing temperature, and water penetrates further into the rock or soil.

In the Pacific Islands, the dominant soil-forming processes are associated with organic matter additions, humification (organic decomposition) and incorporation, mineral transformations, and water movement through the profile. Organic matter production is high, leading to the depositing of significant litter on soil surface, where decomposition soon ensues. Organic matter turnover is usually quite rapid, unless some feature of the vegetation or the location (wetness, elevation, aspect) leads to accumulation.

Water movements through the profile lead to eluviation (removal of materials), illuviation (deposition of material), leaching of weathering products, and the availability of water for mineral transformation reactions. Desilication is common in soils derived from aluminosilicate parent materials, with the accumulation of aluminium and iron oxyhydroxides increasing with time. Evidence of illuviation (such as clay "skins" on the surface of soil structural units) is common in Pacific soils derived from volcanic materials in stable landform positions.

Spodic horizons (caused by the movement of aluminium, iron, and organic matter down the profile in solution) are rare, as the necessary conditions of vegetation, water and parent material occur infrequently. Water movements in profiles are such that the accumulation of carbonates or soluble salts in soils is extremely rare.

## Soils Use and Management

The major factors affecting use are soil properties (for example, depth, slope, drainage, nutrient status), climate, and proximity to potential markets. The proximity of markets is particularly important for food crops, which are grown close to many urban centers for local sale. Export-oriented crops (sugar, cocoa, coffee, tea, and oil palm) are often grown at distances from markets in areas with suitable climate and soils, with the exception of fresh fruit such as papaya, which is exported by air and therefore grown relatively close to the points of export.

For the larger islands (> 1000 km$^2$), climate differences between the windward and leeward sides of the islands are often very important (see Table 5.1). Crops adapted to a period of water stress in their life cycle are grown predominantly on the drier sides of the islands, while drought-sensitive crops are grown on the windward sides. Thus sugar and oil palm are usually found on deep soils in areas with a marked dry season (Viti Levu, Fiji, and Guadalcanal, Solomon Islands, respectively), while taro, rice, and cocoa are found in wetter areas. For the smaller islands, the climate effects are less marked, and on the atolls, there is effectively no rainfall variation.

In the larger islands, there are extensive areas of acid soils (in this context, acid soils are considered as soils with pH in water (1:1) of less than 5.5 and where the exchange complex has significant levels of aluminium present) (Table 5.2). The main factor contributing to this extensive area of acid soils in the region is the hot and wet climate (high rates of weathering and leaching). Some human activities (land clearance and burning) lead to more acid soils while others (mulching, addition of coral sand) may help to maintain the fertility and reduce the rate of acidification.

Overall, Pacific Island acid soils are generally underutilized.

### Table 5.2

**Extent of Acid Soils in Some Pacific Island Countries**

| Country/Territory | Aerial Extent of Acid Soils % | Comments |
|---|---|---|
| American Samoa | 20-40 | Volcanic soils (Mollisols and Andisols) |
| Cook Islands | 40-60 | Volcanic soils |
| Fed. States of Micronesia | 60-80 | Volcanic soils and soils derived from Continental type rocks |
| Fiji | 40-50 | Derived from volcanics and associated sediments |
| French Polynesia | 60-70 | Volcanic soils |
| Guam | 20-25 | Often steepland soils |
| New Caledonia | 40-50 | Derived from metamorphic rocks, volcanic rocks, including ultramafics |
| Northern Marianas | 20-40 | Volcanic soils |
| Palau | 80 | Volcanic soils |
| Papua New Guinea | 8-15 | Mainly wet lowland soils |
| Samoa | 10-20 | Volcanic (basaltic soils) |
| Solomon Islands | 40-50 | Volcanic soils |
| Tonga | 5-10 | Volcanic soils |
| Vanuatu | 30-50 | Volcanic soils |
| Wallis and Futuna | 70-80 | Volcanic soils |

The development of appropriate management strategies could provide the opportunity for many countries to significantly increase their agricultural production potential. Factors to be considered in this context include the use of lime and fertilizers, the introduction or development of acid-tolerant crops, including tree crops, the more efficient use of available water, and the provision of a guaranteed market for the increased production (Morrison et al. 1988; Morrison et al. 1989).

On atolls, soil properties are largely dominated by the calcareous nature of the parent material, even where this has been covered with volcanic ash or other materials. The soils tend to be shallow, alkaline, and coarse-textured, having carbonate mineralogy with a very low silica content. Fertility can be high in undisturbed soils under natural vegetation, but can decrease dramatically as a result of inappropriate cultivation techniques (land clearance and fire).

As for all tropical soils, organic matter in coralline soils performs an important role in the concentration and cycling of plant nutrients. Since Pacific Island carbonate soils are frequently sandy and excessively well drained, organic matter has a second key role—that of moisture retention. The moisture retention in the absence of organic matter is very low (see Figure 5.3). The total amount of water retained in the soil profile often remains low, and plants are subject to water stress unless the rainfall is high and relatively constant, or unless the local groundwater can be tapped.

Soils derived from carbonate materials have a wide range of

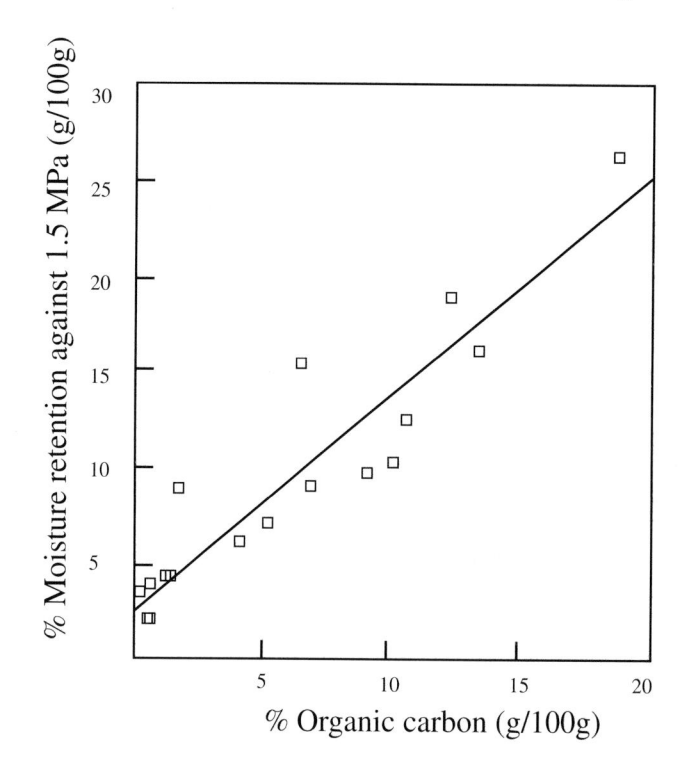

*Figure 5.3.* The variation in moisture retention with organic matter content for some Tarawa soils. 1.5 MPa is the maximum suction force plants can exert (Morrison and Seru 1986).

uses despite their limitations. Such materials are the only soils in several island groups (Tuvalu, Tokelau) and are common soils in other groups (Cook Islands, French Polynesia). Inhabitants of these islands have developed agricultural practices to produce a wide range of crops on such soils. These include coconuts, pandanus, breadfruit, citrus, and vegetables, with the specific practices and crops dependent on local factors, including the rainfall pattern. The use of mulches and pits dug down to the water table are among the practices utilized to achieve significant production (Small 1972, Chase 1992).

## Soil Erosion

In many Pacific islands, environmental conditions (heavy rain, steep slopes) indicate a high potential for soil erosion. Despite the obvious evidence of erosion in rivers (sediment loads) and on the land surface (rills and gullies) there is remarkably little experimental data on erosion rates. There is a dearth of measurements from erosion plots and only a limited amount of information from other techniques, e.g., erosion stakes, sediment loads.

In Fiji, Glatthaar (1988) and Liedtke (1989) measured soil

losses of 22–80 t/ha/yr on slopes of 5°-29°, in a sugarcane growing area north of Nadi. In the Waimanu catchment (also in Fiji), erosion was about 53 t/ha/yr. Landslides are clearly visible on steep slopes of the larger islands. A major rainstorm in April 1986 caused some 620 landslides in the Waimanu catchment alone, corresponding to a soil movement of 92 t/ha/yr or 3.5 mm over the whole catchment. Field observations of soil loss in Fiji using erosion stakes or profile reference points were reported by Clarke and Morrison (1987), who calculated soil losses of 90–300 t/ha/yr for areas where forest or indigenous grassland were converted to intensive sugarcane production.

The factors contributing to soil erosion are rainfall, soils, topography, vegetative cover, and erosion control practices. Erosivity (the ability of the rain to cause erosion), is closely related to rainfall intensity. In the Pacific Islands, rainfall intensity data are very limited. Calculation of erosion index (EI) values (see Hudson 1981) is possible for only a few locations. Examination of rainfall data for Fiji led to the following values of erosion index (Ambika Prasad and J. Morrison, unpublished results):

| | |
|---|---|
| Suva (Laucala Bay) | 1,210 |
| Nadi (Airport) | 930 (utilizing all rains over 10 mm/hr) |
| Sigatoka | 817 |

The limited rainfall intensity information suggests that EI values are > 500/yr for most of the region. These EI values are extremely high when compared with figures of 100–500 throughout the major agricultural areas of the world.

Wischmeier and Mannering (1969) describe erodibility of a soil as "a complex property dependent both on its infiltration capacity and on its capacity to resist detachment and transport by rainfall and runoff." Erodibility is therefore dependent on properties such as particle size distribution, organic matter content, presence of structure-cementing agents (such as iron and aluminium oxyhydroxides), the nature of the clay minerals, and ion chemical balance. These five properties largely determine the stability of soil aggregates. Bulk density, a measure of soil compactness (g/cm$^3$), and air-filled pore space determine the infiltration characteristics.

Much of the region is dominated by steep, mountainous country deeply incised by rivers and streams. Since much of the surface runoff following heavy rain is over steep slopes, the erosivity of the water is markedly increased. Steep slopes lead to frequent landslides following heavy rain. On several sites where indirect studies of erosion have taken place, the rates have been much lower than expected based on site characteristics. One explanation may be very high water infiltration rates, such as those observed by Willatt et al. (1995). On a Typic Humitropept (an Inceptisol), having slopes up to 30°, infiltration rates having an arithmetic mean > 200 mm/h were measured, with only 14 mm runoff out of 1,300 mm of rainfall.

Vegetative cover is an important factor in erosion control since this intercepts much of the rainfall and reduces the energy of its impact on the soil surface. Vegetation has the added advantage (over other types of soil cover) that it is rooted in the soil, and the roots help to keep the soil in place. In the Pacific Islands, plant growth is rapid due to the abundant rain and tropical temperatures. It is unusual for bare soil surfaces to remain so for any length of time under natural conditions. However, the harvesting of crops, the clearing of land for agriculture, logging, and certain construction activities all lead

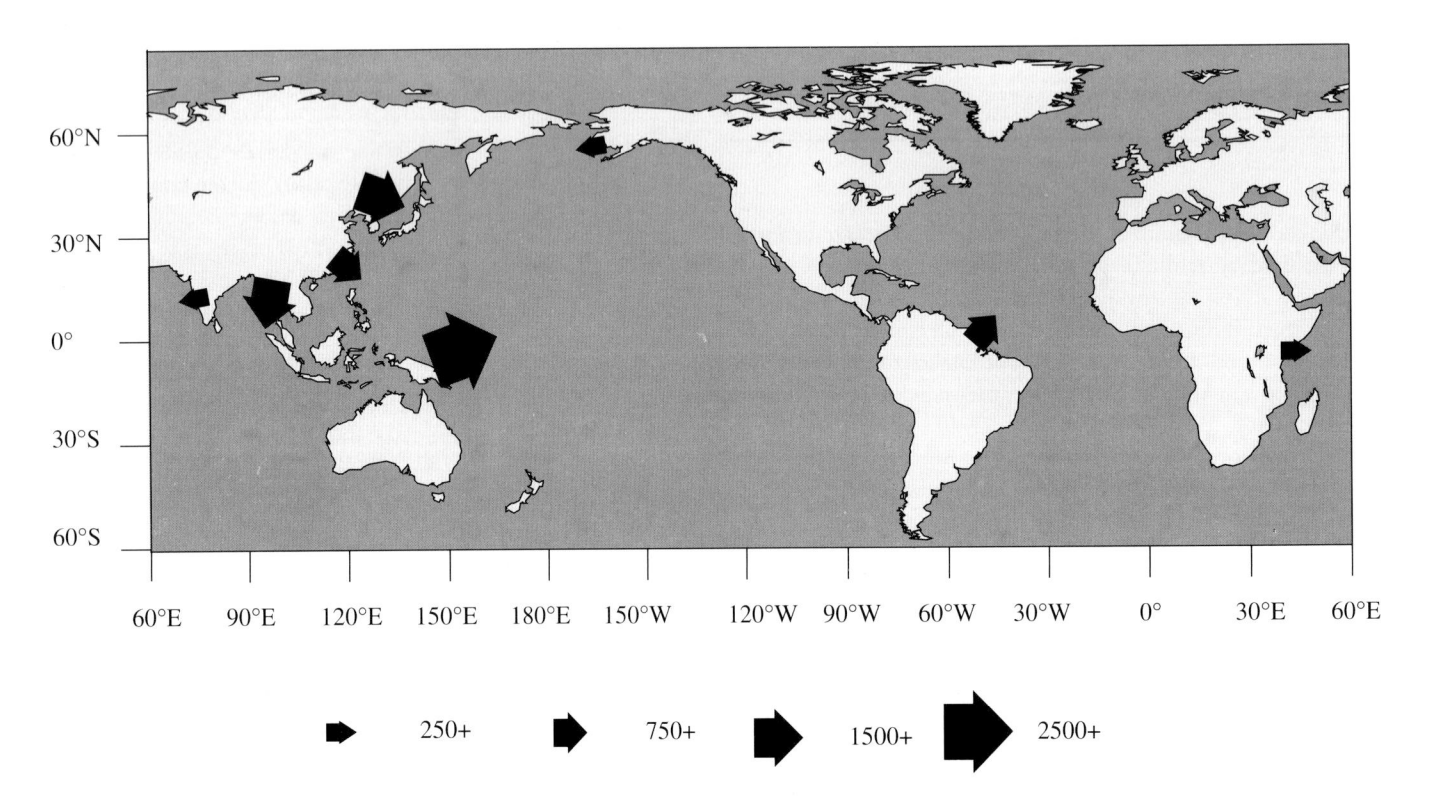

*Figure 5.4.* Outflow of sediment from the world's major rivers; numbers are in millions of tons/year (after Milliman 1990b).

### Table 5.3

**Topsoil and Subsoil Nutrient Data for Two Fiji Pedons** (Data from Morrison et al. 1987b)

| Soil | Depth cm | %C | %N | Ext P mg/kg | Exch. Cations (cmol/kg) K | Ca | Mg |
|---|---|---|---|---|---|---|---|
| SQ2 | 0-15 | 6.67 | 0.41 | 42 | 0.26 | 3.00 | 1.27 |
|  | 15-50 | 0.76 | 0.07 | 8 | 0.03 | 0.16 | 0.05 |
| KBA-S | 0-10 | 8.00 | 0.51 | 28 | 0.25 | 3.90 | 1.84 |
|  | 10-34 | 2.78 | 0.19 | 15 | 0.09 | 0.38 | 0.28 |

to extensive removal of the vegetative cover on the soil, contributing to erosion.

Erosion control measures include biological methods involving maximum cover of the soil surface (mulch, cover crops, and mixed cropping), and mechanical measures (terracing). Biological methods are usually more efficient than mechanical, and the mechanical methods can lead to even greater problems if not properly designed and executed. The use of buffer strips involving vetiver grass or pineapples or legume trees, and tillage along the contour have proved very effective erosion control measures in the region.

A major problem encountered in assessing soil erosion in the Pacific Islands is the absence of data on erosion rates under "natural" conditions. This is understandable given the difficulties in locating suitable situations and attempting to carry out appropriate experiments in such isolated locations. Without such information, conclusions about the impact of people on the rates of erosion must obviously be somewhat speculative.

### Suspended Sediment Loads in Rivers

Another method of examining erosion rates is by studying the movement of suspended sediment in rivers. A survey of sediment loads carried by rivers to the coastal zone in Oceania has been made using available (both published and unpublished) data (Asquith et al. 1994). The method of calculating sediment yield selected was that of Fournier (1960). The results of the sediment yield calculations for the South Pacific Islands indicate a total regional annual sediment load in rivers of $2.49 \times 10^9$ t (with Papua New Guinea producing $2.02 \times 10^9$ t/yr of this total).

The sediment yield value of approximately $2.5 \times 10^9$ tonnes per annum is not unrealistic in the light of the global sediment budgets/flux calculations of Walling and Webb (1987), Milliman and Mead (1983), and Milliman (1990a, b). Milliman (1990b) noted that global fluvial sediment flux estimated by the Fournier method was $32–51 \times 10^9$ t/yr. While this estimate is probably high (current opinion puts the value at more like $15 \times 10^9$ t/yr), there is a general consensus in the literature that the contribution from Oceania represents a considerable proportion of the global value. Milliman (1990b) noted that Southern Asia and Oceania (in this definition including Island Southeast Asia and New Zealand) contribute over 70% of the world's sediment flux, with Oceania discharging $3 \times 10^9$ t/yr of sediment to the ocean (Figure 5.4). This is close to the value obtained independently in the above study.

### Nutrient Losses via Soil Erosion

In addition to the physical damage brought about by soil erosion, the transported materials, being derived mainly from topsoils, carry with them significant quantities of valuable plant nutrients. This is particularly important in the Pacific Islands, where, for many soils, the surface layer represents the "richest" part of the whole profile. This is well illustrated for two Fiji soils by the data in Table 5.3.

This transport of nutrients represents two environmental hazards: the loss of valuable plant growth resources, which is detrimental for agriculture, and the movement of nutrients in the coastal zone, where they may contribute to eutrophication (nutrient overload) and related problems. Nutrient loss contributes to the generally low agricultural yields noted in the region (Morrison et al. 1987a) and the increased agricultural use of marginal land, which further exacerbates the erosion/sedimentation problem (Morrison et al. 1990).

## Conclusions

Soils represent one of the major natural resources of the Pacific Islands. We are fortunate that for many islands, good information on soils is available. In some cases, adequate information is not yet available. Given the fragile nature of Pacific Island environments (small islands separated by substantial stretches of ocean), it is imperative that good soil management be practiced if local inhabitants are to sustain production of food and forest products. The small size of many of the islands is an environmental hazard in this context. Mistakes in environmental management may be extremely difficult to rectify, at least in the short term. Recognizing the importance of soils and the development of national sustainable land use plans is essential for the future well-being of Pacific Islanders.

# Bibliography

Asghar, M., T. J. Davidson, and R. J. Morrison, eds. 1988. *Soil taxonomy and fertility in the South Pacific*. Apia: University of the South Pacific.

Asquith F., M. Kooge, and R. J. Morrison. 1994. *Transportation of sediments via rivers to the ocean and the role of sediments as pollutants in the South Pacific*. Reports and Studies No. 72. Apia: South Pacific Regional Environment Programme.

Buol, S. W., F. D. Hole, and R. J. McCracken. 1980. *Soil genesis and classification*. Second Edition. Ames: Iowa State University Press.

Chase, L. D. C., and J. P. Widdowson. 1983. Sulphur in the agriculture of Pacific high islands. In *Sulphur in S.E. Asian and S. Pacific agriculture*, ed. G. Blair and R. A. Till, 206–217. Armidale: UNE Press.

Chase, R. C., ed. 1992. *Review of agricultural development in the atolls*. Apia: University of the South Pacific.

Clarke, W. C., and R. J. Morrison. 1987. Land mismanagement and the development imperative in Fiji. In H.C. Brookfield and P. M. Blaikie, *Land degradation and society*, 176–185. London: Methuen.

Cowie, J. D. 1980. Soils from andesitic tephra and their variability, Tongatapu, Kingdom of Tonga. *Australian Journal of Soil Research* 18:273–284

Dodson, J. 1992. *The naive lands: prehistory and environmental change in Australia and the Southwest Pacific*. Melbourne: Longman Cheshire.

Fairbairn, T. I. J. 1985. *Island economies*. Suva: Institute of Pacific Studies, University of the South Pacific.

Fiji Meteorological Services. n.d. Information sheets 21, 153, 171.

Food and Agriculture Organization, United Nations. 1990. *Soil map of the world*. Paris: UNESCO.

Fosberg, F. R. 1954. Soils of the Northern Marshall atolls, with special reference to the Jemo series. *Soil Science* 78:99–107

Fosberg, F. R. 1957. Description and occurrence of atoll phosphate rock in Micronesia. *American Journal of Science* 225:584–592.

Fournier, F. 1960. *Climat et erosion: La relation entre l'erosion du sol l'eau et les précipitations atmospheriques*. Presses Universitaires de France, Paris

Glatthaar, D. 1988. The sediment load of the Waimanu River Southeastern Viti Levu, Fiji. In *Report about two research projects in the Republic of Fiji*, ed. H. Liedtke and D. Glatthar, 52–75. Sponsored by the German Research Foundation. Bochum: Geographical Institute, Ruhr University.

Hudson, N. 1981. *Soil Conservation*. Ithaca, New York: Cornell University Press.

Kuhlken, R. 1994. *Tuatua ni Nakavadra*: A Fijian irrigated taro agrosystem. In *The science of Pacific Island peoples*. Vol. 2, *Land use and agriculture*, ed. R. J. Morrison, P. Geraghty, and L. Crowl, 51–62. Suva: Institute of Pacific Studies, University of the South Pacific.

Lal, P. N. 1990. *Conservation or conversion of mangroves in Fiji*. Occasional Paper No. 11. Honolulu: Environment and Policy Institute, East-West Center.

Latham, M., P. Quantin, and G. Aubert. 1978. *Étude des sols dela Nouvelle-Caledonie*. Paris: ORSTOM.

Leslie D. M. 1984a. A proposal for an Oceania Benchmark Sites Network for Agrotechnology Transfer OBSNAT. Proceedings of the International Symposium on Minimum Data Sets for Agrotechnology Transfer, March 1983, 33–54. ICRISAT Centre, India.

Leslie. D. M. 1984b. *Soils of the Koronivia Agricultural Research Station, Viti Levu, Fiji*. New Zealand Soil Survey Report, 75, Soil Bureau, DSIR, Lower Hutt.

Liedtke, H. 1989. Soil erosion and soil removal in Fiji. *Applied Geography and Development* 33:68–92.

Manner, H. I., and R. J. Morrison. 1991. A temporal sequence chronosequence of soil carbon and nitrogen development after phosphate mining on Nauru Island. *Pacific Science* 45:400–404.

Marsden E., G. J. Fergusson, and M. Fieldes. 1958. Notes on the radioactivity of soils with application to Niue Island. Proceedings of the Second International Conference on the Peaceful Uses of Atomic Energy, Geneva 18, 514.

Milliman, J. D. 1990a. *Discharge of fluvial sediment to the oceans: global, temporal and anthropogenic implications*. Washington D.C.: NAS/NRC Press.

Milliman, J. D. 1990b. Fluvial sediment in coastal seas: flux and fate. *Nature and Resources* 26(4):12–21.

Milliman, J. D., and R. H. Meade. 1983. World-wide delivery of river sediment to the oceans. *Journal of Geology* 91:1–21.

Morrison, R. J. 1991. Some Andosols from Savai'i, Western Samoa. *Soil Science Society of America Proceedings J*. 55:159–164.

Morrison, R. J., and D. M. Leslie, eds. 1982. *Proceedings of the South Pacific Regional Forum on Soil Taxonomy*. Institute of Natural Resources, University of the South Pacific.

Morrison, R. J., and V. B. Seru. 1986. *Soils of Abatao Islet, Tarawa, Kiribati*. Envir. Studies Report 27. Suva: Institute of Natural Resources, University of the South Pacific.

Morrison R. J., R. Naidu, and U. Singh. 1987a. Sulphur in the agriculture of Papua New Guinea and the South Pacific Islands. In *Fertilizer sulphur requirements and sources in developing countries of Asia and the Pacific*, 57–66. FADINAP/FAO/Sulphur Institute/ACIAR, Bangkok.

Morrison, R. J., R. Naidu, S. Naidu, and R. A. Prasad. 1987b. *Classification of some reference soils from Viti Levu and Vanua Levu, Fiji*. INR Environmental Studies Report No. 38, University of the South Pacific.

Morrison, R. J., R. Naidu, and U. Singh. 1988. Acid soils of Fiji. Fiji Meteorological Services. n.d. Information sheets 21, 153, 171.

Morrison, R. J., R. Naidu, P. Gangaiya, and Yee Wah Sing. 1989. Amelioration of acid soils in Fiji. In *Soil management and smallholder development in the Pacific Islands*, ed. E. Pushparajah and C.R. Elliot, 255–270. Bangkok: IBSRAM.

Morrison, R. J., W. C. Clarke, N. Buresova, and L. Limalevu. 1990. Erosion and sedimentation in Fiji: an overview. In *Research needs and applications to reduce erosion and sedimentation in tropical steeplands*, ed. R. R. Ziemer, C. L. O'Loughlin, and L. S. Hamilton, 14–23. Wallingford: IAHS Publication No. 192

Morrison, R. J., P. Geraghty, and L. Crowl, eds. 1994. *The science of Pacific Island peoples*. Vol. 2, *Land use and agriculture*. Suva: Institute of Pacific Studies, University of the South Pacific.

New Zealand Soils Bureau. 1979. *Soils of the Cook Islands: an introduction*. Wellington: New Zealand Ministry of Foreign Affairs.

Roe, D. 1989. The Kolevu terraced taro system, west Guadalcanal. In *Soil management and smallholder development in the Pacific Islands*, ed. E. Pushparajah and C. R. Elliot, 205–212. Bangkok: IBSRAM..

Schroth, C. L. 1971. Soil sequences of Western Samoa. *Pacific Science* 25:291–300.

Simonson, R. W. 1959. Outline of a generalised theory of soil genesis. *Soil Science Society of America Proceedings* 23:152–6.

Small, C. A. 1972. *Atoll agriculture*. Tarawa: Agriculture Department, Gilbert and Ellis Islands Government.

Smith, C. W. 1983. *Soil survey of the islands of Palau, Republic of Palau*. Washington, D.C.: U.S. Dept. of Agric. Soil Conservation Service,

Soil Survey Staff. 1975. *Soil taxonomy: a basic system of soil classification for making and interpreting soil surveys*. Washington, D.C.: U.S. Dept of Agric. Handbook No. 436, U.S. Gov. Printing Office.

Soil Survey Staff. 1996. *Keys to soil taxonomy*, Seventh Edition. Washington, D.C.: Natural Resource Conservation Service, U.S. Department of Agriculture.

Soil Survey Staff. 1996. *Keys to soil taxonomy*, Seventh Edition. Washington, D.C.: Natural Resource Conservation Service, U.S. Department of Agriculture.

Southern, W. 1986. The late Quaternary environmental history of Fiji. Ph.D. thesis, Australian National University, Canberra.

Wall, J. R. D., and J. R. F. Hansell. 1976. *Land resources of the Solomon Islands*. Vol. 8, *Outer Islands*. Land Resources Division UK, Surbiton.

Walling, D. E., and B. W. Webb. 1987. Material transport by the world's rivers: evolving perspectives. In *Water for the future: hydrology in perspective*. Proceedings of the Rome Symposium, April 1987. IAHS Publ. No. 164, Wallingford.

Whitehead, N. E., R. G. Ditchburn, W. J. McCabe, and P. Rankin. 1992. A new model for the origin of the anomalous radioactivity in Niue Island South Pacific soils. *Chemical Geology*, Isotope Geoscience Section, 94, 247–260.

Willatt, S. T., J.Q. Suqa, and L. Limalevu. 1995. Water infiltration and implications for soil erosion: a case study at Waibau, Viti Levu, Fiji. *South Pacific Journal of Natatural Science* 14:43–54.

Wischmeier, W. H., and J.V. Mannering. 1969. Relation of soil properties to its erodibility. *Soil Science Society of America Proceedings* 33:131–137.

Wright, A. C. S. 1963. *Soils and land use of Western Samoa*. Wellington: New Zealand Soil Bureau Bull. 22.

Young, A. 1976. *Tropical soils and soil survey*. Cambridge: Cambridge University Press.

Young, F. J. 1988. *Soil survey of the Territory of Guam*. Washington, D.C.: USDA (United States Department of Agriculture) Soil Conservation Service.

# Chapter 6

# Water

*Derrick Depledge*

## Introduction

A supply of fresh water is a prerequisite to any settlement. The needs of the people who first came to the Pacific were met by preexisting supplies, which they either could see or knew where to find. The technology was simple and adequate, perhaps using lengths of bamboo or locally made clay pots as containers for collection.

Rainfall was collected from the trunk of a tree using a thick bush rope. Groundwater was collected from hand-dug wells, usually shallow, but sometimes reaching considerable depth. The location of a village was often dictated by the presence of freshwater springs or the proximity of a stream.

With the arrival of the Europeans, water resource development progressed and benefited from the new technologies and materials available to the particular nation involved over the period of colonization. Those Pacific Island groups with continuing dependence still have ongoing support and sometimes the latest technology from the affiliated country.

Improvements in water supply included the development of previously unknown groundwater resources, the ability to transport and distribute water to consumers, the ability to treat and disinfect surface water that was previously not used or was used with subsequent adverse effects on health and well-being, the availability of large containers, such as tanks and cisterns, and the construction of large dams to store water.

The development of water resources for domestic purposes in the Pacific as well as for other human activities, including agriculture and industry, which are growing in scale, increasingly requires consideration of the effect on the existing ecosystems and the environment in general.

The scattered nature of settlement in the islands of the Pacific has led to a system of land tenure, which is seen to include the water that flows over or under the ground. Access to stream or spring flow may be possible only with the permission and payment of compensation to local landowners. The concept of ownership of water by the state is not widely accepted in the Pacific, although in some countries legislation allows the government to control the allocation of resources.

Modern development of adequate supplies of fresh potable water resources involves some considerable expense. The motto of the (Western) Samoa Water Board is "Water, a Gift from God." Simple messages such as this, although probably meeting the early missionaries' purpose of giving the people a reason to look after their water supply, now obstructs, to some extent, the need to put a value and a cost on the supply of water and to finance the production of clean water and maintenance of supply systems by charging consumers. A 1988 estimate of the value of water resources in New Zealand, including water for supply, hydropower, recreation, freshwater fisheries, gravel replenishment, and waste disposal, was almost NZ$2.5 billion (Mosley 1988).

## Available Water Resources

### Rainfall

Water is taken from every phase of the water cycle. The primary source of fresh water over the Pacific Ocean is from the atmosphere in the form of precipitation. This is used directly or feeds the surface and underground freshwater resources. Most Pacific islands exist as small landmasses in a predominantly oceanic region. The airstreams approaching most coastlines have often traversed large tracts of water and are moisture laden. Mean relative humidity and annual rainfall are, therefore, generally high throughout the Pacific, but the rainfall is variable both spatially and temporally.

Spatially, rainfall available as a water resource is affected by the presence or absence of high ground, the seasonal movement and location of the intertropical and South Pacific convergence zones and the passage of cyclones and troughs of low pressure associated with depressions.

Temporally, rainfall has daily, seasonal, and secular variations that, although predictable to some extent, can never be anticipated sufficiently to prevent drought or flooding from causing some degree of physical hardship. The pattern of late afternoon rain in the tropical areas, rainy seasons, and yearly variations related to global climatic changes such as the El Niño Southern Oscillation all affect the availability of rainwater as a resource.

Effective rainfall, that is, the rainfall contributing to runoff (surface water) and to the groundwater reserves, is limited by the amount of evaporation that occurs and transpiration by plants. These processes remove particularly large volumes in the tropical and subtropical areas of the Pacific and reduce the available water resources. Average annual values for potential evapotranspiration in the tropical Pacific are in the region of 1,700–1,800 mm (Nullet 1987).

### Surface Water

Surface water is found in rivers and other channels, lakes, reservoirs, and wetlands. It is found where there is sufficient rainfall or groundwater discharge to provide the resource and where soils and the underlying geological materials are relatively impermeable. Countries with large landmasses, such as Papua New Guinea (PNG) and New Zealand, have large catchment areas and often long rivers with high mean flows. The three largest rivers in PNG, the Sepik, Fly, and Purari, have a combined catchment area of over 200,000 km², over one-third the area of the whole country (Piliwas 1996). Rivers in New Zealand have smaller but substantial catchment areas (the Clutha, 21,000 km²) and length (the Waikato, 425 km²). Flows can be high, with an estimated total annual discharge for New Zealand rivers of about 415 km³/yr. The Clutha in the South Island of New Zealand has a mean discharge of 563 m³/s (Mosley 1995).

Other high islands in the Pacific have small catchment areas where permeability is low, often with rapid runoff characteristics, giving flash flooding on occasions. The average catchment area on O'ahu in Hawai'i, for example, is only 2.6 km² (Peterson 1991).

Perennial and ephemeral streams are also found on smaller islands where conditions are favorable. The island of 'Eua in Tonga, for example, has constantly flowing water fed from inland cave systems, and there are numerous spring-fed streams on the higher islands of Vanuatu and Solomon Islands.

Lakes vary in size from the large volcanic, glacial, and manmade lakes of New Zealand to small depressions on islands such as Mitiaro in the Cook Islands, containing shallow and sometimes brackish-water reserves.

Because the residence time of water on the Earth's surface is small compared with that of groundwater, surface water resources, particularly rivers and streams, respond more rapidly to variations in the local rainfall pattern and are therefore more limited in their availability.

## *Groundwater*

Groundwater is found throughout the Pacific, with only the smallest islands not having a usable freshwater lens perched above saline water. Available storage ranges from thin fragile lenses, perhaps 1–2 m thick, to large aquifers in limestone, volcanic, or sedimentary sequences on larger islands. Some islands have abundant groundwater resources. The 2,000 or so inhabitants of the elevated coral atoll of Niue have water reticulated to all their houses on the island from a lens (Figure 6.1), which has a maximum thickness, estimated from electrical resistivity soundings, of 50–170 m (Jacobson and Hill 1980).

Groundwater, with a global average residence time of about 1,400 years, is less affected by the temporal and secular variations of rainfall than is surface water. By comparison the global average residence time for water in rivers is 12 days and in lakes 1.2 years. Small island groundwater lenses, however, may have comparatively small residence times. The typical atoll rises little more than 5 m above sea level; generally consists of coral sands and gravels, in which the freshwater lenses are found, overlying a solid limestone formation; and has limited width and area (Figure 6.2).

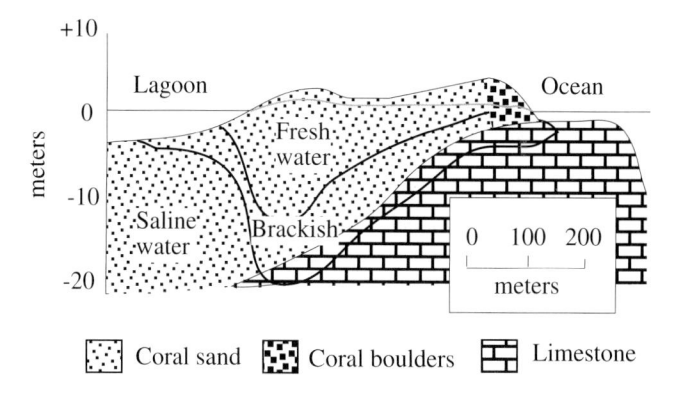

*Figure 6.2. Water sources on Tarawa, Kiribati (after Falkland 1991).*

Atolls are highly responsive to the capricious nature of rainfall. Exploitable water resources may be as low as 20% of the mean annual recharge to the lenses (Anthony 1991). Moreover, vegetation, and coconut trees in particular, act as phreatophytes and are known to consume large quantities of water directly from the shallow groundwater table by transpiration. Recent stem flow measurements on mature coconut trees on the island of Bonriki in Tarawa, Kiribati, indicate that 100–150 liters may be used by a single tree each day (White 1996).

There is a clear distinction between the water-bearing strata on small islands and those on the larger and higher islands. Larger islands can have high-yielding and extensive aquifers in limestone, volcanic, or sedimentary rock sequences (Figure 6.3). Limestone formations are often uplifted reefs that have been

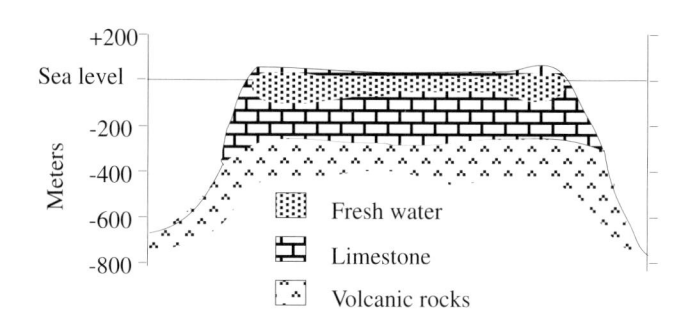

*Figure 6.1. Water sources on Niue (after Falkland 1991).*

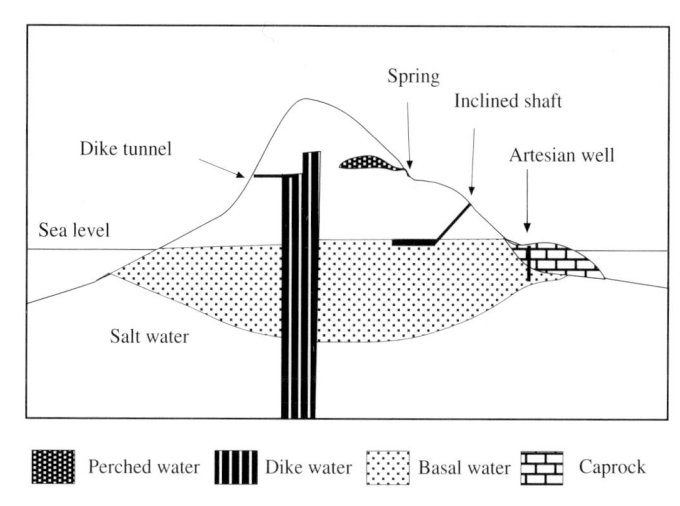

*Figure 6.3. Water sources on a high island.*

subjected to karstification, giving them a secondary porosity that renders them highly permeable. Volcanic sequences forming aquifers may consist of *in situ* lava flows, perhaps faulted and intruded by dikes, and reworked volcanic material in bedded horizons. Alluvial plains of varying permeability are found in many of the larger islands of the Pacific. They consist of sand and gravel with finer materials derived from adjacent mountain chains or other high ground.

At locations adjacent to plate margins, and where recent volcanic activity has taken place, thermal groundwater is often found, either rising from depth or being heated from the elevated ground temperatures in the area. In particular these thermal areas are found adjacent to the Australian-Indian/Pacific plate boundary. There are two main groups of geothermal waters, the low-temperature waters (20°–100°C), associated with active faulting, and the high-temperature waters (> 100°C), associated with areas of active volcanism (Hunt and Bibby 1992).

## Water Quality

### Natural Water Quality

Water, being the "universal solvent," is affected by the medium over which or through which it passes. Rainwater is generally low (<10mg/l) in dissolved solids, although usually a little acidic. Surface waters and groundwater have chemical compositions that reflect their origin. Typical analyses from the Pacific are shown in Table 6.1. As well as picking up harmless elements from the environment, water, in all phases of its natural cycle, also picks up contaminants, both natural and man-made (Gangaiya and Morrison 1988).

Rainfall in places like Hawai'i can be affected by the gaseous emissions from volcanoes, causing the phenomenon of "acid rain," which can leach roof materials and cause metals such as lead to accumulate in the water stored in tanks. Similarly, ash and other particles emitted from volcanoes in New Zealand have affected water supplies in areas surrounding eruptions. In PNG, Rabaul's water supply was destroyed in the 1994 eruption by falling ash.

In the context of small atoll islands and in coastal regions, groundwater supplies can be affected by saline intrusion if the resource is overpumped.

### Man-made Contamination of Water Supplies

A growing waste stream threatens many water supplies, people's health, and the often fragile ecosystems of the Pacific. There are a range of pollutants that affect the water resources. These are derived partly from industrial and agricultural sources, but mostly from urban development and other nuclear settlements (Morrison et al. 1996). In fact, humans have always used water deliberately as a waste-transporting agency. The Pacific, as elsewhere, has many examples of polluted water resources.

Mining is a major potential polluter of surface waterways in the Pacific. Heavy metals used in processing ore, as well as sediment from the catchment disturbance caused by excavation, roading, and tailings dam construction, are a threat to rivers that take the mine discharges in such countries as New Zealand, PNG, and Fiji.

Similarly, forestry operations can be a cause of serious degradation of catchments in the tropical and subtropical countries (Bruijnzeel and Critchley 1994). The high and intense rainfalls experienced in many areas can lead to rapid soil stripping following clear felling of rain forests if codes of practice are not followed diligently. The resulting sedimentation of rivers accompanying deforestation can destroy natural

### TABLE 6.1

**Typical Analyses for Freshwater Resources in the Pacific (mg/kg except for pH and conductivity)**
Source: SOPAC Water and Sanitation section n.d.

| | NIUE<br>Ground Water | NAURU<br>Rain Water | KIRIBATI<br>Ground Water | VANUATU<br>Thermal Spring | VANUATU<br>River Water |
|---|---|---|---|---|---|
| conductivity ($\mu$S/cm) | 321 | 21 | 575 | NR | 350 |
| pH | 7.7 | 6.5 | 8.4 | 7 | 7.25 |
| TDS (total dissolved solids) | 179 | 10 | NR (not recorded) | NR | 190 |
| chloride | 10 | 1 | 17 | 10700 | 48 |
| sulphate | 4 | 0.3 | 6.2 | 170 | 2 |
| carbonate | NR | <0.5 | 6 | NR | NR |
| bicarbonate | 163 | 9 | 346 | NR | 78 |
| potassium | 2 | NR | 0.31 | 200 | 7 |
| magnesium | 9 | 0.6 | 23 | 38 | 2 |
| sodium | 6 | 1 | 9.5 | 4740 | 15 |
| calcium | 44 | 1 | 83 | 2560 | 24 |

water habitats not only in stream but beyond the river mouth onto reefs and coastal areas. Samoa, the Federated States of Micronesia, and most Melanesian countries have all experienced this type of pollution of their water resources (Asquith et al. 1994).

Agricultural use of fertilizers, herbicides, fungicides, and pesticides, except in New Zealand, is not yet widespread (Morrison et al. 1996). The growing of crops such as squash pumpkins in Tonga and Vanuatu and sugarcane in Fiji and Hawai'i is leading to an increased use of these possible water pollutants, but no major problems have been detected to date, largely because the insecticides and fungicides are being used in low quantities and are generally of the "safer" category, which break down rapidly on contact with the soil.

Industry is also limited in the Pacific Island nations, except for New Zealand. The large-scale freezing works (abattoirs), pulp and processing mills, refineries, smelters, and other industrial developments found in New Zealand are rare elsewhere in the Pacific. A nickel smelter in Noumea, New Caledonia, sugar refineries on the main islands of Fiji, and major mining operations in PNG are exceptions.

In both the urban and rural areas of the Pacific there is the problem of liquid and solid waste disposal from domestic sources. Failure to deal with these adequately can have disastrous effects on water supplies from both a health and an environmental point of view (Morrison 1997).

Water-borne diseases spread by fecally contaminated water include the viral diseases infectious hepatitis and poliomyelitis and the bacterial diseases cholera, typhoid, and bacillary dysentery. Diarrheal diseases caused by both viruses and bacteria contribute to the deaths of many children each year in places such as Kiribati (Saito 1995), and throughout the Pacific. Disease-causing biological agents (pathogens) affect the health and well-being of many adults as well, reducing their income-generating capacity and effectiveness in the workplace. They have a large and significant impact on morbidity and mortality rates in the Pacific.

Where water-flushed toilets exist, large quantities of water often may be needed. Pour-flush toilets require a reliable supply. For other sanitation types, water is still needed for hand washing if good hygiene is practiced. Most sanitation facilities have the potential to contaminate water supplies. On small islands, where groundwater is a major source, the ability of effluent from latrines to penetrate to the water table can pollute the groundwater supply and can lead to the spread of disease (Dillon 1996).

Universal access to a safe water supply, coupled with the availability of sanitary means of excreta disposal, would bring about a marked increase in the standard of living and economic well-being of many in the Pacific region. In Honiara in Solomon Islands, for example, in 1993 each child under one year of age on average suffered four incidents of infectious diseases including skin diseases, yaws, red eye, and fever (Solomon Islands Goverment 1993a).

High infant mortality rates in some locations, and the presence of malaria and other vector-transmitted illnesses throughout a large part of Melanesia, are a real concern in the region.

Open tanks, uncovered containers, and other standing water, particularly during rainy seasons, provide breeding grounds for the mosquito larvae that transmit malaria and other diseases such as dengue fever to humans. In PNG in 1990 the infant mortality rate was 57.5 per 1,000 live births, down from 93 in 1975 (Berhane 1994). In the same year the Kiribati infant mortality rate was 65. Inadequate supplies of clean water and poor sanitation are major factors in the prevalence of water-related diseases. In 1992 in Solomon Islands 440 malaria cases per 1,000 population were reported (Solomon Islands Government 1993b). Regular typhoid epidemics have occurred in periurban areas of Port Moresby and other towns in PNG.

### Remedial and Preventative Measures

Where required, most Pacific reticulated urban water supplies are disinfected by the use of chlorine, either in gas or liquid form. This is generally effective in eliminating bacterial contamination.

Water extracted for supply from waterways may also be discolored from time to time by sediment, particularly during heavy rain periods, and require treatment in the form of sedimentation and/or filtration. Sophisticated treatment plants to deal with the suspended and soluble solids are operated in such places as Auckland in New Zealand to provide a clean potable water supply for the city. Simpler treatment facilities are found in smaller urban areas of the Pacific such as 'Apia in Samoa, where a series of slow sand filters and sedimentation tanks are used.

In the village or rural situation, particularly where the

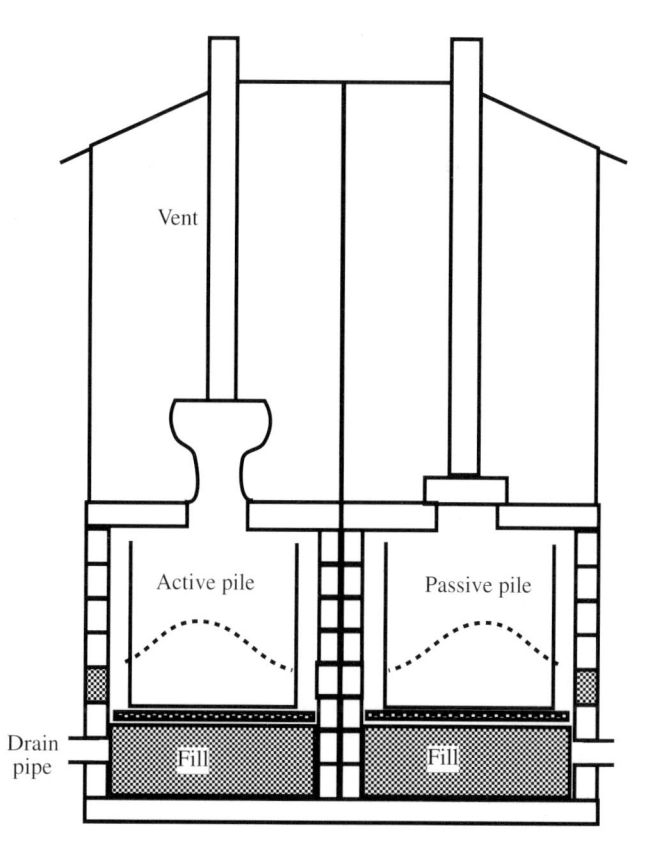

*Figure 6.4. Composting toilet diagram, Kiritimati Island, Kiribati.*

population is increasing, there is a need for improved health and hygiene education related to the processes of water supply, waste disposal, and food preparation. The location of latrines at some distance and downstream from shallow wells would reduce the risk to health from waterborne diseases.

On Kiritimati Island in Kiribati a trial of waterless composting toilets is being undertaken (Figure 6.4). These zero discharge toilets do not contribute effluent to the groundwater and may, in time, result in an unpolluted water lens (Crennan 1996).

There is little legislation in many of the Pacific Island countries regarding the protection of areas of water supply. Only in New Zealand, Hawai'i, and some of the French and American territories are protection zones in evidence. Guam, for example, has an Environmental Protection Agency that administers wellhead protection zones around the 100 wells that supply most of the island, and a designated groundwater management and protection zone. Elsewhere, land tenure problems often preclude a national resolution to protect water resources. Zones have been proposed for the water supply catchment for Port Vila in Vanuatu (Depledge 1994), but without the backing of legislation at present.

Many rivers, lakes, and wetlands in New Zealand have been preserved from development through water conservation orders. Some are in national parks and are regarded as being of recreational value.

# Water Use

## Domestic Use

The demand for water in the Pacific varies greatly. There are urban areas, particularly in those countries consisting of small atolls, where population densities are as high as 10,000 people per km$^2$. However, despite the trend toward urban migration and unlike the world as a whole, the Pacific requires much of its domestic water in a rural setting. PNG has a large population for a Pacific country, but the land area is so great that the overall density of population is only around 8 per km$^2$, which is just below the average density for the whole of the Pacific.

Urban usage ranges in value from lows of 20–40 liters per capita per day (lpcd) in Tarawa, Kiribati, to over 850 lpcd in Rarotonga and 1,090 lpcd in Tahiti. Table 6.2 shows the wide range of consumption per capita throughout the region. It should be noted, for contrast, that European targets for domestic water consumption are now set at 120 lpcd.

## Agricultural and Industrial Use

Agriculture and industry are major contributors to the New Zealand economy. Irrigation alone consumes about 1.1 km$^3$ each year (Mosley 1995), while many of the dairy factories scattered throughout the two main islands use volumes in excess of 1,500 m$^3$ daily. Industrial uses can also be high. The aluminum smelter in Southland, New Zealand, consumes 4,500 m$^3$ per day from groundwater resources derived from the underlying gravels. New Zealand Steel in the North Island uses 1,700 m$^3$ per day. On a lesser scale, in Fiji there are over 1,000 ha of rice with facilities for irrigation (Raj 1996).

On the main island of Viti Levu there are three storage reservoirs for irrigation water with capacities ranging from 1 to 3 million m$^3$; 65 km of canals deliver water to farms; 300 ha are used for sprinkler irrigation of vegetable crops. In Hawai'i, storage of water for agriculture is particularly difficult because of the highly permeable volcanic rocks and soils. Water is therefore transported via a network of ditches and tunnels from wet mountainous areas to the drier lowlands for irrigation of crops such as sugarcane. In 1985 85% of all water use in Hawai'i was for agriculture, mostly irrigation (Dept. of Land and Natural Resources 1987). In Guam, 3.5% of the public water supply is used for irrigation annually.

Stock usage can be high in countries with intensive grazing, such as New Zealand. Free-ranging herds, such as those providing meat for the beef industry in Vanuatu, use less water. In Samoa stock consume an estimated total of about 100 m$^3$ a day. Agricultural water use in rural areas or outer islands in the

### TABLE 6.2
**Domestic Water Consumption in Some Pacific Countries**
Source: SOPAC Water and Sanitation section n.d.

| LOCATION | COUNTRY | WATER USE (lpcd) |
|---|---|---|
| Aitutaki | Cook Islands | 100 |
| Kosrae | Fed. States of Micronesia | 40 |
| Majuro | Marshall Islands | 170 |
| Nauru | Nauru | 160 |
| Rarotonga | Cook Islands | 850 |
| Tahiti | French Polynesia | 1090 |
| Tarawa | Kiribati | 20-40 |
| Ebeye | Marshall Islands | 76 |
| Wellington | New Zealand | 230 |
| Noumea | New Caledonia | 420 |

Pacific varies greatly depending on available resources. In the village, the animals such as pigs, goats, and chickens belonging to a household can create a demand of perhaps an additional 0.5 persons.

## Other Uses

Hydropower is being developed throughout the Pacific, providing 80% of the requirements in New Zealand and providing substantial contributions to the power needs of Samoa, PNG, French Polynesia, Hawai'i, and Fiji. This is not strictly a consumptive use but affects stretches of rivers where diversion or damming occurs.

On the higher islands, fast-flowing perennial rivers have been harnessed for hydroelectric power. Schemes ranging from small micro hep to large-scale power stations have been built in the Pacific.

Also on the larger islands, lakes and rivers are used for recreational purposes, including boating, swimming, fishing, and other aquatic sports. Artificially created lakes, associated with hydropower development, are also used in this way. For example, Lake Karapiro in New Zealand has a rowing course and is used for many boating activities.

Water is used extensively for the disposal of wastes, both in a liquid and a solid form. Rivers, in particular, are the recipients of much of the municipal, sometimes treated effluent from sewage disposal systems.

# Technologies for Water Supply

## Conventional Technology, Rainwater

To collect rainwater a catchment is required and some form of storage must be constructed. On a household scale, tanks are built to collect the rain from roofs, provided the roofs are of suitable material, such as galvanized iron, aluminum, or clay or cement tiles. Tanks in the Pacific are made of ferrocement, steel, timber, fiberglass, and heavy duty polyethylene. Water quality is generally good provided adequate precautions are taken to keep roofs clean and prevent access to the tanks by insects and small animals. In the Pacific, rainwater collection ranges from the simple catchment from house roofs into small containers or tanks to large-scale catchments directing flow to a reservoir or storage tank. This last method can be illustrated by the use of the 30 hectares of the airport runway in Majuro in the Marshall Islands, which provides an average of almost 800,000 m³/year to the water supply for Majuro, assuming 20% of the rainfall is lost to evaporation (Doig 1996). Adjacent reservoirs have capacities to store about 57,000 m³ of raw water and 7,600 m³ of treated water.

## Conventional Technology, Surface Water

Water resources from rivers, streams, and lakes are used throughout the Pacific, specifically on the higher islands. Water may either be impounded behind a dam to create storage or be taken directly from a stream or other intake. In Rarotonga in the Cook Islands, an average of 1,200 m³ per day is taken from 12 filtered or open intakes from the radial streams that flow from the central high area of the island. Eighty-six percent of the population of Fiji receive on average 167,000 m³/day of reticulated water, mainly derived from surface water sources. Ninety-five percent of the reticulated supply in French Polynesia is obtained from river sources.

Small gravity-fed systems, consisting of an intake, a supply line, and either a storage tank or standpipes in the villages, have been installed in many Pacific Island countries, such as Vanuatu, to provide water to one or more villages. These may suffer from intermittent supply, especially during the dry season, and siltation during heavy rains. The major advantage of gravity systems is the economy of operation and maintenance.

## Conventional Technology, Groundwater

The use of groundwater varies from individual household wells to major supplies from large aquifers supplying major cities, such as Christchurch in New Zealand (Figure 6.5).

The simple, shallow hand-dug well on a small island is usually something of a health hazard because of its open condition and the proximity of sanitation facilities or the existence of free-ranging stock. Major improvements have been made by providing a cover, generally a concrete slab, over open wells and installing a hand pump to replace the rope and bucket previously used (Mourits and Depledge 1995). Various projects are under way in such countries as Solomon Islands and Vanuatu to provide hand-pumped wells in the village.

In some locations major projects have been undertaken to relocate wells away from villages and sources of pollution, such as in the outer islands of the Gilbert Group in Kiribati. Here, the UN project is using diaphragm pumps, placed in the villages to pump water from wells located at safe distances of up to 750 m from the dwellings. Beyond 750 m, electric pumps are used, with solar energy as the motive power (Metutera 1996).

Where there is a high demand on the shallow groundwater of small islands, recent projects have used infiltration galleries

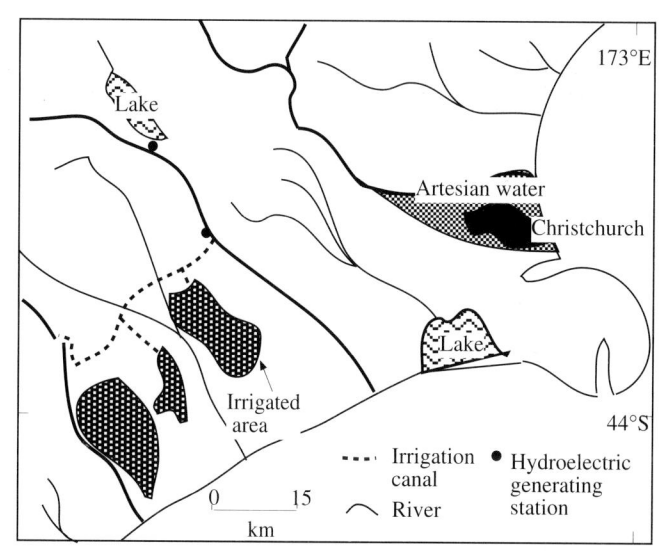

*Figure 6.5.* Water resources in Christchurch, New Zealand (after Soons 1972).

with horizontal, shallow perforated pipes feeding a central well to skim the fresh water from the lenses (Figure 6.6). The galleries use helical rotor pumps to maintain a small and steady extraction of the water resource, limiting the drawdown and thus avoiding localized saltwater intrusion (Falkland 1991). Examples of such galleries in the Pacific can be found in Majuro, Marshall Islands, Tarawa, Kiribati, and Aitutaki in the Cook Islands.

Groundwater resources from volcanic sequences, such as those found in Hawai'i and French Polynesia, can provide high quantities of water from confined conditions. In Tahiti, wells drilled at the base of slopes yield up to 100 liters/second with little drawdown (Guillen 1996). In Hawai'i high-yielding aquifers are located behind dikes and fault structures and are often tapped by horizontal wells or tunnels (Peterson 1991). Basal volcanic sequences around the Hawaiian Islands provide the bulk of the groundwater from skimming tunnels (Maui Tunnels), which are similar to infiltration galleries but on a larger scale.

Groundwater supplies from limestone aquifers for urban areas such as Port Vila in Vanuatu and Honiara in Solomon Islands are generally of good quantity and quality, requiring minimal treatment.

Thermal groundwater is used in the Pacific for cooking, heating, bathing, and recreation. The hot springs of Rotorua in New Zealand are a typical example. Villages adjacent to dormant or active volcanoes, such as Savo in Solomon Islands and Yasur in Tanna, Vanuatu, utilize thermal groundwater.

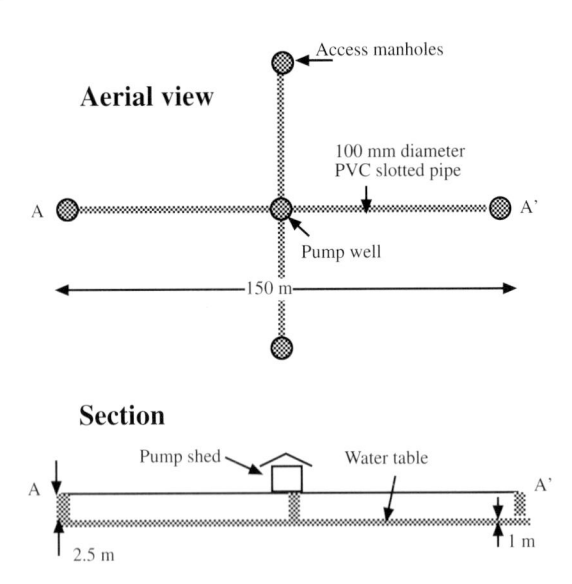

*Figure 6.6. Diagram of infiltration gallery (after Falkland 1991).*

### Unconventional Technology, Importation

Importation of water is practiced in Fiji during dry spells. Water is barged to outer islands or tankered to water-short villages on the main islands by the Public Works Department. This places a large demand on the national budget, with annual costs sometimes exceeding FJ$1 million (UNDHA 1994).

In Nauru, where most of the island has been exploited for phosphate mining, rendering groundwater unsuitable for use, water supply from roof catchments has been supplemented by importing water using the return trips of the ships used to export the ore.

### Unconventional Technology, Desalination

With the end of mining approaching, the Nauru government has installed a desalination plant to provide fresh water for the island nation. This consists of a plant using a distillation process and waste heat from the power station.

Desalination technology has also been used on a small scale in other countries of the Pacific. These include the Marshall Islands (Ebeye), where a multiple-effect distillation plant is currently providing 450 m$^3$/day, and Tuvalu (Funafuti), where a small reverse osmosis plant with an installed capacity of 15 m$^3$/day is used as a standby for the hospital.

### Other Unconventional Technology

To conserve valuable freshwater supplies, salt water has been used for firefighting and sewage disposal systems at some locations, such as Tarawa in Kiribati and Majuro and Ebeye in the Marshall Islands. A total of 189 lpcd of seawater are used in the two urban centers of the Marshalls. In the outer islands people often use seawater for washing to conserve their freshwater supplies.

In the urban context, demand management and other water conservation techniques are used to reduce the amount of water required to be supplied. Various actions are used in the Pacific to promote economy of water use, including metering of all consumers; education in the need to economize on water; promotion of efficient plumbing and sanitary fittings; reduction of unaccounted-for water by leak detection and system rehabilitation (Goodwin 1996); and adjustment of tariffs to reflect true costs and to penalize extravagant use.

In French Polynesia the introduction of a payment system for water reduced consumption to 25% of the previous usage. A 43% reduction in consumption was reported in Honiara, Solomon Islands, following the introduction of metering. Similarly, in Pohnpei in the Federated States of Micronesia a 25% reduction in consumption followed metering and a revised pricing structure for water supply. In American Samoa metering reduced consumption from a maximum of 570 lpcd to an average of 230 lpcd.

## Assessment of Future Needs

### Growing Populations and Urbanization

Fewer than 10 million people live in the Pacific. Growth rates are locally high and are increasing regionally at rates ranging from zero in Samoa to 3.6% in Solomon Islands (World Bank 1990). Much migration from the small island nations to the larger and more affluent neighbors such as New Zealand and Australia accounts for the low growth rates of such places as Samoa and Tonga. There is also migration from the rural areas and from the outer islands to urban centers. The major problems arise in the periurban areas, where squatter settlements develop without the aid of the amenities of the urban area proper, such as power reticulation and a safe water supply.

Urban water supply continues to be a problem for many countries because of the increasing pressure put on the resources. Several methods of alleviating the problem have been tried. Semiprivatization, practiced in such places as Vanuatu, New Caledonia, and French Polynesia, appears to be successful (Alla 1994). Other countries, less convinced that such an important resource should be dealt with by a private company, have opted for some form of corporatization, removing political interference from the water supply operation and giving the organization some form of autonomy, as in the (Western) Samoa Water Authority, the Tonga Water Board, and the Solomon Islands Water Authority.

### *Industrial and Agricultural Growth*

In the world as a whole, agriculture, particularly in the form of irrigation, accounts for a major part of the water usage. In the Pacific, apart from New Zealand and some small areas in a few of the high-island countries, irrigation is little practiced. This may change in the future with the introduction of lucrative food crops such as squash pumpkins for Asian markets.

Water demand is likely to increase with independence of many nations and their drive toward self sufficiency. Tourism, small industries, especially agro-industries such as sugar, oil, and copra, will create demands. Mining activities and logging of the high-value hardwoods of the Pacific tropical forests are likely to expand in the Melanesian countries. There is a clear need to introduce enforceable environmental legislation in these countries as soon as possible.

### *Environmental Needs and Ecosystems*

Land-based activities on the often small habitable landmasses of the Pacific affect both the fragile freshwater resources and the coastal and marine ecosystems surrounding the land. A growing population rate together with the displacement of traditional land practices by introduced agriculture, mining, and forestry developments is seriously stressing the freshwater resources and the land and marine resources. River systems and even shallow groundwater reservoirs receiving pollutants in turn pass these on to the marine environment by the natural gravitation of fresh water to the sea. Thus we have a growing concern for the nearshore waters of many Pacific Island nations and for the reefs that receive much sediment and sometimes toxic wastes from mining, forestry, and other land disturbances via inland waterways. Sewage is a major contributor to pollution in the Pacific. This pollution affects both fresh water and marine waters adjacent to the coast. The septic tanks used extensively in Port Vila, Vanuatu, contribute many nutrients and even microorganisms to the underlying groundwater, the harbor, and lagoons.

### *Water Politics in Hawai'i*

A recent dispute over water diversion on O'ahu illustrates some of the political, economic, and environmental issues relevant to water allocation in Hawai'i. The Waiāhole ditch is a tunnel extending 43 km through O'ahu's main mountain range, channeling water from dikes in the windward side of the island to the dry leeward side. It was built by 1916 by a coalition of sugar planters, pumping an average 107,000 m$^3$/d for irrigation in leeward O'ahu.

In the early 1990s, declines in the profitability of agriculture led the Oahu Sugar Company (largest user of the Waiāhole ditch) to transfer its operations to the Philippines, where labor prices were lower. Thirty-six thousand hectares were released from sugar production, and up to 83,000 m$^3$/d of ditch water was dumped into leeward gulches. Leeward landowners, farmers, and resorts, the state Department of Agriculture, the Honolulu Board of Water Supply, and the U.S. Navy favored continuing the diversion. Waiāhole taro farmers, Native Hawaiian groups, and environmentalists demanded return of water to the windward side.

Those demanding windward restoration argued that the ditch violated traditional Hawaiian water rights, lowered windward stream levels, promoted root rot on windward taro (which requires cool water flow), and endangered native aquatic species in windward streams and Kāne'ohe Bay (formerly an important estuarine fish nursery). They maintained that leeward needs could be served through groundwater. Leeward interests argued that water was needed for agriculture, residential and commercial development, golf courses, aquifer recharge, and urban growth, and that groundwater was too expensive or insufficient.

Hearings by the state Water Use Commission, which controls water use in Hawai'i, began in November 1995. In December 1997, the commission issued its decision (Kreifels 1997). It allocated continued leeward diversion of 53,000 m$^3$/d for use in agriculture, golf courses, and other uses and returned 49,000 m$^3$/d to the windward side to raise stream levels and for use by windward farmers (the latter included 7,500 m$^3$/d as a possible future reserve for leeward agricultural expansion). The issue remains in dispute, but the decision has set an important precedent.

## Conclusions

Pacific Island water use reflects the still-developing nature of the area, with a range of water supply technology from the primitive to the most modern. Each has its merits and its drawbacks. The real need for individual communities, large and small, is an appropriate technology that is also affordable and sustainable. While meeting the basic needs for human beings, that is for drinking, cooking and washing, it must also meet the requirements of maintaining health through hygiene. The future will also bring an increasing demand from the agricultural and industrial sectors. The vital contribution of clean fresh water to the environmental and ecological stability of the Pacific will also take on an increasing importance.

# Bibliography

Alla, P. 1994. Public/private partnership—an optional way of delivering a better service in the water industry. In *Pacific water sector planning, research and training,* 121-124. Honiara:UNESCO/SOPAC/UNDDSMS.

Anthony, S. S. 1991. Case study 7: Majuro Atoll. In *Hydrology and water resources of small islands: a practical guide,* ed. A. Falkland, 368-374. Paris: UNESCO/IHP.

Asquith, F., M. Kooge, and R. J. Morrison. 1994. *Transportation of sediments via rivers to the ocean and the role of sediments as pollutants in the South Pacific.* Reports and Studies No. 72. Apia: South Pacific Regional Environment Programme.

Berhane, D. 1994. Position and issues paper, country background. Water and Sanitation Committee, PNG.

Bruijnzeel, L. A., and W. R. S. Critchley. 1994. *Environmental impacts of logging moist tropical forests.* Paris: UNESCO/IHP Humid Tropics Programme Series No. 7.

Convard, N. 1993. *Land-based pollutants inventory for the South Pacific region.* Apia: SPREP Report and Study Series No. 68.

Crennan, L. 1996. Case study 4: composting toilet trial in Kiritimati, Kiribati. In *Technologies for augmenting freshwater resources in small island developing states.* Suva: UNEP/SOPAC.

Department of Land and Natural Resources. 1987. Water use 1985. Unpublished data, Dept. of Lands and Natural Resources, Hawai'i.

Depledge, D. 1994. *The urban water resources of Port Vila, Vanuatu.* Vila Hydrogeological Report, Dept of Geology, Mines and Water Resources.

Depledge, D. 1996. *Water resources development and management in the Pacific Region.* Keynote presentation, ADB Regional Consultation Workshop, Manila.

Dillon, P. 1996. *Groundwater pollution by sanitation on tropical islands.* A UNESCO/IHP Study. CSIRO Groundwater Studies Report No. 6.

Doig, K. 1996. *Republic of Marshall Islands water and sanitation action plan.* Suva: SOPAC Tech Report 236.

Duncan, M. J. 1992. Flow regimes of New Zealand rivers. In *Waters of New Zealand,* ed. M. P. Mosley, 13-27. NZ Hydrological Society.

Falkland, A. 1991. *Hydrology and water resources of small islands: a practical guide.* Paris: UNESCO Studies and Reports in Hydrology No. 49.

Gangaiya, P., and R. J. Morrison. 1987. Natural waters in the South Pacific Islands. In *Chemistry serves the South Pacific,* ed. J. Bonato, et al., 160–168. Suva: Institute of Pacific Studies, University of the South Pacific.

Goodwin, R. 1996. *A programme of action for the sustainable development of water resources in Micronesia.* Keynote Address, Water Resources Management in the Pacific Rim Conference, Guam.

Guillen, J. 1996. Augmenting freshwater resources in small islands: French Polynesia. In *Proceedings of workshop on maximising and augmenting freshwater resources in small islands,* SOPAC, Fiji, 6-8 Feb. 1996.

Hunt, T. M., and H. M. Bibby. 1992. Geothermal hydrology. In *Waters of New Zealand,* ed. M. P. Mosley, 147-166. Christchurch: NZ Hydrological Society.

Jacobson, G., and P. J. Hill. 1980. Hydrogeology of a raised coral atoll—Niue Island, South Pacific Ocean. *BMR Journal of Geology and Geophysics* 5:271-8.

Kreifels, S. 1997. A state commission decision on Waiahole Ditch will divert millions of gallons. *Honolulu Star Bulletin,* December 24, 1997.

Metutera, T. 1996. Case study 1: augmenting freshwater resources in Kiribati. In *Technologies for augmenting freshwater resources in small island developing states.* Suva: UNEP/SOPAC.

Morrison, R. J., ed. 1997. *Waste management in small island developing states in the South Pacific.* 2 vols. Bangkok: UNEP.

Morrison, R. J., P. Gangaiya, and K. Kosky. 1996. Contaminated soils in the South Pacific Islands. In *Contaminants and the soil environment in the Australasia-Pacific region,* ed. R. Naidu, et al., 659–670. Amsterdam: Kluwer Academic Publisher.

Mosley, M. P. 1988. *Climate change impacts—the water industry.* Chapter 20. Wellington: New Zealand Ministry for the Environment,

Mosley, M. P. 1995. Flow regimes in New Zealand. In *Rivers and people in Southeast Asia and the Pacific—partnership for the 21$^{st}$ century.* Paris: UNESCO/IHP.

Mourits, L., and D. Depledge. 1995. *Handpumps in the S Pacific—a review.* Suva: SOPAC Technical Report No 224.

Nullet, D. 1987. Water balance of Pacific atolls. *Water Resources Bulletin* 23:1125-1132.

Peterson, F. L. 1991. Case study 6: Hawaiian Islands. In *Hydrology and water resources of small islands: a practical guide,* ed. A. Falkland, 362-367. Paris: UNESCO/IHP.

Piliwas, L. 1996. *Papua New Guinea country paper.* Regional Consultation Workshop, Asian Development Bank, Manila, 10-14 May 1996.

Raj, R. 1996. *Fiji country paper.* Regional Consultation Workshop, Asian Development Bank, Manila, 10-14 May 1996.

Saito, S. 1995. *Knowledge, attitudes and practices research on diarrhoeal diseases.* Tarawa: Kiribati Child Survival Project.

Solomon Islands Government. 1993a. Incidence rate of disease in 1993 per 1,000 persons. Honiara: Statistics Unit, Ministry of Health and Medical Services.

Solomon Islands Government. 1993b. The national antimalaria plan of operation, 1994-1998. Honiara: Ministry of Health and Medical Services National Antimalarial Programme, December 1993.

Soons, J. M. 1972. *Modern geography: water, with reference to Australia and New Zealand.* Auckland: Reed Education.

UNDHA. 1994. Assessment of drought problems in Fiji. *Water Resources Journal* 30(12):94-105.

White, I. 1996. Personal communication, Water Research Foundation of Australia, ANU, Canberra.

World Bank. 1990. *Social indicators of development.* Washington, DC: World Bank.

# SECTION 2

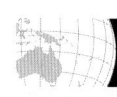

# THE LIVING ENVIRONMENT

The Pacific Islands are home to diverse ecosystems—strand communities on shoreline plains and atolls, montane forests cloaking the interior of high islands, and marine ecosystems extending offshore. Island flora and fauna are distinctive, with high rates of endemism, taxonomic disharmony, and vulnerability to invasion and extinction. Biotic distributions vary considerably in accordance with geotectonic history, ease of dispersal, habitat availability, and human interference. Section 2 explains how Pacific Island biota have spread and evolved, then describes the principal ecosystems. Contributors include E. Alison Kay, Harley I. Manner, Dieter Mueller-Dombois, Moshe Rapaport, and Stephen G. Nelson.

# CHAPTER 7

# Biogeography

E. Alison Kay

## Introduction

*"Biogeographic aims are of two principal sorts: to use distribution as a guide to earth history; and to explain distribution through application of theories of earth history and evolution. The first aim, investigative, seeks pattern; the second, explanatory, seeks to explain pattern by process."* C. Patterson, 1983.

The biotas of islands, and particularly those of the Pacific Ocean, have been of enormous interest since the mid-eighteenth century, when Captain Cook and his ships' companies began the exploration of the Pacific for the western world, returning to Europe with cargoes of strange new animals and plants. A century later, Charles Darwin's (1902) descriptions of finches, iguanas, and tortoises of the Galápagos Islands heightened interest in the biotas of islands, and, in *The Origin of Species*, Darwin (1872) devoted two chapters to biogeography based not just on islands, but in great part on Pacific islands (Kay 1994). Today Pacific Island biogeography contributes in major ways to evolutionary theory. The birds of New Guinea are model organisms for Mayr's (1942) definition of allopatric speciation. The ants of Melanesia are players in MacArthur and Wilson's (1967) *Theory of Island Biogeography*. The achatinelline land snails of the Hawaiian Islands and the partulid land snails of the south and west Pacific are central to concepts of speciation and insular endemism (Gulick 1890, Clarke and Murray 1969). The finches of the Galápagos (Grant 1986) and the Hawaiian honeycreepers (Freed et al. 1987) are classic examples of adaptive radiation. But of all island organisms, the Hawaiian Drosophilidae have been declared "supreme" (Williamson 1981); variation in their chromosome banding spells out their evolutionary history within the island chain.

Despite two centuries of interest in Pacific Island biotas, the deceptively simple questions central to Pacific Island biogeography remain: how do animals and plants arrive on islands and what happens to them over time? In this review, patterns of distribution and the processes that may explain the patterns are distinguished to highlight differences in pattern and process between the biotas of islands and those of the sea surrounding them.

## Patterns

*"To do science is to search for repeated patterns, not simply to accumulate facts, and to do the science of geographical ecology is to search for patterns of plant and animal life that can be put on a map."* Robert H. MacArthur, 1972.

### Patterns of Islands

The Pacific is an ocean of islands. More than a thousand islands rise above the surface of the sea; another ten thousand lie below it. On the east is the American continent. On the west is a series of island chains, the Kuriles, Japan, the Philippines, and Indonesia; Australia, New Guinea, New Caledonia, and New Zealand. The islands of Polynesia and Micronesia lie east of the western borderlands, scattered above and below the equator, their furthest outposts the Hawaiian Islands, the Tuamotus, the Marquesas, the Pitcairn Islands, and Easter Island. Beyond is the East Pacific Barrier, more than 4,000 km of open ocean, and finally the offshore islands of the west coast of the Americas: Clipperton and other small islands above the equator and the Galápagos that lie across the equator 800 km from the coastline of Ecuador.

Micronesia, the Samoas, French Polynesia, and islands to the east of Tonga are on the Pacific Plate, one of 11 rigid plates comprising the crust of the Earth. New Caledonia is on the neighboring Indo-Australian Plate. The Pacific Plate is presently subducting, or moving under, the Indo-Australian Plate, and the boundary is unstable and difficult to delineate. Fiji, Vanuatu, the Solomons, New Guinea, New Zealand, and Tonga lie within the Melanesian borderlands, a broad zone of interaction between the two plates. To the east, the boundary is separated from South America by the Nazca Plate (on which Easter Island lies). North of Baja California, the Pacific Plate assumes a marginal position offshore of the west coast of North America, and northward lies below the Bering Arc and the Kuriles.

All Pacific islands are products of volcanism or tectonic uplift. They include the newly forming volcano Lōihi, 900 m below the sea surface south of the island of Hawai'i; massive active shield volcanoes rising 4,000 m above the sea on Hawai'i itself; the eroded mountains of Tahiti and Samoa; and submerged volcanic banks on which corals have established themselves, forming reefs or atolls as in the Marshall Islands. The islands of the western border of the Pacific Plate, formed as the plate subducts into the Tonga-Kermadec trench, lie in tectonically complex regions, subject to uplift and subsidence, and are in general larger than are the islands in the central Pacific. The mid-ocean islands are the products of hot spots in the plate, magma erupting and forming the volcanoes that are carried away from the hot spot as the plate moves northwest. The results are linear chains of islands, the Hawaiian, Society, Marquesas,

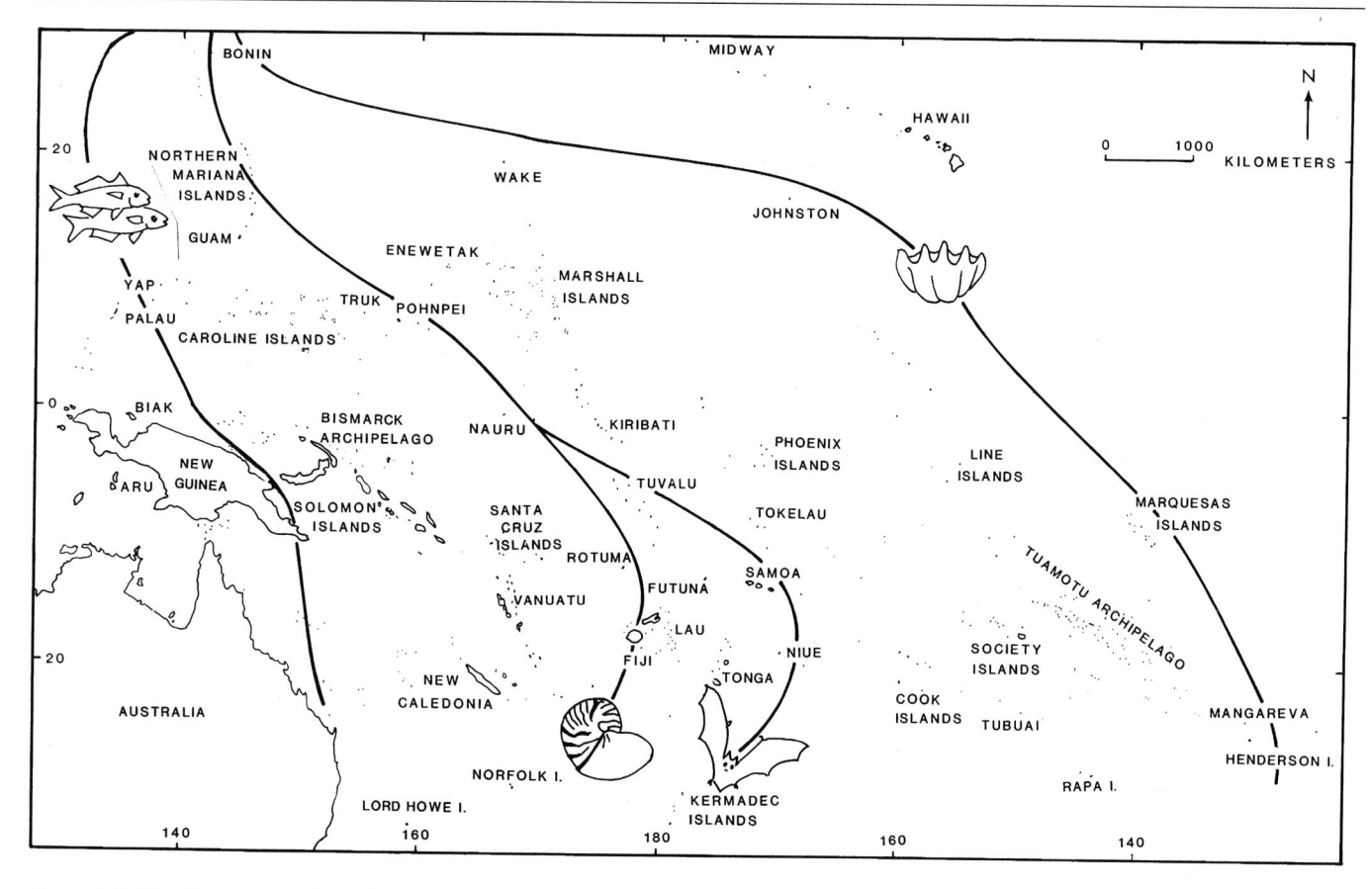

*Figure 7.1.* The distribution of true freshwater fishes, Nautilus, fruit bats, and the giant clam Tridacna *in the Pacific. Dropouts like these animals contribute to species attenuation west to east in the Pacific.*

and Galápagos islands, the youngest island in each chain near the hot spot, the oldest farthest away. The chronological sequence is very clear in the Hawaiian Islands: the high volcanic islands lie nearest the hot spot; and atolls, reefs and shoals built on volcanic bases fall between the volcanic islands and the long ago submerged islands of the Emperor Seamounts.

Island terminology in biogeography remains qualitative. Islands once associated with continents (New Guinea, New Caledonia, and New Zealand) are termed "continental"; those at the western edge of the Pacific Plate (the Solomons and Tonga) and the mid-ocean islands that have never had connections with continents, are "oceanic." "High islands" are of either volcanic or continental rocks (or mixtures of the two); "low islands" are calcareous atolls and reef flats on which sand and coral rubble are piled as high as a wave will reach; and "*makatea*" are composite islands of volcanics and limestone (Nunn 1994) that have been raised above sea level by lithospheric flexure of the ocean floor (Spencer and Benton 1995).

### The Biota of High Islands

The distribution of animals and plants on Pacific islands is not random. Patterns were recognized as observant explorer-naturalists from Europe traversed the ocean two centuries ago, discovering not only an unfamiliar biota, but recognizing some of its peculiarities. Johann Reinhold Forster's (1996) observations on Cook's second voyage of 1772–1775 in the Pacific are especially perceptive: "The countries of the South Sea . . . contain a considerable variety of animals, though they are confined to a few classes only." The only terrestrial mammals he reported were "the vampyre and the common rat," recognizing the latter as "domestic." The birds "are numerous, and form a considerable variety of species. . . . they enliven the woods with their continual songs, and contribute much to the splender [sic] of nature by their varied plumage." But "no countries in the world produce fewer species of insects than those of the South Sea," and, to Forster's apparent delight, "this happy country is free from all noxious and troublesome insects; no wasps, nor mosquitoes." Forster also wrote of the "vegetable kingdom" in the Society Islands, describing mountain summits "wholly covered with forests . . . [in which] all kinds of vegetables . . . thrive with luxuriance," among them "mosses, ferns, epidendra, and the like," in the moisture intercepted from the clouds.

Others of the explorer-naturalists provided details of the patterns described by Forster. Adelbert Chamisso (1821), on the Russian ship *Rurick*, noticing that the greatest diversity of species appeared centered toward the west, said, "the appearance of nature in the eastern lands of the South Seas, reminds us at once of Southern Asia and New Holland, and is wholly dissimilar to America," and the French botanist Lesson (1825) not only recognized that "The vegetable kingdom of the islands of the South Sea is entirely Indian . . . contrary to the course of the winds from east to west," but he also saw that "one loses successively the richness . . . toward neighboring America."

Modern biologists confirm and quantify the observations

The Pacific Islands

of the explorer-naturalists. New Zealand has a mixture of tropical and temperate animals and plants: frogs but no snakes, the lizard-like tuatara, the flightless kiwi, tropical *Metrosideros,* and temperate southern beeches, *Nothofagus.* The Solomon Islands are entirely tropical, with a marsupial mammal, 17 bats, cockatoos and hornbills, snakes and lizards. New Guinea is rich in birds, among them fruit pigeons, kingfishers, birds-of-paradise, and the flightless cassowary; marsupial mammals, and an egg-laying montreme, a spiny anteater, are also found there.

East of the Solomons and New Guinea the only mammals are 17 species of bats, and they are reduced to 4 in Fiji and 1 in the Cook Islands (Wodzicki and Felten 1975) (Figure 7.1). Amphibians are found only as far east as Fiji (Myers 1935), where there are also 4 snakes and large iguanid lizards (Schmidt 1930). Birds have colonized isolated islands and archipelagoes throughout the Pacific, but the number of resident land and freshwater birds falls from more than 500 in New Guinea to 13 in the Marquesas (Stoddart 1992). Butterflies also colonized remote archipelagoes, the number of species falling, as is true of birds, with 61 species in New Caledonia, 2 in Hawai'i, and 3 in the Marquesas (Adler and Dudley 1994). Among the insects, large groups, orders, and families common to all the continents are absent from the oceanic islands: there is neither a single native species of scarab beetle nor are there endemic leaf beetles (Zimmerman 1942). Few if any native ants range east of Rotuma (Fiji Islands), Samoa, and Tonga (Wilson and Taylor 1967), and there are no native anopheline mosquitoes east of 170° (Zimmerman 1942). Weevils are the most widespread group, found on nearly all islands; they have speciated extensively and are often flightless (Gressitt 1956). Land snails are well represented, and 3 of the 15 families and 1 subfamily are endemic (Kay 1995). Of coastal plants, *Desmodium* and *Hedyotis* occur only as far east as Niue, and mangroves, *Barringtonia,* and *Pisonia* reach the Marshall Islands but are not found in Hawai'i.

The pattern of western relationships described by Chamisso and Lesson is essentially repeated for insects (Zimmerman 1948, Gressitt 1956), land snails (Solem 1959), and most higher plants (van Balgooy 1971). There are, however, New Zealand, Australian, American, and Hawaiian elements in the flora of Tahiti (Fosberg 1992) and American elements in the Hawaiian Islands. Four groups of insects (Asquith 1995), the angiosperm *Schiedea* and its relatives (Wagner, et al. 1995), and the silversword alliance, with its apparent ancestor among the tarweeds of North America (G.D. Carr 1990), are prominent members of the Hawaiian biota. The biota of the Galápagos Islands is, in contrast, "remarkably similar to that of neighboring South America" (Darwin 1902), (Figure 7.2) although a land snail (Vagvolgyi 1975) and a true bug (Froeschner 1985) seem to be derived from the western Pacific.

The Cook ships returned to England in 1780 with bird skins, land snails, and pressed plants, the first of hundreds of curious animals and plants that were to be recognized from Pacific islands during the next two hundred years. There were massive araucarias and kauris on the continental islands of New Zealand and New Guinea, and breadfruit, palms, *Pandanus,* and climbing vines such as *Freycinetia* on oceanic islands. Among

*Figure 7.2. The endemic Galápagos Islands hawk, related to hawks in the Americas (photo EAK).*

the strangest birds in the world were the moa, the mythical giant flightless birds in New Zealand that turned out to be real; the kagu in New Caledonia, small birds with a bark like a dog; megapodes on Vanuatu and in Belau, fowl-like birds that deposit their eggs in soil, in hot volcanic ashes, or heaps of decaying leaves; and, in Samoa, tooth-billed pigeons, with their powerful curved bill. Butterflies from New Guinea were described as "bird-winged," the achatinelline tree snails from Hawai'i as "gemlike" (Color Plate 7A-B).

*Figure 7.3–4. The endemic Galápagos Islands iguanas. 7.3. The marine iguana. 7.4. The land iguana (photos EAK).*

Among Pacific Island animals and plants there is also an array of curious features attributed to otherwise familiar plants and animals. In Hawai'i, raspberries lack thorns, and mints lack their usual strong fragrance (Carlquist 1970); on Rarotonga, *Fitchia*, a relative of the sunflower, is a woody tree (Carlquist 1965). In the Galápagos, 1 of the 2 species of iguanas is marine and feeds on seaweeds (Figures 7.3-7.4), and in both the Galápagos and Hawai'i, finch-like birds act like woodpeckers, and others have bills that crush seeds. Flightless birds turned up on islands all over the Pacific: a cormorant in the Galápagos (Figure 7.5), rails on islands from Henderson (Pitcairn Islands) and the Hawaiian Islands west to Guam (Mariana Islands), and the moa and kiwi in New Zealand. Among the most remarkable animals are an extinct flightless goose with teeth, *Thambetochen,* the "astonishing goose," (Olson and Wetmore 1976), and caterpillars that ambush and then devour drosophilid flies (Montgomery 1983), both in the Hawaiian Islands. The remarkable freshwater biotas of fishes, crustaceans, and mollusks on oceanic islands are descended from marine ancestors, but they are confined to fresh water only as adults; their larval lives are spent at sea.

Every island and group of islands is unique in one or more ways. Taxa in an archipelago, on an island, in a stream, on a ridge, or in a valley and found nowhere else, are referred to as "endemic." Species present in an environment as the result of human intervention are termed "introduced" or "alien." Species and higher taxa are distinguished as native or indigenous if they have reached an area without human intervention.

*Figure 7.5. The flightless cormorant from the Galápagos Islands (photo EAK).*

High islands are distinguished by endemic taxa, families (in Hawai'i the bird family Drepaniididae and the land snail family Amastridae) (Color Plate 7B), subfamilies, genera, and species. Genera on high islands have a disproportionately large number of species (Zimmerman 1942): in Hawai'i, where more than 90% of the insects are endemic, the fly genus *Drosophila* exceeds all other organisms, with more than 500 species described and named and another 200–300 to be described (Hardy and Kaneshiro 1981). The average number of species per genus in Hawaiian insects is 9.8 (range 1–218) (Zimmerman 1948). In Tahiti and Samoa, where more than 90% of the land snails are endemic, there are between 10 and 20 species per genus (Kay 1995). It was once said that each valley and ridge in Hawai'i had its own species of land snail (O.P. Emerson 1941); and Garrett (1887) wrote of land snails as "rare and peculiar to one valley in Tahiti."

## The Biota of Atolls and Makatea

One malacologist defined island types by their land snail faunas (Cooke 1966): high islands distinguished by endemic families and genera, raised coral islands (*makatea*) by endemic species, and atolls lacking endemic species but with widespread indigenous species. The definition is generally applicable to other components of the biota, although the grass *Lepturus gasparricensis* is endemic on Pokak and Wake (Marshall Islands) (Fosberg 1955); a loulu palm (*Pritchardia*) is endemic to Laysan (Northwest Hawaiian Islands); a giant gecko is found only on Kapingamarangi (Caroline Islands); and endemic species of rails evolved on Laysan and Wake (Steadman 1995).

Atoll vegetation consists of relatively few widely distributed species, perhaps no more than 150 (Thaman 1992). Among them are purslane (*Sesuvium* and *Portulaca*), morning glory (*Ipomoea*), and *Scaevola* on the beaches; screwpine (*Pandanus*), *Pisonia* (Figure 7.6), tree heliotrope (*Tournefortia*), the grass *Lepturus repens,* and the sedge *Fimbristylis cymosa* inland. Counts of native terrestrial animals indicate equally sparse numbers: atoll insects include perhaps 400 species on Enewetak (Marshall Islands) (Samuelson and Nishida 1987). Only about 10 species of land snails, all widespread, occur on atolls (Cooke 1966). Eighteen to 20 species of wide-ranging sea birds, winter visiting shorebirds, and occasional visitors such as the reef heron (*Egretta sacra*) and the long-tailed cuckoo (*Eudynamis taitensis*) comprise the bird fauna at Enewetak (Berger 1987). Distribution of even cosmopolitan species islands is sometimes patchy: the pink morning glory *Ipomoea pes-caprae* is on French Frigate Shoals (Northwest Hawaiian Islands) but not at Pearl and Hermes Reef; the blue-flowered *I. indica* is at Laysan but not at French Frigate Shoals (Lamoureux 1980).

Henderson Island is a *makatea*, 33.5 m above sea level. The island's flora of 63 indigenous species of vascular plants is larger than those of its neighboring sea-level atolls, Oeno and Ducie, the former with 16 species, the latter with only 2 (Florence, et al. 1995). The Henderson land snail fauna consists of 16 species, of which 8 are endemic (Preese 1995), and there are 180 species of insects including endemic species (Benton 1995), consistent with Cooke's (1966) generalization. Four endemic species of land birds survive on Henderson.

*Figure 7.6. A forest of* Pisonia *on Fanning Atoll (photo EAK).*

## The Pacific Marine Biota

On Cook's second voyage into the Pacific, Forster (1966) commented on "difficulties in the collection" of marine organisms, "not only from our very short stay in many places, but . . . because we were obliged . . . to depend upon the natives . . . there being no expert fishermen on board." Nevertheless, he noted that "The South Sea is rich in fish, and has a great variety of species," and his predecessor on the first Cook voyage, Sidney Parkinson, sketched 66 fish in Tahitian waters (D.J. Carr 1983). R. B. Hinds (1844), on the *Sulphur*, remarked that in the ocean, "large and important groups of mollusks are entirely absent," that the marine shells attenuated in species numbers from west to east across the Pacific, and that marine mollusks seemed to have their origins to the west.

The earlier reports are confirmed by modern observations: the focus of species diversity lies in the west, in New Guinea, Indonesia, the Philippines, and Southeast Asia; diversity decreases with increasing latitude and distance to the east: "to move inwards from the Cook Islands to Tonga is to move . . . from bare, barren reef flats to communities of sea grasses and mangroves, abundant ophiuroids (sea stars) and probably twice as many genera of reef building corals" (Stoddart 1976) (see Figure 7.1). Among the mollusks, the abalones (Haliotidae), vase shells (Vasidae), and giant clams (Tridacnidae) (Figure 7.1, Color Plate 7C) occur as far east as the Marshall and Society islands but are not in Hawai'i. Numbers of species attenuate, from 70 cowrie species in the Philippines to 55 on Guam and 30 in Hawai'i (Kay 1984), and from 300 coral species in Indonesia to 50 in Hawai'i (Veron 1995). In the inshore fish fauna, the numbers range from 1,357 species for the Palau Islands and Yap, 844 for the Mariana Islands, 800 for the Marshall Islands, and 536 for the Hawaiian Islands (Randall 1992). The marine biotas of tropical high islands and atolls are all coral reef biotas, but Chamisso (1821) did note that algae found on the reefs of high islands were absent on low islands. The brown alga *Sargassum* is known from the atolls of Ulithi and Kayangel in the western Pacific arc, but is not found on atolls in the central Pacific (Tsuda 1976).

The patterns of distribution of the marine biota generally follow those of the terrestrial biota with three exceptions: there is relatively little endemism; there are no endemic families or genera, only endemic species; and the number of species per genus is low. Pickering (1854), of the United States Exploring Expedition in Hawai'i in 1841, may have been the first to notice the lack of endemism when he remarked that "the marine shells inhabiting the . . . Hawaiian group . . . are in general very widely diffused," but "each separate island of the Hawaiian group contains land-shells . . . that are not found on the neighboring islands, nor in any part of the whole globe." In Hawai'i, 90% of land snail species are endemic, there is an endemic family, and the many endemic genera average 40 species per genus. In the marine mollusks, about 26% of the species are endemic; endemism is at the species level only (Kay 1984); and there are no more than 1 or 2 endemic species in a genus (Kay and Palumbi 1987). Endemism in marine species in the Society Islands is like that in Hawai'i (Kay 1984), but there is virtually no endemism in the Line Islands (Kay and Switzer 1974), Marshall Islands (Kay and Johnson 1987) or Mariana Islands (Vermeij, Kay and Eldredge 1983).

## Mapping the Pacific Biota

That different regions of the globe are inhabited by entirely distinct animals and plants was suggested by Buffon in 1791 (Lyell 1832), but he may well have been preceded in the concept by Forster (1996), who recognized the plants of the islands of the Pacific as "the Flora of the South Seas" in 1778. The South Seas, or Polynesia, so-called by eighteenth-century French geographers (Simpson and Weiner 1989), was one of Schouw's (1823) six botanical "kingdoms," an early example of the division of the Earth into areas distinguished by their biotas. Zoologists saw things differently, recognizing six "primary regions," corresponding to the six continents, Africa, India, Asia, Australia, and North and South America (Sclater 1858, Wallace 1876), each with its own fauna. Polynesia (here including all Pacific islands except for New Guinea), "without indigenous Mammalia, and very poor in all forms of life," was appended to Australia (then including New Guinea). By the end of the century the Australian malacologist Charles Hedley (1899), recognizing that the biota of the islands of Polynesia was very different from that of Australia, moved Polynesia into Wallace's Oriental Region (Asia south of the Himalayas and Tibet, to the

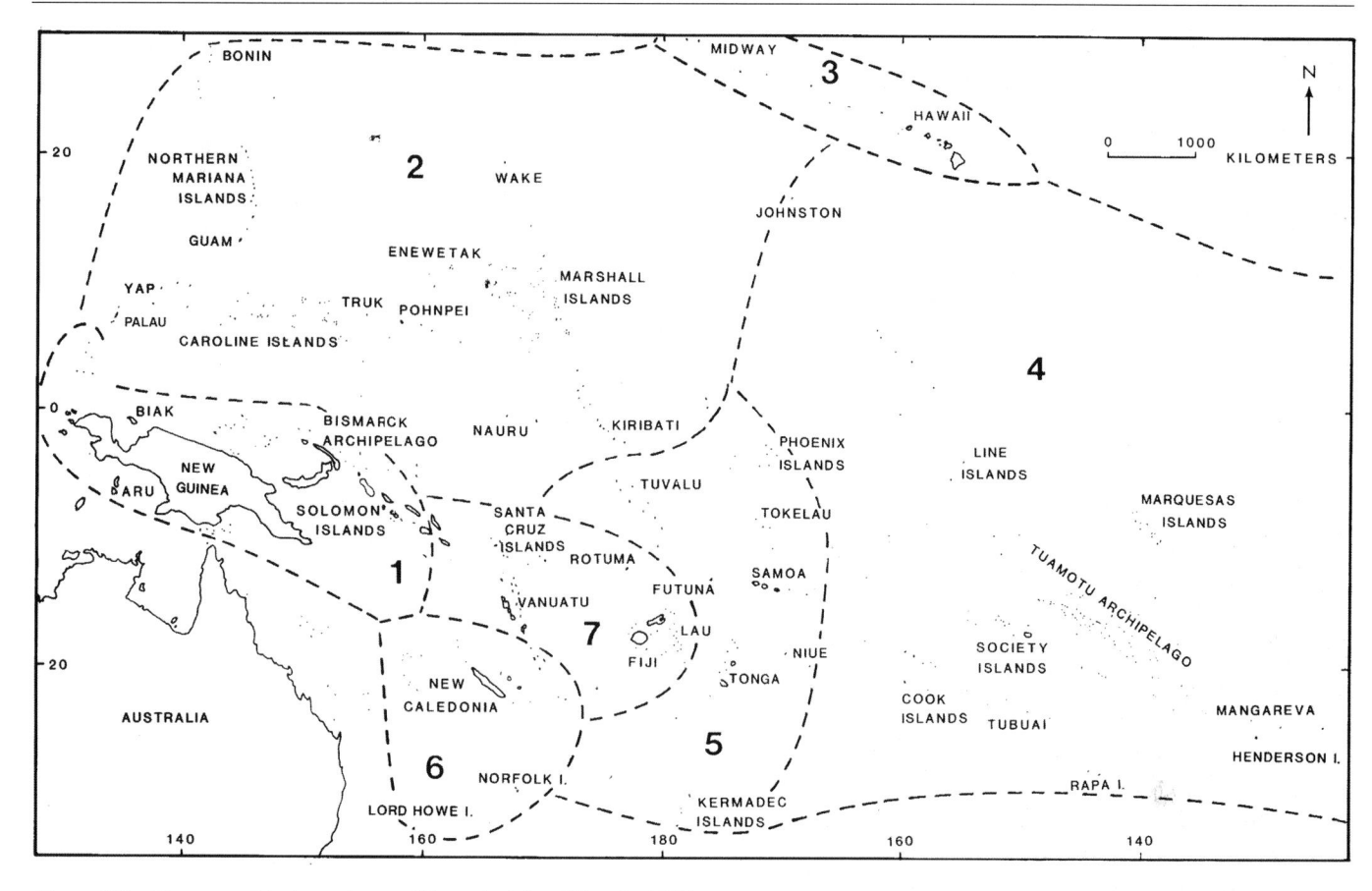

*Figure 7.7a. Biogeographical provinces of Oceania (after Udvardy 1975).*

Philippines, Borneo and Java) (Wallace 1911). That practice has since been followed by botanists (Brownlie 1965, van Steenis 1950), ornithologists (Mayr 1941), and entomologists (Gressitt 1956). A plethora of boundary lines purportedly distinguishing cohesive biotas have also encompassed the islands' biotas within Polynesia (Kay 1980). Land shells were accommodated in four subdivisions (Woodward 1856); insects were fitted into three sections (Gressitt 1961); and birds and plants were distributed in provinces, five for the birds (Mayr 1941) and four for the plants (van Balgooy 1976). Figure 7.7a illustrates an attempt to recognize subdivisions acceptable to most biologists (Udvardy 1975), with an Oceanian Realm (comparable with Oriental, Australian, etc., realms) divided into seven provinces.

The oceans were regionalized by the American geologist James Dwight Dana (1853), who recognized three kingdoms in "a natural geographical arrangement," subkingdoms corresponding to temperate and torrid zones, provinces distinguished by water temperatures, and districts identified primarily by their crustacean inhabitants. The Oriental Kingdom encompassed "the great ocean, from the east coast of Africa to the Hawaiian and Paumotu (Tuamotu) islands, covering two-thirds of the surface of the globe [which] makes one great kingdom, closely related in its species." The "great ocean" was named the Indo-Pacific (Lyell 1854), and the Indian Ocean and the western and central part of the Pacific, with "the greatest wealth of animal life," were further distinguished as the Indo-West Pacific (Figure 7.7b) by the Swedish biogeographer Sven Ekman (1935). Ekman also determined that "the faunistic centre of this region is the Malay archipelago," which he extended to include the Philippines and south China, calling the whole area the Indo-Malay archipelago.

Within the Pacific, Dana recognized three provinces—Polynesian, Hawaiian, and Rarotongan—but as they were "imperfectly indicated" by their Crustacea, he left the boundaries somewhat loose. Other provinces were subsequently recognized, perhaps the most extreme those of the German malacologist Franz Schilder (1961), who accommodated one family of marine mollusks (the Cypraeidae) in eight units. In a very different arrangement, Springer (1982), recognizing the high degree of endemism on the Pacific Plate, proposes the plate as a major subunit of the Indo-Pacific biogeographic region.

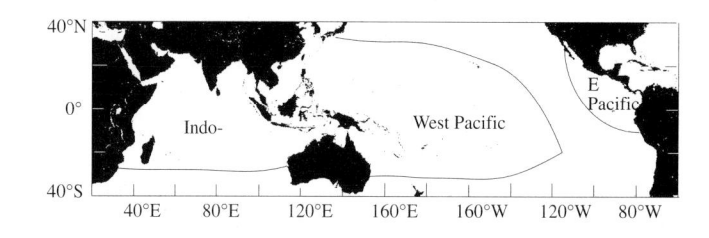

*Figure 7.7b. The Indo-West Pacific and East Pacific marine biogeographic regions (after Paulay 1997).*

The Pacific Islands

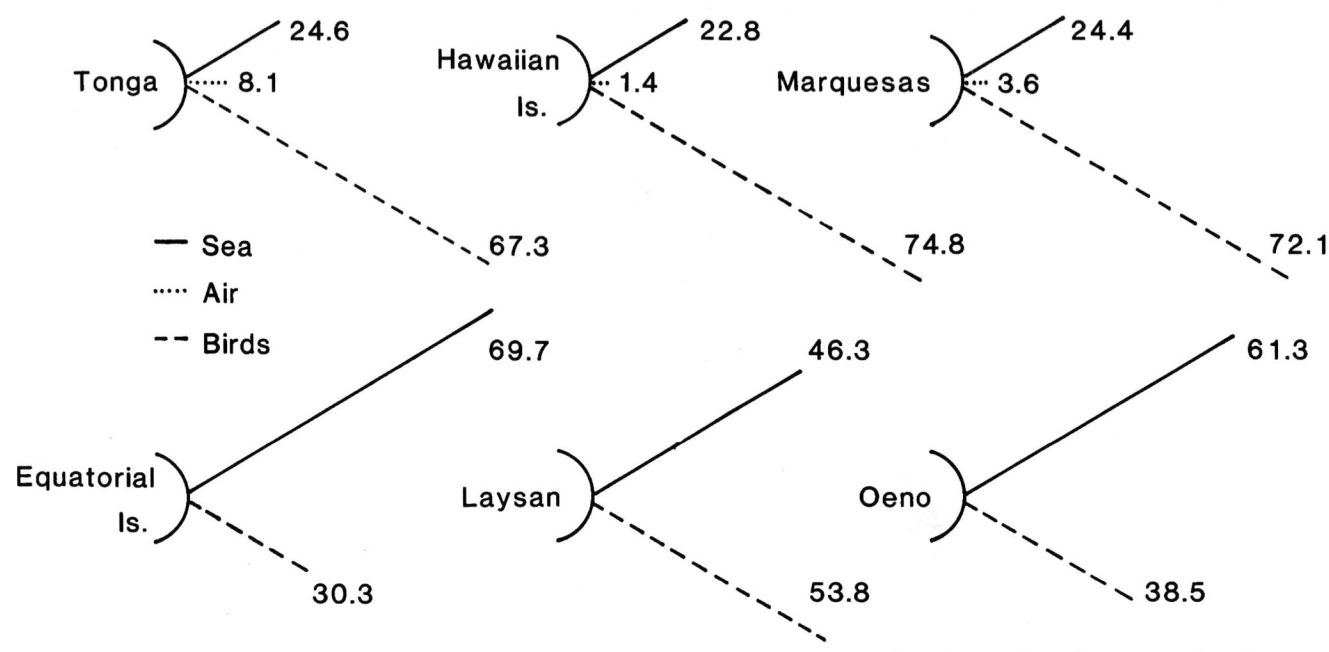

*Figure 7.8.* Diagrams of modes of seed dispersal for some Pacific islands. Percentages calculated from the number of immigrants thought to account for the contemporary native species for each dispersal mode. Adapted from Carlquist (1967).

## Process

*"On looking at a map of the world we inhabit, we find that its surface is divided between land and water, continents and oceans; each . . . inhabited by peculiar sorts of animals. . . . What are the causes that have produced this dissimilarity of creatures? . . . [I]s there method in all this amazing diversity?"* William Swainson, 1835.

### Distribution Patterns Explained

Because all Pacific oceanic islands originate as volcanoes and begin their existence devoid of life forms, every animal and plant on these islands is descended from an ancestor that arrived from somewhere else, that is, an ancestor that arrived by dispersal. The efficacy of various modes of dispersal is shown in Figure 7.8. Predictably, what arrive on islands are plants with barbed or sticky seeds carried by bats and birds with built-in means of dispersal, and, as Gressitt and Yoshimoto (1963) demonstrated by sampling the jet stream high over the Pacific, small insects, spiders and spores. Representatives of 73 insect families were collected in that aerial plankton; 53% of those families are reported in a recent survey of Henderson Island (Benton 1995), where moths and flies make up 50% of the insect fauna. Fourteen percent of the world's fern genera are in the Marquesas and in Hawai'i (Wagner 1991). Predictably, true freshwater fish such as carp and minnows, which cannot withstand high salinities, are absent from the midocean islands, as are amphibians and land snakes, conifers, many large-fruited trees, and bamboos.

The role of dispersal in the distribution of marine organisms in the Pacific is similarly demonstrable: pumice and other lightweight materials raft young corals in the open ocean (Jokiel 1984); long-lived molluscan larvae have been retrieved from central Pacific waters (Scheltema, 1986); and experiments with coral planulae indicate they are viable in the plankton for at least three months (Richmond 1982). The records of pelagic duration of larval fishes of 35 days in the central Pacific in contrast to 45 days in the Hawaiian Islands (Brothers and Thresher 1985) are also evidence for the efficacy of marine larval dispersal. Planktonic larvae must remain competent, that is, able to successfully settle and metamorphose, for periods long enough to allow immigration from a source area to a distant landing, and, as with terrestrial organisms, poorly dispersing species such as baler shells (*Melo*), abalone (*Haliotis*), and anemone fish are absent or there are disproportionately few representatives. Others—cowries (Cypraeidae), cones (Conidae), wrasses (Labridae), and moray eels (Muraenidae)—are overly rich.

*"A new island may not be an Eden, but at least it's empty."* **Hubbell, 1968**

Distance and chance, both factors in long-distance dispersal, take a toll: relatively few dispersal events are successful, and a very few ancestors account for a plethora of species on oceanic islands. A single colonization accounts for the 127 species of partulid land snails (Crampton 1925) of Samoa, Tonga, Tahiti, Belau, and the Mariana Islands and the 500 species of *Drosophila* in the Hawaiian Islands (Kaneshiro 1988). Sixteen successful colonizations resulted in 80 species of land snails in the Galápagos (Peck 1991); and 270–282 successful colonizations gave rise to the Hawaiian angiosperm flora of 956 species (Wagner 1991). In effect, thousands of species of plants, birds, insects, and land snails, many of them endemic to a single island, or to a ridge or a valley on an island, developed *in situ* by autochthonous speciation, literally "springing from the land itself."

Given one or two individuals arriving by chance, reproduction results in small populations sequestered by isolation, leading to the mode of speciation termed "allopatric" by Mayr (1942). The gene pools are but partial representations of ancestral gene pools. Given an island, speciation is fueled by a mosaic environment, hills, valleys, *kīpuka*, lava tubes, and individual islands themselves, each a barrier to gene flow. But there are no barriers to experimenting with form, function, or ecological tolerances and requirements on an island. Continental competitors and enemies that keep an organism in its biological niche have been left behind. Genetic variation with little chance of surviving in the old environment not only survives but is established as organisms move into new niches, adapting to life in a variety of different situations. As the descendants of one ancestral stock after another move into new niches, the landscape is filled by animals and plants doing things very differently from their ancestors.

Changes in ancestral habits, from insect to bird pollination, from shrub to woody tree, from insectivore to woodpecking in a bird, or from feeding on the yeasts of decaying fruits to predation on spiders in *Drosophila*, are termed adaptive shifts. Shifts in habit allow the occupation of new niches. Where there were no large herbivores, tortoises filled that niche in the Galápagos, and geese and the *moa-nalo*, heavy-bodied flightless derivatives of ducks, once filled the niche in Hawai'i (Olson 1991).

If the descendants of a single immigrant ancestor have undergone several adaptive shifts, the evolutionary result is an adaptive radiation. The primary examples of adaptive radiation in the Pacific occur most noticeably on islands at the edge of the dispersal range. In the Galápagos Islands 13 finches and in the Hawaiian Islands 22 honeycreepers, evolved a range of feeding habits, seed cracking, wood pecking, cactus eating, and honey sucking that filled otherwise empty niches. Twenty-eight endemic Hawaiian species of what was a west American tarweed range in form from low-growing tufts of greenery on bare lava on the slopes of the volcano at 75 m to the majestic silverswords of Haleakalā and Mauna Kea at elevations of 4,000 m (G.D. Carr 1987) (Color Plates 7D-F). Relatives of lettuce described by Carlquist (1965) on the Juan Fernandez Islands (Chile) include a rosette shrub with leathery, narrow, smooth-edged leaves in the shade of the rain forest; an ungainly plant with thick succulent stems, leaves more than a foot long, and huge yellow flowers in grassy meadows at sea level; and a single-flowering cone of small white flower heads surrounded by featherlike leaves on a thick, unbranched stem on the steep slopes of the cloud forest.

### Evolutionary Time Scales

Timelines for speciation have been estimated from the age of islands. On Rapa (Austral Islands), five million years old, 67 species of flightless weevils (beetle subgroup *Miocalles*) and 45 achatinellid and 24 endodontoid land snail species have evolved (Paulay 1985, Solem 1982). On Tahiti (Society Islands), one million years old, 70 species of beetles (*Mecyclothorax*) are endemic (Perrault 1987). Twenty-five of the 26 species of picture-wing *Drosophila* evolved on the island of Hawai'i, no older than 600,000 years (Carson 1983). On Henderson Island, 285,000 years old, there are an endemic flightless rail and a fruit dove that co-evolved with 20 fruit species in that period of time (Diamond 1995).

The recent development of molecular techniques involving DNA provide dates for origins and interisland colonization. The ancestors of the Hawaiian Drosophilidae (DeSalle 1995) may have arrived 20 million years ago, somewhere between Nihoa and French Frigate Shoals, and an ancestor of the Hawaiian honeycreepers is estimated to have colonized Kaua'i approximately 3.5 million years ago (Tarr and Fleischer 1995). An "older" island to the northwest, now eroded below the appropriate elevation to support a forest, is proposed as the colonization site of the purple-fruited lobeliad *Cyanea-Rollandia* clades (clade: a taxonomic group containing a common ancestor and its descendants) (Givnish et al. 1995).

Plate tectonic theory adds yet another dimension to the classical story of insular evolution. Each island in the linear chronological series of volcanoes formed as the Pacific Plate passes over the hot spot is colonized by founders from the preceding volcano, and speciation ensues. The process repeats as new islands form and results in a succession of single-island

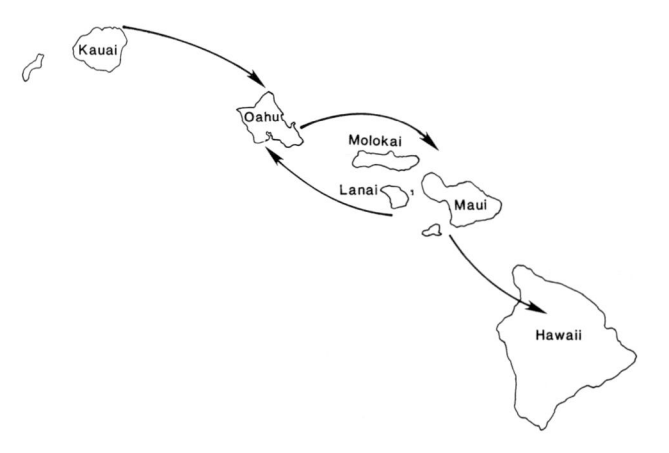

*Figure 7.9.* Interisland dispersal events in the Hawaiian Islands, showing founder species dispersing from older islands to the younger islands, an occasional "backward" jump.

endemic species with the sister species of each taxon on a neighbor island, the basal taxa on older islands (Funk and Wagner 1995) (Figure 7.9), the younger genera on the more recent islands. Recent analyses in Hawai'i of the crickets *Laupala* and *Prognathogryllus* (Shaw 1995), the heteropteran *Sarona* (Asquith 1995), and honeycreepers (Tarr and Fleischer 1995) demonstrate the relationships between phylogenetic order and island age. In the Hawaiian silversword alliance, an ancestral California tarweed was probably externally bird-dispersed to Kaua'i, and 13 interisland dispersals later account for the present distribution of the 28 species (Baldwin and Robichaux 1995).

## Speciation in the Sea

The key factor in the speciation game on oceanic islands is the isolation of gene pools. If gene pools are not isolated, if a continuous flow of immigrants colonizes an island, a necessary element for speciation is absent and the biota remains representative of widespread species, as it is on the beaches of high islands and atolls. Carlquist's (1967) dispersal mode figures demonstrate the point (Figure 7.8). An average of 59% of the seed plants for atolls such as Laysan, Oeno (Pitcairn Islands), and the "equatorial atolls" (Line Islands and Kiribati) are dispersed by ocean drift, but just 25% of seed plants arrive by ocean drift in the high islands closest to those atolls, the Hawaiian and Marquesas islands. Atolls are barely above sea level, and their seed plants are primarily beach or strand plants with fruits that float (Figures 7.10-7.13). The partly endemic biota of *makatea*

*Figure 7.12.* The red-footed booby on Tournefortia at Johnston Island (photo EAK).

*Figure 7.10–7.11.* The beach morning glory Ipomoea pes-caprae. *7.10* In the Galápagos, *7.11* In the Hawaiian Islands (photos EAK).

may result in part because these islands are higher than atolls, with resulting protection from salt spray prevalent on atolls (Fosberg 1974).

The patterns of endemism in marine organisms also reflect a continuous flow of immigrants: 20%–30% endemism for species of marine mollusks and fishes in the Hawaiian and the Society islands; and virtual absence of both species and genus level endemism in marine mollusks (Kay 1984) and shore fishes (Randall 1992, Springer 1982) of the central Pacific. Nor are there species swarms or radiations in the sea comparable with the adaptive radiations of birds and the silversword alliance on land. Species : genus ratios are of the order of 1–2:1 among the corals (Jokiel 1987), other marine invertebrates (Kay and Palumbi 1987), and fishes (Hourigan and Reese 1987), far below the >10–20:1 ratios in the terrestrial biota.

Fossil records in the Pacific also provide evidence for a scenario of continuous immigration and recolonization in marine habitats. Reef-associated limestone from the Eocene in the Marshall Islands records the time when Enewetak, now an atoll, stood above the sea as a high island. Above the Eocene fossil reefs are Miocene marine mollusks, which were associated with sea grass beds and mangrove swamps, neither of which is now present on the atoll; and above the Miocene reefs are shells of *Trochus, Nerita,* and *Littorina* of Pleistocene age, which must have arrived only a few thousand years ago (Kay and Johnson 1987). Fossil corals dredged from the Emperor Seamounts document the occurrence of reef corals in the Hawaiian Archipelago 34 million years ago in the early Oligocene (Grigg 1988). Since the Oligocene extinction, recolonization and changes in coral species composition similar to those at Enewetak have occurred in Hawai'i. The Miocene corals of Midway differ from those of the Oligocene in the Emperor

*Figure 7.13.* The cork-like floating seeds of Scaevola in the Hawaiian Islands (photo EAK).

Seamounts, and the corals of the Hawaiian Islands today are different again from those on Midway's Miocene reefs.

The fossil reefs of Mauke and Niue (Paulay 1990, 1991), all now above sea level, also represent episodes of extinction and recolonization, but reflect cycles of sea-level change over periods of 6,000–8,000 years during the Cenozoic, when large areas of shallow shelf environments, especially those of the inner reef, were stranded during sea-level regressions of the Ice Age. One-third of Pacific shallow water inner reef bivalves may have become extinct during the sea-level changes, and the present modern fauna is interpreted as the result of Post-Pleistocene recolonization, when rising seas flooded inner reef habitats (Paulay 1991). In the Hawaiian Islands, an extinct endemic species of the gastropod *Conus* inhabited an intertidal Pleistocene marine bench on Oʻahu when sea level was higher than it is today. Kohn (1980), comparing the extinct endemic with a present-day congener, the widely distributed *C. chaldaeus*, which it resembles in morphological features and which is now present on Hawaiian benches, concludes that "it probably speciated in Hawaiʻi, perhaps differentiating from an early propagule, . . . thrived during the last interglaciation, and subsequently became extinct."

Both the recent and fossil patterns of endemism are explained if the ocean is considered an open system in which animals and plants come and go, with constant gene flow by dispersal, where isolation is less likely than on land, and marine habitats, rather than being filled by speciation *in situ* as they are on land, are filled by dispersal from other archipelagos. Marine endemics apparently result from single immigrations and single speciation events, each endemic species derived from a different Indo-West Pacific ancestor (Kay and Palumbi 1987).

## The East Pacific Barrier

The expanse of open ocean (5,000–7,000 km) that separates the tropical west coast of America from the Indo-West Pacific is often cited as the major reason for the relatively few fishes, mollusks, and corals with Indo-West Pacific affinities that occur along the western coast of tropical America (Grigg and Hey 1992): 54 transpacific shore fish species (Rosenblatt and Waples 1986), 61 species of marine mollusks (W.K. Emerson 1991), and 56 coral species (Veron 1995). That this segment of the Pacific acts as a substantial dispersal barrier to eastward movement of shallow water marine species is suggested by the analyses of 11 transpacific fishes. Their genetic composition is compatible with the notion that the fishes are either recently dispersed or the results of continuing gene flow from the Indo-Pacific (Rosenblatt and Waples 1986).

## Vicariance Theory: Continental Islands and Insular Speciation

Dispersal alone does not account for all distribution patterns in the Pacific. Unique elements in the biotas of New Zealand, New Caledonia, New Guinea, and Fiji—the tuatara (*Sphenodon*), a small, lizardlike reptile in New Zealand that has been extinct elsewhere in the world for 60 million years, the Antarctic beeches and araucaria pines in New Caledonia that co-occur only in a few parts of Australasia and South America, and iguanas in Fiji that are otherwise restricted to the Americas and Madagascar—are not easily explained by dispersal theory. Nor does dispersal theory alone explain the hundreds of species of drosophilid flies and land snails, traceable to only a few dispersing ancestors on Pacific islands. Explanations for these patterns are the domain of vicariance theory, whereby patterns originate largely as the result of the mobility of land areas: the movement of tectonic plates and their land masses; subsidence and uprise; and the myriad of events that form the hills, valleys, kīpuka, and lava tubes of the mosaic environment of high islands. Vicariance theory requires dispersal in the early history of the taxon, before the imposition of the barriers, the subsequent disruption of a once continuous range of a species by an environmental factor external to the organisms themselves, and speciation.

## Origins of the Insular Biotas

The pattern of the western relationships of the biota of the Pacific Islands remarked on by the early explorer-naturalists is generally acknowledged by botanists, zoologists, and marine biologists, excepting the American biota of the Galápagos and American elements such as the iguanids in Fiji and the silverswords in Hawaiʻi. The western relationships are, however, complex. Much of the biota of New Zealand and New Caledonia, the kauris and araucarias, the amphibians and reptiles, and flightless birds such as the *moa* and the kagu, is an inheritance of their ancient Gondwanaland origin. Other elements of Pacific Island floras and faunas are more recent derivatives of the Oriental and Papuan regions, their ancestors found in Southeast Asia and Australasia.

The marine biota with its diversity focus in the Indo-Malayan Archipelago is recognizably representative of the Indo-West Pacific. But whereas terrestrial biologists do not argue about the nature of presumed source areas, marine biologists ask a fundamental question: Is the Indo-Malayan Archipelago (in its widest sense) a center of origin of the corals, mollusks, and fishes of Pacific islands, or did their ancestors speciate in the central Pacific and accumulate in the Indo-Malayan center of diversity? The Swedish marine biogeographer Sven Ekman (1953) referred to the Indo-Malayan region as "the centre and focus from which the others recruited the main contingent of its fauna." His thesis was based on the notion that a high diversity center would pour out species that were dispersed eastward. The American geologist Harry Ladd (1960) proposed the opposite scenario: speciation occurred in the islands of the central Pacific, and prevailing winds and currents carried species westward into the East Indies. Ladd and others who support his argument for the Indo-Malayan Archipelago as a center of accumulation find the oldest representatives of sea grasses, mangroves, corals, marine mollusks, and barnacles (McCoy and Heck 1976, Kay 1990, Jokiel and Martinelli 1992, and Newman 1986) in the central Pacific rather than in the Indo-Malayan Archipelago.

Alternative explanations have been proposed to explain the center of diversity. Rosen (1985) suggests a "diversity pump," with alternating speciation on outlying islands feeding a center and speciation within the center, both fueled by vicariance associated with geotectonic and glacio-eustatic events. McManus (1985) envisions a dynamic interplay of intermittent land bridges leading to isolation of the tropical waters of the Indian and Pacific oceans as land bridge construction and destruction by tectonics and sea-level change alternately facilitate speciation on land and sea. Pandolfi's (1992) hypothesis involves longitudinal displacement of whole faunas by plate tectonic movement, emergence of land barriers during the Miocene collision of Gondwana-Australia and Southeast Asia, and the Plio-Pleistocene sea-level fluctuations that produced land barriers and fragmented island areas.

## The Equilibrium Theory of Island Biogeography

One of the most perceptive of Johann Reinhold Forster's (1996) observations in the Pacific in 1772 was that "islands only produce a greater or less number of species, as their circumference is more or less extensive." The observation underlies in part MacArthur and Wilson's (1967) extraordinarily heuristic equilibrium theory of island biogeography. Simply put, the McArthur and Wilson theory says that the number of species on an island is in a dynamic equilibrium involving two competing processes, the immigration or addition of new species onto an island and the extinction or removal of species already there. As immigration rate decreases and extinction increases, the two rates meet in equilibrium, with neither gain nor loss of species (Figure 7.14). Two additional inferences are drawn from the equation: if immigration is reduced or extinction increased, the island will equilibrate at fewer species. Thus small islands harbor fewer species than large islands because small islands receive fewer immigrants and more extinction occurs (the area effect), and remote islands harbor fewer species than nearby islands because remote islands receive fewer successful immigrants and undergo as many extinctions (the distance effect). The equilibrium is dynamic: change is continual as one species is extinguished and another takes its place in what is termed "turnover."

The MacArthur and Wilson equations have been criticized because the results of experiments on islands and in island-like situations have not always followed the predictions of the equations. Nor does the model consider the effect of vicariance or of humans on island populations. Nevertheless it continues to serve as a quantitative tool for an understanding of island biogeography both with and without people.

## Extinctions

Fossils associated with Pacific islands date back to the Cretaceous more than 100 million years ago, with records of now extinct species of foraminiferans, coralline algae, corals, rudistids (bivalves), and mollusks from dredgings in the Marshall Islands and Nauru Basin, the Line Islands, the Mid-Pacific Seamounts, and the Emperor Seamounts (Menard and Hamilton 1963, Premoli Silva and Bursa 1981, Grigg 1988). Eocene and Miocene corals different from present reef corals in the Marshall and Hawaiian Islands have been retrieved from reef cores drilled at Enewetak and Midway (Ladd et al. 1967, Grigg 1988). The best-documented extinction events, however, are those of the Quaternary "ice ages" of the last 2 million years, when sea-level fluctuations altered reef environments, extirpating perhaps one-third of the shallow water bivalve fauna in the central Pacific (Paulay 1990).

Sea-level fluctuations also impacted the terrestrial biotas. In an analysis of prehistoric land snail deposits on O'ahu (Hawaiian Islands), initially interpreted (Kirch 1982) as an endemic biota drastically affected by human-induced habitat destruction, Dye and Tuggle (1998) conclude that the decline in the populations "began . . . sometime before 50 B.C.–A.D. 950, perhaps 1,000 years before significant human settlement," and attribute the decline to lowering of the water table, perhaps caused by a drop in local sea level from its mid-Holocene high stand. Fossil pollen grains, long the essential tools of stratigraphy, also signal changes in climate, as they represent *in situ* vegetation. In Hawai'i, pollens from bogs on Kaua'i, Moloka'i, and Maui record changes in mountain vegetation from dominant rain forest vegetation to xerophytic alpine species probably during the last glaciation (Selling 1948, Gavenda 1992). On Mangaia (Cook Islands), pollens dated 6,500–4,000 yr B.P. point to higher sea level, clearance of forests, and the like (Ellison 1994).

Pregill's (1993) succinct summary of the fossil situation for lizards on oceanic islands is apt: "brief . . . in all instances . . . younger than the earliest human occupation." His find of the bones of 3 species of lizards in precultural sediment below a calcite lens dated at ca. 60,000 to 80,000 yr B.P. on 'Eua (southern Tonga) is evidence that two skinks and a gecko colonized 'Eua

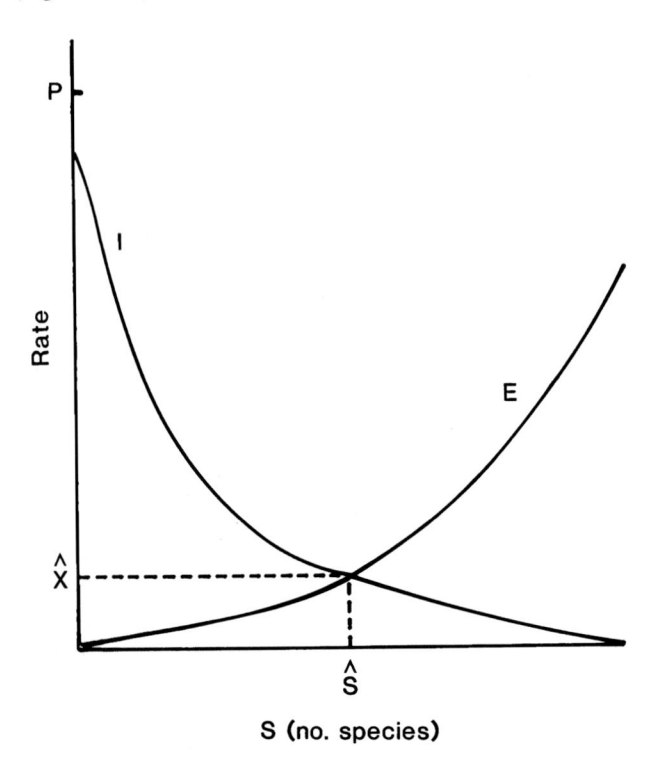

*Figure 7.14.* The equilibrium model of a biota of a single island. The equilibrium species number is reached at the intersection point between the curve of rate of immigration of new species arriving on the island and the curve of extinction of species from the island. After MacArthur and Wilson 1967.

unassisted by humans. Perhaps the oldest terrestrial fossils known from central Pacific islands are the six taxa of Lower Miocene to Late Pleistocene endodontoid land snails from reef core drillings on Bikini and Enewetak (Marshall Islands) and Midway (Hawaiian Islands) (Solem 1976). They represent species that lived in rain forests when the now-atolls were high islands.

## The Human Impact

*"[I]f we are to understand what is likely to happen to ecological balance in the world, we need to examine the past as well as the future." C. S. Elton, 1958*

The Pacific islands described by the naturalist-explorers of the late eighteenth century were not the pristine islands of dreams, but islands that had been inhabited and cultivated for three millenia. Forster (1966) vividly describes the stamp of human settlement in 1774: In the Society Islands "the plains . . . give greater room for cultivation than mountainous exposures [but] the remotest extremities of the vallies [are] covered with plantations"; in the Marquesas "the variety of plants is not . . . so great, owing to the room which the plantations take up in the woods themselves"; and Easter Island had apparently "undergone a great alteration by fire."

The purposeful introduction of cultigens, chickens, dogs, and pigs, as well as the unintentional movement ashore of stowaway rats and weeds in those prehistoric years, is the human version of dispersal, immigration, and colonization, another means by which organisms reached a thousand islands. Alien organisms were purposefully planted, transforming rain forest and dryland ecosystems into economic landscapes of coconut groves and breadfruit plantations. As cultigens increased, the native vegetation was displaced, to the extent that it is said of Pacific atoll vegetation "With the exception of *Pemphis* stands and . . . the mangrove proper, no primitive vegetation types can be recognized today. The original formations have been so thoroughly modified by man that there is no trace left of them"(Catala 1957).

Both purposeful and accidental introductions of animals and plants continue today, far outnumbering the cultigens and stowaways of the prehistoric Pacific. In Hawai'i alone, over 2,000 alien arthropod species and about 30 alien nonmarine mollusks are established in the wild and 20 to 30 new arrivals establish each year (Howarth 1985). Among the introductions in the Pacific in recent years are the brown tree snake on Guam (Mariana Islands), introduced after World War II, which preys on birds, lizards, and small mammals (Savidge 1987); and *Euglandina rosea*, a carnivorous snail, introduced to combat the giant African snail *Achatina fulica* in the 1970s on islands from New Caledonia to Hawai'i. The native vegetation has been equally disrupted by alien ornamentals and forestry plantings such as *Leucaena*, *Albizia*, and *Miconia*.

The discovery of prehistoric bird bones from archaeological sites on island after island throughout the Pacific is key to the enormity of change in the biotas of Pacific islands since humans arrived on them 3,000 years ago. In the 10-year period 1985–1995 Steadman (1995) estimates records of 10 species or populations lost on each of approximately 800 major oceanic islands of the Pacific, for a total loss of 8,000 species or populations. Extinctions attributable to western impact in the Pacific continue today. Andrew Garrett (1887) in the Society Islands writes of collecting "several thousand specimens" of land snails. Almost 50 years after Garrett's death, visiting malacologists wrote "of not finding any live specimens of the critical species reported" (Cooke 1935). And 100 years later, the carnivorous land snail *Euglandina rosea* caused the extinction of the entire remaining partulid snail fauna of Moorea (Society Islands) in less than 10 years after its introduction (Murray et al. 1988). In the Hawaiian Islands all but perhaps 8 or 10 of the 41 species of the tree snail *Achatinella* known in 1900 are still to be seen on O'ahu (Hadfield, pers. comm.). On Guam (Mariana Islands), the brown tree snake has virtually extirpated the native birds (Savidge 1987). Throughout the Pacific, flying foxes, fruit bats, and pigeons are hunted to the point of near extinction (Wiles et al. 1991).

Marine animals are also subject to the effects of humans. Populations have disappeared; others are reported as size-affected and reduced in numbers. Hugh Cuming (ms.) reported no pearl oysters at Ana'a in 1827, although they were found elsewhere in the Tuamotu Archipelago. Within the next 100 years the pearl oyster beds of seven atolls in the Tuamotus (Salvat 1981) and one in the Hawaiian Islands (Galtsoff 1933) were exhausted. Numbers of two species of sea turtles in American Samoa, the green turtle *Chelonia mydas* and the hawksbill *Eretmochelys imbricata*, have declined significantly from historic levels because of habitat loss and subsistence harvests (Tuato'o-Bartley et al. 1993).

Much of the prehistoric bird extinction was apparently human-induced (Steadman 1997). Predation, however, was but one cause. Cultivation of the agricultural landscape meant the removal of native vegetation and forest cover, resulting in displacement of native birds and insects, slope erosion, and deposition of enormous amounts of terrigenous sediment on lowlands and reef flats (J. Allen 1997, M. S. Allen 1997).

The prehistoric bird extinctions premise two major biogeographical implications: the ranges of most living Pacific land bird species are smaller today than at the time of first human contact, and disjunct distributions appear to be due to extinction rather than natural absence (Steadman 1997). Three species of Vini parrots once inhabited islands in the Marquesas; there are none today. Five species of rails coexisted on Mangaia; 3 survive today (Steadman 1995). At least 3 species of endemic lizards and a large skink colonized 'Eua (Tonga); bones are all that remain today (Pregill 1993). Bones of a megapode on To'aga (American Samoa) indicate the presence of megapodes farther east than was previously known (Steadman in Kirch and Hunt 1997). A giant iguana once lived in Tonga (Pregill and Dye 1989) where none lives today. Several genera of land birds on Rota (Mariana Islands) with limited or no range in Micronesia today probably were widespread before human arrival (Steadman 1992).

Extinctions and depleted populations have major ecological effects on oceanic islands, effects that are magnified by the nature of insular organisms and the synergism between and among species. Endemic Hawaiian plants evolved without thorns and fragrance in the absence of herbivores, which today decimate the native flora. The pollinators and seed dispersers in the central Pacific are fruit bats, fruit-eating doves, and pigeons that feed in trees, *Ficus*, *Guettarda*, and *Pipterus* (Cox et al. 1991). The trees are lost to cultivation; the birds are lost for lack of trees; and loss of the birds affects the plants that have co-evolved with them (Craig et al. 1994).

Theoretically, an island population should remain stable, changing only in composition as one species is extinguished and another takes its place, that is, by turnover. Steadman (1985) estimated a prehuman turnover rate of 0–3 vertebrates in approximately 4,000 years on five islands in the Galápagos and 21–24 populations of vertebrates lost in the two centuries since people arrived on those same islands. If those estimates are correct, human-related extinctions are roughly two orders of magnitude greater than prehuman extinction in the Galápagos.

## Conclusions

*"The biogeographer who today proposes to draw final and dogmatic conclusions need only contemplate the changes in geophysical hypotheses in the last decade or two." A.C. Smith, 1970.*

Two questions are central to the biogeography of Pacific islands: how do animals and plants arrive on islands and what happens to them over time? The explorer-naturalists of the eighteenth and nineteenth centuries distinguished patterns of islands and their biotas as they reported the only terrestrial mammals on oceanic islands were fruit bats and rats; and that "the appearance of nature" reminded them of Southeast Asia and the Indo-Malayan archipelago rather than the Americas. Modern biologists find other patterns. West to east across the Pacific various animals and plants drop out; amphibians, for example, are found only as far east as Fiji. The terrestrial biotas of high islands are distinguished by endemic taxa, families, and subfamilies, and genera with disproportionately large numbers of species. Low islands (atolls) share most of their species with neighboring islands. The marine biota differs from the terrestrial pattern in that there is relatively little endemism at the species level, and with only one or two species per genus. The unique terrestrial biotas of the Pacific Islands are mainly related to those of the Oriental Region; the marine biota is part of that of the Indo-West Pacific. The processes that underlie the patterns of distribution involve dispersal, vicariance, speciation, and extinction. As a result of dispersal very few ancestors account for thousands of species of plants, birds, insects, and land snails by authochthonous speciation. Changes in ancestral habits led to adaptive shifts and adaptive radiations in periods from 5 million years to less than 285,000 years. Speciation is enhanced by vicariant events, the movement of continents, and the rise and fall of sea level. In contrast, in the sea, gene pools are not isolated; a continuous flow of immigrants colonizes islands, resulting in at most 20%–30% species endemism in marine mollusks and fishes on isolated islands, such as in Hawai'i. Fossil records of corals dating back more than 30 ma suggest extinctions, continuous immigration and recolonization of marine habitats from the Eocene through the Miocene, and changes in sea level 6,000–8,000 years ago. The focus of diversity is in the Indo-Malayan archipelago and Southeast Asia, but its nature is debated by biogeographers who ask whether that area is a center of origin or a center of accumulation. Extinctions in the Pacific, except for those associated with geotectonic and sea-level changes, appear to be largely human-induced. In prehistoric time, land and sea birds were hunted to extinction; other extinctions resulted as the landscape was altered for agriculture. Alien animals and plants, prehistoric and recent, which decimate susceptible native biotas, were purposefully or accidentally introduced. The effects are additive. The extinctions of the terrestrial biota of oceanic islands has enormous biogeographical implication as fossils indicate that prehistoric distribution patterns were far more extensive than they are today.

**Appendix 7.1.** Geologic time table, showing selected tectonic events and evolution of major taxa

| Era | Period | Epoch | Age (millions of years) | |
|---|---|---|---|---|
| Cenozoic | Quaternary | Holocene | 0.01 | |
| | | Pleistocene | 2 | Ice ages |
| | Tertiary | Pliocene | 5 | Hominids |
| | | Miocene | 24 | Australia/NG collide with SE Asia |
| | | Oligocene | 37 | |
| | | Eocene | 58 | |
| | | Paleocene | 66 | Mammals |
| Mesozoic | Cretaceous | | 144 | Breakup of Gondwana, flowering plants |
| | Jurassic | | 208 | Dinosaurs |
| | Triassic | | 245 | Breakup of Pangaea |
| Paleozoic | Permian | | 286 | |
| | Carboniferous | | 360 | Conifers |
| | Devonian | | 408 | Vascular plants, fish |
| | Silurian | | 438 | |
| | Ordovician | | 505 | |
| | Cambrian | | 570 | Invertebrates |

# Bibliography

Adler, G. H., and R. Dudley. 1994. Butterfly biogeography and endemism on tropical Pacific islands. *Biological Journal of the Linnean Society* 51:151–162.

Allen, J. 1997. Pre-contact landscape transformation and cultural change in windward Oʻahu. In *Historical ecology in the Pacific Islands*, ed. P.V. Kirch and T. L. Hunt, 230–247. New Haven: Yale University Press.

Allen, S. M. 1997. Coastal morphogenesis, climatic trends, and Cook Island prehistory. In *Historical ecology in the Pacific Islands*, ed. P.V. Kirch and T. L. Hunt, 124–146. New Haven: Yale University Press.

Asquith, A. 1995. Evolution of *Sarona* (Heteroptera, Miridae). In *Hawaiian biogeography: evolution on a hot spot*, ed. W. L. Wagner and V. A. Funk, 90–120. Washington, DC: Smithsonian Institution Press.

Baldwin, B. G., and R. H. Robichaux. 1995. Historical biogeography and ecology of the Hawaiian silversword alliance (Asteraceae): new molecular phylogenetic techniques. In *Hawaiian biogeography: evolution on a hot spot*, ed. W. L. Wagner and V. A. Funk, 259–287. Washington, DC: Smithsonian Institution Press.

Benton, T. G. 1995. Biodiversity and biogeography of Henderson Island's insects. *Biological Journal of the Linnean Society* 56:245–259.

Berger, A. 1987. Avifauna of Enewetak Atoll. In *The natural history of Enewetak*, vol. 1, ed. D. M. Devaney, E.S. Reese, B. L. Burch, and P. Helfrich, 215–220. Office of Scientific and Technical Information, U.S. Dept. of Energy.

Brothers, E. G., and R. E. Thresher. 1985. Pelagic duration, dispersal and the distribution of Indo-Pacific coral reef fishes. In *The ecology of deep and shallow coral reefs*, vol. 2, ed. M. Reaka, 53–59. NOAA Symposium Series Undersea Res., Washington, D.C.: U.S. Department of Commerce.

Brownlie, G. 1965. The geographical affinities of the South Pacific island fern floras. *Pacific Science* 19:219–223.

Carlquist, S. 1965. *Island Life*. New York: The Natural History Press.

Carlquist, S. 1967. The biota of long-distance dispersal. Part 5, Plant dispersal to Pacific Islands, *Bulletin of the Torrey Botany Club* 94:129–162.

Carr, D. J. 1983, ed. *Sydney Parkinson*. Honolulu: British Museum (Natural History) and University of Hawaiʻi Press.

Carr. G. D. 1987. Beggar's ticks and tarweeds: masters of adaptive radiation. *Trends in Evolution and Ecology* 2:192–195.

Carr, G. D. 1990. *Argyroxiphium* DC Silversword. In *Manual of the flowering plants of Hawaiʻi*, vol. 1, ed. W. L. Wagner, D. R. Herbst and S. H. Sohmer, 258–262. Honolulu: University of Hawaiʻi Press, Bishop Museum Press.

Carson, H. 1983. Chromosomal sequences and interisland colonizations in Hawaiian *Drosophila*. *Genetics* 103:465–482.

Catala, R. L. A. 1957. Report on the Gilbert Islands: some aspects of human ecology. *Atoll Research Bulletin* 59:1–187.

Chamisso, A. 1821. Remarks and opinions of the naturalist of the expedition. In O. Kotzebue, *a voyage of discovery into the South Seas . . . in the years 1815–1818*. Reprint, New York: Da Capo Press, 1967.

Clarke, B., and J. Murray. 1969. Ecological genetics and speciation in land snails of the genus *Partula*. *Biological Journal of the Linnean Society* 1:31–42.

Cooke, C. M., Jr. 1935. In H. E. Gregory, Report of the Director. *Bishop Museum Bulletin* 133:36–55.

Cooke, C. M. Jr., 1966. In H. W. Harry, Land snails of Ulithi Atoll, Caroline Islands. *Pacific Science* 20:212–223.

Cox, P. A., T. Elmquist, E. D. Pierson, W. E. Rainey. 1991. Flying foxes as strong inter-actors in South Pacific island ecosystems: a conservation hypothesis. *Conservation Biology* 5:448–463.

Craig, P., T. E. Morrell, and K. Soʻoto. 1994. Subsistence harvest of birds, fruit bats, and other game in American Samoa, 1990–1991. *Pacific Science* 48:344–352.

Crampton, H. E. 1925. Contemporaneous organic differentiation in the species of *Partula* living in Moorea, Society Islands. *American Naturalist* 59:5–35.

Cuming, H. Journal of a voyage from Valparaiso to the Society and the adjacent islands performed in the schooner *Discoverer* Samuel Grimwood master in the years 1827 and 1828. Manuscript, Mitchell Library, Sydney.

Dana, J. D. 1853. *Crustacea*. United States Exploring Expedition, Vols. 13–14 (1852–1855). Philadelphia: C. Sherman.

Darwin, C. 1872. *On the origin of species*, 6th ed. London: John Murray. Reprint New York: P. F. Collier & Son, 1909.

Darwin, C. 1902. *Journal of researches into the natural history and geology of the countries visited during the voyage round the world of H.M.S. "Beagle" under command of Captain FitzRoy, R.N.*, 2nd ed. London: John Murray.

DeSalle, R. 1995. Molecular approaches to biogeographic analysis of Hawaiian Drosophilidae. In *Hawaiian biogeography: evolution on a hot spot*, ed. W. L. Wagner and V. A. Funk, 72–89. Washington, DC: Smithsonian Institution Press.

Diamond, J. M. 1995. Introduction to the exploration of Henderson Island. *Biological Journal of the Linnean Society* 56:1–5.

Dye, T. S., and H. D. Tuggle. 1998. Land snail extinctions at Kalaeloa, Oʻahu. *Pacific Science* 52: 111-140.

Ekman, S. 1935. *Tiergeographie des Meeres*. Leipzig: Akad. Verlagsges.

Ekman, S. 1953. *Zoogeography of the sea*. London: Sidgwick and Jackson.

Ellison, J. C. 1994. Palaeo-lake and swamp stratigraphic records of Holocene vegetation and sea-level changes, Mangaia, Cook Islands. *Pacific Science* 48:1–15.

Elton, C. S. 1958. *The ecology of invasions by animals and plants*. London: Chapman and Hall.

Emerson, O. P. 1941. Punahou under Daniel Dole. In *Punahou: 1841–1941*, ed. M. C. Alexander and C. P. Dodge. Berkeley: University of California Press.

Emerson, W. K. 1991. First records for *Cymatium mundum* (Gould) in the eastern Pacific Ocean, with comments on the zoogeography of the tropical trans-Pacific tonnacean and non-tonnacean prosobranch gastropods with Indo-Pacific faunal affinities in West American waters. *The Nautilus* 105:62–80.

Florence, J., S. Waldren, and A. J. Chepstow-Lusty. 1995. The flora of the Pitcairn Islands: a review. *Biological Journal of the Linnean Society* 56:79–119.

Forster, J. R. 1996. In *Observations made during a voyage round the world, on physical geography, natural history, and ethic philosophy*, ed. N. Thomas, H. Guest, and M. Dettelbach. Honolulu: University of Hawaiʻi Press..

Fosberg, F. R. 1955. Pacific forms of *Lepturus* R. Br. (Gramineae). *Occasional Papers, B. P. Bishop Museum* 21:285–294.

Fosberg, F. R. 1974. Phytogeography of atolls and other coral islands. In *Biology and geology of coral reefs*, vol. 3, ed. O. A. Jones and R. Endean. New York: Academic Press.

Fosberg, F. 1992. Vegetation of the Society Islands. *Pacific Science* 46:232–250.

Freed, L. A., S. Conant, and R. C. Fleisher. 1987. Evolutionary ecology and radiation of Hawaiian passerine birds. *Trends in Ecology and Evolution* 2:196–203.

Froeschner, R. C. 1985. Synopsis of the Heteroptera or true bugs of the Galapagos Islands. *Smithsonian Contributions to Zoology*. No. 407:1–84.

Funk, V. A., and W. L. Wagner. Biogeography of seven ancient Hawaiian plant lineages. In *Hawaiian Biogeography: evolution on a hot spot*, ed. W. L. Wagner and V. A. Funk, 160-194. Washington, DC: Smithsonian Institution Press.

Galtsoff, P. S. 1933. Pearl and Hermes Reef, Hawaiʻi: hydrological and biological observations. *Bishop Museum Bulletin* 107:1–49.

Gavenda, R. T. 1992. Hawaiian Quaternary paleoenvironments: a review of geological, pedological, and botanical evidence. *Pacific Science* 46:295–307.

Garrett, A. 1887. On the terrestrial molluscs of the Viti Islands. Part 1. *Proceedings of the Zoological Society of London,* 1887:164–189.

Gibbons, J. R. H. 1985. The biogeography and evolution of Pacific island reptiles and amphibians. In *Biology of Australasian frogs and reptiles,* ed. G. Grigg, R. Shine and H. Ehmann, 125–142. Royal Zoological Society of New South Wales.

Givnish, T. J., K. J. Sysma, J. F. Smith, and W. J. Hahn. 1995. Molecular evolution, adaptive radiation, and geographic speciation in *Cyanea* (Campanullaceae, Lobelioideae). In *Hawaiian biogeography: evolution on a hot spot,* ed. W. L Wagner and V. A. Funk, 288–337. Washington, DC: Smithsonian Institution Press.

Grant, P. 1986. *Ecology and evolution of Darwin's finches.* New Jersey: Princeton University Press.

Gressitt, J. L. 1956. Some distribution patterns of Pacific Island faunae. *Systematic Zoology* 5:11–32.

Gressitt, J. L. 1961. Problems in the zoogeography of Pacific and Antarctic insects. *Pacific Insects* 2:1–94.

Gressitt, J. L., and C. M. Yoshimoto. 1963. Dispersal of animals in the Pacific. In *Pacific Basin biogeography: a symposium,* ed. J. L. Gressitt, 283–292. Honolulu: Bishop Museum Press,

Grigg, R. W. 1988. Paleoceanography of coral reefs in the Hawaiian-Emperor Chain. *Science* 240:1737–1743.

Grigg, R. W., and R. Hey. 1992. Paleoceanography of the tropical Eastern Pacific Ocean. *Science* 255:172–178.

Gulick, J. T. 1890. Divergent evolution through cumulative segregation. *Journal of the Linnean Society of London Zoology* 20:189–274.

Hardy, D. E., and K. Y. Kaneshiro. 1981. Drosophilidae of Pacific Oceania. In *The genetics and biology of Drosophila,* ed. M. Ashburner, H. L. Carson, and J. N. Thompson, 308–348. New York: Academic Press.

Hedley, C. 1899. A zoogeographic scheme for the Mid-Pacific. *Proceedings of the Linnaean Society of New South Wales* 24:391–423.

Hinds, R. B. 1844. *The zoology of the voyage of H.M.S. "Sulphur" under the Command of Captain Sir Edward Belcher . . . during the years 1836–1842.* London: Smith Elder and Co.

Hourigan, T., and E. Reese. 1987. Mid-ocean isolation and the evolution of Hawaiian reef fishes. *Trends in Ecology and Evolution* 2:187–191.

Howarth, F. G. 1985. Impacts of alien land arthropods and mollusks on native plants and animals in Hawai'i. In *Hawai'i's terrestrial ecosystems: preservation and management,* ed. C. P. Stone and J. Michael Scott, 149–179. Honolulu: Cooperative National Park Resources Study Unit University of Hawai'i.

Hubbell, T. H. 1968. The biology of islands. *Proceedings of the National Academy of Sciences* 60:22–32.

Jokiel, P. L. 1984. Long-distance dispersal of reef corals by rafting. *Coral Reefs* 3:113–116.

Jokiel, P. L. 1987. Ecology, biogeography and evolution of corals in Hawai'i. *Trends in Ecology and Evolution* 2:179–182.

Jokiel, P. L., and and F. J. Martinelli. 1992. The vortex model of coral reef biogeography. *Journal of Biogeography* 19:449–458.

Kaneshiro, K. 1988. Speciation in the Hawaiian *Drosophila*. *BioScience* 38:258–263.

Kay, E. A. 1980. Little worlds of the Pacific: an essay on Pacific basin biogeography. *University of Hawai'i Harold L. Lyon Lectures* 9:1–40.

Kay, E. A. 1984. Patterns of speciation in the Indo-West Pacific. In *Biogeography of the tropical Pacific,* ed. F. J. Radovsky, P. H. Raven, and S. H. Sohmer. Bishop Museum Special Publication 72:33–44.

Kay, E. A. 1990. The Cypraeidae of the Indo-Pacific: Cenozoic fossil history and biogeography. *Bulletin of Marine Science* 47:23–34.

Kay, E. A. 1994. Darwin's biogeography and the oceanic islands of the Central Pacific. In *Darwin's laboratory,* ed. R. MacLeod and P. F. Rehbock, 49–69. Honolulu: University of Hawai'i Press.

Kay, E. A. 1995. Diversification and differentiation: two evolutionary patterns in the molluscan fauna of Pacific islands with consequences for conservation. In *Biodiversity and conservation in the mollusca,* ed. A. C. van Bruggen, S. M. Wells, and Th. C. M. Kemperman, 37–53. Leiden: Backhuys Publishers.

Kay, E. A., and S. Johnson. 1987. Mollusca of Enewetak Atoll. In *The natural history of Enewetak,* vol. 1, ed. D. M. Devaney, E. S. Reese, B. L. Burch, and P. Helfrich, 105–146. Office of Scientific and Technical Information, U.S. Dept. of Energy.

Kay, E. A., and S. R. Palumbi. 1987. Endemism and evolution in Hawaiian marine invertebrates. *Trends in Ecology and Evolution* 2:183–186.

Kay, E. A., and M. F. Switzer. 1974. Molluscan distribution patterns in Fanning Island lagoon and a comparison of the mollusks of the lagoon and seaward reefs. *Pacific Science* 28:275–295.

Kirch, P. V. 1982. The impact of prehistoric Polynesians on the Hawaiian ecosystem. *Pacific Science* 36:1–14.

Kohn, A. J. 1980. *Conus kahiko,* a new Pleistocene gastropod from Oahu, Hawaii. *Journal of Paleontology* 54:534–541.

Ladd, H. S. 1960. Origin of Pacific island molluscan fauna. *American Journal of Science* 258A:310–315.

Ladd, H. S., J. I. Tracey, Jr., and M. G. Gross. 1967. Drilling on Midway Atoll, Hawaii. *Science* 156:1088–1094.

Lamoureux, C. H. 1980. In Kay, 1980. Little worlds of the Pacific: an essay on Pacific Basin biogeography. *University of Hawai'i Harold L. Lyon Lectures* 9:1–40.

Lesson, R. P. 1825. Coup-d'oeil sur les Iles Oceaniennes et le Grand Ocean. *Annales des Sciences Naturelles* 172–188.

Lyell, C. 1832. *Principles of geology.* Vol. 2. London: John Murray. (Johnson Reprint Corporation, 1969).

Lyell, C. 1854. *Principles of geology.* 9th ed. New York: D. Appleton & Co.

MacArthur, R. H. 1972. *Geographical ecology.* New York: Harper & Row.

MacArther, R. H., and E. O. Wilson. 1967. *The theory of island biogeography.* Princeton: Princeton University Press.

Mayr, E. 1941. Borders and subdivisions of the Polynesian region as based on our knowledge of the distribution of birds. *Proceedings of the 6th Pacific Science Congress* 4:191–195.

Mayr, E. 1942. *Systematics and the origin of species.* New York: Columbia University Press.

McCoy, E. D., and K. L. Heck. 1976. Biogeography of corals, seagrasses, and mangroves: an alternative to the center of origin concept. *Systematic Zoology* 25:201–210.

McManus, J. W. 1985. Marine speciation, tectonics and sea-level changes in Southeast Asia. *Proceedings of the 5th International Coral Reef Congress* 4:139–144.

Menard, H. W., and E. L. Hamilton. 1963. Paleogeography of the tropical Pacific. In *Pacific Basin biogeography,* ed. J. L. Gressitt, 193–217. Honolulu: Bishop Museum Press.

Montgomery, S. L. 1983. Carnivorous caterpillars: the behavior, biogeography and conservation of *Euplithecia* (Lepidoptera: Geometridae) in the Hawaiian Islands. *GeoJournal* 76:549–556.

Murray, J. E., E. Murray, M. S. Johnson, and B. Clarke, 1988. The extinction of *Partula* on Moorea. *Pacific Science* 42:150–153.

Myers, G. S. 1935. Ability of amphibians to cross sea barriers, with special reference to Pacific zoogeography. *Proceedings of the 7th Pacific Science Congress* 4:38–48.

Myers, A. A., and P. S. Giller. 1990. *Analytical biogeography*. New York: Chapman and Hall.

Nelson, G., and D. E. Rosen, eds. 1981. *Vicariance biogeography: a critique*. New York: Columbia University Press.

Newman, W. A. 1986. Origin of the Hawaiian marine fauna: dispersal and vicariance as indicated by barnacles and other organisms. In *Crustacean biogeography*, ed. R. H. Gore and K. L. Heck, 21–49. Rotterdam: A. A. Balkema.

Nunn, P. D. 1994. *Oceanic islands*. Cambridge: Blackwell.

Olson, S. 1991. Patterns of avian diversity and radiation in the Pacific as seen through the fossil record. In *The unity of evolutionary biology, the proceedings of the Fourth International Congress of Systematics and Evolutionary Biology*, vol. 1, ed. E. C. Dudley, 314–318. Portland, Oregon: Dioscorides Press.

Olson, S. and A. Wetmore. 1976. Preliminary diagnoses of extraordinary new genera of birds from Pleistocene deposits in the Hawaiian Islands. *Proceedings of the Biological Society of Washington* 89 (18):247–258.

Pandolfi, J. M. 1992. Successive isolation rather than evolutionary centres for the origination of Indo-Pacific reef corals. *Journal of Biogeography* 19:593–609.

Patterson, C. 1983. Aims and methods in biogeography. In *Evolution, time and space: the emergence of the biosphere*, eds. R. W. Sims, J. H. Price, and P. E. S. Whalley, 1–28. Systematics Association Special Volume No. 23. New York: Academic Press.

Paulay, G. 1997. Diversity and distribution of reef organisms. In *Life and death of coral reefs*, ed. C. Birkeland, 298–345. New York: Chapman and Hall.

Paulay, G. 1991. Late Cenozoic sea level fluctuations and the diversity and species composition of insular shallow water marine faunas. In *The unity of evolutionary biology: proceedings of the Fourth International Congress on Systematics and Evolutionary Biology*, vol. 1, ed. E. C. Dudley, 184–193. Portland: Dioscorides Press.

Paulay, G. 1990. Effect of Late Cenozoic sea level fluctuations on the bivalve faunas of tropical oceanic islands. *Paleobiology* 16:413–434.

Paulay, G. 1985. Adaptive radiation on an isolated oceanic island: the Cryptorhynchinae (Curculionidae) of Rapa revisited. *Biological Journal of the Linnean Society* 26:95–187.

Peck, S. B. 1991. The Galapagos Archipelago, Ecuador: with an emphasis on terrestrial invertebrates, especially insects; and an outline for research. In *The unity of evolutionary biology: proceedings of the Fourth International Congress on Systematic and Evolutionary Biology*, vol. 1, ed. E. C. Dudley,1319–1336. Portland: Dioscorides Press.

Perrault, G. G. 1987. Microendemisme et speciation de genre *Mecyclothorax* (Coleoptera–Carabidae Psydrini) à Tahiti (Polynesie Francaise). *Bulletin de la Societe de Zoologique de France* 112:419–427.

Pickering, C. 1854. *The geographic distribution of animals and plants*. Boston: Little Brown and Co.

Preese, R. C. 1995. Systematic review of the land snails of the Pitcairn Islands. *Biological Journal of the Linnean Society* 56:273–307.

Pregill, G. K. 1993. Fossil lizards from the late Quaternary of 'Eua, Tonga. *Pacific Science* 47:101–114

Pregill, G. K., and T. Dye. 1989. Prehistoric extinction of giant iguanas in Tonga. *Copeia* 505–508.

Premoli Silva, I., and C. Bursa. 1981. Shallow-water skeletal debris and larger foraminifers from Deep Sea Drilling Project 462, Nauru Basin, Western Equatorial Pacific. *Initial Reports of the Deep Sea Drilling Project* 61:439–453.

Randall, J. E. 1992. *Endemism of fishes in Oceania*. UNEP: Coastal resources and systems of the Pacific Basin: investigation and steps toward protective management. UNEP Regional Seas Reports and Studies No. 147.

Richmond, R. 1982. Energetic considerations in the dispersal of *Pocillopora damicornis* (Linnaeus) planulae. *Proceedings of the Fourth International Coral Reef Symposium* 2:153–156.

Rosen, B. R. 1984. Reef coral biogeography and climate through the Late Cenozoic: just islands in the sun or a critical pattern of islands? In *Fossils and climate*, ed. P. J. Brenchley, 201–262. Chichester: Wiley.

Rosenblatt, R. H., and R. S. Waples. 1986. A genetic comparison of allopatric populations of shore fish species from the Eastern and Central Pacific Ocean: dispersal or vicariance? *Copeia* No. 2:275–284.

Salvat, B. 1981. Preservation of coral reefs: scientific whim or economic necessity? Past, present and future. *Proceedings of the 4th International Coral Reef Symposium Manila* 1:225–229.

Samuelson, G. A., and G. M. Nishida. 1987. Insects and allies (Arthropoda) of Enewetak Atoll. In *The natural history of Enewetak Atoll*, vol. 1, ed. D. M. Devaney, E. S. Reese, B. L. Burch, and P. Helfrich, 147–177. Office of Scientific and Technical Information, U.S. Dept. of Energy.

Savidge, J. A. 1987. Extinction of an island forest avifauna by an introduced snake. *Ecology* 68:660–668.

Scheltema, R. S. 1986. Long-distance dispersal by planktonic larvae of shoal-water benthic invertebrates among Central Pacific islands. *Bulletin of Marine Science* 39:241–256.

Schilder, F. A. 1961. The geographical distribution of cowries (Mollusca: Gastropoda). *Veliger* 7:171–183.

Schmidt, K. P. 1930. Essay on the zoogeography of the Pacific islands. In S. N. Shurcliff, *Jungle Islands*. New York: G.P. Putnam's Sons.

Schouw, J. F. 1823. *Grundzuge einer allegemeinen Pflanzengeographie*. Berlin.

Sclater, P. L. 1858. On the geographical distribution of the members of the Class Aves. *Journal of the Linnean Society (Zoology)* 2:130–145.

Selling, O. H. 1948. Studies in Hawaiian pollen statistics. Part III. *On the Late Quaternary history of the Hawaiian vegetation*. Bernice P. Bishop Museum Special Publication 39.

Shaw, K. L. 1995. Biogeographic patterns of two independent Hawaiian cricket radiations (*Laupala* and *Prognathogryllus*). In *Hawaiian biogeography: evolution on a hot spot*, ed. W. L. Wagner and V. A. Funk, 39–56. Washington, DC: Smithsonian Institution Press.

Simpson, J. A., and E. C. Weiner, eds. 1984. *The Oxford English Dictionary*. Vol. X . Oxford: Clarendon Press.

Smith, A. C. 1970. The Pacific as a key to flowering plant history. *University of Hawai'i Harold L. Lyon Lectures* 1:1–27.

Solem, A. G. 1959. Systematics and zoogeography of the land and freshwater Mollusca of the New Hebrides. *Fieldiana Zoology* 43:1–359.

Solem, A. G. 1977. Fossil endodontoid land snails from Midway Atoll. *Journal of Paleontology* 51:902–911.

Solem, A. G. 1982. *Endodontoid land snails from Pacific Islands (Mollusca: Pulmonata: Sigmurethra). Part II. Families Punctidae and Charopidae, zoogeography*. Chicago: Field Museum of Natural History.

Spencer, T., and T. G. Benton. 1995. Structure, topography and vegetation: the significance of raised reef islands. *Biological Journal of the Linnean Society* 56:11–12.

Springer, V. G. 1982. Pacific Plate biogeography with special reference to shore fishes. *Smithsonian Contributions to Zoology* 376:1–182.

Steadman, D. W. 1985. Fossil birds from Mangaia, Southern Cook Islands. *Bulletin of the British Ornithological Club* 105:58–66.

Steadman, D. W. 1992 Extinct and extirpated birds from Rota, Mariana Islands. *Micronesica* 25:71–84.

Steadman, D. W. 1995. Prehistoric extinctions of Pacific Island birds: biodiversity meets zooarchaeology. *Science* 267:1123–1131.

Steadman, D. W. 1997. Extinctions of Polynesian birds: reciprocal impacts of birds and people. In *Historical ecology in the Pacific Islands*, ed. P. V. Kirch and T. L. Hunt, 51–79. New Haven: Yale University Press.

Steenis, C. G. G. J. van. 1950. *Flora Malesiana*. Ser. 1. Vol. 1. Djakarta: Noordhoff-Kolff N.V.

Stoddart, D. R. 1976. Continuity and crisis in the reef community. *Micronesica* 12:1–9.

Stoddart, D. R. 1992. Biogeography of the tropical Pacific. *Pacific Science* 46:276–293.

Swainson, W. 1835. *A Treatise on the geography and classification of animals*. London: Longman, Green and Co.

Tarr, C. L., and R. C. Fleischer. 1995. Evolutionary relationships of the Hawaiian honeycreepers (Aves, Drepanidinae). In *Hawaiian biogeography: evolution on a hot spot*, ed. W. L. Wagner and V. A. Funk, 147–59. Washington, DC: Smithsonian Institution Press.

Thaman, R. R. 1992. Vegetation of Nauru and the Gilbert Islands: case studies of poverty, degradation, disturbance, and displacement. *Pacific Science* 46:128–158.

Tuato'o-Bartley, N., T. E. Morrell, and P. Craig. 1993. Status of sea turtles in American Samoa in 1991. *Pacific Science* 47:215–221.

Tsuda, R. T. 1976. Occurrence of the genus *Sargassum* (Phaeophyta) on two Pacific atolls. *Micronesica* 12:279–282.

Udvardy, M. D. F. 1975. A classification of the biogeographical provinces of the world. International Union for Conservation of Nature and Natural Resources. Morges, Switzerland. Occasional Papers 18.

Vagvolgyi, J. 1975. Body size, aerial dispersal, and origin of the Pacific land snail fauna. *Systematic Zoology* 24:465–488.

van Balgooy, M. J. J. 1971. Plant geography of the Pacific. *Blumea Supplement* 6:1–122.

Vermeij, G. J., E. A. Kay, and L. G. Eldredge. 1983. Molluscs of the Northern Mariana Islands, with special reference to the selectivity of oceanic dispersal barriers. *Micronesica* 19:27–55.

Veron, J. E. N. 1995. *Corals in space and time. The biogeography and evolution of the Scleractinia*. Townsville: University of New South Wales Press.

Wagner, W. L. 1991. Evolution of waif floras: a comparison of the Hawaiian and Marquesan Archipelagos. In *The unity of evolutionary biology, proceedings of the Fourth International Congress of Systematics and Evolutionary Biology*, vol. 1, ed. E. C. Dudley, 267–284. Portland, Oregon: Dioscorides Press.

Wagner, W. L., S. G. Weller, and A. K. Sakai. 1995. Phylogeny and biogeography in *Schiedea* and *Alsinidendron* (Caryophyllaceae). In *Hawaiian biogeography: evolution on a hot spot*, ed. W. L Wagner and V. A. Funk, 221–258. Washington, DC: Smithsonian Institution Press.

Wallace, A. R. 1876. *The geographical distribution of animals*. 2 vols. London: MacMillan.

Wallace, A. R. 1911. *Island life*. London: MacMillan and Co.

Wiles, G. J., J. Engring, M. V. C. Falanruw. 1991. Population status and natural history of *Pteropus mariannus* on Ulithi Atoll, Caroline Islands. *Pacific Science* 45:76–84.

Williamson, M. 1981. *Island populations*. Oxford: Oxford University Press.

Wilson, E. O., and R. W. Taylor. 1967. An estimate of the potential evolutionary increase in species density in the Polynesian ant fauna. *Evolution* 21:1–10.

Wodzicki, K., and H. Felten. 1975. The peka, or fruit bat (*Pteropus tonganus tonganus*) (Mammalia, Chiroptera) of Niue Island, South Pacific. *Pacific Science* 29:131–138.

Woodward, S. P. 1851–1856. *Manual of Mollusca*. London: John Weale.

Zimmerman, E. C. 1942. Distribution and origin of some eastern oceanic insects. *American Naturalist* 76:280–307.

Zimmerman, E. C. 1948. *Insects of Hawai'i*. Vol. 1. Honolulu: University of Hawai'i Press.

# CHAPTER 8

# Terrestrial Ecosystems

*Harley I. Manner, Dieter Mueller-Dombois, and Moshe Rapaport*

## Introduction

Prior to European contact, virtually all Pacific Islanders lived in rural locations, dependent on the natural environment for basic subsistence needs. This dependence inevitably resulted in large-scale ecosystem conversion. Today, the pace and intensity of exploitation have accelerated. Areas under primary forest, comprising many rare, endemic species of plants and animals, are covered by secondary forest, savannas, agriculture, and urban development. The study of terrestrial ecosystems and their modification has thus become a critical issue in the Pacific Islands. We begin here with the ecosystem concept, and outline the origins and causal factors of ecosystem formation. We then describe each of the major Pacific Island ecosystem types. Vegetation is used as the principal biological component by which terrestrial ecosystems are recognized.

## The Ecosystem Concept

During the seventeenth through nineteenth centuries, geographers, naturalists, and travelers to foreign lands noted the "step-wise changes in pattern from forest to the vegetation near permanent snow fields in the Alps and to the colorful vegetation of distant lands" (Mueller-Dombois and Ellenberg 1974), and began to systematically describe and classify these recurring patterns by life form or growth types and macroclimate-related categories. In the nineteenth and twentieth centuries, there were many attempts to explain the causal interrelationships between biota, climate, soil, and geomorphological development (Fosberg 1963). Given the inadequacies of discipline-based approaches to understanding complexities of environmental relationships and problems, there was a growing realization that a holistic approach was necessary.

In 1928, the limnologist Woltereck introduced the concept of ecological system for aquatic habitats, visualized as a space-limited dynamic system. The vegetation ecologist Tansley (1935) introduced the shorter term "ecosystem" to describe an integrated system formed by terrestrial communities and their specific habitats. Woltereck's and Tansley's systems, consisting of organisms and their inorganic components in a relatively stable equilibrium, were open, that is, dependent on outside energy, and of various kinds and sizes. The central point of these systems is that fundamentally, organisms cannot be considered separately from their specific environments, as both organisms and environment form a functional system in nature (Mueller-Dombois and Ellenberg 1974).

The analysis and description of an ecosystem includes a wide range of interrelated structural and functional characteristics. Structural components of an ecosystem include the quantity and distribution of its biotic and abiotic materials, species structure (species composition, numbers, diversity), organic structure (biomass, nonliving organic matter), habitat, niches, macro- and microclimate, geology and soils (Mueller-Dombois and Ellenberg 1974, Odum 1963). Ecosystem functions include the transfer or cycling of materials, mineral nutrient dynamics, and the flow of energy between the structural components of the ecosystem. Vegetation forms the primary producer component, while other essential biological components are the consumers and the decomposers.

## Origins and Causal Factors of Ecosystem Formation

The origins and factors that determine Pacific island ecosystem development were described by Mueller-Dombois (1992, 1994), and Mueller-Dombois and Fosberg (1998). This relationship, though specifically formulated for vegetation, also applies to other components of ecosystems, including animal biota.

It is here restated in modified form as:

Ecosystems = f (g, cl, d, b, ac, e) time

where
- g = geoposition
- cl = climate
- d = disturbance regimes
- b = biota
- ac = accessibility potential of biota
- e = ecological characteristics of organisms.

The geographic location, geology, geomorphology, and soils (g), and climate (cl) are the major physical environmental components. Disturbance regimes (d) include natural perturbations (such as storms and long-term climatic changes) and anthropogenic habitat modification and introductions. The biota (b) refers to the floral and faunal components of a given ecosystem. The accessibility factor (ac) refers to the ability of a species to reach and become established in the island and in the specific ecosystem. The ecological properties or attributes of a species (e) include its life form, physiological requirements, and natural history strategy. These properties determine the ability of organisms to compete and live with each other in the same or different ecosystems.

Climate, topography, and soils have pronounced effects on the mature structure and long-term functioning of the flora and fauna of an ecosystem. Thus on high islands, ecosystem development is altitudinally differentiated by climate, and ecosystem changes can be studied along an altitudinal gradient, or along a precipitation gradient. Providing that most other factors are kept constant, differences in ecosystem structure and function can be studied as in an experimental design. Under natural conditions, tropical lowland rain forests differ from montane forests and other ecosystems with respect to the diversity of species, life forms, biomass, and vertical layering. For example, in a study of ecosystem structure on Hawai'i Island, both floral and faunal biota were shown to covary along an altitudinal gradient between 1,000 and 3,000 meters (Mueller-Dombois et al. 1981).

## Strand and Atolls

The strand is that portion of the beach or coastline of volcanic rock or coral limestone located adjacent to the seashore but above the high-tide line (Fosberg 1960). The vegetation of the strand is a relatively narrow band of halophytic (salt-tolerant) herbs, shrubs, and tree species, often characterized by fleshy leaves with a salty sap, as well as by stunted and prostrate growth forms along windswept coasts (Figure 8.1). These species are

*Figure 8.1. Strand vegetation on a Micronesian atoll (photo HIM).*

well adapted to the harsh conditions of physical disturbance, salinity, drought, dessication, and rocky, calcareous soils. Most strand species are widespread and indigenous to the tropical and subtropical Pacific Islands. Given the large number of atolls in the Pacific and the high ratio of coastline to land area, this ecosystem is one of the most common in the region.

Atoll ecosystems are strand-like in character and support the relatively few species tolerant of salinity (Figure 8.2). The individual *motu* on an atoll do not always support all species found throughout the atoll. Thus, the *motu* often support only fragmental communities consisting of very few species. But most are indigenous. On large *motu* exceeding a few hectares, natural vegetation tends to be more luxuriant, particularly where the freshwater lens is better developed. Large *motu* usually contain several phreatophytic (reliant on groundwater) species in their interior. Such islets commonly display a zonation of vegetation that coincides with the availability of fresh groundwater. The following zones may be present:

1. A sparse halophytic cover of vines, grasses, and sedges on the upper foreshore of windward coasts. One of the most widespread plant species is the prostrate vine *Ipomoea pes-caprae* (beach morning glory). Also found here are some grasses and shrubs (particularly *Scaevola taccada*). The small tree or arborescent shrub *Pemphis acidula* commonly forms thickets on limestone rock along atoll beaches.

2. A halophytic low forest fringe. This is often dominated by *Tournefortia argentea* (the tree heliotrope) and typically occurs on the beach crest.

3. Littoral forest composed of halophytic, low-statured species. This may include *Pandanus tectorius* and *Casuarina equisetifolia* (ironwood), now mostly displaced by coconut plantations.

4. Mixed forests composed of several phreatophytic species. They may form two layers, with *Pisonia grandis* or *Calophyllum inophyllum* in the upper canopy and *Guettarda speciosa* in a lower subcanopy. Here too, the indigenous species have now become largely displaced.

5. Central depression with marsh or swamp forest vegetation. On the larger islets, these depressions have usually been excavated and enlarged for the cultivation of *Cyrtosperma chamissonis* (swamp taro) and *Colocasia esculenta* (taro). Some depressions may be saline and consequently contain mangroves.

6. Halophytic forest on lagoon shore beaches. Mangroves, including *Bruguiera gymnorhyza* and *Rhizophora* spp., sometimes form small stands fringing lagoon shores.

On smaller *motu* this zonation is often reduced or absent. The vegetation then is composed only of low-lying shrubs,

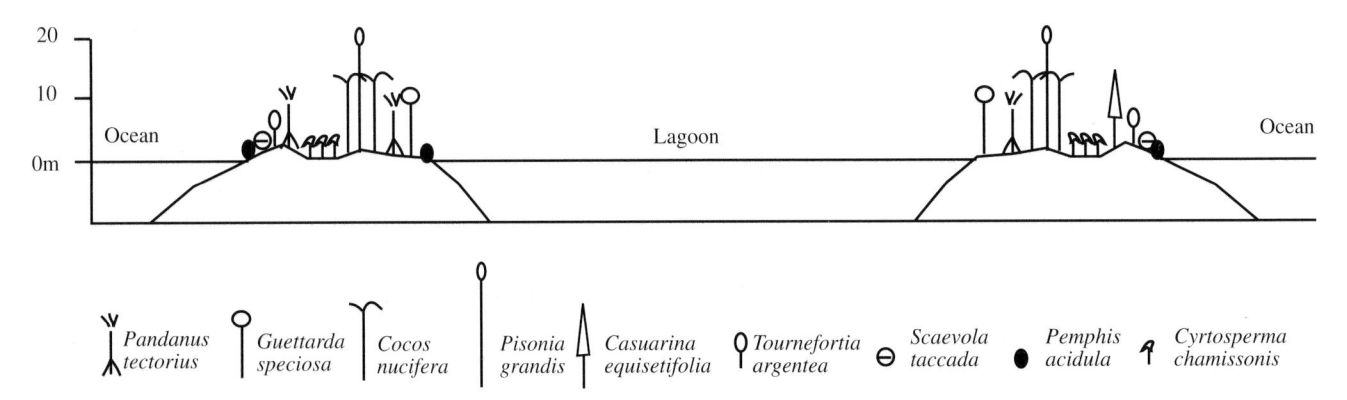

*Figure 8.2. Profile diagram of vegetation on a coral atoll, showing depressions used for growing Cyrtosperma chamisssonis.*

grasses, and sedges (Stoddart 1975). On dry atolls, even where large *motu* are present, the vegetation is likewise restricted and dominated by only a few salt-tolerant and drought-resistant species, often forming monospecific communities (Mueller-Dombois and Fosberg 1998). On Taongi Atoll in the Northern Marshall Islands, the forest and scrub vegetation is dominated by *Tournefortia argentea*. In the Phoenix Islands, pure stands of *Cordia subcordata* can be found (Hatheway 1955). In moister atolls of the Southern Marshall Islands, *Pisonia grandis* grows in species-pure dense stands, in association with guano (Hatheway 1953). These stands of *Pisonia* were formerly widespread features of atolls. Their mono-dominance as forest species may be related to the harsh, salty atoll environment and the very small total number of plant species available, as well as to their dispersal by sea birds. *Pisonia* fruits are sticky and become attached to birds' feathers and feet.

Rainfall has a pronounced effect on species numbers in atoll ecosystems. For example, Canton Island in the Phoenix group, with only 500 mm of rainfall, supports only 14 species of vascular plants, while Arno Atoll in the central Marshalls, with over 4,000 mm, supports about ten times as many (Wiens 1962).

## Mangroves

Mangrove ecosystems are a naturally occurring group of taxonomically unrelated trees and shrubs that grow in the tidal zones of wind-protected deltas, estuaries, and other muddy seashores of the tropics (Ellison 1991). Mangroves are obligatory halophytes and exist only in habitats that are periodically inundated by seawater (Figure 8.3). They are best developed on leeward and protected coastlines and are virtually absent from wind-exposed sandy coasts and headlands where there is an active surf (Hosokawa et al. 1977). The distribution of mangrove species is influenced by a number of factors. They include frequency and duration of seawater flooding, consistency of the soil, the degree of fresh water at river mouths, and the concentration of brackish water (Walter 1971). At the seaward edge, mangroves are represented by very few species, in many cases by only one species. Inland, where fresh water dominates, the variety is greater, but only in areas of high species diversity.

Mangrove species can be divided into two major centers of diversity with little overlap: a western hemispheric group consisting of eight species, and an eastern hemispheric group of 40 species (Tomlinson 1986). Almost all mangrove species in the Pacific Islands belong to the eastern hemispheric group, with a center of diversity between 135°E and 150°E. Mangrove ecosystems are best developed in the western Pacific islands of Palau, Papua New Guinea, and Solomon Islands, and least developed in Polynesia, with Samoa (four species) representing its easternmost extension (Tomlinson 1986, Woodroffe 1987). One species is found as far north as southern Kyushu (31M N) in Japan (Hosokawa, et al. 1977) and as far south as Victoria, Australia, at 38°S latitude (Tomlinson 1986). Likewise, the only mangrove species in New Zealand, *Avicennia resinifera*, extends as far south as 38° (Wardle 1991). *Rhizopora mangle*, from Central America, has a disjunct distribution in the Pacific. Ellison (1991)

*Figure 8.3.* Mangrove forest of Bruguiera gymnorrhiza *in a "mangrove depression" on Puluwat Atoll (photo HIM).*

has suggested that the distribution pattern of *R. mangle* is the result of subsidence of atolls in the central and eastern Pacific, which causes local extinctions.

In Pohnpei, a mangrove species (*Gynotroches axillaris*) is, surprisingly, found growing at 700-m elevation near the dwarf cloud forest on Mt. Nanalaud. Mangrove ecosystems also occur in the Central and Eastern Caroline atolls. In the Marshall Islands, mangrove species can be found in clear water in what has been called "mangrove depressions" (Fosberg 1947). These depressions, some of which are abandoned taro pits (Fosberg 1960:13), are rock lined and relatively mud free. Similar kinds of mangrove depressions can be found in Nauru and Puluwat Atoll. Elsewhere in the Caroline Islands, small areas of mangroves grow in sheltered lagoonal areas on Losap, Mokil, Woleai, and Western Kiribati.

The soils of mangrove ecosystems are often soft, muddy, shallow, anaerobic, acid sulfate clays. In order to survive in such soils, mangrove trees have specialized root systems. These include aerial roots, prop roots, buttress roots, and pneumatophores (breathing roots), root structures that allow for the exchange of gaseous oxygen. These root systems are also effective sediment and litter traps that allow for the succession of mangroves farther offshore and high rates of biological productivity. Mangrove ecosystems also provide protection of coastlines and shore areas from wind and wave action. They are critical habitats for larval and juvenile fishes, crabs, and other faunistic life-forms.

Natural mangrove sites in the Western Pacific have become increasingly endangered by coastal and urban development. Conversely, mangrove species were introduced into Hawai'i for sediment control in 1902, but are now considered pests, displacing native coastal biota in several sheltered lagoon areas.

## Freshwater Wetlands

Marshes and swamps are freshwater wetlands, where the water table fluctuates near or above the land surface, or where the soil surface is permanently saturated (Figure 8.4). Marshes can be considered early successional stages dominated by

*Figure 8.4. Nipa palm (Nypa fruitcans), Talafofo River, Guam. The leaves of the nipa palm were once used for thatch. This mangrove species grows typically at the fresh water end of the brackish- to fresh water gradient in estuaries. Nipa palm was introduced from the Philippine Islands but is naturalized in some rivers on the southeastern side of the island (photo HIM).*

herbaceous vegetation. Under natural conditions marshes can develop into swamps (freshwater wetlands with forest development). Since these ecosystems are associated with impeded drainage, they occur in depressions or low-lying areas adjacent to rivers and streams, at the edges of lakes and volcanic craters, and in coastal lowlands where the sediment accumulation impedes the flow of fresh water to the ocean. Typical tree cover includes *Barringtonia asiatica* and *Hibiscus tiliaceus* (Stemmermann 1981). Wetlands can also form in locations where artesian springs break the land surface.

Because they are important habitats for waterfowl, such wetlands are now often protected from development, but they have been much modified by human settlement. Pacific Islanders have traditionally used many of these wetlands for the cultivation of *Colocasia esculenta* and *Cyrtosperma chamissonis*, converting entire watershed basins for this purpose. Thus in Hawai'i, few wetlands remained in a pristine form by the time of European contact. Colonial settlement brought further changes, as streams were intensively channeled with concrete plumes and low-lying coastal wetlands were permanently drained to accommodate expansion of coastal and urban settlement.

There are many types of freshwater swamp ecosystems. Fosberg (1960) lists several types of grass and sedge marshes in Micronesia, the most prominent of which is the tall cane-like grass *Phragmites karka*. This species, along with *Saccharum spontaneum*, forms extensive grasslands along the intermittently flooded lowlands of Papua New Guinea. It is found between sea level and 2000-m elevation but is less extensively distributed in the other islands of Melanesia. These swampy grasslands occur in poorly drained areas and are maintained by periodic fires. One of the interesting grass species is *Leersia hexandra*, the principal component of "floating islands" in Papua New Guinea rivers and lakes (Leach and Osborne 1985).

The *Metroxylon sago* palm swamp forest is exploited for starch by coastal and riverine peoples in Papua New Guinea, Vanuatu, and Solomon Islands. In Solomon Islands and Fiji, related species are *M. salomonense* and *M. vitiense*, respectively. In Papua New Guinea, sago starch is an important item of barter between sago producers and fisherfolk from the coast and offshore islands (Lea and Irwin 1967). While these palm swamp forests are natural in origin, many are tended, in the sense that trees and the undergrowth are weeded, and individual trees are transplanted. Another related species is *Metroxylon amicarum*, the ivory nut palm. In the high islands of Pohnpei and Kosrae are small patches of these palms within the rain forest. Also notable are peat swamps dominated by *Pandanus* spp. in Fiji and Papua New Guinea, and niaouli (*Melaleuca quinquenervia*) swamps and wetland savannas in New Caledonia.

## Lowland Rain Forests

Primary rain forest was originally the principal lowland ecosystem landward of the strand on most Pacific high islands (Figure 8.5). Lowland rain forests are generally found on the

*Figure 8.5. Tropical rain forest at 300 m on Viti Levu, Fiji. These forests are species rich and contain many endemic plants (photo HIM).*

windward sides of islands where the monthly rainfall exceeds 100 mm and there is no deficiency in soil moisture. In many Pacific islands, these primary forests have been replaced by secondary forests, scrub, savannas, and urban development. However, significant stands of tall, majestic rain forest still remain in the lowlands of Papua New Guinea and Solomon Islands, due to the more extensive areas covered and (with the presence of malaria) relatively sparse populations.

Latitude and elevation are also important in the distribution of rain forests. At low latitudes in the equatorial tropics (0°–10° latitude), the tropical lowland rain forest may range from sea level to 1000 m. In the subequatorial tropics (10°–23° latitude), lowland rain forests are usually restricted to lower elevations (below 600 m) and the windward side of islands (Brookfield with Hart 1971). Lowland rain forests in the Hawaiian Islands (20°N) are likewise restricted to elevations below 600 m (Mueller-Dombois and Bridges 1981). At the fringes of the tropical belt, subtropical rain forests can be found in the Bonins, Lord Howe, Norfolk Island, and the Kermadecs (Mueller-Dombois and Fosberg 1998).

Primary lowland rain forests are typically multilayered, have closed canopies, and are composed mainly of broadleafed evergreen trees (Figure 8.6). Exceptions are found in Eastern

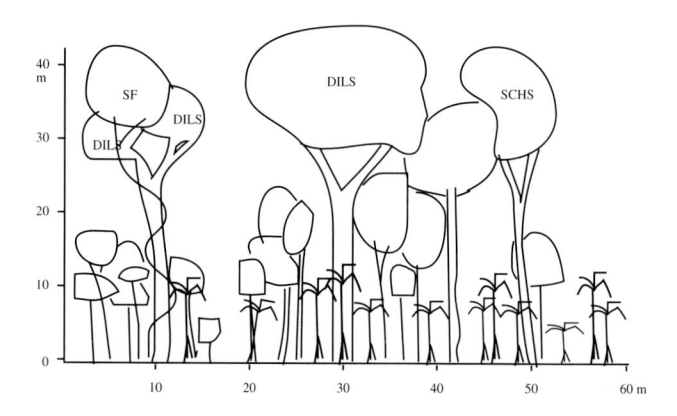

*Figure 8.6. Profile diagram for a diverse, mixed-species lowland rain forest in Kolombangara, Solomon Islands, dominated by the shade bearers Dillenia salomonensis (DILS) and Schizomeria serata (SCHS), and including a strangling fig (SF) and the palm Physokenta insolita (after Whitmore 1974).*

Melanesia (Vanuatu, Fiji, New Caledonia) and on Norfolk Island, where southern hemisphere conifers (mostly araucariads and podocarps) are prominent members of tropical and subtropical lowland rain forests. Additional life-forms of the tropical rain forest are epiphytic ferns and orchids; tall, herbaceous monocots (bananas, gingers); lianas (woody vines); and tall trees with plank buttresses and aerial roots. A groundcover may be absent because most sunlight is intercepted by the tree canopy. The tallest trees exceed 37 m in height (Lea and Irwin 1967, Brookfield with Hart 1971). Rates of organic matter decomposition and nutrient cycling are rapid because of high temperatures and humidities. Tropical rain forests are one of the world's most productive ecosystems because of their almost year-round growth activity. The total above-ground plant biomass in a lowland tropical rain forest can be over 400 metric tons per hectare (Whittaker 1975).

Lowland rain forests are rich in species composition. It is not uncommon to find between 80 and 100 species of trees/hectare in a tropical lowland rain forest (Brookfield with Hart 1971). The richness of tree species in such a diverse forest usually leaves room for only a few individuals of a particular species per unit area. On tropical islands, the lowland rain forest is less diverse in plant and animal life-forms and species relative to the continental tropics and often has smaller-sized populations, but more individuals per species may be accommodated on a given area.

## Montane Rain Forests

With increasing altitude, the tropical lowland rain forest gives way to a simpler structured, less speciose, montane rain forest. Upland species gradually replace lowland forest species. Trees with buttresses disappear, and tree ferns often become dominant in the undergrowth. At these high elevations, orographically uplifted air cools to the condensation point, resulting in cloudiness and frequent, heavy rainfall. Solar radiation is reduced as a consequence. These forests, rich in endemics, are found at elevations varying from 600–2,000 m on most high islands. Certain tree families, such as Myrtaceae (myrtle family), Rubiaceae (coffee family), and Rutaceae (citrus family), are usually well represented.

In New Guinea, montane forest consists of two main types: mixed broadleaved forests, some with tall emerged araucariads; and monodominant forests of southern hemisphere oaks (*Castanopsis*), beech (*Nothofagus*), pines (*Araucaria*), or podocarps. The upper canopy of the broadleaf forests can reach 30 m; that of the conifer forests can be twice that height. In Fiji, Vanuatu, and New Caledonia, conifers—particularly *Araucaria* species—are important forest components; *Agathis* and *Podocarpus* spp. are present as well. *Nothofagus* forests occur in Papua New Guinea, New Zealand, and New Caledonia.

A subtype of montane rain forest is the cloud forest (Hamilton et al. 1995). Clouds moving as fog near ground and through the canopy of such forests precipitate on leaves, branches, and all cooled surfaces including the epiphytes, which serve as condensation surfaces. The resulting drip adds considerable quantities of water to the root system. Soils under cloud forests are often waterlogged or boggy. The vegetation is then characterized by short, gnarled, or stunted trees covered with mosses, liverworts, ferns, and orchids (Figure 8.7). However, on very porous substrates, such as on young volcanic islands, cloud forest trees may be as tall as those in less cloud-frequented areas.

In Papua New Guinea montane rain forest is generally found near and above 2,000 m, as the landmass of this large island results in an upward shift of ecological zonation (also called the *Massenerhebung's* effect). In contrast, on other, smaller high islands in the tropical Pacific, montane rain forest occurs at lower elevations, usually above 500 m. In Pohnpei, montane rain forest starts below 700 m. Small areas of this forest type are also found on Kolombangara, Solomon Islands, at 300–400 m

*Figure 8.7.* Boggy cloud forest at 700 m, Pohnpei. Most trees are stunted, standing only 3 m tall because of high cloud cover and saturated soil. The endemic palm Clinostigma ponapensis is shown here as one of the few tall-growing trees (photo HIM).

(Brookfield with Hart 1971). On Oʻahu these forests occur upward of 460-m elevation, depending on their topographic position relative to cloud frequency (Ripperton and Hosaka 1942). Gagné and Cuddihy (1990) report that they found cloud forests at 1,200–2,000-m elevation on Maui, Molokaʻi and Hawaiʻi.

Bogs may also occur in these cool and moist montane forests. They occur in areas of impeded drainage, generally on flat to gently sloping topography underlain by impervious substrates. These bogs are generally highly oligotrophic (nutrient poor, oxygen starved, and acidic). The accumulation of humus and peat from dead biotic material is often considerable, because of the slow rates of organic decomposition. Bog vegetation is dominated by hummock-forming grasses, sedges (especially *Oreobolus* spp.), and ferns. Shrubs and even stunted trees may also be present, particularly in drier areas. Many of the species in these bogs are endemics. Specialized species found in the montane bogs of Hawaiʻi include dwarf *Metrosideros*, bog greensword (*Argyroxiphium* spp.), *Cheirodendron* spp., and various lobelias (Campanulaceae spp.)

Due to the rugged prevailing conditions, montane forests have experienced less modification than adjacent lowland areas in most parts of the Pacific and provide refugia for many native biota no longer present elsewhere. With the notable exception of highland valleys in Papua New Guinea (densely populated and intensely cultivated for millennia), montane habitats experienced relatively minimal disturbance by indigenous Pacific Islanders. Following European settlement, montane forest has become increasingly displaced by forest clearance, conversion to pasture, and the introduction of species such as guava (*Psidium cattleianum*), exotic birds (displacing pollinators of endemic plants), and European pigs (with a greater tendency to establish feral populations, as compared with indigenous pre-European introductions).

## Leeward Ecosystems

On the leeward sides of high islands in the trade wind zones, rainfall is much reduced because of the rainshadow effect (Figure 8.8). Compressional warming of winds downslope can

*Figure 8.8.* Dry, leeward scrub on Oʻahu, Hawaiʻi. Valley and upper slopes in the background are enclosed in cloud (photo MR).

produce an additional desiccation effect. A wide range of community types has been noted for leeward areas, including dry forests, shrublands, and grasslands (Gagné and Cuddihy 1990). These dry seasonal forests usually have open canopies and contain species that can tolerate several months of drought. Trees and shrubs in such ecosystems are usually scattered in savanna-like formations, but sometimes form thickets. The height of the canopy is lower than that of forests at comparable elevations on the windward side. In Hawaiʻi, remnant dry forests are quite rich, containing at least 30 tree species, adapted to drought through small leaves (as in *Diospyros* and *Santalum* spp.) or deciduous habit (such as *Erythrina sandwicensis*) (Mueller-Dombois and Fosberg 1998). However, most of the natural vegetation on leeward coasts and lower mountain slopes has been destroyed by clearance, conversion to agriculture and pasture, and introduced herbivores, and the land is currently covered by introduced grasses, shrubs, and trees.

## Secondary Forests

Secondary forests and related biota are found in most parts of Oceania where disturbed indigenous forests have been allowed to regenerate after removal of frequent perturbations (Figure 8.9). This process of secondary forest development may be defined as a succession involving mostly fast-growing, short-lived trees that invade following a disturbance of a large area when rainfall is adquate and soil nutrient conditions are still favorable for tree growth and forest formation. Secondary forests follow abandoned farmlands, waste places, logged forests, and areas of shifting cultivation whenever fallow lengths (resting times) are long enough to allow for the return of forest (Clarke 1967, Manner 1981, Fosberg 1960). Secondary forests are thus successional stages that have not yet advanced to primary

**Figure 8.9.** *Secondary forest in a Micronesian rain forest gap. Identifiable components are the kochop palm (Clinostigma ponapensis) and tree ferns. The gap is dominated by heliophytes (photo HIM).*

forest redevelopment. Notably absent are the shade-adapted trees (sciophytes) that characterize primary forests.

For much of Melanesia, where former garden sites are abandoned to fallow for six years or more, the succeeding vegetation is a secondary forest (Manner 1981). If population pressure on land results in shorter fallow, or if areas under fallow are subjected to fire, the succession is curtailed to a bush fallow. With more frequent disturbance by fire, an anthropogenic grassland will follow, even in rain forest environments (Mueller-Dombois 1981a). In the northern limestone plateau of Guam, secondary vegetation consists mainly of shrubs because of short fallow periods, which interrupt the forest succession. Also in Guam, *Leucaena leucocephala* has formed persistent low-stature forests on slopes underlain by limestone. This provides a prominent example of a formerly mixed species habitat reoccupied by an aggressive species, with a tendency to form monodominant stands.

In contrast to primary forest formation, the development of secondary forests is quite rapid. Secondary forests can reach a height of 12 m in three years because of favorable light conditions and their very soft wood (Walter 1971). Unlike primary successions, where species turnovers are often associated with modifications of soils and microclimate (Whittaker 1975), secondary succession is driven more strongly by differential rates of growth and survival of the mostly shade-intolerant pioneer species (Manner 1981). Secondary forest tree species are shorter lived, and the height of the canopy they form is typically lower and less variable than that of the primary forest. Often, the leaves of secondary forest species are lighter in color than those of primary forest species.

The early stages of secondary succession are characterized by an abundance of weedy annuals, grasses, ferns, and shrubs, as well as vines (e.g. *Merremia* spp. in Melanesia), many of which are heliophytes (sun-loving species). As succession proceeds, the fast-growing secondary trees are displaced by the more shade-tolerant species. Eventually, the secondary forest species give way to the longer-lived and taller primary forest species. However, frequent perturbations (including forest clearance and introduction of such species as *Passiflora mollissima* in Hawai'i,

*Miconia calvescens* in Tahiti, as well as feral fauna) can easily shift the balance between these two broad ecological groups of species.

## Savannas, Grasslands, and Shrublands

In Pacific islands with volcanic soils, fern and grass savannas occupy extensive areas in both humid tropical rain forest and seasonally drier climates (Figure 8.10). Savannas in the arid areas of the southern coast of Papua New Guinea and those on the flooded lower reaches of the Snake, Markham, and Sepik rivers (Brookfield with Hart 1971, Haantjens et al. 1965) are believed to be natural in origin. By contrast, in many areas where slash-and-burn agriculture is practiced, there is evidence that repeated human-set fires are responsible for arresting vegetation recovery in the savanna stage (Clarke 1966, Street 1966, Nunn 1994). The

**Figure 8.10.** *Savanna and ravine forest with coconuts, in southern Guam. These savannas are frequently burned, and as a result, these ravine forests have been greatly reduced in area. Remnant ravine forests have been increasingly displaced by coconuts, breadfruit, and other cultivated species (photo HIM).*

conversion of forest to savanna ecosystems is accompanied by a sharp drop in biological diversity. Soils under anthropogenic savannas are chemically and physically degraded forest soils (Street 1966, Brookfield with Hart 1971, Manner 1981).

There are many types of savannas in the Pacific found under a wide range of climates and edaphic conditions. In New Caledonia, the niaouli (*Melaleuca quinquenervia*), or paperbark tree, savanna is very extensive in its distribution throughout the leeward lowlands (Gillison 1983). In the dry, hot savannas of southern Papua New Guinea, woody species display adaptations to fire and drought. These adaptations include small- to medium-sized trees with root suckering; thickened and waxy cuticles; seed adapted to fire or heat shock; thick and deeply fissured bark; or highly inflammable bark consisting of paper-thin laminations (which serve to clear old growth and promote reproduction). On the floodplains of the Ramu, Snake, and Sepik rivers, there are tall grasslands of many species. A unique savanna is found in the Markham and Ramu floodplains, where *Cycas media* is the arboreal component. These fire-adapted tree savannas and low-lying flood plain savannas appear to be of natural origins.

Some savannas previously thought to be anthropogenic may also be natural. Recent palynological evidence in Fiji suggests that the *talasiqa* savannas on the leeward sides of Viti Levu, Vanua Levu, and Lakeba Island predated the arrivals of humans (Latham 1983). Zan and Hunter-Anderson (1987), citing the presence of endemic plant species in Micronesian savannas, suggest that these may have originated during a period of aridity predating the arrival of humans. However, there is evidence that human-set fires are responsible for the maintenance and spread of the Micronesian savannas. The presence of endemic species does not preclude an anthropogenic origin, as these endemics may have invaded the savannas after they were formed (Fosberg 1960). When protected from fire, such savannas are usually invaded by a secondary growth of trees, often by ironwood trees (*Casuarina equisetifolia*) as the first pioneers (Mueller-Dombois and Fosberg 1998).

## High-Altitude Ecosystems

High-altitude ecosystems are found at elevations above the inversion layer in Papua New Guinea, Hawai'i, and Maui. Above the inversion layer, usually coinciding with the orographically formed upper cloud layers, precipitation decreases and the air becomes progressively drier and cooler (Figure 8.11).

In Hawai'i, inversion may occur beween 1,200–2,000 m, depending on slope position relative to the incoming trade

*Figure 8.11. Alpine desert in the crater of Haleakalā, Maui. At between 2500–3000 m, this area lies above the inversion layer and is the habitat of the endemic silversword (Argyroxiphium sandwicense) (photo HIM).*

winds. Where the inversion occurs near the lower level of 1,200 m, and where the trade winds have already lost some of their moisture on the wet slopes, mesophytic (moderately wet) mountain parkland can be encountered (Color Plate 8a). These are typically characterized by *Acacia koa* tree colonies in a matrix or grassland and scrub. At higher elevations, another legume tree, *Sophora chrysophylla*, often along with *Myosporum sandwicensis*, becomes more common. At 2,000 m, mountain parkland merges with subalpine vegetation, characterized by tussock grasses (such as *Deschampsia*, with a tufted growth form, usually golden-yellow in color), scattered *Sophora*, and shrubs.

On Mauna Loa, in Hawai'i Volcanoes National Park, Mueller-Dombois and Bridges (1981) identified the following successive upslope ecosystems: a subalpine open *Metrosideros* scrub forest with scattered trees (2,040 to 2,380 m); a treeline of open *Metrosideros* scrub with scattered trees (up to 2,590 m); an alpine scrub desert dominated by the heath shrubs *Vaccinium* and *Styphelia,* (up to 3,080 m); a *Rhacomitrium* moss desert (up to 3,350 m); and above that a lava stone desert up to the summit at 4,208 m. The summit area is often covered with snow during several winter months.

In Papua New Guinea, which lies within 10° of the equator, subalpine vegetation occurs at higher elevations (3,500–4,000 m). Tussock grasslands can be found at high-elevation intermontane basins and valleys in Papua New Guinea, notably in areas of waterlogged soils (Smith 1975). Such tussocks are interspersed with patches of small trees and shrubs. Also present at these high elevations are savannas with scattered tree ferns, and grasslands dominated by bamboos. Above 4,100 m, woody shubs become increasingly scarce, and short grasses predominate. A tundra zone is reached at about 4,300 m, characterized by a sparse growth of lichens, mosses, and hardy grasses.

Because of their cold climate, remote location, and lack of suitability for agriculture or pasture development, high-altitude ecosystems have been less affected by human perturbation, much more so than montane forests. However, in spite of this protection, displacement by introduced biota poses an important potential threat to native species.

## High-Latitude Ecosystems

New Zealand, in southern Polynesia, represents the most isolated continental island group in the Pacific. In aggregate size, New Zealand is comparable to New Guinea. It represents an ancient fragment of the former Gondwana continent and was historically always positioned at higher latitudes (the "Roaring Forties"), in a much cooler environment than elsewhere in the Pacific Islands region. New Zealand's landmass extends over 1,500 km through three latitudinal climatic zones: warm temperate (most of the North Island), cool temperate (southern half of the South Island), and central temperate (Wardle 1991). At the vertical scale, New Zealand has a range of altitudinal ecosystems comparable to that of the tropical high islands of New Guinea and Hawai'i, but with a biota adapted to the cooler climates.

Due to colder temperatures and lack of surrounding coral reefs, New Zealand's coastal ecosystems lack the characteristic plant assemblages so common in the tropical and subtropical Pacific Islands. However, a mangrove species (*Avicennia marina*) is found on the North Island, varying in size with latitude (ranging from 10 m high at the far north to less than a meter tall at the limits of its distribution, around 38°S). Extensive sand dunes exist inland of the coastal strand, anchored by the sedge *Desmoschoenus spiralis* and sand grass *Spinifex hirsutus*. On rocky beaches and cliffs, succulents are commonly found, adapted to conditions of salt spray. Farther inland, coastal forest begins, including *Metrosideros excelsa* and *M. umbellata*, varying in their distribution with latitude.

The western portions of both main islands lie in the path of the prevailing winds (westerlies), and annual precipitation exceeds 1,000 mm, increasing along a southward gradient. Lowlands in the warm-temperate zone contain many Malesian (Island Southeast Asian) rain forest elements. Central temperate lowlands have elements in common with the montane environment of the warm temperate zone on the North Island, including several *Nothofagus* species. Cool temperate lowlands in the south contain floristic elements of central subalpine zones, such as New Zealand's mountain beech (*N. solandri* var. *cliffortioides*) as well as heath and cushion shrubs. In the extreme south, alpine tussock grasses form the native lowland vegetation.

New Zealand is famous as the center of diversity for the southern hemisphere gymnosperm (conifer) family *Podocarpaceae*. Podocarp species once dominated lowland rain forests, though these have been reduced to remnants. The podocarps occur as towering emergents over lower canopies of angiosperm (flowering plant) hardwoods with tropical relationships. The angiosperm flora is diverse and includes several *Metrosideros* species (*M. excelsa*, *M. robusta*, and *M. umbellata*), roughly coinciding in their distribution with the three latitudinal temperate zones. A native palm (*Rhapalostylis sapida*) and several tree ferns (*Cyathea* spp.) occur in association with podocarp-angiosperm forests. Remnant stands of giant kauri (*Agathis australis*) still survive in the North Island, and pollen records indicate that various *Araucaria* spp. were also once present.

A great variety of wetlands occur in New Zealand. Swamps occur at many of New Zealand's lake margins, representing an ecotone (transitional zone) to dry land, and colonized by reeds (*Typha orientalis*), rushes and sedges, giving way with drier conditions to swamp flax (*Phormium tenax*), ferns, and ultimately tall *Polodcarpus dacrydioides* forest. On flat-topped mountains with poor drainage, bogs are found. Highly specialized plants grow under these harsh conditions, including sphagnum mosses, *Gunnera* spp., *Lycopodium* spp., sundews, and bladderworts (which rely on insects, rather than soil, for their nutrients), dwarfed *Leptospermum* scrub, and bog pine (*Dacrydium bidwillii*).

On the eastern (leeward) sides of New Zealand, rainfall is much reduced throughout the year (to less than 1,000 mm), with a summer low in the North Island. Under natural conditions, leeward slopes included forests, scrub, and tussock grasslands, but most of this had largely been converted to grasslands by the time of European arrival. The endemic low tussock *Poa colensoi* is now widespread throughout both islands due to its ability to withstand grazing pressure. One of the distinctive native species is the cabbage tree (*Cordyline australis*), which regenerates from underground corms even in disturbed landscapes. However, there have been recent reports of epidemic mortality of these trees (Simpson 1993).

Montane forests in New Zealand are dominated by various *Nothofagus* beech species, but scattered tall podocarps emerge above the canopy, particularly at lower levels. Relative to the remnant lowland forests, the montane forests are lower in stature and poorer in species. There are natural disjunctions in montane *Nothofagus* distributions, known as "beech gaps." Where habitat would otherwise be favorable, these gaps have been attributed to slow reinvasion of *Nothofagus* species following glaciation (McQueen 1992). Beech nuts are not eaten by birds and are too heavy for wind dispersal (Enting and Molloy 1992). New Zealand's montane forests are followed upward by a subalpine zone, characterized by a mosaic of mountain beech forest, scrub, and grasslands. Beyond the mountain beech treeline, an alpine zone begins, occupied in the lower potions by scattered heath shrubs, cushion plants, and high tussock grasses (including *Chionochloa* spp.). Wardle (1991) has recognized a "penalpine" zone, so named because northern hemisphere pines have penetrated upward of the native tree line. A similar situation exists now in the summit area of Santa Cruz Island in the Galápagos (Mueller-Dombois and Fosberg 1998). In the upper portion of the alpine zone only specialized biota survive, such as cushion plants (*Raoulia* spp. and others), adapted to severe climatic conditions through such features as small, leathery, silver-gray leaves and strong taproots.

Because of its age, large size, and many habitats, New Zealand is worthy of particular attention by those interested in Pacific Island ecosystem studies. However, a recent government report (1997) draws attention to the declining state of New Zealand's natural biota. According to the report, 85% of the lowland forests and wetlands have vanished since the 1200s, when the islands were first settled by Polynesians. An estimated thousand living species are threatened with extinction, including the kiwi bird, now a national icon. Of 93 birds known to have evolved and existed only in New Zealand 43 are now extinct and 37 are in danger of extinction, due to habitat modification and alien introductions.

For further discussion of New Zealand's terrestrial ecosystems, readers are referred to Enting and Molloy (1982), Gunson (1983), Fleet (1986), and Wardle (1991).

## Ultramafic Maquis

One of the most distinctive ecosystems in the Pacific Islands is the New Caledonian maquis, found in the southern massif, and a few smaller outcroppings of peridotite (exposed mantle rock) and serpentine (metamorphosed peridotite) on New Caledonia, comprising about a third of the island. The substrate rock and soils are poor in phosphorous, potassium, and calcium (normally necessary for plant survival and growth), but with relatively high concentrations of nickel, magnesium, chromium, cobalt, and other metals. This substrate was deposited in the early Tertiary, with the overthrusting of a thick layer of oceanic crust atop a distant fragment of Gondwana (Morat et al. 1981).

Over the course of the past 60 million years, a specialized biotic community has developed, capable of withstanding an edaphic (soil controlled) environment that is toxic to most plant biota (Figure 8.12). The maquis community is comprised of many ancient Gondwana relicts, which have adapted to the otherwise toxic substrate. Variations in rock and soil mineral composition and isolation of ultramafic fragments in distant parts of the island have led to an extraordinary degree of specia-

*Figure 8.12.* Agathis ovata *growing in ultramafic maquis, New Caledonia (photo DMD).*

tion: at least 1,031 species are native species (over half the total number of species in New Caledonia), 91% of which are endemic (Morat 1993).

The name "maquis" derives from certain apparent similarities with the Mediterranean maquis. New Caledonia maquis is found in a variety of climatic conditions, from sea level to the highest mountains (1,600 m), from less than 900 mm of rainfall annually to over 4 m. The typical vegetation is stunted trees (generally up to 2.5 m, though higher is some areas) with tough, waxy leaves, often sparsely grouped in rosettes at the end of branches, amidst a variety of sedges, ferns, and herbs, with emergent southern pines (*Araucaria* spp.) and kauris (*Agathis* spp.). The families Myrtaceae, Rutaceae, Rubiaceae, and Proteaceae are well represented. Spines, succulents, and grasses are absent (Jaffré 1980, Mueller-Dombois and Fosberg 1998).

Growth is remarkably slow in the New Caledonian maquis vegetation, an effect that persists to some extent even if the species are planted in a more fertile environment. There is an exuberant production of flowers, but seeds seldom make it to maturity due to slow growth, recurrent dry periods, and insect predation, and young plants are seldom seen in the maquis. Interestingly, even when a significant perturbation occurs, such as a forest fire, replacement by other species does not occur, apparently because very few other species can thrive given the high concentrations of heavy metals. Instead, the original community structure slowly reestablishes itself (Jaffré 1980).

## Recent Volcanic Ecosystems

Volcanic activity on the island of Hawai'i offers insights into the dynamics of primary succession (Figure 8.13). Every few years, new land surfaces are created by lava flows. In the process of flowing toward the sea, older flows and the vegetation on them are destroyed, while others are left intact, sometimes only in the form of pockets or *kīpukas* (islands of older vegetation) surrounded by more recent volcanic substrate and biota. Various studies conducted in *Metrosideros polymorpha*–dominated forests suggest that this primary successional process is quite predictable within the rain forest environment (Mueller-Dombois 1987).

The initial colonizers of new lava surfaces are blue-green algae. Then ferns and mosses assemble in the fissures. Four to five years later, the lava surfaces are covered by lichens, while *M.*

*Figure 8.13.* Lava flow with young, developing forest of Metrosideros polymorpha, *100 years old, near Kīlauea, Hawai'i Island (photo HIM).*

*polymorpha* seedlings begin to spread across the new lava flows. This stage is associated with invasion of mainly native pioneer shrubs, such as *Dubautia scabra* and *Vaccinium reticulatum*, and scattered tall ferns of *Sadleria cystheoides*. After 50–200 years, the clubmoss *Lycopodium cernuum* and the tall sedge *Machaerina angustifolia* may form a closed groundcover. During this time *Metrosideros* individuals develop from seedlings into saplings. Between 50 and 200 years of substrate age, the sapling stands may be from 3–8 m tall. After 150–250 years, there is a higher, denser canopy of *Metrosideros*, with an undergrowth of *Cibotium* tree ferns, native rain forest shrubs, and other subcanopy species (Mueller-Dombois 1987, Mueller-Dombois and Loope 1990).

This sequence of development is estimated to take as long as 400 years (Atkinson 1970) on lava flows, or 200–300 years on volcanic ash. It may be followed by a synchronous stand-level dieback of the senescing (advanced aging) *Metrosideros* canopy cohort. Dieback may then be triggered by a climatic instability, resulting in physiological shock (this affects even younger trees, but the latter survive, while the old ones succumb). *Metrosideros* then can be expected to regenerate into a new forest, as other native species are not able to become successional dominants. However, invasion by alien heliophytes is entirely possible at this stage if such alien pioneer species are in the neighborhood of dieback stands. In the 1930s, a forest dieback area on Maui Island was partly replanted with alien species for watershed protection. One of the planted species, *Melaleuca quinquenervia*, is actively invading the remaining area and spreading over partially recovered *Metrosideros* scrub on waterlogged ground (Mueller-Dombois 1987).

Other recent volcanic ecosystems in the Pacific Islands occur in the Northern Marianas, Tonga, Vanuatu, Papua New Guinea, New Zealand, and the Galápagos Islands (Mueller-Dombois and Fosberg 1998).

## Limestone Forest and Scrub

Raised limestone islands occur widely across the Pacific, the consequence of reef uplift and accretion at plate boundaries or volcanic loading by midplate islands. Some islands (Nauru) are formed entirely of limestone; in other locations (Mangaia), a limestone *makatea* wall surrounds a volcanic core. In a third variant (parts of Papua New Guinea), pockets of limestone exist on continental or volcanic substrates. The limestone substrate is porous, alkaline (pH 7.5 or above, compared to 6 or below for volcanic substrates), and usually with thin soils. In some areas, extensive solution by water has led to extensive dissection, leaving a rocky, pit-and-pinnacle topography known as karst (*feo* or *makatea* in Polynesia), with almost no soil. Enormous deposits of phosphate rock occur on raised limestone islands.

The vegetation on raised limestone islands may be considered a modified strand type, with transitional stages to a diverse, species-rich forest. In level areas with accumulated soils and adequate rainfall, and where elevation ensures minimal salinity, the forest resembles that of adjacent volcanic or continental islands, but often with many strand species or derivatives. In the southern Marianas, the genera *Ficus* (including banyans), *Pandanus*, *Artocarpus*, and many others are common, along with a scrubby undergrowth of smaller trees and shrubs, and (with adequate moisture) a thick epiphyte cover, especially ferns (*Aplenium nidus* and other species)(Mueller-Dombois and Fosberg 1998). In Micronesia, such limestone forests can still be found in the southern Marianas, the Palau Rock Islands, and Fais. Only remnants remain on Nauru and Banaba (Kiribati), both stripped during past phosphate mining.

Northern Guam, composed of raised limestone, contrasts sharply with volcanic southern Guam. Much of the limestone plateau (mostly a U.S. military base) is still wooded, with a mixture of *Artocarpus*, *Ficus*, *Pandanus*, and other species. In contrast, the southern, volcanic portion of the island is covered by a savanna dominated by tall swordgrass (*Miscanthus*), with forest remaining mainly in ravines and steep slopes. Elsewhere as well, savannas do not occur on elevated limestone islands. Two explanations have been suggested by Mueller-Dombois and Fosberg (1998): 1) volcanic soils are more easily invaded by grasses following fires and agricultural clearing; 2) volcanic terrain tends to be more hilly, and thus more subject to erosion and replacement by grasses.

Limestone forests in Melanesia are exceptionally diverse, probably a consequence of high rainfall, superimposed layers of volcanic ash, and proximity to biotic source areas. For example, the raised limestone island of Pio (off San Cristobal, in the Solomons) is covered by a tropical rain forest with emergents reaching 40 m high, with buttress and stilt roots, abundant lianas (vines) up to half a meter in diameter, epiphytic ferns, orchids, and strangler figs (Pernetta and Manner 1994). Similarly, vast karst areas in the Bismarcks and main island of Papua New Guinea are covered with the same mixed-species lowland rain forest present on adjacent volcanic and continental substrates, though in low-rainfall locales *Casuarina papuana* often dominates (Pajimans 1975).

Limestone forest on the Loyalty Islands and Isle de Pins contains many of the trees present on rain forests of the main island of New Caledonia (*Intsia*, *Albizia*, *Canarium*, and others), with a canopy reaching 20 m, including emergent banyans and *Araucaria columnaris* trees. However, other gymnosperms are absent, and the forest is less luxuriant in diversity relative to the main island.

Limestone forests on Tonga, enriched by a meter or more of volcanic ash deposits, are much degraded, but remnants still exist on some islands, with canopies of up to 30 m high, dominated by *Calophyllum neo-ebudicum*, *Elaeocarpus tonganus*, and a variety of other species (Drake et al. 1993). Inner portions of the *makatea* walls surrounding the Southern Cook Islands (Figure 8.14) contain low, species-rich forests, locally dominated by *Barringtonia asiatica*, *Pandanus tectorius*, and *Elaeocarpus tonganus*. Makatea, in the Tuamotus (devastated by phosphate mining), once had extensive limestone plateau forest composed of *Pandanus tectorius*, *Ficus prolixa*, *Guettarda speciosa*, *Pritchardia vuyltekeana* (an endemic palm), and other species. Farther east, on Henderson Island, a similar limestone forest still survives.

*Figure 8.14.* Limestone forest with *Casuarina* equisetifolia *and other species on the outer edge of the* makatea *of Atiu, Cook Islands, with an understory of* Scaevola *and* Pemphis *(photo MR).*

## Fauna in Ecosystems

Because of their mobility, many animal species range widely across different ecosystems. Moreover, zoogeographical syntheses are lacking for the Pacific Islands as a whole. However, some preliminary generalizations will be offered, primarily concerning birds and mammals. In most cases, birds are the most visible faunal element of the region's terrestrial ecosystems. As with plants, distributions drop sharply with distance from New Guinea. Mammals are limited almost entirely to New Guinea and (to a much lesser extent) some former land-bridge islands. In the more distant Pacific, terrestrial mammals are represented only by bats (rats are thought to have been introduced by humans).

A variety of seabirds frequent strand and atoll ecosystems, particularly in areas where human disturbance is minimal and where natural vegetation is relatively intact. Many species spend most of their life in the open sea, visiting land only when nesting. Other seabirds, such as fairy terns, noddies, frigatebirds, and tropicbirds, prefer more sheltered waters for feeding and are often found along some shore areas. A wide variety of migrating shorebirds, or waders (plovers, sandpipers, and other species) is found in the Pacific, often arriving suddenly after storms (Pratt, Bruner, and Berrett 1985).

Mangroves attract large populations of some birds, for example, the cicadabird and the mangrove flycatcher. Some birds, like the Fiji population of little heron, are virtually restricted to mangroves. There are freshwater wetlands in the coastal lowlands of most Pacific islands with dependent birds highly vulnerable to ecosystems disturbance. Today some of the most significant wetlands in the Pacific are man-modified ponds (including taro pondfields) and reservoirs. These habitats are essential for the survival of ducks, coots, gallinules, stilts, herons, and other species.

Grasslands and savannas provide an important habitat for native birds (for example, rails, hawks, and owls) and mammals (wallabies, spiny anteaters, and rodents in southern New Guinea). Such habitats have become increasingly disturbed; thus exotic birds (such as skylarks and meadowlarks) often predominate. However, some native species have adapted to exotic biota (such as the golden white-eye in *Leucaena* and *Algoroba* stands in Micronesia). A few native birds (such as the lesser golden plover) thrive even in city parks in the urban Pacific (Pratt, Bruner, and Berrett 1985). Similarly, some mammals (especially fruit-eating bats) exist and thrive even in disturbed habitats.

Lowland and montane forests are the most important habitat for Pacific Island landbirds. New Guinea, with its extensive area, diverse habitats, and proximity to continents, has an exceptionally rich assortment of forest birds (Beehler, Pratt, and Zimmerman 1986). The spectacularly colored bird of paradise and hut-constructing bower birds of New Guinea's rain forests have long served as models for evolutionary studies. Hawai'i's honeycreepers show remarkable adaptations to different forest habitats and feeding niches through changes in coloration and beak structure. Some birds appear to have coevolved with particular plant species and remain mutually interdependent.

Studies in New Guinea have shown that altitudinal zonation exists in many forest bird species (Figure 8.15). Fruit pigeons, crowned pigeons, several kingfisher genera, and certain lories, parrots, and birds of paradise species are found almost entirely in lowland forests; other species (some honeyeaters, astrapias, bowerbirds, and the six-wired birds of paradise, for

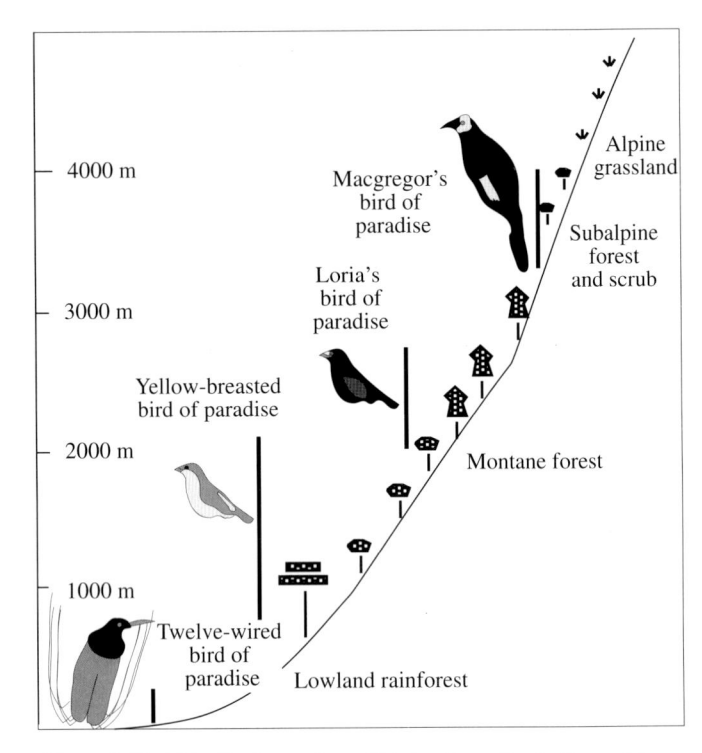

*Figure 8.15. Altitudinal zonation of birds of paradise in Papua New Guinea (after Keast 1996).*

example) are restricted to upland regions. Diversity begins to decline at high elevations (above 1,500 m in New Guinea) as a consequence of reduced land area, cooler temperatures, higher incidence of cloud and fog, lower plant productivity and diversity, and lower canopy height and structural diversity (Beehler, Pratt, and Zimmerman 1986).

The greatest diversity of native mammals occurs in New Guinea, particularly in its montane forests (Flannery 1995, 1995a). Mammals native to New Guinea include marsupials (kangaroos, cuscuses, bandicoots, possums, quolls, and related species), monotremes (spiny anteaters), and murids (rats and mice). Beyond the adjacent landbridge islands, bats (including frugivorous, nectivorous, and insectivorous species) are the only native mammalian fauna currently present. Most mammals (with the notable exception of murids, and bats in Hawai'i and New Zealand) are of Australian origins.

Monotremes evolved well before the time New Zealand and New Caledonia split off from Australia (around 80 Ma), but they became extinct in both areas soon afterward. In New Zealand, periodic underwater submergence apparently selected for species that can fly between islands. Birds thus become "the ecological equivalents of giraffes, kangaroos, sheep, striped possums, long-beaked echidnas and tigers" (Flannery 1995b), including 12 species of moa. The moa, in turn, may have selected for the divaricating growth habit of many New Zealand plants (where the plant exterior is protected by tough, leafless twigs).

Flannery (1995b) suggests that in New Caledonia the challenge was the toxic soils that developed after the oceanic overthrust (formerly more extensive in area), selecting for energy conservative species, such as reptiles. These then underwent an extraordinary adaptive radiation equivalent to that of birds in New Zealand. They included crocodiles, horned turtles, and goannas (relatives of the Komodo dragons). All of these (like most of the large birds of New Zealand) became extinct shortly after the arrival of human colonists. Today, New Caledonia's native reptile population consists solely of geckos and skinks.

## Summary and Conclusions

Figure 8.16 shows an idealized high island with its natural ecosystems in summary form. From the top down, they include high-altitude ecosystems (restricted to the tallest islands), followed by montane rain forest (present on most of the Pacific high islands), and lowland and coastal ecosystems (found even on islands less than 500 m in elevation). We would suggest, following Mueller-Dombois and Fosberg (1998), that altitudinal range (as a surrogate for climate) can be considered a key unifying principle in the study and classification of Pacific Island terrestrial ecosystems or biomes. Physiognomy, structure, and functions of distant islands are often remarkably alike in similar topographic/climatic zones, even though considerable variability exists at the local level.

We have shown that other natural controls also play important roles in shaping Pacific Island ecosystems, including proximity to the ocean, streamflow, and substrate (Table 8.1). These

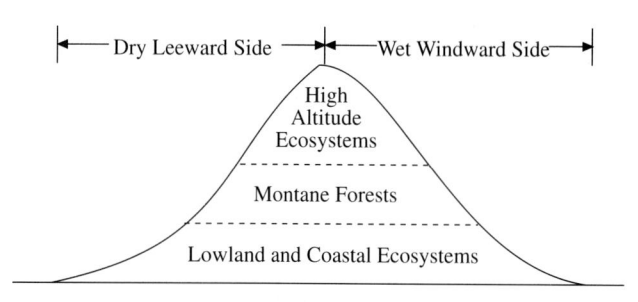

**Figure 8.16.** Ecosystem zonation in an idealized high island (after Mueller-Dombois and Bridges 1981).

controls exert their influence by specific stresses on component plant and animal biota. Thus, only salt-adapted species survive on coral atolls and high island coastal ecosystems. Mangrove, swamp, and bogs species must be adapted to prolonged immersion in standing water. A specialized suite of biota exists on recently cooled lava flows; and yet another highly specialized suite has evolved to withstand the toxic heavy metals present in ultramafic rock substrates.

Since their arrival, humans have made use of natural ecosystems in the Pacific Islands. Many ecosystems have been altered, some purposefully and irrevocably by exploitive practices, such as the release of mammalian herbivores (Cuddihy and Stone 1990, Stone et al. 1992). Most changes reflect a tragedy of the commons (Hardin 1968) and have occurred in the name of progress and civilization. New species are constantly being introduced into the islands, ostensibly to improve the quality of life for humans. In spite of efforts to control importation, pest organisms, such as the brown tree snake on Guam, are often accidentally introduced and become invasive. Aggressive alien

### TABLE 8.1

**Classification of Pacific Island Terrestrial Ecosystems**

| Control | Ecosystem type | Characteristic stress |
|---|---|---|
| Oceanic | Strand and atoll | Waves, salt spray, salt innudation |
|  | Mangroves | Tidal currents |
| Fluvial | Wetlands | Stream flow |
| Climatic/topographic | Lowland rain forests | Shade |
|  | Montane rain forests | Cold, relief, thin soils |
|  | Leeward ecosystems | Aridity |
|  | Secondary forest and scrub | Fire, degraded soils |
|  | Savannas | Fire, degraded soils |
|  | High altitude | Cold, wind |
|  | High latitude | Cold, seasonal changes |
| Edaphic | Ultramafic maquis | Toxicity |
|  | Recent volcanic ecosystems | Porosity, thin soils |
|  | Limestone forest and scrub | Porosity, alkalinity |

plant species with new strategies (such as seed dispersal by alien birds or feral pigs) may outcompete native key species, thereby disrupting natural ecosystems.

Active vegetation management has become a necessary task in these island ecosystems, where their natural maintenance mechanisms have been compromised. The success of controlling alien species through ecosystem management has varied, but there is guarded optimism (Stone et al. 1992). Ecosystem change will continue to rise as human populations increase and make further demands on the remaining natural ecosystem (Figures 8.17 and 8.18). However, not all the indigenous biota of the islands are weak competitors. In the absence of adverse human disturbances, there is a chance that many of the native species that are the key ecosystem builders may survive. Much depends on human attitudes, environmental policy, and adequate resource management.

*Figure 8.17.* Succession on phosphate-mined areas of Nauru Island. This site was mined during the 1950s. The successional development of vegetation is slow. The dominant shrub here (1981) was Scaevola taccada *(photo HIM)*.

We suggest that, for the purpose of biological conservation on islands, where humans determine the doom or survival of indigenous ecosystems to a much greater degree than elsewhere, research efforts with high conservation value be increased (Mueller-Dombois 1981b). Research results in knowledge and understanding. With this comes an awareness of the value of the naturally evolved biodiversity as a self-functioning resource in the dynamics of native ecosystems.

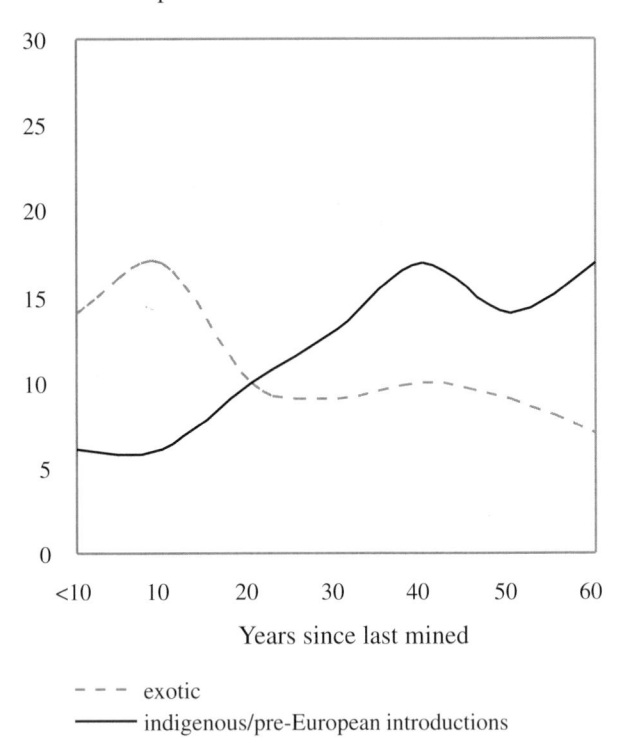

*Figure 8.18.* Successional changes following mining on Nauru (after Manner et al. 1985). The most important tree species in revegetated areas included Calophyllum inophyllum, Ficus prolixa, Morinda citrifolia, *and* Guettarda speciosa.

# Bibliography

Atkinson, I. A. E. 1970. Successional trends in the coastal and lowland forest of Mauna Loa and Kilauea volcanoes, Hawaii. *Pacific Science* 24:387–400.

Beehler, B. M., T. K. Pratt, and D. A. Zimmerman. 1986. *Birds of New Guinea*. Princeton: Princeton University Press.

Brookfield, H. C., with D. Hart. 1971. *Melanesia: a geographical interpretation of an island world*. London: Methuen.

Clarke, W. C. 1966. From extensive to intensive shifting cultivation: an example from central New Guinea. *Ethnology* 5:347–359.

Clarke, W. C. 1977. The structure of permanence: the relevance of subsistence communities for world ecosystem management. In *Subsistence and survival: rural ecology in the Pacific*, ed. T. Bayliss-Smith and R. Feachem, 364–384. London: Academic Press.

Cuddihy, L. W., and C. P. Stone. 1990. Alteration of native Hawaiian vegetation, effects of humans, their activities and introductions. Honolulu: Cooperative National Park Resources Studies Unit, University of Hawai'i.

Drake, D. R., W. A. Whistler, T. J. Motley, and C. T. Smeda. 1996. Rain forest vegetation of 'Eua Island, Kingdom of Tonga. *New Zealand Journal of Botany* 34: 65–77.

Ellison, J. C. 1991. The Pacific palaegeography of *Rhizophora mangle* L. (Rhizophoraceae). *Botanical Journal of the Linnean Society* 105:271–284.

Enting, B., and L. Molloy. 1982. *The ancient islands: New Zealand's natural environments*. Wellington: Port Nicholson Press.

Flannery, T. 1995. *Mammals of New Guinea*. Ithaca: Cornell University Press.

Flannery, T. 1995a. *Mammals of the south-west Pacific and Moluccan Islands*. Ithaca: Cornell University Press.

Flannery, T. 1995b. *The future eaters: an ecological history of the Australasian lands and people*. NY: Brazillier.

Fleet, H. 1986. *The concise natural history of New Zealand*. Singapore: Heinemann.

Fosberg, F. R. 1947. Micronesian mangroves. *Journal of the New York Botanical Garden* 48:128–138.

Fosberg, F. R. 1960. The vegetation of Micronesia. 1. General descriptions, the vegetation of the Marianas Islands, and a detailed consideration of the vegetation of Guam. *Bulletin of the American Museum of Natural History* 119 (1):1–76 and plates 1–40.

Fosberg, F. R. 1963. The island ecosystem. In *Man's place in the island ecosystem. a symposium*, ed. F. R. Fosberg 1–6. Tenth Pacific Science Congress, Honolulu (1961). Honolulu: Bishop Museum Press.

Gagné, W. L., and L. W. Cuddihy. 1990. Vegetation. In *Manual of the flowering plants of Hawaii*, ed. D. R. Wagner, et al., vol. 1, 45–114. Honolulu: Bishop Museum Press.

Gillison, A. N. 1983. Tropical savannas of Australia and the Southwest Pacific. In *Ecosystems of the world*. Vol. 13, *Tropical savannas*, ed. F. Bourliere, 183–243. Amsterdam: Elsevier Scientific Publishing Co.

Government of New Zealand. 1997. *State of New Zealand's environment 1997*. Wellington: Government Printing Office.

Gunson, D. 1983. *Collins guide to the New Zealand seashore*. Auckland: Collins.

Haantjens, H. A., J. A. Mabbutt, and R. Pullen. 1965. Environmental influences in anthropogenic grasslands in the Sepik plains, New Guinea. *Pacific Viewpoint* 6: 215–219.

Hamilton, L. S., J. O. Juvik, and P. N. Scatena, eds. 1995. *Tropical montane cloud forests*. Ecological Studies Series, vol. 110. NY: Springer-Verlag.

Hardin, G. 1968. The tragedy of the commons. *Science* 162: 1243–1248.

Hatheway, W. H. 1953. The land vegetation of Arno Atoll, Marshall Islands. *Atoll Research Bulletin* 16:1–68.

Hatheway, W. H. 1955. The natural vegetation of Canton Island, an Equatorial Pacific atoll. *Atoll Research Bulletin* 43:1–8.

Hosokawa, T., H. Tagawa, and V. J. Chapman. 1977. Mangals of Micronesia, Taiwan, Japan, the Philippines and Oceania. In *Wet coastal ecosystems*, ed. V. J. Chapman, 271–291. Amsterdam: Elsevier Scientific Publishing Co.

Jaffré, T. 1980. *Etude écologique du peuplement végétal des sols dérivés de roches ultrabasiques en Nouvelle-Calédonie*. Paris: ORSTOM.

Keast, A. 1996. Avian geography: New Guinea to the eastern Pacific. In *The origin and evolution of Pacific Island biotas, New Guinea to Eastern Polynesia: patterns and processes*, ed. A. Keast and S. E. Miller, 373–398. Amsterdam: SPB Academic Publishing Company.

Latham, M. 1983. Origin of the talasiga formation. In *The eastern islands of Fiji: a study of the natural environment, its use and man's influence on its evolution*, eds. M. Latham and H. C. Brookfield, 129–141. General Report No 3, UNESCO/UNFPA Man and the Biosphere Project. Paris: ORSTOM.

Lea, D. A. M., and P. G. Irwin. 1967. *New Guinea; the territory and its people*. Melbourne: Oxford University Press.

Leach, G. J., and P. L. Osborne. 1985. *Freshwater plants of Papua New Guinea*. Port Moresby: University of Papua New Guinea Press.

Manner, H. I. 1981. Ecological succession in new and old swiddens of montane Papua New Guinea. *Human Ecology* 9(3):359–377.

Manner, H. I., R. R. Thaman, and D. C. Hassall. 1985. Plant succession after phosphate mining on Nauru. *Australian Geographer* 17:185–195.

McQueen, D. R. 1992. Disjunction of tree species in mountain forests, southern North Island, New Zealand: a review of paleobotanical evidence. *Pacific Science* 4b:269–75.

Morat, P., T. Jaffré, J. M Veillon, and H. S. MacKee. 1981. Végétation. Atlas de la Nouvelle-Calédonie, 28. Paris: ORSTOM.

Morat, P. 1993. Our knowledge of the flora of New Caledonia: endemism and diversity in relation to vegetation types and substrates. *Biodiversity Letters* 1:72–81.

Mueller-Dombois, D. 1981a. Fire in tropical ecosystems. In *Fire regimes and ecological properties*, ed. H. A. Mooney, T. M. Bonnickson, N. L. Christensen, I. E. Lotan, and W. A. Reiners. USDA Forest Service General Technical Report WO–2b, 137–176.

Mueller-Dombois, D. 1981b. Understanding Hawaiian forest ecosystems: the key to biological conservation. In *Island ecosystems: biological organization in selected Hawaiian communities*, ed. D. Mueller-Dombois, K. W. Bridges, and H. L. Carson, 502–520. US/IBP Synthesis Series 15. Stroudsberg, Pennsylvania: Hutchinson Ross Publishing Company.

Mueller-Dombois, D. 1987. Forest dynamics in Hawaii. *Trends in Ecology and Evolution* 2(7):216–220.

Mueller-Dombois, D. 1992. The formation of island ecosystems. *Geojournal* 28(2):293–296.

Mueller-Dombois, D. 1994. Island vegetation of the tropical Pacific: a survey of small areas in a large area. *Colloques Phytosociologiques* 23:103–114.

Mueller-Dombois, D., and K. W. Bridges. 1981. Introduction. In *Island ecosystems: biological organization in selected Hawaiian communities*, ed. D. Mueller-Dombois, K. W. Bridges, and H. L. Carson, 35–76. US/IBP Synthesis Series 15. Stroudsberg, Pennsylvania: Hutchinson Ross Publishing Company.

Mueller-Dombois, D., and H. Ellenberg. 1974. *Aims and methods of vegetation ecology*. New York: John Wiley & Sons.

Mueller-Dombois, D., and F. R. Fosberg. 1998. *Vegetation of the tropical Pacific Islands*. Ecological Studies, vol. 132. NY: Springer-Verlag.

Mueller-Dombois, D., and L. L. Loope. 1990. Some unique ecological aspects of oceanic island ecosystems. *Monographs on Systematic Botany of the Missouri Botanical Gardens* 32:21–27.

Mueller-Dombois, D., et al. 1981. Altitudinal distribution of organisms along an island mountain transect. In *Island ecosystems: biological organization in selected Hawaiian communities,* ed. D. Mueller-Dombois, K. W. Bridges, and H. L. Carson, 77–180. US/IBP Synthesis Series 15. Stroudsberg, Pennsylvania: Hutchinson Ross Publishing Company.

Nunn, P. D. 1994. *Oceanic islands.* Oxford: Blackwell Publishers.

Odum, E. P. 1963. *Ecology.* New York: Holt, Rinehart and Wilson.

Pajimans, K. 1975. *Explanatory notes to the vegetation map of Papua New Guinea.* Land Research Series no. 35. Melbourne, Australia: CSIRO (Commonwealth Scientific and Industrial Research Organization).

Pernetta, J. C., and H. I. Manner. 1994. *The ecosystems of small islands in the Southwest Pacific (the sixth expedition of the SS "Callisto").* UNEP Regional Seas Reports and Studies N. 151 and SPREP Reports and Studies No. 63.

Pratt, H. D., P. L. Bruner, and D. G. Berrett. 1985. *The birds of Hawaii and the tropical Pacific.* Princeton University Press.

Raynor, B. 1994. Resource management in upland forests of Pohnpei: Past practices and future possibilities. *Isla: A Journal of Micronesian Studies* 2(1):47–66.

Ripperton, J. C., and E. Y. Hosaka. 1942. *Vegetation zones of Hawaii.* Hawaii Agricultural Experiment Station Bulletin No. 89. Honolulu.

Schmid, M. 1989. The forests in the tropical Pacific archipelagoes. In *Tropical rain forest ecosystems: biogeographical and ecological studies,* ed. H. Leith and M. J. A. Werger, 283–301. Ecosystems of the World 14B. Amsterdam: Elsevier Science Publishers.

Simpson, P. 1993. The cabbage trees (*Cordyline australis*) are dying: investigations of sudden decline in New Zealand. In *Forest decline in the Atlantic and Pacific regions,* ed. R. F. Huettl and D. Mueller-Dombois, 280–292.

Smith, J. B. 1975. Mountain grasslands of New Guinea. *Journal of Biogeography* 2:27–44.

Stemmermann, L. 1981. *A guide to Pacific wetland plants.* Honolulu: U.S. Corps of Engineers.

Stoddart, D. R. 1975. Vegetation and floristics of the Aitutaki motus. *Atoll Research Bulletin* 190:87–116.

Stone, C. P., C. W. Smith, and J. T. Tunison. 1992. *Alien plant invasions in native ecosystems of Hawaii: management and research.* University of Hawai'i in cooperation with the National Park Resources Studies Unit. Honolulu: University of Hawai'i Press.

Street, J. M. 1966. Grasslands on the highland fringe in New Guinea: localisation, origin, effects on soil composition. *Capricornia* 3:9–12.

Tansley, A. G. 1935. The use and abuse of certain vegetational concepts and terms. *Ecology* 16:284–307.

Thorne, R. F. 1963. Biotic distribution patterns in the tropical Pacific. In *Pacific basin biogeography: a symposium,* ed. J. L. Gressitt, 311–350. Tenth Pacific Science Congress, Honolulu (1961). Honolulu: Bishop Museum Press.

Tomlinson, P. B. 1986. *The Botany of Mangroves.* Cambridge: Cambridge University Press.

Walter, H. 1971. *Ecology of Tropical and Subtropical Vegetation.* (Translated by D. Mueller-Dombois, edited by J. H. Burnett). Edinburgh: Oliver and Boyd.

Wardle, P. 1991. *Vegetation of New Zealand.* Cambridge: Cambridge University Press.

Whitmore, T. C. 1974. *Change with time and the role of cyclones in tropical rain forest on Kolomobangara, Solomon Islands.* Commonwealth Forestry Institute Paper no. 46. Oxford, England: Holywell.

Whittaker, R. H. 1975. *Communities and ecosystems.* Heidleberg. Springer Verlag.

Wiens, H. J. 1962. *Atoll environment and ecology.* New Haven: Yale University Press.

Woodroffe, C. D. 1987. Pacific Island mangroves: distribution and environmental settings. *Pacific Science* 41:166–185.

Zan, Y., and R. L. Hunter-Anderson. 1988. On the origins of the Micronesian "savannahs": an anthropological perspective. In *Proceedings of the Third international Soil Management Workshop for the Management and Utilization of Acid Soils in Micronesia,* February 2–6, 1987, Republic of Palau, ed. J. L. Demeterio and B. DeGuzman, 18–27. Agricultural Experiment Station, College of Agriculture and Life Sciences, University of Guam.

# CHAPTER 9

# Aquatic Ecosystems

*Stephen G. Nelson*

## Introduction

The vast area of the Pacific Islands region is largely underwater and is blessed with a diverse array of aquatic ecosystems: inland fresh waters, mangroves, seagrass meadows, coral reefs, kelp beds and forests, continental shelves and slopes, pelagic ecosystems, and the deep sea.

The focus in this chapter will be on ecosystem function, comparing import, use, and transfer of organic materials and nutrients. Every ecosystem relies on such processes. The inputs upon which consumers and decomposers depend must come from primary producers, or be imported from elsewhere. Examination of such processes provides an informative means of comparing disparate ecosystems.

Natural processes and human activities can have profound effects on aquatic ecosystems. Sediment, excess nutrients, and toxic compounds are carried by the flow of water downhill into rivers, streams, and lakes, and ultimately into estuarine and marine ecosystems. Inflow of terrestrial materials and interactions among aquatic ecosystems complicate the problems of management and conservation.

Many aspects of these ecosystems are poorly known. This, along with my specialization in tropical ecosystems, may render the coverage somewhat uneven. Given the breadth of the subject matter, it is difficult to provide detailed accounts of every case. With those cautions, I will examine some of the major aquatic ecosystems in the region, starting with inland fresh waters and proceeding through oceanic ecosystems, outward and downward.

## Inland Fresh Waters

The numbers and kinds of species found in Pacific Island fresh waters (Figure 9.1) vary considerably, depending on the dominant food sources. For example, the number of aquatic species usually increases from headwaters to estuaries, where fresh water and seawater mix (Maciolek and Timbol 1981). Most Pacific Island streams have few species relative to those of New Guinea (Allen 1991). New Zealand also has a distinctive fresh water biota.

There are striking similarities in Pacific Island stream faunal assemblages. This is the case because relatively few taxonomic groups of organisms have the dispersal abilities and life-history characteristics necessary for traversing oceanic expanses and successfully establishing in insular fresh waters (Ryan 1991, Fitzsimons et al. 1996).

Prominent ichthyofauna of Pacific Island streams include

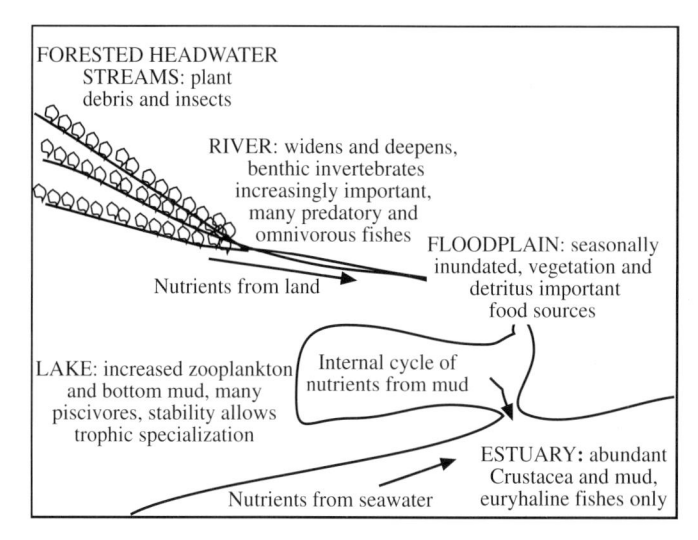

*Figure 9.1. Tropical freshwater ecosystems (after Lowe-McConnell 1977).*

gobies, flagtails, and eels (Maciolek and Ford 1987, Nelson et al. 1997). Stream invertebrates include shrimps, crabs, snails, bivalves, sponges, and even a species of nudibranch. Many fishes and macroinvertebrates (other than insects) are diadromous—spending a stage of their life cycle in fresh water and another stage in the ocean. A few species, such as thiarid snails, spend their entire lives in fresh water.

Primary producers are mainly attached algae that grow on exposed surfaces of rock and submerged roots. Additional organic input is derived from leaf fall, detritus, and other materials derived from the terrestrial communities within the watershed. Nitrogen, phosphorus, and other nutrients run into the stream from the soil. Atmospheric nitrogen becomes available through fixation by blue-green algae. Nutrients regenerated by fishes and shrimps may also be important to the primary producers, especially during periods of low stream flow.

Consumers in inland aquatic ecosystems are numerous. Epilithic (stone-attached) algal films and filamentous macroalgae are consumed by gobies, snails, and other herbivores. Mountain gobies (*Stiphodon* spp.) are often the most abundant of herbivorous fishes, feeding on algal films of bedrock, boulder, or cobble. Some species feed on filamentous algae and larval aquatic insects; others feed on shrimps, snails, or small fishes. Other organisms, such as some aquatic snails, rely mainly on terrestrial organic inputs.

Atyid shrimps are sediment and filter feeders, removing particulate matter with brushlike appendages. These feeding activities result in the removal of sediment from rock surfaces, which allows increased growth of algae on the cleared surfaces (Pringle et al. 1993). Palaemonid shrimps are omnivorous, feeding on plant materials, algae, and invertebrates. Both shrimps are found at high densities throughout island streams in the tropical Pacific and are responsible for most of the secondary productivity (Bright 1982).

New Zealand's stream fauna differs considerably from that of tropical Pacific islands. Few species are herbivores (Huryn 1996). Insects are more important in aquatic food webs than is the case on tropical islands. Invertebrate fauna include many aquatic insects, two types of crayfish, atyid shrimps, and snails. Fishes include galaxids, smelts, eleotrids, graylings, a lamprey, and freshwater eels (McDowall 1990).

The most extensive inland aquatic habitats in the Pacific Islands are the great rivers and swamplands of Papua New Guinea. The Sepik and the Fly are among the world's most powerful rivers in terms of annual water flow. The rivers wind gradually to the sea, often changing course, leaving a trace of lagoons, oxbow lakes, and vast swamplands—which convert into grasslands during the winter dry season. Large chunks of vegetation are periodically torn off the Sepik banks, drifting off as floating islands, often with trees and animals aboard (Wheeler 1988).

Here as well, most inland aquatic fauna have marine affinities. The fauna is diverse, with numerous endemics. Native species include over 200 frogs, 9 turtles, 6 eels, several snakes, and 2 crocodiles (Keast 1996). Catfishes (Ariidae and Plotosidae) are well represented, with 28 recorded species. New Guinea's freshwater fishes (329 species) are large, with over half growing to over 30 cm long; the few small species (such as gobies) are found mainly in small side streams (Lowe-McConnell 1987). A rich variety of food sources are exploited, depending on the zone (Table 9.1).

Inland aquatic ecosystems are highly vulnerable to human activities. Because removal of vegetation increases sediment loads, reduces the input of organic materials, increases stream temperatures, and alters water levels, construction near streams must include precautions to ensure that exposed sediment is not washed into the water. Irrigation runoff may contain herbicides, pesticides, and overly high nutrient levels. Dams can block migrations of diadromous species and (through flow changes) alter the distributions of aquatic organisms.

Many introduced species have become established in Pacific Island fresh waters; these have often had detrimental effects on the indigenous fauna. There are only a few cases in which the introductions are considered to have been a benefit, and some that resulted in complete disaster. On Nauru, for example, introduced tilapia have made it impossible to continue the traditional culture of milkfish, which now must be imported from Guam or Kiribati. In New Zealand, introduced aquatic plants have become a major nuisance (McDowall 1990).

## Mangrove Ecosystems (Mangals)

Of the various near-shore ecosystems discussed below (Figure 9.2), mangroves rise highest above sea level, forming dense forests in estuaries and flooded shores of the tropics and subtropics (Hosakawa et al. 1977), extending as far south as the North Island of New Zealand (Figure 9.3). Mangrove ecosystems are the tropical counterparts of temperate salt marshes.

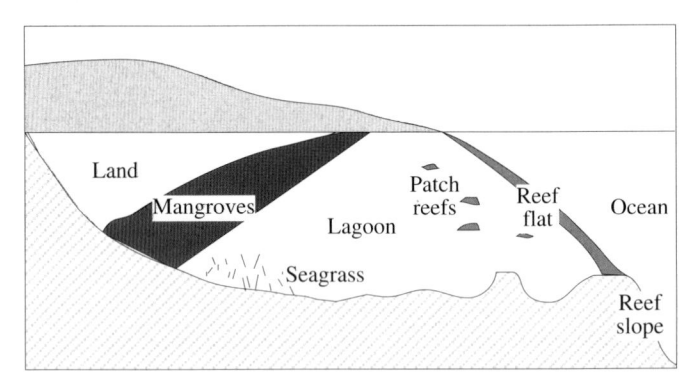

*Figure 9.2. Near-shore ecosystems in the tropical Pacific.*

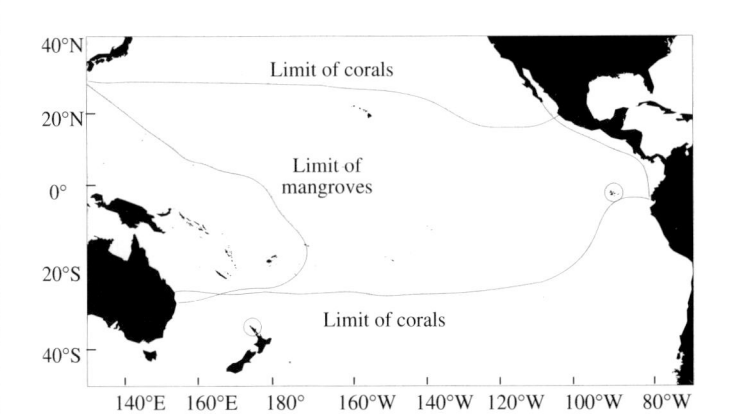

*Figure 9.3. Limits for the distribution of mangroves and coral in the Pacific Islands (after Kay 1980 and Nunn 1994). Outlier populations of mangroves are shown in northern New Zealand and the Galápagos.*

### TABLE 9.1

**Number of Fish Species in Various Trophic Categories in the Purari River, Papua New Guinea**

(after Lowe-McConnell 1987 and sources therein)

| Feeding mode | Small creeks | River | Delta (upper) | Delta (lower) |
|---|---|---|---|---|
| Detritivores | 4 | 8 | 4 | 9 |
| Fructivores | 0 | 3 | 2 | 3 |
| Other plant-eaters | 0 | 3 | 0 | 2 |
| Insectivores | 4 | 5 | 3 | 4 |
| Molluscivores | 0 | 0 | 4 | 4 |
| Prawn-eaters | 0 | 12 | 14 | 20 |
| Crab-eaters | 0 | 0 | 0 | 11 |
| Piscivores | 1 | 6 | 7 | 15 |
| Omnivores | 0 | 3 | 2 | 2 |

Aerial roots serve to trap sediment and fine organic materials. Nutrients are also brought in through tidal action. The rates of nitrogen fixation in the sediments of mangrove swamps are high (ranging from 0.03 to 2.8 g/m$^2$/year) (Howarth et al. 1988).

The leaves of mangrove trees are rich in tannins, which inhibit consumption by terrestrial insects. The palatability of the leaves is also decreased because of high cellulose and fiber and a low nitrogen content. Much of the organic input from mangrove trees requires microbial enrichment and decomposition before it can be of use to aquatic consumers. Microbial activity reduces the C:N ratio from one-third to one-half of that of newly fallen leaves in about eight months, increasing the protein content and nutritional value (Twilly et al. 1986).

Decomposition of organic material is facilitated by the activities of burrowing marine organisms, since material decomposes more rapidly when buried. Decomposition is also facilitated by the high sulfate content of mangrove sediments (Lugo et al. 1988).

Microbial activity is also important in converting dissolved organic matter (DOM) released from decaying vegetation and living plants into particulate organic matter (POM), needed by filter-feeding organisms and detritivores (Mann 1988). Some of the DOM is taken up by bacteria, which form aggregates that can be colonized by other microorganisms. Some aggregates sink to the bottom and are consumed by a variety of crustaceans, including amphipods, isopods, copepods, and shrimps (Camilleri and Ribi 1986).

Consumers are abundant and diverse in mangrove ecosystems. Because the finer organic particles are easily suspended in the water column by tidal action, and because the mangrove roots provide surfaces for attachment, mangroves have an abundance of oysters, shrimps, crabs, and other invertebrates. Oysters often cover the submerged roots of mangrove trees (Braley 1982). Mud crabs, fiddler crabs, and penaeid shrimps are often prominent. Numerous fishes are present, including mudskippers (small gobies) and rabbitfishes.

Mangroves are vulnerable to many anthropogenic disturbances. For example, on Guam, an oil spill from an upstream refinery killed a large portion of the already limited number of mangroves. Replanting of seedlings has restored the mangrove community, although it will be some time before the ecosystem recovers completely. The health of mangroves is dependent on frequent flushing from tidal action, and barriers to tidal flow will result in death of the affected trees. On Babeldaup, in the Palau Islands, construction of a shrimp pond resulted in destruction of a large section of mangrove.

The destruction of mangroves and other coastal ecosystems in areas converted to shrimp farms is considered to be a significant environmental problem throughout the tropics (Lockwood 1997). This concern was expressed clearly in 1996 by a group of 21 nongovernmental organizations calling for a global moratorium on expansion of shrimp farming until the criteria of sustainability could be met. It has been estimated that about 50% of mangrove ecosystems have been transformed or destroyed by human activity (Vitousek et al. 1997).

## Seagrass Meadows

Along shores protected from wave action, seagrasses flourish and form meadows, a source of food and shelter to a wide variety of marine organisms (Brouns and Heijs 1991). Seagrasses grow in soft sediments and stabilize them. Like mangroves, seagrasses evolved from terrestrial plants and have roots that extract nutrients from the sediments in which they grow. Seagrasses provide a habitat for numerous species of marine invertebrates, fishes, and algae. Unlike coral reefs and mangroves, seagrasses are present in both tropical and temperate coastal areas.

Tropical seagrasses have high rates of primary production (Table 9.2). However, since they evolved from terrestrial plants, their blades have a high content of indigestible cellulose and fiber. Some seagrasses contain secondary metabolites that deter herbivorous fishes (Paul et al. 1990). There are reports of undecomposed seagrass blades even in deep-sea environments (Phillips and Menez 1988). Nonetheless, seagrasses provide food for herbivorous fishes, urchins, shrimps, sea turtles, and dugongs (Stevenson 1988). Dugong browsing on seagrasses can result in cleared strips within the beds (Donning 1981).

Early insights into the importance of herbivory in seagrass meadows came from halos, or bare areas around rocks or other shelters in the seagrass meadows, created and maintained by herbivorous fishes and sea urchins. Rabbitfishes and parrotfishes also frequently feed on seagrass. Biomass retained in seagrass meadows is eventually broken down by bacteria and other microorganisms. The organic material is either retained within the bed or exported to other coastal environments.

Human activities that are particularly likely to adversely affect seagrasses include dredging, sewage discharge, thermal pollution, and agricultural runoff (Phillips and Menez 1988). In some areas seagrass consumption has decreased due to overfishing of sea turtles (Stevenson 1988). Increased seagrass growth has been attributed to increasing nitrogen inputs from human activities on a global scale. This increased production is usually associated with decreased species diversity, as some seagrass

### Table 9.2

**Primary Productivity Rates in the Ocean**
(after Sumich 1988 and Barnes and Hughes 1982)

| Location | Average productivity (gC/m²/yr.)* |
|---|---|
| Open ocean (tropical) | 40 |
| Open ocean (temperate) | 120 |
| Continental shelf | 200 |
| Upwelling zones | 300 |
| Seagrasses (temperate) | 600 |
| Mangroves | 800 |
| Coral reefs | 1000 |
| Kelp beds | 1000 |
| Seagrasses (tropical) | 1500 |

*average figures from various studies; much higher maxima frequently occur.

species are better able to use the increased nutrients than others (Vitousek et al. 1997).

## Coral Reefs

Coral reefs are massive biogeological structures characterized by high productivity in areas of low dissolved nutrient concentrations, and by great species diversity, including fish, invertebrates, algae, and other life forms.

The physical structures that constitute the reef framework are composed primarily of calcium carbonate, deposited by reef-building (hermatypic) corals and calcareous algae. Reef-building corals are colonial animals that are able to grow rapidly with the aid of dinoflagellates (single-celled algae). These symbionts, known as zooxanthellae, photosynthesize and translocate nutrients to their host and assist in the deposition of calcium carbonate needed in reef formation (Muller-Parker and D'Elia 1997). The zooxanthellae benefit from receiving nitrogen, excreted as ammonium by the coral polyps (Table 9.3).

The number of symbioses between autotrophic organisms and invertebrates is a striking feature of coral reefs. For example, giant clams (*Tridacna*) also have symbiotic zooxthanthellae in their tissues, and many species of ascidians (filter-feeding sea

### Table 9.3

**Benefits and Costs of Symbiosis Between Corals and Zooxanthellae** (after Muller-Parker and D'Elia 1997)

| Benefits | Costs |
| --- | --- |
| **A. Coral** | |
| Supply of carbon | Regulation of algal growth |
| Increased growth and reproduction | High oxygen tension |
| Facilitation of calcification | Rejection of excess algae |
| Conservation of nutrients | Affected by algal disease |
| Sequestration of toxins by algae | |
| **B. Zooxanthellae** | |
| Supply of carbon dioxide | Translocation of carbon |
| Maintenance in photic zone | Low growth rates |
| Uniform environment | Subject to expulsion by host |
| Protection from grazers | Losses by predators of coral |
| High population density enabled | |

squirts) contain symbiotic algae of the genus *Prochloron*. Many sponges contain symbiotic cyanobacteria. It is these symbioses that allow the high productivity of reef ecosystems to be sustained.

Exogenous sources of nutrients are in relatively short supply in most coral reef ecosystems, especially on atolls (Hatcher 1997). However, rates of nitrogen fixation by benthic (bottom-dwelling) bacteria and cyanobacteria are high, contributing significantly to coral reef nitrogen budgets (Yamamuro et al. 1995).

Nutrients are also brought in from the open ocean.

Even though tropical oceanic waters are low in dissolved nutrients, attached algae and autotrophic symbionts are able to rapidly take up available nutrients. Near schools of fish, ammonium concentrations may be elevated, and coral reef algae can rapidly exploit even brief pulses of nutrients (Nelson 1985). Fishes that feed in the water column and take shelter in the reef transport materials and nutrients from the pelagic (open sea) ecosystems to those of the coral reef. On high islands, nutrient inputs from terrestrial runoff are important. Downwelling is another source of nutrients on some islands. In the northern portion of Guam, which is a raised limestone plateau, the freshwater lens has a relatively high content of nitrate, and seeps provide nutrients that are important to coral reefs. Endo-upwelling may be another source of nutrients on atolls (Figure 9.4).

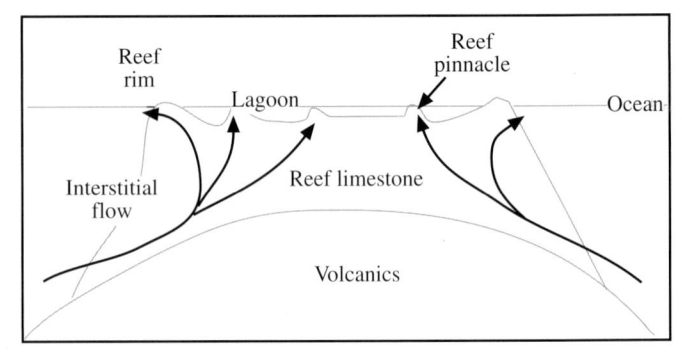

*Figure 9.4.* Idealized section through an atoll showing endo-upwelling (after Rougerie and Wauthy 1993). Deep interstitial nutrient-rich water is warmed by geothermal heat, causing it to rise and exit through cracks in the reef rim and lagoon bottom, facilitating growth of coral pinnacles (patch reefs) and the surrounding reef. Endo-upwelling is also hypothesized to have contributed to phosphate depositions in raised limestone islands.

Because of these numerous sources of nutrients, some feel that coral reef productivity is limited by the surface area available to primary producers (rather than being limited by nutrients) (Longhurst and Pauly 1987). Raising nutrient inputs causes an increase of benthic algae (Hatcher 1997), which can block coral recruitment.

The major primary producers in reef ecosystems are attached macroalgae and symbiotic microalgae. Schools of herbivorous surgeonfishes, parrotfishes, and rabbitfishes roam the reefs, browsing or grazing any sprig of macroalgae not defended by calcification or secondary metabolites (Paul 1992). Thus, the standing crops of macroalgae are usually low, except in areas that are less accessible to herbivorous fishes, such as on shallow reef flats or near river mouths. Some species of damselfish defend patches of algae from other herbivores and remove unwanted algae (Lassuy 1980).

Butterflyfishes, triggerfishes, corallivorous marine snails, and starfishes feed directly on coral polyps. Other fishes harvest the zooplankton that feed on particulate matter. Invertebrate herbivores, particularly sea urchins, also have significant roles in the functioning of coral reef ecosystems (Carpenter 1997). The corals themselves are consumers, obtaining nutrition from

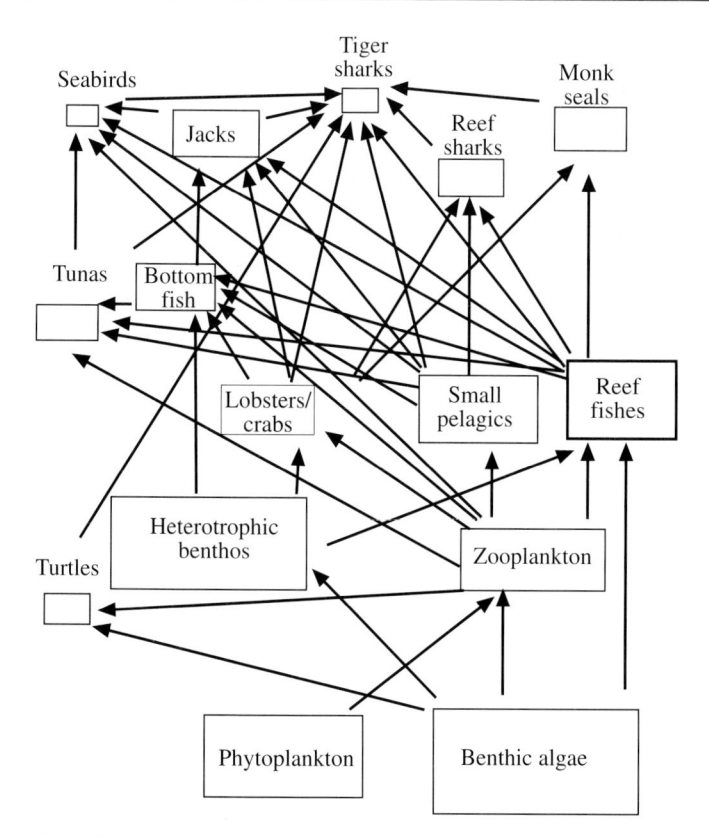

*Figure 9.5. Representation of the foodweb on French Frigate Shoals, Northwest Hawaiian Islands (after Polovina 1984). The area of each box is proportional to the logarithm of the biomass of each group.*

capturing planktonic (floating) organisms and from the uptake of dissolved organic matter. The result is a highly efficient use of organic matter (Figure 9.5).

Organic material falling into bottom sediment is consumed by invertebrates and reef fish (Nelson and Wilkins 1988). Sea cucumbers feed on sediments, selectively ingesting nutrient-rich particles. These organisms can be abundant in some reef habitats, especially in shallow lagoons or reef flats. Sediment-feeding surgeonfish (such as *Ctenochaetus striatus*) are often numerous in coral reef habitats.

While utilization of nutrients and energy in coral reef ecosystems is highly efficient, export of materials to surrounding ecosystems also occurs. Some of this is from predation by pelagic fishes. Most of the export is in the form of particulate organic matter that is carried out to sea by currents. This particulate organic matter consists largely of mucus secreted by corals. Loss of biomass from macroalgae and other organisms also occurs in association with tropical storms, which are frequent and often severe in some areas.

Coral reefs are extensive and most diverse in the western Pacific, with over 400 species recorded, whereas fewer than 100 occur in eastern Polynesia (Paulay 1997). Postulated explanations include differences in oceanographic conditions (cooler waters in the eastern Pacific due to cold currents and upwelling) and geotectonic factors (warm, shallow seas in Southeast Asia; difficulty dispersing against prevailing easterly currents; and closure of Central America during the Pliocene 5-2 Ma, severing the connection with Caribbean corals).

The lack of coral reefs in temperate latitudes has been attributed to lethal effects of low temperature, competition by macroalgae (such as kelp), and the costs of calcification. The deposition of calcium carbonate requires the release of carbon dioxide from solution, as shown:

$$Ca^{++} + 2HCO_3^- \longrightarrow CO_2 + H_2O + CaCO_3$$

In cool, temperate waters, $CO_2$ tends to remain in solution (as with a carbonated beverage), and the above reaction becomes energetically costly. In tropical waters, $CO_2$ (used in photosynthesis by zooxanthellae) tends to come out of solution, and $CaCO_3$ (used for the reef framework) is deposited (Hallock 1997).

Over geological time, reef (and other) limestones have effectively tied up a significant portion of atmospheric $CO_2$, making the Earth a livable planet. (Had this not occurred, atmospheric temperatures would have risen dramatically, due to the sun's natural aging and increasing luminosity.) The evolution of efficient photosynthetic mechanisms in algae and terrestrial plants has had a similar beneficial function. Humans, however, are upsetting this balance by burning vast amounts of fossil fuels and damaging coral reefs (Hallock 1997).

Natural events affecting reefs include typhoons, earthquakes, outbreaks of the crown-of-thorns starfish, ENSO (which can result in elevated temperatures or unusually low tides), and sea-level fluctuations. Human disturbances include reef mining, land clearing, sewage discharge, thermal discharge from power plants, overfishing, and anchor damage. One sign of stress in corals is bleaching, the loss of zooxanthellae or their pigments related to elevated temperatures and exposure to ultraviolet or intense visible irradiance, causing oxidative stress and inhibiting photosynthesis (Lesser 1996).

## Kelp Ecosystems

The temperate nearshore waters of New Zealand have extensive areas of hard substrate ("rocky reefs"), providing a rich benthic environment. Nutrient concentrations around New Zealand coasts are higher than in the tropical Pacific and support a large biomass of macroalgae and phytoplankton. Algae growth in temperate waters is also facilitated because specialized fish herbivores are rare, relative to the tropics (Paulay 1997). Competition can be severe and space availability becomes limiting for benthic algae and dependent organisms.

The shorelines here are often dominated by various kelp (large brown algae) species attached to rocky substrates (Figure 9.6). Kelp occurs in dense stands subtidally, often forming a closed canopy over smaller algae. The giant kelp *Macrocystis pyrifrea*, suspended by air bladders at the base of each leaf, forms undersea "forests" reaching up to 30 m in height and occupying as much as 10 m$^2$ of space per individual in sheltered locations on the South Island (Schiel et al. 1995).

As is characteristic of temperate rocky shores, conspicuous zonation is found in the macroalgae of New Zealand. Schiel (1988, 1994) described an upper zone dominated by *Carpophyllum* spp. (bladder kelp); an intermediate zone with abundant sea urchins but few macroalgae; and a deep zone (>10 m) of monospecific stands of *Ecklonia radiata* (Figure 9.7).

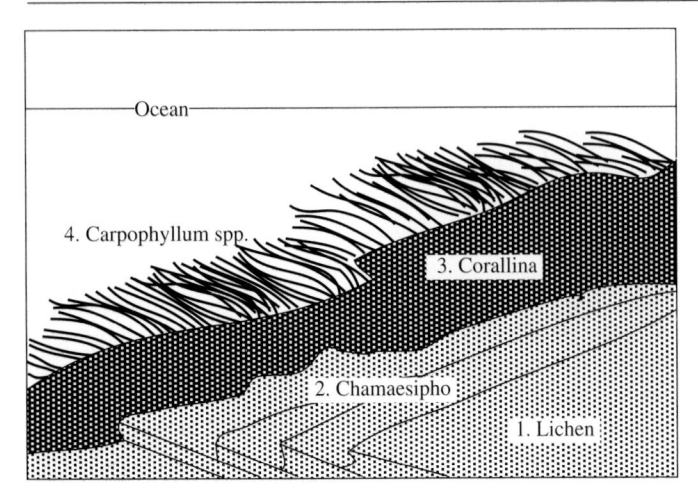

*Figure 9.6. Shoreline zonation in Northeast New Zealand (after Morton and Miller 1968). From top down, the following are shown a lichen encrusted platform, oyster ledges, a coralline algae ledge, and fringing, subtidal kelp.*

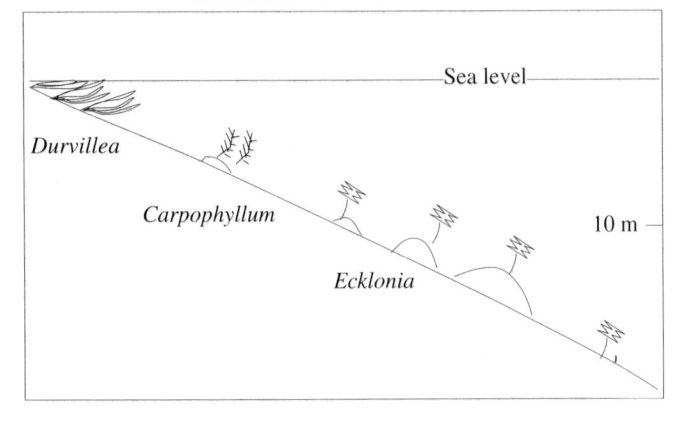

*Figure 9.7. Schematic representation of depth distribution of prominent kelp species in New Zealand (after Schiel 1988).*

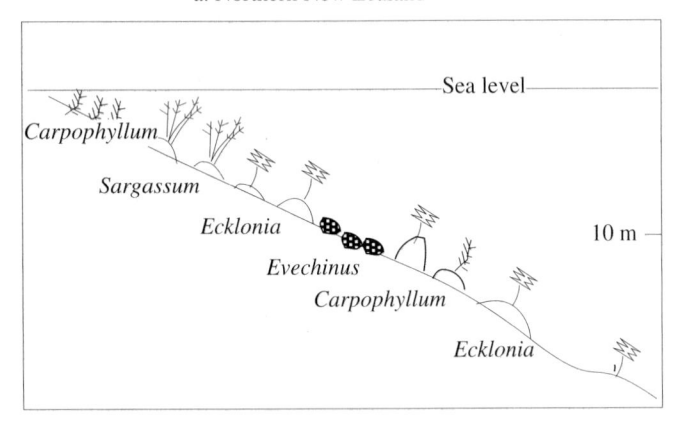

In southern New Zealand, *Carpophyllum* spp. are replaced by *Durvillea antarctica* (bull kelp) at the uppermost level.

Primary productivity is high in kelp ecosystems. Some of this productivity is exported to adjacent ecosystems, as is evident by the piles of drift algae occurring on beaches, particularly following storms. The remaining productivity is stored in the biomass of the algal beds or consumed by herbivores.

Invertebrate consumers are abundant along the shores of New Zealand, while there are few herbivorous fishes. Sea urchins (*Evecinus cloroticus*) and abalone (locally called *paua*) (*Haliotis* spp.) are important herbivores in kelp beds (Schiel et al. 1995). Small herbivores include shrimps, crabs, marine snails, and amphipods. Some herbivores harvest phytoplankton. A conspicuous example of these are the mussels, filter-feeders that often form dense beds. Various fishes and marine mammals feed on the abundant invertebrates or smaller fishes. New Zealand is also the home of several species of diving birds, including penguins.

Kelp ecosystems are highly vulnerable to human activities. Pollution, such as that resulting from the thermal discharges of power plants and oil spills, can cause much damage to shoreline ecosystems. New Zealand's concern over the potential for radioactive pollution by other countries engaged in the transportation or detonation of nuclear materials within the Pacific Ocean region has been clearly articulated and has led to some highly visible political clashes over the years (notably with France and the United States, though these disputes have become less strident in recent years).

## Continental Shelf and Slope Ecosystems

On most Pacific islands, the seafloor slopes sharply downward to several km depth. However, at two locations—New Guinea and New Zealand—the seafloor slopes gradually down to around 200-m depth (the continental shelf) prior to dropping steeply to the ocean floor (Figure 9.8). Large portions of

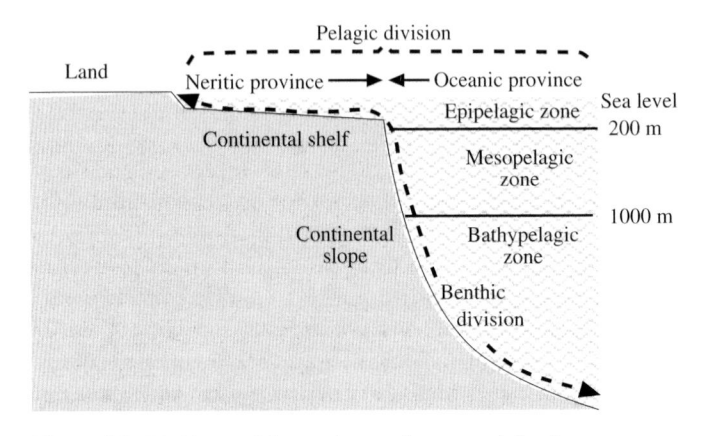

*Figure 9.8. Divisions of the marine environment (after Lowe-McConnell 1977).*

these waters (the neritic marine province) are sufficiently shallow for sunlight to penetrate, supporting phytoplankton and benthic algae. Neritic ecosystems receive abundant nutrients from adjacent land masses. The waters are also well mixed through wind, tidal action, and in some locations upwelling (Barnes and Hughes 1982, Longhurst and Paulay 1987).

Thus, primary productivity is relatively high above continental shelves. The interactions between neritic waters and benthos are numerous. Approximately 20% of the primary productivity is consumed by pelagic herbivores; the remainder sinks to the bottom, enriching the sediments and providing nutrition for detrital feeders and decomposers. Benthic organisms often spend a portion of their lives as larvae in the pelagic zone (as many as 80% of the macrobenthic invertebrates in tropical waters), taking advantage of the rich phytoplankton production (Barnes and Hughes 1982).

Consumers of shelf benthos include clams, oysters, worms, crabs, lobsters, starfishes, sea urchins, sponges, and fishes. Fishes, along with squid, are abundant in neritic ecosystems and are the targets of commercial fisheries, particularly in New Zealand. Fish communites differ depending on the dominant substrate. For example, groupers (Serranidae) and snappers (Lutjanidae) are found in rocky areas, and threadfins (Polynemidae) and grunts (Pomadasyidae) in muddy and sandy areas (Longhurst and Paulay 1987). Surface waters are home to large schools of sardines (Clupeidae) and anchovies (Engraulidae), in turn hunted by mackerels, tunas, and sharks. Temperate waters have a less diverse shelf fauna, but with many species akin to tropical groups.

Slope fauna (below 200 m depth) are more widely distributed (antitropically and circumglobally), relative to shelf species, owing to the homogenous environment. In New Zealand, common species include orange roughy (*Noplostethus atlanticus*), hoki (*Macruronus novazelandiae*), deep sea dories (*Allocyttus* spp., *Pseudocyttus maculatus*), and ling eel (*Genypterus blacodes*). With increasing depth, fish have larger eyes and heads, smaller abdomens, and other adaptations to poor light and dispersed food sources. Evidence elsewhere suggests that slope fauna decrease in abundance and diversity with increasing depth, although narrow strata of high diversity may occur at midslope levels (around 500 m) (Ward and Blaber 1994).

Continental shelves and slopes are subject to damage by oil spills, sewage and thermal discharges, and overfishing. Dams block nutrients from entering the neritic zone, resulting in a potential decline in fisheries. Intense commercial fishing affects continental shelf ecosystems by removing substantial amounts of biomass. Enormous amounts of nontarget species (including 90% of shrimp trawl catch) are discarded every year from commercial marine fisheries (Vitousek 1997, Mangel et al. 1993). Trawls, by dragging along the bottom, also damage the habitats of other species.

In recent decades, the New Zealand fisheries industry has increasingly turned to the deep waters at the edge of the continental shelf (the continental slope), trawling at bottom and midlevel waters down to 1,000 m. Dense concentrations of commercially important fish exist at these depths, yielding a fish catch of several hundred tons annually, unmatched elsewhere in the Pacific Islands. Many of these species (such as the orange roughy) are long lived with up to 100-year lifespans and relatively low recruitment rates. Following intense exploitation, stocks are likely to drop sharply and may have difficulty recovering.

## Pelagic Ecosystems

The ocean is divided vertically into pelagic and benthic components (the water column and the seafloor, respectively). The pelagic division in turn includes an epipelagic zone (0-200 m), a mesopelagic zone (200-1,000 m), and a bathopelagic zone (below 1,000 m).

Sharp gradations of illumination and temperature occur with depth in the epipelagic zone. Diurnal and (in temperate waters) seasonal changes are also marked. Below this, the mesopelagic zone has very little light, a very gradual temperature gradient, and little seasonal variation. Oxygen may be depleted, but there are often high concentrations of phosphates and nitrates. The bathypelagic zone below is characterized by continuous darkness, low temperatures, and high pressures (Lowe-McConnell 1977).

Tropical ocean waters are generally nutrient poor, since nutrient upwelling is less common than in temperate regions. There is an upwelling zone in the eastern Pacific, but this extends westward only as a narrow strip along the equator. Near New Guinea and New Zealand, productivity is raised because of the discharge of groundwater and rivers from large adjacent landmasses. With the above exceptions, however, waters of the open ocean are low in nutrients and primary productivity (Figure 9.9).

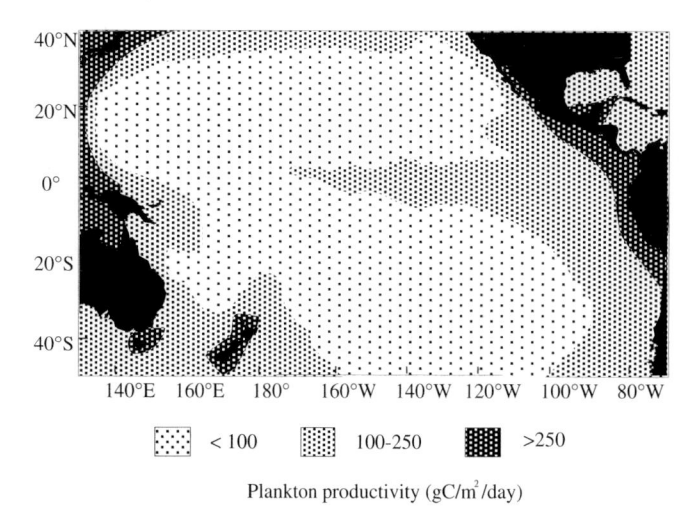

*Figure 9.9.* Phytoplankton productivity in the Pacific Ocean (after Barnes and Hughes 1982, and sources therein).

Primary production occurs only in the photic (or euphotic) layer, where light penetrates sufficiently for photosynthesis to occur. This layer extends to a maximum of 250 m under conditions of full sunlight and clear water. Primary production is accomplished mainly by phytoplankon, carried in the water column but slowly sinking to the depths below. The picoplankton (primarily photosynthetic bacteria) are also a significant source of primary production, especially in nutrient-poor waters.

Phytoplankton and picoplankton are so efficient at taking up nutrients that in some areas the dissolved nitrogen is not easily detectable. Nitrogen and phosphate are regenerated by zooplankton, driving photosynthesis and stimulating the growth of the primary producers. Another source of nutrients in oceanic waters is dissolved organic matter (Tanoue et al. 1996).

Phytoplankton are consumed by herbivorous copepods and other organisms. The copepods are in turn consumed by pelagic jellyfish, larval fish, larval crabs and lobsters, predatory copepods, and other zooplankton. These in turn are preyed upon by large fish and other components of the nekton (active swimmers, as differentiated from the floating plankton).

At the top of the food chain are large nekton, including predatory sharks, tunas, billfishes, and marine mammals. Most of these species feed on fishes, crustaceans, and cephalopods. Others have more restricted diets. One such specialized feeder is the dolphin fish (*Coryphaena* spp.), which preys on flying fish (Longhurst and Paulay 1987). The billfishes, such as marlins, are deep-diving aggressive feeders, with a diet consisting largely of other fishes. Because these nekton are large and highly mobile, they can seek out food-rich patches even in waters of low productivity.

Not all large nekton feed on large prey, however. The huge whale shark, which grows to over 17 m in length, feeds by filtering very small zooplankton from the water column. Another large filter-feeding shark is the megamouth (*Megachasma pelagius*), which supports its 4.5-m-long body by capturing zooplankton on tiny teeth and cartilaginous filters (Longhurst and Paulay 1987).

Nekton productivity is proportional to primary productivity, but at a much attenuated level. Secondary productivity diminishes by roughly an order of magnitude at each additional level in the trophic chain, often represented as an energy pyramid. There are energy losses at each level, resulting from unconsumed individuals (which eventually input to decomposers) and energy lost through metabolic activity. Thus, productivity (and biomass) of top predators is only a fraction of that of herbivorous species (Barnes and Hughes 1982).

Most of the organic material produced in the epipelagic zone of the open sea is consumed there. The remaining 20% sinks to the depths below and enters the mesopelagic zone. Here, low light levels make vision possible to suitably adapted organisms but will not support photosynthesis. There is no primary production, and organic inputs derive from above. Inhabiting this zone are numerous fishes and shrimps. Most of these species do not wait for organic material to fall from above, but make nocturnal migrations into epipelagic areas to forage.

Most theories advanced to explain these daily vertical migrations assume that the main benefit is increased foraging success in the upper waters. However, warmer temperatures and higher dissolved oxygen levels may be more important in explaining this phenomenon (Williamson et al. 1996). Whatever the cause of this migration, the result is the transport of organic materials and nutrients from the shallower areas into the mesopelagic. Materials not consumed in the mesopelagic zone sink into the deep sea.

## Deep Sea Ecosystems

Deep sea ecosystems are oligotrophic, having relatively few available food sources. Most organic particles are consumed and

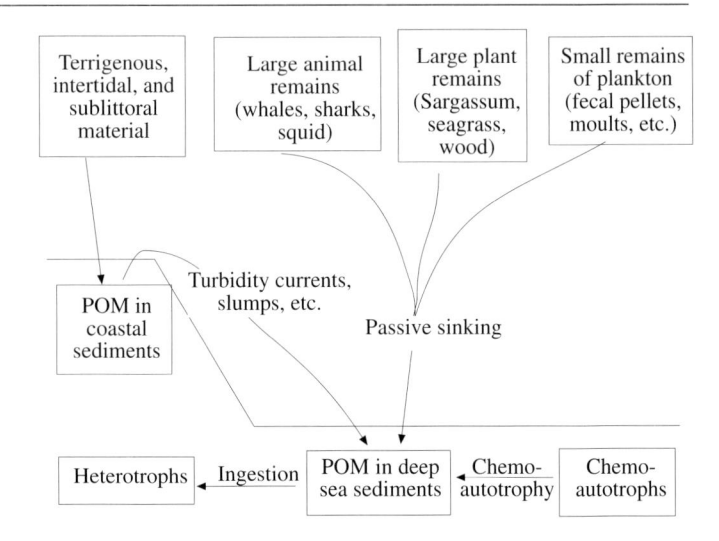

*Figure 9.10.* Conceptual model of the potential sources, transport, and sinks for organic matter to the deep sea (after Gage and Tyler 1991 and sources therein).

mineralized at much lesser depths (Figure 9.10). The amount of organic matter that reaches the ocean floor depends partly on the productivity of the surface water above it, but depth is a major factor (Hobbie 1988). A particle may take months to sink to the bottom, and only around 3% of the particulate organic matter produced in the euphotic zone ever reaches the deep sea. (Jannasch and Taylor 1984). The deep sea is thus low in productivity. Exceptions occur where the carcasses of large fishes or whales sink to the bottom, and at hydrothermal vents, as discussed below.

Deep sea organisms have a variety of adaptations that allow them to survive the severe physical and biological conditions. Light does not penetrate beyond the photic zone, so the only light available is that which is produced by the organisms themselves (bioluminescence) or from the glow of fissures and vents in the ocean floor. Many deep sea fishes, shrimps, and squids have photophores, special organs in the skin for producing light, which aid in species recognition, provide camouflage, and possibly serve in communication.

Deep sea organisms must also contend with high pressure and low temperature, and the enzymes of their metabolic systems have become adapted to these conditions. There is a general decrease in metabolic rate among fishes and invertebrates as depth increases. The decreased metabolic rate is largely the result of the reduced activity levels of deep sea organisms. Reduced levels of activity are presumably an adaptation to the limited and unpredictable supplies of food, conditions that may favor sit-and-wait strategies over active foraging (Somero et al. 1991).

Hydrothermal vents occur at areas of seafloor spreading or near areas of subduction, such as the Marianas Trough (Hessler and Lonsdale 1991). Other hydrothermal vents are located near the Caroline Islands, New Guinea, and New Zealand. In such locations, organisms are exposed to warm waters laden with metals and hydrogen sulfide. These waters would be toxic to most marine organisms, but resident species have evolved physiologically (Hessler and Lonsdale 1991), enabling them to survive and flourish. Warm, chemical-rich water emitted from the vents allows chemosynthesis by bacteria. Bacteria, in turn, support abundant consumer populations (Van Dover and Fry 1994).

Many deep sea organisms are hosts to symbiotic chemosynthetic bacteria. Tube worms, for example, have a specialized feeding structure, the trophosome, which contains dense populations of chemosynthetic bacteria (Robinson and McCavanaugh 1995). Chemosynthetic symbionts are also found in other deep sea organisms (Haygood 1996).

## Conclusion

In this review I have attempted to cover some of the major aquatic ecosystems of the Pacific Island region. Some of their features are summarized in Table 9.4. The aquatic ecosystems of the Pacific Islands region are diverse and of great practical significance and economic value and immeasurable aesthetic value. Their complexity and vulnerability to human activities, on both local and global scales, are now being more fully appreciated (Vitousek et al. 1997), but they are still poorly understood. A greater understanding of the structure and function of these ecosystems will occupy ecologists for decades to come. The endeavors of these scientists will be crucial for resource management in the future (De Leo and Levin 1997). In the meantime, we should be careful in our stewardship of these ecosystems. We must ensure that they remain valuable sources of fascination and practical benefits to the generations that follow.

### Table 9.4

**Comparison of Some of the Major Aquatic Ecosystems of the Pacific Island Region**

| Ecosystem | Input | Primary production | Consumers |
|---|---|---|---|
| Fresh waters | Leaf fall, nutrient run-off from adjacent terrestrial ecosystems | Mostly from attached algae | Fishes, shrimps, snails, eels |
| Mangroves | Organic materials and nutrients from rivers and the sea | Leaf production from mangrove trees, estaurine and marine algae | Fishes, shrimps, crabs, and other invertebrates |
| Seagrass meadows | Nutrients from rivers, sea, and sediments | Seagrasses; benthic marine algae | Fishes, shrimps, crabs, and other invertebrates, dugongs |
| Coral reefs | Nutrients from the rivers and the sea, nitrogen fixation, regeneration by marine organisms | Symbiotic algae; benthic marine algae, phytoplankton | Reef fishes; invertebrates; marine turtles, sea snakes |
| Kelp | Nutrients from the rivers and the sea, nitrogen fixation, regeneration by marine organisms | Macroalgae and other algae, phytoplankton | Invertebrates; fish |
| Continental shelf | Nitrogen fixation, terrestrial runoff, regeneration by marine organisms | Photosynthetic picoplankton; phytoplankton, benthic marine algae | Zooplankton, fishes, invertebrates, and marine mammals |
| Open-ocean, euphotic zone | Nitrogen fixation; regeneration by marine organisms | Photosynthetic picoplankton, phytoplankton | Zooplankton, pelagic fishes, invertebrates, and marine mammals |
| Deep sea | Nutrients and organic materials from zones above | Symbiotic chemo-synthetic bacteria | Slow moving fishes, benthic invertebrates |

# Bibliography

Allen, G. R. 1991. *Field guide to the freshwater fishes of New Guinea*. Publication No. 9 of the Christensen Research Institute.

Barnes, R. S. K. and R. N. Hughes. 1982. *An introduction to marine ecology*. London: Blackwell.

Braley, R. D. 1982. Reproductive periodicity in the indigenous oyster *Saccostrea cucullata* in Sasa Bay, Apra Harbor, Guam. *Marine Biology* 69:165–173.

Bright, G. 1982. Secondary benthic productivity in a tropical island stream. *Limnology and Oceanography* 27:472–480.

Brouns, J., and F. Heijs. 1991. Seagrass ecosystems in the tropical west Pacific. In *Ecosystems of the World 24. Intertidal and littoral ecosystems*, ed. A. C. Mathieson and P. H. Nienhuis, 371–390. New York: Elsevier.

Camilleri, J. C., and G. Ribi. 1986. Leaching of dissolved organic carbon (DOC) from dead leaves, formation of flakes from DOC, and feeding on flakes by crustaceans in mangroves. *Marine Biology* 91:337–344.

Carpenter, R. C. 1977. Invertebrate predators and grazers. In *Life and death of coral reefs*, ed. C. E. Birkeland, 98–229. New York: Chapman and Hall.

Colin, P. L., and C. Arneson 1995. *Tropical Pacific invertebrates: a field guide to the marine invertebrates occuring on tropical Pacific coral reefs, seagrass beds, and mangroves*. Beverly Hills: Coral Reef Press.

De Leo, G. A., and S. Levin. 1997. The multifaceted aspects of ecosystem integrity. *Conservation Ecology* (on line) 1(1):3. http://www/consecology.org/voll/issl/art3.

del Giorgio, P. A., J. M. Gasol, D. Vaque, P. Mura, S. Agusti, and C. Duarte. 1996. Bacterioplankton community structure: protists control net production and the proportion of active bacteria in a coastal marine community. *Limnology and Oceanography* 41:1169–1179.

DiSalvo, L., and H. T. Odum. 1974. Coral reefs. In *Coastal ecological systems of the United States*, ed. H. T. Odum, B. J. Copeland, and E. A. McMahan, 372-441. Washington, D.C.: The Conservation Foundation in cooperation with the National Oceanic and Atmospheric Administration Office of Coastal Environment.

Donning, D. P. 1981. Sea cows and sea grasses. *Palaeobiology* 7:417–420.

Fitzsimons, J. M., R. T. Nishimoto, and W. S. Devick. 1996. Maintaining biodiversity in freshwater ecosystems on oceanic islands of the tropical pacific. *Chinese Biodiversity* 4:23–27.

Keast, A. 1996. Pacific biogeography: patterns and processes. In *The origin and evolution of Pacific Island biotas*, ed. A. Keast and S. E. Miller, 477–512. Amsterdam: SPB Academic Publishing.

Ford, J. I., and R. A. Kinzie III. 1982. Life crawls upstream. *Natural History* 91(12):60–67.

Gage, J. D., and P. A. Tyler. 1991. *Deep-sea biology: a natural history of organisms at the deep-sea floor*. Cambridge: Cambridge University Press.

Grigg, R. W., and J. E. Maragos. 1974. Recolonization of hermatypic corals on submerged lava flows in Hawaii. *Ecology* 55:387–395.

Hallock, P. 1997. Reefs and reef limestones in earth history. In *Life and death of coral reefs*, ed. C. E. Birkeland, 13–42. New York: Chapman and Hall.

Hatcher, B. G. 1997. Organic production and decomposition. In *Life and death of coral reefs*, ed. C. E. Birkeland, 140–174. New York: Chapman and Hall.

Haygood, M. G. 1996. The potential role of functional differences between Rubisco forms in governing expression in chemoautotrophic symbioses. *Limnology and Oceanography* 41:370–371.

Hessler, R. R., and P. F. Lonsdale. 1991. Biogeography of the Mariana Trough hydrothermal vents. In *Marine biology, its accomplishment and future prospect*, ed. J. Mauchline and T. Nemoto, 65–182. Tokyo: University of Tokyo Press, and Amsterdam: Elsevier Science Publishers.

Hobbie, J. E. 1988. A comparison of the ecology of planktonic bacteria in fresh and salt water. *Limnology and Oceanography* 33:750–764.

Hosakawa, T., H. Tagawa, and V. J. Chapman. 1977. Mangals of Microneisa, Taiwan, Japan, the Philippines, and Oceania. In *Ecosystems of the world 1. Wet coastal ecosystems*, ed. V. J. Chapman, 271–291. New York: Elsevier Science Publishers.

Howarth, R. W., R. Marino, and J. Lane. 1988. Nitrogen fixation in freshwater, estuarine, and marine ecosystems: 1. Rates and importance. *Limnology and Oceanography* 33:669–687.

Huryn, A. D. 1996. An appraisal of the Allen paradox in a New Zealand trout stream. *Limnology and Oceanography* 4:243–252.

Jannasch, H. W., and C. D. Taylor. 1984. Deep-sea microbiology. *Annual Review of Microbiology* 38:487–514.

Kay, E. A. 1980. Little worlds of the Pacific: An essay on Pacific basin biogeography. *University of Hawaii Harold L. Lyon Lectures* 9:1–40.

King, M. 1989. *Coastal environments in the South Pacific*. Noumea: SPREP (South Pacific Regional Environmental Program).

Lassuy, D. R. 1980. Effects of "farming" behavior by *Eupomacentrus lividus* and *Hemiglyphidodon plagiometopon* on algal community structure. *Bulletin of Marine Science* 30:304–312.

Lesser, M. P. 1996. Elevated temperature and ultraviolet radiation cause oxidative stress and inhibit photosynthesis in symbiotic dinoflagellates. *Limnology and Oceanography* 41:272–283.

Lockwood, G. 1997. World shrimp production with environmental and social accountability: a perspective and a proposal. *World Aquaculture* 28:52–55.

Longhurst, A. R. and D. Pauly. 1987. *Ecology of tropical oceans*. San Diego: Academic Press.

Lowe-McConnell, R. H. 1977. *Ecology of fishes in tropical waters*. Institute of Biology's Studies in Biology no. 76. London: Edward Arnold.

Lowe-McConnell, R. H. 1987. *Ecological studies in tropical fish communities*. Cambridge: Cambridge University Press.

Lugo, A. E., S. Brown, and M. M. Brown. 1988. Forested wetlands in freshwater and salt-water environments. *Limnology and Oceanography* 33:894–909.

Maciolek, J. A., and J. I. Ford. 1987. Macrofauna and environment of the Nanpil-Kiepw River, Ponape, Eastern Caroline Islands. *Bulletin of Marine Science* 41:623–632.

Maciolek, J. A. and A. S. Timbol. Environmental features and macrofauna of Kahana estuary, Oahu, Hawaii. *Bulletin of Marine Science* 31:712–722.

Mangel, M., R. S. Hofman, and J. R. Twiss, Jr. 1993. Sustainability and ecological research. *Ecological Applications* 3:573–575

Mann, K. 1988. Production and use of detritus in various freshwater, estuarine, and coastal marine ecosystems. *Limnology and Oceanography* 33:910–930.

McDowall, R. M. 1990. Freshwater fishes and fisheries of New Zealand—the angler's Eldorado. *Reviews in Aquatic Sciences* 2:281–341.

Morton, J., and M. Miller. 1968. *The New Zealand sea shore*. London-Auckland: Collins.

Muller-Parker, G., and C. F. D'Elia. 1997. Interactions between corals and their symbiotic algae. In *Life and death of coral reefs*, ed. C. E. Birkeland, 96–113. New York: Chapman and Hall.

Nelson, S. G. 1985. Immediate enhancement of photosynthesis by marine macrophytes in reponse to ammonia enrichment. *Proceedings of the Fifth International Coral Reef Congress, Tahiti*, Vol. 5:65–70.

Nelson, S. G., and L. G. Eldredge. 1991. Distribution and status of introduced cichlid fishes of the genera *Oreochromis* and *Tilapia* in the islands of the South Pacific and Micronesia. *Asian Fisheries Science* 4:11–22.

Nelson, S. G., J. E. Parham, R. B. Tibbatts, F. A. Camacho, T. Leberer, and B. D. Smith. 1997. Distributions and microhabitats of the amphidromous gobies in streams of Micronesia. *Micronesica* 30:83–91.

Nelson, S. G., and S. deC. Wilkins. 1988. Sediment processing by the surgeonfish *Ctenochaetus striatus* at Moorea, French Polynesia. *Journal of Fisheries Biology* 32:817–824.

Nunn, Patrick D. 1994. *Oceanic islands*. Oxford: Blackwell.

Odum, H. T., B. J. Copeland, and E. A. McMahan 1974. *Coastal ecological systems of the United States*. Vol. 1. Washington, D.C.: The Conservation Foundation in cooperation with National Oceanic and Atmospheric Administration, Office of Coastal Environment.

Paul, V. J. 1990. Seaweed chemical defenses on coral reefs. In *Ecological roles of marine natural products*, ed. V. J. Paul, 24–50. Ithaca and New York: Comstock Publishing Associates.

Paul, V. J., S. G. Nelson, and H. R. Sanger. 1990. Feeding preferences of adult and juvenile rabbitfish *Siganus argenteus* in relation to chemical defenses of tropical seaweeds. *Marine Ecology Progress Series* 60:23–34.

Paulay, G. 1997. Diversity and distribution of reef organisms. In *Life and death of coral reefs*, ed. C. Birkeland, 298–353. New York: Chapman and Hall.

Phillips, R. C., and E. G. Menez. 1988. Seagrasses. *Smithsonian Contributions to the Marine Sciences* 94. Washington, D.C.: Smithsonian Institute Press.

Polovina, J. J. 1984. Model of a coral reef ecosystem I. The ECOPATH model and its application to French Frigate Shoals. *Coral Reefs* 3:1–11.

Pringle, C. M., G. A. Blake, A. P. Covich, K. M. Buzby, and A. Finley. 1993. Effects of omnivorous shrimp in a montane tropical stream: sediment removal, disturbance of sessile invertebrates and enhancement of understory algal biomass. *Oecologia* 93:1–11.

Robinson, J. J., and C. M. McCavanaugh. 1995. Expression of form I and form II Rubisco in chemoautotrophic symbioses: Implications for the interpretation of stable carbon isotope values. *Limnology and Oceanography* 40:1496–1502.

Rougerie, F., and B. Waruthy. 1993. The endo-upwelling concept: from geothermal convection to reef construction. *Coral Reefs* 12:19–30.

Ryan, P. A. 1991. The success of the Gobiidae in tropical Pacific insular streams. *New Zealand Journal of Marine and Freshwater Research*. 18:25–30.

Schiel, D. R. 1988. Algal interactions on shallow subtidal reefs in northern New Zealand: a review. *New Zealand Journal of Marine and Freshwater Research* 22:481–489.

Schiel, D. R. 1994. Kelp communities. In *Marine biology*, ed. L. S. Hammond and R. N. Synnot, 345–361. Sydney: Longman Cheshire.

Schiel, D. R., N. L. Andrew, and M. S. Foster. 1995. The structure of subtidal algal and invertebrate assemblages at the Chatham Islands, New Zealand. *Marine Biology* 123:355–367.

Somero, G. N., E. Dahlhoff, and A. Gibbs. 1991. Biochemical adaptations of deep-sea animals: insights into biogeography and ecological energetics. In *Marine biology, its accomplishment and future prospect*, eds. J. Mauchline and T. Nemoto, 39–57. Tokyo: University of Tokyo Press and Amsterdam: Elsevier Science Publishers.

Stevenson, J. C. 1988. Comparative ecology of submerged grass beds in freshwater, estuarine, and marine environments. *Limnology and Oceanography* 33:867–893.

Sumich, J. L. 1988. *An introduction to the biology of marine life*. Dubuque, Iowa: William Brown Publishers.

Tanoue, E., M. Ishii, T. Midorikawa. 1996. Discrete dissolved and particulate proteins in oceanic waters. *Limnology and Oceanography* 41:1334–1343.

Twilley, R. R., A. E. Lugo, and C. Patterson-Zucca. 1986. Litter production and turnover in basin mangrove forests in southwest Florida. *Ecology* 67:670–683.

Van Dover, C. L., and B. Fry. 1994. Microorganisms as food resources of deep-sea hydrothermal vents. *Limnology and Oceanography* 39:51–57.

Vitousek, P. M., H. A. Mooney, J. Lubchenco, and J. M. Milillo. 1997. Human domination of earth's ecosystems. *Science* 277:494–499.

Ward, T. J., and S. J. M. Blaber. 1994. Continental shelves and slopes. In *Marine biology*, ed. L. S. Hammond and R. N. Synnot, 333–344. Sydney: Longman Cheshire.

Wheeler, T. 1988. *Papua New Guinea: a travel survival kit*. Victoria, Australia: Lonely Planet Publications.

Williamson, C. E., R. W. Sanders, R. E. Moeller, and P. L. Stutsman. 1996. Utilization of subsurface food resources for zooplankton reproduction: implications for diel vertical migration theory. *Limnology and Oceanography* 41:224–233.

Yamamuro, M., H. Kayanne, and M. Minagawa. 1995. Carbon and nitrogen strable isotopes of primary producers in coral reef ecosystems. *Limnology and Oceanography* 40:617–621.

## Appendix 9.1. Taxonomic Relationships of Some Common Aquatic Invertebrates

| Phylum | Class | Freshwater species | Marine species |
| --- | --- | --- | --- |
| **Arthropoda** | Crustacea | Crabs, shrimps, crayfishes | Crabs, lobsters, shrimps, amphipods, copepods, barnacles |
| **Mollusca** | Gastropoda | Snails | Snails, sea slugs |
|  | Bivalvia | Clams | Oysters, clams |
|  | Cephalopoda |  | Squids, octopi |
| **Annelida** | Polychaeta | Worms | Bristle worms |
| **Echinodermata** | Holothuridea |  | Sea cucumbers |
|  | Echinoidea |  | Sea urchins |
|  | Asteroidea |  | Starfishes; brittle stars |
| **Coelenterata** | Anthozoa |  | Corals, sea anemones |
|  | Scyphozoa |  | Jellyfishes |
| **Chordata** | Ascidiacea |  | Sea squirts |
| **Poriphera** |  | Sponge (rare) | Sponges |

# SECTION 3

# HISTORY

Pacific Islanders have had varying experiences under colonialism. The impact was especially profound in land-rich islands amenable to agricultural settlement. In the worst situations, islanders have become outnumbered, deprived of their land, marginalized, or assimilated into the dominant society. Fewer settlers arrived on very small islands, but traditional sociopolitical, economic, and religious systems have been severely challenged. Section 3 explores Pacific Islands history, with chapters on prehistory, the postcontact period, politics, race relations, and literature. Contributors include Frank R. Thomas, David A. Chappell, Terence Wesley-Smith, RDK Herman, and Selina Tusitala Marsh.

# CHAPTER 10

# The Precontact Period

*Frank R. Thomas*

## Introduction

As the pace of European exploration of the Pacific quickened in the second half of the eighteenth century, an increasing number of insular societies were drawn into the various processes of culture contact, often with disastrous consequences. Thus ended what may be considered the prehistory of an area, archipelago, or specific island and the beginning of the historic period. The history of the region is of course known to us from the written sources left by a variety of individuals (explorers, traders, missionaries) who interacted with Pacific Islanders. The former were also responsible for providing the outside world with the first accounts on the origin of Oceania's inhabitants.

Prehistory, as defined by most contemporary scholars, draws on several disciplines, including, but not limited to, linguistics, biological anthropology, the study of oral tradition, and archaeology. As Chappell (this volume) points out, these approaches may also provide important information and offer alternative perspectives on the nature of early Euro-American and Pacific Islander encounters. Clearly, no single approach for understanding the past can claim supremacy. Conflict between disciplines may be a source of healthy skepticism that allows us to look at our methods and theories in a more critical way.

This chapter attempts to present a synthetic view of the Pacific Islands before European contact by examining data gathered from a range of disciplines and showing how various methods and theories have led to explanations or interpretations. Several themes, reflecting the diversity and unity of recent investigations in the region, are addressed. They include 1) origins and direction of settlement; 2) subsistence strategies; 3) long-distance exchange; 4) demography; 5) sociopolitical evolution; 6) warfare; and 7) human impact on island ecosystems.

The review relies largely on western scientific approaches. This is not to deny the significance of indigenous perspectives and understanding. While conflicts over the ownership and control of remains and interpretation of the past (and the present!) are not expected to be resolved anytime soon (e.g. Cachola-Abad 1993, Graves and Erkelens 1991), there is a need for continued dialogue between native voices and those who study them.

## Origins and Direction of Settlement

### Pleistocene Occupation of Greater Australia and Beyond

The settlement of the Pacific may be divided into two broad phases: 1) a Pleistocene (the last ice age from about 3 million to 10,000 years ago) occupation of Sahulland (also called Sahul—Greater Australia, including New Guinea) and islands of Near Oceania (Bismarck to Solomon Archipelagoes) and 2) a late-Holocene colonization past the main Solomon Islands into Remote Oceania. Two biogeographical boundaries are thought to have played a significant role in the human settlement of the Pacific: the Wallace-Huxley Line and the boundary between Near and Remote Oceania (Figure 10.1).

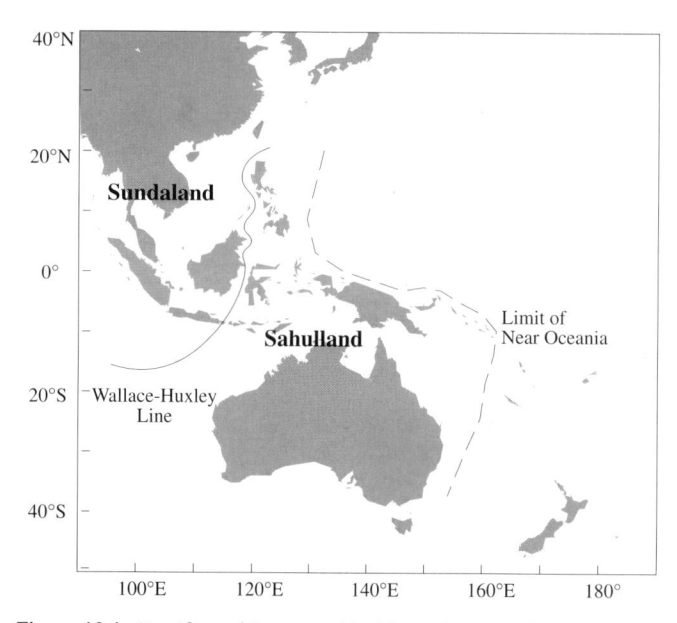

*Figure 10.1. Significant biogeographical boundaries in the southwest Pacific (after Bellwood 1993).*

East of the Wallace-Huxley Line lies Wallacea, which comprises the islands between the continental shelves of Sundaland (mainland Southeast Asia, western Indonesia, and the adjacent continental shelf) and Sahulland. Dispersal into Wallacea from Sundaland (where human antiquity is presumed to be greater in view of the presence of the pre-modern hominid *Homo erectus* in Java), could only be accomplished by crossing stretches of open ocean (even at lowest sea level), although from this region to San Cristobal at the end of the main Solomons chain, most islands are intervisible.

It is reasonable to assume that with falling sea level, the frequency of successful voyaging and colonization would have been high. But also, with rising postglacial seas, marine resources gained in importance for some populations, promoting seafaring skills. There are few reliably dated Pleistocene sites in Wallacea. On Sulawesi, evidence of occupation may stretch as far back as 30,000 B.P. ("Before Present," or prior to A.D. 1950, from which radiocarbon dates are measured) (Clark 1991). In the northern Mollucas, coastal caves are known to have been occupied by 33,000 B.P. (Bellwood 1997).

Sites dating to between 30,000 and 20,000 B.P. are known from throughout Australia, as are some even older sites, including startling new evidence for human occupation of the northwestern part of the continent by at least 116,000 years, according to thermoluminescence dating (Fullagar et al. 1996, Smith and Sharp 1993). Australia's cultural evolution appeared to have had only minor influence on subsequent developments elsewhere in the Pacific. The northern part of Sahulland, however, presented greater opportunities for economic transformations, setting the stage for expansion farther east.

In the New Guinea Highlands, Kosipe and Nombe are the two oldest known sites, having been occupied by at least 25,000 B.P. (Allen 1993). The Huon peninsula in northeastern New Guinea yielded waisted axes dating back to more than 40,000 years (Groube et al. 1986). Several cave, rock shelter, and open-air Pleistocene sites, associated with the local exploitation of chert (a flintlike quartz) and obsidian (volcanic glass), are known east of New Guinea (Figure 10.2). They include sites on New

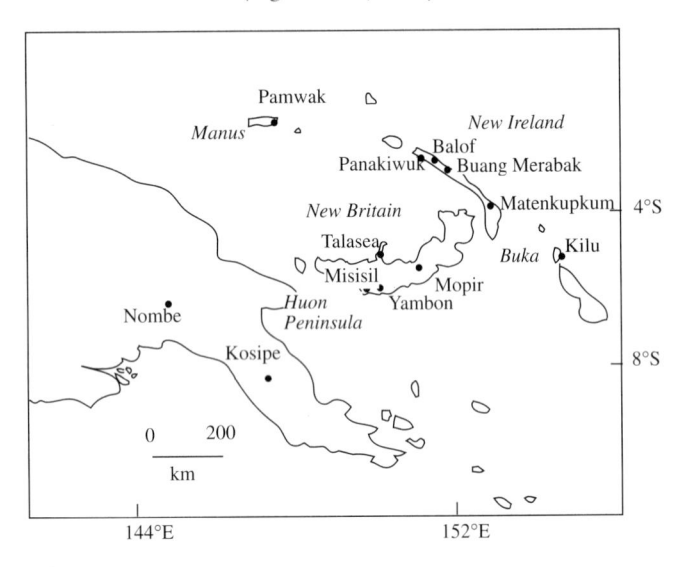

*Figure 10.2. Pleistocene sites in the southwest Pacific (after Gosden 1993).*

Britain, New Ireland, Manus (Admiralty Islands), and Buka (northern Solomons) (Allen 1993, Frederiksen et al. 1993, Pavlides and Gosden 1994, Specht 1981, Spriggs 1993a, Summerhayes and Allen 1993). Evidence of cultural activities in the region goes back to 35,000 B.P.

### The Holocene and the Lapita Phenomenon

As the glaciers retreated worldwide and sea levels rose and then stabilized, important cultural transformations were underway. Probably the most notable change involved the first attempts at plant domestication, which would later have tremendous impacts on human demography and social evolution.

By the early Holocene, New Guinea and most if not all the islands of Near Oceania displayed rich cultural, linguistic, and human biological diversity.

Suddenly (within a few centuries), a well-marked cultural horizon appeared, from the Bismarcks to Samoa (Figure 10.3).

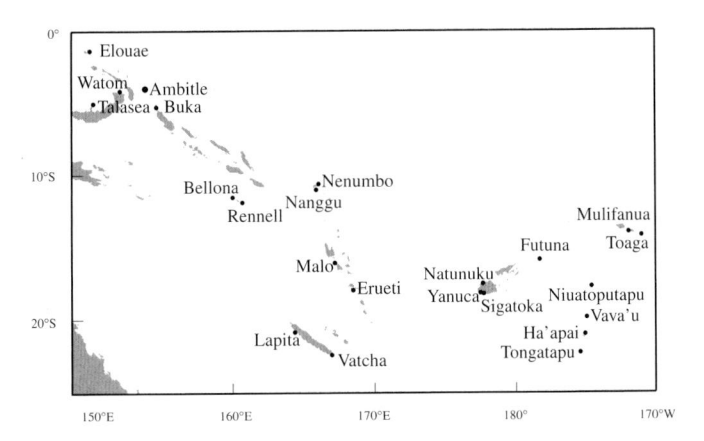

*Figure 10.3. Major Lapita sites (after Bellwood 1993).*

On present evidence, this Lapita horizon was the first to have reached the islands of Remote Oceania (Green 1979). The most diagnostic trait associated with this horizon consists of a distinctive dentate-stamped pottery style, Lapita, named after a site on the west coast of New Caledonia and related to earlier findings on the northeastern tip of New Britain. This pottery is known from various localities, as far away as Samoa. Because of the absence of pre-Lapita occupation in Remote Oceania, it has been suggested that further expansion into the Pacific required substantial improvements in navigational skills and technology, not available to Pleistocene and early Holocene seafarers, even at times of lower sea level (Irwin 1992:43, but see Nunn [1993:20] for the opposing viewpoint).

Alternatively, factors of biogeography (limited plant and animal resources on more distant islands) rather than limitations in seafaring technology could effectively have prevented early settlement of Santa Cruz, Vanuatu, and New Caledonia unless "an economy based on cultivation or at least a developed form of wild plant-food production involving transportation of many useful plant species" was already established (Spriggs 1993b:141).

Lapita may be looked at in terms of continuities and discontinuities with the preceding period. Cases for continuity include the expansion of an exchange system identified archaeologically in the form of obsidian and a trend toward increasing exploitation of marine resources (Spriggs 1993a). Although there is no convincing evidence for pre-Lapita animal and plant domestication (with the exception of *Canarium*), agriculture (probably taro) was practiced in the New Guinea Highlands some 9,000 years ago (Hope et al. 1983). The notion that Lapita colonists carried cultigens and agricultural techniques from Southeast Asia has been modified by genetic research showing that some of these cultigens are native to wider areas, including New Guinea (Table 10.1) (Yen 1985).

Perhaps the most compelling piece of evidence in favor of

### Table 10.1

**Major Pacific Island Plant Foods**

| Species | Origin |
| --- | --- |
| **Trees and shrubs** | |
| *Artocarpus altilis* (breadfruit) | New Guinea |
| *Cocos nucifera* (coconut) | IndoPacific |
| *Metroxylon* spp. (sago) | New Guinea |
| *Musa sapientum* (banana) | Southeast Asia |
| *Musa troglodytarum* (Australimusa banana) | New Guinea |
| *Pandanus tectorius* | IndoPacific |
| *Piper methysticum* (kava) | Melanesia |
| *Syzigium maaccense* (mountain apple) | Southeast Asia |
| **Tubers** | |
| *Alocasia macrorrhiza* | Southeast Asia |
| *Colocasia esculenta* (taro) | Southeast Asia |
| *Cyrtorsperma chamissonis* (swamp taro) | Southeast Asia |
| *Dioscorea* spp. (yam) | Southeast Asia |
| *Ipomoea batatas* (sweet potato)* | Americas |
| *Tacca leotopetaloides* (arrowroot) | Southeast Asia |
| **Other plants** | |
| *Oriza sativa* (rice)-Marianas only* | Southeast Asia |
| *Saccharum officinarum* (sugarcane) | New Guinea |

* use uncertain prior to European contact

discontinuity is the sudden appearance of a highly decorated ceramic style in the Bismarcks and the almost instantaneous (in archaeological terms) spread of Lapita east to Santa Cruz (Solomon Islands), Natunuku (Fiji), Niuatoputapu (Tonga), and To'aga (Manu'a, American Samoa), beginning about 4000 B.P. and covering a distance greater than 4,000 km in perhaps 300 years or less (Kirch et al. 1990). On present evidence, settlement of the Marianas took place about 3500 B.P., probably from the Philippines. It is possible that both Yap and Belau were also occupied during that period, but so far there is no evidence of human occupation prior to about 2000 B.P (Irwin 1992:127, Rainbird 1994).

Other elements that seem to be associated with the initial appearance of Lapita include a distinctive adz kit; shell ornaments; animal husbandry of pig, dog, and chicken; the first convincing evidence of plant domestication as revealed by macrofossils; a new settlement pattern of stilt houses over lagoons or on small offshore islands; and the expansion in the distribution of New Britain and Admiralty (Lou) Island obsidian westward to Sabah (Borneo) and eastward to Fiji (Spriggs 1993a).

In sum, Lapita emerges as a blend of external and indigenous elements. The linguistic evidence supports the view that there was a movement of people from Island Southeast Asia into the Bismarcks and beyond. Language remains one of the most powerful links between Oceanian and Southeast Asian populations (Pawley and Ross 1993). In Near Oceania, the new migrants found previously established populations who spoke non-Austronesian languages, presumably the descendants of the first Pleistocene inhabitants, and interacted with them to produce the rich linguistic, biological, and cultural types found in the region today (Bellwood 1993).

Small founding populations who ventured farther into the eastern Pacific underwent a series of genetic changes (Houghton 1991, Serjeantson and Gao 1995). However, there is clear evidence for a genetic trail leading back into Southeast Asia (Pietrusewsky 1994; Serjeantson and Hill 1989).

### Toward the Sunrise and the Margins

An important issue confronting prehistorians studying Lapita is the chronological gap between the settlement of Samoa and islands farther east (Cook Islands, Societies, Marquesas, and other archipelagoes). It may be that the people who settled Samoa required some time to adapt to its geological and faunistic elements, in contrast to the better-endowed islands in the southwest Pacific. According to Irwin (1992:83), however, there appears to be no navigational threshold between the so-called western and eastern Polynesian islands to warrant a long pause in colonization.

It may be that the earliest sites east of Samoa have simply not yet been located. Likewise, there is no firm evidence of human occupation from Kiribati to the high islands and atolls of the Carolines prior to about 2000 B.P. (Irwin 1992:130-131). Subsidence of Pacific Plate islands and coastal progradation (deposition and cementation of beach sand) would probably hinder the discovery of early sites in those regions (Kirch 1988b). To this evidence may be added the low archaeological visibility of sites in the paucity of ceramics (Irwin 1981). The evidence from liguistics suggests a period of unified development on the order of 1,000 years, presumably in Western Polynesia, to account for the innovations in Proto-Polynesian before the divergence of the Eastern Polynesian branch (Pawley 1996).

New navigational problems had to be overcome in the settlement of Remote Oceania. As one moves away from the sailing corridor in the western Pacific that brings westerlies into Near Oceania (during the southern summer monsoons), southeast trade winds become more pronounced, making it more difficult to sail eastward. Terrell (1986:86) suggests that in the process of expansion into the eastern Pacific, and before a successful landfall was made, "many human lives were lost at sea"; Irwin (1992:88-89), however, argues that these failures resulted in relatively few deaths, but were part of an exploring strategy of "upwind, uplatitude method of search and return."

Continued expansion toward the extremities of the "Polynesian Triangle" or "Marginal Polynesia" brought ancient voyagers to lands lying outside the tropics (e.g., Easter Island, New Zealand). The peculiar climate of those regions, the great distances separating the various archipelagoes and the attendant reduction in the frequency of contacts, together with the challenges and opportunities offered by the new environments contributed to further divergence among scattered communities. Evidence for human activity in Hawai'i is allegedly present by about 2000 B.P. (Hunt and Holsen 1991), on Easter Island between 2000 and 1700 B.P. (Kirch 1984:267), and in New Zealand perhaps as early as 1700 B.P. (Sutton 1987). However, more conservative estimates continue to be ardently defended (Anderson 1996, Spriggs and Anderson 1993). A landfall on the South American coast remains a distinct possibility, but so far the evidence for such contact is limited to the sweet potato (*Ipomoea batatas*) (Yen 1971).

## Subsistence Strategies

### Terrestrial Resources and Production

In the vast territory stretching across the southern portion of Sahulland (Australia), cultural communities were able to disperse in their search for food. Indeed, the landscape provided an array of animal resources, while the coasts supplied fish and shellfish. Wild plants were also exploited, but true agriculture did not develop to an extent comparable to that of New Guinea.

Groube (1989) proposed a sequence for the emergence of food production in northern Sahulland. From initial forest foraging and hunting, people began to select and promote certain plants, through both minimal clearance and expansion of the forest fringes. As group territories stabilized, forest management led to permanent or semipermanent promoted stands (e.g., sago) in the wet forested regions and the management of scattered natural stands in areas with a dry season. In the latter case, the system evolved into forest gardens. Between 10,000 and 5,000 years ago, intergroup competition and perhaps the introduced Asian pig may have played key roles in the development of this strategy. The final stage was achieved by the creation of fenced or ditched gardens to keep growing pig populations out of cultivated areas.

The presence of waisted axes in New Guinea and Australia by at least 40,000 years ago may provide indirect evidence of forest clearance associated with food plant promotion rather than as the sole result of hunting practices.

Carbonized particles from several New Guinea highland sites, including the Baliem Valley (Irian Jaya), Kosipe, and Telefomin, demonstrate that humans were actively manipulating the environment at different times during the last 30,000 years. The overall impact appeared to have been minimal, however, possibly due to low population densities in the late Pleistocene (Haberle 1993). It is not until 7000 B.P that we begin to have clear evidence for human impact on the vegetation from the Baliem Valley.

Beyond Sahulland, evidence for late Pleistocene and early Holocene environmental and plant manipulation remains scanty. Remains of *Canarium* nuts from Pamwak and Kilu may indicate deliberate planting, tending, and harvesting of these comparatively nonperishable resources, which were possibly introduced from New Guinea, and could assist in modeling a pathway to agriculture based on energetically efficient arboriculture in the depauperate forests on the smaller islands (Clarke et al. this volume, Spriggs 1993b). A successful colonizing strategy would also include the deliberate introduction of wild animals such as the bandicoot (*Echymipera kalubu*) at Pamwak, cuscus (*Phalanger orientalis*), and wallaby (*Thylogale brunii*), whose remains have been found in New Ireland caves (Flannery and White 1991). Other introductions, particularly rat species, were more likely accidental byproducts of human colonization of the islands.

In sum, one could interpret changes in the archaeological record after 20,000 B.P. as an attempt to mimic the greater biological diversity of New Guinea—in effect, bringing resources to people rather than moving people to resources. This was accompanied by the transfer of materials such as New Britain obsidian (Gosden 1993). According to Gosden, this new strategy may have started when growing populations restricted mobility. By the time humans penetrated into Remote Oceania, it would be fair to say that the Indo-Pacific tuber/root/tree crop complex (Table 10.1) had developed to a degree that enabled the biogeographically depauperate islands to support relatively large social units.

Coconuts and pandanus, being salt tolerant, may have been established on coasts before the arrival of humans. The coconuts, whose floating ability has been documented, would have encouraged people to settle in the face of uncertain water resources. Coconuts and irrigated taro could be relied upon perennially and, together with breadfruit and pandanus, could be preserved (Alkire 1978:30). In some locations, early ethnographic descriptions and recent archaeological research suggest the absence of precontact dogs, pigs, and fowl, perhaps because of the lack of sufficient food or water (particularly on atolls) and the direct competition with humans. Birds would have been relatively abundant, however, at least in the initial stages of human settlement.

At higher latitudes, a number of tropical crops simply could not thrive. In New Zealand, horticulture was dominated by the sweet potato, supplemented by yam, taro, gourd, and *Cordyline terminalis*. Because of a more benign climate, food production had achieved greater success on the North Island compared with the South Island. However, the long coastline and vast land area of both islands provided ample opportunities for a hunting-gathering-fishing economy that included the exploitation of fern root, large sea mammals, and gigantic flightless birds (Davidson 1983). Other islands lying outside the tropics, such as the Kermadecs, Chathams, Norfolk, Rapa, and Easter, would have posed similar challenges to the establishment of introduced crops and animals.

Data on prehistoric food production are varied and include both direct and indirect evidence such as food preparation tools; large-scale anthropogenic burning and concomitant erosion; anthropophilic land snails; the recovery of pig and chicken bones and their strong association with horticultural systems; pondfields and other forms of irrigation; garden soils under mounds; desiccated, waterlogged, and carbonized plants; and trace elements in bone.

## Marine Exploitation

Fish and marine invertebrates constitute a significant portion of the protein diet of many Pacific Island societies. It is apparent from the archaeological record that the general patterns of marine resource exploitation, particularly nearshore faunas, extend far back into the prehistoric record (Butler 1988, Nagaoka 1988).

Environments characterized by broad reef flats led to the development of fishing gear and techniques quite distinct from those employed around islands lacking such features.

The study of the marine component of prehistoric insular societies was first dominated by the typological approach, examining fishhooks and other gear to infer migration paths and to establish the relative age of sites in the same way pottery and other artifacts were examined. More recently, the focus has shifted toward ecologically oriented work that includes the analysis of tool function, the recovery and quantification of faunal remains, collection of environmental data on the marine habitats, and ethnoarchaeological inquiries to develop and test hypotheses regarding prehistoric fishing behavior and to answer questions of long-term change in fishing and shell-gathering practices (Allen 1992, Anderson 1981, Kirch and Dye 1979).

## Intensification of Production

In his seminal work on subsistence agriculture, Barrau (1965) described two basic environments: "the wet and the dry." Taro fits into Barrau's first division, while yams, sweet potato, and a range of other crops belong in the second. Indigenous systems were of two types: extensive and intensive. The former characterized shifting cultivation, in which the garden plots were left fallow after cropping to allow for soil regeneration, while the latter featured changes in hydrologic and edaphic (soil related) conditions to increase yields (Kirch 1979).

A good example of studies of agricultural intensification is provided by research in Hawai'i. Taro pondfields (Figure 10.4) were particularly numerous on windward sides of islands. Irrigation technology and coordinated water use were cited by Allen (1991) as having played crucial roles in fostering political complexity by producing large surpluses for the ruling classes to further legitimize their position of authority. On O'ahu, production of taro surpluses was achieved by A.D. 1400, reflecting the centralized control of agriculture. However, it appears that the most complex and militarily most powerful chiefdoms arose in dry, leeward sections (Kirch 1994:318-319).

On leeward Maui and Hawai'i Island, sweet potato, sugarcane, gourds, and banana were grown, perhaps as early as A.D. 1350 (Kirch 1985:224-225, 230). At European contact, dense human populations inhabited leeward districts, including those on O'ahu, where sweet potato and fishponds provided a suitable resource base (Thomas 1995). Indeed, the Hawaiian Islands offered a unique form of intensified use of certain marine resources achieved by the construction of fishponds to raise milkfish and mullet, capable of producing more than 900,000 kilograms of fish annually (Kirch 1985:211-214).

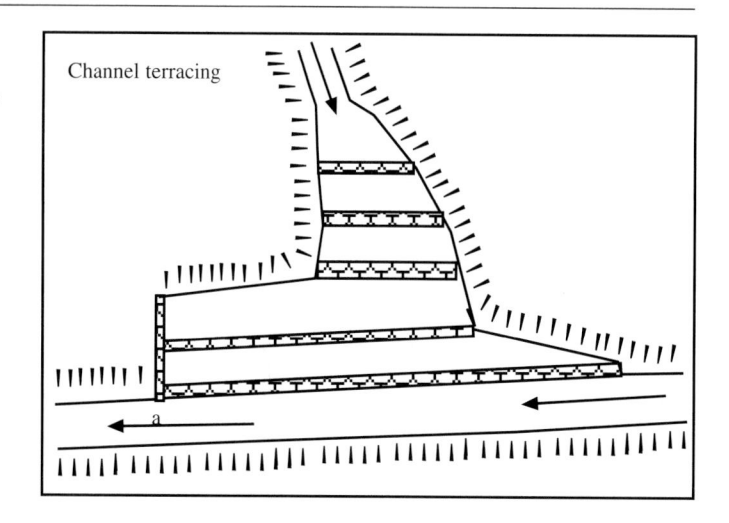

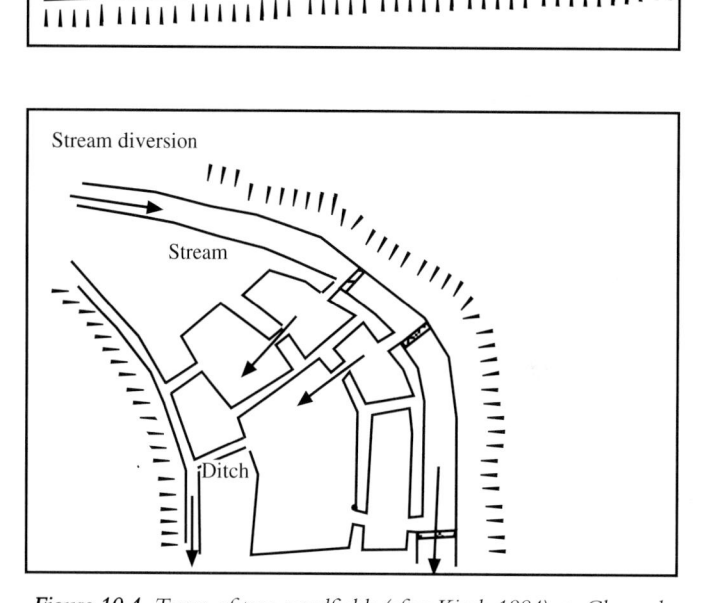

*Figure 10.4.* Types of taro pondfields (after Kirch 1984). **a.** Channel terracing **b.** Stream diversion

## Long-distance Exchange

### Pleistocene and Lapita Exchange Systems

The transfer of "small but continuous amounts" of obsidian is clearly attested in Pleistocene and early Holocene sites on both New Britain and New Ireland, beginning at least 20,000 years ago (Allen 1993:145). The wild animal transfers from New Guinea to the smaller islands may also have been incorporated in exchange networks.

With the appearance of Lapita, there was a corresponding expansion in trade, both geographically and in the quantity of material being moved. New Britain Talasea obsidian has been found as far as the Reef Islands (2,000 km from the source) and Fiji, some 3,700 km distant (Kirch 1991:147). In the Reef-Santa Cruz islands, evidence for imports also includes chert, oven stones, stone adzes, and ceramics over a period of 700 years. These findings suggest that trade may have been carried out through 1) direct access and local reciprocity at distances of less than 30 km; 2) one-stop reciprocity with groups 300–400 km distant; and 3) down-the-line exchange over greater distances (Green 1982). The Lapita system clearly differed from the more specialized and geographically constricted systems described ethnographically in the western Pacific.

Within the Bismarck Archipelago, recent investigations have documented the presence of both Talasea and Lou obsidian at a number of Lapita sites (Figure 10.5). Of particular interest are the changes in the frequency of materials over time. In the Mussau Islands, roughly equal amounts of Talasea and Lou obsidian give way to a dominance of Lou material. Watom Island shows the opposite trend, while sites in southwest New Britain have very occasional Lou pieces, yielding instead numerous Talasea and Mopir imports (Kirch 1991:148).

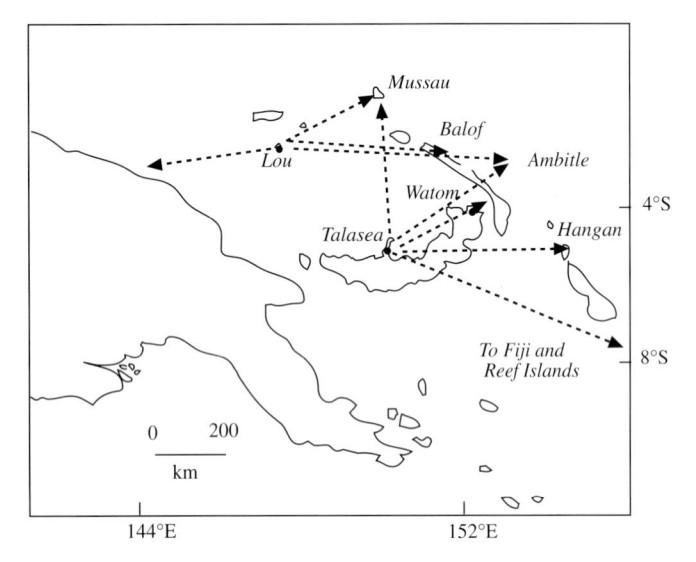

*Figure 10.5.* Directions of obsidian exchange in the Southwest Pacific (after Lacey 1982).

### Some Interaction Spheres within Remote Oceania

Kirch (1978) expressed the view that cultural adaptation in Remote Oceania must have evolved through a trajectory of increasing isolation. While this model may hold for specific localities such as the Hawaiian Archipelago, Easter Island, and New Zealand, there is at present no solid basis that such a process was under way in the Fiji/Tonga/Samoa region (Davidson 1977, Green 1981).

Little is known about the intensity of trade between the island of Tongatapu and the northern Tongan outliers, Fiji, and Samoa prior to about 500 years ago—when Lapita pottery had long since disappeared. The ethnographic evidence shows that trade was entrenched within an intricate system of alliances, as reflected in the exchange of status items (Kirch 1984:239, 322).

Farther out in the eastern Pacific, physical distance and perhaps the relatively greater physical uniformity of islands "offered fewer possibilities for development of distinctively localized production, and hence for complementary goods-focused exchange" (Oliver 1989:564). Nevertheless, given recent conclusions regarding the nature of ancient navigation skills (Irwin 1992), it would seem reasonable to suggest the possibility of engaging in regular trade with mother communities after settlement (cf. Terrell et al. 1997). Where there is ethnographic evidence for extensive networks, such as between the Tuamotu and Society archipelagoes, Yap and Belau (as exemplified by limestone money), or Yap and coral islands to the east (the *sawai* system), there is good reason to use archaeology to trace the evolution of those systems.

As our knowledge improves, we can expect to fill some of the gaps in our understanding of exchange in the vast region of Remote Oceania. For example, recent geochemical studies have confirmed the transfer of basalt artifacts from Tutuila in American Samoa to Mangaia in the Southern Cooks from A.D. 1000–1500 (Weisler and Kirch 1996). Henderson, an elevated limestone island in the southeast Pacific, which was uninhabited at European contact, yielded imported basalt, volcanic oven stones, volcanic glass, and pearlshell, suggesting an interaction sphere that included Pitcairn and Mangareva and ended about A.D. . 1400–1450 (Weisler 1994).

The abandonment of Henderson and other "mystery islands" (Bellwood 1979:352) could be related to a breakdown in communication with other communities.

### Explaining Exchange

Exchange among insular communities provided several benefits, including access to resources that were either absent or in short supply as a result of geologic/biogeographic differences; access to resources subjected to environmental hazards; access to mates in situations of demographic instability; and access to certain "prestige" items to enhance the position of elites. Part of the success of the Lapita expansion into Remote Oceania could be attributed to the maintenance of ties with communities on the better-endowed islands of Near Oceania. This strategy was undoubtedly of great benefit in the initial stages of settlement before local resources could be properly assessed (cf. Kirch 1988b).

Because of their overall marginality, atolls occupy a prominent position in discussions centered on exchanges (Williamson and Sabath 1984). Alkire (1978) described several examples of interisland ties in the form of clusters and complexes. One of the most celebrated cases of extensive networks was the *sawai*, which hierarchically linked Gagil District on Yap to outer atolls stretching for 1,000 km. The importance of these contacts is best illustrated by the fate of those communities that did not survive as a result of distance, relative isolation, and productive potential (Thomas 1993).

Kirch (1991) commented on both the ceremonial and symbolic component of Lapita exchange, based on his Mussau data. Elaborately decorated, labor-intensive ceramics were traded in high volumes and appeared to have been exchanged for shell artifacts. The pottery did not show evidence of having been used in a utilitarian context, such as food preparation. Plainware ceramics, however, were locally manufactured and distributed apart from the decorated sherds, and thus may have functioned differently. Analyses of several vessel attributes of Santa Cruz plain ware (Thomas 1989) suggested a utilitarian function, possibly associated with cooking.

The general conclusion then would be that the production and exchange of decorated pots, shells, and perhaps other items was monitored by elites. In the western Pacific, the collapse of long-distance trade in prestige goods led to increasing trade density over a more restricted space and big-man competitive feasting at the local level. The same process of collapse may have been a factor in the development of theocratic feudalism in some eastern Pacific societies (Friedman 1981).

## Demography

It has long been assumed that rapid population growth generally followed settlement of a pristine ecosystem (*r*-selection). Through time, the intrinsic growth would level off at or near carrying capacity because of increased mortality as density rises (Figure 10.6). Such growth is termed logistical or *K*-selected (Diamond 1977).

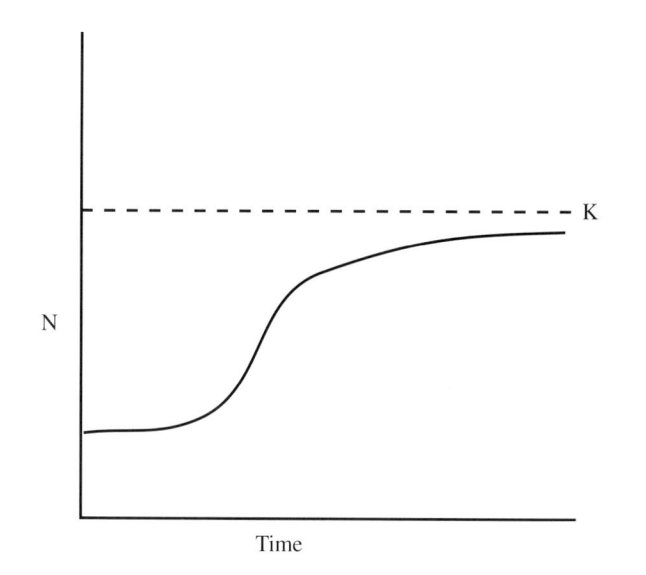

*Figure 10.6. Logistic growth curve (after Kirch 1984).*

There has been much debate concerning the concept of carrying capacity (Dewar 1984). The ethnographic data presented by Birdsell (1968) suggest that the budding-off process would begin before optimum local population is reached (on the order of 60%–70% of the predicted carrying capacity). Bayliss-Smith (1978) emphasized the importance of subjective states of mind, including impressions of overcrowding, excessive workload, and unpleasant diet, in assessing the degree to which populations would disperse or resort to various forms of population control (e.g., infanticide, warfare).

Paleodemography continues to challenge prehistorians. Protohistoric estimates are often widely divergent, since they were not generally based on detailed surveys. Moreover, as populations quickly succumbed to disease, displacement, and intensified warfare in the wake of European intrusion, later censuses often reflected demographic trends quite unlike those that prevailed in the past. Even if reliable estimates could be obtained initially, we would still need to reconstruct the appropriate population growth curve (see Kirch [1984:102] for an illustration of several models of population growth).

In most cases, we are limited to data that take into account a small founding population (of 80 or fewer people), the length of an occupation sequence, and an estimate of population at contact (Green 1993).

Kirch (1984:103) initially favored a logistic or sigmoid process to characterize "population growth on all Polynesian islands," but following criticisms of methods for estimating demographic change and of density-dependent vs. density-independent models (e.g. Sutton and Molloy 1989), he conceded that biological and cultural controls on fertility and mortality could well operate outside conditions of ecological stress (Kirch 1994:310).

Exchange may be examined as a response to risk and uncertainty affecting local resources. Sustained contacts would not only confer advantages in situations of environmental instability, but would also ensure the transfer of people to counter demographic instability, particularly during early stages of colonization (Hunt and Graves 1990). It may be that with the establishment of more stable demographic levels and a more secure subsistence base, the need to pursue long-distance voyaging would have diminished (Kirch 1990).

## Warfare

Open conflicts and warfare may be linked to a variety of circumstances, including the notion that organized aggression may reflect ecological disequilibrium (Sponsel et al. n.d.).

There appears to be a correlation between territoriality and densely distributed, predictable resources. This correlation can be attributed to the fact that such resources are the most economically defendable. In other words, the benefits of maintaining exclusive access to certain resources within an area outweigh the costs of defending them (Dyson-Hudson and Smith 1978). At the same time, such resources constitute the most attractive objects of competitive aggression. In such environments, one might expect to find organized groups bent on defending and acquiring territory.

Carneiro's (1970) theory of "environmental circumscription" argues that warfare was encouraged when an expanding population was constrained either by environmental barriers or competing social groups. Losers of a conflict might be assimilated into the winner's society as a lower class. In this way, a number of independent chiefdoms would eventually be brought under a single hierarchical military government. The adaptive advantages of a successful military operation quickly led to its institutionalization in the form of an early state. The state grew in size as a result of external conquests.

Refinements of Carneiro's theory have included the changing patterns of "artificial" circumscription resulting from anthropogenic degradation (Dickson 1987) and the importance of time depth to account for differences in the level of political organization achieved among the three largest Pacific chiefdoms—New Zealand, Hawai'i, and Tonga (Kirch 1988a).

Conflict over resources, including arable land, has left numerous traces in the archaeological record throughout the Pacific Islands. These comprise the actual weapons and fortified sites, such as those found in Fiji, New Zealand's North Island, and Rapa (Figure 10.7). Other indicators of aggressive behavior

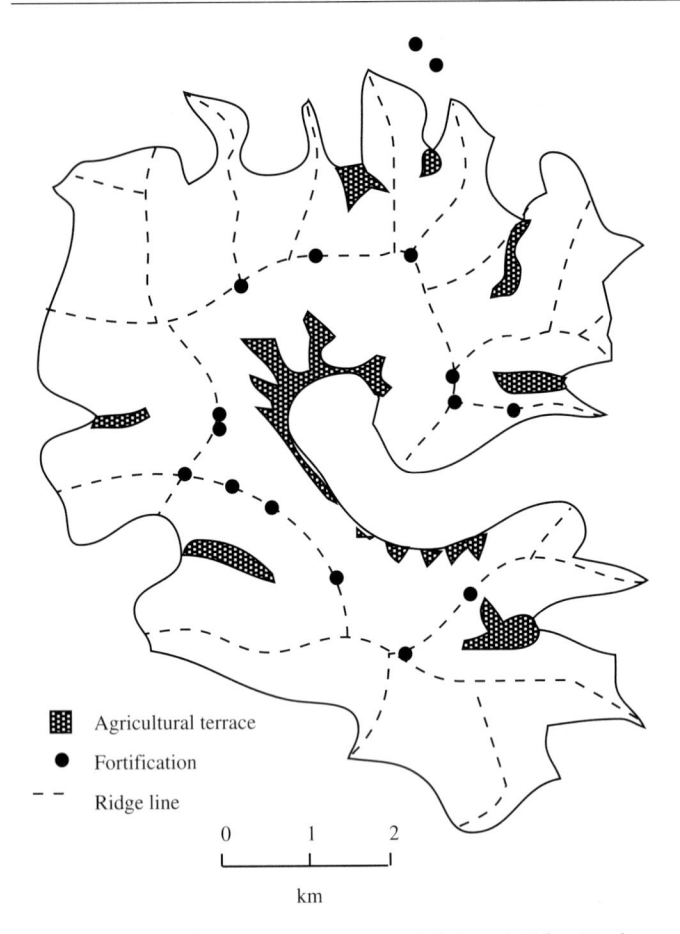

*Figure 10.7. Fortifications on Rapa, French Polynesia (after Kirch 1984).*

include mortuary remains showing death by violent means and wholesale destruction of property and religious sites such as the famous *moai* statues of Easter Island.

Conflict obviously cannot be reduced to underlying ecological principles of competition. Goldman's (1970) thesis that status rivalry had affected the history of all Polynesian societies (and by extension Proto-Oceanic communities) is instructive here. As Kirch writes:

> Population increase and land shortage did not cause endemic warfare in Polynesian islands; they provided a context and stimulus wherein *ariki* [chief] and *toa* [warrior], striving for domination over people and resources, created through conflict, alliance, subversion, and persuasion, social and political systems never before realized in Polynesia.(1984:216)

While atoll societies have generally been depicted as more egalitarian than high-island societies, violent conflict was not absent. In Kiribati wars were waged primarily to compete for fame and secondarily for acquiring land (Baraniko et al. 1979). However, limited and fluctuating resources may have led many atoll societies to quickly grasp environmental constraints and thus establish tight controls over population growth (Bayliss-Smith 1974).

## Sociopolitical Evolution

Kirch (1984) argued that chiefdoms tended to arise in large and densely settled agrarian societies (Figure 10.8). Pressure on environmental resources (see below) stimulated storage of foods, which enhanced the managerial role of the chief and allowed for surplus in time of abundance. Intensification of production is likely to have been stimulated by increasing population, but power rivalries and warfare were ancient features of Pacific Island cultures, and the development of hierarchies may have occurred without population pressure. As Kirch has recently argued:

> Chiefs and the kinship groups they headed took advantage of surplus production to continually renegotiate the relations of asymmetry, hierarchy, dominance, and hegemony both within and without the local group. . . . Hence the importance of social production to an understanding of the processes of agricultural innovation and intensification. (1994:313)

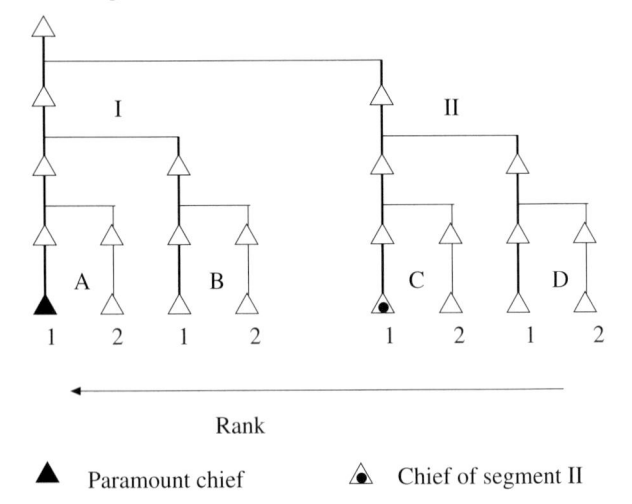

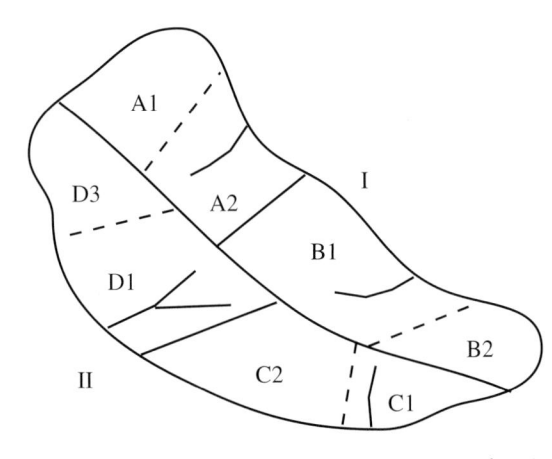

*Figure 10.8. Apical clan segmentation, chiefly succession, and territorial fissioning in a hypothetical island (after Kirch 1984).*

Green (1980) described the prehistory of Makaha Valley on O'ahu to demonstrate increasing stratification in the area. The earliest settlement dates to about A.D. 1100. Within one or two centuries, there is evidence of modification on the valley slopes for dryland farming and the appearance of temporary field shelters. Between A.D. 1400 and 1500, permanent dwellings were built. Irrigation complexes increased the types of production, and a major religious temple (*heiau*) was built (correlating with chiefs who could extract a surplus and mobilize the labor). About A.D. 1650, a Lono-class *heiau* was converted into a *luakini* temple (where human sacrifice was practiced). A large irrigation ditch indicates intensification of production.

By European contact, commoners had lost their genealogies and land and were organized under lateral kin relationships. The *ali'i* (chiefs) were divided into conical clans whose pinnacle was the paramount chief. Tribute was paid to the high chief and used for his organization of advisors and priests, and others who were his immediate support. Large quantities of food were allocated for the construction of irrigation systems, fishponds, temples, chiefs' tombs, and craft specialists (as in Tonga and Tahiti). Chiefs supported commoners through ritual and provision of subsistence in times of shortage. Hawaiian social organization pushed chiefdoms to their structural limit.

## Human Impact on Island Ecosystems

### Influence on Native Vegetation

Data in support of prehistoric human-induced vegetation change in the Pacific come from a variety of sources. Two oceanic islands that have become objects of extensive paleoenvironmental research are briefly reviewed (for other examples, see Kirch [1984:139-146]).

Pollen cores taken from volcanic crater lakes on Easter Island suggest a decline in forest cover in the last millennium, resulting in the grasslands that have characterized the island ever since. Trees would have been felled not only for the purpose of land clearance associated with horticulture and settlements, but also to provide the material needed to transport and raise the numerous megalithic statues. The construction and removal of the statues would have considerably disturbed the surrounding vegetation, causing an increase in soil erosion (Bahn and Flenley 1992).

Recent interdisciplinary work on Mangaia has documented the beginning of significant environmental changes by about 1000 B.P., as evidenced by forest clearance and conversion into fernlands (Figure 10.9); burning, with corresponding increases in charcoal influx; increased soil erosion and alluvial deposition in valley bottoms; remains of domesticated plants and animals, as well as inadvertently introduced rats and landsnails; and avifaunal extinctions (Kirch 1997).

It is important to keep in mind the potential significance of natural phenomena—the effects of climate, sea level, and tectonic forces—to account for environmental change on many islands during their postsettlement history (see Nunn 1992). With the advent of the little Climatic Optimum, beginning about 1200 B.P. and lasting to 650 B.P., much of the tropical

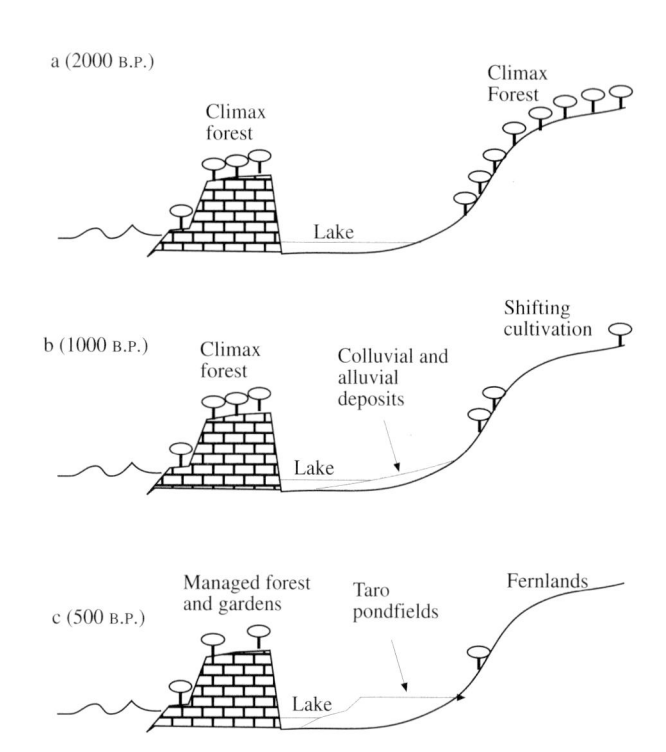

*Figure 10.9. Forest clearance over time in Mangaia, Cook Islands (after Kirch 1997).*

Pacific was warmer and drier than at present, promoting erosion and fires. Forest clearance would have aggravated landscape instability. The Little Ice Age that followed may have put an end to long-distance voyaging as temperatures fell and storminess increased.

Climate-related disruption of cropgrowing systems would have been an important source of social stress. In Fiji, beginning about 850 B.P., there is a proliferation of fortified structures, which may be related to changing climate (Nunn 1992 and this volume). On Easter Island, reduction of trees to build canoes and statues, and perhaps the decline of navigational knowledge following the breakdown in long-distance voyaging, left no escape. Oral traditions and archaeological evidence indicate a period of warfare from A.D. 1300 to 1650, coinciding with the Little Ice Age. Abandonment of some of the "mystery" islands might also be tied to the issue of climate change (McCall 1994).

Careful analysis and interpretation of the paleoenvironmental record should assist future researchers in their assessments of the relative contribution of humans and natural phenomena in bringing about environmental changes (cf. Haberle 1993).

### Impacts on Native Fauna

Human disturbance of island vegetation resulted in the reduction or extinction of several bird species through habitat destruction or fragmentation. Direct predation was another cause for changes in faunal composition, as were the destructive activities of stowaway rats (cf. Cassels [1984] for an overview). While every species is capable of withstanding certain levels of predation, some are more susceptible to overexploitation and extinction than others because of slow reproductive rates and few natural enemies, resulting in restricted mobility and the lack of effective defensive mechanisms. Insular terrestrial fauna, such as flightless birds, are a case in point (Anderson 1989).

Since the discovery of extinct New Zealand *moa* remains, the number of human-induced bird extinctions throughout the Pacific has expanded considerably (Steadman 1997). Large-bodied lizards, such as the extinct iguana from Lifuka, Tonga, also suffered at the hands of human predators. Turtles were also greatly reduced following a period of intense exploitation coinciding with early human presence on several Pacific islands (Dye and Steadman 1990, Kirch 1984:146-147).

A number of studies have examined the long-term effects of human exploitation and environmental change on fish, invertebrate, and sea mammal populations resulting in a decline in species diversity and reduction in average age and size (Allen and Schubel 1990, Anderson 1979, Shawcross 1975, Smith 1989, Spennemann 1987, Swadling 1986).

Catterall and Poiner have studied life history and habitat information to assess resilience among selected intertidal mollusks, finding that species exhibited differences in their ability to withstand similar levels of predation. They cautioned that apparent balance between traditional societies and their resources may be more closely related to a species' biological properties than to deliberate conservation (Catterall and Poiner 1987, Poiner and Catterall 1988).

## Conclusion

The prehistory of the Pacific Islands has been shown to be a complex mix of external influences and local processes of cultural change against the background of a dynamic environment in a variety of settings. Humans did not simply adapt to changing conditions; they also manipulated their social and natural environments, sometimes leading to their demise and sometimes providing themselves with new adaptive options and evolutionary trajectories.

## Acknowledgments

I wish to thank A. Pawley, M. Rapaport, and M. Spriggs for their comments and suggestions for improving this chapter.

## Bibliography

Alkire, W. H. 1978. *Coral islanders*. AHM: Arlington Heights.

Allen, J. 1993. Notions of the Pleistocene in Greater Australia. In *A community of culture: people and prehistory of the Pacific*, ed. M. Spriggs, D. E. Yen, W. Ambrose, R. Jones, A. Thorne, and A. Andrews, 139–151. Occasional Papers in Prehistory No. 21. Canberra: Department of Prehistory, Research School of Pacific Studies.

Allen, M. S. 1992. Temporal variation in Polynesian fishing strategies: the Southern Cook Islands in regional perspective. *Asian Perspectives* 31:183–204.

Allen, M. S., and S. E. Schubel. 1990. Recent archaeological research on Aitutaki, Southern Cooks: The Moturakau Shelter. *Journal of the Polynesian Society* 99:265–295.

Anderson, A. 1979. Prehistoric exploitation of marine resources at Black Rocks Point, Palliser Bay. In *Prehistoric man in Palliser Bay*, ed. B. F. Leach and H. M. Leach, 49–65. Bulletin No. 21. Wellington: National Museum of New Zealand.

Anderson, A. 1981. A model of prehistoric collecting on the rocky shore. *Journal of Archaeological Science* 8:109–120.

Anderson, A. 1989. Mechanics of overkill in the extinction of New Zealand moas. *Journal of Archaeological Science* 16:137–151.

Anderson, A. 1996. Adaptive voyaging and subsistence strategies in the early settlement of east Polynesia. In *Prehistoric mongoloid dispersals*, eds. T. Akazawa and E. J. Szathmáry, 359–373. Oxford: Oxford University Press.

Bahn, P., and J. Flenley. 1992. *Easter Island, earth island*. London: Thames and Hudson.

Baraniko, M., T. Taam, and N. Tabokai. 1979. Strife: the civil wars. In *Kiribati: aspects of history*, ed. A. Talu et al., 65–95. Suva/Tarawa: Institute of Pacific Studies and Extension Services, University of the South Pacific; Ministry of Education, Training and Culture, Kiribati Government.

Barrau, J. 1965. L'Humide et le sec: an essay on ethnological adaptation to contrastive environments in the Indo-Pacific Area. *Journal of the Polynesian Society* 74:329–346.

Bayliss-Smith, T. P. 1974. Constraints on population growth: the case of the Polynesian outlier atolls in the precontact period. *Human Ecology* 2:259–295.

Bayliss-Smith, T. P. 1978. Maximum populations and standard populations: the carrying capacity question. In *Social organisation and settlement: contributions from anthropology, archaeology and geography*, Part 1, ed. D. Green, C. Haselgrove, and M. Spriggs, 129–151. Oxford: BAR International Series (Supplementary) No. 47(1).

Bellwood, P. S. 1979. *Man's conquest of the Pacific: the prehistory of Southeast Asia and Oceania*. NY: Oxford University Press.

Bellwood, P. S. 1993. The origins of Pacific peoples. In *Culture contact in the Pacific: essays on contact, encounter and response*, ed. M. Quanchi and R. Adams, 2–14. Cambridge: Cambridge University Press.

Bellwood, P. S. 1997. Ancient seafarers: new evidence of early Southeast Asian sea voyages. *Archaeology* 50(2):20–22.

Birdsell, J. B. 1968. Some predictions for the Pleistocene-based equilibrium systems among recent hunter-gatherers. In *Man the hunter*, ed. R. B. Lee and I. Devore, 229–240. Chicago: Aldine.

Butler, V. L. 1988. Lapita fishing strategies: the faunal evidence. In *Archaeology of the Lapita cultural complex: a critical review*, ed. P. V. Kirch and T. L. Hunt, 99–115. Thomas Burke Memorial. Research Report No. 5. Seattle: Washington State Museum.

Cachola-Abad, C. K. 1993. Evaluating the orthodox dual settlement model for the Hawaiian Islands: an analysis of artifact distribution and Hawaiian oral traditions. In *The evolution and organisation of prehistoric society in Polynesia*, ed. M. W. Graves and R. C. Green, 13–32. Auckland: New Zealand Archaeological Association.

Carneiro, R. 1970. A theory for the origin of the state. *Science* 169:733–738.

Cassels, R. 1984. Of New Zealand and other Pacific islands. In *Quaternary extinctions: a prehistoric revolution*, ed. P. S. Martin and R. G. Klein, 741–761. Tucson: University of Arizona Press.

Catterall, C. P., and I. R. Poiner. 1987. The potential impact of human gathering on shellfish populations, with reference to some NE Australian intertidal flats. *Oikos* 50:114–122.

Clark, J. T. 1991. Early settlement in the Indo-Pacific. *Journal of Anthropological Archaeology* 10:27–53.

Davidson, J. M. 1977. Western Polynesia and Fiji: prehistoric contact, diffusion and differentiation in adjacent archipelagoes. *World Archaeology* 9:82–94.

Davidson, J. M. 1983. Maori prehistory: the state of the art. *Journal of the Polynesian Society* 92:291–307.

Dewar, R. E. 1984. Environmental productivity, population regulation, and carrying capacity. *American Anthropologist* 86:601–614.

Diamond, J. M. 1977. Colonization cycles in man and beast. *World Archaeology* 3:249–261.

Dickson, D. B. 1987. Circumscription by anthropogenic environmental destruction: an expansion of Carneiro's (1970) theory of the origin of the state. *American Antiquity* 52:709–716.

Dye, T. S., and D. W. Steadman. 1990. Polynesian ancestors and their animal world. *American Scientist* 78(3):207–215.

Dyson-Hudson, R., and E. A. Smith. 1978. Human territoriality: an ecological reassessment. *American Anthropologist* 80:21–41.

Flannery, T. F., and J. P. White. 1991. Animal translocations: zoogeography of New Ireland mammals. *National Geographic Research and Exploration* 7:96–113.

Fredericksen, C., M. Spriggs, and W. Ambrose. 1993. Pamwak rockshelter: a Pleistocene site on Manus Island, Papua New Guinea. In *Sahul in review: Pleistocene archaeology in Australia, New Guinea and Island Melanesia*, eds. M. A. Smith, M. Spriggs, and B. Fankhauser, 144–152. Occasional Papers in Prehistory No. 24. Canberra: Department of Prehistory, Research School of Pacific Studies, Australian National University.

Friedman, J. 1981. Notes on structure and history in Oceania. *Folk* 23:275–295.

Fullagar, R. L. K., D. M. Price, and L. M. Head. 1996. Early human occupation of northern Australia: archaeology and thermoluminescence dating of Jinmium rock-shelter, Northern Territory. *Antiquity* 70:751–773.

Goldman, I. 1970. *Ancient Polynesian society*. Chicago: University of Chicago Press.

Gosden, C. 1993. Understanding the settlement of the Pacific Islands in the Pleistocene. In *Sahul in review: Pleistocene archaeology in Australia, New Guinea and Island Melanesia*, ed. M. A. Smith, M. Spriggs, and B. Fankhauser, 131–136. Occasional Papers in Prehistory No. 24. Canberra: Department of Prehistory, Research School of Pacific Studies, Australian National University.

Graves, M. W., and C. Erkelens. 1991. Who's in control? method and theory in Hawaiian archaeology. *Asian Perspectives* 30:1–17.

Green, R. C. 1979. Lapita. In *The prehistory of Polynesia*, ed. J. D. Jennings, 27–60. Cambridge: Harvard University Press.

Green, R. C. 1980. *Makaha before 1880 AD*. Pacific Anthropological Records No. 31. Honolulu: B. P. Bishop Museum.

Green, R. C. 1981. Location of the Polynesian homeland: a continuing problem. In *Studies in Pacific languages and cultures: in honour of Bruce Biggs*, ed. J. Hollyman and A. Pawley, 133–158. Auckland: Linguistic Society of New Zealand.

Green, R. C. 1982. Models for the Lapita cultural complex. *New Zealand Journal of Archaeology* 4:6–19.

Green, R. C. 1991. Near and Remote Oceania—deestablishing "Melanesia" in culture history. In *Man and a half: essays in Pacific anthropology and ethnobiology in honour of Ralph Bulmer*, ed. A. Pawley, 491–502. Auckland: Polynesian Society.

Green, R. C. 1993. Tropical Polynesian prehistory—where are we now? In *A community of culture: the people and prehistory of the Pacific*, ed. M. Spriggs, D. E. Yen, W. Ambrose, R. Jones, A. Thorne, and A. Andrews, 218–238. Occasional Papers in Prehistory No. 21. Canberra: Department of Prehistory, Research School of Pacific Studies, Australian National University.

Groube, L. 1989. The taming of the rain forests: a model for late Pleistocene forest exploitation in New Guinea. In *Foraging and farming: the evolution of plant exploitation*, ed. D. R. Harris and G. C. Hillman, 292–304. London: Unwin Hyman.

Groube, L., J. Chappell, J. Muke, and D. Price 1986. A 40,000-year-old human occupation site at Huon Peninsula, Papua New Guinea. *Nature* 324:453–455.

Gumerman, G. J. 1986. The role of competition and cooperation in the evolution of island societies. In *Island societies: archaeological approaches to evolution and transformation*, ed. P. V. Kirch, 42–49. Cambridge: Cambridge University Press.

Haberle, S. 1993. Pleistocene vegetation change and early human occupation of a tropical mountainous environment. In *Sahul in review: Pleistocene archaeology in Australia, New Guinea and Island Melanesia*, ed. M. A. Smith, M. Spriggs, and B. Fankhauser, 109–122. Occasional Papers in Prehistory No. 24. Canberra: Department of Prehistory, Research School of Pacific Studies, Australian National University.

Hope, G. S., J. Golson, and J. Allen. 1983. Palaeoecology and prehistory in New Guinea. *Journal of Human Evolution* 12:37–60.

Houghton, P. 1991. The early human biology of the Pacific: some considerations. *Journal of the Polynesian Society* 100:167–196.

Hunt, T. L., and M. W. Graves. 1990. Some methodological issues of exchange in Oceanic prehistory. *Asian Perspectives* 29:107–115.

Hunt, T. L., and R. M. Holsen. 1991. An early radiocarbon chronology for the Hawaiian Islands: a preliminary analysis. *Asian Perspectives* 30:147–161.

Irwin, G. 1981. How Lapita lost its pots: the question of continuity in the colonisation of Polynesia. *Journal of the Polynesian Society* 90:481–494.

Irwin, G. 1992. *The prehistoric exploration and colonisation of the Pacific*. Cambridge University Press, Cambridge.

Kirch, P.V. 1978. The Lapitoid period in West Polynesia: excavations and survey in Niuatoputapu, Tonga. *Journal of Field Archaeology* 5:1–13.

Kirch, P.V. 1979. Subsistence and ecology. In *The prehistory of Polynesia*, ed. J. D. Jennings, 286–307. Cambridge: Harvard University Press.

Kirch, P. V. 1984. *The Evolution of the Polynesian chiefdoms*. Cambridge: Cambridge University Press.

Kirch, P.V. 1985. *Feathered gods and fishhooks*. Honolulu: University of Hawai'i Press.

Kirch, P. V. 1988a. Circumscription theory and sociopolitical evolution in Polynesia. *American Behavioral Scientist* 31:416–427.

Kirch, P.V. 1988b. Long-distance exchange and island colonization: the Lapita case. *Norwegian Archaeological Review* 21:103–117.

Kirch, P.V. 1990. Specialization and exchange in the Lapita complex of Oceania (1600–500 B.C.). *Asian Perspectives* 29:117–133.

Kirch, P.V. 1991. Prehistoric exchange in Western Melanesia. *Annual Review of Anthropology* 20:141–165.

Kirch, P.V. 1994. *The wet and the dry: irrigation and agricultural intensification in Polynesia*. Chicago: University of Chicago Press.

Kirch, P.V. 1997. Changing landscapes and sociopolitical evolution in Mangaia, Central Polynesia. In *Historical ecology in the Pacific Islands: prehistoric environmental and landscape change*, ed. P. V. Kirch and T. L. Hunt, 147–65. New Haven: Yale University Press.

Kirch, P. V., and T. S. Dye. 1979. Ethno-archaeology and the development of Polynesian fishing strategies. *Journal of the Polynesian Society* 88:53–76.

Kirch, P.V., T. L. Hunt, L. Nagaoka, and J. Tyler. 1990. An ancestral Polynesian occupation site at To'aga, Ofu Island, American Samoa. *Archaeology in Oceania* 25:1–15.

Lacey, R. 1982. Archaeology and early man. In *Atlas of Papua New Guinea*, ed. D. King and S. Ranch, 4–5. Port Moresby: University of Papua New Guinea.

McCall, G. 1994. Little Ice Age: some proposals for Polynesia and Rapanui (Easter Island). *Journal de la Société des océanistes* 98:99–104.

Nagaoka, L. 1988. Lapita subsistence: the evidence of non-fish archaeofaunal remains. In *Archaeology of the Lapita cultural complex: a critical review*, eds. P. V. Kirch and T. L. Hunt, 117–133. Thomas Burke Memorial. Research Report No. 5. Seattle: Washington State Museum

Nunn, P. D. 1992. *Keimami sa vakila na liga ni kalou (feeling the hand of god): human and nonhuman impacts on Pacific Island environments*. Occasional Paper No. 13. Honolulu: East-West Center Program on Environment.

Nunn, P. D. 1993. Beyond the naive lands: human history and environmental change in the Pacific Basin. In *The margin fades: geographical itineraries in a world of islands*, eds. E. Waddell and P. D. Nunn, 5–27. Suva: Institute of Pacific Studies, University of the South Pacific.

Oliver, D. L. 1989. *Oceania: the native cultures of Australia and the Pacific Islands*, Vol. I. Honolulu: University of Hawai'i Press.

Pavlides, C., and C. Gosden. 1994. 35,000-year-old sites in the rainforests of West New Britain, Papua New Guinea. *Antiquity* 68:604–610.

Pawley, A. 1996. On the Polynesian subgroup as a problem for Irwin's continuous settlement hypothesis. In *Oceanic culture history: essays in honour of Roger Green*, ed. J. Davidson, G. Irwin, F. Leach, A. Pawley, and D. Brown, 387–410. Special Publication. Dunedin, New Zealand Journal of Archaeology.

Pawley, A., and M. Ross. 1993. Austronesian historical linguistics and culture history. *Annual Review of Anthropology* 22:425–459.

Pietrusewsky, M. 1994. Pacific-Asian relationships: a physical anthropological perspective. *Oceanic Linguistics* 33:407–429.

Poiner, I. R., and C. P. Catterall. 1988. The effects of traditional gathering on populations of the marine gastropod *Strombus luhuanus* linne [sic] 1758, in Southern Papua New Guinea. *Oecologia* 76:191–199.

Rainbird, P. 1994. Prehistory in the Northwest Tropical Pacific: the Caroline, Mariana, and Marshall islands. *Journal of World Prehistory* 8:293–349.

Serjeantson, S. W., and X. Gao. 1995. *Homo sapiens* is an evolving species: origins of the Austronesians. In *The Austronesians: historical and comparative perspectives*, ed. P. Bellwood, J. J. Fox, and D. Tryon, 165–180. Canberra: Department of Anthropology, Research School of Pacific and Asian Studies, Australian National University.

Serjeantson, S. W., and A. V. S. Hill. 1989. The colonization of the Pacific: the genetic evidence. In *The colonization of the Pacific: a genetic trail*, ed. A. V. S. Hill and S. W. Serjeantson, 286–294. Oxford: Oxford University Press.

Shawcross, W. 1975. Some studies of the influences on prehistoric human predation on marine animal population dynamics. In *Maritime adaptations of the Pacific*, ed. R. W. Casteel and G. I. Quimby, 39–66. The Hague: Mouton.

Smith, I. W. G. 1989. Maori impact on the marine megafauna: pre-European distributions of New Zealand sea mammals. In *Saying so doesn't make it so: papers in honour of B. Foss Leach*, ed. D. G. Sutton, 76–108. Monograph No. 17. Dunedin: New Zealand Archaeological Association.

Smith, M. A., and N. D. Sharp. 1993. Pleistocene sites in Australia, New Guinea and Island Melanesia: geographic and temporal structure of the archaeological record. In *Sahul in review: Pleistocene archaeology in Australia, New Guinea and Island Melanesia*, eds. M. A. Smith, M. Spriggs, and B. Fankhauser, 37–59. Occasional Papers in Prehistory No. 24. Canberra: Department of Prehistory, Research School of Pacific Studies, Australian National University.

Specht, J. 1981. Obsidian sources at Talasea, West New Britain, Papua New Guinea. *Journal of the Polynesian Society* 90:337–356.

Spennemann, D. H. R. 1987. Availability of shellfish resources on prehistoric Tongatapu, Tonga: effects of human predation and changing environment. *Archaeology in Oceania* 22:81–96.

Sponsel, L. E., M. Rapaport, and F. R. Thomas. n.d. The ecology of war and peace in the Pacific prior to Europeans. Unpublished manuscript.

Spriggs, M. 1985. Prehistoric man–induced landscape enhancement in the Pacific: examples and implications. In *Prehistoric intensive agriculture in the tropics*, Part 1, ed. I. S. Farrington, 409–434. Oxford: BAR International Series No. 232.

Spriggs, M. 1993a. Island Melanesia: the last 10,000 years. In *A community of culture: the people and prehistory of the Pacific*, ed. M. Spriggs, D. E. Yen, W. Ambrose, R. Jones, A. Thorne, and A. Andrews, 187–205. Occasional Papers in Prehistory, No. 21. Canberra: Department of Prehistory, Research School of Pacific Studies, Australian National University.

Spriggs, M. 1993b. Pleistocene agriculture in the Pacific: why not? In *Sahul in review: Pleistocene archaeology in Australia, New Guinea and Island Melanesia*, ed. M. A. Smith, M. Spriggs, and B. Fankhauser, 137–143. Occasional Papers in Prehistory No. 24. Canberra: Department of Anthropology, Research School of Pacific Studies, Australian National University.

Spriggs, M., and A. Anderson. 1993. Late colonization of East Polynesia. *Antiquity* 67:200–217.

Steadman, D. W. 1997. Extinctions of Polynesian birds: reciprocal impacts of birds and people. In *Historical ecology in the Pacific Islands: prehistoric environmental and landscape change*, eds. P. V. Kirch and T. L. Hunt, 51–79. New Haven: Yale University Press.

Summerhayes, G. R., and J. Allen. 1993. The transport of Mopir obsidian to Late Pleistocene New Ireland. *Archaeology in Oceania* 28:144–148.

Sutton, D. G. 1987. A paradigmatic shift in Polynesian prehistory: implications for New Zealand. *New Zealand Journal of Archaeology* 9:135–155.

Sutton, D. G., and M. A. Molloy. 1989. Deconstructing Pacific palaeodemography: A critique of density dependent causality. *Archaeology in Oceania* 24:31–36.

Swadling, P. 1986. Lapita shellfishing: evidence from sites in the Reef/Santa Cruz Group, Southeast Solomons. in *Traditional fishing in the Pacific: ethnographical and archaeological papers from the 15th Pacific Science Congress*, ed. A. Anderson, 137–148. Pacific Anthropological Records No. 37. Honolulu: B. P. Bishop Museum.

Terrell, J. 1986. *Prehistory in the Pacific Islands: a study of variation in language, customs, and human biology*. Cambridge: Cambridge University Press.

Terrell, J. E., T. L. Hunt, and C. Gosden. 1997. The dimension of social life in the Pacific: human diversity and the myth of the primitive isolate. *Current Anthropology* 38:155–195.

Thomas, F. R. 1989. Vessel function of the plain ware assemblages from Santa Cruz, Southeast Solomon Islands and Culture Historical Implications. *Crosscurrents* 3:55–77.

Thomas, F. R. 1993. Successes and failures on atolls: a review of prehistoric adaptations and contemporary lessons. In *Culture and environment, a fragile coexistence: Proceedings of the Twenty-fourth Conference of the Archaeological Association of the University of Calgary*, ed. R. W. Jamieson, S. Abonyi, and N. A. Mirau, 423–430. Calgary: University of Calgary Archaeological Association.

Thomas, F. R. 1995. Excavations at Maunalua Cave, Hawai'i Kai, O'ahu. *Hawaiian Archaeology* 4:17–26.

Weisler, M. I. 1994. The settlement of Marginal Polynesia: new evidence from Henderson Island. *Journal of Field Archaeology* 21:83–102.

Weisler, M. I., and P. V. Kirch. 1996. Interisland and interarchipelago transfer of stone tools in prehistoric Polynesia. *Proceedings of the National Academy of Sciences of the United States of America* 93:1384–1385. Washington, D.C.

Williamson, I., and M. D. Sabath. 1984. Small population instability and island settlement patterns. *Human Ecology* 12:21–34.

Yen, D. E. 1971. Construction of the hypothesis for distribution of the sweet potato. In *Man across the sea: problem of Pre-Columbian contacts*, ed. C. L. Riley, C. Kelley, C. W. Pennington, and R. Rands, 328–342. Austin: University of Texas Press.

Yen, D. E. 1985. Wild plants and domestication in Pacific islands. In *Recent advances in Indo-Pacific prehistory*, ed. V. N. Misra and P. S. Bellwood, 315–329. Leiden: E. J. Brill.

# Chapter 11

# The Postcontact Period

*David A. Chappell*

This chapter traces historical changes in Oceania from early Euroamerican contacts through colonial rule into the post-1945 era of decolonization. The reader should be aware, however, that history is never separate from the present, because each generation reinterprets the past in light of its own priorities. The written history of the Pacific Islands was produced mainly by Euroamericans until very recently, and as an academic subject that is taught in universities the field really dates only to the 1950s. Foreign explorers, missionaries, traders, and colonial officials kept many records, but their accounts were often biased, privileging the "civilizing" influence of outsiders. Colonial historians tended to perpetuate these one-sided impressions, while critics stressed the negative effects of outsiders on indigenous societies, from deaths caused by introduced diseases to cultural losses when native peoples adopted Christianity or metal tools and weapons. For example, Alan Moorehead's *The Fatal Impact* describes the decline of native peoples and customs in Tahiti and Australia after contact.

This Eurocentric historiography of the islands began to change in the 1950s, when J. W. Davidson of the Australian National University recommended what came to be called an "island-centered" or "islander-oriented" approach. He and his followers urged scholars to do fieldwork, rather than simply researching in colonial archives, and to consider other sources of data, such as oral traditions, archeology, ethnobotany, linguistics, and anthropology. The goal was to focus on the historical interplay between indigenous and foreign actors, to reveal participation by native peoples in making their own history (Howe 1984). Greg Dening (1980) and Marshall Sahlins (1985) blended histories of culture contact with anthropological data, creating "ethnographic history." Other scholars warned that a Euroamerican-run capitalist "world system" created economic exploitation and dependency (Howard and Durutalo 1987), and indigenous nationalists spoke of past and ongoing victimization by outsiders (Trask 1993, Walker 1990). As more Oceanians joined the ranks of academic historians, they added their voices to these debates (e.g. Meleisea 1987).

## Early Interactions with Euroamericans

Before Ferdinand Magellan named and crossed the Pacific in 1520–21, the ocean basin was divided into subregions by an equilibrium of disinterest. For thousands of years, sheer distance had limited contact between Oceania and the Pacific Rim to sporadic interaction with insular Southeast Asia and, probably, South America. Oceania was a self-contained, culturally diverse maritime world linked together by its own exchange networks and canoe migrations, but like the Americas it hovered just out of reach of global trends. In 1513, however, Portuguese and Spanish explorers arrived at the western and eastern shores of the Pacific, respectively, and soon other explorers began to cross Oceania on missions for the emerging world economy. European monarchs sought to bypass Middle Eastern middlemen and gain direct access to Asian spices and silks. In the process, Columbus stumbled upon the Americas, where Spain reaped a windfall of gold and silver by enslaving native peoples (Hezel 1983, Howe 1984).

Ferdinand Magellan, a Portuguese sailing for Spain, left Europe in 1519 with five ships to finish the job that Columbus had set out to do—reach Asia by sailing west. By the time the expedition rounded Cape Horn, the stormy tip of South America, the sea beyond looked relatively peaceful, hence the name "Pacific" (by a lucky coincidence, it was not hurricane season). Magellan next accomplished two things: his ships were the first to cross the Pacific Ocean, and they did so without seeing anyone until they reached Guam. Unfortunately, the latter feat meant that his crews were starving and ill when they encountered the Chamorro people of the Marianas. Moreover, two systems of property were colliding: the Spanish believed in private ownership (and knew they were only halfway around the globe), while the Chamorros, like most Oceanians, emphasized communal property sharing and expected to assimilate new arrivals, including their material possessions. The Chamorros went out to the Spanish ships in sailing canoes to exchange gifts.

Antonio Pigafetta, Magellan's chronicler, wrote that they "boarded the ships and stole one thing after another, to such an extent that our men could not protect their belongings" (Paige 1969). Violence resulted, and Magellan labeled Guam the Island of Thieves, beginning a process of (mis)naming that would persist for centuries. He himself died in another conflict in the Philippines, but one of his ships managed to return home with enough cloves to make a profit, thus encouraging more Spanish adventures across the Pacific (Rogers 1995). These included three expeditions from Peru to Melanesia in search of ancient King Solomon's gold mines, but violence similar to that on Guam left only a few place-names like "Solomon Islands" as a lasting legacy. More significant was the establishment of the first trans-Pacific shipping route: from the sixteenth to the eighteenth centuries, Spanish treasure galleons traded Mexican silver for Asian luxury goods at Manila. Yet they still missed most of the Pacific Islands, since they sailed by a northerly route (Howe 1984).

On Guam, however, Spanish priests arrived with an armed escort in 1668. Jesuit father Diego Luis de San Vitores (Figure 11.1) set out to convert the Chamorros to Catholicism, baptizing young children whom he befriended by giving them sugar from his pockets. Some Chamorros, such as Kipuha (a statue of

*Figure 11.1. Statue of San Vitores outside Catholic cathedral, Agana, Guam (photo LEM).*

him stands in Agana today), welcomed the Spanish, but others opposed the foreign intrusion by force. After San Vitores himself took up arms and was killed, fighting between pro-Spanish forces and rebels almost depopulated the Marianas. Combat deaths, relocation to Guam, and diseases reduced the epidemiologically vulnerable Chamorros by about 90% in a single generation (Rogers 1995). This holocaust would be repeated on other Pacific islands exposed to intensive foreign contact, just as it occurred on the American mainland.

Meanwhile, British and French raiders attacked Spanish treasure ships in the Pacific as well as the Atlantic. The Dutch made brief excursions into the South Pacific in the 1600s but soon decided to devote their colonizing energies to spice-rich Southeast Asian islands. They left a few place-names, like Tasmania and New Zealand on maps.

Up to this time, European contacts with Pacific Islanders had been rather fleeting and tragic. Serious attempts at communication came only after a peace treaty between Britain and France in 1763 enabled their navies to explore Oceania more systematically. Expeditions carrying scientists and artists set out to test geographic theories that a Northwest Passage might link the Atlantic and the Pacific, or that a Terra Australis Incognita (unknown southern continent) was balancing the Eurasian landmass. The problem of obtaining adequate provisions of food and water still haunted ships until British explorer Samuel Wallis found Tahiti in 1767. Tahiti's reputation for hospitality, nurtured by the Pomare family, helped to foster a myth of the South Pacific as a paradise, where people never had to work hard, loved freely, and lacked the material greed of Western culture. In fact, that myth derived from a deliberate strategy devised by indigenous leaders. After their first violent encounter with Wallis, Tahitian elders sent young women out to the ships to offer sexual favors in return for such rare treasures as iron—at the unexpected price of venereal disease (Moorehead 1966).

When French explorer Louis Antoine de Bougainville arrived at Tahiti in 1768, he and his crew were entranced. He even took a man called Ahutoru to Paris as a specimen of a "noble savage." French Enlightenment writers like Denis Diderot lamented the fate of Tahitians now that European ships began to frequent the island, but the Pomares and other ambitious chiefs added foreign trade contacts to traditional power dynamics in their quest for supremacy. Pomare I presented himself as a king to James Cook, and organized the sale of pork to feed the convicts in the new British colony of Australia (founded in 1788). Pomare II welcomed English Protestant missionaries in 1797, and by 1815 he had conquered Tahiti with their help as gunrunners—combining this assistance with shrewd political marriages with other chiefly families (Howarth 1985, Howe 1984). A similar process occurred in Hawai'i, where Kamehameha I united the islands using both indigenous alliances and trade contacts with foreigners who were buying local sandalwood or transhipping furs from Northwest America to China (Howe 1984).

Explorers paved the way for missionaries and traders by gathering information about resources in the Pacific basin. In 1789, H.M.S. *Bounty* went to Tahiti to collect breadfruit trees to feed African slaves on Jamaica; despite the famous mutiny, William Bligh finally completed his task on a second voyage in 1792. The London Missionary Society arrived in 1797 with a Tahitian vocabulary compiled by a *Bounty* mutineer. On his third expedition to the Pacific (Figure 11.2), Cook purchased furs from Native Americans on the northwest coast, and after his death in Hawai'i, his crew sold those furs for a great profit in China. A New Englander from Cook's crew persuaded American ships to enter the trade. Some recruited Hawaiian sailors, one of whom was Henry Opukahaia, whose death in New England inspired the first American Protestant missionaries to come to Hawai'i in 1820. Those missionaries arrived just after Kamehameha's death, when American whaleships were beginning to hunt the Japan grounds and winter in Hawai'i. The native *kapu* (law) system had declined as foreigners and those who traded with them broke the rules, so the missionaries found Hawai'i ready to transform into a Christian state like Tahiti (Sahlins 1981). By 1850, the land systems in both kingdoms had been privatized, much to the disadvantage of most indigenous people (Scarr 1990, Newbury 1980).

In the early stages of the nineteenth century, a precarious balance existed between indigenous leaders and foreign traders and advisors. Beachcombers, who deserted from Euroamerican vessels or were shipwrecked, earned acceptance by offering linguistic and technical skills to chiefs while adopting local customs. Some were kidnapped, like Isaac Davis and John Young, whom Kamehameha I rewarded handsomely for their services. Those on Pohnpei acquired a monopoly over trade with ships, while other beachcombers died in local wars or left the islands to become tattooed carnival curiosities in Europe. Hundreds of

........ Cook I 1768-71     — — — Cook II 1772-75     Cook III 1776-80

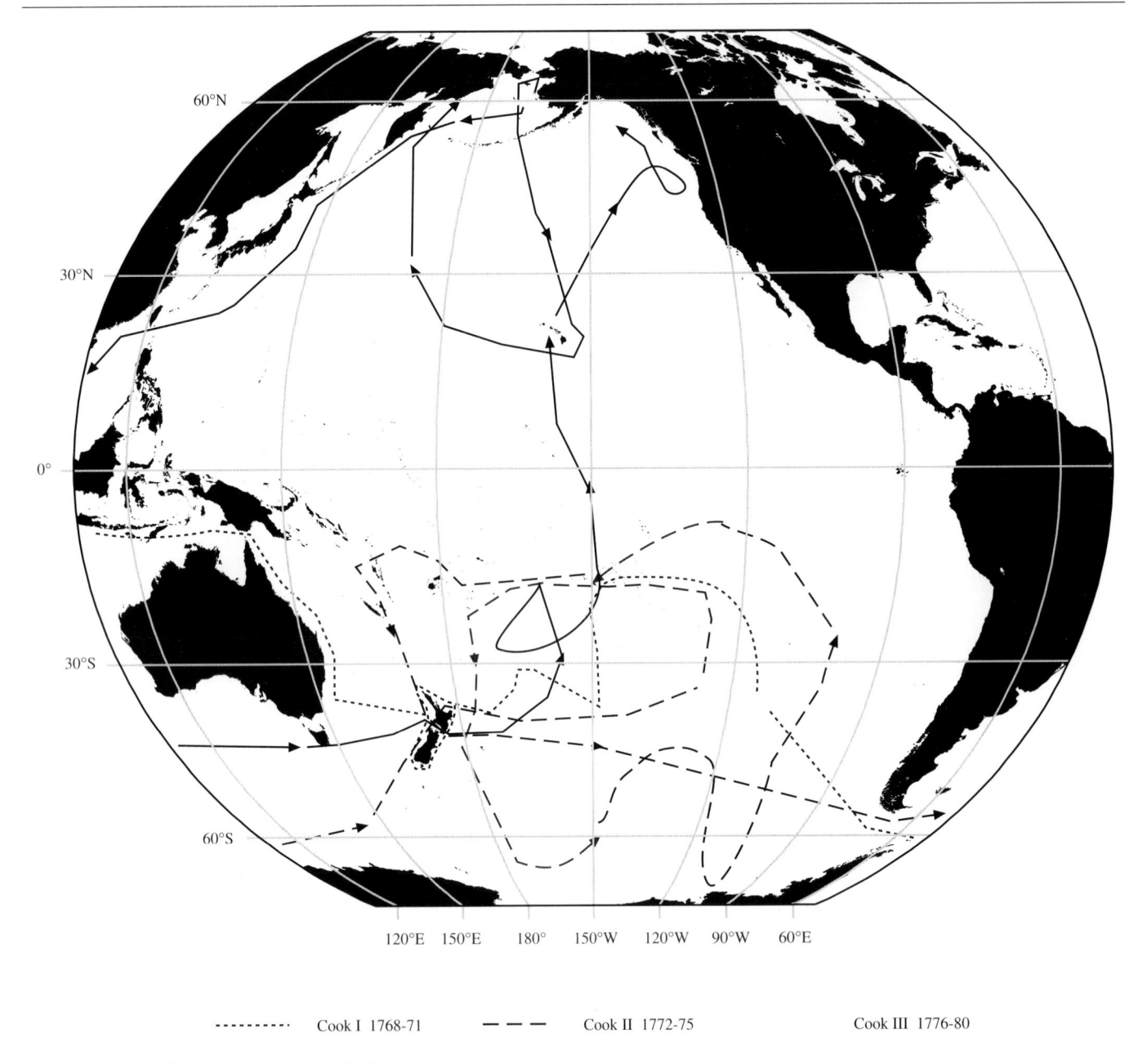

*Figure 11.2.* Pacific voyages of Captain Cook.

indigenous islanders also played this role, as ships that recruited them as sailors dropped them off on any generic island before leaving the region. By 1846, there were four hundred Hawaiians in Tahiti and two hundred Tahitians in Hawai'i. As whaling ships developed seasonal circuits around the region, nearly every island traded with foreign vessels and sent out or received seamen. The Tuamotus sold pearls, and Micronesia exported tortoiseshell, copra and bêche-de-mer. Fiji had both sandalwood and bêche-de-mer to offer, and New Caledonia and Vanuatu began to export sandalwood and receive missionaries by the 1840s (Howe 1984, Maude 1968).

Native teachers (indigenous missionaries) played a major role in the conversion of islanders to Christianity (Howe 1984). English and American missionaries pursued a "Polynesian strategy" by winning over the chiefs of Hawai'i, Tahiti, and Tonga so that the masses of commoners would follow. They then sent new converts westward to other islands, assuming that indigenous teachers would be able to communicate better and pave the way for white missionaries. Yet half the native teachers died prematurely, because the farther west they went, the graver the risk for Polynesians: in Melanesia they encountered many different languages and customs, frequent warfare between small polities, and deadly malaria. Gradually, however, Oceanians "indigenized" Christianity, sometimes blending it with their own beliefs. In Samoa, Siovili returned from travels overseas to create his own quasi-Christian church. Meanwhile, becoming a Protestant pastor was similar to being a *matai*, or titled chief. In 1850, Samoan teachers went on strike to demand equal pay with whites and succeeded (Howe 1984).

By the mid-1800s, the balance of contact increasingly tilted in favor of industrialized foreign powers. As Oceanians bought more imports, traders shrewdly sold manufactured goods on credit, adding interest until they could call on their country's warships to demand payment—or land. Like Guam, Tahiti, and Hawai'i, New Zealand became a focal point of Euroamerican expansion. The Maori had begun to grow potatoes and wheat and cut trees to sell to whalers and sealers from the British colony in Australia. Maori men worked on foreign ships, and English missionaries began to preach Christianity with help from Maori teachers. In 1820, Chief Hongi Hika visited London, where King George IV gave him a shotgun and a suit of armor that he used in wars against his old enemies. By 1840, British agents persuaded Maori chiefs to sign the Treaty of Waitangi, which was supposed to be a model arrangement that would protect Maori rights while allowing English colonists to settle in New Zealand. But the Maori version did not use *mana* to describe the "sovereignty" that the Maori chiefs ceded, and disputes over the Treaty's meaning and over land sales led to wars. The Maori impressed the English with their military skills and in 1858 even elected their first king to unite their efforts, but they finally lost the wars and over three million acres (Howe 1984, Walker 1990).

In the 1840s, France was competing with Britain for influence in the islands and began to seek secure "ports of call" for its ships. Using the pretext that Catholic missionaries had not been welcomed in Tahiti (where English Protestants had already converted most of the population), the French navy conquered the Society Islands and nearby archipelagoes beginning in 1842. France also established missionary control over Wallis and Futuna and in 1853 took New Caledonia, despite local resistance. In Tahiti and Wallis and Futuna the French allowed Polynesian rulers to retain symbolic authority, but in Melanesian New Caledonia, which had thirty indigenous language groups, they seized land and punished resisters by forcing them onto crowded reserves. By 1900, the Kanaks of New Caledonia retained only ten per cent of their land, they had to perform forced labor, and their chiefs were appointed by French police. Meanwhile, France brought 20,000 convicts, as well as ranchers and coffee farmers, to New Caledonia between 1864 and 1894; descendants of those European migrants today comprise one third of the territory's population (Henningham 1992).

As foreign business expanded in Oceania, labor supply became a serious issue. During the sandalwood trade in Melanesia in the 1840s, it proved easier to control workers if they were removed from their home island so they would be at the mercy of their employers. By the 1860s, the blockade of southern cotton in the American Civil War caused a Pacific plantation boom, so recruiters sought workers mainly in populous Melanesia, where they already had sandalwood contacts. By the early 1900s, 120,000 Oceanian workers left their home islands on contract to plantations in Queensland (Australia) or islands like Fiji and Samoa. At first, ships often kidnapped laborers, a practice known as "blackbirding." In 1862-64, for example, Peru seized 3,500 islanders from as far west as the Gilbert Islands to work in mines and plantations; few of the captives returned home, and epidemics killed many of those left behind. Another notorious case was that of the *Carl*, an Australian-based vessel that lured canoes alongside and then kidnapped the islanders in 1871; when their captives tried to rebel, the crew fired into the hold and killed a hundred. Such incidents led to Australian attempts to regulate labor recruiting in the 1870s, so that the process became more voluntary (Howe 1984, Maude 1981).

Labor migration and planter ambitions helped to prepare the way for colonial rule. In 1877, Britain created the Western Pacific High Commission, which sent naval patrols to Melanesia not only to regulate labor recruiting but also to protect traders and missionaries. In 1887, France and England signed a joint naval agreement to patrol the New Hebrides, effectively transforming it into a labor reserve for New Caledonia and Australia. Native "passage-masters" gathered recruits before ships arrived, and returnees brought back trade-boxes full of manufactured goods they could use to get married or pay debts. Asians also labored on plantations in Oceania, changing the demography of places like Hawai'i and Fiji. Sugar planters in Hawai'i benefited from the Mahele of 1848-50, which privatized land, and pressure from creditors and planters forced Fijian chiefs to cede their sovereignty to Britain in 1874. Gov. Arthur Gordon set aside 83% of the land for Fijians, but imported indentured laborers from India to grow sugarcane. His dual policy would create an ethnic crisis in Fiji, which like New Caledonia became an ethnically bipolar society (Scarr 1990).

## Colonialism and Resistance

By the 1880s, competition among imperial powers around the world was intensifying, partly for prestige and partly for strategic or economic gain. A scramble for colonial real estate began, usually rationalized by claims that Euroamericans would "civilize" the natives (or else prevail through Darwinian "survival of the fittest"). When foreign contact bolstered indigenous leaders, as in Hawai'i or Tahiti, they might be coopted or later overthrown, but trade could also destabilize indigenous societies. In Samoa, traders sold guns to opposite sides in local wars and then demanded land in payment for debts, while in parts of Melanesia, guns brought back by overseas laborers increased warfare to the point where local leaders sometimes asked to be "pacified." In 1887, King David Kalākaua of Hawai'i tried to forge a last-ditch alliance with High Chief Malietoa Laupepa of Samoa, but German warships prevented the pact. Not even the destruction of six foreign warships in 'Apia harbor by a hurricane could keep Samoa from being partitioned by Germany and the United States. Britain also partitioned New Guinea with the Dutch and Germans and attempted to share the New Hebrides with France in a very problematic "condominium" arrangement. Because of its early base in Sydney, Britain and its settler surrogates (Australia and New Zealand) acquired a dozen colonies in the South Pacific (Howe, Kiste, and Lal 1994, Rodman and Cooper 1983).

The northern Pacific saw old and new imperial actors in competition. Spain laid claim to Micronesia because of its early bases in the Marianas and Philippines, but American missionaries and German copra traders were more active in the Carolines and Marshalls. In 1885, Germany annexed the Marshalls and Carolines. Spain protested, so Pope Leo XIII arbitrated, awarding the Carolines to Spain politically but permitting German traders and American missionaries to continue operating. Spain tried to establish a garrison on Pohnpei, but indigenous chiefs resisted so strongly that the Spanish hid in their fort and finally sold the Carolines to Germany in 1898. By that year, the upstart United States had defeated Spain in the Spanish-American War, seizing Guam and the Philippines. Meanwhile, American residents in Hawai'i had overthrown the monarchy of Queen Lili'uokalani in 1893, with intimidating support from the U.S. ambassador and warships in Honolulu harbor. An American-dominated "republic" willingly ceded Hawai'i to the U.S. empire in 1898 as a strategic naval base from which to control Guam and the Philippines. Pago Pago harbor in eastern Samoa was also annexed in 1899 (Hezel 1995, Hanlon 1988, Howe, Kiste, and Lal 1994).

By 1900, then, every island in Oceania had come under foreign colonial rule, through destabilization and cession or outright conquest. Even Easter Island was seized by the Chilean navy in 1888. When a treaty was signed, as the Berlin Convention of 1884-85 required, it was usually misunderstood by the indigenous chiefs, who often regarded it as a friendship agreement or just another paper to sign for a passing warship. Warships had developed a habit of threatening islanders to pay their debts and often bombarded villages, as when a missionary had been chased off Tanna in 1865. But now the foreigners came to stay. Even inland New Guinea encountered patrols by Australians and Germans who enforced their authority, collected taxes, recruited labor and took land for plantations or gold mines. On small islands like Nauru and Banaba, British mining companies began to plunder the environment by digging up phosphate ore (Figure 11.3), using laborers from other islands or from Asia (Howe, Kiste, and Lal 1994, Hezel 1995).

*Figure 11.3. Phosphate mining operations on Nauru (photo LEM).*

Colonial rule was the most unequal form of contact with outsiders yet, since the indigenous peoples became subjects of distant governments and, in varying degrees, lost control of their own destiny. They would experience new economic activity, but the majority of profits usually went into other hands and left the islands. Whatever wages or rents remained perpetuated the consumption of imports, so economic dependency on outsiders only increased. The education provided by mission schools tended to produce clerks for the colonial administration, who in effect became collaborators in the redirection of their futures toward the capitalist world economy (Howard and Durutalo 1987). In some cases, the new rulers used indigenous elites to legitimize their policies, but there was a general colonization of native minds, as white *mastas* insisted on their own cultural superiority (Wolfers 1975, Lal 1992).

Nevertheless, Pacific Islanders tested the limits of colonial power in order to preserve a degree of sovereignty. Their resistance took a variety of forms, from armed force to alternative churches and economic cooperatives, to sly noncompliance. In 1900, Britain signed a Treaty of Friendship with King Taufa'ahau Tupou II of Tonga. This arrangement respected the 1875 monarchical constitution but stipulated that a British Resident would give advice in all cabinet decisions. Would the advice have to be followed? Tupou II took a stand on the issue of the Tonga Ma'a Tonga Kautaha, a copra-marketing cooperative created in 1909 to bypass British traders, who charged Tongans twice as much as Europeans for their imports. Most Tongans joined the *kautaha* and began to transport their copra directly to Sydney for better prices, so the British traders complained. The British Resident confiscated *kautaha* property on the charge of misappropriation of funds by its expatriate manager, but Tupou won his case in the court of the Western Pacific High Commission and had the Resident recalled to London. In contrast, the Fijian Great Council of Chiefs cooperated with Britain, as in 1912, when Apolosi Nawai formed a cooperative called the Viti Kabani. His vociferous advocacy on behalf of his fellow *taukei* (commoners) against both chiefs and colonizers led to his being charged with embezzlement and sedition. Despite repeated arrests, he continued protesting—even creating his own church and calling himself king until he was finally deported for good (Hempenstall and Rutherford 1984).

Varying colonial contexts inspired different forms of resistance. The German governor of western Samoa, Wilhelm Solf, closed down a native economic cooperative and deported chiefs who opposed his administration, but Albert Hahl of German New Guinea responded to revolts by trying to protect native lands while at the same time recruiting labor for planters. In 1910, Pohnpeians of Sokehs district took up arms against a brutal German governor, but warships soon defeated them. The rebel leaders were lined up and shot on the beach and their families deported to an outer island. In World War I, Germany lost its colonies to Japan north of the equator and to Britain, Australia, or New Zealand in the South Pacific. Palauans soon organized a protest against the Japanese: the Modekngei movement advocated a return to Palauan values and survived repression. In western Samoa, a nonviolent Mau movement arose in 1926 in opposition to the heavy-handed policies of the New Zealand military governor. Despite a massacre of peaceful protestors in 'Apia in 1929, known as Black Saturday, the Mau was legalized in 1935 and won almost every seat in the subsequent Fono election (Hempenstall and Rutherford 1984, Meleisea 1987).

Melanesia, where colonizers tried to rule very diverse, small-scale societies, produced many examples of resistance. In 1927, Basiana, a *ramo* (bounty hunter) on Malaita in Solomon

Islands, organized the ambush of British governor William Bell, who had tried to collect taxes and confiscate firearms on his patrols. A destructive punitive raid by British militia and rival Solomon Islanders captured Basiana and hanged him (Keesing 1992). Two years later, police and boat operators in Rabaul (New Guinea) went on strike for better wages, but they put their trust in local missionaries, who refused to help. The Australian administration sentenced Sumsuma and other ringleaders to years of hard labor in the Wau goldfields (Gammage 1975). Perhaps the most imaginative protests came from so-called "cargo" movements led by local prophets, who often combined Christian rituals and indigenous beliefs in new churches that promised millennial change and material rewards. A so-called Vailala "madness" in Papua in 1919 was explained by a government anthropologist as a sign that modernization was causing mental breakdown among natives. Actually, Papuans were subtly mocking the Australians by shaking violently when near them. Some rocked in chairs on verandas, sipping drinks and commenting on how lazy white men were since they did no apparent work (Worsley 1968).

World War II was a turning point in Pacific history, as islanders encountered more destruction, larger numbers of outsiders, and more dramatic innovations than ever before. Apart from Pearl Harbor, most actual fighting occurred in the western Pacific, but even in the eastern islands, the United States established supply bases that had economic and cultural impact on the indigenous peoples. In 1942, Japan advanced from its Micronesian bases as far south as New Guinea and Solomon Islands and began to bomb northern Australia. At the first warnings of Japanese invasion, most Europeans fled, leaving islanders to wonder what had happened to their much-vaunted superiority. Only a few coast-watchers remained behind to report on troop movements, so islanders from Guam to Guadalcanal had to face a new invader alone. At times, relations with the Japanese were positive, but as the war continued, their demands grew more ruthless. Most of the people of Nauru were relocated to Chuuk as laborers, for example, and when food supplies became limited, Japanese troops generally considered natives expendable. The American liberation was very destructive, due to massive bombing and fighting from bunker to bunker. The United States paid $100 compensation for each islander killed.

Oceanians played several roles in the war and gained new insights into the outside world. Many served as wage laborers at military bases, and in New Guinea, they carried supplies and wounded. The Australians gratefully nicknamed them "fuzzy wuzzy angels" and commemorated their services in song, but the carriers later complained they had not been compensated for their efforts. Other islanders fought as soldiers, notably the commandos recruited in Fiji at the request of Ratu Lala Sukuna (Figure 11.4), who like Maori leaders urged his people to prove their loyalty to Britain in order to gain political rewards later. Islander encounters with common soldiers from the United States and Australia were relatively egalitarian compared with previous race relations. Despite colonial orders not to share food or supplies with natives, the soldiers fraternized with them. Black American troops impressed the islanders because their

*Figure 11.4.* Statue of Ratu Sukuna outside government buildings, Suva, Fiji (photo LEM).

segregation in supply services made them look like "big men" in charge of material wealth. On Malaita, U.S. troops also fueled local protest efforts by advising natives that the United States too had once been a British colony but had won its independence. This helped to inspire the Maasina Rule Movement, which set up local councils, customary courts, and cooperatives that defied the British. Because of exposure to greater quantities of imported goods, more "cargo" churches evolved, and islanders aspired to better wages and new dietary preferences like corned beef and Spam (White and Lindstrom 1989, Howe, Kiste, and Lal 1994, Keesing 1992).

## Challenges of Decolonization

Despite United Nations support for self-determination after 1945, decolonization in the Pacific Islands is still far from complete, for strategic and economic reasons. World War II was followed by the Cold War, a global competition between the United States and the Soviet Union and their allies that divided the world into two rival camps. In the Pacific, the United States wanted to avoid another Pearl Harbor by maintaining advanced bases around Communist powers in Asia. After taking over Micronesia from Japan, it acquired formal control over those islands from the United Nations (UN) in 1947 as a "strategic" Trust Territory. By 1952, the United States formed a defensive alliance with Australia and New Zealand called ANZUS, effectively denying the whole region to Communist intrusion. The United States and Britain also demonstrated their nuclear capabilities in over seventy atomic tests, mainly in the Marshall

Islands and the Australian desert between 1946 and 1962. Just as those tests came to an end, France began hundreds of nuclear experiments of its own in the Tuamotu atolls, from 1966 to 1996 (Thompson 1994).

This legacy of nuclear testing in Oceania is a bitter one for many islanders. The people of Bikini in the Marshall Islands were exiled from their atoll in 1946 (Figure 11.5) and have

*Figure 11.5. Chief Juda with American naval officers, Rongrik Atoll, Marshall Islands (photo U.S. Navy).*

never been able to return to their radioactive homeland, except for a temporary sojourn in the 1970s. Despite monetary compensation from the United States, Marshallese still complain about ruined islands, leukemia, thyroid cancer, and "jellyfish" babies as a result of their being treated like "guinea pigs" by a colonial power. The residents of Kwajalein Atoll were evicted in 1951 in favor of U.S. military personnel who continue to run missile tests there. French testing has aroused more protest because from 1966 to 1974 it occurred aboveground, in violation of the 1963 test-ban treaty, and even after the tests were moved underground, questions remained about the safety of setting off atomic blasts in coral atolls. In 1985, self-governing Oceanian countries signed a treaty that created a South Pacific Nuclear Free Zone, banning all testing and storage of nuclear weapons. Only in 1996, after performing another series of hotly protested blasts, did France (along with the United States and Britain) sign the S.P.N.F.Z. treaty (Firth 1987, *Pacific Islands Monthly*, May 1996). Perhaps "nuclear colonialism" is finally coming to an end.

Unlike the United States and France, Britain chose to scale back its colonial empire after India gained independence in 1947. The British withdrawal "east of Suez" spurred decolonization in Australian and New Zealand territories as well. The UN played a more active role in this process after its 1960 resolution that non–self-governing peoples should be offered three choices: independence, free association, or incorporation—i.e., equal rights within the colonizing country, such as Hawai'i's statehood in 1959 (Roff 1991). In 1962, Western Samoa was the first country to regain its independence, with the provision that only *matai* be allowed to vote or run for office.

Nauru won control of its phosphate industry and became independent in 1968, and by 1980, Tonga, Fiji, Papua New Guinea, Solomon Islands, Kiribati, Tuvalu, and Vanuatu also voted for independence. Vanuatu (formerly New Hebrides) owed its sovereignty to British support, since co-administrator France actively opposed independence to protect planter interests. These new states formed the Pacific Forum in the 1970s to pool their resources and gain more regional clout. In the 1980s, three western Pacific states formed the Melanesian Spearhead with a similar purpose (Thompson 1994).

Nation-building has been a challenge for many of these states, since their boundaries and government structures are legacies of colonialism. In culturally diverse Melanesia, national elites brought up through the colonial educational and administrative systems have tried to enforce unity and develop their considerable mineral resources. But secession movements on Bougainville in Papua New Guinea (PNG), the western Solomons, and on Santo and Tanna in Vanuatu have tested such visions. Some Melanesian leaders have tried to build consensus around *kastom* (custom), "Melanesian socialism," or the "Melanesian Way," but these concepts have not replaced local loyalties. Even the wealth from mining is limited by demands from multinational companies to keep wages, taxes and environmental protection to a minimum or else they will relocate. Urban centers like Port Moresby face growing crime problems from unemployed migrants, and the vote-of-no-confidence system borrowed from Britain makes it hard for a coalition government to last for very long. Half of PNG's Parliament is voted out in every election (Wanek 1996).

Fiji became independent in 1970, after negotiations between Fijian and Indian leaders. Indians had organized labor unions and long pushed for elected representation, but Fijian chiefs had relied on British protection. In 1959, chiefs had broken up a multiethnic strike by urging their commoners not to listen to "sweet-talking" Indians, and in 1963, when Fijian commoners received the right to vote for the first time, they supported their chiefs instead of Indian opponents of the power elite. At independence, each ethnic group was guaranteed 22 seats in the lower house of Parliament, and Fijian land and customary rights could only be changed with approval by six of the eight high chiefs in the upper house. For seventeen years, an Alliance led by Ratu Sir Kamasese Mara held power with votes from Fijians, Muslim Indians (who feared the Hindu majority), and other minorities. In 1987, however, a coalition of Hindu Indians and western and urban Fijians outvoted Mara's Alliance. The new government of Timoci Bavadra, a western Fijian, was soon overthrown in a military coup by Sitiveni Rabuka, who is now Fiji's Prime Minister. Thousands of Indians have emigrated, but the constitution has gone through two revisions, first very pro-Fijian and then more moderate (Lal 1992, Dawn of a new era 1998).

Fijian nationalists control their army, but elsewhere native sovereignty movements wage uphill struggles against immigrant power. In Hawai'i, Guam, and New Zealand, the indigenous peoples are minorities in their own islands and face what some activists call "ethnocide," or cultural assimilation by the majority. Since the 1970s, activists have revived their languages and cultures and had limited success at recovering land. The U.S. Navy stopped bombing practice on Kahoʻolawe, and the U.S. Congress admitted complicity in the overthrow of the Hawaiian monarchy; it also returned some military land on Guam to the local government, but it tabled a Guam Commonwealth proposal. A Waitangi Tribunal is slowly redressing Maori grievances about land, water, and fishing rights. France abolished forced labor and granted French citizenship in its Pacific territories in 1946, but it also jailed nationalist leaders in Tahiti and New Caledonia during unrest in the late 1950s. Nuclear testing in French Polynesia and French immigration to New Caledonia during a nickel boom stirred new protests, but aid money from Paris (and the loyalty of European settlers in New Caledonia) has kept nationalists from gaining a democratic majority. The 1980s were very violent in New Caledonia, but Accords reached in 1988 and 1998 postponed votes on independence in return for a gradual devolution of powers to the territory (Robie 1989, Henningham 1992, Chappell 1998).

Five resource-poor Pacific Island countries have chosen to decolonize by voting for free association, which allows self-government but also continued economic (and military) ties to the colonizing power. In the North Pacific, the Marshall Islands, the Federated States of Micronesia, and Palau have all signed a Compact of Free Association with the United States. They are self-governing members of the UN and the Pacific Forum but receive millions of dollars in "strategic rent" from the United States, which retains military options. Palau at first had an antinuclear clause in its constitution, but after years of economic pressure from the United States, it removed that and approved the Compact. Micronesians are not U.S. citizens (except in the Northern Marianas, which became a Commonwealth), but as "habitual residents" they can migrate freely to the United States. In the South Pacific, the Cook Islands and Niue opted for free association with New Zealand, which grants them self-government at home but also New Zealand citizenship and subsidies. Most people in those two states have now moved to New Zealand for better jobs and schooling. Three very small island groups, Tokelau, Pitcairn, and Easter Island, remain dependencies of New Zealand, Britain, and Chile, respectively (Roff 1991, Hayes 1991). Table 11.1 shows the current political status of Pacific Island groups.

Economics has thus compromised sovereignty in Oceania. Today at least 500,000 anglophone islanders have migrated to the United States, Australia, and New Zealand, and within the French circuit, more than half of Wallis and Futuna's population has moved to mineral-rich New Caledonia for jobs. This process has received an acronym, MIRAB, for migration, remittances (money and goods sent home to families), aid and bureaucracy (government salaries are often paid by foreign aid grants) (Bertram and Watters 1985). Returnees who have lived abroad and received Western educations sometimes challenge traditional elites and push for democratic reforms, as in Samoa and Tonga (Campbell 1992). Some observers see MIRAB as neocolonial dependency, while others regard it as the continuation of an ancient voyaging dynamic (Hayes 1991, Hauʻofa 1994). Small island countries can also benefit from the United Nations Law of the Sea, which grants exclusive economic zones for 200 miles around their shores. The Pacific Forum, for example, has negotiated a collective tuna fishing agreement with the United States. Saipan, Fiji, and American Samoa are developing garment industries for export, while Kiribati still sends laborers to the Nauru mines or foreign ships. Tuvalu lives mainly off stamp sales and a trust fund, and Hawaiʻi relies almost entirely on tourism (Fairbairn et al. 1991). In the so-called "Pacific century," Oceania is generally pursuing a path of interdependence.

## The Past As Prologue

The past five hundred years in the Pacific Islands have witnessed accelerating change. During the first half of that period, the impact of Euroamericans was minimal, except on Guam, which Spain colonized brutally. By the late 1700s, local chiefs began to exploit growing contacts with foreign explorers and traders to enhance their own status. In the mid-1800s, however, such interaction began to favor outside powers, who had industrialized, until by 1900 sovereignty itself was lost.

Imperialism has been studied from various angles, ranging from the Euroamerican "cores" of a global system to resistance and negotiation by indigenous peoples in the outer "periphery" (Doyle 1986). Despite the superficial transformations on political maps, colonialism in the Pacific Islands varied greatly from place to place. In the Marianas, Hawaiʻi, New Zealand, and New Caledonia, native people were marginalized and dispossessed of most of their lands, but in Fiji, Tonga, and Samoa, traditions survived more or less intact, as did their land ownership systems. Nicholas Thomas has argued that colonialism was not really monolithic and should be studied as a series of projects undertaken by many actors, including missionaries, traders, planters, administrators, and anthropologists, who sometimes disagreed with each other. This plurality, when combined with the diversity of native societies and also differing strategic and economic values of the islands to outsiders, makes it difficult to assess the impact of foreign rule in a general way (Thomas 1994).

Recent studies of "subaltern" (colonized) peoples suggest that their quest for full independence is limited by subtle cultural, social, and economic changes that complicate their visions of the past and future (Prakash 1994). Hence the preference by many Pacific Islanders for incorporation into the excolonizing country as a commonwealth, state, or territory, or for the negotiated, relative autonomy of "free association." Postcoloniality is thus an elusive concept, even in supposedly sovereign countries.

Robert Jackson has called many excolonies quasi states, because their structures and borders are rather artificial colonial creations that exist mainly in international law and hence need ongoing subsidies and policing from abroad (Jackson 1990). The rebellion of Bougainville and frequent changes of government leadership in PNG have led some observers to call it a neocolonial state whose national elite is really replicating expatriate rule over diverse local "nations" (Wanek 1996). Meanwhile, in Fiji, Tonga, and Samoa, challenges to chiefly leaders by urbanized or well-traveled indigenous critics have led to strident debates over who benefits from "traditionalism" (Lawson 1996). Epeli Hauʻofa of Tonga has accused Western-educated

### Table 11.1 — Political Status of Pacific Island Groups

| Colonial power | Incorporated into colonial power | Still dependent | Self-governing in free association | Independent |
|---|---|---|---|---|
| United Kingdom and France | | | | Vanuatu (1980) |
| United Kingdom | | Pitcairn | | New Zealand (1907) |
| | | | | Fiji (1970) |
| | | | | Tonga (1970) |
| | | | | Tuvalu (1978) |
| | | | | Solomon Is. (1978) |
| | | | | Kiribati (1979) |
| France | | French Polynesia | | |
| | | New Caledonia | | |
| | | Wallis & Futuna | | |
| New Zealand | | Tokelau | Cook Is. (1965) | Samoa (1962) |
| | | | Niue (1974) | |
| Australia | | Norfolk Is. | | Nauru (1968) |
| | | | | Papua New Guinea (1975) |
| United States | Hawaii (1959) | American Samoa | Marshall Is. (1986) | |
| | Northern Marianas | Guam | Federated States of Micronesia (1986) | |
| | | | Palau (1994) | |
| Chile | | Easter Island | | |

chiefs of manipulating traditions in a two-faced way to keep power for themselves while they actually adopt rather untraditional lifestyles (Hau'ofa 1987).

Pressures and temptations from the outside continue to test indigenous identities. Sovereign Nauru is so "hooked" on imports that the people are developing diabetes from eating too much junk food, while subaltern Maoris, Hawaiians, and Chamorros are relearning their own languages in schools to resist total assimilation. Regional cooperation in the Pacific Forum or Melanesian Spearhead offers hope for small island states to band together in a competitive world arena, while out-migration is developing transnational networks through which Oceanians can explore new frontiers of opportunity and change. The quest for truly self-sustaining nation-states may be illusory, since even the United States is the largest debtor country on the planet right now, yet there remains considerable dynamism in Pacific societies, even if outsiders fail to recognize grassroots initiatives.

In fact, outsiders never have understood Oceania very well, from Magellan's violent encounter with Guam, to the myth of South Seas "paradise" invented by Tahitians (and perpetuated by modern tourism), to the ways that Oceanians "indigenized" Christianity and corned beef, to today's experiments in free association and migratory transnationalism. Cultures are never static. Despite all the tragic loss of life from alien diseases, colonial conquest, world wars, and nuclear testing, and other traumas such as foreign immigration, racial discrimination, and exploitative capitalism, Pacific Islanders are survivors. That is how they became Oceanians in the first place.

As Hau'ofa (1994) puts it,

> Oceania is vast, Oceania is expanding, Oceania is hospitable and generous, Oceania is humanity rising from the depths of brine and regions of fire deeper still. . . . We must not allow anyone to belittle us again, and take away our freedom.

# Bibliography

Bertram, I. G., and R. F. Watters, 1985. The Mirab economy in South Pacific microstates. *Pacific Viewpoint* 26(3):497–519.

Campbell, I. C. 1992. *Island kingdom: Tonga, ancient and modern.* Christchurch: University of Canterbury Press.

Chappell, D. 1998. Finally, Wallisians get recognition. *Islands Business* 24:9, 22–23.

Dawn of a new era. 1998. *Islands Business* 24:9, 23.

Dening, G. 1980. *Islands and beaches.* Melbourne: Melbourne University Press.

Doyle, M. 1986. *Empires.* Ithaca: Cornell University Press.

Fairbairn, T., C. Morrison, R. Baker, and S. Groves. 1991. *The Pacific Islands: politics, economics and international relations.* Honolulu: University of Hawai'i Press.

Firth, S. 1987. *Nuclear playground.* Honolulu: University of Hawai'i Press.

Gammage, B. 1975. The Rabaul strike 1929. *Journal of Pacific History* 10(3):3–29.

Hau'ofa, E. 1987. The new South Pacific society: integration and independence. In *Class and culture in the South Pacific,* ed. A. Hooper, S. Britton, R. Crocombe, J. Huntsman and C. Macpherson, 1–12. Suva: University of the South Pacific.

Hau'ofa, E. 1994. Our sea of islands. *The Contemporary Pacific* 6(1):148–161.

Hayes, G. 1991. Migration, metascience and development policy in Island Polynesia. *The Contemporary Pacific* 3(1):1–58.

Hempenstall, P., and N. Rutherford. 1984. *Protest and dissent in the colonial Pacific.* Suva: University of the South Pacific.

Henningham, S. 1992. *France and the South Pacific.* Honolulu: University of Hawai'i Press.

Hezel, F. 1983. *The first taint of civilization: a history of the Caroline and Marshall Islands in precolonial days, 1521-1885.* Honolulu: University of Hawai'i Press.

Hezel, F. 1995. *Strangers in their own land: a century of colonial rule in the Caroline and Marshall Islands.* Honolulu: University of Hawai'i Press.

Howard, M., and S. Durutalo. 1987. *The political economy of the Pacific Islands to 1945.* Townsville: James Cook University Press.

Howarth, D. 1985. *Tahiti: a paradise lost.* New York: Penguin.

Howe, K. R. 1984. *Where the waves fall: a new South Sea Islands history from first settlement to colonial rule.* Honolulu: University of Hawai'i Press.

Howe, K. R., R. Kiste, and B. Lal. 1994. *Tides of history: the Pacific Islands in the twentieth century.* Honolulu: University of Hawai'i Press.

Jackson, R. 1990. *Quasi-states: Sovereignty, international relations and the Third World.* NY: Cambridge.

Keesing, R. 1992. *Custom and confrontation: the Kwaio struggle for cultural autonomy.* Chicago: University of Chicago Press.

Lal, B. 1992. *Broken waves: a history of the Fiji Islands in the twentieth century.* Honolulu: University of Hawai'i Press.

Lawson, S. 1996. *Tradition versus democracy in the South Pacific: Fiji, Tonga and Western Samoa.* NY: Cambridge.

Maude, H. E. 1968. *Of islands and men.* Melbourne: Oxford University Press.

Maude, H. E. 1981. *Slavers in paradise.* Canberra: Australian National University Press.

Meleisea, M. 1987. *The making of modern Samoa.* Suva: University of the South Pacific.

Moorehead, A. 1966. *The fatal impact: an account of the invasion of the South Pacific, 1767–1840.* New York: Dell.

*Pacific Islands Monthly.*

Newbury, C. 1980. *Tahiti nui: change and survival in French Polynesia.* Honolulu: University of Hawai'i Press.

Paige, P. S., ed. 1969. *The voyage of Magellan: the journal of Antonio Pigafetta.* Englewood Cliffs, NJ: Prentice-Hall.

Prakash, G. 1994. Subaltern studies as postcolonial criticism. *American Historical Review* 99(5):1475–1490.

Robie, D. 1989. *Blood on their banner: nationalist struggles in the South Pacific.* London: Zed Books.

Rodman, M., and M. Cooper, eds. 1983. *The pacification of Melanesia.* New York: University Press of America.

Roff, S. 1991. *Overreaching in paradise: United States policy in Palau since 1945.* Juneau: Denali Press.

Rogers, R. 1995. *Destiny's landfall: a history of Guam.* Honolulu: University of Hawai'i Press.

Sahlins, M. 1981. *Historical metaphors and mythical realities.* Ann Arbor: University of Michigan Press.

Sahlins, M. 1985. *Islands of history.* Chicago: U. Chicago.

Scarr, D. 1990. *The history of the Pacific Islands.* Melbourne: Macmillan.

Thomas, N. 1994. *Colonialism's culture.* Princeton.

Thompson, R. 1994. *The Pacific Basin since 1945.* NY: Longman.

Trask, H. K. 1993. *From a native daughter: colonialism and sovereignty in Hawai'i.* Monroe, ME: Common Courage.

Walker, R. 1990. *Ka whawhai tonu matou: struggle without end.* Auckland: Penguin.

Wanek, A. 1996. *The state and its enemies in Papua New Guinea.* Richmond, UK: Curzon.

White, G., and L. Lindstrom, eds. 1989. *The Pacific theater: island representations of World War II.* Honolulu: University of Hawai'i Press.

Wolfers, E. 1975. *Race relations and colonial rule in Papua New Guinea.* Sydney: University of Sydney Press.

Worsley, P. 1968. *The trumpet shall sound: a study of cargo cults in Melanesia.* New York: Schocken.

# Chapter 12

# Changing Patterns of Power

*Terence Wesley-Smith*

## Doomsday in the Pacific Islands?

Until relatively recently the Pacific Islands region appeared as a haven of stability and modest affluence in a Third World rife with bloodshed and poverty. The post–Word War II transfer of power from colonizer to colonized was, in general, an orderly one, and remarkably free of the violence that characterized the process elsewhere. Even in the troubled French territory of New Caledonia, the 1988 Matignon Accords promised peace and reconciliation between warring settler and indigenous communities, although the Accords put the issue of independence on hold for at least a decade. Furthermore, things seemed to be going relatively well in island nations that achieved independence or self-government after 1962. Despite occasional signs of strain, the democratic constitutional structures adopted at independence appeared to be holding up quite well. Political power changed hands peacefully and by constitutional means, and there was no sign of the sorts of serious human rights abuses that plagued the newly independent countries of Asia and Africa. Most important, material standards of living remained relatively high, bolstered by large village-based sectors of "subsistence affluence" as well as generous aid transfers from the metropolitan powers active in the region.

However, a series of events in the late 1980s served to dampen the prevailing mood of optimism. Most dramatic were two military coups in Fiji in 1987, which ousted the duly-elected government and installed a new constitution that discriminated heavily against citizens of Indian descent, some 50% of the population. In the same year, a domestic power struggle erupted in Vanuatu that would lead eventually to a breakdown in constitutional order, rioting in the streets of Port Vila, and a threatened intervention by regional security forces led by Australia. Observers were also increasingly concerned with developments in Papua New Guinea, by far the largest island state, where parliamentary politics had become turbulent and unpredictable, official corruption was surfacing as a major issue, and a wide range of domestic groups, including criminal "raskol" gangs, routinely flaunted the authority of the state. Their worst fears were realized in late 1988 when landowners on the island of Bougainville set out to close down the giant copper and gold mine at Panguna, sparking a bloody and destructive secessionist conflict with the Papua New Guinea security forces that continues to this day.

By the early 1990s there was also mounting concern—even alarm—about the state of island economies. A series of reports drew attention to the fact that most island economies were growing only slowly, if at all, despite relatively high inflows of development assistance, a phenomenon dubbed the "Pacific paradox" by the World Bank (World Bank 1993). In a much discussed monograph published in 1993, a group of researchers at the Australian National University warned that continuing slow rates of economic growth coupled with high rates of population growth in some parts of the region could lead to general socioeconomic collapse, or "doomsday," within two decades (Cole 1993). In 1997 a leaked official Australian brief described the economic outlook for some island countries as "bleak" and argued that there was "a question mark over whether the smallest, resource-poor countries will be able to maintain current standards of living (or indeed be viable) without external assistance" (FEMM 1997).

The doomsayers tend to lay the blame for these problems squarely at the feet of island governments, routinely citing "poor governance and economic mismanagement" as key contributing factors (FEMM 1997). However, this is, at best, only part of the explanation for the islands' current woes. After all, the structural features of island economies are well known, many economies have been slow-growing or even stagnant for years, and in most cases current development policies and practices have been in place since independence. The most significant change since the late 1980s has not been the performance of island economies, or even the stewardship of island leaders, but rather the willingness of external powers to subsidize those economies. During the Cold War, security and strategic interests mattered most to the United States, Great Britain, Australia, New Zealand, and France, who were particularly concerned to exclude the Soviet Union and its allies from the region. Aid flows and policies reflected this preoccupation with strategic denial, which was thought to depend on helping island leaders meet their development needs and expectations—and keep them firmly oriented to the Western world. It is no coincidence that the concern with economic performance, governance, and self-sufficiency has increased at the same time that the Cold War strategic imperative has fallen away.

The events of the last decade have stripped away some of the layers of illusion that have tended to cloud perceptions of political and economic development in the Pacific Islands. The political crises in Fiji, Vanuatu, and especially Papua New Guinea serve as sobering reminders that the institutions and assumptions of the nation-state have been exported to the Pacific from their European homelands relatively recently and that democracy is a "foreign flower" that has not automatically taken root in some Pacific soils. The recent concern with economic crisis reminds us that the capitalist market economy is a relative newcomer to the region as well, and that its establishment has been highly problematic and traumatic everywhere, including in Europe, where it first emerged.

What we are witnessing in the Pacific Islands in the 1990s

are troubling symptoms of rapid and comprehensive social change, a process that clearly has its origins in the disruptions and innovations of the colonial period. According to Arturo Escobar, this process, often euphemistically called "development" or "modernization," has produced instead "massive underdevelopment and impoverishment, untold exploitation and oppression" throughout the Third World (Escobar 1995). The doomsayers fear that Pacific Island societies are heading down this path as well, but, curiously, see salvation in increasing rather than decreasing the pace of change. Their critics argue that the prescription of rapid economic growth and further integration into the global economy may well make matters worse, and actually create the doomsday conditions it seeks to avoid.

## The Role of the State

Today a growing number of students of Third World development wonder why the leaders of the global movement for decolonization, who promised to rid the world of the scourge of European colonialism, so readily adopted Western institutions and models of development when independence was finally achieved. Arturo Escobar, for example, is puzzled by the fact that a handful of industrialized nations provided the "indubitable models" for hundreds of newly independent societies of the Third World, which were expected to "catch up" with the industrial world, "perhaps even become like them" (Escobar 1995). In particular, the state model of political organization, although "an artifact of a small segment of human history," was universally embraced and quickly became "the focal point for hopes of achieving broad goals of human dignity, prosperity, and equity; it was to be the chisel in the hands of the new sculptors" (Migdal 1988).

Just as the state was central to the aspirations of Third World leaders at the time of independence, so it is at the center of contemporary efforts to explain why these noble goals have generally not been achieved. Prominent historian of Africa Basil Davidson, for example, blames much of the catastrophe that has befallen African countries since independence on the "curse of the nation-state" (Davidson 1992), while Joel Migdal notes that the vast majority of Third World states are what he calls "weak states," seemingly incapable of "changing their societies in particular ways" (Migdal 1988).

The debate about the role of the state in the development of the newly independent nations of the Pacific is relatively new. As Peter Larmour notes, political analysts have been "preoccupied with written constitutions and the achievement of independence," while leaving unchallenged the assumption that a European-style nation-state was the most appropriate—perhaps even the only—vehicle to achieve desirable change in Pacific Island societies (Larmour 1994). Such a debate has emerged in recent years in the wake of the political and economic crises of the last decade, especially at the Australian National University, where a research team was assembled in 1996 to investigate issues of "State, Society and Governance" in neighboring Melanesian countries. "State" in this context is generally used to refer to a hierarchical network of official institutions "that has the ability or authority to make and implement the binding rules" for all people residing in a particular territory (Migdal 1988). "Society" refers to other forms of social organization that exist within the territory, which may compete with the state for the right to make "binding rules." Less familiar is the concept of "governance," which is generally used "to refer to the manner in which power is exercised in the management of a country's economic and social resources" (Larmour 1996). This notion of governance is interesting precisely because it does not assume the predominance of state institutions in the production of outcomes, but tries to explain how power is actually exercised and decisions made in developing countries. Although a focus on governance serves to decenter the role of the state, it does little to challenge the wider assumptions about "development" in which the whole governance debate is embedded. For most writers in this genre, the industrial countries still provide the "indubitable models" for economic development that trouble Escobar and others; their dominant concern is how to achieve those goals, rather than how the goals themselves might be rethought.

Obviously the many and complex issues associated with contemporary state, society, and governance in the Pacific Islands cannot be addressed in any comprehensive way here. However, it is possible to identify some key historical factors that have contributed to the present situation, factors that are sometimes forgotten in the rush to judgment about development problems and prospects in the region. The first task is to discuss how power was exercised in island societies before Europeans introduced their own notions of state and government, and to note some important variations across the region and over time.

## Pre-European Patterns of Power

We know much about the spatial and chronological dimensions of the human settlement of the Pacific Islands, but relatively little about the social and political characteristics of the early settlers. We assume that the earliest arrivals, who entered the Australia–New Guinea region from Southeast Asia at least 50,000 years ago, were loosely organized, impermanent, and relatively unstratified bands of hunters-and-gatherers. It is unclear what structural changes, if any, occurred as these Papuan-speaking populations expanded over the main landmasses and occupied adjacent islands as far east as Solomon Islands over the next 20,000 years or so. Since everybody had more-or-less equal access to the material necessities of life, there would have been few economic levers of control available to ambitious individuals. Power relations probably revolved around age and gender differences.

The potential for using economic means to exercise power would have expanded with the independent development of agriculture in one or more parts of the Western Pacific some nine thousand years ago and its spread and intensification over subsequent millennia. The ethnographic record for New Guinea and adjacent islands suggests a useful distinction between political systems in which men's power was based on their control of wealth and those in which it rested on the control of knowledge or ideas (Harrison 1993). Maurice Godelier, for example, proposed that the term "big-man," first generalized for all of Melanesia by Marshall Sahlins in an influential article (Sahlins 1963), be reserved for those societies, mainly in highland New Guinea, where wealth exchanges had become essential to social reproduction. He argued that other societies, where the available "points of power" were limited to ritualized activities, particularly male initiation, were better described as "great man" societies (Godelier 1991). Godelier's classificatory scheme implies some sort of evolutionary link between the two systems. However, there is little direct evidence that big-man societies actually emerged over time from great-man societies and, even if they did, the factors that might have propelled such a transition remain obscure. It was clearly not a universal process, since many different patterns of leadership and degrees of stratification were apparent among the thousands of Papuan-speaking societies by the time Europeans arrived. It is worth noting, however, the absence from these societies of concepts of genealogically based rankings of persons or descent groups.

Differences among Papuan-speaking groups were almost certainly less significant than differences between these groups and a second wave of migrants from Southeast Asia that arrived in coastal New Guinea and adjacent islands some 4,500 years ago. It seems likely that these early Austronesian-speaking groups brought an ideology of ascribed hierarchy with them, or at least developed it in the process of expansion. Certainly, there is strong evidence of stratification among the Austronesian-speaking groups that began to expand rapidly from the Bismarck Archipelago, through Island Melanesia, and on into the uninhabited reaches of Western Polynesia about 3,500 years ago. According to Patrick Kirch (1984), these groups were rank-organized, with seniority based upon genealogical distance from a founding ancestor, and ruled by hereditary chiefs (Figure 12.1). These groups were, of course, the ancestors of the present-day Polynesians, and of most Micronesian populations.

The degree to which such principles were elaborated and emphasized over time in particular Austronesian societies appears to be a product of a whole range of local environmental, social, and economic factors. Some societies in Polynesia, such as Pukapuka in the Cook Islands, remained relatively egalitarian, while others, such as Hawai'i, Tonga, and the Society Islands, developed elaborate, hierarchical, and centralized political systems. Still others, like Easter Island, may have been highly stratified at some point in their histories, but had returned to less elaborate forms of organization by the time Europeans arrived (Kirch 1984). In Micronesia, the highest degree of stratification occurred on Pohnpei and Yap in the Caroline Islands (Figure 12.2), with the Southern Gilbert Islands and Nauru among those places that had relatively egalitarian social and political structures when Europeans arrived.

The general argument here is that Austronesian and Non-Austronesian societies followed fundamentally different trajectories

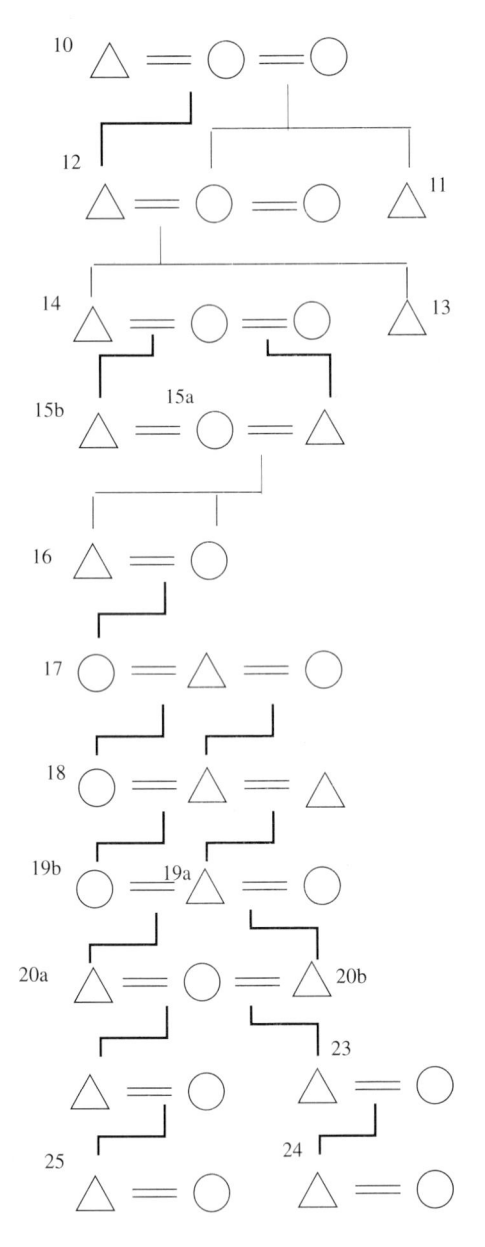

*Figure 12.1. Genealogical relationships of paramount chiefs on Hawai'i Island. Males are designated by triangles, females with circles. Numbers indicate the sequence of succession from Liloa (10) to Kamehameha (25) (after Kirch 1984).*

*Figure 12.2. Chiefs' meeting place, Map Island, Yap (photo LEM).*

146     The Pacific Islands

of political development in Oceania, with Austronesian societies producing many variations on the theme of genealogically based rank. Non-Austronesian societies were no less varied, but the structures of power had more to do with individual control of strategic resources than with heredity. The major problem with this conceptual scheme is, of course, that by no means all of the Austronesian-speaking groups in the southwestern part of the region had hereditary forms of leadership when Europeans arrived. Some analysts have argued that these Austronesian-speaking big-man or great-man societies had somehow "devolved" over time from earlier hierarchical forms. However, the situation can also be explained in terms of historical interactions between Austronesian interlopers and resident Papuan populations. Peter Bellwood, for example, suspects that a great deal of the postulated deconstitution of chieftainship may instead be the result of the "strong influence and even cultural takeover by Papuan speakers of Austronesian social networks" (Bellwood 1990). In this process of "Papuanization," numerically superior resident groups might have adopted the language of the visitors in order to join their productive regional trade networks or colonizing expeditions. Both forms of leadership may have coexisted for a while, with the Papuan model eventually becoming dominant.

## The Colonial State

Indigenous trajectories of political change were rudely interrupted by the arrival of Europeans into the region and the eventual establishment of colonial rule over all Pacific Island societies. Colonialism was everywhere a powerful force, but it was by no means a monolithic one. Its impact on a particular population depended upon a variety of factors, not least the length of the colonial experience. Spain established colonial rule in Guam and the rest of the Marianas as early as 1668, but most Pacific islands were not formally incorporated into foreign empires until the second half of the nineteenth century. Some Pacific populations, most notably in the highlands of New Guinea, did not come under external government control until the second half of the twentieth century. One island group, Tonga, felt the pressure of external interests, but managed to avoid direct colonial rule altogether (Figure 12.3). A significant number of Pacific Island places experienced a succession of at least two different colonial masters over the years, most notably as a result of the defeat of Germany in World War I and of Japan in World War II, and the subsequent loss of their respective island territories to other powers.

The process of political change precipitated by colonial rule took many different forms and can only be fully understood on a case-by-case basis. However, for all Pacific places, colonization ultimately meant the establishment of that most fundamental unit of Western political organization, the state, that "official hierarchy of legislative, administrative and judicial bodies (each vested with delegated and defined authority)" designed to create and maintain order among a population occupying a particular territory defined by geographical boundaries (Lawrence 1971).

The closest indigenous approximations to the Western state

*Figure 12.3.* The royal palace, built in 1867 by George Tupou I, Tongatapu, Tonga (photo LEM).

were the elaborate and stratified chiefdoms in the Austronesian-speaking societies of Polynesia and Micronesia. In Hawai'i, for example, Europeans found complex, hierarchical decision-making structures, involving members of the chiefly class (*ali'i*), their stewards (*konohiki*), and a "considerable body of councilors, priests, executants, and other retainers who formed a 'court' of the paramount chief" (Kirch 1984). The boundaries of these polities expanded and contracted over time, but often incorporated whole islands. The political system in Tonga was even more elaborate, with dual paramount chiefs of the Tui Tonga and hau lines controlling the entire Tongan archipelago and beyond, ultimately extending their influence to Samoa and Eastern Fiji (Kirch 1984).

It is tempting to categorize these entities as pre- or proto-states, suggesting that, given time, they would have evolved or developed into European-style states. However, the historical circumstances surrounding the evolution of states in Europe were really quite specific, especially in their economic dimensions, and there is no reason to believe that Pacific entities would have followed that particular trajectory rather than an almost infinite number of other possibilities. What we do know is that in the nineteenth century chiefs in Hawai'i, Tahiti, and Tonga used their connections with European interlopers to expand these structures into full-blown states "complete with public governments and public law, monarchs and taxes, ministers and minions" (Sahlins 1963).

In some ways the more centralized, unified, and stratified Pacific polities were better placed to resist the colonial advance. However, only the Tongan state survived for any length of time, and chiefly structures were more typically used to further colonial ends. Britain, for example, ruled Fiji by attaching itself to the top of a hierarchical network of chiefly power, and Spain, Germany, and Japan all attempted to use chiefly structures to govern their possessions in Micronesia. In other cases, the colonial power bypassed, and eventually undermined, the chiefly establishment, as occurred in French Polynesia after the collapse of the Pomare dynasty, and in Hawai'i after the overthrow of the monarchy in 1893, as well as in the Cook Islands and northern and central parts of the Gilbert Islands.

Pacific Island places with smaller-scale, less permanent, and more diffuse big-man or great-man political systems were more difficult for colonial powers to govern effectively, providing more opportunities for the persistence of indigenous political institutions and practices. With no suitable preexisting political structures to work through, colonial authorities in New Guinea, Solomon Islands, and New Hebrides (later Vanuatu), were forced to construct entirely new administrative units and institutions, and create a new class of native officials to occupy their lower levels. Even by the end of the colonial era, state structures in these places tended to be rudimentary, fragmented, and inefficient.

European colonization forged political boundaries that were significantly different from preexisting ones. In the vast majority of cases, colonial boundaries created much larger political units than before, bringing often disparate communities together for the first time. The colonial boundaries of French Polynesia, for example, joined five different archipelagos whose inhabitants had few traditional cultural or political links, and each colonial entity in Melanesia encompassed hundreds of previously autonomous groups. While traditional political boundaries were often fluid and sometimes relatively open, colonial boundaries were usually clearly defined, permanent, and impermeable. The division of the Pacific Islands into colonial entities sent neighboring groups off on quite different trajectories of change.

*Figure 12.5.* Meeting of the toeaina *(council of elders) on Fakaofo, Tokelau (photo MR).*

The nature and extent of Western-style government structures established in a territory usually reflected the perceived interests of the colonial power. In extreme cases, such as Dutch New Guinea and British (later Australian) Papua before World War II, where the only significant interest was strategic control, a token government presence was sufficient. Subject populations living away from easily accessible coastal areas were often left largely to their own devices between the infrequent visits of government patrols. On the other hand, in settler colonies like New Zealand, Hawai'i, and New Caledonia, or resource-rich places like Nauru, indigenous populations were confronted with much more extensive, comprehensive, and intrusive government structures.

In most Pacific places before World War II, colonial government was largely about controlling native populations and regulating their activities to facilitate colonial interests. It involved varying degrees of violence, domination, exploitation, and racism (Hanlon 1994). Colonial policies were often justified as serving native interests as well, as part of some wider civilizing mission. Such ideas were, no doubt, sincerely held by principled colonial officials, but they rested squarely on European notions of racial and cultural superiority, progress, and manifest destiny. Some colonial officials, like Lt. Gov. Hubert Murray in Papua or Sir Arthur Gordon in Fiji, even placed native interests above foreign ones at times. But their ability to decide what was best for the native population, and which aspects of native life should and would be protected, reveals much about the essential nature of the colonial system (West 1968, Lal 1992).

Colonization took political power away from local Pacific

*Figure 12.4.* Chief in custom village on Tanna, Vanuatu (photo LEM).

Island communities and put it in the hands of resident colonial officials and, ultimately, of decision-makers in remote capital cities in Europe, the United States, Australia, or New Zealand. The instrument of imperial control was the colonial state, which defined new, enduring territorial configurations and installed alien administrative mechanisms. The extent to which the daily lives of particular Pacific populations were affected by these developments depended largely on which colonial jurisdiction they found themselves in, and the interests and policies of the administering power at the time. The persistence of indigenous political forms and structures (Figures 12.4 and 12.5) may, in some cases, have resulted from local resistance or the intrinsic qualities of those institutions, or both. But more often they endured because they were allowed or even encouraged to do so by the colonial power in furtherance of its own interests.

## Power Returned, Power Retained

Europe's mighty global empires have disintegrated in the second half of the twentieth century under nationalist pressures in the colonies that proved increasingly difficult to contain. The political face of the Pacific has been transformed over the last forty years as well. Starting with Western Samoa (now Samoa) in 1962, nine island entities have achieved full independence, and most Pacific Islanders now live in independent states. However, more than half of all island colonies have not acquired this status and retain constitutional or other significant links to the colonial power. The key question of which island colonies would become independent and which would remain dependent was not determined by the physical or economic characteristics of the colony or even the expressed desire of the people, although these factors were important in some cases. Instead, the critical variable was the interests of the colonial power.

Stewart Firth argues that "the greater the strategic value of an island territory, the less likely that territory has been to proceed to sovereign status" (Firth 1989). This argument works well for the Pacific territories governed by the United States. According to Robert Kiste, from the beginning "American involvement in the Pacific Islands has predominantly been motivated by strategic and security concerns" (Kiste 1994). These considerations were certainly important in determining the political status of Hawai'i, Guam, and the Northern Marianas, all of which became permanently integrated into the United States political system. The Federated States of Micronesia, the Marshall Islands, and Palau are now self-governing nations (Figure 12.6), but their compacts of "free association" with the United States effectively trade control of military and security matters in return for massive financial subsidies from Washington. Nor has independence ever been a real option for those Pacific Islanders colonized by France, which remains determined to maintain a global presence (Aldrich 1989). In 1954 France unilaterally removed New Caledonia, French Polynesia, and Wallis and Futuna from the United Nations' list of non–self-governing territories on the grounds that they "enjoyed self-government within the French

*Figure 12.6.* Nitijela (National Parliament), Majuro, Marshall Islands (photo LEM).

Republic" (Maclellan and Boengkih 1996). Since that time, France has consistently maintained that its Pacific territories are not colonies but integral parts of the French state.

On the other hand, independence was the only option presented to other Pacific Islanders. This was the case for residents in colonies of Great Britain, whose reduced capacity to maintain global interests dictated a deliberate policy of withdrawal from the region. Fiji, Solomon Islands, and the Gilbert and Ellice Islands Colony (which split into two independent entities, Kiribati and Tuvalu), were all granted full independence in the 1970s, with the New Hebrides (Vanuatu) eventually following suit in 1980, despite resistance from France, Britain's partner in the condominium government. This was a staged withdrawal, with local leaders exerting significant influence on events, especially in the final stages (Macdonald 1994). Nevertheless, for these people, as for the peoples of the American and French territories, the decolonization process was controlled by the colonial power and ultimately reflected its interests.

New Zealand was keen to withdraw from its island dependencies as well. The few economic and strategic benefits yielded by direct control of Western Samoa, the Cook Islands, Niue, and Tokelau were more than offset by the diplomatic costs of defying growing anticolonial sentiment in the international community. Its decolonization policy was shaped soon after the end of the Pacific war in response to nationalist demands in Western Samoa, when it was decided to prepare the territory for independence as soon as possible. The possibility of integration with New Zealand was effectively ruled out for the Cook Islands, and later for Niue and Tokelau, on constitutional grounds, even though this might well have been the preferred option for these Pacific Islanders. Eager to maintain their connections with and access to New Zealand, Cook Islanders, Niueans, and more recently, Tokelauans agreed to accept New Zealand's preferred option, self-government in free association with New Zealand. These entities retain the option of withdrawing from the agreement at any time in favor of full independence (Wesley-Smith 1994).

Unlike New Zealand, Australia was in no hurry to decolonize its Pacific territories, where it had real interests at stake.

However, its best efforts to retain control of Nauru's lucrative phosphate resources were ultimately defeated by a combination of factors, including astute local leadership, pressure from the United Nations, and the disunity of Australia's partners in the trusteeship agreement, New Zealand and Great Britain. Australia recognized that the strategically important territories of Papua and New Guinea, which it administered together after World War II, would eventually achieve self-government, but envisaged a very long period of preparation. However, mounting pressure from the United Nations in the 1960s persuaded Australia to adopt an accelerated program of decolonization that resulted in independence in 1975. The option of integration into the Australian federation as a state, which would have addressed Australia's strategic concerns directly, was considered, but quickly abandoned on the grounds that the overwhelmingly white Australian public would never accept large numbers of Melanesians in their midst.

The global decolonization movement liberated many Pacific Islanders from direct colonial rule, but left others dependent and dissatisfied. Dissidents in Irian Jaya, for example, a Dutch colony inhabited by more than a million Melanesians incorporated into Indonesia in 1962, continue to wage a guerrilla war against Indonesian sovereignty under the banner of the Organisasi Papua Merdeka (OPM), or Free Papua Movement. In New Caledonia, the Front Libération Nationale Kanak et Socialiste (FLNKS) heads the kanak struggle for independence against the opposition of settlers, who represent a majority in the territory, as well as the French state. Meanwhile, indigenous minorities in other settler colonies, most notably New Zealand and Hawai'i, are also demanding redress of historical grievances and the right to sovereignty or self-determination.

## Making States and Nations

It was perhaps inevitable that where political power was returned to Pacific Islanders it was returned in the form of a European-style nation-state. This was, after all, the fundamental unit in the existing global political system, from which all international status, legitimacy, and protection from external aggression would be derived. The process of decolonization itself was orchestrated in important ways by the United Nations, an institution committed by its charter to preserving the notion of state sovereignty. Furthermore, Third World leaders generally saw this as the appropriate instrument to achieve their goals. It is important to remember that what they had in mind was radical transformation of societies that in most cases had already been profoundly altered by the forces of capitalism and colonialism. The "humpty-dumpty" of indigenous political and economic forms had long since fallen off the wall, and the challenge was to put the pieces together again in what were seen as new and progressive ways (Migdal 1988).

However, putting the basic elements of the nation-state together in the Pacific and elsewhere in the Third World has been difficult, to say the least. Theorists usually distinguish between the state, an administrative-legal structure with sovereignty over citizens within a bounded territory, and the nation, a group of people who feel as if they belong together by virtue of some perceived shared cultural characteristics or common heritage. Ideally the boundaries of the two will coincide, and the process of political development in the Third World is often referred to as "nation-building." This is misleading because usually both nation and state have to be created, and assembling viable state structures is almost always the first order of business. It is also misleading because this rather bland architectural metaphor masks the contested and often violent nature of the process.

Some Pacific Island places have experienced a relatively smooth transition to nation-statehood. In the Kingdom of Tonga, for example, the essential ingredients of statehood had been in place since the nineteenth century, and when it terminated its protectorate arrangement with Britain in 1970, a strong sense of Tongan national identity was already well established. Although all the inhabitants of the Samoan archipelago shared many cultural values, the essential locus of political power and identity had always been at the village level. Samoan nationalism was largely a colonial phenomenon, forged in opposition to New Zealand's administration of the western islands, which may explain why incorporating (or reincorporating) the eastern islands, which remain a territory of the United States, has never emerged as a significant political issue (Meleisea 1987, 1988).

Both Tonga and Samoa have had to struggle with thorny political issues in recent decades, but these have involved the nature and operation of state institutions, rather than the fundamentals of nation-statehood. In Tonga a pro-democracy movement has argued that the present concentration of political power in the monarch and a handful of noble families is no longer appropriate and advocates a shift to more broadly based representative institutions (Helu 1992). In Samoa, the tension between centralized state institutions established at independence and local centers of power based on traditional chiefly *matai* titles was softened somewhat by limiting suffrage and parliamentary participation to holders of *matai* titles. Although the shift to universal suffrage in 1990, coupled with the recent proliferation of *matai* titles, represents a significant shift toward a more "modern," democratic form of politics, it has by no means put paid to central-local tensions (Le Tagaloa 1992, Leiataua and Alailima 1994).

As in Tonga and Samoa, the existence and jurisdiction of Fiji's state structures have not been seriously challenged, although two military coups in 1987 significantly altered the way access to political power is managed. The difficulty in Fiji has always been imagining a political community that embraces the approximately equal number of citizens of Fijian descent and those whose ancestors were brought from India to work the sugar plantations in the late nineteenth and early twentieth centuries. Furthermore, there have been problems of unity on both sides of the Fijian-Indian ethnic divide. Indo-Fijian leaders have attempted to foster a common identity in the face of significant internal religious and cultural differences, with limited success. Fijian leaders have had more success creating a strong sense of belonging among indigenous Fijians using entrenched chiefly structures and more-or-less subtle invocations of "the Indian threat." However, Fijian unity has been severely challenged since the mid-1980s by factions in the western part of the main island of Viti Levu who object to the historical dominance of Eastern chiefs and confederacies; by an assertive Methodist church advocating an extreme version of ethnic politics; and by a political movement intent on reducing the political dominance of the chiefly establishment, which it portrays as self-serving and corrupt, in favor of a more open politics serving grassroots interests.

The debate regarding the causes of and justifications for the 1987 coups still goes on (see e.g. Lal 1988, Scarr 1988, Robertson and Tamanisau 1988, Ravuvu 1991). However, it is clear that the widespread public support for the first coup in the Fijian community was largely based on the perception that the indigenous way of life was somehow threatened by the rise of the recently elected coalition government that was portrayed as "Indian-dominated." The argument for Fijian paramountcy was championed by a well-organized Taukei (people of the land or indigenous people) Movement, whose determined opposition to a political compromise proposed by Gov.-Gen. Ratu Sir Penaia Ganilau prompted a further military intervention in September 1987. Taukei aims were effectively realized in 1990 with the installation of a new constitution that explicitly discriminated against citizens of Indian descent in the electoral process and guaranteed that Fijians would continue to control the levers of political power. The polarizing effect of events since 1987 makes a single, overarching Fijian nation more difficult than ever to imagine, while centralized state structures survive essentially intact.[1]

Problems of both state- and nation-making remain even more acute in the other independent Melanesian countries of Vanuatu, Solomon Islands, and Papua New Guinea. The peculiar legacy of dual colonial rule in Vanuatu was parallel state administrative structures, one erected by the British and one by the French, which actively competed with each other for influence throughout the archipelago, especially in the run up to independence. Although it was a relatively simple matter to merge these bureaucratic structures when the colonial powers finally withdrew, the legacy for national identity was much more profound and divisive. British support for and French opposition to independence served to further polarize national political communities already mobilized on either side of the francophone-anglophone divide. A key event in this process of polarization was the secessionist rebellion on the large northern island of Santo in 1980, actively supported by the French authorities as a last-ditch attempt to reduce anglophone dominance in politics and disrupt the transition to independence (Beasant 1984).

The politics of exclusion, with the anglophone "nation" led by Prime Minister Father Walter Lini fully in control of state structures, persisted for nearly a decade after independence (Van Trease 1995a, Arutangai 1995). By the late 1980s, however, the solidarity of the governing Vanua'aku Pati had begun to crumble. Things began to unravel after Prime Minister Walter Lini was incapacitated by a stroke early in 1987, opening the way for the first direct challenge to his leadership since he was elected president of the party (then called the New Hebrides National Party) in 1974. His challenger was Barak Sope, the founding Secretary-General of the party, and the ensuing bitter struggle for power split the party into three competing factions, led to rioting in the streets of Port Vila, and precipitated a constitutional crisis when the president of the republic, Ati George Sokomanu, was arrested after trying unsuccessfully to install a rebel government led by Sope.

The leadership crisis of the late 1980s shattered the hegemony of the Vanua'aku Pati and marked the decline of the anglophone-francophone politics forged in opposition to French policies in the late colonial period. In many ways, the new politics, built around smaller, more personalized and locally based political factions, better reflects the archipelago's extremely fragmented cultural landscape. However, this situation is even more problematic than the earlier one because, in a sense, Vanuatu has been de-nationalized. Raised anew is the challenge of forging a viable ni-Vanuatu identity out of myriad competing local and regional identities based on vernacular language and kastam (Van Trease 1995b, c).

Like Vanuatu, the neighboring Solomon Islands consists of a collection of small-scale traditional communities loosely tied together by emerging market forces, rudimentary state institutions, and perhaps most important, church networks, none of which predate the colonial era. Unlike in Vanuatu, there was no oppositional external force, no common enemy, to help forge a common identity among these disparate colonial subjects. Independence was given by the British, not wrested from them, and while it bequeathed common citizenship on all inhabitants of the colony, it did not bestow a common national identity. As Christine Jourdan points out, nationalism in Solomon Islands is essentially an urban phenomenon, created by those citizens "who have to shape a future for themselves away from custom and tradition," and encouraged by pragmatic state officials concerned "to hold the country together." It is transmitted to the hinterlands by educational institutions and is part of an emerging popular culture that incorporates elements of both tradition and modernity; it gains much of its strength from Pijin, a lingua franca that, because of its relatively recent origin, belongs to no one and everyone at the same time (Jourdan 1995).

The postcolonial state lacks the coercive capacity of its colonial predecessor and has little economic hold over ordinary citizens, most of whom remain firmly attached to village economies that are still largely self-sufficient. Whatever legitimacy it enjoys must be earned through the provision of desired modern services such as health and education and by meeting the demands of rural people for "development." This is a virtually impossible task, given the limited financial and other resources available to the state and the escalating claims on them by a rapidly growing population. The situation is further complicated by a decentralized system of provincial government ostensibly established to reflect the diversity of the country and make state institutions more responsive to the needs of the people. These have become important sites in the competition for state resources, reinforcing regionalism but doing little to strengthen nationalism. Furthermore, the rise of provincial government has not been accompanied by improved delivery of services, which in many parts of the country have deteriorated over time. After two decades of independence, according to Ian Frazer, the Solomon Islands state is "no closer to the kind of legitimacy required for stability and unity in the future" (Frazer 1995).

In many ways the problems of state- and nation-making in Solomon Islands are mirrored on a much larger scale in its giant western neighbor, Papua New Guinea. As in Solomon Islands, the national state lacks both legitimacy and the resources to coerce recalcitrant citizens into submission. Attempts to win allegiance through the delivery of essential services and "development" projects to local constituencies have not proved particularly successful and may even have been counterproductive. The evidence suggests that state resources and the bureaucratic institutions that deliver them are often captured by local forces and made to serve local, quasi-traditional institutions and values rather than centralized, modern ones (Jacobsen 1995). This process, a type of reverse colonization, attests to the resilience of indigenous ways of life and economy, but reduces the effectiveness of the state and confounds its modernizing mission. Attempts to create a sense of nationhood, which must of necessity emphasize a common future rather than a common past for the country's diverse citizens, have met with some success in urban areas. But even in town, local or ethnic identities remain important signifiers, and in some rural parts of the country there is little or no sense of belonging to the nation or identifying with its mission (see e.g. Clark 1996).

Also like the Solomons, Papua New Guinea recognized some of the difficulties inherent in governing such a diverse and fragmented physical and cultural landscape and installed a decentralized system of government shortly after independence. The provincial government system further frustrated the ambitions of the bureaucratic national state by creating competing local centers of political power and patronage and was effectively legislated out of existence in 1995. The recentralization of political power in Papua New Guinea was, of course, strongly resisted by those in control of provincial government structures, and several provinces, especially in the Islands region, threatened to secede. The threats subsided as some dissident leaders were enticed into important positions in the new administrative structures and others adopted a wait-and-see attitude to the reforms. However, such disintegrative tendencies will remain significant until such time as centralized state structures command more legitimacy and ordinary people begin to feel a sense of attachment to the nation. This is not likely to occur anytime soon.

One part of Papua New Guinea, the island province of Bougainville, has made a concerted attempt to break away from the state. Secessionist sentiments were apparent there in the late 1960s, when the social and economic disruption associated with the construction of a massive copper and gold mine at Panguna fueled the emergence of a strong sense of Bougainvillean nationalism. In 1975, just before Papua New Guinea's own independence, a group of Bougainvilleans declared an independent Republic of the North Solomons. Unable to win international recognition, the secessionists agreed in 1976 to be part of the new Papua New Guinea state in return for a degree of political autonomy to be exercised through a provincial government. However, periodic protests over the adverse environmental and social impacts of the mine continued and in late 1988 erupted into violence (Oliver 1991, Wesley-Smith 1992). Landowners in the vicinity of the mine embarked on a campaign of sabotage that forced its closure six months later, by which time the Bougainville Revolutionary Army had emerged with independence its declared goal. The evidence suggests that the transition from local protest to secessionist war was largely precipitated by the heavy-handed response to the crisis by state security forces (Connell 1991).

The ongoing Bougainville crisis, which has caused enormous bloodshed and suffering, is the most troubling example so far of the hazards of state-making in the Pacific Islands, and the destructive potential of development or modernizing processes generally. For nearly a decade, state officials have been unable either to negotiate a settlement to the crisis or force compliance by military means. In a dramatic move to break the impasse before the 1997 general elections, the national government of Sir Julius Chan hired foreign mercenaries to spearhead a military operation designed to crush the rebel force and retake the Panguna mine. The plan backfired when military commander Brig. Gen. Jerry Singirok broke ranks to publicly condemn the scheme and demand its revocation. He argued that the planned use of sophisticated counterinsurgency equipment would produce many casualties and implied that Prime Minister Chan and other senior officials were benefiting financially from the $36 million mercenary contract. In the face of a massive public outcry and clear signs that most of the military were sympathetic to Singirok's position, Chan and two of his senior government colleagues agreed to step down from office pending the results of a commission of inquiry into the charges of corruption.

## Future Prospects: Beyond the Nation-state?

Decolonization efforts in the Third World since World War II have centered on the institutions of the nation-state, itself an artifact of an expansive nineteenth century European colonialism. In the Pacific Islands, as elsewhere in the colonized world, liberation from colonialism has come to mean gaining control of a European-style state structure and then creating a coherent national community out of the various groups enclosed by its boundaries. Some Pacific Island peoples have yet to achieve political independence, while those that have now realize that this is only the beginning of a long and often arduous process of state- and nation-building (Figure 12.7). The ongoing struggle to transform indigenous cultural practices and institutions to fit the needs and assumptions of "modern" state structures has produced mixed results in the islands. Nowhere in the region could the process be regarded as complete, although in some parts of Polynesia "modern" and "traditional" structures manage to coexist relatively peacefully. This is not the situation in some parts of Melanesia, where the transition has been effectively subverted by resilient local forces or, in the case of Bougainville, has precipitated extended violent confrontation.

Global developments in the late twentieth century make the process of making states and nations even more problematic. Ironically, political power has been restored to colonized peoples at a moment in history when the global significance of

*Figure 12.7.* French and Tahitian administrators on a joint visit to the Tuamotus, French Polynesia (photo MR).

the sovereign nation-state is in decline. Today, it is global forces, often diffuse and invisible, that most affect our lives, and nation-states—even the most powerful—are increasingly incapable of controlling them. The Cold War masked this emerging reality somewhat, not least in the Pacific where Western powers generously subsidized state- and nation-building efforts essentially to counter an assumed "Soviet threat." In the 1990s, with the Cold War a thing of the past, Pacific Island states operate in a new, less forgiving international environment. Perhaps the clearest example of the new reality is in Micronesia, where American security interests have changed dramatically in recent years and the Federated States of Micronesia and Marshall Islands face the possibility of a much less generous financial settlement when their compacts of free association come up for renewal in the year 2001.

With the possible exception of Tonga, all Pacific Island states are what Migdal calls weak states, in that their leaders simply do not have the capacity to engineer fundamental social and economic changes in their societies. Furthermore, this situation is unlikely to improve as already besieged states continue the battle against erosive domestic forces, while increasingly having to confront damaging global forces as well. Yet fundamental change is ultimately what "modernization" and "development" are all about, and what donor countries and agencies increasingly require as a condition for continued support.

Pacific Island states may be weak, but their societies are generally strong. They remain strong precisely because the effects of capitalism and colonialism were generally less damaging here than in other parts of the world. In conventional development frames this is regarded as an undesirable condition, to be rectified, almost at any cost. However, nearly fifty years after these ideas were first translated into development policies and practices throughout the Third World, the results are hardly encouraging. While the dream of development—embraced by Western theorist and Third World leader alike—has turned into a nightmare, some of the most influential development agencies and experts in the Pacific Islands appear to be advocating more of the same (Escobar 1995).

The challenge is to imagine alternative, more flexible, forms of political organization that are better able to deal with global forces and more accommodating of local needs and demands. Under these new circumstances, and especially in Pacific places bypassed by major global circuits of exchange, indigenous political forms and values may enjoy a new lease on life.

## Notes

[1] Fiji's constitution was revised in 1997–98, partly as a requirement for rejoining the British Commonwealth. The new constitution includes a bill of rights and restores some electoral rights to Indo-Fijians (Seneviratne 1997).

## Bibliography

Aldrich, R. 1989. France in the South Pacific. In *No longer an American lake: alliance problems in the South Pacific*, ed. J. Ravenhill, 76–105. Berkeley: Institute of International Studies, University of California at Berkeley.

Arutangai, S. 1995 Post-independence developments and policies. In *Melanesian politics: stael blong Vanuatu*, ed. H. Van Trease, 59–91. Christchurch and Suva: Macmillan Brown Centre for Pacific Studies, Canterbury University and Institute for Pacific Studies, University of the South Pacific.

Beasant, J. 1984. *The Santo Rebellion*. Honolulu: University of Hawai'i Press.

Bellwood, P. 1990. Hierarchy, founder ideology and Austronesian expansion. Paper given at Hierarchy, Ancestry and Alliance conference, Australian National University.

Clark, J. 1996. Imagining the state, or tribalism and the arts of memory in the highlands of Papua New Guinea. In *Narratives of the nation in the South Pacific*, eds. T. Otto and N. Thomas, 65–90. Amsterdam: Harwood Academic Publishers.

Cole, R. V., ed. 1993. Pacific 2010: challenging the future. Pacific Policy Paper #9. Canberra: National Centre for Development Studies, Australian National University.

Connell, J. 1991. Compensation and conflict: the Bougainville copper mine, Papua New Guinea. In *Mining and indigenous peoples in Australasia*, ed. J. Connell and R. Howitt, 55–75. Sydney: Sydney University Press in Association with Oxford University Press, Australia.

Davidson, B. 1992. *The black man's burden: Africa and the curse of the nation-state*. New York: Times Books.

Escobar, A. 1995. *Encountering development: the making and unmaking of the Third World*. Princeton, New Jersey: Princeton University Press.

FEMM. Forum Economic Ministers' Meeting. 1997. Australian Delegation Brief. Cairns, 11 July. Typescript.

Firth, S. 1989. "Sovereignty and independence in the contemporary Pacific." *The Contemporary Pacific* 1(1&2): 75–96.

Frazer, I. 1995. "Decentralization and the postcolonial state in Solomon Islands." In *Lines across the sea: colonial inheritance in the postcolonial Pacific*, ed, B. V. Lal and H. Nelson, 95–109. Brisbane: Pacific History Association.

Godelier, M. 1991. An unfinished attempt at reconstructing the social processes which may have prompted the transformation of great-man societies into big-man societies." In *Big-men and great-men: personifications of power in Melanesia*, ed. M. Godelier and M. Strathern. Cambridge: Cambridge University Press.

Hanlon, D. 1994. Patterns of colonial rule in Micronesia. In *Tides of history: the Pacific Islands in the twentieth century*, ed. K. R. Howe, R. C. Kiste, and B. V. Lal, 93–118. Honolulu: University of Hawai'i Press.

Harrison, S. 1993. "The commerce of cultures in Melanesia." *Man* 28:139–159.

Helu, I. F. 1992. Democracy bug bites Tonga. In *Culture and democracy in the South Pacific,* ed. R. Crocombe, et al., 139–152. Suva: Institute of Pacific Studies, University of the South Pacific.

Jacobsen, M. 1995. Vanishing nations and the infiltration of nationalism: the case of Papua New Guinea. In *Nation making: emergent identities in postcolonial Melanesia*, ed. R. J. Foster, 227–249. Ann Arbor: The University of Michigan Press.

Jourdan, C. 1995. "Stepping stones to national consciousness: the Solomon Islands case." In *Nation making: emergent identities in postcolonial Melanesia*, ed. R. J. Foster. Ann Arbor: The University of Michigan Press.

Kirch, P. V. 1984. *The evolution of Polynesian chiefdoms*. Cambridge: Cambridge University Press.

Kiste, R. C. 1994. United States. In *Tides of history: the Pacific Islands in the twentieth century*, ed. K. R. Howe, R. C. Kiste, and B. V. Lal, 227–257. Honolulu: University of Hawai'i Press.

Larmour, P. 1994. Political institutions. In *Tides of history: the Pacific Islands in the twentieth century*, ed. K. R. Howe, R. C. Kiste, and B. V. Lal, 381–405. Honolulu: University of Hawai'i Press.

Larmour, P. 1996. Models of Governance and Development Administration: State, Society and Governance in Melanesia, Discussion Paper 96/2. Canberra: Research School of Pacific and Asian Studies, Australian National University.

Lal, B. V. 1988. *Power and prejudice: the making of the Fiji crisis*. Wellington: New Zealand Institute of International Affairs.

Lal, B. V. 1992. *Broken waves: a history of the Fiji Islands in the twentieth century*. Pacific Islands Monograph Series, No. 11. Honolulu: University of Hawai'i Press.

Lawrence, Peter. 1971. Introduction to *Politics in New Guinea*, eds. R. W. Berndt and P. Lawrence, 1–34. Nedelands, Western Australia: University of Western Australia Press.

Le Tagaloa, A. F. 1992. The Samoan Culture and Government. In *Culture and democracy in the South Pacific*, ed. R. Crocombe, et al., 117–137. Suva: Institute of Pacific Studies, University of the South Pacific.

Leiataua, V., and F. Alailima. 1994. Restructuring Samoa's Chiefdom. In *New politics in the South Pacific*, ed. W. vom Busch, et al., 247–269. Rarotonga and Suva: Institute of Pacific Studies, University of the South Pacific, in association with the Pacific Islands Political Studies Association.

Macdonald, B. 1994. Britain. In *Tides of history: the Pacific Islands in the twentieth century*, ed. K. R. Howe, R. C. Kiste, and B. V. Lal, 170–194. Honolulu: University of Hawai'i Press.

Maclellan, N., and J. Boengkih. 1996. *France's decolonisation process in New Caledonia: conflict on the path to self-determination*. Pacific Series Working Paper No. 1. Melbourne: Centre for Asia-Pacific Studies, Victoria University of Technology.

Meleisea, M. 1987. *The making of modern Samoa: traditional authority and colonial administration in the history of Western Samoa*. Suva: Institute of Pacific Studies, University of the South Pacific.

Meleisea, M. 1988. *Change and adaptations in Western Samoa*. Christchurch: Macmillan Brown Centre for Pacific Studies, University of Canterbury.

Migdal, J. S. 1988. *Strong societies and weak states: state-society relations and state capabilities in the Third World*. Princeton, New Jersey: Princeton University Press.

Oliver. D. 1991. *Black islanders: a personal perspective of Bougainville, 1937–1991*. Honolulu: University of Hawai'i Press.

Ravuvu, A. 1991. *The facade of democracy: Fijian struggles for political control, 1830-1987*. Suva: Reader Publishing House.

Robertson, R. T., and A. Tamanisau. 1988. *Fiji—shattered coups*. Sydney: Pluto Press.

Sahlins, M. D. 1963. Poor man, rich man, big man, chief: political types in Melanesia and Polynesia. *Comparative Studies in Society and History* 5(3):285–303.

Scarr, D. 1988. *The politics of illusion: the military coups in Fiji*. Kensington: University of New South Wales Press.

Seneviratne, K. 1997. "South Pacific: Fiji's new constitution promises racial harmony." Inter Press Service (IPS), July 20, 1997. http://www.oneworld.org/ips2/jul/fiji.html

Van Trease, H. 1995a. The colonial origins of Vanuatu politics. In *Melanesian politics: stael blong Vanuatu*, ed. H. Von Trease, 3–58. Christchurch and Suva: Macmillan Brown Centre for Pacific Studies, University of Canterbury and Institute for Pacific Studies, University of the South Pacific.

Van Trease, H. 1995b. Years of turmoil, 1987–91. In *Melanesian politics: stael blong Vanuatu*, ed. H. Von Trease, 73–118. Christchurch and Suva: Macmillan Brown Centre for Pacific Studies, University of Canterbury and Institute for Pacific Studies, University of the South Pacific.

Van Trease, H. 1995c. The Election. In *Melanesian politics: stael blong Vanuatu*, ed. H. Von Trease, 119–158. Christchurch and Suva: Macmillan Brown Centre for Pacific Studies, University of Canterbury and Institute for Pacific Studies, University of the South Pacific.

Wesley-Smith, T., ed., 1992. A legacy of development: three years of crisis in Bougainville. Special Issue, *The Contemporary Pacific* 4(2).

Wesley-Smith, T. 1994. Australia and New Zealand. In *Tides of history: the Pacific Islands in the twentieth century*, ed. K. R. Howe, R. C. Kiste, and B.V. Lal, 195–226. Honolulu: University of Hawai'i Press.

West, F. J. 1968. *Hubert Murray: the Australian pro-consul.* Melbourne: Melbourne University Press.

World Bank. 1993. *Pacific Island economies: toward effective and sustainable growth.* Vol. I: *Overview.* Washington D.C.: World Bank.

# CHAPTER 13

# "Race," Identity, and Representation

*RDK Herman*

## Conceptualizing Identity

The Pacific Islands form a cultural mosaic comprising not only many islander peoples, but peoples of European descent ("Westerners") and of Asian descent as well. The geography of these many peoples, though never stable, has changed dramatically in the past few hundred years as Westerners and Asians have, at different times and in different places, entered the region, and as islanders themselves have increasingly migrated both within and outside the Pacific.

Among the results of contact among and juxtaposition of different peoples is the arising of *representations*—categorizations and images by which members of one group distinguish others from themselves. This chapter considers the role of such representations and aims to present tools by which they may be understood. While much of the terrain is specific to the local level, the aim here is to elucidate the broader principles at work.

There are several vectors of representation that come into play: inter-islander representations; islander representations of Europeans and of Asians; and European and Asian representations of islanders and each other. Not all of these vectors have the same power, nor the same relevance to Pacific Island studies. This chapter considers a limited scope within the broader subjects of "race," identity, and representation, and paints with broad strokes. Detailed local observation and consideration are necessary to understand any given situation.

The two major arenas to be considered include, first, Western representations of islanders. This comes earlier because this is the first arena in which a literature developed, brought on by European exploration. Later, particularly with the growth of anthropology, literature on interislander representations became available. But this literature, too, is a product of European penetration. And because that penetration substantially altered cultures, economies, and demographies, and to the extent that interislander representations are often mediated by a Western scientist/observer, it is difficult to consider them as representing "pre-European contact" modes.

More important, Western representations of islanders form a powerful battery that has come to characterize the islands as we have come to know them. Such representations have been intimately linked with the exercise of power. The science of "race," as a way of classifying humans, developed simultaneously with outward conquest from the European heartland and was used to justify the conquering of outlying territories and the subjugation of their peoples. For the Pacific, this began with the Spanish, who had already used Aristotelian notions of "natural slavery" in regard to Native Americans. Religious dictum was also employed. "Heathenism" was linked with "savagery" and "barbarism" and became another justifying motive for conquest of non-European others. Representation of islanders henceforth involved "racial" classification using a variety of biological indicators and correlated with behavioral characteristics said to be "in the blood."

At the time that Western explorers entered the Pacific, most island societies were small and fragmented. Island groups were characterized more strongly by kinship-based groups, or perhaps island-wide identity, than by any overarching archipelagic identity. The early historical period bears a record of warfare and conquest within most island chains, often with some Western support, technology or advice being provided to one or more sides. The emergence of archipelagic nations such as Hawai'i, Tahiti, Fiji, Tonga, and so on was the result of conquest and influence by one or more Western powers.

When Pacific islands were brought into the emerging global economic order, a new force became dominant Pacific-wide: capitalism. This Western economic form, and its associated social and cultural institutions, was not a monolithic or unified phenomenon, but nonetheless constituted a political economy qualitatively and quantitatively different from those existing in island societies at the time. In different ways and at different times, all Pacific Island societies eventually had to cope.

Western representations of islanders have served colonial penetration and the expansion of capitalism since Western ships entered the Pacific. Because of the unequal distribution of power in favor of the "West"—virtually all Pacific Island economies were taken over and transformed by Western capital, often with overt political colonization as well—the power of Western representations is strongly disproportionate to the representations islanders have of each other or of Westerners. Western representations have achieved global circulation through various media of reproduction: print, photography, art, film, documentaries, and so on.

A few guiding principles must be kept in mind. First: these Western representations come from a diversity of materials. They collectively present a picture that, though unstable and fluctuating from source to source, is a product of the discourse on islanders as a whole. A second and related principle is that there is no unitary "Westerner" who holds such an image. Each of us is our own person, and while we participate and live within the field of discourse, we accept or reject parts of it in accordance with our own ideas.

Third, while these overall representations are the building blocks and products of racism, to most Westerners these were simply "truth" or "science" (see Gould 1981, Stepan 1982), without the conscious awareness of racism and power that we espouse today. Western history of the Pacific Islands generally shows a positive image of Westerners as helpers, transformers, movers, and shakers who aided the islanders during difficult transitions. Many must have understood themselves in this light. And there are representations that are distinctly laudatory of the islanders.

The second part of this chapter considers islander representations, and ways in which islander identity is constructed. Because islanders did not share in the broad and politically functional discourses of "race" specific to the West, identity among island communities has been constructed differently. The differential impact of colonialism on different islander groups, however, has posed situations in which identities are being reconstituted to cope with new political circumstances.

## Economies of Western Representation

JanMohamed (1986) has suggested that in colonialism, representations of a colonized people form a currency: a coherent body of symbology in which the ideologies of colonization are inscribed, and the products of which are circulated. Others have since argued that colonial ideology is written "on the body" of the colonized people: they are described, represented, hence "defined" in terms that justify colonial practices. And as these practices change, so too do the representations. Hence representations form an "economy" of symbols that serve the aims of the larger political economy.

The topic of representations of islanders within Western imperial practices is voluminous and controversial. Within any of these representations, there is diversity and contradiction. We can, as a shorthand, speak of "missionary representations," because all of these operate out of a particular economy. This does not mean that missionary representations form a uniform body without contradiction or difference. But there was a power relationship in which even well-intentioned Westerners were often patriarchal and patronizing. Representations of islanders thus facilitated, or justified, imperialism in the Pacific, whether they preceded, accompanied, or followed overt practices.

The major areas in which colonial economies of representation have arisen include 1) the exploration literature, in which contact with the islanders was usually brief and good relations were important for survival; 2) the missionaries in the Pacific, who were the first major gatherers of knowledge in this unknown (to the West) territory, and who had their own particular agendas that depended on particular representations of islanders; 3) capitalist forces such as plantations and the colonial governments that backed them, who were dependent on islander labor and/or access to (or control of) land; 4) military forces concerned with acquiring strategic bases; and 5) tourism, dependent on the "exotic" to attract visitors. There are many other voices as well, such as beachcombers, travel writers, journalists, novelists, and filmmakers. While these voices are influential and sometimes contradictory, they tend to embellish the major economies and draw from their images.

It is likely that the invocation of "difference" by one group toward another knows no geographic or temporal limits. But the use of scientific observation and classification of people that would become racial science in the nineteenth century has its roots in European colonial expansion. Spanish rule in the New World coupled with the enslavement of Native Americans had already evoked an argument of "natural slavery" based on Aristotelian ideas (Pagden 1982). This posited races of people as distinct varieties in the scale of nature; that is, distinct "species" independently created. The idea of "species" was not sufficiently developed until much later, but the differentiation of humans had already begun.

Skin color had not originally been a major issue, as seen in the variety of European slaves taken by the Spanish. But by the eighteenth century the slave trade had become almost exclusively black (Stepan 1982). This fused with literary traditions to the effect that white represented purity, innocence, goodness, and the like, while black represented evil, pollution, and so on. The result was that black skin became a "natural" sign of inferiority. "Difference" then came to be sought in anatomy: if persons were biologically alike, then they all deserved equal rights and privileges. However, if they could be shown to be anatomically different, then inequality was justified instead.

In the Pacific, this color-based scale fused with a differentiation of social and political structures, which in turn led to differences in Western colonial attitudes and policies. The resulting differentiation of "levels of civilization" as determined by skin color, physiognomy, and social forms was first outlined by Johann Reinhold Forster on Cook's second voyage and mapped by French navigator Dumont d'Urville in 1832 (Thomas 1989). The boundaries of Polynesia, Micronesia, and Melanesia identified differences in social and political structure: lighter-skinned Polynesians were said to constitute a uniform family with highly developed political hierarchies, while darker-skinned Melanesians had more fragile tribal systems prone to arbitrary tyrannical rule. Melanesian cultures were said to be generally more degraded and savage (Australian aborigines being perhaps rock bottom with their alleged destitution of technological and social forms).

At the time of Cook, one theme in European philosophy posed islanders as "natural men," "noble savages" whose proximity to nature made them morally pure. As European society advanced technologically, nature was often seen as degraded, dirty, impure, and brute. Humanity being more divine than lower animals by virtue of being able to improve upon nature, those cultures that remained closer to nature were deemed closer to animals than to civilized people (Smith 1985). With the increasing technology gap, native peoples were seen more and more as "backward." But during the Age of Exploration, the footing was more level, and explorers came to know and appraise islanders as people not too unlike themselves.

### *Explorers*

Many of our contemporary images of the Exotic South Pacific derive directly or indirectly from the journals of the early explorers. The Age of Exploration combined scientific endeavor with more overtly imperialist purposes. The instructions for explorers clearly called, on the one hand, for the appropriation of land wherever possible— theoretically "with consent of the natives," if there were any (see e.g. Beaglehole 1967, III:ccxxiii; La Pérouse 1799: 24-6; D'Urville 1987:II: 284-5; and Wilkes 1845, I:xxvi-xxvii). On the other hand, the scientific gaze of the explorers was directed explicitly at the bodies of native peoples, as seen in Cook's instructions for all three voyages: "You are likewise to observe the Genius, Temper, Disposition and Number of the Natives, if there be any, and endeavour by all proper means to cultivate a Friendship and Alliance with them" (Beaglehole 1955). The "nature" of an islander group would directly affect the kind of relationship that group would come to have with Western powers in the ensuing years. Hence understanding these "natures" and their roots is critical.

The explorers were often dependent, both in their observational tasks and in reprovisioning their ships, on amicable relations with the peoples they encountered. The Pacific Islands were often controlled by powerful local figures whom the explorers and their crews came to know as individuals, as fellow human beings with strange customs, but as more or less equals. Dening (1986) highlights the dual nature of exchange and possession involved with early European contact in Tahiti. Smith (1992) explains how for the artists accompanying the voyagers, portraiture in particular required the subject (usually of the local elite) to sit for some time, thus requiring a friendly relationship between the subject and the artist.

While a sense of European superiority underlies the literature of this period, there is nonetheless often an open admiration for certain islanders who demonstrated a dignity and stateliness with which European officer-gentlemen identified. There are also admissions of islander superiority in certain skills, particularly those involving strength, agility, and anything to do with the ocean. Admiration for technological feats, such as irrigation systems and boat design, are also present. And the physical beauty of certain persons received high praise. Thus the complexity of interpersonal relations and experiences made for a rich picture of Pacific Island peoples, not easily reduced to the types of generalizations found in racial science. Still, this did not preclude the drawing of generalizations regarding different peoples.

The extent to which violence formed representations of islanders must not be overlooked. Campbell (1990) writes that only in a few cases of contact between explorers and islanders had violence or threat not been present, that men on both sides "came from militaristic societies in which recourse to violence was a traditional solution to conflict, or in which strangers were held to be outside the usual ethical and legal limits," and that much of the bloodshed was due to "European arrogance and pride." But more often we know of the islanders', not the explorers', tendencies towards hostility. European hostility either disappears, as in the case of Tahiti (Pearson 1969), or is overshadowed by islander violence, as in Cook's death (Herman 1996).

Pearson (1969) asserts that there was a pattern, begun with Quiros and repeated after the incidents at Tahiti:

first, "pacification," the intimidation of the home population by means of superior weapons, and then the imposition of a European system of justice, administered without distinction to inhabitant and visitor, followed by demonstrations of conditional benevolence. On the Polynesian side the series of events was resistance, or . . . initial welcome, then resistance after a breach of whatever understanding was implied in the welcome, followed by defeat, intimidation, appeasement, and finally acceptance of European sovereignty in those questions which concerned both parties. (p. 211)

It is from this, Pearson asserts, that the pastoral imagery of Polynesia developed. The socio-racial distinctions between Polynesians and Melanesians were in turn affected by the resultingly friendly reception the explorers had gotten from the Polynesians and the often hostile and violent reception from the Melanesians (Thomas 1989).

"Promiscuity" is an important component of the pastoral imagery from this period. Pearson notes that the "first clear evidence of the offer of sexual accommodation for the visitors is . . . eight days after arrival and after drastic military defeat." Furthermore, the "girls themselves at first seemed uneasy, and it was the senior men who directed them to it." (1969). He concludes that the use of women to pacify Western men became an intentional strategy for coping with threat. Bougainville and later Cook's crews, arriving after the pacification, took this state of affairs to be "natural," and the myth grew. The result is a sustaining image from this period of islanders as "promiscuous." This is the foundation for an eroticization of the South Seas that persists today.

There is no doubt that Pacific Islanders had different senses of sexual propriety, and that Westerners found these "shocking" at the same time that they indulged in them. Virtually all explorers—the officers—visiting the Hawaiian Islands condemned outright the wanton displays of sexuality whereby the women attempted to entice them, while the crewmen were busy taking advantage of the opportunity. It can further be seen that sex constituted a means of trade whereby islanders obtained Western goods in the initial contact periods, including the intangible exchange of essence the women accrued through intercourse with these powerful strangers. Yet the hope of discouraging this "free sex" would become one motivation for missionaries to enter the Pacific.

## *Missionaries*

Missionaries' representations played an important role in establishing Western understandings of the islanders. As the only *resident*, literate, Western-trained observers, missionaries served as the eyes and ears of geography, their writings being incorporated in geography compendia of the times. Thomas (1994) notes that missionary visions and ideas were widely circulated through periodicals, books, and photographic media.

Missionary representations were formed during the state of social, cultural, and demographic upheaval that followed in the explorers' wake. The devastating impact of introduced diseases was a major factor, augmented by the undermining of traditional guilds and sciences by new technology, the shattering of world view brought by the intrusion of aliens with powerful and deadly weapons, the introduction of spiritous liquors, and the exploitation of islanders by beachcombers and unscrupulous merchants.

The extent of these ills varied throughout the Pacific, but all variously played roles in missionary representations. In particular, missionary discourses tended to argue that islanders had brought these troubles on themselves through sinfulness, and though nonmissionary Westerners were certainly aggravating the situation, Western intrusion was not fundamentally at fault. Blame was placed on the islanders and their traditions, a tactic that provided impetus and justification to transform islander societies.

Especially for Protestant missionaries from Great Britain and the United States, islanders were represented as needing to be socially and culturally transformed in conjunction with being converted to Christianity. This was due to the perceived link between humans' divine aspect and the ability to overcome "nature." "Savage" tendencies had be to transformed to "civilized" behavior, which often meant the imposition of Western cultural forms such as clothing, etiquette, food, gender roles, and political forms. Though it was asserted that these "forgotten" peoples would rise quickly in their level of civilization under Western tutelage, the less-heard counterargument did exist, namely that islander lifestyles and cultures, not to mention their lands and even their lives, would be lost through the introduction of things European. Social decay and depopulation from sickness set in early, and did evoke criticism at home of European intrusion.

The economy of missionary representations must therefore be understood in its diversity. There were the harshest critics, who characterized islanders as destitute of all knowledge whatsoever (as demonstrated by their lack of written language and numbers) and those who took a more measured view. There were those who saw islanders as "children of God," with all the same (if not more) positive qualities as their European counterparts. There was even the occasional missionary who himself "converted" and went native, such as Thomas Kendall in New Zealand. Overall, three streams emerge from missionary representations.

First, though their uncivilized characteristics were pointed out, islanders were not posed as essentially different from Europeans. Thomas (1993, 1994) argues that missionaries actually sought to downplay difference, as the missions were dependent on the belief—by themselves and their sponsors—that island peoples could be converted. Customs, not biology, were the problem. Missionary representations thus focused on images of conversion—islanders in clean white clothes, neatly groomed, living in tidy villages and attending church or school—that helped to emphasize the success of the missions (1993).

Second and related is the necessarily paternalistic view of missionaries themselves as pastors of the flocks, father-figures to the "childlike" islanders. Semicivilized island communities were shown as proof of missionary success and efficacy. That is, it is the missions, not the people, who are the real subject of such representations. Referring to grown men as "boys," calling them by first names, or omitting their names altogether furthered this paternalistic relationship.

Third, the success of the mission would rarely be represented as "complete." Here the missions, in their later years, tended implicitly toward agreement with biological notions of racial difference. Converted islanders were sometimes said to still be lacking a certain ineffable "something" that would make them "real" Christians. This justified the continuation of the mission. If the islanders succeeded in their transformation to Christianity, the missionaries would be out of a job. The resistance to making islanders into ministers of the church had similar logic.

Therefore, whereas the missionary approach started out with a view that all persons were fundamentally equal under God, as the nineteenth century moved on it tended in some areas toward the racial ideas of the times, seeing peoples as having essential differences that could not be rooted out.

While responsible for a share of cultural and political colonialism, missionaries generally militated against the abuse and exploitation of islanders by other Westerners. Hence missionary representations differed from other Western themes. The emphasis on an ultimate sameness and the mission of cultural "assimilation" ran directly contrary to the search for the "exotic" by travel writers and adventure seekers, the forerunners of tourism. Missionary images de-emphasized the erotic and exotic, tending more to emphasize the mothering or domestic roles of fully clothed women and the ability of islanders to be "civilized." Westerners who today come to the Pacific expecting free sex, bare-breasted women, and "cannibal tours" often bemoan the fully clothed legacy of the church fathers. Furthermore, missionary goals sometimes involved retaining indigenous sovereignty—hoping to achieve independent, Christian nations—where other colonial forces sought to displace it.

## Colonial Rule

Imperialism in the Pacific, even into the late nineteenth century, was at best hodge-podge and haphazard rather than a coherent policy by any of the European powers (Hempenstall 1994). The reasons for Western intrusion were various, but whether economic or political, they all required some justification, and this could be (and was) located in any of several representational motifs of Pacific Islanders. As Western policies in the nineteenth century came increasingly to include the acquisition, or direct political colonization, of Pacific Islands, the racio-cultural hierarchy set forth earlier was more fully developed and used to justify a diverse range of colonial policies.

The idea of "varieties of the human species" or racial "types" put forth by Forster gained strength between 1800 and 1850. Stepan states that by the 1850s in Britain, "the notion that the races formed a graded series, with the European at the top and the Negro invariably at the bottom, had become one of the cornerstones of racial science" (1982). According to Thomas, British policy responded to the indigenous peoples on the basis of social evolutionary criteria: "the rights of those near the bottom of the ladder, such as Australian aborigines, received extremely scant notice, while indirect rule was appropriate for peoples with more developed technologies and recognizable hierarchical social institutions," for example the institutionalization of "custom" and land tenure in Fiji but not in Solomon Islands (1994:109). In Australia the doctrine of Terra Nullius effectively represented aboriginal peoples at least as without society or land tenure of any recognizable form, at worst as subhuman.

Hanlon (1994) states that colonizing powers required a more benevolent justification within their own societies to "cloak the self-interest that usually underlay the colonization process." Lèvy-Bruhl's concept of "primitivism" was one such tool for defending empire. This scientific but less pejorative notion postulated such peoples as "pre-logical," without "intellectual, social, political, and religious structures that would allow them to cope with modernity." Each of Micronesia's colonizers, according to Hanlon, "explained their mission as an effort to overcome this disinclination toward rational thought and to help integrate the islands' populations into the modern world" (1994).

Inasmuch as Polynesians were said to be closer to Europeans, the Polynesian migration literature, from Fornander's work (1878-1885) to Buck (1930s) moved eagerly toward postulating Polynesians as "long lost Aryan cousins." Treagar's "Aryan Maori" was the most blatant and far-fetched attempt. The premise was widely accepted and appeared in a range of texts, from natural histories to tourist and military handbooks, into the twentieth century. As the lighter-skinned, allegedly more socially and politically developed Polynesians had traveled the farthest, while the darker-skinned and more "tribal" Melanesians were thought to have remained fairly close to the Australasian homeland, the hierarchy of dark-skinned/nature to light-skinned/civilization was reinforced. That Polynesians had made such remarkable journeys long before Columbus was even more reason to conclude that they were really Europeans—for no mere savage peoples could have achieved such a feat.

The implications of this discourse for colonialism were readily utilized. To the extent that Polynesians were the "long lost Aryan brothers" of the West, it was the duty of the West to educate them, to bestow upon them the birthright of civilization that they missed by wandering off in the other direction. And this would be best brought about through two prongs of colonization: Western political rule, as these peoples were in too early a stage of civilization to properly govern themselves and fully develop their island economies; and cultural change, as they needed to be raised in their level of civilization to catch up to their "birthright."

At the same time, posing islanders as different and inferior, whether in degree of civilization (Polynesians) or biology (Melanesians), was useful in mobilizing labor. This is true for both on-island plantations where indigenous workers were needed and off-island plantations where labor needed to be imported. Colonial policies varied considerably, from Fiji, where local "custom" was to be protected from plantation life through the importation of Indian labor, to Hawai'i, where labor was seen as a cure to islander "indolence." This representation of the "lazy islander" deserves critical scrutiny. Island economies required far less labor than expected in industrial societies, but this did not mean that laziness was condoned. The eight- or ten-hour work day was twice what was necessary within the indigenous economy, so missionary or plantation-owner ideas of a full work day ran counter to generations of local practice. Also, the wages paid by the plantations did not, in cases such as Samoa and Hawai'i, seem worthwhile.

But the representation of laziness aided policies aimed toward providing labor for capitalist enterprises. Labor was postulated as positively transforming the islanders, raising their level of civilization and promoting Christianity. Gibson (1993) notes an Australian company's 1932 remarks about inducing the islanders "to make more copra, and be more energetic, rather than spending so much time loafing under coconut trees, or paddling about in canoes." Missionaries had posed the identical line of reasoning earlier.

The manipulation of racial traits for political purposes is exemplified by the 1893 overthrow of the Hawaiian monarchy by Westerners. Where earlier the great strides of the islanders away from "barbarism" had been lauded, by the late nineteenth century writers were remarking that the "stain" of savagery could not be eliminated. Hawaiian rulers reacting to increasing white hegemony by reinvigorating indigenous ways were seen by whites as degenerating backward, proving their indelible savage tendencies. One U.S. writer of the time summed up a number of popular arguments when he stated,

> The natives have proved themselves to be incapable of governing and unfitted for the condition of civilization, as is shown by their rapid decline in numbers and their inability to adapt themselves to changed conditions.... Indolent and easy-going, they are perfectly content with any form of government which allows them to sun themselves, bedecked with flowers.... It is natural that the white man should become the governing power. (See *The American Monthly Review of Reviews* 17 (January 1898):76.)

On the positive side, islanders were represented as "happy natives," childlike, musical and loving, a pleasure to meet—but not appropriate for positions of power.

The interbreeding of "races" was often adamantly denounced. The missionary Keesing's 1934 study on Samoa states that "half castes can never be expected to rise as a class to the ordinary European level.... The half-caste must be left to sink to his own level in the scale of humanity and become in time a hewer of wood and drawer of water for the rest of the community" (cited in Shankman 1989:230). Racial categorization variously defined Westerner-islander "half-castes" as either "native" or European, depending on whether such offspring were seen positively or negatively in the scale of humanity. In the Hawaiian Islands as late as 1950, a child was generally classified according to the race of the father, except that children with one Hawaiian parent were classed as Part-Hawaiians, and children with only one Caucasian parent were classified according to the race of the non-Caucasian parent. This preserved both a growing "Hawaiian" community and a biologically distinct white identity.

Overall, colonial representations used difference, defined biologically and associated with social and cultural traits, to explain and justify inequality that resulted from the introduction of capitalism. Islanders, as well as imported laborers, were kept "in their place" through policies that allocated specific roles to different groups within a socioeconomic hierarchy. Segregation of groups was implemented to preserve and promote difference. Mamak & Ali (1979) thus argue for a coalescence of race and class, especially in cases of islander rebellions. Though the correlation between "race" and class is not clear-cut—as class differentiation within groups was promoted and resulted in ethnic elites who facilitated colonial rule—race can nonetheless be seen as a manifestation based on and reifying economic difference. "Yellow scare" racist attitudes toward Chinese populations that became economically competitive with Westerners further point up this class basis for racial distinction.

### Contemporary Representations

Representations of Pacific Islanders in the twentieth century build strongly on the themes of the nineteenth. While the "happy native" images of the late nineteenth century prevail, the images of strength and pride from the times of the explorers are in some cases reasserted, but not associated with the contemporary islanders. Rather, they become symbols of a noble past in Polynesia, or of exotic savagery for tourist consumption in Melanesia. There are also new themes, and new variations on old themes, that predominate in the twentieth century. These reflect both social and cultural changes in the West and new economies of representation involved in film, music, and tourism.

The War in the Pacific served to bring the islands more fully into Western consciousness and popular culture. But generally the resulting images presented the islands and their peoples as the backdrops for Western adventures and historical episodes, the struggles between "super powers," in which the islanders themselves were bystanders caught in the crossfire. In Papua the "fuzzy wuzzy angels" retain a positive perception as aids to the Australian war effort, with photos emphasizing these peoples as carrying wounded Aussie soldiers to safety and medical attention.

Westerners are the producers of such images. Newsreels, photographs, movies—these were not produced by the islanders themselves, but by British, American, and Australian efforts. As such, they emphasize the Western engagement with the war, "our boys" over *there*. A dependent relationship for the islanders is reinforced, as is the positioning of the islands as battlegrounds or playgrounds for Westerners against the Japanese. The islands themselves changed hands from one colonial power to another across both wars, maintaining the position of colonies.

The "savagery" that was to be feared and transformed in the last century is mobilized as a resource for tourism today. The rapid social and technological changes that moved the West further from nature have increased the desire to see and briefly experience "native" peoples who remain closer to nature. Islanders thus become spectacles, usually presented in safe and comfortable venues that promote neither fear of real danger nor inconvenience for the visitor.

Such representations have a long history. Burns Philp & Co Ltd, an Australian trading firm in Melanesia, engaged in "exoticism" to promote a blossoming tourist trade in the 1910s (Gibson 1993). These representations, not unlike the missionary representations, suggested "savagery" that had been brought under rule, "either through law-keeping regimes, or through the guarantee of the native's light skin and his (implicitly related) adeptness at cultivation" (Gibson 1993). A visit to the islands meant an adventure from which the visitor would return unscathed. Some critical theorists now interpret these maneuvers as "feminizing" the islanders. This term refers to a masculine image of what constitutes "femininity," and not to any essential nature of women.

Several distinct themes combine to produce "feminization." The first suggests that islanders are "not real men." Missionaries referred to them as "boys" or as "children." The discourse of "indolence" contained a theme according to which islanders were unable to "stand on their own two feet like men." In the case of tourism, this feminization means that there is no threat—as Gibson said, the islands are open to (white) masculine endeavor and romance. Second, it positions the islanders as receptive, subservient. Here too the historical tendency toward turning islanders into laborers resurfaces, but now it is transposed as "hospitality." In their care, you will be revivified, healed, soothed. Another device is posing the islanders and their cultures as "not speaking," as not having genuine meaning. Indigenous languages and cultures are quaint curiosities, childlike and simple. Islanders "chatter" but do not "speak"; they have no real information to share. Finally, there is a distinct historical trend, beyond the scope of this study, that links the representations of female islander bodies with a feminization of Pacific Islands themselves, linking the "exotic" with the "erotic" (Jolly 1997).

Examples of these themes abound in today's tourist promotion literature. A 1996 Executive Destinations advertisement for Fiji, entitled "Rise Above Reality," states,

> Escape to the utopia of Fiji and experience the healing powers of an unspoilt culture blessed within a pristine environment.
>
> Explore your heart as you feel your spirits soar at the hands of exquisite hosts to whom the most intimate hospitality is second nature.

A century of colonial policies that contained and codified "custom" while eliminating the "savage" tendencies suddenly becomes an "unspoilt culture," the subservient position of the islanders "second nature." A 1996 Venture Holidays advertisement, in which a photograph shows two male Fijian musicians in wraps ("skirts") entertaining an elderly white couple, states,

> There are still special corners of the South Pacific and Toberua is one of them. Legend has it that Toberua was named after a Fijian maiden who brought love and romance to the island. They would like to share that with you!

An advertisement for P&O cruises reads,

> The South Pacific is a melting pot of unique and unusual cultures. One thing they all have in common is the desire to make sure you have a great time!

A critical counterpart to the feminization of islander cultures in Western representations concerns the positioning of islander women in Western ethnography. In all phases of colonial discourse—explorer, missionary, planter, colonizer, tourist—island women have been seen through the lens of Western gender roles taken to be the norm. Island ethnographies written by Western academics, even in the late nineteenth and early twentieth century, are strongly flavored by this Western bias, as researchers focused their attentions on men and derived masculine world views taken as universal for those cultures. Consequently negative symbolic representations of womanhood are often prominent, such as the *tapu/noa* dichotomy in which "sacredness" (*tapu*) is aligned with "male" and "profane" (*noa*) with "female." Ralston (1992) has shown that much ethnography and historiography, based on interviews with men, has emphasized certain island societies as strongly patrilineal, where evidence suggests these tendencies were much less pronounced.

Inasmuch as economic motives underlie much of Western representation, the position of Pacific Islands in the global economy maintains a negative perception from the West. The majority of islands are resource-poor and reliant on international aid, often from their former colonial "masters." Others are subsidized in return for providing strategic location for Western military bases. As subsistence economy is not seen as having value in its own right, the focus on economic nonviability or dependency perpetuates a sense of Pacific Islanders as "little brown children" dependent on a paternal West.

## Identity and Representation Among Islanders

Understanding how Pacific Islanders construct identity is highly problematic. All literature on the subject is an after-product of colonial encounters, and much of it is Western interpretation. Historical statements of islanders themselves were mediated by the Western writers who reported them. We also know that islanders often spoke in ways that (they felt) were expected of them or that would not give offense, or that they had been taught the white man's ways were "correct" and their own ways "savage" or "backward." Indigenous ethnographers such as David Malo were strongly influenced by their missionary teachers to the point of denigrating their own cultures, and some were taught versions of the "scale of humanity" in mission school textbooks.

Understanding contact-era islander representations of Westerners is also problematic. There has been much debate over the traditional interpretation of Captain Cook's being perceived as a "god" by Hawaiians. Certainly Westerners in their large ships were understood as technologically superior, but studies show that inasmuch as early explorers saw islanders as essentially equals, so too did the islanders understand these foreigners. New Caledonians are said to have initially welcomed European settlers as long-lost ancestors who had returned from the past (Ataba 1973, cited in Mamak and Ali 1979: 128). According to Oliver's study of Bougainville, where some Europeans treated islanders with fairness and humanity while many others "considered them to be subhuman and handled them fraudulently and brutally," whites earned a bad reputation that tainted all dealings between them and the islanders. Thus Bougainvillian representations of whites as hostile complemented the white representations of the islanders as hostile to whites (1991: 29).

The translation of technological superiority into "ethnic" superiority could well have been one brought about through Western ideologies and their imposition through colonial practice and policy. Howard (1970) says of Rotumans that a sense of European superiority was still manifest at the time of his study, characterized by a "felt inability to participate successfully in European society."

Islander identity and the development of ethnic consciousness is a contentious topic. Recent collections of studies compiled by Howard (1989) and particularly by Linnekin and Poyer (1990) suggest that islander identity does not follow Western notions of "ethnicity" or race. Rather than being essentialist or biologically rooted, identity is derived from external situations and experiences. Individuals are understood according to their "social placement" or relationships. Shared identity derives from sharing food and water, physical environment, mode of production, spirits, and social activities. Other people "do other things" because they live in different physical and social worlds (Linnekin and Poyer 1990).

This principle is said to differ across the Pacific, and the extent to which it marks a distinct divergence from Western notions of identity is debatable. In Lieber's (1990) study of Kapingamarangi and Pohnpei, hereditary descent does delineate boundaries among people, but these boundaries have limited meaning when behavior becomes a critical issue. In the case of Kapingamarangi raised on Pohnpei, it is their behavior that ultimately determines whether or not they are accepted by their "kin" as being Kapingamarangi. This means there are attributes that the Kapingamarangi identify as "Pohnpeian," but also that being Pohnpeian is a matter of being "from Pohnpei," from that place and its environment and practices. An "ethnic" Pohnpeian raised, say, in the United States would not qualify, as his or her language and behavior would be quite different.

Linnekin and Poyer's and Howard's volumes both assert that islander identities cannot be understood outside of the colonial experience. Linnekin and Poyer write that "the formation of ethnic groups in the island Pacific characteristically reflects the influence of Western (and in the Micronesian case Japanese) categories and institutions. We believe that ethnic group organization was absent in the precolonial Pacific." This is not to suggest that islanders did not postulate cultural differences and group identities, but that factors such as context, situation, and performance operated in lieu of or in conjunction with "racial" or "ethnic" categories.

This argument stands in opposition to those of other theorists on ethnicity, who take a more universalist view of identity and ethnic formation. Smith (1981) poses a universalist definition of ethnicity as being constituted by a shared sense of common origins, a claim to a common and distinctive history and destiny, one or more distinctive cultural characteristics, and a feeling of collective uniqueness or solidarity. His argument, however, is rooted deeply in a study of European cultures, with no empirical consideration of Pacific Islanders. Van den Berghe is noted for posing a view based on sociobiology: that all humans are genetically predisposed to prefer members of their own kin (blood group) over anyone else (the common practice of adoption among some islander societies would seem to belie this). The tension between the universalists and those who see a distinctive situation in the Pacific Islands is one that is not easily resolved. The universalist argument is particularly appealing to those who wish to assert that "they" (islanders) are no less racist than "we" (Westerners), a position that, regardless of any validity, glosses over the structural inequality of the colonial contexts in which racial differentiation has been employed.

Colonists failed to distinguish the pluralities of identity among native peoples. In New Caledonia, where there were perhaps 36 different and sometimes mutually unintelligible dialects, there was no common national identity. The French treated the islanders as a homogenous group, though divided into "collaborators" and "resisters" (Winslow 1989). Terms such as "Maori" in New Zealand and "aboriginal" in Australia encompassed and unified disparate groups for purposes of colonial policies. Shared identity emerged from shared treatment under colonial policy, as well as from resistance to it.

Indigenous ethnic political consciousness, emerging from colonization, exists increasingly with increased levels of disenfranchisement. Lieber, among others, argues for a hierarchy of Oceanic categorizations of identity. The independent island states have more circumstantial and plural notions. Flinn (1990) shows nested identities for Pulapese in Chuuk (Truk), upward from the atoll, to the island group, to a collective status for "outer islanders" in regard to those from Moen. This nesting of identities mollifies an overarching identity as "Trukese." On the other hand, in the ongoing colonies (such as Hawai'i, New Zealand, French Polynesia, and Australia) indigenous groups responded to colonists by distinguishing them into new cultural domains: *haole, pakeha, mehnwaii*, etc. (Lieber 1990).

In these latter situations indigenous identity is polarized in opposition to the ongoing colonial presence. Indigenous discourse in these cases may produce bifurcated stereotypes aimed to point out the ills, illegality, and disenfranchisement of colonization. In extreme cases, a noble-savage vision of indigenous peoples is opposed to colonizing, genocidal, nature-raping, racist white culture—with all of what may be perceived as the ill behavior of the Westerners during the previous two centuries lumped onto Westerners of today. Walker's (1989) article on New Zealand presents such a polarized view of "two basic cultures in the world, namely the culture of indigenous people and the culture of metropolitan society," which are "polar opposites in human organization" (1989). Some contemporary Hawaiian nationalists speak of the "Missionary boys' club" as being the oppositional colonial presence, even though capital and power in Hawai'i has moved largely into the hands of off-island multinational corporations personally unrelated to the historical white elite and in some cases nonwhite owned.

Such a polarized distinction, enhanced and mobilized, aids in producing a united identity in order to resist or combat colonization. Nationalist movements follow Anderson's notion of "imagined community," wherein a new, unified identity is forged where none previously existed, to serve the struggle for independence. In other situations there is the matter of state benefits and programs aimed at the indigenous population and which demand a legal definition of identity in order to determine who qualifies. Here flexible and circumstantial definitions do not suffice, yet biological definitions prove equally problematic. Definitions such as 50% "by blood" lead to the disenfranchisement of members of the next generation who are children of "mixed" marriages. Such biological definitions reflect the legacy of Western ideas regarding race and identity.

An oppositional situation also faces transplanted communities, such as Banabans on Rabi (Fiji) or immigrant populations throughout the Pacific. Cultural identity becomes objectified, polarized, and mobilized because it stands in opposition to other identities and cultural groups. Asian groups in the Pacific have likewise found themselves uniting into previously nonexistent shared identities, as Indians in New Zealand (Leckie, 1989); or have been represented with a range of negative characteristics (especially amoral sexuality) when they pose economic threat to white hegemony. The 1997 attacks on and looting of Chinese merchants during antigovernment riots in Port Moresby, on the other hand, show the resentment by indigenous Melanesians against these more economically successful people (the part-Chinese heritage of Prime Minister Julius Chan was also an ostensible reason for the attacks).

The legacy of colonialism is, therefore, a diversity of political and ethnic situations across the Pacific, from formerly distinct peoples who have been lumped together in sovereign states, to transplanted communities of islanders and Asians, to ongoing colonies. Social relations between and among islanders have been transformed in varying degrees by capitalism, new modes of production, urbanization, and increased transportation and communications. At the same time the promulgation of Western representations of islanders through film, literature, and advertising has presented strong images against which islanders must compete in order to claim their own identities within the arena of Western discourse. Representational devices that have served to "feminize," or which still promote a sense of inferior Otherness based on biology, make it difficult for islanders to speak and be heard, to be taken seriously. Tourism promotions reassert and enhance this position of islanders within the global cultural economy.

For those from the West, then, the task is a difficult one of awakening to the heritage of representations that have formed images of Pacific Islanders, and the ongoing relationship between these images and power. For those who are from the islands themselves, the challenge may be to decolonize, to steer clear of accepting Western definitions of island cultures, and to assert one's own identity in the world.

# Bibliography

Beaglehole, J. C., ed. 1967. *The journals of Captain James Cook on his voyages of discovery.* Vol. III. *The voyage of the Resolution and Discoverer 1776–1780.* London: Cambridge University Press/The Hakluyt Society.

Campbell, I. C. 1990. *A history of the Pacific Islands.* St. Lucia: University of Queensland Press.

Dening, G. 1986. Possessing Tahiti. *Archeology in Oceania* 21(1):103–118.

D'Urville, J. S-C. D. 1987. *An account in two volumes of two voyages to the South Seas.* Ed. and trans. H. Rosenman. Honolulu: University of Hawai'i Press.

Flinn, J. 1990. We still have our customs: being Pulapese in Truk. In *Cultural identity and ethnicity in the Pacific*, ed. J. Linnekin and L. Poyer, 103–126. Honolulu: University of Hawai'i Press.

Gibson, R. 1993. I could not see as much as I desired. In *Pirating the Pacific: images of trade, travel and tourism*, ed. A. Stephen, 22–43. Sydney: Powerhouse Museum.

Gould, S. J. 1981. *The mismeasure of man.* New York: Grove Press.

Hanlon, D. 1994. Patterns of colonial rule in Micronesia. In *Tides of history: the Pacific Islands in the twentieth century*, ed. K. R. Howe, R. C. Kiste, and B.V. Lal, 93–118. Sydney: Allen & Unwin.

Hempenstall, P. 1994. Imperial manoeuvres. In *Tides of history: the Pacific Islands in the twentieth century*, ed. K. R. Howe, R. C. Kiste, and B.V. Lal, 29–39. Sydney: Allen & Unwin.

Henningham, S. 1994. France in Melanesia and Polynesia. In *Tides of history: the Pacific Islands in the twentieth century*, ed. K. R. Howe, R. C. Kiste, and B.V. Lal, 119–146. Sydney: Allen & Unwin.

Herman, RDK. 1995. Kālai'āina—carving the land: geography, desire and possession in the Hawaiian Islands. Ph.D. dissertation, University of Hawai'i.

Herman, RDK. 1996. The dread taboo, human sacrifice, and Pearl Harbor. *The Contemporary Pacific* 8(1):81–126.

Howard, A. 1970. *Learning to be Rotuman: enculturation in the South Pacific.* New York: Teachers College Press.

Howard, M. C., ed. 1989. *Ethnicity and nation-building in the Pacific.* Tokyo: The United Nations University.

Howe, K. R., R. C. Kiste, and B.V. Lal, eds. 1994. *Tides of history: the Pacific Islands in the twentieth century.* Sydney: Allen & Unwin.

Jolly, M. 1997. From Point Venus to Bali Ha'i: eroticism and exoticism in representations of the Pacific. In *Sites of desire /economies of pleasure: sexualities in Asia and the Pacific*, ed. M. Jolly and L. Manderson, 99–122. Chicago & London: University of Chicago Press.

Lal, Brij V., ed. 1992. *Pacific Islands history: journeys and transformations.* Canberra: The Journal of Pacific History.

La Perouse, J. F. G. [1799] 1968. *A voyage round the world, performed in the years 1785, 1786, 1787, and 1788, by the Boussole and Astrolabe, under the command of J. F. G. de la Perouse.* Vol. I. Reprint. New York: De Capo Press.

Leckie, J. 1989. From race aliens to ethnic group—Indians in New Zealand. In *Ethnicity and nation-building in the Pacific*, ed. M. C. Howard, 168–197. Tokyo: The United Nations University.

Lieber, M. D. 1990. Lamarckian definitions of identity on Kapingamarangi and Pohnpei. In *Cultural identity and ethnicity in the Pacific*, ed. J. Linnekin and L. Poyer, 71–102. Honolulu: University of Hawai'i Press.

Linnekin, J., and L. Poyer, eds. 1990. *Cultural identity and ethnicity in the Pacific.* Honolulu: University of Hawai'i Press.

Mamak, A., and A. Ali. 1979. *Race, class and rebellion in the South Pacific.* Sydney: George Allen & Unwin.

Pagden, A. 1982. *The fall of natural man: the American Indian and the origins of comparative ethnology.* Cambridge: Cambridge University Press.

Pearson, W. H. 1969. European intimidation and the myth of Tahiti. *Journal of Pacific History* 4:199–217.

Ralston, C. 1992. Colonised women: writing about Polynesian women. In *Pacific Islands history: journeys and transformations*, ed. B.V. Lal, 167–183. Canberra: The Journal of Pacific History.

Shankman, P. 1989. Race, class, and ethnicity in Western Samoa. In *Ethnicity and nation-building in the Pacific*, ed. M.C. Howard, 218–243. Tokyo: The United Nations University.

Smith, A. D. 1981. *The ethnic revival.* Cambridge: Cambridge University Press.

Smith, B. 1985. *European vision and the South Pacific.* 2d ed. Sydney: Harper and Row.

Smith, B. 1992. *Imagining the Pacific.* New Haven and London: Yale University Press.

Sorrenson, M. P. K. 1979. *Maori origins and migrations: the genesis of some Paleha myths and legends.* Auckland and Oxford: Auckland University Press and Oxford University Press.

Stepan, N. 1982. *The idea of race in science: Great Britain 1800–1960.* Hamden, Connecticut: Archon Books.

Stephen, A., ed. 1993. *Pirating the Pacific: images of trade, travel and tourism.* Sydney: Powerhouse Museum.

Thomas, N. 1989. The force of ethnology: origins and significance of the Melanesia/Polynesia division. *Current Anthropology* 30(1):27–34.

Thomas, N. 1993. The beautiful and the damned. In *Pirating the Pacific: images of trade, travel and tourism*, ed. A. Stephen, 44–61. Sydney: Powerhouse Museum.

Thomas, N. 1994. *Colonialism's culture: anthropology, travel and government.* Carlton, Victoria: Melbourne University Press.

Walker, R. J. 1989. Colonisation and development of Maori people. In *Ethnicity and nation-building in the Pacific*, ed. M. C. Howard, 152–168. Tokyo: The United Nations University.

Wilkes, C. [1845] 1970. *Narrative of the United States Exploring Expedition during the years 1838, 1839, 1840, 1841, 1842.* Vols. I and IV. Reprint. Ridgewood, New Jersey: The Gregg Press.

Winslow, D. 1989. Independence and ethnicity in New Caledonia. In *Ethnicity and nation-building in the Pacific*, ed. M. C. Howard, 259–284. Tokyo: The United Nations University.

# Here Our Words

*Selina Tusitala Marsh*

> Inside me the dead
> woven into my flesh like the music
> of bone flutes:
>
> my polynesian fathers
> who escaped the sun's wars, seeking
> these islands by prophetic stars,
>
> emerged
> from the sea's eye like turtles
> scuttling to beach their eggs
>
> in fecund sand, smelling
> of the sea—the stench of dead
> anemone and starfish,
>
> eyes
> bare of the original vision, burnt
> out by storm and paddles slapping
>
> the hurricane waves on, blisters
> bursting blood hibiscus
> to gangrened wounds salt-stung . . . .
>
> Albert Wendt, "Inside us the Dead" (Wendt 1976)[1]

Rotuman playwright and scholar Vilsoni Hereniko argues that scholarly disciplines studying the Pacific have often been limited by a one-dimensional focus on external reality (Hereniko 1995). Many outside "experts" believe they can understand a culture by examining surface details objectively. Such a stance is critiqued by Tongan poet, satirist, and anthropologist Epeli Hauʻofa in his poem "Blood in the Kava Bowl" (Wendt 1980, 239-240):

> In the twilight we sit
> drinking kava from the bowl between us.
> Who we are we know and need not say
> for the soul we share came from Vaihi.
> Across the bowl we nod our understanding of the line
> that is also our cord brought by Tangaloa from above,
> and the professor does not know.
> He sees the line but not the cord
> for he drinks the kava not tasting its blood.

The metaphorical umbilical cord connects all Pacific peoples genealogically to their spiritual parent, the Polynesian god Tangaloa. The familial relationship between those of common spiritual, mythological parentage means shared identities and knowledge of which the professor is ignorant. The professor does not know that the cup he holds to his mouth is the "cup of the soul and the sweat of our people." Nor that the kava he drinks is "mixed with blood from . . . the mouths of all oppressed Tongans . . . ." Hauʻofa's professor is unqualified to read the metaphorical map charted by this Tongan kava ceremony. Whether the professor would consider relinquishing his authoritative status in order to learn is another matter, as hinted at in the third stanza:

> The professor still talks
> of oppression that we both know
> yet he tastes not the blood in the kava
> mixed with dry waters that rose to Tangaloa
> who gave us the cup from which we drink
> the soul and the tears of our land.

Traditional academe has often maintained that there is only one truth, and the more qualified an expert is (judged by the number of his or her "registered reputations" [see Petaia 1980]), the more likely he or she is to possess truth. Hereniko explains that this narrow focus on facts marginalizes internal realities, or what he calls emotional truths, defined by a spectrum of human experience that is resistant to capture by quantitative analysis. These truths exist in thought, feeling, imagination, heart, spirit, and soul.

Such emotional truths form the very essence of oral and written literatures in the Pacific (Hereniko 1995). This discussion covers indigenous literature in English and the light it sheds on the history and geography of the region.

## Orature: Living Breath of Past

Orature breathes. Nigerian author and theorist Ngugi wa Thiongo (1986, 1993) uses the term "orature" to describe oral tradition in all its forms: chant, song, dance, speech. Literally, Pacific orature can be sung in celebration, chanted in honor, prayed in worship, and spoken in reverence and remembrance. Figuratively, as demonstrated in Wendt's poem, oral traditions exhale past into present, inhale future into past. The common Pacific adage "We face the future with our backs" indicates that appreciation and knowledge of the past is vital for shaping a future. In the realm of creative writing, oral traditions are a formative influence in writers' works. Even when oral traditions are not overtly acknowledged or consciously devised, Wendt (1980) argues that Pacific Island artists absorb oral aesthetics by osmosis. Samoan author Wendt pays homage to the *fagogo* told by his grandmother in his childhood (*fagogo* are stories told at night, equivalent to fairy tales, usually with a moral, or instructive element to them) (Crocombe 1973); Tongan poet Konai Helu Thaman's later verse and rhythmic structure echo Tongan song and chant composition (pers. comm.); Tupou Posesi Fanua stylistically mimics Tongan legends in her contemporary legends (Fanua 1975); the epic poems of Cook Island and New Zealand poet Alistair Campbell are influenced by Pacific mythology; the poetry of Gilbertese Maunaa Itaia is informed by translated oral traditions (see Letters, *Pacific Islands Monthly*, June, 1973, 30); and the influence of metaphorical devices embedded in Pacific proverbs and riddles can be seen throughout Pacific literature.

The Pacific has a great canon of its own—its oral traditions. Not only is this canon a source of inspiration, but it also comes complete with its own form of literary criticism (see e.g. Dunlop 1985 on Wendt, Edmund 1990 on Hau'ofa, and Enos 1972 on literature in Papua New Guinea). Indigenous aesthetics, often invisible to the outside eye, allow an appreciation and understanding of this canon and the contemporary literature that springs from it. The recognition of these internal aesthetic principles, alongside incorporated Western aesthetics,[2] has been the driving force in recent movements to theorize Pacific literature.[3] Investigating critical ways of thinking about indigenous literatures is crucial in their validation and promotion.[4]

But orature is more than a vehicle for assessing and inspiring creative expression. Generational words (I use that term to refer to words that have been passed down through generations) reveal and transmit Pacific ways of knowing and being. For example, many creation chants recount genealogies that connect humanity with the gods. These gods often originated from sky and sea and from cosmic forces of dark and light, and frequently personified forms of nature.[5] This creation defines Pacific identity. Wendt's poem "Inside Us the Dead" demonstrates this interconnectedness as he merges living with dead, past with present, and humanity with creation.

Ancient premises inform metaphorical constructions in contemporary Pacific literature. Nature is commonly invested with historical, social, and spiritual significance. Our Polynesian fathers and mothers voyaged Oceania, died in storms at sea, fought "sun's wars," suffered "blisters/bursting blood hibiscus," read "prophetic stars," and lived to nestle in the arms of Papa (Mother Earth) and Rangi (Sky Father) once more.[6] Here, they became caretakers of the *whenua, fonua, fanua, fenua, honua, henua* (translations for the word "land" in Maori, Tongan, Samoan, Tahitian, Hawaiian, and Marquesan languages respectively).

To Maori, *whenua* (like its counterpart in many other Pacific Island languages) is more than just a physical piece of earth—it is familial. Papa is a primal parent from which all humanity originates. She is the Earth Mother, while Rangi is the Sky Father. Papa is to be nurtured, worshipped, and respected. In turn she sustains and supports her children with food and shelter (Orbell, 132). *Whenua* also refers to afterbirth. Traditionally, the placenta was buried in the land (returning it to Papa) or thrown into the sea. The placement of human tissue from which life was sustained into the earth to rejuvenate life thus continues the cyclical revolutions of life through death through life.[7]

Embedded symbolically and metaphorically within contemporary Pacific literature is the understanding that the *whenua* breathes life; people; culture; spirit.

## Black Volcanic Stone

Ni-Vanuatu poet and politician Grace Mera Molisa and Hawaiian poet, sovereignty leader, and scholar Haunani-Kay Trask both use volcano images to symbolize the political context of the indigenous people and the sacred connection to the *vanua/'āina*

Molisa's primary metaphor for the new nation-state of Vanuatu (formerly the New Hebrides) provides the title for her first collection, *Black Stone* (Molisa 1983). It alludes to the volcanic foundations in Vanuatu, as well as to the immovable spirit of indigenous people. The very term "Vanuatu" evokes within its people reminders of their timelessness of spirit, despite colonialism, and counsels them to remain steadfast in their identity embedded in the *vanua*. Molisa's poem "Vanuatu" follows in part:

> Ageless Vatu
> primeval source
> of creative forces
> ad infinitum . . .
>
> . . . Vatu offspring
> born of oblivion
> in vexing rebellion
> stay steadfast
> Vanuaaku Vanuatu.

Analogous metaphors are used in Molisa's poem "Black Stone," simultaneously describing the volcanic rock of Vanuatu and its newly independent people.

> Black Stone
> Molten lava
> solidified . . .
>
> . . . Eternal essence
> of immortal soul's
> steadfast fixture
> founding Man's
> physical cosmos . . .
>
> Threshold
> of the spirits
> transfixed
> to the stable
> equilibrium
> of constancy
> and permanence . . .

The rest of the poem uses such adjectives as "solidified," "coagulated," and "obstinate" to evoke permanence and stability of the *vanua* and of its people. The final stanza,

Black Stone
immovable
immobile
Black Stone

through repetition, alliteration, and adjective exhorts Ni-Vanuatu to stand strong in the immortal past while dealing with a postcolonial present.

Similarly, Trask uses the imagery of the volcano to symbolize the political quest of Native Hawaiians. In contrast to Molisa's solid, immobile imagery, the cover of Trask's poetry collection *Light in the Crevice Never Seen* portrays a volcano that is alive, scalding, in transition, liquefying, dangerous, and precarious. The light in the crevice of volcanic rock scalds the darkness with its scorching yellow and red flowing lava. In "E Pele e, fire-eater from Kahiki," Trask (1994) recalls Pele, Hawaiian deity of the volcano, a goddess traditionally worshipped in pre–European contact Hawaiian religion, a practice that continues today. She is "fire-eater" and, according to hula legend, is god-woman-hag. Like lava, she is fiery, unstable, unpredictable, and destructive when burning with jealousy.

Breath of Papa's life
miraculously becomes
Energy, stink with

sulfurous sores. Hi'iaka
wilting in her wild home:
black *lehua*, shriveled
*pukiawe*, unborn *ali'i*.

Far down her eastern flank
the gourd of Lono dries
broken on the temple wall.

Cracked lava stones
fresh with tears, sprout
thorny vines, thick
and foreign.[8]

"Energy" alludes to the proposals of ever-present geothermal development projects upon Native Hawaiian lands. Worshippers of Pele view such developments as a desecration of the sacred site of worship of their goddess and an assault (rape) on Papa (earth mother).[9] In the poem, the indigenous offspring of Hi'iaka (deity of the forest) dies.[10] The *lehua*, a flower believed to cause rain when picked, conveys the image of warrior, beloved friend, relative, sweetheart, and expert fisher. Introduced vines and plants, which often overgrow and choke indigenous plants, are an ever-present problem in Hawai'i.

## Colonial Transformations

The West also has a tradition of personifying the land. In the popular travel literature of European explorers, the land is described as a female body, and the image is often one of sexualized violence. Land is commonly described as virgin territory waiting to be controlled, penetrated, and subdued. "Land" popularly connotes real estate, a commodity, a property to be bought, owned, and sold. Land is perceived as an entity outside of the self. One philosophy intimately connects humanity to the land in language, epistemology, and physical and spiritual terms; the other desires not just connection, but domination.

*Whenua*, a generational word, spoken from a cosmogenic world-view that reflected an interconnected relationship between humanity and creation, was generally neither recognized nor valued by colonizers. The Western/English definition of "land" lacks the *kauna* (Hawaiian for "hidden meaning") of its Pacific counterparts. The conceptual differences between land and people's relationship to the land can be generalized as one of ownership versus stewardship.[11]

As colonialism took effect, many indigenous peoples found themselves ousted from occupation and use of land.[12] Landlessness and limited access to land resources led to dependency upon foreign goods and political powerlessness. Powerful colonial ideologies came to suppress and influence indigenous peoples, their concepts, and in some cases, their languages. In many islands, *whenua* had become "land." The differences in meaning of this one word—land—demonstrate the difference between two peoples with widely varying and inevitably conflicting, world views. It is this conflicting point of divergence that underpins the main tone of protest in first wave Pacific literature.

Regaining the *whenua* from former colonial powers and resulting neocolonial governments forms the foundation of sovereignty and independence movements throughout the Pacific. Returning spiritually and physically to the *whenua* is an indigenous imperative. In contemporary postcolonial literature the *whenua* as more than just a physical entity is being revived and used in the struggle for independence and decolonization.[13]

Pacific literature laments, celebrates, confronts, encounters, and contends with such reconnections with the *whenua*, along with re-visioning spiritual, cultural, and political aspects of indigenous cultures previously negated. Indo-Fijian scholar and author Subramani notes that, given the political context from which Pacific literature arises:

> It is not surprising that the major concerns of a large part of this literature are an indictment of colonialism and neo-colonialism, on the one hand, and the concomitant aspiration to rehabilitate the indigenous cultures "tainted" by colonialism, on the other. (Subramani 1985, xiii)[14]

The wholesale indictment of colonialism as evil incarnate may be criticized as overly simplistic and polarized. With European contact came literacy, modern medicine, introduced foods, and metal technology. It is also important to recognize the complex agendas at work between native and colonizer and native agency at contact. For these reasons, Subramani favors a dialectical approach toward Pacific literature and its relationship with colonialism (Subramani 1992).

However, it is clear that in many cases, the trade-off for such goods was costly and had long-term effects. Although many Pacific Islanders experienced some cultural and technological reciprocity upon contact, this tended to be short-lived. The price of literacy was often an indoctrination into Western religious belief systems and covert or overt schooling in ideologies that privileged things of the West over things indigenous (see Thaman 1992). The value of orature was overshadowed by the written text. Introduced medicine did relatively little to halt the infection of introduced diseases. Metal technology and gun warfare increased the number of indigenous casualties in battles, in both intertribal warfare and wars against European forces.

The damaging and enduring effects of colonialism overwhelm the benefits of contact in the first wave of postcolonial Pacific literature (Subramani 1985). The writing is polemic in tone, outlining a clearly delineated colonial oppressor versus an indigenous oppressed. This political, emotional, and cultural dualism between native versus colonizer is indicative of first-wave literature of postcolonial societies elsewhere. It is arguably a necessary stage of recovery and recuperation from former colonialisms.

Without an understanding of such cultural, social, and political context and subtext, the *kauna* within creative writing is lost. Intended value and meaning become buried beneath literal meanings measured by and against eurocentric aesthetics. Consequently, Pacific literature was often not appreciated on its own terms, but subject to Western norms and value judgments that often rendered it as substandard literature.[15] The need to write and be read appreciatively has become the impetus for many South Pacific writers and critics.[16]

## "Breach Birth"

*Tangata Tangata* (People People) was one of the first films to express and examine colonization and decolonization of the Pacific from the perspective of Pacific Islanders.[17] At its debut at the Second Annual Pacific Islands Images Film Festival in Hawai'i (1995), Samoan filmmaker Poumau Papali'i described contact with white colonialism as a "breach birth."[18] This is an apt description. It avoids the simplistic dualism of early indigenous reactions to colonialism and is indicative of some of the complexities of European contact.

As a noun, "breach" is defined as "the breaking or neglect of a rule or agreement" (Hawkins 1988). The violation of indigenous laws and ways of living proved to be the cornerstone of many colonial invasions and overthrows—regardless of the formal establishment of a treaty.[19] A second definition describes the act as "an opening made by a breakthrough" (Guralnik 1984). This meaning connotes rape metaphors used to describe colonial invasions that forcefully penetrated native lands and people's lives. The breakthrough was furthered by material and ideological means through trade and patrons or brokers of Christianity. Other definitions describe some of the effects: an estrangement (Guralnik 1984), a broken place, a gap (Hawkins 1988). In some islands, the disease and the musket warfare that accompanied colonialism literally broke indigenous populations.[20]

To compare colonial contact in the South Pacific with a breech birth acknowledges the blood and pain of our colonial history born out of differing forms of oppression. Despite the relatively short time-span of the reign of colonialism in many islands, it has been, in the majority of cases, the most devastating, life-changing event in history, wreaking irrevocable change in the lives of indigenous people. But Papali'i's metaphorical extension also acknowledges the infusions of new beginnings and different birthings. When contextualized in the entire history of the Pacific, colonial history is only part of a Pacific history spanning thousands of years. In other words, the Pacific

> eludes
> precludes
> concludes
> stasis
>
> tis "anti-stasis"
>   ever-moving
>   ever-grooving
>     to beaten drum of lali soothing
>     voices in fagogo telling
>     tales of old and new
>
> ever-revolving
> ever-solving
> mysteries of itself
>   with itself
>   by itself
>
> ever-growing
> ever-knowing
>   of itself and other worlds
>     incorporating
>       investigating
>         revitalizing
>           unto itself
>             indigenizing
>               outside selves . . . .
>                 (Marsh 1997)

Pacific peoples continue to absorb different experiences, realities, and influences, adopting, growing, and birthing new possibilities. Literacy was one of these adopted influences.

## Writing and Critiquing: Tools in Decolonization

Sharing words, telling stories, and retelling histories and mythologies is part of a contemporary cultural revitalization in the Pacific. Reclaiming orature through writing allows the healing of past silences and invisibilities to take place in the wake of colonization. Multitudinous aspects of the indigenous self were overtly and covertly negated through colonization. Samoan-American poet and scholar Caroline Sinavaiana maintains that through the telling of stories we come to know and perpetuate "something essential about who we are ... " (Sinavaiana 1995, see Saaga et al. 1990). In Sinavaiana's case, self-knowledge came through listening to stories and learning about Samoan identity largely through myths and legends. Her poetry realizes the common Pacific maxim that the future is formed by looking into the past.

Stories can revive present identity by retrieval of past histories. Stories can validate identities to the self and the world by providing models of strength and empowerment. Talk story (Pidgin Hawaiian for storytelling or catching up on the news in someone's life) can thus be a powerful tool of decolonization inside the classroom, boardroom, village, and home. The imposition of other stories and dominant realities is a common tool of imperialism. One blatant way control was enforced from the outside was demonstrated when indigenous languages were banished from the public arena. Conversely, control can be enforced from within on a subconscious level as observed in the black skin/white masks neocolonial syndrome popularized by Algerian theorist, psychiatrist, and revolutionary Frantz Fanon (1968) in his seminal anticolonial text. Such stories are used to colonize and assimilate indigenous minds into Western ways of thinking and being. In the process they often denigrate indigenous identities.

Sinavaiana describes the Americanization of eastern Samoa as another "rudely imposed story about who we are." However, the story remains unfinished. Such oppressive, imposed metanarratives have

> yet to be challenged, corrected, and re-told. Instead, the twisted plot continues to unwind in a classically destructive cycle of colonial violence: first bloodshed and forced treaties; then, alcohol, cash and commodities; now, substance abuse, domestic violence and other stress related diseases.
>
> Having internalized the dynamics of this embattled plot—as have all colonized peoples—I now look for words that can reconcile the combatants. I look for stories that can cut through the veils of shadow that flutter across our faces, threatening to smother the spirit, to extinguish the breath. (Sinavaiana 1995)

Edward Said (1994) argues that "The power to narrate or to block other narratives from forming or emerging is very important to culture and imperialism, and constitutes one of the main connections between them . . . ." Unblocking our stories is one of the many ways of exposing, exploring, and deconstructing the various ideological colonizations of the mind. Writing and storytelling are an integral part of "decolonizing the mind."[21]

## Literature "on" and "of" the Pacific

There is a difference between literature "on" the Pacific and literature "of" the Pacific. Before the 1960s, the bulk of literature on or about the Pacific and its peoples was written by nonindigenous authors. Such writings and imaginings played a significant part in the ideological colonization of the Pacific by the western world.

Since the mid 1970s, an increasing number of scholars have documented how Maori and Pacific Islanders were contained, categorized, and, to a certain extent, controlled through various stereotypes. (See Wendt 1976, 1980, 1995, Subramani 1975, 1978, 1985, 1989, Grace and Ihimaera 1978. Sharrad 1993, Pearson 1968, 1984, Sinclair 1992, and Krauth 1978, although nonindigenous, have made valuable contributions to this area.) Perpetrated from early first-contact voyage accounts (such as the original and edited travel logs of Cook, Bougainville, Byron, Carteret, and Wallis, and also, as Pearson [1984] points out, through the bias of editors like John Hawkesworth [esp. Chapter One]), to the literature and art produced by canonical masters of the West (such as writers Herman Melville, Robert Louis Stevenson, Somerset Maugham, James Michener, and Jack London, and artist Paul Gauguin), such racist and stereotypical constructions of islanders tended to reflect changing trends in European thought rather than actual Pacific realities. Wendt (1976) argues that this writing provided a forum for "papalagi fantasies and hang-ups, dreams and nightmares, prejudices and ways of viewing our crippled cosmos, [rather] than [views] of our actual islands." In his seminal essay "Towards a New Oceania," Wendt (1980) meanders through the canon of major authors and issues that have affected the reading of Pacific Islanders:

> Oceania has been written by papalagi and other outsiders. Much of this literature ranges from the hilariously romantic through the pseudo-scholarly to the infuriatingly racist; from the "noble savage" school through Margaret Mead and all her comings of age, Somerset Maugham's puritan missionaries/drunks/saintly whores and James Michener's rascals and golden people, to the stereotyped childlike pagan who needs to be steered to the Light.

Often, literature on the Pacific revealed what Said called the orientalizing eye/I, where, according to the norms and categories of knowledge of the West, indigenous peoples are constructed as different, as the exotic Other (Said 1978). African-American feminist critic bell hooks notes that many Western ideologies have enough influence to penetrate our self-perceptions: "They had the power to make us see and experience ourselves as 'Other'" (hooks 1992). An ocean away, Wendt acknowledges this forced "otherness" and subsequent self-alienation in terms of language: "To some extent, I am still a stereotyped tourist wandering through the stereotyped tropical paradises, a cliché viewing the South Seas through a screen of clichés" (Wendt 1976).

First-wave writing from the Pacific reacted against the negative influence of colonialism. Eurocentric ideologies inherent in colonial education and religion were often the subject of derision, as demonstrated by Ruperake Petaia's satirical poem "Kidnapped" (Petaia 1980):

> I was six when
> Mama was careless
> she sent me to school
> alone
> five days a week
>
> One day I was
> kidnapped by a band
> of Western philosophers
> armed with glossy-pictured
> textbooks and
> registered reputations ...
>
> ... Each three-month term
> they sent threats to
> my Mama and Papa
>
> Mama and Papa loved
> their son and
> paid ransom fees
> each time
> Mama and Papa grew
> poorer and poorer
> and my kidnappers grew
> richer and richer
> I grew whiter and whiter ...

Popularized European fiction (Subramani 1985, esp. Chapter 4), travel/adventure literature (popularized in the Western world by authors like Melville, Stevenson, Maugham, and Michener; see Pearson 1984), and nonfiction (as seen in publications from missionaries like Vicesimus Knox, who wrote the influential "On the Savage Manner of South Sea Islanders and the Best Means of Improving Them"; see Subramani 1985) were seen as ideological vehicles for perpetuating colonialism's racist attitudes (see Subramani 1985). In such texts Pacific Islanders are either exoticized (more than human, as seen in the notion of the Noble Savage, Golden People); demonized (less than human, as demonstrated in the Children of Nature or Black Devils stereotypes; see Wendt 1976); or part of an exotic backdrop.

The ability of the Empire to write back (a play on words by Salman Rushdie; see Introduction to Ashcroft et al. 1989) enabled the voicing of a Pacific consciousness in the public literary realm. Literature "of" the Pacific not only allowed a critiquing of literature on the Pacific, but aided in creating and affirming indigenous cultural production. Gramsci defines "hegemony" as a consensual domination through the influence of ideas and institutions (see also Said 1994). The majority of English Departments (the institution) in the Pacific, and literature (the medium of ideas) being taught within these departments, generally continue to affirm eurocentric hegemony. In spite of being superseded by the United States and Russia in international political and economic power, Britain remains the center of cultural production within commonwealth countries (see Ashcroft et. al. 1989).

Destabilizing that eurocentric canon in the Pacific is as vital today as it was thirty years ago. Today, Pacific children are still being colonized through a solely eurocentric education that has little relevance to their lives. In "Reality," a poem by Tongan poet and scholar Konai Helu Thaman, a young boy has achieved success in Western education, yet upon returning to his island, discovers that the books and blackboards have little use. The last stanza compares images of Western education with decay, in contrast with "Pacific-ness" and growth:

> ... I see my teacher
> Sitting on a sterile rock
> Near the beach
> Selling green coconuts
> What do I do now?
> An old man close-by whispers,
> "Come fishing with me today
> For you have a lot to learn yet." (Thaman 1987)

Trained as a teacher, Thaman relates how she felt part of the conspiracy of colonialism while teaching Tongan children English realities:

> I know Shakespeare was/is a great writer ...
> and Wordsworth too—but can you tell me
> why 13-year-old Tongan children should
> memorize "Daffodils" when they do not
> even have any idea what daffodils are, or look
> like? (Hereniko 1992)

Thaman saw it as her responsibility as an educator to place culturally relevant and affirming material into the hands of Tongan schoolchildren—thus beginning her career as one of the most prolific and well read poets in the Pacific. Many authors began writing in an attempt to fill the great need for indigenous texts. Thaman claims she simply wrote what she wanted to read.[22]

## The Rewriting of Dominant Discourses

In 1973, Cook Islander Marjorie Tuainekore Crocombe, a member of the South Pacific Creative Arts Society, proudly launched *Mana*, the Pacific's first international literary publication. A pivotal journal of creative writing, it has been instrumental in fostering and disseminating writing in and around the South Pacific. As founding editor, she wrote,

> The canoe is afloat. The flow of creativity in poetry, drama, storywriting, as well as other forms of creative expression from painting to wood sculpture has expanded enormously (in Oceania). Hidden talents are being developed, ideas are being expressed, confidence is growing, and the volume and quality increases all the time. (Crocombe 1973)

By 1974, the literary canoe was indeed afloat. As the waves of change in power and technology beat upon the shore, increasingly more indigenous writers began voyaging in literary canoes. More gained similar shoreline access as foreign writers. However, compared with the literature of other indigenous peoples around the globe, this Pacific literature is comparatively recent, since the Pacific is one of the last regions in the world to receive literacy. Prior to 1960 there was virtually a complete absence of published fiction.[23]

Political upheaval and decolonization predominated during the late 1960s and 1970s in the Pacific, causing an indigenizing of social institutions from politics to education to religion. Crocombe notes the effects on literature:

> People all over the Pacific were wanting to express themselves and to have their thoughts communicated to others in their own countries and through the Pacific—even beyond it if there was an interest. (Crocombe 1973)

As the globe shrank, anticolonial struggles for self-determination by indigenous peoples the world over provided a source of strength and comradeship and set models in place for self-determination. Tertiary institutions established in the islands became the centers in mediating anticolonial consciousness. Universities were also the largest facilitators of writing in English. These institutions enabled a fertile milieu in which people gathered, shared and developed ideas about the decolonization movements occurring throughout the Pacific. Notably, the universities of Papua New Guinea and the South Pacific in Fiji became two of the most influential centers of political thought and change.[24] These institutions produced and consumed much Pacific writing—fiction and nonfiction.

Several important events led to the movement of Pacific literature among the island nations. Ulli Beier arrived at the University of Papua New Guinea in 1967 and led the first local writing workshops and conferences. Eventually the Institute of Papua New Guinean Studies (which doubled as a publishing outlet) was formed (Wendt 1980). The Beiers were also instrumental in organizing writing outlets, ventures that led to the formation of *Papua Pocket Poets*, *New Guinea Writing* and the journal *Kovave*. Early recognition of this emergence of writing occurred in 1969 when Alan Makay, manager of Collins Ltd in Auckland, New Zealand, offered a prize for Pacific writing in order to stimulate it. Raymond Pillai has won the prize once (Pacific Island Writers workshop video 1986, opening comments). In 1972 Ken Arvidson established the Writers Society, which, with the input of Crocombe and Wendt in 1973, became the South Pacific Creative Arts Society, based at the University of the South Pacific in Suva, Fiji. The Society consisted of volunteers, among whom were Joe Nabola, Raymond Pillai, Howard Van Trease (Vanuatu Center), Konai Helu Thaman, Ken Arvidson, and Ron Crocombe.

"Mana," the Society's four-page literary section in the *Pacific Islands Monthly*, eventually became independent due to the overwhelming response from the public. The launching of *Mana* as a literary biennial in English occurred in 1976. *Mana* was (and continues to be) instrumental in fostering and disseminating writing in and beyond the Pacific. By 1974/5, the University of the South Pacific had employed Wendt, who began organizing and teaching courses in Creative Writing at the English Department. The various publishing outlets and creative writing courses provided the necessary stimulus and impetus for creative writing to emerge.[25]

In 1980 Wendt gathered together representative poems, short stories, and excerpts of novels and edited *Lali: A Pacific Anthology*, the first collection of Pacific literature written in English. A *lali* is a hollowed-out log, beaten with one (or two) heavy sticks, used to gather, summon, and inform people of impending events. This collection contains some of the first "drum beats" of voices sounding out through the Pacific *to* the Pacific—calling islanders to listen to and read the writings of their own people. Realizing that many of the works published were the first works of the writers, Wendt stated his intention to "capture the essence and spirit of the beginnings of our literature before it ages, divides, branches into more 'sophisticated' journeys and forms and techniques." The literary beginnings of the Pacific possessed the "raw power of innocent anger, joy, and lament" (Wendt 1980). The writing addressed what Wendt called the *aitu* (evil spirits) of colonialism: racism, oppression, corruption, and societal changes wrought by rapid modernization.

Fervent excitement, expectation, and hope surrounded this first wave of literature. As noted, first-wave writing tended to vilify "the colonizer," reacting against racist stereotypes and a history of domination that worked to silence indigenous voices. According to Subramani (1985), this reaction formed "an inner dialectic of the new literature." As evidenced in other writings that emerged out of similar colonial contexts, early Pacific literature was characteristically "nationalistic, angry, protesting, lamenting a huge loss" (Wendt 1995). Albert Leomala's poem "Kros" best exemplifies this stage. From the then New Hebrides (now Vanuatu), Leomala prioritizes Pidgin, the local language of Ni-Vanuatu, and uses it to protest missionization in a bare, direct, and confrontational manner:

> *Kros mi no wandem yu*
> *Yu kilim mi*
> *Yu sakem aot ol*
> *We blong mi*
> *Mi no wandem yu Kros . . .*
>
> (Cross I hate you
> You are killing me
> You are destroying
> My traditions
> I hate you Cross . . . .) (Wendt 1980)

Colonial and indigenous people were often seen in "irreconcilable opposition." As a result, much of the fiction from the Pacific Islands espoused unwavering "political and social commitment, with a heavily tragic, pessimistic vision of our times." Much of the writing vented individual political awakening and assertion against colonial domination and exploitation. Other poetry attempted to reconstruct past losses and is thus "a fabulous storehouse of anthropology, sociology, art, religion, history, dance and music" (Wendt 1995).

A lull in the writing occurred in the middle of the 1970s. Wendt points out that the fledgling writers who began the literary movement were also the urban educated of the islands. These people became the new leaders in government, education, and business, rapidly filling positions of authority and power in their growing and independent island nations. As such, the demands of either attaining self-determination or administering it quickly consumed their time and focus. Some authors wrote later through a different outlet (Beier 1980). Others never wrote again (Wendt 1980).

Ironically, some writers became the embodiment of the type of colonialism they had earlier rejected and protested in their writing. Despite colonial administrators' giving way to native sons, the structure of oppressive power relations remained the same. In many situations, the process of colonialism merely saw a change of skin color of those in power. To borrow an image from Fanon, although the new civil servants had black skins, many continued to wear white masks (Fanon 1968). For many, independence held a "false gleam" (a common metaphor of postcolonial writers; see Achebe 1958, Thiongo 1986). Neocolonialism became the subject of derision in much poetry, as in "Uncivil Servants," by Konai Helu Thaman:

> Many of my friends
> Are civil servants
> With uncivil thoughts ...
>
> ... But they cannot erase my existence
> For my plight chimes with the hour
> And my blood they drink at cocktail parties
> Always full of smiling false faces
> Behind which lies authority and private interests ....
> (Thaman 1980)

Samoan poet and artist Momoe Malietoa von Reiche personifies the town while metaphorically connecting human obesity with internal corruption and material consumption in her poem "This Town." The experts—both indigenous and foreign—work to the detriment of her people:

> This town is puffing with faalavelaves,
> Panting with a brain overload of
> Experts and crooked lawyers,
> Wheezing with conniving politicians and
> Gregarious customs officers.
> This town is going to die suddenly
> Of constipation. (Von Reiche 1988)

Two years later Maori produced their own anthology with *Into the World of Light: An Anthology of Maori Writing* (W. Ihimaera, D. S. Long, eds, 1982) which surveyed literature from the previous ten years. Maori writing began to flourish from 1970, a decade during which Maori were published in all the literary genres (see Ihimaera and Long 1982). Like the Hawaiians, Maori, despite being *tangata whenua*, found themselves a minority in their own country, forming 10% of the total New Zealand population in 1960 (Ihimaera & Long 1982). Like the Hawaiians, they refused to be marginalized. While mourning the losses of the past, Maori, with their indomitable spirit, are determined to shape their own future, as seen in Rowley Habib: Nga Pitiroirangi's poem "Orakau":

> Again the storming of the troops of the palisades.
> Again the repulse.
> Again the storming.
> And yet again the repulse. Wave upon wave.
> Through a day and a night and another day ...
>
> And the women and children in battle.
> Again the use of sticks for bullets.
> And still the invaders come
> Their numbers seem limitless.
> For every man who falls two move up to take his place.
> They seem indestructible.
> The spirit of the defenders fails.
>
> Yet through the ordeal, the sinking morale
> These words are still able to be uttered.
> 'Friend, this is the word of the Maori.
> *Ka whawhai tonu, ake, ake, ake.*'
> We will fight for ever and ever and ever. (Ihimaera and Long 1982)

Literature was one way of processing the past, asserting identity, and validating experiences that were previously denigrated. The noticeable absence of a glossary in this anthology indicated that despite popular opinion, New Zealand was not a monolingual, monocultural society. Maori literature, and its steady growth, argued for the need to reconsider New Zealand's national identity as bilingual and bicultural. The bulk of this urban literature centered on Maori/Pakeha relations and race conflicts.

What could be considered a second wave of writing began subsequently, and is manifested in a second anthology, *Nuanua: Pacific Writing in English Since 1980*, in 1995 also edited by Wendt. The *nuanua* (rainbow) imagery symbolizes

> the diversity of cultures and languages, of fauna
> and flora found in Polynesia, Melanesia and
> Micronesia ... also ... the richness and variety
> of our literatures, both oral and written. (Wendt
> 1995)

Issues surrounding decolonization still occupied Pacific literature as much as they did peoples lived realities. Wendt writes:

> Colonialism, racism, modernization, and their effects on us remain major preoccupations in our literature. A sense of profound loss still pervades that writing. At the same time in those countries struggling for their independence the writing is full of anger and hope. (Wendt 1995)

Other themes include loss of pride and self-esteem; loss of traditional skills due to urbanization; alienation from a Westernized society; the effects of modernity and materialism on local cultures; corruption of indigenous elite; and internal forms of oppression within society.

In this second wave, writers veered away from vilifying colonists or attacking simplified power oppositions and turned criticism inward. Hereniko observes "more experimentation in language as writers become confident enough to speak in their own unique voices, sometimes critically about their own cultures or leaders" (Goetzfridt 1995, Foreword). Writing that critiqued patriarchy and women's disempowerment surfaced. Jully Makini (Sipolo) of Solomon Islands and Grace Mera Molisa of Vanuatu are two leading Melanesian poets who critique the position of women within their own societies and also, for the first time in this medium, publicly proffer "a woman's views" (Sipolo 1981). They challenged the use of the bases of traditional societies as strongholds to keep women from becoming empowered in rapidly modernizing societies. Molisa critiques *kastom* and argues that it is often used as a patriarchal tool to keep women (and other less privileged groups) oppressed. Her often quoted poem "Custom" notes:

> Inadvertently
> misappropriating
> "Custom"
> misapplied
> bastardised
> murdered
> a Frankenstein
> corpse
> conveniently
> recalled
> to intimidate
> women
> the timid
> the ignorant
> the weak. (Molisa 1983)

Molisa's deliberate use of the English word "custom"—as opposed to its Vanuatu dialect *kastom*—subtly critiques the seemingly sanctified belief that all *kastom* stems from unadulterated, untainted, pure forms of tradition. Using the word "custom" signifies the modern influence and manipulation inherent in the shaping of seemingly traditional belief systems.

In her second collection of poetry, *Colonised People*, Molisa parallels the oppressive power relations behind colonialism with that of patriarchy and sexism. Molisa states in the introduction:

> In a state of oppression Women are multiply oppressed compared with Men. Such is clear in Vanuatu. Vanuatu is now free of foreign colonial domination but NiVanuatu Women are still colonised. (Molisa 1987)

With stronger, more confident developments in theme came more indigenous shifts in literary style. Despite the anger voiced in blatant antiwhite, anti-Western, anticolonial, anti-Christian content in the first wave, Hereniko notes the irony in the use of structures and forms used to express this anger, which in some ways worked against itself (Goetzfridt 1995, Foreword). Wendt (1995) notes the commonly used modernist style of writing imitating the realist mode adopted by English canonical writers such as Eliot, Yeats, Pound, and the like. He describes the style as containing "deliberate ambiguity and complexity, irony, unified structures and characterization, the search for originality and uniqueness, and the concealment of artifice in the hope of transcending time and place." It became apparent that decolonization was a process, not a step. Writers like Molisa and Makini currently lead the way for others to use creative writing as a vehicle for voicing other forms of internal oppressions.

Recent Pacific literature leans toward more personal explorations of the Pacific psyche. Increasingly, contemporary writing focuses on a pan-Pacific identity brought about by frequent physical and educational mobility, rapid urbanization, and the influx of modern technology. For example, Fijian Joseph Veramu's latest work, *Moving Through the Streets* (1994), allows a creative glimpse into the lives of youth in the rapidly urbanized and intensely integrated city of Suva.

One particularly interesting current of writing is being produced by young urban second- or third-generation Pacific Islanders born or raised in the country to which their parents migrated. A common focus here is the exploration of multicultural identities and the migrant experience. Banaban–Gilbertese–African-American Teresia Kieuea Teaiwa states in her collection *Searching for Nei Manoa* (1995), that her poetry is a means through which she navigates her way through life with "the joys and pains of a mixed cultural identity and a feminine gender" (Teaiwa 1995). Niuean born John Puhiatau Pule's *Shark That Ate the Sun* (1992) weaves song, legend, chant, myth, and poetry—in prose and epistolary form in both English and Niuean—in his tale of a Niuean family's migrant experience in New Zealand. And most recently, Samoan-born, New Zealand–educated performance poet and author Sia Figiel's novel *Where We Once Belonged* (1996), lyrically examines Samoan life and transforming identities through the eyes of a young adolescent girl. Figiel's novel won the 1997 Booker Prize for First Book in the Asia/Pacific region and was a finalist for the Commonwealth Writers Prize.

Others, like dynamic Samoan-born, New Zealand–grown filmmaker Sima Urale, explore different mediums of storytelling that are becoming more accessible—namely film and video. Maori filmmaker Merata Mita views film as a natural progression from oral storytelling:

> History contains stories and therefore stories are very important. It doesn't surprise me that there's a reaching towards film and video which is strongly a visual kind of storytelling from a people who have strong oral traditions. I mean, we didn't go in for writing. We had carefully coded inscriptions that became carving or koro patterns which the keepers of that knowledge would decipher .... (Marsh 1996)

Urale has gained international recognition for her work. Like Pule, she also explores the experience of a Polynesian family who has migrated to New Zealand. Urale privileges the view of the child in O Tamaiti (The Children). The film, with its sharp, black-and-white images, relies heavily on visual and aural effects rather than on dialogue. In silence, Urale gives voice to the often voiceless.

The Pacific Islands Film Festival organized by Pacific Islanders in Communications, based in Hawai'i, holds yearly film festivals that showcase films by indigenous people. Increasing numbers of Pacific Islanders are writing, directing, and producing their own stories on film and video. The organization grows stronger every year. As computer technology becomes increasingly available, the future holds endless possibilities as the Internet increases in accessibility. Writing and storytelling, art and literature will continue to permeate all forms of communication with each new generation.

## In/Site into a Place

No one can ever really know a site, place, or location despite the authoritative tones of those with "registered reputations." However, to have in/site into a place means not only having an understanding of its environment, but also insight into the hearts and minds of its people. If, with the humility of the learner, we listen, then we come a little closer to understanding and appreciating others.

The three main waves of Pacific literature offer a glimpse into the hearts, minds, and spirits of the indigenous peoples of Oceania. (This delineation is not intended to be read as strict categories. Rather, the intention is to convey general movements of thought in the writing of the Pacific.) The first wave of writing largely represented a "cultural clash" that produced reactionary writing. In the second wave of writing, indigenous and foreign cultures began to integrate. The third wave leans toward the exploration of multicultural identities and pan-Pacific nationalities. Mediums of storytelling expand as far as the technology and the imagination allow. However, like literal waves, these figurative "waves" flow in, through, over, and under each other, surging backward and forward.

In 1994, Subramani, the first to produce a comprehensive survey of Pacific literature in this stated region, initiated one of the few courses of Pacific literature taught at the University of the South Pacific in Fiji. Its course book advocated: "Reading imaginative literature is one of the ways of breaking geographical and cultural barriers and participating in the larger universe and understanding the human condition" (Subramani 1994).

Samoan author and scholar Albert Wendt has often promoted the idea that Pacific literature should be read side by side with texts of history and other disciplines (unpub. comm.). Wendt's suggestion does not seek to proffer any anthropological truth, but aims to catch a glimpse of some of the humanity of the object—thus seeing it as subject. Breaking down strict demarcations allows insight into the imagination, experience, and emotional reality of a place through some of its people. Such an exercise would render a whole and more informed understanding of the people and places of the Pacific. For literature—song, chant, dance, oratory, proverb, myth, legend, poetry, short story, novel, play, autobiography, biomythography, film—is embedded with the histories, values, epistemologies, and humors of a people.[26]

If creative writing is visualized as a metaphorical map tracing spiritual and cultural landscapes, the reader, alongside the author, may explore the valleys and ravines of the human experience. Insight takes place from the emotional truths as well as the scientific ones—each shedding light on the other. We come to know a little more about other people and ultimately about ourselves as we continue to express, to examine. This visualization is, thus, an open invitation for ongoing dialogue:

> ... Therefore,
> friend,
> before the wind shakes
> and the sky gathers
> let us sit a moment
> by the hum's edge
> and the fringe of light,
> the quiet water under
> the bullfrog's assertion
> where the finger of water
> points into silence.
>
> There our words
> will find the delicate filaments
> that anchor brain to belly or heart,
> words to tease other words
> and words
> that bear unseen
> the source
> which we must touch
> to see.
>
> ("Invitation," Pio Manoa, in Wendt 1995)

# Notes

[1] Hauʻofa's poem appears with an explanatory note: "Takalaua, the twenty-third Tuʻi Tonga, was killed by two men, whom his son caught, took to a special kava ceremony, forced to chew the dry roots of the kava plant for the king's kava bowl, and then had butchered for distribution to the assembled chiefs of the realm."

[2] Any written form of indigenous creativity cannot escape the inherent influence of Western aesthetics; indeed many have embraced it and indigenized writing to suit their own purposes—for example, Wendt's indigenizing of English (1995, 3) and Enos' concept of Niuginian English (1972, 47).

[3] In 1994, the first conference to "Theorize Pacific Literature: From the Inside Out" was held at the University of Hawaiʻi at Mānoa. Although not the first conference to theorize about Pacific Literature, it was one of the first international conferences to do so "from the inside out," enabling a significant number of Pacific Island writers and scholars to participate. Dr. Vilsoni Hereniko, member of the conference board, along with several supportive staff at the Center for Pacific Island Studies, actively sought a high level of indigenous participation.

[4] Common aesthetics and content considerations found in oral storytelling and prevalent in contemporary Pacific literature include heavy use of analogy, metaphor, proverb, and allusion. Often the *kauna* (Hawaiian for hidden meaning) is encapsulated within Nature, mythology, history, and the lives and events surrounding royalty or chieftainship. The entertainment factor (the use of humor, wit and satire), is also important, for it guarantees the storytellers' ability to hold the attention of a reading or listening audience and increases the liability factor of the storyteller with whom people must feel some link, sympathy or empathy, identification with or interest in.

[5] One of the most widely published creation chants is the Hawaiian *Kumulipo*, made available to the English-speaking world when, under house arrest by an illegal government in 1897, Queen Liliʻuokalani translated the manuscript into English. The widely accepted version was authored by the then King David Kalākaua, whose genealogy and link to the gods is reinforced within the chant (thus politically strengthening and justifying Kalākaua's ties to royalty). Two thousand lines long, with a pre–European contact artistic style, it contains Hawaiian cosmology, genealogy, and philosophy. It is a noted Hawaiian treasure. See Beckwith 1981.

[6] Orbell (1995, 10, 133) notes that the mythological figures of Papa and Rangi are widespread throughout the Pacific and therefore are some of the most ancient personifications created when the first migrants were in one place and then dispersed throughout the Pacific.

[7] Often a tree will be planted above the placenta, which in turn continues nourishing creation. See Patricia Grace's *Potiki* (1986) and the circumstances surrounding Mary's birthing of Toko in the sea. This familial relationship is often embedded in everyday language. Hawaiians exhort each other to *malama ʻāina* —to care for the land as one would a parent.

[8] In "Hawaiʻi" Trask (1994) notes that Hiʻiaka is sister of Pele and deity of the forest. Pele and her family were originally from Kahiki in the South Pacific. Lono is one of the four major Hawaiian gods representing fertility. He was also god of the Makahiki season, when war was prohibited and games and feasting continued for four months.

[9] While I was in Hawaiʻi during 1994–96, vehement protests were staged in protest to geothermal drilling and penetrating Diamond Head Crater and other sites.

[10] The full name translates as "Hiʻiaka-from-the-breast-of-Pele." Pele raised Hiʻiaka as a sister, but in actuality fulfilled the role of a mother.

[11] Although I use the term "stewardship" to highlight the caretaker role of people on the land, it does not signify the importance of the familial aspect of the people-*whenua* relationship.

[12] The concept of total ownership was arguably foreign to islanders. Thus, the selling of land was often perceived as merely relinquishing the rights to use the resources of the land for a set period of time. Such misunderstandings have been at the center of much historical and contemporary conflict.

[13] While "postcolonial" is a useful term for delineating an era, there is a continuing debate over whether there can truly be a postcolonial society. Some Maori activists argue that colonialism is still alive and well in Aotearoa (New Zealand) as long as the Treaty of Waitangi remains unrealized. "Postcolonial" connotes an end to formal colonialism that is far from being realized in many peoples' lives. Wendt's definition highlights this predicament and seems more accurate in describing actual experiences around the world: "For me the *post* in post-colonial does not just mean *after*, it also means *around, through, out of, alongside,* and *against* . . . ." (1995, 3).

[14] The advocation of a manichean world view of "evil colonist" vs. "good native" is not the intention here. There were varying degrees of reciprocal exchange as natives eagerly sought out foreign technology. Natives were active agents, sometimes taking or accepting what was needed or wanted and trading or sacrificing what they had. Cultures have always been subject to internal and external change and conflict—the South Pacific is no exception.

[15] This can be seen as recently as 1992 in the Faber controversy, involving the appointment of C. K. Stead, New Zealand writer and critic, as editor to *The Faber Book of Contemporary South Pacific Writing* (London: Faber & Faber). Several of the main writers—Albert Wendt, Keri Hulme, Witi Ihimaera, and Patricia Grace—withdrew their consent to be included because they felt that, considering much of Stead's past uninformed and unsympathetic eurocentric criticism of Pacific Island literatures, he was not suitable to edit such a collection. In both form and structure, indigenous voices were yet again being framed (and validated) by authorial Pakeha voices. Both Wendt and Ihimaera (who have produced excellent anthologies) were passed over for Stead. See Hereniko and Shwartz 1994, and Hereniko's foreword to Goetzfridt 1995.

[16] To be "read appreciatively" means to be read *with* those who have knowledge of the social, cultural, and political contexts of the writer from the Pacific and *who* use this information to enlighten the text. This is by no means a position exclusively held by indigenous people of the Pacific, nor do Pacific bloodlines guarantee such a position.

[17] Indigenous peoples are increasingly turning to film as an effective oral and visual medium with which to retell their histories and take back their voices. Recently, Hawaiians produced *Act of War* (1993), recounting the overthrow of the Hawaiian monarchy, which aired on public television and also at various film festivals, while the Pueblo peoples produced *Surviving Columbus* (1994), a film that explored the effects of colonization on Pueblo culture.

[18] Breech birth is a medical term describing a delivery in which a full-term baby is not naturally positioned head first in the birth canal, thus making the birth extremely painful for the mother and distressing and dangerous for the baby.

[19] As seen in the legalized Treaty of Waitangi, in which *tino rangatiratanga* (equal partnership) has still yet to be implemented.

[20] For example, Rapanui (formerly Easter Island) lost an estimated 98% of its population. *Tangata, Tangata*. Dir. Poumare Papaliʻi.

[21] A term coined by African author and theorist Ngugi wa Thiongo (1986).

[22] Due to gender, race, class, religious beliefs, etc., many writers who find themselves on the margins of society have made similar claims (e.g. African-American author Toni Morrison).

[23] For the purposes of this article, my definition of literature makes the distinction between published fiction and indigenous writing. There were numerous nineteenth century indigenous writers, but I am referring only to published fiction and other expressions of creativity. One exception to the general absence of published fiction prior to 1960 was Florence "Johnny" Frisbie's autobiographical story of a Cook Island girl and her *papaʻa* father entitled *Miss Ulysses of Puka Puka* (New York: Macmilllan, 1948). Perhaps this anomaly can partly be attributed to the heavy influence and involvement of Frisbie's *papaʻa* father in the writing and editing of the book.

[24] The University of the South Pacific now has several island extensions in Western Samoa, Tonga, the Solomon Islands, the Cook Islands, Fiji, Niue, and Kiribati.

[25] The first wave of writing was spearheaded by Tom and Lydia Davis from the Cook Islands in 1960 with *Makutu*. In 1965 Colin Johnson's *Wild Cat Falling* became the first novel written by an Aborigine. Vincent Eri became the first Papua New Guinean to publish a novel, in 1970, with *The Crocodile*. Three years later Albert Maori Kiki's autobiography, *Ten Thousand Years in a Lifetime,* was published. In 1972 Maori writer Witi Ihimaera published the first in a trilogy about life in rural Maori communities with *Pounamu, Pounamu* (1972), *Tangi* (1973), and *Whanau* (1974). A second trilogy appeared in 1977 with *A New Net Goes Fishing*. In 1978 Grace's prolific career as author began with the publication of *Mutuwhenua: The Moon Sleeps*. Meanwhile, Wendt published *Sons for the Return Home* (1973), *Leaves of the Banyan Tree* (1979), and *Pouliuli* (1977). These instrumental works inspired and encouraged others to write. For more detailed accounts of the development of this literature, see the introductions to *Lali* (Wendt 1980) and *Nuanua* (Wendt 1995). Also see the introduction to Tiffen (1978).

[26] Tongan satirist Epeli Hau'ofa once said that if you know what makes a people laugh, then you know the people (unpublished communication).

# Bibliography

Achebe, C. 1958. *Things fall apart*. London: Heinemann.

Ashcroft, B., G. Griffiths, and H. Tiffin. 1989. *The empire writes back: theory and practice in post-colonial literatures*. London and New York: Routledge.

Beckwith, M. W. 1981. *The Kumulipo: a Hawaiian creation chant*. Honolulu: University of Hawai'i Press.

Beier, U., ed. 1980. *Voices of independence: new black writing from Papua New Guinea*. New York: St. Martin's Press.

Crocombe, M. T. 1973. Pacific personality. Samoa's Albert Wendt. poet and author. *Mana: A South Pacific Journal of Language and Literature* 1:45–47.

Crocombe, M. T. 1976. Introduction. *Mana: A South Pacific Journal of Language and Literature* 1:1.

Dunlop, P. 1985. Samoan writing: searching for the written *fagogo*. *Pacific Islands Communication Journal* 14:1:41–69.

Edmund, R. 1990. Kiss my arse! Epeli Hau'ofa and the politics of laughter. *Journal of Commonwealth Literature* 25(1):142–155.

Enos, A. 1972. Niugini literature: a view from the editor. *Kovave* 4(1):46–49.

Fanon, F. 1968. *Black skins, white masks*. London: MacGibbon and Kee.

Fanua, T. P. 1975. *Po fananga: folk tales of Tonga*. San Diego: Tofua Press.

Figiel, S. 1996. *Where we once belonged*. Auckland: Pasifika Press.

Goetzfridt, N. 1995. *Indigenous literature of Oceania: a survey of criticism and interpretation*. Westport, Connecticut: Greenwood Press.

Grace, P. 1978. *Mutuwhenua: the moon sleeps*. Auckland: Longman Paul.

Grace, P. 1986. *Potiki*. Auckland: Viking.

Grace, P., and W. Ihimaera. 1978. The Maori in literature. In *Tihe Maori ora: Aspects of Maoritanga*, ed. M. King, 80–85. Wellington: Methuen.

Guralnik, D. B., ed. 1984. *Webster's New World dictionary of the American language*. New York: Warner Books and Simon & Schuster.

Hawkins, J. M. 1988. *The Oxford paperback dictionary*. 3rd ed., Oxford University Press.

Hereniko, V. 1992. Interview with Konai Helu Thaman. *Mana: A South Pacific Journal of Language and Literature*. 9:2.

Hereniko, V. 1995. Indigenous knowledge and academic imperialism. Unpublished paper presented at Contested Ground: Pacific History Conference. Honolulu, Hawai'i.

Hereniko, V., and S. Shwartz. 1994. Talking chief: the role of the critic in a colonized Pacific. Unpublished paper.

hooks, bell. 1984. *Feminist theory: from margin to center*. Boston: South End Press.

hooks, bell. 1992 *Black looks: race and representation*. Boston: South End Press.

Ihimaera, W., ed. 1992. *Te Ao marama: contemporary Maori writing*. Auckland: Reed.

Ihimaera, W., and D. S. Long, eds. 1982. Into the world of light: an anthology of Maori writing. Auckland: Heinemann.

Krauth, N. 1978. Politics and identity in Papua New Guinean literature. *Mana: A South Pacific Journal of Language and Literature* 2(2):45–48.

Manoa, Pio. 1995. "Invitation." In *Nuanua: Pacific writing in English since 1980*, ed. Albert Wendt, 73. Auckland: University of Auckland Press.

Marsh, S. T. 1997. Statued ('stat you?) traditions. *Wasafiri* 25.

Mita, M. 1996. Issues of cultural diversity. Pacific Island Images Film Festival, Pacific Islanders in Communication, University of Hawai'i at Mānoa Art Auditorium, August 2, 1996.

Molisa, G. M. 1983. *Black stone: poems*. Suva: Mana.

Molisa, G. M. 1989. *Black stone II: poems*. Vanuatu: Black Stone Publications, and Vanuatu USP Centre.

Molisa, G. M. 1989. *Colonised people: poems*. Port Vila, Vanuatu: Black Stone Publications.

Orbell, M. 1995. *The illustrated encyclopedia of Maori myth and legend*. Christchurch: Canterbury University Press.

Pearson, B. 1968. The Maori and literature 1938–65. In *The Maori people in the nineteen-sixties: a symposium,* ed. E. Schwimmer, 217–256. New York: Academic Press.

Pearson, B. 1984. *Rifled sanctuaries: some views of the Pacific Islands in western literature*. Macmillan Brown Lectures 1982. Auckland: U. of Auckland Press.

Petaia, R. 1980. *Blue rain*. Apia, Western Samoa: U. of South Pacific Centre, Western Samoa, Mana Publications.

Pule, J. P. 1992. *The shark that ate the sun: ko e ma'go ne kai e la'*. Auckland: Penguin Books.

Saaga, E., C. Sinavaiana, and J. Enright. 1990. *Three Tutuila poets*. Pago Pago, American Samoa: Le Siuleo o Samoa.

Said, E. 1979. *Orientalism*. New York: Vintage Books.

Said, E. 1994. *Culture and imperialism*. New York: Vintage Books.

Sharrad, P. 1993. A rhetoric of sentiment: thoughts on Maori writing with reference to the short stories of Witi Ihimaera. In *New Zealand literature today*, ed. R. K. Dhawan and W. Torentto, 60–72. New Delhi: Indian Society for Commonwealth Studies.

Sharrad, P., ed. 1993. *Readings in Pacific literature*. Wollongong: New Literatures Research Centre.

Sinavaiana, C. 1995. Storytelling as healing. Summer Institute for Pacific Women. Unpublished paper.

Sinclair, K. 1992. Maori literature: protest and affirmation. *Pacific Studies* 15(4):283–309.

Sipolo, J. 1981. *Civilized girl: poems*. Suva: South Pacific Creative Arts Society.

Sipolo, J. 1986. *Praying parents: a second collections of poems*. Honiara, Solomon Islands: Aruligo Book Centre.

Subramani. 1975. Review of *Best stories of the South Seas*. *Journal of the Polynesian Society* 84(4):523-536.

Subramani. 1978. Images of Fiji in literature. In *South Pacific images*, ed. C. Tiffin, 43–52. St. Lucia, Queensland: U. of Queensland, 1978.

Subramani. 1985. *South Pacific literature: from myth to fabulation*. Suva: University of the South Pacific.

Subramani. 1989. Indo-Fijian writing. *Ethnies* 4:41–47.

Subramani. 1992. *South Pacific Literature: from myth to fabulation*, revised edition, Suva: IPS, University of the South Pacific.

Subramani. 1994. LL102 Pacific Literature in English: introduction and assignments, Semester 2, 1994. Suva, Fiji: Department of Literature and Language, School of Humanities, The University of the South Pacific.

Teaiwa, T. 1995. *Searching for Nei Manoa*. Suva, Fiji: Mana Publications.

Thaman, K. H. 1987. *Hingano: selected poems, 1966–1986*. Suva, Fiji: Mana Publications.

Thaman, K. H. 1980. *You, the choice of my parents*. Suva, Fiji: Mana Publications.

Thaman, K. H. 1992. Cultural learning and development through cultural literacy. In *Voices in a seashell: education, culture and identity*, ed. B. Teasdale and J. Teasdale. Suva: IPS, USP, UNESCO.

Thiongo, N. wa. 1986. *Decolonising the mind: the politics of language in African literature*. Portsmouth, N.H.: Heinemann.

Thiongo, N. wa. 1967. *A grain of wheat*. London: Heinemann.

Thiongo, N. wa. 1993. *Moving the centre: the struggle for cultural freedoms*. Portsmouth, N.H.: Heinemann.

Tiffen, C., ed. 1978. *South Pacific images*. Brisbane: South Pacific Association for Commonwealth Literature and Language Studies.

Trask, H. 1994. *Light in the crevice never seen*. Corvallis, Oregon: Calyx Books.

von Reiche, M. M. 1988. *Tai: heart of a tree: a collection of poems*. Auckland: New Women's Press.

Wendt, A. 1976. *Inside us the dead: poems, 1961–1974*. Auckland: Longman Paul.

Wendt, A. 1976a. Towards a new Oceania. *Mana: A South Pacific Journal of Language and Literature* 1(1):49–60.

Wendt, A. 1980. *Lali: a Pacific anthology*. Auckland: Longman Paul.

Wendt, A. ed. 1995. *Nua Nua: Pacific writing in English since 1980*. Auckland: Auckland University Press.

# SECTION 4

# CULTURE

Pacific Island cultures are rich and diverse, ranging from the numerous ethnolinguistic groupings of Melanesia, to the spatially extended cultures of Micronesia, to the remarkably homogenous cultures characteristic of Polynesia. Traditional cultures have altered significantly following external contact, but have remained resilient. Even where indigenous islanders are minorities, cultural revivals are currently under way. Section 4 explores Pacific Islands cultures, with chapters on language, social relations, tenure, law, religion, and art. Contributors include Andrew Pawley, Lamont Lindstrom, Ron Crocombe, Richard Scaglion, John Barker, and Deborah Waite.

# Language

*Andrew Pawley*

## Introduction

More than 20% of the world's languages are packed into the Pacific Islands, a region that contains less than one percent of the world's land mass and population.[1] The 1300–1400 distinct languages[2] spoken by its indigenous peoples belong to at least twenty distinct genetic stocks.[3] The present chapter examines the geographical and historical contexts of this formidable linguistic diversity.

Can anything be learned about the geography of the Pacific by studying the languages of its peoples? The answer, surely, is yes. From careful study of their languages we can, at the very least, learn much about how different communities describe their environments and can compare their views with those of scientists. Languages can be thought of as codes for talking about and interpreting the world—indeed, as codes for constructing conceptual worlds. To learn a language is to learn, among other things, a vocabulary of concepts and a body of formulas for talking about different subject matters. In fact, a large part of becoming competent in any science or other field of conventional knowledge or belief is learning how its participants talk about their subject matter.

Traditional Pacific Island societies have developed rich and elaborate terminologies for certain aspects of their natural and man-made environments.[4] But more significant than the sheer size of terminologies is their content and structure—the nature of the concepts and the way these are ordered, for example, into taxonomies or hierarchical systems of inclusion and contrast. In any Pacific language, a good deal of the vocabulary speakers use for talking about their surroundings will translate readily into English and other languages and, to a lesser extent, into the technical lexicons of scientists. However, one also finds terms without close translation equivalents, and some of these reveal insights that have escaped western ecologists.

An example is the term *abn,* used by the Kalam people of the Schrader Ranges, Papua New Guinea. *Abn* are systems of natural tunnels or cavities, often extending into large galleries, that are present underneath the forest floor in certain places. Such underground tunnel systems occur above about 1,500 m on the wet slopes of the midmontane rain forest and are used by many animals that the Kalam hunt. Ralph Bulmer glossed *abn* by a neologism, "undercroft (of the forest)," and comments:

> To ecologists these [spaces] are just part of the "litter layer." But to English-speakers who are not biologists, "litter" suggests loose leaves and compost, and gives no inkling of the complexities of this underground world.... The absence of a technical biological term for *abn* perhaps reflects the limited extent to which ecologists have focussed on genuinely primary forests, climax vegetation of a sufficient antiquity to create and sustain such subterranean tunnel systems. (Majnep and Bulmer 1990, vol. I, p.9)

After presenting some basic facts about language families and their distributions, we proceed with a case study on how a Pacific Island language community talks about parts of their environment. Finally, we ask what can be learned from comparative linguistics about the prehistory of the various cultures, economies, and ecological adaptations of Pacific societies.

## The Language Families of the Pacific, Their Distribution and Internal Relations

The distribution of Pacific Island languages and language families (stocks of languages sharing a common ancestor but having no established genetic relationship to other stocks) is compactly indicated in *Ethnologue* (Grimes 1992) and is mapped in detail in the two-volume *Language Atlas of the Pacific Area* (Wurm and Hattori 1981–83). The three-volume *Atlas of Languages of Intercultural Communication in the Pacific, Asia and the Americas* (Wurm, Mühlhausler, and Tryon 1996) also treats nonindigenous languages.

When scanning the maps in these works one is overwhelmed by the dense concentration of languages in Melanesia (Table 15.1). The island of New Guinea is not much bigger than France, but linguistically speaking it is the equivalent of a continent, with nearly one thousand languages falling into some twenty distinct genetic stocks and isolates.[5] Another three hundred or so languages are spoken in Island Melanesia, from the Bismarck Archipelago to Vanuatu, and these belong to several different stocks.

By contrast, the area made up of Micronesia, Fiji, and the Polynesian Triangle is relatively homogeneous, containing fewer than forty languages, all belonging to the Austronesian family. Whereas in Melanesia the norm is many languages per island group or large island, in the Polynesian Triangle and in Micronesia each well-defined island group generally has a single language.

Few of the languages in Melanesia have more than five thousand speakers. The largest indigenous Pacific Island language communities (figures very approximate and excluding emigrants) are Standard Fijian (330,000), Samoan (170,000), Tahitian (140,000), and Tongan (100,000), plus several in Papua New Guinea—Enga (170,000), Melpa (130,000)—and Irian Jaya: Western Dani (150,000) and Lower Grand Valley Dani

### Table 15.1

**Approximate Number of Indigenous Languages and Unrelated Families in Pacific Regions**
(after Grimes 1992, Wurm and Hattori 1981-83)

| Region | Land area (sq. km) | Languages | Families |
|---|---|---|---|
| Irian Jaya | 415,000 | 248 | 4 + |
| Papua New Guinea mainland | 406,650 | 728 | 12 + |
| Admiralty Is. | 2,098 | 29 | 1 |
| New Britain & offshore is | 35,862 | 45 | 3 + |
| New Ireland & Mussau | 9,615 | 18 | 2 |
| Bougainville | 9,329 | 28 | 2 |
| Solomon Islands | 29,800 | 63 | 3 |
| Vanuatu | 12,190 | 112 | 1 |
| New Caledonia & Loyalties | 19,100 | 25 | 1 |
| Fiji-Rotuma | 18,270 | 3-6 | 1 |
| Micronesia | 3,750 | 11-17 | 1 |
| Polynesian Triangle excluding NZ | 25,050 | 15 | 1 |
| New Zealand | 268,500 | 1 | 1 |

### Table 15.2

**Some Austronesian Cognate Sets**

| | "eye" | "liver" | "louse" | "rain" | "eight" |
|---|---|---|---|---|---|
| Proto Austronesian | *maCa | *qatay | *kutu | *qudaL | *walu |
| Paiwan (Taiwan) | maca | qatsay | kasiw | qudal | alu |
| Tagalog (Philippines) | mata | atay | kuto | ulan | walo |
| Toba Batak (Indonesia) | mata | ate-ate | hutu | udan | walu |
| Manam (N. New Guinea) | mata | | kutu | ura | |
| Kwaio (Solomons) | maa | l/ae/fou | 'uu | uta | kwalu |
| Lolomatui (Vanuatu) | mata | ate | kutu | uhe | welu |
| Puluwat (Micronesia) | maah | ya/ya | uuw | wut | waluw |
| Bauan (Fiji) | mata | yate | kutu | uca | walu |
| Tongan (Polynesia) | mata | 'ate | kutu | 'uha | valu |

(130,000). Social change and the spread of English, French, and the pidgins as prestige languages are seriously weakening the position of many indigenous languages in the Pacific, including Chamorro (spoken in the Marianas), Hawaiian and Maori, and Tahitian, and many of them may not survive the twenty-first century.

## The Austronesian Family

Most of the language families present in Melanesia have no relatives outside this region. There is, however, one that is clearly intrusive. The vast Austronesian family (formerly often called "Malayo-Polynesian") is spread two-thirds of the way around the tropical world from Madagascar to Easter Island (Figure 15.1). In the Pacific, it extends from Taiwan and Hawai'i in the north to New Zealand in the south.

Recent estimates place the number of languages in the Austronesian family at around 1,200 (Grimes 1992, Tryon 1995, Wurm and Hattori 1981-83), far ahead of any other generally accepted language family in the world except the African family sometimes called Niger-Congo. About 40% of the Austronesian languages are found in Melanesia, Micronesia, and Polynesia. The remainder lie farther west, in Indonesia (about 400), Malaysia (108), and the Philippines (165), with smaller numbers in Taiwan (22), Vietnam (9), Thailand (1), and Madagascar (3).

It is easy to find cognates (words inherited from a common ancestor) between the most widely separated Austronesian languages. See Table 15.2. A star before a form indicates that it is reconstructed, not directly attested.[6]

Arriving at a reliable subgrouping or family tree for a large family of languages is usually much harder than merely establishing genetic relatedness. The most reliable method of subgrouping is by shared innovations. To show that a family has subgroups A, B, and C, we should demonstrate that the members of each subgroup share a significant body of common changes to the protolanguage exclusively of the others. There is a certain amount of disagreement about the higher branches of Austronesian, but the following classification (a modified version of that developed by Blust 1978, 1982, 1993–94, 1996) has a fair degree of general acceptance.

It is a striking fact that all the Austronesian languages of Melanesia east of 136° E, plus the Polynesian languages and all the languages of Micronesia except Chamorro and Belau, fall into a single subgroup (probably a fourth-order subgroup) of Austronesian, known as "Oceanic."[7] The boundary between Oceanic and the rest of Austronesian runs through western New Guinea and curves northwest through Micronesia east of Belau and the Marianas. The immediate relatives of Oceanic are the Austronesian languages of south Halmahera and Cenderawasih Bay, at the northwestern end of Irian Jaya. Oceanic and the South Halmahera–West New Guinea group form a large subgroup known as Eastern Malayo-Polynesian (Blust 1978).

Figure 15.3 shows a fairly conservative view of the high-order subgroups of Oceanic.[8]

## Structural Characteristics of Oceanic Austronesian Languages

Five thousand years of diversification within the Austronesian family has produced a range of grammatical systems comparable in diversity to that exhibited across the Indo-European subgroups: Romance, Germanic, Slavic, etc. However, there are certain characteristics common to many Austronesian languages of the Oceanic subgroup. Among these are

• Words typically consisting of two or three open syllables (without consonant clusters or final consonants), e.g. Hawaiian *wahine* (woman).

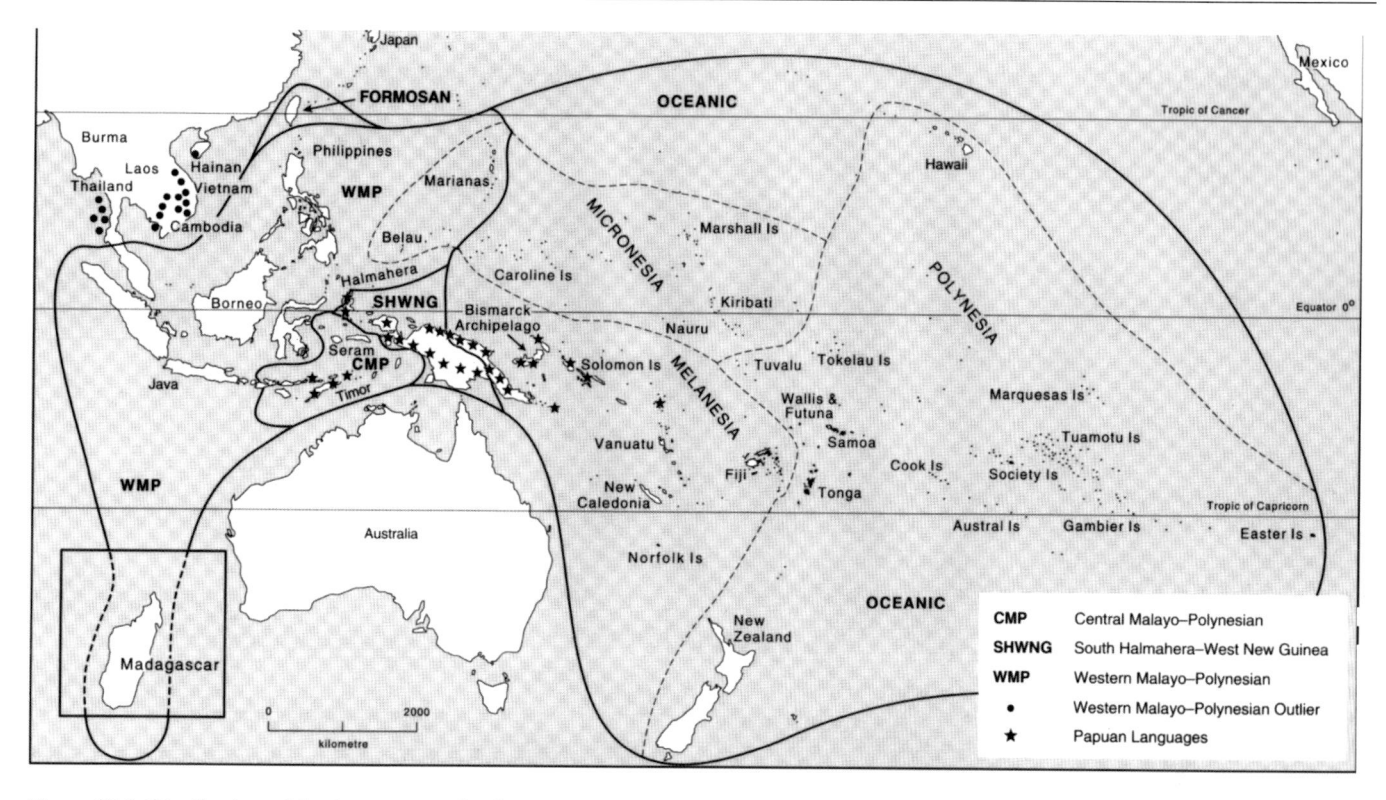

*Figure 15.1.* Distribution of the Austronesian family and its major subgroups (Madagascar shown as inset).

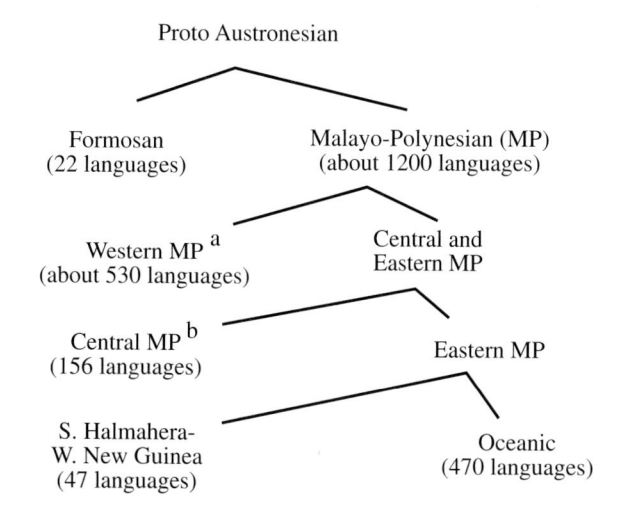

*Figure 15.2.* High-order subgroups of Austronesian (after Blust 1995). Notes: [a]Western Malay-Polynesian comprises chiefly the languages of Madagascar, the Philippines, Malaysia, and Indonesia as far east as mid-Sumbawa and including Sulawesi. [b]Central Malay-Polynesian includes the languages of the islands of eastern Indonesia east of Sulawesi and mid-Sumbawa, excluding South Halmahera and the Non-Austronesian languages of Timor and Halmahera. Some Central Malay-Polynesian languages are spoken on the Bomberai Peninsula, on the Bird's Head of New Guinea.

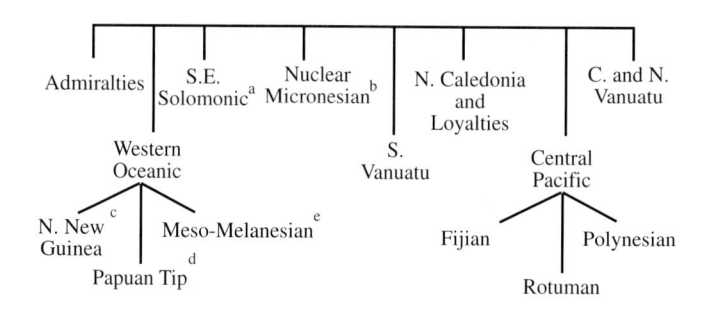

*Figure 15.3.* Probable high-order subgroups of Oceanic. Notes: [a]Roughly Guadalcanal, Malaita, San Cristobal. [b]Micronesian languages excluding Chamorro, Belau, and Yapese. [c]From Sepik to Morobe. [d]Central, Milne Bay, and Northern Provinces of Papua. [e]Roughly, New Britain from Willaumez Peninsula east, New Ireland, and W. Solomons.

- A distinction in first person plural pronouns between "we, excluding the addressee," and "we, including the addressee."
- The obligatory marking of nouns, when possessed by a pronoun, to distinguish kinds of possessive relationships: inalienable (body part and kinship terms), edible, drinkable, or general; e.g. Fijian *tama-na* (his father), *ke-na ika* (his fish [as food]), *me-na bia* (his beer [to drink]), *no-na vale* (his house [general]).
- Word order in which the verb precedes the direct object and the noun precedes its modifier. (New Guinea languages, influenced by their Papuan neighbors, are an exception.)

The Pacific Islands

• An elaborate transitivity system, in which transitive verbs are derived by a short or long transitive suffix (Proto Oceanic *-i and *-akini) and the direct object slot may be filled by nominals standing for a wide range of semantic roles: undergoer, place, goal, stimulus, cause, concomitant, instrument, beneficiary.

• A number of other verb-deriving affixes (e.g. *paka- causative, *paRi- collective action or reciprocal relation and *ta- spontaneous stative) and several affixes that derive nouns from verbs (*i- , *-in- ,and *-an).

For further information on Oceanic languages see Crowley et al. (forthcoming), Geraghty (1983), Sebeok (1971), Ross (1988), Tryon (1976, 1995), Tryon and Hackman (1983).

### The Non-Austronesian or Papuan Families of Melanesia

Although they do not form an established genetic unit, the indigenous Non-Austronesian languages of Melanesia are usually collectively referred to as "Papuan." It is now thought that in mainland New Guinea there are a dozen or so distinct families (often called "phyla") of Papuan languages plus several isolates (Figure 15.4). In Island Melanesia, in the region from New Britain to the Solomons, there are several more such families. There are also non-Austronesian languages spoken in Timor and Halmahera.

One very large Papuan stock has been identified. The Trans New Guinea (TNG) family contains almost 500 of the more than 750 or so Non-Austronesian languages of Melanesia (Wurm 1975), making it the third largest language family in the world (in number of members). The family completely dominates the central cordillera that runs the length of New Guinea, and it covers large parts of northern and southern New Guinea.

The precise membership and the subgrouping of the very diverse Trans New Guinea family remain controversial. Only a small number of cognate sets—around 100—have been securely identified as being shared by widespread subgroups of TNG.

### TABLE 15.3

#### Some Cognate Sets of the Trans New Guinea Family

|  | "breast" | "eat" | "louse" | "name" |
| --- | --- | --- | --- | --- |
| Proto TNG | *amu | *na- | *niman | *ibi |
| Asmat (S. Irian Jaya) |  | na- |  | yipi |
| Kati (W. PNG) | ane- |  | im |  |
| Kiwai (SW coast, PNG) | amo |  | nimo |  |
| Kewa (W. Highlands, PNG) |  | na "food" |  | ibi |
| Kuman (C. Highlands, PNG) | aemu |  | numan |  |
| Kube (Morobe Prov., PNG) | namu | ne- | imiŋ |  |
| Katiati (Madang Prov., PNG) | ama |  | ñima | nimbi |
| Aomie (Central Prov., PNG) | ame |  | ume | ihe |

### Structural Characteristics of Trans New Guinea Languages

Although there is considerable variation in the grammatical typology of TNG languages, certain features are very widespread (Foley 1986, Wurm 1975). These include the following, illustrated by examples from the Kalam language (see also the discussion in the section following this on Kalam language and the environment):

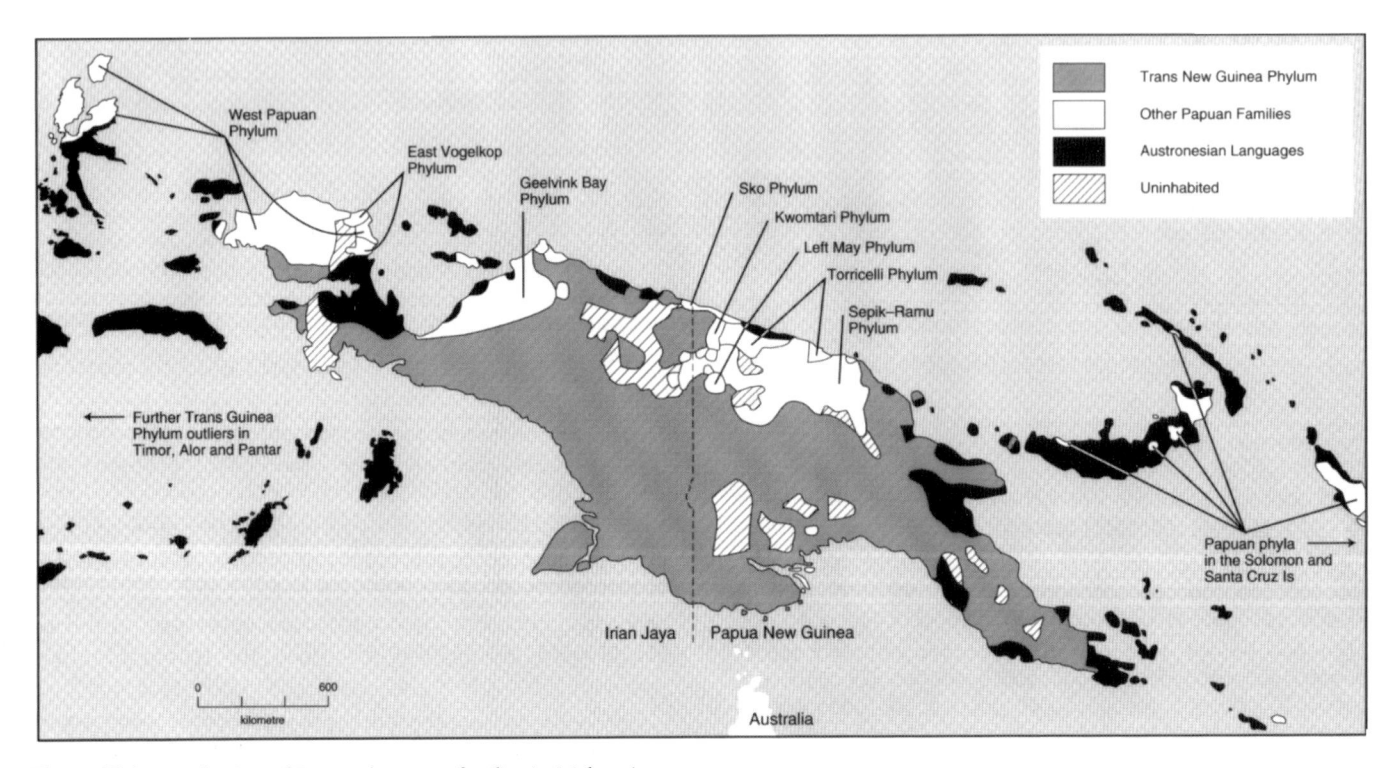

*Figure 15.4.* Distribution of Papuan language families in Melanesia.

- Quite complex verb morphology, with suffixes on main verbs that mark the person and number of the actor or subject and mark tense, aspect, or mood.
- Word order in which the direct and indirect object precede the verb and a modifying clause precedes the noun it modifies, e.g. "I shot the pig that ate my sweet potatoes" will be expressed in Kalam as "I pig the sweet potatoes my ate-it shot-I."
- Serial verb constructions, consisting of a string of consecutive bare verb stems that describe conventional sequences of actions in a highly analytic way, e.g. "to taste" is expressed as "eat perceive," "to feel" as "touch perceive," and "to fetch" as "go get come."
- Small inventories of verb stems, compensated by use of standardized serial verb sequences and/or by phrasal verbs consisting of a nominal adjunct(s) + verb, e.g. "to see" is "eye perceive," "to hear" is "ear perceive," "to dream" is "sleep perceive."
- In sentences consisting of two or more clauses there is "switch-reference" and "relative tense" marking on nonfinal clauses. The verb in a nonfinal clause carries a suffix or suffixes that indicate 1) whether that verb has the same actor or subject (SS) as the verb in the final clause in the sentence or a different actor or subject (DS) and 2) whether the event denoted by the medial verb is prior to (PRIOR), simultaneous with (SIM), or future to (FUT) that of the final verb, as for example, the Kalam sentence:

| Nad wog g-na-k-nŋ | You work do-you-past-DS.SIM |
| cn kmap | we song |
| ag-ig. | utter-SS.SIM |
| amn-nu-k | go-we-past |

"While you were working we were going along singing."

### Other Papuan Families

The greatest concentration of other Papuan families (or phyla) and isolates is on the northern side of New Guinea, from the Bird's Head to the Sepik-Ramu basin and especially in the Sepik region (Figure 15.4). Most of these families have received little comparative study, and their validity is by no means secure (Wurm 1975, Foley 1986 ).

The Sepik-Ramu phylum is a problematic grouping of about 100 languages spoken on the Sepik River and in the western part of Madang Province. The Torricelli phylum consists of about 48 languages centred in the Torricelli Ranges between the Sepik River and the north coast and extending into NW Madang Province. The West Papuan phylum comprises about 24 languages spoken at the western end of New Guinea, on the northern part of the Bird's Head and on N. Halmahera Island.

Several smaller families have been identified, including Sko (spoken on the north around the PNG–Irian Jaya border), Kwomtari (northwest part of Sandaun or West Sepik Province), Left May (south of Kwomtari around the May River, a tributary of the Sepik), and Amlo-Musiai (between Kwomtari and Left May). At the western end of New Guinea there is the Geelvinck Bay phylum, spoken on the coast of Cenderawasih (fomerly Geelvinck) Bay and on Yapen Island, and the East Bird's Head phylum. In addition there are a number of individual languages with no established relatives scattered about New Guinea, especially in the Sepik area.

Several pockets of Papuan languages are found in Island Melanesia. New Britain contains an uncertain number of stocks. There is an isolate on New Ireland, a small phylum in South Bougainville, another in the Central Solomons and another in Santa Cruz.[9]

### On the Number and Size of Language Communities in Melanesia

For the Eurocentric observer a natural question is Why so many languages and language families in Melanesia? Why are the language communities so small? But a Melanesian might equally well ask Why so few languages and language families in Europe? The fact is that, in its linguistic diversity, Melanesia is not very different from North America up until the nineteenth century and from many areas of contemporary southern Asia, sub-Saharan Africa, Central America, and Amazonia. Before the rise of city states and empires, political units everywhere were small, probably seldom larger than a collection of kinship groups or a village containing a few hundred or at most a few thousand people. No unit had the political and economic power to dominate a large area. Neighboring polities were often hostile. Given these severe limits on the size of sociopolitical groups, and given that all languages are constantly changing, the dispersal of a language community was bound to lead to linguistic fragmentation.

In the Pacific Islands, small polities and hostile neighbors were not the only constraints on size of speech communities. In New Guinea and New Britain, in particular, heavily forested mountain ranges and extensive swamps imposed natural limits to communication. Substantial ocean gaps between islands everywhere provided natural points of linguistic fission. In Micronesia and Polynesia, the position of boundaries between languages and dialects correlates closely with the length of voyages by canoe (Marck 1986, 1997).

The larger territorial range and population size of most languages in Polynesia (one language per island group) and Micronesia compared with New Guinea and Island Melanesia (many languages per island group of comparable size) can be attributed to a combination of factors: 1) Eastern Polynesia and certain parts of Micronesia were settled by Austronesian speakers much later than most parts of Island Melanesia. There has been less time for local diversification. 2) Unlike New Guinea and most of Island Melanesia, Polynesia and Micronesia were uninhabited before the arrival of Austronesian speakers. The founding colonizers of each island group, therefore, could occupy the whole region rather than being confined to residual pockets of territory around established communities. 3) Sailing skills were better developed or better maintained in Micronesia and Polynesia than in most parts of Melanesia and 4) the existence of powerful hereditary chieftainships within island groups such as Hawai'i, Tonga, Samoa, and the Societies provided social and political bases for regular interisland voyaging.

## European and Other Recently Arrived Languages

Co-existing with the indigenous languages in almost every part of the Pacific are various languages that have been brought by European and Asian settlers in the last few centuries (Sebeok 1971). French is the first language of most people in New Caledonia and many on Tahiti and is an important second language throughout French Polynesia (the Society Islands, Marquesas, the Tuamotus, etc.) and in Vanuatu. English is the now the first language of most people in Hawai'i and New Zealand and is an important second language throughout the Pacific Islands except in the French-speaking territories. On Easter Island, Spanish coexists with the indigenous Polynesian language. In Fiji, several Indian languages are spoken, Hindi being the most important lingua franca among Indian Fijians. In Hawai'i, Japanese and a number of Chinese and Filipino languages are spoken by sizable subgroups of the community. Chinese languages are spoken by small populations of Chinese settlers in most Pacific nations.

## Recently Developed Languages: The Pidgins and Creoles

Several important lingua francas have been been created as a result of contact between Europeans and Pacific Islanders. In Papua New Guinea, Tok Pisin (also called New Guinea Pidgin) is the popular "grassroots" interethnic language. It is spoken by perhaps two million people as a second language and is now the first language of many thousands of urban dwellers (Mühlhäusler 1979). In the Solomons, Pijin (Keesing 1988) and in Vanuatu, Bislama (Crowley 1990) play similar roles. These three languages are all regional developments from nineteenth-century South Pacific Pidgin, which began as an unstable contact jargon used by English speakers with Australian aborigines and Pacific Islanders but later became a fully functional language, developed by Melanesians first in plantation contexts in the South Pacific and then transported to various parts of Melanesia by returning plantation workers (Keesing 1988, Wurm et al. 1996). The Melanesian pidgins are mixed languages in that they use forms largely derived from English, but in many cases the meanings and pronunciations of these forms have been radically changed under the influence of indigenous (mainly Austronesian) languages.

For example, the pronouns of Tok Pisin use elements taken from English that have been completely reworked to create a pronominal system with four persons and three numbers and no gender and case distinctions, identical in structure to that of many Oceanic languages. The singular pronouns are: *mi* (I/me), *yu* (you), *em* (he/him, she/her). The dual pronouns are *mitupela* (we/us two excluding the addressee), *yumi tupela* (we two including the addressee), *yutupela* or *tupela* (you two) and *tupela* (they/them two). The plural pronouns are *mipela* (we three or more excluding the addressee), *yumi* (we/us three or more including the addressee), *yupela* (you three or more) and *ol* (they three or more). Hawaiian Pidgin has largely independent origins, having been developed in the plantations of Hawai'i.

## Languages As Encoding Environmental Knowledge: A Case Study

The fifteen thousand or so speakers of Kalam occupy several mountainous valleys around the junction of the Schrader and Bismarck ranges, in southwest Madang Province, Papua New Guinea.[10] Two of these valleys, the Simbai and Kaironk, contain the only large continuous corridor of grasslands in the rugged, heavily forested ranges between the northern lowlands and the extensive grasslands of the Jimi Valley lowlands and the main valleys of the Central Highlands beyond the Jimi Valley. The Kalam share many cultural features in common with peoples of the Middle Ramu Valley to the north and the Central Highlands to the south.[11] For most Kalam populations, first contact with government patrols did not come until the middle 1950s.

The present discussion focuses on the Kalam living in the Upper Kaironk Valley. Most live on the steep lower slopes of the V-shaped valley at altitudes of between about 1,500–1,600 m and 2,000 m, but people cultivate land up to 2,350 m. They also exploit resources present at higher altitudes up to the forested crests of the Schrader Range at over 2,700 m and down to below 500 m in adjacent lowland grasslands and forests.

The Kalam practice shifting agriculture, with sweet potato as the staple, although taro and yams are the important foods for ceremonial purposes. Pig herds have become of increasing importance in recent generations. Hunting of mammals and birds is pursued as a recreation and a source of meat, feathers and pelts. The largest social groups are small named local kin groups, usually consisting of between forty to eighty people, whose members live in scattered hamlets containing an extended family. Typically, each person and family has primary rights to patches of land on a strip on one or both sides of the valley extending from down near the river up to the crests of the mountain range, thus giving its members access to resources from various altitudinal zones.

### Kalam Ecological Zones

We are fortunate to possess an extensive body of writings by a member of Kalam society about his people's knowledge and use of their environment. During the mid-1960s Ian Saem Majnep was the young field assistant of the social anthropologist and ethnobiologist Ralph Bulmer. Later he became the senior author of several joint works about the ethnobiology of the Upper Kaironk (Majnep and Bulmer 1977, 1983, 1990, Majnep et al. n.d.).[12]

In *Kalam Plant Lore* (Majnep et al. n.d.) Majnep describes the way the Upper Kaironk people divide their territory into ecological zones. For instance, the altitudinal cline is divided into four main zones distinguished chiefly by vegetation and climate but also taking account of associated animals. Brief extracts from Saem's account follow. Editorial additions (other than Latin names) are enclosed in square brackets.

> Marking [ecological] zones is important to us in the first place because we need to know

how particular crops will grow in particular places.... Let me begin with the highest zone, which we call the *kamay* or southern beech zone. There [on the mountain crest ridges from about 2,300 m upward] the dominant trees are *kamay* (small-leafed southern beech, *Nothofagus pullei*). Other plants common in this southern beech zone are the mountain pandanus (*Pandanus julianetii + brosimus*) and a Eugenia tree ... and a kind of wild ginger [*Alpinia* sp. with important ritual uses]. The common birds include the Orange-billed Mountain Lory and Belford's Meledictes. A marsupial, Edwards' Silky cuscus, *Phalanger gericeus,* also lives there. This high zone is not good for gardens. The ground is cold and wet and unsuitable for crops.

In the zone we call *sugun* [from about 2,300–2,400 m down to about 2,000 m] the characteristic trees are *sugun* (*Garcinia schraderi*) and *kuam* (*Garcinia archboldiana*), *kalap db* (*Dacrydium elatum*) and *bbolmol* (*Monimiaceae* sp.). Other plants include the pandans *gudi* [*Pandanus antaresensis*, whose leaves are used to thatch houses], *kumi* [a cultivar of *Pandanus julianettii*, whose nuts are eaten] and *jjak* [a wild *Pandanus* sp., similar to *gudi*, whose leaves are used to make sleeping mats] and the bamboo called *wdn-kubsu* [used for bowstrings, fire thongs, water containers, and baskets]. Several birds are rare higher up in the beech forest but common in the garcinia zone: the *nol* (Reichenow's Meledictes), the *gulgul* (Greater Sicklebill Bird of Paradise), and also the *ñopd* (King of Saxony Bird of Paradise). In this warmer region sweet potato, sugar cane and other crops grow well.

Lower down [from about 2,000 m down to the Kaironk River at 1,500-1,600m] is the oak zone, known as *kabi* or *sawey*, where most of us live. The dominant trees in the patches of forest that survive here are the oaks *sawey* (*Castanopsis acuminatissima*) and *kabi* (*Lithocarpus* sp.) and also the broad-leafed southern beech (*Nothofagus carrii*), *Podocarpus theritifolia*, *Helicia nontana* and *Ficus augusta*. Wherever the *sawey* oaks grow, taro, yams, sweet potatoes, bananas and sugar cane flourish. The ancestors mainly made their gardens on ridges, clearing the forest there and later this turned into grassland .... Nowadays we plant casuarinas all over this zone.

The zone that we call *tmen* [after the Lawyer cane that grows there] includes the warmer country in the lower parts of the mountain ranges [below about 1,500 m] and also the flat lowlands of the Ramu and Jimi Valleys). Certain trees ..., birds ... and game mammals ... are characteristic of the *tmen* zone.... There are various crops that won't grow well in our area because it is cold, which down there grow to a large size. (Majnep et al. n.d. 1-2).

The Kalam also distinguish various other microenvironmental zones or biotopes, including *mon wog* (primary forest), *wog salm* (secondary forest regrowth in old gardens), *mseŋ* (grassland, open country), and *ñg bak* (banks of streams). Majnep's writings show that knowledge of the environment involves more than assigning names; it also involves understanding processes and relationships. An intimate knowledge of which plants go together is of course of prime importance to successful agriculture and foraging, and an intimate knowledge of which plants and animals go together is crucial to hunters.

### Kalam Classification of Animals and Plants

About 400 vertebrate categories (taxa) are distinguished by name, of which the Kalam eat about 200. The largest group falls under the primary taxon *yakt* (flying birds and bats). There are about 230 *yakt* taxa, representing 5 species of bats and 204 species of birds, of which 140 occur in the Upper Kaironk Valley and another 60 within a day's walk. Forty-five mammal taxa are distinguished. Most fall in the category *kmn* (game mammals), several under *as* (very small mammals), and three under *kopyak* (rats considered to be dirty and not eaten). There are over 120 invertebrate taxa, of which at least 40 (including grubs, caterpillars, grasshoppers, spiders, and snails) are eaten.

Kalam primary taxa of birds and mammals (Figure 15.5) differ markedly both from zoologists' and from English folk taxonomies.

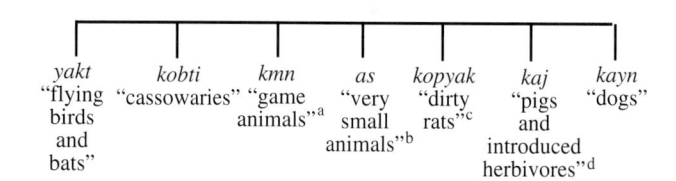

| *yakt* "flying birds and bats" | *kobti* "cassowaries" | *kmn* "game animals"[a] | *as* "very small animals"[b] | *kopyak* "dirty rats"[c] | *kaj* "pigs and introduced herbivores"[d] | *kayn* "dogs" |

*Figure 15.5. Kalam primary taxa of birds and mammals. Notes:* [a]*Wild mammals, such as wallabies, possums and giant rats.* [b]*Very small marsuipals and bush rodents.* [c]*Includes any rat species found close to human settlements.* [d]*Includes cattle and horses.*

There is, of course, no reason to expect a close match between zoologists' higher order taxa, which are based on evolutionary considerations, and those in a folk taxonomy, which one might expect to be based on "common sense."[13] What, then, is the common sense behind the Kalam high-order classes? The short answer is that this is a combination of things, ranging from morphological characteristics to cultural values: what counts as prized game, what methods of capture are used, what is considered unclean or dangerous to people at certain stages of life, and so on.

At the level of species, Kalam categories for wild mammals and birds match rather well with those of Western zoologists (Bulmer 1967, 1970). This reflects the fact that to close observers of nature most vertebrate species and genera are marked by multiple characters of morphology and behavior. In a number of cases, the Kalam appear to have observed facts about animal behavior and recognized taxonomic distinctions that have only belatedly been acknowledged by zoologists.

About 1,500 terms, or 15% of the recorded lexicon of Kalam, name kinds of plants. Plants are of paramount importance in Kalam economic and social life.[14] The Upper Kaironk people eat about 28 species of domesticated food plants, which they divide into 170 named cultivars. They also eat another 40 species of plants seldom or never cultivated, and they cultivate more than 30 other species for other purposes—medicines, rituals, ornamentals, flavoring and wrapping food, and technology. Another 150 wild species are used in technological or ritual functions. Many other plants are important to them as the known feeding and nesting sites of different kinds of birds and animals that are hunted.

Although Kalam high-order categories of plants (Figure 15.6) bear no resemblance to the evolutionary-based classification of botanists, they are quite like those of everyday English, though there are some differences. There is no Kalam term for

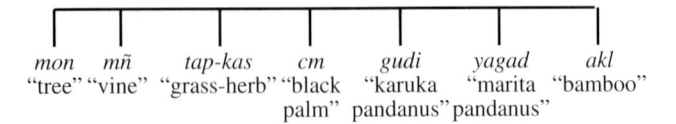

| mon | mñ | tap-kas | cm | gudi | yagad | akl |
|---|---|---|---|---|---|---|
| "tree" | "vine" | "grass-herb" | "black palm" | "karuka pandanus" | "marita pandanus" | "bamboo" |

*Figure 15.6. Some Kalam primary taxa of plants.*

"plant." The primary taxon *mon* (tree) does not include pandans (there is no generic for pandans) or palms (no generic). The taxon *mñ* (vine, creeper) includes certain woody trees, which the Kalam acknowledge can also be called *mon*. *Tap-kas* is used as a loose generic for all herbs and soft-stemmed grasses, though its main use is for green vegetables.

When distinguishing between closely related trees and other plants, Kalam use many different diagnostics, including characteristics of the stems (woody, vine, etc.); hardness, color, durability, and burning characteristics of the wood; shape, color, and other features of the bark or skin, the leaves, the fruit and the flowers; characteristics of the sap; and typical parasites. There is considerable agreement between western botanists' taxa at the level of genus and species and Kalam lower-order taxa.

### Terms for Direction, Location and Times

The Kalam have an elaborate stock of directional and locative terms adapted to their mountain environment. Directional terms are relative. There are no Kalam terms for the four cardinal directions. Instead, a speaker assumes as his frame of reference a V-shaped valley, with directions formulated in relation to the direction of flow of the stream: *neŋ* (upriver direction), *im* (downriver direction), *doŋ* (across-river direction) or in terms of relative height on a hillside: *yoŋ* (up[hill]), *yaŋ* (down[hill]). Because the streams run down quite steep valleys, "upriver" also means "the upper valley, at higher altitudes," and "downriver" means "the lower valley, at lower altitudes." The valley-based directionals can be modified by prefixes indicating, e.g., close or distant location, approximate vs. precise location, orientation in relation to addressee, and the angle of movement in relation to the ground (steep or vertical vs. horizontal). The directional system is transportable. It can be applied to smaller valleys within valleys and (with some difficulty) extended to flat valleys and coastal flats (with the sea being "downriver" and the inland "upriver").

Locatives give absolute positions. A locative consists of 1) a landmark term—a place name or description of a particular landscape feature, optionally modified by 2) a relation marker, marking, e.g., top or bottom, near or far side of the item named. A name is given to every small stream, hill, ridge, patch of flat land, area of forest, and land cleared at the edge of the forest. The average adult can name most of these landmarks within several kilometers of his home.

The seasons are divided into "dry" and "wet," and other points in the annual cycle are named for characteristic events, such as the times when certain trees are in fruit or when certain birds appear, and for positions of the sun between winter and summer solstices. As everywhere, perhaps, Kalam distinguish terms for time of the day based on the presence or absence of light and the movement of the sun. But there are other terms that draw more distinctively on features of the local environment, as when the Kalam speak of the *ñugl ñagl* (dawn and evening chorus of insects and frogs in the grassland) and the *gub mañmod* (dawn and evening chorus of animals from the edge of the forest), as events that signal dusk is approaching.

### Does Traditional Knowledge of the Environment Have Long-term Value?

We have looked, however superficially, at the ways in which a Pacific society describes and talks about its environment. One question that has engaged anthropologists is Why do people in traditional societies classify certain parts of their natural surroundings in such detail? Two opposing views have been proposed (Berlin 1991, Hayes 1991). The "intellectualist" hypothesis holds that people are simply intellectually curious and demand order in their understandings of the world. The "utilitarian" (or "adaptational") view is that people pay attention only or mainly to what is useful to them. The latter view is intuitively appealing but it is not satisfactory unless we can show a systematic relation between uses and classifications.

At any rate, it seems that both views contain elements of truth. The extremely detailed taxonomies of plants and animals that are important to a people can be partly explained in terms of economic value and other practical considerations. However, we find that the depth and detail of classifications sometimes go beyond the call of practical needs. The Kalam and other peoples could plant and gather and hunt just as well without constructing some of the higher-order categories they have constructed.

Do "folk" understandings of the environment have any value in a modernizing world? Ralph Bulmer comments:

> The knowledge of people who still live or recently have lived traditional ways of life is important for two reasons. First, scientific investigation of plants and animals can be speeded up enormously

if proper advantage is taken of what local people already know. Second, a respect for this knowledge and its cultural contexts can itself perhaps be a conservational force.... Knowledge is much more than being able to name things. It is knowing precisely where [the plants and animals] are to be found, ... how they make their nests or dens, what they feed on, what their seasonal movements are, and many other details of their behavior. Such information is very pertinent to local conservation programs. (Bulmer 1980:72)

We may note in passing that Kalam notions of conservation, like most peoples', are self-interested. Land is fallowed, trees are planted or protected, and prime hunting or fishing spots are reserved, but for the purpose of maximizing yields and catches within the near future or within the lifetimes of the owners and their children.

## Historical Context

Reconstructions of human prehistory in the Pacific have relied chiefly on three disciplines: archaeology, linguistics, and biological anthropology. The archaeological record contains little direct evidence of perishable artifacts and the intangible elements of culture. In these matters comparative linguistics can be a rich source of information. However, the central method of historical linguistics tells detailed stories only in cases where language families show numerous cognate sets. The set of surviving cognates diminishes with time, so that after a few thousand years the evidence grows very thin.

Archaeological evidence (Thomas, this volume) shows that humans reached the Australia-New Guinea continent upward of 40,000 years ago and by 30,000 years ago or earlier had settled New Britain and New Ireland and the main Solomons group. By contrast, there are no sites in the Pacific Islands beyond the Solomons group known to be older than 1300 B.C. These remoter islands evidently remained uninhabited by humans until the Austronesian diaspora.

The presence in western Melanesia of so many apparently unrelated language families, with no external relatives, points to a period of human occupation and local diversification upward of 10,000 years. It is not possible to be more precise than this, although one can speculate that some of the diverse language stocks of both the New Guinea mainland and Island Melanesia continue the languages of the earliest late Pleistocene settlers in these regions. As Australia and New Guinea were connected as recently as about 8,000 years ago, one might expect to find traces of old connections with Australian languages, but no solid evidence has been found (see Foley 1986 for some speculations).

The lexical diversity of the TNG languages is considerably greater than that exhibited by the Austronesian or Indo-European famiies, two families that probably broke up some 5,000 to 6,000 years ago. Indeed some of the larger subgroups of TNG appear themselves to be internally just as disparate as Indo-European or Austronesian (an example is the Madang subgroup, comprising over one hundred languages located mainly between the central coast of Madang Province and the Bismarck and Schrader Ranges). These facts suggest that the common ancestor of the TNG family probably broke up at least 6,000 years ago. Another clue resides in the distribution of borrowings by certain TNG languages of the Madang subgroup from an early stage of the Oceanic branch of Austronesian, indicating contact upward of 3,000 years ago between an already well differentiated branch of TNG and Austronesian languages.

TNG languages appear to have dispersed very early along the central highland spine of New Guinea. There we find many subgroups that are only very remotely related. By contrast, some of the TNG groups of the southwestern plains and swamplands of Irian Jaya are more closely related to each other and to the Ok family found in the Highlands and foothills around the Irian Jaya–Papua New Guinea border, pointing to a fairly recent expansion of TNG languages into this southwestern region, perhaps initially from the border Highlands area.

It seems clear that the large Trans New Guinea family expanded at the expense of other non-Austronesian families. What cultural advantage could have underpinned such an expansion? The development of agriculture is a possible explanation. By 9,000 to 6,000 years ago some New Guinea Highlands societies had begun to cultivate root crops (Golson 1977), and if TNG speakers were the first agriculturalists in the region it is likely that, like farmers elsewhere, they would have come to enjoy a considerable population advantage over peoples dependent on foraging (Bellwood 1996). But this hypothesis remains speculative. The widespread occurrence of forms like *ma* for "taro" is suggestive, but does not provide conclusive evidence for early cultivation of taro by TNG speakers. A similar term occurs in some Austronesian languages of the New Guinea area (though not elsewhere), and borrowing might have gone in either direction (and more than once).

Many groups in the Central Highlands use a special "pandanus language," with a vocabulary completely different from ordinary speech, when gathering and cooking the nuts of the mountain pandanus (*Pandanus julianetti* + *P. brosimus*). The wide use of such a language implies an earlier and longstanding importance of mountain pandanus nuts as a food source, perhaps going back to preagricultural times.

### *The Austronesian Dispersal: Continuity and Change in Culture and Environment*

We turn now to the history of the Austronesian family, which dominates the Pacific Islands outside of the New Guinea mainland. Where did the family originate? What factors enabled Austronesian languages to spread so widely? Was the dispersal everywhere associated with the gradual modification of an ancestral Austronesian material culture and social structure or did the colonists often undergo rapid cultural change after settling in new environments and/or after coming into contact with alien peoples? Were Austronesian languages often adopted by other peoples with whom the colonists traded or intermarried?

The most economical hypothesis places the dispersal center of any language family in the region of its greatest genetic diversity, i.e., where its primary branches or subgroups come together. The currently favored Austronesian subgrouping (Figure 15.3) points to the Taiwan-Philippines region as the probable dispersal center of Proto Austronesian, with Taiwan the more likely. Although they are few, the Taiwan languages appear to fall into several primary subgroups, coordinate with a single subgroup comprising the rest of Austronesian.

Proto Oceanic, the stage immediately ancestral to almost all the Austronesian languages of the southwest and central Pacific, was probably located in the Bismarck Archipelago and/or the facing north coast of New Guinea, perhaps at first based mainly on small islands because the large islands were already inhabited by non-Austronesian speakers. A northwest Melanesian location is indicated by the subgrouping pattern—the closest relatives of Oceanic are found at the western end of New Guinea—and by certain lexical reconstructions for fauna, which include names of animals confined to western Melanesia and eastern Indonesia (Blust 1982), e.g. *kasuari (cassowary), *kadroRa (cuscus, phalanger), and *mwaja (bandicoot).

The rake-like Oceanic family tree (Figure 15.3), with a scattering of high-order subgroups local to different parts of Melanesia, suggests that once Oceanic speakers began to disperse they quickly established colonies in various parts of the southwest Pacific. There were, however, considerable delays before Austronesian speakers reached their present limits. The island groups of Polynesia east of Samoa were probably not settled until the first millennium A.D. New Zealand was reached only about 1,000 years ago.

The archaeological record is consistent with linguistic evidence concerning the nature of early Austronesian directions of dispersal and material culture (see Bellwood 1985, 1996, Kirch 1997, Spriggs 1993, 1995). Several commentators have argued that key elements in the Austronesian diaspora must have been 1) possession of sophisticated watercraft and navigational abilities, allowing rapid dispersal across ocean gaps, and 2) an agricultural "package" involving crops and domestic animals, enabling Austronesian immigrants to dominate and marginalize or absorb nonfarming populations throughout Island Southeast Asia and to survive on islands with impoverished biota in the central Pacific.

In South China and Taiwan, sites with large, permanent villages, showing a range of ceramic vessels often with incised and stamped decorations, sometimes containing residues of grains, appear before 3000 B.C. These assemblages have forebears elsewhere on the East Asian mainland, especially in the Yangzi area. Sites with comparable features appear in the Philippines, Borneo, and Sulawesi only after about 2000 B.C (Bellwood 1985). Before the arrival of Austronesian horticulturalists, the Philippines and much of the Indo-Malaysian archipelago were, presumably, occupied exclusively by foraging peoples or small-scale horticulturists.

In the mid–second millennium B.C., sites with a range of ceramic pots, jars, and bowls, some showing distinctive, elaborate dentate-stamped and incised patterns, and with an elaborate suite of shell artifacts, appear suddenly in the Bismarck Archipelago, north of New Guinea. Some of these sites are associated with large villages having stilt houses. Within three or four centuries of its appearance in the Bismarcks, close relatives of this Lapita cultural complex, as it is known, turn up in various parts of the southwest Pacific, reaching 6000 km eastward across as far as Fiji, Tonga, and Samoa (Kirch 1997, Thomas, this volume). Lapita sites east of the main Solomons chain show some differences, e.g. a shift from stilt houses to houses built on the ground and some reduction in variety and degree of decoration of ceramic vessels.

One point of dispute among archaeologists is whether the various elements attributed to the Lapita culture were 1) introduced as a complete package by Austronesian speakers coming from the west, 2) mainly the product of long periods of local development or 3) the outcome of a mixture of introduced and local elements.

The linguistic evidence runs strongly against position 2). Lapita assemblages have a geographic distribution that strongly connects them to the Oceanic subgroup of Austronesian languages. And Oceanic languages show continuities in vocabulary indicating that Proto Oceanic speakers had an economy and technology similar to that attributed to the bearers of the Lapita culture. Furthermore, much of the Proto Oceanic economic and technological vocabulary goes back at least to Proto Malayo-Polynesian. It is hard to escape the conclusion that early Lapita was primarily an imported "Austronesian" culture. That does not, however, rule out the possibility that Lapita culture owed some elements to local innovation and to borrowing from "Papuan" speech communities. Subsequently, in some regions of western Melanesia, Oceanic and Papuan-speaking communities had upward of 3,000 years of trade and intermarriage, often with far-reaching effects on their languages and cultures.

There is a large body of cognate vocabulary that yields lexical reconstructions (see footnote 5) bearing on questions of continuity and change in culture and environment associated with the Austronesian diaspora.[15] This material leaves little doubt that the Austronesian expansion into and across the Pacific was, for the most part, carried out by colonists who imported their culture with them and whose linguistic descendants, in many cases, maintained many features of the ancestral culture. Upward of thirty terms to do with seafaring can be reconstructed for Proto Oceanic (Pawley and Pawley 1994). These terms are continued in widely scattered daughter languages from New Guinea to Micronesia and Polynesia and most of them continue Proto Malayo-Polynesian prototypes. Table 15.4 gives a sample.

Terms for double canoe are not reconstructible for Proto Oceanic, but are attributable to Proto central Pacific, suggesting that the double canoe may have been developed by Oceanic speakers as they moved into the central Pacific.

Lexical comparisons show that Proto Austronesian speakers had a cluster of terms for rice and millet: *pajay (rice plant, paddy), *beRas (husked rice), *Semay (cooked rice), *ZaRami (rice straw) and *zawa (millet), as well as *qumah (garden, cultivated field) (Blust 1995, n.d.). A group of terms for root crops

### Table 15.4

**Some Proto Oceanic Terms for Canoe Parts and Seafaring**

| | |
|---|---|
| *waga | outrigger canoe (generic); large sailing canoe |
| *tola | kind of large canoe |
| *baban | plank; canoe plank or strake |
| *soka(r) | thwart |
| *(q)oRa | washstrake, probably topstrake |
| *pataR | platform (over hull and outrigger) |
| *saman | outrigger float |
| *kiajo | outrigger boom |
| *patoto | connective sticks attaching float |
| *kata(q)e, kate(q)a | free side of canoe, opposite the outrigger |
| *layaR | sail |
| *jila | boom or yard of (triangular) sail |
| *ŋuju | projecting headboard of prow |
| *pose | (canoe) paddle |
| *lima(s), nima(s) | bailer |
| *laŋon | rollers |
| *laŋoni | place rollers under a boat |
| *ujan, *lujan | to load (a boat); cargo, freight |
| *quliŋ | to steer; rudder |

### Table 15.5

**Some Proto Oceanic Terms for Horticulture and Food Plants**

| | |
|---|---|
| *quma | garden, plantation |
| *poki | to clear ground for planting |
| *talo(s) | taro, *Colocasia esculenta* |
| *piRaq | elephant ear taro, *Alocasia macrorrhiza* |
| *bulaka | swamp taro, *Cyrtosperma chamissonis* |
| *qupi | greater yam, *Dioscorea alata*; yam (generic) |
| *up(e,a) | taro seedling |
| *pudi | banana, *Musa* cultivars |
| *joRaga | banana, *Australimusa* group |
| *topu | sugarcane, *Saccharum officinarum* |
| *laqia | ginger, *Zingiber officinale* |
| *kuluR | breadfruit, *Artocarpus altilis* |
| *Rabia | sago, *Metroxylon* spp., mainly *Metroxylon sagu* |
| *sag(u) | sago starch |
| *talise | Java almond, Indian almond, *Terminalia catappa* |
| *qipi | Tahitian chestnut, Pacific chestnut, *Inocarpus fagifer* |
| *[ka]ŋaRi | canarium almond, *Canarium* spp. |
| *kapika | Malay apple and rose apple, *Eugenia* spp. |
| *ñonum | *Morinda citrifolia* |
| *tawan | *Pometia pinnata* |
| *quRis | Polynesian plum, hog plum, Tahitian apple, *Spondias cytherea* |
| *ñatu(q) | tree with avocado-like fruit and hard wood, *Burckella obovata* |

are attributable to Proto Malayo-Polynesian but not (on present evidence) to Proto Austronesian: *tales (taro: Colocasia sp.), *qubi (yam: Dioscorea sp.), *biRaq (giant arum: Alocasia sp.). Whereas all the root crop terms persist in Proto Oceanic, none of those for grain crops do, indicating that rice and millet were not part of the Proto Oceanic economy. It it is likely that cereals were less suited than root and tree crops to the tropical environments encountered by the Austronesian colonists. Table 15.5 lists a selection of Proto Oceanic terms having to do with horticulture and food plants, based on Ross (1996a).

Although they came to dominate the Philippines and Indonesia, Austronesian languages had much less impact in mainland New Guinea, where they are mainly confined to certain patches along the north coast and southeast Papua. This distribution suggests either that some of the non-Austronesian peoples of the north coast were already practicing agriculture when the Austronesians arrived or at least had an economy capable of supporting high population densities. At any rate, they had the numbers and organization to hold their ground. There are abundant signs that the Austronesians at first had a similar, marginal distribution in Halmahera, Timor, New Britain, New Ireland, Bougainville, and the Solomons. However, in due course a large part of these regions became Austronesian-speaking, though not without a good deal of linguistic and cultural exchange between immigrants and aboriginal populations (Dutton and Tryon 1993).

The Pacific Islands

## Notes

[1] I am indebted to Ann Chowning, Margaret Florey, Robin Hide, Malcolm Ross, Matthew Spriggs, and Gerard Ward for useful comments on the first draft. Research reported here on the Kalam language and ethnobiology was supported by grants from the Wenner Gren Foundation for Anthropological Research, the NZ University Grants Committee, and the Papua New Guinea Biological Foundation. For present purposes the Pacific Islands are defined as consisting of Melanesia, Micronesia and Polynesia, i.e. "Oceania." However, it will be necessary to touch on relationships with languages of contiguous regions. Within Melanesia a distinction is made between New Guinea and what is often termed "Island Melanesia."

[2] These are fairly conservative estimates. Linguists usually regard two speech traditions as different languages if connected speech in the two is mutually unintelligible for most practical purposes. This criterion leaves a considerable residue of unclear cases, where a parent language has given rise to a chain of dialects that continue to diverge, as in the case of the Romance languages, where there is still some mutual intelligibility between (Castillian) Spanish, Portuguese, Catalan, Italian, Romansch, Sardinian, and others.

[3] Two language families (like two people) are spoken of as "unrelated" if they are not known to share a common ancestor. It is not possible to prove that two languages are not, ultimately, genetically related; one can only show that there is no good evidence for positing a genetic connection. To establish that languages are related one needs to demonstrate that they share resemblances that must be attributed to direct inheritance rather than to other causes—borrowing, chance, or universal characteristics of human speech. Among the kinds of resemblances indicating common descent are systematic sound correspondences in words with related meanings.

[4] We find striking differences between languages in the domains that are elaborated. It is common for small communities to distinguish by name over one thousand different wild plants and for horticultural communities to name fifty or more varieties of a single plant species when it is a staple crop. The Kaluli of Papua New Guinea, who live surrounded by wet rain forest near Mt. Bosavi, have more than ninety words for different kinds of noises made by water (S. Feld pers. comm.).

[5] One way of measuring the linguistic diversity in a region is simply to count the number of different languages—comparable to reckoning diversity of fauna, say, by counting the number of species. But if all the languages—or bird species—of a region were to belong to a single family, the genetic diversity in these domains would be shallow, no matter how large the number of languages or species. A measure of deep genetic diversity is the number of distinct genetic stocks (language groups that have no established relationships to any other groups).

[6] Linguistic "reconstructions" are elements (sounds, words, etc.) attributed to a prehistoric language on the basis of inference, as opposed to observation. For a reconstruction to be reliable it must be based on systematic agreements between elements in recorded languages, following the procedures of the genetic comparative method, which rests crucially on the principle of regularity of sound change. See also footnote 3.

[7] The Oceanic group is defined by a number of common innovations in sound system and grammar. Evidence for Oceanic was first put forward by Dempwolff (1934–38), and subsequent research (e.g. Ross 1988) has refined his arguments and generally strengthened the case.

[8] This subgrouping is based on many sources, summarized in Pawley and Ross (1993, 1995). Less conservative subgroupings would lump together certain of these subgroups.

[9] Wurm (1975) wishes to lump all the Papuan languages from New Britain to the Solomons in an East Papuan phylum, together with Yeletne of Rossel Island. This remains a highly problematic proposal.

[10] Kalam society, ethnobiology, and language are described in various works by Ralph Bulmer and his associates, including Bulmer (1967), Bulmer and Majnep (1977, 1983, 1990), Bulmer and Pawley et al. (n.d.).

[11] The speech traditions we now call Kalam consist of various named dialects, which belong to two main subgroups known as Etp language and Ti language, which are about as different from each other as Italian and Spanish.

[12] Since 1978 Majnep has written all his works in Kalam, with English translations by his collaborators.

[13] When comparing indigenous and "Western" views of Nature we need to keep in mind that there is no one view common to the Western world. Scientific taxonomies of plants and animals differ profoundly from the taxonomies of laypeople, and folk taxonomies vary considerable from one Western society to another.

[14] For all New Guinea peoples plant resources are the most important single natural resource, far outweighing animal resources. Powell (1976) lists over two hundred New Guinea plant species that are used for medicinal and technological purposes.

[15] More than 5,000 lexical reconstructions have been attributed to early stages of Austronesian (Blust n.d.). A Proto Polynesian lexical file has grown to over 3,000 reconstructions (Biggs n.d.). A Proto Oceanic lexicon and thesaurus with perhaps 2,000 lexemes is in preparation at the Australian National University.

## Appendix 15.1

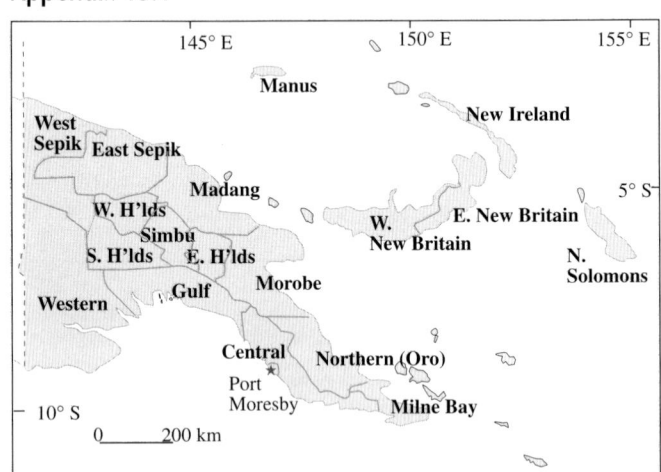

*Major provinces of Papua New Guinea*

# Bibliography

Bellwood, P. 1985. *Prehistory of the Indo-Malaysian Archipelago.* New York/Sydney: Academic Press.

Bellwood, P. 1996. The origins and spread of agriculture in the Indo-Pacific region. In *The Origins and Spread of Agricuture and Pastoralism in Eurasia,* ed. D. Harris, 465-498. London: UCL Press.

Bellwood, P., J. J. Fox, and D. Tryon, eds. 1995. *The Austronesians: historical and comparative perspectives.* Canberra: Department of Anthropology, Research School of Pacific and Asian Studies, Australian National University.

Berlin, B. 1991. The chicken and the egg-head revisited: further evidence for the intellectualist bases of ethnobiological classification. In *Man and a half: essays in Pacific anthropology and ethnobiology in honour of Ralph Bulmer,* ed. A. Pawley, 57-66. Auckland: Polynesian Society.

Biggs, B. n.d. Proto-Polynesian lexical file (POLLEX). Computer file. [1994] Department of Maori Studies, University of Auckland.

Blust, R. A. 1978. Eastern Malayo-Polynesian: a subgrouping argument. In *Second International Conference on Austronesian Linguistics: Proceedings,* ed. S.A. Wurm and L. Carrington, 181-234. Canberra: Pacific Linguistics C-61.

Blust, R. A. 1982. The linguistic value of the Wallace Line. *Bijdragen tot de Taal-, Land en Volkenkunde* 138:231-250.

Blust, R. A. 1993-94. Central and Central-Eastern Malayo-Polynesian. *Oceanic Linguistics* 32: 241-293.

Blust, R. A. 1995. The prehistory of the Austronesian-speaking peoples: a view from language. *Journal of World Prehistory* 9(4): 453-510.

Blust, R. A. 1996. The position of the Formosan languages: method and theory in Austronesian comparative linguistics. In *Papers for International Symposium on Austronesian Studies Relating to Taiwan,* ed. P. J-K. Li, C-H. Stang, and Y-K. Huang, 585-650. Tapei: Institute of Historical Philology, Academia Sinica.

Blust, R. A. 1996. Austronesian comparative dictionary. Computer file. Department of Linguistics, University of Hawai'i.

Bulmer, R. N. H. 1967. Why is the cassowary not a bird? *Man* (new series) 2: 5-25.

Bulmer, R. N. H. 1970. Which came first: the chicken or the egghead? In Echanges et communications: mélanges offerts à Claude Levi-Strauss à l'occasion de son 60ēme anniversaire," ed. J. Pouillon and P. Miranda, 1069-1091. Mouton: The Hague

Bulmer, R. N. H. 1980. Traditional conservation practices in Papua New Guinea. In *Traditional conservation practices in Papua New Guinea: implications for today,* ed. L. Morauta, J. Pernatta, and W. Heaney, 39-77. Institute for Applied Social and Economic Research, Boroko, Papua New Guinea.

Bulmer, R., and A. Pawley, with J. Kias, I. S. Majnep, and S. P. Gi. n.d. A dictionary of the Kalam language, Papua New Guinea. Printout. Dept. Linguistics, Research School of Pacific Studies, Australian National University.

Clark, R. 1997. Proto Central and North Vanuatu reconstructions. Computer file, Department of Anthropology, University of Auckland.

Crowley, T., 1990. *From Beach-la-Mar to Bislama: the development of the national language of Vanuatu.* Oxford: Oxford University Press.

Dempwolff, O. 1934-38. *Vergleichende Lautlehre des austronesichen Wortschatzes.* Vols. 1 (1934), 2 (1937), 3 (1938). Berlin, Dietrich Reimer.

Dutton. T. E. and D. T. Tryon, eds. 1993. *Language contact and change in the Austronesian world.* Berlin: Mouton de Gruyter.

Foley, W. F. 1986. *Papuan languages.* Cambridge University Press.

Geraghty, P. 1983. *Topics in Fijian language history.* Oceanic Linguistics Special Publication 18. Honolulu: University of Hawai'i Press.

Golson, J. 1977. No room at the top: agricultural intensification in the New Guinea Highlands. In *Sunda and Sahul: prehistoric studies in Southeast Asia, Melanesia and Australia,* ed. J. Allen, J. Golson and R. Jones, 601-638. London/New York/San Francisco: Academic Press.

Green, R. C., and A. Pawley (in press). Early Oceanic architectural forms and settlement patterns: linguistic, archaeological and ethnological perspectives. In *Archaeology and language III: artefacts, languages and texts: building connections,* ed. R. Blench and M. Spriggs. London: Routledge.

Grimes, B., ed. 1992. *Ethnologue: languages of the world.* 12th ed. Dallas: Summer Institute of Linguistics.

Hayes, T., 1991. Interest, use and interest in uses in folk biology. In *Man and a half: essays in Pacific anthropology and ethnobiology in honour of Ralph Bulmer,* ed. A. Pawley, 109-114. Auckland: Polynesian Society.

Irwin, G. 1992. *The prehistoric exploration and colonisation of the Pacific.* Cambridge: Cambridge University Press.

Keesing, R. C. 1988. Melanesian languages and the Oceanic substrate. Stanford University Press.

Kirch, P. V. 1997. *The Lapita peoples.* Oxford: Blackwell.

Lynch, J., and F. Pat, eds. 1996. *Oceanic studies: proceedings of the First International Conference on Oceanic Linguistics.* Canberra: Pacific Linguistics C-133.

Lynch, J., M. Ross, and T. Crowley, eds. (forthcoming). *The Oceanic languages.* London: Curzon Press.

Majnep, I. S., and R. Bulmer. 1977. *Birds of My Kalam country.* Auckland and Oxford University Presses.

Majnep, I. S., and R. Bulmer. 1983. *Some wild food plants of the Kalam people.* Auckland University Working Papers in Anthropology no. 63.

Majnep, I. S., and R. Bulmer. 1990. *Kalam hunting traditions.* vols. 1-6. (ed. A. Pawley). Auckland University Working Papers in Anthropology nos 85-90.

Majnep, I. S., A. Pawley, and R. Bulmer. 1996. Kalam plant lore. Printout. Dept. of Linguistics, Research School of Pacific Studies, Australian National University.

Marck, J. 1986. Micronesian dialects and the overnight voyage. *Journal of the Polynesian Society* 95(2):253-258.

Marck, J. 1997. Polynesian language and culture history. Ph.D. thesis, Department of Linguistics, Research School of Pacific and Asian Studies, Australian National University.

Mühlhäusler, P. 1979. *Growth and structure of the lexicon of New Guinea Pidgin.* Canberra: Pacific Linguistics C-52.

Paijmans, K., 1976. Vegetation. In *New Guinea vegetation,* ed. K. Paijmans, 23-104. Canberra: CSIRO.

Paijmans, K., ed. 1976. *New Guinea vegetation.* Canberra: CSIRO in association with Australian National University Press.

Pawley, A., ed. 1991. *Man and a half: essays in Pacific anthropology and ethnobiology in honour of Ralph Bulmer.* Auckland: Polynesian Society.

Pawley, A., and R. C. Green. 1984. The Proto Oceanic language community. In *Out of Asia: peopling the Americas and the Pacific,* ed. R. Kirk and E. Szathmary, 161-184. Canberra, Dept. Pacific History, Australian National University.

Pawley, A., and M. Pawley. 1994. Early Austronesian terms for canoe parts and sailing. In *Austronesian terminologies: continuity and change,* ed. A. Pawley and M. Ross, 329-361. Canberra: Pacific Linguistics C-127.

Pawley, A., and M. Ross. 1993. Austronesian historical linguistics and culture history. *Annual Review of Anthropology* 22:42-5-59

Pawley, A., and M. Ross. 1995. The prehistory of the Oceanic languages: a current view. In *The Austronesians: historical and comparative perspectives,* ed. P. Bellwood, J. Fox and D. Tryon, 39-74. Department of Anthropology, Research School of Pacific and Asian Studies, Australian National University.

Pawley, A., and M. Ross, eds. 1994. *Austronesian terminologies: continuity and change.* Canberra: Pacific Linguistics C-127.

Powell, J. M. 1976. Ethnobotany. In *New Guinea vegetation,* ed. K. Paijmans, 106–183. Canberra: CSIRO.

Ross, M. D. 1988. *Proto Oceanic and the Austronesian languages of Western Melanesia.* Canberra: Pacific Linguistics C-98.

Ross, M. D. 1996a. Reconstructing food plant terms and associated terminologies in Proto Oceanic. In *Oceanic Studies: Proceedings of the First International Conference on Oceanic Linguistics,* ed. J. Lynch and F. Pat, 165-223. Canberra: Pacific Linguistics C-133.

Ross, M. D. 1996b. Proto Oceanic terms for pottery. In *Studies in Oceanic culture history: essays in honour of Roger Green,* ed. Davidson et al., 67-82. Dunedin: Journal of New Zealand Archaeology special publication.

Sebeok, T. E. 1971. *Current trends in linguistics, vol. 8 . Linguistics in Oceania.* The Hague: Mouton.

Spriggs, M. 1993. Island Melanesia: the last 10,000 years. In *Community of culture: the people and prehistory of the Pacific,* ed. M. Spriggs, D. Yen, W. Ambrose, R. Jones, A. Thorne, A. Andrews, 187-205. Canberra: Prehistory Department, Australian National University.

Spriggs, M. 1995. The Lapita culture and Austronesian prehistory in Oceania. In *Austronesian terminologies: continuity and change,* ed. A. Pawley and M. Ross, 112-133. Canberra: Pacific Linguistics C-127.

Tryon, D. 1976. *New Hebrides languages: an internal classification.* Canberra: Pacific Linguistics, Series C-50.

Tryon, D., and G. Hackman. 1983. *Solomon Islands languages: an internal classification.* Canberra: Pacific Linguistics C-72.

Tryon, D., ed. 1995. *Comparative Austronesian dictionary.* (5 vols.). Berlin: Mouton de Gruyter.

Williams, N. M. & G. Baines, eds. 1993. *Traditional ecological knowledge. wisdom for sustainable development.* Centre for Resource and Environmental Studies, Australian National University.

Wurm, S. A., ed. 1975. *New Guinea area languages and linguistics* vol. 1. Canberra: Pacific Linguistics C-39.

Wurm, S. A., and L. Carrington, eds. 1978. *Second International Conference on Austronesian Linguistics: Proceedings.* Canberra: Pacific Linguistics C-61.

Wurm, S. A., and S. Hattori, eds. 1981-83. *Language atlas of the Pacific area.* Vol. 1 (1981). vol. 2 (1983). Canberra: Pacific Linguistics C-66, C-67.

Wurm, S. A., P. Mühlhäusler, and D. Tryon, eds. 1996. *Atlas of Languages of Intercultural Communication in the Pacific, Asia and the Americas.* (3 vols). Berlin: Mouton de Gruyter.

# Social Relations

*Lamont Lindstrom*

Alexander Selkirk, marooned in the Juan Fernandez Islands of the southeastern Pacific between 1704 and 1709, inspired one of literature's most enduring sociological horror stories. In *Robinson Crusoe*, Daniel Defoe retold Selkirk's castaway experience to explore the individual's relations with society. By the end of the story, after surviving several years of horrible and desperate isolation, Crusoe builds a new society on his desert island beginning with his Man Friday. Enduring debates about the "individual" and whether or not individuals can exist outside society, and also about humanity's estrangement from nature, have ensured the lasting popularity of Defoe's novel (one of the prototypes of the genre).

These issues began to take on a particular urgency in Defoe's eighteenth century as capitalism and a system of economic classes developed, reshaping long-standing social relational patterns. Humans are all social animals, but understandings of the person and the group differ from place to place, and change from time to time. Early European explorers, expecting distant Pacific islands to be deserted like Crusoe's sanctuary, were surprised to find them inhabited. We now know that, apart from odd castaways like Selkirk, the human occupation of the Pacific Islands has been a social endeavor. External observers have frequently turned to Pacific Island societies to explore the nature of individuality and sociability. They have also turned to Pacific societies to understand the connections between social structure and the environment.

## Social Relation, Identity, Role

A variety of interests have motivated European efforts to map out Pacific social orders, including the colonialist imperatives of governance and control. Ongoing concern to make sociological sense of the Pacific has mirrored Western debates over the definition and scope of individuality and society, and questions about how individuals fit into that larger social order. Over the past two centuries, Pacific cultures have provided data for alternative constructions of individuality and society that Western critics have used to either justify or to challenge their own social orders. The romantic South Seas or, alternatively, the savage South Seas (see Herman, this volume) both acquired their peculiar character in a contrastive relationship with a Europe imagined to be enervated and dreary or a Europe celebrated as admirably evolved and civilized.

Like those fabulous blind men who grasp different parts of the elephant, scholars have approached Pacific social orders at several different levels. For some, the basic unit of analysis is the individual and then the network of social relationships. Others start with the social relationship as the fundamental social unit—a dyad that relates two persons into larger groups and institutions. And others begin with those groups (clans, lineages, villages, chiefdoms) and institutions (the economy, religion, moiety systems, and so forth) as primary units of analysis. Whether focused at the level of person, relational dyad, or institution, a common conclusion is that Pacific Islanders are, even today, less individualistic and more embedded within their social relationships than are, say, most Americans, Europeans, or Australians.

Before surveying social relations in the Pacific, we should first recollect the standard sociological model of a relationship. This, simply, is a dyad comprising two endpoints ("social identities") joined together by culturally organized exchange behavior (a "role"). This schema of identity and role attempts to capture the basics of how people relate in culturally patterned ways. Every social relation involves a pair of social identities, or capacities or positions, that people must assume in order to relate together. Most important social identities are labeled, e.g. parent/child, brother/sister, teacher/student, chief/commoner, lover/lover, friend/friend. Children born into a society learn the inventory of locally recognized social identities (see Ochs 1988; Schieffelin 1990).

Along with paired identities, children also learn local expectations of the "roles," or the appropriate behavior, or culturally scripted interaction, associated with related identities. The minimal exchange expectations of "roles" must be met, or else the claim to the associated identity may be lost. If I do not treat my children right, my identity as a proper father may be impugned. If I behave unexpectedly, my identity claims may lose social legitimacy. "Treating someone right," or "relating" in general, always involves some form of exchange. Social behavior thus can be rephrased largely as exchange. For relationships to endure, the people in them must at least occasionally exchange something. And important relations—those beyond the casual or passing—require ongoing and repeated acts of exchange. When interaction ceases, relations fade away.

There are four basic sorts of relational exchange tokens: communications (words and nonverbal signals); acts of body contact such as petting, touching, kissing, blows, and beatings; things, goods, or material items, some of which are animate (pigs, for example, along with other animal and plant species are important Pacific exchange items); and, occasionally, other human beings. One's "role" comprises expectations about the exchange of these tokens within a social relationship, given one's identity therein as, say, a "chief" or a "mother" or a "husband."

During any day, people take on many social identities, some simultaneously, to engage in (i.e. to communicate or exchange within) one or another social relationship. Most relationships are context-dependent, associated with particular times and places.

Risi, for example, who lives in Port Vila, Vanuatu, waking in the morning finds herself engaged mostly within child/parent relations. Walking to school highlights her friend/friend identities. Then, within schoolroom context, student/teacher relations come to the fore, interpolated with ongoing student/student, friend/friend, and perhaps girlfriend/boyfriend connections. After school, she takes on economic identities of co-worker/co-worker and employee/boss in the small trade store where she works. In the evening, she returns home and her kin identities once again become predominant.

A few social identities, notably those of gender and age, and also identities of race and kin-group membership, are less tied to specific contexts in most Pacific societies. Instead, people carry these fundamental (although still culturally recognized) social capacities around within them throughout the day, wherever they are. Identities of age, gender, and kinship often influence other sorts of social relations in which that person takes part, be these economic, political, or religious.

The diversity of cultures across the immense spread of the Pacific Ocean makes difficult attempts to generalize or summarize Pacific social relations. One can describe as many differences as commonalities among Pacific cultures. Life, and the social relations that structure it, on O'ahu, Tanna, Fais, Viti Levu, and Guam differ in remarkable ways. Moreover, many of the sorts of social relations in which islanders engage in the year 2000 are unlike those their ancestors enjoyed in 1900 and before, and this is as true of isolated West Futuna as it is of metropolitan Honolulu or Auckland. And social relations in Pacific towns and cities, where people are more firmly tied into global economic networks, are no longer the same as those back in rural villages or outer-island hinterlands.

This chapter, which takes a rural ("traditional") rather than urban perspective, explores general features of Pacific social relationships. It reviews basic Pacific understandings of the "person" and the means by which islanders define, create, cultivate, and repair their social relations. In so doing, however, it must neglect much of the diversity and complexity of social life in the islands.

# Personhood

The tenor and organization of a social relationship obviously have much to do with the "persons" involved. And the Pacific person—at least in traditionalist regions—may not be necessarily the same as the "individual," as this has developed in the West. Many have suggested, in fact, that the individual (as we know ourselves to be today) appeared rather recently in European history, an artifact of modernity, of the Enlightenment, and of an industrialized, capitalist mode of production. Everyone conceives of "persons." All languages have words for "me," and "you" and also various permutations of "he and/or she," "we," "you all," and "they." Everyone also has a notion of a "self"—some intellectual and emotional consciousness of being. But people may not conceive of their persons and their selves as individualistic, at least not to the same degree.

Those of us who know ourselves as individuals have absorbed a set of values and expectations about that individuality (even if our life experiences and emotions do not always measure up to the ideal). The Western person (and self)—at least if this person is normal and "balanced"—should live within his or her skin. The person is bounded, autonomous, and unique. Individual identity does not spill over to incorporate other, also presumably autonomous, individuals. Nor does personal identity include parts of the landscape. Zen-like experiences of *satori*, in which the boundaries of individual personality melt away and one is now just One-with-Nature, are seemly only for mystics, the insane, and drug abusers. Furthermore, individuals should strive for a unified knowledge of self, so that life becomes a dramatic journey with a satisfactory beginning, middle, and end, and (if all goes well) a purpose as well.

Those who have concerned themselves with personhood here and there about the Pacific have argued that many islanders conceive of themselves—and therefore of their social relations in general—in less individualistic terms. In many island cultures, sense of self goes beyond the skin to incorporate other people and also aspects of objects and landscape. Some may also have less coherent, less unified, and less singular conceptions of selves, as analyses of the person and its ontology in different Pacific cultures have suggested. (See, for examples, accounts of Pacific ethnopsychologies in White and Kirkpatrick 1985.)

## Polysided Polynesians

The constitution of the Samoan "person" has been debated since the early work of Margaret Mead in the 1920s. (Mead, like many American anthropologists of her day, was interested in the fit between personality and cultural patterns; see also Levy 1973.) Bradd Shore (1982) has argued that Samoans expect behavior to reflect people's multiple "sides" rather than some singular and integrated inner self. The Samoan person, like a prism, is faceted:

> While the European concept of the integrated, coherent, and "rounded" personality suggests the metaphor of a sphere, the most perfectly "integrated" of objects, the contrasting Samoan metaphor implicit in the Samoan conception of person is a many-faceted gem. (1982:141)

The person differs depending on which facet of personality is turned to the fore—which side is then socially engaged. This gem metaphor emphasizes the several surfaces of personality rather than supposing some inner depth where the truth, or authenticity, of a person might be sought.

Samoan personality facets include one's kinship and political identities and also a set of character traits. People may have complex and changeable characters as well as multiple social identities. Shore notes:

> Samoans on the whole do not focus on a temperamental or behavioral consistency within a person, although they may recognize one or more traits as strong within that person. The emphasis for evaluating people is not the

consistency of behavior with behavior, or of trait with trait, but rather the appropriateness of a trait to a given situation. (1982:140)

People do not conceive of an integrated, consistent self inhabiting a body over the long term. Promising, for instance, has different weight in Samoa than it does in the West insofar as there is no internally consistent person to guarantee that the promise will be fulfilled from one context to the next. Also, Samoans, like most Pacific Islanders, do not value privacy (or at least do not admit liking to be alone, as this would be impolite and suspicious). Shore suggests that, alone, people may lose grasp of who they are, since their personality depends on and reflects their relations with others, rather than welling upward from a sense of having a coherent inner self that inhabits their bodies. It is a commonplace that islanders almost everywhere fail to appreciate Western demands for individual privacy—time alone that helps shore up the boundaries of our personalities when these become frayed. Privacy, in the Pacific, menaces rather than protects the self.

## Melanesian Dividuals

Drawing partly on her research near Mt. Hagen, in the Highlands of Papua New Guinea, Marilyn Strathern (1988; see also Read 1955) has suggested that Melanesians are "dividuals" rather than individuals. The latter term, from the Latin for "indivisible," clearly reflects Western notions of the bounded, unified, and autonomous self. Strathern proposes that Papua New Guineans know themselves to comprise divisable parts, each of which reflects their participation in various social relationships, particularly kin relations. She writes:

> A Melanesian model of the person would already incorporate the fact of connection or relation. The person is not axiomatically "an individual" who, as in Western formulations, derives an integrity from its position as somehow prior to society. (1988:93)

Strathern argues that people conceive of their bodies as a "microcosm of relations" (1988:131). The body, too, and not just the self, is built up of different bits and pieces, the residue of past and present exchanges with others. People in a relationship exchange goods, and these "things are conceptualized as parts of persons" (1988:178). I, as a person, include part of you—my mother—because of the direct impact your presence has had on me, and also because the food and other objects that you give me remain part of you as I take them into my body.

A conception of dividuated persons whose parts are composed of personalized objects they receive from other dividuated persons obviously challenges the simple Western model of a social relationship. In this model, recall, two independent individuals exchange tokens (objects, words) that they believe to be disconnectable from the self. We might still use the standard sociological model of two identities linked by exchange, however. If Strathern is correct, then this does not in Melanesia represent two autonomous individuals swapping alienable objects. Rather, the relational dyad comprises a side or part (or Samoan facet) of one person that incorporates—on the opposite side of the relationship—some part of *another* person as well as the inalienable items, words, and goods that flow within (and not between) this particular facet of joint personality.

## Micronesian Insides

Islanders on Ifaluk, according to Catherine Lutz (1988), share the Samoan and New Guinean concept of the person as fundamentally social: "The person is first and foremost a social creature and only secondarily, and in a limited way, an autonomous individual" (1988:81). The Ifaluk have weak notions of personal boundaries and "it is considered natural that one person's thought should influence another's" (1988:88). A person's "internal processes are seen as acquiring their significance in relation to social processes" (1988:96). Because Ifaluk boundaries between self and other are porous, people understand their feelings mostly to originate externally rather than to emerge from internal emotional processes: "their emotional lives *are* their social lives" (1988:101). Again, aspects of the Pacific self are located at least partly outside the body.

These analyses of Pacific understandings of the person as faceted, multiple, and not completely contained within the body help explain a number of other aspects of Pacific cultures. Some, for example, have noted difficulties in eliciting coherent life histories from islanders. If people do not conceive of themselves as an autonomous and unique personality, they may be unaccustomed to talking about themselves as if they have only one long story. Only those who believe that they remain essentially the same through time and space—who imagine that they are engaged in some life journey that has a beginning, middle, and an end—are accustomed to telling coherent, developmental life stories. Moreover, in places such as Fiji, chiefs and important storytellers may use the first-person pronoun "I" to recount what some ancestral namesake accomplished in the past (Lindstrom 1982). One's personality, here—at least in the ways people have of talking—can incorporate dead personages and historic feats.

Many islanders have several personal names, furthermore, that key various facets, or sides, of their personality. They may have various names simultaneously and they also may change their names throughout their lives, as different aspects of their personality emerge, or as they change character altogether. My Vanuatu friend Sating, for example, was first called by another name. Arguing over a boy, she by mischance killed a girl by knocking her down and smashing her head against a tree. After a lengthy dispute-settlement process, her father gave her to the family of the dead girl. She then took the name of her victim, Sating, in order to replace (or impersonate) the girl within her grieving family.

Thus we can understand how many islanders believe that unbalanced or otherwise unsettled social relations can make them sick. Social discord (which we would see as external) leads to imbalance, or illness, in the body. Thinking and feeling—

processes that we believe to occur within the body—in many island ethnopsychologies emanate from a person's matrix of relationships (which islanders might experience as part of the self). In most Pacific societies, there is little use for a language of individual creativity to explain the origins of new ideas. Rather, a rhetoric of inspiration and of learning from others is used to account for novelty. Knowledge comes from the dead, or from parents or elders (Lindstrom 1990). Here, as with disease, islanders look beyond the body to assign responsibility and to explain ideas that we might see as originating within individuals.

But one must resist the temptation to draw overly rigid oppositions between faceted, dividual islanders, on the one hand, and unified, coherent Westerners, on the other. Several excellent life histories of islanders have been compiled, for example, despite their supposed lack of coherent selves. These are people who can and do think of their lives as organized developmentally from time to time and event to event (see e.g. Keesing 1978; A. Strathern 1979). Sating's new family, too, never completely accepted her as a replacement for their dead daughter. Nor did the first Sating's boyfriend welcome the new Sating's continuing amorous advances. Although Sating had acquired the personality of her dead rival, her original personality—or perhaps even her individuality—was not forgotten.

Moreover, people everywhere today are engaged, to one degree or another, in global communicative and exchange networks that circulate notions of the autonomous and responsible individual. The image of the normally autonomous person in the West can also be a caricature. Many of our neighbors may be as many-sided as the ordinary Pacific person, as depicted in the above analyses.

In summary, the constitution and interplay of social relations depends on local understandings of the "person." The standard sociological model of a relationship comprising autonomous individuals linked by communication and exchange distorts Pacific notions of the constitution of personhood, and how persons relate themselves together into larger social units. These units, in the islands, most commonly are kinship groups.

## Kinship

Kin relations structure most islanders' everyday lives (Figure 16.1). Residence groups are based on kinship. Kinship determines the membership of many economic enterprises as well as political and religious associations. Most people live, work, politic, and worship with kin, and these relations define much of who they are. The extended family is common throughout the region, except among the most cosmopolitan. Even in urban centers, such as Papeete, Noumea, and 'Apia, and among those communities (e.g. the Hawaiians and New Zealand Maori) that are now encapsulated within settler states, kinship remains important. The Hawaiian *'ohana* ("family") and the Maori *whaanau* ("family"), *hapuu* ("subtribe"), and *iwi* ("tribe") remain in various ways socially and symbolically powerful today.

Various descent and marriage patterns occur in Pacific societies today. Kinship structures before the colonial era may

*Figure 16.1.* Father and son construct a new house in Samaria village, Tanna, Vanuatu (photo LL).

have been even more diverse. Monogamy and polygyny both were customary marriage practices in Pacific societies. Although monogamy has spread to become the standard marriage form, especially since most islanders today are Christian, polygyny also is not uncommon, especially in parts of Melanesia, where some successful men may marry more than one wife. Jimmy Stephens, for instance, a political leader involved in the independence of Vanuatu, was partly renowned for the number of his wives.

All the major types of descent reckoning occur in one Pacific society or another. Matrilineal rules of descent determine kin-group membership in parts of Melanesia (e.g. northern Vanuatu, the Trobriand Islands, parts of Bougainville) and Micronesia (e.g. Pohnpei, Chuuk, Palau). In these societies children become members of their mother's (and mother's brothers') lineages and clans. Elsewhere, people follow patrilineal or cognatic rules to define the bounds of their descent groups. In patrilineal systems, children share the father's kin-group affiliations. With cognatic (or "bilateral") descent rules, individuals may choose which of their various kin connections, through their mother's or father's side, to activate and therefore which local kin-groups to join.

Other traditional kin practices persist as well. In many Pacific societies, particularly in Polynesia, brother/sister ties are emphasized in one fashion or another. In some communities, as in Tonga and Fiji, older sisters command their brothers' respect. These traditional sibling ties continue to affect contemporary political relations among the ruling families of Tonga and Fiji. Brothers and sisters and also, in some places, sons-in-law and mothers-in-law must avoid certain topics of discussion (such as those involving sexuality and pregnancy) and sometimes avoid one another altogether. This ritual avoidance may relate to marriage practices: unless a sister marries into a certain kingroup, her brother may be unable to marry a woman from that group. Ritualized "joking" relations sometimes parallel these avoidance relations. Men who stand to each other in the kin category "brother-in-law," for instance, in some societies must joke around. Brother/brother relations, too, are politically and economically important throughout the Pacific (see Marshall 1983).

Whatever descent rule locally applies, kin-groups such as extended families, clans, and lineages are significant units within the social fabric. In rural areas, people's land and sea rights continue to derive from their kin-group memberships. Even in regions where land has been commodified or otherwise alienated from customary land-tenure systems, people may still assert rights to that property based on their kin identities. In urban areas, migrants typically employ kin connections to acquire places to live and also often employment. Neighborhoods and settlements of people all from the same region have emerged in or around most Pacific cities. Islanders prefer to live with kin, or at the least with people from home areas. In Papua New Guinea, for example, the term "*wantok* ('same language') system" describes the ongoing resilience of rural kin and regional ties within urban areas and within the nation's political and economic organizations.

### *Relatedness*

A person's membership in this or that kin-group depends on local cultural notions of descent and relatedness. Although all island cultures recognize "blood" and other shared substances as meaningful for the creation of kin identities, these ideologies of shared substance may be less important than they are in the West (see Linnekin and Poyer 1990). Children also become related to parents through acts of exchange or environmental influences as much as they do by virtue of their birth. I may become a member of my father's lineage because people believe that I have inherited his blood, or bones, or some other natural substance from that man. But I may also become a member of that group if he has nurtured me, or named me, or if I have grown up on his land. These acts of exchange, in fact, make me into his son as they make him my father.

It follows, then, that adoption and fosterage are common in almost all Pacific societies (see Brady 1976). The Hawaiian word for adopted child, *hanai*, comes from "feeding." An exchange of children among families functions to distribute people over sometimes limited landscapes. It also deepens political relations between relatives and neighbors who adopt or foster each other's children. Adoption is facilitated by cultural beliefs that nurture—not just nature—creates kinship. Pacific definitions of the person that incorporate one's social relations also come into play here. My identity, who I truly am, depends on who has cared for me. I become not just what I have eaten, but part of who has fed me, as they become part of me. People establish relations and create kinship through regular acts of exchange in addition to simpler facts of birth or marital alliance.

## Geography and Identity on Tanna

There is also an important relationship between personal identity and geographic place in many Pacific cultures. This may involve origin myths that have local clans and lineages emerging from particular places. It may also involve associations people make between living off the food and other resources of a place and the growth of their bodies and personalities. Customary sympathies between land and identity have been valorized in Pacific independence movements, such as in Vanuatu, French Polynesia, and New Caledonia. Hawaiian nationalists similarly evoke identity in land in their phrase *aloha 'āina,* "love for the land." Just as personal and group identities may be naturalized in landscape, so is landscape often humanized, or at least inspirited. Important mountains, rock formations, and other distinctive geographic features, in many traditional religious systems are alive or once were alive, and they may continue to be helpful or dangerous to humans.

In some societies, such as Tanna (Vanuatu), people link places with personal names. Most men receive a name from a finite stock of available names. This personal title provides membership in a local kin-group and also rights to particular plots of land. Personal and group identities are rooted in land. Names connect people with territory, with an "estate," that provides both nurture and identity. Men's names entitle them to land and also other rights, including two sorts of chiefly status. Women's names have no attendant land rights. The Tannese recycle their names from generation to generation. As individuals are born they receive local names and thereby embody the set of social "personalities" associated with each island neighborhood (Lindstrom 1985). Land, and personal names, therefore, circumscribe individuals, rather than vice versa:

> Land is not a possession, it is a being; one can hold it only if one identifies with it. A right of origin represents a right of land tenure, and a man's customary name or title proves his identification with land. Therefore the "real man" or *man ples* is the individual who actually lives on the land of his ancestors from the era of magical stones, and who carries their real, or original names. (Bonnemaison 1994:303)

Local groups on Tanna resemble typical Pacific lineages, but as they are based ultimately on nomination, rather than on descent *per se*, they might better be called "name-sets." Children become members of their father's group only if they receive a personal name associated with that group. In some parts of the island, a third of all children are named by men who are not their fathers. Although most of these children continue to live with their parents, they are members of different lineages (or name-sets), inheriting the land and social identities of their namers. Widespread adoption of this sort is facilitated by Tannese (and broader Pacific) notions about the power of nurture to effect sentiments of kinship, and of land associations to define personal identity.

Women receive names from one name-set or another, but are less attached to land than are men. Most women, at marriage, move to their husband's place of residence. This, commonly, is also the place of residence of his father and/or namer. Men through their names inherit rights to live near one of several hundred kava-drinking grounds on the island, called *nakamals*. These are circular clearings always shaded by at least one magnificent banyan tree. People also meet at these clearings to debate important issues, resolve disputes, dance, and exchange goods.

Men and women remain spatially segregated throughout much of their daily lives. Customarily, men and circumcised boys (boys are ritually circumcised between six and twelve years of age) lived apart in a men's house at their kava-drinking ground. Women, girls, and young boys lived in family houses in the circling hamlets. Nowadays, thanks to a century of Christian influence on the island, most men have moved back into the villages and sleep with their families, but the sexes continue to sleep separately within family houses. People rarely have sex inside their houses; instead, they go off to their gardens or to the forest. When a women menstruates, her husband avoids her, since the Tannese share a common Melanesian belief that menstrual blood can make men sick. Menstruating women do not cook nor do they go work in their gardens. They relax in the village during their period, taking care not to drip any blood that a man might walk on. As a woman ages, however, and stops menstruating, she becomes symbolically more masculine and gains increasing influence within her family and village.

The dominant spatial pattern on Tanna is that male is to center as female is to periphery. This pattern reflects a fundamental sexual inequality on the island. Local leaders are men. A few woman gain political influence as religious leaders or healers, but these are uncommon. Men own land. Women have access to land only through their fathers or husbands. Men have rights to speak in public. Women have no rights of public speaking—or therefore to influence public decision-making; they must communicate through male spokesmen. Men have the right to drink kava and thereby receive inspirations and other important knowledge, while drunk, from ancestral spirits. But they deny women the right to get drunk.

Village and kava-drinking ground architecture reflects this basic center/periphery pattern, although it did so more clearly in the past, when men and circumcised boys lived on central kava-drinking grounds while women and children remained in the peripheral hamlets. This center/periphery pattern also structures the seating arrangement of public discussions. The Tannese argue frequently about land, the planning of upcoming exchanges and dances, marriage negotiations, exchange imbalances, and so on, but they are usually able to solve their problems peaceably in lengthy debate and discussion on kava-drinking grounds. Men, women, and children all attend these debates, but only men speak. Men sit around the circumference of the kava-drinking ground itself, and an orator, taking his turn, moves toward the center of the ground. The clearing's center signifies power, efficacy, speech, and masculinity. Women sit behind men between the kava-drinking clearing and the edge of the forest as befits their less cultured, more natural essence—according to island gender prejudices. They may complain loudly and talk among themselves, but a woman, even one directly involved in a problem under discussion, cannot rise to her feet to take the floor. Instead, she must find a male to speak for her to the assembled crowd.

The center/periphery pattern also governs dance style on the island. The Tannese celebrate many life-cycle events with ritual exchanges of kava, pigs, food, woven baskets and mats, bark skirts, and lengths of imported cloth and blankets that they buy in trade stores. After an exchange, men drink kava and people eat, and, at night, everyone returns to the kava-drinking ground to dance until dawn. The typical style is a circle dance that spins counterclockwise. Men dance in a tight group in the middle of the clearing. Women, dancing in pairs, form a periphery around the central male dancers. As the inner male circle spins, women, farther out, have to skip to keep up with the rotating center. Men dance together in larger groups, symbolizing their broader sociability. Women dance two-by-two, denoting their more limited and particular relationships.

This symbolic and spatial opposition between central males and peripheral females also patterns the way that people plant their farm plots, or gardens. These gardens, like kava-drinking grounds, are circular clearings cut from the green forests of the island. Human agency—or culture—involves hacking away the natural, lush tropical forest. The center of a clearing in the landscape is the most cultured and most masculine space. Women, conversely, occupy the edges of clearings, in that they are more closely connected with the forest—at least in terms of island dualism that opposes culture and nature, men and women.

When the Tannese plant their two most valuable root crops—yams and taro—they reproduce these spatial gender conceptions. Yams (Diascorea spp.), which can grow six feet long or more, are symbolically masculine. These are long, hard, good to eat, and the most appreciated vegetable food on the island. People plant symbolically male yams in the center of their garden clearings. Around these yams, they plant taro—a plant that is symbolically feminine. In gardens, the spherical, feminine taro corm contrasts with and surrounds the long, harder masculine yam. Again, central masculinity contrasts with peripheral femininity. This gender imagery perhaps partly derives from the natural positions of heterosexuality itself, as the hard male penis is encompassed and surrounded on all sides by the soft female vagina. If so, the Tannese have endowed this sexual arrangement with a series of cultural meanings and understandings of central men and peripheral women. These symbolic oppositions support political inequality between cultured, speaking central men and natural, mute peripheral women.

There are unequal constraints on the movement of men and women in space. Actually, everyone's mobility on the island is constrained according to an individual geography based on personal name, kinship, and friendship links. A traditional network of inherited name-associated exchange relationships, or "roads," links place with place (Bonnemaison 1994). Many of these roads are actual trails through the forest, although some are only metaphorical, marking long-standing connections between people living at two different kava-drinking grounds. Men move easily along the roads they own, traveling from place to place. They are more nervous, however, traveling for the first time to places to which they have not inherited any rights of mobility or association.

Men travel more than women. They move along their roads to visit kin and exchange partners at other kava-drinking grounds. Women tend to stay in home villages. As the island has become involved in the cash economy, many men have left Tanna for work and school in the capital city, Port Vila, on Efate Island, or for other northern islands. Women also find work and go to school in Vila and elsewhere, but their numbers are fewer.

Women make one socially important move when they marry. Almost always, a woman moves to her new husband's village. A series of marriage feasts and exchanges marks her passage from her mother and father's village to that of her new husband's. During one of these passages, her father, or another leading man from her village, takes her by the arm, moves her across the kava-drinking ground, and gives her to the father of her new husband. This ritual physical movement across a kava-drinking clearing signals her transfer from family to family. The Tannese practice "sister-exchange marriage," and eventually a woman from her husband's name-set will move across, in the opposite direction, to her father's group to balance out the marriage exchange.

Some lovers violate this pattern with a different sort of movement in space. They run away and elope to avoid the control of their elders. This wild movement breaks the pattern of ritual female crossing of the kava-drinking ground. Village leaders and parents, of course, get angry at the elopement and sometimes try to break up the couple; otherwise they have to deal with the marriage's effect on local exchange relations and attempt to restore exchange balance after the fact. Elopement, to a degree, empowers the woman involved, in that she at least chooses whom to run off with and when to run. Most of the time, however, the island's patterned spatial movement circumscribes people's identities.

## Exchange

Islanders create, maintain, and repair their social relations through acts of exchange. Exchange ceremonies, often keyed to important points in a person's life cycle, remark changing positions within a network of kin relations (Figures 16.2–16.3, Color Plates 16A–16F). The birth of a baby, the circumcision of a son, the first menstruation of a daughter, the marriage of a child, and the death of a parent all commonly demand the exchange of goods between at least two extended families. Some anthropologists have attempted to model Pacific social structures as the effect of concatenated individual acts of exchange (see e.g. Schwimmer 1973, Schieffelin 1976).

*Figure 16.2.* Man killing pig to be given to an exchange partner in Tanna's nakwiari ritual dance cycle (photo LL).

*Figure 16.3.* Rauaua wraps tuber pudding for baking in an earth oven; this is later given to guests at a funeral feast (photo LL).

Tokens of exchange everywhere in the Pacific include foodstuffs—here again is the symbolic connection between feeding and relatedness. The pig, especially, is a ubiquitous and valued exchange token in almost every Pacific society (except for those, like New Caledonia, that traditionally lacked pigs). Islanders, depending on local ecosystem, also exchange fish, fowl, turtles, dogs, cassowaries, flying foxes—the gamut of larger, available Oceanic animals, wild and domesticated. They also have elaborated a variety of other exchange tokens, ranging from the shell bead and red-feather "moneys" of Solomon Islands to the shell armbands and necklaces of the Trobriands, whale teeth in Fiji, and the large stone disks of Yap. Cash, nowadays, is as common as pigs in lubricating social relations, as are various market commodities that people give one another alongside traditional exchange goods.

Marriage brings into existence new, affinal relations of kinship between two families and is everywhere celebrated with exchange of goods. Marriage patterns differ, however, from urban areas, where men and women may choose whom to marry, and to marry in church, to rural areas, where traditional marital ritual obtains. In Vanuatu, for instance, courts recognize three sorts of marriage: civil, religious, and "customary." Even in urbanized areas, sometimes onerous exchanges of goods that anthropologists have called "brideprice" or "bridewealth" remain common in many Pacific societies. In Port Moresby, for example, urbanites jokingly refer to young women as "Toyotas," since that is what their families will demand from prospective suitors. In some Melanesian cultures, like Tanna, people arrange "sister-exchange" marriages. A woman marries into one family, which then must provide a second woman in return (Figure 16.4).

*Figure 16.4.* Men from one family give one of their daughters to a man from a second, who must provide a daughter in return (photo LL).

*Figure 16.5.* Man ritually breaks off a branch from a kava plant he is giving away as part of a dispute settlement exchange (photo LL).

Islanders exchange goods to repair, as well as to create, social relations. When relations become "entangled" (see Watson-Gegeo and White 1990), people attempt to settle their disputes in formal or informal courts, or at village meetings where they talk out the problem. Among Hawaiians, for example, families in conflict may come together to "set things right" (*ho'oponopono*) by discussing the issue at hand. Pacific dispute-settlement procedures typically attempt restitution rather than punishment of guilty individuals. Sating, as noted above, took on the personality of her victim in order to restore a family's loss. This, too, speaks of people's concern to preserve the social fabric of relationships rather than the rights or responsibilities of autonomous individuals. Traditionally, where settlement procedures failed, kin and village groups might go to war. Given Pacific conceptions of the person as socially embedded, killing or injuring *any* relative of the wrongdoer could satisfy honor and balance affairs.

Where dispute-settlement works, however, both parties to a conflict exchange gifts (Figure 16.5), although one side may give more than the other. In Samoa, for example, if someone seriously offends another, to repair relations the chiefs from his or her family apologize (*ifoga*) by visiting the highest chief of the injured family. They humble themselves by sitting outside his house, their heads bowed and covered with fine woven mats. If apology is accepted, they present fine mats and also money to the injured family (and may also receive food and small gifts in return). Exchange of this sort functions to restore social relations, just as other acts of exchange once brought these relationships into being and sustained them through time.

## Violence

Compared with American or European norms, violence in the Pacific is modest. No Pacific society was, in fact, pacific, in that violence both within groups, and between groups, occurred traditionally. Wars of territorial aggression and violent chiefly competition for paramount status shaped the history of most Polynesian and Micronesian societies. In Melanesia, people also fought over land as well as exchange and marital imbalances and other sore points of conflict (see Gardner and Heider 1968, Knauft 1990).

Colonialization and missionization efforts dampened warfare for several generations throughout much of the Pacific. Recently, however, intergroup conflict has returned in new political form in a number of Pacific states. A rebellion on Bougainville during the 1980s and 1990s, for example, has cost several thousand lives. There has also been passing but still deadly violence in New Caledonia and French Polynesia associated with political efforts to acquire independence from France. Fears of potential violence between the indigenous and Indo-Fijian communities of Fiji also constrain politics in that state. Violence is increasing in urban areas, such as Port Moresby and other cities in Papua New Guinea, associated with the emergence of urban youth gangs (*raskols*, in Pidgin English) (Harris 1988). In Chuuk, too, fighting among young men, usually drunk, became a serious social problem in the 1970s (Marshall 1979).

Whereas intergroup violence declined during the twentieth century, intragroup violence—particularly domestic conflict—has increased in many Pacific societies. Recurrent domestic violence occurs in many island families between husbands and wives, between parents and children, and among siblings. "Many Pacific societies consider a certain level of family violence to be normal and acceptable" (Counts 1990). Patterns and frequencies of "normal" violence differ from society to society. In much of Melanesia, for example, parents strike children only reluctantly, and siblings observe rules that permit younger to strike older, but not vice versa. In some Polynesian societies, on the other hand, parents more freely discipline children with slaps and blows (see, for Samoa, Freeman 1983:205).

Domestic violence has worsened in some Pacific towns and cities as migrant families live apart from their extended kin whose presence once would have provided various sorts of support and also restraints to keep violence from getting out of hand. Migrants to urban areas come under financial and interpersonal stress, some of which manifests itself in wife beating and child abuse. Alcohol use is commonly associated with domestic violence, especially since in many Pacific cultures, such as Palau, drunks are partially absolved of responsibility for their actions (Nero 1990). In Chuuk, alcohol-related violence between men and women and also between village youths became such a problem that women successfully campaigned for a prohibition on alcohol sales (Marshall and Marshall 1990).

Rates of violence directed against the self, including suicide, have also increased in the Pacific. In various island societies, different categories of people are more or less likely to kill themselves given the play of social forces and everyday stress. Throughout much of Melanesia, the typical suicide is a young woman. These women often endure painful pressure to marry against their will, and marriage pulls them into a series of new relationships with husband and his kin in which they are subordinated. Although people on Tanna, for example, aver that a woman has ultimate rights to refuse any man that her parents have selected to become her husband, it may be very difficult for her to resist this choice. Some woman attempt (and sometimes succeed) to kill themselves by climbing and jumping from trees in order to signal the seriousness of their opposition to an unwanted engagement.

In Micronesia and Polynesia, conversely, boys and young men are most likely to kill themselves. Typical mechanisms of suicide include hanging and drinking herbicide. Many of these boys and adolescents kill themselves "in a state of anger at having been scolded or punished by a parent or some other elder" (Freeman 1983:220; see also Hezel, Rubinstein and White 1985). Suicide patterns reflect local cultural concepts of power, guilt, and compensation. "In different ways, all of these cultural conceptions are concerned with the dilemmas of anger and other intense emotions felt by persons in low status positions who have limited avenues for expressing these emotions and promoting moral claims" (White 1985:12).

## Equivalence and Hierarchy

Very few human relations are egalitarian. Most of the time people must deal with others who, in important ways, are not their equals, as often do parents and children, men and women, and chiefs and followers. Exchange patterns within such relationships work to sustain hierarchy and inequality. Unbalanced gift-giving may strengthen the political capital of those who give vis-à-vis those who receive. Or it may mark the status of a chief and the duty of others to support the highborn.

In some parts of the Pacific, relations between adult men, and between kin-groups, ideally are egalitarian. An ethos of economic and political equivalence characterizes many Melanesian societies. People strive to sustain balance in their exchange relationships. On Tanna, for example, to celebrate the successful circumcision of his son, a man will publicly present a heap of exchange goods (pigs, kava, mats, baskets, bark skirts, lengths of cloth, blankets) to one of his wife's brothers. He expects, eventually, to receive everything back when that brother-in-law gives him goods in return, celebrating the circumcision of one of his own sons. People nowadays write down exact numbers of exchanged objects to ensure a balanced exchange. If someone falls ill, people may suggest that he has left his exchange relationships unbalanced too long. Positive and negative reciprocity are equally important in the maintenance of relational equivalence. It is important to pay back gifts that one has received, but also to return injury for injury, insult for insult (see Trompf 1994).

Despite an ethos of interpersonal equivalence, leaders direct the affairs of Pacific villages, families, lineages, and clans. Contrasts between the chiefly systems of Polynesia and Micronesia and the more egalitarian political systems of Melanesia have often been noted. The position of chief is an ascribed status. Men, and in some cases women, from certain descent groups succeed to the position of chief because of their genealogical identity—they descend from other chiefs. Inherited chiefly status in Polynesia often comes with attributions of *mana*, or a personal power or efficacy that ordinary people lack. In some societies, such as Tonga, a single chiefly lineage sits atop the social pyramid. In others, a coterie of leading families controls the various districts of an island. In addition to chiefly and common lineages, a class described as "slaves" existed in some Eastern Polynesian societies. Comparative theory has attempted to explain these hierarchical variations as caused by the distribution of environmental resources (Sahlins 1958) or as an evolutionary outcome of aristocratic status competitions (see Goldman 1970).

In much of Melanesia, on the other hand, leaders (or "big-men"—a term that Pacific Studies has borrowed from Melanesian Pidgin English)—achieve their positions on the basis of individual abilities to organize economic exchange, settle disputes, demonstrate wisdom, and otherwise influence community opinion. The distinction between the Melanesian big-man and the Polynesian and Micronesian chief is too simple in that it obscures the fact that chiefs also exist in various Melanesian societies and that Polynesian (and Micronesian) chiefly leadership is based in individual ability as well as genealogical position. In Samoa, for example, all families control chiefly (*matai*) titles that they bestow on those family members who promise to serve kin-group interests.

## Class

Traditional hierarchies of chief and commoner or big-man and follower are increasingly sliding into modern inequalities based on class. Whereas kinship once structured and colored political relationships between leaders and followers (the chief or big-man leading his kin-group), economic inequalities of class nowadays increasingly underlie political authority in the Pacific. Many local leaders, in addition, today base their authority on the state rather than solely in custom (see White and Lindstrom 1997).

In some places, state constitutions have been designed that recognize traditional systems of hierarchy. In Samoa, for example, only *matai* (those with chiefly titles) may run for Parliament. Chiefly families are also very influential within the political systems of Tonga, the Cook Islands, and Fiji. However, customary limitations on chiefly authority that once worked to mute social inequality have often broken down. In Tonga and also in the Marshall Islands (where chiefly control of land has provided certain families the lion's share of U.S. military land rents), for example, people today criticize chiefs who have taken advantage of their positions to enrich themselves, neglecting traditional social and economic responsibilities.

As Pacific Islanders have become engaged in the global marketplace, inequalities based on economic position have increased. Hierarchies of class now overlay those of kinship and status, especially in those states where some families are enriched by their control of land, forests, minerals, and other resources being exploited by multinational corporations. Ben Finney undertook one of the first studies of class formation in two Tahitian communities in the early 1960s (Finney 1973b). He wrote then of "the emergence of a South Seas type of urban proletariat" that was appearing "virtually overnight" (1973b:140). Since that time, urban migration has accelerated. Every Pacific state has at least one city—or a sizable town—that is the political, economic, and cultural focus of the nation (see e.g. Connell and Lea 1995 for Polynesia, Haberkorn 1989 for Vanuatu).

Urbanization, wage labor opportunities, limited access to secondary education, and the growth of state bureaucracies have all accentuated class formation in many Pacific nations. Many families now depend on wage labor rather than on subsistence farming or gardening. Labor unions have been established in most Pacific states, and workers—particularly government employees—have gone on strike in Solomon Islands, Vanuatu, and elsewhere (see Howard 1986).

The growing importance of class over kinship is not limited to urban areas. Finney (1973a) also studied local business entrepreneurs around the town of Goroka in the Papua New Guinea Highlands. In the 1960s, big-men, or traditional village leaders, had begun to apply their organizational and managerial skills to create successful coffee plantations and trucking businesses. Twenty years later, he returned to study "a new elite of wealthy business leaders."

On Ambae Island, Vanuatu, similarly, "a category of relatively rich individuals is emerging ... through inequalities of customary land distribution that allow a few large landholders to earn incomes at least four times as large as the average copra [dried coconut] producer.... The wealthy operate more and more as capitalists" (Rodman 1987:162; see also Hooper 1987). However, given the continuing importance of kin-groups and other sorts of customary relationships, Western labels of class (bourgeois and proletarian, big and small peasants) hide much of the complexity of Pacific economic and political relationships.

## Ethnicity

We encounter some of the same difficulties when we apply Western notions of "ethnicity" to Pacific Island societies. We typically base our definitions of ethnic identity in shared "blood" (or race), custom, language, and so forth. Linnekin and Poyer, however, exploring various Pacific understandings of identity, argue that in many Pacific societies, group identities, ethnic or otherwise, are less essentially part of one's nature but are based, rather, in a person's behavior (1990:4–5; see Howard 1989, Crocombe 1993). According to Linnekin and Poyer, Pacific perceptions of personal and group identity admit that

> people can voluntarily shift their social identities, that a person can maintain more than one identity simultaneously, and that behavioral attributes—such as residence, language, dress, participation in exchanges—are not only significant markers but are also effective determinants of identity. (1990:9)

Western notions of ethnicity, however, do inform identity and politics in Hawai'i (the most ethnically complex Pacific archipelago) and New Zealand, where individuals must define themselves in terms of powerful ethnic categories of Maori, (other) Pacific Islander, or Pakeha (European) (see King 1991). Ethnic politics is also underway in other island states with European and Asian settler populations, notably New Caledonia, French Polynesia, Guam, and the Marianas (Ward 1992).

Fijian politics since independence have been shaped by a serious ethnic divide between indigenous Fijians and the Indo-Fijian community descended from laborers recruited by the British to work sugarcane plantations. Until 1987, a party that represented mostly indigenous Fijians ran the state. That year, elements within Fiji's military staged two coups after the Fiji Labour Party won national elections for the first time. Many blamed these coups on ethnic tensions, insofar as the Labour Party had attracted mostly Indo-Fijian support (see Ewins 1992). The military, in this view, overthrew the government in order to reestablish indigenous Fijian domination of Parliament. Others, however, have argued the greater significance of class: The military restored ruling families (which were of both indigenous and Indo-Fijian ancestry) to a position of state domination (see e.g. Howard 1991).

In Papua New Guinea some have explained, and sometimes justified, the attempt by secessionists on Bougainville to achieve independence in ethnic terms. The "black skins" of

Bougainville, in this rhetoric, differ ethnically from the "red skins" who inhabit the rest of the country (Nash and Ogan 1990; see also Larmour 1992). People's use of ethnic categories, in this case, is not necessarily identical with ways ethnicity gets constructed beyond the Pacific. And in contemporary Hawai'i, a second system of group identity that contrasts "local" with "nonlocal," relying on behavioral attributes such as residence, language, and dress, overlaps mainland understandings of ethnic identity as based in essential features of race or ancestry.

As more people move to Pacific towns and cities and come to rely on wage labor rather than the land to eat, their identities are less and less defined by local kin-group memberships. Here, islanders are becoming more individualistic in the sense that they are now more money-oriented and less dependent or interested in their extended families. At the same time, they are reaching out beyond their traditional kin-groups to join new communities and associations that are defined by shared economic position (class), or by broader identities of shared geographic origin, language, religion, and so on (ethnicity). Creeping economic modernity, increasing individuality, and also growing class and ethnic differentiation, however, do not necessarily anticipate an impending disintegration of kinship and other customary Pacific social relations.

## Changing Relationships

Once-current theories that everyone in the world, eventually, as they develop economically and politically, will come to resemble Europeans and Americans are clearly wrong. Although, nowadays, global economic and communication systems move ideas, images, goods, and people around the world with increasing felicity, local cultural orders do manage to survive. If the world system did indeed result in nothing but cultural homogeneity, then Japan today would be no different from, say, Oklahoma. People, as active participants in these global networks, maintain significant ability to choose what to consume and what to refuse, what to listen to and what to tune out. Furthermore, they can decide to use products and ideas in novel ways that make sense of the global in local terms. The local, in this fashion, redirects and reshapes incoming social and cultural forces.

Undoubtedly, however, Pacific Islanders today are increasingly involved in global networks that are affecting the shape of their everyday social relationships. Selkirk, or his literary avatar Robinson Crusoe, was an eighteenth-century allegory. A castaway existence is no longer feasible or even creditable as a South Pacific romance. Even the few families surviving on isolated Pitcairn Island get mail and radio transmissions. People on Tanna, Aitutaki, and Easter Island, and in Honolulu, Los Angeles, and Sydney are increasingly interrelated.

New exchange flows, new identities of class and ethnicity, and new, perhaps, conceptions of responsible, autonomous, and coherent persons will no doubt have an increasing impact on island social relationships. Notably, debate is under way at the moment in many Pacific communities about the changing roles of women and men within island families (see Jolly and Macintyre 1989), and also about proper relations between chiefs (and big-men) and their onetime followers within island states. Social relations such as these are today increasingly unsettled by the opportunities and challenges of economic and political development in the islands.

# Bibliography

Amarshi, A., K. Good, and R. Mortimer. 1979. *Development and dependency: the political economy of Papua New Guinea.* Melbourne: Oxford University Press.

Bonnemaison, J. 1995. *The tree and the canoe: history and ethnogeography of Tanna.* Honolulu: University of Hawai'i Press.

Brady, I. 1976. *Transactions in kinship: adoption and fosterage in Oceania.* ASAO Monograph No. 4. Honolulu: University Press of Hawai'i.

Connell, J., and J. P. Lea. 1995. *Urbanisation in Polynesia.* Canberra: National Centre for Development Studies, Australian National University.

Counts, D. A. 1990. Introduction. Special Issue: Domestic Violence in Oceania. *Pacific Studies* 13(3):1–5.

Crocombe, R. 1993. Ethnicity, identity and power in Oceania. In *Islands and enclaves,* ed. Garry Trompf, 195–223. New Delhi: Sterling Publishers.

Ewins, R. 1992. *Colour, class, and custom: the literature of the 1987 Fiji coup. Regime change and regime maintenance in Asia and the Pacific,* No. 9. Canberra: Australian National University.

Finney, B. R. 1973a. *Big-men and business: entrepreneurship and economic growth in the New Guinea Highlands.* Honolulu: University Press of Hawai'i.

Finney, B. R. 1973b. *Polynesian peasants and proletarians.* Cambridge, MA: Schenkman Publishing Company.

Finney, B. R. 1987. *Business development in the Highlands of Papua New Guinea.* Pacific Islands Development Program Research Report, No. 6. Honolulu: East-West Center.

Freeman, D. 1983. *Margaret Mead and Samoa: The making and unmaking of an anthropological myth.* Cambridge, MA: Harvard University Press.

Gardner, R., and K. G. Heider. 1968. *Gardens of war: life and death in the New Guinea stone age.* New York: Random House.

Goldman, I. 1970. *Ancient Polynesian society.* Chicago: Chicago University Press.

Haberkorn, G. 1989. *Port Vila: transit station or final stop?* Pacific Research Monograph No. 21. Canberra: National Centre for Development Studies, Australian National University.

Harris, B. M. 1988. The rise of rascalism: action and reaction in the evolution of rascal gangs. IASER Discussion Paper No. 54. Port Moresby: Institute of Applied Social and Economic Research.

Hezel, F. X., D. H. Rubinstein, and G. M. White. 1985. *Culture, youth and suicide in the Pacific: papers from an East-West Conference.* Honolulu: Center for Pacific Island Studies, University of Hawai'i.

Hooper, A. ed. 1987. *Class and culture in the South Pacific.* Auckland: Centre for Pacific Studies, University of Auckland; Suva: Institute of Pacific Studies, University of the South Pacific.

Howard, M. C. 1986. History and industrial relations in the South Pacific. *South Pacific Forum* (special issue, Labour History in the South Pacific) 3:1–10.

Howard, M. C. 1989. Ethnicity and the state in the Pacific. In *Ethnicity and nation-building in the Pacific,* ed. M. C. Howard, 1–49. Tokyo: United National University Press.

Howard, M. C. 1991. *Fiji: race and politics in an island state.* Vancouver: University of British Columbia Press.

Jolly, M., and M. Macintyre. 1989. *Family and gender in the Pacific: domestic contradictions and the colonial impact.* Cambridge: Cambridge University Press.

Keesing, R. M. 1978. *'Elota's story: the life and times of a Solomon Islands big man.* New York: St. Martin's Press.

King, M. 1991. *Pakeha: the quest for identity in New Zealand.* Auckland: Penguin Books.

Knauft, B. M. 1990. Melanesian warfare: a theoretical history. *Oceania* 60:250–311.

Larmour, P. 1992. The politics of race and ethnicity: theoretical perspectives on Papua New Guinea. *Pacific Studies* 15(2):87–108.

Levy, R. I. 1973. *Tahitians: mind and experience in the Society Islands.* Chicago: University of Chicago Press.

Lindstrom, L. 1985. Personal names and social reproduction on Tanna. *Journal of the Polynesian Society* 94:27–45.

Lindstrom, L. 1990. *Knowledge and power in a South Pacific society.* Washington, DC: Smithsonian Institution Press.

Linnekin, J., and L. Poyer. 1990. *Cultural identity and ethnicity in the Pacific.* Honolulu: University of Hawai'i Press.

Lutz, C. A. 1988. *Unnatural emotions: everyday sentiments on a Micronesian atoll and their challenge to Western theory.* Chicago: University of Chicago Press.

Marshall, M. 1979. *Weekend warriors: alcohol in a Micronesian culture.* Palo Alto, CA: Mayfield Publishing Company.

Marshall, M. 1983. *Siblingship in Oceania: studies in the meaning of kin relations.* ASAO Monograph No. 8. Lanham: University Press of America.

Marshall, M., and L. B. Marshall. 1990. *Silent voices speak: women and prohibition in Truk.* Belmont, California: Wadsworth Publishing Company.

Nash, J., and E. Ogan. 1990. The red and the black: Bougainvillean perceptions of other Papua New Guineans. *Pacific Studies* 13(2):1–17.

Nero, K. L. 1990. The hidden pain: drunkenness and domestic violence in Palau. Special issue: domestic violence in Oceania. *Pacific Studies* 13:63–92.

Ochs, E. 1988. *Culture and language development: language acquisition and language socialization in a Samoan village.* Cambridge: Cambridge University Press.

Read, K. 1958. Morality and the concept of the person among the Gahuku-Gama. *Oceania* 54:233–282.

Rodman, M. C. 1987. *Masters of tradition: consequences of customary land tenure in Longana, Vanuatu.* Vancouver: University of British Columbia Press.

Sahlins, M. 1958. *Social stratification in Polynesia.* Seattle: University of Washington Press.

Schieffelin, B. B. 1990. *The give and take of everyday life: language socialization of Kaluli children.* Cambridge: Cambridge University Press.

Schieffelin, E. L. 1976. *The sorrow of the lonely and the burning of the dancers.* New York: St. Martin's Press.

Schwimmer, E. 1973. *Exchange in the social structure of the Orokaiva: traditional and emergent ideologies in the Northern District of Papua.* London: C. Hurst.

Shore, B. 1982. *Sala'ilua: a Samoan mystery.* New York: Columbia University Press.

Strathern, A. 1979. *Ongka: a self-account by a New Guinea big-man.* London: Duckworth.

Strathern, M. 1988. *The gender of the gift: problems with women and problems with society in Melanesia.* Berkeley: University of California Press.

Trompf, G. W. 1994. *Payback: the logic of retribution in Melanesian religions.* Cambridge: Cambridge University Press.

Ward, A. 1992. The crisis of our times: ethnic resurgence and the liberal ideal. *Journal of Pacific History* 27:83–95.

Watson-Gegeo K., and G. M. White. 1990. *Disentangling: conflict discourse in Pacific societies*. Stanford: Stanford University Press.

White, G. M. 1985. Suicide and culture: island views. In *Culture, youth and suicide in the Pacific: papers from an East-West Center conference*, ed. F. X. Hezel, D. H. Rubinstein, and G. M. White, 1–14. Honolulu: Center for Pacific Island Studies, University of Hawai'i.

White, G. M., and J. Kirkpatrick. 1985. *Person, self, and experience: exploring Pacific ethnopsychologies*. Berkeley: University of California Press.

White, G. M., and L. Lindstrom 1997. *Chiefs today: traditional Pacific leadership and the postcolonial state*. Stanford: Stanford University Press.

# Chapter 17

# Tenure

*Ron Crocombe*

Land and water tenures are shaped by the environment, by past experiences and present circumstances of the people who live by them, and by external forces. Tenure systems also influence ecology, society, and economy in a continuing process of interaction.

Tenures used to be guided only by diverse traditional customs and precedents. Today they are also covered by laws—lots of laws—of the fourteen independent nations and twelve dependent territories of the region.

The larger and more valuable the unit of land or water, the more important law is likely to be; and the smaller and poorer the unit, the more significant custom is likely to remain. Custom tends to be more important in rural communities, but at the national level and in situations of intense use and heavy investment, formal law is usually dominant. In practice, however, it is not a case of some areas being covered by law and others by custom, because most land and water is influenced by both in varying degrees.

## Traditional Precedents

Pacific Island tenure systems were diverse, but shared some common elements. All evolved to facilitate allocation of rights of access for subsistence agriculture (the dominant food source in most places), sea foods (which were important in coastal areas and predominant in a few), and hunting and foraging (which was supplementary except in a few infertile pockets where it was the main food source).

*Figure 17.1.* Land under intensive sweet potato cultivation in the Sepik region, Papua New Guinea, still under customary tenure (photo RS).

Rights to land were in all cases multiple, conditional, and negotiable. What was owned was not the land or water so much as rights to it—rights vis-à-vis other people. No rights were absolute. Some rights to land and water were held by individuals, but there were many shades of difference between the rights of even close relatives. Rights of males differed from (and were generally superior to) those of females. Rights of older brothers, and cousins of more senior lines, were often superior to those of juniors. Resident rightholders took precedence, other things being equal, over nonresidents. Labor strengthened rights, so those who worked the land enhanced their claims over those of equal blood right who did not. And more forceful personalities and more persuasive arguments could tilt balances, for multiple principles could be called upon and given varying degrees of emphasis to benefit those relying on them.

No one person held all rights to any one plot of land (nor do people anywhere, incidentally, including in commercialized, industrialized societies). As well as interacting laterally with the rights of one's peers, individual rights were nested with those of extended families, lineages, clans, tribes—and now of course, of governments, banks, insurance systems, and other institutions. Wives (or in some cases in-marrying husbands) held rights contingent on the marriage. The land rights of adoptees varied greatly even within communities, for much depended on the circumstances of the adoption and the relationship of the adopting parents and the adoptee. Refugees and others with special needs were often accommodated under negotiated arrangements, but the rights of refugees and adoptees were often vulnerable once the person who granted the rights died.

As Guiart (1996) observes, "there is no formal ownership of land in Western terms [but] systems regulating access to land for each individual in each generation." Day to day decisions were based on broad customary principles modified by pragmatism, as different customs could be used to justify different actions. For example, seniority might of itself give priority over juniors, but persons with outstanding records of military or community service might rate higher.

As there was no writing or mapping, rights and boundaries relied on memory. The memories of specialists in this art were at times prodigious. Although memory is selective and tends to deflect in the interest of the person remembering, it allows flexibility and adaptation. Tuimaleali'ifano's (1997) study of the competing and often radically different memories of Samoan experts in relation to the same land and chiefly titles—always deflected to the service of the "remembering" party—is an excellent example of a Pacific-wide (and humanity-wide) tendency.

Most land rights were transferred by inheritance from a parent or other close blood relative, but in the process many factors came into play. These included the needs of individuals, the harmony or conflict between potential heirs and heritors, the extent to which heirs had used that land, who provided for the elders in their declining years, what payments were made at funerary feasts (this was particularly important in some Vanuatu and Solomon Islands cultures), and other considerations.

Warfare was more important in transferring land rights than is often recognized. Wars were usually triggered by disputes over pigs or other property, over women, insults, or compensation. But as a consequence of war, land rights often changed hands. A New Zealand Maori proverb observed that the deaths of men were caused by land and women, and Ballard (1996) notes that although Papua New Guineans often deny that wars were fought over land, many resulted in land acquisition. He notes that Huli people deny they fought for land, but the oral history of three thousand plots there showed that wars "reconfigured the social landscape on a massive scale." Those who lose in such conquests seldom relinquish their claims to the land or their hope that eventually they will get it back. Examples could be presented from throughout the region.

Every household needed access to several kinds of land for different purposes, so soils and crops influenced tenures. Even on atolls, with their apparent uniformity, plots were usually narrow slices running from the lagoon to the ocean to give the holder access to different microenvironments. Most people have rights in more than one such "slice," because that facilitates exchange of use rights with others in a complex pattern of mutual obligation and reciprocity that broadens options and enhances social security (Clarke 1994, Crocombe 1968).

Rights in multiple plots of land were necessary because most crops required seven to fifteen years of fallow after harvest due to the leaching of soils by rain and heat and the rapid concentration of pests and weeds in gardens. Fallowing facilitates flexible allocation of land, adapted to the needs of those involved at the time the land is ready to plant again. But taro (*Colocasia*) and *puraka* (*Cyrtosperma*) can be grown continuously in fertile swamps, and thus rights to them were strictly defined. At the other extreme, medicinal plants, fibers, trees, birds, and animals were scattered in the wild and accessible to all members of the large community.

Climate is a vital determinant. Most plants brought by the Maori from tropical Polynesia to New Zealand would not grow, so they relied more on hunting and gathering, which necessitated rights to large areas being shared by many people.

Demography influenced tenures, with denser populations recognizing more precise and detailed rights than sparser populations, except when self-propagating species provided much of the diet (as in a few fertile and densely populated estuaries of coastal Papua). Likewise, the more labor needed for production, the more individualized the tenure tended to be, so the intensive cultivation and longer storage feasible for the staple yams on Tonga's rich soils led to a more individualized system, with households spread across the countryside. Samoa, on the other hand, with rocky soil that was difficult to cultivate, relied more on self-propagating breadfruit and bananas, which required minimal effort and facilitated village living and communal tenures.

For most of the region, about one-tenth of a hectare of land per person was needed under cultivation at a time, although this varied with soils and crops. Because of the long fallow, half to two hectares of gardening land per person (up to ten hectares per family) was needed in addition to land for hunting and foraging.

## Traditional Rights to Water

Polynesians and Micronesians were among the world's most skilled mariners, navigators and fishermen for many centuries. As might be expected among people who depended so heavily on the resources of the sea, their marine tenures were among the world's most complex, and included different categories of rights (to reefs, shoals, passages, swamps, etc.) being held by communities, descent groups, and individuals; rights to use of surface waters being differentiated from those of bottom waters; rights to particular fish being separate from those of other fish and from the waters they swam in; and sometimes seasonal changes in rights. Some atoll cultures had rules for the allocation of rights to logs and other things that floated offshore or drifted on shore.

Culture, values, and knowledge should not be overlooked. Some Papua New Guinea people (such as the Koitabu) lived near the sea for centuries but made little use of it, while others (such as the Motu) who arrived later with intimate understanding of marine environments used it intensively. Similar juxtapositions of communities with skills to exploit different environments were common in Melanesia, often leading to trade between the two economies.

Where waters are extensive and foods plentiful, there will be little subdivision, many rights being held by the community. Several communities may have rights of access through a reef passage, even though only the community where it is located will have rights to fish in it. Those who invest labor, such as in making fish weirs, will have stronger rights of use than those who do not (see e.g. Atanraoi 1995).

Salt water in lagoons, estuaries, and the open sea was usually a more important source of food and other resources than fresh water. The degree to which rights were divided by area varied enormously, with some cultures making detailed provision for individual rights to highly valued fishing sites. The number of persons sharing rights was generally larger the farther the site was from the village and the more difficult it was to mark. Thus open sea was often accessible to all whose community lands bordered it, whereas shallow waters and fringing reefs were more clearly demarcated.

Even far inland where fresh water is plentiful, customary rights to it are very detailed (see e.g. Popisil 1965, Kalinoe 1998). The rights cover who may draw drinking water from where, who may bathe and where, who may catch fish and prawns and where and when, who may divert water for irrigation or other use, access rights, and so on.

## External Influences

All the ancient systems have been radically modified, and today's customary tenures are very different from yesterday's. Yet elements of the ancient traditional systems outlined above are still evident—more markedly in isolated areas.

New technology, from steel tools to bulldozers, radically alters the amount of land one person can farm, and the terms of its tenures. High technology and a money economy lead to global markets and the attraction or seduction to turn Melanesian forests into Japanese toilet paper, the chiefly beverage kava (*Piper methysticum*) into a herbal medicine, coconut oil into "health" soap, and bêche-de-mer (trepang, or sea cucumber) into aphrodisiacs for the international market. The demand for imports leads Kanaks to grow coffee for Europe, Tongans to replace yams for subsistence by pumpkins for Japan, and Micronesians to work in hotels rather than gardens.

New products require different land types. Coconuts had been grown in small quantities for subsistence, but commercial production requires larger areas. Most attempts to farm cattle have been abandoned, or reduced to a few, because farmers cannot get sufficiently exclusive rights to a large enough area to make it economical; and when they do, they are often obliged to give the cattle away to provide feasts at community functions. Moreover, many Pacific people are averse to fences, which may imply mistrust. Many fences have been chopped down.

Central governments brought substantial change. Most Melanesian communities recognized no authority over more than a few hundred people, and few Polynesian communities contained more than a few thousand. In both cases, leaders at the top did not usually interfere in the day to day allocation of land rights. Change wrought by central governments is often thought to be due to their being colonial, but it is an inevitable by-product of technological development. The Kingdom of Tonga, which was never a colony, introduced the most extensive tenure reforms of any government in the region (Crocombe 1975, Maude and Sevele 1991).

Another action of any national government is to stop warfare—or at least to try. No one doubts the virtue of stopping warfare, but it was done without adequate understanding of the longer-term function of warfare in adjusting land to population. So no adequate alternative access was provided for those who outgrew their former areas, or whose needs changed due to cash cropping or other new uses.

Demography is closely related to tenure. Last century many Pacific populations were decimated by introduced diseases to which they had no immunity, by more lethal weapons, and by labor migration. This century, growing immunity and better medical services led to booming populations, so in many situations there are five times more people to be accommodated than the traditional tenures were designed for. The proud claim that every islander has customary rights to land is hollow when, as for a growing proportion, their rights are minuscule, fragmented, restricted, badly located relative to today's opportunities, or shared with hundreds of others.

Density of people per square kilometer of land ranges from only 9 in Melanesia to 140 in Micronesia, but with great variations within both. Moreover, much of Melanesia is too mountainous for human habitation. But despite population increase, much land is used less and less effectively, as tenure problems and preference for urban occupations attract people away.

Moreover, the last decade has seen more immigration into the region than ever before, particularly Chinese and Filipino immigration to the Marianas, Palau, Papua New Guinea, and Fiji. This too has implications for tenure.

Indigenous people no longer live where they used to. Whereas traditional systems evolved in a context where most people spent their whole lives in one locality, mobility has been growing for over a century. The first change, in the 1800s, involved young men working on foreign ships, plantations, and mines, as missionaries, or in other capacities. New medical, educational, commercial and religious services led to concentration in villages and towns of people who were formerly spread more evenly across the landscape. This process continues, but tenure adaptations have in most cases been inadequate to accommodate them satisfactorily.

Motor transport and the abolition of warfare expanded the range over which rights could be effectively maintained. Traditionally, few people held rights more than five kilometers from home, and most considerably less. Now, in many islands (e.g. American Samoa, the Cook Islands, French Polynesia, Niue, and many outer islands of Fiji), most "owners" live on another island in that country, or abroad.

## Risks and Benefits of Codification

Since customs are often disputed, does it help to codify them? Not necessarily, for codification changes custom by cementing it in place, whereas flexibility was one of its key elements. It would be impossible to implement a law that said, as customary systems provided, that rights fade over time to the extent they are not used and relative to the needs of others who use or want to use them more, that those who fulfill community obligations best usually receive stronger support for rights, and that good memory, persuasive power, and physical force enhance de facto land rights.

Land customs have been codified in a few places such as Kiribati and Tuvalu, where populations are small and the atolls relatively uniform. Each of those countries has one main language and similar land customs. More commonly, custom is not defined, and in cases of dispute, the courts decide what accords best with custom for that case. Most land courts of the region, however, have vastly more cases than they have the time or resources to resolve. Where judgments are given, many are ignored, as many governments lack the administrative capacity to enforce the decisions of their land courts.

In most of the rural Pacific the law states that custom shall prevail, but it is always with qualifications. Many customary systems accepted that serious offenders be killed, banished, deprived of land rights, or have their homes burned, their animals confiscated, or property destroyed. Most such actions are prohibited by law today. Even where custom has been completely replaced by law officially, custom often "invades" the law. Thus governments that nationalized all seawater are not always able to implement that law and will not force legal rights over the (legally former) customary owners who have votes in the next election.

# Land Registration—When, What, and How?

Registration aims to define who owns what rights in order to resolve disputes as well as enhance stability, productivity, and environmental protection. These goals, however, will not necessarily be achieved. A major difference between most tenures in Europe and Asia today on the one hand, and traditional Pacific tenures on the other, leads to much misunderstanding. In customary Pacific tenures (as in earlier customary systems in Europe and Asia), land and water rights waxed and waned at different phases of life from birth through to death, in response to personal, family, and community needs, and to political and economic forces. This constant living process gave flexibility, which has negative attributes as well as positive. In capitalistic and communistic societies, on the other hand, rights are precisely defined in area and time. A seller's rights are extinguished, and the buyer acquires them in total. It is the same with gift or inheritance, or joining a commune. This was not so in Pacific societies, where one who gave, lent, or sold land rights to another did so as part of a continuing relationship. Rights were never fixed, but constantly strengthened or weakened, and the rights of those away too long faded out or were superseded.

Registration was resisted where people feared it might facilitate forced sale, but in most situations registration was welcomed in order to confirm one's rights, for land disputes were common.

When lands commissions were set up to register land, people usually insisted that they register the traditional boundaries recognized at that time for subsistence purposes. But the small, fragmented lots into which lands were divided for subsistence often differed in size, shape, and location from what would be best suited to the commercial farming or other occupations many of them were then going into.

In any case, registration is a long and expensive process. The governments of Fiji and the Cook Islands decided one hundred years ago to register all land, expecting it would take a few years, but neither has completed the process. The decision more than twenty years ago to register all land in Papua New Guinea has been followed by almost no progress, and Lakau (1995) is one of many who caution against hasty or extensive registration of customary land in rural Papua New Guinea. Public trust in the government is low, its funds and skills limited, and change in rural communities is too complex for systems to keep up with in the present sociopolitical climate.

After registration, in most Pacific Island countries land rights can be acquired only by accident of birth—that is, by inheritance from parents. This is a poor basis for allocating what is in many cases their most valuable resource. Those who originate from isolated islands or remote areas find it difficult to get effective access to land near towns, ports, markets, or jobs. Likewise, many whose grandparents had adequate land but large families now have nominal rights to such infinitesimal plots, or share the rights with so many others, that the plots are of little but symbolic value. Traditional mechanisms of gift, permissive occupancy, adoption, voluntary reallocation, and warfare have not been adequately substituted for, even though a mobile population in a modern economy needs much more flexibility of land transfer.

Sale of land is prohibited in most Pacific Island countries, or if allowed is strictly controlled. This ensures that families do not lose their rights, but the prohibition should be adapted to current need. In the Cook Islands, Nauru, Niue, Tokelau, and Tonga, for example, it is against the law to sell land rights, even to close relatives. American Samoa allows sale between blood kin. In the Cook Islands, Nauru, and New Zealand, once a name is on the register it stays there, and those who by customary processes would have retained rights in some lands and dropped out of others, remain in perpetuity—and their children and grandchildren ad infinitum.

In most of Polynesia, land rights were inherited primarily through the father, but could be inherited through the mother. Rights through both were seldom activated for long. Once land is registered, however, no one wants to "fade out" of any plot, so tiny plots now have hundreds of legal owners. Many individuals in Nauru now "own" one thousandth or less of a share in a plot less than a hectare.

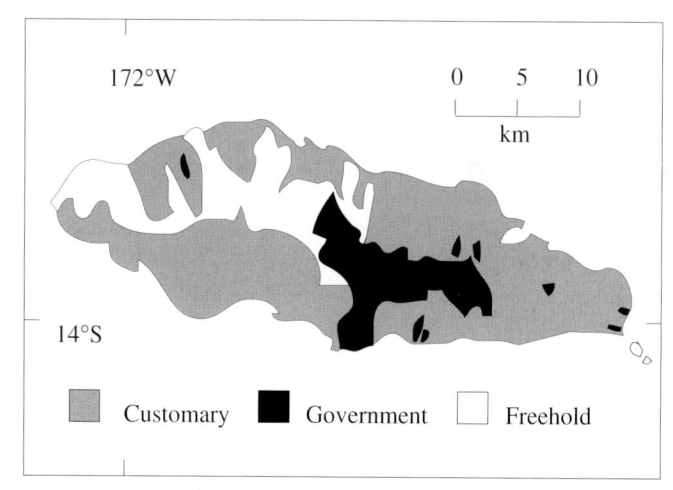

*Figure 17.2.* 'Upolu, Samoa, showing customary, government, and freehold land (after Asghar 1988).

These problems are not caused by traditional systems, none of which enabled such ridiculous results. Partly they were caused by colonial governments that understood the way rights were acquired better than the way they withered if not activated. Even more, today they are caused by those who insist on every descendant inheriting a share of every piece. If land is registered and sale is forbidden (as in much of the region), and all offspring inherit equal rights from both parents, the number of "owners" in each plot more than doubles every generation. Many Polynesian and Micronesian people accept it as their established custom, which it is now, although very different from earlier traditions (see e.g. Crocombe 1975b, Crocombe and Meleisea 1994, France 1969, Ward and Kingdon 1995 and many others).

In Fiji and Samoa (see Figure 17.2), freehold land may be sold, but freehold comprises only 4% of the area in each (it was 8% in Fiji until the government returned some land to indigenous ownership). In Kiribati, land may be sold to other I-Kiribati if the buyer can prove that he or she has no land on that island and needs it for housing or other approved purposes, and if the seller can prove that the land being sold is surplus to the requirements of the seller and his or her family. However, the rule is often overlooked in Tarawa, where one-third of the national population lives, and where some people are landless. In Papua New Guinea, land can be sold "in accordance with custom," which provides some flexibility but also leaves the process open to accumulation of large areas by entrepreneurs.

In most countries, land transfer is restricted to leasing, often subject to heavy restrictions. It is also very cumbersome in situations such as in French Polynesia or the Cook Islands, where leasing a house site may require the approval of dozens or hundreds of individuals with rights in it.

## Land Alienation

In Melanesian societies with complex monetary systems, land could be bought using traditional currency (see e.g. Pospisil 1963), but where this occurred it was in a context of ongoing social relationships. Outright sale of land was unfamiliar to most Pacific peoples, and when European entrepreneurs purchased large tracts (most sales took place between 1840 and 1900), there was often misunderstanding on both sides about what rights changed hands and for how long. Europeans familiar with freehold thought they had bought all rights unconditionally, whereas many islanders thought equally genuinely that they had provided land to immigrants in need with the customary understanding that it would revert to them if the "buyer" did not use it, and that they would receive periodic help and tribute from those to whom they supplied land.

There were also many instances of cheating and fraud on both sides. The worst European speculators deceived Vanuatu people of enormous areas (Sope 1976, Van Trease 1987), and Samoans sold Europeans three times the total area of Samoa (Meleisea 1990, Schoeffel 1996). Some lands were taken by force by colonial governments, as in New Zealand (Kawharu 1977, Ward 1974), New Caledonia (Saussol 1979), and Hawai'i (Meller and Horwitz 1987), or by local chiefs, as in Tonga (Rutherford 1977), Fiji (Routledge 1985), and Kiribati (Namai 1987). Figure 17.3 shows the current extent of indigenous reserves in New Caledonia (most of the remainder was taken by force). Figure 17.4 shows current land tenure in Maui, Hawai'i (the picture is similar for the neighboring islands as well), where a majority of the land has been acquired by large landowners and federal and state governments.

Nevertheless, in the region as a whole, expatriates generally found plenty of people willing to sell their land. The view often heard today, that Pacific Islanders would never sell their lands, was not the case. They wanted money or things it would buy, but often also hoped that plantations or other facilities built on alienated land would facilitate employment, trade, roads, wharves, and even education or medical services. These hopes were often not realized, or inadequately achieved, and many regretted having sold. However, foreign buyers had little difficulty buying much more land throughout the region than they were ever able to use over the ensuing hundred years. Capital and labor were much harder to get than land. One of the few

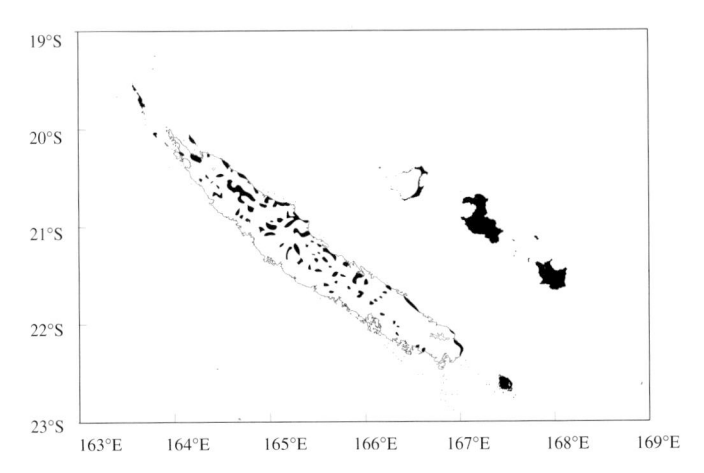

*Figure 17.3. Extent of indigenous reserves (shown in black) on New Caledonia (after Angleviel et al. 1992).*

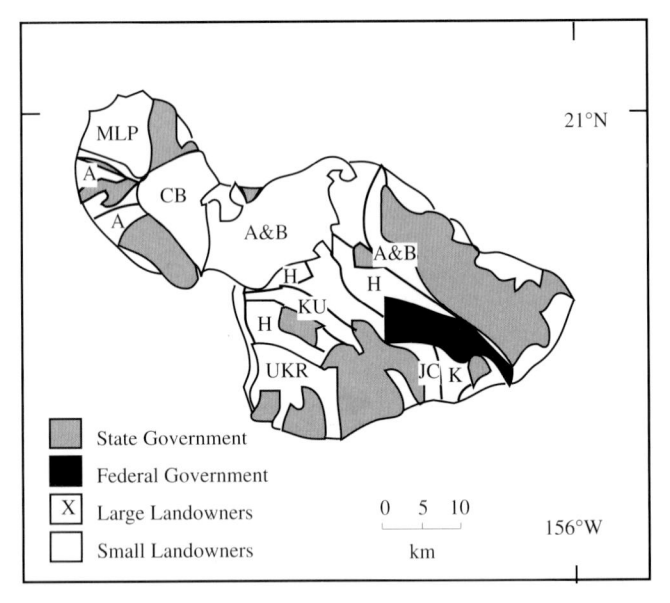

*Figure 17.4. Maui, Hawai'i, showing land distributed almost entirely between government and large landowners (after Decker 1983).*

places where all alienated land was used was Micronesia from 1914 to 1945, when Japanese settlers outnumbered indigenous people (Peattie 1988, Yanaihara 1940).

Where land sale was stopped it was often due to the influence of missions, colonial governments, or local chiefs who had become aware of problems caused by alienation elsewhere. Because of the wars over land between Maori and European in New Zealand, the United Kingdom forbade sale of land in Fiji and annulled most of the sales that had taken place before it became involved. The United Kingdom allowed New Zealand to administer the Cook Islands only on condition that land sale was forbidden. Germany refused to recognize most land purchases by Europeans in Samoa before it took control.

Leasing therefore became the common way immigrants acquired land rights from the beginning of this century. It was better, because the original owners earned rent and got the land back at the end of the lease—usually sixty-six or ninety-nine years. However, the erosion of the fixed rents due to inflation and the massive rise in populations made leasing less popular. As a result, the world-wide trends for lease terms to be shorter, for rents to be reviewed regularly, and for benefits to be shared more widely (e.g. shares of turnover or profit, and participation in ownership and management of enterprises on leased land), are now apparent in the Pacific.

Much of the formerly alienated land has gone back to the descendants of its former owners. Vanuatu cancelled all freehold titles and declared all land to be owned by indigenous people under custom, though immigrants could lease lands they were actually farming (Alatoa 1984, Arutangai 1987). Papua New Guinea and Solomon Islands adopted similar but less comprehensive policies. The proindependence party in New Caledonia has a similar goal. The Fiji government recently decided to return to indigenous ownership about half of the land it then owned (which it had acquired because it had been declared "ownerless," or because the owning clans had died out). This amounts to about 4% of the total land area of Fiji. All Japanese were repatriated from Micronesia after World War II, and most of the lands they occupied are now held by Micronesians. Kiribati bought back the alienated Line Islands. The government or individuals in Western Samoa acquired almost all foreign-owned land. Now very little land is owned by immigrants in the tropical South Pacific except in the French territories and Irian Jaya, where massive immigration from Java and other parts of Indonesia has been accompanied by confiscation, intimidation, and forced sales, reinforced by the fact that the Indonesian government does not recognize indigenous rights except to land that is currently under cultivation.

Even where immigrants outnumbered indigenes, and where most of the land was alienated to Europeans or Asians (as in Guam, Hawai'i, the Northern Marianas, New Caledonia, New Zealand, Palau, and Pohnpei), large areas have been returned to indigenous ownership in recent years due to political and economic action. More is likely to return. However, the proportion of national income deriving from land is reducing, so some of the gains are more symbolic than real. And given current trends in the region, it will not be surprising if that which is acquired from Europeans by the end of this century will be controlled by new Asian investors within a generation or two.

One of the ironies is that where no land was ever alienated (as in Tonga, Niue, the Cook Islands, Wallis and Futuna, and with trivial exceptions Tokelau and Tuvalu), or where alienated land has long since been returned (as in Samoa), the desire of people to emigrate permanently is very strong. To the maximum extent that they can gain access, the countries they want to settle in are those where most land was alienated and converted to tenures and uses that enabled those countries to generate vastly higher incomes. As a result, many more Polynesians now live in New Zealand, Australia, the United States, Chile, France, and elsewhere than in island Polynesia, and many Micronesians emigrate to the United States since access was granted in 1986. They have no qualms about buying freehold land where they settle.

Every nation wants (and has) roads, public buildings, port facilities, and airports. Many need space to resettle disadvantaged people. Moreover, every Pacific Islands government has a policy of attracting capital to generate income and employment. Hotels, factories, plantations, even the Japanese spaceport that is planned for Kiritimati Island (Kiribati), all need land and modify tenures in practice—even if there is no change in law or stated principle.

Public facilities necessitate acquiring rights from private interests. This does not mean that only one form of tenure is suitable for public lands, but some change to the former systems is inevitable. I assumed before independence that land acquisition in the public interest would be easier after independence, but it is harder, due to growing populations, the increasing value of land, and a visible decline in the 1990s in public confidence in the elected governments.

Other intensive uses are beset by similar contentions. Disputes over the relative benefits to lessees and landowners have seen resorts, factories, and other enterprises burned or closed. Even tiny, isolated, government-owned telecommunications repeater stations on remote peaks that had never been used by anyone have amazingly high values attributed to them by a range of claimants, a range that gets wider as the payouts increase. Many national facilities in Papua New Guinea, including airports, have been seized, smashed, or threatened in the ongoing battle for more compensation.

In subsistence societies the needs of the community took precedence over those of individuals. The community is now the nation, and land rights increasingly need to be allocated according to public need. But cultural change takes place at different speeds, and land is always an area of cultural lag, so it may take time before the systems of land allocation catch up with the current needs of the people they are intended to serve.

## The Continuing Evolution of Marine Tenures

Customary rights to coastal waters and tropical lagoons tended to shrink after contact with industrial technology. Reliance on the sea was reduced, due to population losses last century, the growth of paid employment, emigration, commercial agriculture, and imported proteins. Today, however, the sea is becoming more intensively used due to rising populations, new marine products (e.g. cultivated seaweed and shellfish, tropical fish for foreign aquariums, octopus exported to Japan), and tourist diving.

Many governments declared a century ago that all water, and land below high-water mark, were henceforth government property and available equally to everyone. In practice, however, customary rights usually continued to be recognized in varying degrees.

Even in countries where laws provide that coastal waters belong to the customary owners and that custom shall determine their use, much has changed. If what was a quiet village becomes a town and harbor, the water rights and practices are going to adapt, whatever the law or custom says. Likewise, when people who fished for subsistence begin fishing commercially, or when products formerly regarded as rubbish (such as sea cucumber) become commercial products, then the tenure of the water where it is harvested may change in practice if not in principle.

Some governments are giving greater recognition to customary rights. Indigenous Fijians assert traditional claims to water vis-à-vis Indian and other immigrants. Traditional rights were acknowledged by both the independent government since 1970 and the colonial government before that, but not implemented much in practice. Growing populations, more commercial fishing, and heightened ethnic tensions have led to closer definition and stricter enforcement of such rights. Likewise, in Manus (Papua New Guinea), increased population and commercialization, including tuna boats catching bait fish, have extended claims and intensified competition for coastal waters (Carrier 1983).

The technology for culturing pearls enhanced the value of suitable lagoons. Customary claims were reasserted or reinterpreted. Pearl farmers wanted exclusive rights to an area (see Figure 17.5). As the best spaces filled up, competition became keener. And as some people were going to be rich, jealousy sharpened disputes over access, even though there was no precise customary precedent for commercial use of lagoon space. Many atoll people who worked in town now came back, along with some who had never been on their "home" atoll (but whose forebears came from there), to claim water for pearls and land for living. And some strangers from other islands arrived because in law the lagoon was public property for any citizen of the nation—not just the island (and in French Polynesia lagoon space is allocated by the government). Pearl farming has changed the de facto tenure and use of the lagoons and exacerbated disputes in the Tuamotu Islands (Rapaport 1996) and the northern Cook Islands (Newnham 1997), as well as generating enormous differences in incomes. It is likely to have similar effects in Tuvalu, Kiribati, the Marshall Islands, and other places that are beginning pearl culture. What to do about lagoon rights is constantly discussed, but progress in resolving the problems is slow.

More extensive use of reefs, particularly commercial use, naturally enhances claims to them. Outboard motors and new fishing technology, including refrigeration, extend the distance over which rights can be effectively exercised (and claimed or stretched!).

Catching octopus for export from the outer reefs of Tarawa and Maiana is a profitable new industry. It, and the commercial production of selected seaweeds, may lead to stronger assertions of traditional rights to reefs, and their more precise definition. Other new reef products being explored, and in some cases exploited, include pharmacological extracts from marine plants and animals. Tourism and sand for construction are leading to more disputes over rights between low- and high-tide marks and to beaches. For case studies on current directions in traditional marine tenures, see South et al. (1995).

The United Nations Law of the Sea Convention arose out of disputes between nations of North and South America. Although the origin was incidental to the Pacific Islands, the islands are the greatest beneficiaries from the new regime. LOS recognizes a 12-nautical-mile territorial zone and a 188-nautical-mile exclusive economic zone (EEZ). This new marine tenure is the basis for the largest source of earnings (mainly from tuna and snapper) for Kiribati and Tuvalu, and for a potential bonanza for the Cook Islands, which has vast deposits of seabed minerals in its EEZ.

Although national governments control the EEZs, they may make concessions to component units. In the Federated States of Micronesia and Papua New Guinea, there are different formulae for marine rights to be shared between the national government and state or provincial governments. The United States seems likely to grant the economic benefits (not the sovereignty) from waters around Guam and the Northern Marianas to their local governments. And in some Pacific Island nations, the claims of local landowning communities to adjacent waters are recognized in varying degrees.

Beyond the EEZ lie the international waters, which are coming under increasing international control, including the International Seabed Authority, which leases mining rights to seabed minerals to member nations of the United Nations. The rights in the Clarion-Clipperton zone southeast of Hawai'i were the first to be so allocated.

## The Influence of Fresh Water Sources on Tenure Forms

Crops like irrigated taro enabled higher productivity, denser populations, more elaborate social and leadership systems, and more complex rights to land and water. Where irrigated taro is the main starch food, the whole valley was the primary traditional political unit in which a chief or council of chiefs controlled people and water. Within the valley, smaller clans and families controlled the water they drew off for their taro. Watersheds were the main boundaries (in contrast to localities where irrigation is not used, where the watercourse rather than the watershed is often the boundary). Taro requires hard labor, so the right to it almost always lay with the household that did the work.

On atolls there are no valleys and no running water. Fresh water is scarce and therefore more valuable than on high islands, where it is generally plentiful. On atolls, access to water requires different technology and results in different patterns of social

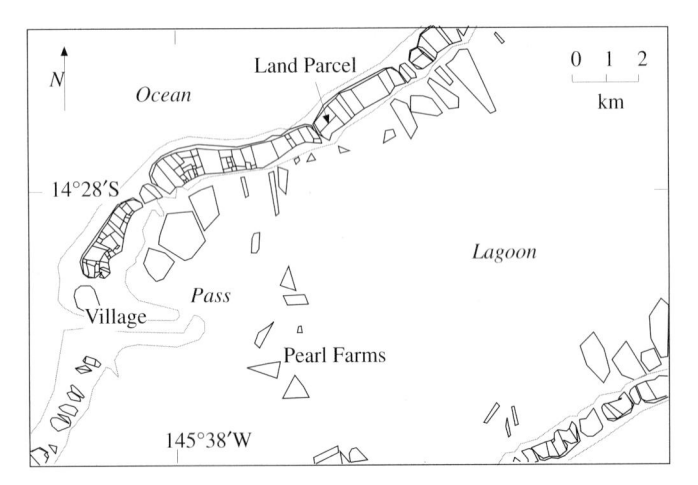

*Figure 17.5. Takaroa, Tuamotus, showing land parcels and adjacent pearl farms.*

organization, even among atoll people who came from high-island origins (which most did).

The main root crop on many atolls (*Cyrtosperma*) required irrigation. Atolls often evolved more egalitarian leadership systems because there is no need for central control of water. Even more work is required than with taro on high islands, so the household that supplies the labor has strong rights to the land and the tubers. There are exceptions to these generalizations for other reasons, but it was commonly so.

Fresh water is obtained by digging down through the porous coral to the fresh water that floats on the salt, causing the salt water to sink in a curve, which is deepest at the center of the land on the islet. So land in the center is more fertile and more valuable than that at the edges. Digging wells for domestic water is hard work—and was even harder before the introduction of metal tools last century—so wells are valuable assets of those who dug them. It was harder still to dig pits to create gardens deep enough that tubers reach the freshwater lens. Because there is only sand and coral rock at that level, soil is created from leaves, food remains, and surface soil from elsewhere. Each tuber is cultivated by hand, with soil and mulch packed around it as it grows. This exceedingly hard work is reflected in the value of that crop and the concentration of rights to it in the planter.

## Rights to the Bowels of the Earth, and Up to the Skies

Like subsistence agriculturalists everywhere, Pacific peoples seldom used more than a few centimeters of soil. There was surface mining of stone for tools, salt for cooking, and ochre for painting, but no awareness of the existence or value of gold, copper, nickel, and other minerals.

Colonial governments usually followed their metropolitan principle, which in many cases meant that minerals belonged to the state and that income should be used for public benefit. In practice, unfortunately, this benefit was often for the colonial public more than the indigenous public. Since independence, much of the income has been absorbed by the central bureaucracy rather than used for national development. Former or present landowners were usually compensated for disturbance, although France did not compensate for the nickel mines in New Caledonia, nor Indonesia for the gold and copper mines in Irian Jaya, nor Japan for Angaur in Palau.

Independent governments followed the principle of national ownership of minerals. Responding to the public demand for employment and income, they increasingly sought investment, much of it foreign because of the low propensity to save in most Pacific communities. This national interest, however, conflicts with the interest of the landowners. The most spectacular case is Bougainville, where the civil war which has raged since 1989 was triggered by the dispute between landowners and the national government over benefits from the copper mine—then the government's largest source of revenue. Smaller disturbances over the same issue have occurred at most mines, at the only producing oil fields, and other developments.

Consequently the Papua New Guinea government decided to give landowners much more of the benefit. That does not stop the trend, however, which applies whether the enterprise is owned nationally or from abroad. Where landowners see an opportunity for more benefits, they or their lawyers can build a sense of grievance and maximize claims. Some, like Donigi (1994), believe that all benefits belong to the traditional landowners and that governments have no right to them. The share for those who supply capital and expertise is also a matter of contention. But most elected governments consider that most of the massive benefits derived from such "unearned increment" should accrue to them to provide public services. The principle that all parties should benefit is generally accepted, but what constitutes a fair share is one of the most contentious issues in much of the region today (Larmour 1989).

The Fiji government had a long dispute with the United States because its military aircraft flew through the Nadi Flight Information Zone, which includes not only Fiji, but all air space above a certain altitude over much of Tuvalu, Nauru, and Kiribati, east to Samoa and south to the New Zealand zone. Finally, the dispute was made quiescent by giving Fiji additional aid. Since then the Small Islands States group (the Cook Islands, Kiribati, Nauru, Niue, and Tuvalu), has been investigating the possibility of charging aircraft (including all aircraft between Australia and New Zealand and the Americas) to fly through their air space—in the way that Japan pays Russia for the same privilege. Maori claimed to own all radio waves in New Zealand and demanded compensation for their use by broadcasters (the main one at the time was the government). The claim was rejected by the Supreme Court, but is still being pursued.

## The Land Rights of Women

In 90% of Melanesia, all of Polynesia, and part of Micronesia, tenure rights were inherited mainly through men. Even in the 10% of cultures where they were transmitted predominantly through women, land management was performed largely by men. The colonial governments were from patrilineal cultures of Europe, and Christianity is a male-dominated religion. When Japan, whose culture and religions were likewise patrilineal, was the colonial power in Micronesia, this further reduced traditional matrilineal principles there. In the part of Fiji (Bua) where matrilineal principles prevailed, the United Kingdom government absorbed them into the predominant patrilineal pattern. But even without pressure from governments or religions, commercial agriculture had a similar effect, so it became common for Tolai men in Papua New Guinea and Ifira men in Vanuatu to transfer lands they derived from their mothers, on which they had planted coffee, cocoa, or other commercial crops, to their sons rather than their sisters' sons as they would have under custom.

Change has been radical in some countries, minimal in others. Thus in Hawai'i, French Polynesia, the Cook Islands, Niue, and New Zealand, where land rights and chiefly titles were the prerogative of men, they are now just as commonly held by women. The change came about as a result not of policy or activism, but of largely imperceptible shifts in behavior in response to such technologically driven innovations as women gaining control of reproduction, labor-saving devices, and a related world ethos including equal education and opportunity. In Guam and the Northern Marianas, where the traditional matrilineal systems changed during Spanish, German, and Japanese colonial eras to patrilineal, now both inherit equally. A trend toward greater equality in land rights is discernible in Kiribati and Samoa, but there is little sign of it in Tonga or most of Melanesia. Islamic influence from Indonesia in Irian Jaya will reinforce patrilineal tendencies there.

## "Local" and "Foreign" Ethnicity Remain Important

What constitutes the "in-group" or the "out-group" in the Pacific is largely determined by ethnicity. This always was the case, with people of other tribes (particularly if they spoke another language or showed differences of culture) being generally placed in the "foreign" category. The categories have expanded with mobility and with immigration of Europeans and Asians, but they are still important.

Citizenship in a Pacific nation does not give equal access to land. In most countries, ultimate title is reserved for people indigenous to the nation, but often those indigenous to a locality within it. These titles are reinforced by traditional logic of blood and history and by Old Testament theology. Thus the land rights of Indians who have lived five generations in Fiji and are citizens, or equivalent Europeans and Chinese in Solomon Islands and Papua New Guinea, or Solomon Islanders in Tonga and Samoa, and many others, are constrained by both law and custom.

The trend is intensifying rather than relaxing, with recent constitutional reviews and changes in Papua New Guinea and Solomon Islands recommending more discrimination rather than less. In Fiji since the 1987 coups, the rights of indigenous Fijians have strengthened relative to those of other categories.

Those who claimed traditional rights to areas that have become towns and cities are in many cases reasserting those rights against both people originating from other countries and those from other parts of the same country. With towns expanding and income gaps widening, demands by former landowners for a greater share of benefits are growing. Some get it, others lose the lot as aggressive squatters take over land and neither landowners nor governments are able to enforce "landowners'" rights.

## Relations Between Tenures and Productivity

Much of the most fertile and best located land is not under customary tenures. It is in freehold, leasehold, occupation rights, or other tenures that give more secure rights to producers. Even where these lands lie side by side with lands under customary tenures of equal fertility, the former are markedly more productive. There are various reasons for this, but tenure is an important one (Acquaye 1987, Overton 1988).

Socialization and value systems are also vital factors in productivity and lead to radically different outputs from the same tenures. The way in which some New Guinea highlanders migrate to coastal areas and outproduce coastal neighbors whether immigrant or local, despite insecure tenure, parallels the way Chinese farmers in Tahiti and Fiji outproduce Tahitians and Fijians despite insecure tenures.

Converting subsistence farmers into factory or hotel workers is relatively easy. They enter a new motivational context with clear directions, time frames, and goals, and immediate incentives like hourly pay. Converting subsistence farmers (who have been shown in many islands to require only twelve hours of work a week to produce their needs) into commercial farmers, however, is difficult and slow. I know of no example, anywhere in the region, of the rapid or highly successful conversion of whole communities of subsistence farmers into commercial farmers, although in most places there is some commercial cropping. Aporosa Rakoto's (1973) study of Fijian sugar farmers showed that those who were successful were self-selected (which no established community can be), had moved sufficiently far from their place of origin to be able to avoid undue calls on their time and resources, and had individual tenure. The productive farmers met customary obligations more selectively, though often more generously. (Rakoto's full study was unfortunately never published, as he died prematurely.)

Where increased productivity is a goal, farmers need to be able to move from their community of origin, and those not highly motivated to farming (a large percentage in any human community that has much choice), should be encouraged to seek other occupations to the extent that they are available. As Rusiate Nayacakalou pointed out a generation ago, the disadvantages of rigidly tying land to social groups now outweigh the advantages. Doing so reduces flexibility, constrains opportunity, and inhibits productivity. Such rigidity was not characteristic of customary systems.

Tying land to social groups is more problematic when the only way one can join is by accident of birth. In situations of pure subsistence, minimal mobility, and social organization by kinship, accident of birth (i.e. sex, order of birth, seniority in a clan or family, etc.) is one useful principle on which to allocate land rights. It was commonly the primary ideological principle, but extensively qualified in practice by need, use, numbers in a family, contributions to family and community activities, extensive adoption, multiple marriage, acceptance of refugees, gift, permissive occupancy, and the ability to defend it from others.

Accident of birth simplifies record-keeping and minimizes short-term disputes, but rigidly applied it inhibits people's goals for higher productivity and freer mobility and is neither equitable nor economical. Imagine if only the sons of doctors were allowed to be doctors, and the sons of farmers had to be farmers. Such inherited employment was common in Europe, Asia, and the Pacific in ancient times. It can be done in today's context at the price of keeping people poor. Yet many Pacific countries still allocate land on criteria that reduce their income and opportunities and encourage young people to seek livelihoods elsewhere.

Whereas it was common for basic rights to large areas to be

associated with a local or descent group, rights to component plots for cultivation were held by individuals and households. For administrative convenience, however, some colonial tenures registered only the group rights, leaving internal allocation to its leaders. With increasing population and commercialization, however, individuals and households need more clearly defined rights. These can be provided by leasing (practiced extensively in Fiji in relation to non-native Fiji Islanders, and to a lesser extent in Tonga and elsewhere) or by occupation rights (common in French Polynesia, the Cook Islands, and Niue). Occupation rights are cheaper and easier to administer, longer term (perpetual if used), and tied to usage. They are also closer in principle to the traditional custom. Occupation rights and leases are associated with much higher productivity than lands under customary tenures.

Tenures are adapting to the fact that many people now live in towns, or elsewhere doing "urban-type" work in resorts, mines, military or fishing bases, or logging camps, or as transient administrators, nurses, teachers, extension workers, church ministers, storekeepers or pensioners. This is true for the great majority in American Samoa, the Cook Islands, Easter Island, French Polynesia, Guam, Hawai'i, the Marshall Islands, Nauru, New Zealand, New Caledonia, Niue, Norfolk, the Northern Marianas, and Palau—and for about half in Fiji. Traditional customs require radical modification to be of optimum use to such people.

The Federated States of Micronesia, Samoa, Tonga, Tokelau, Pitcairn, Tuvalu, and Wallis and Futuna fall into another category. Most indigenous people who remain in those countries live on their land and derive much of their livelihood from it. But most of the people derived from most of those countries now live in metropolitan countries. And most goods and services in all those countries are financed by salaries, wages, contract work, and transfer payments from abroad (intergovernment and NGO aid, remittances from absent relatives, etc.).

Land and water remain the sources of livelihood for the majority in Irian Jaya, Papua New Guinea, Solomon Islands, Vanuatu, and Kiribati. This small number of countries nevertheless contains most Pacific Islanders. But even for them, tenure conditions are radically different from those of the self-sufficient, subsistence past. Mobility is increasing, and intensifying interaction with commerce and government leads to standardizing influences on land policy and practice from the capital and from abroad.

Most Pacific governments aim to promote rural development and minimize urbanization. However, practice is often contrary to policy. The many positive adaptations to urbanization include better land-utilization planning, specific tenures for commercial, industrial, residential, public service, and other uses, and strata titles for intensive uses (see e.g. Crocombe et al. 1981.

## Most "Landowners" in Most Countries Are "Absentee Landlords"

Only in Nauru and Niue does one island constitute a nation. Both are sufficiently small for everyone to live at home and drive to work each day. So everyone has access to lands they traditionally identify as theirs. But in neither case is land the main source of livelihood. Most Nauruans remain on Nauru, but depend on paid work, phosphate royalties, and government services. By contrast, about 90% of Niueans live overseas, and many who remain on Niue work for the government (Richmond-Rex 1995). Many services are paid for by aid and remittances.

Even in nations with extensive rural areas, there is increasing concentration on main roads, harbors, airports, and commercial centers. This worldwide trend will intensify. How far should the land rights of the growing number of "absentee landowners" be recognized? One possibility is to cancel them, but it is more easily said than done, for absentees value their rights at "home," even if they never return there. Fiji law allows any clan to delete from joint ownership of clan land any person who had been absent for two years. Yet no clan has ever done so, even though probably most men have left their clan land for at least two years. Some islands in Kiribati had a traditional rule that a man absent for seven years was "lost at sea" and his lands reallocated. That law was applied to those who chose to resettle in the Phoenix Islands in the 1930s and then to Solomon Islands in the 1950s and 1960s, and Washington and Fanning Islands more recently. Niue introduced legislation to cancel the rights of Niueans who had lived abroad more than twenty years, but the absent majority living in New Zealand and Australia, who contribute to relatives back home, protested so strongly that the legislation was withdrawn.

Nevertheless, the rights of absentees are modified, reduced, compromised, or made conditional by social as well as legal processes. Others are often allowed to use the land of absentees. While it would be impolite to cancel legal rights of absent clan members, most absentees realize that there is competition for land at home and do not try to exercise such rights. Many absentees who return are made so unwelcome that they move out again, and some who try to derive benefit from the land in their absence are persuaded to desist.

Ambiguity adds flexibility, but it can also reduce rural productivity, which is very low in most island states. Where governments or the public want to increase it, the rights of absentees must be addressed. In many islands the rights of absentees frustrate both those who remain and those who go. A higher degree of predictability is needed, so all parties are clearer as to their rights and responsibilities, to improve security and productivity. This may include prescribing periods of absence before one's land rights are reduced (e.g. restricted to enough for retirement) or made conditional (such as allowing succession only to those retaining citizenship—as was the case in Tonga until the High Court reversed the policy by a new interpretation of law), or making long-term absentees return and convince authorities of their intention to remain (as some Land Court judges in the Cook Islands have required). Other conditions might include making inheritance conditional on appropriate contributions to community needs (as is common in many societies in practice), or on the approval of resident kin.

## The Land Rights of Chiefs

The word "chief" (and such other terms as "big-men") is used to describe many different kinds of customary leaders. In the subsistence past, the land rights of chiefs were fused in varying degrees with those they led, but in today's money economy there is no precedent to determine the "proper" monetary or fractional share for a chief—that is, assuming people want such benefits to be allocated on criteria fitted to another era. It is tempting for chiefs to claim money benefits as theirs alone, or largely. The income gap between chiefs and commoners has in many cases widened alarmingly. Chiefs generally rationalize this as a traditional entitlement, whereas more equitable distribution would reflect prior custom more accurately.

This trend is visible in many countries (although chiefly power is waning in others), and accentuated by the fact that investors find it easier to deal with single chiefs than with numerous clansmen. Corruption, too, is easier the more power is concentrated.

## Potentials for the Future

Needs have changed radically, and some tenures have changed too, but in the Pacific as elsewhere, tenure change lags behind social and economic change. Resistance to conscious changes in land tenure are often reinforced by the assumption that the traditional system was God-given and should remain for ever. Caution is compounded by the history of land alienation in some countries, and by the insecurity of paid work, for alternative social security systems are minimal and jobs precarious. Nevertheless, amazing changes are acceptable, even insisted on (often reinterpreted as traditional) if people assume they will benefit from them.

Change cannot be achieved by laws or policies if there is strong resistance to them—as in the case of the Mau rebellion in Samoa (in response to attempts to individualize land), Fiji's ineffective provisions to cancel the rights of absentees (described above), and the short-term lease provisions in the Cook Islands, which aimed to boost productivity but which met with apathy.

Because changes in tenures lag behind other changes in society, increasing the mismatch between customary principles and current aspirations reinforces other motives leading the more enterprising and innovative to seek livelihoods off the land. That tendency will remain. For those who stay on the land, the discrepancies themselves generate slow but imperceptible change (see e.g. O'Meara 1990).

In Fiji, where 14,000 long-established Indian settlers lease farms from indigenous Fijians, conflict is high over rents and political issues. Some lessees have been harassed into abandoning the farms. How many others will be renewed and on what terms is still being negotiated. Whatever the outcome, the insecurity will reduce productivity and national income for some time.

Water rights are no less contentious. In New Zealand, some Maori claim 100% of the 200-mile EEZ. In a recent settlement the government gave Maori claimants half of the national fishing quota. Other Maori claim all rivers, which are now public assets, as tribal property. If current experiments with wave energy and ocean thermal energy conversion succeed, they will have implications for tenure of suitable reefs throughout the region.

The only places in the world where comprehensive land reforms have been quickly implemented is where someone holds absolute power (or close to it) and forces the changes. The only comprehensive reform in the Pacific was in Tonga, where a conquering warlord introduced a new system as part of a package designed to retain his power. It worked. His descendants still rule Tonga a century and a half later.

Nowhere in the Pacific today do such conditions exist. Radical change is not an option, but progressive, incremental improvements are feasible. Tenure change seldom takes place until the problems are acute, but in many islands they are. Even so, meeting the challenges head on can lead to violent resistance and become counterproductive. De facto change often takes place long before de jure change is feasible. Tenures take longer to adjust than most aspects of life, so the tendency is to get on with other activities. Some improvements are taking place, but the Pacific will not be alone in the world if many rural communities become stagnant backwaters occupied by apathetic people, while more rapid adaptations take place in towns.

## Acknowledgments

Linda Crowl, Peter Larmour, Moshe Rapaport, and Howard van Trease kindly made very helpful comments on the draft, but they are not responsible for remaining errors and omissions.

## Bibliography

Most geographical and anthropological studies in the Pacific include some information on land tenure. In addition, an extensive range of publications focuses on land tenure. For land tenure studies of the Pacific Islands region generally, see Acquaye et al. 1987, Bartlett et al. 1981, Crocombe et al. 1991, Lundsgaarde et al. 1974, Waigani Seminar 1971, and Ward and Kingdon 1995.

It is hard to know what to cite from the vast volume of published and unpublished material on land and water tenure systems in the region. Items included were determined as much on the basis of what was at hand at the time of writing as on assessment of relative importance.

Acquaye, E., et al. 1987. *Land tenure and rural productivity in the Pacific Islands*. Suva: University of the South Pacific.

Akimichi, T. 1991. Sea tenure and its transformation in the Lau of North Malaita, Solomon Islands. *South Pacific Study* 12(1):7–22.

Alatoa, H., et al. 1984. *Land tenure in Vanuatu*. Suva: University of the South Pacific.

Angleviel, F., et al. 1992. *Atlas de Nouvelle Caledonie*. Noumea: ORSTOM.

Arutangai, S. 1987. Vanuatu: overcoming the colonial legacy. In *Land tenure in the Pacific*, ed. R. Crocombe, 261–302. Suva: University of the South Pacific.

Asghar, M. 1988. Land use in Western Samoa. In *Soil taxonomy and fertility in the South Pacific*, ed. M. Asghar, T. Davidson and R. J. Morrison, 376–390. Apia, Western Samoa: University of the South Pacific.

Atanraoi, P. 1995. Seeking security and sustainability in a situation of high mobility. In *Customary land tenure and sustainable development*, ed. R. Crocombe, 55–74. Noumea: South Pacific Commission.

Ballard, C. 1996. *The politics of resource ownership in Papua New Guinea*. National Centre for Development Studies Seminar. Canberra: Australian National University.

Bartlett, A., et al. 1981. *Land, people and government: public lands policy in the South Pacific*. Suva: University of the South Pacific.

Carrier, J. G. 1981. Ownership of productive resources on Ponam Island, Manus Province. *Journal de la Société des Océanistes* 37:205–217.

Carrier, J. G. 1983. Profitless property: marine ownership and access to wealth on Ponam Island. *Ethnology* 22:133-51.

Clarke, W. C. 1994. Traditional land use and agriculture in the Pacific Islands. In *The science of Pacific Island peoples*, Vol. 2, ed. J. Morrison, P. Geraghty, and L. Crowl, 11–38. Suva: University of the South Pacific.

Crocombe, R. 1964. *Land tenure in the Cook Islands*. Melbourne: Oxford University Press.

Crocombe, R. 1968. Observations on land tenure in Tarawa. *Micronesica* 4:27–37.

Crocombe, R. 1975a. Land tenure in Tonga. In *Land and migration*, ed. S. H. Fonua, 43–61. Nuku'alofa: Tonga Council of Churches.

Crocombe, R. 1975b. Pre-contact traditional land tenure: the ideological base. *South Pacific Quarterly* 25(3):13–19.

Crocombe, R., ed. 1981. *Land, people and government: public lands policy in the Pacific Islands*. Suva: University of the South Pacific.

Crocombe, R., ed. 1991. *Land tenure in the Pacific*. Suva: University of the South Pacific.

Crocombe, R., and M. Meleisea, eds. 1994. *Land issues in the Pacific*. Christchurch: University of Canterbury.

Decker, B. 1983. Land tenure. In *Atlas of Hawaii*, ed. R. W. Armstrong, 152. Honolulu: University of Hawai'i Press.

Donigi, P. 1994. *Indigenous or aboriginal rights to property: a Papua New Guinea perspective*. Port Moresby: University of Papua New Guinea Press.

Elders of Nukunonu. 1987. Customary principles in Nukunonu. In *Land tenure in the atolls*, ed. R. Crocombe, 110–113. Suva: University of the South Pacific.

EMPAT (Economic Management Policy Advisory Team). 1996. *Economic use of land in the FSM: a review and description of land tenure systems in the FSM*. Asian Development Bank Occasional Paper no. 6, Manila.

Falanruw, M. 1994. Traditional fishing in Yap. In *Science of Pacific Islands peoples*, vol. 1, ed. R. J. Morrison, et al., 41–58. Suva: University of the South Pacific.

Fonua, P. 1991. Consequences of return migrants to a Tongan village. In *In search of a home*, ed. L. Mason and P. Hereniko, 3–23. Suva: University of the South Pacific.

France, P. 1969. *The charter of the land: custom and colonization in Fiji*. Melbourne: Oxford University Press.

Guiart, J. 1996. Land tenure and hierarchies in eastern Melanesia. *Pacific Studies* 19(1):1–29.

Hooper, A., and J. Huntsman. 1987. Tenure, society and economy. In *Land tenure in the atolls*, ed. R. Crocombe, 117–140. Suva: University of the South Pacific.

Hudson, R. 1996. Pitcairn Island lands. Unpublished report to Pitcairn Council.

Hviding, E. 1996. *Guardians of Marovo lagoon: practice, place and politics in maritime Melanesia*. Honolulu: University of Hawai'i Press.

Johannes, R. E. 1981. *Words of the lagoon: fishing and marine lore in the Palau District of Micronesia*. Berkeley: University of California Press.

Johannes, R. E. 1994. Pacific islands people's science and marine resource management. In *Science of Pacific Islands peoples*, ed. R. J. Morrison, et al. Suva: University of the South Pacific.

Kalauni, S., et al. 1977. *Land tenure in Niue*. Suva: University of the South Pacific.

Kalinoe, L. K. 1998. Customary water rights and water law: a case study of the Upper Sepik River. *Melanesian Journal of Land Studies* (in press).

Kamikamica, J. 1987. Making native land productive. In *Land tenure in the Pacific*, ed. R. Crocombe, 226–239. Suva: University of the South Pacific.

Kawharu, H. 1977. *Maori land tenure*. London: Oxford University Press.

Knudsen, K. 1964. *Titiana: a Gilbertese community in the Solomon Islands*. Eugene, Oregon: University of Oregon.

Lakau, A. 1995. Options for the Pacific's most complex nation: Papua New Guinea. In *Customary land tenure and sustainable development*, ed. R. Crocombe, 95–118. Noumea: South Pacific Commission.

Larmour, P., ed. 1979. *Land in Solomon Islands*. Suva: University of the South Pacific.

Larmour, P., ed. 1984. Alienated land and independence in Melanesia. *Pacific Studies* 8(1):1–47.

Larmour, P. 1989. Sharing the benefits: customary landowners and natural resource projects in Melanesia. *Pacific Viewpoint* 30(1):56–74.

Larmour, P. 1991. *Customary land tenure: registration and decentralization in Papua New Guinea*. Port Moresby: National Research Institute.

Lawrence, P., and I. Hogbin. 1967. *Studies in New Guinea land tenure*. Sydney: Sydney University Press.

Leupena, T., and K. Lutelu. 1987. Providing for the multitude. In *Land tenure in the atolls*, ed. R. Crocombe, 143–165. Suva: University of the South Pacific.

Lundsgaarde, H. 1974. *Land tenure in Oceania*. Honolulu: University of Hawai'i Press.

Mason, L. 1987. Tenures from subsistence to star wars. In *Land tenure in the atolls*, ed. R. Crocombe, 3–27. Suva: University of the South Pacific.

Maude, A., and F. Sevele. 1987. Tonga: equality overtaking privilege. In *Land tenure in the Pacific*, ed. R. Crocombe, 114–142. Suva: University of the South Pacific.

McPhetres, S. 1993. The history of land issues in the Commonwealth of the Northern Marianas. *Umanidat* 1(1):14–19.

Meleisea, M. 1980. *O tama uli: Melanesians in Samoa*. Suva: South Pacific Social Sciences Association.

Meleisea, M. 1990. *The making of modern Samoa*. Suva: University of the South Pacific.

Meller, N., and R. Horwitz. 1987. Hawaii: themes in land monopoly. In *Land tenure in the Pacific*, ed. R. Crocombe, 25–44. Suva: University of the South Pacific.

Namai, B., et al. 1987. The evolution of Kiribati land tenures. In *Land tenure in the atolls*, ed. R. Crocombe, 30–39. Suva: University of the South Pacific.

Nayacakalou, R. 1965. The bifurcation and amalgamation of Fijian lineages over a period of fifty years. *Proceedings of the Fiji Society for 1960 and 1961*, Suva, Fiji.

Nayacakalou R. 1992. *Leadership in Fiji*. Suva: University of the South Pacific.

Newnham, R. T. 1996. Social impact of pearl culture on Manihiki. Manuscript, Rarotonga.

O'Meara, J. T. 1990. *Samoan planters: tradition and economic development in Polynesia*. Fort Worth: Holt, Rinehart and Winston.

Overton, J., ed. 1988. *Rural Fiji*. Suva: University of the South Pacific.

Panoff, M. 1964. *Les structures agraires en Polynesie Francaise*. Papeete: ORSTOM.

Peattie, M. 1988. *Nan'yo: the rise and fall of the Japanese in Micronesia 1885–1945*. Honolulu: University of Hawai'i Press.

Pospisil, L. 1963. *Kapauku Papuan economy*. New Haven, Connecticut: Yale University Publications in Anthropology No. 67.

Pospisil, L. 1965. A formal analysis of substantive law: Kapauku Papuan laws of land tenure. *American Anthropologist* 67(5):186–21.

Prasad, B., and C. Tisdell. 1996. Getting property rights "right": land tenure in Fiji. *Pacific Economic Bulletin* 11(1):31–46.

Rakoto, A. 1973. Can custom be custom-built? Cultural obstacles to Fijian commercial enterprise. *Pacific Perspective* 2(2):32–35.

Rapaport, M. 1996. Between two laws: tenure regimes in the Pearl Islands. *The Contemporary Pacific* 8(1):33–49.

Ravault, F. 1980. Land problems in French Polynesia. *Pacific Perspective* 10(2):31–65.

Richmond-Rex, F. 1995. Seeking security and sustainability in a situation of high mobility. In *Customary land tenure and sustainable development*, ed. R. Crocombe, 75–94. Noumea: South Pacific Commission.

Rodman, M. 1987. *Masters of tradition: consequences of customary land tenure in Longana, Vanuatu*. Vancouver: University of British Columbia Press.

Rogers, G., ed. 1986. *The fire has jumped*. Suva: University of the South Pacific.

Routledge, D. 1985. *Matanitu: the struggle for power in early Fiji*. Suva: University of the South Pacific.

Rutherford, N. 1977. *Friendly islands: a history of Tonga*. Melbourne: Oxford University Press.

Saussol, A. 1979. *L'Héritage: essai sur le problème foncier Mèlanesien en Nouvelle Caledonie*. Paris: Société des Océanistes, Musée de l'Homme.

Schoeffel, P. 1996. *Sociocultural issues and economic development in the Pacific Islands*. Manila: Pacific Studies Series, Asian Development Ban

Sope, B. 1976. *Land and politics in the New Hebrides*. Suva: South Pacific Social Sciences Association.

South, R.. et al., eds. 1995. *Traditional marine tenure and the sustainable management of marine resources in Asia and the Pacific*. Suva: International Ocean Institute.

Tabira, N., et al. 1990. Traditional fishing rights in Papua New Guinea, *Occasional Papers* no. 20. Kagoshima, Japan: Kagoshima University Research Center for the South Pacific.

Tonkinson, R. 1968. *Maat village: a relocated community in the New Hebrides*. Eugene, Oregon: University of Oregon.

Tuimaleali'ifano, M. 1997. Fa'a Samoa: history and process of traditions. Ph.D. thesis, University of the South Pacific, Suva.

Van Trease, H. 1987. *The politics of land in Vanuatu*. Suva: University of the South Pacific.

Waigani Seminar. 1971. Land tenure and indigenous group enterprise in Melanesia, collected papers of the Waigani Seminar (unpublished). Port Moresby: University of Papua New Guinea.

Waiko, J. 1995. *Land: customary ownership versus state control in Papua New Guinea and Australia*. Sydney: University of New South Wales Centre for South Pacific Studies.

Ward, A. 1974. *A show of justice: racial amalgamation in nineteenth century New Zealand*. Canberra: Australian National University Press.

Ward, A. 1982. *Land and politics in New Caledonia*. Canberra: Australian National University.

Ward, R. G., and E. Kingdon, eds. 1995. *Land, custom, and practice in the South Pacific*. Cambridge: Cambridge University Press.

Yanaihara, T. 1940. *Micronesia under the Japanese mandate*. Oxford: Oxford University Press.

# Law

*Richard Scaglion*

One of the most striking characteristics of "law" in most contemporary Pacific Island nations is what legal scholars call "legal pluralism." Legal pluralism is the simultaneous existence of different types of legal systems within a single setting. In the contemporary Pacific, legal pluralism most often derives from legal heritages that combine "custom" law and "introduced" law in various ways. However, in any given country, there also can be multiple and sometimes contradictory forms of customary law, the simultaneous existence of which creates even more difficulties for Pacific nations as they struggle to create unified and equitable national legal systems.

In Papua New Guinea, there are upward of 850 distinct language groups (Grimes 1992:877), each of which represents a different cultural group with its own customary legal system. The problems in reconciling these many different and sometimes conflicting systems of customary law have been profound. Vanuatu also has more than 100 customary legal systems (Grimes 1992:897), and in addition must reconcile all of these with two very different introduced systems: British and French. Even where "custom law" is relatively homogeneous, colonial legacies can create problems in legal pluralism. American Samoa and Samoa, for instance, are separate countries with similar customary systems. However, they must contend with very different introduced systems that, in the former case, stress the Constitution and laws of the United States, and, in the latter, the rules of English common law and equity as developed in English and New Zealand courts.

The existence and importance of legal pluralism in contemporary Pacific nations is a reflection of historical and ongoing tensions in island life: conflicts between customary ideas and Christian teachings; between traditional notions of group-based or corporate responsibility and introduced concepts of individual legal responsibility and rights; between customary approaches, in which disputes cannot be isolated from the broader social context, and introduced legal systems, in which courts attempt to deal with offenses as discrete occurrences; between the authority of local leaders and that of the regional and national courts and governments. Thus the story of contemporary legal institutions in the Pacific is very much a story of negotiation and reconciliation between and among competing models of law, authority, and morality.

This chapter briefly reviews the nature of indigenous Pacific legal systems, concentrating on the nature of authority and the processes of dispute management. I argue that there are two different basic models of indigenous law: one found in hierarchical societies, the other based on the dispute process of egalitarian societies. I then turn to an examination of how these two models condition the research paradigms social scientists have applied to studies of Pacific legal systems. Finally I examine the nature of legal pluralism in the contemporary Pacific, focusing on the dialectic between "traditional" and "introduced" legal systems, and consider the negotiation of various conflicting legal issues for contemporary island life.

## Indigenous Legal Systems

The numerous and diverse peoples of the Pacific Islands, who arguably constitute nearly a quarter of all societies known to anthropologists, can be divided into two basic groups. The first group migrated to the Pacific Islands fifty thousand years or more ago, but inhabited only Australia, New Guinea, and a few nearby islands. The other group, whom I will call the Austronesians, also settled parts of Melanesia, but alone colonized all of the previously undiscovered areas of Micronesia and Polynesia within the past five thousand years or so (see Thomas, this volume). The Austronesian language family is one of the largest in the world, numbering around twelve hundred languages spread widely throughout Southeast Asia and the Pacific (see Pawley, this volume). During the past two thousand years, Austronesians have been the premier seafaring peoples in the world, discovering most of the far-flung islands of the vast Pacific Basin. Because of their presumably common background and relatively rapid dispersal throughout the Pacific Islands, the contemporary Austronesian peoples of the Pacific all have relatively similar languages and cultures.

In contrast to the Austronesians, the earlier Pacific migrants, who presumably did not speak Austronesian languages, today have very diverse cultures and languages. As a result, they constitute a group more in opposition to the Austronesians than because of any clearly distinguishing characteristics of their own. Because of this, they are often referred to simply as "Non-Austronesians." Despite their cultural diversity, however, a few generalizations can be made about the Non-Austronesian peoples of the Pacific. They were certainly less enthusiastic seafarers than were the Austronesians. Most groups lived in the interior of larger islands or on the Australian continent, practicing horticulturally based subsistence techniques or foraging, whereas the Austronesians were more likely to live in coastal areas and to combine fishing and maritime exploitation with horticultural techniques. However, the most important contrast for our purposes here is that Austronesians tend to have hierarchically organized social structures, whereas Non-Austronesians almost uniformly have egalitarian social organizations based on reciprocal relationships. The result is widely different types of customary political and legal organizations (Scaglion 1996).

Contrasts are often drawn between the people and cultures

of "Melanesia" on the one hand, and "Polynesia" and "Micronesia" on the other. As we shall see, one such example is the classic contrast between the "Polynesian Chief" and the "Melanesian Big-Man" (Sahlins 1963) as models of indigenous political leadership. Such contrasts are often of limited utility because they do not pay adequate attention to the distinction between Austronesians and Non-Austronesians, and to the fact that both types of peoples live within the boundaries of "Melanesia." Hence, chiefly authority is strong among the Austronesian-speaking Trobriand Islanders of Papua New Guinea, but virtually nonexistent among the Non-Austronesian highlands tribes of the interior of this same country. Because of its cultural heterogeneity, Melanesia defies easy classification and thwarts a geographically based division between hierarchical and egalitarian systems of authority.

In order to better understand competing models of law in the contemporary Pacific, we must consider how different types of societies conceptualize authority and power. Legal scholars have long recognized that the presence or absence of legitimized power, or authority, in any given society is critical to an analysis of conflict resolution. Complex societies, having some form of centralized government, usually also have very well developed notions of authority. In socially stratified, hierarchical cultures, legal authorities can use their legitimate power in order to force compliance with rules or laws. Hopefully (but certainly not always), these laws reflect local notions of right and wrong and have been constructed for the greater good of society. Whether or not this is the case, legal systems in hierarchical societies give considerable "weight" to rules of behavior, thus privileging formalized laws and procedures.

It follows that legal scholars or social scientists who study complex societies gravitate toward research paradigms emphasizing formal "rules." However, in the egalitarian, decentralized tribal societies found in many parts of Melanesia, there are no formal legal authorities, and formal rules are much less important. Disputes between people are handled on a case-by-case basis, sometimes through consensus solutions based on notions of fairness or "equity," sometimes by various sorts of political maneuverings. Thus, scholars working in these types of societies often adopt a "processual" paradigm, focusing on the processes through which disputes actually become resolved. Studying the processes of dispute resolution rather than formal legal rules helps such researchers to better explain what goes on in acephalous societies.

As an example of these different approaches, we might profitably compare Riesenberg's (1968) study of the hierarchically organized (Austronesian) polity of Ponape (now Pohnpei, in the Federated States of Micronesia) with Koch's (1974) study of the Non-Austronesian Jalé people of highland New Guinea. Riesenberg spends much time describing the formal structure of Pohnpeian society. He takes up the nature of promotion and succession; the types of titles and the honorific forms associated with them; the positions of Nahnmwarki and Nahnken, the two supreme chiefs of each tribe; the nature of political councils, courts and trials; punishments meted out by chiefs, supernatural sanctions bolstering chiefly authority, and the prerogatives of chiefs. Only after the formal structure is described does he examine the nature of prestige competitions in which social statuses are contested. Although he sees rules as flexible, Riesenberg stresses that an understanding of formal rules is necessary for understanding the dialectic between rules and processes that together constitute Pohnpeian law:

> Thus, when an informant relates the theory of political advancement he is essentially giving the rules of descent-group seniority; but the case histories related in this work reveal how these rules must be accommodated and compromised in applying them to a complex political system. And it is the application of them and their delicate balancing against all the other principles previously mentioned that result in a flexible but stable and workable state. (Riesenberg 1968:111)

Likewise, in examining social relations on the Polynesian island of Rapa, Hanson (1970) chose first to describe the rules or norms of behavior, which he likened to "maps," afterward describing how actual practice departs from this ideal set of rules:

> Norms governing many important social relationships in Rapa have been mapped out, but these provide only the bare outlines of expected behavior. They neither delineate each detail, nor are they observed with mechanical precision. Rapans adhere to them like a vessel to the shipping lanes in a broad swath of ocean, not like a train confined to its rails. In this and the following two chapters are numerous examples of how Rapans observe, bend, or controvert these norms. (Hansen 1970:116)

In both cases, the researchers chose to focus on "rules" of behavior as a point of departure from which actual behavior was measured. In contrast is Koch (1974), who focuses on conflict resolution among the Non-Austronesian Jalé and a social context in which there are no legal norms at all:

> Jalé society lacks not only forensic institutions like courts and offices whose incumbents exercise a delegated judicial authority, but even more rudimentary institutions such as forums convened to discuss a dispute. Nor do the Jalé have positions of political leadership that empower their incumbents to exercise control over a local community and to adjudicate disputes among its members.
>
> Furthermore, although my own observations of behavior and informants' descriptions of customary modes of conduct could be collated in a catalog of rules, the Jalé themselves do not formulate any legal norms.

> Rather, they speak of their behavior either as "what we do," which describes a right and approved course of action, or as "what is not done," which refers to wrong and reprehensible conduct. (Koch 1974:31)

> Every social group must cope with conflicts among its members and between itself and other social groups. Rather than being something pathological, enmity and disputes are a normal part of social life. A conflict arises when a person or group suffers or believes it has suffered an infringement of a right. Whether or not a right constitutes a legal claim or a customary expectation may be an interesting problem in jurisprudence; for the Jalé such a distinction is meaningless. (Koch 1974:26)

In my own studies of the customary law of the Non-Austronesian Abelam peoples of the Sepik area of Papua New Guinea (Scaglion 1976, 1981), I found that Abelam also were disinterested in formulating or even discussing abstract "rules" of behavior:

> Most informants not only showed a distinct lack of interest in my attempts to formulate any general statements about traditional conflicts, but also displayed a frustrating refusal to make any definite statements about cases in the abstract. "Someone might do it that way," "someone would do that if he felt like it," were common responses to abstract hypothetical cases. Thus even abstract hypothetical cases had to be described using specific individuals and situations: "What if X's pig ruined six yams from Y's garden?" (Scaglion 1981:30)

Perhaps the differences between these two basic models of dispute management—one rule-governed, one situation-specific—can best be illustrated by reference to actual "trouble cases," or instances of dispute. The first case I will examine involves a dispute over succession to a title on the hierarchically organized island of Pohnpei, as described by Riesenberg (1968:19). As I mentioned previously, Riesenberg found it necessary to first explain the "rules" of succession (before showing how these rules were contested and manipulated). In Pohnpei society, there are two "lines" of chiefs, one headed by the Nahmwarki (which Riesenberg calls the "A-line") and one headed by the Nahnken (the "B-line"). The titles in the A-line are all ranked, and Riesenberg refers to them as A1 (the Nahmwarki himself), A2, A3, etc. The B-line is similarly organized. Ideally, the highest titles of the A-line are held by the senior males of a single "royal" clan, whereas the highest titles of the B-line are held by the senior males of another "noble" clan. Again ideally, male titleholders in the A-line marry B-line females and vice-versa, thus assuring that all high chiefs would carry royal blood on one side and noble blood on the other. Ideally, rules of primogeniture apply. In fact, however, the system is even more complicated. Descent is matrilineal, and high-ranking men were often polygamous, having secondary wives from "commoner" clans. Therefore, they might have "commoner" sons older than their "noble" sons. Also, they often adopted children, who were distinguished from "real" children. Furthermore, all children born to the Nahmwarki or Nahnken before they ascended to their titles are called *tiekepe*, or "true" children, but those children born after they assumed their titles are called *ipwin pohn warawar*, or "born upon the ditch," referring to the chasm separating these men of greatest honor from all other people. Those "born upon the ditch" receive the greatest deference.

The above rules seem very complicated, and, indeed, they are. When a high chief dies, if the holder of the next highest title is a capable individual, an eldest son, born of both "royal" and "noble" blood, and "born upon the ditch," then the line of succession is usually clear. But this is rarely the case, and two or more individuals frequently have conflicting claims, which they pursue by stressing the importance of one rule over another. In the case that Riesenberg describes, the B2 titleholder wished to ascend to the B1 title upon the death of the titleholder. But there was contestation and conflict, and a rather surprising outcome in which rules were manipulated. Riesenberg describes this as follows (see Figure 18.1):

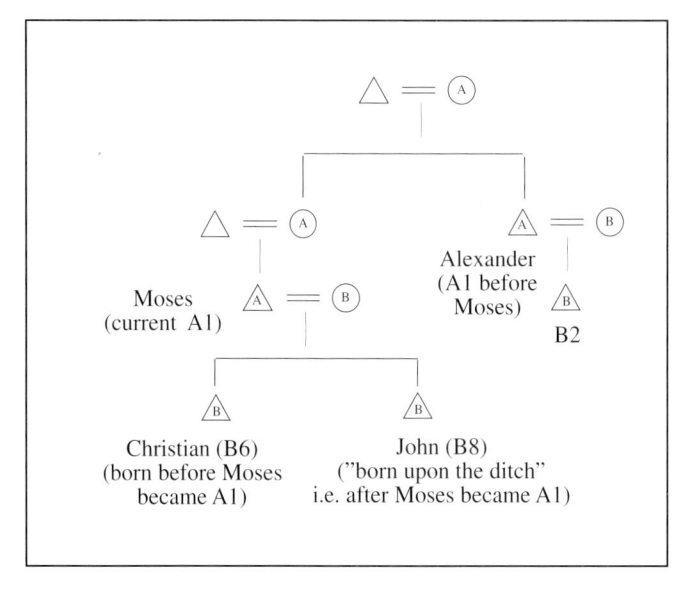

*Figure 18.1.* Genealogy of contestants mentioned in text (based on data in Riesenberg 1968).

> The B1 of Madolenihmw, Sali by name, died in 1959 or 1960. The A1, Moses, had a son, John, who was Born Upon the Ditch. John, the 8th of his children, had the title of B8. Moses did not want to promote the B2 to B1 but wished instead to elevate his own oldest son, Christian, who was B6.... At the promotion feast Moses arose, with the traditional cup of kava, made a speech that dwelled on

Ponapean customs concerning those Born Upon the Ditch, then called his son John up, gave him the cup, and proclaimed him B1. John, in his twenties, was a victim of tuberculosis (he died soon after). He made a speech that mentioned his own inadequacies, inexperience, and illness, then he called on his brother, Christian, gave him the cup, and said that Christian would be B1 instead of him. All of this had been rehearsed ahead of time. The A1 would have found it a delicate and difficult matter to promote the B6 to B1 ahead of the B2, but by using the device described here he got around the problem.

This case illustrates the centrality of rules in hierarchical societies: even when rules are broken, their breaking is most often framed and legitimized according to other rules. It can be contrasted with a trouble case that occurred among the egalitarian, Non-Austronesian Abelam people, which I witnessed in 1975 (adapted from Scaglion 1976:94-95):

> Kaprélép and Paal, who lived in the same ceremonial group, were having affairs with each other's wives. Each knew, but for a time neither said anything. Finally one day they met and had some words. Kaprélép, who was especially angry, picked up a stone and hit Paal over the head, knocking him semi-conscious. Paal's cousin (father's brother's son), who was in the same clan, but who had moved into a different ceremonial group from the disputants, happened to be nearby. He grabbed Kaprélép by the throat and began strangling him. Other bystanders pulled them apart.
>
> Nyamio, a big man from the ceremonial group of the disputants, heard the noise and set out to investigate. When he arrived, he succeeded in calming down the disputants, including Paal, who had by then revived. They then had an informal meeting or "moot," attended by the many onlookers who had gathered. After much discussion, both principals agreed to end their affairs and forget the trouble. In order to formalize this mediated settlement, Nyamio suggested that they exchange shell rings in a formal, therapeutic ceremony of reconciliation called *ngwayé kundi*.
>
> Later that day, Kaprélép and Paal each gave a shell ring to Nyamio, who held one in each hand. Each disputant held a small quantity of lime on the leaves of the *narandu* plant (a symbol of peace), and each smeared the lime on his counterpart's chest. Nyamio then chanted a special conciliatory *ngwayé kundi* song, after which he gave each man the other's shell ring, thus "killing" the trouble.

In our studies of customary law in the decentralized Jalé and Abelam societies, which lack formal "rules" of behavior, Koch and I focused on the actual processes of negotiation and mediation through which conflicts are managed (see e.g. Scaglion 1983). We, like many other legal scholars who work in similar situations, were interested in how leaders like Nyamio, who did not actually possess legitimized authority, managed to sway people's opinions and settle disputes. Such leaders, called big-men, achieve influence and exercise power through their individual accomplishments. Unlike the chiefs of many Pacific societies, whose power depends upon succession to ascribed, hereditary office, big-men are free-enterprising individualists whose charisma and accomplishments earn them a following. In such societies, individual leaders rise and fall, and the social groups over which they have influence are likewise constantly shifting. However, big-men rarely exercise influence beyond a small group of kin and supporters, and, in these cultures, there are no traditional forms of authority transcending the local level.

## Reconciling Customary and Introduced Law at the National Level

Well before European contact, some Pacific societies were hierarchically organized whereas others were decentralized. Given these two different forms of political and judicial organization, what forms of law have emerged from the meeting of colonial and customary legal systems? When Pacific peoples came into contact with Europeans during the colonial era, European nations were all hierarchically organized. Where European powers came into contact with hierarchically organized, rule-oriented Pacific societies, customary and introduced legal models have shared certain basic characteristics. Colonial governments, recognizing the ascribed power of chiefs, often made efforts to co-opt, complement, or build upon existing legal authority. Introduced legal and political structures in such contexts (mainly in Micronesia and Polynesia) often reflected, or worked in concert with, traditional forms of authority in some fashion or another. Though power was often contested, because traditional and introduced structures were based on similarly hierarchical models, similar sets of expectations applied. Colonial powers often found it easier to try to modify existing systems rather than to attempt to replace them entirely.

Other Pacific societies (mostly in Melanesia), however, were acephalous, lacking in any forms of centralized authority recognizable to colonial governments. Traditional forms of conflict management in egalitarian societies, while effective in the smaller, more personal contexts in which they developed, were thought to be largely untenable in the colonial and postcolonial context of a developing nation-state. They were often regarded as "uncivilized" by colonial authorities, and efforts were made to replace indigenous legal systems or to supersede them with hierarchical models of law. Consequently, contemporary national law in these countries has tended to fit less comfortably with traditional forms than in contexts in which indigenous Pacific peoples employed hierarchical models. Although colonial authority has been contested in both contexts, the fields of contestation have varied.

Because of their structural similarity to European models of authority, Austronesian legal systems have been co-opted, modified, and/or changed by colonial administrations over a very long period of time. Some Polynesian hierarchies took on British- or American-style governments well over one hundred years ago. While Tonga remains a hereditary monarchy, today there is a Constitution, formal written statutes passed by a Legislative Assembly, and a Parliament, which is controlled by hereditary chiefs. In other Polynesian hierarchies, chiefs share influence with introduced forms of authority. The Territorial Council of Wallis and Futuna comprises the three traditional chiefs and three other members appointed by the Chief Administrator. In still other locations, traditional chiefs act in an advisory capacity. In the Cook Islands, the House of Ariki advises on matters related to custom; in the Republic of the Marshall Islands, the Council of Iroij may request consideration of statutes affecting customary law.

It took much longer for non-Austronesian, "egalitarian" methods of conflict resolution to be formally recognized and integrated into national legal systems. In Papua New Guinea, the first Village Courts, designed to apply local customary law, were established in 1975 (Figures 18.2-18.4). In contrast to this is the Land and Chiefly Titles Court of hierarchically organized Samoa, a court established by Germany nearly three-quarters of a century earlier, in 1903, to hear disputes related to *matai* (chiefly) titles and local land matters by applying local custom. Although the German colonial government in Samoa recognized and empowered local chiefs very early, the German colonial government's reaction to local leadership in German New Guinea was quite different. Realizing that no one was really "in charge" at the local level, the colonial government attempted to establish local nontraditional authorities by setting up introduced titles of leadership (Luluai and Tultul) in village contexts. Not surprisingly, the authority of these "leaders" was generally not recognized by local people.

A comparison of legal development in Papua New Guinea and Samoa provides an interesting contrast. During the Australian colonial era, Papua New Guinea's formal court structure was established in much the same form as it exists today. The formal courts use the rules and procedures of introduced Western law, primarily by applying Australian law and British common law to given fact situations. There are few if any of the mediation and consensus settlement procedures that characterize much of Papuan customary law. At the top of the formal court structure is the Supreme Court, which hears appeals from the National Court. The National Court has exclusive original jurisdiction over major criminal and civil matters. Each major region has a District Court, with more limited civil and criminal trial jurisdiction, and several Local Courts, the lowest level of formal courts, originally designed to serve people at the local level.

Before the introduction of Village Courts, this formal court structure operated with little or no regard for local custom.

*Figure 18.2-3.* Maprik court houses (photos RS). (Note: all photos among the Abelam, in the Sepik area of Papua New Guinea.)

Disputes within villages were usually handled in informal village meetings, or moots, as they had always been, and there was very little interaction between these traditional "remedy agents" and the introduced courts (Scaglion 1976). It has been only recently, in an attempt to better integrate customary and introduced law, that Village Courts were established by the *Village Courts Act* 1973 (No. 12 of 1974). The primary function of a Village Court is to "ensure peace and harmony in the area for which it is established by mediating in and endeavoring to obtain just and amicable settlements of disputes" by applying local customs (s. 18). In this way, Papua New Guinea has been able to subsume its multiplicity of customary legal systems into a single structure. Local leaders, serving as Magistrates, can follow local procedures and apply local custom with the weight of law. Village Court compromise solutions and decisions are recognized and usually upheld by the Local Courts.

In Samoa, where customary law has long been applied in courts, local leaders have had a far longer involvement in formal legal structures. The nearly 100-year-old Land and Titles Court, for example, is often considered to be the most influential court in Samoa today. The court comprises Samoan Judges (chiefs appointed for three-year terms) and Assessors (senior chiefs appointed from a panel). The Chief Justice or a Judge of the Supreme Court acts as President of the court and provides

**Figure 18.4.** *Village Court meeting (photo RS).*

guidance on legal and procedural matters, but only rarely actually presides over hearings, where unwritten Samoan custom and usage are followed exclusively. The court holds three almost continuous and concurrent sittings: two on 'Upolu and one on Savai'i. The Court has exclusive jurisdiction over matters involving *matai* (chiefly) titles and land matters. There is no provision for review. No decision can be challenged in any other court, nor can any other court hear matters of chiefly titles or land (Anesi and Enari 1988).

Today both Samoa and Papua New Guinea have what legal scholars would call "similar sources of law." Both countries have a constitution and recognize formal acts or statutes of a national parliament. Both recognize the laws and statutes of their pre-Independence colonial powers (New Zealand and England in the case of Samoa; Australia and England in the case of Papua New Guinea) that were in force before Independence (1962 for Samoa, 1975 for PNG), to the extent these are not inconsistent with statute or inappropriate to the circumstances of the country. Both recognize local custom and usage within certain limits, and both recognize the principles and rules of English common law and equity that are not in conflict with any of the above sources of law.

Yet even in Samoa, tensions between introduced and customary law exist, and the relative influence of each continues to be negotiated. Surprisingly, the Samoan Fono, or Village Council, perhaps the most institutionalized local, customary law court in the Pacific Islands today, has only recently (Village Fono Act, 1991) been recognized by law. As Sapolu (1988) points out, there has been a gradual erosion of the influence of the Fono. Although the Constitution expressly recognizes Samoan custom and usage as applied to local government, it also vests judicial power in the formal courts: The Court of Appeal, Supreme Court, Magistrates' Courts, and the Land and Titles Court. Thus, to the extent that formal courts apply case-law decisions derived from other common law countries, and Parliament passes statutes adopted from or modeled upon Western law, it is likely that the Fono's influence will continue to decline.

Papua New Guinea and Samoa are both independent countries that have never had large numbers of outside settlers. But in many industrialized Pacific locales, such as Australia, Hawai'i, and New Zealand, the descendants of outside settlers today outnumber indigenous Pacific Islanders. Accommodating the needs of these diverse populations through legal pluralism has been yet another challenge in the contemporary Pacific. An innovative experiment in reconciling the legal systems of the indigenous New Zealanders (Maori) with the descendants of the mostly British settlers (Pakeha, or white New Zealanders) is the Waitangi Tribunal. The Tribunal was established in New Zealand (Aotearoa) in 1975 by the Treaty of Waitangi Act, the object of which was "to provide for the observance and confirmation of the principles of the Treaty of Waitangi" (Ward 1991:98).

The Treaty of Waitangi itself was signed in 1840 by the first British governor and some five hundred Maori chiefs. But the intentions of the signers, and the interpretation of the treaty itself, have been highly controversial virtually from the outset, owing largely to the existence of both English and Maori language versions of the treaty. The first major area of controversy is over the parties involved in the treaty: do "the Maori" constitute a singular collectivity or are they in fact separate ethnic groups and therefore multiple treaty partners? Maori activists seeking coequal power with Pakeha prefer the former formulation. An alternative interpretation regards treaty agreements as having been made with a number of separate groups. Article 1 of the English version, for example, states that "The Chiefs of the Confederation of the United Tribes of New Zealand, and the separate and independent Chiefs who have not become members of the Confederation" cede to the Queen of England "all the rights and powers of Sovereignty" that the "Confederation or the Individual Chiefs" exercise over their respective territories, suggesting an agreement with separate groups.

Even more controversial is the meaning of the "sovereignty" that the Maori chiefs ceded to the British in 1840. In the Maori language version, the chiefs agreed to give up *kawanatanga*. This is a neologism derived from the transliteration of *kawana* (governor) and the critical idea of "authority," the importance of which I have described at length earlier in this chapter. The new word implied some sort of novel, national, overarching authority, which the Maori chiefs no doubt thought would help protect their chieftainships and land. The chiefs (*rangatira*) expressly did NOT give up either their own *rangatiratanga* or their *mana*, words denoting chiefly authority. Article 2 in the English version seems to concede this, confirming the chiefs and tribes in "the full exclusive and undisturbed, possession of their Lands and Estates, Forests, Fisheries and other properties" so long as they wished to retain them. However the Maori version seems to go even further than this, confirming for the chiefs and the people the *tino rangatiratanga* of their lands and their *taonga* (a broad term meaning "valued possessions"). Whatever the Maori understanding(s) of the agreement may have been, and before the interior or southern chiefs had even signed the treaty, the British declared sovereignty over the entire North Island by cession, and the South Island and Stewart Island by right of discovery (Ward 1991: 91). It quickly became clear that, to the British, "sovereignty" meant something much more sweeping than the Maori chiefs ever imagined *kawanatanga* might encompass.

Today the Waitangi Tribunal, chaired by the chief judge of the Maori Land Court, and comprising a bicultural and interdisciplinary membership, has broad powers to interpret the treaty. The tribunal can review and make recommendations on any act, regulation, policy, or practice of the Crown that a Maori complainant feels has injured his or her rights under the treaty. It can also, by its own initiative, challenge any law it deems likely to breach the treaty. In certain cases it is empowered to make "binding recommendations," although it has not yet done so (Durie 1996). The tribunal has made wide-ranging recommendations on issues ranging from industrial pollution of rivers to the status of the Maori language as a *taonga*, or valued thing.

According to the chairman of the tribunal, Chief Judge Edward Taihakurei Durie (1996), contemporary claims involve "resource management policies, the impact of development works, Maori language, land administration, Maori participation in economic development, judicial systems, administrative structures, Maori land law, the alienation of state assets by the Crown, education, immigration, the status accorded Maori women, intellectual property rights, cultural maintenance, fishing, hunting, foraging, and a range of laws and regulations." However, not everyone views the tribunal in a positive light. Critics point to the slowness of the tribunal process, the failure of Maori to regain surplus Crown land, and the negative impact of economic reforms on Maori communities as evidence of its lack of effectiveness. Some see the very existence of the tribunal as an agency of suppression of the Maori people. Whether or not this is the case, the tribunal has had some successes in reconciling the customary practices of the Maori people with the authority of the modern nation-state.

Although specific details vary greatly, most contemporary Pacific Island nations currently have some form of "custom" law existing side by side with "introduced" law (Powles and Pulea 1988, Table). Most often, customary law governs land, and sometimes succession, local government, and marriage and divorce. Introduced law typically governs criminal matters, cash-oriented economic transactions, and the activities of the central government. Yet the spheres of customary and introduced law often overlap and intersect, leaving quite a bit of room for legal maneuvering, as the cases of Papua New Guinea, Samoa and New Zealand all suggest.

## Negotiating Law in the Local Context

What is "authority"? What is "custom law"? Such terms are not easy to define. In the discussions above, I have drawn sharp contrasts between chiefs and big-men, hierarchical and egalitarian societies for analytic purposes. However, such simplistic dichotomies do not adequately convey the complexity and richness of the legal process in any given local situation. The authority of chiefs is often questioned, negotiated, and limited. Big-men sometimes exercise considerable influence, and can wield a certain amount of power. Although I have argued that rules are more formally inscribed in hierarchical societies, egalitarian tribal societies do not lack notions of morality and fairness. Many egalitarian societies have quite complicated normative orders, which play important parts in shaping how cases actually get resolved (Color Plates 18A-F). Furthermore, while many legal scholars believe that the rules of law in complex societies are clear and predictable and determine the outcomes of cases, legal realists and legal anthropologists see "law" as much less certain, with rules that are highly variable, sometimes vague, and often contested and manipulated.

A brief examination of the nature of leadership in the contemporary Pacific will serve as an example. A recent volume (Feinberg and Watson-Gegeo 1996) entitled *Leadership and Change in the Western Pacific* suggests that chiefs and big-men may not really be so different after all, since "prevalent stereotypes of ascribed leadership markedly fail to reflect the actual processes and struggles of political life" (Whitehouse 1996:393). Chiefly authority emerges as amorphous and fluid, no easier to pin down or clearly describe than are more decentralized forms of leadership. Niko Besnier's article "Authority and Egalitarianism: Discourses of Leadership on Nukulaelae Atoll" describes how "Nukulaelae people reminisce longingly about the days when any command issued by a chief or the council would be cheerfully complied with by everyone" (1996:103). Such a "discourse of nostalgia," however, is in dialectic opposition to a "discourse of egalitarianism," which surfaces in the manipulation of symbolic tools associated with counterhegemonic action, such as ridicule, gossip, contempt, and spoofing. Ironically, leaders are reproached for being leaders, because they are too "bossy" and set themselves above others. One of the most common ways in which Nukulaelae leaders negotiate their difficult position is by not presenting themselves as speaking or acting on their own behalf. Rather, they present themselves as the *sui*, or representative of a group, thus being "noble," and placing the concerns of the group above their own selfish priorities. In so doing, they emerge as persons worthy and deserving of positions of leadership.

Such strategies are not really very different from those used by big-men in egalitarian societies. In one conflict case I recorded (adapted from Scaglion 1976:158–159), Abelam big-men acted in comparable fashion:

> Kwumun had land near another village. One day he discovered one of his pigs speared to death, lying putrefied on the other village's land adjacent to his own. After bringing a few men to see the pig, he buried it, and went to see Nyamio, his group's leading big-man, to discuss the problem. Together with some big-men who would act as representatives of the adjoining village, Nyamio arranged for a "moot" (informal village meeting for the purposes of conflict resolution) to be held in Kwumun's hamlet next week in order to discuss the problem with all principals to the dispute.
>
> In what was widely perceived to be a power play by Kwumun's antagonists, the visiting delegation, which was expected to arrive

in the morning, did not come until 12:30 p.m. When all were finally seated, Kwumun stated his case. Why had his pig been killed? Had it ruined any gardens? If so, why hadn't he been told? His speech was answered by a big-man representing the other group, who stated that the two men who speared the pig had gone to a nearby village and he wasn't sure why they had done it. Nyamio then countered with a speech designed to embarrass the opposing big-men. What kind of big-men were they anyway, if the young men didn't even listen to them? Couldn't they control their followers? After this, a few other speeches were given, but the absence of the principals made settlement impossible.

Another moot was set for the next week at the other village, so that the principals would be more likely to be present. When the morning of the scheduled day dawned, a heavy rain the previous night had made the paths slippery, and Kwumun's group decided not to go. Nyamio sent word that the other group's big-men should settle the case by themselves, and, if acceptable, he and the others would abide by their decision.

About a week later, word was returned that the two guilty men refused to admit killing the pig, but everyone knew they had done it. The big-men, acting as representatives of their group, proposed that a piglet would be designated and raised for Kwumun. Members of their group would all contribute a little, and when the piglet reached the size of the slaughtered pig, it would be given to Kwumun, who was satisfied with this resolution.

This case demonstrates not only the importance of corporate responsibility above individual liability, but also the use of the same sorts of discursive strategies contrasting authority and egalitarianism that were described by Besnier. Nyamio, in an attempt to discredit the big-men from the rival village, stressed their lack of authority. If they had power, they should be able to control their followers. If they couldn't, they were ineffective leaders. His rivals, on the other hand, played on the egalitarian principle, portraying themselves merely as representatives of their group. By putting aside their own self-interests and agreeing to make restitution to preserve the honor of the group, they reinforced their legitimacy as leaders in the eyes of their followers.

The power of local people to manipulate, contest, and redefine various aspects of law has not always been recognized by social scientists. Scholars have often seen "law" in colonial contexts as a vehicle for encoding and perpetuating power relationships. Even in postcolonial situations, asymmetrical power relationships have often been stressed, particularly in situations where traditional chiefs attempt to maintain power or where emerging elites attempt to exercise it. Consideration of the politics of dominance and resistance and the articulation between national and local legal systems has led some researchers to take what Galanter (1981:1) has called a "legal centralism" perspective, also called the "command" model of law (cf. Kidder 1979). In this approach (heavily influenced by dependency theory), law is regarded as an instrument of domination by a ruling class over an essentially powerless peasantry (see e.g. Fitzpatrick 1980). Thus Paliwala (1982:191), in an analysis of Papua New Guinea's Village Courts, sees these local-level courts as bringing about "greater involvement and control by the state and a degree of authoritarianism on the part of court officials. The result is relatively alienated dispute settlement with relatively little scope for community involvement and party consensus." However, other researchers in Papua New Guinea take a "legal interactionism" approach, which sees local people not so much as an oppressed peasantry, but rather as local innovators with the agency to affect their own affairs. Examples of studies supporting this perspective include Strathern (1972), Westermark (1978), Scaglion (1979, 1990), Rodman and Rodman (1984), Rodman (1985), and Zorn (1990). These studies demonstrate how Pacific Islanders consciously and creatively affect local-level legal development.

Perhaps the most dramatic example of this is Rodman's (1985) study of legal innovation in Ambae, Vanuatu. When the national government effectively withdrew from participation in local legal affairs at the end of the colonial era, local people, particularly in the district of Longana, employed this context for legal innovation:

> They set about creating a new legal order for themselves in a systematic, self-conscious manner. . . . they codified a set of laws that covered most causes of dispute and the most likely breaches of the law that occur in everyday life. The laws and schedules of fines in the code were specific and detailed. [The code] served as a basis for decision making in court. Finally, the new legal order in Longana, in which written codes play a vital role, became well-established. (Rodman 1985:620)

While the Ambae example is particularly striking, it is not unique. In often less dramatic ways, local people throughout the Pacific continually shape their own legal destinies. In a study of changing patterns in Village Court use in a rural area of Papua New Guinea (Scaglion 1990), I noticed that the proportion of women plaintiffs had increased dramatically. In seemed that, rather than submitting disputes to a little-understood introduced court, or attempting to have them settled in the male-dominated forum of village politics, women were increasingly choosing a forum in which local custom is recognized, but where changing social patterns and women's rights are also being acknowledged. A wider study of conflict cases throughout rural Papua New Guinea (Scaglion and Whittingham 1985) found that Village Courts were the single most successful remedy agent in resolving women's grievances. By channeling disputes to the remedy agent of their choice, Papua New Guinean women have made progress toward achieving some measure of legal equality with men. Zorn (1990) reports similar findings in her analysis of Village Courts in an urban context, examining how magistrates innovatively interpret law to respond to changing social circumstances.

Clearly, national governments, ruling elites, and the relatively powerless all seek to further their own ends. Increasingly, discourses of cultural authenticity and indigenous rights frame these efforts. Studies of interactive legal pluralism thus fit broadly within a growing awareness of the "politics of culture" in the Pacific Islands (cf. Feinberg 1995). Increasingly, culture itself is seen as an entity that can be self-consciously manipulated to suit individual and group interests. Keesing and Tonkinson's (1982) volume on reinventing traditional culture in Island Melanesia demonstrated the power of "kastom" as a symbol of identity, the indigenous past(s) constructed in the present for political purposes (see also Hanson's controversial 1989 article on Maori custom). Because custom is fluid and difficult to codify, it can be interpreted and used for various purposes: to justify certain practices or actions, to shape and reshape cultural identities, and to redefine and recreate the past to suit contemporary political agendas (White and Lindstrom 1993). Studies of language use within disputing contexts in the Pacific reinforce this position (see e.g. Brenneis and Myers 1984, Watson-Gegeo and White 1990, Goldman 1983, Brison 1992). As Duranti (1994:174) says of speech in the Samoan Fono:

> The constitution of a moral world in which people and other entities are characterized as willful instigators of certain events—that is, Agents—is an essential part of political discourse as well as of everyday speech. In the fono context, it is the village hierarchy and the meaning of rank that are discussed and reassessed. What does it mean to be a chief? What does it mean to show respect? Who should be in charge of making important decisions for the community? What are the values implied by the concrete actions of the members of the village council? In answering these questions, sometimes indirectly and sometimes directly, fono members continuously redraw not only a political but also a moral map of their community.

# Appendix 18.1    Customary Law in the Pacific Islands

| Political Entity | Legally Recognized Aspects of Customary Law | Role of Traditional Leaders in Administration of Justice |
| --- | --- | --- |
| American Samoa | Customs of the Samoan people not in conflict with the laws of American Samoa or the U.S. are recognized (Am. Sam. Code Annotated, Sec. 1.02); mainly in relation to land, chiefly titles and local government. | Senate consists of matai (chiefs). Associate Judges are matai, Village Courts administer customary law, presided over by a matai (Associate Judge). |
| Australia | Customs of the aboriginal and Torres Strait Island people are recognized in limited areas. Land rights of aboriginal peoples recognized. | In the Torres Straits, Queensland's Community Services (Torres Strait) Act 1984 (as amended 1986) empowers Island Courts to hear matters of custom. |
| Cook Islands | The ancient custom and usage of the people of the Cook Islands is recognized in relation to customary land (Cook Islands Act 1915 [NZ], S. 422, S. 446) | House of Ariki (chiefs) acts in an advisory capacity in relation to custom. |
| Federated States of Micronesia | Micronesian customs and traditions are recognized (Constitution of the F.S.M., art. XI, s.11). | Local-level litigation (in local languages) takes place in Village Courts presided over by justices chosen for respect and knowledge of custom. |
| Fiji | Customs of the indigenous people of Fiji relating to the holding of customary land and aspects of chiefly authority and local government are recognized. | Council of Chiefs has privileged representation in the Senate |
| Guam | Customary law of Chamorros (indigenous people of Guam) is not recognized. | |
| Hawai'i | Local customary law, with particular regard to property rights, is recognized. | |
| Kiribati | Local custom of the people of Kiribati, particularly in relation to land, marriage, and adoption, to the extent that it is not inconsistent with natural justice, equity, and good conscience, or any statute, is recognized (Magistrates' Courts Ordinance s. 42). | Magistrates' Courts are presided over by individuals with knowledge of local custom. |
| Marshall Islands, Republic of | Customary law of the Marshall Islands, particularly in relation to land, marriage, and the holding of chiefly titles, is recognized. | Council of 12 Iroij (chiefs) is selected by custom. The Council may request reconsideration of statutes affecting customary law. Chiefs also resolve local disputes and maintain order according to custom. |
| Nauru | The institutions, customs and usages of the Nauruan people are recognized in relation to land, personal property, and succession. | |

| Political Entity | Legally Recognized Aspects of Customary Law | Role of Traditional Leaders in Administration of Justice |
|---|---|---|
| New Caledonia | Customs and usages of the Kanak people that relate to civil matters (such as land, succession, marriage and divorce, and adoption) are recognized for French citizens of ethnic Melanesian origin (unless expressly renounced). | |
| New Zealand | Customs of the Maori people in regard to land matters are recognized. | Maori Land Court has jurisdiction over Maori land; appeals to the Maori Appellate Court. Maori Wardens have local disciplinary and welfare responsibilities. Waitangi Tribunal hears matters related to the treaty. |
| Niue | The customs and usages of the people of Niue in relation to land and fishing rights are recognized. | |
| Norfolk Island | Customary law not recognized except by specific statute. | |
| Northern Mariana Islands, Commonwealth of | The customs of the indigenous people (Chamorro and Carolinian), particularly in relation to domestic relations, land tenure, wills, and traditional methods of healing are recognized. | |
| Palau | Traditional laws of Palau are recognized; in cases of conflict, statutes prevail only to the extent that they do not conflict with the underlying principles of traditional law (Constitution, art. V s. 2). | Council of Chiefs advises the president on traditional laws and customs. |
| Papua New Guinea | The customs of the people are recognized to the extent that they do not conflict with constitutional law or statute, and are not repugnant to the general principles of humanity. | Village Courts, presided over by groups of Magistrates who are local leaders knowledgeable in customary law, exercise limited primary jurisdiction in most local matters. |
| Pitcairn | Customary law not formally recognized. | |
| Samoa | Samoan custom and usage recognized in relation to the holding of matai (chiefly titles), customary land, and the rules of village government. | Laws are made by a Parliament comprising mostly matai. Local justice is administered in Village Fonos (councils), which have become institutionalized. |
| Solomon Islands | The rules of customary law prevailing in specific areas of the Solomon Islands are recognized subject only to the Constitution and statutes of Parliament. | Local Courts in areas defined by language and custom have unlimited jurisdiction in customary law matters and exclusive jurisdiction in customary land matters. |

| Political Entity | Legally Recognized Aspects of Customary Law | Role of Traditional Leaders in Administration of Justice |
| --- | --- | --- |
| Tokelau | In principle, custom is almost totally overridden by specific legislation except in land matters. | In practice, village daily life is ruled by custom. |
| Tonga | As an independent monarchy, the King of Tonga is the highest traditional leader, and the Constitution and statutes of the Legislative Assembly reflect customary law. | Parliament is controlled by hereditary chiefs. |
| Torres Strait Islands | See Australia | See Australia |
| Tuvalu | Recognized are principles expressing Tuvalu values, culture and tradition as set out in the Preamble to the Constitution of 1986 and adopted as the basic law of Tuvalu; with regard to land, succession and adoption, Tuvalu custom and tradition are largely codified in the Lands Ordinance and Lands Code 1956. | Island Councils receive bills "for consideration and comment" between sessions of Parliament. |
| Vanuatu | The customary law of the people of Vanuatu is recognized, and, in particular, custom in relation to the ownership and use of land and to institutions and procedures for resolving disputes concerning ownership. | A National Council of Chiefs is advisory, has certain powers of appointment, and is consulted on national land law. Custom chiefs are represented on regional councils and Island Courts. |
| Wallis and Futuna | The customs of the people of Wallis and Futuna (particularly in relation to property held in accordance with custom (Law 61.814 arts 3 and 4) that do not contradict general legal principles are recognized. | The Territorial Council, comprising the three traditional chiefs of Wallis and Futuna, and three members appointed by the Chief Administrator, advise and review bills. At the local level, Assessors of the Court of First Instance are local-born and generally have knowledge of local custom. |

# Bibliography

Anesi, T., and A. F. Enari. 1988. The land and chiefly titles court of Western Samoa. In *Pacific courts and legal systems*, ed. G. Powles and M Pulea, 107–111. Suva: University of the South Pacific.

Besnier, N. 1996. Authority and egalitarianism: discourses of leadership on Nukulaelae Atoll. In *Leadership and change in the Western Pacific*, ed. R. Feinberg and K. A. Watson-Gegeo, 93–128. London: Athlone.

Brenneis, D., and F. R. Myers. 1984 (1991). *Dangerous words: language and politics in the Pacific*. Prospect Heights, IL: Waveland Press.

Brison, K. J. 1992. *Just talk: gossip, meetings and power in a Papua New Guinea village*. Berkeley: University of California Press.

Duranti, A. 1994. *From grammar to politics: linguistic anthropology in a Western Samoan village*. Berkeley: University of California Press.

Durie, E. T. 1996. Speech delivered at a conference on Indigenous peoples: rights, lands, resources, autonomy at the Vancouver Trade and Convention Centre, British Columbia, Canada, March 20–26.

Feinberg, R., ed. 1995. *The politics of culture in the Pacific Islands*. Special issue of *Ethnology* 34(2 and 3).

Feinberg, R., and K. A. Watson-Gegeo, eds. 1996. *Leadership and change in the Western Pacific: essays presented to Sir Raymond Firth on the occasion of his ninetieth birthday*. London: Athlone, London School of Economics Monographs on Social Anthropology No. 66.

Fitzpatrick, P. 1980. *Law and state in Papua New Guinea*. New York: Academic Press.

Galanter, M. 1981. Justice in many rooms: courts, private ordering and indigenous law. *Journal of Legal Pluralism* 19:1–47.

Goldman, L. 1983. *Talk never dies: the language of Huli disputes*. London: Tavistock.

Grimes, B. F., ed. 1992. *Ethnologue: languages of the world*, 12th ed. Dallas: Summer Institute of Linguistics.

Hanson, F. A. 1970. *Rapan lifeways: society and history on a Polynesian island*. Boston: Little, Brown and Co.

Hanson, F. A. 1989. The making of the Maori: culture invention and its logic. *American Anthropologist* 91:890–902.

Keesing, R., and R. Tonkinson, eds. 1982. *Reinventing traditional culture: the politics of custom in Island Melanesia*. Special issue of *Mankind* 13.

Kidder, R. L. 1979. Toward an integrated theory of imposed law. In *The imposition of law*, ed. S. Burman and B. Harrell-Bond, 289–306. New York: Academic Press.

Koch, K. F. 1974. *War and peace in Jalémó: the management of conflict in Highland New Guinea*. Cambridge: Harvard University Press.

Paliwala, A. 1982. Law and order in the village: the village courts. In *Law and social change in Papua New Guinea*, ed. D. Weisbrot, A. Paliwala and A. Sawyer, 191–217. Sydney: Butterworths.

Powles, G., and M. Pulea. 1988. *Pacific courts and legal systems*. Suva: University of the South Pacific.

Riesenberg, S. H. 1968. *The native polity of Ponape*. Smithsonian Contributions to Anthropology 10. Washington: Smithsonian Institution Press.

Rodman, W. L. 1985. A law unto themselves: legal innovation in Ambae, Vanuatu. *American Ethologist* 12:603–624.

Rodman, W. L., and M. C. Rodman. 1984. Rethinking kastom: on the politics of place naming in Vanuatu. *Oceania* 55:242–251.

Sahlins, M. 1963. Poor man, rich man, big-man, chief: political types in Melanesia and Polynesia. *Comparative Studies in Society and History* 5:285–303.

Sapolu, F. 1988. Adjudicators in Western Samoa. In *Pacific courts and legal systems*, ed. G. Powles and M. Pulea, 60–64. Suva: University of the South Pacific.

Scaglion, R. 1976. *Seasonal patterns in western Abelam conflict management practices*. Ph.D. Thesis, University of Pittsburgh.

Scaglion, R. 1979. Formal and informal operations of a village court in Maprik. *Melanesian Law Journal* 7:116–129.

Scaglion, R. 1981. Samukundi Abelam conflict management: implications for legal planning in Papua New Guinea. *Oceania* 52:28–38.

Scaglion, R. 1983. The effects of mediation styles on successful dispute resolution: The Abelam Case. *Windsor Yearbook of Access to Justice* 3:256–269.

Scaglion, R. 1990. Legal adaptation in a Papua New Guinea Village Court. *Ethnology* 29:17-33.

Scaglion, R. 1996. Chiefly models in Papua New Guinea. *The Contemporary Pacific* 8:1-31.

Scaglion, R., and R. Whittingham. 1985. Female plaintiffs and sex-related disputes in rural Papua New Guinea. In *Domestic violence in Papua New Guinea*, ed. S. Toft, 120–133. Port Moresby: Papua New Guinea Law Reform Commission, Monograph No. 3.

Strathern, M. 1972. *Official and unofficial courts: legal assumptions and expectations in a Highlands community*. New Guinea Research Unit Bulletin No. 47. Canberra: The Australian National University.

Ward, A. 1991. Interpreting the Treaty of Waitangi: the Maori resurgence and race relations in New Zealand. *The Contemporary Pacific* 3:85–113.

Watson-Gegeo, K. A., and G. M. White, eds. 1990. *Disentangling: conflict discourse in Pacific societies*. Stanford: Stanford University Press.

Westermark, G. 1978. Village courts in question: the nature of court procedure. *Melanesian Law Journal* 6:79–96.

White, G. M., and L. Lindstrom. 1993. *Custom today*. Special issue of *Anthropological Forum* 6(4).

Whitehouse, H. 1996. From possession to apotheosis: transformation and disguise in the leadership of a cargo movement. In *Leadership and change in the Western Pacific*, ed. R. Feinberg and K. A. Watson-Gegeo, 376–397. London: Athlone.

Zorn, J. G. 1990. Customary law in the Papua New Guinea village courts. *The Contemporary Pacific* 2:279–311.

# CHAPTER 19

# Religion

*John Barker*

What is "Oceanic religion"? Until recently many scholars restricted the term to the religions of Pacific Islanders as they existed before extensive European contact. They wrote of mission Christianity as an intrusive force and sought to explain a variety of postcontact religious movements as indigenous responses to colonialism. Today, with Christianity entrenched across the region and with colonialism outside the French and Indonesian territories a receding memory, a sharp distinction between indigenous and foreign religions is no longer viable.

For most Pacific Islanders, the religion of the present is a complex and ever-changing mix of local and imported elements. In some cases, especially where missionaries have only recently been at work, the "traditional" and "Christian" may be readily distinguished. More often one encounters situations such as on Ujelang in the Marshall Islands (Carucci 1993). The people of this isolated atoll dedicate four months each year to competitive singing, dances and games, and feasts. The ritual season climaxes on December 25 and the first Sunday of the new year. On these days the community lavishes food upon their minister, whom they expect, as with the chiefs of old, to keep some for his own use and redistribute the rest among the congregation. Laurence Carucci shows that the Ujelang way of celebrating Christmas parallels pre-Christian rituals meant to assure prosperity. But this Christmas celebration also incorporates and speaks to the Ujelang people's experience of successive colonial regimes; of displacement during the War and nuclear testing years; of a commitment to Congregational Christianity; and of a desire to be culturally distinct within Micronesia. Christmas on Ujelang turns out to be about a lot of things.

Such mixings and fusions are common across the Pacific Islands (Figure 19.1). On the surface at least they reflect a remarkable willingness to try out Western ideas and practices. At a deeper level, however, they are the living productions of a profoundly experiential and flexible appreciation of the spiritual that long pre-dates the exploration and conquest of the region by Europeans. Spectacular instances of religious transformation in indigenous religious practices are well known. Many New Guinea people, for instance, traded magic, mythologies, and even whole ritual complexes with their neighbors (Harrison 1993). From premissionary Hawai'i we have the fascinating example of Queen Ka'ahumanu, who in 1819 instigated the overthrow of the elaborate system of ritual prohibitions that had previously separated men from women, nobles from commoners (Swain and Trompf 1995:172). Early observers often portrayed islanders as slaves to unchanging customs. This stereotype suited the colonial project (see Thomas 1994). More careful historical

*Figure 19.1. Atiu island woman, dancing in church New Year celebration (photo MR).*

and ethnographic work, however, has revealed the highly innovative, often performative quality of Oceanic religions (e.g. Schieffelin 1976, Wagner 1972). Paradoxically, this very openness has allowed many aspects of older indigenous religions to continue into the present, insinuated into Christian forms and more visibly syncretic religious movements such as the famed Melanesian "cargo cults."

There is no aspect of Oceania more difficult to generalize about than religion. In part, this has to do with the cultural diversity, the mix of historical influences, and the inventiveness of local religious expressions across the region. But it also has to do with the extraordinary attention outsiders have paid to Oceanic religion over the years. Turn to any standard regional bibliography and you will find thousands of articles and books dealing with religion (e.g. Fry 1987, Taylor 1965). There is a staggering amount of detailed information on virtually every aspect of religion from every corner of this vast region.

There have been few published overviews of religion in Oceania. The most comprehensive is a recent essay by Garry Trompf, the preeminent scholar of Oceanic religions today, which surveys traditional religions, "cults of intrusion," and Christianity and provides a very useful annotated bibliography (Swain and Trompf 1995). Excellent entries on Micronesian,

Melanesian, Polynesian and Oceanic religions, as well as a historic overview of religious scholarship in the region, can be found in Mircea Eliade's *Encyclopedia of Religion* (Eliade 1987). John Garrett (1982, 1992) and Charles Forman (1982) have written the most comprehensive surveys of missionary efforts and contemporary Christianity in Oceania. Attempts at theoretical synthesis above the level of local culture are very rare, with the singular exception of cargo cult studies (Lindstrom 1993). Hence, mention needs to be made of Trompf's (1994) recent ambitious study, *Payback*, in which he attempts an understanding of Melanesian religions, past and present, in terms of a common moral logic of retribution.

I do not attempt a synthesis of Oceanic religion here. Instead, I confine myself to some general observations and themes, although along somewhat different lines than those pursued by Trompf (Swain and Trompf 1995). For convenience, I define three roughly distinguished historical contexts: indigenous religions as they existed around the time of contact with Europeans; religious practices and beliefs after contact, particularly as influenced by Christian missionaries and indigenous religious leaders; and the contemporary situation, simultaneously marked by a renewal of ancient religious forms and a new wave of Evangelical missionaries. Readers should be aware that this is at best a useful fiction. Oceanic peoples experienced European contact in vastly different circumstances over a time period ranging from the sixteenth century to the late 1960s. Further, indigenous peoples in settler colonies like New Zealand, Hawai'i, and New Caledonia had a markedly different and more brutal experience of colonialism than people elsewhere who remained majorities in possession of their own lands. Finally, the religious expressions described here under the three "periods" may all be witnessed today, often in the same places.

Before launching into a survey of Oceanic religion, past and present, it will be useful to briefly consider the historic background of interest in the subject itself. From the early years of exploration to the present, outsiders have been fascinated by Oceanic religions, recognizing that ideas about the sacred, or the supernatural, form part of the very fabric of life in this part of the world. Divining what religion "means" for Pacific Islanders, or how their religious experiences and understandings compare with other peoples', however, has proven far from easy. The twists and turns of scholarly approaches to Oceanic religion form a fascinating subject in its own right. More important, it provides a cautionary tale of the strengths and weaknesses in human studies and helps us better understand why religion occupies such a prominent position in the larger study of Pacific societies.

## The Study of Oceanic Religion

On April 22, 1770, the *Endeavour* began its explorations of the uncharted eastern coast of Australia. Captain James Cook and his men occasionally spied groups of people along the shore or fishing off canoes. These people appeared to take no notice at all of the 106-foot ship. They only reacted when the Englishmen boarded boats and made their way to shore. The story became famous. Years later observers attributed the puzzling lack of response from aborigines to a cognitive inability to "see" the ship. There was simply nothing in their highly integrated worldview that would allow them to make sense of, to put a name to, the strange object offshore (Moorehead 1966:67–68).

This interpretation has been rightly disputed by contemporary scholars who feel it is too sweeping and based on inadequate evidence. In any case, we know that the aborigines grasped the murderous implications of the European visitors quickly enough. However, the story does have a moral: All people tend to understand new experiences in terms of what is already familiar to them. We cannot know for sure how aborigines made sense of the *Endeavour*, but we have considerable written evidence on how Europeans made sense of them and other people they encountered. They did so in reference to standards from their own "civilization."

This is especially apparent in the case of religion. Oceanic religions generally lacked the more visible features of institutionalized Christianity, upon which Europeans based most of their assumptions concerning religion. Religion was integrated into the fabric of social life in Oceanic societies. Early European visitors recognized a resemblance between the ancestral religions of the ancient Mediterranean societies and the rituals, temples, and priesthoods of Polynesia. But the religious assumptions upon which these visible manifestations were based were as invisible to early European observers as the *Endeavour* was said to be to the aborigines. Consider an advertisement put out by the Anglican Board of Missions in 1909 in support of work in New Guinea:

> What the Missions in New Guinea do NOT do.
> They do not destroy any religion or form of truth. The fetish worship of the Papuan cannot be dignified with the name of religion. There is nothing to destroy except superstition. The native lives in a world in which Nature takes beautiful forms, and he is not slow to rise to the moral beauty of Nature's God.[1]

It is easy enough to take cheap shots at such sentiments. They strike most of us today as bigoted, patronizing, and destructive. All of this is true, but it is important to bear in mind that the women and men holding these beliefs about their own and other people's religious lives were sincere. All human thought is conditioned by social experience. Cultural relativism—the willingness to explore other people's lives in their own terms—is a very recent human invention, a product of an increasingly multicultural world. The early observers of the Pacific Islanders had to draw upon their prior inferences about religion to make sense of what they were seeing. To make matters more complicated, these assumptions were themselves increasingly under attack in the West.

The European invasion of Oceania broadly corresponded to an intellectual revolution in the West in which biblical interpretations of natural and human history were challenged and largely displaced (at least among the educated elite) by "scientific" ones that drew upon empirical evidence (Langness 1987).[2] Interpretations of non-Western peoples occupied a large place in these arguments. The European public was fascinated by Cook's descriptions of Pacific Islanders, particularly the Tahitians (see Smith 1960). To many, the Tahitians seemed to embody the state of "Natural Man," freed from the constraints of church and government. To followers of the philosopher J. J. Rousseau, the Tahitians seemed to exemplify the dignified qualities of the Noble Savage. To others, like the directors of the newly formed London Missionary Society, the Tahitians marked the degraded state of humankind without Christianity. (They promptly sent a crew of missionaries to save the Tahitians from themselves.)

From the late eighteenth century to the present, the study of Oceanic religion has been guided by controversies over the nature and place of religion in human experience, controversies largely originating and carried on outside of the region itself. During the latter nineteenth century, scholars labored to fit data from Oceanic societies into grand, and often incredibly simplistic, sequences of world history to "prove" variously that all humans were the sons and daughters of Adam or that religion itself was primitive illusion destined eventually to fade away in highly evolved industrial society. These constructions gave way to often equally fanciful attempts to show historic links between the "high civilizations" of the ancient Near East and Oceanic cultures. In the twentieth century, interest shifted to the mechanics of society. Small-scale cultures in Oceania and elsewhere were seen as "natural laboratories," simple societies in which the basic functions of cultural institutions could be more easily viewed than in large-scale, complex states. Scholars explored the ways religion in Oceanic cultures functioned to meet human needs, maintain social harmony, and, most recently, govern the relations between men and women.[3]

Many of the past theories about Oceanic religion appear questionable and even ridiculous to us today. As critics often point out, they provided an insidious rationale for colonialism: As "primitives" lacking the higher forms of civilization, including "true" religion, Pacific Islanders needed the strong guiding hand of "civilized men" who could control their murderous passions and break the lock of unchanging custom over their lives. Such assumptions, which if unfashionable never seem to entirely disappear, justified a magnitude of crimes and imposed untold pain upon Oceanic peoples, not least in the crusade against indigenous religious beliefs and practices.

However, there has been some compensation. Several long-term European residents, concerned that all knowledge of the past might soon disappear, made careful records of what they observed and recorded sacred texts and memories of past ritual life from knowledgeable elders. The best known of these early works are George Grey's *Polynesian Mythology and Ancient Traditional History of the Maori as Told by Their Priests and Chiefs* (1855), an important collection of Maori narratives, and R. H. Codrington's *The Melanesians* (1891), a wide-ranging survey of religious beliefs and practices in Solomon Islands. Some missionaries encouraged literate converts to undertake their own research. We owe a great deal of our understanding of precontact Hawaiian religion to the work of students at the Lahainaluna seminary on Maui (see Sahlins 1985). Careful works such as these remain invaluable resources in their own right. In addition, they allow scholars to make better sense of more fragmentary records on Oceanic religions.

As data accumulated on Oceanic religions, the quality of studies also improved. The real breakthrough came with the establishment of long-term ethnographic fieldwork as the basic methodology of anthropology. Bronislaw Malinowski demonstrated in *Argonauts of the Western Pacific* (1922), the first of several dazzling monographs on the Trobriand Islands, that apparently irrational beliefs about witches, the events of creation, or magic make sense when viewed in the wider context of a people's social life. One can gain an appreciation of this wider whole only by living with people, sharing in their lives, and understanding their language. This insight has remained the basis for most studies of Oceanic religion since, including ethnohistoric reconstructions of Polynesian and Micronesian religions that may no longer be directly observed.

While Malinowski put his own ethnographic observations to work in support of functionalist hypotheses about religion in general, students have been increasingly interested in studying Oceanic religions as systems of ideas in their own right. This is not easy to do—as already mentioned, "traditional" Oceanic religions lack written exegesis. There are no authorized accounts. Scholars make sense of particular religious elements by looking for more general cultural and social patterns. There is lots of room here for interpretation. Thus, while there might be general agreement on the existence and nature of, say, sorcery beliefs among Melanesians, there are considerable differences in how scholars account for its cultural logic. Is sorcery best understood as a political tool, does it reflect a deeper epistemology, or is it part of a moral code that holds a community together? Beyond this lies a more vexing issue: How systematic are (or were) Oceanic religions? Should practices such as sorcery be understood as reflections of a deeper imbedded system or as creative reactions to the challenges, expected and unexpected, people encounter in their lives?

Such questions are hardly specific to Oceanic religion. I have written here about the ways that prior conceptions of religion shaped European perceptions of Oceanic beliefs and rituals. The converse is also true. Increasingly reliable knowledge about Oceanic religion has challenged and reshaped scholarly assumptions about religion in general. If we gain a deeper appreciation of Oceanic religions by viewing them in the context of social life, shouldn't the same insight apply to Christian, Jewish, or Moslem believers elsewhere? The more we learn about the religious lives and beliefs of ordinary people, the smaller the gap between "world" and "local" religions. Increasing knowledge about Oceanic religion has led scholars to challenge some of the most entrenched assumptions about "primal" religions in "simple" societies. The assumption that "traditional" Oceanic religions were intensely conservative, changing slowly if at all, and had to be almost entirely displaced by Christianity has been strongly disputed by modern scholarship. Mounting evidence shows that Oceanic religions were and are for the most part very flexible and inventive and that many indigenous concerns and structures continue in Christian forms, giving them a strongly Oceanic cast (Barker 1990). There has been a marked shift of attention toward history in studies of Oceanic religions. This is reflected in Trompf's recent survey, two-thirds of which deals with postcontact religious movements and Christianity (Swain and Trompf 1995).

Studies of Oceanic religion reflect the social ideologies and structures of their time. But they also contest them. Because of this dialectic movement, the study of Oceanic religions offers students something other than a record of exotica. We are challenged to rethink the fundamentals of our being: What is religion? How common are religious experiences? How does the consumer culture of the global economy affect religious sensibilities? These are perennial questions, but we are also challenged by new questions that reflect the changing contours of the postcolonial world. Pacific Island religious leaders and scholars are making their voices heard, contesting not only Western constructions imposed on Oceanic religions but the ability of modern scholars, the vast majority of whom are of European descent, to sympathetically understand Oceanic epistemologies and aspirations (see e.g. Borofsky 1997). Religion has always occupied a central place in Oceanic studies. The liveliness of the present debates, backed by ever more meticulous research, indicates that religion will remain a central concern for many years to come.

## Oceanic Religions at Contact

In this section and the next I use the "ethnographic past" voice to indicate that most of what I'm describing belongs to the past. However, as I have already noted, many aspects of "traditional" religions continue into the present.

Different as the religious systems were, most elaborated a few basic themes:

### Intimacy of the Spiritual World

Everywhere in Oceania people lived in intimate proximity to spiritual influences and entities (Figure 19.2). No one has described the "enchantment" of the Oceanic landscape with greater elegance than the missionary-ethnographer Maurice Leenhardt, who studied the relationships between myth and the land in New Caledonia (Leenhardt 1979 [1947]). His observations are broadly applicable. The Maisin people of Oro Province in Papua New Guinea, with whom I have worked, sacrificed to the ancestors whenever they started new gardens; walked quietly around certain pools, glades and swamps, the continuing residences of the heroes of their myths; told of encounters with monsters in the deep forest; and manipulated certain foods and materials to attain or avoid spiritual powers. This is not to say that Maisin, any more than other Oceanic people, walked in fear of ghosts, sprites, and things that go bump in the night. The numinous was an expected part of everyday life—not good or bad, but simply an unavoidable reality. One day when walking to a remote garden, I observed to a Maisin friend that we had come a long way from other people. He replied flatly that we were hardly alone; we were entirely surrounded by spirits.

*Figure 19.2. In the Tuamotus, interatoll voyages always begin with a prayer (photo MR).*

And so we were.

In Polynesia and eastern Melanesia spiritual intimacy was conveyed most powerfully in the related concepts of *mana* and *tabu*. *Mana* can be understood as the manifestation of godly power in this life. Entities that generate or that order may be described as having or enacting *mana*. In Polynesia, *mana* proclaimed itself in images of abundance, of which perhaps the most spectacular were the chiefs themselves, whose "beauty" was marked by bright costumes, brilliant rituals, generous gifts to the people, and often marked corpulence (Shore, 1989:138-39). People throughout the region associated "chiefly" with agricultural fecundity in a wide variety of ways. In Tikopia, as elsewhere, a chief received the first fruits of gardens in community ceremonies and enjoyed precedence in eating as he was "terrestrial agent for the god—bestowing food, and hence . . . 'owner' of all resources" (Firth, 1936:482). A person, thing or place manifesting *mana* was surrounded and constrained by ritual prohibitions (*tabu*), meant to prevent contagion from (and to) less sacred entities. By virtue of their godly *mana*, chiefs not only proclaimed *tabu*s over resources, such as coconuts, but they also were *tabu* themselves to less sacred persons. Hawaiian chiefs, for instance, maintained an elaborate system of food and etiquette restrictions meant to protect their *mana* from the deleterious effects of commoners and members of the other gender.

There was no clear line between the spiritual and human in indigenous religions. Those engaging or encountering spiritual powers took on aspects of the spiritual themselves. In Melanesian societies, those wishing to use magic for hunting, gardening, healing, or attacking enemies had to prepare by avoiding foods and substances that might "cool" their bodies and undergoing disciplines to "heat" themselves up. Once prepared, they themselves became spiritually dangerous to others. Since serious illness or accident in most places was understood to have spiritual causes, humans—acting as sorcerers and witches—were widely believed to have the ability to bring illness, accidents, and death to others (Fortune 1932). The sorcerer's power, however, was not entirely willful. In the southern Papuan society of Mekeo and elsewhere, one could get very sick merely by approaching a sorcerer without proper precautions. The sorcerer, witch, shaman, and magician acted as visible entry points for spiritual power in human society, power which as humans they could influence but not completely control. The greatest sorcerers/healers in Mekeo were called "men of sadness," in part because of the toll that constant engagement in the spiritual took upon their social relations and their bodies. They were simultaneously terrifying and tragic (Stephen 1995; cf. Young 1983).

## The Autonomy of Spirits

Early missionaries sometimes accused Oceanic peoples of "worshiping" spirits and gods. Everywhere, however, attitudes toward spiritual beings were far more ambivalent than this would suggest. On the tiny Micronesian atoll of Ifaluk, people openly spoke of their hate for and fear of the ghosts that bedeviled their lives (Spiro 1952). In communities on Manus Island in Papua New Guinea, "Sir Ghost," the spirit of a recently departed father, maintained a brooding watch over the economic activities of every household (Fortune 1936). In Hawai'i, commoners welcomed the annual return of Lono with orgiastic rites, only to witness the slaying of the god by their human king (Sahlins 1985). In these different cases we witness a desire to influence spiritual entities that are recognized as having powers beyond human understanding or control.

Students of Oceanic religion distinguish between a variety of spiritual entities. We can roughly arrange these into a continuum ranging from those closest to those furthest away from living humans roughly as follows: ghosts, ancestral spirits, nonhuman spirits, culture heroes, gods. In many places, ghosts would hang around villages following a death both helping and hurting individuals and households. Among the Maisin, for instance, a recently deceased father might visit a daughter in a dream to advise her of a good place to plant a garden or to request a certain name for a baby; but the same ghost feeling lonely might just as easily take the soul of a new baby. Ancestral spirits or gods could be just as capricious and unpredictable, but because they had far greater power than ghosts, they had to be appealed to in larger communal ceremonies. Given the common experiences of violence and uncertainty of health and food in many areas, many communal rituals were directed at the fickle deities influencing war and fertility (Mageo and Howard 1996).

Scholars have long noticed the general correspondence between social organization and cosmology. In the hierarchically organized societies of Polynesia, religious worldviews were "vertically" oriented, focused upon deities who created the world and founded the chiefly lines of descent (Swain and Trompf 1995). Trompf cautions us not to draw too strong a contrast with the small-scale societies elsewhere in the Pacific, noting the presence of high gods in several Melanesian and Micronesian communities. Still, in general, Melanesian cosmologies tended to have a more "lateral" emphasis, in which ancestral and nonhuman spiritual forces occupied the near landscape rather than the sky or distant horizon.

## The Transformative Power of Ritual

Ritual can be defined as a set of formalized behaviors that, when used properly, harnesses spiritual power in such a way as to bring about a transformation in the empirical world. Ritual is thus often somewhat provisional—open to modification and experimentation.

Magic and sacrifices were probably the most common rituals carried out in daily life. Islanders gathered special substances and chanted incantations to aid the growth of food in the gardens, to strengthen the abilities of dogs to track game, to attract fish into nets, and to undertake a wide variety of other necessary subsistence activities (Malinowski 1954). In most places, people also made use of magic to deal with the uncertainties of romances and conflicts. In colonial times, Melanesians adapted magic to aid and protect their teams during soccer or cricket matches. Everywhere, islanders made sacrifices of food and wealth to spirits and gods, mirroring the exchanges that guided human morality. In giving tribute to their chiefs, Polynesians gave to the gods. In turn, the gods, through the chief, should redistribute the blessings of the land and sea back to their sources, thus assuring bounty in the new year (Firth 1970, Williamson 1933).

The most common communal rituals in villages centered on transformations in the life cycle: birth, sexual maturity, marriage, and death. Such occasions were often marked by massive feasts and exchanges as well as spectacular ceremonials (Figure 19.3 and Color Plates 19A–19C). Weddings between aristocratic families in Tonga, for instance, occasioned huge celebrations during which meters upon meters of tapa cloth were presented

*Figure 19.3.* Traditional dancing by Maisin youth, Papua New Guinea. The distinctive decorations worn by the dancers are believed to have been set at the time of creation. Each clan has its own distinct tapa cloth designs and arrangements of shells and feathers. As they dance, the Maisin see and merge with their ancestors, bringing mythic memory to life (photo JB).

as gifts. In Melanesia, life transition ceremonies called for years of careful planning on the part of ambitious leaders: the planting of special gardens, the raising of suitably fat village pigs, the careful cultivation of allies who might be induced to make contributions. The elaborate male initiation ceremonies among the Ilahita Arapesh in the Sepik region, to take one example, thus also presented an opportunity for not-so-covert competition between political rivals (Tuzin 1980). The "secular" politics of ritual, however, should not blind us to their religious aspects. The beautiful mourning and memorial ceremonies performed for years after the death of important women and men in parts of New Britain and New Ireland, for instance, served to revitalize the people's connections with the ancestors by giving them a physical form among the living. One would first hear the unearthly "voices" of the ancestors from the bush before their eruption into the village clearing in the form of elaborate masked dancers. The death feasts comprised a communal sacrifice to the ancestors, assuring not only the safe passage of the recently deceased into the spiritual world but also the continuing reproduction and prosperity of human society (Errington 1976).

The work of spiritual transformation was often hard and dangerous. Public rituals could require huge outlays of labor, food, and wealth; last for weeks or months at a time; and impress observers and participants alike with spectacular art and performances. Much of the Oceanic "art" in museums today provides mute testimony to the creative forces of island rituals. What the art cannot reveal is how islanders themselves became physically transformed in the larger public spectacles, particularly initiations and rites connected to warfare (Herdt 1984). In different places novices underwent terrifying hazings; participants permanently incised their bodies with exquisite tattoos and raised lacerations; and, most notoriously, initiates consumed portions of the bodies of diseased relations or murdered enemies, seeking to imbibe something of their spiritual essence (Bateson 1958, Barker and Tietjen 1990, Zegwaard 1959). The stakes involved in the larger rituals were extraordinarily high. Failure could bring the wrath of gods and ancestral spirits upon a people, leading to famine, dissension, or massacre at the hands of enemies (see e.g. Keesing 1992).

Rituals are the most visible and ordered of religious phenomena. For that reason, scholars have long been interested in their more general social functions in traditional societies. In the Trobriand Islands of Papua, to take a well-studied example, Annette Weiner (1976) has argued that the elaborate exchanges of male and female wealth in mortuary ceremonies served to reproduce kin groups and gender distinctions over time, giving that society a marked cultural stability. In ancient Tahiti, on the other hand, virtually every kin, occupational, and political group "had its own more or less distinctive set of spirit tutelars, and a specific place, a *marae*, for interacting with them" (Oliver, 1989:907). In effect, Tahitian commoners typically owed allegiance both to the spirits of their natal kin groups and to the gods of their chief. The ornate rituals at chiefly *marae*s secured a chief's following while virtually guaranteeing conflict as he fought to gain other chiefs' "congregations." Such contests were thus at once secular and religious. Priests and others who had special knowledge of the invisible world of the spirits and gods wielded extraordinary power.

Some students have looked for even wider functions. One of the best-known studies of ritual from Oceania is Roy Rappaport's (1984) *Pigs for the Ancestors*. Drawing on meticulous ethnographic detail, Rappaport argued that warfare and peacemaking rituals among the Maring of New Guinea, at which large numbers of pigs were slaughtered and eaten, formed a cycle that kept the human population in balance with the carrying capacity of their mountain environment. The argument was provocative and is still controversial. Still, no one would disagree with Rappaport's primary insight: religion, including ritual, formed part of the fabric of traditional Oceanic societies. As such, it should be viewed as an integral component of a total ecological system.

## Power and Knowledge

Religious attitudes are fostered not only in practices but through what people know and imagine (Herdt and Stephen 1989). Knowledge of the spiritual was stored and passed on to new generations in a variety of forms and media. These included narratives (mythologies, legends, entertaining tales), songs and chants, magical incantations, and prayers. Corresponding to Western notions of literature, such forms were relatively easy to record and thus occupy a large part of the published works on Oceanic religions. In recent years, scholars have worked hard to understand this material in terms of the cultures that produced it (e.g. LeRoy 1985, Valeri 1985). But many religious narratives, such as the powerful Maori creation stories of Rangi (heaven) and Papa (earth), have a universal appeal and through the work of popular writers like Joseph Campbell have become widely known. The Papua New Guinea scholar John Waiko (1981) reminds us that knowledge of the spiritual was not confined to linear forms in traditional societies. Knowledge of the spiritual was conveyed through all the senses. It became manifest in material culture, in rituals, in the experience of mishaps, and in the very geography of one's surroundings. Some of the most innovative work on Oceanic religion today explores the myriad ways such knowledge was created, communicated, and remembered (Battaglia 1990, Barth 1987, Wagner 1986).

In a classic article on the Baloma spirits of the Trobriand Islands, Bronislaw Malinowski (1954) observed that knowledge of the spiritual was not distributed evenly. People differed in their particular interests; as important, certain people developed specialized esoteric knowledge. As Lamont Lindstrom (1990) shows in a fascinating study, the lineaments of knowledge and power often run in parallel courses. The small-scale societies of Melanesia are famed for the relative weakness of leaders, particularly compared with the ranked and sometimes stratified societies that formed in parts of Micronesia and Polynesia. Melanesians almost universally embraced ethics based upon the common practice of reciprocal exchange (Mauss 1954). Anthropologists have sometimes called Melanesian societies "egalitarian," a confusing description that obscures the fierce competitive spirit and resulting inequalities that characterized much of the region. In the never-ending game of exchanges, the man or woman who gardens better, gives away more food, speaks eloquently, fights fiercely, or, especially, possesses esoteric knowledge, gains important advantages. At the same time, he or she becomes vulnerable to the attacks of competitors. Sorcerers and witches were the great levelers in Melanesian societies, since they tended to attack individuals who stood out from others in possessions or abilities (Fortune 1932). In some places, however, leaders known to be sorcerers achieved almost despotic power through terror (Young 1983).

The elaborate male initiation rites carried out in many Melanesian societies also often involved secret knowledge, sometimes revealed to initiates only after they had passed through six or seven stages and had become old men themselves (Barth 1975, Gell 1975, Tuzin 1980). The male cults clearly ordered males into ranks based on their degree of initiation. They also clearly articulated a distinction between male and female. There has been much discussion among scholars, however, as to whether the gender distinction is best understood as a form of inequality or difference (Errington and Gewertz 1987). The lineaments of power were clearer in the ranked societies of Polynesia and high-island Micronesia. Here priestly specialization, which reached its climax in the temple complexes of Tahiti and Hawai'i, reinforced an essentialized difference between the aristocratic elite and everyone else (Goldman 1970).

Religious assumptions did not merely reinforce political structures in Oceania; they formed one set of elements in ever-shifting political arrangements, constantly subject to modification. Not only might the whims of the gods change during a war, but new gods or spiritual forces might reveal themselves. This explains why the arrival of Europeans in the Pacific Islands simultaneously posed a political and a religious challenge to Oceanic peoples. The Hawaiians identified Captain Cook with their god Lono, but in a new and unpredictable guise (Sahlins 1985). Some interior peoples of New Guinea had myths warning of spirits that would enter the land from the south and bring about the destruction of the world; when the Hides patrol struggled through the area in the 1930s, these people faced the stark choice of beating back these harbingers of doom or fleeing (Schieffelin and Crittenden 1991). For their part, a large contingent of Europeans—the Christian missionaries—were indeed committed to bringing a new religious "truth" to the islanders, one which they hoped would displace indigenous understandings of the spiritual. They did not entirely succeed, but their efforts changed the religious life of Oceanic peoples forever.

## Mission Christianity and Postcontact Religious Movements

Apart from early Spanish missionary efforts in Guam and some of the Carolines, the mission era began in 1798 when the newly formed London Missionary Society sent a shipload of lay missionaries to Tahiti (Gunson 1978). Over the course of the next century, virtually all of the major denominations of Western Europe and its settler colonies staked claims in the Pacific Islands. Roman Catholic and Protestant orders competed to win souls, but for the most part the Protestants respected each other's zones of influence, resulting in a geography of denominational affiliations that is reflected in the national churches of today. Missionaries were among the first whites to settle in the islands, often years before colonial powers took control.

As they became familiar with local political alignments and learned the vernacular, missionaries became brokers manipulated by the factions struggling to control the islands. In Tahiti, Tonga, and Fiji, newly "Christian" chiefs found their alliances with the newcomers useful in conquering their rivals and unifying the islands for the first time (Howe 1984). After the colonial powers took over, the missionaries continued to play the role of broker. In most places, they provided the basic social services of schooling and medicine. Colonial administrators, always stretched for cash, regarded missions as a necessary if not always entirely reliable part of the apparatus needed to control and "civilize" native populations (Thomas 1994). And, indeed, missions were instrumental in passing on to converts, particularly the school children in their care, basic Western orientations to time, space, and authority (Smith 1994).

A small number of Europeans directed and consolidated mission work in most places. The main bearers of the new religion, however, were almost always Pacific Island converts. In 1821, John Williams of the London Missionary Society began the "native agency," a small group of trusted converts who were sent out to settle in non-Christian areas, often at great risk to their own lives. Over the succeeding decades of the nineteenth and early twentieth centuries, Tongans preached the gospel to Fijians, Samoans found converts in Tuvalu, and Hawaiians spread American Congregationalism across central Micronesia. In a massive effort, hundreds of Polynesian and eastern Melanesian missionaries introduced Christianity in the small coastal communities of Papua New Guinea under the banners of a half dozen denominations (Garrett 1982, 1992). Many of these dedicated men and women were buried there, victims of disease, poor nutrition and sometimes violence (Crocombe and Crocombe 1982).

As each new mission base was consolidated, another army of indigenous teachers, evangelists, and clergy set out for the next village, valley, or island. Most New Guinea highlanders thus heard of Christianity from coastal converts who settled among them (Radford 1987). The ever-growing mission networks created a conduit for the diffusion of plants, domesticated animals, technologies, and cultural practices from the central Pacific to the peripheries (Latukefu 1978). It is not correct, then, to see conversion in Oceania simply as an encounter between indigenous and Western culture. Almost everywhere, islanders acted as mediators (Crocombe 1983:18). While the cultural cast that, say, a Polynesian pastor gave to Christian practice might be jarring for a congregation in Papua New Guinea, it was nevertheless a distinctly Pacific interpretation (Wetherell 1980).

Compared with other mission fields, Christianity spread across Oceania with amazing rapidity. This is not to say, however, that the path of conversion was necessarily easy or smooth.

Depending upon their theological and cultural backgrounds, missionaries found much to object to. There was universal condemnation of cannibalism, head hunting, human sacrifice, and other ritual expressions of warrior culture. Missionaries also frowned upon polygyny, sorcery, and many of the more elaborate rituals that they tended to see as expressions of "idolatry." Particularly before the establishment of colonial control over the islands, however, missionaries had limited abilities to do much more than condemn. The effective agents of change were, again, often the core group of first converts. In many parts of Polynesia, the arrival of missionaries coincided with massive social and political turmoil, wars, and loss of population through introduced diseases. Such disasters weakened faith in the traditional deities while strengthening the position of those chiefs who aligned themselves with the new Christian god.

Elsewhere, converts used their intimate knowledge of local beliefs to stage "power encounters" to demonstrate the superior power of the Christian god over ancestral spirits (Tippett 1967). Converts desecrated ancestral shrines in parts of Solomon Islands, gathered and destroyed magical materials in public bonfires in Papuan villages, and broke into men's cult houses to reveal sacred masks and carvings to uninitiated boys and women. The extraordinary first-hand account of the conversion of the Cook Islands written by the evangelist Maretu in 1871 reveals the importance of confrontation, coercion, and fear in the missionary campaign (Crocombe 1983). However, one should not paint too negative a picture. Missionaries found much to admire in Oceanic cultures, which they compared favorably with the social ills of Europe (Thomas 1994); the early island proselytizers won over many converts through persuasion and dedication and are remembered fondly today; and, finally, for many, Christianity presented some protection from the more oppressive demands of indigenous religion and the disruptions of colonial change.

Even where new Christians cast off the visible signs of the old religion, there were continuities as they translated their new faith into culturally familiar terms (Color Plate 19C). Thus Samoans and Tongans transformed the theologically egalitarian Congregationalist and Methodist missions into vehicles of hierarchy in which the pastor assumed the exalted place of the old chiefs and priests. Congregations showered their pastors with lavish gifts as a visible token of their devotion to God (Roach 1987). In Melanesia and Micronesia, people identified local sacred sites with biblical events—as Eden, the site of Christ's crucifixion, or Jerusalem. The old ancestral and bush spirits lived on in the guise of "devils"; Mary and other Christian figures come to people in dreams to warn of future events and to heal sickness; and even God could be reconfigured as a kind of super sorcerer (see Barker 1990, 1992; Boutilier, Hughes and Tiffany 1978).

On the mission and colonial frontiers, and often behind them, indigenous prophets inspired independent religious movements that often merged aspects of indigenous religions with elements of Christianity and Western practices in response to the various crises brought on by contact. In New Zealand, conflicts between Maori and the growing white population, especially over the expropriation of land, led certain prophets to reject missionary readings of the Bible in favor of interpretations more in accord with their own epistemology and experience. Te Ua Haumene gained the first large following. Inspired by the angel Gabriel, Te Ua taught that the Maori were the true chosen people of Jehovah, whom they could call upon to defeat the Europeans. Many of his followers believed that the prophet's rituals and spells would grant them immunity from European bullets, a belief they put into practice (with disastrous results in the Maori Wars of 1864-65). Te Ua's Pai Marire ("good and peaceful") movement inspired the later King movement and the Ringatu Church (Clark 1975). Since Te Ua's day, Maori prophets have continued to inspire new movements and churches, the most important being the Ratana church begun in the 1920s. Strongly separatist, such movements and churches have drawn upon Maori culture and distinct readings of the Bible, framing the political and social challenges Maori face in religious terms (Sinclair 1993).

Similar, if smaller, religious movements occurred in Tahiti, Samoa, Fiji, and elsewhere. They were almost always countered by colonialist reprisals. Missionaries and government officials usually regarded independent religious movements as retrograde descents into "superstition," as forms of collective "madness" and, worst, serious challenges to their own authority. In an important study of the Fijian prophet Navosavakadua, of the 1880s "Tuka Cult," Martha Kaplan (1995) directs our attention to the roles colonialists played in the shaping of religious movements. In the case of the Tuka movement, the prophet and his followers shaped their message and actions partly in the face of unrelenting hostility on the part of the colonial authorities and their chiefly allies. More important over the long term, the authorities committed their reified understanding of the Tuka "cult" to the official record. This resulted in the temporary removal of Navosavakadua's followers to a distant island and close surveillance of their activities after their return. It also led scholars to misread the Tuka as an early form of a cargo cult.

The reality that religious movements emerged and dissolved along the colonial frontier, pushed and pulled by a multitude of different influences, challenges any easy interpretation. At the same time, it adds to their exotic and dramatic appeal. This is especially apparent with the so-called "cargo cults" of Melanesia. Early in the twentieth century, colonial observers began to report strange behavior and beliefs from coastal New Guinea. The best known was the "Vailala Madness," so described by the Papuan government anthropologist F. E. Williams (1923), who conducted the first of several detailed ethnographic studies of religious movements in the region. In the Gulf of Papua, prophets convinced large numbers of people that their ancestors could be induced to return to life if the proper preparations were made. They would come in ships bearing vast quantities of the material goods—"cargo"—enjoyed by European colonialists. To hasten the event, villagers performed rituals mimicking European actions. They held marching drills, erected "radio masts" to receive messages from the ancestors, and constructed wharfs. Most disturbing to Williams, people also fell into ecstatic writhing trances.

The "Madness" was suppressed, but reports of apparently similar "cults" continued to be filed in succeeding years. Cargo

The Pacific Islands 241

figured in only a minor way in several of these, notably the "Taro cult" in Papua and Maasina Rule in Solomon Islands (Williams 1928, Laracy 1983). With the end of World War II and the repulsion of the Japanese from northern Melanesia, religious movements like that at Vailala broke out in several widespread regions. It was around this time that some unknown resident invented the memorable phrase "cargo cult," which quickly entered into common parlance (Lindstrom 1993). The most important movements centered on the prophets Yali in Madang, Paliau on Manus island, and Yaliwan in the East Sepik—all in Papua New Guinea—and the mysterious figure of Jon Frum on Tanna island in Vanuatu. These and other movements received considerable attention, not least from the postwar generation of anthropologists who made them into their special study (e.g. Gesch 1985, Lawrence 1964, Schwartz 1962).

No subject in Oceanic religion has attracted as much attention and exercised as many intellectual muscles as the cargo cults. Most administrators thought that the cults reflected an ignorance of the workings of the capitalist economy and would fade as education and experience improved. Anthropologists detected in the patterns of the movements deeper inherent rationalities. Peter Worsley (1968) saw the cults as, in part, protests against European hegemony that in some cases, notably Maasina Rule, functioned to draw people from different cultural and linguistic backgrounds into emergent nationalist movements. In a superbly detailed study of Yali, Peter Lawrence (1964) argued that the cults should be understood as modern expressions of a traditional ideology that would remain convincing to Melanesians until the rural economy underwent serious change. Kenelm Burridge (1960, 1969), writing about the same area, understood cargoism in more religious terms, as a redemptive quest to reestablish the moral reciprocities between white men and Melanesians that, according to indigenous myths, existed at the beginning of time. Developing an earlier line of argument advanced by V. Lanternari (1965), Lattas (1992) has analyzed cargo narratives as symbolic representations of the experience of oppression, while Trompf (1994) has argued that the movements should be understood as native reprisals against colonial domination.

Even as cargo cult studies proliferated at a pace with the "cults" themselves, scholars began to express some doubt about the concept. Some worry about its empirical fitness: many different kinds of religious movements, some of which have little explicitly to do with cargo, get lumped into the category; there is also a tendency to see every local economic endeavor, from trade stores to regional cooperative societies, as nascent cargo cults. Others consider the term itself a slander demeaning Melanesian peoples. The most serious challenge to cargo cult studies comes from a recent book by Lamont Lindstrom (1993), which convincingly illustrates the ways that Western obsessions and desires about commodities, mixed with assumptions about cultural "others," have insinuated themselves into discussions about cargoism. Whatever we might choose to call them, religious movements continue to emerge in Melanesia. Cargo cults and other variants of indigenous religious movements will continue to challenge understanding for the foreseeable future.

## Oceanic Religion in a Global Context

Today Christianity is "traditional religion" for many Pacific Islanders in two senses. In sheer numbers, the vast majority of people consider themselves Christian. In Papua New Guinea more than 90% of the population has declared membership in a church in recent censuses. Outside and excluding New Zealand, the number rises to a staggering 99% (Ernst, 1994:21). As important, indigenous Christians now head and staff most of the old missions, which have, in turn, become national churches (Figure 19.4 and Color Plate 19D).[4] Second, in rural areas where most people still live, Christianity and a range of indigenous religious attitudes and practices have long been accom-

*Figure 19.4.* Minister of Congregationalist Church, Atiu, Cook Islands (photo MR).

modated to each other (see e.g. White 1991). When a person falls seriously ill in many Melanesian societies, to take one example, her concerned kin will typically turn to the local medical orderly, to villagers knowledgeable of medicines from the bush, to healers who can detect the ghosts or sorcerers that have inflicted the sickness, and to the village pastor, who will pray for God's intercession (Frankel and Lewis 1989). These juxtapositions may jar the outside observer, but they strike most village people as common sense.

There are very few places left in Oceania that have not been visited by missionaries. Apart from remote corners of Papua New Guinea and Irian Jaya, the few pockets of traditionalists include people like the mountain Kwaio of Malaita in Solomon Islands, who have determinably held their Christian kin on the coast at bay for more than half a century (Keesing 1992). Elsewhere, people have rediscovered, or brought out of hiding, long-suppressed religious beliefs and practices, often, as is the case in New Caledonia, New Zealand, and Hawai'i, as expressions of cultural identity in the struggle for political rights and autonomy. A renewed interest in ancestral culture, particularly on the part of the emerging intellectual elites, has brought with it considerable reflection on the activities and excesses of the early missionaries. Many church leaders have made efforts to restore (in modified form) many of the cultural practices and arts that their predecessors worked so hard to end. These innovations range from the addition of traditional drumming and chants in services to monuments such as the stunning Roman Catholic cathedral in Port Moresby in the form of a Sepik *haus tambaran*. Perhaps more important in the long run, many clergy and theological students have dedicated themselves to creating specifically Pacific theologies (Trompf 1987). Ironically, villagers who have long heard about the time of "pagan darkness" are often very reluctant to accept such changes imposed from above (Arbuckle 1978, Keesing and Tonkinson 1982).

Autonomous religious movements continue to emerge, especially in Melanesia. As with the Maori churches in New Zealand, a few of the Melanesian cargo cults have evolved into more stable associations, cooperatives, and independent churches (see e.g. Whitehouse 1995). One of the more accessible of the "cults," the Jon Frum movement in Vanuatu, has even become something of a tourist beacon (Lindstrom 1993). The main challenge to the traditional churches comes not from indigenous religious leaders but from a "third wave" of missionary activity (Ernst 1994). The Mormons and other regionally established conservative churches are growing rapidly, and new missionaries, mostly conservative evangelicals from the United States and Australia, are pouring into the region. The new missionaries often see the established churches as little better than the "pagan" religions they replaced and do not hesitate to denounce them. Many people in rural areas are attracted by the ecstatic worship style of Pentecostal Christianity, which often takes on "cargoist" overtones in Melanesia. But the new missionaries are making their biggest conquests among the better educated, rapidly urbanizing sectors of the population. Increasingly, church elders find themselves defending their Christian "traditions" to younger members of the community who question old compromises with local customs as well as the social privileges enjoyed by the established clergy.

In many ways, widespread missionary influence has made Oceania a less religiously diverse area. Different as the Christian denominations are, they vary far less in ritual and belief than the religions they mostly replaced. From the perspective of Pacific Islanders, however, the religious world has almost certainly become more diverse and more fragmented. Even in remote areas, people increasingly have the choice of joining one or another denomination or none at all. It is far easier to travel than in the past. When young people leave their communities, often for years at a time to go to school or to work, they do not experience the local spirit-filled landscape that so shaped their ancestors' spiritual perceptions. With weakened links to their home communities, young people are exposed to a wide range of products available in the global religious marketplace. Radio, television, and video machines have at the same time made it easier for new sects to communicate with even remote locations. Less anchored to place, religious symbols and organizations can be employed in national and even international campaigns and movements. The results can be both beneficial and destructive. Across the Pacific, Christian activists have formed associations to battle a host of modern threats: alcoholism, sexual abuse, violent crime, poverty in urban areas, land theft, and the abuse of land and waters through military programs, overfishing and industrial mining, logging, and farming (Swain and Trompf 1995:213-20). On the other hand, some of the Fijian elite have come to embrace a dangerous type of religious nationalism, combining cultural parochialism with an exclusionary Christianity that has bolstered racism against Fijians of Indian descent (Rutz 1995). Religion, as Burridge (1969) observed some years ago, is ultimately about power in this world as well as beyond. It should not be surprising, then, that the pro-democracy movement in Tonga parallels a struggle for dominance between minority and majority churches (Marcus 1993).

From the time of earliest human settlement, Oceania has been a meeting place for cultures. As this chapter demonstrates, religious insights and experiences formed an essential part of indigenous life in the past and will continue to form a key lens through which Pacific peoples understand and shape their destiny for the foreseeable future. Research on religion has always held a fundamental priority in Oceanic studies, resulting in a massive database of ethnographic, historical, literary, and artistic productions. Oceanic religious experience has been too complex and diverse to be accommodated within a single academic discipline. Anthropology, history, psychology, missiology, religious studies, and geography, among others, have all made their contributions. Much of this material, in the form of books, films, and recordings, has made its way back into Pacific communities, where it is adding yet another dimension to religious understandings and creativity. Ironically, and sadly, the voices of outside scholars have dominated discourse on Oceanic religions, often drowning out the voices of the people themselves. As Pacific Islanders, scholars and lay people alike, reappropriate their religious traditions, we can look forward to the emergence of new insights into the spiritual dimensions of human existence. The literature on Oceanic religion has reached that point of richness where one can begin to appreciate how much more there is to learn.

## Notes

[1] Ironically, this ad appears on the flyleaf of one of the more sympathetic accounts of indigenous religion by a pioneering missionary (Stone-Wigg 1909).

[2] I place "scientific" in quotes simply to indicate that the new views were by no means free of ideology and thus objective. However, insisting that empirical evidence must be the final arbiter of disputes, the critics of biblically based anthropology forced themselves and their opponents to record more detailed and systematic observations. The body of data that emerged, in turn, provided the most powerful ammunition for those who later challenged evolutionary approaches to human religion.

[3] See Jorgensen (1987) for a more detailed account of changing fashions in the study of Pacific religion.

[4] The main exception is the Roman Catholic Church, whose celibacy rule bedevils efforts to replace European clergy.

## Bibliography

Arbuckle, G. A. 1978. The impact of Vatican II on the Marists in Oceania. In *Mission, church and sect in Oceania*, ed. J. A. Boutilier, D. T. Hughes, and S. W. Tiffany, 275–99. Ann Arbor: University of Michigan Press.

Barker, J., ed. 1990. *Christianity in Oceania: ethnographic perspectives*. ASAO Monograph No. 12. Lanham, New York: University Press of America.

Barker, J. 1990. Female facial tattooing among the Maisin of Oro Province, Papua New Guinea: the changing significance of an ancient custom. *Oceania* 60:217–34.

Barker, J. 1992. Christianity in Western Melanesian ethnography. In *History and tradition in Melanesian anthropology*, ed. J. Carrier, 144–173. Berkeley: University of California Press.

Barth, F. 1975. *Ritual and knowledge among the Baktamin of New Guinea*. New Haven: Yale University Press.

Barth, F. 1987. *Cosmologies in the making: a generative approach to cultural variation in inner New Guinea*. Cambridge: Cambridge University Press.

Bateson, G. 1958. *Naven*, 2nd edition. Stanford: Stanford University Press.

Battaglia, D. 1990. *On the bones of the serpent: person, memory, and mortality in Sabarl Island society*. Chicago: University of Chicago Press.

Boutilier, J. A., D. T. Hughes, and S. W. Tiffany, eds. 1978. *Mission, church, and sect in Oceania*. Ann Arbor: University of Michigan Press.

Burridge, K. O. L. 1960. *Mambu: a Melanesian millennium*. New York: Harper and Row.

Burridge, K. O. L. 1969. *New heaven, new earth: a study of millenarian activities*. London: Blackwell.

Carucci, L. M. 1993. Christmas at Ujelang: the politics of continuity in the context of change. In *Contemporary Pacific societies: studies in development and change*, ed. V. S. Lockwood, T. G. Harding, and B. J. Wallace, 304–20. Englewood Cliffs, NJ: Prentice Hall.

Clark, P. 1975. *"Hauhau": The Pai Marire search for Maori identity*. Auckland: Auckland University Press.

Crocombe, M. 1983. *Cannibals and converts: radical change in the Cook Islands*. Suva: Institute of Pacific Studies, University of the South Pacific.

Crocombe, R., and M. Crocombe, eds. 1982. *Polynesian missions in Melanesia*. Suva: Institute of Pacific Studies, University of the South Pacific.

Eliade, M., ed. 1987. *Encyclopedia of religion*. New York: Macmillan.

Ernst, M. 1994. *Winds of change: rapidly growing religious groups in the Pacific Islands*. Suva: Pacific Conference of Churches.

Errington, F. 1974. *Karavar: masks and power in a Melanesian ritual*. Ithaca: Cornell University Press.

Errington, F., and D. Gewertz. 1987. *Cultural alternatives and a feminist anthropology: an analysis of culturally constructed gender interests in Papua New Guinea*. Cambridge: Cambridge University Press.

Firth, R. 1936. *We the Tikopia: a sociological study of kinship in primitive Polynesia*. London: Allen and Unwin.

Firth, R. 1970. *Rank and religion in Tikopia*. Boston: Beacon Press.

Forman, C. W. 1982. *The island churches of the South Pacific*. Maryknoll, New York: Orbis Books.

Fortune, R. F. 1932. *Sorcerers of Dobu*. London: Routledge and Kegan Paul.

Fortune, R. F. 1936. *Manus religion: an ethnological study of the Manus natives of the Admiralty Islands*. Philadelphia: American Philosophical Society.

Frankel, S., and G. Lewis, eds. 1989. *A continuing trial of treatment: medical pluralism in Papua New Guinea*. Dordrecht: Kluwer Academic Publishers.

Fry, G. W., and R. Maurico. 1987. *Pacific Basin and Oceania*. Vol. 70. World Bibliography Series. Oxford: Clio.

Garrett, J. 1982. *To live among the stars: Christian origins in Oceania*. Geneva: World Council of Churches.

Garrett, J. 1992. *Footsteps in the sea: Christianity in Oceania to World War II*. Suva: Institute of Pacific Studies.

Gell, A. 1975. *Metamorphosis of the Cassowaries*. London: Althone.

Gesche, P. 1985. *Initiative and initiation: a cargo cult–type movement in the Sepik against its background in traditional village religion*. St. Augustin, West Germany: Anthropos-Institut.

Goldman, I. 1970. *Ancient Polynesian society*. Chicago: University of Chicago Press.

Gunson, N. 1978. *Messengers of grace: evangelical missionaries in the South Seas, 1797–1860*. Melbourne: Melbourne University Press.

Handy, E. W. C. 1927. *Polynesian religion*. Bulletin No. 34. Honolulu: Bernice P. Bishop Museum.

Harrison, S. 1993. The commerce of cultures in Melanesia. *Man* 28:139–58.

Haynes, D. E., and W. L. Wuerch. 1995. *Micronesian religion and lore: a guide to sources, 1526–1990*. Westport, Connecticut: Greenwood Press.

Herdt, G., and M. Stephen, eds. 1989. *The religious imagination in New Guinea*. New Brunswick, NJ.

Herdt, G. H., ed. 1984. *Rituals of manhood: male initiation in Papua New Guinea*. Berkeley: University of California Press.

Howe, K. R. 1984. *Where the waves fall: a new South Sea Islands history from first settlement to colonial rule*. Honolulu: University of Hawai'i Press.

Jorgensen, D. 1987. Oceanic religions: history of study. In *Encyclopedia of religion*, ed. M. Eliade. New York: Macmillan.

Kaplan, M. 1995. *Neither cargo nor cult: ritual politics and the colonial imagination in Fiji*. Durham: Duke University Press.

Keesing, R. M. 1992. *Custom and confrontation: The Kwaio struggle for cultural autonomy*. Chicago: University of Chicago Press.

Keesing, R. M., and R. Tonkinson, eds. 1982. *Reinventing traditional culture: the politics of kastom in island Melanesia*. Mankind 13(4).

Langness, L. L. 1987. *The study of culture*. Novato, CA: Chandler & Sharp.

Lanternari, V. 1963. *The religions of the oppressed: a study of modern messianic cults*. New York: New American Library.

Laracy, H. 1983. *Pacific protest. the MAASINA RULE movement. Solomon Islands, 1944–1952*. Suva: Institute of Pacific Studies, University of the South Pacific.

Lattas, A. 1992. Skin, personhood, and redemption: the doubled self in West New Britain cargo cults. *Oceania* 63:27–54.

Latukefu, S. 1978. The impact of South Seas Islands missionaries on Melanesia. In *Mission, church, and sect in Oceania*, ed. J. A. Boutilier, D. T. Hughes, and S. W. Tiffany, 91–108. Ann Arbor: University of Michigan Press.

Lawrence, P. 1964. *Road belong cargo.* Manchester: Manchester University Press.

Leenhardt, M. 1979 [1947]. *Do kamo: person and myth in the Melanesian world.* Chicago: University of Chicago Press.

LeRoy, J. 1985. *Fabricated world.* Vancouver: University of British Columbia Press.

Lindstrom, L. 1990. *Knowledge and power in a South Pacific society.* Washington, D.C.: Smithsonian Institution Press.

Lindstrom, L. 1993. *Cargo cult: strange stories of desire from Melanesia and beyond.* Honolulu: University of Hawai'i Press.

Mageo, J. M., and A. Howard, eds. 1996. *Spirits in culture, history, and mind.* New York/London: Routledge.

Malinowski, B. 1922. *Argonauts of the Western Pacific.* New York: Dutton.

Malinowski, B. 1954. *Magic, science and religion and other essays.* New York: Doubleday.

Marcus, G. E. 1993. Tonga's contemporary globalizing strategies: trading on sovereignty admidst international migration. In *Contemporary Pacific societies: studies in development and change,* ed. V. S. Lockwood, T. G. Harding, and B. J. Wallace. Englewood Cliffs, NJ: Prentice Hall.

Mauss, M. 1954. *The gift.* London: Cohen and West.

Moorehead, A. 1966. *The fatal impact: an account of the invasion of the South Pacific, 1767–1840.* London, Hamish Hamilton.

Oliver, D. L. 1989. *Oceania: the native cultures of Australia and the Pacific Islands.* Honolulu: University of Hawai'i Press.

Radford, R. 1987. *Highlanders and foreigners in the Upper Ramu: The Kainantu Area 1919–1942.* Melbourne: Melbourne University Press.

Rappaport, R. A. 1984. *Pigs for the ancestors,* 2nd ed. New Haven: Yale University Press.

Roach, E. 1987. From English mission to Samoan congregation. Ph.D. dissertation, Columbia University.

Rutz, H. J. 1995. Occupying the headwaters of tradition: rhetorical strategies of nation making in Fiji. In *Nation making: emergent identities in postcolonial Melanesia,* ed. R. Foster, 71–94. Ann Arbor: University of Michigan Press.

Sahlins, M. 1985. *Islands of history.* Chicago: University of Chicago Press.

Schieffelin, E. L. 1976. *The sorrow of the lonely and the burning of the dancers.* New York: St. Martin's Press.

Schieffelin, E. L., and R. Crittenden. 1991. *Like people you see in a dream: first contact in six Papuan societies.* Stanford: Stanford University Press.

Schwartz, T. 1962. The Paliau Movement in the Admiralty Islands, 1946–1954. *Anthropological Papers of the American Museum of Natural History* 49:211–421.

Shore, B. 1989. Mana and tapu. In *Developments in Polynesian ethnology,* ed. A. Howard and R. Borofsky, 137–73. Honolulu: University of Hawai'i Press.

Sinclair, K. P. 1993. The Maori tradition of prophecy: religion, history, and politics in New Zealand. In *Contemporary Pacific societies,* ed. V. S. Lockwood, T. G. Harding, and B. J. Wallace, 321–34. Englewood Cliffs: Prentice Hall.

Smith, B. 1985. *European vision and the South Pacific.* Oxford: Melbourne University Press.

Smith, M. F. 1994. *Hard times on Kairiru Island: poverty, development, and morality in a Papua New Guinea village.* Honolulu: University of Hawai'i Press.

Spiro, M. E. 1952. Ghosts, Ifaluk, and teleological functionalism. *American Anthropologist* 54:497–503.

Stephen, M. 1995. *A'aisa's gifts: a study of magic and the self.* Berkeley: University of California Press.

Stone-Wigg, M. J. 1909. *The Papuans: a people of the South Pacific.* Melbourne: Shipping Newspapers, Ltd.

Swain, T., and G. Trompf. 1995. *The religions of Oceania.* London: Routledge.

Taylor, C. R. H. 1965. *A Pacific bibliography,* 2nd ed. London: Oxford University Press.

Thomas, N. 1994. *Colonialism's culture: anthropology, travel and government.* Princeton: Princeton University Press.

Tippett, A. R. 1967. *Solomon Island Christianity. a study in growth and obstruction.* London: Lutterworth.

Trompf, G. W., ed. 1987. *The gospel is not western: black theologies from the Southwest Pacific.* Maryknoll, New York: Orbis.

Trompf, G. W. 1994. *Payback: the logic of retribution in Melanesian religions.* Cambridge: Cambridge University Press.

Tuzin, D. F. 1980. *The voice of the tambaran: truth and illusion in Ilahita Arapesh religion.* Berkeley: University of California Press.

Valeri, V. 1985. *Kingship and sacrifice: ritual and society in ancient Hawai'i.* Chicago: University of Chicago Press.

Wagner, R. 1972. *Habu: the innovation of meaning in Daribi religion.* Chicago: University of Chicago Press.

Wagner, R. 1996. *Asiwinarong: ethos, image and social power among the Usen Barok of New Ireland.* Princeton: Princeton University Press.

Waiko, J. D. 1981. Binandere oral tradition: sources and problems. In *Oral traditions in Melanesia,* eds. D. Denoon and R. Lacey, 11–30. Port Moresby: University of Papua New Guinea Press.

Weiner, A. B. 1976. *Women of value, men of renown: new perspectives on Trobriand exchange.* Austin: University of Texas Press.

White, G. M. 1991. *Identity through history: living stories in a Solomon Islands society.* Cambridge: University of Cambridge Press.

Whitehouse, H. 1995. *Inside the cult: religious innovation and transmission in Papua New Guinea.* Oxford: Clarendon.

Williams, F. E. 1923. *The Vailala Madness and the destruction of native ceremonies in the Gulf Division.* Port Moresby: Territory of Papua, Anthropology Reports No. 4.

Williams, F. E. 1928. *Orokaiva magic.* Oxford: Oxford University Press.

Williamson, R. W. 1933. *The religious and cosmic beliefs of Central Polynesia.* Cambridge: Cambridge University Press.

Worsley, P. 1968. *The trumpet shall sound.* London: McGibbon and Kee.

Young, M. 1983. *Magicians of Manumanua.* Berkeley: University of California Press.

Zegwaard, G. A. 1959. Headhunting practices of the Asmat of West New Guinea. *American Anthropologist* 61:1020–41.

# Chapter 20

# Art

*Deborah Waite*

Pacific art occupies many categories and dimensions that, in turn, have regional distribution. Architecture, anthropomorphic and zoomorphic images, masks, ceramics, bowls, lime spatulas, canoes, shields, and weapons may be ascribed to the category of art. Two-dimensional visual expression such as painting, low-relief carving, tattooing, scarification, and plaited fiber designs also qualify. Art may be produced to last permanently or exist only for the duration of a ritual. It may be collectively owned by a social group or privately owned and displayed. There are traditional gender associations: many types of image-making are created by men and may not be viewed by women. Much art from the Pacific designates or defines the regional and social identity of the owner or wearer. Much of what we call art was not thought of as art by its makers or users, at least until recent times. The removal of objects from the Pacific and reinstallation in Western museum cases has recontextualized them to a degree unimaginable to many of their initial makers and users.

The three broad regional divisions of Melanesia, Micronesia, and Polynesia have been already introduced in this text, together with linguistic and cultural differences. It is not surprising that comparable distinctions may be observed in the visual arts. Masks, for example, predominate in Melanesia (including Irian Jaya). By contrast, only one island in Micronesia (Satawan in the Mortlocks) has a masking tradition. Face masks worn by people are uncommon in Polynesian traditions, although architectural gable masks are a feature of structures in New Zealand. The rich Polynesian tradition of barkcloth (*tapa*) production has produced barkcloth that differs in appearance and use from Melanesian barkcloth.

## Prehistory

Prominant among prehistoric art traditions of the Pacific is the Lapita Cultural Tradition. Lapita ceramics appear to have been a major, widespread, and early ceramic tradition in the Pacific, but by no means the only one. The origins of the Austronesian-speaking Lapita peoples may lie within Southeast Asia, but more than likely, they developed in northeastern Melanesia among pre-existing peoples. Archaeological evidence makes possible the definition of Lapita as a cultural tradition based primarily on a fishing economy with occasional evidence of possible long distance trade between settlements. Sites with the earliest dates occur in western Melanesia, with dates for the Lapita dispersal across the Pacific occurring within the fourth millennium B.P. (Spriggs 1984:207).

Lapita ceramics, remains of which have been found from Manus (Admiralty) Islands to Western Polynesia, consist primarily of high-fired friable sherds of bowls; some small figurines have been found at Lapita sites on Fiji (Green 1979:17, 29). Ceramic bowls, evidently produced in several sizes, would have displayed elaborate surface decoration around the upper bowl surface. The repetitive curvilinear and angular designs were rendered with a dentate stamping instrument on the damp clay surface. In both Melanesia and Polynesia, there was a tendency through time toward gradual design simplification as well as a trend from more complex to simpler bowl types. This plainware tradition was transported to the Marquesas Islands and appears in the earliest sites there (c. 2000 B.P.). In Melanesia, plainware ceramics date from c. 2900 to 200 B.P. (Spriggs 1984:213–214).

Lapita ware would appear to be ancestral to later Melanesian and Polynesian art, but so also are other ceramic traditions. The Mangaasi ceramic complex of Vanuatu and Tikopia and ceramic production at sites in the New Guinea Highlands (Wanlek - 4000 B.P.), Bougainville, and Solomon Islands are examples of Lapita-related ceramic traditions (e.g. Reeve 1990:2–13). Geometric designs also predominate on ceramic sherds found in these areas, but decorative techniques emphasize incision, appliqué, and paddling over dentate stamping.

Prehistoric art from the Pacific Islands includes rock art, as well as three-dimensional stone carvings. On the eastern half of the island of New Guinea, rock shelters in the Sepik River Basin contain stenciled images of the human hand, cassowary bone daggers, and *kina* shell. Particularly notable is Pundimbung Shelter, a sixty-meter long gallery of rock art shelters located along one of the southern tributaries of the Sepik (Swadling et al. 1988, Figures 45–46). Sites in the New Guinea Highlands have yielded carved stone images, mortars, and pestles (grinding stones). Mortars frequently bear images of anthropomorphic faces; pestles represent a variety of birds and animals (Swadling et al. 1988, Figures 56-63; Newton 1979:32-57). Polynesian petroglyphs also belong to a prehistoric Pacific, though not exclusively so. Their production continued well into historic times. The definition of "history" varies from one area to another and primarily refers to the time of first European contact.

Implications of prehistoric art for later art forms in the Pacific are problematic. Pottery produced within historic times in eastern New Guinea would appear ultimately to have traceable origins in the oldest ceramic production from this island. However, design-making in the Lapita tradition died out centuries before it recurred in various historic arts, so caution must be urged for those who seek the seeds of Melanesian and Polynesian art in Lapita.

## Artists Past and Present

Pacific artists are and have always been specialists, in that they were (and are) recognized for their skills. Among Polynesian and Micronesian peoples, experts in image-carving, tattooing, and barkcloth-making coexisted with specialists in canoe-building, net-making, architecture, navigation, herbal medicine, sorcery, and other institutions. These specialists underwent long and systematic training in their technical skills as well as in the history, mythology, and genealogy of their peoples. Inheritance could play a role. The son of an expert tattoo artisan, for example, might follow that profession.

In the islands of Melanesia, the role of an artist is perhaps less classificatory than in Polynesia. There may be several artists in a village. Among the Asmat people of southeast New Guinea (West Irian),

> There is no word in Asmat for art or for artist; a good carver is referred to as a *tsjestsju ipitsj*, a clever man, or *wow ipitsj*, design man. Good carvers in Asmat have the kind of prestige usually reserved only for great headhunters. Every village, no matter how small it might be, has its own group of carvers. There is no family tradition of carvers and no one is chosen or forced to become a carver. Asmat carvers turn to art from some inner drive or instinct. The young sit at the feet of the older artists and wait to be asked to do a whole piece by themselves. (Schneebaum 1990:29-30)

Philip Dark recorded that among the Kilenge of West New Britain (Papua New Guinea)

> recognition of a man as an artist carries with it recognition of his competence in a variety of spheres such as carver, painter, canoe maker and house constructor.

But

> it is acknowledged that certain artists excel at certain artistic activities and not in others. Very few are considered to be pre-eminent in all the arts, but old man Marakos was one and was called *namos tame*, master artist. . . . A person becomes *namos tame* because everyone recognizes his skill. (Dark 1974:19)

In these and other similar recorded instances, the artists are men and primarily woodcarvers. For many years, women artists in the Pacific were not given similar acknowledgment in Western literature, largely because the focus of attention was woodcarving, and especially image-making, largely executed by men. Women, on the other hand, have distinguished themselves in ceramics and as fiber artists. *Bilum* bags utilized by both sexes in Papua New Guinea (and most recently in Solomon Islands) were fabricated by women whose looping techniques provided clues to the place of origin and identity of the artist (Thomas 1991:117–124). Weaving and plaiting executed by women also played a vital role within Micronesian cultural traditions (Feldman and Rubenstein 1986). Barkcloth production in Polynesia and Fiji was also women's work, as were the fine mats worn and exchanged at major ceremonial occasions. The Tongan *ta'ovala* and other waist mats represent a particular example of women's fiber work in Tonga (Color Plate 20A); a recent development of grave art in Tonga is also the work of women (Teilhet 1990:222–243, 1992a:44–52, 1992b:40–65). Maori women have long been famous for the feather and other fiber garments as well as tattooing (for other women) (Nga Puna Roimata o te Arawa 1993).

## Art and Environment

Many if not most of the materials from which art is fashioned come directly from the environment. Volcanic islands covered with rain forest possess abundant trees and plants for wood and fiber constructions. Melanesian and Polynesian high islands belong to this category. Atolls are generally less well endowed with heavy forestation. In some instances, e.g. Easter Island, stone carving became a major form of sculpture in part because of the availability of volcanic rock and the relative scarcity of plant life.

The species of wood or plant utilized for certain artifacts has among many peoples specific symbolic value. Images of Tu, god of breadfruit in Mangareva (French Polynesia), were carved from the breadfruit tree. Similarly, in Hawai'i three of the large wooden images allegedly representing Kū, also once associated with agriculture, were carved from breadfruit wood (see Kaeppler, Starzecka, and Rudall 1993:41).

The Asmat of southwest New Guinea live in a forest environment and are sedentary hunters and gatherers in the forests surrounding their villages. Their mythology links man with tree. The trunk may be equated with the body of a man; branches with arms, roots with legs. The fruit of a tree corresponds with the human head. Asmat myths about the transformation of tree into man or man from wood thus provide justification for the representation of ancestors as carved trees (Schneebaum 1990:20, 42–43, Thomas 1995:80–83).

The importance of the environment as revealed in materials used for making art and, by extension, the people who procure or cultivate them, becomes obvious in art objects comprising several elements. Hawaiian featherwork, for example, utilized bird feathers for the outer visible surfaces of capes, cloaks, and helmets. Feathers were attached to a backing of *olonā* netting (*Touchardia latifolia*), while rootlets from the *'ie'ie* plant (*Freycinetta arborea*) were employed to make the basic structure of feather helmets and images. Within a given land division, or *ahupua'a*, some or all of the desired materials could be found in the mountains or near the sea. Certain sections of islands within the Hawaiian archipelago were widely recognized as ideal cultivation or collection sites for plants. Well-known planting localities for *wauke*, or paper mulberry

(*Broussonetia papyrisera*), the inner bark of which was one major source for Hawaiian *tapa*, or barkcloth, were the eastern coast of Maui and the Kona district of Hawai'i Island (Handy and Handy 1972:209).

Changes in an environment can radically affect the production of traditional artifacts. The logging industry is producing the most radical alterations of the ecosystem in rain forest areas and is a matter of grave concern. The Maisin people, who live on the northeastern coast of New Guinea Island, have been repeatedly approached by forestry officials and outside logging interests for rights to their forests. The production of barkcloth, a longstanding tradition among the Maisin, has been adapted by them as a form of protest against the logging industry. An exhibition called *Jumping Lines: Maisin Art and Rainforest Conservation* was organized and held at the University of California, Berkeley, in 1996 as a protest statement (sponsored by Greenpeace and the university). Maisin artists traveled to Berkeley to speak about their art and this motive for their barkcloth production (Thompson 1996:11–13).

## Parameters of Space and Time

Two types of parameters, chronological and iterative, may be used separately and interchangeably in discussing the context that is so critical for the study of Pacific art. Chronological parameters provide a time framework employed to assess the age of archaeological finds as well as historical and anthropological information.

Iterative parameters comprise those ritually celebrated events that continually reiterate or restate aspects of the life cycle. Birth, initiation into adulthood, marriage, and death are principal rites of passage or transition within the life cycle of the individual. Public rituals marking commemoration of these events are repeated successively within a given community and often involve the presence and utilization of artifacts. Their performance reiterates elements of the life cycle for people and ensures continuity. The larger life cycle is referenced and celebrated in major public rituals, especially at stages in the process of agricultural cultivation. Both types of life cycle, that of the individual and that of growing plants, demarcate time in an iterative rather than a strictly chronological manner.

Both sets of parameters, chronological and iterative, combine to create the space and time within which visual and performing arts exist.

## Art and the Body

Throughout the Pacific, the human body has been an object of marking. Two-dimensional body surface marking refers to tattooing, scarification, and body painting, as well as designs rendered on clothing. Three-dimensional marking includes attached ornaments and garments wrapped and folded around the body. All have been viewed as recognizable signs of individual and social identity.

Body marking has been a traditional means of permanently confirming status within the life cycle and, accordingly, the community. Tattooing has been the dominant body marking process in Polynesia and parts of Micronesia and Melanesia. A tattooed body indicated maturation—eligibility for marriage and full social responsibility within a community. In Hawai'i and the Society Islands, tattoos were also executed to connote specific events such as battle victories and to indicate major social positions.

The tattooing procedure was performed by specialists, who punctured the skin with small serrated bone blades attached to wooden handles. In pigmented tattooing, the blades, or combs, were dipped in a bluish-black dye (made from *kukui* nut or sugarcane charcoal); puncturing of the skin was accomplished by tapping the handled comb, or blade, with a mallet. The unserrated blades of Maori tattoo instruments left an incised or carved impression on the skin. Most tattooing is pigmented, leaving a bluish-black permanent design. In Solomon Islands, unpigmented tattooing results in finely-incised designs that are barely visible.

Both sexes were tattooed, but usually with significant differences. The broad linear patterns employed in Samoan men's tattooing, for example, contrasted sharply with small radial designs for Samoan women. It was important that the right hands of Marquesan and Samoan women be tattooed so that they might mix and serve the traditional *kava* drink. Regional and historical changes in tattooing designs reflected movements of people and other historical events. This is particularly evident in tattooing from the north and south islands in the Marquesas island group (Von den Steinen 1925, vol. I; Herring 1973). Tattoo designs correlated rather closely with designs rendered on other artifacts and, in so doing, served as direct referents to these other socially significant objects.

Scarification is a particularly Melanesian form of body marking for both men and women. Raised scars rendered in rows or patterns are obtained by rubbing charcoal into knife wounds so that they will heal in a permanently raised state. Puberty initiation rites were and still are a principal context for scarification among the Chambri and others living along the Sepik River of New Guinea. The process took place during the seclusion period of puberty initiation (Bateson 1936, 1958:130–131, plates X and XI; Williamson 1990:389). For Australian Brian Taylor to become a member of Chambri society, ritual scarification was necessary in 1981 (Errington and Gewertz 1990:316–317). This is but one of several examples of an outsider undergoing local puberty rituals in order to obtain recognition as a complete adult from the islander perspective.

Body painting is the practice of painting designs on the body at times of social importance, such as war or rites of passage (Color Plate 20B). This practice is particularly common among Melanesian peoples (for example, Schneebaum 1990:59). Unlike scarification and tattooing, body painting is impermanent. Both genders may employ the practice, making use of designs that correspond to patterns carved on the surfaces of wooden images or painted on modeled skulls.

Ornaments made of shell, bone, teeth from whales, porpoises, and dogs, plaited grasses, and flowers served (until today in some areas) as social signification, as did direct body marking. These ornaments may indicate rank, leadership, or social maturation or serve as protective amulets. The material from which they are fashioned frequently enabled them to be categorized as wealth. These functions were seldom singular. Neck pendants, ear and nose ornaments, even arm and leg bands usually conveyed several messages as to the status and identity of the wearer. The tridacna clamshell ring, *eringi* or *bakeha*, once worn by important males in the Western Solomon Islands, indicated high status and, at the same time, ranked as the most valuable item within the system of shell currency, or exchange media (Russell 1948:320, Somerville 1897:363–364).

Subtle yet definite gender distinctions could be made evident in body ornaments. Ear ornaments worn by high-ranking men and women in the Marquesas Islands were fashioned from whalebone. They comprised two sections: a disk that appeared in front of the earlobe and a curved section extending behind the ear. The latter portion of men's ornaments, *ha'akai*, terminated in a tiny anthropomorphic figure, or *tiki*; one or more similar images might be carved along the shank. The shank of women's ear ornaments, *taina*, was fashioned into an intricate figural grouping that referenced social customs regarding birth confinement as well as social behavior with respect to guests (Von den Steinen 1925:23–25, 138–139, 140–147). It was evidently the role of women to be the discreet bearers of these significant visually recorded messages.

One of the most prominent types of ornament common to people living in Melanesia and Polynesia is the *kapkap* (Melanesian term), a clamshell disk to which is attached a turtleshell disk perforated into a radial design (Color Plate 20C). Regional preferences dictated whether *kapkaps* were worn as pendants or fastened to forehead bands. The latter were slightly smaller in size that the former. In Melanesia, *kapkaps* were worn in the New Guinea Highlands, the Bismarcks, and the Western Solomon Islands. The Marquesas Islands represent the main locus of this ornament in Polynesia. Here, several disks were attached to a forehead band; the whole, termed *uhikana*, was worn by high-ranking males.

Colonialization, missionaries in particular, fostered, or required, adoption of Western clothing instead of traditional barkcloth garments. Another effect of Western contact has been the substitution, within a traditional matrix, of Western-imported cotton threads and cotton material, as well as chemical dyes for locally produced materials. The effect of World War II on the adoption of these and many things Western should not be overlooked.

Two principal types of traditional garments are common to the Pacific: barkcloth and loom-woven fabric. Loom-woven fabric has a much more limited distribution than barkcloth, being confined primarily to Micronesia, in particular the Caroline Islands. Weaving was done on a backstrap loom similar to those of Indonesia; banana and hibiscus fibers were the most favored ones (Feldman and Rubenstein 1986:47).

Barkcloth is still produced in parts of Melanesia (as in the north coast of New Guinea and Fiji) and in Polynesia. It was once a widespread phenomenon throughout the islands of Polynesia, but with the arrival of European ships in the eighteenth century, European cloth made inroads. Barkcloth production for local use declined and even disappeared in many areas, but is now being produced for ritual use and for the tourist trade.

Barkcloth was (is) made by beating fermented strips of the inner bark of the paper mulberry plant (*Broussonetia papyrifera*). Other plant species such as breadfruit have been used, but paper mulberry appears to have been a consistent favorite. The bark strips were beaten with wooden mallets or beaters grooved so as to separate the fibers and expand them as much as possible. Overlapped edges of the expanded strips could then be beaten together to form larger pieces. These were decorated through immersion dyes, stenciling, stamping, printing, and rubbing. Traditional dyes were obtained from local plants, nuts, and tree bark (Kooijman 1972, Pritchard 1984). Barkcloth production methods were similar in Melanesia, but certain uses differed radically from Polynesian custom. The large sheets of barkcloth utilized in Polynesia as presentation gifts on ritual occasions did not have Melanesian counterparts other than on Fiji. Conversely, barkcloth provided a major material for mask-making in Melanesia.

Prior to the adoption of European cloth at different periods during the nineteenth century, barkcloth clothing was widely worn wrapped or draped around the body. In the Society Islands, for example, both sexes wore a *pareu*, or wraparound, from waist to knee (male) or from breasts to below knee (female). Both also wore a poncho-like upper garment, *tiputo*, tied at the waist by a sash or girdle, *tatua*. Women also, on occasion, wore a cloak, or *'ahu*. Tahitian women were depicted wearing expansive ritual skirts or costumes of barkcloth to which feather tassels were appended (Oliver 1974 vol. I:152–153). On the Melanesian island of Erromanga in southeastern Vanuatu, a woman of the nineteenth century wore a barkcloth upper garment with fifteen or more leaf skirts and a painted pandanus outer skirt. So form-concealing was this garment that missionary-introduced clothes were revealing by contrast (Lawson 1994:37–38, 145).

New Zealand, Hawai'i, and the Society Islands are the only three areas in Polynesia where feather garments were traditional insignia for the upper classes. In Hawai'i, the outer surfaces of feather capes, *'ahu'ula*, as well as cloaks, consisted of bird feathers. The highest-ranking capes and cloaks bore red feathers from the *'i'iwi* bird (scarlet honeysucker—l'estiaria coccinea) and yellow feathers taken from the tips of the *'o'o*, or black honeyeater (*Acrulocercus*) amd *mamo*, or black honeycreeper (*Drepanis pacifica*) birds. Professional feather catchers procured the feathers by trapping the birds on branches coated with a sticky substance. Feathers were sorted and tied to a backing, or *nae*, of *olonā* netting. This backing consisted of several pieces of *olonā*. A. Kaeppler has suggested that protective *mele*, or chants, were recited during the production of this netting, giving protective *mana* (spirit power) to garments worn in battle as well as on other important occasions (Kaeppler 1985:119). Helmets, or *mahiole*, were plaited from the *'ie'ie* vine (*Freycinetia arborea*) covered with *olonā*, to which were tied the feathers.

Kiwi, pigeon, and parrot feathers attached to a flax backing predominated among Maori feather cloaks (*kahu kura* in New Zealand. *Kuri* (dog) hair was attached to another special Maori cloak, *mahiti*. Brown, white, and yellow prevailed among

Maori cloaks, while red and yellow were the highest-ranking colors in Tahiti and Hawai'i. The oldest Maori *kahu*, however, first recorded by Europeans in 1769, comprised red parrot feathers like the *'ahu* of Hawai'i (see Mead 1969:56). The signifying process was comparable in all three regions: enhancing the visibility of the high-ranking wearer in all circumstances.

## Art and Warfare

Warfare in the Pacific could be said to provide an arena for the human body extended. That is, all visible attributes definitive of social and regional identity for an individual (body surface markings, ornaments, and garments) are extended toward the enemy through the ornamentation of weapons and shields. Carving details, painting, shell inlay, and attachment of shells or feathers may convey the appropriate messages for the enemy, or the Other, but at the same time, are the very features that have allowed for reclassification of weapons and shields as art.

Warfare had many motives. Headhunting, suspicion of witchcraft, and revenge all provided motives, but paramount is land acquisition, ranging from relatively small disputes over land to large-scale colonization. The uniting of all Hawaiian islands into a single kingdom by Kamehameha I by 1810 is a major example of large-scale land acquisition. The Wahgi people, in the New Guinea Highlands, differentiated between fighting (*nganmal*) and warfare (*opo*) and used different weapons in each. Weapons used in fighting confined to a group (clan, tribe) were restricted to long staves and parry shields. Warfare involved the use of spears, bows and arrows, and large battle shields (O'Hanlon 1995a:473).

Headhunting raids were conducted as a form of ritual regeneration required for supplying the needs of a community at times of initiation and in conjunction with other socially creative events such as marriage or the inauguration of a new canoe. The end of the nineteenth century saw the cessation of headhunting in the Solomons; just before 1930 and as late as the 1960s are closing dates for the Iatmul and Asmat of New Guinea, respectively.

A war canoe (Color Plate 20D) could be evidence of approaching or returning warriors. War canoes from the Western Solomon Islands have long been described by outsiders in a manner that indicated the impact on the viewer. Fleichman describes a large war canoe, *tomako*, from the Roviana Lagoon, New Georgia Island, as

> a magnificent affair about fifty-five feet long and with a seating capacity of thirty-five. Its ornamented prow was twelve feet high and its stern fourteen feet, both being studded with mother-of-pearl designs which ran all the way up to their tops. On the prow was a grotesque figurehead in the shape of an animal also inlaid with mother of pearl, while surmounting it, as its topmost decoration, were two tiny figures of humans—so out of proportion that they were as grotesque as the figurehead. Strings of evenly-matched white shells hung on both bow and stern, augmenting that feeling of . . . power which the whole canoe possessed. (Fleichman 1935:122, Plate IV)

This account postdates the period of time during which headhunting actively prevailed in the Western Solomons (see Thomas 1991:47), but it is one of the fullest outsider accounts that indicates the vivid impressions made by the canoes. Fleichman's use of terms such as "grotesque" and "head of an animal" in denoting the long-jawed (but still anthropomorphic) *nguzunguzu* prow figurehead is not uncommon and, despite the misinterpretation, the strangeness of this head appears to have made it a conspicuous marker. The head allegedly represented a spirit that protected the canoe from storms at sea caused by other spirits. The highly visible shells could have served to recall to the insider viewer the shell currency possessed by the canoe owner and other canoe occupants, as well as the offerings of shell rings made to spirits to solicit and acknowledge their aid (see Waite 1990:44–66).

In this part of Solomon Islands, standard warriors' shields were fashioned of coiled cane and fiber and had a flat oval shape. Black-painted lines on the obverse surface delimit sections of the shields; other designs may represent stylized bird wings. The patterns are subtle and do not cover the surface of a shield (approximately the distance between the mid-thighs and shoulders of a shield bearer). Shells and beads attached to shields borne by important individuals were relatively small in scale. Only a relatively few shell-inlaid or -incrusted shields from this area (see Waite 1983) bore surface ornament large and striking enough to make a visible impression (see O'Hanlon 1995b:74–88). It would seem, judging from written accounts, that it was the shield and weapon manipulated by the moving warrior that conveyed the immediate message of aggression, that is, the body extended.

In the Micronesian islands of Kiribati, well into the nineteenth century, warriors wore full armor, the only armor in the Pacific region. Each "suit" comprised a jacket with high protective back, collar, and trousers made of knotted coconut fiber. Designs representing stylized dolphins created by inserting supplementary threads of human hair into the fiber constituted the only surface designs. The stomach area was reinforced by hardened stingray skin. Two types of helmets, one of plaited twine with interwoven tufts of human hair on helmet top and ear guards, and the other comprising the "puffed-out hardened skin of a blowfish," protected the head. The ensemble was so heavy and unwieldy that attendants were necessary to aid the warriors and hand them their weapons (Feldman and Rubenstein 1986:21).

Warriors from Kiribati bore daggers, swords, or long spears of coconut wood. Sharks' teeth were lashed along the lengths of these weapons. The horrific effect of these objects as weapons is countered by their grace of form, which has led them to be recontextualized as art objects. *Arts of the South Seas*, an exhibition held in 1946 at the Museum of Modern Art in New York, included Micronesian swords, navigation charts, and other Pacific artifacts that had not previously been exhibited in a Western art museum (Linton and Wingert 1946:71).

Hawai'i is another region in the Pacific where shark-tooth weapons were once utilized in fighting. The weapons included daggers and clubs that could be used for close-in fighting and possibly for "ritual dissection of the bodies of killed victims." Ancient Hawaiians also made use of a wooden handle to which a dagger made from swordfish bill or stingray spine was attached. Like the shark-tooth weapons from Micronesia, these fiercely effective weapons have been recontextualized as art objects, a phenomenon also true of the Hawaiian feather garments and helmets (Buck 1964:443–455, Wardwell 1994:242–251).

Large wooden war clubs figure prominently on other Polynesian islands up until the introduction of European firearms. The Marquesan *'u'u* is a distinctive Polynesian war club (Figure 20.1). The standard type produced up until c. 1890 has a length of from four to five feet and is made of *toa* or ironwood (*Casuarina*). The density and weight of ironwood makes it an appropriate choice for a weapon; the bulk of that weight is concentrated in the flared upper part of the Marquesan club, intricately carved to represent two back-to-back (Janus-like) anthropomorphic faces, their juncture visible only in profile (Ivory 1994:53-65). The manner of carving has repercussions on numerous Marquesan artifacts, e.g. carved wooden bowls, stilts, and ear ornaments. Freestanding images and tattooing incorporate the same means of handling form and surface design. A tattooed warrior holding an *'u'u* projected an obvious visual statement about personal and regional identity and status (see Thomas 1995:94–95)—still another example of the extended body in battle context. Implements of war—shields, armor, clubs, and spears—appear to have attained their effectiveness as extensions of the bodies of their users, conveying all the messages—social, spiritual—that that relationship could imply.

## Art and Ritual

Ritual may be defined as repeated systemic actions always performed in the same way but in association with a variety of events. E. Vilasa writes that among the Phosamogo and Thavia people of Santa Isabel island, Solomon Islands, *fafara*, a form of ritual sacrifice to the spirits, was performed before and following tribal wars, fishing and hunting trips, after an unsuccessful harvest, and "on any occasion when it was necessary to ask forgiveness of the spirits and bring about reconciliation after relationships with them had been disturbed" (Vilasa 1986:56). Rituals like these would be executed on behalf of a large social group, but other rituals are more individual and private.

In ritual, art objects may be utilized to effect a boundary crossing between the world of men and the spirit world. In addition to a metaphorical boundary crossing, the physical movements of ritual participants and objects through a ritually prescribed geographical space are a common feature of many ritual performances. In the *fafara*, for example, a pig to be sacrificed, accompanied by a priest and principal leader, was moved to a *phadagi*, or place of sacrifice where this action was accomplished along with verbal supplication to spirits requesting forgiveness as well as future pigs and fruit for the people. Dancers, who had remained in a cleared area outside the sacred space until granted permission to enter, moved into the sacred area, each carrying a shield and an axe (Vilasa 1986:56–61).

Tattooing in Polynesia was traditionally executed in a ritually consistent manner and, thus, belongs in any consideration of art and ritual. In Samoa, the Marquesas, and elsewhere in Polynesia, tattooing constituted an initiation for young people and, characteristically for ritual, involved prescribed sequential acts including feasts, speeches, the presence of specific participants (specific relatives and, above all, the tattoo artisan) and, in keeping with the formulae of ritual, prescribed tattoo motifs executed in sequence (Tapu 1986:160–170, Herring 1973:83–109, Thomas 1995:106–108).

Carved *mbis* poles of the Asmat of southwest New Guinea play a significant social role within a single collective ritual. These ancestor poles are produced in central Asmat and in Bisman region villages along the Casuarina Coast. Each pole is an inverted mangrove tree with one buttress root left intact. A pole is carved into superimposed female and male figures; the outward-extending buttress root, perforated with meaningful designs, branches out from the torso of the uppermost figure. *Mbis* were carved to commemorate or avenge deaths within a village. Headhunting was once a prominant cause of such deaths, but today accidental deaths and other communal disasters or imbalances such as an inadequate fish supply in local rivers justify *mbis* production. The carving of a *mbis* pole may take four or five months, but its ritual "life" if short; after the *mbis* ritual, the poles are taken from the village and returned to

**Figure 20.1.** *Detail of head of war club, Marquesas Islands. Honolulu Academy of Arts 4396.1, Honolulu, Hawai'i (photo HAA).*

the forests from which they came (Schneebaum 1990:42–43; Thomas 1995:80–88).

*Malangan* images from another Melanesian island, New Ireland, reference the deceased in a different manner (Figure 20.2). Produced only in northern New Ireland, *malangan* carvings have a distinct appearance that distinguishes them from other Pacific images. Vertical anthropomorphic images, male and female, exhibit blocky heads that project in front of bodies; these are frequently surrounded by a cage-like assemblage of curving and straight pieces of wood, some carved in the form of birds, fish, or snakes. Small plaited designs cover large portions of a *malangan* carving, visually fragmenting the sculptural whole.

Land-sharing for gardening and other functions is a necessary fact of life in northern New Ireland and results in extended land ownership. A family may work garden plots located in several villages, resulting in ritual confederations among people. Regulations over land working may be completely independent of clan identity and marriage and are articulated through participation in mortuary ceremonies culminating in the production of *malangan* sculpture. Since the images are produced only for a single ceremony, it is the memory of an image once seen at a *malangan* ceremony that constitutes the connecting link.

Masks may be viewed as one type of image that serves as a receptacle or vehicle for ancestral spirits. Masks are worn with partial or complete body coverings of leaves or fiber. The entire ensemble, mask and body covering, is regarded as the spirit presence, not just the mask alone. For the most part, masks are made and worn by men. The construction process takes place under conditions of privacy in the men's house or outside the village away from the eyes of women and children who are as yet uninitiated into the presence of masks and the spirits that they embody. There have been exceptions to this seemingly all male institution: one is the *siveritki* mask traditionally worn by older women of the Baining peoples of New Britain, Papua New Guinea (Corbin 1988:236–237). Masks appear at rituals performed in association with rites of passage and other commemorative events, e.g. food harvest. Among many people, masks have and still may enforce social regulations or restrictions. Mask-wearing members of the Dukduk society on New Britain and neighboring areas collected fines of shell currency from transgressors of social norms (Color Plate 20E).

In Satawan (Micronesia), mask-wearing had a single function: warding off of typhoons in order to protect the breadfruit trees, a major source of food supply on this small island. The wooden masks, *tapuanu*, were produced by male members of the *soutapuanu* society and were carved from breadfruit wood—a readily available wood not without obvious symbolic import. Small wooden figures as well as carved architectural relief masks in the *soutapuanu* communal house reiterated the features of the masks (Feldman and Rubenstein 1986:29–31).

In appearance, *tapuanu* masks epitomize the minimalist approach to design characteristic of Micronesian art. Large, flat anthropomorphic faces with straight tops and pointed chins display linear features. Beneath prominent, projecting straight eyebrows, horizontal eye slits flank a long two-sided nose (Figure 20.3). The mouth is executed as a lozenge or diamond-shaped form horizontally extended. Certain masks display a hair knot projection at one side of the flat-topped skull. Faces are painted white: mouth, eyebrows, and hair knot are accentuated in red and/or black. These sparingly used design motifs, evenly positioned within the large white expanse of the face, create an expression of ominous serenity.

Barkcloth masks made and worn by the Baining people, New Britain, contrast in many ways with masks from Satawan (Color Plate 20F). The Baining live in the interior forests of the Gazelle Peninsula and have always depended heavily upon the forests. Northern and Central Baining have longstanding traditions of barkcloth effigies and masks. All but the female *Siveritki* mask (Figure 20.4) are worn by men in elaborate day and nighttime rituals (and also today in other commemorative, sometimes Christian-related contexts). Traditional rituals celebrate growth and fertility (daytime) and young men's initiations (nighttime). Daytime masks recall plant growth processes, while nighttime masks represent animals, insects, even plants of the forest (Corbin 1979:159–179).

Ritual contexts for masked presences and other images and artifacts may involve a traditionally designated section of

**Figure 20.2.** Malangan *figure, Northern New Ireland. L.34 1/2". Honolulu Academy of Arts, 4373.1. Honolulu, Hawai'i (photo HAA).*

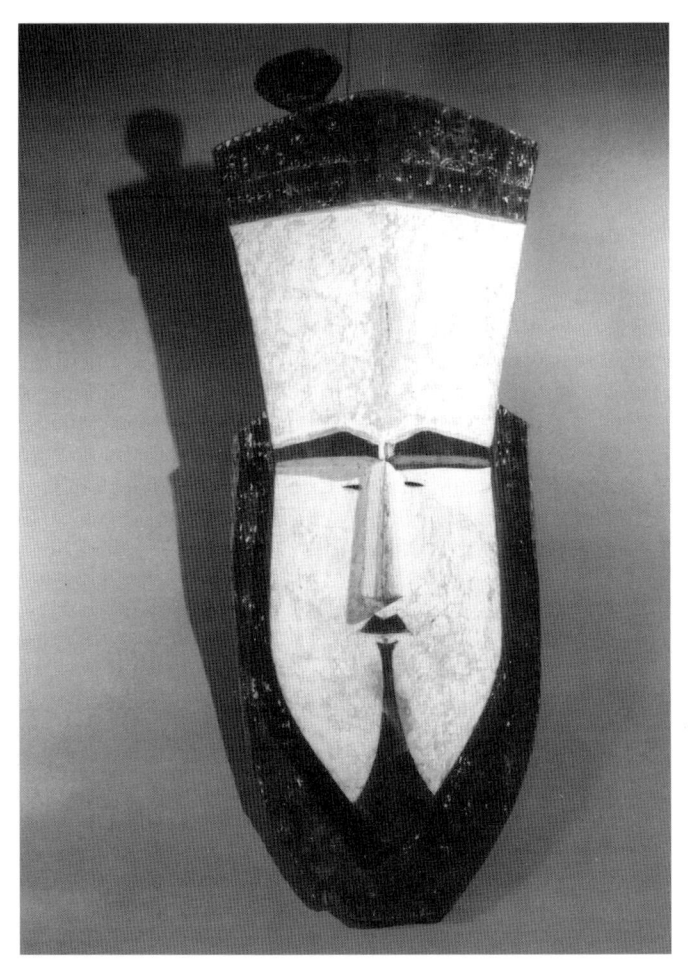

**Figure 20.3.** Tapuanu mask, Satawan Island, Mortlock Islands. Honolulu Academy of Arts 4436.1 L.33 3/8", Honolulu, Hawai'i (photo HAA).

the natural environment, as in, for example, the *fafara* ritual of Santa Isabel, Solomon Islands. They may also take the form of men's ceremonial houses (Melanesia and Micronesia); the Polynesian rectangular (usually) stone-walled enclosures termed *marae* in East Polynesia; *heiau* in Hawai'i and *ahu* on Easter Island; and in New Zealand, the chief's house on the *marae*. The elaborately carved and painted Maori houses differ from their counterparts in East Polynesia in the use of wood as the main building material and in the carved wooden imagery. Melanesian men's houses and the *bai*, or men's house once common in the Belau Islands of Western Micronesia, also display carved and painted images that refer to or contain spirits of the ancestors and associated animals or birds. In Melanesia, these images may be represented in the form of canoe prows, masks, drums, gongs, freestanding anthropomorphic images, and other artifacts. Portable artifacts are often used ritually within the men's house, were often carved there, and, in many cases, stored there. In New Guinea, the region traversed by the Sepik River as well as the interior mountain regions abound in richly decorated men's houses (see Bowdon 1990:480–490, Smidt and McGuigan 1993:121–141).

In the Palau Islands of Micronesia, the richly carved and painted *bai* have largely been replaced by smaller, less significant structures. The old *bai*, of which over 150 were documented between 1908 and 1910, were destroyed by typhoons and during World War II (Thomas 1995:168–180). The traditional *bai* were distinguished by rows of low-relief carved and painted scenes from mythology and history executed on the facades and on a series of horizontal tie beams that stretched across the *bai* interior. In the 1930s, a Japanese doctor taught Palauans to carve individual portable "story boards" replicating the architectural beams but detached and smaller in size—destined for sale to tourists (see Thomas 1995:168–180; Robinson 1983:176).

The Eastern Polynesian *marae*, Easter Island *ahu*, and Hawaiian *heiau* served as foci for ritual, but their stone walls were not decorated in a Melanesian or Palauan manner. Large stone statues of important ancestors once stood on or near a *marae* and atop the image *ahu* in Easter Island. In Hawai'i, wooden images of ancestors or *akua* (deities) were set up within *heiau* for ritual purposes. Missionaries brought an end to these customs in Polynesia during the early decades of the nineteenth century.

**Figure 20.4.** Sivertiki mask, Baining, New Britain. Pacific Pathways Collection, Honolulu, Hawai'i (photo DCY).

The Pacific Islands

# Contemporary Art

Much of the art mentioned in the course of this chapter is traditional. There are, however, definite modifications, changes, and omissions. Modification in materials used and less time for both preparation and the holding of rituals (due, for example, to road-building) has affected the production of what we call art throughout the Pacific. The recognition of objects as art and their recontextualization for sale to outside visitors is, and has long been, one mark of contemporaneity, although the chronological time period for this development ranges from the nineteenth century to the 1990s. In 1893, a British navy lieutenant on a surveying ship in the Marovo Lagoon, Solomon Islands, was told that the altered features of one type of anthropomorphic image indicated its spirit identity, whereas images depicted more proportionately were made for traders (Somerville 1897:378).

In 1961, the Dutch anthropologist Adrian Gerbrands travelled to do research among the Asmat and, specifically, to study the work of woodcarvers in Amanamkai village and to collect specimens of their work. For Gerbrands, artists carved freestanding anthropomorphic images in contrast to their own, which were largely an integral part of posts. The artist Matjemos brought to him a carved buttress, or mangrove root like those atop the *mbis* poles, only this was a separately carved object for sale. The artist Bishur produced "pseudo-canoe prows" for sale to Gerbrands (Gerbrands 1967:79, 95, 164).

The Asmat, with sponsorship of resident Crosier Fathers, built a museum for their art in the village of Agats in 1973 (Schneebaum 1990:v–viii). The Crosier Fathers and Brothers, missionaries whose home base lies in Hastings, Nebraska, were far removed in ideology from the missionaries who destroyed so much of Polynesian art during the first decades of the nineteenth century.

The Iatmul and neighbors living along the banks of the Sepik River in New Guinea continue to maintain traditional men's houses, associated masks, and other carvings, while producing carvings for sale that may resemble, yet differ in minor details (such as body painting or headgear) from ritually sanctioned carvings.

Since becoming an independent nation in 1978, Solomon Islands has witnessed an increase in the production of art for sale to its growing numbers of tourists. The Western Province, where art was once created largely in association with the ritual needs of war and prestige, has become a center for tourist art production.

What would once have been war canoe prow figureheads now line the shelves of shops in Honiara, the capital city of the Solomons. These *nguzunguzu* come in several sizes and may be adapted for new purposes, such as bookends and keyrings. The new products recall the old traditions, however, and information available at shops and in tourist brochures makes clear their past associations, now viewed as part of the collective history of the nation.

Tourist art has also been a prominent feature for several decades in Micronesia and Polynesia. The style and form of older ancestor images reappears in smaller sizes and far greater numbers for sale. *Tapa* production for tourist consumption in the form of small Western-style table mats and other artifacts are a feature of Fijian and Polynesian markets. Small mats, baskets, and pocketbooks plaited in traditional ways are available for the outsider.

Tattooing, once banned, has been rejuvenated, especially in association with annual festivals, such as the annual Tahitian Bastille Day fête, which demonstrates a fusion of colonial with indigenous histories. The revival of *moko,* tattooing traditions in New Zealand, and *kakau,* tattooing in Hawai'i, is becoming increasingly vital as a means of reasserting identity and relinquishing foreign alliances.

Training in European art techniques such as printmaking and bronze casting has become increasingly valued as a means through which traditional designs and themes can be communicated to an ever-widening audience and integrated with European-derived features of style and imagery. It was outsiders, however, who initially implemented this learning process. In the 1960s, Ulli and Georgina Beier developed art courses at the University of Papua New Guinea. Many of the first Pacific Island artists to become recognized as individual artists outside the communities from which they came and beyond the perimeters of the ritual contexts within which art was normally produced were trained in this institution (Thomas 1995:184–208).

Islanders are increasingly appropriating Western-derived themes for their own imagery, even in ritual contexts. Masks of the Sulka people of New Britain (Melanesia) currently integrate Roman Catholic imagery of saints, mitred bishops, and the like (as in the film, *The Drum and the Mask*, 1995). Pacific art, in short, continues to challenge the expectations of an ever-widening audience.

# Bibliography

Bateson, G. 1936. *Naven.* 2nd ed. Stanford: Stanford University Press.

Bowdon, R. The architecture and art of Kwoma ceremonial houses. In *Sepik heritage: tradition and change*, ed. N. Lutkehaus, 480–490. Durham, N.C.: Carolina Academic Press.

Buck, P. (Te Rangi Hiroa). 1964. *Arts and crafts of Hawaii*, Bernice P. Bishop Museum Special Publication 45.

Coombe, F. 1911. *Islands of enchantment: many-sided Melanesia seen through the eyes and recorded by F. Coombe.* London: MacMillan.

Corbin, G. 1979. The art of the Baining, New Britain. In *Exploring the visual art of Oceania*, ed. S. Mead. Honolulu: University of Hawai'i Press.

Corbin, G. 1988. *Native arts of North America, Africa and the South Pacific.* New York: Harper and Row.

Dark, P. K. 1974. *Art and life, a look at a New Guinea people.* London: Academy Editions.

Errington, F., and D. Gewertz. 1990. The chief of the Chambri: social change and cultural permeability among a New Guinea People. In *Sepik heritage: tradition and change in Papua New Guinea*, ed. N. Lutkehaus. Durham, N.C.: Carolina Academic Press.

Feldman, J., and D. Rubenstein. 1986. *The art of Micronesia.* Honolulu: University of Hawai'i Art Gallery, University of Hawai'i.

Fleichmann, J. 1935. *Footsteps in the sea.* New York: Putnam.

Gerbrands, A. 1967. *Wow-Ipits. eight Asmat woodcarvers of New Guinea.* The Hague and Paris: Mouton and Co. Publishers.

Green, R. 1979. Early Lapita art from Polynesia and island Melanesia: continuities in ceramic, barkcloth and tattoo decorations. In *Exploring the visual arts of Oceania*, ed. S. Mead, 13-31. Honolulu: University of Hawai'i Press.

Handy, E. S. C., and E. G. Handy. 1972. *Native planters in old Hawaii, their life, lore, and environment*, Bernice P. Bishop Museum Bulletin 233. Honolulu: Bishop Museum Press.

Herring, E. 1973. Tatu. In *Dimensions of Polynesia*, ed. J. Teilhet, 83–109. San Diego: Fine Arts Gallery of San Diego.

Ivory, C. 1995. Late nineteenth century Marquesan clubs. *Pacific Arts*, the Journal of the Pacific Arts Association, Numbers 11 and 12, July, 1995, 20-28.

Kaeppler, A. 1985. Hawaiian art and society: traditions and transformations. In *Transformations of Polynesian culture*, ed. A. Hooper and J. Huntsman, 105–131. Auckland: The Polynesian Society.

Kaeppler, A., with D. Starzecka and J. Rudall. 1993. Wood analysis and historical contexts of collecting Hawaiian wooden images. In *Artistic heritage in a changing Pacific*, ed. P. Dark and R. Rose, 41–46. Honolulu: University of Hawai'i Press.

Kaeppler A., C. Kaufmann, and D. Newton. 1993. *L'art oceanien.* Paris: Citadelles and Mazenod.

Kooijman. S. 1972. *Tapa in Polynesia.* Bernice P. Bishop Museum Bulletin 234. Honolulu: Bishop Museum Press.

Kuchler, S. 1992. Making skins: Malangan and the idiom of kinship in Northern New Ireland. In *Anthropology, art, and aesthetics*, ed. J. Coote and A. Shelton, 94–112. Oxford: Clarendon Press.

Lawson, L. 1994. *Collecting curios: missionary tales from the South Seas.* Montreal: McGill University, Fontana Monograph Series III.

Linton, R., and P. Wingert. 1946. *Arts of the South Seas.* New York: Museum of Modern Art.

Mead, S. 1969. *Traditional Maori clothing. a study of technological and functional change.* Wellington/Auckland/Sydney: A. H. and A. W. Reed.

Newton, D. 1979. Prehistoric and recent art styles in Papua New Guinea. In *Exploring the visual arts of Oceania*, ed. S. Mead, 32–57. Honolulu: University of Hawai'i Press.

Nga Puna Roimata o Te Arawa. 1993. *Te papa Tongarewa.* Museum of New Zealand. Wellington: Aotearoa New Zealand.

O'Hanlon, M. 1995a. Modernity and the "graphicalization" of meaning: New Guinea Highland shield design in historical perspective. *Journal of the Royal Anthropological Institute (n.s.)* 1(3):469–493.

O'Hanlon, M. 1995b. Medusa's art, interpreting Melanesian shields. In *Protection, power and display: shields of island Southeast Asia and Melanesia*, ed. A. Tavarelli, 74–88. Chestnut Hill, Mass.: Boston College Museum of Art, October 6–December 10, 1995.

Oliver, D. 1974. *Ancient Tahitian society.* 3 volumes. Honolulu: University of Hawai'i Press.

Pritchard, M. Siapo. 1984. *Bark cloth of Samoa.* American Samoan Council on Culture, Arts and Humanities Special Publication No.1.

Reeve, R. 1990. The early history of the western provinces. results of recent investigation. *O'O, a Journal of Solomon Islands Studies*, 2(2): 2–13.

Robinson, D. 1983. The Decorative motifs of Palauan clubhouses. In *Art and artists of Oceania*, ed. S. Mead and B. Kernot, 163–178. Palmerston North (N.Z.): Dunmore Press.

Russell, T. 1948. The culture of Marovo, British Solomon Islands. *Journal of the Polynesian Society* 57(4): 307–329.

Schneebaum, T. 1990. *Embodied spirits: ritual carvings of the Asmat.* Salem, Mass. Peabody Museum. A Traveling Exhibition from the Gajdusek Collection of the Peabody Museum of Salem and the Crosier Asmat Museum Collection of Hastings, Nebraska.

Smidt, D., and N. McGuigan. 1993. An Emic and Etic role for Abelam art (Papua New Guinea); the context of a collecting trip on behalf of the Rijksmuseum voor Volkenkunde, Leiden, in artistic heritage. In *A changing Pacific*, ed. P. Dark and R. Rose, 121–141. Honolulu: University of Hawai'i Press.

Somerville, B. T. 1897. Ethnographical notes in New Georgia, Solomon Islands. *Journal of the Royal Anthropological Institute* 26:412.

Spriggs, M. 1984. The Lapita cultural complex. *Journal of Pacific History.* 19(4): 202–223.

Swadling, P., B. Hauser Schaubling, P. Goracki, and F. Tiesler. 1988. *The Sepik-Ramu: an introduction.* Boroko, New Guinea, Papua New Guinea: National Museum

Tapu, T. 1986. Tattoo ritual in Samoa. In *Pacific rituals: living or dying.* Institute of Pacific Studies of the University of the South Pacific, 56–65.

Teilhet, J. 1990. Tongan grave art. In *Art and identity in Oceania*, ed. A. and L. Hanson. Honolulu: University of Hawai'i Press

Teilhet, J. 1992. Clothes in Tradition: The Ta'ovala and Kiekie as social text and aesthetic markers of custom and identity in contemporary Tongan Society, Parts I and II. In *Pacific Art, Journal of the Pacific Arts Association*, no.5, January, 1992, 44-52; no.6, July, 1992, 40–65.

Thomas, N. 1991. *Entangled objects: exchange, material culture and colonialism in the Pacific.* London/Cambridge, Mass.: Harvard University Press.

Thomas, N. 1995. *Oceanic Art.* World of Art Series. New York/London: Thames and Hudson.

Thompson, L. 1996. The Maisin's Logging Alternative. *Pacific Islands Monthly* 66(2):11–13.

Vilasa, E. 1986. The Fafara ritual of Santa Isabel. In *Pacific rituals, living or dying.* Institute of Pacific Studies of the University of the South Pacific, 56–65.

Von den Steinen, K. 1925. *Die marquesaner und ihre kunst.* Berlin: Dietrich Reimer.

Waite, D. 1983. Shell-inlaid shields from the Solomon Islands. In *Art and artifacts of Oceania*, ed. S. Mead and B. Kernot, 114–136. Palmerston North (N.Z.): Dunmore Press.

Waite, D. 1990. Mon canoes of the Western Solomon Islands. In *Art and identity in Oceania*, ed. A. H. Hanson, 44–66. Honolulu: University of Hawai'i Press.

Wardwell, A. 1994. *Island ancestors: Oceanic art from the Masco Collection*. Seattle/Detroit: University of Washington Press in Association with the Detroit Institute of Arts.

Williamson, M. 1990. Gender and the cosmos in Kwoma Culture. In *Sepik heritage: tradition and change in Papua New Guinea*, ed. N. Lutkehaus, 385–394. Durham, N.C.: Carolina Academic Press.

# SECTION 5

# POPULATION

Population growth—rapid in independent countries, slow or even negative in dependent entities and urbanized societies—is a critical concern in the contemporary Pacific. Burgeoning towns and cities are dealing with unemployment, housing shortage, and social malaise. Demands for education, health services, and gender equality are increasing, yet the relevance of existing programs has been questioned. These issues are explored in Section 5, with chapters on demography, mobility, health, education, women, and urbanization. Contributors include Jean-Louis Rallu, Dennis A. Ahlburg, Moshe Rapaport, Nancy J. Pollock, Sitaleki A. Finau, Glenda Mather, Camilla Cockerton, Jean-Pierre Doumenge, John Connell, and John P. Lea.

# Chapter 21

# Demography

*Jean-Louis Rallu and Dennis A. Ahlburg*

Pacific Island populations were among the last to come into contact with the Western world in the late eighteenth century and early nineteenth century. After World War II, they experienced rapid population growth and economic development. Population growth remains rapid in many island groups, while economic development has been very slow. This is likely to hamper development efforts. Accommodating increasing numbers of people will pose significant challenges to governments and societies, most importantly in areas of education, health services, jobs, and protection of the environment.

## Historical Background

Prior to European contact, Pacific populations were in contact with each other through networks based on religion, kinship, or warfare, but (except for sporadic interactions in the region's margins) were isolated from major Pacific Rim civilizations. Because of this isolation, Pacific Islanders lost immunity against diseases common on the continents (see McNeill 1976 on continental populations and immunity to epidemic diseases). Following the precipitous contact by Europeans, various epidemics (at first) and tuberculosis (later on) resulted in widespread morbidity and, in some cases, decimation of island populations.

Estimates of island populations made at the time of European contact were unreliable. However, retrospective studies of Marquesan genealogies between 1886 and 1945 have shown a regular decline of around 2% yearly in the absence of epidemics (Rallu 1990). The causes of negative growth were extremely high death rates (above 60 per 1,000) due to infectious diseases (mainly tuberculosis), and low fertility (with TFR[1] of 3.0) as a result of widespread venereal diseases. For instance, 25% of Marquesan females born in 1876–1885 had no live births. Negative growth of this order results in a halving of the population in thirty-four years. Allowing for the effect of epidemics and famine, the Marquesas probably had a population around 45,000 at the end of the eighteenth century. By 1931, at its lowest point, the population was only one-twentieth this size.

The experience of Tahiti was probably similar, with wars and epidemics at the end of the eighteenth century and the first half of the nineteenth century. Wilson, an English missionary, reported a constant population decline in Taiarapu (Tahiti) similar to that in the Marquesas. Since medical facilities were introduced earlier in Tahiti, the population size stabilized around 1880. Consequently, the population decline was lower than in the Marquesas (by a factor of 10 rather than 20). In the Western Society Islands, less frequently visited by Europeans than Tahiti, population decline was even lower, on the order of a quarter to a half of the precontact population. This was also likely the case in Central Polynesia.

It is difficult today to imagine the population impact of disease on susceptible populations (our closest recent experience being HIV/AIDS). Whereas the death rate increased by between 5% and 10% in Europe during the 1918 influenza epidemic, it grew five-fold in Tahiti and reached 191 per 1,000, and 196 per 1,000 in Western Samoa (current mortality rates are 5 and 8 per 1,000 respectively). The spread of disease was most rapid in small islands, but even in large Pacific islands, disease had a significant impact. For example, in New Zealand the population decline upon contact was around 50%. The impact of the 1918 flu among Maori was, however, less important than in Tahiti and Samoa. Thus, population decline was unequal throughout the Pacific Islands. The timing of recovery also varied, with stabilization in the mid-nineteenth century in Polynesia, but continuing decline until the 1920s or 1930s in Melanesia.

## After World War II

After World War II, most island populations experienced a demographic boom. Sanitation improved, infertility was reduced, and mortality dropped, as it did in most other developing countries. Population growth rates often rose to over 3% annually. Melanesia and non–U.S.-affiliated Micronesian islands differed from this pattern, since mortality remained higher due to less rapid improvements in sanitation. Fertility differentials linked with traditional sexual behavior also had an important impact on growth rates. Breastfeeding and postpartum abstinence were of longer duration in Melanesia relative to Polynesia, resulting in lower TFRs. French Polynesia, the Cook Islands, and New Zealand, with relatively permissive sexual behavior, had earlier childbearing than Central Polynesia or Micronesia.

### Demographic Transition

Increases in fertility after World War II (with TFR rising up to 7 on many islands) raised concerns about population pressure in small Polynesian islands, and family planning programs were implemented. The effects spread rapidly. By the early 1970s, TFR declined to around 5 in most of Polynesia. Fiji and several Micronesian groups experienced a similar change in fertility, but Western Melanesia, Wallis and Futuna, the Marshall Islands, and Nauru did not undergo significant fertility decline before the 1980s. Notwithstanding the early decline in fertility, population growth rates remained high in Polynesia, due to fertility still well above replacement level and the very young population structures (following two decades of rapid population growth). Most Polynesian populations stabilized in the 1970s and 1980s due to strong continued outmigration.

## Migration

Migration plays a critical role in the Pacific: it was responsible for the initial peopling of the islands; it made possible the colonial policy of labor supply (varying from savage recruitment in the nineteenth century to contracts in the twentieth century); and provided a demographic, economic, and social safety valve throughout the 1970s and 1980s. The colonial economy based on plantations (Fiji, Hawai'i, and on a smaller scale in Tahiti, New Caledonia, Samoa) and mines (New Caledonia, Banaba, and Nauru) created a few inmigration centers in the region. However, some of these centers ceased to attract migrants by the early twentieth century,[2] due to closures of mines (Banaba and Makatea) and declines in plantation production.

Among the most important long-term consequences of colonial labor migration is the establishment of significant Asian populations in the Pacific Islands, most notably Chinese, Japanese, Koreans, and Filipinos in Hawai'i (359,000 by 1931); Indians in Fiji (62,000 by 1920); and smaller numbers of Asians in New Caledonia (diverse sources, including Chinese, Vietnamese, and Javanese) and French Polynesia (Chinese). Additional discussion of, and references for, the historical and demographic aspects of European and Asian migration to the Pacific Islands can be found elsewhere in this volume.

The establishment of regional organizations in Fiji (location of the University of the South Pacific and the South Pacific Forum) and New Caledonia (location of the Secretariat of the Pacific Community) was another source of migration flows. The French territories continue to attract European migrants, related to periodic nickel booms in New Caledonia and nuclear testing in French Polynesia.[3] New Caledonia remains a migration destination for Europeans and Wallisians and, secondarily, Ni-Vanuatu and Tahitians. In Guam and the Marianas, economic booms have led to inmigration by Micronesians and Asians. New Zealand and Hawai'i attract migration from both inside and outside the Pacific Islands.

The main direction of migration since 1945 has been outmigration to the Pacific Rim in response to relatively better economic prospects. Periodic deterioration of the economic situation of these host countries, passage of restrictive legislation on migration, and expulsions of overstayers in the 1970s only marginally reduced emigration from islands. This was because the economic gap remained large and because an illegal migration strategy was now being widely employed: entry with a short-term visa, settlement and job-finding through relatives in the country, and subsequent application for residency or citizenship status.

Migration streams followed colonial links. One network linked New Zealand to its former colonies, followed by Tonga and later Fiji (primarily Indo-Fijians). Another network linked the United States with American Samoa and U.S.-related Micronesian islands, along with Samoa. A third network is that between France and its territories, as well as with Vanuatu (formerly a condominium between England and France). Kiribati and Tuvalu, previously under British administration, experience little outmigration, despite severe population pressure on resources. The Solomon Islands and Papua New Guinea also experience little outmigration.

Table 21.1 shows how population growth has declined in countries affected by migration in the postwar period, with negative growth being frequently observed in the smallest populations. Readers should bear in mind that natural increase[4] was around or slightly above 2% yearly in most of the region in the 1980s.

### TABLE 21.1

**Rates of Population Growth in Main Emigration Countries of the Pacific Islands (in %)**

| Periods[1] | Samoa | Cook Is. | Niue | Tokelau | Tonga | Wallis & Futuna | Amercan Samoa |
|---|---|---|---|---|---|---|---|
| 1951–1956 | 2.8 | 2.1 | 0.7 | 0.6 | | -1.6 | 1.0 |
| 1956–1961 | 3.3 | 2.0 | 0.7 | 2.8 | | | -0.1 |
| 1961–1966 | 2.8 | 0.9 | 1.3 | 0.3 | 3.1 | 0.0 | |
| 1966–1971 | 2.2 | 2.1 | -0.8 | -3.4 | | 1.1 | 3.0 |
| 1971–1976 | 0.7 | -3.2 | -5.1 | -0.3 | 1.5 | | 1.6 |
| 1976–1981 | 0.6 | -1.0 | -3.1 | 0.0 | | 4.3 | 1.8 |
| 1981–1986 | 0.1[2] | -0.7 | | 1.5 | 0.5 | | 1.9 |
| 1986–1991 | 0.5[2] | 1.1 | -1.4 | | | 1.2 | 3.7 |

[1] Census dates are for Samoa, Cook Is. Niue, Tokelau, as shown above; for Wallis et Futuna, 1953, 1961, 1969, 1976, 1983, 1990, for American Samoa, 1950, 1956, 1960, 1970, 1974, 1980, 1985, 1990 and for Tonga, 1956, 1966, 1976, 1986.

[2] Calculated using census figures. Data of rim countries show that population growth was probably negative in 1986–1990.

The Pacific Islands

## The 1980s and Beyond

Pacific Island demography has undergone considerable change during the 1980s, as discussed below:

### Fertility

By the 1980s, fertility decline[5] had begun in Solomon Islands, Vanuatu, Wallis and Futuna, and Papua New Guinea, and by the 1990s in the Marshall Islands as well. Despite these declines, fertility levels in the Solomon Islands and the Marshall Islands remain among the highest in the world (Table 21.2). The TFR appears to have leveled off between 4.5 and 5.0 in areas that experienced an earlier demographic transition (as in Tonga, Kiribati, Fiji, and Samoa). Fertility is declining in the French territories and the Cook Islands. In contrast to parts of Asia, in no island population (except among New Zealand Maori) has fertility declined to replacement level.

One reason why fertility in the Pacific remains high is the relatively low rate of contraceptive use. The percentage of contraceptive use among women varies from 3%-4% in Melanesia to 10%-30% in Polynesia (in many developing countries the rate is between 30 and 70). During the mid-1970s, almost 60% of Fijian women were reported to be using contraception. It is not clear whether low current use reflects insufficient supply, as in Melanesia and remote Polynesian islands (Lucas and McMurray 1994), or insufficient demand, related to the perceived high value and relatively low cost of children (with support from the extended family and the state).

Further contributory factors are opposition by churches (which are very strong in the Pacific); low levels of education,

### Table 21.2

**Demographic Indicators for Pacific Island Countries and Territories** (Cole 1993, CPS 1994, UNDP 1994, World Bank 1993 and 1995)

| | Population mid-1995,000 | Land area | Population density | Urban population (percent) | Largest city 1,000[1] | Birth rate | Death rate[2] |
|---|---|---|---|---|---|---|---|
| Fiji | 774.8 | 18,272 | 42 | 39 | 141 | 25(1993) | 5 |
| New Caledonia | 182.2 | 19,103 | 10 | 70 | 65 | 24(1993) | 6 |
| Papua New Guinea | 4,042.4 | 462,243 | 8 | 15 | 193 | 33(1992) | 11 |
| Solomon Islands | 367.8 | 28,370 | 13 | 13 | 30 | 42(1986) | 10 |
| Vanuatu | 164.1 | 12,190 | 14 | 18 | 19 | 38(1989) | 9 |
| | | | | | | | |
| FSM | 105.7 | 701 | 149 | | | 35(1994) | 8 |
| Guam | 149.3 | 541 | 276 | 38 | 50 | 30(1992) | 4 |
| Kiribati | 78.4 | 811 | 97 | 35 | 25 | 36(1990) | 13 |
| Marshall Islands | 54.7 | 181 | 302 | 65 | 28 | 49(1988) | 9 |
| Nauru | 10.5 | 21 | 472 | 100 | 10 | 24(1992) | 5 |
| Northern Marianas | 56.7 | 471 | 120 | 53 | 23 | 30(1991) | 3 |
| Palau | 16.5 | 488 | 34 | 69 | 10 | 22(1990) | 8 |
| | | | | | | | |
| American Samoa | 54.8 | 200 | 274 | 33 | 16 | 38(1992) | 4 |
| Cook Islands | 19.1 | 237 | 80 | 25 | | 27(1991) | 8 |
| Wallis and Futuna | 14.4 | 255 | 56 | | | 31(1990) | 6 |
| Niue | 2.0 | 259 | 8 | | | 16(1991) | 5 |
| French Polynesia | 218.8 | 3,521 | 62 | 57 | 69 | 28(1990) | 5 |
| Tokelau | 1.5 | 10 | 158 | | | | |
| Tonga | 98.2 | 747 | 131 | 31 | 29 | 23(1993) | 4 |
| Tuvalu | 9.5 | 26 | 365 | 42 | | 29(1991) | 11 |
| Samoa | 163.4 | 2,935 | 56 | 21 | 34 | 31(1991) | 8 |
| | | | | | | | |
| New Zealand | 3,527.9 | 267,800 | 13 | 85 | 896 | 17(1993) | 8 |
| Hawai'i | 1,316.0 | 16,637 | 79 | 89 | 836 | 16.5(1994) | 6 |

[1] at latest census (prior to 1996), [2] same year as birth rate, [3] ratio of 0-17 + 60 and over / 18-59.

particularly female education in Melanesia; and often a lack of government support for family planning policies. A high level of contraceptive use in Fiji in the late 1970s was observed at a time when both churches and the government actively promoted family planning. This is no longer the case.

High teenage fertility is prevalent, particularly in Eastern Polynesia, Solomon Islands, and most of Micronesia (Figure 21.1).

## Mortality

Life expectancies at birth have risen markedly over the last twenty-five years throughout the Pacific. In many island groups, life expectancy is well above sixty-one years (the average for developing countries), and a few have life expectancies close to or over seventy years. Kiribati and Papua New Guinea, which have life expectancies around fifty years, are two important exceptions.

There are two distinct patterns of mortality in the Pacific. A "traditional" pattern exists in high-mortality countries: a significant proportion of deaths are due to infectious diseases. A "modern" pattern exists in low-mortality countries: cardiovascular diseases and cancer account for a large portion of deaths. Papua New Guinea, Solomon Islands, Vanuatu, Kiribati, and the Federated States of Micronesia exhibit the traditional pattern, with infectious diseases responsible for over 20% of deaths. Fiji, most of Polynesia, and eastern Micronesia exhibit the modern pattern, with over 25% of deaths attributed to heart disease (Taylor, Lewis, and Levy 1989).

Infant mortality estimates vary considerably. A major cause

| Growth rate | Total fertility rate | Life expectancy at birth | Enrollment- primary | Enrollment-secondary | GNP /capita 1991 | Dependency ratio[3] |
|---|---|---|---|---|---|---|
| 1.7 | 3.2 | 63(1986) | 100 | 55 | 1,930 | 75 |
| 1.9 | 2.4 | 72(1993) | | | 3,530 | 66 |
| 2.1 | 5.1 | 56(1992) | 73 | 11 | 830 | 85 |
| 3.1 | 5.8 | 61(1986) | 48 | 11 | 690 | 109 |
| 2.1 | 5.3 | 63(1989) | 87 | 12 | 1,150 | 98 |
| | | | | | | |
| 3.4 | 5.1 | 65(1994) | 100 | 57 | 1,554 | 92 |
| 2.5 | 3.5 | 74(1992) | | | 21,000 | 58 |
| 1.8 | 3.8 | 60(1990) | 63 | 32 | 720 | 85 |
| 3.6 | 7.2 | 61(1988) | 95 | 53 | 1,610 | 124 |
| | 7.5 | 56(1981) | 88 | 71 | | 83 |
| 9.6 | 5.6 | 68(1991) | | | | |
| 1.0 | 3.1 | 67(1990) | 100 | 77 | 3,289 | 64 |
| | | | | | | |
| 3.8 | 4.5 | 70(1984) | | | 21,000 | 77 |
| 1.1 | 3.5 | 70(1988) | 98 | | 3,416 | 72 |
| 1.3 | 4.6 | 68(1990) | | | | 96 |
| -3.5 | 3.5 | 66(1987) | 100 | 87 | 3,051 | 87 |
| 3.0 | 3.1 | 70(1992) | | | 3,530 | 70 |
| -1.3 | 3.6 | 68(1986) | 100 | | | 113 |
| 0.5 | 4.5 | 68(1993) | 99 | 87 | 1,280 | 89 |
| 1.7 | 3.3 | 67(1991) | 100 | 89 | 1,068 | 78 |
| 0.4 | 4.8 | 65(1991) | 99 | 82 | 960 | 88 |
| | | | | | | |
| 1.0 | 2.1 | 76(1993) | 100 | 99 | 12,800 | 63 |
| 3.5 | | 79(1990) | | 95 | 27,107 | 58 |

The Pacific Islands

*Figure 21.1.* Young mother in rural Solomon Islands (photo JLR).

of illness and death among infants and children is gastrointestinal disease, particularly diarrhea, linked to impure drinking water and inadequate sanitation. These problems are greatest in Melanesia and are especially serious in rural areas (Figure 21.2). Child survival appears to be closely related to availability and use of maternal and child health services. Unfortunately, these services are threatened by economic difficulties and budget cuts experienced by many countries over the last decade.

*Figure 21.2.* Housing conditions in Malakula, Vanuatu (photo J-LR).

By late 1995, about eight hundred cases of HIV/AIDS had been reported in the island nations of the Pacific. The actual number of cases is likely ten to one hundred times higher. The health care costs of a person with HIV/AIDS are over ten times the average expenditure on health care per capita and several times the national income. If a sizable epidemic occurs in the Pacific (and this is a possibility in at least some areas), mortality rates could rise substantially, with significant economic and social consequences (Ahlburg, Larson, and Brown 1995, United Nations 1996).

Life expectancy is positively related to income, foreign aid per capita, level of education, and provision of health services (Taylor, Lewis, and Sladden 1991). Many Pacific Island states and territories spend two to three times as much of their budgets on health care, relative to other developing countries. This investment has contributed to a reduction of mortality levels, but there are notable exceptions. For example, Papua New Guinea spends twice the proportion of its national budget on health than the average for developing countries, yet its life expectancy is 13% lower, and its maternal mortality rate is over three times the average (Ahlburg 1996).

## Population Growth

Due to persistent high fertility and declining mortality, most Pacific Islands have experienced moderate to high rates of natural increase.[6] In a few cases, international migration has prevented this high rate of natural increase from being translated into high rates of population growth (Tonga, Samoa, the Cook Islands, Niue, and Fiji during the late 1980s). However, rates of annual population increase are often higher than the 2% average for developing countries. With a 2% growth rate, population size will double in thirty-five years; and with a 3% growth rate, in twenty-four years.

*Figure 21.3.* King Tupou IV of Tonga, presiding over baptism (photo J-LR).

In a study of eighteen Pacific island groups, Ahlburg (1996) reported eleven to have population growth rates of 2% or more and six of 3% or more. Rapid population growth, whether due to natural increase (as in Melanesia and parts of Micronesia) or to inmigration (as in the Northern Marianas) has resulted in social and economic pressure throughout the region.

## Migration

Migration data for the Pacific are sketchy because many countries do not have a reliable way of estimating inflows and outflows. Migration in the 1980s for four island groups with substantial outmigration (Samoa, Tonga, Cook Islands, and Fiji) was estimated using census and immigration data from New Zealand, Australia, the United States, and Canada (Table 21.3). A number of patterns and trends are discernible.

International migration is clearly a Polynesian and

### Table 21.3

**Net Migration of Island-born Populations in Countries of the Pacific Rim in the 1980s Based on Census and Migration Statistics (Rallu 1996)**

|  | W Samoa | Tonga | Cook I. | Fiji |
|---|---|---|---|---|
| **1986–1991** | | | | |
| **New Zealand** | | | | |
| census | 9,250 | 5,850 | -270 | 9,470 |
| migration[1] | 11,400 | 5,620 | | 11,375 |
| **Australia** | | | | |
| census | 2,800 | 1,730 | 850 | 15,350 |
| migration | 5,380 | 2,110 | 875 | 18,220 |
| **American Samoa** | | | | |
| census | 5,030 | 510 | | |
| **1981–1986** | | | | |
| **New Zealand** | | | | |
| census | 9,950 | 1,990 | 1,830 | 870 |
| migration[1] | 9,290 | 1,520 | | 1,695 |
| **Australia** | | | | |
| census | 2,200 | 1,856 | 820 | 5,394 |
| migration | 2,280 | 2,300 | -127 | 8,078 |
| **USA and Canada 1980–1990** | | | | |
| USA (census) | -1,000 | 5,500 | | 8,400 |
| USA (migration[2]) | 2,743 | 5,442 | | 9,209 |
| Canada (census) | | | | 10,350 |
| **Totals (all the above Pacific Rim countries)** | | | | |
| **1980s** | | | | |
| census | 28,230 | 17,436 | 3,230 | 49,834 |
| migration | 32,380 | 17,560 | | 58,118 |
| **1986–1991** | | | | |
| census | 16,080 | | 580 | |
| migration | 23,471 | | | |

[1] New Zealand migration data are by citizenship
[2] Migration data for the USA were based on immigration, rather than net migration, since departure data were not available until recently.

Micronesian phenomenon (Figure 21.4). In parts of Polynesia, there are more people resident overseas than there are in the home islands. This applies equally to islands with large populations (Tonga and Samoa) and those with small populations (Niue, Tokelau, Wallis and Futuna, and the Cook Islands). In 1991, 42% of Tongans and almost 50% of Samoans lived overseas. Migration from these countries in the 1980s appears to have been so great that population size declined, with net losses over 2% yearly in 1986–1990, outweighing the effect of natural increase.

*Figure 21.4. Departure of Wallisians to Noumea (photo J-LR).*

Tongan and Samoan migration is mainly to New Zealand, the United States, and Australia. Fiji has experienced significant outmigration since the two coups d'etat in 1987 and now provides the largest flows in the region, losing skilled workers and professionals to North America, Australia, and New Zealand. This migration was so large that the Indo-Fijian population declined in the second half of the 1980s. Guam, Saipan, and the Northern Marianas have received large numbers of Micronesians, as well as large numbers of Asian migrants. It is thought that large numbers of Micronesians will eventually move on to Hawai'i and the mainland United States.

The primary motive for migration in the Pacific, as elsewhere, is economic improvement for migrants and their families, although regulative changes and cultural considerations also affect flows. Young adults find better-paying jobs overseas, and their families benefit from their remittances. Migrants distributed in different countries "insure" the family against economic crises and unemployment. Pressure on governments to address rapid population growth and job creation for young adults is reduced by migration and the associated remittances. The removal of many young, educated people from the population also slows the pace of social change.

In New Zealand, the relaxation of restrictive migration policies introduced in the 1970s (culminating in December 1986 with a visa-waiver for stays of less than three months for Tongans, Samoans, Fijians, I-Kiribati, and Tuvaluans) led to a significant migration influx and was quickly changed. The reintroduction of restrictive migration policies in New Zealand and Australia resulted in negative net migration to New Zealand by Tongans and Samoans in 1990–1994 (Bedford 1992),[7] and in stable or slightly declining migration to Australia. In consequence, Samoan migration to American Samoa increased, in the hope of gaining entry to the United States.

However, stricter U.S. migration policy kept many prospective migrants in American Samoa, leading to a 45% population increase in the 1980–1990 period (mainly Samoans, Tongans, and also some Asians). A tightening of requirements in Australia and economic developments in New Zealand led to step-migration of Samoans to Australia. In 1986–1990, 74% of Samoan arrivals in Australia occurred through the Trans-Tasman

Agreement between New Zealand and Australia. In contrast, most Fijian and Tongan immigrants in Australia came directly from their home islands.

Remittances sent by migrants are of critical importance in islands of origin. In Tonga and Samoa remittances per migrant are roughly 80% of GNP per capita and in aggregate more than three times the total value of exports (Brown and Connell 1993, Ahlburg 1991). Remittances have raised the standard of living and have made the distribution of income more equal. The conventional view is that remittances are primarily spent on consumption, particularly on imported goods (Ahlburg 1991). However, Brown and Connell (1993) argue, based on new survey data from Tonga and Samoa, that most households save or invest domestically a substantial part of the remittances. If this is the case, remittances may play a significant role in economic development.

## Age Structures

Migration has had important effects on age structure and dependency ratios.[8] (Figure 21.5) Emigration, which is concentrated among young adults of both sexes, offsets natural increase in age groups 20–24 and 25–29 and cause the typical "hourglass" age pyramids in island groups with high outmigration. Thus high fertility, low mortality, and outmigration of young adults combine to produce very high dependency ratios in most Pacific countries (see Table 21.2); this places a heavy burden on societies.

*Figure 21.5. High dependency rates are common in Vanuatu (photo J-LR).*

Although overall numbers will continue to grow, declining fertility and proportionate increases in numbers of working-age adults should ensure declining dependency ratios. Providing that productive employment can be created for the region's growing labor force, the pressure of caring for the young and old should diminish. Recent slowdowns in outmigration and the possibility of return migration could reduce dependency ratios. Simulations show that reduced migration of young adults combined with even small return migration of middle-aged adults, such as occurred in the Cook Islands in 1986–1991, can rapidly reduce age dependency.

The question remains: will island labor markets be able to provide a sufficient number of jobs? Data from the Cook Islands show that labor force participation rates slightly declined in the 1986–1991 period. A similar trend occurred in the formal sector in Samoa throughout the 1980s, despite sustained emigration. Small island countries may well continue to have difficulties creating jobs for larger generations entering the labor market, and young adults who can no longer migrate may be compelled to remain in the subsistence economy.

## Ethnic Composition

Ethnic diversity among indigenous populations is significant in Melanesia, especially in Papua New Guinea. Of these groups, the most numerous and most diverse are Papuan-speaking communities, present on Papua New Guinea and Solomon Islands. Linguistic data, while not a perfect marker for ethnicity, suggest that Papuans and Austronesians comprise approximately 87% and 14% of the indigenous population in the above two countries, respectively (Wurm and Hatori 1981).

Islands with large proportions of Europeans include New Zealand, Hawai'i, Guam, New Caledonia, and French Polynesia (Table 21.4). In New Zealand and New Caledonia (both with large land area and attractive agricultural opportunities) this is a consequence of settlement programs launched during the early nineteenth century; in Hawai'i, Guam, and French Polynesia it is a more recent phenomenon. Many French settlers were formerly present in the New Hebrides (Vanuatu), but most left following independence (likewise with many Australian settlers in Papua New Guinea).

Fiji, Hawai'i, and the Northern Marianas have populations with large proportions of Asians (Figure 21.6). In Fiji, these are mainly Indians, descended from labor migrants during the colonial period. In Hawai'i, Asians include Japanese, Filipinos, and Chinese, also a consequence of labor migration. In the Northern Marianas, Asian migration is a more recent phenomenon, primarily from China and Southeast Asia.

### TABLE 21.4

**Ethnic Composition of the Population in Selected Pacific Islands***

| | % European | % Asians | % Other non-indigenous | % Pacific Island migrants |
|---|---|---|---|---|
| American Samoa | 2 | 2 | 3 | 4 |
| F. Polynesia | 12 | 5 | 1 | 0 |
| Fiji | 1 | 47 | 3 | 0 |
| Guam | 14 | 30 | 14 | 4 |
| Hawai'i | 33 | 45 | 8 | 2 |
| N. Caledonia | 35 | 4 | 4 | 12 |
| N. Marianas | 2 | 49 | 0 | 15 |
| New Zealand | 80 | 2 | 4 | 4 |

*Includes all Pacific Island groups with over 10% non-indigenous population, based on the most recent censuses

*Figure 21.6. Hindu temple in Nadi, Fiji (photo J-LR).*

Pacific Island migrants are present in significant numbers in the Northern Marianas, New Caledonia, New Zealand, American Samoa, Guam, and Hawai'i. This migration wave is of relatively recent origin, part of the search for employment and better economic opportunities. It is difficult to generalize about the "Other" category, as census definitions vary in this regard. In Guam, for example, it reflects the large military contingent. In other areas it may reflect persons of mixed origin, or specially designated minority groups (Blacks or Hispanics in the United States).

Ethnic diversity creates a volatile situation in island societies—particularly so in Fiji, site of two political coups. The native Fijian population wavers around 50% and fears loss of political power to Indians and others. In Bougainville, a revolutionary army has brought copper mining to a halt, demanding an end of control by Papua New Guinea. In New Caledonia, native Kanaks lost most of their land during the nineteenth century to French colonists and are now outnumbered by Europeans and other groups; the situation remains highly volatile.

In Hawai'i and New Zealand, native groups are minorities, but there are increasing demands for indigenous rights, including land return, cash payments, and some form of self-government.

# Population and Development

## Labor Force

The proportion of the labor force in the formal sector[9] is low compared with that in developed countries, but high relative to developing countries. In Samoa, Tonga, Kiribati, and Tuvalu, the male labor force in the formal sector is respectively 34%, 53%, 59%, and 60%. In Melanesia and the Central Pacific, the majority of the population works in agriculture (including subsistence agriculture). Less than 20% of the work force is employed in industry, with higher numbers in New Caledonia, French Polynesia, American Samoa, and the Cook Islands. The latter groups often have large public sectors, ranging from 28% of formal employment in New Caledonia to 52% in the Cook Islands (before halving of the public sector following economic restructuring in 1996).

Due to outmigration, a large proportion of adults of working age are overseas, on the order of 50% for island groups with significant emigration. Most island-born migrants work in industry, with over 75% being production workers in New Zealand and Australia (except for Fiji-born), and around 50% in the United States. The proportion of migrants who are managers, professionals, and technicians are less than 10% in Australia and New Zealand (except for Fiji-born, 26%) and around 15% in the United States.

## Island Economies

Melanesian economies are based on agricultural exports (copra, cocoa, cattle), mining (in Papua New Guinea, Fiji, and New Caledonia), forestry (in Vanuatu, Solomon Islands, Papua New Guinea), and fisheries. Natural resources, except fisheries, are very limited or nonexistent in Micronesia, which has to import fresh vegetables and wood. Kiribati and Tuvalu, which rely on short-term contract work migration, lag behind the Polynesian countries in regard to housing and the general standard of living.

Sustained economic development in Polynesia in the 1960s and 1970s has been explained (Bertram and Waters 1985) as primarily due to inflows of foreign aid and remittances (Figure 21.7). Fiji also experienced significant economic development, based mainly on the exploitation of resources and trade. By the end of the 1970s, several island groups had a higher GDP/capita than most developing countries. In the 1980s, economic growth in the Pacific Islands was sluggish, with an average rate of 0.1% per year, well behind rates in developing Asia and other island regions (3.7% for the Caribbean and 2.4% for the Indian Ocean) (World Bank 1993).

*Figure 21.7. Storefront in 'Apia. Relative high consumption is enabled through remittances and aid (photo J-LR).*

The causes of the recent poor economic performance include a failure to invest in the private sector and an overexpansion of the public sector, fueled by foreign aid. The large inflow of aid and remittances also likely led to an increase in the value of the exchange rate and a rise in wages, which decreased the competitiveness of exports and import-replacement industries (Ahlburg 1991). Foreign aid seems to have had similar impacts in the French territories and U.S.-related islands.

Economic prospects of the island nations appear bleak when considering the generally limited agricultural land and natural resources, high production costs, great distance to markets, the need for significant restructuring of their economies, and impending declines in migration, remittances, and aid. The key to a successful future is investment in human resource development. Although many Pacific nations and territories spend more on education and health than the average for developing countries, the quantity and quality of services produced is not equal to the resources spent.

Education systems need to be made more efficient, teacher training must be improved and curricula made more relevant to national human resource needs in order to stimulate economic development. Similar improvements need to be made in the delivery of health services (Ahlburg 1996).

## Health and Environment

Access to health services in the Pacific is generally much better than the average for developing countries, but the level of health often does not match the resources expended. Pacific Island countries and territories have more doctors (except in Western Melanesia) and more nurses per capita than the average for developing countries. Yet provision of family planning lags behind other countries; this has important negative impacts on child and maternal health and contributes to high rates of population growth. Without access to contraception, women have difficulty spacing births adequately and achieving their desired family size (Figure 21.8).

*Figure 21.8. Women's gathering in Vanuatu (photo J-LR).*

The prevalence of breastfeeding is low in the Pacific. Malnutrition affects 20% of children under five years of age in Vanuatu and 35% of children in Papua New Guinea. Wasting and stunting (respectively, low weight in relation to height and low height in relation to age) are a significant problem for older children in Solomon Islands and Vanuatu, a reflection of inadequate nourishment. Child malnutrition is both a human rights issue and an economic concern. In preventing individuals from reaching their physical and intellectual potential, malnutrition threatens a nation's development prospects.

The environment is also a matter of great concern in small islands. The land is threatened by a rise in sea level. Water pollution, including fresh water and lagoons, is likely to rise. Increases in pesticide and fertilizer use have been significant, along with the promotion of commercial agriculture and domestic use, even in areas with low or no population growth (such as the Cook Islands, Tonga, and Samoa). The environment is further threatened by mining and logging operations that can pollute water and reef resources, upon which many livelihoods depend.

## Urbanization

Most island groups have low urbanization levels, although rates of urban growth have recently risen in Solomon Islands, the Marshall Islands, Papua New Guinea, and Tonga. Rates of urban growth are 4.3% in Papua New Guinea and 6.6% in Solomon Islands (compared with 5% average for low-income countries in 1985-1990). If these rates persist, they will lead to a rapid doubling of the urban population. For example, the population of Port Moresby would double within sixteen years (from 190,000 in 1993).

It is often thought that population growth causes urbanization (this is clearly the case in Fiji, and may be the case in Papua

*Figure 21.9. Downtown Suva, Fiji (photo J-LR).*

New Guinea as well—see Connell and Lea 1993). However, recent research has indicated that more important factors are government policies that preferentially subsidize living costs, reduce the return to agriculture (largely by controlling the price of food), and concentrate public services (health care facilities, safe drinking water and sanitation, and higher education) in urban areas. This has apparently already occurred in South Tarawa (Kiribati) and Funafuti (Tuvalu), leading to environmental stress.

Urbanization and population density need not necessarily result in environmental degradation. Urbanization can benefit the economy by providing a market large enough to encourage the local production of goods and services. Whether increasing concentration of population adversely affects the environment depends heavily upon government land-use and pricing policies and enforcement of regulations.

## Population Forecasts

The populations of most Pacific Island groups are projected to grow over the next thirty-five years. Expected increases in population range from a low of 20% for Nauru to around 100% for Papua New Guinea and the Northern Marianas, 150% for Solomon Islands, and about 300% for the Marshall Islands. These population projections are based on assumptions that fertility will decline, life expectancy will increase, and international migration will decline, in many cases to net levels of zero.

These projections ignore the impact of HIV/AIDS, which could considerably increase mortality and slow (but probably not reverse) population growth. Because population projections are based on predictions concerning human behavior (which is very difficult to predict, particularly up to twenty or thirty years into the future) they are uncertain. Despite the possibility of inaccuracies, population forecasting is an important planning tool, allowing policymakers to work through the implications of various assumptions concerning future fertility, mortality, and migration.

Population projections indicate that the very high dependency ratios in the Pacific will fall until 2020 or even 2030 because lower fertility will decrease the proportion of the population under age twenty. However, the proportion of persons over sixty years is projected to increase, from around 5% currently to around 10% in most of Melanesia and Micronesia by 2030, and over 15% in Fiji, French Polynesia, New Caledonia, and Tonga.

A main concern in the near future is rapid growth of young adult age groups, as job creation has been slow in the recent past. Population projections suggest that job creation will be an enormous challenge. For many island groups, the number of new jobs needed over the next thirty-five years will more than double.

Papua New Guinea will face a formidable challenge in educating large, remote, and culturally diverse populations. For most island groups, there will be a need for two to four times as many places in primary school; and an even greater increase will be required to enroll 60% of children in secondary school. Across the Pacific, there will be a need to improve education systems and upgrade the quality of teaching.

Population growth will also necessitate an increase in the number of doctors, nurses, and hospital beds, solely in order to maintain the quantity and quality of care.

## New Zealand and Hawai'i

New Zealand and Hawai'i are distinctive with regard to demography and economy. While they have sizable populations of native islanders as well as Pacific Island migrants, the majority of inhabitants are of European and American origin. Their economies also have more in common with continental societies than with other Pacific Island societies.

### Demography

New Zealand and Hawai'i have both passed through the demographic transition, with fertility low, around replacement level, and high life expectancy (see Table 21.2). Rates of natural increase are moderate, around 1% yearly. Age structures reflect populations in the posttransitional phase, with proportions of children under fifteen years well below 25%, and high proportions of elderly aged sixty and over (15%). Future demographic problems relate to the social costs of aging: pension funds and health expenditures.

New Zealand Maoris, including part-Maoris, were 12.9% of the New Zealand population in 1991 and (foreign born) Pacific Islanders 2.9% of the population. In Hawai'i, a large proportion of the population are of Asian ancestry. Native Hawaiians constitute a similar proportion of the population to Maoris in New Zealand, while Pacific Islanders are less than 1% of the population, not counting American Samoans.

Native populations in Hawai'i and New Zealand have a much younger age structure and higher natural growth than the total populations.[10] However, due to variations in reporting ethnicity at civil registration and at the census (especially for part-Maoris), precise levels of fertility and life expectancy are debated in New Zealand. Fertility is not very different from that of the total population, and life expectancy at birth is estimated at around three and four years lower than that of the non-Maori population (Pool 1991).

Asia is increasingly becoming a source of migrants to New Zealand, and has long been important for Hawai'i. Despite schemes for islanders to enter New Zealand, Asians succeed better through current "point" systems. They are also comparatively well educated and find jobs easily.

### Socioeconomic Characteristics

The GDP/capita in Hawai'i and New Zealand is much higher than elsewhere in the Pacific Islands, and the economy is based on production and services, rather than on agriculture and aid. In Hawai'i, 1.4% of jobs are in the primary sector (agriculture) and 8% are in the secondary sector (industry). In New Zealand, the primary sector accounts for 10% of the workforce and the secondary sector somewhat more than 20%. In Hawai'i, tourism is the dominant area of employment; New Zealand has a comparatively diversified economy. In both cases, the economy is much less dependent on the public sector relative to other island economies.

There are important socioeconomic differentials among ethnic groups. Native Hawaiians have higher unemployment rates and lower incomes relative to other demographic groups, with 18.8% of Hawaiians below poverty level (twice the value for the total population). In New Zealand, unemployment rates of Maoris and Pacific Islanders are twice as high as for the total population. Island-born workers, and to a lesser extent their New Zealand-born offspring, are most frequently production workers. However, there appears to have been some upward occupational mobility between the 1986 and 1991 censuses.

## Conclusion

Pacific Island populations will face formidable economic and demographic challenges in the following decades. Because of generally high rates of population growth, ways must be found to provide education, jobs, and health services. As the number of elderly grows, new services will be required. These developments will strain the resources of the region's governments and families, and consideration of population policies is urgently needed.

Opinions differ on the potential for economic growth. Some, including the World Bank, think that by exploiting opportunities in agriculture, fisheries, tourism, and small manufacturing, Pacific Island populations can generate moderate and sustained economic growth. To do so, however, they need to provide a stable political and economic environment, improve economic and human infrastructure, reward initiative and competitiveness, and broaden trade and investment links. Others doubt that these objectives can or should be pursued. Rather, it is argued that a moderate level of well-being can be maintained by a judicious combination of migration, remittances, and foreign aid.

It is not clear which development path should be chosen since each entails considerable risk. What is clear is that population growth and the demands of human development require increased mobilizing of additional resources from whatever source and/or more efficient use of existing resources.

## Notes

[1] Total fertility rate: average number of children per woman in her lifetime

[2] Even from the end of the nineteenth century with the closure of the Atimaono plantation in Tahiti

[3] Nuclear testing stopped in early 1996 in French Polynesia.

[4] The difference between births and deaths, which constitutes population growth without considering the effect of migration

[5] Data on fertility and mortality are mainly derived from indirect methods because civil registration is not complete in most island countries (except French territories, U.S.-affiliated islands, the Cook Islands, and, to a lesser extent, Tonga). Most Melanesian countries (including Fiji) and Samoa did not achieve much progress in registration of vital events since independence.

[6] The excess of births over deaths

[7] In 1995 and 1996 (years ending 31 March), net migration of Tongans, Samoans, and Fijians to New Zealand has been strongly positive again. However, islanders will still have difficulties entering through selective point systems.

[8] The ratio of young and old to the working-age population

[9] The formal sector is defined as "work for cash" or "work for money" in most countries, as opposed to the subsistence economy.

[10] For instance, 37.5% of the New Zealand Maori population is below age fifteen and 4.3% above age sixty; natural growth rate is just below 1.5%.

## Bibliography

Ahlburg, D. 1991. Remittances and their impact: a study of Tonga and W. Samoa. Pacific Policy Paper No. 7, National Center For Development Studies. Canberra: Australian National University.

Ahlburg, D. 1996. Demographic and social change in the island nations of the Pacific. Asia-Pacific Population Research Reports No. 7, East West Center, Hawai'i.

Ahlburg, D., and M. J. Levin. 1990. The North-East Passage, Pacific Research Monograph No. 23, National Center For Development Studies. Canberra: Australian National University.

Ahlburg, D. A., H. J. Larson, and T. Brown. 1995. Health care costs of HIV/AIDS in the Pacific. Pacific Health Dialog 2(2).

Baudchon, G., and J. L. Rallu. 1993. Evolution démographique récente dans les TOM du Pacifique, 1970–1990. Population, No. 4, 1993, INED, Paris.

Bedford, R. D. 1991. Migration and development in the Pacific Islands: reflections on recent trends and issues. In *The South Pacific: problems, issues, prospects*, ed. R. Thakur, 145–68. London: Macmillan.

Bedford, R. D. 1992. International migration in the South Pacific. In *International migration systems: a global approach*, ed. M. M. Kritz, L. L. Lim, and H. Zlotnik, 41–62. Oxford: Clarendon Press.

Bertram, G., and R. F. Watters. 1985. The MIRAB economy in the South Pacific microstates. Pacific Viewpoint 26(3):497–519.

Brown, R. P. C., and J. Connell. 1993. Migration and remittances in Tonga and Western Samoa. Vol.1, Main Report. Bangkok: International Labour Organization.

Brown, R. P. C., and J. Connell. 1995. Migration and remittances in the South Pacific. Asia Pacific Migration Journal 4(1):1–34.

Chapman, M. 1991. *Pacific Island movement and socioeconomic change*. Population and Development Review 17(2):263–292.

Chapman, M., and P. S. Morrison, ed. 1985. *Mobility and identity in the Islands Pacific*. Wellington, New Zealand: Victoria University Press.

Cole, R. V. 1993. *Pacific 2010: challenging the future*. National Center for Development Studies. Canberra: Australian National University.

Commission du Pacifique Sud (CPS). 1994. Pacific Island Populations, Rapport de la Commission du Pacifique Sud à la Conférence Internationale sur la Population et le Développement (Le Caire 1994). Nouméa: CPS.

Connell, J., ed. 1991. *Migration and development in the South Pacific*, Pacific Research Monograph No. 24, National Center for Development Studies. Canberra: Australian National University.

Connell, J. Various dates. *Migration, employment and development in the South Pacific*, Country Reports, SPC/ILO. Noumea: Commission du Pacifique Sud.

Connell, J., and J. P. Lea. 1993. *Planning the future: Melanesian cities in 2010*. National Center for Development Studies. Canberra: Australian National University.

ESCAP 1993. *Pacific Island countries: economic performance and selected issues in policy management and adjustments*. NY: United Nations.

Haberkorn, G. 1995. Prioritising priorities: Pacific Island population developments and their implication for public policy. New Zealand Population Review 21(1–2):1–26.

Hayes, G. 1991. Migration, metascience, and development policy in Island Polynesia. The Contemporary Pacific 3(1):1–58.

Hayes, G. 1992. Polynesian migration and the demographic transition: a missing dimension of recent theoretical models. Pacific Viewpoint 33(1):1–35.

Levin, M., and R. Retherford. 1986. *Recent fertility trends in the Pacific Islands*, Papers of the East West Population Institute, No. 101. Honolulu: East-West Center.

Lucas D., and C. McMurray. 1994. Family planning in the South Pacific. In *Fécondité et insularité*. Conference organized by C. Ory. St. Denis, 403–414. Reunion: Conseil General de la Reunion.

Masey, D. S. et al. 1993. Theories of international migration: review and appraisal. Population and Development Review 19(3):431–466.

McCall, G., and J. Connell, eds. 1993 *A world perspective on Pacific Islanders migration: Australia, New Zealand and the USA*. Pacific Studies Monograph No. 6. Centre for South Pacific Studies. Sydney: University of New South Wales.

McNeill, W. H. 1976. *Plagues and peoples*. NY: Doubleday.

Pool, I. 1991. *Te Iwi Maori: A New Zealand population, past, present and projected*. Auckland: Auckland University Press.

Rallu, J. L. 1990. *Les Populations océaniennes aux XIXème et XXème siècles*. Paris: INED.

Rallu, J. L. 1996. Recent trends in international migration and economic development in the South Pacific. Asia-Pacific Population Journal 11(2):23–46.

Taylor R., N. D. Lewis, and S. Levy. 1989. Societies in transition: mortality patterns in Pacific Island populations. International Journal of Epidemiology 18:634–46.

Taylor R., N. D. Lewis, and T. Sladden. 1991. Mortality in Pacific Island countries around 1980: geopolitical, socioeconomic, demographic and health service factors. Australian Journal of Public Health 15:207–221.

Trlin A. D., and P. Spoonley, eds. 1992. *New Zealand and international migration*, Vol. 2, Dept of Sociology, Massey University, Palmerston North, New Zealand.

UNDP 1994. *Pacific human development report*. Suva, Fiji: United Nations.

United Nations 1996. *Time to act: the Pacific response to HIV and AIDS*. Suva, Fiji: United Nations.

World Bank. 1993. *Pacific Island economies: toward efficient and sustainable growth*. Washington D.C.: World Bank.

World Bank. 1995. *Pacific island economies: building a resilient economic base for the twenty-first century*. Country Dept. III, East Asia and Pacific Region. Washington D.C.: World Bank.

# Chapter 22

# Mobility

*Moshe Rapaport*

## Introduction

Mobility—the study of population movement—is a vast and labyrinthine area of research at the interface between several scholarly disciplines (geography, anthropology, economy, history, and population studies). Mobility is vital for any society, particularly in small islands characterized by limited land, natural resources, and economic opportunities and high rates of natural increase. Since the earliest settlement of the Pacific Islands, mobility has been associated with opportunity, but new challenges and necessary adjustments have inevitably ensued, along with competition and conflict.

This chapter provides a broad overview of mobility, beginning with patterns evident in oral traditions, followed by the historical transitions in mobility pattern among island communities in various parts of the Pacific. The movements of European settlers and associated labor migrants are then discussed, along with the displacements that ensued. The final section considers contemporary migration, based on census data and ethnographic studies, focusing on trends, rationales, impact, and sustainability.

## Mobility in History

### Ancestral Journeys

The extent and time depth of oral tradition vary significantly across the Pacific Islands region. Oral traditions are most extensive in the case of large and culturally homogenous populations, hierarchical political systems, and societies in which lineage and primogeniture were important. Genealogies and related traditions in Polynesia are especially well developed, reaching up to thirty-six generations in Tonga, and even longer in Hawai'i and the Marquesas. Voyaging traditions are numerous in New Zealand, where first colonization was relatively recent. In Melanesia, oral traditions generally span shorter periods; however, traditions extending several hundred years exist and have been corroborated in some cases by archaeologists.

Several caveats need to be kept in mind. Tradition foreshortens time, telescoping several generations into a single heroic figure or episode. Its telling is often selective, eliminating previous occupiers. In Pukapuka, Cook Islands, historical knowledge is conditioned by cultural concerns over status and competence (Borofsky 1987). In general, perceptions of historical truth are pragmatic, serving social and political ends. Historical events are not easily disentangled, given the varied purposes of the narrators, frequent rearrangement, and heavily veiled symbolic references.

While decoding such accounts may be difficult, an unsupported literalist approach is equally hazardous (Scarr 1990).

Voyaging traditions constitute a special subset of oral history. Such accounts encompass multiple locations, lending themselves to comparisons (particularly in the case of two-way travel). Details of crews and itineraries are frequently contradictory—perhaps expectedly so, since the traditions are critical to the establishment of first arrival, genealogies, and land claims. The feasibility of particular itineraries can be evaluated against climatic, oceanographic, and archaeological data or by contemporary reenactments such as the voyage of the *Hōkūle'a* (Finney 1979). Even in the absence of supportive data, such traditions can illustrate the scope, variety, and multiple purposes of precontact journeys.

Prior to European contact, travel was often difficult and hazardous. The perils of open sea navigation and the dangers of warfare were both significant challenges. Voyagers throughout the Pacific would have shared the sentiment of the Maori *ariki* (chief) who, leaving ancestral Hawaiki behind, chanted, "The only tie which unites us is the fleecy cloud drifting hitherward"

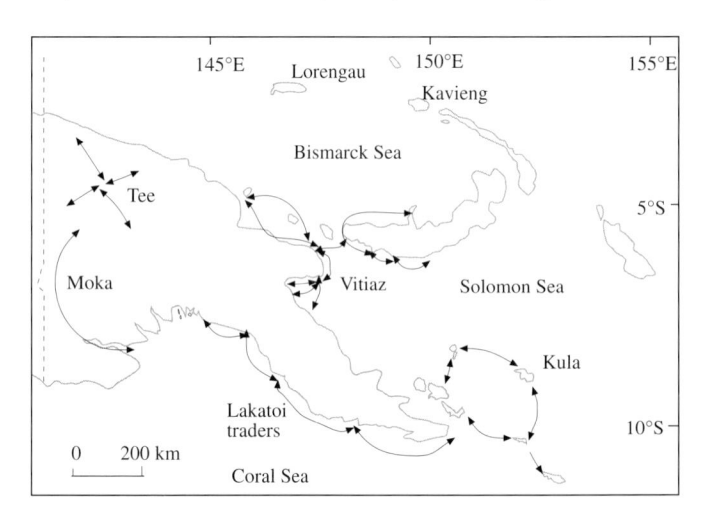

*Figure 22.1.* Pre-European trading networks in the Papua New Guinea area (after Lacy 1982).

(Luomala 1955). But they also would have shared the excitement of the early discoverers of Aotearoa (New Zealand), finding a country that produced *moa* and greenstone in abundance.

Oral tradition preserves the details of the voyages; each *iwi* (tribe) has its own traditions (Evans 1997 provides a referenced review). Kupe came aboard the *Matahorua* (see Figure 22.2). The *Arawa* was built from a *totara* tree in Rarotonga by Tamatekapua. The *Arawa*'s navigator, the wise Ngatoroirangi, was carried off unwittingly with his wife while performing the rites of departure (he was originally to have sailed with the *Tainui*). Such narratives have been called founding journeys (Lacey

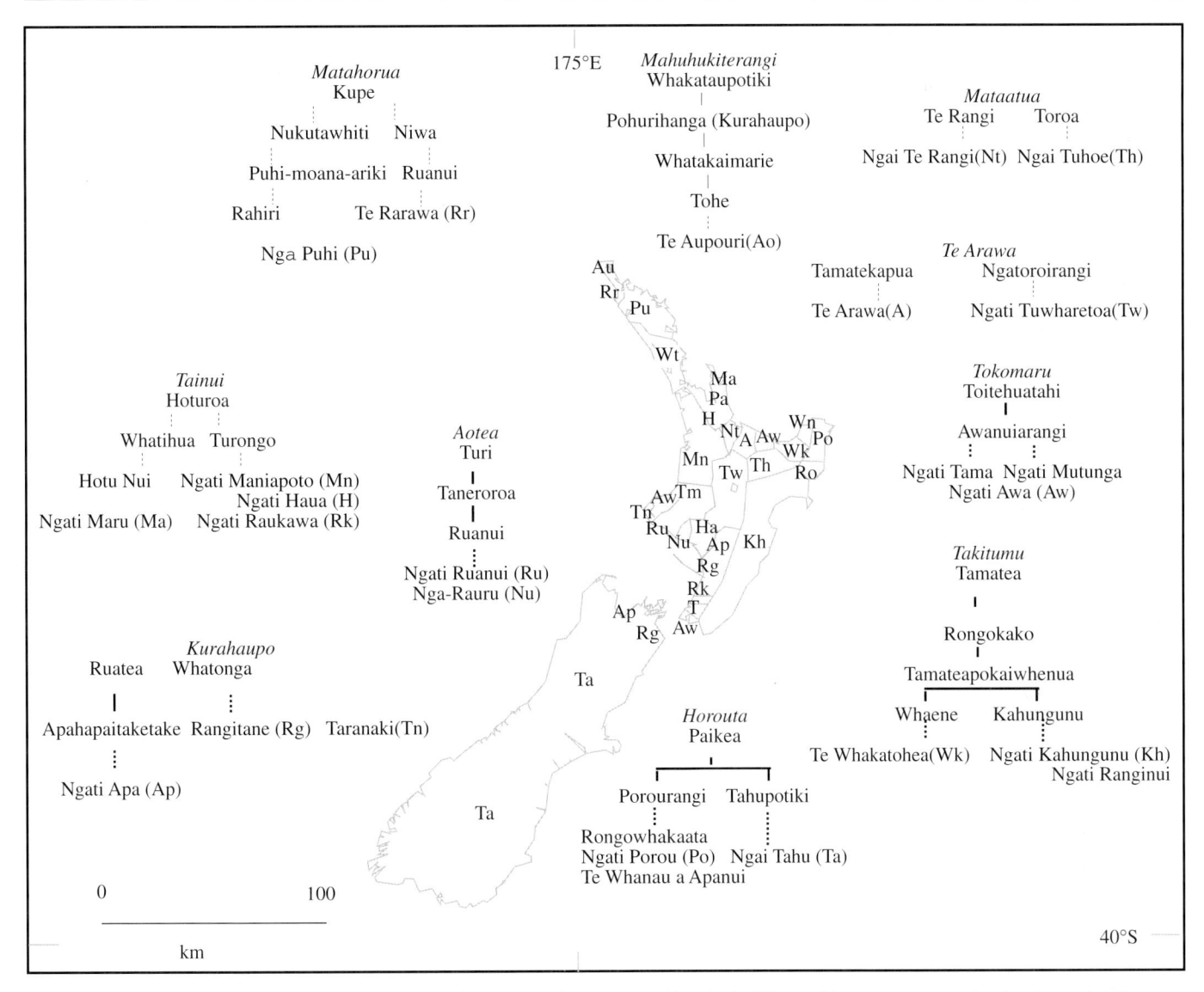

*Figure 22.2.* Approximate iwi *(tribal) distribution in the nineteenth century, with principal lines of descent to ancestral* waka *(canoes) (after McKinnon 1997 and Ward 1995).*

1985), providing a link to the ancestors, a legitimating charter, and validation of the rights to particular locations.

Mala, founder of the Vitiaz Strait trade, was driven off his home island following an alleged misdemeanor with his sister-in-law. Edai Siabo, founder of the Motu trading network, learned how to construct his *lagatoi* (sea-going canoes) through the tutelage of a *dirava* (spirit) under the sea. For the people of the Vitiaz Straits and the Motu, such accounts are founding journeys (as are the ancestral colonizing voyages for the Maori). Such stories also illustrate another pattern in traditional mobility, particularly characteristic of Melanesia: journeys of exchange and trade.

The Vitiaz Strait trade carried obsidian, live pigs, dogs' teeth, bows and arrows, net bags, pottery, and taro in exchange for boar's tusks, live dogs, mats, disc beads, betel nut, red ochre, and sago. Other such networks included the Kula cycle and the Motu trade. A long-distance exchange network connected islanders on fifteen atolls in the Western Carolines (Figure 22.3), who voyaged 700 km annually to the high island Yap with tribute of woven cloth, twine, and shell valuables to "partner/parents," receiving counter-gifts of food and turmeric (Alkire 1978, Bellwood 1979).

Related to journeys of exchange were journeys for marriage partners. The Tuamotuan *kaito* (warrior) Moeava traveled 500 km eastward to Napuka to find his wife Huarei (and an equal distance to Makemo to fight his rival, the giant Patira) (Audran 1918). Pele, the Hawaiian volcano goddess, dispatched her sister to fetch her lover Lohi'au from Kaua'i, though things didn't work out as expected. Sinilau traveled from Samoa to Tonga to meet high-born Hina, climbing eight fences and extinguishing a hundred watchfires to avoid the guards (Luomala 1955).

In Melanesia, journeys of initiation were common. In the New Guinea Highlands, young initiates journeyed to a secret area, experiencing seclusion, purification, fasting, trials, and transmission of ancient knowledge, often involving daring

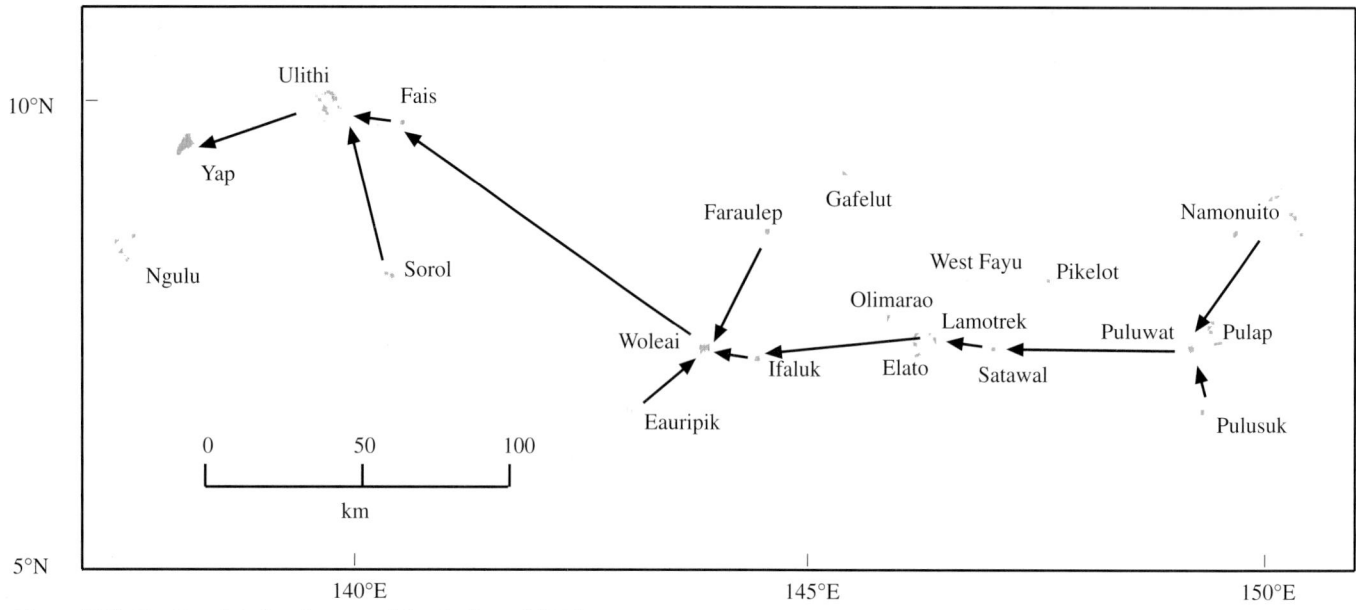

*Figure 22.3.* Yap Sawei *(tribute) system (after Bellwood 1979).*

journeys to procure the necessary sacred plants and the appropriate chants (Lacey 1985). Men from Malakula, in central Vanuatu, would voyage once in a lifetime in pilgrimage to neighboring Aoba, island of Tagaro, conducting ceremonies and exchanges with local islanders (Bonnemaison 1985a, 1985b).

The *marae* (temple) Taputapuatea on Raiatea, French Polynesia, attracted worshippers from a reputed radius of around 700 km. By the time of European contact, long-distance voyaging had declined significantly, but pilgrims continued to arrive from neighboring islands bearing annual tribute to Oro and to be instructed at the *fare vanaa* (house of sacred wisdom). A highly respected group of entertainers, the *arioi*, traveled throughout the Society Islands providing songs, dances, athletics, acting; recitations of poetry, history, and folklore; and even social critique of local *ari'i* (chiefs) (Luomala 1955).

There were also journeys of exile and refuge. Mala, founder of the Vitiaz Strait trade, is said to have fled his home island, as mentioned above. In New Zealand, in at least some versions of the accounts, several of the ancestral voyaging canoes are said to have fled Hawaiki following warfare (originally ignited by either theft, insults, or land disputes). Warfare with established groups following landfall precipitated new rounds of exile and resettlement (Evans 1997, McKinnon 1997, Scarr 1990).

## Traditional Mobility and Its Transformation

In most parts of the Pacific, mobility patterns have altered significantly, so that it is difficult to know what earlier forms of mobility were like. Not surprisingly, studies of traditional mobility have often focused on remote parts of Melanesia, especially the subsistence cultures of New Guinea. Watson (1985) catalogued the variety of mobility patterns among the Northern Tairora in the Eastern Highlands of Papua New Guinea, at altitudes of 1,220–3,350 m. The description is in the ethnographic present and includes coverage of recent decades, but is meant to describe mobility prior to European contact.

Tairora local groups are small independent political units, typically with fewer than 200 residents. Surrounding each of the groups are areas of bush, used for hunting and gathering and as buffer zones against adjacent hostile groups. Few Tairora ever travel farther than about 10–12 km, the main exceptions related to leading men, trade, and refugee movements (Table 22.1). Refugee, connubial, and disaffection movements may be classified as either migration (a change in residence) or circulation (visits, hunting, trade, etc.), depending on the aim and outcome; intraterritorial shifts are considered migration. The remaining movements are circulatory.

Bonnemaison (1985a, 1985b) describes territorial mobility in Vanuatu and its contemporary transformation. Traditionally, each local group was linked to a particular sacred or magical place and to one or more *nakamal* (kava-drinking places). Extraterritorial movements were usually short, infrequent, and dangerous. Access to the sea for inland groups was possible only after delicate negotiations and payment in pigs and women, and along a narrow track. In Aoba and Pentecost where to "be a man" involved a lifelong ascent up a hierarchy of social grades, mobility was essential in procuring sponsorship (by grade members) and the tusked pigs and mats required for ritual transactions. In southern Vanuatu, rank was inherited genealogically, and mobility correspondingly less extensive.

Traditional society was heavily impacted by waves of sandalwooders, blackbirders, missionaries, planters, and traders. The termination of warfare and weakening of traditional power structures led to a lifting of taboos on unauthorized journeys and to a dramatic increase in mobility, particularly in the rank-competitive northern islands (Figure 22.4). Movement was also accelerated by population growth and reduction of available land. Between the end of the nineteenth century and the end of World War II, circular migration to plantations became the dominant form of mobility. More recently, young people are increasingly moving to urban areas.

It should also be noted that initially, European contact often resulted in a decline in mobility (J-L. Rallu, pers. comm.).

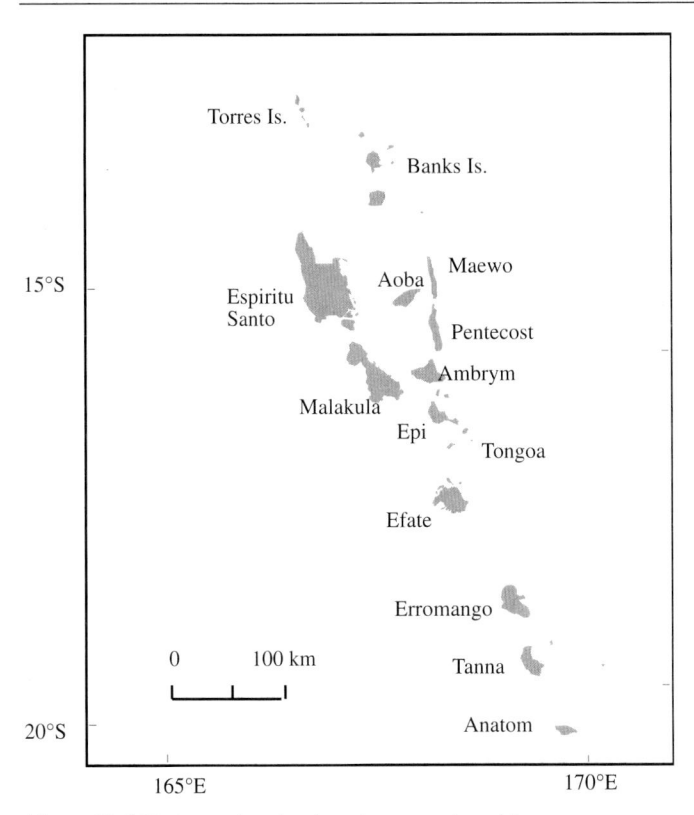

*Figure 22.4.* Vanuatu, showing locations mentioned in text.

### TABLE 22.1

**Tairora Movements, Characterized by Purpose and Participation** (after Watson 1985)

| Movement type | Frequency | Participation |
|---|---|---|
| Circulation (C) | | |
| Migration (M) | | |
| Shift of residential site (M) | 5–15 years | 1–10 households |
| Refugees (C, M) | 25–50 years | 1–12 households |
| Connubial flows (C, M) | Up to 1 year | Individual females |
| Disaffected males (C, M) | Variable | Individual males |
| Strong man's travels (C) | Varies with distance | Outstanding strong men, solitary or with entourage |
| Trade (C) | Once or twice a year | Lesser strong men, in small parties |
| Intraphratric visits (C) | Once a month | Varies |
| Warfare (C) | Several times a year | 6 men or more |
| Ambushes (C) | As above | Individuals or very small parties |
| Sorcerer's travels (C) | Variable | Individual, always covertly |
| Hunting (C) | Depends on need | 1–2 men |
| Gathering (C) | As above | Variable, may include children |
| Affinal visits (C) and distance | Depends on age | Family group |

Missionaries were reluctant to let new Christians go to areas still under pagan influence. Since islanders increasingly used European vessels, the construction of large traditional interisland sailing vessels came to an end (greatly limiting the potential destinations). Interisland voyaging was also limited by population decline and erosion of traditional sociopolitical structures (necessary for organizing large-scale interisland voyages).

Historical mobility transformations among the Siwai, of Bougainville, are discussed by Connell (1985). Prior to European contact the population lived in small hamlets on the land of matrilineage elders called *mumis* (big men). Population movement occurred either for marriage or changing status of *mumis*; less frequently, entire hamlets were relocated. Germany occupied the northern Solomons, including Bougainville, in 1886, partly to facilitate labor recruitment for its plantations in Samoa and New Guinea. Plantations were also begun on Bougainville, with rubber, cocoa, cotton, copra, and other tropical crops.

Around 1914, when the Australian administration took over, labor migration became increasingly common. Inducement for plantation labor was provided by an imposed head tax, from which contract laborers were exempt. Contracts were for three years, but work was hard, and few signed on for a second contract. Following World War II, plantation labor shortage led to reduction in hourly requirements and a tripling of the minimal wages. Returning plantation workers increasingly began to undertake cash cropping on their own, engaging in short-term plantation work mainly in periods when crop sales were inadequate.

In 1960 enormous copper ore deposits were discovered in Panguna, where there had previously been a small gold mine. Mining operations commenced by Bougainville Copper Limited (BCL) in 1972, providing easy access to jobs and high wages, attracting many Siwai migrants. Related work opportunities also became available at nearby Panguna and Arawa towns. By 1976, the total time of Siwai workers with BCL averaged 3.1 years, suggesting the slow emergence of an "urban-industrial proletariat," a decline in circular mobility, and long-term migration (Connell 1985).

Mobility transformations in Tuvalu (Figure 22.5) are discussed by Munro (1990). Prior to European contact, individual islands were autonomous and economically self-contained. Since the atolls all have the same limited range of resources, there was little scope for interisland trading links, though institutionalized visits between islands did involve the reciprocal exchange of goods. The first significant external contacts occurred in the 1820s with passing whaleships, exchanging iron, fishhooks, bottles, and knives for coconuts and mats. Whalers were superseded by resident traders, institutionalizing a trade in coconut oil and, later, copra.

The London Missionary Society entered Tuvalu in 1865, installing Samoan pastors on each atoll. The need for cash rose with competitive church-building, Western clothing, and education. In 1892, Britain declared a Protectorate over the then Ellis and Gilbert islands, and in 1901, following the discovery of phosphates on Ocean Island (Banaba), the first contingent of labor migration was recruited, mainly young men on two-year

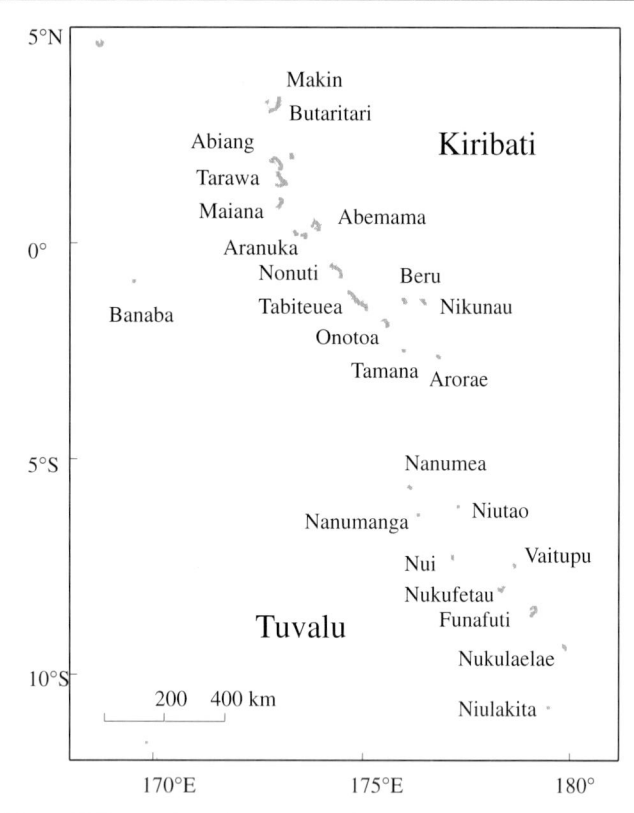

*Figure 22.5. Tuvalu and western Kiribati, showing locations mentioned in the text.*

contracts. Returning labor migrants brought outbreaks of infectious disease and a population decline, reversed only after the installation of medical officers on each atoll.

Urban development on Tarawa began in 1946; by 1963 over seven hundred Tuvaluans were living in Tarawa, employed predominantly in administrative and clerical capacities. In 1975, Tuvalu separated from the British colony, and mass repatriation of its civil servants ensued, many of whom became employed in Funafuti, the new capital. Today, Tuvaluans rely heavily on remittances from overseas workers in Nauru and foreign ships, along with British grant aid. Tuvaluans are hoping to wean themselves from dependence through an $A26 million dollar trust fund established with British participation in 1987 (Munro 1990).

## Settlement and Displacement

Extensive European settlement in the Pacific Islands and the associated influx of Asian migrant labor was most prominent in island groups with relatively large landmasses. Small pockets of European settlement occurred throughout the Pacific, but the magnitude and impact of settlement were greatest in New Zealand, Hawai'i, and New Caledonia. Asian settlement was extensive in Hawai'i and Fiji, with smaller groups in New Caledonia, French Polynesia, and (more recently) New Zealand, Guam, and the Commonwealth of the Northern Marianas (Table 21.4).

Sinclair (1980) has concisely summarized the sequence of events that led to European settlement of New Zealand:

In the European history of New Zealand, trade came second, close in the wake of the first navigators.... [I]ndustry and commerce brought the missionaries. Mission and trade led to a residence which became settlement; and the flag followed the settler.

New Zealand was settled in a hundred ways. Some towns were "military establishments," garrison towns. Some were laid out and sold by entrepreneurs.... Some towns grew up around Maori villages. The settlement of some districts began when a squatter drove in his sheep. And traders, missionaries, whalers, gold-diggers, or dairy farmers were the pioneers in others.

The influx of European settlers in New Zealand was intense (45,730 arrived in 1863 alone), the result of population increase in Britain and the frustration and poverty that accompanied the industrial revolution (Sinclair 1980). In other island groups the demographic influx was smaller, but the presence of even a few determined foreigners could have significant consequences. Planters such as Claus Spreckels, who used their capital to "get a toehold, then a foothold, then a near stranglehold" in the islands (Daws 1983) could cause considerable upheaval. Even a trickle of traders, missionaries, and planters, compounded with an influx of migrant labor, could have a significant impact.

Labor migration, primarily from Asia, was initiated by planters. Some migrants were recruited as "indentured workers" under several-year contracts. Migrants elsewhere came as indentured workers (though sometimes by deceit and outright kidnapping) and also as "free emigrants," with kinsmen or businessmen providing tickets in exchange for delayed payment. Some migrated for adventure, but most left through necessity, due to population pressure, social upheaval, famines, or wars. Emigrants came from all classes, but most often the small cultivating classes, tenants, and laborers (Wilson et al. 1990).

Colonial settlement, assisted by "guns, germs, and steel" (Diamond 1997), led inevitably to displacement of native populations. One of the largest and most egregious displacements occurred in New Caledonia. Between 1860 and 1894, over 40,000 French prisoners were sent to the island, many of whom settled subsequently. In 1864, nickel ore was discovered; this along with settler demands for agricultural land and cattle ranching led to a policy of *cantonnement* (reserves). Indigenous Kanaks were relocated and confined to reservations comprising around 10% of the land in Grand Terre (see Figure 17.2), giving rise to guerrilla wars in 1878 and 1917, ultimately suppressed (Ward 1982, Oliver 1989). The reservations still exist in New Caledonia (though many Melanesians now live elsewhere).

Elsewhere, islanders were displaced through individual purchases and government claims to "unused land." In Hawai'i during the 1840s, American advisors persuaded King Kamehameha III to effect the "Great Mahele," legislation transforming the land to individualized (and alienable) property ownership, in which commoners received less than 1%. Sugar planters and ranchers found it easy enough to purchase

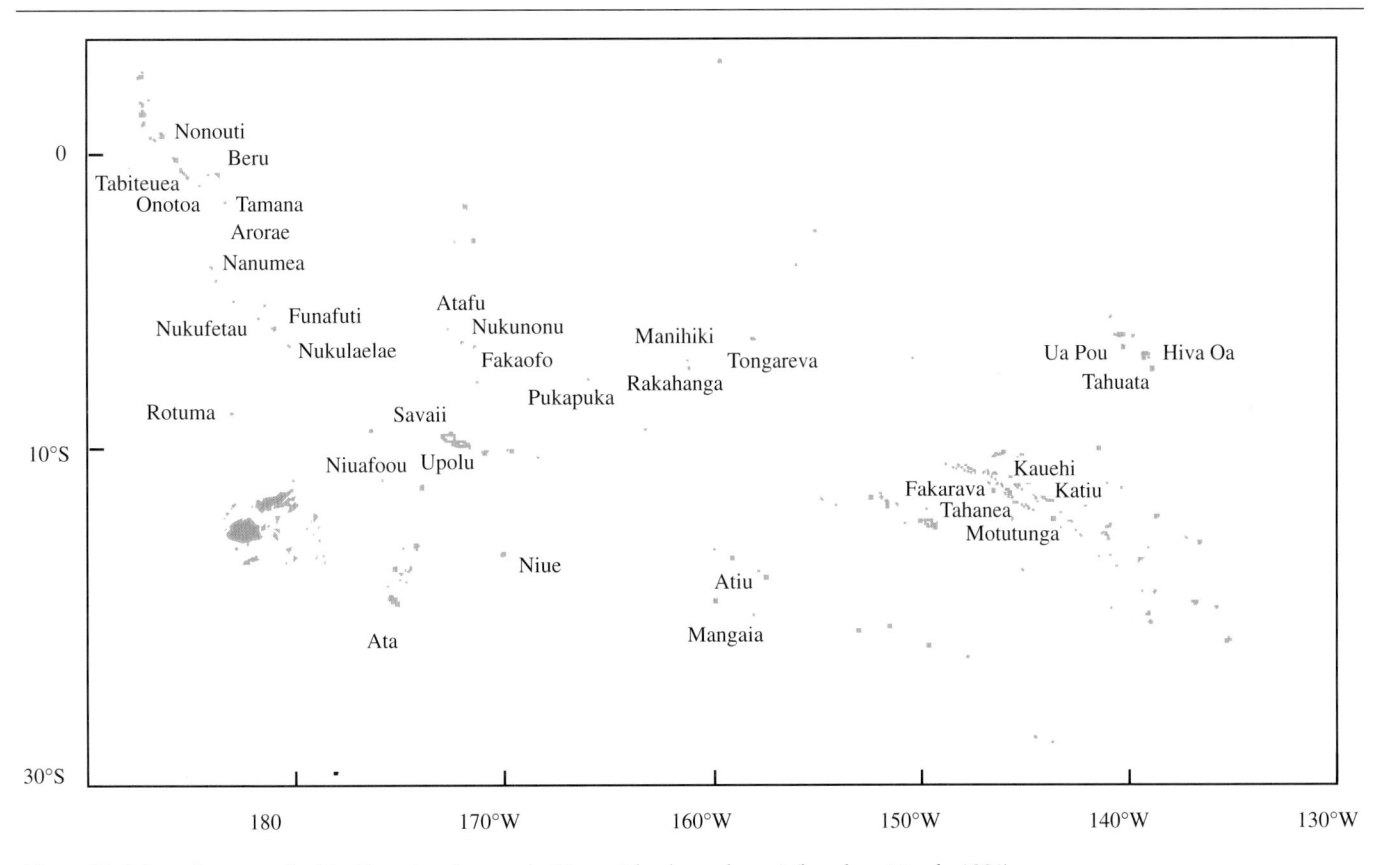

*Figure 22.6. Locations recruited by Peruvian slave trade (Easter Island not shown) (based on Maude 1981).*

immense tracts from the king and land-rich chiefs. In New Zealand, overwhelming settler numbers and warfare with resentful Maori ended with the confiscation of 7.5 million hectares of land. Maori survivors "were pushed back into unwanted corners or allowed to drift along in town slums" (Oliver 1989).

On several atolls and small islands, catastrophic displacement ensued during the Peruvian slave raids of 1862–3 (Figure 22.6), striking with the force of a great "tsunami" (Maude 1981). In many islands, only a fragment of the original community remained (Table 22.2). An estimated 3,634 islanders were taken to Peru, the majority by deceit or kidnapping by sheer force. In Peru, the islanders were classified by the government as colonists, but they were sold and treated as slaves for plantation labor and domestic service at wealthy haciendas. Lonely, miserable, and overworked, they died with rapidity. Following political pressure, an attempt was made to repatriate 1,009 recruits, but only 157 reached the islands alive, due to neglect, disease, or being thrown overboard.

Nuclear testing by the United States led to evacuation of four atolls in the Northern Marshalls (Figure 22.7). Inhabitants of Bikini were evacuated in 1946 to Rongerik, but (due to

### TABLE 22.2

**Islands Most Heavily Affected by Peruvian Slave Trade**
(Maude 1981)

| | Estimated population 1862 | Percent recruited |
|---|---|---|
| Tongareva | 570 | 83 |
| Nukulaelae | 315 | 79 |
| Nukunonu | 140 | 54 |
| Funafuti | 317 | 54 |
| Fakaofo | 261 | 54 |
| Ata | 350 | 41 |
| Easter Island | 4126 | 34 |
| Rakahanga | 340 | 34 |
| Atafu | 140 | 26 |
| Pukapuka | 600 | 24 |
| Niue | 5021 | 2 |

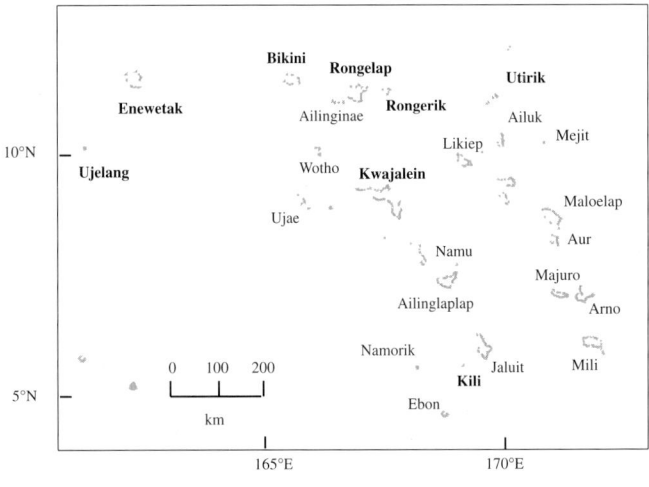

*Figure 22.7. The Marshall Islands, showing islands mentioned in text.*

The Pacific Islands

inadequate resources there) had to be resettled on tiny Kili. Some islanders returned to Bikini in 1972 following an attempted cleanup, but were reevacuated six years later following evidence of nuclear toxicity, resulting in lawsuits and multimillion dollar settlements by the United States. Enewetak (Eniwetok) Islanders were evacuated in 1947 to Ujelang; many returned in 1980 following a cleanup there, but parts of Enewetak remain unsafe. Rongelap and Utirik Islanders were evacuated in 1954 to Kwajalein; they were permitted to return subsequently, but many left again due to radiation exposure (Firth 1994).

## Mobility Today

### Trends

Pacific-wide demographic comparisons are subject to many problems, including varying census dates, assumptions, reliability, and definitions. With this important caution in mind, selected demographic trends relevant to migration will be presented and discussed, based on census and vital statistics data (Table 22.3). A striking observation is the population decline experienced on the very small island groups, such as Pitcairn (reflecting migration to Australia and the United States), Tokelau, and Niue (reflecting migration from both to New Zealand).

The magnitude of annual net migration is computed from the difference between the rates of population growth and natural increase. Net outmigration (indicated by negative values)

### Table 22.3

**Selected Demographic Indices for the Pacific Islands Relevant to Mobility** (DBEDT 1994, SPC 1995, SNZ 1996)

| | Total Population | % Urban | Annual rate of total population growth (%) | Annual rate of natural increase (%) | Annual net migration* (%) | Annual rate of urban growth (%) | Net urban growth* (%) |
|---|---|---|---|---|---|---|---|
| **MELANESIA** | | | | | | | |
| Fiji | 713,375 (1986) | 39 | 2 | 2 | 0 | 2.6 | 0.6 |
| New Caledonia | 164,173 (1989) | 70 | 2 | 1.8 | 0.2 | 2.1 | 0.1 |
| Papua New Guinea | 3,607,954 (1990) | 15 | 2.3 | 2.3 | 0 | 4.1 | 1.8 |
| Solomon Islands | 285,176 (1986) | 13 | 3.4 | 3.2 | 0.2 | 6.2 | 2.8 |
| Vanuatu | 142,419 (1989) | 18 | 2.8 | 2.9 | -0.1 | 7.3 | 4.5 |
| **MICRONESIA** | | | | | | | |
| FSM | 10,4724 (1994) | n.d. | 2.6 | 3 | -0.4 | n.d. | n.d. |
| Guam | 133,152 (1990) | 38 | 2.3 | 2.6 | -0.3 | 1.9 | -0.4 |
| Kiribati | 72,335 (1990) | 35 | 2.3 | 2.3 | 0 | 3.1 | 0.8 |
| Marshall Is. | 43,380 (1988) | 65 | 4.2 | 4 | 0.2 | 8.2 | 4 |
| Nauru | 9,919 (1992) | 100 | 2.9 | 1.9 | 1 | 2.9 | 0 |
| N. Marianas | 43,345 (1990) | 53 | 9.5 | 2.7 | 6.8 | 9.4 | -0.1 |
| Palau | 15,122 (1990) | 69 | 2.1 | 1.4 | 0.7 | 2.7 | 0.6 |
| **POLYNESIA** | | | | | | | |
| American Samoa | 46,773 (1990) | 48 | 3.7 | 3.4 | 0.3 | 8.2 | 4.5 |
| Cook Islands | 18,617 (1991) | 58 | 1.1 | 1.9 | -0.8 | 2.4 | 1.3 |
| French Polynesia | 188,814 (1988) | 57 | 2.5 | 2.4 | 0.1 | 2.2 | -0.3 |
| Hawai'i | 1,108,229 (1992) | 89 | 1.4 | 1.1 | 0.3 | 1.7 | 0.3 |
| New Zealand | 3,618,302 (1996) | 85 | 1.4 | 0.8 | 0.6 | 0.7 | 0.7 |
| Niue | 2,239 (1991) | 30 | -2.4 | 1.1 | -3.5 | -2 | 0.4 |
| Pitcairn Is. | 53 (1993) | 0 | -9.1 | n.d. | n.d. | n.a. | n.a. |
| Samoa | 161,298 (1991) | 21 | 0.5 | 2.3 | -1.8 | 1.2 | 0.7 |
| Tokelau | 1,577 (1991) | 0 | -1.3 | n.d. | n.d. | n.a. | n.a. |
| Tonga | 94,649 (1986) | 31 | 0.5 | 2.5 | -2 | 2.5 | 2 |
| Tuvalu | 9,043 (1991) | 42 | 1.7 | 1.8 | -0.1 | 4.8 | 3.1 |
| Wallis and Futuna | 13,705 (1990) | 0 | 1.3 | 2.5 | -1.2 | n.a. | n.a. |

*see text for derivation

occurs in several territories and former territories of New Zealand (Niue, Tonga, Samoa, and the Cook Islands) and the United States (Guam and the Federated States of Micronesia). Net inmigration flows occurred in the Northern Marianas, Palau (reflecting migration from Micronesia, the Philippines, and East/Southeast Asia), and Hawai'i.

Hayes (1985, Table 22.4) has compared migrant flows based on U.S., New Zealand, and Australian censuses, which classify residents by place of birth. Guamanians and Samoans are the most numerous Pacific Rim immigrants, followed by Fijians (mainly Indo-Fijians), Tongans, Cook Islanders, and American Samoans, and considerably smaller numbers of Micronesians, Melanesians, Tokelauans, and Niueans. The majority of Melanesia-born (notably from Papua New Guinea) in Australia are assumed to be nonindigenous settlers who left at the time of independence or subsequent periods.

### Table 22.4

**Pacific Island–born Populations Overseas**
(Hayes 1985)*

| Place of birth | USA | NZ | Australia |
| --- | --- | --- | --- |
| Fiji | 7,538 | 6,372 | 9,357 |
| Melanesia n.c. | 7 | 957 | |
| New Caledonia | 144 | | 896 |
| Papua New Guinea | 425 | | 18,695 |
| Solomon Islands | 97 | | 721 |
| Vanuatu | 30 | | 676 |
| | | | |
| FSM | 1,401 | | |
| Guam | 36,782 | | |
| Kiribati | 106 | | |
| Marshall Is. | 1,197 | | |
| Micronesia n.c. | 1,551 | 186 | |
| N. Marianas | 2,137 | | |
| Nauru | 27 | | |
| Palau | 1,003 | | |
| | | | |
| American Samoa | 9,361 | | |
| Cook Islands | 130 | 13,851 | |
| French Polynesia | 1,014 | | |
| Niue | 0 | 94 | |
| Pitcairn Is. | 27 | | |
| Polynesia n.c. | 125 | 7,013 | |
| Samoa | 12,582 | 24,141 | |
| Tokelau | 61 | 1,284 | |
| Tonga | 5,619 | 5,232 | 2,615 |
| | | | |
| Oceania n.c. | | | 16,898 |

* Ward (1996) reports a ca. 1990 estimate of 16,700 Pacific Islanders in Canada (mainly Indo-Fijians) and 21,900 in Metropolitan France.
Note: n.c.: non-classified

The relatively large numbers of Polynesian migrants in New Zealand (Color Plate 22A) and absence of Melanesians has been explained as a consequence of former colonial administration and continuing political and economic relationships. Polynesian migrants are seen as close relatives to the New Zealand Maori, facilitating their absorption. Similar arguments could be made for Polynesian populations in Hawai'i (Color Plate 22B). Another factor may be traditional patterns of long-distance voyaging, especially prevalent in Polynesia and Micronesia. However, "it is difficult to avoid the conclusion that ethnocentrism has also played a role" (Hayes 1985).

Comparative data on internal migration are scarce. Walsh (1982) provides internal migration rates (defined as the percent of urban residents not born in the urban area—note that this is a proportion rather than an annual rate) for nine Pacific Island groups, based on censuses from 1976–1979. Highest values were found in Solomon Islands (97.3%), followed by Kiribati (77.7%), Tuvalu (67.2%), Fiji (50.3%), Samoa (43.3%), the Cook Islands (29.9%), and Tonga (20.6%). The exceptionally high rate for the Solomons occurred because Honiara was a new town, having begun from a U.S. army base during World War II.

Net urban growth (in Table 22.3) is derived from the difference between urban and total population growth rates and provides an indicator of internal migration. This is only an approximation, as differential urban/rural rates of population increase and external migration can also affect relative growth rates (see Walsh 1987). The data suggest net rural-to-urban migration on most Pacific Islands, with highest rates in Vanuatu, the Marshall Islands, American Samoa, and Tuvalu. Negative values, suggestive of net counterstream (urban-to-rural) migration occur in French Polynesia (due to a black pearl boom), Guam, and the Northern Marianas.

### Explaining Migration

Several analytical models have been proposed to explain migration, some based on structural economic and demographic dynamics, and others emphasizing the motives of individual migrants (see Bedford 1980). Some of these models originated as ways to explain circular migration, but they are also relevant to the study of migration in general, given that many migrants begin with short-term circulatory moves. The emphases of the various models (some of which are discussed below) are different, but they are not necessarily in conflict; rather, each attempts to explain a different facet of migration behavior.

One model suggests a balancing between the centripetal power of kinship ties, social relationships, and village obligations and the centrifugal attractions of wage employment and commercial, social, and administrative services (Chapman 1976, Chapman and Prothero 1977). Movement is thus a way of rationalizing a territorial separation between social ties, goods, and services, all of which may be dispersed between several locales. The composition and relative power of these opposing forces change over an individual's lifetime, and circular migration may give way to permanent settlement or return to home.

A second model ("transnational corporation of kin") suggests that migration be viewed as a collective decision by migrant family units (rather than an individual decision by migrants), as a "rational allocation of labor units" with potential long-term benefit to migrants and the sending community (Bertram and Watters 1985). Movement of individuals occurs without severing links with the kin group of origin. Home kin provide long-term security and resources to help send and support migrants in the initial stages, while migrants reciprocate with remittances and help with visiting relatives and potential new migrants.

Dependency theory provides a third model for explaining migration, based on the structural factors at work. According to this model, which Hayes (1991) attributes to Connell (1987), Pacific Island migrants are characterized as "discontent, oversocialized victims of the global capitalist system wrenched from their islands and families by the destructive forces of monetization, individualism, and consumerism" (Hayes 1991). Migration is seen as a destructive force that undermines the culture, social system, and demographic balance of the home society.

A fourth model situates migration in demographic transition theory and has been termed the "multi-phasic demographic response theory" (see Hayes 1991, and sources therein). According to this model, rising population eventually results in increasing pressure upon resources; rural populations respond through absorption (agricultural intensification), reductions in fertility (through culturally available means), urbanization, and migration. This model has been described as a "modified Malthusian framework," though Hayes (1991) cautions that decisions are based on perceptions of need, rather than population pressure "in any absolute sense."

The relationship between expanding pressure, fertility reduction, and migration is illustrated by Hayes (1991) through a Cook Islands case study. In the early twentieth century (stage 1), birthrates and death rates were both relatively high, with no natural population increase. Beginning around 1915 (stage 2), the death rate began a long-term, though fluctuating, decline. Since birthrates remained the same, population size began to expand. At around 1960 (stage 3), birthrates began to drop, and death rates leveled off as well, so that the rate of natural increase began to decline (Figure 22.8).

Up until the 1970s, population growth was continuous, reaching a peak of over 21,000 in 1972, almost three times the population in 1900. By the mid 1960s, real GDP per capita increased at an exceptionally high rate of 9.2% annually, despite rates of natural increase exceeding 3%. An alternative measure of social welfare (the "Physical Quality of Life Index") confirms the rise in standards of living. It is thus apparent that the population increase was successfully "absorbed" (presumably through use of additional land and new technology) (Hayes 1991).

It is significant that the drop in birthrate that occurred in the 1960s began prior to the introduction of modern family planning methods by the Cook Islands Department of Health. Family planning clinics have apparently helped facilitate a transition that had already begun to occur. By 1986, over 50% of women of childbearing ages were reported to be using some kind of modern contraception. At the same time, the proportion of celibate women has increased by over 10% compared with that of a generation earlier (Hayes 1991).

The scope for rural-to-urban movement within the Cook Islands is extremely limited, due to traditional land tenure arrangements and few employment opportunities in the capital, Rarotonga. Yet the urban center has continued to grow, with 56% of the population residing on Rarotonga in 1986 (compared with 47% in 1961). This growth has been accomplished through expansion of tourism, offshore banking, and clothing factories established earlier. Simultaneously, there has been a major shift away from agriculture and fishing, with only 19% of the population so occupied in 1986 (Hayes 1991).

External migration, primarily to New Zealand, was already significant during the 1940s, but picked up substantially in the following decades, reaching a peak of 10% of the population in 1974, offsetting the high rates of natural increase. Following that year, however, years of emigration resulted in substantial decline in the population size, and net migration began to reverse, with net immigration occurring in several years during the 1980s. By the 1980s, population levels remained relatively stable, oscillating between 17,000 and 18,000.

The demographic behavior of the Cook Islanders over the past three decades appears to match the expectations of demographic response theory, involving a combination of absorption, fertility reduction, urbanization, and external migration. While particular responses waxed and waned, they were effective overall in reducing population pressure in culturally acceptable ways. The "stalling" of the demographic transition (with birthrates still well above death rates) is explained by the availability of emigration to New Zealand under existing political arrangements (Hayes 1991).

## Impact

As in other parts of the world, migration has led to significant changes in Pacific societies (Connell 1987, 1990). It is not always possible to separate those consequences that derive from migration and those that derive from the spread of capitalism and modernization (partly because migration itself derives to a large extent from economic disparities). Moreover, the demographic, economic, and social changes associated with migration differ from rural to urban areas, and from place to place, particularly in Melanesia, where substantial cultural divides exist

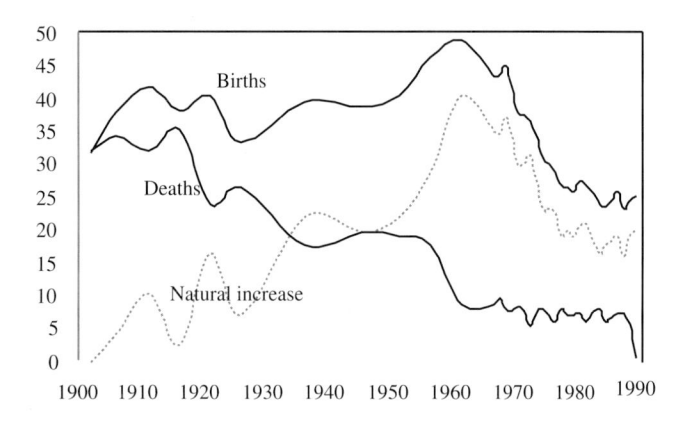

*Figure 22.8.* Demographic transition in the Cook Islands (after Hayes 1991).

between adjacent areas. Obviously, the impact will differ in sending and receiving communities.

Boyd (1990) has discussed the way the Iraqi Awa, of the Eastern Highlands of Papua New Guinea, deal with returning migrants and their earnings. First contacted by an Australian exploratory patrol in 1947, the Iraqi Awa are subsistence-oriented cultivators. Since 1963, they have also grown coffee. However, marketing the crop involves a five-hour walk to the nearest road, and profits are often minimal due to fluctuating prices, so coffee does not meet local cash needs. Consequently, virtually all men seek wage labor in the Highlands or farther at some time in their lives, though only a portion are successful.

For nonmigrants among the Iraqi Awa home community, returning migrants are perceived to be in a state of indebtedness, which requires distribution of some portion of the savings. Parents and older siblings stake their claim on the basis of prior care for the migrant during the years of childhood. The community reminds migrants of their obligations before they leave home by mourning their departure and through gifts of food and magical protection items, including the killing of pigs. While the migrants are absent, wives may be chosen for them, and relatives at home may make betrothal payments. If a married migrant is absent, relatives care for his wife, children, pigs, and coffee trees.

On reentering the village, returnees are subject to much attention and hospitality, along with welcoming feasts and pigs, and

> [t]he returnees strut about in the village in their urban dress playing transistor radios at full volume and regaling listeners with stories of their adventures. At the same time they gradually distribute goods and money to those they favor.

During the reentry period, which may last up to a month, returnees must observe certain restrictions because of the foreign spirits adhering to their bodies. They are not permitted to enter subsistence gardens or spend time with their wives. At the end of the period, the migrants are taken by older nonmigrant matrilineal kin to ceremonial sites where special exorcist rituals are performed, including nose bleeding, cane swallowing, and penis laceration. Those who perform these rituals all can expect some compensation. Migrants compensate by departing secretly, or with other expressed intentions (Boyd 1990).

In the Tuamotus, French Polynesia, a recent black pearl boom (Figure 22.9, Color Plates 22C–D) has led to urban-to-rural migration, with consequent social impact (Rapaport 1995). Migration began in the 1980s following pioneering maricultural initiatives by government scientists and private pearl farmers, based on earlier work by the Japanese. By the 1980s, pearl farming had begun on some sixteen atolls in the Tuamotus, leading to waves of migration from Tahiti and population increases of up to 20% per year. Most of the migration comprises returning migrants, including many who had been absent for two or three generations.

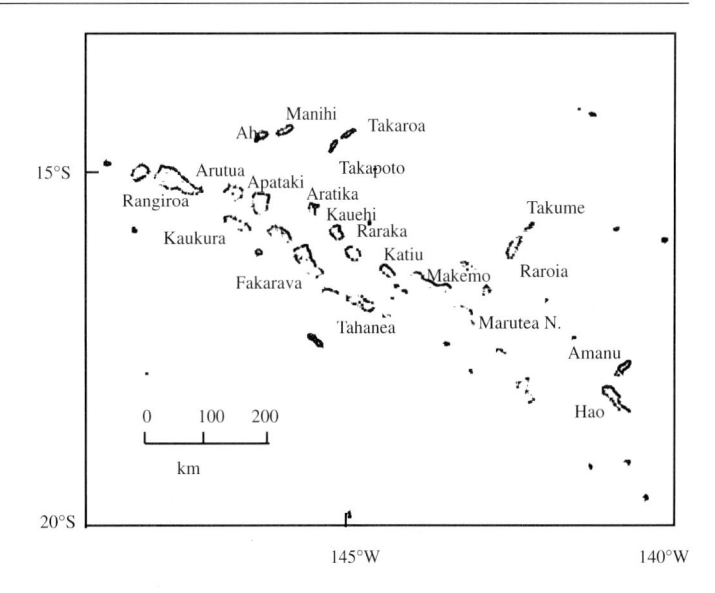

*Figure 22.9.* The Tuamotu Archipelago, showing pearl farming islands.

The Tuamotus had been relatively depopulated in recent decades, and the migrants were generally welcomed, though small quarrels inevitably ensued over access to land, associated lagoon space, and government-allocated pearl farming concessions. The most significant problem, however, developed over *ona* (businessmen), mainly Chinese-Tahitians who had received concessions and established pearl farms many times larger than anyone else; but opposition also emerged toward all pearl farmers lacking roots on the atoll, including migrants from other atolls with questionable claims to local ancestry.

Conflict was most severe on Takaroa, an atoll with the most abundant natural pearl oyster stocks (Rapaport 1996). An association of protection was formed by Mahinui Pou, a return migrant from New Caledonia, aimed at reserving Takaroa's lagoon for the *taata tumu* (those indigenous to the atoll). The association reacted with petitions, confiscations, and demonstrations, modeling these efforts after nineteenth-century protests against similar incursions by foreigners. However, the Tahitian administration intervened and managed to quiet the population, promising to be more vigilant with concession allocations.

The problems of Polynesian migrants in New Zealand have been reviewed by Spoonley (1990). Recruitment (by individual employers and family members) began in the 1950s and became oriented toward semiskilled and unskilled employment in Auckland and Wellington. In 1981, only 2% of Samoan and Cook Island males were employed in professional and technical capacities, compared with 18% of English migrants (and 39% of American migrants). Following a 1970s recession, Pacific Islanders were increasingly perceived as responsible for a variety of problems ranging from unemployment to a decline in law and order.

A political reaction began in 1974, with crackdowns on overstayers, including random street checks and dawn raids, with prosecutions and deportations continuing into the 1980s. The National Party portrayed islanders as a "racial threat, as people who took jobs, acted illegally and were violent." A hasty treaty was concluded with Samoa to ensure Samoans did not claim New Zealand citizenship (as was their right according to a prior legal decision). Work migration laws were rewritten, moving New Zealand toward a rigidly controlled contract labor scheme, with a maximum eleven-month duration.

In the 1980s, previous difficulties have been compounded by economic restructuring and devolution of government services. The problems of Pacific Island migrants have also become overshadowed by nationalist politics among the Maori and the emergence of biculturalism. The priorities of addressing past land grievances have thus become opposed to priorities of citizenship, and there is even some suspicion that the government is trying to encourage competition between ethnic groups, in the hope of diminishing the force of both claims (Spoonley 1990).

### Sustainability

The Cook Islands, Niue, Samoa, Tonga, and other Polynesian groups have become dependent on external migration for remittances and to relieve population pressure, but there is debate concerning the sustainability of this migration. The premises of dependency theory would suggest that migration is ultimately unsustainable (Brookfield 1985). Bertram and Watters (1985) argue that migration is sustainable and appropriate given local economic constraints, and that small island economies can be best classified as "MIRAB" economies (reliant on migration, remittances, aid, and bureaucracy).

According to this view, the village economy helps assure that control over natural resources is not threatened by any competing mode of production and provides the "floor" below which real incomes will not fall. This village economy is complemented and overlapped by the cash economy, in the sense that wage earners and entrepreneurs retain access to land and participate in village activities even if absent for long periods. Investment of kin-group labor in agriculture is just one of several strategies by the transnational corporations of kin, alternating with opportunities in government work or overseas work.

In support of this argument, Bertram and Watters show that remittances over two decades in the Cook Islands, Niue, Kiribati, Tokelau, and Tuvalu have not declined, and have actually increased significantly. To arguments that migrant remittances will inevitably decline with length of absence and identification with new locations and social ties, they reply that the continuing flow of new migrants would make up for any depreciation in the existing stock of "human capital" in regional growth poles. However, migration opportunities do clearly depend on migration policies of metropolitan countries, and the recent trend in New Zealand has been to cut down on migration.

## Conclusion

Given the "anastomosing" pattern of contemporary migration in the Pacific Islands, in which remittances and trade flow through transnational household economies, Ward (1996) suggests that the fundamental premises of nationhood and sovereignty may have to be examined. It is possible that many of the region's perceived economic problems arise as a consequence of outmoded ideas of what constitutes the boundaries and definitions of "Tonga" or "Samoa." As transnational ethnic communities, Pacific Islanders may appear to have considerably more expanded resources, populations, and opportunities (Ward 1996).

However, Pacific societies were anastomosing with each other well before the modern period. Genealogies throughout Polynesia intertwine, joining and departing after several generations. Pāʻao from Kahiki, unsatisfied with the unruly forgetful descendants of early colonists, brought the land an unsullied chief from the ancestral lineage and reinstalled what he perceived to be the proper rites and social order (Malo 1976). Early voyagers moved back and forth between Hawaiki and Aotearoa even without the jet plane. Today, new methods are being used, but old patterns may be reasserting themselves.

# Bibliography

Alkire, W. H. 1978. *Coral islanders.* Arlington Heights, Illinois: AHM Publishing Corporation.

Audran, H. 1918. Tradition of and notes on the Paumotu (or Tuamotu) Islands. *Journal of the Polynesian Society* 27(105):26–35.

Bedford, R. 1980. Overview of recent research on the variety and forms of population mobility in Southeast Asia and Melanesia: the case of circulation. Paper presented to the 1980 Development Studies Centre Conference "Population, Mobility & Development," 8–10 October 1980.

Bellwood, P. 1979. *Man's conquest of the Pacific: the prehistory of Southeast Asia and Oceania.* New York: Oxford University Press.

Bertram, I. G., and R. F. Watters. 1985. The MIRAB economy in South Pacific microstates. *Pacific Viewpoint* 26(3):497–519.

Bonnemaison, J. 1985a. The tree and the canoe: roots and mobility in Vanuatu societies. *Pacific Viewpoint* 26(1):30–62.

Bonnemaison, J. 1985b. Territorial control and mobility within ni Vanuatu societies. In *Circulation in population movement: substance and concepts from the Melanesian case,* ed. M. Chapman and R. M. Prothero, 57–80. London: Routledge and Kegan Paul.

Borofsky, R. 1987. Making history: Pukapukan and anthropological constructions of knowledge. Cambridge: Cambridge University Press.

Boyd, D. J. 1985. New wealth and old power: circulation, remittances, and the control of inequality in an Eastern Highlands community, Papua New Guinea. In *Migration and development in the South Pacific,* ed. J. Connell, 97–106. Canberra: National Center for Development Studies, Research School of Pacific Studies, Australian National University.

Brookfield, H. C. 1985. Communication (quoted), in I. G. Bertram and R. F. Watters. 1985. The MIRAB economy in South Pacific microstates. *Pacific Viewpoint* 26(3):497.

Buck, P. 1972. *Vikings of the sunrise.* Chicago: University of Chicago Press.

Chapman, M. 1976. Tribal mobility as circulation: a Solomon Islands example of micro/macro linkages. In *Population at microscale,* ed. L. A. Kosinski and J. W. Webb, 127–142. Christchurch: New Zealand Geographical Society.

Chapman, M., and R. M. Prothero. 1977. Circulation between home places and towns: a village approach to urbanization. Paper prepared for the working session on urbanization in the Pacific, Association for Social Anthropology of Oceania, Monterey, California, 2–6 March.

Connell, J. 1985. Copper, cocoa and cash: terminal, temporary, and circular mobility in Siwai, north Solomons. In *Circulation in population movement: substance and concepts from the Melanesian case,* ed. M. Chapman and R. M. Prothero, 119–148. London: Routledge and Kegan Paul.

Connell, J. 1987. *Migration, employment and development in the South Pacific.* Noumea: South Pacific Commission.

Connell, J. 1990. Modernity and its discontents: migration and change in the South Pacific. In *Migration and development in the South Pacific,* ed. J. Connell, 1–28. Canberra: National Center for Development Studies, Research School of Pacific Studies, Australian National University.

Daws, G. 1983. History. In *Atlas of Hawaii,* ed. R. W. Armstrong, 97–106. Honolulu: University of Hawai'i Press.

Department of Business, Economic Development, and Tourism (DBEDT). 1994. *The State of Hawaii data book; a statistical abstract.* Honolulu: DBEDT.

Diamond, J. 1997. *Guns, germs, and steel: the fates of human societies.* NY: W. W. Norton and Company.

Evans, J. 1997. *Nga waka o nehera: the first voyaging canoes.* Auckland: Reed Books.

Finney, B. R. 1979. *Hokulea: the way to Tahiti.* NY: Dodd and Mead.

Firth, S. 1994. Strategic and nuclear issues. In *Tides of history: the Pacific Islands in the twentieth century,* ed. K. R. Howe, R. C. Kiste, and B. V. Lal, 283–299. Honolulu: University of Hawai'i Press.

Hayes, G. R. 1985. *International migration in the Pacific Islands: a brief history and a review of recent patterns.* Asian Population Studies Series No. 64. Bangkok: ESCAP.

Hayes, G. R. 1991. Polynesian migration and the demographic transition: a missing dimension of recent theoretical models. Paper prepared for XVII Pacific Science Congress, Honolulu, Hawai'i 27, May–2 June 1991.

Lacey, R. 1982. Traditional trade. In *Atlas of Papua New Guinea,* ed. D. King and S. Ranck, 8–9. Port Moresby: University of Papua New Guinea.

Lacey, R. 1985. Journeys and transformations: the process of innovation in Papua New Guinea. *Pacific Viewpoint* 26(1):81–105.

Luomala, K. 1955. *Voices on the wind: Polynesian myths and chants.* Honolulu: Bishop Museum Press.

Malo, D. 1976. *Ka mo'oleo Hawaii: Hawaiian antiquities.* Honolulu: Bishop Museum Press.

Maude, H. E. 1981. *Slavers in paradise: the Peruvian slave trade in Polynesia, 1862–1864.* Stanford, California: Stanford University Press.

McKinnon, M. ed. 1997. *New Zealand historical atlas: ko papatuanuku e takoto nei.* Auckland: Department of Internal Affairs.

Munro, D. 1990. Migration and the shift to dependence in Tuvalu. In *Migration and development in the South Pacific,* ed. J. Connell, 29–41. Canberra: National Center for Development Studies, Research School of Pacific Studies, Australian National University.

Oliver, D. 1989. *The Pacific Islands.* Honolulu: University of Hawai'i Press.

Rapaport, M. 1995. Pearl farming in the Tuamotus: atoll development and its consequences. *Pacific Studies* 18(3):1–25.

Rapaport, M. 1996. Between two laws: tenure regimes in the pearl islands. *The Contemporary Pacific* 8(1):33–49.

Scarr, D. 1990. *The history of the Pacific Islands: kingdoms of the reefs.* Melbourne: Macmillan.

Sinclair, K. 1980. *A history of New Zealand.* London: Allen Lane.

South Pacific Commission (SPC). 1995. *Statistical Bulletin of the South Pacific No. 42.* Noumea: South Pacific Commission.

Spoonley, P. 1990. Polynesian immigrant workers in New Zealand. In *Labour in the South Pacific,* ed. C. J. Moore, J. Leckie, and D. Munro, 155–164. Townsville: James Cook University of Queensland.

Statistics New Zealand (SNZ). 1996. *1996 census of population and dwellings.* Wellington, NZ: Statistics New Zealand.

Walsh, A. C. 1981. Some questions on the effects of migration in the Pacific Islands, with particular reference to source areas. Paper presented at the Conference on the Consequences of Migration, East-West Center, Honolulu, Hawai'i, August 25–31, 1981.

Walsh, A. C. 1982. *Migration, urbanization and development in South Pacific countries.* New York: ESCAP.

Walsh, A. C. 1987. *Migration and urbanization in Papua New Guinea: the 1980 census.* Papua New Guinea Research Monograph No. 5. Port Moresby: National Statistics Office.

Ward, A. 1995. *A show of justice: racial "amalgamation" in nineteenth century New Zealand.* Auckland: Auckland University Press.

Ward, A. W. 1982. *Land and politics in New Caledonia.* Canberra, Australia: Research School of Pacific Studies, Australian National University.

Ward, G. W. 1996. Expanding worlds of Oceania: implications of migration. Paper delivered at National Museum of Ethnography, Osaka, March, 1996.

Watson, J. B. 1985. The precontact northern Tairoroa: high mobility in a crowded field. In *Circulation in population movement: substance and concepts from the Melanesian case,* ed. M. Chapman and R. M. Prothero, 15–38. London: Routledge and Kegan Paul.

Wilson, M., C. Moore, and D. Munro. 1990. Asian workers in the Pacific. In *Labour in the South Pacific,* ed. C. J. Moore, J. Leckie, and D. Munro, 78–107. Townsville: James Cook University of Queensland.

# Chapter 23

# Health

*Nancy Pollock and Sitaleki A. Finau*

In tracing the development of health issues in the Pacific, we are faced with three broad concerns. First, what do we include in the concept of health? Does it refer just to medical diagnosis, or to general issues of well-being? Second, health was part of community caring and sharing in the Pacific long before Western ideas of health and medicine were introduced. Traditional healers have been marginalized, but are now playing a larger part in modern healing and policies. Third, a debate about past practices and intentions in health care poses the question whether health has improved or deteriorated since European contact. There are arguments for both stances. We will outline the arguments and raise questions about health status, policy, and programs today.

Health is a major concern, though often a low priority, in any society, and there are many cultural ways of maintaining it. In Samoa, as elsewhere in the Pacific, health is integral to society's worldview (Macpherson and Macpherson 1990). It is based on spiritual as well as social, mental, and physical aspects (Finau 1996). Maintaining health is not just about keeping individuals alive. It is about sustaining the *wairua* ("essence" in Maori) of the community, from ancestors to the newest grandchild. Health is holistic.

The Yanuca Island Declaration for health in the Pacific adopted the goal of "Healthy Islands" by the twenty-first century. Ministers of Health from seventeen Pacific Island groups agreed on several programs to carry out the shared ideas. A multisectoral approach with strong community participation was a major foundation block, including the following basic principles: children are nurtured in body and mind; environments invite learning and leisure; people work and age with dignity; and ecological balance is a source of pride (Dever and Finau 1995, WHO 1995, 1997).

The "Healthy Islands" goal has commenced implementation in Fiji on the island of Kadavu "with a view towards applying this experience to other islands in Fiji, as well as modeling the approach for other islands in the Pacific" (Han 1996). This approach builds upon Pacific experiences and provides a basis for the new problem-based learning approach in training environmental health professionals and doctors in Fiji, Hawai'i, and Pohnpei (Samisoni 1994, Dever et al. 1997, Ireland, et al. 1996, Finau 1992/93).

This chapter presents an overview of issues in health as Pacific countries and territories prepare themselves for life in the twenty-first century. It does not aim to provide detailed analysis of the many issues debated in other forums. The primary aim is to provide scholars with pointers to the diverse topics relevant to health in the Pacific Islands.

## Health Concept

Health is a broad topic that overlaps many disciplinary areas of discourse. It ranges from a sense of general well-being to freedom from specific diseases. It includes social as well as medical parameters. Some consider care of the body a collective, community responsibility; others consider it a matter of individual care and control. Health policies have been formulated in particular ways based on the underlying principles and have altered over time.

The medicalization of health over the last 150 years has been a gradual process whereby disease phenomena have become the central feature. What is termed "biomedicine" refers to a mechanistic paradigm whereby the circulation of blood, or the functioning of the brain, or some other cause has been given priority in identifying diseases. These diseases could then be treated largely mechanistically, in order to restore health.

Four assumptions have been associated with the biomedical paradigm, founded on the science and rationality of medicine. First, disease is seen as a deviation from a hypothetical standard for normal biological functioning. Second, each disease is assumed to be mediated by a specific pathogenic agent. Third, diseases are assumed to be generic, sharing similar symptoms and locations. Fourth, biomedical attention has been directed at curing rather than preventing (Curtis and Tarkett 1996).

On the basis of these four assumptions, Western medicine has addressed itself to improving the world's health. Through identification of significant epidemic diseases, then coronary heart disease, diabetes, and cancer, and more recently HIV/AIDS and mental diseases for target treatment, biomedicine has sought to stem the severity of these diseases for the societies of the world. One resulting outcome has been reduced mortality—with rapid population growth as a consequence.

Medicine has been designed to rectify anomalies in health. As the anthropologist Hocart (1954) noted, medicine is a specialized form of ritual for promoting life. Health pertains to more than just maintaining life; it promotes well-being and involves moral concerns. What is good and desirable can be labeled healthy; what is bad or undesirable can be termed sick, diseased, or ill. In this sense, health is an ultimate human good and a necessary state for achieving other goals (Finau 1993).

Health covers the total lifestyle of a community. It includes the healthy and the sick, as well as the healers, and those concerned to bring about a more healthy state of that community. In this sense it is holistic. Health is a subjective notion, reaching into all aspects of people's lives. The World Health Organization (WHO) declaration defines health as "a state of complete physical, mental and social well-being" (WHO/UNICEF 1978). Spiritual well-being may be added to this definition (Table 23.1).

### TABLE 23.1

#### Definitions and States of Health

Health: a state of complete physical, social, mental, and spiritual well-being, not just the absence of disease and infirmity

**Four States of Well-being:**

| | |
|---|---|
| Physical well-being | e.g. sickness (morbidity), death (mortality), life expectancy, work satisfaction, happiness and other "feel-good" indicators |
| Social well-being | e.g. housing, literacy, employment, poverty, and population growth |
| Mental well-being | e.g. mental illness, abuse, crime, violence, and delinquency |
| Spiritual well-being | e.g. religiosity and creed |

## Traditional Health and Healing

Our knowledge of health practices prior to the arrival of Western medicine is sparse. We have a few detailed accounts by early explorers, in which islanders were reported as "robust and healthy" and "living on healthy islands" (Howe 1984). It was also observed that "diseases were few in number and comparatively simple in their character," though such observations "may point to a poor medical awareness in the missionaries, or to the low expectations they held" (Lange 1984). Lange notes that in Polynesia, yaws, filariasis, and intestinal parasitism were endemic, but not fatal. He concludes that "accurate retrospective diagnosis is difficult and often impossible" (Lange 1984).

The historical interface between traditional health and introduced standards of health is being reassessed today (Parsons 1985). It is likely that we may never know the full extent to which health was good or bad, though archaeologists and medical historians offer us pieces of the picture for consideration. As several scholars argue, the political agenda behind the early writings must always be taken into account (Arnold 1993).

Nicholson's analysis of nineteenth-century Maori health considers four images of indigenous peoples: the Noble, the Romantic, the Amalgamative, and the Dying Savage. These alternative approaches color the accounts of health and medicine for the early contact period. He argues that the representations of biological and cultural inferiority of non-European peoples were structured by convention and ideology, in accordance with the audiences addressed (Nicholson 1993).

Bushnell (1993) also suggests two pictures, one that Hawaiians were so inbred that they were predisposed to suffer from contagious diseases, the other that Hawaiians had been spared the ravages of epidemics, due to their isolation. A general picture of well-being emerged when writers contrasted islanders' health status with that in their homelands. Of course they may not often have seen the sick or disabled or witnessed death, so had a rather rosy picture in their minds. They are also not likely to have recognized unfamiliar symptomatologies and diseases.

Irregularity of food supply may have been apparent only to those who stayed long enough to witness and experience the problem (Pollock et al. 1989). Missionaries, with relatively long stays, often provide incisive comments on stature, birthing practices, and the large amount of food eaten, particularly at celebrations, by some sectors of the population. Warfare was condemned, as were practices of widow strangulation and infanticide, and "strange" birthing customs. Venereal disease was occasionally mentioned. The use of turmeric (which can be considered a spiritual healing practice) was noted, but not explained.

Sicknesses prevalent in precontact times included yaws in many Pacific Island societies, malaria in inland New Guinea and Solomon Islands, and widespread filariasis. As Bligh recorded: "We already see them with dreadful Cancers, Consumptions, Fevers, Fits and the Scropula (sic) in a Shocking degree, and we may infer many incidental diseases besides" (quoted in Howe 1984:49). Degenerative diseases such as arthritis have been detected from skeletal material. Infant and maternal mortality varied from society to society, but came to be accepted culturally. For example, in the Marshall Islands, children were not traditionally named or welcomed into society with a *kemeem*, or party, until one year after birth.

Since major disorders were believed to be caused by the gods (Parsons 1985), they had to be propitiated at the same time healers assisted the sick person. Medicine was an integral part of the belief system, and as such was treated ritually. It is thus not surprising that many modern-day Polynesians, for whom the Christian faith is very strong, continue to consult their traditional healers, with simultaneous prayers, often along with medical treatment (Finau 1994a).

Traditional healing as practiced before the arrival of Western medicine in the Pacific was generally considered less efficacious for the diseases that followed European contact. As Macpherson and Macpherson (1990) demonstrated, Samoans have particular ways of thinking about and explaining an illness, as defined by their culture. These attitudes have changed over time, but still shape the ways in which Samoans explain and react to illness today.

Food is a central feature in Samoan health beliefs, as in the proposition that "people who eat well are less likely to get sick" (Macpherson and Macpherson 1990). This is an important issue to consider before labeling Samoans (and other Polynesians) obese. To attempt to remedy an illness, such as heart disease, by asking a Polynesian to eat less may be counterproductive. Understanding the place of food in the culture necessitates that it be seen as more than just material input. Eating is a symbolic act that is integrated with generosity and the social well-being of the group (Pollock 1992).

Local plants used in healing have been recorded for many Pacific societies and remain useful compendia of one part of health practice. Seemann's account in 1860 of plant uses in Fiji indicates that many of these plants had multiple uses, with medicinal uses overlapping for various illness categories. Similarly, Biggs appends a list of plants to his discussion of traditional medicine in East Futuna with the heading Pharmacopoeia Futunensis (Biggs 1985). Many plants held curative properties for a range of ailments; and many ailments could be cured with a range of plants. Several such lists exist for Pacific societies. The pursuit of the chemical properties of many plants used in Pacific healing has become a subdiscipline in its own right—ethnopharmacology—and an issue of intellectual property ownership (Parsons 1985).

Healing methods in Pacific societies took four general forms: a beverage prepared from a mixture of leaves or bark in liquid form; insertions of crushed leaves and other material into various orifices of the body; massage, particularly of the limbs or trunk, using oils and other lubricants made from local plant and animal materials; and surgery and manipulation, using trephining, bone setting, wound closure, and pus drainage to treat many physical conditions (Ludvigson 1985). The practice of massage has continued into the present more noticeably than the others, in part because it offers the bodily contact that is so important in the healing process (MacDonald 1985). All these treatments are forms of social acceptance, as opposed to the social marginality associated with a period of sickness promoted by Western medicine.

Our assessments of non-Western health care have been revised over the last twenty years as we examine traditional health practices with more care. Local practices were downgraded following European contact (Denoon 1988), but have subsequently become acceptable. This change in attitude is being reinforced both by the promotion of traditional medicine as a legitimate and efficacious alternative in modern Pacific health care systems, as well as by our increased understanding of the cultural foundations of these non-Western healing beliefs and practices (Finau 1994a).

## The Impact of Western Intrusion

Historically, island communities were linked into a "sea of islands," which was traversed frequently. As contacts with a wider world increased, so the scale of health concerns also increased. New diseases followed soon after contact. Influenza, measles, leprosy, diarrheal diseases, tuberculosis, and poliomyelitis each took its toll of the population, not always fatally, but certainly in very debilitating ways (Lange 1984). Islanders had few medicines for their own use and quickly exhausted their supplies in the face of major epidemics such as the influenza outbreaks of 1877 and 1919. (The first outbreak was said to have been introduced to Fiji by one of Sir Arthur Gordon's staff.) Similar problems with measles led to a loss of about 40% of the Fijian population in the 1880s (Cliff and Hagget 1985). Local medicines were not considered adequate to deal with the new diseases.

New forms of treatment and medicine were needed for introduced epidemic diseases. MacLeod and Lewis (1988) have argued that medicine became a new tool of empire, enabling colonial governments to assert their influence more deeply into the fabric of Pacific societies. Indeed, Lavelua Queen Amelia of Wallis asserted her requirement that the new representative of French power after 1888 must be a naval doctor. Dr. Maxime Viala (1919) was the second medical resident to fill the post, carrying out his work in Wallis between 1906 and 1910. He recorded the high incidence of filariasis (and the local means of excising the offending swelling), as well as leprosy, tuberculosis, and yaws.

Many people died from these disease outbreaks, but the degree of impact is uncertain. We do know that some populations, such as the Marquesans, were severely decimated; mothers in child-birth were particularly heavy casualties (Rallu 1990). The reduced fertility of a number of populations such as the Marquesan eventually gave way to a gradual increase in fertility, until another influenza or measles epidemic arrived.

Rallu's (1990) historical demographic analysis of Marquesan and Melanesian data has given us a picture of how contacts on particular islands affected morbidity and fertility. His analysis of Marquesan medical records for the period 1886 to 1945 shows an early decline in the population size (with a mean of 2% annually), followed by an intense crisis of mortality between 1911 and 1925. Thereafter, mortality rates halved and fecundity levels increased, leading to a new stabilization of the Marquesan population.

Rallu's parallel assessment of Melanesian populations in the nineteenth century draws on data for the northern Vanuatu islands. Rapid depopulation occurred at the end of the nineteenth century at a time of frequent contact with new arrivals. When the majority of survivors became immunized, the population stabilized, assisted by new programs of sanitation and other health protection measures.

Data to validate this period of infectious diseases are drawn from medical records of the times. But these were likely to be incomplete and inaccurate, since systems for reporting sickness and deaths, particularly from rural areas, were not well established. Causes of death, or the diagnoses of some diseases, were also subject to inaccuracies. For example, dengue was "often clinically diagnosed as influenza" (Lewis and Rapaport 1995). The degree of error cannot be assessed, but we must nevertheless remain alert to building major schema on the basis of unverifiable data.

McArthur's demographic reconstruction of the Pacific in the eighteenth and nineteenth centuries (1967) is used frequently as a baseline for health assessment, along with estimates of deaths and births and Annual Medical Reports. Data for Fiji and Papua New Guinea are perhaps the most inclusive, though all colonies and dependencies were expected to include a report on health status in their annual reports. Since independence this data has become more scattered. The Secretariat of the Pacific Community requests annual health reports from all its member countries, but it has no "teeth" with which to enforce its request, and the quality of data across the Pacific remains inconsistent (Finau 1994b, O'Leary 1995).

Summary reviews of disease incidence and health in the Pacific, however, provide useful syntheses of the reports and personal research available thus far. Marshall's "Disease Ecology of Australia and Oceania" (1990-91) provides a detailed assessment of some twenty diseases, ranging from leprosy, upper respiratory infections, and pertussis to syphilis, gonorrhea, and alcohol and tobacco use. This assessment is an excellent reference for a scholar seeking to find a few initial leads for research. It is clear that the range of diseases affecting Pacific populations has increased. For example, only seven diseases were reported for Nauru in the League of Nations Report for 1923, whereas Marshall included some twenty commonly occurring diseases a decade ago.

Malaria is a communicable disease that is still a serious concern. In New Guinea it is hyperendemic in the hot, wet lowlands (Marshall 1990). The proximity of large village units that resulted from colonial administrative edicts facilitated the spread of the disease from the lowlands to the highlands. The development of strains resistant to established drugs is a further complication. Malaria is becoming more common in Fiji, and cases have occasionally appeared in western Polynesia; the eastward spread is expected to continue with global warming (Hales and Woodward 1995). Malaria is a major health concern for mothers and young children, not only because of the resulting anemia, but also because the fevers are so debilitating.

Medical systems were introduced into Pacific Island colonies in the nineteenth century, alongside missionary activities. Hospitals were built in port towns, staffed with doctors and nurses drawn from either the missions or the colonial governments (e.g. Viala 1919). Rural populations were poorly served, other than by a nurse who was a missionary. With rapid urbanization since 1945, rural populations have continued to be distanced from health services, though health clinics in rural areas became more numerous in the 1950s. In contrast with the hospitals, these clinics were staffed by local people, mainly male, trained for two or three months initially, and provided with minimal facilities and drugs. Pregnant women had to travel considerable distances if they needed specialist attention. In the face of such minimal access to Western health care, it is not surprising that traditional systems of health care have been maintained.

A distinction between communicable and noncommunicable diseases is commonly made, with communicable diseases being superseded by noncommunicable diseases (Coyne 1984, Taylor et al. 1989). This "epidemiological transition" is paralleled by a demographic transition: a lowering of death rates, followed by a lowering in birthrates. According to this framework, most of the Pacific Islands are in a transitional phase, with varying life expectancies and high birthrates (Table 23.2).

Transition theory does not explicitly include the role of indigenous healing, cultural views of the body, the role of healers and hospitals, and non-Western beliefs about the causation of illness and maintenance of health. Since before colonial interventions no statistics were available, this latter-day picture cannot include the long earlier period during which populations managed their health. Nor does it anticipate or account for the reemergence of infectious diseases such as tuberculosis and HIV/AIDS.

## Diseases of Modernization?

The period following World War II has been labeled by health transitionalists as the beginning of the modernization of health, though this label may be contested. The emergence of "diseases of modernization" has been associated with the transition from communicable to noncommunicable diseases (Baker et al. 1986, Lewis and Rapaport 1995, Zimmet et al. 1990). Foremost among these diseases are diabetes, coronary heart disease, and various cancers (Bloom 1987).

### TABLE 23.2

**Pacific Island Populations Classified According to Their Positions Along the Demographic and Epidemiological Transitions** (after Taylor, Lewis, and Levy 1989)

| Early | Transitional | Completed |
|---|---|---|
| Papua New Guinea | New Caledonia | Hawai'i |
| Solomon Islands | Fiji | New Zealand |
| Vanuatu | Western Samoa | Guam |
| Kiribati | Tonga | Cook Islands |
| FSM | Marshall Islands | American Samoa |
|  | French Polynesia | Northern Marianas |
|  | Wallis & Futuna | Niue |
|  | Nauru | Palau |
|  | Tuvalu |  |

Diabetes mellitus (particularly the non–insulin-dependent form, or maturity-onset diabetes) has been closely studied under the auspices of WHO. Rates of diabetes ranged from 0.8% for a rural Papua New Guinea group to 30.3% for Nauruans (Zimmet et al. 1990, Taylor and Thoma 1985). Rural populations showed a generally much lower level of diabetes than migrant and urban populations (Coyne 1984). Obesity is a targeted factor, associated with a high-calorie but poor nutritional intake and reduced energy expenditure (Zimmet and King 1985). The role of genetics is the subject of much debate (Pollock 1995).

Cardiovascular disease has been reported as the leading cause of death in several populations in the 1970s (Bloom 1987). But since causes of death are not appropriately recorded in many Pacific Island countries, the information may be inaccurate. A Tokelau study (Prior et al. 1995) has followed the incidence of heart disease among those on the home atoll and emigrants in New Zealand since 1967. This epidemiological team also studied heart disease in two Cook Island populations, as well as a Maori and Pakeha New Zealand population, noting rising levels of heart disease and hypertension in urbanized communities (Fleming and Prior 1981).

Levels of hypertension range from "none" in Pukapuka and the Western Highlands of Papua New Guinea to about 35% in American Samoa, Hawai'i, Guam, and Nauru. Circulatory diseases are an increasing problem in Fiji, with the recorded growth rate most marked over the last twenty years. Male deaths in Fiji attributed to hypertension are in a 3:1 ratio with female deaths, yet twice as many women (often diagnosed in association with pregnancy admissions) are being treated as men (Ripley et al. 1996). Environmental and genetic causal factors are both postulated. Diets comprising high salt and fat and low fiber, as found in many processed imported foods, are commonly blamed. Stress and lack of exercise are two other related factors (Coyne 1984). Bloom (1987) adds cigarette smoking.

Dietary change and reduced exercise patterns are considered to contribute significantly to increasing levels of cardiovascular disease, hypertension, and diabetes, particularly in urban populations. Obesity has been cited as an important risk factor for maturity-onset diabetes and cardiovascular disease, even though cardiovascular disease incidence levels are low in Pacific countries (Hodge et al. 1996). However, recommending against obesity strikes at the heart of Pacific Island peoples' values regarding food, as discussed above (Pollock 1995). Furthermore, Swinburne et al. (1994) have shown that the Body Mass Index (widely used as a measure of obesity) may not be appropriate to the body size of Polynesians.

Cancers are significant as a health concern, because they not only cause death, but also can be disabling and can devastate the lives of individuals and their caretakers. Data on cancer in the South Pacific are sparse (Bloom 1987), with types of cancers often not recorded (Coyne 1984). In Tonga, for example, cancer was the second leading cause of death, accounting for 16% to 18% of all deaths recorded (Bloom 1987). But deaths on outer islands may not be clearly identified as to cause, and thus these figures apply only to deaths for urban Tongans.

Liver cancer in men and cervical and breast cancers in women are the most frequently reported cancers (Coyne 1984). Oral cancer incidences are high in Papua New Guinea, associated with betel chewing.

Mental health has been considered by a few specialists. Levy's monograph on Tahitians provides an incisive examination of Tahitian personal organization using psychoanalytic theories (Levy 1973). He found similarities in personality forms between the societies of Polynesia and Micronesia that he surveyed. Their responses to stresses of change were of acceptance rather than resistance. Models of personality and psychological structure were simplistic, he noted. He questioned whether the similarities were "artefacts of shared emphases of the common intellectual subculture of Micronesian and Polynesian specialists" (Levy 1972).

Gallimore's study of the psychological aspects of the Nānākuli community in Hawai'i also raised issues of Polynesian personality, particularly with relation to education performance. Graves and Graves (1975) conducted several studies of the impact of modernization on the personality of Cook Island people, both in Rarotonga and in New Zealand; they subtitled one report "How to make an Up-Tight, Rivalrous Westerner out of an Easy going, Generous Pacific Islander." A review of mental health in the Pacific concluded that mental illness is relatively rare, but with rising incidence of schizophrenia, depression, and anxiety among Westernized and migrant populations (Allen and Laycock 1997).

Disability in Pacific societies is a much neglected topic. The role of culture in the definition of disability is discussed in a forthcoming volume, which includes "disability stories" (Fitzgerald and Armstrong 1996).

## Mortality and Life Expectancy

Death registration, like morbidity data, is deficient in most Pacific countries. There have been attempts to adjust for under-enumeration by applying indirect methods to census or survey data. However, this has not improved the identification of cause of death. The causes of death vaguely defined or not recorded at all are estimated to be about 25% to 50% of overall mortality. Table 23.3 shows the status of mortality information in the Pacific.

### TABLE 23.3

**Status of Mortality Information in the Pacific Islands**
(after Taylor, Lewis and Levy 1985)

| Islands in which mortality information is generally reliable | Islands in which mortality information is unreliable or suspect |
|---|---|
| American Samoa | Federated States of Micronesia |
| Cook Islands | Fiji |
| French Polynesia | Kiribati |
| Guam | Marshall Islands |
| Hawai'i | Papua New Guinea |
| Nauru | Samoa |
| New Caledonia | Solomon Islands |
| New Zealand | Tonga |
| Niue | Tuvalu |
| Northern Mariana Islands | Vanuatu |
| Palau | |
| Tokelau | |
| Vanuatu | |
| Wallis and Futuna | |

Hospital mortality is disproportionately represented in the existing information. It is thus not surprising that reported mortality and morbidity statistics mainly reflect the experience of the urban dwellers. The leading causes of death include both infectious diseases (especially respiratory diseases) and noninfectious diseases (like cardiovascular diseases, cancer, endocrine, nutritional, and metabolic diseases), as well as accidents, injuries, and congenital/perinatal problems (Taylor et al. 1989).

Relatively low life-expectancies and high infant mortality rates occur among peoples exposed to malaria, and on islands distant from medical expertise. Higher life-expectancy rates have been associated with dependent territories, such as the Cook Islands, French Polynesia, Niue and American Samoa, where metropolitan powers maintain the health care system and offer medical evacuation services (Taylor et al. 1989).

Longer-lived populations are clearly placing a new stress on island social systems (Figure 23.1). Old people today are more active and require both food and some level of hospital or medical care. They also may want to work and to retain their autonomy. This is a new challenge because there are no precedents for such long-lived populations in the Pacific, and new social mores

### Table 23.4 — Demographic and Service Variables for the Pacific Islands (UNICEF 1993, DBEDT 1994, SNZ 1996)

| | Total Population 1992 | Annual growth rate % | Population <15 years % | Crude birth rate % | Life expectancy at birth in years | Access to safe water % | Access to adequate sanitation % | Access to health services % | Access to electricity % |
|---|---|---|---|---|---|---|---|---|---|
| American Samoa | 50,900 | 3.7 | 38.1 | 39.3 | 70.3 | 99 | 97 | 95 | 94 |
| Cook Islands | 19,500 | 1.0 | 37.0 | 27.0 | 69.8 | 99 | 96 | 100 | 87 |
| Federated States of Micronesia | 114,800 | 3.6 | 46.8 | 37.9 | 64.1 | 30 | 61 | 75–80 | - |
| Fiji | 752,700 | 0.6 | 38.2 | 24.4 | 63.1 | 92 | 99 | 98 | 48 |
| French Polynesia | 205,800 | 2.5 | 36.0 | 27.5 | 69.0 | 98 | 98 | - | 91 |
| Guam | 140,100 | 2.3 | 30.0 | 27.2 | 72.1 | 100 | 99 | 100 | 98 |
| Hawai'i | 1,200,000 | 1.4 | 21.5 | 17.2 | 78.0 | - | - | - | - |
| Kiribati | 76,000 | 2.3 | 40.3 | 29.4 | 60.2 | 65 | 53 | 85 | - |
| Marshall Islands | 50,000 | 4.2 | 51.0 | 49.2 | 61.1 | 50 | 74 | 95 | 59 |
| Nauru | 9,800 | 1.6 | 46.6 | 41.0 | 55.5 | 90 | 97 | 100 | 99 |
| New Caledonia | 176,900 | 2.0 | 32.6 | 25.3 | 69.1 | 90 | 88 | - | 85 |
| New Zealand | 3,618,302 | 1.4 | 23.0 | 15.5 | 76.5 | - | - | - | - |
| Niue | 2,200 | 2.5 | 36.7 | 22.8 | 66.0 | 100 | 100 | 100 | 98 |
| Northern Mariana Islands | 54,000 | 9.5 | 23.8 | 38.0 | 66.8 | 99 | 96 | 100 | 91 |
| Palau | 15,900 | 2.2 | 30.1 | 22.0 | 67.0 | 88 | 98 | 75 | 97 |
| Papua New Guinea | 4,056,000 | 2.3 | 41.8 | 34.2 | 49.6 | 23 | - | 88 | 39 |
| Pitcairn | 100 | - | 31.8 | - | - | - | - | 100 | - |
| Samoa | 163,000 | 0.2 | 41.1 | 28.7 | 63.1 | 70 | 100 | 100 | 38 |
| Solomon Islands | 337,000 | 3.5 | 47.3 | 38.3 | 60.7 | 61 | 12 | 80 | 61 |
| Tokelau | 1,600 | 0.0 | 42.6 | 32.0 | 68.0 | 100 | 65 | 100 | 100 |
| Tonga | 97,400 | 0.5 | 40.6 | 34.2 | 69.0 | 100 | 72 | 100 | 93 |
| Tuvalu | 9,100 | 1.7 | 34.7 | 31.0 | 67.2 | 100 | 78 | 100 | 39 |
| Vanuatu | 156,500 | 2.5 | 44.1 | 38.0 | 62.8 | 87 | 91 | 75 | 14 |
| Wallis & Futuna | 14,100 | 1.3 | 41.9 | 28.1 | 68.0 | 96 | 55 | 100 | 77 |

*data for urban area only

*Figure 23.1. A Tokelau migrant in New Zealand has returned to visit her disabled mother on Fakaofo, Tokelau (photo MR).*

may be required. Postmenopausal care has not been widely addressed. Can we thus consider increased life expectancy a measure of improved health care?

Saving the lives of infants and mothers has been reasonably successful in Pacific societies, as the drops in infant mortality indicate. But it has also contributed to rapid population growth. This in turn has led to the introduction of methods to control women's fertility, but with low acceptance rates (7%–30%) (Haberkorn 1995). Many women have expected to have a baby every two years, and their husbands also expect this (Pollock fieldnotes 1996); thus there are strong deterrents to reducing the population growth.

With 50% or more of many Pacific populations under the age of fifteen, many public health concerns arise. Immunizing all those children, monitoring their dental care—let alone their nutritional status—and overseeing the health of school children are all expenses on the public purse. With funds extremely limited, and little private care, what is the future of the health of these populations?

## Diet and Nutrition

Food-related problems have been identified as important contributing factors to morbidity and mortality. Most of the problems lie in the system of food provisioning, rather than at the level of digestion, absorption, and excretion (Pollock 1992). Health care planners need to take on board the cultural importance of food in order to offer nutrition education programs

**TABLE 23.5**    **Mortality and Nutritional Status Among Pacific Children (UNICEF 1993, DBEDT 1994, SNZ 1996)**

| | IMR 1980 | IMR "latest" | CMR 1980 | CMR "latest" | % Breast feeding at 12 mos. | Weight/age '80 %, 0–4 yrs. | Height/age '80 %, 0–4 yrs. | Weight/Height '80 %, 0–4 yrs. |
|---|---|---|---|---|---|---|---|---|
| American Samoa | 18 | 11 | - | 16 | - | - | - | - |
| Cook Islands | 28 | 26 | - | 32 | - | 1 | 1 | 1 |
| Federated States of Micronesia | - | 52 | - | 72 | 59 | 13 | 10 | 1 |
| Fiji | 41 | 22 | 86 | 41 | - | 15 | - | 15 |
| French Polynesia | 23 | 11 | - | 14 | 10 | - | 2 | 1 |
| Guam | 12 | 12 | 15 | 15 | - | - | - | - |
| Hawai'i | - | 6 | - | - | - | - | - | - |
| Kiribati | 82 | 65 | 132 | 88 | - | 15 | 2 | 8 |
| Marshall Islands | 60 | 63 | - | 92 | 62 | 20 | 7 | 24 |
| Nauru | 31 | - | 42 | - | - | - | - | - |
| New Caledonia | 21 | 11 | - | 14 | - | - | - | - |
| New Zealand | - | 8 | - | 8 | - | - | - | - |
| Niue | 12 | 12 | - | 12 | 17 | 2 | 2 | 1 |
| Northern Mariana Islands | 21 | 19 | 33 | - | - | - | - | - |
| Palau | 27 | 25 | 39 | 35 | 53 | - | - | - |
| Papua New Guinea | 72 | - | 114 | - | 95 | 38 | - | 6 |
| Samoa | 33 | 28 | 51 | 35 | 53 | 17 | - | - |
| Solomon Islands | 46 | 38 | 86 | 65 | 91 | 23 | 12 | 3 |
| Tokelau | - | 30 | - | 30 | - | - | - | - |
| Tonga | 40 | 26 | 44 | 31 | 53 | 2 | 2 | 1 |
| Tuvalu | 42 | 40 | 77 | 56 | 66 | - | - | - |
| Vanuatu | 94 | 45 | - | 58 | 77 | 23 | 7 | 13 |
| Wallis & Futuna | 49 | 13 | 74 | - | - | - | - | - |

IMR: Infant mortality rates/1,000 live births, CMR: Child mortality rates (<5 yrs.)/1,000 live births

that are locally appropriate. Food availability, affordability, and acceptability are cultural issues with health consequences. Food imports have been considered as political and economic concerns more than for their health implications. An increasing number of island states have Food and Nutrition Committees in place with a range of expertise to offer health-promoting political advice.

A study of diet on a small outer atoll in the Marshalls in the late 1960s showed that the main local food, breadfruit, was complemented by imported rice when the former was out of season (Pollock, 1970 and 1974). Flour and sugar were purchased as money was available. Very sweet tea was the popular drink, and when mixed with rice was the major weaning food for infants (Pollock 1970). The increasing use of sugar is of particular concern for the wider health issues of dental caries and "empty" calories.

Diets of rice, or breadfruit and tea, perhaps with some fish once or twice a week are still eaten on Namu today. In Samoa, Bindon (1982) recorded a list of some forty foods that Samoans ate from time to time, at least partly reflecting an increase in imported foods. An ongoing study of the diet of Naduri Fijians over ten-year periods since 1953 also indicates similar trends. Sugar intake is noticeably increasing over this period (Parkinson, pers. comm.).

Despite increased use of imported foods, local foods retain a place in the diet (Figure 23.2). They have a value beyond that of "just food." They symbolize identity with a traditional lifestyle, appealing particularly to the tastes of older Pacific people, particularly those who have resided away from home. Despite their expense, they continue to be desired and used alongside Western foods (Pollock 1975 and Pollock et al. 1989).

Dietary studies need to be correlated with maturity-onset diabetes studies in order to pinpoint more closely the particular foods that lead to the onset of diabetes. The daily pattern of eating may be important, as Pacific peoples move from only one meal during an active day on their home island to a "grazing"

*Figure 23.2.* The islanders of Atiu, a makatea *island in the Southern Cooks, are relatively well fed with taro, bananas, and ocean produce (photo MR).*

pattern of eating four or five times a day while working or sedentary in an urban environment (Pollock 1995a).

Dietary studies have shown that caloric intakes vary from 7,200 for Nauruan males (Zimmet 1985) to 1,870 calories on Namu atoll, and less during times of food scarcity (Pollock 1970). How food is distributed among household members, such as women's consignment to eating "leftovers," is a vital question for assessments of diet and health. Women's anemia has been attributed in part to low dietary intake, particularly of protein, which may be scarce in everyday diets.

Hankin et al. (1970) discovered some severe deficiencies in Chamorro diet that led to recommendations for supplementation through Guam and CNMI (Commonwealth of the Northern Mariana Islands) health services. Urban populations have begun to show signs of severe nutritional deficiencies in the 1980s due to high intake of processed foods, which have taken on high status along with their high cost (Bloom 1987, Pollock 1992).

Reduced breastfeeding and the availability of powdered milk infant feeding substitutes have led at least two Pacific nations, Papua New Guinea and the Marshall Islands, to "ban the bottle" in an attempt to give children a better nutritional start to life. The impact of this new regime not only on the health of the infants, but also on working mothers will need to be assessed.

## Women's Health

Women have demanded more attention to their personal health problems since 1981, when they raised health as a key topic at the first Pacific Regional Women's Conference. The lack of female health staff in the rural and outer island clinics deters women from seeking assistance when they have internal or genital pains. The WHO emphasis on Primary Health Care has drawn more women into the health scene (WHO/UNICEF 1978). Programs for upgrading Maternal and Infant Care have been established, but women have a variety of health needs that still need attention (Seniloli 1995).

The place of women in the community as the first-line caregivers has not been recognized adequately (Schoeffel 1986, Pollock 1995b). Women spend a lot of their energy attending to the needs of the wider family and community group. Women are the main healers, whose skills are called on when no other help is available. Their incorporation into primary health care provisioning at the village or district level strengthens their position in society and takes account of what has been significant but overlooked for too long (Pollock 1995b).

More women are needed in health policymaking. They have wide personal knowledge of this sector, but have been denied opportunities to contribute to the health plans and policies at the national level (Pollock 1993b). Nursing has attracted a number of Pacific women, who gain recognition for the intensity of their caring skills. But nurses are secondary to doctors (Finau 1990). In the medical section of health, women doctors need to be actively supported to enable them to complete the long training period apart from their families.

## Smoking, Alcohol, and Other Health Concerns

The use of tobacco has increased markedly, especially in the last thirty years. Rates of 88% for males and 51% for female Fijians have been recorded (Collins et al. 1996). The links between smoking and lung cancer and heart disease are widely publicized; despite educational health programs in schools, the number of young islanders taking up smoking continues to increase. In New Zealand, Maori women are increasing their use of tobacco while use by other sectors of the population is declining.

A study of smokers in rural and urban Viti Levu, Fiji, in 1994 found that 55% of adult males and 20% of adult females smoked. This has severe negative implications for reducing cardiovascular disease in Fiji. While smokers in this study saw limiting their smoking as desirable, they also associated smoking positively with leisure and relaxation, particularly with kava drinking (Meo et al. 1996).

Tobacco is widely cultivated throughout the Pacific, making it readily available. "Rope" tobacco is smoked more in rural areas than are preprepared cigarettes, which are costly; and despite the cost, cigarettes carry considerable positive status value among young people today (Figure 23.3). The correlation of high levels of smoking with low educational achievements has been widely noted, as have the health implications of smoking.

A conference to examine tobacco control in Micronesia looked at legislation options, including prohibiting sales to minors, but enforcement is difficult if not impossible. Education programs with schools and young people have been considered the best option (Durand and Abraham 1996). In the Pacific, there have thus far been minimal resistance and few counter messages to the tobacco industry's powerful lobbying and

**Figure 23.3.** Smoking is widespread among adult males in the Tuamotus (photo MR).

marketing. Indeed, governments often support the establishment of cigarette factories for "economic benefits."

Alcohol use has increased steadily in the last thirty years, particularly among urban populations. Attempts to keep districts "dry" have faced real battles, some of which have become decidedly political. Marshall's *Weekend Warriors* (1979) traced a campaign by the women of Chuuk to reduce the amount of alcohol the men of the community consumed, as this consumption was costly and led to violence. Yet the positive masculine image associated with alcohol consumption proved difficult for the women to counteract. The campaign had some successes and some failures.

Alcohol has been widely linked with road deaths due to drunken driving. Taylor et al. (1985) found that alcohol was a major factor in road accident deaths, significantly lowering the life expectancy for males. A study of alcohol consumption by young males on Wallis and Futuna revealed that young people were concerned about their drinking habits, particularly where these led to serious road accidents. But there are few other ways to socialize in this traditional, sex-segregated society (Pollock and Tafili 1988 and 1991).

HIV and AIDS data from WHO show that the Pacific Islands region has a much less acute problem than elsewhere (Sarda and Harrison 1995). Governments are trying to keep the figures low by raising awareness, but discussions of sexuality are notoriously circumscribed culturally. Papua New Guinea had 247 reported HIV cases in 1995, whereas American Samoa reported none and Samoa reported one case of AIDS and one of HIV. These infections are likely to result in a significant demand for treatment and supportive health services (Sarda and Harrison 1995).

Ciguatera fish poisoning has become an important concern in several islands and appears to be at least partly a consequence of reef perturbation. Regionally specific health problems include "pig bel" and kuru in Highland Papua New Guinea, achromatopsia in Pingelap, and lytica-bodig in Guam and Rota. Youth suicide and kava overindulgence are problematic in some areas. Ways of accommodating the ill effects of these occurrences are present in local lore, though not often reported in the medical literature.

## Environmental and Sociopolitical Context

Environmental health issues are of increasing concern in the Pacific. In Papua New Guinea and Solomon Islands, logging has led to pollution and erosion. Waste disposal is especially problematic on crowded atolls, such as Tarawa, Kiribati. The regularity of natural disasters (such as cyclones) undermines development efforts and worsens the biological environment (Finau 1987c). Rising sea levels (possibly as much as 1 m per 40 years) are a serious worry for many atolls (Hales and Woodward 1995). Geographical distance between communities makes development and infrastructure maintenance difficult and expensive (Finau 1993).

Past nuclear testing by Britain, France, Australia, and the United States has been highly politicized (Finau 1987a). The health effects have not adequately been studied, though high incidences of goiter have been reported in the Marshall Islands. The level of local awareness of these concerns is low (Pollock 1996 fieldnotes, Wotje), but a few spokespeople have been able to seek compensation for their people (Pollock in press). Whether Tuamotuans will achieve such compensation for fallout from Moruroa and other French nuclear testing remains to be seen.

Economic limitations take their toll on health. In a global economy based on large scale, it is very difficult for small Pacific islands to achieve and sustain relative economic independence (Bertram and Watters 1985). A possible solution may lie in appropriate technologies that dissolve the constraints of smallness, fragmentation, and remoteness (Thomason et al. 1991). In order to take such a leap, innovative and entrepreneurial leaders must be available. These leaders must have multiple skills and be able to work in isolated areas. Health services need to keep pace with such developments.

In several Pacific Island societies, diverse ethnic groups are present, with differing health status and needs. Ethnic plurality may be due to immigrants (e.g. Fiji) or the diversity of the indigenous population (e.g. Papua New Guinea with 700 languages) (Finau et al. 1991). This pluralism has led to political instability and ethnic inequality. Indigenous populations have a disproportionately low share of wealth and power in Hawai'i, New Zealand, Fiji, and other island groups. Such ethnic disparities create differential morbidity and mortality expressions (Taylor et al. 1989).

Health also has political dimensions (Thomason et al. 1991). Many Pacific Island groups have achieved political independence. However, the presence of lingering colonialism (nuclear, educational, trade, and cultural) has led to the creation of satellite states (Hearn 1981). Pacific peoples find it increasingly difficult to shed the expectations of high material and status reward from Western academic qualifications, as well as the perception that Western goods are essential to a good life, even in remote Pacific islands (Finau 1987a and b and 1988).

## Health Care Issues

Health care systems have been formalized under Western colonial influence in order to respond to new concerns of illness, disease, and health. Today they are directed mainly at coping with diseases. They offer a range of options that may include: self-care by treating one's child or oneself; seeking care from others who will provide treatment or advice, whether in the form of traditional healing or Western medicine; or doing nothing because no solution is apparent. Health care decisions are frequently made jointly by members of the extended family (Chambers and Chambers 1985).

Traditional medicine and health practices require further attention (Finau 1994a, Pollock 1990). For example, do the practices work? Are they doing more harm than good? Are these practices available, accessible, acceptable, and affordable to communities? Are these practices effective, efficient, and equitable? The answers to these questions provide potential criteria for the continuation or termination of both Western and traditional medicine practice.

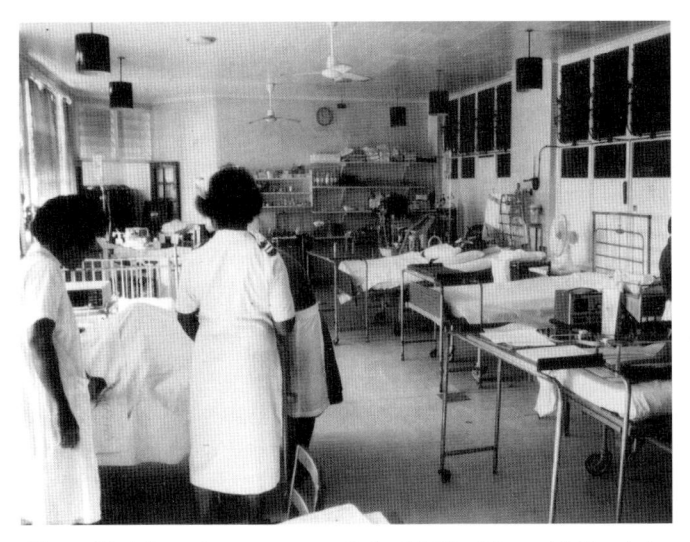

*Figure 23.4. Intensive care room, Colonial War Memorial Hospital, Suva, Fiji (photo LEM).*

For an appropriate health care system in the modern Pacific, both traditional medicine and Western scientific medicine have essential roles. Each can contribute, with traditional medicine focusing on holistic health care and Western scientific medicine specializing in mechanistic organ repairs. The former needs to be seen and revived as an integral part of culture and another vehicle for self-reliance and self-determination. The latter must be controlled to serve communities' needs and not vice versa.

Primary health care (Figure 23.5) attempts to address the main health problems in the community by providing a wide range of promotive, preventive, curative, and rehabilitative services in an affordable and appropriate fashion (WHO/UNICEF 1978, WHO 1981). This is to be accomplished with initiatives from the community and within existing resource constraints; the health care system must be very close to the people and within the boundaries of their worldview (Finau 1987a and b).

The important components implicit in the primary health care approach (WHO/UNICEF 1978, WHO 1981) may be summarized as

- dependence on community participation for planning and implementation
- low cost and affordability for communities
- equitable distribution of resources
- inclusion in primary health care of the following elements: education, food supply and nutrition, water supply and basic sanitation, maternal child health, immunization, prevention of endemic diseases, treatment of common diseases, and provision of essential drugs

Primary health care has been widely advocated. However, accumulated experience shows that several important constraints exist (Finau 1987b):

Lack of vision. There is a paucity of understanding of the dream, vision, or philosophical underpinning that shapes the choices made. Such vision is necessary in making decisions on family planning; the attack on poverty and social injustices versus the provision of curative medical facilities (Navarro 1981); and the preservation of life versus the slowing down of the aging process (Milio 1985). The visions of the average islander will differ considerably from those of the elites.

Managerial problems. Centralization of decision making and sluggish bureaucracy hinder appropriate response and resource allocation to community needs. The control and supervision of the peripheral activities are poor, sectorial coordination almost nonexistent, and total program evaluation practically nil. This produces poor motivation and threatens the credibility of health workers. The information systems are insufficient to be useful to evaluate and monitor health projects.

Political commitment. Available resources are dependent on aid rather than a fair entitlement of the common resources of the global community (Hau'ofa 1985). Rhetoric is not adequately backed with resource allocation. Provision of health services often occurs without an equitable distribution of existing public resources. Governments are building hospitals, attracting more technology, increasing medical specialization, and minimally reorienting the medical curriculums for doctors and nurses, while often neglecting the needs of rural people.

Opposition of the health profession. Physicians and other health professionals are worried that primary health care will decrease their income, status, and influence. A common claim is that the quality of service will be threatened; but this can be a subterfuge. Health professionals generally have a disproportionate ownership of and access to both wealth and power and are in the self-gratifying position of being consumers of public funds and controllers of the health market (Finau 1987a).

To overcome these constraints, communities must be informed and educated in a manner appropriate to Pacific Island environments and cultures. They must be enabled to articulate their problems and express themselves in terms understandable to others. Health professionals must be socialized to community-based health services. Nonclinical personnel must improve their training to counter the current monopoly of the medical profession in the health industry.

*Figure 23.5. A nurse dispenses primary health care in the clinic of Fakaofo, Tokelau (photo MR).*

## Has Pacific Health Improved or Worsened with Western Inputs?

Two papers dissenting over interpretations of acculturation and health in the Highlands of New Guinea highlight the temporal framework within which we view health. Wirsing (1985) suggests that isolated traditional societies, such as those in the Highlands of New Guinea, managed to survive and reproduce over two or three thousand years and must have been relatively healthy. In response, Dennett and Connell (1988) argue that acculturation toward a money economy has had a positive effect on nutritional status. Neither of these positions makes claims to meeting an absolute standard of health. Rather both arguments claim that the status of health of earlier populations differs from that in the present day. The validity of making judgments from present-day criteria is left open to question.

Similar questions relate to other parts of the Pacific. Using the notion of "modernization" and opposing it to "traditional societies," various authors (e.g. Fleming and Prior 1981, Baker et al. 1986, Zimmet et al. 1990) suggest that the modern era is distinguished by a high rate of noncommunicable diseases in contrast with the "traditional" era marked by high rates of infectious diseases causing high mortality. But is high mortality a good measure of health? A far greater number of people are affected today by epidemics of influenza, measles, or dengue because populations are larger. Also today the consequences of ill health may have greater social consequences, such as loss of income, and thus inability to provide for the family. Where family size is reduced, the level of dependency increases health concerns. (see Table 23.6).

Nutritional standards, like disease patterns, are based on Western medical criteria. These are not necessarily appropriate to Pacific populations. As we have seen with measures of obesity, worldwide standards may not be applicable. Cultural views of food must be taken into consideration, as they provide the mental as well as the physical satisfactions. Dietary adequacy has to meet cultural as well as biological criteria.

An assessment of health that includes a strong cultural component is a different exercise from measuring disease or medical status. In the past, populations were undoubtedly healthy, since their health criteria were part of their social values and fitted their own cultural and biological needs; they adjusted to innovations as they occurred. But Western diseases, medicine and health systems were founded on very specialized cultural criteria drawn from another social system.

The distance between local health criteria and Western medical standards has narrowed over time. Traditional healing persists, although in forms adjusted to modern-day living. Local foods are still valued. Western medical practitioners have come to appreciate the contributions of local healers, local herbal treatments, and community support for sick persons.

A Healthy Islands goal for the next century will need to rely on both local health and Western medicine, as only a combination of the two will be a culturally and economically feasible means of maintaining the well-being of peoples in the Pacific region.

### Table 23.6

**A Summary of the Health Effects of Development**
(after Finau 1993)

| | |
|---|---|
| **Direct health effects** | **Examples** |
| Occupational hazards | Injuries in construction, poisoning in leather tanning, or dust inhalation in saw mills |
| Overindulgent hazards | Alcohol abuse, stress and tiredness |
| **Indirect health effects** | |
| Lifestyle | Overeating, no exercise, drug abuse, promiscuity |
| Migration and Westernization | Dislocation, family breakdown, etc. |
| Other intermediate factors | Inability to handle cash, poverty, unemployment, and affluence |
| **Health assessment effects** | |
| Absence of impact assessment | Due to increased disease |
| Absence of health monitoring | Undetected poisoning |
| **Health service effects** | |
| Increase in use | Due to increased disease |
| Relocation of services | When mines close or open |
| Competition for resources with other sectors | |

# Bibliography

Allen J. S., and J. L. Laycock. 1997. Major mental illness in the Pacific: a review. *Pacific Health Dialog* 4(2):105–118.

Arnold, D., ed. 1993. *Imperial medicine and indigenous societies*. Manchester University Press.

Baker, P., J. M. Hanna, and T. S. Baker. 1986. *The changing Samoans: behaviour and health in transition*. New York: Oxford University Press.

Bertram, G. F., and R. F. Watters. 1985. The MIRAB economy in the South Pacific microstates. *Pacific Viewpoint* 27(1):47–59.

Biggs, B. 1985. Contemporary healing practices in East Futuna. In *Healing practices in the South Pacific*, ed. C. D. F. Parsons, 108–128. Laie, Hawai'i: The Institute for Polynesian Studies.

Bindon, J. 1982. Breadfruit, bananas, beef, and beer: modernization of the Samoan diet. *Ecology of Food and Nutrition* 12:49–60

Bloom, A. 1987. Health and nutrition in the Pacific: problems and policy issues. In *Human resources development in the Pacific*, ed. C. D. Throsby, 53–88. Canberra: National Centre for Development Studies, Pacific Policy Papers No. 3.

Bushnell, O. A. 1993. *The gifts of civilization: germs and genocide in Hawaii*. University of Hawai'i Press.

Chambers, A., and K. S. Chambers. 1985. Illness and healing in Nanumea, Tuvalu. In *Healing practices in the South Pacific.*, ed. C. D .F. Parsons, 16–50 Laie, Hawai'i: The Institute for Polynesian Studies.

Cliff, A., and P. Haggett. 1985. *The spread of measles in Fiji and the Pacific*. Canberra: ANU Dept. of Geography HG/18.

Collins, V. R., G. K. Dowse, and P. Zimmet. 1996. Smoking prevalence and trends in the Pacific. *Pacific Health Dialog* 3(1):87–95.

Coyne, T. 1984. *The effect of urbanization and western diet on the health of Pacific Island populations*. Noumea: South Pacific Commission Technical Paper No. 186.

Curtis, S., and A. Tarkett, 1996. *Health and Societies*. London: Arnold.

Dennett, G, and J. Connell. 1988. Acculturation and health in the Highlands of Papua New Guinea: dissent on diversity, diets and development. *Current Anthropology* 29(2):273–299.

Denoon, D. 1988. Medical services in Papua New Guinea, 1884–1984. In *Papua New Guinea: a century of colonial impact, 1884–1984*, ed. S. Latukefu, 317–332. Port Moresby: University of Papua New Guinea.

Department of Business, Economic Development, and Tourism (DBEDT). 1994. *The State of Hawaii data book: a statistical abstract*. Honolulu: DBEDT.

Dever, G. J., and S. A. Finau. 1995. The Yanuca Island Declaration: Pacific health in the twenty-first century. *Pacific Health Dialog* 2(2):70–74.

Dever G. J., S. A. Finau, and R. Hunton. 1997. The Pacific medical education model: introducing the process of innovation. *Pacific Health Dialog* 4(1):177–190.

Durand, A. M., and I. J. Abraham. 1996. Tobacco control: a Pacific conference. *Pacific Health Dialog* 3(1):74–76.

ESCAP/SPC. 1982 *Report of the ESCAP/SPC Conference Seminar on Population Problems of Small Island Countries of ESCAP/SPC Region*. New Caledonia: Asian Population Studies Series.

Feinberg, R. 1979. *Anutan concepts of disease: a Polynesian study*. Laie, Hawai'i: Institute for Polynesian Studies, Monograph No. 5.

Finau, S. A. 1981. Traditional medicine in the Pacific health service. *Pacific Perspective* 9:92–93.

Finau, S. A. 1987a. Health science of the South Pacific: the challenges. *New Zealand Journal of Agricultural Science* 21:2–5.

Finau, S. A. 1987b. Primary health care, community development, and the South Pacific. *SSED Review* 8(15):62–63.

Finau, S. A. 1987c. Community priorities following disaster: a case study from Tonga. *Social Science and Medicine* 28(11):961–966.

Finau, S. A. 1988. Bureaucracy and the Pacific health services. *Pacific Studies* 14:131–144.

Finau, S. A. 1990. Pacific doctors and nurses: union or divorce towards the year 2000. *SSED Review* 18:54–57.

Finau, S. A. 1992/1993. Pacific health: an analysis for training new leaders. *Asia Pacific Journal of Public Health* 6(2):46–53.

Finau, S. A. 1993. Health and development in the Pacific: which way to die? *Papua New Guinea Medical Journal* 36(4):324–336.

Finau, S. A. 1994a. Traditional health practices in the modern Pacific: blessing or dilemma? *New Zealand Medical Journal* 107:14–17.

Finau, S. A. 1994b. National health information systems in the Pacific : in search of a future. *Journal of Health Planning and Policy* 9(2):161–170.

Finau, S. A. 1995. Pacific women: development for better health. *Pacific Health Dialog* 2(1):98–103.

Finau, S. A. 1996. Health, environment and development: towards a Pacific paradigm. *Pacific Health Dialog* 3(2):266–278.

Finau, S. A. 1997. From the Yanuca Declaration to the Rarotonga Agreement: verbiage on Pacific health en route to the 21st Century. *Pacific Health Dialog* 4(2):52–58.

Fitzpatrick, M., and J. Armstrong. 1996. *Disability in the Pacific*. MS - pers. comm.

Fleming, C., and I. Prior, 1981. *Migration, adaptation and health in the Pacific*. Wellington, NZ: Wellington Postgraduate Medical Society.

Graves, T. D., and N. B. Graves. Stress and health: modernization and health in traditional Polynesia. *Medical Anthropology* 3(1):23–59.

Haberkorn, G. 1995. Fertility and mortality in the Pacific Islands. *Pacific Health Dialog* 2(1):104–112.

Hales, S., and A. Woodward. 1995. Climate change in the South Pacific region: priorities for public health research. *Australian Journal of Public Health* 19(6):543–545.

Han, S. T. 1996. New horizons in health: a perspective for the 21st century. *Pacific Health Dialog* 3(2):253–258.

Hankin J., et al. 1970. Dietary and disease pattern among Micronesians. *American Journal of Clinical Nutrition* 23(3):344–352.

Hau'ofa, E. 1985. Aid: a South Pacific perspective. *South Pacific Forum* 2(2):182–188.

Hearn T. J., ed. 1981. *New Zealand and the South Pacific the papers of the Fifteenth Foreign Policy School*. Dunedin, New Zealand: University of Otago.

Hocart, A. M. 1954 *Social origins*. London: Watts & Co.

Hodge, A. M., G. K. Dowse, and P. Zimmet. 1996. Obesity in Pacific populations. *Pacific Health Dialog* 3(1):77–86.

House, W. 1995. The role and significance of population policies in the Pacific Islands. *Pacific Health Dialog* 2(1):35–44.

Howe, K. 1984. *Where the waves fall*. Honolulu: University of Hawai'i Press.

Ireland, J., B. Powis, and N. Litidamu. 1996. Roots and wings of Healthy Islands: the history and potential of environmental health in the Pacific. *Pacific Health Dialog* 3(2):259–265.

Lange, R. 1984. Plagues and pestilence in Polynesia. *Bulletin of the History of Medicine* 58:325–346.

Levy, R. 1973. *Tahitians: mind and experience in Society Island*. Chicago: University of Chicago Press.

Lewis, N., and M. Rapaport. 1995. In a sea of change: health transitions in the Pacific. *Health and Place* 1(4):211–26.

Ludvigson, T. 1985. Healing in Central Espiritu Santo, Vanuatu. In *Healing practices in the South Pacific*, ed. C. D. F. Parsons, 51–64. Laie, Hawai'i: The Institute for Polynesian Studies.

McArthur, N. 1967. *Island populations of the Pacific*. Canberra, Australia: ANU Press.

MacDonald, J. 1985. Contemporary healing practices in Tikopia, Solomon Islands. In *Healing practices in the South Pacific*, ed. C. D. F Parsons, 65–86. Laie, Hawai'i: The Institute for Polynesian Studies.

MacLeod, R., and M. Lewis. 1988. *Disease, medicine and empire*. London: Routledge.

Macpherson, C., and L. Macpherson. 1990. *Samoan medical belief and practice*. Auckland: University of Auckland Press.

Marshall, L. 1990–91. Disease ecology of Australia and Oceania. In *Cambridge history and geography of human diseases*. Cambridge: Cambridge University Press.

Marshall, M. *Weekend warriors: alcohol in a Micronesian culture*. Palo Alto: Mayfield Publishers.

Meo L., D. Phillips, and R. Brough. 1996. Smoking in Viti Levu. *Pacific Health Dialog* 3(2):41–42.

Milio, N. 1985. Creating a healthful future. *Community Health Studies* 9(3):270–280.

Navarro, V., ed. 1981. *Imperialism, health and medicine*. New York: Baywood Publishing Co.

Nicholson, M. 1993. Medicine and racial politics: changing images of the New Zealand Maori in the nineteenth century. In *Imperial medicine and indigenous societies*, ed. D. Arnold, 66–104. Manchester University Press.

O'Leary, M. J. 1995. Health data systems in Micronesia: past and future. *Pacific Health Dialog* 2(1):126–132.

Parsons, C. D. F., ed. 1985. In *Healing practices in the South Pacific*. Hawai'i: Institute for Polynesian Studies.

Pollock, N. J. 1970. *Breadfruit and breadwinning on Namu atoll, Marshall Islands*. Ph.D. dissertation in Anthropology, University of Hawai'i.

Pollock, N. J. 1974. Breadfruit or rice: dietary choice on a Micronesian atoll. *Ecology of Food and Nutrition* 3:107–115.

Pollock, N. J. 1975. The risks of dietary change: a Pacific atoll example. In *Gastronomy*, ed. M. L. Arnott. The Hague: Mouton. World Anthropology Series.

Pollock, N. J. 1986. Food classification in three Pacific societies. *Ethnology* 25(2):107–117.

Pollock, N. J. 1990. More than health services: health for Pacific peoples. Comment in *Regional Development Dialogue* 11(4):103–107.

Pollock, N. J. 1992. These roots remain. *Institute of Polynesian Studies* and University of Hawai'i Press.

Pollock, N. J. 1993a. Food dependency in the Pacific revisited. In *Development that works!*, ed. C. Walsh, C8.1–C8.7. Palmerston North: Massey University Amokura Publications.

Pollock, N. J. 1993b. Understanding and addressing women's health needs in the Pacific. In *Development and planning in small island nations of the Pacific*, 173–184. Nagoya, Japan: United Nations Centre for Regional Development.

Pollock, N. J. 1995a. Introduction. *Social aspects of obesity*, ed. I. de Garine and N. Pollock. N.Y.: Gordon & Breach.

Pollock, N. J. 1995b. Gender issues in Pacific health. MS - paper read at Gender and Health in the Pacific conference, Canberra 1995.

Pollock, N. J., with A. AhMu, S. Asomua, and A. Carter. 1989. Food and identity: food preferences and diet of Samoans in Wellington, New Zealand. In *Migrations et identité Actes du Colloque*, C.O.R.A.I.L., Publications de L'Université Française du Pacifique, Vol. l, fascicules 3 & 4, Noumea, New Caledonia.

Pollock, N. J., with M. Tafili. 1988. Wallis and Futuna Reports To New Zealand Medical Research Council, Auckland, and the Department du Sante, Wallis Island.

Pollock, N. J., with M. Tafili. 1991. Report on *Use of alcohol by young people on Wallis and Futuna*. Report to New Zealand Health Research Council, Auckland.

Pollock, N. J., with M. Tafili. 1995. Introduction. *Social aspects of obesity*, ed. I. De Garine and N. Pollock. New York: Gordon and Breach.

Pollock, N. J. In press. Fall out from nuclear testing in the Marshall Islands. In Endangered peoples, ed. J. Fitzpatrick. *Cultural Survival*.

Prior, I. A. M., and C. Tasman-Jones. 1981. New Zealand Maoris and Pacific Polynesians. In *Western diseases: their emergence and prevention*, ed. H. C. Trowell and D. P. Burkitt, DP. London: Edward Arnold.

Rallu, J-L. 1990. *Les Populations Océaniennes aux XIXe et XXe siècles*. Institut National d'Etudes Démographiques. Travaux et Document, Cahier No. 18.

Ripley R., M. Imo, and D. Phillips. 1996. The management of hypertension in Fiji: is current practice effective? *Pacific Health Dialog* 3(2):47–49.

Richardson, J. 1987. Health and health care in Papua New Guinea. In *Human resources development in the Pacific*, ed. C. D. Throsby, 25–52. Canberra: National Centre for Development Studies, Pacific Policy Papers No. 3.

Samisoni J. 1994. Old school new programme: the Fiji School of Medicine 1994. *Pacific Health Dialog* 1(2):67–71.

Sarda, R., and G. Harrison. 1995. Epidemiology of HIV and AIDS in the Pacific. *Pacific Health Dialog* 2(2):6–13.

Schoeffel, P. 1986. Dilemmas of modernization in primary health care in Western Samoa. *Social Science and Medicine* 13(3):209–216.

Seeman B. 1860. Viti: government mission to the Fijian Islands. Reprint 1973 by Dawsons of Balmoral, London.

Seniloli, K. 1995. Perspectives on Pacific women and children. *Pacific Health Dialog* 2(1):121–125.

South Pacific Commission (SPC). 1994. *State of Pacific children: special theme of the 33rd South Pacific Conference*. Noumea, New Caledonia: South Pacific Commission.

Statistics New Zealand (SNZ). 1996. *1996 Census of population and dwellings*. Wellington: SNZ.

Swinburne, B., P. Craig, B. Strauss, and R. Daniel. 1994. Body mass index: is it an appropriate measure of obesity in Polynesians? In *Proceedings of the Australasian Society for the Study of Obesity*, 18.

Taylor, R., P. Bennett, R. Uili, et al. 1985. Diabetes in Wallis Polynesians. *Diabetes Research and Clinical Practice* 1:169–178.

Taylor, R., N. Lewis, and S. Levy. 1985. *Mortality in Pacific Island countries: a review circa 1980*. Noumea: South Pacific Commission.

Taylor, R., N. Lewis, and S. Levy. 1989. Societies in transition: mortality patterns in Pacific Island populations. *International Journal of Epidemiology* 18(3):634–646.

Taylor, R., and K. Thoma. 1985. Mortality patterns in the modernized Pacific Island nation of Nauru. *American Journal of Public Health* 75(2):149–155.

Thaman, R. 1982. The foods that came first. *Alafua Campus Agricultural Bulletin* 7(3):105–116.

Thomason, J., W. C. Newbinder, R. L Kolehmainen-Aitken. 1991. *Decentralization in a developing country: the experience of Papua New Guinea and its health service*. Canberra: National Centre for Development Studies.

UNICEF. 1993. State of Pacific children. Unpublished data.

Viala, M. 1919. Les Iles Wallis et Horn. *Bulletin de la Société Neuchateloise de Géographie* 28.

WHO. 1981. *Analysis of the content of the eight essential elements of PHC*. WHO Document No. HPC/PHC/REP/81.1 Geneva.

WHO/UNICEF. 1978. *Report by the director-general of WHO and executive director of UNICEF. International Conference on Primary Health Care,* Alma-Ata, USSR.

WHO. 1995. *Yanuca Island Declaration on health in the Pacific in the 21st century.* Meeting of the Ministers of Health for the Pacific Island Countries. WPRO Office, Manila.

WHO. 1996. *Discussion paper on healthy islands.* WPR/HRH/DHI(1)/97.3 Rarotonga WHO Meeting of the Directors of Health for Pacific Island countries.

Wirsing, R. 1985. The health of traditional societies and the effects of acculturation. *Current Anthropology* 26:303–22.

Zimmet, P., G. K. Dowse, and C. Finch. 1990. The epidemiology and natural history of NIDDM: lessons from the South Pacific. *Diabetes/Metabolism Review* 6:91–124.

Zimmet, P., and H. King. 1985. The epidemiology of diabetes mellitus: recent developments. *The Diabetes Annual* 1:1–15.

# Chapter 24

# Education

*Glenda Mather*

> The earth is in effect one world, in which empty, uninhabited spaces virtually do not exist. Just as none of us is outside or beyond geography, none of us is completely free from the struggle over geography. That struggle is complex and interesting because it is not only about soldiers and cannons but also about ideas, about forms, about images, and imaginings. (Said 1994, 6)

## Introduction

Western education and literacy were eagerly accepted in Hawai'i, Tahiti, and many other Pacific Islands during the early contact period, and are even more eagerly accepted today. Educational systems built during the colonial period have made considerable advances in literacy, numbers of schools and universities, and other measures. However, there is considerable diversity in educational services in various parts of the Pacific. Distance, fragmentation, lack of resources, and in some cases linguistic diversity pose important challenges for many of the newly independent island groups. The utility and purpose of current educational systems have been increasingly brought into question. Island communities are attempting to reintroduce traditional culture into educational curricula. This chapter provides an outline of the above issues and indicates the complexity of educational policy and planning in the region.

## Traditional Education

Traditional forms of education involved the teaching of roles and obligations within small communities. Informal learning involved direct participation in community activities, such as farming, fishing, sailing, and hunting, along with the preparation of food, cloth, and mats (Figure 24.1). Formal learning included initiation rites and responsibilities. Specialized activities such as building, tattooing, and medical training involved intensive processes of apprenticeship (Murray-Thomas 1993). Oral traditions were the main method of transmitting history, folklore, religion, and personal-social values from one generation to the next.

In precontact Pohnpei, men's education and work was largely in the public domain, with emphases on politics, warfare, and feasting. Women tended to focus on productive knowledge and skills, such as weaving textiles, and utilization of various natural materials for subsistence, exchange, and status. Women's roles included those of medical practitioner, midwife, and therapeutic masseuse (Kihleng 1992). Boughton (1992) describes

*Figure 24.1. Students and master craftsman, Colonia, Yap (photo LEM).*

education of young men in a traditional Marianas society. Male children were educated in a men's house, where they learned the customs and traditions of their maternal clan. Once this apprenticeship was completed, they were sponsored by one of their maternal uncles in rites of passage to adulthood, leading to membership in one of several status levels.

In Polynesia, the spread of knowledge and information was regulated by concepts of *mana* and *tapu*. Priests, or "experts," possessed knowledge of divine matters (*mana*) in addition to knowledge of horticulture, navigation, and tool making, which meant they acted as intermediaries between higher realms and earthly activities. Rules of access and behavior (*tapu*) were used to maintain this separation between different sectors of society. Ritual education was also important in other parts of the Pacific. In Melanesia, for example, daily activities as well as major social events were carried out after a prolonged consultation with supernatural deities. Gardening, tribal fighting, or feasting were never embarked on without such a process taking place. Such rituals could only be successful with approval of the gods.

## Historical Transformations

Missionary education was devoted to "civilizing" the local population, relegating traditional cultural practices to a "time of darkness" or ignorance (Hereniko 1994).

The acquisition of knowledge moved from community-based situations to a more formal venue where students memorized the alphabet, read the Bible, and recited sums and passages of scripture. Christian missionaries introduced Western concepts of literacy to oral societies via books and hymns translated into local languages. They also established churches where islanders were trained in roles of pastors, deacons, and catechists. Adults and children studied "Christian doctrine, reading and writing, calculating, geography and world history" at a fairly elemental level at Sunday schools and village day schools. Girls learned sewing and boys carpentry (Murray-Thomas 1993). Missionaries continued to run educational institutions until government agencies stepped in.

Education was generally seized on in terms of social advantage. While all island conversions might not be directly attributable to a desire for literacy, it certainly was a major motivating factor. This presumed link between social prestige and the adoption of Christianity was reported by a Solomon Islander in 1939:

> How are you [white men] different? Because you can read books. [That is why] you can buy axes, knives, clothing, ships and motor-cars . . . . you do not have to work hard; you pay us little money and we work for you, carrying heavy boxes on our backs. All this we know comes from books. If we understood books, we could do this. If we could read your books we would have money and possessions. (Hogbin 1939)

The introduction of literacy resulted in a transformation of oral societies where traditional chiefs, big-men, and spiritual diviners had previously held authority to social organization based on "silent, visible" forms of communication (Topping 1992). Such transformations helped erode traditional cultural practices and industries throughout the Pacific, while strengthening the influence of missionaries and the colonial process in general. (Yet somewhat paradoxically, introduced systems of education and language would be used later on as equally powerful tools in the struggle against colonialism and the reinvigoration of indigenous languages and cultures.)

Colonial governments entered reluctantly into the field of education. The initial educational developments focused on the training of clerks and public servants to fulfil the demands of colonial administration; a much later phase became responsive to the needs of self-governance and independence. While colonial education operated differently in every colony and school, some forms of European language and moral education were commonly taught. The British resident in the Cook Islands in the 1920s advocated that education be closely aligned with industrialization—a concept that was far removed from local needs at the time. British colonial government in Fiji was established according to indirect rule, where administration followed Fijian lines, and education had an agricultural/manual work focus.

Postwar decolonization resulted in an increasing demand for Western education incorporating an academic curriculum. Political and educational institutions in the region were developed, with a centralization of schools and other infrastructure. Successive phases of tertiary-level educational development in the region include the extension of tertiary options and focus on theological training (1920s), medical training (1920s–1940s), overseas scholarship phase (1940s–1960s), and the establishment of regional universities (1960s–1980s) (Crocombe 1988).

The University of the South Pacific in Suva, Fiji, was established in the 1960s with appointed colonial directors of education. This institution was designed to serve British and New Zealand Pacific territories, with extension centers in other island groups (Figure 24.2). Several seminaries and bible colleges were also established in Suva. During the same decade the University of Papua New Guinea (UPNG) was established, with campuses in Port Moresby and Goroka in the Highlands, along with a University of Technology (UNITECH).

The establishment of centralized infrastructure has led to population movements and urban drift, evident in many other

*Figure 24.2. University of the South Pacific, Port Vila Campus, Vanuatu (photo GM).*

parts of the region but most noticeable in the American colonies. In Micronesia, American-style education has become a major industry (Figure 24.3). Students from U.S. territories have access to educational facilities and scholarships in Hawai'i and the U.S. mainland, while the University of Guam has provided regional facilities from 1968. A French Pacific university has also recently been established, with branches in New Caledonia and Tahiti.

Pacific Island governments still often have their policy and planning options defined externally. Yet schooling can play a vital role in the creation of new "national identities, economic reconstruction, and (the) inculcation of new values and attitudes

*Figure 24.3. Agriculture and Technology School (PATS), Pohnpei (photo LEM).*

*Figures 24.4–5. Primary school and classroom, Fakaofo Atoll, Tokelau (photo MR).*

in people" (Zachariah 1985). Educational institutions often inherit responsibilities for the integration of migrant cultures, the promotion of religious doctrines, the spread of local languages, and the development of a strongly defined national identity and national culture.

Educational options for small island societies are limited by factors of size, scale, and isolation of island communities (Figure 24.4–5). Distance educational facilities are already providing some islands with direct access to satellite and distance education programs, including two-way voice communications, fax, and electronic data transmission. Such facilities include Peacesat (serving the South Pacific) and Micronet (serving U.S.-affiliated groups) (Crocombe 1995, see also Ogden 1997). Early U.S.-funded educational television in American Samoa in 1964 proved to be an expensive failure. This medium of education is now being extensively developed in Australia.

Comparative data on literacy and schooling for selected Pacific Island groups are shown in Table 24.1. The wide variation in educational achievement is evident, with highest levels of schooling and literacy in Polynesia. Lower levels of attainment in Melanesia are a reflection of the greater landmasses and populations; challenging environments and climates; diverse cultures; and relative recency of culture contact and infrastructural establishment, particularly in remote areas.

## Educational Development in Two Island Groups

An illustrative perspective on the development of existing educational systems is provided through a brief historical overview of education in Papua New Guinea and the Cook Islands.

### *Papua New Guinea*

Papua New Guinea is one of the largest island groups in the Pacific in terms of area and population. It is endowed with rich resources, but lacks road and other infrastructure and has an enormous degree of cultural diversity. Expenditure on education must compete with many other aspects of its emerging economy. Issues facing the design and provision of education in Papua New Guinea parallel those of other Melanesian islands (Vanuatu, Solomon Islands); high costs of education are reflected in a high dropout rate from secondary and tertiary levels of education. These problems exist despite a shortage of skilled labor and continued reliance on expatriates for specialist positions.

Australia controlled all aspects of educational policy and planning from 1946 onward, subsequent to British colonial rule. The Australian colonial approach focused on a "blending of cultures"—an approach that was increasingly challenged by pro-independence nationals during the 1950s who thought

### TABLE 24.1 Pacific Human Development Indicators – Selected States.
(adapted from *Pacific Human Development Report*, 1994, UNDP, Suva, Fiji)

| Country | Life Expectancy at Birth | Adult Literacy Rate (15+) | Mean Years of Schooling | GDP per Capita (US$) |
|---|---|---|---|---|
| **Melanesia** | | | | |
| Fiji | 63.1 | 87 | 6.8 | 1991 |
| PNG | 49.6 | 52 | 2.1 | 999 |
| Solomon Islands | 60.7 | 23 | 2.8 | 529 |
| Vanuatu | 62.8 | 64 | 4.0 | 1020 |
| **Micronesia** | | | | |
| FSM | 64.1 | 81 | 7.6 | 1474 |
| Marshall Islands | 61.1 | 91 | 8.5 | 1576 |
| Palau | 67.0 | 98 | 9.6 | 3289 |
| **Polynesia** | | | | |
| Cook Islands | 69.8 | 99 | 8.4 | 3416 |
| Niue | 66.0 | 99 | 8.3 | 3051 |
| Samoa | 63.1 | 98 | 9.1 | 722 |
| Tonga | 69.0 | 99 | 7.1 | 1396 |

they should have some control over the educational framework. English language instruction was consolidated during this period as a resolution of conflict between "inward looking" community-based education and the more outward looking form of education based on "empire and nation building" (Delpit and Kemelfield 1985).

Colonial education and mission-run schools operated independently of each other. Attempts to unite these separate systems did not take place until 1970. From this time district education boards and national government were required to produce education plans. When Papua New Guinea achieved independence in 1975, rates of educational achievement were low, and a high priority was set on expanding all levels of education. Yet local political demands for decentralization challenged the establishment of a national education system, particularly in North Solomons Province, which claimed a degree of autonomy from central government (Bray 1984).

The desire to amalgamate aspects of traditional society with contemporary Western lifestyles underlies an alternative educational movement, *Viles Tok Ples Skul* (VTPS), including basic classes in reading, writing, and counting in vernacular languages, alongside classes on local customs, values, and behavior. Today hundreds of "barefoot instructors" operate community-wide "critical literacy projects." These projects typically involve instructors moving between villages to attend classes in approximately 1,500 rural communities. The critical literacy programs follow Paulo Freire's objectives, attempting to provide an understanding of social and political conflicts (Maslen 1994).

Since independence, factors of slow economic growth, rising unemployment, and increased urban violence have challenged educational policies. While there have been gains in access to basic education over the last decade, levels of educational attainment remain low, and considerable regional variation exists in educational equity. An important concern is that education limited to the primary level might create, rather than solve employment problems.

## *Cook Islands*

The Cook Islands are one of the smallest countries in the region, with a population of 18,617 scattered across fifteen atolls and islands. A dependency on tourism and agricultural production indicates the limited resource base, with the islands being one of the most aided countries in the world. The islands are miniscule in size and population, but are culturally homogeneous, closely related to other Polynesian societies. The population of this island group has been in decline for the last two decades, with a larger number of Cook Islanders now living abroad, the majority in New Zealand.

New Zealand and Fiji established primary education during the missionary and colonial period of influence (1923–1964), with small numbers of Cook Islanders benefiting from overseas scholarship programs. After self-governance in 1965, the Cook Islands faced a shortage of trained and skilled workers for government services. Expatriate islanders were repatriated to join the workforce, and overseas scholarship programs were expanded. The 1968 Education Act declared primary education should be free, secular, and compulsory for all children for a nine-year period.

The 1975 Cook Islands Education Policy Statement proclaimed the urgent need for workplace skills and national priorities for promoting higher education. More recently (1979–1989) an "Education at Home" initiative has resulted in educational facilities and support services with a local base, enabling students to undertake tertiary studies at the Cook Islands Extension Center of the University of the South Pacific. While some students have continued to go abroad for their studies, there are now many students who undertake distance education in Rarotonga.

Today, education is compulsory for all children between the ages of five and fifteen years, with preschool education available on all islands. Use of the Cook Islands Maori language is encouraged during preschool education and at early levels of primary schooling. At secondary schooling level, national syllabus education is provided, culminating in the Cook Islands School Certificate. Successful students are eligible to take the New Zealand School Certificate examination, apply for overseas scholarships, or enroll for distance education courses locally.

## Language and Curriculum Options

The role of local language in education is often limited, but there is increasing recognition of the importance of "language of initial literacy." Tongan is the chief medium of instruction in Tonga, and Samoan is used in both American Samoa and Samoa in lower grades of schooling, with increasing English at higher levels. Micronesian languages follow a similar pattern, although the variety of local languages presents a challenge. The Cook Island Maori language is used for early instruction in the Cook Islands, while Fijian education follows native tongue (Fijian or Indian) in the first three years, followed by English (Thomas and Postlethwaite 1984).

The impacts of globalization and tourism will continue to favor the use of languages of wider communication such as English and French, but different strategies can be identified. Metropolitan France is eager to maintain colonial links in the region; thus French economic, ideological, and political ties have been artificially stimulated, often at the expense of local indigenous languages. In Micronesia, the United States has funded a progression from instruction in local vernacular languages to major regional languages and English.

In New Zealand, English is the dominant language in education, but Maori language now has the same legal status as English and is taught in a number of schools. "Language nests" (*Kohanga Reo*) allow preschool children to participate in Maori culture and language from birth. The state education system has launched several bicultural policy documents in the 1980s that stress recognition of a Maori dimension or perspective, which now provides an underlying philosophical base for all curriculum developments (Taskforce to Review Education Administration 1988, NZ Ministry of Education 1990).

Language policies in Melanesia are complicated by the existence of bilingual or multilingual populations. Policymakers and governments in New Caledonia, Vanuatu, and Papua New

Guinea tend to favor the choice of a language of "wider communication" in preference to the mother tongue. With increasing levels of intervillage and interisland communication and migration, Pidgin dialects often replace local languages. (Benton 1981).

Curriculum inputs and design often function as unchallenged products of Western education; however, they inevitably embody certain theoretical models. For example, Western mathematics has been accepted as a universal form of learning and "a culturally neutral phenomenon in the (otherwise) turbulent waters of education and imperialism" (Bishop 1990). However, mathematics, along with technology, can be seen to play a critical role in the control and domination of imperial power as perpetuated through trade, administration, and education.

Local knowledge systems in Pacific societies are orally based and rely on memory, talk, and oratory. Young people traditionally learned their history and culture through listening to adults "relate legends, quote proverbs, recite lineage of ancestry and that of chiefs of the village and region" (Murray-Thomas 1993). In addition, strict controls over access to certain forms of knowledge determine how and when these forms of knowledge may be revealed. Education is seen as inspiration revealed to the student, rather than two-way interaction between student and teacher (Lindstrom 1990).

The provision of formal education in the region has typically involved 95% imported skills, materials, and perspectives. Educators are increasingly suggesting some local-level adaptations. Despite an increase in indigenous inputs and a critical approach that challenges the validity of imported knowledge, regional considerations are not always recognized in the design and development of education. For example, the World Bank acknowledged the importance of social and cultural factors in its 1991 country-based study of Pacific economies, but it virtually ignored the practical realities of incorporating these factors in planning and administration (Hooper 1993).

Many problems involved with the provision of foreign educational aid have been attributed to "chronic failures of cultural empathy" (Thaman 1993). By way of improvement, Fry and Thurber urge educational consultants and planners to acquire increased sensitivity to local conditions (Fry and Thurber 1989). Foreign consultants often embrace values that conflict with those of their host community. Too often, consultants see only a small part of the problem, overlooking cultural and attitudinal factors and imposing alien and often inappropriate values and preferences on the direction and form the curriculum eventually takes.

Forms of educational "resistance" occur as nation-building exercises in colonial settings (New Caledonia) and demands of indigenous minority groups for some control over policy and planning options (Hawai'i and New Zealand). There have been recent moves to develop education incorporating aspects of *rangatiratanga* (sovereignty/autonomy) and Maori or *iwi* (tribal group) development. These policies are based on Treaty of Waitangi guarantees of protection of unqualified chieftainship and recognition of Maori interests, land claims, political rights, and customs (Penitito 1988, Smith 1991, Simon 1992). Hawaiian Studies programs are also now offered at the University of Hawai'i.

There is increasing recognition of indigenous science, technology, and belief systems. The first Science of Pacific Islands Peoples Conference was hosted by the University of the South Pacific in July 1992. The conference indicated a concern for the protection, control, and distribution of all forms of traditional knowledge. Local peoples allege that successive "settler" governments have dispossessed them of their controls over spiritual, cultural, and scientific resources. There is a desire to broaden a previously limited Western conception of science and legal "ownership" to include cultural and spiritual practices, definitions, and inputs (Morrison, Geraghty, and Crowl 1994).

Planning and delivery of education systems in the region now recognize questions of culture and identity, the development of a relevant local education system (usually combining traditional learning with Western education), and the implications of loss of traditional knowledge. The establishment of formal institutions of education has effectively provided Western technology and education throughout the region. The challenge now is to incorporate the impacts of Western learning with particular reference to the economic, cultural, and social aspects of Oceanic life.

## Conclusions

Two contradictory trends are evident in approaches to education and development. The first focuses on similarities between societies and suggests that some degree of "standardization of services is desirable" within a world system (Vedder 1994). Another contemporary approach emphasizes social diversity, seeking to achieve a blending of traditional and modern aspects of curricula and learning. Official government policy options continue to reflect conventional academic and vocational attitudes toward the provision of workforce skills and qualifications (often despite the lack of employment options and opportunities).

Cultural diversity and population movement between islands and farther afield complicate educational choices and opportunities. The establishment of the South Pacific Board of Educational Assessment (SPBEA) in 1981 indicates attempts to move away from colonial models of syllabus and examination. However, no one model of education can fulfill all requirements and meet the needs of every island population. Demands for recognizing local realities in educational policy reflect wider challenges for overall global control and manipulation of "developing regions." The balancing exercise between language and curriculum options has no easily determined outcome.

Just as national symbols and ideology represent a blending of traditional and modern elements, truly relevant education for small island states might embrace some blend of traditional and modern forms of learning and knowledge. A contemporary form of cultural survival might rely on the adaptation of various tools and devices from the West including "education . . . books and libraries; research and its application," in addition to "traditional ways." The use of knowledge created by a combination of these methods should retain valued aspects of island cultures for active use in the twenty-first century (Ward 1993).

Appendix 24.1.

# An Overview of Pacific Educational Institutions
(adapted from Douglas 1994, Population Statistics 1995)

| State/Population | Primary Schools | Secondary | Tertiary | Postsecondary/vocational |
|---|---|---|---|---|
| American Samoa (1990) 46,773 | 29 elementary schools (22 public); 85 early childhood centers (80 public). | 8 secondary schools (6 public) | Govt. scholarship program to US, Mormon college | American Samoa Community College – trades, business skills, teacher education |
| Cook Islands (1991) 18,617 | Preschool; 29 primary schools, 24 govt.-operated and 5 private | 7 colleges: (3 on Rarotonga, 1 each on other islands) | USP extension courses at degree & diploma level, also vocational & community level | Teachers Training College, Rarotonga, open sporadically; various tech courses at secondary schools, local apprenticeship scheme |
| FSM (1994) 104,724 | 177 primary/elementary schools, 164 state-operated, 13 private | 10 public and 7 private schools | College of Micronesia established in 1987 – Community, Nursing, Agric. & Science; Tertiary degree Guam, Hawai'i or Fiji | Vocational training integrated into basic education – business studies, agriculture, tech & indust. arts |
| Fiji (1986) 715,375 | 680: (14 Ministry of Education; Committees run 510; Christian 76; Hindu/Muslim 65; other specialist commercial admin | 140 schools (11 govt.) | University of the South Pacific - (serving 12 countries of region) | Fiji Inst. Tech.; School Maritime Studies, Hotel/Catering, Teacher Training. Fiji School of Nursing, Medicine, Pac. Theological College, Pac. Regional Seminary |
| French Polynesia (1988) 188,814 | 259 government primary schools, 19 private schools | 23 govt. secondary schools, 9 private schools | French University of the Pacific, 1987 – liberal arts, law & sciences to public admin. & tourism; DEUG foundation for further studies in France | Teachers Training College; Chamber of Commerce & Industry – business courses; |
| Guam (1990) 133,152 | About 25 elementary schools | Several high schools operated by government and Catholic Church (11,386 enrolled public; 2,739 private) | University of Guam – Agriculture & Life Sciences; Business & Public Admin; Education, Arts & Sciences | Guam Community College 1977; apprenticeship training, high school education, certificates & associate degrees |
| Hawai'i (1995) 1.18m | 239 public schools (elementary, intermediate & high schools) 129 private schools | | University of Hawai'i (3 campuses); Brigham Young Univ. (private) | 7 community colleges, 3 private colleges |
| Kiribati (1990) 72,335 | 110 government-run schools, 2 private church schools | 10 secondary schools (8 church operated) | USP extension on Tarawa, plus students at Suva, NZ, Aust. & other Pacific locations | Tarawa Technical Institute – tech & admin. courses; Teachers College; Nursing School; Maritime Training School. |
| Marshall Islands (1988) 43,380 | 76 public primary schools; 26 private primary schools | 6 private secondary schools; 2 public secondary schools | Member of USP with extension center in Majuro | College of Micronesia – trade and vocational skills |

The Pacific Islands

| State/Population | Primary Schools | Secondary | Tertiary | Postsecondary/vocational |
|---|---|---|---|---|
| New Caledonia (1989) 164,173 | 280 primary schools (one-third private) | 41 (18 public, 23 private) | Melanesian students at USP (Suva) & UPNG; summer school in French –Noumea | 4 institutions offering teaching, technology, trades, prelim. law and economics, teacher training |
| New Zealand (1996) 3.38m | Maori, Pakeha & Island community kindergartens; 2,340 primary (85 private) | 38 bilingual; 711 schools (19 private) | 7 universities | 25 polytechnics - vocational education program, trades |
| Niue (1991) 2,239 | 384 primary pupils in 1990; 28 teachers | 1 secondary school with 279 pupils in 1990, 25 teachers | Partner in USP – extension center in Alofi, students at USP in Fiji | Trade and professional colleges in NZ, Fiji and Samoa |
| PNG (1990) 3.7m | 2,606 primary, 29 expatriate primary schools | 4 national high schools; 135 secondary, 7 expatriate | UPNG (1966), medicine, arts, science, agriculture, education & law | Technical colleges, commercial and vocational training centers |
| Samoa (1991) 161,298 | 24,745 pupils in govt. primary schools, 3,908 in mission schools (1990) | 9,180 students in intermediate; 11,268 in secondary (1990) | USP second campus at Alafua near 'Apia, Agriculture; Nat'l Univ. of Western Samoa (1984) education, arts, science, commercial | Vocational training at technical institute – admin., auto repairs; training college for primary & secondary |
| Solomon Islands (1986) 285,176 | 423 government primary schools, 54 church-operated schools | 8 National schools (academic), 6 of which church operated; 15 provincial schools (vocational) | University in Fiji, Australia, PNG. USP extension center in Honiara | College of Higher Education (SICHE) in Honiara – commerce, basic trades, fisheries, admin., teaching, nursing, surveying, primary teacher training |
| Tonga (1986) 94,649 | 102 govt., 11 mission | 7 govt. and 37 private | USP extension, scholarships to USP, NZ, Aust. & UK | 18 post-secondary institutions - 8 church run, 8 govt. training centers & private Atenisi Institute |
| Tuvalu (1991) 9,043 | Primary schools on all islands | 2 high schools, 1 govt.-operated on Vaitupu Island; second church administered at Fetuvalu | USP extension center at Funafuti – also Fiji, NZ or Australia | Maritime training school, fully operational since 1983; 9 community training centers offering vocational subjects |
| Vanuatu (1989) 142,419 | 173 English medium schools (16,000 pupils); 99 French medium schools (10,500 pupils) | 17 secondary schools, 11 English medium; 4 French medium also 2 bilingual schools | USP extension center since 1989; f/time degree, diploma & certificate courses; USP Pacific languages & law unit | Vanuatu Institute of Tech. & Vocational Education on Efate; Ecole Technique de Saint Michel on Santo. Vanuatu Teachers College, Nurse Education |

Adapted from *South Pacific Yearbook*, 1994, ed. N. and N. Douglas; *Fiji Times*, Suva, Population Statistics, 1995; *Statistical Bulletin of the South Pacific*, #42 (compiled by D. Carter-Gau and G. Haberkorn); South Pacific Commission.

# Bibliography

Baba, T. L, I. J. Cokanasiga, and J. B. Caballes. 1992. *South Pacific education profiles: a sourcebook on trends and developments*. Suva: Institute of Education, University of the South Pacific.

Baldauf, R. B., and A. Luke, eds. 1990. *Language planning and education in Australasia and the South Pacific*. Avon, England: Clevedon; Philadelphia: Multilingual Matters.

Benton, R. A. 1981. *The flight of the Amokura: Oceanic languages and formal education in the South Pacific*. Wellington: Council for Educational Research.

Bishop, Alan J. 1990. Western mathematics: the secret weapon of cultural imperialism. *Race and Class* 32(2):51–65.

Boughton, G. J. 1992. Revisionist interpretation of precontact Marianas society. In *Pacific history: papers from the 8th Pacific History Association conference*, 221–224. Mangilao: University of Guam.

Bray, M. 1984. *Educational planning in a decentralised system: the Papua New Guinean experience*. Port Moresby, Sydney: University of Papua New Guinea Press/University of Sydney Press.

Burton, J. W. 1930. *Missionary survey of the Pacific Islands*. London: World Dominion Press.

Crocombe, R. 1995. *The Pacific Islands and the USA*. Rarotonga/Suva/Honolulu: Institute of Pacific Studies, University of the South Pacific/Pacific Islands Development Programme, East-West Center.

Crocombe, R., and M. Meleisea. 1988. *Pacific universities: achievements, problems and projects*. Suva: Institute of Pacific Studies, University of the South Pacific.

Delpit, L., and G. Kemelfield. 1985. Building on Melanesian foundations: Viles Tok Ples Skuls in the North Solomons. In *From rhetoric to reality: PNG's 8-point plan and national goals after a decade* (15th Waigani Seminar), ed. P. King, W. Lee, and V. Warakai, 421–430. Port Moresby: University of Papua New Guinea Press.

Douglas, N. and N. eds., 1994. *South Pacific yearbook*. Suva: Fiji Times.

Flinn, J. 1992. *Diplomas and thatch houses: asserting tradition in a changing Micronesia*. Ann Arbor: University of Michigan Press.

Forman, C. W. 1978. Foreign missionaries in the Pacific Islands during the twentieth century. In *Mission, church and sect in Oceania*, ed. J. A. Boutilier, D. T. Hughes, and S. W. Tiffany, 35–64. Ann Arbor: University of Michigan Press.

Freire, Paulo. 1985. *The politics of education: culture, power and liberation*. Massachusetts: Bergin & Garvey Publishers, Inc.

Fry, W. G., and C. E Thurber. 1989. *The international education of the development consultant*. Oxford: Pergamon Press.

Gannicott, K., and C. D. Throsby. 1992. Educational quality in economic development: ten propositions and an application to the South Pacific. *International Review of Education* 38(3):223–239.

Hannerz, U. 1992. *Cultural complexity: studies in the social organization of meaning*. New York: Columbia University Press.

Hereniko, V. 1994. Representations of cultural identities. In *Tides of history: the Pacific Islands in the twentieth century*, ed. K. R. Howe, R. C. Kiste, and B. Lal, 406–434. North Sydney: Allen & Unwin.

Hogbin, H. 1939. *Experiments in civilization: the effects of European culture on a native community of the Solomon Islands*. London: Routledge and Kegan Paul.

Hooper, A. 1993. Socio-cultural aspects of development in the South Pacific. In *The future of Asia-Pacific economies. Pacific Islands at the crossroads?* ed. R. V. Cole and S. Tambunlertchai, 314–342. Canberra: Asian and Pacific Development Centre and National Centre for Development Studies.

Kihleng, K. S. 1992. Pohnpei women in the nineteenth century. In *Pacific history: papers from the 8th Pacific History Association conference*, 169–176. Mangilao: University of Guam.

Lindstrom, L. 1990. Local knowledge systems and the Pacific classroom. *Papua New Guinea Journal of Education* 26(1):5–17.

Maslen, G. 1994. A new word order: weekend Australian. *Good Weekend Magazine*, December 10, 1994, 18–27.

Morrison, J., P. Geraghty, and L. Crowl, eds. 1994. *Science of Pacific Island peoples. Vol. IV. Education, language, patterns and policy*. Suva: Institute of Pacific Studies, University of the South Pacific.

Murray-Thomas, R. 1993. Education in the South Pacific: the context for development. *Comparative Education* 29(3):233–248.

Ntiri, D. W. 1993. Africa's educational dilemma: roadblocks to universal literacy for social integration and change. *International Review of Education* 39(5):357–372.

New Zealand Ministry of Education. 1990. *Tihe Mauri ora: Maori language: Junior classes to Form 2*. Wellington: Government Printer.

*Pacific human development report*. 1994. Suva, Fiji: UNDP.

Penetito, W. 1988. Maori education for a just society. In *The April report: social perspectives. Vol. IV. Te Komihana mo Nga Ahuatanga-a-Iwi*, Report of the Royal Commission on Social Policy. Wellington: Government Printer.

Pettman, Jan. 1984. Schooling, stratification and resocialization in Papua New Guinea. In *Social stratification in Papua New Guinea*, Working Paper No.5, ed. R. J. May, 133–151. Canberra: Department of Political and Social Change, Research School of Pacific Studies, Australian National University.

Population statistics. 1995. *Statistical Bulletin of the South Pacific*. #42 (compiled by D. Carter-Gau and G. Haberkorn). Noumea: South Pacific Commission

Said, E. 1993. *Culture and imperialism*. London: Chatto & Windus.

Simon, J. 1992. *State schooling for Maori: the control of access to knowledge*. AAREINZARE Conference Proceedings. Australia: Deakin University.

Smith, G. 1991. *Tane-Nui-a-Rangi's legacy . . . Propping up the Sky: Kaupapa Maori as resistance and intervention*. AAREINZARE Conference Proceedings. Australia: Deakin University.

Taskforce to Review Education Administration. 1988. Report. *Administering for excellence: effective administration in education*. Wellington: NZ Government Printer.

Tavola, Helen. 1991. *Secondary Education in Fiji: A Key to the Future*. Suva, Fiji: Institute of Pacific Studies, University of the South Pacific.

Teasdale, R., and J. Teasdale, ed. 1992. *Voices in a seashell: education, culture and identity*. Suva: Institute of Pacific Studies, University of the South Pacific in association with United Nations Educational, Scientific and Cultural Organization.

Thaman, K. H. 1993. Culture and the curriculum. *Comparative Education* 29(3):249–260.

Thomas, R. M., and T. N. Postlethwaite. 1984. *Schooling in the Pacific Islands: colonies in transition*. Oxford: Pergamon Press.

Tryon, D. T., and J-M. Charpentier. 1989. Linguistic problems in Vanuatu. *Ethnies* 4(Spring):13–17.

Vedder, Paul. 1994. Global measurement of the quality of education: a help to developing countries?. *International Review of Education* 40(1):5–17.

Ward, R. G. 1993. South Pacific Island futures: paradise, prosperity or pauperism? *The Contemporary Pacific* 5(1):1–21.

World Bank. 1986. *Financing education in developing countries: an exploration of policy options*. Washington, D.C.

World Bank. 1991. *Pacific Islands economies: toward higher growth in the 1990s.* Washington, D.C.

World Bank. 1993a. *Sustaining rapid development in East Asia and the Pacific.* Washington, D.C.

World Bank. 1993b. *Pacific regional post-secondary education study.* Washington, D.C.

World Conference on Education for All. 1990. *Meeting basic learning needs: a vision for the 1990s.* New York: Inter-Agency Commission (UNDP, UNESCO, UNICEF, World Bank, UNICEF).

Zachariah, M. 1985. Lumps of clay and growing plants: dominant metaphors of the role of education in the Third World, 1950–1980. *Comparative Education Review* 29(1):549–556.

# Women

*Camilla Cockerton*

## Introduction

Writings on women and international development rarely mention Pacific women (e.g. Young 1989, Momsen 1991, Shiva 1994). Prior to 1975, academic literature on the Pacific region in general was devoted almost exclusively to men's experiences. Women, studied primarily by feminist scholars, entered Pacific academic literature in the 1980s as a separate and legitimate focus of study. Influenced by second-wave feminism of the 1970s, many of these scholars were women. Feminist scholars criticized the gender-blindness of the existing literature and called for a new research agenda, with women at the forefront of the analysis. The geographical coverage of this exciting new body of literature is, however, uneven.

Much of the research on Pacific women has been conducted by nonindigenous women researchers and writers, but this trend is changing. The voices of Pacific women, speaking individually and as members of women's organizations, are increasingly heard. One of their greatest contributions has been to insist that the values, opinions, and objectives of Pacific women be respected and used as the basis for development initiatives. Women's oral histories, biographies, and stories—a growing body of work—give women the space to represent themselves and their cultures (Ne 1992). They provide a sharp contrast to previous accounts of Pacific women, mostly written by European men.

Pacific researchers and writers now recognize the immense diversity of women's experiences across this region. The situations of Pacific women are extremely diverse, reflecting differences in social class, geographical region, ethnicity, religion, sexuality, and age. Just as international feminist critiques challenge the unity of the category "woman," so too do Pacific women deny the homogeneity of the category "Pacific woman."

Much of the recent literature on Pacific women is written from a feminist perspective, focusing on gender (the cultural construction of sexual difference). It challenges androcentric narratives by recovering women's roles in history and taking fuller account of women's views and experiences. For instance, the study of initiation in the Pacific remained largely the study of male initiation for one hundred years, until a 1995 text focused squarely on female initiation rites (Lutkehaus and Roscoe 1995). Feminism stresses the initiative and agency of women and their impact upon dominating structures. Feminism also challenges the ahistorical, essentialist, and biological determinist assumptions behind some analyses of women's subordination.

Anthropologists specializing in the Pacific have devoted considerable attention to gender relations from an ethnographic perspective (e.g. MacKenzie 1991, Lepowsky 1993). Early writings on Pacific women go back to the anthropological work of Bronislaw Malinowski, Margaret Mead, and Gregory Bateson in the 1920s and 1930s (Ralston 1992). After World War II, when anthropological research intensified throughout the Pacific, researchers were drawn to Melanesia. They wanted to build on these early pioneers and to work in societies that had experienced little or no contact with the non-Melanesian world (O'Brien and Tiffany 1984).

Even today, this research continues to dominate the literature on Pacific women and gender. Initially, the research aimed to dispel the myth that gender inequalities are universal (Errington and Gewertz 1987, Gewertz 1988). Papua New Guinea in particular has been extensively researched. Most notably, Frederick Errington and Deborah Gewertz (1987) reanalyzed Margaret Mead's influential study of the gender relations of the Chambri of Papua New Guinea. They argued that, instead of constituting a matriarchy, Chambri women neither dominate men nor vice versa.

From the 1920s until the late 1970s, much of the literature on women and gender in the Pacific was anthropological. The early 1980s marked an abrupt shift in disciplinary focus, with a focus on development issues (e.g. ACOA 1986, Cole 1985, Fahey 1986, Griffen 1987, Lee 1985, Levy et al. 1988, Pickering 1983, Seniloli 1989, Thomas 1986). Issues raised included family planning, female extension workers, contraception, fertility, labor relations, barriers and opportunities, and empowerment. From the perspective of Pacific Islanders, even by 1988 the status of women was one of the most controversial issues in the contemporary Pacific (Tongamoa 1988). The 1990s witnessed a divergence in the literature on women and gender in the Pacific, away from purely anthropological or development studies toward theoretically informed, comparative (e.g. Drage 1995), and interdisciplinary research.

Overall, there are two main theoretical frameworks of gender in the Pacific region. The first links gender to systematic inequality and power and studies gender in relation to colonialism, global capitalism, race, and class (e.g. Fahey 1986). Theories about the social, economic, and political subordination that often accompany Westernization have influenced this body of research.

Within this theoretical framework, some writers discuss the intersection of precolonial with colonial gender and economic relations (e.g. Lockwood 1995). Others link female/male relations to Marxist models of production and reproduction (e.g. Gailey 1987). Some studies analyze how women's status decreased with colonial development (e.g. Gailey 1980). Feinberg (1986) attributed women's declining status in eastern

Papua New Guinea to the changing economic system this century, especially "European commodities and wage labor." Linnekin (1990) argues instead that Hawaiian women maintained their access to land and power during the early colonial period. Similarly, Kihleng (1996) explores how Pohnpei women maintained, and perhaps enhanced, their power and authority with colonialism and capitalist penetration.

The second main theoretical framework depicts gender as continually contested, changing across time and space (e.g. Lepowsky 1993). For instance, most Micronesian societies are matrilineally organized, with less patriarchal control of women. From this perspective, men and women have multiple roles, statuses, and positions within particular cultures. This framework challenges the binary nature of gender and questions the search for universal hypotheses. These studies prefer ethnographic, localized, historicized approaches to gender.

This chapter, in the face of this immense diversity, presents only wide generalizations about Pacific women, taking examples from various island groups. The first section explores women's changing experiences under colonialism in the Pacific. The next section examines women's economic contributions, followed by a discussion of other social and political issues particularly relevant to women.

## Colonialism

Colonialism had a diverse effect on Pacific women, and, certainly, men and women were differentially affected by colonial rule (Etherington 1996, Jolly 1994). The impact of colonialism on women depended on many factors, such as types of export crops introduced, the control of land, the nature of colonial rule, and cultural traditions about the division of labor.

Researchers are now interested in understanding how the arrival of foreign missionaries and colonial administrators complicated traditional gender relations. For instance, in Hawai'i missionary practices and alliances empowered certain groups of women (Linnekin 1990). Most missions in the Pacific were founded by men, with men in leadership positions. The South Sea Evangelical Mission in Solomon Islands, founded by Florence Young, was one exception. At this mission, women had status and roles comparable to men's (Little 1993). Missionaries disapproved of particular aspects and practices of indigenous cultures and took direct actions to change or eradicate them. In Fiji, for instance, missionaries abhorred polygamy and infant betrothal to old men (Vakadewavosa 1992).

European men brought with them their own notions of the proper social and economic roles for women. The Victorian ideal was that women should stay at home and concentrate on child-rearing and domestic labor (feminine tasks such as cooking, sewing, and housekeeping). European policies did not challenge the strong traditions of patriarchal control of women in Pacific societies; indeed, such policies often strengthened those traditions.

New production systems needed by the expanding colonial powers, such as cash cropping, induced new divisions of labor. In the Pacific, as elsewhere, men became the main participants in cash cropping and were largely in control of the new cash economy (Rennie 1991). For example, in Solomon Islands, traditionally both men and women shared in subsistence gardening. After the introduction of cash cropping, women had almost total responsibility for subsistence crop production, in addition to assisting in cash cropping (Rennie 1991).

Similarly, in Tonga, cash cropping has altered the traditional division of labor. Traditionally, women and men shared many tasks, including child care, house-building, traditional medicine, and bartering. Women also produced coconut oil, fished in lagoons, produced bark cloth, wove, and cooked special chiefly dishes. Men did all the farming and most of the cooking, deep-sea fishing, canoe-building, and weapon-production. After European trade contact, Tongan men abandoned their domestic work in favor of copra cash cropping (Rennie 1991).

Even after colonial rule, Pacific women continue to suffer disadvantage and discrimination in many facets of their personal lives, though male domination varies enormously across the region. Regardless, women should not be seen as merely passive victims. Women play vital roles in development, and struggle in various ways to improve their lives. For instance, women take an active role in church activities (Figure 25.1), often forming women's church groups for a variety of community tasks.

**Figure 25.1.** *Woman addressing congregation during Sunday church service, Vairaatea, Tuamotus (photo MR).*

## Economy

Women make substantial contributions to Pacific economies. Their contributions are often to subsistence agriculture, though this varies across the Pacific. Pacific women also provide labor input for cash crops. Their agriculture work suffers from lack of technical support and advice on food crop cultivation, such as intensive cultivation techniques, marketing, and business opportunities (Avalos 1995). Women's role in fishing is also much larger than is generally acknowledged (Davis and

Nadel-Klein 1992). In Papua New Guinea, women catch at least 25% of the annual catch weight (Avalos 1995). Women are dominant in the processing stage of small-scale fisheries and in the marketing of fish.

The importance of Pacific women's economic contributions, especially their contributions to agriculture and the domestic economy (Figures 25.2-25.5), has tended to be forgotten and ignored. In part, this is because development planners and policymakers class much female economic activity as housework or subsistence. Hence, it is not recorded in such macro-scale measures of economic activity as the gross national product.

*Figure 25.2.* Preparation of taro on Atiu, Cook Islands (photo MR).

*Figure 25.3.* Two women transporting bananas to village, Atiu, Cook Islands (photo MR).

*Figure 25.4.* Massive tapa cloths in Tonga, produced by women's groups (photo LEM).

*Figure 25.5.* Preparation of "collectors" for pearl farming, Takaroa, Tuamotus (photo MR).

In Samoa, for example, census data exemplifies the inability of statistical formulas to account for women's work. People are classified as either "economically active" or "economically inactive," and 81% of Samoan women are classified as "economically inactive" (Fairbairn-Dunlop 1991). Of these, 57% are listed as "home-makers." This data fuels the belief that homemaking is not an economic activity. Yet women's contributions to smallholder subsistence and commercial farming (which provide the livelihood for 70% of the population in Samoa) is significant.

National Statistics Offices in some Pacific Island countries have embarked on the development and improvement of sex-desegregated data to reflect the participation of both men and women in key sectors of the economy (Fairbairn-Dunlop 1991). Regional workshops and forums over the past twenty years have stressed the need for research and data on Pacific women's needs.

Pacific women make significant contributions to the household economy by participating in formal and informal sector employment, including self-employment. Most of the traders in marketplaces are women. Many of the goods that women sell also have been produced, processed, and transported to market by women. Women, especially rural women, engage in small-business activities as a means of contributing to income for family needs. Women experience unique difficulties in marketing their products and obtaining credit for their businesses. Of 2,039 loans by the Agriculture Bank of Papua New Guinea in January 1991, only 91 were provided to women (Booth 1991 in Avalos 1995).

Women in urban areas, particularly those with education, are beginning to face new economic challenges. In recent decades, many women work as teachers, health-service personnel, and government employees. Most of these formal-sector jobs are considered very desirable, although many do not command especially high rates of pay.

Overall, formal employment constitutes a very small percentage of the total economic activities of Pacific women. In Papua New Guinea, only 18% of formal-sector employees in 1990 were women (Avalos 1995). Women are generally clustered in particular kinds of jobs. In Hawai'i, women (especially immigrant women) are generally concentrated in low-paying, traditionally female clerical, sales, and service occupations (Fan 1996). Ethnic and social-class backgrounds complicate their labor force participation.

Women also contribute to Pacific economies from overseas. Remittances from America, New Zealand, Australia, and other countries play a huge role in Pacific economies, and women migrants are important remitters. Overall, women migrants send larger remittances to their home countries than men, despite their lower incomes (Vete 1995).

## Politics

Women's contributions to political institutions and processes have varied across the Pacific region. Generally, there are few opportunities and little encouragement for female political activism in contemporary, Western-modeled political institutions (Figure 25.6). While many countries have appointed female cabinet ministers, only a few have made serious attempts to involve women in the political process. Pacific women's electoral success is very low when compared with other regions (Drage 1995). In most public spheres of activity, women have minimal access to top decision-making positions (Avalos 1994).

*Figure 25.6.* Former mayor of Takapoto, Tuamotus (photo MR).

Following the international decade for women, from 1975 to 1985, culminating in the Nairobi Conference in 1985, several Pacific Island countries have set up Ministries of Women or Women's Divisions. These offices initiate legislation on women's rights, encourage women to run for elective office, nominate women for appointment to government agencies, and actively promote women's information networks. However, only seven exist in the region, and these receive minimal support by government agencies (Drage 1995).

Recent years have witnessed a growth of women's political activity in nongovernmental organizations and community groups operating at all levels (Drage 1995). These groups may be more effective than government programs in alleviating women's burdens and are helping to initiate a feminist transformation in the way in which women's development is done. Even in small communities, Pacific women are adopting strategies that are at least implicitly feminist. Women are forming their own local organizations to address needs that they themselves have identified as important (Scheyvens 1995).

National councils of women are nongovernment umbrella organizations that coordinate women's activities on a national level. In recent years, these groups have broadened their interests from family issues and "female crafts" training to health, education, economics, nuclear testing, skills training, politics, and violence against women (ACOA 1986). Some of the groups represent a large portion of the population. For instance, a third of the population of Tokelau belongs to the Tokelau National Women's Association, Fatupaepae (Drage 1995).

International nongovernment organizations (NGOs) commonly provide funds to national councils of women for administration costs and for training and leadership courses. Fairbairn-Dunlop (1991) warns that Pacific women need to clearly identify and understand the assumptions underlying programs offered by donors. International agencies have drawn Pacific NGOs into strong worldwide networks of ideas, including certain assumptions of women's status and ideal roles. These assumptions may include Western feminist concepts of women's rights, basic human rights, and women's roles as preservers of cultural tradition or providers of welfare.

Pacific women are becoming more united in their opposition to militarization and the incorporation of the Pacific into the global nuclear system (Ishtar 1994). Polynesian and Micronesian women are increasingly alarmed at the connections between the French and American nuclear test programs and the increasing incidence of miscarriages, deformed births, infant mortality, skin diseases, and cancers, particularly thyroid cancer. At the first Pacific Women's Conference in 1975 and subsequent conferences, women protested over nuclear testing and proposed nuclear waste dumping in the region (Griffen 1991). Some women's groups, such as the Chamorro women organizers in Guam (Souder 1990), play crucial roles in promoting a nuclear-free Pacific.

## Education

Across the Pacific region, men achieve higher levels of education than women. However, there are exceptions. In

Micronesia, a recent national report reveals men's literacy rate at 67% as opposed to 87% for women (PWRB 1997). Women's relatively lower educational participation and lower literacy rates in most of the region contribute to their limited political participation and particular social problems. For instance, teen pregnancy is a growing problem (Davis and Rapaport 1995), and there is often inadequate education on family planning and contraception (Jayaraman 1995, Levy et al. 1988, Seniloli, 1989).

In Papua New Guinea, for example, in primary school (first to sixth grade), the number of girls roughly equals the number of boys. After Grade 6, the proportion of women enrolled in vocational schools is less than 30% of the total enrollment of these schools (Avalos 1995). Almost equal numbers of male and female students complete Grade 10 in Port Moresby, yet few women move on to upper-secondary education. The average proportion of girls accepted in further studies after Grade 10 is 35%, compared with about 70% of the boys (Avalos 1995). Even fewer women, one in five, participate in the distance alternative for secondary education (Phillip 1993, Seta 1993).

The low retention of girls in high schools is a complex issue. Some researchers identify problems of school fees, marriage and pregnancy, distance from home and school, and pressures associated with domestic activities (Seta 1993). The attitude of parents, particularly fathers, may be a particularly important factor affecting the retention of female high school students (Avalos 1995). Women remain even more underrepresented as university students, high school teachers, administrative staff, and university lecturers and staff (Flaherty 1993). In 1990, only 23% of students at the University of Papua New Guinea were women (Avalos 1995).

However, Pacific Island groups have explicitly recognized the importance of women's education. The University of the South Pacific offers distance education courses to women in Melanesian countries (Bolabola and Wah 1995). International agreements have also been made to increase educational opportunities for Pacific women (Grandea and Gibb 1995). The education of women also makes sound economic sense (Gannicott and Avalos 1994). High levels of women's education also result in higher levels of gross national product. Women's education can also help limit population growth and improve infant and child health and welfare (Gannicott and Avalos 1994).

## Domestic Violence

Domestic violence is a widespread and serious problem in many regions of the Pacific. Papua New Guinea has the world's second highest incidence of violence against women, according to a 1994 UNICEF report (Waram 1995). Sixty percent of women have reported incidence of domestic violence; this figure is undoubtedly much lower than actual incidence. In 1982 the National Council of Women in Papua New Guinea successfully pushed the Law Reform Commission to investigate domestic violence and recommend legal and other means of protecting women. In Samoa, almost 30% of women surveyed said they had been victims of bashing or sexual abuse (Peteru 1996). The extent of the problem elsewhere in the Pacific remains underresearched.

Some researchers have explored domestic violence from a geographical perspective. In Papua New Guinea, researchers found that domestic violence is significantly higher among the urban elite than among low-income urban households (Zimmer-Tamakoshi 1995). Social and professional pressures are greater among the elite, and elite women are more likely to be dependent upon their husbands' earnings. Other research considers how women's experiences of male violence change in different contexts, particularly during women's migration from rural to urban places (e.g. Cribb and Barnett 1999, Cribb 1995).

Throughout the world, assaults on women by their husbands or partners are the most common form of violence. Most victims find it difficult to leave their violent family situations because of lack of money, the responsibility of children, and the accompanying emotional, psychological, and financial abuse. Researchers are beginning to explore the wider context of family violence (e.g. Olson 1994, Lepowsky 1994). Violence occurs between different family members and on many different levels (not just physical abuse, but emotional, financial, and psychological abuse). Violence against men, children, and the elderly is becoming more openly discussed.

Pacific women's groups are publicly addressing the issue of male violence against women. Since the early 1980s, Pacific Island NGOs have been active in combating domestic violence. Some countries have initiated violence control programs against male violence (Merry 1995). The Hawaiian legal system in particular has adopted a more activist stance by initiating batterers' treatment programs and the criminalization of spouse abuse. A women's refuge in Suva, Fiji, has proved enormously successful (Rashid 1995). The Fiji Women's Crisis Centre now trains women from other Pacific islands in establishing and managing crisis counseling services and organizations.

Women's groups across the Pacific are calling for more research on the many forms of violence against women. Researchers have begun to explore some of the reasons for this violence (Counts 1990). Some writers cite modernization as exacerbating violence in the Pacific. In Palau, alcohol is implicated in wife beating, and people are not held responsible for actions while drunk (Nero 1990). Violence may also paradoxically play a role in social conformity and cohesion. In some regions, male violence is a means of controlling female sexuality. For example, among Indo-Fijians, beating is a strategy to preserve the virtue of unmarried girls (and hence family honor) and the modesty and subordinate status of married women (Latieff 1990).

Another strand of research on domestic violence in the Pacific depicts gender as a fluid social construct. Sally Merry's research (1995) shows how both women's and men's gender identity is transformed by the criminalization of spouse abuse in Hawai'i. For instance, battered women are offered legally endowed, autonomous selves who can choose to stay or to leave a violent man. In a special issue in *Pacific Studies* (1990) devoted to domestic violence, gender and violence are depicted as fluid and contestable. Some authors suggest a "violence ethos," in which the person is socially constituted, with violence and aggression as aspects of personhood.

# Development

Development programs have affected distinct groups of Pacific women in different ways (Dickerson-Putman 1994). Women are still seen as having their needs often ignored by development programs and projects, relative to men (Avalos 1994). Women make indispensable contributions to subsistence, yet they are excluded from direct participation in the development of commercial farming and fishing because of official perceptions that women's work is not "real farming" or "real fishing" (Cole 1985, Davis and Nadel-Klein 1992).

Rural women in particular have been the victims of development processes and outcomes. Evidence for this includes the increasing duration of their workday, the widening gap between male and female incomes, and women's greater responsibility in household management (Stephens 1991). Improvements to rural extension services for women are needed for rural women to participate in development efforts (Gabriel 1990, Pickering 1983).

Structural adjustment policies, implemented by the World Bank to improve developing countries' economies and reduce debt, have had a differential impact on women and men. Reductions in social services and promotion of income-generating activities have undermined women's subsistence activities. Other negative effects of international development policies include intensification of women's unpaid and paid work, feminization of the manufacturing sector, increased female participation in the informal sector, biases in female health and education, and increased domestic violence (Aiomanu 1996, Burman 1995).

The events of the United Nations Decade for Women (1975–1984) greatly influenced the attitudes and policies of international agencies and governments. However, there has been a perception in most Pacific government offices and NGOs that the promotion of "Women in Development" means the support for separate, in many cases small, welfare-oriented projects for women. These have usually assisted women with their domestic responsibilities and, in more recent years, with the establishment or strengthening of small income-earning projects (ESCAP 1995).

Perhaps the most successful development programs for women are those initiated by local women for themselves (Lee 1985). For instance, in the Highlands of Papua New Guinea, Wok Meri is a successful savings and exchange system created by women (Sexton 1986). The transactions include small loans from members of many groups to each other at a public ceremony. Wok Meri is women's collective response to the dramatic economic changes of the last fifty years.

A new development tool to open up dialogue on women's issues is theater (PWRB 1997). For example, the Fiji-based drama group Women's Action for Change (WAC) empowers people by encouraging them to devise solutions to everyday issues. The group focuses on themes of women's fight to gain a political voice, youth problems, and struggles in the home and workplace.

The majority of aid recipients in women-and-development schemes have been small women's groups that do not survive more than two years (Small 1989). Analyses attribute this short lifespan to problems in conception and organization (i.e. the local and unconnected nature of women's small-group rural projects) or implementation (i.e. the resistance of men).

# Women in Western Areas

Some parts of the Pacific region are more "Westernized" than others. These include New Zealand, Hawai'i, Guam, and urban centers in many island groups. Much of the literature covers issues particularly pertinent to these locations, including discrimination in employment (Olsson 1992), occupational segregation (Fargher and Maani 1992), women executives (Smith and Hutchison 1995), women socialists (Damousi 1994), gender bias in legal aid (Office of Legal Aid and Family Services 1994), sport (Cameron 1993), and even women hitchhikers (Bell 1990). Research in such areas is often more concerned with theoretical issues than is literature on other Pacific islands' women (e.g. De Plessis and Bunkle 1992, James and Saville-Smith 1994, Grimshaw 1994).

The situations of women in New Zealand and Hawai'i sharply differ from most women's experiences in the other Pacific islands. This is due to a wide range of factors, including different colonial histories and cultures, and the preponderance of European descendants in their populations. However, even in these areas women are by no means an undifferentiated group. In particular, native islanders and Pacific Islander migrants have distinct social and economic differences from their European counterparts.

# Conclusion

Many current writers now argue for change at all levels of government to address the status of Pacific women and to achieve full participation of women in the development process. In order for this to happen, it must be recognized that women's status is not uniform nor static across the Pacific. Rather, the constructions of gender and patriarchy are fluid across time and space. Women's experiences have varied and continue to vary enormously across Pacific regions (Polynesia, Micronesia, and Melanesia) and between individual countries and smaller localities. They cut across a myriad of lines including class, race, ethnicity, sexual orientation, age, and time.

Women and gender are increasingly being addressed in conference sessions, papers, and publications on the Pacific. However, at a recent conference in Singapore on Women in the Asia-Pacific Region: Persons, Powers and Politics (1997), Pacific Island women were rarely mentioned. Of the ninety conference papers, one focused on New Zealand (Longhurst 1997) and three on other Pacific islands (e.g. Cockerton 1997, Leckie 1997, Scheyvens 1997). Rather than being marginalized or ignored, the experiences of Pacific women should be included in future texts on women and international development.

Literature on women and gender is not just important in its own right; it can engage with wider sociopolitical dialogues. As Ralston (1992, 171–173) writes, studies on Pacific women and gender can contribute to broader debates on ethnicity, identity, tradition, and colonialism, and within many disciplines. Unfortunately, this integration does not always occur. For instance, some texts on "identity" completely ignore gender, defining "identity" only as "ethnic identity" (e.g. Tuimaleali'ifano 1990, Chapman and Morrison 1985). Gender studies can open up new ways of thinking about the Pacific region.

*Figure 25.7.* Nurse attends child on Takaroa, Tuamotus (photo MR).

*Figure 25.8.* Village matriarch and repository of oral tradition (right) on Vairaatea, Tuamotus (photo MR).

# Bibliography

Aiomanu, K. 1996. A feminist analysis of gender-differentiated impacts of structural adjustment policies in Fiji as a case study. Unpublished M.Sc. London: Gender and Development, London School of Economics and Political Science.

Australian Council for Overseas Aid (ACOA). 1986. *Development in the Pacific: what women say.* Canberra, A.C.T.: Australian Council for Overseas Aid.

Avalos, B. 1994. Women and development in Papua New Guinea. Economics Division Working Papers, South Pacific 94(2). Australian National University, Research School of Pacific and Asian Studies.

Avalos, B. 1995. Women and development. *Pacific Economic Bulletin* 10(1):73–83.

Bell, K. S. 1990. Making tracks: gender relations and tramping. Unpublished master's thesis. Christchurch: Geography Department, University of Canterbury.

Bolabola, C., and R. Wah. 1995. *South Pacific women in distance education: studies from countries of the University of the South Pacific.* Suva: USP University Extension and the Commonwealth of Learning.

Burman, E. 1995. The abnormal distribution of development: policies for southern women and children. *Gender, Place and Culture: A Journal of Feminist Geography* 2(1):21–36.

Cameron, J. 1993. Gender in New Zealand sport: a survey of national sport administrators. Unpublished report. Christchurch: Sociology Department, University of Canterbury.

Chapman, M., and P. S. Morrison, eds. 1985. Mobility and identity in the island Pacific. A special issue of *Pacific Viewpoint* 26(1).

Cockerton, C. 1997. Unpacking domestic violence as a spatial image. Paper presented at the International Conference on Women in the Asia-Pacific Region: Persons, Powers and Politics, 11–13 August. Singapore: RELC.

Cole, R. V. 1985. Women in development in the South Pacific: barriers and opportunities. Papers presented at a conference held in Port Vila, Republic of Vanuatu, 11–14 August 1984. Canberra: Development Studies Centre, Australian National University.

Cribb, J., and J. R. Barnett. 1999 (forthcoming). Being bashed: Western Samoan women's attitudes towards domestic violence in Western Samoa and New Zealand. *Gender, Place, and Culture.*

Damousi, J. 1994. *Women come rally: socialism, communism and gender in Australia, 1890–1955.* Melbourne: Oxford University Press.

Davis, D. L., and J. Nadel-Klein. 1992. Gender, culture, and the sea: contemporary theoretical approaches. *Society and Natural Resources* 5(2):35–147.

De Ishtar, Z. 1994. *Daughters of the Pacific.* North Melbourne: Spinifex Press.

Dickerson-Putman, J. 1994. Women, development and stratification in the Eastern Highlands Province of Papua New Guinea. *Urban Anthropology* 23(1):13–38.

Drage, J. 1995. The exception, not the rule: a comparative analysis of women's political activity in Pacific Island countries. *Pacific Studies* 18(4):61–93.

Du Plessis, R., and P. Bunkle, eds. 1992. *Feminist voices: women's studies texts for Aotearoa/New Zealand.* Auckland: Oxford University Press.

Errington, F., and D. Gewertz. 1987. *Cultural alternatives and a feminist anthropology: an analysis of culturally constructed gender interests in Papua New Guinea.* Cambridge: Cambridge University Press.

ESCAP, United Nations Economic and Social Commission for Asia and the Pacific. 1995. Pacific women NGO Programme of Action for the Beijing UN Conference.

Etherington, N. 1996. The gendering of indirect rule: criminal law and colonial Fiji, 1875–1900. *The Journal of Pacific History* 31(1):42–57.

Fahey, S. 1986. Development, labor relations and gender in Papua New Guinea. *Mankind* 16(2):118–131.

Fairbairn-Dunlop, P. 1991. "E au le inailau a tamaitai": women, education and development, Western Samoa. Unpublished Ph.D. thesis. Macquarie University.

Fairbairn-Dunlop, P. 1993. Women and agriculture in Western Samoa. In *Different places, different voices: gender and development in Africa, Asia and Latin America,* ed. J. H. Momsen and V. Kinnaird, 211–223. London: Routledge.

Fan, C. C. 1996. Asian women in Hawai'i: migration, family, work, and identity. *National Women's Studies Association Journal* 8:70–84.

Fargher, S., and S. Maani. 1992. The gender gap in New Zealand: evidence of income differential occupational segregation. Working paper in economics no. 109. Auckland: University of Auckland.

Feinberg, R. 1986. Market economy and changing sex-roles on a Polynesian atoll. *Ethnology* 25(4):271–282.

Fife, W. 1995. Models for masculinity in colonial and postcolonial Papua New Guinea. *The Contemporary Pacific.* 7(2):277–302.

Fincher, R., and R. Liepins. 1997. Placing action: geographies of Australian women's activism. Proceedings of the International Conference on Women in the Asia-Pacific Region: Persons, Powers and Politics, 11–13 August. Singapore: RELC.

Flaherty, T. A. 1993. Educational opportunities for high school girls in Milne Bay and East Sepik province: female teachers making a difference. In *Participation and education change: implications for educational reform in Papua New Guinea,* ed. C. Thirlwall and B. Avalos, 237–248. Port Moresby: University of Papua New Guinea Press.

Gabriel, T. 1990. Pest management, women and rural extension. *Tropical Pest Management* 36(2):173–176.

Gailey, C. W. 1980. Putting down sisters and wives: Tongan women and colonization. In *Women and colonization: anthropological perspectives,* ed. M. Etienne and E. Leacock, 294–322. New York: Praeger.

Gailey, C. W. 1987. *Kinship to kingship: gender hierarchy and state formation in the Tongan Islands.* Austin: University of Texas Press.

Gannicott, K. G., and B. Avalos. 1994. *Pacific 2010: women's education and economic development in Melanesia.* Pacific Policy Paper No. 12. Canberra: Australian National University.

Gewertz, D. ed. 1988. *Myths of matriarchy reconsidered.* Oceania Monograph No. 33. Sydney: University of Sydney.

Grandea, N., and H. Gibb. 1995. *What's in a job? equity in human resource development in Asia-Pacific economies.* Ottawa: North-South Institute.

Griffen, V., ed. 1987. *Women, development and empowerment: a Pacific feminist perspective.* Report of a Pacific women's workshop, Naboutini, Fiji, 23–26 March, 1987. Kuala Lumpur: Asia and Pacific Development Centre.

Griffen, V. 1991. *Caring for ourselves: a health handbook for Pacific women.* Suva: Oceania Printers.

Grimshaw, P. 1994. *Colonialism, gender and representations of race: issues in writing women's history in Australia and the Pacific.* Parkville: University of Melbourne.

House, W. J. 1994. Gender issues for investigation in labor markets in the Pacific: some data and research prerequisites for policy formulation. Discussion paper No. 11. Suva: UNFPA Country Support Team Office for the South Pacific.

James, B., and K. Saville-Smith. 1994. *Gender, culture and power: challenging New Zealand's gendered culture.* Auckland: Oxford University Press.

Jayaraman, T. K. 1995. Demographic and socioeconomic determinants of contraceptive use among urban women in the Melanesian countries in the South Pacific: a case study of Port Vila town in Vanuatu. Occasional Paper No. 11. Asian Development Bank, Economics and Development Resource Center.

Jolly, M. 1994. *Women of the place: kastom, colonialism and gender in Vanuatu*. Switzerland: Harwood Academic Publishers.

Jolly, M., and M. Macintyre, eds. 1989. *Family and gender in the Pacific: domestic contradictions and the colonial impact*. Cambridge: Cambridge University Press.

Keef, S. P. 1990. Commerce matriculants: gender and ability. Working paper No. 4/90. Wellington: Victoria University of Wellington.

Kihleng, K. 1996. Women in exchange: negotiated relations, practice, the constitution of female power in processes of reproduction and change in Pohnpei, Micronesia. Unpublished Ph.D. thesis. Mānoa: University of Hawai'i at Mānoa.

Latieff, S. 1990. Rule by the Danda: domestic violence among Indo-Fijians. *Pacific Studies* 13(3):43–62.

Leckie, J. 1997. The limits to re-negotiating gender and work in Fiji. *Proceedings of the International Conference on Women in the Asia-Pacific Region: Persons, Powers and Politics, 11–13 August*. Singapore: RELC.

Lee, W. 1985. Women's groups in Papua New Guinea: shedding the legacy of drop scones and embroidered pillowcases. *Community Development Journal* 20(3):222–236.

Lepowsky, M. 1993. *Fruit of the Motherland: gender in an egalitarian society*. New York: Columbia University Press.

Lepowsky, M. 1994. Women, men, and aggression in an egalitarian society. *Sex Roles* 30(3/4):199–212.

Levy, S. J., R. Taylor, I. L. Higgins, and D. A. Grafton-Wasserman. 1988. Fertility and contraception in the Marshall Islands. *Studies in Family Planning* 19(3):179–185.

Lewis, D. N., and M. Rapaport. 1995. In a sea of change: health transitions in the Pacific. *Health and Place* 1(4):211–226.

Linnekin, J. 1990. *Sacred queens and women of consequence: rank, gender and colonialism in the Hawaiian Islands*. Ann Arbor: The University of Michigan Press.

Little, J. 1993. *And God sent women: women in the South Sea Evangelical Mission*. Unpublished M. Theol. Thesis. Pacific Theological College.

Lockwood, V. S. 1995. *Tahitian transformation: gender and capitalist development in a rural society*. Boulder and London: Lynne Rienner Publishers.

Longhurst, R. 1997. Flexible labor: bending over backwards. *Proceedings of the International Conference on Women in the Asia-Pacific Region: Persons, Powers and Politics, 11–13 August*. Singapore: RELC.

Lutkehaus, N. C., and P. B. Roscoe, eds. *Gender rituals: female initiation in Melanesia*. New York and London: Routledge.

MacKenzie, M. A. 1991. *Androgynous objects: string bags and gender in central New Guinea*. Chur, Switzerland: Harwood Academic Publishers.

Merry, S. E. 1995. Gender violence and legally engendered selves. *Identities* 2(1–2):49–73.

Momsen, J. H. 1991. *Women and development in the Third World*. London and New York: Routledge.

Ne, H. (collected and prepared by G. L. Cronin). 1992. *Tales of Molokai: the voice of Harriet Ne*. Laie, Hawai'i: Institute for Polynesian Studies, Brigham Young University–Hawai'i. University of Hawai'i Press.

Nero, K. L. 1990. The hidden pain: drunkenness and domestic violence in Palau. *Pacific Studies* 13(3):63–92.

O'Brien, D. and S. W. Tiffany eds. 1984. *Rethinking women's roles: perspectives from the Pacific*. Berkeley, London, Los Angeles: University of California Press.

Office of Legal Aid and Family Services. 1994. *Gender bias in litigation legal aid: issues paper*. Australia: Office of Legal Aid and Family Services, Attorney-General's Department.

Olson, E. 1994. Female voices of aggression in Tonga. *Sex Roles* 30(3/4):237–248.

Olsson, S. ed. *The gender factor: women in New Zealand organisations*. Palmerston North: Dunmore Press.

Perkins, F. 1993. *Integration of women's concerns into development planning: market interventions*. Reprint Series No. 8. Australian National University, Research School of Pacific Studies, National Centre for Development Studies.

Peteru, C. 1996. Breaking the silence. *Pacific Islands Monthly* 66(6):26–27.

Phillip, A. 1993. Trying to cope: the struggle of women in Port Moresby to continue their education by distance. In *Participation and education change: implications for educational reform in Papua New Guinea*, eds. C. Thirlwall and B. Avalos, 263–278. Port Moresby: University of Papua New Guinea Press.

Pickering, R. H. 1983. The role of the female extension worker in Vanuatu agriculture. *New Zealand Agricultural Science* 17(3):256–258.

PWRB (Pacific Women's Resource Bureau). 1997. *Women's News* 12(1).

Ralston, C. 1992. The study of women in the Pacific. *The Contemporary Pacific* 4(1):162–175.

Rashid, Y. 1995. Dealing with domestic violence. *Pacific Islands Monthly* 65(6):32.

Rennie, S. J. 1991. Subsistence agriculture versus cash cropping—the social repercussions. *Journal of Rural Studies* 7(1/2):5–9.

Scheyvens, R. 1995. Would the hand that rocks the cradle dare to rock the boat? feminism in the Solomon Islands. *New Zealand Geographer* 51(1):6–9.

Scheyvens, R. 1997. *The disempowerment of women through logging and mining activities in Melanesia*. Paper in the International Conference on Women in the Asia-Pacific Region: Persons, Powers and Politics, 11–13 August. Singapore: RELC.

Seniloli, K. 1989. *Family planning in Fiji*. Islands/Australia Working Paper 90/2. Australian National University, Research School of Pacific Studies, National Centre for Development Studies.

Seta, T. 1993. Why low female retention in secondary schools? an East Sepik experience. In *Participation and education change: implications for educational reform in Papua New Guinea*, ed. C. Thirlwall and B. Avalos, 249–262. Port Moresby: University of Papua New Guinea Press.

Sexton, L. 1986. *Mothers of money, daughters of coffee: the Wok Meri movement*. Monograph No. 10. Studies in Cultural Anthropology. Ann Arbor: UMI Research Press.

Shiva, V. ed. *Close to home: women reconnect ecology, health and development worldwide*. Philadelphia: New Society Publishers.

Small, C. 1989. *From the ground up: an anthropological version of a women's development movement in Polynesia*. Working paper No. 182. East Lansing: Office of Women in International Development, Michigan State University.

Smith, C., and J. Hutchinson. 1995. *Gender: a strategic management issue*. Chatswood: Business and Professional Publishing.

Souder, L. 1990. Guam update: Chamorro self-determination and militarisation of Guam: U.S. violates spirit and intent of United Nations declaration. *Pacific News Bulletin* 5(6):8–10.

Stephens, A. 1991. Poverty and gender issues. *Asian-Pacific Journal of Rural Development* 1(1):62–74.

Thomas, P. 1986. Women and development: a two-edged sword. In Women and development: what women say, 1–17. Canberra: Australian Council for Overseas Aid.

Tongamoa, T., ed. 1988. *Pacific women: roles and status of women in Pacific societies*. Suva: Institute of Pacific Studies of the University of the South Pacific.

Tuimaleali'ifano, M. A. 1990. *Samoans in Fiji: migration, identity and communication.* Suva: Institute of Pacific Studies, Fiji, Tonga and Western Samoa Extension Centres of the University of the South Pacific.

Vakadewavosa, T. D. R. 1992. *The changing role of women and ministry in the Methodist church in Fiji.* Unpublished B.D. thesis. Pacific Theological College.

Vete, M. F. 1995. The determinants of remittances among Tongans in Auckland. *Asian and Pacific Migration Journal* 4(1):55–68.

Waram, R. 1995. Tragedy strikes home. *Pacific Islands Monthly*, March, 12–13.

Young, K. ed. 1989. *Serving two masters: Third World women in development.* Bombay: Allied Publishers Ltd.

Zimmer-Tamakoshi, L. 1993. Nationalism and sexuality in Papua New Guinea. *Pacific Studies* 16(4):61–97.

Zimmer-Tamakoshi, L. 1995. Passion, poetry, and politics in the South Pacific. *Ethnology* 34(2):113–27.

# Urbanization

*Jean-Pierre Doumenge*

## Introduction

The development of urban centers is usually associated with organized political and administrative power, durable construction materials, transport and communication networks, water and energy supplies, and well-developed manufacturing, storage, and trade. Urban centers differ in size, plan, demography, and economies. The emergence, development, and transformation of towns and cities can be termed urbanization. During recent centuries, this process has intensified—in the Pacific as in other parts of the world.

Urbanization in the Pacific was closely linked to the colonial process, and subsequently to the introduction of a cash economy, reinforced by the influence of Christian missions. Today, urbanization is present in most Pacific Island groups but varies considerably in scale and pattern. Throughout the region, the proportion of island population living in urban centers has been increasing over recent decades, bringing changes in lifestyle and environment and posing new challenges for the future.

## Historical Emergence of Urban Centers

Prior to European contact, Pacific Island societies lived in hamlets, villages, and, occasionally, larger nucleated centers, such as Nan Madol in Pohnpei. However, due to the reliance on tubers, roots, and fruits, storage on a large scale was not very feasible. Hence, few people could be separated from subsistence agricultural and fishing activities. Moreover, political power was generally dispersed between a multitude of small-scale tribal groups or chiefdoms. Their military, administrative, and technological capacities were not sufficiently expanded to give rise to concentration of population, diversification of activities, and creation of towns and cities.

Europeans entered the Pacific in the early sixteenth century, but it was much later before the Pacific Ocean was explored to any great extent. A Spanish maritime route (the "galleon trade") joining Acapulco to Manila was established from the sixteenth to the eighteenth century across the Micronesian area, periodically stopping at Guam. South of the equator, the discoveries of Mendana and Tasman were without direct consequences, for a long time, for the majority of Pacific Island groups.

In the years following the extensive voyages of British and French explorers in the late eighteenth century up to the early nineteenth century, contacts between island societies and external countries were still sporadic. Local communities were visited only by small-scale expeditions searching for pearls, whale oil, sandalwood, and other products. These expeditions were linked with trading companies based in Sydney and San Francisco, at the periphery of the Pacific region.

Around the same time, Christian missionaries (beginning with the London Missionary Society) began to establish nucleated settlements in the Pacific Islands, but without initially transforming existing systems of economy, social organization, and land tenure. On several islands, however, land was acquired by missionaries and other settlers, and warehouses and workshops were built to accommodate new demands. By the mid-nineteenth century, the first Pacific Island towns began to emerge. These were Papeete (Tahiti), Honolulu (Hawai'i), Kororareka (New Zealand), Levuka (Fiji), and 'Apia (Samoa) (Ralston 1978).

Trading contacts intensified after the 1840s. Fur traders from San Francisco disembarked regularly at O'ahu on route to China. Traders from California, Australia, and other Pacific Rim locations arrived in Hawai'i and Tahiti to purchase fresh food for miners and hunters. Others sought fresh produce in the ports of New Zealand. The Sydney penal colony, for example, regularly received vegetables from New Zealand or Fiji and pork from Tahiti (Doumenge 1966).

Missionaries and traders needed the protection of island chiefs. But chiefs were in permanent competition with others, and alliances frequently shifted. Increasingly, support was solicited from European governments to stabilize local alliances. Beginning around 1840, European powers entered into competition over the Pacific region, dispatching naval forces and eventually taking possession of most island groups. Urbanization facilitated both necessary services and control of island populations.

Naval officers protecting colonial interests required ports easy to protect from ocean surges and storms. Ideally, these ports had wide and deep harbors, without reefs. Naval and trade ships required passes deeper than those used by traditional canoes. New settlements also needed protection against attack, and for this reason were often situated on defensible islets, peninsulas (Port Moresby, Suva, and Wellington), or sheltered bays (Honolulu, Pago Pago, and Auckland).

During the 1860s, European trading companies began to preserve copra (used in the production of margarine, soap, and cosmetics) for export to Western Europe and North America, initiating an extensive spread of coconut plantations. In the 1870s and 1880s, plantation economies became more diversified. The introduction of a variety of new crops, including cotton, sugar, coffee, cocoa, pineapple, and vanilla, stimulated trade and the growth of plantations and contributed to the emergence of towns.

By the late nineteenth century, expatriate miners, ranchers, and planters had become numerous and well established in several island groups. Organized public and private services were required in the main ports and agricultural centers. On Viti Levu, Fiji, small towns were created by the Colonial Sugar Refining Company to administer the immigrant labor force (Connell and Curtain 1982). In New Caledonia, nuclei were built up at various points along the west coast (generally at the estuary of a local river) to supply ranchers, miners, and the French penal colony.

The largest gold mining towns, with at most 2,000 people, were located in Papua New Guinea and Fiji. Nickel and manganese mining towns were established in New Caledonia. Phosphate extraction on Nauru and Makatea led to some nucleation, but these towns were of a temporary nature. Mining did not generate large centers prior to the mid-twentieth century, except where metallurgical processing operations were present, notably gold in Dunedin (New Zealand) and nickel in Noumea (New Caledonia).

Colonial urban and regional centers initially had a limited effect on hinterland societies. Outlying areas served primarily as reserves for labor and raw materials. In Papua New Guinea, lack of road connections made contact with the densely populated highlands particularly difficult. In many areas, transport of goods and people was limited to sea traffic. Over time, however, the influence of ports began to radiate to the periphery; towns increasingly served as centers of diffusion for new products and new ideas.

Colonial towns were initially planned and administered by and for European expatriates. Christchurch ("the most English city out of England") was planned from England; Dunedin ("Edinburgh of the Southern Hemisphere"), from Scotland (Bacconnier 1988). Nouméa was built on a wide grid, on leveled hills and drained swamps (Doumenge 1966). Honolulu was developed on hills and taro marshes (Huetz de Lemps 1977). Melanesian towns under German, British, and Australian rule reflected patterns in the metropolitan country.

In Australian Papua, towns sprawled over large distances, as in Australia, and urban planning was often negligible. Colonial towns were not always elegant or attractive places; they were generally small-scale, peripheral endeavors. Nineteenth and early twentieth century Melanesian towns, for example, have been described as "seedy and dusty outliers of largely uninterested colonial powers" (Connell and Lea 1994).

At the end of the colonial era, the usual pattern for Pacific towns was of the following form:

a) A core grid of roads surrounded by rows of one- or two-story buildings, serving as stores, warehouses, private and public offices, hotels and bars, and private houses. These were generally constructed with wooden walls and corrugated iron roofs. In New Zealand and Hawai'i, stone, brick and concrete buildings were present as well.

b) A periphery, spreading in accordance with the surrounding landscape and composed of expatriate residential estates and indigenous villages.

Colonial towns were essentially places where Europeans exchanged, stored, and sometimes processed plantation and mining products. Some expatriate families lived in the regular grid, but many preferred to live along coastal plains, on low hill slopes, and in valleys converging on the harbor and central business districts. Asians could be found along or inside the grid street pattern, often as small shop owners.

Colonial towns generally remained enclaves of the outside world, reflecting, with some differences, the respective metropolitan society. Islanders generally stayed in nearby villages, close to the towns where they worked, but were socially and spatially marginalized (Connell and Curtain 1982). In New Zealand, most towns were separated intentionally from Maori villages. In Hawai'i, Tahiti, and Samoa, intermarriage between expatriates and islander women was common, but it was infrequent elsewhere.

## The Demographic Influx

Nineteenth-century towns were built by and for Europeans and Americans, serving as nodal points for economic activity and political control. By 1865, 172,000 British settlers were in New Zealand, mostly engaged in sheep ranching. French settlers established ranches in Western New Caledonia. Other settlers began to farm tropical crops, including sugar and coffee, in Hawai'i (Americans); Micronesia, Samoa, and Northern New Guinea (Germans); Tahiti (French); and Papua and Fiji (British).

Competition between Europeans and Pacific Islanders soon led to conflict (violently in the case of the Maori land wars and Kanak revolts) and to rising concern over the implications of European settlement. In Solomon Islands, Vanuatu, Tokelau, Easter Island, and some of the Cook Islands, relations were further strained by blackbirding; islanders were compelled to work on Queensland sugar plantations and Latin American mines, sometimes by force, under conditions of semislavery.

With economic, administrative, and missionary activity increasing, the need for labor grew steadily, and islanders began to settle near plantations, towns, and ports. Head taxes were imposed in New Caledonia and Papua New Guinea. To obtain the necessary cash for required taxes and rising material aspirations, islanders began to settle and find work in plantations, and eventually (when colonial restrictions on migration and urban settlement were relaxed) in towns as well.

Where local labor was insufficient or regarded as inadequate, laborers were recruited from Asia. Most were unmarried males, generally with five-year contracts; however, women quickly became part of these migration streams (Doumenge 1966). Migrant laborers began their stay in plantations and had the option of returning home upon expiration of their contracts, or when plantations and mines began to decline, but many stayed on in the islands, moving to towns for educational, economic, and other opportunities.

In Hawai'i, 359,000 migrants arrived from Asia, originating in successive waves from China, Japan, Okinawa, Korea, and the Philippines, to work in sugar plantations and mills and in Honolulu industries (Lind 1980). In Fiji, 62,837 Indians were recruited for plantations in Viti Levu and Vanua Levu and the public works department in Suva (Connell and Curtain 1982); with their descendants, Indians constituted half the population by 1944. Japanese, Vietnamese, and Javanese were recruited to New Caledonia for plantations and mining and were more numerous than Europeans prior to World War II.

Smaller numbers of Asians arrived in other locations. Between the world wars, there was considerable migration from Japan to Micronesia (then a Japanese colony). In Palau and the Marianas, Japanese outnumbered Micronesians. By 1939, 540,000 Asians and 140,000 Europeans were living in the tropical Pacific Islands (Doumenge 1966). During World War II, the U.S. military build-up contributed to urban employment and business. However, the number of Asians fell substantially following the war, with many (particularly in New Caledonia and Micronesia) repatriated to their home countries.

Pacific Islanders were seldom part of the urban world. Even in Honolulu, where intercultural relations were "numerous and friendly," islanders gradually became second-class citizens (Ralston 1978:214). In Melanesia prior to World War II, islanders were permitted in towns only with employment contracts for a limited duration, were housed by their employers, and were otherwise segregated. Intergroup assimilation, sexual relations, and marriage were discouraged. In Port Moresby, curfews were in effect (Connell and Curtain 1982).

For islanders, the situation began to change following contact with the American army and participation with Allied Forces during World War II. There was an increasing demand for schools, hospitals, and government jobs. Access to citizenship rights accelerated this change, along with the desire for a better standard of living and some decline in racial discrimination. Existing towns acted as demographic pumps, stimulating a migration influx by islanders.

Circular migration (and, later, long-term migration) became a permanent component of urbanization, initially for young men and later for young women. Increasingly, rural families made the choice to move to or closer to towns to earn wages and educate children, returning to villages of birth only for holidays and traditional feasts. This process began in Polynesia and later extended to Melanesia and Micronesia as well.

During the 1960s and 1970s, colonial powers increased their expenditures as part of preparation for independence, giving rise to an economic boom. The rush to urban areas, and in particular to capital cities, then became sustained. Introduction of modern airports and jets facilitated global linkages, invigorating urban centers and stimulating international migration by islanders. By then, material expectations had increased among islanders, and urban life offered opportunities (not always fulfilled) for a higher standard of living.

In recent decades, urban economic opportunities in Hawai'i, New Zealand, and, on a smaller scale, New Caledonia have attracted migration from other Pacific Islands. From independent and free-associated entities of Polynesia and Micronesia, there has been significant emigration to New Zealand, Hawai'i, and the United States. In Papua New Guinea, Solomon Islands, and Vanuatu, urban influx is internal, especially to capital cities. In French and American territories, mobility varies in accordance with the prevailing economic, employment, and infrastructural situation.

With a relatively strong economy and a strategic position on the route to North America, Honolulu attracts migrants from Micronesia and American Samoa. Western Samoans and other Polynesians often work at fish canneries in Pago Pago before moving to Hawai'i (and California), assisted by extended-family networks. Similarly, Micronesians often stay temporarily in Guam, working in construction, transport, and tourism and later moving to Hawai'i.

New Zealand's urban centers attract migrants from Tokelau, the Cook Islands, Niue (all of whom are considered New Zealand citizens), Samoa, and (more recently) Tonga and Fiji (an exodus triggered by the 1987 military coup in Fiji). In 1991, there were over 150,000 Pacific Islanders in New Zealand, particularly in Auckland. Considering its Pacific Islander residents as well as approximately a half million local Maoris, Auckland has become the "Polynesian capital of the world."

Nouméa has been a destination of migrants from Tahiti, Wallis and Futuna, and (formerly) Vanuatu. The result is often work competition between Polynesians and Melanesians. Notwithstanding government attempts to counterbalance Nouméa's urban primacy, Melanesians continue to arrive in Nouméa from the hinterland and outer islands. By the 1970s, 80% of the average income of New Caledonia Melanesians (previously confined to rural reservations) derived from urban employment and remittances (Doumenge 1982).

## Contemporary Towns and Cities

Contemporary Pacific towns and cities are multifunctional, polyethnic, and dominated by tertiary activities. Government, administrative, and military functions are prominent in capital cities. Business and administrative offices congregate in an urban core. Nearby are hospitals, hotels, restaurants, and other valued facilities. Resorts, golf clubs, and leisure places extend along the coastline; yacht clubs and marinas sit in sheltered bays; warehouses and manufacturing plants are located near ports. Barracks and naval bases may be located centrally (as in Papeete) or peripherally (as in Honolulu).

Residential suburbs extend up valleys or along beaches, and more broadly on shore plains or plateaus, along with shopping, recreation, and cultural centers. New suburbs colonize hillslopes, conforming to the relief. Well-built houses and neighborhoods are found on hilltops or near the shore. Lower-class housing is found in low-lying areas, near industrial parks or mangroves. Subdivisions sprawl outward where land is available, as in Auckland or Nouméa; otherwise (as in Port Moresby, Suva, and Papeete), squatter settlements occur.

In small Pacific Islands, towns (confined to the capital) extend in a thin coastal band on either side of the port. On volcanic islands, the interior is covered by forest and scrub; the coastal plain, covered by coconut and other crops, is often the locus of urban expansion. Where agriculture and fishing are dominant, as in Tonga or Solomon Islands, capitals are a cluster of small concrete houses beyond the coastal commercial axis. Such towns are often a mosaic of villages, with many trees and gardens.

On atolls, narrow islets and a lack of garden vegetation

lend a different appearance to towns. In the Federated States of Micronesia, around 20,000 people live on Moen Islet, in Truk district. This nucleus aggregates several small villages, but without significant infrastructural services. Larger towns have emerged in Majuro (Marshall Islands) and Tarawa (Kiribati). There, capital city political and administrative functions have generated industrial, commercial, and service activities in recent years.

Small towns are generally highly dependent on government spending and associated services. In some towns, industrial sectors have developed, oriented both for exports and local markets. For example, Fongafale (on Funafuti, Tuvalu) produces biscuits and soap for residents, freezes tuna fish, and produces shirts for export. However, most small towns in the Pacific are overshadowed by the economic and cultural attractions of the main island centers and Pacific Rim cities.

The emergence and development of urban centers depends critically on access to land. Land has posed a problem since first external contact, as indigenous landowners are often reluctant to alienate (and sometimes even to lease) valued family land. In Kwajalein Atoll (Marshall Islands), where residents have been relocated for military purposes and now resettled on crowded Ebeye Islet, there are demands for increased royalties and improved living conditions.

Governments are often unwilling to expropriate land for residential and industrial uses. In Samoa, it is illegal to sell or mortgage customary land unless authorized by Act of Parliament (Connell 1995). Similar restrictions exist in most Pacific Island groups. In Fiji (where native land was protected by the British colonial administration), over 80% of the land is

### Table 26.1 Urban Populations in the Pacific Islands During the 1990s

Data were obtained from the following sources: Bureau of the Census, Washington, DC, for Guam and Hawai'i; Bureau of Statistics, Suva, for Fiji; Department of Statistics, Wellington, for New Zealand; Department of Statistics, Port Moresby, for Papua New Guinea; ITSTAT, Papeete, for French Polynesia; ITSEE, Noumea, for New Caledonia; South Pacific Commission, Noumea: *Statistical Bulletin*, 1994 (for all South Pacific countries); United Nations, New York City: *Statistical Year Book for Asia and the Pacific*, 1994 (for all Pacific countries); The Economist Intelligence Unit, London: *Papua New Guinea, Pacific Countries Annual Reports*, 1996; Europa Publications, Rochester: *The Far East and Australasia*, 1996.

| | Total population | Population of main town | Reference | Density per sq km | urban pop./ total pop. (%) |
|---|---|---|---|---|---|
| **Melanesia:** | | | | | |
| Fiji | 796,000 | Suva : 200,000 | estimate 1993 | 43 | 38 |
| New Caledonia | 196,836 | Nouméa : 118,823 | census 1996 | 10 | 64 |
| Papua New Guinea | 3,922,000 | Port Moresby : 250,000 | estimate 1993 | 8 | 15 |
| | | Lae : 120,000 | | | |
| Solomon Islands | 366,000 | Honiara : 36,000 | estimate 1994 | 13 | 10 |
| Vanuatu | 165,000 | Port Vila : 20,000 | estimate 1994 | 14 | 18 |
| **Micronesia:** | | | | | |
| Guam | 149,000 | - | estimate 1995 | 272 | 93 |
| Federated States of Micronesia | 104,724 | Kolonia: 12,000 | census 1994 | 150 | 40 |
| Kiribati | 78,400 | Tarawa : 29,000 | estimate 1995 | 97 | 37 |
| Marshall Islands | 52,000 | Majuro : 25,000 | estimate 1993 | 287 | 60 |
| Nauru | 10,200 | - | estimate 1994 | 479 | 100 |
| Northern Marianas | 56,700 | Saipan: 45,000 | estimate 1995 | 124 | 95 |
| Palau | 16,500 | Koror: 10,000 | estimate 1994 | 33 | 62 |
| **Polynesia:** | | | | | |
| American Samoa | 54,800 | Pago Pago: 25,000 | estimate 1995 | 281 | 40 |
| Cook Islands | 19,100 | Avarua: 6,000 | estimate 1994 | 81 | 28 |
| French Polynesia | 219,521 | Papeete : 115,759 | census 1996 | - | 61 |
| Hawai'i | 1,186,800 | Honolulu : 700,000 | estimate 1995 | 71 | 80 |
| New Zealand | 3,541,600 | Auckland : 929,300 | estimate 1994 | 13 | 85 |
| | | Wellington : 329,000 | | | |
| | | Christchurch : 318,100 | | | |
| Niue | 2,321 | - | census 1994 | 9 | 25 |
| Pitcairn | 55 | - | estimate 1995 | 13 | - |
| Samoa | 164,000 | 'Apia: 37,000 | estimate 1994 | 58 | 23 |
| Tokelau | 1,577 | - | census 1991 | 156 | - |
| Tonga | 98,400 | Nuku'alofa : 25,000 | estimate 1994 | 132 | 25 |
| Tuvalu | 9,500 | Funafuti : 3,500 | estimate 1995 | 365 | - |
| Wallis and Futuna | 14,166 | - | census 1996 | 5 | - |

currently under traditional tenure. To enlarge cities and towns, planners and developers must negotiate with a Native Land Trust Board acting for local *matakali* (clans).

In Noumea and Papeete, most of the urban area is freehold, but negotiations can be difficult. Landowners tend to speculate, creating a shortage of supply. On O'ahu and Guam, speculation has raised land prices and there have been demands for releasing military territory following the Vietnam War and in the 1990s. Migrant families manage by informal renting in overcrowded conditions (Connell 1995). Rapid growth has led to squatter settlements, presenting a strain on water, sanitation, electricity, and other services.

In planning for urban expansion, governments need to provide access to basic services and employment and, ideally, low-cost urban housing. There is an evident contradiction between the need for employment and better services and the concurrent reluctance to modify traditional tenure patterns. Reclamation of lagoons and wetlands (as has occurred in Waikīkī, O'ahu, permitting tourist development) provides a partial solution.

A population density of 1,000 per sq km is often considered a minimum standard for a town. However, the presence of a developed infrastructure is also important, as large villages may include 5,000 inhabitants, while lacking the infrastructure and commercial activities characteristic of urban centers. In newly independent countries, the urban process is still embryonic, and towns include pockets of traditional villages.

Contemporary urban populations range from around 3,000 in Tuvalu to 1.5 million in New Zealand (Table 26.1). The proportion of the total population residing in urban areas is high in Micronesia, Hawai'i, New Caledonia, Tahiti, and New Zealand (Figure 26.1). Elsewhere in the region, the proportion is lower, due to the recency of urban attraction (in recently independent Melanesian countries) and continuing emigration outflow (in several Polynesian countries).

With the exception of New Zealand (where Auckland is the largest city and Wellington the capital), the largest urban centers are the political capitals. The largest cities comprise at least two-thirds of the urban population, except for New Zealand and Papua New Guinea (Table 26.2); the primacy of main cities is in turn a function of their economic and political vitality. Only two urban centers are sufficiently large to be considered "metropolitan cities"—Honolulu and Auckland, both with populations exceeding a half million.

Processing and manufacturing are present in Honolulu and Auckland, and to a lesser extent in Port Moresby, Suva, and other locations. Mining has generated a large town on Bougainville and small towns elsewhere in Papua New Guinea, New Caledonia, and Fiji. Tertiary activities are common in urban areas of all scales. Tourism is a leading sector in the economy of Hawai'i, Guam, the Northern Marianas, and Palau. Tourism has resulted in the expansion of urban areas, but it has not generally resulted in new towns.

Urbanization is shaped by a combination of political, cultural, and environmental factors. Papeete, for example, was molded by over a century of French colonial administration; yet in its narrow coastal fringe development (related to steep topography and the absence of mangroves) it resembles

### TABLE 26.2 — Relation Between Urban Primacy and the Economy (see Table 26.1 for sources)

| | Main city population / urban population (%) | GDP / capita (US $) 1993 |
|---|---|---|
| **Melanesia:** | | |
| Fiji | 66 (Suva) | 2,070 |
| New Caledonia | 94 (Nouméa) | 15,360 |
| Papua New Guinea | 35 (Port Moresby) | 980 |
| Solomon | 98 (Honiara) | 770 |
| Vanuatu | 67 (Port Vila) | 1,090 |
| **Micronesia:** | | |
| Guam | - (Agana-Tamuning) | 14,240 |
| F. S. M. | 75 (Kolonia) | - |
| Kiribati | 100 (Bairiki/Tarawa) | 750 |
| Marshall Islands | 80 (Majuro /D.U.D) | - |
| Nauru | 100 - | 10,100 |
| Northern Marianas | 100 (Saipan) | 9,300 |
| Palau | 100 (Koror) | - |
| Tuvalu | - | 720 |
| **Polynesia:** | | |
| American Samoa | 100 (Pago Pago) | 7,200 |
| Cook Islands | 100 (Avarua) | 1,600 |
| French Polynesia | 87 (Papeete) | 15,200 |
| Hawai'i | 97 (Honolulu) | 24,800 |
| New Zealand | 31 (Auckland) | 12,100 |
| Samoa | 100 ('Apia) | 690 |
| Tonga | 100 (Nuku'alofa) | 1,350 |
| Wallis-Futuna | | 3,720 |

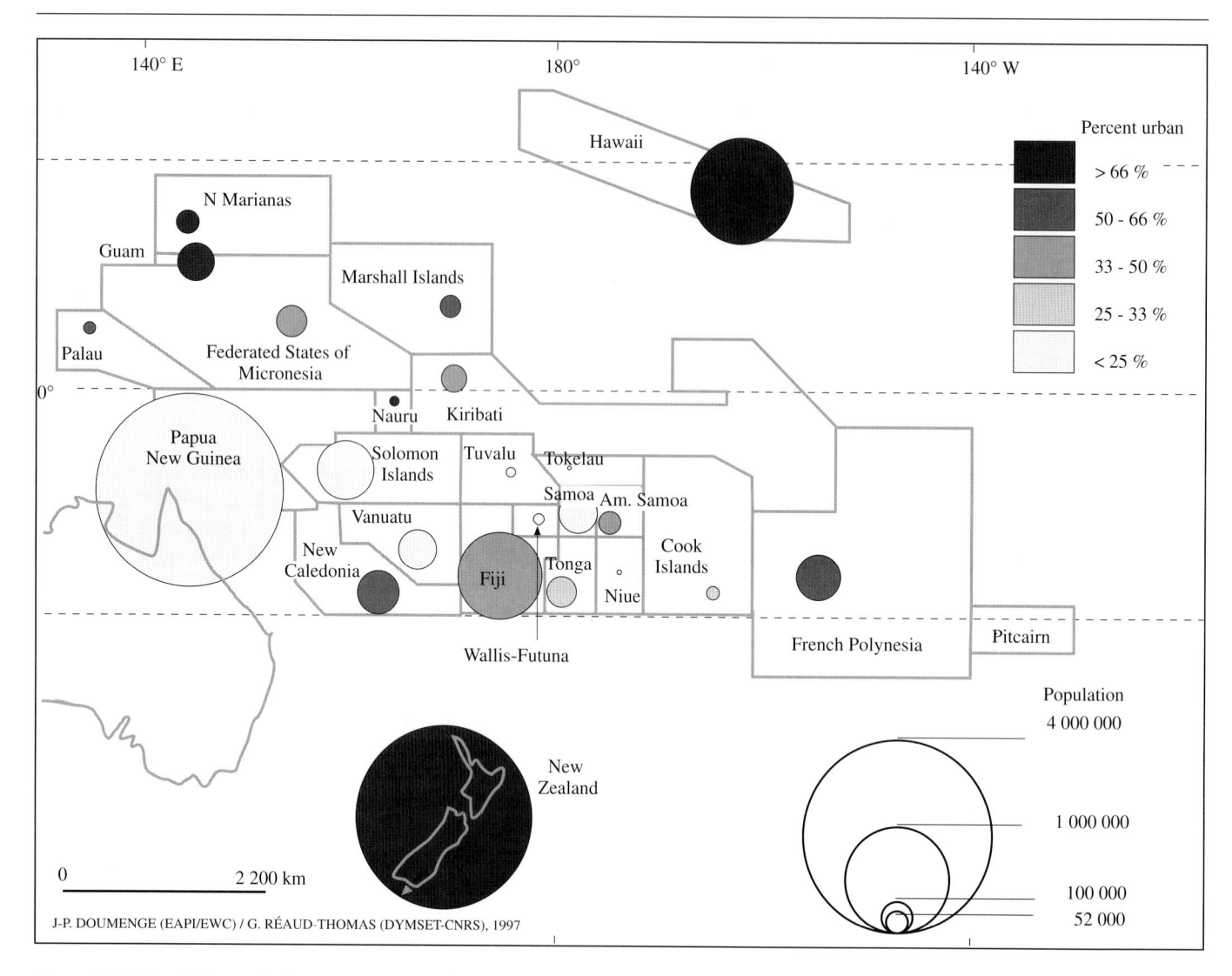

*Figure 26.1. Population and urban percentage in the Pacific Islands in the 1990s (census and official estimates).*

Honolulu rather than Nouméa. Honolulu and Papeete are also alike in the degree of integration between Europeans and indigenous populations, relative to urban centers in Melanesia.

## Illustrative Cases

Space precludes detailed discussion of urbanization by island group throughout the Pacific. However, patterns of urban growth will be outlined through several illustrative cases, along with color maps based on field studies by the author (Color Plates 26A–D).

### Hawai'i

Urbanization in Hawai'i is dominated by Honolulu (see Figure 26.2 and Color Plate 26A), situated on a fairly sizable stretch of O'ahu's leeward coastal plain, including reclaimed wetlands. A more narrow, linear pattern of urbanization and tourist development is found on Maui and Kaua'i. On Hawai'i Island (the "Big Island"), towns include Hilo, Waimea, and Kona. Hawai'i's urban population is ethnically diverse, including Caucasians, Japanese, Chinese, other Asian groups, and Native Hawaiians.

Initially a whaling town, Honolulu grew rapidly with the rise of the sugar and pineapple industries. Trade and industry flourished in a large central business district with diverse service activities. Multistory buildings were progressively built up in

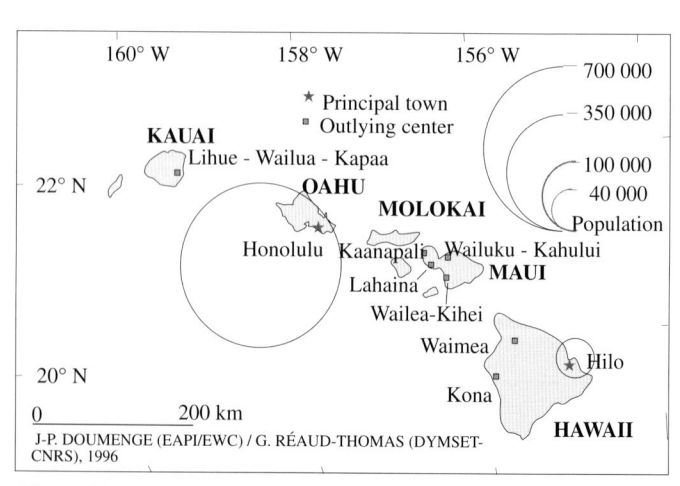

*Figure 26.2. Urban population in Hawai'i (1995 estimate).*

this central area, including a small Chinatown. U.S. military bases, mainly located around Pearl Harbor, became predominant during World War II, then during the Cold War. (These bases form one of the largest military complexes in the world, with 60,000 military and 20,000 civil employees in the 1980s.)

In 1959, the status of Hawai'i changed from U.S. territory to state. Jet air transport made O'ahu an attractive destination for American and Japanese tourists. By the mid 1990's, tourism comprised 35% of the $26,800 million GDP (compared to only 3% for agriculture). Asian economic difficulties have recently resulted in a slowdown in tourism, which has hurt the economy. Most of the tourist population is located in Waikīkī, but the urban residential sector has spread to half the island of O'ahu.

Honolulu's skyline is currently dominated by high-rise hotels, condominiums, and office buildings, built largely during the heyday of the tourist industry. Factories and docks are situated between the city and the bases and heavy industry at Campbell Industrial Park. Large commercial malls serve the metropolitan area. Traffic has become an increasing problem during rush hours, despite the construction of several major highways. The attempted establishment of a "second city" at Kapolei has thus far failed to meet expectations (Goss and McGranaghan 1996).

Neighborhoods differ in ethnicity and socioeconomic stratification, and a variety of combinations exist. Upper-income neighborhoods can be found on the slopes overhanging the coastal plain, in downtown and midtown skyscrapers, and in other exclusive areas. Low-income neighborhoods occur in valleys near the city's center. Middle-income neighborhoods occur in the periphery of Honolulu, around Pearl Harbor, Mililani, and Wahiāwā, or on the windward side, linked to Honolulu by freeways.

## French Polynesia and New Caledonia

Urbanization in both French Polynesia and New Caledonia is overwhelmingly dominated by the capital cities (Figures 26.3-4 and Color Plate 26B)—much as France is dominated by Paris—the consequence of a long period of colonial centralization.

Papeete comprises a 50-km-long agglomeration in Tahiti, French Polynesia, where over half the territory's population resides. Smaller towns occur at Taravao, on the isthmus joining Tahiti's two volcanoes; and in northern Moorea. Smaller yet is Uturoa, regional center for the Leeward Islands. The few towns in the Tuamotus, the Australs, and the Marquesas include only a few hundred inhabitants, with minimal infrastructure and services.

Nouméa is equivalent in size and urban primacy to Papeete, comprising two thirds of New Caledonia's population. Likewise, Nouméa dominates the territory economically and politically. Bourail, situated on the west coast at the junction of two main roads, is the only urban center of significance outside the Nouméa area. The small towns of La Foa, Koumac, and Poindimie can be considered distant extensions of Nouméa and Bourail.

Urban development in both territories accelerated in the

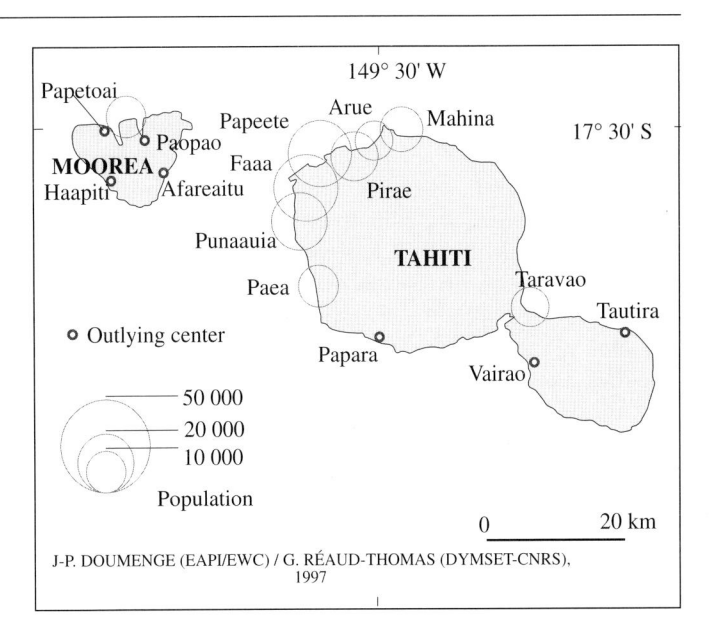

*Figure 26.3.* Urban population in Tahiti and Moorea (1996 census).

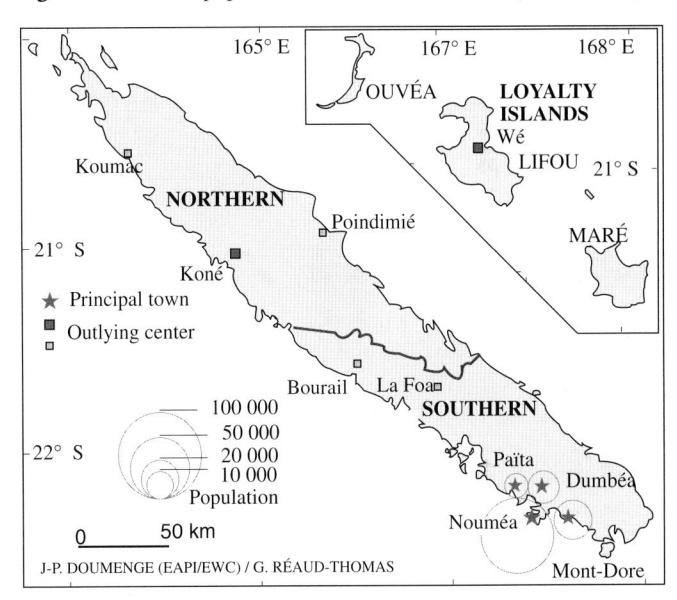

*Figure 26.4.* Urban population in New Caledonia (1996 census).

1960s. Papeete expanded following nuclear weapons testing in the Tuamotus (1963). From 1964 to 1992, the CEP (Centre d'Expérimentation du Pacifique), through military and related expenditures, was the main economic stimulant for urban growth. Growth in Nouméa was linked to the Société le Nickel. Noumea served as a base for allied military forces in 1942, providing a further growth stimulus. Rapid expansion began around 1958. By 1993, industry and services accounted for the largest segment of the GDP in Papeete and Nouméa.

Urban growth has been rapid during recent decades. Noumea had been 15 sq km by 1969; it was double in area by 1992. Papeete had been 15 kilometers long in 1963; it was three times as long in 1992. The central business districts of Papeete and Nouméa now have multistory buildings in addition to older double story stores. Commercial ports have been extended by lagoon reclamations. Marinas and international hotels are located on the periphery of both locations.

In Papeete, the city follows a relatively narrow coastal strip. Wealthy subdivisions occur on the coastal plain and volcanic slopes overlooking the city. Middle-income dwellings occur in the periphery. Low-income housing and small shantytowns are found in downtown valleys, near industrial parks, and behind the airport. These are populated largely by outer-island migrants, especially from the Tuamotus (though reverse migration has recently occurred, attributable to government funding and a black pearl boom).

Nouméa's residential plan is distinctive. The town is built along a narrow peninsula, near a large nickel-melting plant and industrial parks. Low-income housing occurs nearby, occupied mainly by Melanesians and migrant Wallisians. Middle-income dwellings occur in the east and other parts of the city, with diverse ethnic groups. Upper-income neighborhoods occur in the tourism and leisure area to the south, populated mainly by Europeans, Asians, and Tahitians.

The populations of Papeete and Nouméa have increased considerably in recent decades. There are now more outer islanders and mainland French in both locations. In Nouméa, Europeans, Polynesians, and Asians together make up 80% of the population. Melanesians, confined to rural reservations until 1946, are now moving to the Nouméa outskirts and comprise a fifth of the city's population. Papeete is populated mainly by Tahitians and part-Tahitians, followed by Europeans and outer-island migrants.

## Fiji and Papua New Guinea

Urbanization in Fiji and Papua New Guinea is dominated by the country capitals Suva and Port Moresby (Figures 26.5–6 and Color plate 26C). Papua New Guinea, with a vast landmass and population almost 4 million, has sizable secondary towns.

Suva serves as the center of administration and business, followed by Lautoka, center of the sugar belt, and the two regional centers of Nadi and Ba, all on Viti Levu. An international airport, large hotels, and major tourist resorts are located near Nadi. Ba is a central marketplace for Indian farmers. Singatoka is a comparable center for Melanesian villagers. Labasa, on Vanua Levu, is a main sugar processing center, with a predominant Indian population. Levuka, on Ovalau Island, once the capital, but now a minor town, specializes in freezing and canning fish.

By 1881, following Fiji's annexation by the British, Suva had become the capital and main urban center, replacing Levuka. Today, Suva extends from a peninsular central business district near the harbor for some 15 km inland. Its population includes approximately equal numbers of Fijians and Indo-Fijians; the remaining 10% comprises migrant Pacific Islanders, Europeans, and Chinese.

Suva's economic importance (accounting for nearly half the country's gross domestic product) has resulted in significant migration from outer islands (Bayliss-Smith et al. 1988). A government housing authority has attempted to provide modest dwellings and plots of land for low-income wage earners. However, space is insufficient, shantytowns are growing, and there are increasing concerns over urban poverty (Bryant 1992).

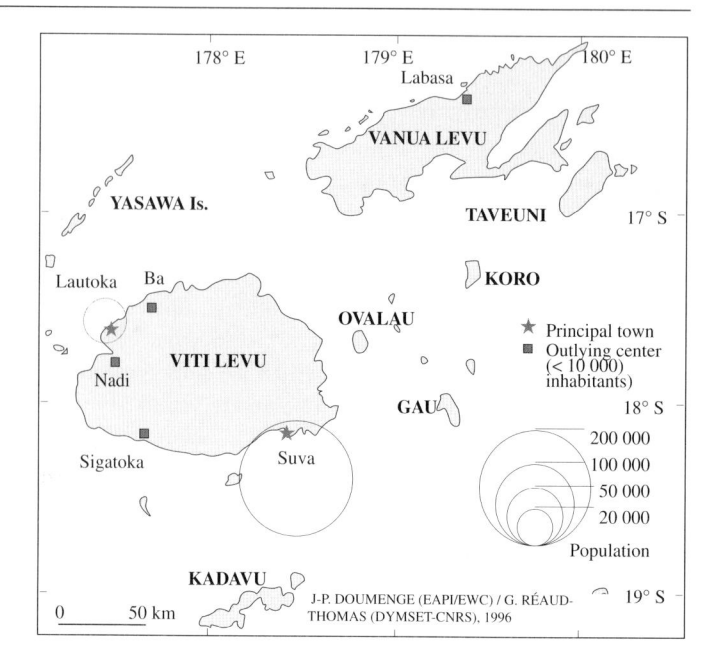

*Figure 26.5.* Urban population in Fiji (1990 estimate).

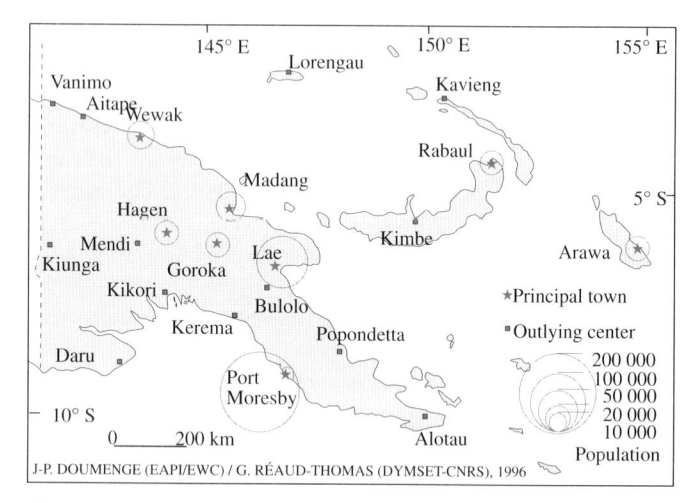

*Figure 26.6.* Urban population in Papua New Guinea (1990 census).

Port Moresby, in Papua New Guinea, has been the territorial capital since the period of British and Australian administration. Though Port Moresby remains the lead city, urban hierarchy is less stratified than elsewhere in the Pacific. Sizable towns are also found in Lae, Madang, Wewak, Goroka, and Mount Hagen in the highlands, none of which are connected by road with Port Moresby. This fragmentation creates problems of coordination and service provision for government and business.

Port Moresby's population rose fourfold between 1970 and 1990. Since it is not yet connected to its hinterland, a majority of the population comes from diverse, often antagonistic ethnic groups in remote districts. Migrants generally assimilate on the basis of partnerships with local clans in the Port Moresby area. Migrants generally group themselves residentially by tribal origin, or wantok ("one talk"), affiliations. However, this grouping is opposed to the policy of the Housing Commission, which discourages ethnic segregation.

As in Suva, Port Moresby extends inland from a commercial

port, but the city lacks a well-defined CBD, and a multinuclear pattern has developed. Public services and industries are spread across inland slopes. Each neighborhood has an autonomous life, with separate commercial and service arrangements. Expatriate and national elites live in expensive villas or multi-story condominiums overlooking the harbor. Land, housing, and employment shortages have repeatedly resulted in tensions between ethnic groups and between long-term residents and squatters.

### Kiribati and the Marshall Islands

Urbanization on Kiribati and the Marshall Islands, both coral atoll groups, is constrained by shortage of land, water supply, and other resources. Yet the capitals Tarawa and Majuro are both fairly sizable towns, with over 20,000 inhabitants each (Figure 26.7 and Color Plate 26D). These towns continue to increase in size, due to an influx by outer-island migrants. Provision of adequate water and sanitation has been difficult to achieve, leading to periodic water contamination and disease outbreaks.

Tarawa's importance grew during World War II, when its Betio Islet was intensively fortified (including a military airstrip) under Japanese occupation. Following the end of the war, Tarawa became the center of administration (succeeding phosphate-rich Banaba, or Ocean Island). Tarawa became the country's capital following independence in 1979. By then, however, phosphates were exhausted, and (with few natural resources) Kiribati remains heavily dependent on aid, overseas earnings by islanders, and a trust fund (based on prior phosphate revenues).

Most of the population is aggregated along a 24-km ribbon of islets linked by causeways. Betio, astride a deep channel between the ocean and the lagoon, serves the country's main port and commercial center, with close to a thousand residents on 1.6 sq km. Most government offices are housed in adjacent Bairiki. The adjacent string of islets is also densely populated. An international airport has been built at Bonriki at the eastern end of the atoll. Despite existing crowding, the population on Tarawa has increased dramatically in recent decades.

Causeway construction now blocks ocean inflow, and wastes accumulate in cut-off sections of the lagoon. This, along with nearby lagoon reclamation, has resulted in the loss of over 200 hectares of mangroves, a breeding area for marine life. Most of the drinking water is still obtained by rain collection from corrugated tin roofs on an individual basis. In contrast to high islands with more abundant fresh water sources, dense atoll populations often find it easier to set up electric and phone connections than to supply safe water and sanitation.

Tarawa's crowding problems are among the most severe in the Pacific region, reflecting both environmental and political factors. Natural resources are limited to reefs (ecologically fragile), seabed mineral deposits (too expensive to exploit at the present time), and phosphates (present only on a few atolls and mostly exhausted during colonial administration). Because of Kiribati's independent political status, overseas migration is not an option for most i-Kiribati.

Darrit-Uliga-Delap (DUD), on Majuro, Marshall Islands, began its growth with the arrival of American forces during World War II, along with the construction of airstrips and stationing of naval units. It then became the territory's administrative center (replacing Jaluit), and today the capital. DUD comprises three islets—about 5 km long, but only 200 m wide—joined by causeways and roads. The town serves as home to some 20,000 Marshallese and is a center for business and government services.

Aid from the United States, granted for a fifteen-year period as part of the 1983 Compact of Free Association, accounts for some two-thirds of the Marshallese budget (other funding comes from military rentals and compensation for nuclear tests). Revenues are also obtained through international fishing licenses (mainly to Japan), passport sales (providing open-access entry to the United States after five years' residence), and ship registries. Much of this money is spent in Majuro, where half the country's population resides.

Fragmentation of traditional landholdings results in multiple

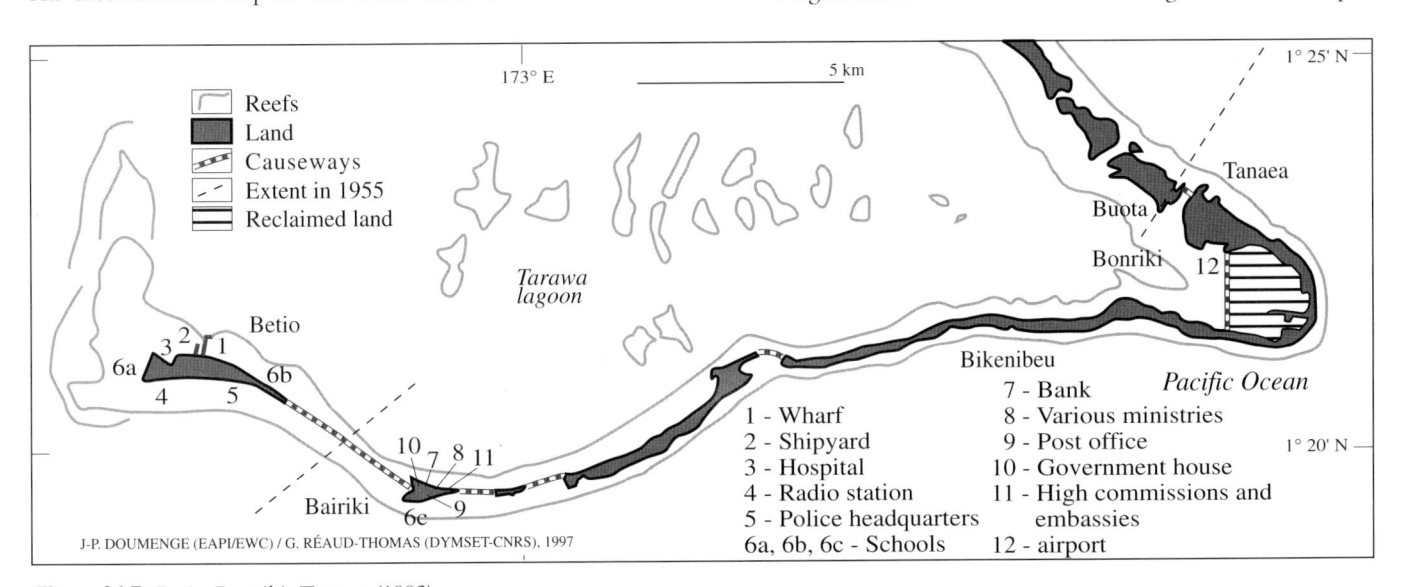

*Figure 26.7. Betio-Bonriki, Tarawa (1992).*

The Pacific Islands

claims to residential areas. Individual claims are typically for a hectare. Several families often reside on these plots, generally in small houses. Land has been allocated for commercial use and public services in central DUD, government buildings and principal public services have been built up on the way to the airport, and schools have been established in each of the three districts. Fresh foods are in scarce supply, and both water supply and sewage remain problematic.

## Impact on Environment and Society

Urban population pressure has had both environmental and social impacts. Mangrove clearance is destroying fish nurseries in Nouméa, Suva, and Tarawa. On Tarawa, landholding lineages have claimed compensation, since the lagoon was under the same tenure as the adjacent land. In most independent countries' urban areas, but particularly so in atolls, important tensions exist between outer-island migrants (who desperately need space) and central island residents (who fear losing their land).

Steep hill construction increases the risk of landslides, particularly in the case of suburbs in Papeete and Honolulu. Water pollution poses an even more pressing problem in some areas. Cities in Hawai'i and New Zealand are well supplied with fresh water and sewerage, but in other island groups, sewerage networks and even water supply are often inefficient or nonexistent. According to Connell (1993), just half of Papua New Guinea's urban households had water supplies and 11% had access to sewerage system in 1990.

Shortage and disruptions in water supply are still usual in most urban centers. International hotels usually must provide water and sewage arrangements on their own. Because of scarce land, high concentrations of people on coastal plains, and the cost of incinerators, it is also difficult to safely dispose of household and industrial rubbish. These issues are particularly problematic for atoll towns, highly constrained in land.

Providing adequate road infrastructure and electricity supplies is frequently a problem. Traffic jams occur daily in Guam, Nouméa, Suva, and Papeete. In Honolulu, freeways facilitate traffic across long distance, but parts of the city are still congested during rush hours. Air pollution is beginning to become worrisome in downtown urban areas. Gas shortages and breakdowns of oil-based power stations occasionally cause problems for both residents and industries.

Urban life generates health and nutritional problems. Food expenses can represent 30% to 40% of the total consumption of city dwellers. In some neighborhoods, traditional crops are grown. Still, urban diets are poor in protein, calcium, and some vitamins. Hunger and malnutrition are appearing among low-income families, hypertension and related diseases are on the rise, and high sugar consumption leads to dental problems. Alcoholism is widely responsible for road accidents and domestic violence.

Urban social stresses result in elevated rates of crime, drug abuse, and suicide. People are often caught in a social jam incomprehensible by reference to traditional roles. In centers as different in size and organization as Honolulu, Papeete, and Port Moresby, suicide and violence are common, particularly among outer-island migrants. In Papua New Guinea, unemployed "raskals" perpetrate robbery and attacks. Security guards and barbed wire fences around middle- and upper-class homes are proliferating.

Traditional social relations lose much of their efficiency in urban centers. Yet individuals of diverse cultural groups must somehow learn to work together, whether in Honolulu or Port Moresby. One form of social network is based on common places of origin. In Nouméa, for example, young men play soccer and young women cricket in traditional district associations. On weekends, meetings and feasts give life to these associations.

Other ways of bridging diverse cultures include neighborhood solidarity, church affiliation, or connections with a political leader. Women's associations invest in a variety of solidarity networks and may recreate the same associations when returning to traditional villages. When necessary, custom is reinterpreted, or adapted to new conditions of life. Pacific Island identities are so strong that custom is seldom totally lost.

Fragmentation is not a constraint when geographical and social mobility are well managed. Continental countries currently help by extending aid and receiving migrants. For the near future, movement of island populations to cities in Australia, New Zealand or America is likely to continue. As migrant communities grow, their members will be increasingly cognizant of their double identity, fashioned jointly by origin and residence.

## Conclusion

Urbanization has brought the Pacific into contact with global modernity. New goods, ideas, and lifestyles have been introduced to cities and surrounding villages, attracting and mixing diverse populations and offering the promise of increased incomes. To benefit from modernity, islanders have tended to move to capital cities (in many cases, the only real cities). Hence, urbanization is almost invariably concentrated in a single place.

For migrants, urban centers are a "promised land," a better life. In all islands, lack of economic opportunities and services displaces people from their villages, in some places creating shantytowns. Island towns and cities are often relays to prosperous Western countries such as Australia, Canada, and the United States. The smallest islands are becoming leisure areas for Japanese, American, and Australian tourists and visiting out-migrants.

Considerable diversity in demography, land use, and activities will probably continue to exist. Nouméa and Suva, for example, are both multiethnic, yet very different in economy and urban policy. Pacific Islanders do not wish to lose their identity—the feeling of being different from the outside world— but they do desire material comfort and education. Reconciling modern individualistic and urbanized lifestyles with traditional culture is likely to be the main challenge for Pacific Islanders in the twenty-first century.

# Bibliography

Antheaume, B., and J. Bonnemaison. 1988. *Atlas des Îles et États du Pacifique Sud*. Paris: PUBLISUD.

Bacconnier, G. 1985. Les villes de Nouvelle-Zélande. *Cahiers d'Outre-Mer* 38:207–234.

Bacconnier, G. 1988. Grandes villes et industries en Nouvelle-Zélande. Thèse de Doctorat d'État, Université de Lyon III.

Bonnemaison, J. 1977. *Système de migration et croissance urbaine à Port-Vila et Luganville (N.H)*. Paris: ORSTOM.

Bryant, J. J. 1977. Urbanization in Papua New Guinea: problems of access to housing and services. *Pacific Viewpoint* 18(1):43–57.

Bryant, J. J. 1992. Poverty in Fiji: who are the urban poor? *Singapore Journal of Tropical Geography* 13(2):90–102.

Buchholz, H. J. 1983. The role of small cities in spatial development in South Pacific island countries. *Malaysian Journal of Tropical Geography* 4(8):1–9.

Connell, J. Various years. *Migration, employment and development in the South Pacific*. Vols. 1–24. Nouméa: South Pacific Commission.

Connell, J., and R. Curtain. 1982. The political economy of urbanization in Melanesia. *Singapore Journal of Tropical Geography* 3(2):119–136.

Connell, J., and J. Lea. 1993. *Planning the future: Melanesian cities 2010*. Canberra: National Centre for Development Studies, Research School of Pacific Studies, Australian National University.

Connell, J., and J. Lea. 1994. Cities of parts, cities apart: changing places in modern Melanesia. *The Contemporary Pacific* 6(2):267–309.

Connell, J., and J. Lea. 1995. *Urbanisation in Polynesia*. Canberra: National Center for Development Studies, Research School of Pacific Studies, Australian National University.

Crocombe, R. 1992. *Pacific neighbours: New Zealand's relations with other Pacific islands*. Suva: University of the South Pacific.

Doumenge, F. 1966. *L'Homme dans le Pacifique Sud*. Paris: Société des Océanistes (Mémoire No. 19).

Doumenge, F. 1990. *La dynamique géopolitique du Pacifique Sud*. *Cahiers d'Outre-Mer* 43: 113–186.

Doumenge, J-P. 1982. *Du Terroir . . . à la Ville: les Mélanésiens et leurs espaces en Nouvelle-Calédonie*. Bordeaux-Talence: CEGET-CNRS-TDGT No. 46.

Doumenge, J-P. 1988. Demographic, economic, socio-cultural and political facts nowadays in the French Pacific Territories. *GeoJournal* 16(2):143–156.

Doumenge, J-P. 1995. L'urbanisation à Guam. *Cahiers d'Outre-Mer* 48:347–380.

Force, R. W., and B. Bishop, ed. 1975. *The impact of urban centers in the Pacific*. Honolulu: Pacific Science Association.

Goss, J., and M. McGranaghan. 1996. Urbanization. In *Hawai'i: a unique geography*, ed. J. Morgan, 143–60. Honolulu: Bess Press.

Guilcher, A. 1969. *L'Océanie*. Paris: PUF.

Harré, J., and C. Knapman. 1977. *Living in town: urban planning in the South Pacific*. Suva: University of the South Pacific.

Howard, M. C. 1989. *Ethnicity and nation-building in the Pacific*. Tokyo: United Nations University.

Howe, K., R. R. Kiste, and B. V. Lal. 1994. *Tides of history: the Pacific Islands in the 20th century*. Honolulu: University of Hawai'i Press.

Huetz de Lemps, C. 1977. Les Îles Hawaii: étude de géographie humaine. Thèse de Doctorat d'État, Université de Bordeaux III.

Huetz de Lemps, C. 1989. Un exemple de macrocéphalie touristique, les îles Hawaii. In *Îles et tourisme*. *Îles et Archipels* No. 10, 195–222. Bordeaux: CRET-CEGET.

Huetz de Lemps, C. 1991. Une métropole dans le Pacifique: Honolulu (Hawaii). In *La grande ville, enjeu du XXI siècle*. Paris: PUF, 255–269.

Jackson, R. 1977. The growth, nature and future prospects of informal settlements in Papua New Guinea. *Pacific Viewpoint* 18(1):22–42.

King, D. 1983. Functionnal deficiencies and constraints in small towns in Papua New Guinea. *Malaysian Journal of Tropical Geography* 4(8):33–39.

King, D. 1991. Contradictions in policy making for urbanization and economic development: planning in Papua New Guinea. *Cities* 12(1):44–53.

Lind, A. W. 1967. *Hawaii's people*. Honolulu: University of Hawai'i Press.

Low, J. 1981. *L'urbanisation et ses incidences sur l'environnement océanien*. Nouméa: South Pacific Commission.

Matwijiw, P. 1982. Urban land problems in Port Moresby, PNG. *Journal of Economic and Social Geography* 73(5):286–294.

Morauta, L., and D. Ryan. 1982. From temporary to permanent townsmen: migrants from the Malamau district, Papua New Guinea. *Oceania* 1:39–55.

ORSTOM. 1981. *Atlas de la Nouvelle-Calédonie*. Paris: ORSTOM.

ORSTOM. 1993. *Atlas de la Polynésie française*. Paris: ORSTOM.

Poirine, B. 1994. L'émigration océanienne: une théorie socio-économique. *Espace, Population, Sociétés* 2:213–224.

Rallu, J-L. 1994. Tendances récentes des migrations dans le Pacifique Sud. *Espace, Population, Sociétés* 2:201–212.

Ralston, S. 1978. *Grass huts and warehouses: Pacific beach communities of the nineteenth century*. Honolulu: University of Hawai'i Press.

Tetiarahi, G. 1983. Papeete, un exemple de croissance urbaine accélérée. *Cahiers d'Outre-Mer*, 36:343–371.

Van Trease, H. 1993. *Atoll politics: the republic of Kiribati*. Suva: University of the South Pacific.

Walsh, C. 1984. Much ado about nothing: urbanization, predictions and censuses in Papua New Guinea. *Singapore Journal of Tropical Geography* 5(1):73–87.

Wanek, A. 1996. *The state and its enemies in Papua New Guinea*. Richmond: Curzon Press.

Ward, G., and M. Ward. 1980. The rural-urban connection, a missing link in Melanesia. *Malaysian Journal of Tropical Geography* 1(1):57–63.

# Chapter 27

# Urban Dilemmas

*John Connell and John P. Lea*

In most Pacific Island groups urbanization has become important as, without exception, towns and cities are growing faster than total populations. In some places—particularly the atoll states of Kiribati, Tuvalu, and the Marshall Islands—this growth has resulted in exceptionally high population densities, comparable with those in the most highly populated Asian cities. Urban migration, rapid growth, and high densities in countries where economic growth has been slight have posed problems of poverty and urban management. As the President of Fiji, Sir Ratu Kamisese Mara, has said:

> It does not require any great genius to figure out the consequences of this urban drift. Quite apart from the basic strains placed on limited infrastructure, we have seen an erosion of cultural values, growing unemployment and the attendant restlessness, increased crime and other ills which plague large urban centres. . . . But in our case we have the additional constraints of limited resources, small land areas, isolation caused by distance and the consequences of the great social and cultural changes wrought by the new realities that our traditional ethos was not equipped to handle. (1994:9)

Contemporary Pacific towns and cities are quite different from their colonial predecessors: they are larger, more evidently home to Pacific Islanders, of greater social and economic importance, and constantly changing.

## Expanding Populations

The movement of people within and between islands has intensified in volume, increased in distance, and become more complex in pattern and purpose since the war years. Internal and international population flows are now the major regulators of demographic change in many of the small Pacific Island groups and are significant influences on urbanization. With the development of modern transportation and particularly air transport, the opportunity for migration has increased in a region that has historically been characterized by high mobility. Whereas in the past, migration tended to be circular or repetitive—often seasonal and usually over short distances—permanent and relatively long-distance migration has, in recent years, become a more general feature. Throughout the Pacific there are a number of general trends in population movement, although not all are necessarily present. First, international migration extends beyond the region; second, small islands are being depopulated as people move to large islands; third, mountain populations are moving to lowlands, usually along the coast; and fourth, urban populations are continuing to grow. In the past quarter of a century these trends have intensified and been accentuated to the extent that it is no longer possible to regard the Pacific as characterized by rural populations. Within and on the fringes of the Pacific, urban islander populations have grown substantially.

The rationale for urbanization and increased population concentrations is evident throughout the Pacific: employment opportunities and services (especially education and health) are concentrated in the urban centers. In small island states, where the labor force and capital are often limited, this urban concentration is inevitable to some extent, hence rural-to-urban migration follows. Urbanization is proportionally least in Melanesia—though towns and cities are larger—since modernization has been belated. It is greatest in Hawai'i and New Zealand, yet even in Kiribati and Tuvalu, urbanization has become significant and development problems have resulted. Almost everywhere, urbanization has been accompanied by rapid population growth (heightened through the limited impact of family planning), with the result that natural increase has become as important an influence on urban growth as rural-to-urban migration.

In Melanesia and the very smallest island groups elsewhere, fewer than a quarter of the population live in towns or cities, and, in at least five cases, more than half the population now live in the towns. As late as 1960 only Suva and Noumea within the colonial Pacific had populations of over 25,000; hence the expansion of urbanization is a dramatic and very recent change in the history of the South Pacific, except in Hawai'i and New Zealand, where there were substantial towns and cities in the prewar years, a function of the pervasiveness of European settlement and the role of trade. By contrast, for Melanesia on the eve of independence:

> The rapid growth of towns equals in significance any of the changes that have swept across Melanesia since World War II. In its consequences for the integration of colonies into new nations, it may even be the most far-reaching of all changes, yet these places are still essentially communities of migrants. (Brookfield with Hart 1971:384)

Rapid urban expansion mainly followed postwar and, later, postindependence expansion in government activity and spending, and with it came a boom in bureaucratic job opportunities for the educated elite and skilled workers. Over time, more and more of this service sector employment became located in the urban areas.

In the prewar years, urbanization was officially discouraged in the colonial Pacific, and towns were primarily European trading and administrative centers. Even in New Zealand before the 1940s the ethnic European administration and also Maori traditionalists sought to discourage migration to towns on the grounds that Maoris would best preserve their cultural identity and improve their economic prosperity by being incorporated within the rural economy (Watson 1985). As discrimination declined and labor demands increased postwar, towns and cities grew and their populations became more permanent. Factors discouraging permanence of the urban population, including the lack of social security, and insecure land tenure, were steadily offset by economic criteria such as higher urban wages, and an actual decline of income-earning opportunities in some rural areas.

Circular or return migration has become of less relative importance, and rural-to-urban migration is permanent or at least long-term. As children are born in towns this permanence is enhanced, while, increasingly, migrants prefer or at least become used to urban rather than rural life. A quarter of the children born in the large Papua New Guinea towns of Port Moresby and Lae, for example, have never visited their "home" villages and, if they were to do so, would find acceptance there difficult (Connell 1997a). It is in this context, above all, that the towns of the South Pacific are increasingly becoming more like those in other parts of the world, as second, third, and further generations of urban dwellers emerge with, at best, only tenuous ties to rural areas. This is significant not merely for the breakdown of traditional social organization that it implies but because it effectively ensures that these second- (or more) generation migrants are destined to remain and raise families in urban areas.

Inhabitants of villages are increasingly being incorporated into urban areas, such as Hanuabada in Port Moresby. Alongside them are migrants and their children from some of the poorer rural areas; for example, the migrants originating from the Gulf Province of Papua New Guinea (Ryan 1989) are firmly established in Port Moresby. There are also bureaucrats and other elite workers outside the towns who have skills unused in rural areas and socioeconomic expectations beyond the capacity of rural areas to meet. Increasingly, differentiation has occurred between those permanent urban residents who are relatively poor—often employed in the informal sector—and bureaucrats and others who are relatively well-off. Only the latter group are mobile, and in the Pacific, as elsewhere, it is the least mobile who tend to be the least successful. They lack capital for travel, cannot distribute money and gifts in the rural villages, and must retain their precarious urban commitment.

Access to land is a crucial influence on the duration of urban residence, and individual ownership of land has resulted in considerable urban permanency in New Zealand and Hawai'i. There are marked differences between social groups in the intention to remain in town. As Nair (1980) has found in Suva, for example, two-thirds of Indo-Fijians have claimed they would remain permanently in the city, while less than one-third of Fijian migrants said they would do likewise despite the greater number having already spent more than half their working lives in Suva. This difference between the two groups was matched in terms of home ownership: only 30% of migrant Fijian heads of household owned a house in Suva, while a further 29% owned dwellings in both Suva and their home village. In contrast, 61% of Indo-Fijian household heads owned their houses in Suva, and only 13% also had a place in the rural area. Similarly, more Fijians visited their rural place of origin, remitted money, and contributed to rural projects when compared with Indo-Fijians of rural origin. The key factor in explaining the difference stemmed from the continuing ownership and access to rural land open only to the Fijians:

> For Fijians in particular, urban centres are regarded as locations of employment and modern amenities, and rural communities primarily as locations that offer opportunities for a better social and cultural life and the chance of a peaceful retirement.... It is conceivable that fewer Indo-Fijians would reside for long periods in the city and more would wish to return to rural settlements if land was available for cash cropping, since many indicated this was the reason they went to Suva. (Nair 1980:89, 92)

The original relationship to the land established by the colonial authorities over one hundred years ago remains an important factor influencing the very different degree of commitment to permanent urban residence. Thus the Indo-Fijians of Suva exhibit some similarities with the poorest migrants in Port Moresby, who may have limited opportunities for access to land at "home." In general, those most likely to remain in urban areas are migrants from remote places where income-earning opportunities are few. Where rising expectations are combined with increasing pressure on rural resources and static job opportunities in the formal sector, migration from rural areas is more likely to be permanent either in Pacific urban areas or in the cities of metropolitan nations on the Pacific Rim.

Urbanization represents, for many, an intended long-term change of residence. Increasingly, migration has been of families rather than single males, while independent female migration is important in some areas; female and family migration to urban areas assists in balancing sex ratios in most towns where, until recently, there were considerable gender imbalances. In Port Moresby the masculinity ratio (males per hundred females) fell from 185 in 1966 to 125 in 1990. By contrast that of Lae was 130 and the mining town of Tabubil was 150. Similar changes were recorded much earlier in Fijian and Vanuatuan urban areas where sex ratios are now evenly balanced. In Polynesia and Micronesia there have never been significant gender imbalances. It is only in the mining towns of Papua New Guinea that sex ratios remain particularly lopsided. The movement toward more balanced sex ratios demonstrates that natural increase has become more important as a determinant of urban population change. Thus, although ambivalent attitudes to urban life and residence persist, migrants are staying longer in town, women have come in increasing numbers, either with their husbands—thus producing and raising families in town—or, less frequently, to seek employment or access to improved services.

A distinctive form of urbanization has appeared in the Pacific associated with the rights, and the lack of rights, of residents to land in urban areas. Cities and towns are characterized by rapidly growing uncontrolled fringes of periurban customary land, settlements on marginal lands—such as swamps and hillsides—beyond the reaches of the formal housing sector, and pockets of traditional villages swallowed up in the expanding modern town. Only in New Zealand and Hawai'i, and to a lesser extent Noumea, Papeete, and Guam, are there extensive tracts of modern suburban low-density development. Otherwise, new offices and tourist establishments and the expensive dwellings of the elite (still largely expatriate in parts of the region) coexist uneasily with low-income suburbs and place huge demands on poorly developed networks of infrastructure and services. This complex and increasingly differentiated townscape is rarely under the jurisdiction of a single municipal authority. Management problems are visible in environmental degradation, traffic, and housing problems. Social and physical variations within towns reflect the availability and provision of housing. Within the towns enormous differences in residential standards occur.

Towns and cities, though now largely indigenous in most cases, retain colonial layouts but have acquired new housing estates, squatter settlements, supermarkets, airports, and multi-lane highways (rather than pavements or bicycle tracks). Ethnic compositions in the towns and cities of Hawai'i and New Zealand are different from those of the regions and nations of which they are part: indigenous populations are disproportionately rural (though in both Hawai'i and New Zealand urbanization has been rapid in recent decades). Though the informal sector is relatively inconspicuous, poverty and urban unemployment have become more visible.

## Constrained Economies

The economies of Pacific Island states and territories are constrained by various factors linked to their small size. These include remoteness and isolation, diseconomies of scale, scarce natural and human resources, and vulnerability to external shocks and natural hazards. Their urban economies are similarly limited. All towns have administrative and service sectors—the principal reasons for their establishment—and these are often the only real contemporary economic functions in the smaller centers.

In the transition from colonial towns, urban economies diversified, but the manufacturing sector is small throughout the Pacific and the informal sector almost absent. Most urban economies are dominated by national governments because of the significance of the public sector, even in areas such as fisheries. Efforts to privatize and to increase competition are being made throughout the region, but the effects on urban unemployment have usually been negative; hence the struggle for jobs is a constant urban preoccupation.

Industry is relatively well developed in New Zealand and Hawai'i, but poorly developed elsewhere. Most manufacturing activities involve the processing of local agricultural and fisheries produce, and (with the exception of fish canneries in Papua New Guinea and American Samoa) these are of limited extent. Although breweries have recently been constructed in the Marshall Islands and Vanuatu, the phase of import substitution has largely passed; hence there has been a declining rate of urban job creation. Beyond food processing, industrial activity centers on the small-scale production of wood and metal products and on engineering. However, there are some exceptions.

In Papua New Guinea the mining town of Tabubil is distinct in its formal layout and has an entirely migrant population. The few other mining towns of the Pacific are tiny. Several states have sought to develop industrial estates; only Fiji has had long-term success because of its concessional trade with Australia and New Zealand, but overall, fewer skills and the absence of raw materials have hindered contemporary industrialization. Employment in the Northern Marianas is dominated by clothes production because of tariff-free entry to the mainland American market. Most of the workforce, who are paid minimum wages below American norms, are Asian women migrants. Industrial employment otherwise accounts for only a small proportion of the urban workforce. Among the indigenous population urban unemployment levels are high.

Urban employment is concentrated in the bureaucracy and service sector. The former is generally privileged, its higher wages and better job security and fringe benefits ensuring that it is the most sought after area of employment, second only to being a politician. In recent years public sector employment has stabilized and contracted, posing problems for urban economies. In those countries where tourism is important (see Fagence, this volume), many tourism facilities are in, or close to, the urban areas—as in Honolulu, Noumea, Papeete, Vila, and Rarotonga—and this labor-intensive industry employs a substantial proportion of the urban workforce (Lea 1996). Otherwise, urban employment is dominated by the visible evidence of retailing and other tertiary services.

*Figure 27.1. Honolulu skyline, University of Hawai'i in the foreground (photo MR).*

The combination of migration, growing urban permanence, few new urban employment opportunities, and the lack of industrialization might have been expected to result in the emergence of a strong informal sector (where wages and working conditions are unregulated). However, there is an almost complete absence of handicraft workers, small-scale traders, and repair establishments that provide such a large proportion of urban employment in many developing countries. In some towns—particularly Port Moresby—the most visible elements of the informal sector include marketing (mainly of betel nuts) and bottle collecting; crime and prostitution are rather less visible. The absence of informal sector activities is partly due to restrictive legislation (especially on food sellers), small markets, limited skills, and comparable earnings in the rural sector.

Markets are conspicuous features of most Pacific towns, though they are relatively small and intermittent where subsistence agriculture and fisheries are weak or remote. Many separate markets are found in the largest towns, and in a few towns specialized fish and betel nut markets exist. Urban residents, many of them self-employed, purchase a substantial proportion of their food (and other goods) in the markets. In larger towns middlemen link urban markets with rural production.

Urban employment is often a primarily male phenomenon, most obviously in Melanesia, and women are generally

*Figure 27.2.* Marketplace, Nuku'alofa, Tonga (photo WA).

employed by government or in the service sector. Women are concentrated in the less skilled parts of the workforce and "glass ceilings" prevent movement out of the relatively unskilled and poorly paid occupations. In most towns the formal sector workforce is youthful. Access to urban employment, even in the public service, is influenced by kinship ties, and in the larger island groups many enterprises are dominated by workers from a particular language group or region, a circumstance that may reduce productivity.

Unemployment is visible in most towns, though the concept of being without a job has little real meaning in most places because of the viability of the subsistence sector. Consequently, there are few adequate measures of employment in use in the region. In the larger towns it is apparent however that unemployment is increasing. In the early 1990s a third of the population of Port Moresby was searching for work, with most of the unemployed being in the 15–19 age group, many of them with little or no education (Connell 1997a:196). Various estimates suggest that unemployment levels are frequently above 10% and that many urban households do not include wage and salary earners, but rely on distant kin or on subsistence production on the edge of town. The extent of urban unemployment has contributed to social disorganization.

Just as unemployment is increasing, especially among those born in towns, so too is urban poverty. Again, there have been few measures of poverty in the Pacific other than Fiji, but the increased extent of begging and crime in some countries suggests that poverty is of growing significance, especially in the larger towns. The popular and romantic view of an urban safety net provided by the extended family, ensuring through redistribution that kin are never hungry or destitute, is no longer valid (Monsell-Davis 1993). In squatter settlements, especially, hunger and poverty are no longer unusual.

By the early 1990s more than a third of the households living in urban settlements in Fiji were considered to be poor, compared with less than half that proportion a decade earlier (Bryant-Tokelau 1995:110). Poverty is equally apparent in squatter settlements elsewhere, some of which have deteriorated into urban slums, even in Papeete and Noumea, where economies are relatively developed. A further consequence of difficult urban conditions is the growth of suicide and domestic violence, though neither are exclusively urban phenomena, and the increase in the number of female-headed households that follows on the heels of family breakdown and social disorganization.

## Urban Management

As the towns and cities of the Pacific have grown, popular concerns have mounted over urban problems: rising urban unemployment, the growth of shantytowns (or squatter settlements), increasing urban crime rates, and the inability to manage and provide effective urban services. Of special importance here are the "brown" environmental problems of sewage and solid waste disposal. Just before independence, the then Prime Minister of Papua New Guinea, Michael Somare, asked:

> Do we really want to become a country of big cities? In all the 700 languages of our country we have never needed words for slum, for unemployment, for air pollution. Do we really wish to build the kind of country that needs those words? (1973:2)

Since then, all those words have become useful and necessary, and poverty has become an urban phenomenon in the same time period, and not only in Papua New Guinea.

Few towns and cities are growing because of an increased demand for industrial labor; nor is their growth fueled by an increasingly productive agricultural sector. Urban growth is principally stimulated by government expenditure on infra-

*Figure 27.3.* Papeete, French Polynesia (photo J-LR).

*Figure 27.4.* DUD, Marshall Islands (photo LEM).

structure and administration and through the centralization of the bureaucracy; the financing of this expenditure is dependent in part on profits from the sale of commodities, but more often through a reliance on external aid and loans. Urban economic development has in effect failed to keep pace with the rate of urban growth. In Melanesia the weak national and urban economic base has placed urban managers (and there are few enough of them) in a desperate race to cope with uncontrolled squatter settlements and to mount an increasingly expensive search for water and fuel in order to adjust to the growing dependence on imported food and energy. Consequently, there is little time for the consideration of the long-term effects of economic planning decisions on the physical environment and for the stability of the towns themselves (Bryant 1993).

There are few parts of the region (apart from New Zealand, Hawai'i, and the largest cities in Melanesia) where physical planning exists, let alone where it has begun to come to terms with long-term social and ecological issues. However, the situation has improved in the late 1990s in Vanuatu and Kiribati, where new urban management strategy plans have been prepared with funding from the Asian Development Bank. The new plans for Port Vila and South Tarawa include recommendations on the provision of urban infrastructure, new housing, and strengthened institutional capacity to control development.

The complexities of land tenure have emphasized social divisions within urban areas, between the "true" people and recent migrants, and have complicated and made more expensive the tasks of urban planning and management. In many urban areas there is an acute shortage of land, and land acquisition—especially for locating garbage dumps or sewage disposal areas—has become extremely difficult, especially in the atoll towns. In a few places, most evidently in Majuro (Marshall Islands), there is no public land whatsoever; hence urban planning, even of the most basic kind, is virtually impossible. Land shortages have contributed to high, but localized, population densities, especially in the atoll states, where space is particularly limited.

On Ebeye (Kwajalein), the second town in the Marshall Islands, around 8,000 people live at a density of 23,000 per square kilometer (60,000 per square mile). In many towns urban land issues are complicated by the structure of traditional ownership. For example, Motu-Koitabu people, the traditional residents of the Port Moresby area, are the sole owners of a third of the city area but live in scattered patches (Lea 1983). Such owners fear the loss of their land, which is the historic basis for their means of existence; hence, in Port Moresby, there are frequent land disputes and basic problems in attempting land-use zoning.

Most Pacific towns are characterized by some spatial inequality in the provision of social and physical infrastructure. Attempts to modernize urban planning and management by introducing land-use zoning have often been resisted, as in Tonga:

> If you zone towns with the best will in the world, and a government made up of angels, you are still going to end up with better services to those areas which are wealthy than you would provide to those areas which are not. (Crown Prince Tupouto'a of Tonga, reported in *Matangi Tonga*, March–April 1993:11)

These sentiments relate closely to the paternalistic basis of traditional power and the way in which it is exercised in Tonga. There is little evidence of equity in urban incomes and service provision in Nuku'alofa, the capital city, and problems exist in planning adequate water and sanitation services. Under such circumstances, the introduction of land-use planning legislation is seen as a means of removing control over land from traditional authority and placing it in the hands of government and the bureaucracy. The fact that government and bureaucracy in the region are also dominated by tradition does not make such a transfer any easier and has resulted in the formal enactment of town planning legislation in the region outside Melanesia being quite rare.

The persistence of village-based settlement within urban areas, particularly in Polynesia, has resulted in the attachment of group loyalties to centers of local power, rather than to any kind of urban governance structure. Urban planning, where it exists, often takes place in the absence of a political structure that coincides with its area of operation, and hence has acquired little legitimacy. Moreover, it is only recently that demands for urban planning have emerged in small island states that have just begun to experience the problems and pressures of urban growth. Ironically, urban planning was most evident in colonial times, when there were few urban problems of the kind experienced today.

## Shantytowns

The most visible sign of rapid urbanization—and the failures of urban management—is the growth of shantytowns, especially in Melanesian cities where migrants contribute to their own economic and social welfare through the provision and improvement of housing. Shantytowns have often been regarded by long-term urban residents as a form of visual pollution and a place of crime and have influenced government decisions either to discourage such settlements or to provide only basic facilities through "site and service" schemes. "Accommodationist" policies found great acceptance in the 1960s and 1970s and were in keeping with early concerns over the social, rather than the economic aspects of urban growth. However, while the provision of amenities for migrants enabled both a reduction in visual pollution and a smoothing of the transition of rural-to-urban migration, it had the inevitable if perhaps paradoxical effect of stimulating further migration (particularly since few rural areas received similar benefits). The more that basic needs are satisfied in urban areas the greater the incentive for others to move to town and hence put pressure on living space.

More recently, urban development policies have given less attention to housing and service provision for squatter settlements. With the reduced focus on rural development that has followed independence and the emergence of economically weak states, migration has continued and heightened the perception of depressed urban living conditions. Government expenditure in urban areas has tended to be disproportionate to urban population sizes and has focused on grand schemes—office blocks, prestigious apartment complexes, highways, and airports—rather than on housing for the poor or basic water supplies. Consequently, socioeconomic inequalities in most towns have grown substantially in recent years.

National housing policies have rarely been able to cater adequately to the needs of the urban poor and have, in practice, favored middle- and upper-income groups. Housing authorities have usually given preference to those best able to pay. In most towns formal housing is expensive, good quality rental accommodation is often scarce, and rents are high, because demand exceeds supply. Housing policies have rarely focused on low-cost or self-help housing; hence informal dwellings account for a substantial proportion of the accommodation in Melanesian cities and characterize the more rapidly growing towns everywhere.

Informal settlements possess considerable advantages, especially for recent migrants, since rents are likely to be low or nonexistent. People are often able to find somewhere to squat near their workplaces and live with kin from their home areas; this enables costs to be shared and increases collective security. Settlers are also able to produce housing appropriate for their immediate needs, which can be transformed without concern for legal problems as these needs change. This is the normal village situation in the Pacific.

Settlers use mainly local or recycled building materials and thus reduce the costs of providing housing. They often locate on marginal sites that are inappropriate for formal housing and, overall, their self-help industry reduces demands on the formal housing market. Few governments in the Pacific are prepared to construct formal housing for subsidized rental today, and where such housing stocks were acquired at the time of independence, as in Papua New Guinea, the dwellings have been given away or sold to their occupants (Connell and Lea 1994). Housing provision and standards remain a problem everywhere.

Shantytowns maximize self-reliance in the use of indigenous human and natural resources and house high proportions of the urban population. But residents often suffer from tenurial insecurity and poor access to services. Over time, many have secured long-term residence, gained access to water and electricity supplies, and improved the quality of their houses. Often this has been in the face of government opposition, officially on amenity grounds and, at least in Papua New Guinea, has resulted in forced removals and repatriation of settlers (Connell and Lea 1994). Nonetheless, shantytowns have appeared in urban areas all over the region and will remain a permanent feature of contemporary urbanization in the Pacific.

## Homelessness in Paradise

Urban populations in Hawai'i and New Zealand are economically better off than elsewhere in the region by the standard statistical measures. Yet residents of large cities have their own sets of problems to contend with, of which arguably the most important is the need for adequate and affordable housing. In recent decades, sizable numbers of individuals and families are finding it exceedingly difficult to cope with housing needs at the margins of "paradise" (Kearns et al. 1991, Smith et al. 1992).

Media attention has focused on the visibly homeless, usually defined as those without any shelter (sleeping on beaches or city streets, in parks or homeless shelters). However, such homeless are only the tip of an iceberg of incipient homeless, including those in inadequate housing (such as trailers or cars), temporarily with relatives and friends, or threatened with eviction. Many of the incipient homeless are only an additional domestic crisis away from being on the streets (Kearns et al. 1991, SMS Research 1992).

Up to the present, the rate of home ownership in New Zealand is one of the highest in the world (over 70% of all households). Yet beginning in the 1980s, economic difficulties led to the establishment of a serious housing need priority for subsidies granted by the Housing Corporation of New Zealand (HCNZ). By the end of the 1980s, the number of New Zealanders in the serious need category was estimated at between 17,000 and 20,000, with up to 100,000 of incipient

*Figure 27.5. Auckland, New Zealand (photo LEM).*

homeless (Kearns 1991).

A survey by Kearns et al. (1991) based on applicants to the HCNZ found that Maori, Pacific Islanders, other ethnic groups (presumably Asians), and women-headed households were overrepresented. Health problems aggravated or caused by inadequate dwellings, identified by some 50% of all respondents during interviews, included colds (particularly among Pacific Islanders), asthma, physical ailments (rheumatism, headaches, backache), mental illness or stress (most common among Europeans), and accidents.

In Hawai'i, an estimated 5,353 were homeless and as many as 300,000 incipient homeless in 1992; only 64% of households were deemed comfortably housed (SMS Research 1992). The data cannot be directly compared with those of New Zealand studies, due to widely differing definitions of homelessness. However, the problem is likely to be more severe than in New Zealand, where as long ago as 1936 the government had committed itself to providing adequate housing for all, regardless of ability to pay (Kearns et al. 1991).

Most likely to be totally homeless in Hawai'i were the unmarried, males, the less educated, recent arrivals, Caucasians, and part-Hawaiians. Asians (over a third of the population) were underrepresented. Perceived reasons for homelessness (in descending order) included economic problems, family disruption, drug and alcohol use, mental illness, commuter homelessness, and personal choice. The most important "needs" were money, shelter, medical care, dental care, clothing, and mailing address (SMS Research 1992).

Up until the 1980s, homelessness in Hawai'i had mainly been the concern of churches and the city government. By 1990, the state government became involved, with plans to house 500 homeless families in temporary villages, along with stipends (for shelters), outreach programs (for medical and social services), and grants (to help individuals secure a home). Other funding is allocated for preventive services to at-risk families and individuals (Homeless Aloha 1994).

Many problems remain. The temporary villages, funded in large part by private foundations, have been much criticized over crowding, lack of privacy, and stigmatization, and the children are often teased at school. In many cases, the construction of temporary villages have been stridently opposed by local communities. In several areas, tent shantytowns have sprung up. Native Hawaiians can apply for federal Hawaiian Homestead land, but few manage to clear the administrative hurdles (Modell 1997). Even in affluent cities, problems of unemployment, homelessness, and inequality are considerable.

## Social Divisions

Most urban residents are either migrants born outside the city or their relatives and speak vernacular languages that possess a cultural resonance and complexity that the imported colonial or recently constructed languages lack. Most live with fellow migrants, identify with their social concerns, and experience city life via a world of kinship contacts. In many spheres, access to employment is gained through kinship ties. Even elements of the "modern" sector, such as the hundreds of buses that ply the roads of Port Moresby, are owned and operated by kin groups. Few organizations cut across such social connections. Unions are few and rarely militant, and are often associated with the upper echelons of employment such as bureaucrats and mine workers. Class consciousness remains weaker than ethnic or regional affiliations, even in the more homogeneous and hierarchical Polynesian towns. Organizations such as churches and sports clubs tend to subsume social groups rather than cut across them. All this emphasizes the "village" organization of most urban places in the Pacific.

Most urban residents in Melanesia choose to live the bulk of their lives as members of their own cultural group. Ties with "home" and kin are vastly more important than links to neighbors from other cultural groups, though these links may be mobilized for particular reasons. Even for those in formal-sector employment, urban life is rarely intended to be permanent. For most migrants, urban residence is a "rural-oriented" strategy designed to generate income and prestige for a successful return to the security of rural areas where land rights exist.

The intention to return reinforces group affiliation in town. Encounters with those from other cultural groups are often fraught with uncertainty and potential conflict. Disputes between social groups have sometimes resulted in violence. Insecurity inevitably reinforces identity. At the same time, connections with others are generally considered advantageous and prestigious but difficult to obtain, retain, and trust. Encounters between Melanesians and Europeans (and other inmigrant groups, such as Asians) are almost entirely generated in the context of employment and commerce.

Where informal squatter settlements characterize towns, these settlements have increasingly come to resemble rural villages, as kinship ties in towns become more elaborate, residential patterns replicate village life, trees and gardens reach fruition, rituals are enacted in the urban setting, incomes are turned to social objectives, urban leaders emerge, and "village" courts provide social control. The physical enactment of rituals—often with music and dance—usually generates a crowd, or at least a widespread recognition that a particular cultural group retains its traditions in some form, thus emphasizing the identities and distinctiveness of others. In this way many urban residents retain close ties with "home," and relatively weak links—other than through employment—with the towns.

A handful of mainly elite Pacific Islanders, especially those who have married out of their particular cultural group, have tended to form a more permanent urban population. This is particularly true of bureaucrats—with long employment tenure—who, if not already in capital cities, seek to migrate there. Similarly, most university students seek to, and do, remain in the Melanesian capitals or, in the case of Polynesia, may search for jobs overseas. Of the bureaucrats, at least in Papua New Guinea:

> Their presence in urban areas not only deprives rural areas of what skills they possess, but ensures a continuing urban bias to the economy through their greater purchasing power and their ability to influence decision-making. The children of urban-dwelling public servants are the first of a truly urban generation of Papua New Guineans. They cannot support themselves in a rural environment; they are committed to towns and may not carry the sympathies most adult Papua New Guineans now feel for village life. (Allen 1983:228)

Even so, such elite urban residents do not see their ethnic identity as diminished by development, education, or monetary success; rather they incorporate these elements into their ritual and political life. They remain in opposition to other ethnic groups through competition for land, political influence, and economic progress.

Notwithstanding the continued significance of subsistence in the Pacific, trading and price fluctuations (whose terms of trade disadvantage commodity producers) have embedded the towns, cities, and villages in a global economic, cultural, and political system. Global culture, economy, and society have arrived in the capital cities of the Pacific, where night clubs have introduced new musical styles, restaurants purvey imported foods, and satellite dishes introduce overseas television channels. In cities where social and cultural life remains bound up with local events and relationships, external ties are shaping new identities (Connell and Lea 1994). And slowly, despite their village origins and divisions, Pacific towns are becoming more like those elsewhere in the world.

## Safety Issues

Social disorganization and crime flow from inequalities in the cities and have grown in concert with the increasing size of the urban populations. In Papeete there have been riots over inadequate urban employment and quality of life. Security concerns among the elite are prevalent in Port Moresby and accentuate topographical divisions in the city, with the better-off occupying the higher ground. In this way neocolonial towns have begun to revert to something akin to the segregated colonial outposts of the past, with an increasing separation of the elite from the poor. It would be misleading to suggest that the situation characterizing Port Moresby in recent years is found everywhere in the urban Pacific, but increases in poverty and a continuation of substantial inmigration elsewhere in Melanesia and in parts of Micronesia form the preconditions for such trends to emerge.

In recent years the environmental aspects of urbanization have received greater prominence as informal dwellings no longer meet the rigorous standards of colonial times, as traffic problems worsen and rivers, streams and urban open spaces become polluted with the wastes of consumer society. In extreme cases like the Tarawa (Kiribati) and Chuuk lagoons (Federated States of Micronesia), the disposal of sewage in places where shellfish are an important food resource has precipitated outbreaks of cholera. There has been inadequate investment in service provision in many key areas: water supplies, sewage facilities, and waste disposal. Provision of open space, transport, health centers, roads, and power supplies are similarly inadequate apart from a very few exceptions. Even then, as in the case of the recent corporatization of the Pohnpei State power supply in the Federated States of Micronesia, the consequence of providing an efficient supply has been to greatly raise prices via a "user pays" approach, throwing into question accessibility to services by the urban poor (Connell and Lea 1998).

Urban water supplies are rarely adequate, and in several towns—particularly in Micronesia—services cannot be guaranteed. Problems have intensified as the public works systems installed in colonial times creak and rust into obsolescence. Leaks, storm overflows, shortages in dry weather, aging and damaged assets (including tadpoles in the water pipes in Honiara), illegal connections, and failures to collect revenue have all exacerbated the basic problems. Few towns possess proper sewage treatment facilities. Neither Port Vila nor any of the other urban areas in Vanuatu, for example, possess a reticulated collection and treatment system. Only Honiara in Solomon Islands has partial coverage, and several plants are inoperative in the Micronesian countries. The small township of Maprik in Papua New Guinea had to be "closed" for several weeks in 1992 when the whole system overflowed. What was adequate for small towns of colonial times cannot now cope with the growing demands of a new era.

Public health is an increasingly significant policy issue in the urban Pacific. One outcome of high unemployment and the inability of many to pay for urban services (such as clean water) is the poor status of nutrition and health in some of the towns. Some of the worst health and mortality problems are experienced in squatter settlements in and around Port Moresby (Connell 1997b) and also in the urban areas that have grown up on coral atolls. The "epidemiological transition" (see Pollock and Finau, this volume) is particularly linked to urbanization; such lifestyle diseases as cancer, cardiovascular problems, and diabetes are associated with more sedentary urban lifestyles combined with increased alcohol and tobacco consumption and inadequate nutrition, overcrowding and poverty. These problems are evident not only in the larger towns but also in centers such as Majuro and South Tarawa, where population densities are high, access to fresh food is restricted, incomes are low, and

*Figure 27.6. Tumon Bay, Agana, Guam (photo LEM).*

costs high. In the region as a whole, increased costs of living have made urban residence more difficult for the majority and more frustrating as expectations rise.

## The Urban Future

Over time, town and city life has appeared more attractive as urban wages and salaries have increased and rural income-generating opportunities have declined relative to those in the towns. Throughout the region, urban populations are growing faster than those in the villages. Yet cities have rarely become physically attractive: social and economic divisions are more apparent and are usually spatially demarcated; urban unemployment, along with social disorganization and crime, has risen, alongside the growing visibility of the informal sector; and urban management has failed to cope. Even in the small towns, urban service provision is fragmented among numerous activities. Tension between landowners and migrants exists in the face of land shortages, and bureaucratic ineptitude and political corruption have contributed to disarray and division, hastening privatization.

Yet urbanization has many positive characteristics. Urban life enables individuals to obtain higher education and technical training and gain access to limited amounts of skilled employment and good housing. Migration may also reduce population pressure on scarce rural resources (especially in atoll economies) and, through remittances, lead to an improved quality of life in rural areas. Cities are centers of political and economic power and sometimes symbols of nationhood and places of economic opportunity.

The Pacific has a significant urban future, and its towns and cities are essential to social and economic development; it is not inevitable that urbanization should be unmanageable and that the problems should worsen. Strategies that emphasize integrated rural development and stress both economic advancement and social services will be important (not merely to minimize the problems but to improve agricultural output, which, along with fisheries, is the core of economic development in most of the countries). However, as more children are born in town and remain there, more urban jobs will have to be found. And as long as urban employment appears more prestigious and city life is perceived as being of higher quality than rural life, the population pressures in urban areas will increase. The social, economic, and environmental future of the region depends to a great extent on how successfully these problems can be solved.

Although new attempts are being made in several countries to formulate coherent urban policy, present approaches toward the management of urbanization are still generally piecemeal and directed toward individual projects and particular towns. Coordination is conspicuous by its absence, a situation (directly reflecting the condition of urban government across the region) that is unlikely to change until the structure of government alters. The future of urban management is also bound up with the ability of urban authorities to become more self-sufficient. The potential for achieving this self-sufficiency depends on income-generating capacity, but taxes and fees are difficult to collect and grants hard to obtain. Solutions materialize in episodic and expensive responses to crisis conditions without reference to the wider context of urban service provision. Urban management is often crisis management rather than the good housekeeping that might avert the worst crises.

Although official concerns over unmanaged urbanization exist alongside an expressed focus on rural development, few real attempts have been made to constrain urban development. Urbanization has been limited primarily because of the continuation of reasonable rural income-earning opportunities. Recognition of urban development problems prompted some attempts to stimulate a counter-balancing rural development and reverse migration flows, but these have rarely been concerted. Two related policies have sought to reduce urbanization: decentralization and the establishment of rural settlement schemes.

Although almost every development plan in the South Pacific identifies "decentralization," as well as "self-reliance," there are few places where the rhetoric resembles reality. Invariably, shortage of capital and skilled labor and inertia in the private sector and bureaucracy have hampered efforts at decentralization. Settlement schemes have, however, been established in a number of countries in an attempt to open up new land for agricultural export production rather than to decentralize the population. Papua New Guinea especially and also Vanua Levu in Fiji have achieved some success in both these aims, although the settlement schemes have proved extremely expensive and land constraints now preclude new settlements. The new growth centers have failed to draw populations away from primate capital cities, and the disappointments of rural development ensure that urban growth will continue throughout the region, especially in Melanesia, where there are few opportunities for international migration. Future towns and cities in the island Pacific are likely to be much larger and more difficult to manage than they are today.

# Bibliography

Allen, B. J. 1983. Paradise lost? rural development in an export-led economy: the case of Papua New Guinea. In *Rural development and the state: contradictions and dilemmas in developing countries*, ed. D. A. M. Lea and D. P. Chaudhri, 215–240. London: Methuen.

Brookfield, H. C., with D. Hart. 1971. *Melanesia: a geographical interpretation of an island world*. London: Methuen.

Bryant, J. 1993. *Urban poverty and the environment in the South Pacific*. Armidale, New South Wales: University of New England.

Bryant-Tokelau, J. 1995. The myth exploded: urban poverty in the Pacific. *Environment and Urbanization* 7:109–129.

Connell, J. 1997a. *Papua New Guinea: the struggle for development*. London: Routledge.

Connell, J. 1997b. Health in Papua New Guinea: a decline in development. *Australian Geographical Studies* 35:271–293.

Connell, J., and J. P. Lea. 1993. *Planning the future: Melanesian cities in 2010*. Canberra: National Center for Development Studies, Australian National University.

Connell, J., and J. P. Lea. 1994. Cities of parts, cities apart? changing places in modern Melanesia. *The Contemporary Pacific* 6:267–309.

Connell, J., and J. P. Lea. 1995. *Urbanisation in Polynesia*. Canberra: National Center for Development Studies, Australian National University.

Connell, J., and J. P. Lea. 1998. *Island towns: managing urbanization in Micronesia*. Honolulu: Center for Pacific Island Studies.

Homeless Aloha. 1994. *The Homeless Aloha report*. Honolulu: Homeless Aloha.

Kearns, R. A., C. J. Smith, and M. W. Abbott. 1991. Another day in paradise? Life on the margins in urban New Zealand. *Social Science and Medicine* 33(4):369–79.

Lea, J. P. 1983. Customary land tenure and urban housing land: partnership and participation in developing societies. In *Land for housing the poor*, ed. S. Angel, et al., 54–72. Singapore: Select Books.

Lea, J. P. 1996. Tourism, realpolitik and development in the South Pacific. In *Tourism, crime and international security issues*, ed. A. Pizam and Y. Mansfeld, 123–142. Chichester: Wiley.

Mara, R. 1994. *The Pacific Islands in the year 2010: a vision from within*. Honolulu: East-West Center.

Modell, J. 1997. (Not) in my back yard: housing the homeless in Hawaii. In *Home in the islands: housing and social change in the Pacific*, ed. J. Rensell and M. Rodman, 194–221. Honolulu: University of Hawai'i Press.

Monsell-Davis, M. 1993. Urban exchange: safety-net or disincentive? Wantoks and relatives in the urban Pacific. *Cultural Anthropology* 16:45–66.

Nair, S. 1980. *Rural-born Fijians and Indo-Fijians in Suva: a study of movements and linkages*. Canberra: Australian National University.

Ryan, D. 1989. Home ties in town: Toaripi in Port Moresby. *Canberra Anthropology* 12:19–27.

Smith, C. J., R. A. Kearns, and M. W. Abbott. 1992. A tale of two cities: the experience of housing problems in Auckland and Christchurch. *New Zealand Geographer* 48(1):2–10.

SMS Research 1992. *Homelessness and hunger in Hawaii*. Honolulu: SMS Research.

Somare, M. 1975. New goals for New Guinea. *Pacific Perspective* 2:1–4.

Watson, M. 1985. Urbanization. In *Population of New Zealand*, 118–251. NY: ESCAP.

# SECTION 6

# ECONOMY

Pacific Island economies are constrained by factors of scale, distance, limited resources, and the vicissitudes of global political economy. Substantive development has occurred in New Zealand, Hawai'i, and, to a lesser extent, the large, resource-rich islands in Melanesia. Most island economies remain partially dependent on external aid and/or remittances. Topics covered in this section include agriculture and forestry, ocean resources, mining, tourism, communications, and external dependence. Contributors include Geoffrey Bertram, William C. Clarke, Harley I. Manner, Randolph R. Thaman, Tim Adams, Paul Dalzell, Esaroma Ledua, Glenn Banks, Frank McShane, Michael Fagence, Michael R. Ogden, and Suzanna Layton.

# CHAPTER 28

# Economy

*Geoffrey Bertram*

## Introduction

Pacific Island economies are small and isolated, but except for Papua New Guinea (Booth 1995:208) they are not poor by the usual standards of world poverty. Provision of basic needs has seldom been under threat for the indigenous populations of the islands, and living standards across much of the region continue to be underwritten by official transfers and private remittances. There is considerable geographic mobility of individuals, which makes migration a central issue for economic policy and ensures that most of the region's labor markets are open, with wages in the islands indexed to wage rates obtainable in the outside world.

Smallness brings with it relative insignificance on the global scale. In 1994, Melanesia, Micronesia, and Polynesia, excluding Papua New Guinea and Hawai'i, had a combined population of 2.5 million, only 0.04% of the world population of 5,630 million. Adding in those two larger entities brings the total to 7.6 million, still only 0.13% of the world total (United Nations 1995, Table 1). Including New Zealand as part of the island Pacific adds another 3.5 million people.

Almost all of the Pacific Island states have, since the nineteenth century, been colonies, associated territories, or integrated parts of larger industrialized countries. (The term "state" is used here to refer to any politically defined entity, including dependent territories as well as sovereign nations.) Trade flows, capital flows, asset ownership, official languages, government structures, and currencies in use have been determined over the past century by the existence of eight main spheres of influence—British, French, U.S., Australian, New Zealand, Chilean, Japanese, and German, the last two of which became absorbed by the others during and after the two world wars of the century. A revival of Japanese influence, in the context of rapidly increasing linkages between the island Pacific and the East Asian economies in general, is a major trend of the 1990s.

The ongoing importance of close links between individual island economies and their out-of-region metropolitan patrons is evident in Table 28.1, which provides some basic data.

The characterization of Pacific Island communities as economic units is problematic. This is reflected in the nature of the economic data that are available, as well as in the political status of the islands and the general tone of outside commentary on economic development prospects in the region. Of the twenty-five entities apart from New Zealand listed in Table 28.1, only nine (Papua New Guinea, Samoa, Fiji, Kiribati, the Solomon Islands, Tonga, Vanuatu, Nauru, and Tuvalu) are independent nation states; only six (Papua New Guinea, Samoa, Fiji, the Solomon Islands, Tonga, and Vanuatu) have their own currencies; and only nine (Papua New Guinea, Samoa, Fiji, the Solomon Islands, Tonga, Vanuatu, the Marshall Islands, the Federated States of Micronesia, and Kiribati) are members of the World Bank and IMF. Major parts of the regional economy, such as Hawai'i, New Caledonia, and French Polynesia, as well as the smallest units (Tokelau, Easter Island, and Norfolk Island) are politically integrated parts of larger countries whose metropolitan economies are located around the Pacific Rim or in Europe. Several other island states are constitutionally "self-governing in free association" with larger countries to whose currency areas they belong.

Pacific Island economies are embedded in wider markets; to only a limited extent are they national market arenas in their own right. The internationalization of markets for goods, services, and factors of production during the 1980s and 1990s was less of a change for Pacific Islanders than for the inhabitants of most of the world's non-OECD (Organization for Economic Development) countries, because of the Pacific's pre-existing freedom of trade and capital flows and its long history of labor migration both within the region and to metropolitan economies. (The OECD is a grouping of the world's wealthy industrial economies.)

To explain income levels in the Pacific it is advisable to use only with great caution, if at all, the two most familiar "modernization" models of economic development: the classical closed-economy model of industrialization on the basis of domestic capital accumulation (Lewis 1954, Rostow 1960); and the outward-oriented export-led growth model pursued by the Asian "tigers" and widely advocated in recent years by agencies such as the World Bank (for example World Bank 1991). The past half century's economic development in most of the island Pacific has been import led, and it has been the struggle to finance rising imports without incurring unsustainable indebtedness that has dictated the various economies' structural evolution.

## Output, Trade, and the Balance of Payments

The usual benchmark statistic used to rank economies in the world scene is Gross Domestic Product per head. For only some of the Pacific Island economies is this available on a consistent basis over time, and for many of the smaller ones the statistical concepts underlying GDP are less applicable than for large "developing economies" because of the importance of external sources of income and the extent to which modern-sector economic activity has moved offshore to the neighboring metropolitan economies. Nevertheless, the data on GDP and the balance of payments do have a story to tell.

The Pacific Islands

## Table 28.1

### Background Data on Twenty-Six Pacific Economies

| Territory | Population | Political classification | Currency | GDP/GNP US$m | Per capita US$ |
|---|---|---|---|---|---|
| **US Pacific** | | | | | |
| Hawai'i | 1,186,000 | Integrated | US$ | 32,724 | 27,592 |
| Guam | 153,700 | Integrated | US$ | 3,128 | 20,351 |
| Northern Marianas | 63,000 | Integrated | US$ | 550 | 8,733 |
| Federated States of Micronesia | 109,200 | Associated | US$ | 203 | 1,860 |
| Palau | 16,900 | Associated | US$ | 98 | 5,813 |
| Marshall Islands | 59,800 | Associated | US$ | 96 | 1,598 |
| American Samoa | 58,900 | Integrated | US$ | 253 | 4,295 |
| Total | 1,647,500 | | | 37,052 | 22,490 |
| **French Pacific** | | | | | |
| French Polynesia | 229,200 | Integrated | Pacific franc | 3,418 | 14,914 |
| New Caledonia | 196,800 | Integrated | Pacific franc | 3,017 | 15,330 |
| Wallis and Futuna | 14,800 | Integrated | Pacific franc | 25 | 1,689 |
| Total | 440,800 | | | 6,460 | 14,656 |
| **Australian Pacific** | | | | | |
| Papua New Guinea | 4,141,800 | Sovereign | Kina | 4,600 | 1,111 |
| Kiribati | 82,400 | Sovereign | Australian $ | 55 | 662 |
| Solomon Islands | 395,200 | Sovereign | Solomons $ | 209 | 529 |
| Vanuatu | 173,900 | Sovereign | Vatu | 187 | 1,078 |
| Nauru | 11,200 | Sovereign | Australian $ | 81 | 7,205 |
| Tuvalu | 10,200 | Sovereign | Australian $ | 4 | 373 |
| Norfolk Island | 2,367 | Integrated | Australian $ | | |
| Total | 4,817,067 | | | 5,135 | 1,066 |
| **New Zealand Pacific** | | | | | |
| New Zealand | 3,480,000 | Sovereign | NZ$ | 50,777 | 14,591 |
| Samoa | 170,000 | Sovereign | Tala | 170 | 1,000 |
| Cook Islands | 19,600 | Associated | NZ$ | 51 | 2,596 |
| Niue | 2,500 | Associated | NZ$ | 7 | 2,825 |
| Tokelau | 1,800 | Integrated | NZ$ | 1 | 667 |
| Total | 3,673,900 | | | 51,006 | 13,883 |
| **Independent Central Pacific** | | | | | |
| Fiji | 800,500 | Sovereign | Fiji $ | 1,801 | 2,250 |
| Tonga | 99,000 | Sovereign | Pa'anga | 125 | 1,262 |
| Total | 899,500 | | | 1,926 | 2,141 |
| **South American Pacific** | | | | | |
| Easter Island | 27,770 | Integrated | Chilean | n.a. | |
| Galapagos Islands | 15,000 | Integrated | Ecuadorean | | |
| Total | 2,770 | | | | |

Main Source: Bank of Hawai'i "Pacific Facts Sheet"

## Table 28.2

### Per Capita GDP by Political Status, US$

| | All | Excl PNG | Excl PNG and Hawai'i |
|---|---|---|---|
| Sovereign territories* | 1,229 | 1,510 | 1,510 |
| In free association | 2,187 | 2,187 | 2,187 |
| Dependent | 22,615 | 22,615 | 14,423 |
| Region average | 6,351 | 11,979 | 5,046 |

* Excluding New Zealand.

Source: Table 28.1.

The first outstanding stylized fact to emerge is that with the exception of New Zealand (an OECD member better classified as part of the metropolitan Pacific Rim economy for reasons discussed below), the GDP per head of island economies listed in Table 28.1 tends to be inversely related to their degree of political independence. Table 28.2 shows that the collective per capita GDP per head of fully sovereign island territories is only 5% that of politically integrated or dependent territories. Exclusion of the very large (by regional standards), very poor sovereign state Papua New Guinea raises this only to 7%. Further exclusion of Hawai'i, the largest and highest-income nonsovereign territory, raises the figure to 10%. Only tiny Tokelau, fully integrated with very low estimated GDP per head, breaks the pattern.

The figures in Tables 28.1 and 28.2 show each economy's GDP converted to US$ at current market exchange rates. This procedure tends to understate the recorded GDP of the poorest countries, because it undervalues their production of nontraded goods, which sell locally at prices well below the prices of equivalent goods and services in rich economies and have to be revalued to "purchasing power parity" in order to make like-with-like comparisons across countries (World Bank 1996:225). Adjusting the GDP of Papua New Guinea, Fiji, the Solomon Islands, Vanuatu, and Samoa on this basis roughly doubles their estimated GDP per head (World Bank 1996:222, Table 28.1a; Booth 1995:210, Table 28.3), whereas Hawai'i, as part of the benchmark U.S. economy relative to which the revaluation is carried out, would be unaffected. The French Pacific territories, in which prices for many nontraded services are inflated by French wage and salary policies (Poirine 1994b), would also be little changed.

Adjusting the poorer island economies' per capita GDP using purchasing power parity might thus raise them only from 5% to 10% of the dependent territories' GDP per head, or to just over 20% with both Hawai'i and Papua New Guinea excluded. Measurement error, in other words, contributes only marginally to the pattern revealed by Table 28.2.

While the data in Table 28.2 show a correlation between political integration and economic prosperity, they do not prove causality: does political integration lead to relative economic prosperity, or does relative poverty result in decolonization? The cases of French Polynesia and the Federated States of Micronesia—both extremely resource-poor but with high incomes because of official transfer payments—provide support for the first hypothesis. Kiribati, decolonized by Britain in the year its phosphate resource was exhausted, gives some credibility to the other.

Provisionally, it seems reasonable to regard political connections as the source rather than the consequence of economic welfare. This proposition, that in the Pacific relative wealth flows from "dependency," and relative hardship from independence, has seemed paradoxical to many social scientists familiar with the larger developing economies of Latin America and Asia. It is nevertheless a feature of small-island economies not only in the Pacific but also in the Caribbean, Atlantic, and Indian oceans.

A second main stylized fact about Pacific Island economies is that across the region, economic growth as measured by GDP during the past two decades has been slow and often outpaced by population growth, so that per capita incomes have been flat or falling slightly according to the official statistics. The region-wide pattern of slow output growth is common across a wide variety of income levels, political regimes, and trade orientations. It represents a significant slowdown compared with the rapid material progress of the region up until the early 1980s and is attributable directly to the end of a period in which government was a strongly growing "leading sector" for the island economies. From the World War II until the late 1970s, with the international political spotlight focused on issues of development and decolonization, the dominant metropolitan powers (particularly the United States, Britain, France, and New Zealand) financed and organized the project of extending to their island dependencies many of the attributes of their own welfare states, especially in the fields of education, health, and public works. However once the dependent territories had been raised to levels of material welfare consistent with the desire of the metropolitan governments to emerge with credibility from the decolonization process, the impetus of state expansion slackened (except in French Polynesia, where the nuclear testing program resulted in a continuing economic boom through the 1980s). Decolonization was usually followed by a drop in or leveling-off of ongoing aid funding provided by former metropolitan powers and a corresponding loss of the previous momentum of public-sector expenditure.

The era of government-led growth left a valuable legacy of physical infrastructure (roads, ports, energy and telecommunications systems, public buildings, education and health), and economies with employment heavily concentrated in the externally financed public sector. However, as public expenditure leveled off, there was no subsequent takeoff of private-sector-led growth in GDP except in Fiji, where sugar, tourism, and manufacturing provided high-linkage export sectors. In most island economies, private investment has remained concentrated in nontraded goods and services such as commerce, construction, transport, communications, and financial services. Because local markets are small, the growth potential of these sectors is limited, and hence investment opportunities are limited.

The slow growth of GDP is certainly not due to any lack of finance for investment. The Pacific Islands do not have a "savings gap"; on the contrary, a common theme in the literature on island finance is the existence of excess liquidity due to the shortage of bankable projects (Nagai 1996). It is low capital absorption capacity, due partly to small scale and geographical isolation, that limits the possibilities for textbook growth models based on large-country experience.

A third stylized fact is the lack of economic integration, as usually understood, among the Pacific Island economies. Trade statistics show the Pacific to be the least-integrated region in the world, with trade between the island states amounting to less than 2% of their total exports (McGregor et al. 1992:20–21). Each island economy trades mainly with bilateral partners outside the region, with former or actual metropolitan patrons the preferred trading partners. Only in nontradable economic activities—government, education, scientific research, transport, communications—is there a tendency toward integration among the island states.

A fourth major feature of the region is its unusual combination of very large trade deficits with a generally healthy current account on the balance of payments. Figure 28.1 plots for fifteen Pacific Island economies the balance of trade in goods and services over the two decades to 1994. This balance, sometimes termed the "commercial balance," is calculated by adding together all of a territory's foreign-exchange earnings from the sale of exported goods and services including tourism, transport, and communications, and then subtracting all foreign-exchange payments for imported goods and services, including services such as transport and insurance that enter into the cost of imported goods. This gives a measure of the extent to which the sale of local output on world markets enables an economy to pay for its import needs. For purposes of cross-country comparison, the data for each economy have been averaged for each five-year period between 1975 and 1994 and expressed as a percentage of merchandise imports (that is, imports of goods, excluding services purchased overseas). Only one of the fifteen economies, Fiji, has shown a positive commercial balance over two five-year periods. The remainder show deficits ranging from around 10-20% of imports (Hawai'i, American Samoa, New Caledonia) to around 100% or more (Tuvalu, the Marshall Islands, French Polynesia, the Federated States of Micronesia).

Because of the very open nature of these economies, the trade deficits are also large relative to GDP. Across the six countries surveyed in detail by the World Bank in 1991, Fiji, Papua New Guinea, Vanuatu, Kiribati, Samoa, and Tonga (World Bank 1991:12), exports averaged 55% of GDP and imports averaged 67%, so that their collective commercial deficit was 12% of GDP—a very high ratio by international standards.

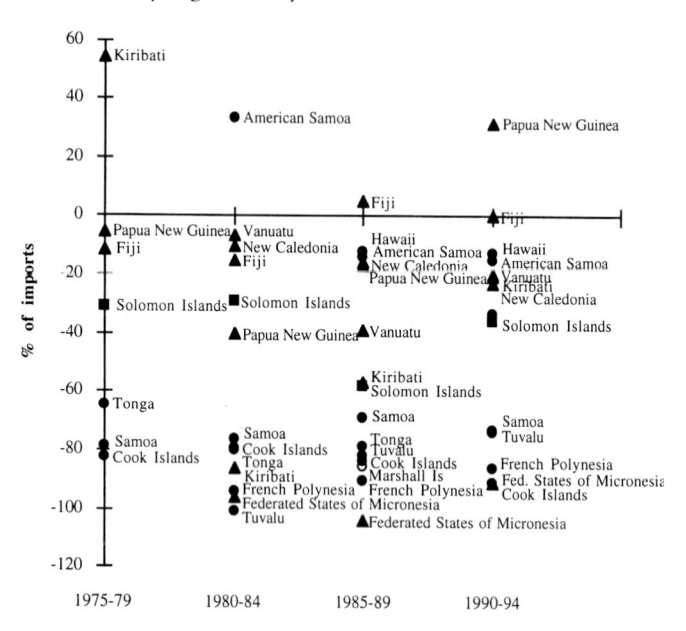

*Figure 28.1.* Goods and services balances of fifteen Pacific territories.

Some possible classifications suggest themselves in Figure 28.1. Melanesia and Hawai'i, with larger land masses and populations, have relatively "strong" commercial balances (small deficits). Small-island Polynesia and Micronesia have conspicuously large deficits. With the exception of Hawai'i and American Samoa, the Polynesian and Micronesian microstates shown in Figure 28.1 have commercial deficits between 50% and 110% of imports, which means that more than half the imports to those economies are financed either by current transfers (repatriated overseas earnings, private remittances, and official aid) or by capital inflow (borrowing plus direct foreign investment).

These two possible means of financing trade deficits have radically different implications for economic sustainability. Economies with trade deficits financed by capital inflows face rising overseas indebtedness over time and so must eventually raise their export revenues to the level required to service that debt, or reduce their imports sufficiently to move their current accounts back to surplus. This is a familiar situation in Africa and Latin America, but does not apply to Pacific Island economies, whose overseas debt has never been allowed to rise above modest levels. A recent World Bank study (World Bank 1996:240-241) classified the degree of indebtedness of 210 economies, including 13 Pacific Island economies. No Pacific Island states were among the 53 "severely indebted low and middle income" economies. Only 2 (Samoa and Papua New Guinea) appeared among the 31 "moderately indebted" countries. The other 11 Pacific economies covered were ranked "less indebted" or had no classifiable external debt. As Table 28.3 shows, the level of public overseas indebtedness in the seven economies for which data are readily available is seldom more than one-third of GDP except for Samoa, which moved into the "moderately indebted" category from the late 1980s, partly because of the heavy public cost of repairing cyclone damage in the early 1990s.

**TABLE 28.3**

**Public and Publicly Guaranteed Overseas Debt of Seven Pacific Economies**

| Country | Debt US$m | GDP US$m | Debt as % of GDP |
| --- | --- | --- | --- |
| **Fiji:** | | | |
| 1989 | 301.6 | 1,254.4 | 24.0 |
| 1994 | 195.2 | 1,869.4 | 10.4 |
| **Kiribati:** | | | |
| 1990 | 3.4 | 32.4 | 10.5 |
| 1994 | 9.3 | 34.3 | 27.1 |
| **Papua New Guinea:** | | | |
| 1989 | 1,314.2 | 3,558.9 | 36.9 |
| 1993 | 1,571.5 | 5,088.5 | 30.9 |
| **Samoa:** | | | |
| 1989 | 71.9 | 109.0 | 66.0 |
| 1992 | 117.8 | 120.0 | 98.2 |
| **Solomon Islands:** | | | |
| 1989 | 99.4 | 167.6 | 59.3 |
| 1993 | 94.9 | 245.0 | 38.7 |
| **Tonga:** | | | |
| 1989 | 38.1 | 115.8 | 32.9 |
| 1992 | 42.6 | 147.1 | 29.0 |
| **Vanuatu:** | | | |
| 1989 | 20.8 | 147.9 | 14.1 |
| 1993 | 39.4 | 181.8 | 21.7 |

Sources: UN Statistical Yearbook 1994, Table 28.81; Asian Development Bank 1994.

The Micronesian/Polynesian combination of large trade deficits and low overseas debt has been sustained for several decades now by large flows of current-account transfer payments into the island economies. These transfers come from three main sources. First is the payment of interest and dividends on financial assets held overseas—income from overseas investments such as Kiribati's Revenue Equalization Reserve Fund, Nauru's large portfolio (both derived from saved phosphate revenues) and Tuvalu's Trust Fund. Second is the flow of remittances sent home by migrants living and working in metropolitan economies such as Australia, New Zealand, the United States, and Canada. Third is official aid provided in the form of "unrequited transfers"—that is, payments for which no subsequent repayment is required, so that the local government budget can be funded with no weakening of the government's balance sheet.

Table 28.4 assembles some figures that demonstrate the various ways in which Pacific Island economies maintain strong current accounts in their balance of payments despite having generally large commercial deficits. Only two of the twelve countries in Table 28.4 have strong trade balances. Fiji, as already seen in Figure 28.1, is an economy that does not have a significant trade deficit and so pays its way on the basis of export earnings. Papua New Guinea is the largest single aid recipient

## TABLE 28.4

### Financing of the Current Account in Twelve Pacific Economies (Annually in US$ Millions)

| Country | Exports: goods & services | Imports: goods & services | Commercial balance | Interest, dividends, etc. | Remittances | Official transfers | Current account balance |
|---|---|---|---|---|---|---|---|
| **American Samoa** | | | | | | | |
| 1985-89 | 292.33 | 337.67 | -45.33 | na | na | na | na |
| 1990-93 | 331.50 | 390.00 | -58.50 | na | na | na | na |
| **Cook Islands:** | | | | | | | |
| 1985-89 | 20.43 | 29.66 | -9.23 | na | na | na | na |
| 1990-92 | 25.85 | 50.37 | -24.52 | na | na | na | na |
| **Federated States of Micronesia:** | | | | | | | |
| 1985-89 | 16.83 | 83.74 | -66.91 | a | 6.53 | 113.75 | 53.36 |
| 1990 | 50.30 | 170.70 | -120.40 | a | 2.40 | 114.93 | -3.07 |
| **Fiji:** | | | | | | | |
| 1985-89 | 581.46 | 565.78 | 15.68 | -25.22 | -10.42 | 24.04 | 4.04 |
| 1990-94 | 905.08 | 922.84 | -17.76 | -13.70 | 8.28 | 34.32 | 11.14 |
| **Kiribati:** | | | | | | | |
| 1985-89 | 20.42 | 41.41 | -20.99 | 7.43b | 2.10 | 19.67 | 8.21 |
| 1990-94 | 29.18 | 62.76 | -33.58 | 15.62b | 7.08 | 25.38 | 14.48 |
| **Marshall Islands:** | | | | | | | |
| 1986-89 | 22.26 | 57.96 | -35.70 | a | 6.01 | 52.80 | 23.10 |
| 1990 | 35.14 | 78.61 | -43.46 | a | 5.68 | 64.12 | 26.34 |
| **Papua New Guinea:** | | | | | | | |
| 1985-89 | 1303.74 | 1494.34 | -190.60 | -150.30 | -105.46 | 214.08 | -232.28 |
| 1990-94 | 2256.36 | 1867.98 | 388.38 | -305.22 | -96.22 | 228.64 | 245.92 |
| **Samoa:** | | | | | | | |
| 1985-89 | 32.85 | 71.01 | -38.16 | 0.08 | 32.41 | 12.92 | 7.25 |
| 1990-94 | 42.60 | 113.03 | -70.43 | 2.61 | 33.37 | 13.78 | -21.36 |
| **Solomon Islands:** | | | | | | | |
| 1985-89 | 92.60 | 137.34 | -44.74 | -7.18 | -0.54 | 26.77 | -25.69 |
| 1990-92 | 116.09 | 167.25 | -51.16 | -8.06 | 3.06 | 35.40 | -20.77 |
| **Tonga:** | | | | | | | |
| 1985-89 | 24.99 | 57.05 | -32.07 | 3.23 | 21.57 | 5.65 | -1.61 |
| 1990-93 | 33.26 | 74.33 | -41.07 | 3.25 | 30.70 | 6.95 | -0.17 |
| **Tuvalu:** | | | | | | | |
| 1985-89 | 4.35 | 7.86 | -3.52 | a | c | 3.53 | 0.02 |
| 1990-93 | 6.55 | 10.54 | -3.99 | a | c | 6.17 | 2.18 |
| **Vanuatu:** | | | | | | | |
| 1985-89 | 51.10 | 84.82 | -33.72 | -0.45 | 6.84 | 25.81 | -1.52 |
| 1990-94 | 86.43 | 100.11 | -13.68 | -24.52 | 11.16 | 15.58 | -11.26 |

a) Included in export and import data. b) Reserve Equalization Reserve Fund income. c) All transfers included in aid column.

Sources: IMF Balance of Payments Yearbook and International Finance Statistics; United Nations Statistical Yearbook 1994; Asian Development Bank Key Indicators of Developing Asian and Pacific Countries 1994; UNCTAD Handbook of International Trade Statistics.

in the region, reflecting its very low income and large population; but aid funding is only about 10% of export earnings and serves mainly to offset the outflow of dividends, interest, and repatriated earnings. (Private remittances flow out from Papua New Guinea because of the large number of expatriates employed there. The small number of Papuan migrants overseas means that remittances in the other direction are small.)

The Federated States of Micronesia, the Marshall Islands, Tuvalu, and the Solomon Islands all have heavy commercial deficits financed by large official transfers. French Polynesia (not included in Table 28.4) also funds its commercial deficit in this way. These economies can be described as aid-driven. In contrast, Tonga and Samoa rely mainly on private remittances to fund their trade deficits; in both these economies remittance flows are on a par with export earnings, and aid provides a top-up. The Cook Islands, Niue, and Tokelau (not included in Table 28.4) all have similar dual reliance on private remittances and official aid. This group of economies can be described as driven by migration and remittances.

A third funding pattern is that of Kiribati, with its large inflow of dividends and interest from offshore financial assets, although official aid remains an important component of its financing. Nauru (not in Table 28.4) has an even stronger role for investment income in its current account and receives only a trickle of aid. These economies can be described as rent-led.

The relative stability over time of these various models of current-account financing is demonstrated in Figure 28.2, which compares the current accounts of Fiji, Tonga, Samoa, Kiribati, and the Federated States of Micronesia from the mid-1970s to the early to mid-1990s. In each chart the solid line shows the funding required in each year to pay for imports of goods and services, including interest and dividends on overseas investment in the local economy. The sources from which funding was obtained are shown by the vertical columns, with exports of goods and services forming the bottom segment of each bar, and other sources of current-account financing added on top. So long as the columns stand higher than the imports line, the current account is in surplus and the economy is able to pay for its full import needs without having to borrow overseas. (Gaps in the charts for Kiribati and the Federated States of Micronesia represent years for which data was not available.)

To a first approximation it is convenient to regard these economies as operating under a foreign-exchange constraint represented by the requirement to keep the current account in balance, so that expenditure on imported goods and services (including outflow of profits and expatriate incomes) exhausts the current financing available in each period. This means not only that any increase in aid, remittances, or export earnings flows through directly to increased imports, but that the opposite is also true: any reduction in external sources of funding places an immediate squeeze on imports and living standards.

The comparison between Fiji and Samoa in Figure 28.2 is instructive. Fiji's current account is financed almost entirely by exports of goods and services, with the current account virtually in balance throughout the two decades shown. Samoa's current account is more than half financed by transfers, with private remittances moving ahead of official aid over the two

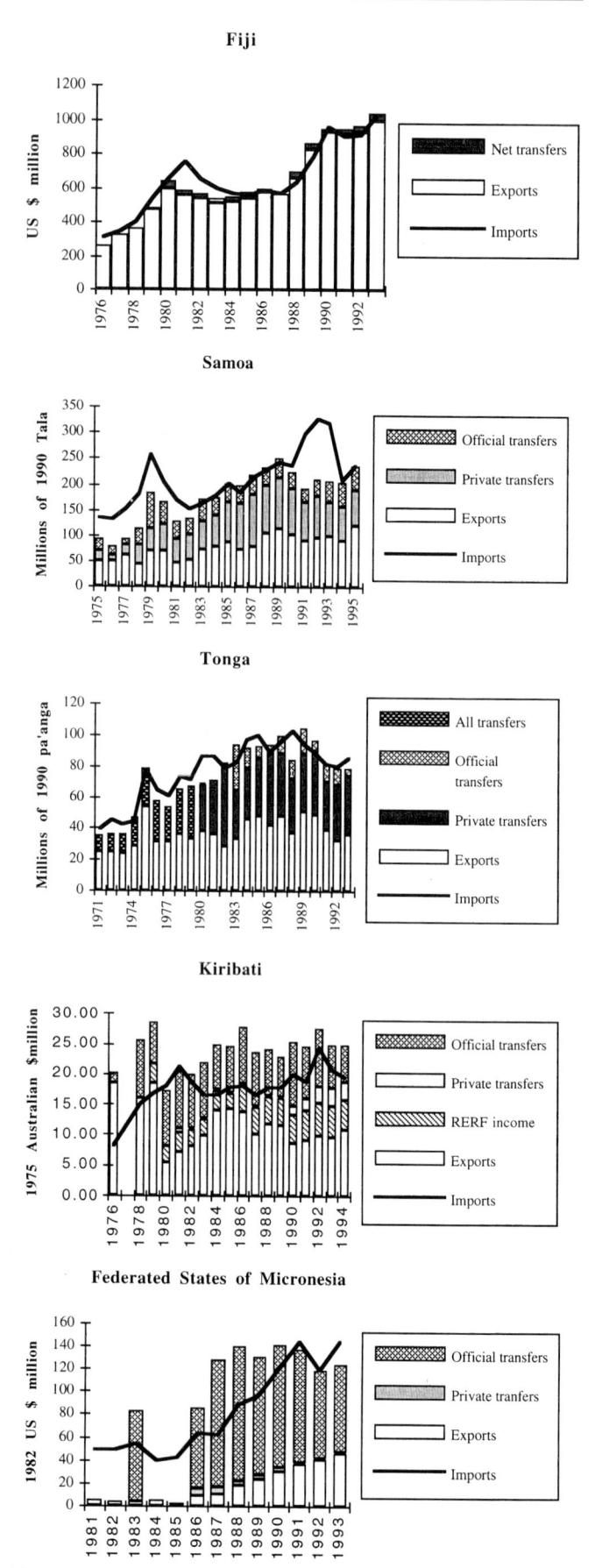

*Figure 28.2.* Current account balances of five Pacific economies: financing of import expenditures including factor payments.

decades, and with exports static from the late 1980s to the mid 1990s. (More recently Samoa's manufactured exports have risen, due to the success of the Yazaki auto-loom plant.)

The current account structures shown in Figure 28.2 imply the absence of a binding link between expenditure and output. Growth statistics commonly focus on the trend of domestic product; but what determines living standards is the ability of ordinary people to purchase goods and services. This is measured in national income accounting not by GDP, but by Gross National Expenditure, GNE. To measure Gross National Expenditure we have to adjust the published GDP statistics by adding imports of goods and services (which supplement local living standards) and subtracting exports (which take goods and services away from local use). Figure 28.3 shows the result of doing this for a number of Pacific economies. Fiji's material living standards are clearly tied to output; Kiribati's are not—indeed, only half the absorption of goods and services in Kiribati is supported by domestic production. Similarly, in the 1980s Samoa's expenditure ran steadily about one-third above product, and in the first half of the 1990s it moved up to a 60% margin.

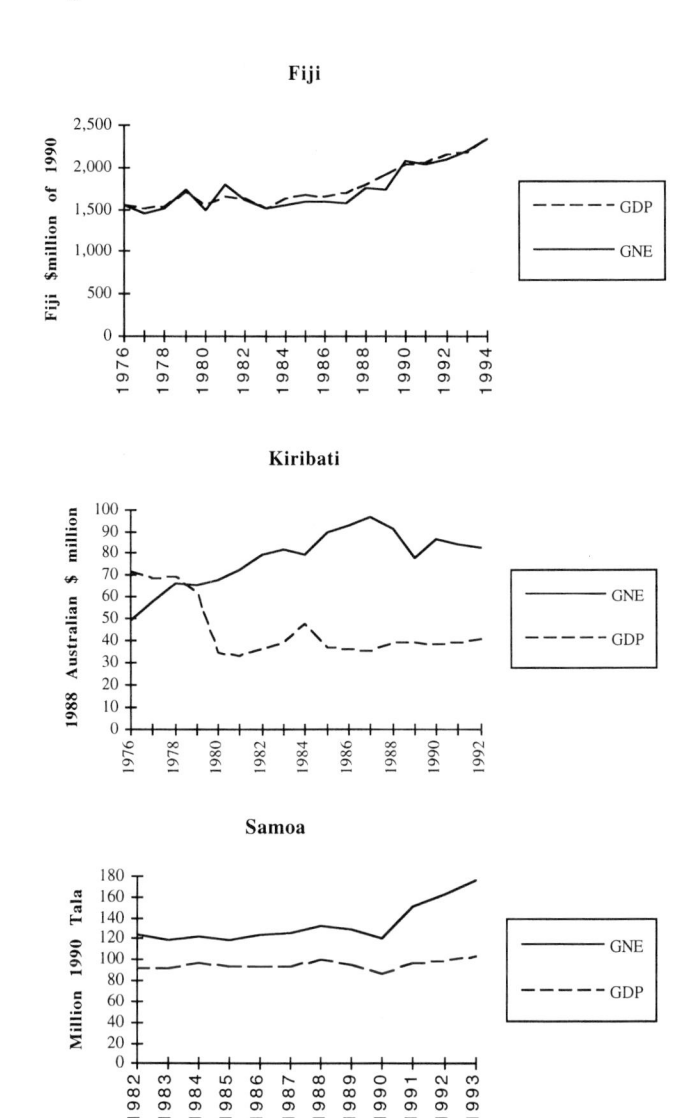

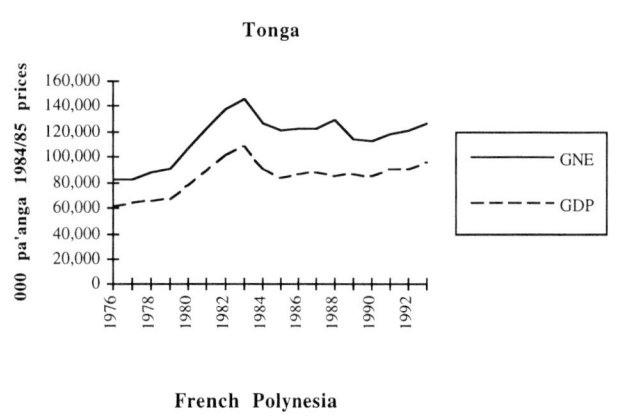

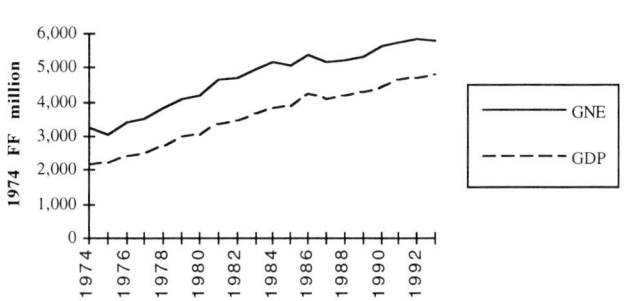

*Figure 28.3.* National expenditure and domestic product.

## Island Economies and Economic Development Theory

The theoretical literature on so-called "microstates" and their economic status has burgeoned in recent years. The debate can be traced back to the end of the 1950s, when the newly established field of development economics turned its attention to the issue of whether the size of a nation-state influenced its economic development. Two books of collected papers from that period (Robinson 1960, Benedict 1967) set the framework for most work until the 1980s and presented a puzzle that still lies at the heart of the microstate literature. This can be stated in the following terms:

Modernization theories predict that small size should be a handicap for growth and development. Yet the world's very smallest autonomous political units are not located at the bottom of the development ladder, nor is there any robust statistical evidence that small size correlates with low standards of living (Milner and Westaway 1993). Considering the countries in Table 28.1, the contrast between tiny Nauru and large Papua New Guinea makes the point nicely.

The conventional economic wisdom further predicts that physical isolation should, other things equal, result in weaker economic performance; yet it has not been possible to show statistically that small-island economies in the world economy are less "developed" than those of states of the same size located on continents (Armstrong and Read 1997).

Theoretical interpretation of these empirical regularities is clearly important for policymaking purposes. By the early 1990s the literature on growth, trade, and migration in the Pacific Islands could be characterized in terms of the emergence of two competing paradigms (Hayes 1991). The dominant mainstream paradigm regards the observed economic success of island microstates as an anomaly that cannot persist unless a "big push" is mounted to promote investment, output, and commodity exports; otherwise, it suggests, in the long run the theoretical disadvantages of smallness must assert themselves. An alternative paradigm is built around the idea that the observed economic condition of island microstates should be seen as normal rather than anomalous and that the mainstream theory should be revised accordingly. Thumbnail sketches of the two paradigms may clarify their essential areas of divergence.

## The Classical Modernization Model

In the modernization approach, development is treated as synonymous with the achievement of economic and political autonomy by means of a self-sustaining, endogenously driven process of economic growth. In turn this requires strong investment, either by local capitalists or by the state, to increase domestic productive capacity and hence achieve sustainable growth of output and employment. On the basis of such capital accumulation, sustained by domestic savings effort, the expected outcome of development is a balanced economic structure, comprising both tradable goods and services that can be sold on world markets and nontradable goods and services, including the infrastructure for a modern economy.

The modernized economy is thought of as being incorporated into the world economy by commodity trade, with outward-oriented "leading sectors." Internally, the mass of the population is incorporated into the development process by means of the payment of wages by modern enterprises, with the real wage rate reflecting an equilibrium balance between population and local production; real wages and living standards thus rise in step with modern-sector output. Population growth is seen through Malthusian spectacles; if it continues unchecked, diminishing returns will eventually force wages and living standards down.

Policies drawn from the modernization model have been highly influential over the past half-century. Political independence from "colonial" attachments is encouraged, and self-reliance based on local capital accumulation thus becomes a goal in its own right. Because of perceived inefficiencies in state-owned production of traded goods, the government sector is frequently assumed to be a drag on growth performance, so that reducing its share of economic activity should favor growth. Recent examples of major Pacific Island studies conducted within this paradigm are Browne and Scott (1989), World Bank (1991), McGregor et al. (1992), Asian Development Bank (1995), and Fairbairn and Worrell (1996). The Malthusian model is presented with stark simplicity in Tisdell and Fairbairn (1984). Growing unease over the limitations of the paradigm when applied to Pacific Island microstates is apparent in Brookfield (1972), Shand (1980), and Connell (1988).

When economic development is seen through this theoretical window, smallness and distance both appear to be disadvantages. From Adam Smith on, most economic theorists have considered that large economic units able to trade with each other at low cost should have the edge in economic performance because of their ability to gain economies of scale while sustaining diversified economies. In contrast, small economies that lack a large enough local market to achieve scale economies in production for that market will be forced to overspecialize in one or two tradable activities, with consequent high exposure to instability and lack of intersectoral spillovers. Isolation raises transport costs and thus reduces the exporter's share of the revenues from sales to outside markets. In combination, these factors would be expected to reduce the economy-wide economic surplus and so limit investment and growth.

A clear statement of this view is Streeten (1993). Similar ideas for the Pacific Islands are in Chapter 1 of Shand (1980). The problem of economic development for small islands is therefore perceived by agencies such as the World Bank as more acute than for larger states; and relatively high living standards supported by means other than domestic production, based on local capital accumulation, are almost automatically characterized as unsustainable.

## The MIRAB Model

The modernization approach to Pacific development summarized above lays heavy emphasis on export promotion and private investment, both of which have rather poor track records in the island Pacific over the past half-century, with a few exceptions.[1]

The main alternative paradigm of Pacific Island development shifts the theoretical spotlight to three other types of economic activity that have performed more strongly in many Pacific Island economies: international sale of factor services rather than produced goods and services; long-term sustained financial transfer flows; and domestic production of nontraded goods. The acronym MIRAB encapsulates this trinity: Migration (of factors of production), Remittances/Aid (financial transfers), and Bureaucracy (nontradables production)(Bertram and Watters 1985; Bertram 1986; Poirine 1994b). The underlying proposition is that globalization of the Pacific economy has been well advanced for several decades now and has rendered the model of self-contained, territorially bounded national economies increasingly inadequate to explain economic performance.

The starting point for the MIRAB analysis was the observed empirical anomaly noted above (that small-island economies exhibited higher standards of living than predicted by the classical model), combined with a critique of the common assumption that economies based on migration, remittances, and aid are inherently unsustainable. In relation to development planning and economic policymaking, the MIRAB approach highlights the extent to which conventional plans and analyses limit themselves to the goal of stimulating the economically marginal tradables sectors, while downplaying the main existing economic locomotives in much of Polynesia and Micronesia. A good example of this tendency is the study of private-sector development options in the Pacific by McGregor et al. (1992), which restricts its definition of "private sector activity" entirely to domestic (that is, local) productive activity and regards export earnings as the sole sustainable source of foreign exchange.

Having acknowledged the dominant role of labor remittances in the Tongan and Samoan balances of payments, the authors dismiss the entire topic of factor exports in a single sentence (McGregor et al. 1992:10): "[R]eliance on remittances is precarious should barriers to migrant labor arise and as ties to home become weakened through time." Yet barriers to migration have proved consistently easier for Polynesians and Micronesians to overcome than the barriers to successful entry into export markets (McGregor et al.'s preferred strategy), and remittance flows have been empirically more sustained and more stable than export proceeds (Brown 1997).

The essential issue addressed by the MIRAB model is the ability of many island economies to sustain levels of expenditure (i.e., standards of living) that run consistently, and apparently sustainably, ahead of local productive activity as measured by GDP. The MIRAB model suggests that external sources of financing that do not leave a residue of debt—that is, current account transfers—are the key to the economic performance of small islands.

In a MIRAB economy the indigenous population maximize their material well-being by means of globalization. Subsistence production from land, most of which remains unalienated under customary tenure, puts a floor under living standards by providing for basic needs and possibly also for some modest cash sales of produce to urban or export markets. However, it is the release of family members and family savings from village agriculture and fishing, and their outward movement not merely to other sectors, but to other islands and other countries, that opens the way to securing higher incomes and wealth. Released factors and cash are allocated across whatever geographical and economic space the local population has access to, with the resulting income shared between migrants and their home communities by means of remittances. This process includes employment in the large aid-supported government sectors, which puts cash into the hands of all households with members engaged in such employment.

The size and persistence of financial flows into island economies from overseas, and of labor migration out, has the effect of making capitalist private-sector activity unprofitable in traded-goods production (especially manufacturing and agriculture) because of the resulting combination of strong exchange rates and high wages.

### Aid and Decolonization

A historical perspective makes it easy to "explain" the high levels of per capita expenditure in small Pacific islands by reference to the character of colonialism in the region. In all colonial Pacific spheres of influence from mid-century on, the living standards of indigenous island populations were raised and maintained by financial transfers from the metropolitan powers. The fear that decolonization might go hand in hand with "aid fatigue" among donors underlay a widespread ambivalence toward political independence and contributed to a general willingness of island populations to retain a high level of political tutelage. As Brookfield (1972:141-142) noted in the midst of decolonization:

> [I]f the available local resources in these countries are inevitably insufficient to support either the transformation or maintenance of welfare at present and desired levels, then there is no alternative to dependence but stagnation and retrogression. Independence may give a nation self-respect, . . . but it is a self-respect that must be severely constrained by awareness that the power of economic decision making is greatly limited. To maximize self-respect [in this sense] is not accordant with maximization of either income or welfare.

Poirine (1995, Ch. 5) has developed, and investigated statistically, a model of the factors determining per capita aid flows (including government budgetary support) to a developing economy and hence its ability to sustain expenditure levels in excess of domestic production. His three hypotheses are that, controlling for other factors:

i) islands receive more aid than nonisland economies because of their greater geostrategic importance and greater per capita control over territory (including sea and air space);
ii) aid per capita is inversely related to island population (consistent with diminishing returns on an aid flow determined by territorial factors);
iii) aid per capita varies inversely with the degree of political autonomy of the territory.

In contrast to models that view aid flows as altruistic transfers subject to "donor fatigue," Poirine argues that financial transfers are generally determined by maximization of self-interest on the part of donors and hence will change only as the margin of donor calculation shifts. Aid donors to small island territories are in effect purchasing a valued service in the form of a geostrategic footprint, the loss of which would have negative spillover effects on the metropolitan country.

Aldrich (1993, Ch. 3) gives a similar account of French aid motivations. Gaffaney (1995:50), addressing the issue "why didn't the United States completely abandon Micronesia after the development of detente and the ICBM?," makes a similar argument but with a subtly different flavor: international moral and political pressure made it impossible for the United States to abandon prior commitments without offending international opinion. Gaffaney suggests that

> even great powers in the international state of nature become bound to commitments and may change their policies towards their dependencies for reasons other than the great powers' own interests. . . . [S]uperpowers may not be completely autonomous agents, but have become involved in a complex web of international norms and standards for the treatment of nonthreatening states.

## Applicability of the MIRAB Model

Casual inspection of the size of aid flows and degree of mobility of labor and financial capital suggests that the MIRAB approach is likely to apply more to Polynesia and Micronesia than to Melanesia. The Melanesian economies are characterized by large size and natural resource endowments and by low international labor mobility. Melanesian island populations do, however, reproduce internally via interisland movement the patterns of migration and remittances found on an international scale in Polynesia (Hayes 1990, Flinn 1992).

Outside the New Zealand sphere of influence where it was formulated (Tokelau, Niue, the Cook Islands) the MIRAB model seems applicable to French Polynesia (Poirine 1994b, 1995, Blanchet 1996); the Federated States of Micronesia (Cameron 1991, Gaffaney 1995, Hezel and Levin 1996); the other small U.S.-associated former Pacific Trust Territories; Tonga and Samoa; Chile's Pacific outpost of Easter Island, outlying islands of Papua New Guinea and the Solomon Islands (Hayes 1993, Friesen 1993); Tuvalu and Kiribati.

The relative importance of remittances, aid, and staple export earnings varies from case to case and from period to period. For a very small economy, the transition from staples export economy to MIRAB economy and back again is an easy one. Consider, for example, the small twentieth-century phosphate economies, Nauru and the preindependence Gilbert Islands (now Kiribati). Both of these exhibited the classic colonial export-economy pattern of a staple-based trade surplus, with the resulting foreign-exchange surplus being the object of a growing struggle between indigenous and metropolitan claimants. Neither economy industrialized on the basis of diversification from the staple—another classic colonial pattern. Both have, however, confronted phosphate depletion by engineering partial (Kiribati) or complete (Nauru) transitions to postphosphate MIRAB systems supported by rent income from overseas investment of retained phosphate earnings rather than the more usual factor, labor.

For larger island states, MIRAB status is harder to establish and sustain because international labor and financial flows reach a critical mass at which political and economic resistance arises. Large-island economies, even when fully politically integrated, like Hawai'i's, require strong per capita export performance in addition to financial transfers to sustain living standards. Those that lacked the leverage to become politically integrated have, of necessity, been forced to attempt the orthodox transition from staple exports to industrialization. This is the situation for most of Melanesia, given neighboring Australia's lack of interest in political integration and constraints on per capita aid availability. Only Fiji has been successful in making the modernization transition; apart from rentier Nauru, the other independent Melanesian states (Vanuatu, Papua New Guinea, and the Solomon Islands) have struggled to establish any sustainable economic dynamic and remain dependent on export sectors with limited backward and forward linkages. New Caledonia, in contrast, exhibits the material benefits of its political integration with France (note its GDP per capita figure in Table 28.1, compared with the rest of Melanesia).

## Settler Colonies

The causal association of external political integration with relatively high material living standards raises important and controversial issues about the roots of economic "success" and "failure" in the Pacific. Observers of New Zealand (or Hawai'i) are sometimes inclined to attribute the relative prosperity and historically strong growth performance of the economy to factors such as the large nonindigenous components of the population, higher skill levels of the labor force, and the establishment of an autonomous capitalist dynamic. By drawing a contemporary cross-sectional contrast between the region's "lead" economies and the rest, a case is then made for encouraging autonomy and capital accumulation in the "follower" economies in order to achieve economic development on a stand-alone basis.

An important theme of this chapter is that comparisons of this sort are fundamentally misdirected because they do not address the long-run historical sequencing of economic development. Rather than drawing comparisons with present-day New Zealand, Pacific analysts ought to be casting back to the New Zealand economy of a century ago for clues to economic success. By the last decade of the nineteenth century, New Zealand was already among the world's top three or four economies in terms of real income per head, a status from which it has since slipped, but to which it was originally driven by a particular combination of circumstances among which three deserve special mention.

First was the high degree of political integration with Great Britain, of which New Zealand was still a colony, although progressing through the stages of formal decolonization. The special political access that New Zealand enjoyed in British government circles remained formidably effective through the Great Depression of the 1930s (when at the 1932 Ottawa Conference New Zealand secured preferential markets for its agricultural exports at the expense of South American export economies) and on into the 1970s. Only in the last two decades has the political linkage failed in the face of European integration; this coincided with a pronounced slowdown in New Zealand's growth performance.

Second was the very open and fluid labor market, which caused real wage rates in New Zealand to be indexed to rates both in Britain and in the other "settler capitalisms" of Australia, South Africa, Chile, Uruguay, and Argentina, as well as with the west coast of the United States (Denoon 1983). (The same effect might apply to Hawai'i, though it is not included in Denoon's study.) Even once British migration to New Zealand slowed down after the 1960s, a close migration nexus has continued to bind together the New Zealand and Australian labor markets, with large numbers of New Zealand–born workers resident in Australia on a long-term basis. This extreme openness of the labor market renders closed-economy modernization models as inapplicable to New Zealand economic history as they are today to most other Pacific Island economies.

Third, New Zealanders were always intensely conscious of their economic dependence and hence torn culturally between the desire to stand more on their own feet, and the recognition that continuing prosperity hinged on preserving the terms of their country's integration into the world economic system. "Colony or nation?" has been a recurring theme in New Zealand literature and political discourse, and only in the past two decades has a more self-confident national identity entrenched itself.

The lesson of New Zealand is not, therefore, that growth can be induced by independence, but rather that economic prosperity can be secured under conditions of dependence, laying foundations for a possible later transition to greater autonomy. For settler capitalism in general, Denoon (1983:228) concludes:

> From their inception, settler states were dominated by social classes committed to an imperial link, and to the production of export staples. State institutions reflected that fact, and in turn influenced the manner in which different social classes interacted upon each other. That strategy could generate tremendous wealth, and rapid demographic growth, which naturally created dangerous tensions within each of the societies.

New Zealand is differentiated from the other Pacific economies included in this book primarily by the timing of its breakthrough to prosperity. In terms of the institutions of the world economic system of the 1990s this translates into OECD membership and inclusion in the "Pacific Rim," both of which give New Zealand, for the moment at least, separate status even from U.S. outliers such as Guam and Hawai'i, which enjoy OECD and Pacific Rim status at one remove. The Rim concept however is theoretically problematic, suggesting as it does that a geoeconomic core can be created out of a geographic periphery. Both New Zealand and the South American members are likely to be reperipheralized as the Asian economic core coalesces and draws in its boundaries from the Rim to the island economies of the North Pacific.

## Migration

Economic development is conventionally defined (see section on Island Economies and Economic Development Theory, p. 343) in terms of the output produced by the resident population of a territory. For many Pacific Islanders, however, development means capitalizing on economic opportunities across a wider international arena. The migrant can plug in to income-earning opportunities, investment opportunities, and educational and lifestyle opportunities that are not available in the home territory and which could be provided there only at unwarranted cost. Wherever they are not restrained by legal barriers, Pacific Islanders are geographically mobile in pursuit of economic opportunity.

A feature of many of the small-island economies, especially those of Polynesia, therefore, is that a significant proportion of their indigenous population reside and work away from their home islands. Correspondingly, an important feature of larger regional economies such as New Zealand's and Hawai'i's is the presence of large communities of migrants who retain strong ties with their home communities. Other Pacific Rim economies such as Australia, California, and British Columbia also have substantial Pacific Islander communities living and working there. Most host countries unfortunately lack detailed census data on these migrant communities; only New Zealand has consistent census data on its islander population by place of birth since the 1950s.

Hayes (1991:3-9) assembled figures from a range of sources to construct an estimate of the geographic distribution of several Polynesian ethnic groups in about 1986. Of his total 500,000 ethnic Polynesians, excluding the indigenous peoples of New Zealand, Hawai'i, and French Polynesia, nearly 40% were resident in the three main metropolitan destinations New Zealand, Australia, and the United States (including Hawai'i). The proportion of these ethnic Polynesians resident outside their homelands in 1986 ranged from 22% for Tongans to 78% for Niueans. Migration has continued in the decade since 1986, and it is probable that the proportion of externally resident Polynesians from the islands covered by Hayes (1991) is now approaching 50%.

Ahlburg and Levin (1990, Ch. 1) found that of 83,000 islands-born migrants living in the United States in 1980, about 27,500 were from Polynesia. The other two significant migrant communities were Guamians (36,782) and Fijians (7,538, mainly Indo-Fijians). Relative to the home populations, over one-third of Guam's indigenous population was living in the metropolitan United States in the early 1980s. Fiji-born migrants in the United States, New Zealand, Australia, and Canada totalled over 33,000.

Ahlburg (1996:8-10) notes that in the 1990s the Federated States of Micronesia, Guam, Palau, and the Northern Marianas all became major host countries for in-migrants from Asia, while the migration of Micronesians themselves continued, resulting in an increasingly complex and dynamic demographic picture in that part of the Pacific. Within Micronesia, large-scale migration movements from smaller to larger islands have reproduced internally the wider pattern of movement; Hezel and Levin (1996:95) estimated 6,330 citizens of the Federated States of Micronesia residing in Guam in 1994 and a further 2,420 in the Northern Marianas—a total of nearly 10% of the FSM population.

Economic interactions between the home-resident and the migrant parts of each islander community remain important, especially as sources of remittance income and of potential employment opportunities for the home residents. Migrants have colonized selected economic sectors and residential neighborhoods of major Pacific Rim cities such as Auckland, Sydney, and Los Angeles, and as their numbers have grown, the links between standards of living in those metropolitan economies and the feasible expectations of island residents have been reinforced and multiplied, effectively indexing many of the economic parameters of the islands to the economies of their larger patrons.

The typical Pacific migrant does not become separated from the home community simply by virtue of migration. On the contrary, migrants exhibit strong tendencies to retain close ties with their home kin groups and to maintain patterns of return visiting and remittances in cash and kind, which continue to bind them to their places of origin and to enable kin groups to live and earn on the international, rather than the national, stage.

Economic development for islander communities is thus not restricted to economic development of island territories. Economic research on these globalized communities, which began with Marcus (1981), is still in its infancy but has been progressing rapidly during the past decade (Loomis 1990, Ahlburg and Levin 1990, Ahlburg 1996a, Brown 1995, Brown and Foster 1995, Brown 1997). One outstanding point to emerge is the sustainability of migrant remittances. Many writers have predicted that remittance effort by migrants should tend to decline over time as ties to the home community wither away; but the evidence from the Pacific Islands does not support this prediction. As Connell and Brown (1995:17-18) remark:

> [W]hat is striking in every case, and well-documented in the case of Tongans and Cook Islanders overseas, is just how long and at what levels remittances are maintained, with only slight evidence of the anticipated decay. From their econometric analysis of recent cross-sectional data from a survey among Tongan migrants in Brisbane, Walker and Brown found that while the propensity to remit was negatively related to the age of the migrant, it was positively related to the migrant's length of absence from home.

Because the economic activities of Pacific Island communities span multiple geographical locations, the analysis of key aspects of economic behavior such as saving, investment, employment, and income has to be conducted in terms of an integrated, internationalized household model. Many islanders plan and act transnationally, either as individuals or as members of more or less organized kin groups; and they allocate their available resources across geographical niches with an eye to maximizing the life chances for themselves and their kin. The "modern sector" of many island economies is located offshore and hence is missing from the usual statistical indicators; yet the individuals who participate in this externally located modern sector remain part of the aggregate productive and spending behavior of their home communities. It is not clear to what extent skills and assets acquired offshore are later returned to the island economies. Brown and Foster's survey work in Australia, for example, supports earlier suggestions that return migration of human capital is not a major feature of the island communities they studied. But this does not remove the basic fact that as capital is acquired in metropolitan economies by individuals who continue to regard themselves as islanders, the balance sheet of the islander population as a whole is increased accordingly and repatriation of assets is not necessary (nor, probably, economically sensible) given the relative rates of return to real investment in the islands as compared with those in the metropolitan host economies.

Anthropologists have recognized, more readily than economists, the ability of communities and kin groups to maintain their organic unity and identity as they become geographically dispersed across geographic space, within island nations as well as internationally. Flinn, writing of migratory links between the islands of Pulap and Moen in Micronesia, captures the essence of this process (Flinn 1992:13):

> In many cases, the social structure spans more than one location. People who leave a home village can nonetheless operate within one social structure, especially with ties they can activate or create when they move. Rather than a geographic focus, we need to take a sociocultural one. As people move in space, they may remain within one social structure. In fact, they can culturally construct geographical space to correspond with social space. Social structure thus adjusts to accommodate movement, and interpretations of place shift to fit social structure.

Social structure here includes both formal and informal economic activity.

## Macroeconomic Management

The governments of independent or self-governing small-island economies typically have less room to maneuver in their economic policymaking than do the fiscal and monetary authorities of large countries. Fiscal prudence is inescapable because these small resource-poor economies are not able to sustain large external debts; the mid-1990s fiscal crisis in the Cook Islands demonstrated the very limited ability of governments to sustain deficit financing. Governments thus must operate within their current income, which rises and falls with the flow of external aid, since the local tax base does not change much. The usual instruments of monetary policy are available in few of the countries of the region. Even countries with their own currencies, such as Papua New Guinea, Vanuatu, Fiji, and Tonga, tend to peg these to the main metropolitan currencies so that the typical exchange rate regime is fixed or quasifixed. Economies that use metropolitan currencies are bound to the purchasing power of those currencies in their countries of issue. The quantity of money in circulation within most island economies is determined by the combination of fiscal policy (including government overseas borrowing) and the balance of payments.

To evaluate problems of macroeconomic management in small-island economies one must therefore begin from a model of the very small open economy with free capital mobility, a fixed exchange rate, and an open labor market. The goals that government can pursue within this framework are limited. On the demand side, fiscal policy sets the level of domestic activity and incomes, with the money supply adjusting passively. Government, in other words, sets the level of income for the local population subject to its externally determined budget constraint. Because that constraint changes only when aid flows change, fiscal policy is in effect controlled by the aid donors rather than the local governments. No crowding-out mechanisms are operative, since the interest rate is externally fixed and the domestic price level is set by the purchasing power of the externally issued or pegged currency.

Many commentaries on the Pacific Island economies appear to assume that crowding-out of private activity by government occurs, which implies that a reduction of the size of the government sector should be a sufficient condition for expansion of private activity (see e.g. Fairbairn and Worrell 1996). The theoretical basis for this position is seldom spelled out, however. The only transmission channel through which government could adversely affect private sector employment and investment is the tax rate, to the extent that taxes represent a deduction from private sector saving and diversion of this purchasing power to consumptive purposes. There is, however, no evidence that shortage of private savings is a constraint on investment levels in any of the Pacific Island economies; most studies suggest that capital absorption capacity presents the binding constraint on private investment (e.g. Connell and Brown 1995:25).

Government can borrow prudently only to the extent that it has reasonable certainty of a future increase in the local tax base to fund servicing and repayment or assurance by aid donors of willingness to underwrite those debt-servicing costs. While in the short run some island governments may escape from this discipline to the extent that lenders are willing to bear the resulting high default risks, over the longer haul government borrowing is not a means of sustainably raising the government sector's permanent income and expenditure. Fiscal policy in the Pacific is revenue-driven and revenue-constrained.

On the supply side, the main determinant of the structure and profitability of private sector output is international competitiveness, as measured by the real exchange rate. Anything that lowers the cost of local products relative to competing suppliers overseas represents a lowering of the real exchange rate and will provide a spur to the growth of the local economy. In larger economies this can be done by lowering the exchange rate of the currency or by lowering real wages or profit markups in those sectors producing tradable goods in competition with other countries. Nominal exchange rate changes are possible only for those economies that have their own currencies, such as Papua New Guinea (which until the 1990s held the exchange rate of the kina high to support anti-inflation objectives, probably contributing to slow growth) and Fiji (which gained rapid advantage from devaluations of the Fiji dollar in the late 1980s). For most small-island economies, however, the nominal exchange rate is not available as an instrument.

With the nominal exchange rate fixed, local costs—especially wage costs—are the main means of changing the real exchange rate. However, in those island economies whose labor markets are flexible and open to migration flows, real wage reductions are more likely to cause outmigration of the most productive workers than increased local output. Raising the productivity of labor at existing wage rates is then the only means of lowering the real exchange rate.

Under these conditions the real exchange rate is determined almost entirely by forces that are exogenous to the typical island economy, with no necessary tendency to settle at a long-run level consistent with the hypothetical equilibrium that seems to be in the minds of most outside observers and aid donors. There is no obvious reason to suppose that real exchange rates will automatically fall to levels at which export activities become the profitable leading sectors for a private-sector-financed takeoff.

## Limited Dualism

As in most developing countries, the central microeconomic issues in the Pacific Islands arise out of the interplay between small-scale local production and consumption systems and the forces of the wider market. The dualism that has characterized twentieth-century developing economies in Latin America, Africa, and Asia is, however, muted in the Pacific except for Papua New Guinea, where the gap between primitive and modern remains stark and large segments of the pre-capitalist economy remain relatively little modified.

Elsewhere, the pre-European economic order has long vanished, to be replaced by a neotraditional village economy built on the pillars of kinship, reciprocity, subsistence affluence, the missionary impact, and trade in simple goods (copra, taro, handicrafts, fish, and similar products exchanging for basic imported consumption goods such as flour, rice, sugar, alcohol, and tobacco). Alongside this village economy but not separate from it have arisen various activities usually classified as in the "modern sector"—government services, plantations, mines, manufacturing, tourism.

In the Pacific, the modern and neotraditional economies are generally integrated rather than separate and tend to become more rather than less integrated over time. Modern activities involve fully monetized transactions in the context of formal markets for labor and goods, together with the deployment of relatively advanced technology. Neotraditional activities include nonmonetary transactions mediated by networks of social relationships and deployment of economic resources on the basis of a combination of market and nonmarket calculations. However, the technological level of the two sectors is not diverging over time. Village fishing is done from motorboats with nylon lines and nets; people and goods are transported in the village sector by motorbikes, cars, and bicycles; radio and television penetration of the village sector is high. Most important, and associated with high literacy rates in most island economies, intersectoral labor mobility is high, and most kin groups have individual members at each end of the modern-neotraditional spectrum.

The articulation of modern formal-sector activities such as government administration with the informal village economy has inevitably produced a degree of social stress. Writing on developments on the Tokelau atoll Fakaofo, Hooper (1993:242, 256, 262-263) notes that

> Between 1967 and 1981 Fakaofo was transformed from a cohesive community based on traditional economic exchange and an established customary order, to one dominated by salary and wage incomes, and two openly conflicting principles of social order....
>
> Wages, salaries, remittances and copra receipts are distributed fairly widely among close relatives ... so that marked discrepancies in income become evened out to some extent. Nevertheless, they do not become completely equalized....
>
> [A]lthough public servants live in the village, retain access to land, and participate in village activities, this has also altered the village economy, since the public servants' participation is very much on their own terms.... With their material base thus altered, many traditional village social relationships have been leached of their former significance ...
>
> In these ways, then, both the neo-traditional mode of production and "way of life" have been altered, probably irrevocably.

The result of this interpenetration of the two poles of the developing economy is that the modern sector in most Pacific Island states has a distinctive flavor attributable to the incomplete proletarianization of the labor force. Wage workers have other dimensions to their economic lives as members of village-based kin groups, with access to land and a variety of life opportunities. Possibilities for the exploitation of labor are limited both externally by migration opportunities (especially in Polynesia and Micronesia) and internally by the scope for involution offered by the neotraditional village economy. The fluidity of the labor market, indeed, is probably the characteristic of Pacific Island economies that most clearly sets them apart from their continental counterparts.

Fundamental to this flexibility is the persistence of "traditional" land tenure, with most cultivable land retained in family ownership and used for subsistence agriculture (including production of foodstuffs for exchange). Commercial plantation agriculture, mainly for copra and sugar, has existed in the region since the late nineteenth century, but has never become a sufficiently dominant rural sector to dissolve the integrity of smallholder subsistence cultivation. On the contrary, outside Hawai'i, both copra and sugar production have tended to slide back toward small-scale cultivation due to an apparent lack of scale economies under Pacific Island conditions.

The high degree of labor market flexibility puts a perennial squeeze on the rate of profit in capitalist enterprises. Hemmed in from above by fixed or semifixed nominal exchange rates and high transport costs, the private sector capitalist can obtain no relief from below by downward pressure on the real wage, because labor costs are indexed to opportunity costs of labor at the involution and migration thresholds. Not surprisingly, private sector entrepreneurship encounters substantial obstacles within the island economies (see e.g. the case studies in Fairbairn 1988) and succeeds best when it modifies capitalist rationality to fit the demands of customary practices and traditions (Fairbairn 1988:273). Many of the most talented entrepreneurial individuals from Pacific Island communities are drawn out to the metropolitan economies around the rim of the Pacific where there are wider opportunities for profitable enterprise and investment. Vancouver, Los Angeles, Auckland, and Sydney contain a growing number of successful Pacific-Islander-owned businesses—a pattern foreshadowed in Marcus's (1981) study of the outward movement of Tongan economic activity.

## Conclusion

This chapter has traversed a range of economic issues that define a substantial research agenda for economists working in the Pacific region. The rapidly improving statistical coverage of Pacific Islanders' economic activities, due both to major database development by international agencies and to a growing body of census material and questionnaire research on the migrant communities, has opened the way for a new round of empirically grounded theoretical work on the characteristics and history of economic development in these globalized, flexible, and much-underestimated economic systems.

## Notes

[1] Fiji is the only small-island economy in the Pacific whose performance to date has lived up to the modernization image of locally financed, export-led industrialization on a primary-commodity export base. New Zealand has long been one of the world's developed economies, structurally more akin to the other metropolitan industrial economies of the Pacific Rim than to those of the island Pacific. Like Australia, the United States, and Canada, New Zealand hosts large communities of migrants from the islands and in doing so provides those island economies with an offshore modern sector. New Zealand is a source, not a recipient, of remittance and aid flows and has its own internal economic dynamic.

## Bibliography

Ahlburg, D. 1991. *Remittances and their impact: a study of Tonga and Western Samoa.* Pacific Policy Paper No. 7, Centre for Development Studies. Canberra: Australian National University.

Ahlburg, D. 1996a. *Demographic and social change in the island nations of the Pacific.* Asia-Pacific Population Research Report No.7. Honolulu: East-West Center.

Ahlburg, D. 1996b. Remittances and income distribution in Tonga. *Population Research and Policy Review* 15(4):391–400.

Ahlburg, D., and M. J. Levin. 1990. *The northeast passage: a study of Pacific Islander migration to American Samoa and the United States.* Pacific Research Monograph No. 23 Canberra: Australian National University.

Aldrich, R. 1993. *France and the South Pacific since 1940.* Honolulu: University of Hawai'i Press.

Armstrong, H. W., and R. Read. 1997. The economic performance of microstates: an inter- and intra-regional comparison. Forthcoming in *World Development.*

Asian Development Bank. 1994. *Key indicators of developing Asian and Pacific countries 1994.* Vol. 25. Manila: Asian Development Bank.

Asian Development Bank Office of Pacific Operations. 1995. *Cook Islands: economic performance, issues and strategies.* Manila: Asian Development Bank.

Benedict, B., ed. 1967. *Problems of smaller territories.* London: Athlone Press.

Bertram, G. 1986. "Sustainable development" in Pacific micro-economies. *World Development* 14(7):809–822.

Bertram, G. 1987. The political economy of decolonization and nationhood in small Pacific societies. In *Class and culture in the South Pacific,* ed. A. Hooper, et al., 16–31. Suva: Institute of Pacific Studies.

Bertram, G. 1993. Sustainability, aid, and material welfare in small South Pacific island economies, 1900–1990. *World Development* 21(2):247–258.

Bertram, G., and R. F. Watters. 1985. The MIRAB economy in South Pacific microstates. *Pacific Viewpoint* 26(3):497–512.

Bertram, G. and R. F. Watters. 1986. The MIRAB process: some earlier analysis and context. *Pacific Viewpoint* 27(1):47–57.

Blanchet, G. 1985. *L'Économie de la Polynésie Francaise de 1960 à 1980.* Tahiti: ORSTOM Travaux et Documents 195.

Blanchet, G. 1996. Quel avenir pour la Polynésie Française? *Journal de la Société des Océanistes* 102(1):31–46.

Booth, A. 1995. Development challenges in a poor Pacific economy: the case of Papua New Guinea. *Pacific Affairs* 68(2):207–230.

Briguglio, L. 1995. Small island developing states and their economic vulnerabilities. *World development* 23(9):1615–1632.

Brookfield, H. C. 1972. *Colonialism, development and independence: the case of Melanesian islands in the South Pacific.* Cambridge: Cambridge University Press.

Brown, R. P. C. 1994. Migrants' remittances, savings and investment in the South Pacific. *International Labor Review* 133(3):1–19.

Brown, R. P. C. 1995. Hidden foreign exchange flows: estimating unofficial remittances to Tonga and Western Samoa. *Asian and Pacific Migration Journal* 4(1):35–54.

Brown, R. P. C. 1997. Estimating remittance functions for Pacific Island migrants. *World Development* 25(4):613–626.

Brown, R. P. C., J. Foster, and J. Connell. 1995. Remittances, savings, and policy formation in Pacific Island states. *Asian Pacific Migration Journal* 4(1):169–185.

Browne, C., and D. Scott. 1989. *Economic development in seven Pacific Island countries.* Washington, DC: International Monetary Fund.

Cameron, J. 1991. Economic development options for the Federated States of Micronesia at independence. *Pacific Studies* 14(4):35–70.

Campbell, I. C. 1992. An historical perspective on aid and dependency in Tonga. *Pacific Studies* 15(3):59–75.

Connell, J. 1987. *Migration, employment and development in the South Pacific.* Noumea: South Pacific Commission.

Connell, J. 1988. *Sovereignty and survival: island microstates in the Third World.* Sydney: University of Sydney Research Monograph 3.

Connell, J., and R. P. C. Brown. 1995. Migration and remittances in the South Pacific: towards new perspectives. *Asian and Pacific Migration Journal* 4(1):1–34.

Denoon, D. 1983, *Settler capitalism: the dynamics of dependent development in the Southern Hemisphere.* Oxford: Clarendon Press.

Fairbairn, T. I. J., ed. 1988. *Island entrepreneurs: problems and performances in the Pacific.* Honolulu: East-West Center.

Fairbairn, T. I. J., and D. Worrell. 1996. *South Pacific and Caribbean island economies.* Brisbane: Foundation for Development Cooperation.

Fleming, E., J. B. Hardaker, and J. Delforce. 1991. Smallholder agricultural economy at the crossroads: policy priorities for sustained agricultural development in South Pacific Island nations. *Journal de la Société des Océanistes* 92–93(1&2):119–126.

Fleming, E. M., and J. B. Hardaker. 1995. *Pacific 2010: strategies for Polynesian agricultural development.* Canberra: Australian National University National Centre for Development Studies.

Flinn, J. 1992. *Diplomas and thatch houses: asserting tradition in a changing Micronesia.* Ann Arbor: University of Michigan Press.

Foster, J. 1995. The relationship between remittances and savings in small Pacific Island states: some econometric evidence. *Asia Pacific Migration Journal* 4(1):117–138.

Friesen, W. 1993. Melanesian economy on the periphery: migration and village economy in Choiseul. *Pacific Viewpoint* 34(2):193–214.

Gaffaney, T. J. 1995. Linking colonization and decolonization: the case of Micronesia. *Pacific Studies* 18(2):23–59.

Hardaker, J. B., ed. 1975. *The subsistence sector in the South Pacific.* Suva: University of the South Pacific.

Hardaker, J. B., and E. M. Fleming. 1994. *Pacific 2010: strategies for Melanesian agriculture for 2010: tough choices.* Canberra: Australian National University National Centre for Development Studies.

Hayes, G. 1991. Migration, metascience, and development policy in island Polynesia. *The Contemporary Pacific* 3(1):1–58.

Hayes, G. 1992. Polynesian migration and the demographic transition: a missing dimension of recent theoretical models. *Pacific Viewpoint* 33(1):1–35.

Hayes, G. 1993. "MIRAB" processes and development on small Pacific islands: a case study from the southern Massim, Papua New Guinea. *Pacific Viewpoint* 34(2):153–178.

Hezel, F. X., and M. J. Levin. 1996. New trends in Micronesian migration: migration to Guam and the Marianas, 1900–1993. *Pacific Studies* 19(1):91–114.

Hezel, F. X., and T. B. McGrath. 1989. The great flight northward: FSM migration to Guam and the Northern Mariana Islands. *Pacific Studies* 13(1):47–64.

Hooper, A. 1993. The MIRAB transition in Fakaofo, Tokelau. *Pacific Viewpoint* 4(2):241–264.

Hooper, A., S. Britton, R. Crocombe, J. Huntsman, and C. Macpherson, eds. 1987. *Class and culture in the South Pacific*. Suva: University of the South Pacific.

James, K. 1991. Migration and remittances: a Tongan village perspective. *Pacific Viewpoint* 32(1):1–23.

James, K. 1993. The rhetoric and reality of change and development in small Pacific communities. *Pacific Viewpoint* 34(2):135–152.

Kakazu, H. 1994. *Sustainable development of small island economies*. Boulder, Colorado: Westview Press.

Kim, I., E. Sidgwick, and M-H. Duprat. 1995. *Kiribati: recent economic developments*. Washington, DC: IMF Staff Country Report 95/117.

Lewis, W. A. 1954. Economic development with unlimited supplies of labor. *The Manchester School of Economic and Social Studies* 22:139–191.

Loomis, T. 1990. Cook Island remittances: volumes, determinants and uses. In *Migration and development in the South Pacific*, ed. John Connell., 61–81. Pacific Research Monograph No. 24, Centre for Development Studies. Canberra: Australian National University.

Marcus, G. 1981. Power on the extreme periphery: the perspective of Tongan elites in the modern world system. *Pacific Viewpoint* 22(1):48–64.

Mayo, L. W. 1988. U.S. administration and prospects for economic self-sufficiency: a comparison of Guam and select areas of Micronesia. *Pacific Studies* 11(2):53–75.

McGregor, A., M. Sturton, and S. Halapua. 1992. *Private sector development: policies and programs for the Pacific Islands*. Honolulu: East-West Center, University of Hawai'i.

Milner, C., and T. Westaway. 1993. Country size and the medium-term growth process: some cross-country evidence. *World Development* 21(2):203–211.

Nagai, S. 1996. *Background paper on monetary control instruments in the South Pacific*. IMF Staff Country Report 96/76. Washington, DC: International Monetary Fund.

Ogden, M. R. 1989. The paradox of Pacific development. *Development Policy Review* 7:361–373.

Poirine, B. 1992. *Tahiti: du melting pot a l'explosion?* Paris: Editions L'Harmattan.

Poirine, B. 1994a. *Tahiti: la fin du paradis?* Papeete, Tahiti: Imprimeries STP Multipress.

Poirine, B. 1994b. Rent, emigration and unemployment in small islands: the MIRAB model and the French overseas departments and territories. *World Development* 22(12):1997–2010.

Poirine, B. 1995. *Les petites économies insulaires: théories et stratégies de développement*. Paris: Editions l'Harmattan.

Poirine, B. 1996. La contribution de la substitution d'importation ñ la croissance dans les Dom-Tom. *Revue Française D'economie* 11(4):167–190.

Rapaport, M. 1995. Pearl farming in the Tuamotus: atoll development and its consequences. *Pacific Studies* 18(3):1–26.

Robinson, E. A. G., ed. 1960. *Economic consequences of the size of nations*. London: Macmillan.

Rostow, W. W. 1960. *The stages of economic growth: a non-Communist manifesto*. Cambridge: Cambridge University Press.

Shand, R. T., ed. 1980. *The island economies of the Pacific and Indian Oceans: anatomy of development*. Development Studies Centre Monograph No. 23. Canberra: Australian National University.

Streeten, P. 1993. The special problems of small countries. *World Development* 21(2):197–202.

Tisdell, C., and T. I. J. Fairbairn. 1984. Subsistence economies and unsustainable development and trade: some simple theory. *Journal of Development Studies* 20(2):227–241.

United Nations 1995. *UN statistical yearbook 1994*. New York: United Nations.

United Nations 1995. *Demographic yearbook 1994*. New York: United Nations.

Walker, A. M., and R. P. C. Brown. 1995. From consumption to savings? interpreting Tongan and Western Samoan survey data on remittances. *Asian and Pacific Migration Journal* 4(1):89–116.

World Bank. 1991. *Pacific Island economies: towards higher growth in the 1990s*. Washington, DC: World Bank.

World Bank. 1996. *World development report 1996*. New York: Oxford University Press.

CHAPTER 29

# Agriculture and Forestry

*William C. Clarke, Harley I. Manner, and Randolph R. Thaman*

The environments where agriculture is practiced in the Pacific Islands range from frost-prone but gardened mountain slopes at 2,600 m in Papua New Guinea through temperate-latitude New Zealand to tiny atoll islets lying scarcely above the reach of the waves in the always warm equatorial ocean. A comparable dissimilarity exists in rainfall—from virtual desert to constantly humid—and in soils, with some young volcanic and alluvial soils being highly fertile, whereas on atoll islets the only natural soil material may be no more than rough, highly alkaline coral rubble.

Traditional Pacific Island agriculturalists adapted to this wide range of conditions with an even wider range of agronomic techniques and crop combinations, which enabled food production on all but the most barren islets or at the highest elevations of the larger islands. Outside of Hawai'i and New Zealand, the majority of today's Pacific Island families still work the land with a wide variety of agricultural practices that continue to provide many of their daily needs, a significant portion of their cash income, and the economic and cultural foundation of a relatively benign and bountiful existence.

## The Cultural and Social Significance of Land and Food Production

The roots of the connection between Pacific peoples, their land, and their agriculture extend deep into Pacific prehistory and myth. Even today, garden magic remains important in places (Bonnemaison 1994, Ch. 12), and agriculture continues to be far more than a mere economic or agronomic matter. As Fijian anthropologist Asesela Ravuvu has written of his own culture :

> Food and the food quest are central to most of our traditional social and economic activities. No ceremonial function is considered complete without a presentation of food or *magiti*. . . . It is shameful if people go hungry. . . . The *magiti* or food gifts should always be the best and the most one can afford. (Ravuvu 1983:41,42)

Aside from the great significance of the production of food for social purposes in Pacific societies, the land itself has much greater social meaning than it does in Western societies. In a Pacific community, agricultural and land-use activities are always social acts; never can planting a garden, cutting down a tree, or establishing a tree garden of breadfruit and pandanus, a grove of coconuts, or an excavated taro garden on an atoll islet be carried out solely as isolated acts of land management. Most modern land tenure systems in the Pacific carry on in modified forms the traditional patterns, all of which were based on the idea that kinship groups held communal rights to land. Within the communal land, individuals or extended families hold rights of use, either generally or to specific plots, because of prior use or because they have planted trees there. No individual, however, has absolute rights over land; all use and users remain bound into a community, tied together by reciprocal rights and obligations.

This integration of community and land is well expressed in the Fijian term *vanua* (and similar words in other Pacific languages), which literally means "land," but includes the social, spiritual, and political aspects of the physical environment identified with a particular social group.

> It does not mean only the land area one is identified with, and the vegetation, animal life, and other objects on it, but it also includes the social and cultural system. . . . The *vanua* contains the actuality of one's past and the potentiality of one's future. It is an extension of the concept of the self. (Ravuvu 1983:70)

## Origins

No longer is indigenous Pacific agriculture seen to be the result of a simple transfer into the islands of an agriculture developed outside the region—with Southeast Asia commonly believed to be the hearth. Although many domesticated and wild plants and animals of Southeast Asian origin and domestication were transferred to New Guinea and beyond to the insular Pacific without significant change (certain species of yam, for instance), it can now be argued that the peoples who settled western Melanesia 30,000 to 40,000 years ago gradually developed their own distinctive indigenous agricultural and land-use systems and domesticated a variety of plants, including sago, one type of *Colocasia* taro, *Canarium* nut, one kind of banana, sugarcane, kava, the *Pandanus* nut of high-elevation New Guinea, several fruit trees, and other plants (Clarke 1994, Yen 1990). The earliest dates for agriculture in New Guinea can be traced back to at least 9,000 years ago (Bayliss-Smith and Golson 1992).

Brief mention must also be made of the sweet potato, which originated neither in Melanesia nor Asia but in the American tropics. The widespread presence of the sweet potato in indigenous (pre–European-contact) Pacific agriculture—where it became extremely important in places such as highland New Guinea and New Zealand—has been explained by various theories of prehistoric migration or as the result of Spanish and Portuguese introductions during the fifteenth and sixteenth centuries. Recent archeological evidence from Mangaia in the Cook Islands of the crop's presence there around AD 1000 (Hather and Kirch 1991), together with linguistic evidence, supports earlier assumptions of its pre-European introduction into central Polynesia from the east, directly from tropical America (Scaglion and Soto 1994, Yen 1974).

Based on crop plants and associated wild plants (e.g. indigenous or naturalized exotic weeds, trees, and fallow vegetation) from these three sources—the Pacific Islands themselves, Southeast Asia, and tropical America—a range of indigenous Pacific forms of agriculture evolved in response to varying environmental conditions, local agronomic innovations, the levels of available labor supply and basic demand for food that depend on population dynamics, and the diversity of deep cultural attributes often assigned to food and food production—as exemplified, for instance, by the "uneconomic" effort and attention put into growing the highly esteemed greater yams *(Dioscorea alata)* (e.g. Bonnemaison 1994:172-176).

## Production Systems

One way to classify agriculture is to subdivide it on the basis of the purposes and the socioeconomic organization of production. Such a classification of Pacific Island production systems, or "modes of production," has been provided by Ward (1980) and Yen (1980). The oldest of these is the integral subsistence system, in which virtually all the requirements of the community are produced locally, cash cropping is absent, and the producers and consumers are the same set of people. The integral subsistence system is now rare in its pure form and would be found, if at all, only in the remoter parts of the island of New Guinea. Elsewhere, it has given way to mixed subsistence–cash cropping, which began shortly after the coming of the first permanent European settlers. Under this system, islanders added introduced commercial crops to their traditional inventory of crops so as to have at least some access to the expanding economy based on money.

The plantation or estate production system was introduced by Europeans in the last century. Foreign-owned and -managed, plantation production was directed almost entirely toward export crops. Unlike in traditional agriculture, the units of production were large, and monocropping predominated. Spatially, coconut palms quickly became the major plantation crop across the coastal lands of most Pacific Islands. Although plantations remain important in parts of the Pacific, they are no longer a favored form of production. Because independent Pacific Island governments and their people see foreign-owned plantations as a remnant of colonial exploitation, the balance of ownership has shifted toward individual nationals or groups of nationals.

The most recently emerged system of production involves a "plantation mode of management." The economies of scale claimed for plantations are achieved through the aggregation of smallholder production under centralized marketing and management control. The most outstanding example of this approach is the sugar industry of Fiji. With the collapse in the second decade of the twentieth century of the indentured labor scheme, whereby Indians had been brought to Fiji to work on plantations, the industry converted to a system of smallholder tenant farmers. General direction is provided by the sugar millers (now the Fiji Sugar Corporation, a largely government-owned enterprise), with the FSC providing economies of scale in credit facilities, research, extension, and transportation as well as some agronomic inputs and large-scale processing.

Modern privately owned or controlled commercial farms and pastoral properties now exist in Hawai'i, New Zealand, Fiji, and Papua New Guinea, and to a lesser extent in some other island countries. These enterprises vary in size and include, for example, the vast cattle ranches and sugar plantations of Hawai'i, the extensive sheep runs of New Zealand, market-garden plots and small-scale ginger or pineapple farms in Fiji, and the coffee groves of indigenous capitalists in the Papua New Guinean Highlands.

## Traditional and Semi-traditional Agriculture

Traditional (subsistence) and semitraditional agriculture in the Pacific can be classified in accordance with the methods of cultivation and land use (e.g. Kirch 1991, Manner 1993, Falanruw 1993 and 1994, Brookfield with Hart 1971). Expectably, classifications vary depending on criteria used or the region treated but they all suggest the Pacific-wide distribution of five cultivation systems and animal husbandry (which also may involve crop production). Each cultivation system has its specific cultivation techniques, cropping frequency, crop inventory, and other features. The six traditional systems are not, of course, necessarily spatially segregated. Often most or all six of them are or were found on a single community's land holding. The six systems are

1) shifting cultivation in forest or bush, sometimes alternating with tree gardens or agroforests;
2) arboriculture (tree gardens or mature fallow forests) and agroforests;
3) water control: irrigation and drainage, including wetland taro systems and drainage for sweet potatoes;
4) intensive dryfield, open-canopy cultivation, including cultivation systems in fern and grass savannas;
5) houseyard gardens; and
6) animal husbandry.

### Shifting Cultivation

Shifting cultivation—other names include swidden and slash-and-burn cultivation—is often held to be the archetypal form of traditional agriculture in the tropics (Figures 29.1–2, Color Plate 29A). In the Pacific Islands, it is found on almost all high islands and raised limestone islands where at least some secondary forest or productive grassland-savanna remains. As Brookfield with Hart (1971:116) notes for Melanesia, all the more technically elaborate forms of agriculture exist within an integument of shifting cultivation, coupled with the extensive use of wild foods. Simple though shifting cultivation may be

*Figure 29.1. A six-month-old slash and burn garden (swidden) on 'Upolu, Samoa. The cultivated plants are banana (Musa spp.), edible hibiscus, true taro (Colocasia esculenta), and kava (Piper methysticum). The trees, Leucaena leucocephala, in the background were recently defoliated by a psyllid fly outbreak (photo HM).*

*Figure 29.2. A bush fallow subsistence garden at Buma, Kwara'e District, Malaita, Solomon Islands. Cultivated plants in the photo are sweet potato, pineapple, Alocasia macrorhiza taro, and yams (Dioscorea spp.) climbing on poles. Colocasia taro is no longer grown here because of Phytophtora colocasiae disease (photo HM).*

technically, it can be very sophisticated, biologically as well as intellectually, in that its management often involves a manipulation not only of a diversity of annual or near-annual crop plants but also of the intervening forest fallow.

More specifically, cultivating crops for a few years in forest clearings and then leaving the land to revert to forest fallow for a longer period suppresses weeds, crop pests, and diseases and renews the soil with organic matter and nutrients. The cultivators, through selective weeding and planting, thereby encourage some tree species and discourage others so that a highly useful tree-garden fallow results. What to the inexperienced eye looks like spontaneous secondary forest proves to be a human-created swidden-fallow agroforest (e.g. Clarke 1971:80–82, 136–139, Thaman 1993a:63–84). Case examples of shifting cultivation in the Pacific include Clarke (1971) for Papua New Guinea, in Melanesia; Falanruw (1993 and 1994) for Yap, in Micronesia; and Kirch (1978 and 1994) for Uvea and Futuna, in Polynesia.

## Arboriculture and Agroforestry

A distinguishing characteristic of the earliest agriculture of the western Melanesian region is the presence of arboriculture—the culture of trees, domesticated following a history of use during a pre-agricultural hunting-gathering stage dating back well beyond 10,000 years BP (Yen 1996). Archeological evidence for arboriculture at least 3,500 years ago comes from the Mussau Islands, north of New Ireland, where tree species included coconut, two or three species of *Pandanus*, the "Tahitian chestnut" *(Inocarpus fagifer)*, the *Canarium* "almond" *(Canarium* spp.), the vi-apple *(Spondias dulcis)*, and several hardwoods prized for carving (Kirch 1989). Many of these trees and others such as breadfruit—which perhaps also has origins in western Melanesia (Ragone 1991, 205)—were transported Pacific-wide, carried by voyaging colonist-cultivators, begetting the rich and beautiful tree groves and orchards that typify Pacific villages and landscapes almost everywhere (Clarke and Thaman 1993, Falanruw 1994, Thaman 1993a, Walter 1994).

In Micronesia, tree gardens still are one of the most conspicuous vegetation formations, a relatively permanent system of land use that provides a wide range of subsistence needs. In its simplest form, the tree gardens consisted of a canopy of timber, food, medicinal, and other multipurpose trees, with an understory of useful annual and perennial plants. It was also a habitat for wild and domesticated animals and a source of many culturally valued items, including traditional medicines, building materials, and firewood. Tree garden composition and structure vary greatly with habitat and island. Along the coast and on atolls, they are relatively simple, dominated by coconuts together with other salt-tolerant species. Farther inland and on the higher slopes, the structure and species composition of these mixed forests are more complex and diverse, with breadfruit (*Artocarpus altilis* and *Artocarpus mariannensis*) the dominant tree species. A detailed description of agroforestry on Pohnpei has been provided by Raynor and Fownes (1993).

## Water Control: Irrigation and Drainage

Of the three main tuber- or corm-bearing starchy staples that dominated indigenous Pacific cultivation systems—aroids (the taro family), several species of yams, and the sweet potato—the taros are the most water-tolerant (Figure 29.3 and Color Plates 29B–C). Yams grow only under dryland conditions and require a dry season. The sweet potato, which tolerates a greater range of soil type and climate than yams, grows well in fertile swampland soils if provided with adequate drainage. Massive systems of ditches to provide drainage for sweet potatoes were constructed in the swamplands of highland New Guinea (e.g. Barrau 1958). On a smaller scale, sweet potatoes and sometimes yams were planted in mounds, ridges, or ditched beds to provide better drainage as well as to loosen heavy soils. Throwing ditch spoil onto the bed maintained fertility. In some places, the contrasting moisture tolerances of taro compared with yams and sweet potato were complementary, with taro grown in the pits excavated to make mounds or ridges for the other two crops.

Widespread across the Pacific were a variety of techniques

*Figure 29.3.* Hydroponic cultivation of Colocasia and Cyrtosperma taro on Falalop Islet, Ulithi Atoll, Yap. Growing taro in these tanks lessens the damage to taro from saltwater intrusion of the freshwater lens and storm wave surges (photo HM).

for irrigating true taro *(Colocasia esculenta)*. True taro is also planted in dryland shifting gardens, given moderately high rainfall, but yields better, more permanently, and with greater freedom from weeds and some insect pests when grown in water (Spriggs 1990). Irrigation techniques included the use of natural ponds, the construction of small dams to pond a stream, the erection of bamboo aqueducts to carry trickles of water to hillside sites, making taro "islets" in swampy areas (Manner 1994), and the construction of extensive canal systems for elaborate hillside terrace systems, such as those of New Caledonia, Fiji, and Hawai'i (Barrau 1958 and 1961, Handy et al. 1972, Kuhlken 1994, Kirch 1977, 1991, 1994). In Palau, *Colocasia* taro was the traditional prestige staple, with many myths and rituals associated with its cultivation. The taro swamps were labor intensive, with fields being visited daily and green manures added to the soil to improve fertility, and were traditionally said to be the "mother of life" (McKnight and Obak 1960).

The other traditional aroid that was particularly subject to irrigation is the giant swamp taro *Cyrtosperma chamissonis*. Not of great importance in Polynesia except on coral atolls, *Cyrtosperma* taro was present in Melanesia in coastal swamps from northern New Guinea to Fiji, where it was a significant traditional staple in the densely populated Rewa Delta on the island of Viti Levu. *Cyrtosperma* came to be of greatest importance on coral atolls (Small 1972). In those harsh agricultural environments almost without soil, often with low rainfall, swamp taro was capable of producing sustained yields of staple food. A pit was excavated to reach the freshwater lens, and soil was created by adding composted leaves of *Guettarda speciosa*, *Tournefortia argentea*, breadfruit, and several other trees, as well as seaweed, pumice, and other materials (Thaman 1990b). The "seed" corm is planted together with the compost of leaves in a bottomless basket that reaches below the water level in the pit. The pit continues to be composted at least four times a year until harvest, two or three years after planting. Some varieties, grown mainly for prestige and ceremonies, may be cultivated for ten to fifteen years.

Rice, also grown in pondfields (paddies), is traditionally grown for subsistence among ethnic Indians in Fiji (Color Plate 29D), and among the Chamorro in the Marianas (though whether rice was introduced to the Marianas prior to European contact is uncertain).

## Intensive Dryfield, Open-canopy Cultivation

Given a choice between practicing shifting cultivation in the forest or cultivating in open grasslands, tropical cultivators worldwide will generally choose to cut the forest and garden for the newly cleared land because, compared with grassland soils, forest soils are relatively more fertile, more friable, and freer of pathogens and pertinacious weeds. But as the human population grows and the density of shifting gardens increases, the forest inevitably diminishes, until, if the pressure continues, it is replaced by grass-fernland-scrub complexes. In dryfield, open-canopy cultivation, the polycultural richness of species and varieties found in forest-fallow shifting gardens usually declines sharply, with many fewer crops planted and crop segregation becoming the rule. Fallow times also diminish, often being shorter than or equal to the cultivation period. Tillage, which requires labor, almost always increases compared with the minimum of soil working and disturbance typically associated with shifting gardens in the forest.

In Yap, in the Federated States of Micronesia, the savannas of the interior are known as the *tayid* or *ted* (Hunter-Anderson 1991). Here, sweet potatoes are grown in a manner similar to those grown in extensive open fields in ditched and sometimes mounded beds in the Eastern Highlands of Papua New Guinea. The Yapese ditched beds, or *milai* (Mueller 1917), are rectangular and surrounded by ditches closed at the ends. The beds are prepared by slashing the grass cover or merely flattening it with a layer of grass cut from around the perimeter of the bed. Blocks of soil and grass are dug up around the perimeter of the garden bed and placed upside down on the bed, and then covered with a layer of soil excavated from the ditches (Falanruw 1993, Hunter-Anderson 1991). Soil accumulations in the ditches are also added to the mound. Other vegetative litter from the surrounding area may be added. Clumps of clay soil from the ditch bottoms are sometimes piled around the perimeter of the garden bed to reduce erosion.

Dryfield-intensive systems like that described for Yap were widely spread across the Pacific, for instance, in Hawai'i, New Zealand, and isolated, treeless Easter Island (Handy et al. 1972, Leach 1984, Metraux 1940:151–152). Such systems are assumed to have developed out of a process of intensification from shifting cultivation (Clarke 1966, Kirch 1991:120–121, 1994). Such a developmental sequence has been demonstrated archeologically for the Kohala Field System on the island of Hawai'i (Rosendahl 1972, Tuggle and Griffin 1973, Kirch 1994). When the Polynesian Maori reached temperate-latitude New Zealand, they developed special techniques to produce dryland sweet potato as a staple under the nontropical conditions. In many islands, following European contact and the decline of indigenous populations and changes in the economy and settlement patterns, the intensive dryfield systems have undergone disintensification or fallen wholly out of use, a process that also happened to most irrigated taro terraces—and to many excavated pit gardens in atoll Micronesia.

### Houseyard Gardens

Houseyard gardens, which may also be named kitchen gardens, dooryard gardens, or backyard gardens, were traditionally present throughout Oceania and remain of great significance today (Landauer and Brazil 1990). Such gardens contain a wide assemblage of trees, shrubs, herbaceous plants, and vines that contribute a wide variety of products, including staple foods, fruits, spices, medicines, stimulants, ornamentation, shade, and perfumes (Thaman 1990a). Often disregarded in assessments of agriculture, houseyard gardens are important spatially, nutritionally, and with regard to aesthetic amenity. Today, a walk through any Pacific Island town or village immediately reveals the wealth of productive beauty created by the ubiquitous plantings of mangoes, breadfruit, coconuts, citrus, bananas, hibiscus, *Cordyline* and *Codiaemum*, the annatto tree, betel nut in places where that habit prevails, fig species, bamboo, soursop, lemongrass, peppers, sugarcane, the paper mulberry, trees and shrubs with edible leaves or colorful leaves, plants with fragrant bark or flowers, taros and yams, cassava, beans, cabbages, and much, much more.

Thaman (1993b) points out that people in towns also make great use of undeveloped or idle lands for planting in addition to their home gardens. In Port Moresby, over one-third of all households were found to have gardens on idle land. On the urbanized Suva Peninsula in Fiji, it was estimated that approximately 5 sq km (over 70%) of the undeveloped area was under this type of cultivation. Thaman (1993b:150) also notes how the gardens vary from house to house:

> Whereas some households have only a few scattered fruit-trees and vegetables, many cultivate food crops on over 50 per cent of their allotments. . . . [I]n some cases in Nuku'alofa, up to 75 per cent of 500–1,000 sq m allotments were under food cultivation, mainly root crops such as taro, tannia, and cassava, amongst *Musa* spp. and scattered trees. Trees become increasingly dominant in long-settled areas, as cash incomes increase, soils decline in fertility, and tree seedlings mature and increasingly shade garden areas.

### Animal Husbandry

The Pacific's pre-European domestic animals were only three, the pig, dog, and chicken, all of Southeast Asian ancestry (although the cassowary native to New Guinea was tamed to some extent). All three were not present everywhere. The pig and dog were absent from Easter Island, the pig and chicken absent from New Zealand, and one or another absent from various atolls, indicating either a failure of initial dispersal or a failure to survive in harsh environments. Generally, the dog and chicken occupied a scavenging or foraging niche and were not important agriculturally. The pig was often of great significance, as communities devoted more and more effort to building up herds for ceremonies and presentations until a large part of food production, especially of sweet potatoes, was directed toward the pigs.

Waddell (1972) reported that up to 63% of the weight of the tubers harvested by a group in the Papua New Guinea Highlands was fed to their pigs (also see Brookfield with Hart 1971:87). A demand for food for pigs at this level requires a considerable expansion or intensification of agriculture. The increasing numbers of marauding pigs cause increased damage to gardens. Caring for and feeding the animals brings a disproportionate increase in women's work, at least in Melanesia. In many forested areas, feral pigs remain an important food resource and are highly esteemed.

Since European contact, other domestic animals, notably horses, cattle, and goats, have been introduced to most larger South Pacific islands but to few atolls. Where cattle have been introduced, they have sometimes caused considerable dislocation to cultivation systems (Grossman 1981, Ward 1994:138).

## The Dynamic Character of Pacific Agriculture

The cultivation systems described above suggest that there is great variation in approaches to agriculture from place to place in the Pacific. In practice, these systems often occurred very close together in a diverse mosaic, the parts of which shifted frequently. Figure 29.4 attempts to show schematically the sort of landscape that results from such a mixture. This is a landscape

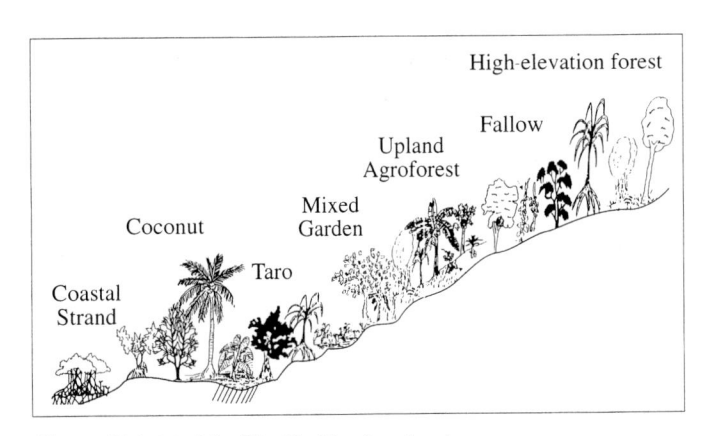

**Figure 29.4.** Model of Pacific Islands polyculture.

rich in agricultural biodiversity, containing a wide range of domesticated and quasi-domesticated plants, varied in what and when they yield. It has an amorphous spatial organization that conceals a complexity designed for producing and maintaining the rich subsistence sector of rural communities. It is difficult to assess in terms of yield and productivity, so that where it survives, the economic and nutritional significance of such diverse production systems is often undervalued.

Such landscapes came into being through incremental additions and long-term experimentation with trees and annual plants and with different methods of cultivation—that is, evolution over many generations of villagers (Clarke and Thaman

1997). Because the evolution took place on many isolated islands or in separate valleys of the larger islands and because each set of gardeners had a different history, arrived with a different stock of plants, and carried out their experimentation in different environments under different densities of population, diverse subsistence production systems developed. There was, however—with the exception of the processing of sago starch from wild or semiwild trees in the swamplands of New Guinea—a common dependence on horticulturally produced high-starch staple foods (taros, sweet potatoes, yams, bananas, and breadfruit), an absence of grains, and an animal protein supplementation to the diet gained by some combination of hunting, pig husbandry, and fishing.

In the history of changes in Pacific agriculture the process of agricultural intensification has long been significant (see Brookfield 1984). Briefly, intensification refers to the increasing application of labor (such as by mulching or by more thorough weeding) or the products of labor (such as agricultural terracing or the construction of drainage ditches) to land in order to increase output of crop from a given area of land over time. In various forms, intensification occurs widely in the Pacific, often mixed with low-input, low-intensity systems such as long-fallow shifting cultivation. Intensification, which often leads to a diminishing return of harvest per unit of labor—even while the yield per hectare increases—is not carried out solely because of population pressure. For example, an increased yield may be desired for presentations of large high-prestige yams or taro or to feed an increasing pig herd needed for purely ceremonial reasons. Building terraces may also have the purpose of counteracting soil erosion on steep slopes.

At the other end of the spectrum is a process of agricultural disintensification. Disintensification may be defined as the abandonment of intensive agricultural practices and the reduction in the amount of labor devoted to agriculture. Sweet potatoes, *Cyrtosperma chamissonis* taro, and the introduced tropical American crop cassava (Figure 29.5) require less labor for their production than yams and true *Colocasia esculenta* taro and are more tolerant of inferior environments. In many Micronesian atolls, *Cyrtosperma* has replaced taro as the dominant aroid because it is more tolerant of salt than *Colocasia esculenta*, produces larger corms, and is longer-lived. On many atolls, *Colocasia* taro is no longer grown or persists as an insignificant crop. In some parts of Fiji and other island groups, particularly in urban areas, cassava has replaced yams and taro as the staple food because it requires less work and produces more on infertile soils (Thaman and Thomas 1985).

Abandonment of taro patches has also occurred in response to changes in the socioeconomic conditions of the Pacific Islands. Since the mid-1800s, the development of the copra plantations and a cash economy in many atolls led to the abandonment of many taro pits as people grew coconuts for cash. On many atolls, up to 70% of the total land area was converted to coconut woodlands (Hatheway 1953). In the mid-1950s on Kapingamarangi Atoll, 57% of the land area was dominated by coconuts, 27.5% was under coconuts and breadfruit, 6.6% under breadfruit, and only 9% in *Cyrtosperma* taro pits (Wiens 1956).

A process named agrodeforestation (Thaman 1992) is currently diminishing the richness of the humanized forests that make up so much of the Pacific landscapes. Reasons for this include the growing significance of imported foods, but also the ignorance among the younger generation of the ecological, economic, and cultural importance of trees. Many trees are not being replaced or protected by a present generation that commonly knows neither the vernacular names nor the uses of such species.

Akin to agrodeforestation is the process of simplification going on in agriculture generally (Ward 1986). Even though many new crops have been introduced into Pacific agricultural systems over the past century, the net effect has been to reduce the diversity of species, cultivars, and methods that characterized traditional agriculture. Some of the most significant introductions have been the native American crops *Xanthosoma* taro, cassava, or manioc *(Manihot esculenta)*, white potato, maize, and the peanut. The reasons for the rapid adoption of these crops are many. Some of them fill in what were gaps in food production—maize, for instance, becoming ready for harvest earlier than the root crops. *Xanthosoma* taro and cassava require less labor and grow better on infertile soils than taro or yams and can be left in the ground until needed.

Several fruit trees—mangoes, oranges, and others—have also been valuable introductions, supplementing the diet with additional energy and important micronutrients. The same is true of a wide variety of vegetables. Also introduced have been high-yielding cultivars of traditional crops, such as bananas and sweet potatoes. These have spread widely, replacing the many traditional cultivars.

## Commercial Agriculture

The history of commercial export agriculture in the tropical Pacific Islands is that of export agriculture everywhere in the tropical world: success and set-back, boom and collapse, enthusiasm and disenchantment. Commercial agriculture

*Figure 29.5. Cassava or tapioca cultivation under coconuts on Rotuma, Fiji. One citrus tree is also present. Cassava is replacing taro as a staple crop in many islands because it is easy to grow and has high yields (photo HM).*

*Figure 29.6.* Commercial dryland taro (Colocasia esculenta) *cultivation near Talafofo, Guam. Agricultural production has not kept pace with the island's economic growth. Despite efforts by the government to increase food production, Guam imports 90% of its foods, and agriculture remains the smallest economic sector (photo HM).*

*Figure 29.7. Sugarcane agriculture near Sigatoka, Fiji. Most sugarcane is grown on small plots, often less than 6 hectares in area, and mostly by manual labor. Infrastructural support, including seed, fertilizer, and technical expertise to small cane farmers in Fiji, is provided by the Fiji Sugar Corporation. Sugar is the backbone of the Fijian economy (photo HM).*

*Figure 29.8. Commercial intercropping of pineapples and* Colocasia *taro near Pago Pago, American Samoa. Plastic and organic mulches are used for moisture conservation and weed control (photo HM).*

(Figures 29.6–8 and Color Plate 29E) remains important in the increasingly monetized Pacific Island economies; and, although many governments see tourism as their countries' economic support in the future, almost all still say that export agriculture must be further developed and diversified, particularly in Vanuatu, the Solomon Islands, Tonga, Samoa, and Papua New Guinea, where most people still rely on agriculture for their livelihood.

The production of many long-term export items has declined in recent years, most significantly copra, but also cacao, bananas, and specialty crops such as oranges and pineapples from the Cook Islands. The reasons are many, including persistently low commodity prices, cyclones, disease, poor marketing, transportation delays, storage problems, and a disinclination on the part of farmers to increase crop output and improve its quality. Since smallholders predominate in the agriculture of the tropical Pacific, the question becomes how to vitalize smallholder agriculture so as to expand food production, employment, and incomes. The issue of management was mentioned above in the description of the "plantation mode of management," whereby smallholder producers receive the economies of scale of centralized processing, marketing, and agronomic advice (Ward and Proctor 1980).

Another aspect of farmer success or failure is motivation. Are Pacific farmers enjoying such "subsistence affluence" that they are not motivated to work hard for cash? Certainly, people sometimes have target sums for particular expenses and will work hard, for example, to produce copra until achieving their goal and then stop. Basically, agricultural labor is not rewarding enough to make people want to engage in it as a full-time occupation. A common outcome of government and aid schemes in the Pacific to intensify, improve, and increase smallholder commercial production is that people accept the seed money and the subsidies to plant or experiment with manufactured, external inputs but drop the enterprise when these monies stop (Asian Development Bank 1996a, Ch. III). A related aspect is that Pacific land-tenure systems militate against the granting of loans for agriculture because the individual farmers do not hold title to the land.

On the other hand, most rural people in the tropical Pacific Islands have access to land and enjoy the security of subsistence production and the ability to produce tubers, tree crops, and pigs or cattle to meet kinship obligations for presentations at weddings or funerals or welcoming celebrations. This approach to the use of land and labor can be seen as efficient and practical, even if it does not lead to maximum commercial production. To some extent, Pacific Island governments and aid agencies are coming to realize the value of subsistence production. A recent assessment of the Vanuatu economy noted that more than 80% of the people rely on subsistence agriculture for their livelihood (Fallon 1994:37). An Asian Development Bank (1996b:3) review of Fiji's agricultural sector noted similarly that the contribution to GDP of subsistence crops grown in the country was similar to that of sugar, the country's main agricultural product.

In export agriculture there is a growing focus in ministries and departments of agriculture on niche products suitable as

Pacific export crops—that is, specialized, high-quality, high-priced products. Current and potential niche products include ginger, spices, and kava from Fiji; vanilla and off-season high-quality vegetables such as squash (butter pumpkin) from Tonga; coffee, kava, and currently an expansion of squash production from Vanuatu; flowers, mangoes, and asparagus from Samoa; and *Eucheuma* seaweed from Kiribati, whence coconut products have previously been the only significant agricultural export. Large-scale production of some crops remains important, such as the estate production of palm oil in the Solomon Islands, the smallholder "umbrella" management system of sugar production in Fiji, and the coffee and tea of Papua New Guinea.

However, even major crops can quickly disappear from exports; for example, after two severe tropical cyclones (hurricanes) badly damaged Samoa's agricultural output in the early 1990s, in 1993 a fungal leaf blight *(Phytophthora colocasiae)* virtually wiped out the production of taro, a crop that was the favored staple food of Samoans and had during the 1980s and into the 1990s become the country's major export crop (worth over US$2 million), supplying the demand for the food among the islander-immigrant population in New Zealand. Natural disasters and disease outbreaks (many of which are at least partly culturally induced) encourage island governments to seek further export diversification, including the niche products mentioned above. Table 29.1 provides recent data showing the major export products from the tropical Pacific Islands. As suggested above, it is best to consider this information as a slice in time. In later years, the situation may well be quite different.

One crop of great importance spatially, if not always economically, is the coconut palm (Color Plate 29F). Once a major export crop and significant industry, coconuts have been planted in immense numbers covering the coastal areas of most Pacific Islands since the Europeans came. Although copra continues to be the main commodity export from Vanuatu and, generally, the only cash crop available to the inhabitants of the outer islands of Kiribati and Tuvalu, coconut products are now generally in decline, except, again, for a few specialized products such as high-quality coconut soaps, a coconut cheese from Fiji, and coconut cream. There is also the suggestion that simply processed coconut oil could provide a substitute for diesel fuel (Morton 1993). Otherwise, the millions of often senile and poorly tended trees are the despair of development planners, who forget the food use of coconuts. What Brookfield (1985:117) describes for Fiji would be applicable across the Pacific:

**TABLE 29.1** Pacific Islands Exports, in US$ '000 *(Far East and Australasia 1995–96)*

| | Minerals & ores | Fish & seafood | Sugar & molasses | Coffee, tea cocoa, vanilla | Wood & byproducts | Coconut & palm oil | Pearls | Copra & coconuts trochus | Shell, coral | Root crops | Fruits & vegetables | Others[1] | Total |
|---|---|---|---|---|---|---|---|---|---|---|---|---|---|
| Papua New Guinea 1990 | 582,011 | 7,716 | | 148,989 | 64,002 | 41,193 | | 9,367 | | | | 398761 | 1252039 |
| French Polynesia 1990 | | | | 675 | | 1,662 | 37,827 | | 12,090 | | 171 | 693234 | 745659 |
| New Caledonia 1992 | 352,670 | | | | | | | | | | | 57155 | 409825 |
| Fiji 1993 | 43,265 | 27,400 | 156,120 | | | 2,378 | | | | | 928 | 151538 | 381629 |
| American Samoa 1989 | 80 | 297,050 | | | | | | | | | | 10400 | 307530 |
| Northern Marianas 1992 | | | | | | | | | | | | 279000 | 279000 |
| Solomon Islands 1993 | | 25,939 | | | 72,690 | | | | | | | 30436 | 129065 |
| Nauru 1988 | 67,600 | | | | | | | | | | | | 67600 |
| Vanuatu 1992 | | | | 1,455 | 1288 | | | 7,293 | 1,243 | | | 12383 | 23662 |
| Tonga 1993 | | 1,589 | | 2,023 | | 72 | | | | 72 | | 13221 | 16977 |
| Western Samoa 1986 | | | | 1,263 | 349 | | | 473 | | 1922 | 17 | 6478 | 10502 |
| Kiribati 1992 | | 354 | | | | | | 3,199 | | | 210 | 388 | 4151 |
| Cook Islands 1992 | | | | | | | | | | | 792 | 2453 | 3245 |
| Marshall Islands 1991 | | | | | 4 | 1396 | | 18 | 176 | | | 1296 | 2890 |
| Niue 1993 | | | | | | | | 6 | | 256 | | 26 | 288 |
| Tuvalu 1989 | | | | | | | | 58 | | | | 5 | 63 |
| Tokelau 1982-3 | | | | | | | | 33 | | | | 6 | 39 |
| FSM 1991 | | | | | | | | | | | | | 0 |
| Guam 1992 | | | | | | | | | | | | | 0 |
| Wallis & Futuna 1985 | | | | | | | | | | | | | 0 |
| Palau | | | | | | | | | | | | | 0 |
| Pitcairn Island | | | | | | | | | | | | | 0 |
| | 1,045,626 | 360,048 | 156,120 | 154,405 | 138,333 | 46,701 | 37,827 | 20,447 | 13,509 | 2250 | 2118 | 1656780 | 3634164 |

[1] Includes the following: scented coconut oil (French Polynesia), handicrafts (Tokelau and Tuvalu), meat (Vanuatu), rubber (Papua New Guinea), pet fish (Kiribati)

In the coconut regions almost every cooked meal employs coconut milk (*lolo*) derived by grating the meat and straining the product. Data collected in the rural areas show that families with good stands of palms might consume about 600 nuts/capita/yr, and a reasonable estimate of average consumption might lie between 300 and 400. . . . Actual consumption varies greatly, but on certain islands it may absorb nuts equivalent to from ten to thirty per cent of normal copra production.

With regard to modern animal husbandry, in many countries there is now battery production of chickens (for meat and eggs) and pigs, based on imported or partly locally produced feeds and on improved imported poultry and pig breeds. In some countries, such as Papua New Guinea, New Caledonia, Vanuatu, and Fiji, large-scale cattle ranching based on improved breeds and pasture, for both local and export sale, has been successful.

### Agriculture in Hawai'i and New Zealand

In Hawai'i, traditional agriculture, dependent on extensive culvert-fed irrigated taro systems and dryland agriculture of sweet potatoes (Kirch 1985b, see also the discussion above on traditional agriculture), went into a long-term decline by the mid–nineteenth century, a consequence of depopulation, land alienation, and commercial cultivation of sugar and pineapple. Sugar and pineapple (together with large-scale cattle grazing) continue to dominate the agricultural sector, but are losing ground, pineapple to cheaper foreign production, and sugar to a combination of low prices, competition from other sources of sweetening, and sugar lands' being priced out of the market by land-use changes from agricultural to urban. As the acreage used for plantation agriculture declines, smaller-scale diversified production has gained ground. Macadamia nuts have been a marked success. Other crops include papaya, flowers, bananas, passion fruit, coffee, vegetables, avocado, and guavas (Daws 1968, Armstrong 1983).

A high-value crop that does not enter the official statistics is *pakalolo* (marijuana or *Cannabis sativa*), which is grown widely, concealed in sugarcane fields, state forests, and other public lands, as well as in backyards and greenhouses. Estimates have placed its turnover above that of any other crop, another example of the success of niche marketing. Illegal cropping of marijuana is also known to be important in Fiji and Papua New Guinea and, most likely, many other Pacific islands.

Agricultural transformation in New Zealand was equally dramatic. Precontact societies were dependent on the cultivation of sweet potatoes and flax, and in suitable locations, taro, yams, and other crops. Here too, depopulation and land alienation led to a decline of traditional agriculture. Much of the landscape was transformed by the late nineteenth century into an enormous pasture land of native grasses or introduced alien grasses and clovers upon which there came to graze huge numbers of sheep and cattle. Farming landscapes continue to change as crops fail or succeed and as the modern trend toward a decrease in the number of farms and an increase in the size of individual farms takes place. Market gardening dominates in the Auckland vicinity, supplying the country's largest, and growing, urban market. Orchards of citrus, Chinese gooseberry ("kiwifruit"), apples, peaches, apricots, or fields of corn, beans, and other vegetables are scattered from north to south according to the suitability of climate and soils and access to land, transport, and processing.

Recent changes in New Zealand agriculture include a decline in sheep numbers (down from 70 million in 1983 to 50 million in 1993) because of the withdrawal, with economic restructuring, of agricultural support in the form of fertilizer subsidies and minimum prices, especially in the face of a depressed international market for sheep meat. Beef and dairy cattle numbers, on the other hand, have increased. The recent success of the New Zealand wine industry has gained the country much notice overseas as growers have concentrated on premium varieties in demand in export markets. Mention may also be made of the remarkably extensive afforestation efforts that have taken place in New Zealand, leading to the largest planted forests in the world, composed of exotic conifers, especially radiata pine (Britton et al. 1992, Cumberland and Whitelaw 1970, Le Heron and Pawson 1996).

## Logging in the Southwest Pacific

Export logging has become an important component of economies in the Southwest Pacific. Logging is currently the largest industry in the Solomon Islands, accounting for over 50% of all export revenues and 31% of all government revenue (Frazer 1998). In Papua New Guinea, logging accounts for only 5%–10% of total exports, but with an estimated 15 million hectares of "operable" forest, there are over 1 million m$^3$/yr of harvested timber (Saulei 1998). In Vanuatu, forest area and diversity are smaller, but logging is nonetheless significant; current licenses (totaling 300,000 m$^3$/yr) exceed the calculated sustainable yield (52,000 m$^3$/yr) by several times (Regenvanu, Wyatt, and Tacconi 1998).

The dominant logging companies in Melanesia are foreign, centered in Japan, Korea, Malaysia, Singapore, and China. Lured by the attraction of export revenues, island goverments encourage investment by subsidizing infrastructure (roads and utilities), granting access to large areas, and offering tax concessions. Forestry exports are undersold, since they are exported mainly in the form of unprocessed logs, and royalty payments are often underestimated, delayed, or underpaid. Worst of all, the process tends to be a "boom and bust" operation, with local populations experiencing the smallest benefits and the greatest harm. Following a brief period of jobs and income, they are left with an impoverished environment, with an increased number of the unskilled laborers already swelling urban areas (Barlow and Winduo 1998).

In most cases, logging of natural rain forests triggers a progressive, irreversible conversion to agriculture, grasslands, and severely devastated landscapes. Governments generally lack the resources or will to mount expensive reforestation (or fertilization) campaigns. Existing schemes to replace logged forests with commercial agricultural projects such as oil-palm plantations (sometimes framed as "agroforestry"), in any case result in drastic reductions in both biodiversity and the potential for subsistence use (Barlow and Winduo 1998).

Government attempts to regulate logging vary considerably. In Vanuatu, landowners have strongly resisted exploitive logging, and the industry has been brought into some measure of control. In the Solomon Islands, cabinet members attempting to increase regulation of the logging industry were forced out of office, replaced by a government that advocated large-scale logging (headed by Prime Minister Solomon Mamaloni, director of a log-exporting company). Papua New Guinea has passed a number of regulatory measures, but rhetoric is often not matched by practice (Barlow and Winduo 1998).

Forestry is very important in New Zealand's economy, ranking as the country's third largest export earner (behind meat and dairy) and accounting for 10% of total exports. However, only about 2% of total exports derive from natural forests (around 6 million hectares), and this is well regulated. Natural forests must be capable of regeneration, preserving the original appearance and diversity. Ninety-eight percent of exports (around 10 million $m^3$/yr) derive from over 1 million hectares of plantation forests, primarily *Pinus radiata* (MFNZ 1998). The logs are in most cases processed locally (to timber, plywood, pulp and paper, etc.), and subsequently exported to Australia, Japan, and Southeast Asia.

On a smaller scale, commercial plantation forests exist in Hawai'i, Fiji, Samoa, and a few other Pacific Island groups. *Pinus caribaea* in Fiji has already formed the basis of a profitable industry. Elsewhere, however, success has been elusive due to impoverished soils and lack of expertise, development funds, and regulatory ability. On most Pacific Islands, development of commercial forestry is precluded by the demands of existing subsistence agroforestry, watershed maintenance, dwindling reserves of biodiversity, and political and economic constraints (Richardson 1985, Barlow and Winduo 1998).

## Sustainability Issues

The agroforests, humanized woodlands, and polycultural gardens of traditional Pacific agricultural systems were all protective of the soil, imitating natural forest. Intensive agriculture on irrigated terraces or the mulched ditched systems acted to lessen erosion and maintain soil fertility. This is not to say that the early agriculturalists were "in harmony" with their environments. At times, like all settlers in new environments, they caused considerable damage—such as by felling forest on steep slopes or an indiscriminate use of fire—but then made mitigating adjustments, such as developing swampland agriculture, terraces, and agroforests that sustained their agriculture for centuries or millennia (Clarke 1994:15,16).

Over the past several decades in the tropical Pacific Islands an environmental threat has been the great expansion in area of land in agricultural use. The causes of the expansion come from several directions. First is the rapid population growth in some countries (notably the Solomon Islands, Vanuatu, and Papua New Guinea) where shifting cultivation is practiced. Such growth leads quickly to a shortening fallow period, which in turn leads to loss of forest biodiversity, agrodeforestation, soil degradation, and declining yields. Another cause is the increase in cash cropping and the development of pastures for cattle. Both these ventures "freeze" what is often the best and flattest land in the community into permanent uses, forcing shifting gardens to be concentrated on steeper, poorer land, bringing soil degradation and erosion. Frazer (1987:ii) noted in his long-term study of a community on Malaita Island in the Solomon Islands that between 1971 and 1985 the area of tree crops doubled, production of cocoa tripled, and copra production quadrupled. This resulted in land shortages, a reduction in bush fallow periods, declines in crop yields, and land degradation.

Thistlethwaite and Votaw (1992:192) note that in 1981, 60% of Pacific Island countries reported soil erosion problems associated with the expansion of agriculture, intensification on land already cropped, timber extraction, and road construction. In 1991 a similar percentage of countries reported soil erosion as a significant environmental problem, listing the same causes but with more emphasis on intensification and accompanying shorter bush or grass fallow. A dramatic example occurred on Mangaia and Atiu in the Cook Islands, where pineapples were planted straight up steep fernland slopes. Massive, spectacular gully erosion resulted in some locations, with the resultant heavy sedimentation and change in water runoff badly affecting the wetland taro grown downslope (Thistlethwaite and Votaw 1992:13).

Another factor in the rapid expansion of clearing for agriculture is that families and individuals can claim land for their individual use by clearing it and planting it with coconuts or other cash crops, thus giving permanent individual control of what is nominally communally held land. This process has led recently to much of the forest remaining in Samoa falling to chain saws, with the cleared land used mainly for the expansion of export taro cropping in the 1980s and 1990s, prior to the 1993 taro leaf blight (Ward 1995, Paulson 1994).

Nor is the Pacific free of polluting agricultural chemicals, with Samoa, for instance, known as a heavy user of weedicides (Fairbairn 1993). Thaman, in his paper "The Poisoning of Paradise" (1984) chronicles the indiscriminate and careless use of pesticides from Hawai'i to Papua New Guinea. In the countries and territories of the Pacific Islands, there is only limited control over the imports of pesticides; some of the pesticides in use have been banned as too dangerous for use in the countries where they were produced.

Pacific Islanders do not generally use fertilizers to the extent that some developed countries do, but on atoll islets, even frugal use of fertilizer can lead to dangerous contamination of the underground freshwater supply. On larger islands, fertilizer runoff has been a significant contributor to eutrophication and clogging of waterways with aquatic weeds. On any Pacific island with a high percentage of coastal area and adjoining reef relative to land area, agricultural chemicals and soil erosion pose a particular threat because of their rapid flow-on effects on the productivity of coasts and reef.

To avoid degradation in the face of the several pressures for an expansion of area under agriculture and an increase in local and export production will require far more attention to sustainability requirements. One approach is to use lands that have already been cleared, farming them more intensively using traditional subsistence and agroforestry practices (Thistlethwaite and Davis 1996, Clarke and Thaman 1997). This approach would maintain marginal lands under protective forest as well as counter the loss of managed biodiversity as crop species and varieties succumb to the uniformity that characterizes market-directed production (Yen 1980:86–87). There are, however, difficulties in operationalizing this prescription.

Governments are less interested in agriculture than in alternative cash-earning ventures such as mines in Papua New Guinea, logging and fisheries in the Solomon Islands, offshore financing in Vanuatu, industrialization in Fiji, and tourism wherever it seems at all possible. Even if sustainable intensification were given serious policy consideration, national institutional capacities are inadequate to the task of providing the information on degradation necessary for environmental planning. Nor are there agencies now capable of monitoring trends or enforcing practices that would lead to sustainability. Further, intensification requires additional inputs, either in the form of imported chemicals or human labor. The first are expensive and can be environmentally damaging; the second is often difficult to mobilize because agricultural effort, if directed toward many of the traditional cash crops, has such a low priority among Pacific Islanders. As Penelope Schoeffel argues (Asian Development Bank 1996a:69):

> In most Pacific island countries the return on a full day of work by an individual on cocoa or copra or coffee will barely cover the cost of 1 kg rice and a can of mackerel—hardly enough to feed a family for a day. Understandably, when a day's labor purchases so little and does not feed a family, smallholders turn their attention away from cash crops and concentrate on subsistence activities that ensure their survival.

If niche products are found that bring good prices, many farmers will be ready to incur environmental degradation for the sake of temporary profit. Possibilities for reasonable returns and more organized environmental management exist under centralized forms of management, such as the organization of smallholder producers in the Fiji sugar industry, but, under centralization, the primary motivation may remain export production, not conservation (Clarke and Morrison 1987).

## Conclusion

Despite the problematic situation described here, there are possibilities for a more cheerful outlook. All three authors of this chapter have in the course of recent research had the pleasure of walking in durable, beautiful, and productive gardens created by today's Pacific Islanders in all three of the Pacific's major cultural divisions: Polynesia, Micronesia, and Melanesia. These are not the integral subsistence systems described earlier in this chapter. All contain some production for cash as well as subsistence, and all their creators have other interests than agriculture, but the gardens themselves possess some of the components of sustainability evolved early on in Pacific agriculture—such as polycultural diversity and continued production without the need for external inputs. Certainly, a return to the independence of the integral subsistence way of life that existed in the Pacific's past is unlikely (Yen 1980:88). But there is the possibility and challenge for Pacific men and women who work the soil and tend the trees to evolve hybrid systems that combine commercial and subsistence agriculture and that will endure productively to meet the needs of future generations.

# Bibliography

Armstrong, R. W., ed. 1983. *Atlas of Hawaii.* Honolulu: University of Hawai'i Press.

Asian Development Bank. 1996a. *Sociocultural issues and economic development in the Pacific Islands.* Manila: Asian Development Bank.

Asian Development Bank. 1996b. *Fiji agriculture sector review: a strategy for growth and diversification.* Manila: Asian Development Bank.

Barlow, K., and S. Winduo. 1998. Introduction (special issue on logging). *The Contemporary Pacific* 9(1):1–22.

Barrau, J. 1958. *Subsistence agriculture in Melanesia.* Honolulu: Bernice P. Bishop Museum Bulletin 219.

Barrau, J. 1961. *Subsistence agriculture in Polynesia and Micronesia.* Honolulu: Bernice P. Bishop Museum Bulletin 223.

Bayliss-Smith, T., and J. Golson. 1992. A Colocasian revolution in the New Guinea Highlands? Insights from Phase 4 at Kuk. *Archaeology in Oceania* 27:1–21.

Bonnemaison, J. 1994. *The tree and the canoe: history and ethnogeography of Tanna.* Honolulu: University of Hawai'i Press.

Britton, S., R. Le Heron, and E. Pawson, eds. 1992. *Changing places in New Zealand: a geography of restructuring.* Christchurch: New Zealand Geographical Society.

Brookfield, H. C. 1984. Intensification revisited. *Pacific Viewpoint* 25(1):15–44.

Brookfield, H. C. 1985. An historical and prospective analysis of the coconut districts. In *Land, cane and coconuts: papers on the rural economy of Fiji*, ed. H. C. Brookfield, 111–247. Department of Human Geography Publication HG/17. Canberra: Research School of Pacific Studies, The Australian National University.

Brookfield, H. C., with D. Hart. 1971. *Melanesia: a geographical interpretation of an island world.* London: Methuen.

Clarke, W. C. 1966. From extensive to intensive shifting cultivation: a succession from New Guinea. *Ethnology* 5:347–359.

Clarke, W. C. 1971. *Place and people: an ecology of a New Guinean community.* Berkeley: University of California Press.

Clarke, W. C. 1994. Traditional land use and agriculture in the Pacific Islands. In *Land use and agriculture*, vol. II of *Science of Pacific Island peoples*, ed. J. Morrison, P. Geraghty, and Linda Crowl, 11–37. Suva: Institute of Pacific Studies, University of the South Pacific.

Clarke, W. C., and J. Morrison. 1987. Land mismanagement and the development imperative in Fiji. In *Land degradation and society*, ed. P. Blaikie and H. C. Brookfield, 176–185. London: Methuen.

Clarke, W. C., and R. R. Thaman, eds. 1993. *Agroforestry in the Pacific Islands: systems for sustainability.* Tokyo: United Nations University Press.

Clarke, W. C., and R. R. Thaman. 1997. Incremental agroforestry: enriching Pacific landscapes. *The Contemporary Pacific* 9(1):121–148.

Connell, J. 1994. Beyond the reef: migration and agriculture in Micronesia. *Isla: A Journal of Micronesian Studies* 2(1):83–101.

Cumberland, K., and J. Whitelaw. 1970. *New Zealand.* London: Longman.

Daws, G. 1968. *Shoal of time: a history of the Hawaiian Islands.* New York: Macmillan.

Doty, M. S. 1954. Part 1. Floristic and ecological notes on Raroia. *Atoll Research Bulletin* 33:1-41.

Fairbairn, T. I. J. 1993. *Western Samoa's census of agriculture: major features and implication for development.* Pacific Studies Monograph No. 7. Sydney: Centre for South Pacific Studies, University of New South Wales.

Falanruw, M. V. C. 1993. Micronesian agroforestry: evidence from the past, implications for the future. In *Proceedings of the Workshop on Research Methodologies and Applications for Pacific Islands Agroforestry*, Technical Coordinators B. Raynor and R. Bay, 37–41. General Technical Report PSW-GTR-140. Pacific Southwest Research Station, US Forest Service.

Falanruw, M. V. C. 1994. Food production and ecosystem management on Yap. *Isla: A Journal of Micronesian Studies* 2(1):5–22.

Fallon, J. 1994. *The Vanuatu economy: creating conditions for sustained and broad based development.* Canberra: Australian International Development Assistance Bureau.

Frazer, I. 1987. *Growth and change in village agriculture: Manakwai, North Malaita.* Occasional Paper 11, South Pacific Smallholder Project. Armidale, NSW, Australia: University of New England.

Frazer, I. 1998. The struggle for control of Solomon Island forests. *The Contemporary Pacific* 9(1):39–72.

Grossman, L. 1981. The cultural ecology of economic development. *Annals of the Association of American Geographers* 71(2):220–236.

Handy, E. S. C., E. G. Handy, and M. Pukui. 1972. *Native planters in Old Hawaii: their life, lore and environment.* Honolulu: Bernice P. Bishop Museum Bulletin 233.

Hather, J., and P. V. Kirch. 1991. Prehistoric sweet potato (*Ipomoea batatas*) from Mangaia Island, Central Polynesia. *Antiquity* 65:887–893.

Hatheway, W. H. 1953. The land vegetation of Arno Atoll, Marshall Islands. *Atoll Research Bulletin* 16:1-68.

Hunter-Anderson, R. 1991. A review of traditional Micronesian high island horticulture in Belau, Yap, Chuuk, Pohnpei, and Kosrae. *Micronesica* 24(1):1–56.

Kirch, P. V. 1977. Valley agricultural systems in prehistoric Hawaii: an archaeological consideration. *Asian Perspectives* 20:246–280.

Kirch, P. V. 1978. Indigenous agriculture on Uvea (western Polynesia). *Economic Botany* 32:157–181.

Kirch, P. V. 1985a. Intensive agriculture in prehistoric Hawaii: the wet and the dry. In *Prehistoric intensive agriculture in the tropics*, ed. I. S. Farrington, 435–454. BAR International Series 232.

Kirch, P. V. 1985b. *Feathered gods and fishhooks.* Honolulu: University of Hawai'i Press.

Kirch, P. V. 1989. Second millennium B. C. arboriculture in Melanesia: archaeological evidence from the Mussau Islands. *Economic Botany* 43:225–240.

Kirch, P. V. 1991. Polynesian agricultural systems. In *Islands, plants, and Polynesians: an introduction to Polynesian ethnobotany*, ed. P. A. Cox and S. A. Banack 113–133. Portland, Oregon: Dioscorides Press.

Kirch, P. V. 1994. *The wet and the dry: irrigation and agricultural intensification in Polynesia.* Chicago: University of Chicago Press.

Kuhlken, R. 1994. Tuatua ni Nakauvadra: a Fijian irrigated taro agrosystem. In *Land use and agriculture*, vol. II of *Science of Pacific Island peoples*, ed. J. Morrison, P. Geraghty, and Linda Crowl, 51–62. Suva: Institute of Pacific Studies, University of the South Pacific.

Landauer, K., and M. Brazil, eds. 1990. *Tropical home gardens.* Tokyo: United Nations University Press.

Leach, H. 1984. *1,000 years of gardening in New Zealand.* Wellington: A. H. and A. W. Reed.

Le Heron, R., and E. Pawson, eds. 1996. *Changing places: New Zealand in the Nineties.* Auckland: Longman Paul.

Manner, H. I. 1993. A review of traditional agroforestry in Micronesia. In *Proceedings of the Workshop on Research Methodologies and Applications for Pacific Islands Agroforestry*, Technical Coordinators B. Raynor and R. Bay, 32–36. General Technical Report PSW-GTR-140. Pacific Southwest Research Station, US Forest Service.

Manner, H. I. 1994. The taro islets (*maa*) of Puluwat Atoll. In *Land use and agriculture*, vol. II of *Science of Pacific Island peoples*, ed. J. Morrison, P. Geraghty, and Linda Crowl, 77–87. Suva: Institute of Pacific Studies, University of the South Pacific.

Marten, K. D. 1985. Forestry in Melanesia and some Pacific Islands. In *Environment and resources in the Pacific*, 115–128. UNEP Regional Seas Reports and Studies No. 69. Geneva: UNEP.

Massal, E., and J. Barrau. 1956. *Food plants of the South Seas.* Technical Paper 94. Noumea: South Pacific Commission.

McKnight, R. K., and A. Obak. 1960. Taro cultivation in the Palau District. In *Taro cultivation practices and beliefs. Part I. The Western Carolines. Anthropological Working Papers*, No. 6. Guam: Staff Anthropologist, Trust Territory of the Pacific Islands.

Metraux, A. 1940. *Ethnology of Easter Island*. Honolulu: Bernice P. Bishop Museum Bulletin 160.

Ministry of Forestry, New Zealand (MFNZ). 1998. *The forestry sector in New Zealand*. http://www.maf.govt.nz/MAFnet/sectors/forestry/forind/httoc.htm

Morton, B. 1993. Coconut power. *Pacific Islands Monthly* 63(12):37.

Mueller, W. 1917. Yap. In *Ergebnisse der Sudsee Expedition. II Ethnographie: Band 2*, ed. G. Thilenius. Hamburg: L. Friederichsen & Co.

Paulson, D. 1994. Understanding tropical deforestation: the case of Western Samoa. *Environmental Conservation* 21(4):326–332.

Ragone, D. 1991. Ethnobotany of breadfruit in Polynesia. In *Islands, plants, and Polynesians: an introduction to Polynesian ethnobotany*, ed. P. A. Cox and S. A. Banack, 203–220. Portland, Oregon: Dioscorides Press.

Ravuvu, A. 1983. *Vaka i Taukei: The Fijian way of life*. Suva: Institute of Pacific Studies, University of the South Pacific.

Raynor, B., and J. Fownes. 1993. An indigenous Pacific Island agroforestry system. In *Proceedings of the Workshop on Research Methodologies and Applications for Pacific Islands Agroforestry*, Technical Coordinators B. Raynor and R. Bay, 42–58. General Technical Report PSW-GTR-140. Pacific Southwest Research Station, US Forest Service.

Regenvanu, R., S. W. Wyatt, and L. Tacconi. 1998. Changing forestry regimes in Vanuatu: is sustainable management possible? *The Contemporary Pacific* 9(1):73–98.

Richardson, D. 1985. Forestry in the South Pacific: how and for whom? In *Environment and resources in the Pacific*, 107–114. UNEP Regional Seas Reports and Studies No. 69. Geneva: UNEP.

Rosendahl, P. H. 1972. Aboriginal agriculture and residence patterns in Upland Lapakahi, Island of Hawaii. Ph.D. dissertation, University of Hawai'i, Honolulu.

Saulei, S. 1998. Forest exploration in Papua New Guinea. *The Contemporary Pacific* 9(1):25–38.

Scaglion, R., and K. A. Soto. 1994. A prehistoric introduction of the sweet potato in New Guinea? In *Migration and transformations: regional perspectives on New Guinea*, ed. A. Strathern and G. Sturzenhofecker, 257–294. Pittsburgh: ASAO Monograph No. 15.

Schoeffel, P. 1994. Where are all the farmers? agriculture, land tenure and development in the Pacific islands. In *Land issues in the Pacific*, ed. R. Crocombe and M. Meleisea, 35–42.

Small, A. C. 1972. Atoll agriculture in the Gilbert and Ellice islands. Tarawa: Department of Agriculture.

Spriggs, M. 1981. Vegetable kingdoms: taro irrigation and Pacific prehistory. Ph.D. dissertation, Australian National University, Canberra.

Spriggs, M. 1990. Why irrigation matters in Pacific prehistory. In *Pacific production systems: approaches to economic prehistory*, ed. D. E. Yen and J. M. J. Mummery, 174–189. Canberra: Department of Prehistory, Research School of Pacific Studies, The Australian National University.

Thaman, R. R. 1990a. Mixed home gardening in the Pacific Islands: present status and future prospects. In *Tropical home gardens*, ed. K. Landauer and M. Brazil, 41–65. Tokyo: United Nations University Press.

Thaman, R. R. 1990b. Kiribati agroforestry: trees, people and the atoll environment. *Atoll Research Bulletin* 333:1–29.

Thaman, R. R. 1992. Agrodeforestation as a major threat to sustainable development. Box 19.4 in *Environment and development: a Pacific Island perspective*, ed. R. Thistlethwaite and G. Votaw, 194–195. Manila/Apia: Asian Development Bank/South Pacific Regional Environment Programme.

Thaman, R. R. 1993a. Fijian agroforestry at Namosi and Matainasau. In *Agroforestry in the Pacific Islands: systems for sustainability*, ed. W. C. Clarke and R. R. Thaman, 63–84. Tokyo: United Nations University Press.

Thaman, R. R. 1993b. Pacific Island urban agroforestry. In *Agroforestry in the Pacific Islands: systems for sustainability*, ed. W. C. Clarke and R. R. Thaman, 145–156. Tokyo: United Nations University Press.

Thaman, R. R., and P. M. Thomas. 1985. Cassava and change in Pacific Island food systems. In *Food energy in tropical ecosystems*, ed. D. J. Cattle and K. H. Schwerin, 191–228. New York: Gordon and Breach.

Thistlethwaite, R. and D. Davis. 1996. *A sustainable future for Melanesia? natural resources, population and development*. Canberra: National Centre for Development Studies.

Thistlethwaite, R., and G. Votaw, eds. 1992. *Environment and development: a Pacific Island perspective*, ed. R. Thistlethwaite and G. Votaw. Manila/Apia: Asian Development Bank/South Pacific Regional Environment Programme.

Tuggle, H., and P. Griffin. 1973. *Lapakahi, Hawaii: archaeological studies*. Asian and Pacific Archaeology Series 5. Honolulu: Social Science Research Institute, University of Hawai'i.

Waddell, E. 1972. *The mound builders: agricultural practices, environment, and society in the Central Highlands of New Guinea*. Seattle: University of Washington Press.

Walter, A. 1994. Knowledge for survival: traditional tree farming in Vanuatu. In *Fauna, flora, food and medicine*, vol. III of *Science of Pacific Island peoples*, ed. J. Morrison, P. Geraghty, and Linda Crowl, 189–200. Suva: Institute of Pacific Studies, University of the South Pacific.

Ward, R. G. 1980. Agricultural options for the Pacific islands. In *The island states of the Pacific and Indian oceans: anatomy of development*, ed. R. T. Shand, 23–39. Canberra: Development Studies Centre Monograph No. 23, The Australian National University.

Ward, R. G. 1986. Reflections on Pacific Island agriculture in the late 20th century. *Journal of Pacific History* 21(4):217–226.

Ward, R. G. 1995. Deforestation in Western Samoa. *Pacific Viewpoint* 36(1):73–93.

Ward, R. G. and A. Proctor, eds. 1980. *South Pacific agriculture: choices and constraints. South Pacific agricultural survey 1979*. Manila/Canberra: Asian Development Bank/Australian National University.

Wiens, H. J. 1956. The geography of Kapingamarangi Atoll in the Eastern Carolines. *Atoll Research Bulletin* 48:1-93.

Yen, D. E. 1974. *The sweet potato and Oceania: an essay in ethnobotany*. Honolulu: Bernice P. Bishop Museum Bulletin 236.

Yen, D. E. 1980. Pacific production systems. In *South Pacific agriculture: choices and constraints. South Pacific agricultural survey 1979*, ed. R. G. Ward and A. Proctor, 73–106. Manila/Canberra: Asian Development Bank/Australian National University.

Yen, D. E. 1990. Environment, agriculture and the colonisation of the Pacific. In *Pacific production systems: approaches to economic prehistory*, ed. D. E. Yen and J. M. F. Mummery, 258–277. Canberra: Department of Prehistory, Research School of Pacific Studies, The Australian National University.

Yen, D. E. 1991. Polynesian cultigens and cultivars: the questions of origins. In *Islands, plants, and Polynesians: an introduction to Polynesian ethnobotany*, ed. P. A. Cox and S. A. Banack, 67–95. Portland, Oregon: Dioscorides Press.

Yen, D. E. 1996. Melanesian arboriculture: historical perspectives with emphasis on the genus *Canarium*. In *South Pacific indigenous nuts*, ed. M. L. Stevens, R. M. Bourke, and B. R. Evans, 36–44. ACIAR Proceedings No. 69. Canberra: Australian Centre for International Agricultural Research.

# CHAPTER 30

# Ocean Resources

*Tim Adams, Paul Dalzell, and Esaroma Ledua*

## Introduction

The resources of the sea play a greater part in the lives of the inhabitants of the Pacific Islands than they do in the lives of almost any other section of humanity. This dependency on marine resources not only is of historical significance but also continues to shape perceptions to the present day. Pacific Islanders eat much more fish than people in the rest of the world, and many states and territories place their main hope for future economic development in marine resources.

We can consider marine resources according to their distinctive uses by human beings in the Pacific Islands region as follows:

I. Extractive uses
  A. Oceanic fisheries (largely commercial and industrial)
  B. Coastal fisheries (largely subsistence and small-scale)
  C. Seabed minerals and marine chemicals (mainly potential, at present)
II. Nonextractive uses
  A. Tourism (both traditional beach-lounging and modern "eco"-tourism and diving)
  B. Renewable energy generation (mainly potential at present)

In this chapter we will concentrate on extractive uses, particularly fisheries. Nonextractive uses are either considered in other chapters or are not yet of major importance.

### Ocean Resources in the Economic and Social Context

It is the smallest islands that tend to be most dependent on marine resources. In the Pacific Island nations and territories that might be considered the most "terrestrially challenged" (Belhadjali 1996)—the Cook Islands, the Federated States of Micronesia, French Polynesia, Kiribati, the Marianas Islands, the Marshall Islands, Nauru, Niue, Tokelau, and Tuvalu—planners have no great expectation of further developing commercial agriculture as a major source of foreign exchange and, in many cases, cannot rely on agriculture to fulfill even local protein needs. For these small islands it has been marine resource usage that has set many of the limits to human population interaction and expansion, and it will probably be marine resource usage, in the form of subsistence fishing, commercial fishing, tourist enjoyment, and possibly mineral or power extraction, that will continue to define the shape of Pacific small-island societies in years to come.

Although the sea plays a less crucial role in the lives of the inhabitants of the larger islands (Table 30.1), most populations (with the exceptions noted below) are still spread along the coast, and very much influenced by the sea. Under most definitions of the term, the "coastal zone" in the Pacific Islands actually covers the entire settled land area. Exceptions to the above generalizations are New Guinea, with large highland populations, and New Zealand and Hawai'i, with large urban populations.

To help place Pacific Islands marine resource usage into the global context, here are some key points:

• Pacific Islanders rank among the highest marine food consumers in the world, and the region as a whole has a considerably greater per capita fishery product consumption than other regions, except perhaps the traditional Inuit regions of the far north and some of the Indian Ocean islands. Few comprehensive studies have been done on seafood consumption in the Pacific Islands, and apparently none that can consistently compare one country with another and with the rest of the world. Per capita annual seafood consumption figures of over 200 kg are regularly and reliably quoted for remote Pacific atolls (e.g. Coyne et al. 1984), and even a comparatively urban/agricultural Pacific Island population like Fiji's consumes 40–50 kg of seafood per annum per capita on average (calculated from data in Fiji Fisheries Division Annual Reports 1978–94).

• As well as eating a lot of fish, Pacific Islanders also catch a lot of fish. This may seem like a superfluous distinction, but the fact that almost every member of the community takes part in fishing is an important characteristic of Pacific Island subsistence lifestyles (fishery methods are depicted graphically in Appendices 30.1–30.2). Even in the more developed Pacific Islands, people maintain strong links with the sea through boat ownership and sport fishing. In many parts of the Pacific, women (often with the help of children) are charged with maintaining the day-to-day food supply of the community and do most of the nearshore fishing and reef-gleaning, while men are responsible for discharging (and creating) external obligations and fishing for cash. In Fiji, over 90% of rural households go fishing at least once a week (Rawlinson et al. 1995). For the region as a whole, it is likely that up to 80% of the weight of fishery products caught by Pacific Islanders does not enter the cash economy and only around 10% of the catch is exported (Adams and Dalzell, in press).

• Despite their limited scale by world standards, and despite the fact that only a small fraction of total domestic fishery production enters the commercial sector, marine resources may occupy a major, even a primary place in some Pacific Island economies. For example, trochus shell is the only visible export from the French territory of Wallis and Futuna; black pearls are French Polynesia's most valuable export, canned tuna is

### TABLE 30.1 — The Relative Importance of Coastal Fisheries in the Pacific Islands

| | Land area km2 | EEZ area km2 | % of EEZ area as land | Population No. | Population per 100 km2 of EEZ No. | Total coastal fish catch tonnes | Coastal fish catch/capita kg | GDP/capita A$ | Aid/capita A$ |
|---|---|---|---|---|---|---|---|---|---|
| American Samoa | 201 | 390,000 | 0.052 | 54,800 | 14.1 | 293.6 | 4.87 | 6,660 | 2,117 |
| Cook Islands | 240 | 1,830,000 | 0.013 | 19,100 | 1.0 | 1080.1 | 51.41 | 5,195 | 912 |
| Fiji | 18,274 | 1,290,000 | 1.417 | 774,800 | 60.1 | 25576.9 | 30.01 | 2,716 | 64 |
| French Polynesia | 3,521 | 5,030,000 | 0.07 | 218,000 | 4.3 | 6647.3 | 27.72 | 19,622 | 1,657 |
| FSM | 701 | 2,978,000 | 0.024 | 105,700 | 3.5 | 7568.0 | 65.09 | 3,400 | ... |
| Guam | 541 | 218,000 | 0.248 | 149,300 | 68.5 | 650.4 | 3.96 | 12,356 | 878 |
| Hawai'i (USA) | 16,641 | 2,381,000 | 0.699 | 964,700 | 40.5 | 13423.8 | 12.65 | 35,500 | ... |
| Kiribati | 690 | 3,550,000 | 0.019 | 78,400 | 2.2 | 13457.8 | 156.05 | 600 | 421 |
| Marshall Islands | 181 | 2,131,000 | 0.008 | 54,700 | 2.6 | 2606.0 | 43.31 | 1,995 | 1,386 |
| N. Marianas Is. | 478 | 777,000 | 0.062 | 56,700 | 7.3 | 3262.6 | 52.31 | 12,941 | ... |
| Nauru | 21 | 320,000 | 0.007 | 10,500 | 3.3 | 413.6 | 35.81 | 22,418 | 27 |
| New Caledonia | 19,103 | 1,740,000 | 1.098 | 182,200 | 10.5 | 3830.0 | 19.11 | 17,970 | 1,901 |
| New Zealand | 268,103 | 6,148,000 | 4.361 | 3,190,124 | 51.9 | 668455.4 | 190.49 | | ... |
| Niue | 259 | 390,000 | 0.066 | 2,000 | 0.5 | 126.5 | 57.5 | 3,946 | 4,034 |
| Palau | 488 | 629,000 | 0.078 | 16,500 | 2.6 | 1633.5 | 90 | 4,163 | 907 |
| Papua New Guinea | 462,840 | 3,120,000 | 14.835 | 4,042,400 | 129.6 | 28102.8 | 6.32 | 1,882 | 127 |
| Pitcairn Island | 5 | 800,000 | 0.001 | 50 | 0.0 | 8.8 | 160 | ... | ... |
| Samoa | 2,831 | 120,000 | 2.359 | 163,400 | 136.2 | 3837.4 | 21.35 | 1,305 | 160 |
| Solomon Islands | 28,370 | 1,340,000 | 2.117 | 367,800 | 27.4 | 12266.9 | 30.32 | 947 | 174 |
| Tokelau | 12 | 290,000 | 0.004 | 1,500 | 0.5 | 210.1 | 127.33 | 478 | 3,750 |
| Tonga | 780 | 700,000 | 0.111 | 98,200 | 14.0 | 2597.9 | 24.05 | 1,815 | 389 |
| Tuvalu | 24 | 900,000 | 0.003 | 9,500 | 1.1 | 1019.7 | 97.58 | 1,256 | 694 |
| Vanuatu | 12,190 | 680,000 | 1.793 | 164,100 | 24.1 | 2763.6 | 15.31 | 1,678 | 337 |
| Wallis and Futuna | 255 | 300,000 | 0.085 | 14,400 | 4.8 | 1008.7 | 63.68 | ... | 75 |

Solomon Islands' main export (or at least its main currently sustainable natural resource export), and fresh tuna has recently become the Federated States of Micronesia's most valuable export. Much of the export of fish from Palau is unquantified, being carried out of the country to Guam as airline checked baggage, but even without taking this into account, fish is still Palau's most important official export.

• The most startling characteristic of Pacific Islands marine resources, at least from the external perspective, is just how little quantitative information is actually available for most areas. As a result of this lack of accurate statistical information, the pressing need for more effective management intervention (resulting from the changes from subsistence toward cash economies, and from traditional to urban lifestyles) has led to the formal promotion of a new management paradigm that devolves responsibility, wherever possible, to the level of the community rather than the level of national government, and which permits action based on local, rather than purely scientific, systems of information (Johannes 1998). This management paradigm (sometimes called "co-management," (Pomeroy and Williams 1994) is "new" of course only to Western minds, and much is based upon traditional systems tested over the course of centuries in the Pacific Islands (Adams 1996).

## Ocean Resources in the Oceanographical and Ecological Context

While Australia and the Pacific Islands comprise a major part of the world in terms of geographical area, and fish is of major importance to the inhabitants, the waters of the region provide only 2% of the total world fishery production (FAO 1997), and half of this regional fishery production is from the pelagic (surface-associated) tuna fishery of the western tropical Pacific. The vast majority (more than 80%) of the remainder comes from the continental shelves of Australia and New Zealand. The overall fishery harvest in most of the region is limited not because the Pacific Ocean itself is not productive, or is grossly underexploited, but because most of the harvestable productivity is available only on the rich upwelling systems of the continental margins of the ocean.

Most Pacific Islands lack the broad, shallow shelves characteristic of most continental margins and of other major island archipelagos in Southeast Asia and the Caribbean. Apart from New Guinea and New Zealand, Pacific Island coastal zones are characterized by comparatively narrow coral shelves sitting on steep island slopes. It is not uncommon to find depths of 3,000 m within 2 km of shore. The relatively small area of shallow water and the general inability of small-island profiles to induce much upwelling of nutrient-rich colder abyssal water mean that most Pacific Island coasts have a lower potential fishery yield than tropical continental areas per unit length of coastline.

Tropical Pacific Island coasts are also characterized by the comparative preponderance of coral reefs. There is much less of the "soft-bottom" habitat common on continental shelves, which are subject to large volumes of terrestrial runoff. Many Pacific islands are surrounded by barrier reefs, almost all have fringing reefs (Color Plate 30A), and the surface area of some Pacific Island nations consists entirely of reefs in the form of atolls (Figure 30.1). The Great Barrier Reef of Australia is the most extensive series of reefs in the world, but the barrier reef around New Caledonia and the Great Sea Reef that straddles

*Figure 30.1.* Patch reef on Fakaofo Atoll, Tokelau (photo MR).

the two main islands of Fiji are also impressive structures. Hermatypic (reef-building) coral structures are not so developed around geologically young island groups like Hawai'i, the Marquesas, Vanuatu, and the Northern Marianas, and barrier reefs are virtually absent, but coral is still the dominant nearshore substrate. The general scarcity of soft substrates is underlined by the almost total lack of bottom-trawl fishing around Pacific Islands (apart from New Zealand). Many independent trials have shown that the main harvest from coastal trawling in this region is ripped fishing nets.

This massive living matrix of coral reefs locks up a lot of the biomass in Pacific Island nearshore waters. Although coral reef ecosystems are among the most complex on Earth, the proportion of the biomass that is useful to human beings, in the form of fish and edible invertebrates, is lower than in most other marine ecosystems. In view of the fact that coral is such an important determinant of life in the Pacific Islands, it is unfortunate that there is as yet no accurate estimate of its extent around most islands or in the region as a whole. Smith (1978) made a very rough first estimate of coral reef area, but this was based mainly on calculating areas of shallow-water shelf from navigational charts and not on the actual presence or absence of coral. However, efforts are currently under way to improve this estimate, particularly through the World Conservation Monitoring Centre (Cambridge, UK) and the International Center for Living Aquatic Resources Management's REEFBASE database (Manila, Philippines).

Other shallow-water marine ecosystems are present in the Pacific Islands, but all except for New Zealand are more or less dominated by coral. Mangroves are an important feature of coasts in the western Pacific, although mangroves are not found naturally much to the east of Samoa, in line with the general massive decline in natural species biodiversity from west to east across the Pacific. Researchers from other regions are often surprised to see mangroves growing adjacent to, or actually upon, coral reefs in the Pacific. Seagrasses also contribute structural components to shallow marine ecosystems and, like mangroves, are particularly significant as "nursery habitat" for the juveniles of many of the living resources that are important to humans, as well as food for the green turtle *Chelonia mydas*. Much of the seagrass growth in the western Pacific is made possible by the sheltering effect of barrier reefs.

Not very far offshore from most islands, the sea bed plunges steeply into abyssal depths. There is as yet no fishery for ocean-bed organisms in the Pacific Islands region apart from some localized patches of precious coral near Midway and Hawai'i and continental shelf fisheries of New Zealand and (to a lesser extent) Papua New Guinea. Trials are occasionally carried out on other island groups to see if there is commercial potential in relatives of the orange roughy (*Hoplostethus* spp). By far the major harvest of the oceanic areas of the Pacific Islands region comes from the pelagic zone, from waters close to the ocean surface, and by far the major component of this zone is made up of tuna, particularly skipjack tuna (*Katsuwonus pelamis*) (Figure 30.2).

*Figure 30.2.* Tuna unloaded for market (photo SPC).

The zone of greatest abundance of tuna in the Pacific is in the west, around the equator from approximately 10°N to 10°S, although the eastward extent of the surface fishery varies with the El Niño southern oscillation (ENSO) index. Much of this area has a relatively low primary productivity, so it seems paradoxical that it can support such a high biomass of tuna (the western tropical tuna fishery currently lands around 1,000,000 tonnes of fish per year (SPC 1996). Recent work at the Secretariat of the Pacific Community (Lehodey et al. 1997) suggests that this high density of tuna is supported by the higher primary productivity at higher latitudes and the subsequent movement of nutrients through the food chain toward the equator. The pelagic large marine ecosystem (LME) of the western tropical Pacific is not yet well researched, but understanding it will be extremely important in the future economy of Melanesia and much of Micronesia.

Economically important tuna species are oceanic in distribution as adults, but tuna larvae are found in high concentrations close to islands (e.g. Leis 1993), and smaller tuna are particularly common in the neritic waters of the Philippines and Indonesia. Politically, much is made of the international nature of tuna resources (see Herr 1990 and FAO 1997), and the slogan "fish without a country" has been used in the past by certain distant-water fishermen to justify the avoidance of management measures by coastal states, but it is clear that tuna are somewhat coastally dependent in their early life.

Another point to note in passing is that dolphins are rarely associated with tuna schools in the western tropical Pacific, unlike in the eastern Pacific close to the Americas, and purse seine nets (see Appendix 30.2) are set either around free schools or very commonly around schools associated with floating logs (this attraction of tuna schools to floating logs is not yet adequately explained). Purse seining in the western Pacific can justifiably be dubbed a "dolphin-friendly" fishing method. If deforestation in Melanesia and Southeast Asia continues at the present rate, it may have some long-term effect on the western tropical Pacific tuna fishery catch (Caddy and Majkowski 1996).

The offshore industrial tuna fishery takes very few species of fish, and only skipjack tuna (*K. pelamis*), yellowfin tuna (*Thunnus albacares*), big-eye tuna (*Thunnus obesus*), and albacore (*Thunnus alalunga*) are normally landed. By contrast the Pacific Island coastal fishery takes a wider diversity of species than just about any other fishery in the world. A creel (fishing catch) sampler in Fiji, for example, would need to be able to recognize at least one hundred species of finfish and at least fifty species of invertebrates. This is partly because coral reefs support a wide diversity of species compared with other shallow marine ecosystems (although this diversity thins out toward the eastern Pacific), but also because Pacific Islanders are extremely dependent on the sea and have developed a culture over millennia based on using almost everything that is edible. Only in areas like the Philippines, with a huge coastal subsistence population and a very high natural biodiversity, does the diversity of everyday catches exceed that of the Pacific Islands.

## Ocean Resources in the Historical Context

The extensive unbroken history of reliance upon marine resources in the Pacific Islands has led to the evolution of diverse and elaborate traditions of utilization of these resources. We hesitate to use the word "management" in reference to these traditions since there is some debate about whether traditional societies place restrictions on the usage of marine resources in order to preserve those resources or to preserve the balance of power in society (Ruddle 1995). It might appear that any tradition that does not lead to the conservation of a particular resource will itself die out along with the resource to which it refers. However, when a culture relies upon a large range of resources covering hundreds of species, it may not threaten community survival if one of them becomes extinct. Certainly, the marine resource usage traditions that are observable in present-day Pacific Island societies have both conservative and exploitative aspects.

The tradition that certain vulnerable (long-lived and erratically recruited) resources like giant clams and turtles are subject to restricted usage, being eaten only on special occasions or by chiefs, is widespread and obviously conservative in effect. One of the most widely practiced forms of traditional marine resource "usage manipulation" in the Pacific Islands is the moratorium or *tabu (tapu)*—a complete ban on the taking of a species, or range of species, for a certain period. Sometimes a *tabu* may be declared after the death of a chief, such as in Fiji. The usual explanation is that resources are built up during the *tabu* to enable a large commemorative feast after one hundred days. *Tabus* may also be declared by individual reef-owners in Solomon Islands in order to build up a large enough stock of trochus shells to enable an occasional economically useful harvest (e.g. Foale 1996). Moratoria are one of the most widespread and traditionally acceptable methods available for small-scale fisheries management in the Pacific.

However, the existence of a strongly traditional culture has not necessarily prevented the massive overexploitation of certain species in certain parts of the Pacific. It is very hard to find a dense population of any salable species of sea cucumber in any Melanesian island at present, and the declaration of endangered status for the larger species of giant clams is certainly justified. The usual explanation for this overexploitation is that the need for cash has overridden traditional constraints.

It is likely that overexploitation occurred in the past as well. The giant clam *Hippopus hippopus* was very common in Fiji in Pleistocene times, judging by its occurrence in fossil reefs, and was possibly present when the first humans came to those islands. Yet today it is completely extinct in Fiji. *H. hippopus*, being confined to reef tops and relatively large in size, is possibly the most vulnerable giant clam species to overexploitation, but possibly also one of the most readily available protein sources for a newly established human population. Less conjectural pointers toward historical overexploitation of other species come from shells in ancient middens. Such archaeological records can demonstrate a significant reduction in average shell size over time, with changes in relative species composition, consistent with heavy exploitation (Dalzell and Adams 1997).

Apart from being of critical nutritional importance in the initial establishment of human populations, marine resources were also important in historical times in attracting further waves of immigration to the Pacific Islands. Although sandalwood was the first major Pacific Island trading commodity to be exploited, the first permanent European and American settlements on several Melanesian islands in the nineteenth century were established as bases for processing and trading bêche-de-mer (dried sea cucumber—*holothurioidea*—or *trepang*), and pearls and pearl shell were a major attraction in the atolls of eastern Polynesia. In the early twentieth century, it was the attraction of marine resources that helped extend Japanese influence into Micronesia, and later, the Japanese distant water fishing fleet was the major factor in the expansion of the Pacific tuna fishery.

An event of significance for Pacific Island marine resources in recent times was the declaration of the 200–nautical-mile Exclusive Economic Zone (EEZ) around each nation and territory (Figure 30.3). Although the first 200-mile zones were proclaimed by certain Pacific coast South American countries in 1940s and 1950s, the first major national "exclusive economic zone" was probably the geographical box (from 15°S to 25.3°S and from 173°W to 177°W) declared by Tonga in 1887 (Petelo et al. 1995). The Pacific Islands played a major political role in developing the concept of the EEZ within the United Nations in the 1970s. Fiji was the first country to ratify and adopt the International Law of the Sea Convention (LOSC) in 1982. Under this Convention, although the exact interpretation

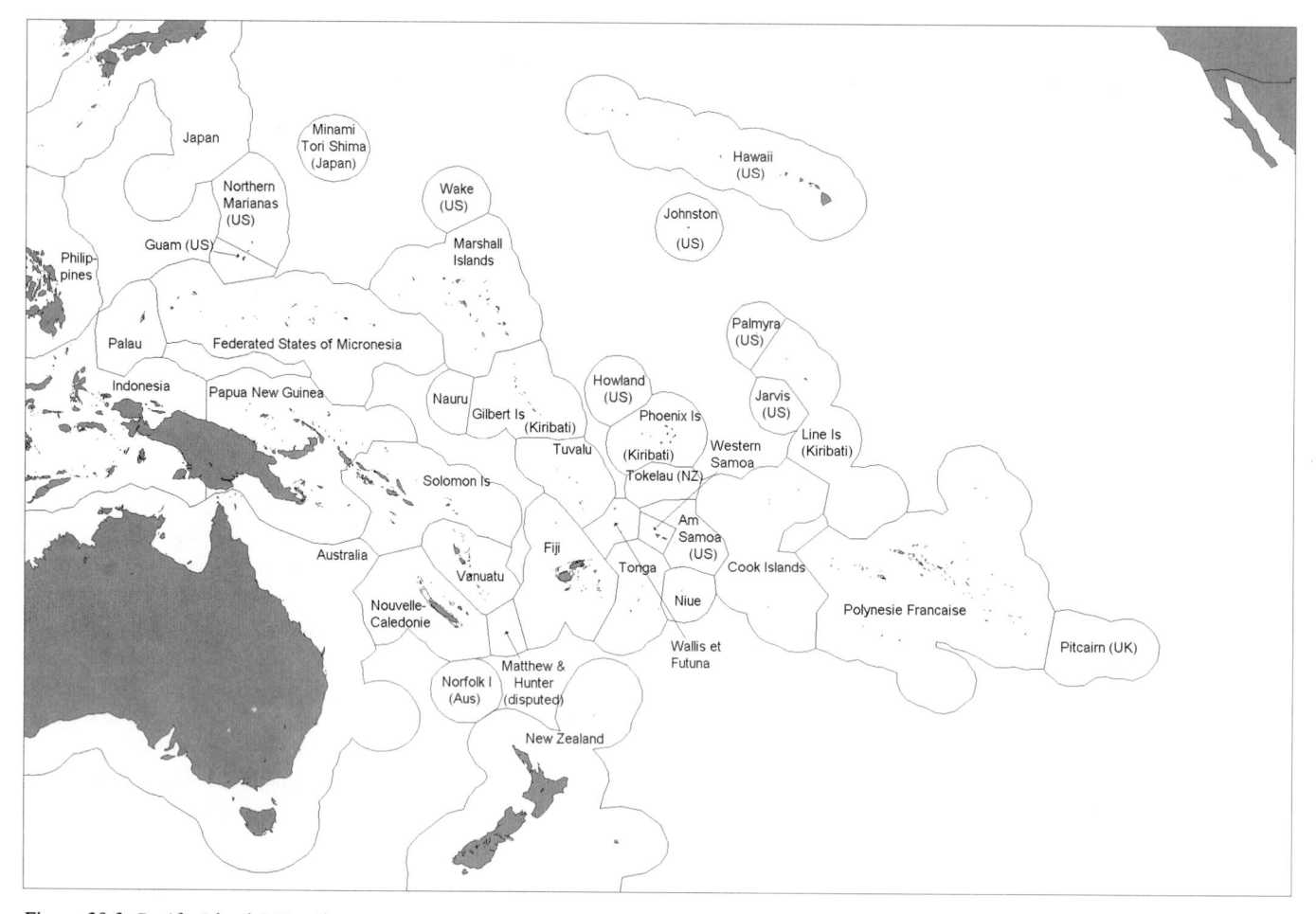

**Figure 30.3.** Pacific Island 200-mile zones.

of some of its articles is still subject to debate, coastal states accepted the responsibility of managing the exploitation of resources from the 12-mile limit of territorial waters out to 200 nautical miles. Incidentally, LOSC is not concerned with coastal fisheries and coral reefs, which usually fall within the 12-mile limit of territorial waters and are thus not part of the EEZ.

To help manage the highly migratory living resources within their EEZs, independent Pacific Island nations set up the Forum Fisheries Agency in 1979, in partnership with Australia and New Zealand. The jurisdiction, and even the existence, of this intergovernmental tuna management agency has been contested by certain distant-water fishing nations, who contend that they should have full and equal membership in any organization that intends to manage the exploitation of any highly migratory species of which they are the chief exploiters. Now that the International Law of the Sea Convention has come into force (on 16 November 1994), the debate is starting to crystallize, but the outcome is still uncertain. The coming five years will be interesting times in Pacific Island marine resource politics.

## Oceanic Fisheries

As pointed out in the introduction to the chapter, the oceanic fisheries of the Pacific Islands region are qualitatively different from the coastal fisheries. At present these oceanic fisheries are for highly migratory pelagic species. (New Zealand, the only Pacific Island group with a significant demersal and midwater trawl fishery, is discussed separately below. Papua New Guinea has an offshore trawl industry based on shrimp, but is of much smaller extent relative to New Zealand shelf and slope fisheries.) The oceanic pelagic fisheries are carried out mostly by industrial fleets owned by Pacific Rim nations and developed-country capital.

The fisheries for tuna in the western tropical Pacific took approximately 1 million tonnes in 1995 (Figure 30.4), and this

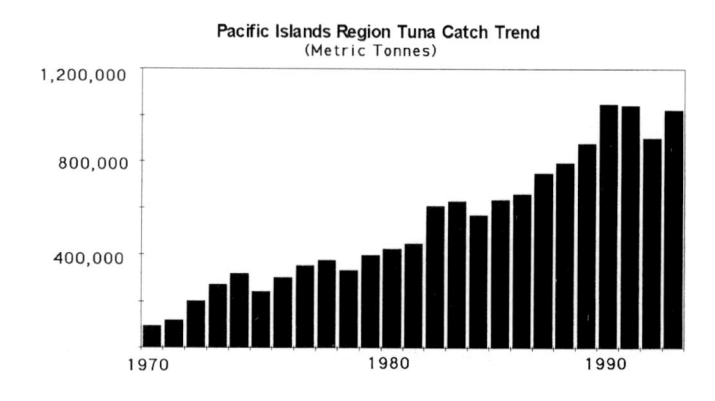

**Figure 30.4.** Pacific Islands region tuna catch trend (1970-1994).

catch appears to have reached some sort of equilibrium following a decade of steady increase. By global standards, the Pacific regional tuna fishery is a fairly new fishery, and a proportion of the recent increase has been a result of absorbing fishing effort by relocation from other global fisheries, particularly the far eastern Pacific. The overall western tropical Pacific tuna fishery is not considered yet to be fully exploited (SPC 1996), and the current plateau in catch is more a result of economic constraints than of resource constraints.

Most of the catch consists of skipjack and yellowfin tuna caught as schools on the sea surface by the purse seine fishing method and destined for canning. Longlining is the other major fishing method, targeting deeper-swimming tunas such as albacore and larger yellowfin and ranging to higher latitudes than purse seining. Some of the longline catch, particularly the albacore, is destined for canning, but large yellowfin and big-eye tunas can command much higher prices on the sashimi market in East Asia, particularly if landed fresh to the marketplace. Pole and line fishing for surface-swimming skipjack and yellowfin tuna, while important in decades past, has now been almost entirely replaced by purse seining, except where pole and lining, with its lower capital cost and higher labor requirement, is still economically viable for supplying local canneries. A breakdown of the catch by different fleets, fishing methods, and species is contained in Tables 30.2–30.4.

The value of the tuna catch in the SPC statistical area (Figure 30.5), at the point of landing, is approximately US$1.6 billion (FFA 1996). Note that approximately 7% of the total catch, by weight, is taken by Pacific Island fishing vessels. There have been several attempts by Pacific Island governments to increase local participation in these tuna fisheries, but only Fiji and Solomon Islands have had much success in operating industrial-scale fishing vessels to supply skipjack and yellowfin to nationally based canneries. Recently, with the development of markets in East Asia for fresh big-eye and yellowfin tuna, other Pacific Island nations are developing their capacity for small-scale longlining, although there is also aggressive competition from large fleets of Asian vessels, especially in Micronesia.

One fishing method that saw a rapid increase in the late 1980s and an equally rapid decline in the early 1990s in the South Pacific was oceanic driftnetting for southern albacore tuna. This was carried out in international waters in the Tasman Sea and around the subtropical convergence zone east of New Zealand (around 40°S), but many Pacific Island nations, particularly those toward the south of the region, feared that the taking of large numbers of juvenile albacore by high-seas driftnetters would affect the longlining fishery for adult albacore. With additional concerns by environmentalists about the large

## TABLE 30.2

**Tuna Catch by National Fleets[1]**
(Catch in metric tonnes within the SPC Statistical Area as a whole)

|  | 1989 | 1990 | 1991 | 1992 | 1993 | 1994 |
|---|---|---|---|---|---|---|
| Australia (Ll, Pl, Ps) | 2,448 | 8,278 | 11,452 | 9,339 | 7,430 | 3,426 |
| China (Ll) | - | - | 721 | 2,350 | 5,391 | 12,425 |
| Cook Islands (Ll) | - | - | - | - | - | 45 |
| Fiji (Ll, Pl) | 5,148 | 3,792 | 5,263 | 4,732 | 4,023 | 4,652 |
| Fed Stat Micronesia (Ll, Fsm) | - | - | 11,322 | 15,451 | 17,328 | 21,472 |
| Hawai'i (Longline Only) | 4,474 | 5,813 | 8,909 | 9,600 | 11,354 | 8,177 |
| Indonesia (Ps) | 12,856 | - | - | - | - | - |
| Japan (Ll, Pl, Ll)[2] | 302,135 | 282,650 | 268,846 | 263,578 | 239,566 | 251,683 |
| Kiribati (Pl, Ps) | 2,282 | 595 | 224 | 551 | 293 | 125 |
| Republic Of Korea (Ll, Ps)[2] | 137,127 | 204,403 | 248,941 | 208,539 | 147,425 | 224,496 |
| Marshall Islands (Ll) | - | - | - | 14 | 69 | 70 |
| Mexico (Ps) | - | - | - | - | - | - |
| New Caledonia (Ll, Pl) | 838 | 1,658 | 1,469 | 860 | 1,237 | 1,300 |
| New Zealand (Ll, Ps, Tr) | 6,939 | 7,653 | 9,200 | 4,995 | 5,037 | 7,845 |
| French Polynesia (Ll, Pl, Tr) | 844 | 1,099 | 1,045 | 1,160 | 2,119 | 2,371 |
| Papua New Guinea (Ll,, Pl, Ps) | - | - | - | - | 8 | 30 |
| Philippines (Ps) | 24,258 | 23,775 | 26,321 | 33,340 | 33,340 | 33,340 |
| Palau (Pl) | 77 | 88 | - | 75 | 75 | 75 |
| Samoa (Ll) | - | - | - | - | 26 | 26 |
| Solomon Islands (Ll, Ps) | 35,916 | 29,547 | 48,578 | 32,773 | 29,813 | 35,299 |
| Russia (Ps) | 4,935 | 2,126 | 3,715 | 2,126 | 8,714 | 6,722 |
| Tonga (Ll) | 234 | 190 | 198 | 223 | 330 | 860 |
| Tuvalu (Pl) | 149 | 90 | 29 | 8 | - | - |
| China (Taiwan) (Ll. Ps)[2] | 117,033 | 145,514 | 192,419 | 258,990 | 196,506 | 210,880 |
| United States (Ll, Ps, Tr) | 142,072 | 167,652 | 219,478 | 206,239 | 203,787 | 208,160 |
| Total | 799,765 | 884,923 | 1,058,130 | 1,054,943 | 913,871 | 1,033,479 |

[1]Refers to combined tuna catch by industrial-scale high-seas fleets of purse seiners (Ps), pole-and-line vessels (Pl), trollers (Tr) and longliners (Ll), for cannery production or for export to markets outside the SPC area

[2]Totals for Japan, Korea, and Taiwan between 1989-1991 include some driftnet catches. Driftnetting was discontinued after 1991.

### Table 30.3 — Tuna Catch by Species

(Catch in metric tonnes of each major tuna species in the SPC fisheries statistical area)

| Year | Albacore Catch | Bigeye Catch | Skipjack Catch | Yellowfin Catch | Total Catch |
|---|---|---|---|---|---|
| 1970 | 31,759 | 17,733 | 10,768 | 32,569 | 92,829 |
| 1975 | 27,785 | 34,006 | 136,363 | 42,541 | 240,695 |
| 1980 | 39,806 | 41,642 | 211,824 | 104,471 | 397,743 |
| 1985 | 27,296 | 40,488 | 371,213 | 129,358 | 568,355 |
| 1990 | 30,888 | 52,824 | 586,395 | 209,003 | 879,110 |
| 1994 | 37,250 | 53,035 | 668,224 | 266,793 | 1,025,302 |

### Table 30.4 — Tuna Catch by Gear

(Catch in metric tonnes of all tuna species by each major fishing method in the SPC statistical area)

| Year | Driftnet Catch | Longline Catch | Pole-and-Line Catch | Purse Seine Catch | Troll Catch | Total Catch |
|---|---|---|---|---|---|---|
| 1970 | - | 81,863 | 10,510 | 456 | - | 92,829 |
| 1975 | - | 98,077 | 133,825 | 8,147 | 646 | 240,695 |
| 1980 | - | 167,145 | 176,684 | 52,446 | 1,468 | 397,743 |
| 1985 | 1,928 | 108,106 | 138,013 | 317,055 | 3,253 | 568,355 |
| 1990 | 7,426 | 114,919 | 82,451 | 667,532 | 6,782 | 879,110 |
| 1994 | - | 128,040 | 72,590 | 819,697 | 4,975 | 1,025,302 |

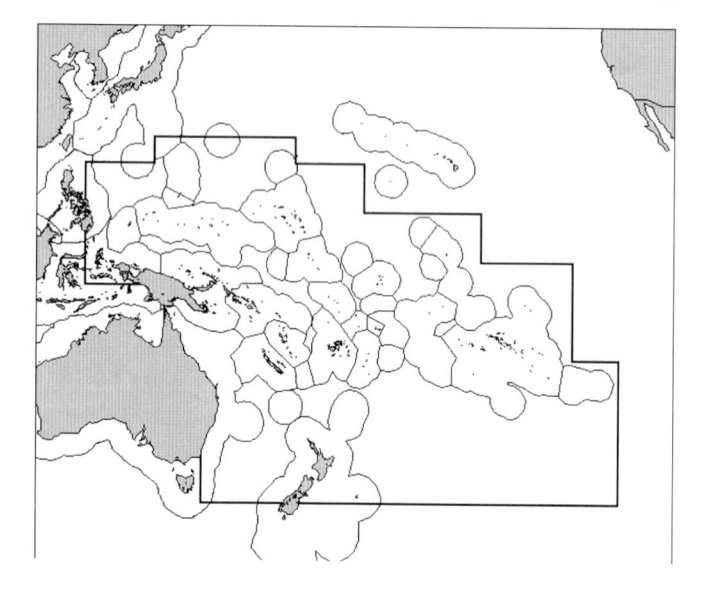

*Figure 30.5.* SPC Fisheries statistical area.

bycatch of commercially unusable species, the potential of driftnets to snare marine mammals, turtles, and seabirds, and vociferous complaints by United States albacore trolling vessels, a considerable political lobby against driftnetting has built up over a short space of time.

The debate over driftnetting took place between distant-water fishing nations and Pacific Island coastal states and territories at a series of consultations organized jointly by the Forum Fisheries Agency and the South Pacific Commission (now the Secretariat of the Pacific Community) between 1989 and 1991. Pacific islands insisted that a large-scale fishery should not be opened up without adequate evidence that it would not damage resources. The distant-water fishing nations argued that a fishery should not be closed down without definite evidence that the fishery was damaging resources. The Pacific Islands' unanimous resolve over oceanic driftnetting provided the final impetus for a subsequent global resolution entirely banning the use of long driftnets. This was one of the first definitive applications of the "precautionary principle" to international finfisheries. However, it may be difficult to continue a long-term ban on a fishing method that may be the only effective way of catching certain high-volume, high-latitude, oceanic species needed for feeding expanding global populations.

Although tuna is the only pelagic fishery of any significance in the Pacific Islands region at present, this was not always the case, and may not continue to be the case in the future. The tuna fishery is a comparatively recent development in the Pacific; prior to this the main fishery was for the great whales. Whales follow migration routes through the islands that are often locally well known (particularly where a beached whale is a valuable source of teeth, of huge ceremonial importance in countries like Fiji), and, though few quantitative sightings records were kept in years past, most observers feel that their numbers have been on the increase for some time now.

The form of a future international management regime for Pacific Island regional tuna fisheries will probably be settled over the next five years or so, but the final outcome is hard to predict. The legal mandate for the development of such an international regime comes from the International Law of the Sea and from the status of these tunas as "highly migratory species" whose range can encompass more than one national exclusive economic zone. Although tuna are the archetypal highly migratory species in the Pacific, there are other widely migratory species for which an international level of management may be desirable. Turtles, for example, range almost as widely as tuna, as do some of the oceanic sharks, and even crayfish can be carried many thousands of miles during their extensive larval stage. Whales are already subject to international management, but other species are not yet considered important enough for concerted regional attention. Perhaps some will be in the future.

## Coastal Fisheries

There are two main types of coastal fishery in the Pacific Islands: export fisheries and the multispecies reef and lagoon fisheries that supply much of the domestic protein requirement.

### Export Fisheries

Pacific Island groups do not export many fishery products from their coastal zones, or large volumes of these products, and those that are exported are primarily commodities aimed at specific niche markets. Chief among these, in terms of volume, are dried sea cucumbers (Figure 30.6), of which the vast majority

*Figure 30.6. Display of undersize holothurians (photo SPC).*

are consumed in China and Southeast Asia. Mother-of-pearl shells (*Trochus niloticus*, *Pinctada margaritifera*, *Turbo marmoratus*, in decreasing order of volume) are also exported for natural shirt buttons and, to a lesser extent, furniture inlays. Recently, with improving transport, the export of chilled and live fish is becoming important. However, the deep reef-slope commercial fishery for eteline snappers that was developing in several countries during the 1980s has given way, in most cases, to small-scale tuna longlining because the economic returns are more consistent from the tuna longline fishery.

Another valuable export product, resulting from the cultivation of primarily wild stocks, is black pearl from the blacklip pearl shell *Pinctada margaritifera*. However, black pearls are currently important only to the economies of French Polynesia and the Cook Islands, since eastern Polynesia is the only part of the region where dense populations of wild broodstock are found (for reasons that are still not well understood ecologically). At the time of writing, pearl farming is still the only commercially significant application of aquaculture in the Pacific Islands. The success of shrimp farming in a number of Melanesian countries continues to vary, and most other aquacultural developments are still at the experimental, or backyard, level.

Most export-oriented coastal fishing is sold to middlemen or exporters, often of foreign origin and capitalization. The occasional availability of commercial exporters in the area results in a characteristic type of exploitation called pulse fishing. Some organisms (such as trochus, smaller aquarium fish, and shallow-water holothurian species) are resilient enough to cope with such pulse fishing, but other species (such as grouper, giant clam, green snail, and pearl oyster in the central and western Pacific) are often fished far beyond their capability for short-term recovery.

There is increasing realization that reef fishery resources are not an inexhaustible attraction for foreign investment and that traditional resource custodianship alone cannot cope with the conflicting values of the cash economy. Stock assessments and controls are gradually being instituted, albeit far too late in some cases. The most appropriate way of managing these export-oriented fisheries appears to be islandwide or nationwide moratoria interspersed with short open seasons.

In general, across the Pacific Islands region, little is known about the volumes being extracted, let alone the status of stocks.

Export categorization is often confused, coastal fishery stock assessment is virtually nonexistent, and most of the information used in policymaking is anecdotal in origin. Accurate figures are few and far between, and the only current comprehensive overview, limited as it is, is contained in Dalzell et al. (1996). The following graphs (Figures 30.7 and 30.8) illustrate trends in some of these fisheries. These particular examples are among the few extended time-series available on these commodities. Note

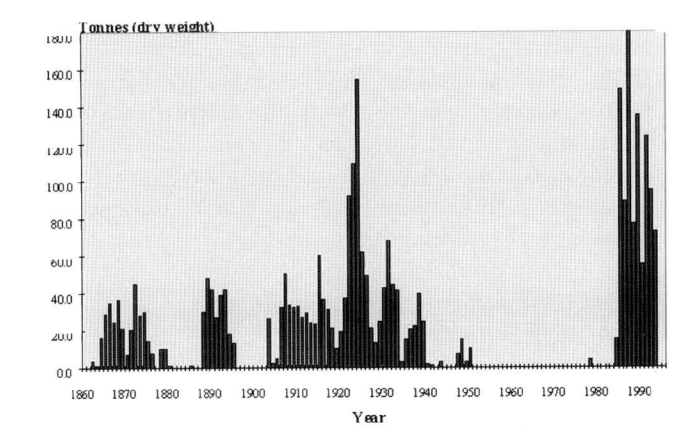

*Figure 30.7. Bêche-de-mer exports from New Caledonia.*

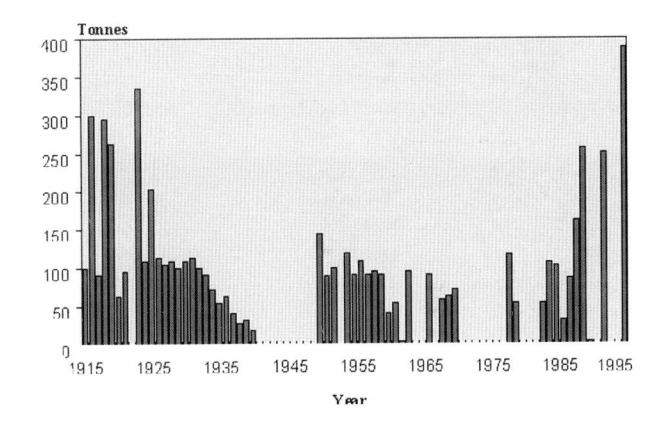

*Figure 30.8. Trochus shell exports from Palau.*

the decline of the bêche-de-mer after World War II, up to the recent reopening of trade with the People's Republic of China, when bêche-de-mer became a useful barter item in the face of currency restrictions. This hiatus was a feature of the bêche-de-mer trade from most Pacific islands.

Figure 30.8 illustrates the hiatus in production during World War II that was felt by all Pacific Island trochus exporters. However, in most countries, this hiatus continued up until the late 1970s, when the world trochus shell commodity price began to rise again as natural pearl buttons began to come back into fashion for high-quality men's shirts. Note also that the recent practice in Palau of restricting trochus harvests to once every two or three years, instead of every year, appears to have enabled much larger individual harvests to be sustained. The increased relative volume of these rarer harvests gives Palauan fishing communities a better economic bargaining position on the world mother-of-pearl shell market.

## Domestic Fsheries

Many of the small range of high-value products that are taken for export, such as deepwater snapper and sea cucumbers, are not traditional local food sources. Some of the export species that are locally used, like giant clam, have generally been scarce enough to be considered traditional luxuries. The Pacific Islands have not yet started to export their staple marine food sources, although this could be changing with the advent of high-value live market possibilities for certain reef fishes.

Most Pacific islands still depend utterly on coastal marine sources for protein. This dependency has come about because of both the lack of land mammals and the limited prospects for agriculture on small islands. Although (or perhaps because) there is a great dependency on coastal fisheries, the marine food base of most Pacific islands appears to be currently secure. There are fears of subsistence overfishing around several capitals. Most Pacific islands are subject to urban drift, and there have been changes in species and size composition of catches in areas with large human populations. Currently, the coastal waters of most islands are not subject to heavy overall fishing pressure. As human populations increase, the degradation of reefs and a consequent reduction in carrying capacity, coupled with increased fishing pressure, will increasingly impact domestic food fisheries.

Nearly all Pacific islands appear to have the sustainable resource capacity within their borders to feed their populations, even at present high rates of consumption. Those territories that import reef food-fish, like Guam and the Northern Marianas, do so not only because of dense populations per unit area of available reef, but because of the high-quality food demands of a large tourism industry and comparatively high wage rates, which make it expensive to use locally caught fish.

Table 30.6 is based on data from various sources, with a wide range of reliability. Many of the data points are based on an average of several estimated from recent years, and some of the subsistence estimates are based on only one survey. It would be impossible to construct a meaningful time-series for most of these areas, but this "snapshot" provides a baseline for comparison between countries.

It is difficult to separate domestic fishery production into commercial and subsistence components, since most Pacific Island fishing communities both consume and sell part of their catch. It is possible to judge community priorities from the observation that it is usually the lower-value, excess portion of the catch that is traded, while the more sought-after fish are consumed by the community. This should be borne in mind when trying to estimate the potential cash value of the subsis-

### Table 30.6 Pacific Island Coastal Fisheries Production (sources: Dalzell et al. 1996, FAO 1997, NZSIC 1998, NMFS 1998)

|   | Subsistence fisheries production (mt) | Nominal value (US$) | Commercial fisheries (mt)[1] | Value (US$) | Total coastal (mt) fisheries production | Nominal value (US$) |
|---|---|---|---|---|---|---|
| American Samoa | 215 | 814,238 | 52 | 178,762 | 267 | 993,000 |
| Cook Islands | 858 | 3,047,863 | 124 | 314,491 | 982 | 3,362,174 |
| F.S. Micronesia | 6,243 | 11,237,400 | 646 | 1,502,296 | 6,889 | 12,739,696 |
| Fiji | 16,200 | 40,117,924 | 6,506 | 18,979,880 | 22,706 | 59,097,804 |
| French Polynesia | 3,108 | 12,432,000 | 2,891 | 15,573,555 | 5,999 | 28,005,555 |
| Guam | 472 | 1,935,632 | 114 | 433,894 | 586 | 2,369,526 |
| Hawai'i[2] | 2182 | 9,173 | 4091 | 17,200 | 6273 | 26,373 |
| Kiribati | 9,084 | 13,373,667 | 3,240 | 4,770,000 | 12,324 | 18,143,667 |
| Marshall Islands | 2,000 | 3,103,213 | 369 | 714,504 | 2,369 | 3,817,717 |
| Nauru | 98 | 219,600 | 279 | 628,605 | 377 | 848,205 |
| New Caledonia | 2,000 | 7,344,417 | 1,032 | 4,833,410 | 3,032 | 12,177,827 |
| New Zealand[3] | 37,972 | 82,855,744 | 511,000 | 655,111,111 | 548,972 | 1,483,688,555 |
| Niue | 103 | 471,504 | 12 | 54,720 | 115 | 526,224 |
| N. Marianas | 202 | 826,685 | 120 | 493,601 | 322 | 1,320,095 |
| Palau | 750 | 1,805,192 | 736 | 2,412,071 | 1,486 | 4,217,263 |
| Papua N. Guinea | 20,588 | 41,176,000 | 4,966 | 22,096,908 | 25,554 | 63,272,908 |
| Pitcairn Islands | 8 | 16,000 | 0 | 0 | 8 | 16,000 |
| Samoa | 3,281 | 5,070,074 | 219 | 319,066 | 3,500 | 5,389,140 |
| Solomon Islands | 10,000 | 8,405,660 | 1,150 | 4,343,811 | 11,150 | 12,749,471 |
| Tokelau | 191 | 104,509 | 0 | 0 | 191 | 104,509 |
| Tonga | 933 | 1,901,208 | 1,429 | 2,806,641 | 2,362 | 4,707,849 |
| Tuvalu | 807 | 657,781 | 120 | 97,811 | 927 | 755,592 |
| Vanuatu | 2,045 | 1,953,360 | 467 | 1,514,364 | 2,512 | 3,467,724 |
| Wallis and Futuna | 862 | 4,310,000 | 138 | 1,285,400 | 1,000 | 5,595,400 |
| Total | 120,202 | 243,188,844 | 539,701 | 738,482,101 | 659,903 | 1,727,392,274 |

[1] Excludes landings from industrial-scale high-seas purse seine, longline and pole-and-line fleets fishing for cannery production or for export markets

[2] Hawai'i subsistence catch refers to recreational catch. Commercial production does not include Hawai'i longline fishery production (see Table 2), although some catch is marketed locally. Commercial figures also include production from a small 5–6-vessel pole-and-line boat fleet that markets fresh catch locally.

[3] The New Zealand domestic catch includes extensive industrial-scale fishing (mainly trawling) on continental shelves. Subsistence catch for New Zealand does not refer to catch that is for consumption only and does not enter the economy, but is that portion of the commercial catch retained for domestic consumption, while the balance is exported.

tence fishery, since it is often assumed that it is the lower-value portion of the catch that is kept for subsistence consumption (e.g. World Bank 1995).

The extreme biological diversity of the catch in these Pacific Island food fisheries (Adams and Dalzell, in press) is overlain by high cultural diversity, both in local preferences for different species and different fishing methods (Figure 30.9, Color Plates 30B–E). Pacific Island traditional fishing methods are the subject of considerable interest and ethnological research (see Ruddle 1996) and, although the use of modern fishing gear (monofilament lines and nets and outboard-powered boats) has become widespread, Pacific Island fishing methods retain a high degree of innovation. The bêche-de-mer "bomb," for example, used in parts of Solomon Islands, is not an explosive but a length of barbed spear fixed in a stone weight that is lowered on a line to spear sea cucumbers on the lagoon floor without the necessity for diving.

*Figure 30.9. Fish trap in Tonga (photo WA).*

Not all community and traditional fishing methods would necessarily be considered "ecologically sound" by modern Western standards. The use of traditional stupefacients like *Derris* and *Barringtonia* is still quite common, and laws completely prohibiting the use of traditional methods are not readily complied with. Such stupefacients are extremely nonselective and, while formerly used mostly on special occasions under chiefly edict, their usage has now spread throughout the population in some societies, with increasing impact near densely populated areas. Even so, these botanical stupefacients are much less damaging than the modern poisonous substitutes of weedkillers and household bleach, which can have a much longer-lasting effect, particularly on coral.

In some of the Cook Islands, no household inventory would have been considered complete in decades past if it did not possess an implement closely resembling a crowbar, used to break open the pockets in the reef inhabited by the small giant clam *Tridacna maxima*. However, in general, traditional fishing methods are less efficient than modern, or more selective (to catch a smaller range of species), and require more skill either in their use or in the fabrication of the gear, which leaves traditional fisheries less vulnerable to overexploitation.

The diversity of preference for different species or families of seafood among different Pacific Island societies is also remarkable and is becoming more obvious as casual mobility increases. Some species (particularly sharks) are formally forbidden to certain clans, but the preference for other species appears to be purely a matter of cultural taste. For example, the dolphin fish, or mahi mahi (*Coryphaena hippurus*), is almost unsalable in the Northern Marianas, but considered a very good food-fish in most parts of the region. Certain species of parrotfish are among the most highly prized components of the catch in the Cook Islands, but rarely targeted in neighboring Niue.

In other cases, justifiable prejudice may evolve against species in certain places because of ciguatera poisoning. Ciguatera occurs when fish ingest the microscopic algal dinoflagellate *Gambierdiscus toxicus*. While ciguatera poisoning is rarely fatal, it is uncomfortable enough for a considerable local system of customs to have grown up around the avoidance of certain species in certain places at certain times of year, particularly larger fish that have a greater chance of accumulating a large dose of toxin.

Even greater respect used to be accorded the turtle (particularly the leatherback, *Dermochelys coriacea*) in certain areas, since turtle poisoning is often fatal and occasionally wipes out whole villages. Even so, preference can often override a known risk of poisoning. It appears that in most Pacific Island societies the risk of ciguatera poisoning is not considered grave, and periodic ciguatera "hot-spots" are usually quickly identified and avoided. But major problems can arise in cash economies, where fish are transported to markets distant from the point of catch. In this case the best strategy may be to avoid certain species entirely. Municipal markets in Fiji ban the sale of certain species, and in New Caledonia many supermarket customers will not purchase any species of reef fish, however slight the risk.

## Some Current Issues in Coastal Fishery Management

The concept of local resource ownership is a common principle across most of the Pacific Islands. In some island groups there have been attempts by governments to assume full rights over resource allocation and to suppress tradition, but most island governments now accept that recognition of, and support for, community management responsibility is one of the strategies most likely to be successful in sustaining coastal fisheries. Traditional concepts of resource use do not necessarily coincide exactly with Western concepts of continuous sustainability, and in some communities the cash economy has severely eroded traditional authority. Still, community tenure of nearshore marine areas and fisheries has been unbroken for centuries and forms varied examples of how marine resource ownership works in different situations. Ironically, the Kingdom of Tonga, which is the only major Pacific Island group never subject to colonial rule, is one of the places where traditional resource allocation systems have substantially broken down.

Unfortunately, most of the intimate knowledge that Pacific Island fishing communities developed about the behavior and seasonality of reef fishes and invertebrates is unwritten, and much has been lost over the course of the twentieth century (Johannes 1980). In addition, the pace of social change is currently so rapid that much of the justification for traditional management—the preservation of fishable resources for the next generation—is undermined by the expectation that the next generation will be urban wage-earners. The need to export marine resources to generate the cash to pay the school fees to achieve these aspirations is immediate. If effective traditional management practices are to be maintained or revived, then Pacific Island governments and institutions are faced with the tasks both of supplementing the traditional knowledge lost and compensating for the erosion of traditional motivation for conservative resource management.

There is a growing view, particularly among environmentalists, that marine protected areas and reserves are the most essential, even the only, requirement for resource maintenance. However, there is still no good proof that marine reserves can help sustain surrounding fisheries, particularly for species whose larvae do not drift very far (in fisheries terms, which are "locally recruited"). Indeed, in areas subject to very heavy subsistence fishing pressure it is possible that excluding fishermen from some areas may increase fishing activity in surrounding areas to such an extent that ecological thresholds are exceeded and the surrounding fishery collapses (John Munro, pers. comm.).

Also, the societal integrity of "no-fishing" reserves is fragile. The build-up of high-value species in reserves is tempting to poachers, and considerable resources have to be put into patrolling reserves. Just one night of relaxed vigilance might destroy years of effort. Sometimes, the resources put into protecting limited areas might be more effectively spent on other methods of fisheries management, such as gear restrictions, size limits, trade-route policing, or moratoria. Marine protected areas are undoubtedly the only way of preserving pristine ecosystems and the best way of providing protection for endangered species, but they may not be the only, or necessarily the wisest, choice for the maintenance of sustainable fisheries.

Because of the longstanding tradition of marine tenure, many Pacific islands are a fine-grained patchwork of small-scale clan or family ownership. Where an ownership unit has jurisdiction over only a small area of reef, it can be difficult for a government to persuade an owner to relinquish that reef. A system of state-owned marine reserves is not an easy concept for most Pacific Islanders to come to terms with. However, most Pacific Islanders are familiar with the concept of voluntary temporary suspension of fishing activity, and in many cases this voluntary suspension of activity can be sustained for much longer periods than an outsider might expect.

The moratorium, or *tabu*, has much the same benefit as a state marine protected area, but has the added advantage of harmonizing better with tradition and promoting compliance by local people rather than needing enforcement against them. It is possible that the *tabu* will be violated, but most state-owned marine reserves in the Pacific Islands are already regularly violated, and in many cases ignored. Public education about the potential benefits of reinforcing traditional community control is probably a much better use of public money than expenditure on compensation for government-induced loss of fishing rights in setting up a marine reserve. If reserves or *tabu* areas are to be effective in helping sustain or replenish nearby areas, presuming that the larvae of target species have sufficient "spillover" characteristics, then the area must be upstream of target reefs. Knowledge of local current patterns is very limited, and many nearshore Pacific Island reefs are not yet even accurately mapped. This is an area of research that needs considerable attention in the near future.

One further issue that is currently topical is that, despite all the plans and guidelines for fisheries to be exploited "sustainably," the current lack of knowledge about Pacific Island marine resources is so profound that we have little idea what level of exploitation is actually "sustainable," and under what conditions, for the vast majority of fisheries.

## Fisheries in New Zealand

Fisheries in New Zealand are distinctive, a consequence of the extensive, temperate continental shelves, along with an industrial economy capable of fully exploiting such resources. Temperate continental shelf fisheries have lower biodiversity, but much higher biomass-per-species, than coral reefs, and they account for 90% of all world fisheries (Rothschild 1996). As in other urbanized societies, New Zealand's fisheries are almost entirely commercial or recreational, with a minimal subsistence component. Relatively few people depend directly on the sea, and the catching of fish is confined to a small minority. New Zealand's fisheries are also distinctive in the application of a fairly comprehensive management system.

Up until 1978 New Zealand's fisheries were nearshore-based, using small trawlers and other vessels. Beginning in 1978 with the international acceptance of EEZs, New Zealand's fisheries began a significant expansion (NZSIC 1998). Fisheries in New Zealand currently comprise about 0.5% of the total world catch, and provide the country with a vital source of exports and foreign cash revenues. The catch from New Zealand waters is roughly equivalent to the entire western tropical Pacific tuna catch (FAO 1997).

New Zealand's fisheries exploit a diverse range of habitats and stocks, using sophisticated technology. Inshore fisheries (such as snapper, caught from the surface to about 200 m depth) were a primary component of New Zealand's fisheries up until 1978. Following this, midwater and deepwater trawl fisheries (heke, roughy, and squid on the continental slope, at 200–1,200 m depth, depending on the species) became more important, currently accounting for the majority of fishery exports. New Zealand fisheries also include pelagic fish (tuna, mackerel, and sharks), shellfish (rock lobster, oysters, scallops, and abalone), and aquaculture (green mussels and salmon).

During the twelve-month period ending June 1996, fisheries were valued at over $NZ1 billion, about 5.6% of the country's total exports (superseded in value only by dairy, meat, forestry, and wool). Finfish account for approximately 65% of seafood exports in New Zealand; shellfish, around 26%. Seafood exports are marketed to Japan (29%), the United States (20%), Australia (11%), and over forty other countries (NZSIC 1998). The top ten export species, including the approximate annual catch and export values, are listed in Table 30.7. In addition, diverse other fish are caught by the recreational and commercial fisheries sectors.

### Table 30.7 — Main Seafood Export Species in New Zealand (data from NZSIC 1998)

| Species | Method obtained | Approx. annual catch (metric tonnes) | Export value ($NZ mil.) 12 mos. ending June 1996 |
|---|---|---|---|
| 1. Hoki (*Macruronus novazelandiae*) | Midwater trawling | 250,000 | 136.8 |
| 2. Orange roughy (*Noplostethus atlanticus*) | Deep sea trawling | 20,000 | 127.8 |
| 3. Squid (*Notodarus spp.*) | Surface trawling and jigging | 120,000 | 117.9 |
| 4. Rock lobster (*Jasus edwardii*) | Potting | 3,000 | 114.5 |
| 5. Greenshell mussel (*Perna canaliculus*) | Longline farming | 60,000 | 97.6 |
| 6. Paua (abalone) (*Haliotis iris*) | Diving | 1,000 | 52.2 |
| 7. Ling eel (*Genypterus blacodes*) | Bottom longlining and trawling | 20,000 | 48.3 |
| 8. Snapper (*Chrysophrys auratus*) | Longlining and trawling | 5,000 | 47.4 |
| 9. Salmon (*Oncorhynchus tshawytscha*) | Cage farming | 7,000 | 37.3 |
| 10. Deep sea dory (*Allocyttus spp., Pseudocyttus maculatus*) | Deep sea trawling | 25,000 | 34.0 |
| 11. Other | | | 365.3 |
| Total | | 511,000 | 1,179.2 |

To safeguard stocks and improve economic efficiency, the New Zealand government instituted an innovative quota management system (QMS). Each year, research is conducted to assess stock sizes of commercial species in specific quota management areas (QMAs). An annual total allowable catch (TAC) limit is then set for each QMA. A certain percentage of the TAC is set aside for recreational and Maori fisheries, and the remainder constitutes the total allowable commercial catch (TACC). This is in turn divided into a number of individual transferable quotas (ITQs), the right to catch a specified fish by weight in a limited area, which can be traded.

The introduction of the QMSs was roughly coincident with a national reassessment of public obligations under the Treaty of Waitangi, which enabled the government to "buy back" large quota shares for the indigenous Maori. In 1992, a final settlement guaranteed Maori 10% of all existing ITQs, 20% for any additional species governed by the QMS, and funding to purchase a 50% share of a fisheries company holding a third of all quotas, valued at NZ$350 million). In addition, a Treaty of Waitangi Fisheries Commission was established, charged with assisting Maori in fisheries and responsible for allocating lease quotas (calculated at well below market rates) to specific tribal groups. Today, it is estimated that the majority of New Zealand fishing quotas are owned by the commission or Maori-controlled fishing companies (Sir Tipene O'Regan 1997).

## Nonliving Resources

One point that has been made many times in reference to natural resources, but particularly to Pacific Island nonliving resources, is that occurrence does not signify a resource. There are hundreds of thousands of tons of polymetallic nodules and crusts on the bed of the Pacific Ocean, but nobody has yet succeeded in retrieving them in more than experimental quantities, due to the extreme depths at which they are found. The costs of retrieval and processing outweigh any potential income, at present. However, the future potential is so great that worries by major industrial nations over access to ocean floor minerals were one of the main reasons why the United Nations Convention on the Law of the Sea took so long to come into force (Kimball 1996).

Pacific Island nonliving marine resources, like the living resources, fall into two main categories: coastal and oceanic.

### Coastal Nonliving Resources

These are resources obtained in shallow water, and thus more cost-effectively obtained and used by Pacific Islanders themselves. The resource most commonly extracted is beach or lagoon sand and gravel for use as aggregate in construction projects, and such usage occurs in every country of the region. Sand and gravel are low–unit-value, high-bulk materials, and thus almost always have to be locally sourced. It is not economical to transport them large distances, particularly from island to island, or internationally. However, availability varies greatly from island to island, and thus there are some remarkable differences in price, from US$6 to US$50 per cubic m (Muller 1993). Sand is a particularly valuable resource in the smaller atoll countries.

The demand for aggregate from Pacific Island coastal waters is increasing alongside economic development, particularly around capital cities and tourist hotel zones. An increasing proportion of this supply will probably have to come from lagoon dredging, in place of the current reliance on beach mining. Lagoon dredging is also the means by which the cement factory in Fiji obtains its source of raw material: coral sand. Shallow water dredging and sand mining are activities that are increasingly seen to interact with traditional fisheries and customary fishing rights. In Fiji a long-established assessment and tribunal system compensates users toward the loss or diminution of fisheries of customary fishing rights owners.

With land-based Pacific Island phosphate sources nearing (Nauru) or having reached (Banaba) exhaustion, increasing attention is being turned to possible phosphate deposits beneath lagoon floors. Prospecting is going on in several atoll countries at the moment, and one of the most economically viable phosphate prospects is said to be beneath the lagoon of Mataiva Island in French Polynesia, buried by up to 7 m of lagoon sediment (Muller 1993). Phosphate is used principally in fertilizers.

One additional and longstanding use of nonliving nearshore resources is as coral boulders and blocks, for lining septic tanks for private sewage mitigation in urban areas and for constructing walls and landscaping gardens. The recent growing export trade in "live rock" from the Pacific Islands utilizes a very similar resource, but at a much lower volume. "Live rock," which can fetch up to US$5 per lb. retail in the United States, is coral rubble that has been colonized by a variety of useful or interesting organisms, such as sponges, calcareous algae, and tube worms, and that is sold as a substrate for seawater reef aquaria. Although the export of live rock requires a considerable amount of skill and capital, this is a much higher-value, lower-volume way of using coral rubble than construction.

### *Oceanic Nonliving Resources*

Polymetallic nodules have been known to occur on the deep-ocean bed of the Pacific (from 4,000 to 6,000 m depth) for over one hundred years. A great deal of time and money has been spent on prospecting and developing methods of recovery, but no economically viable operation has yet emerged. Nodules are generally potato-shaped and porous, 3–6 cm in diameter, and composed, on average, of 20% manganese, 0.75% nickel, 0.5% copper, and 0.25% cobalt (Muller 1993). Polymetallic crusts are a more recent discovery. They are found in slightly shallower water, encrusting hard volcanic rocks on the slopes of seamounts and atolls, at depths of 1,000–1,500 m, but little is known about them

Although polymetallic nodules cover much of the Pacific Ocean floor, they are more highly concentrated in some areas than others, and the Cook Islands government in particular is paying attention to the future possibility of exploiting this resource. Muller (1993) notes, however, that the average prospecting coverage for nodules is on the order of one sample per 4,000 sq km, even in the better-known areas, and it is thus difficult to prove the resource.

Polymetallic massive sulphides are another deep–ocean-bed nonliving potential resource, containing some precious metals, although they still have the status of a scientific curiosity (Muller 1993). These sulphide deposits occur in "black smoker" environments in volcanically active areas (such as the Lau Basin between Fiji and Tonga, and the Manus Basin north of Papua New Guinea).

So far, the only economically viable hydrocarbon (oil) resources to be found in the Pacific Islands region are in Papua New Guinea, despite considerable exploration carried out in Fiji, Tonga, the Solomon Islands, and Vanuatu.

In summary, not a great amount of marine nonliving resources is currently taken out of the Pacific Ocean. Of far more significance, in a negative economic sense, are the large amounts of terrestrial nonliving resources that find their way into the Pacific Ocean, in the form of eroded soil, agricultural chemicals, and urban pollutants.

Appendix 30.1. **Subsistence Fisheries Methods in the Pacific Islands Region**

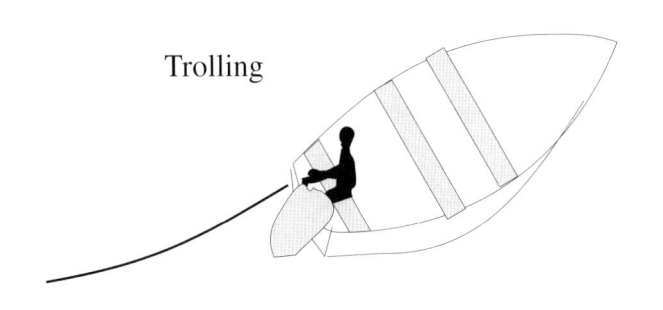

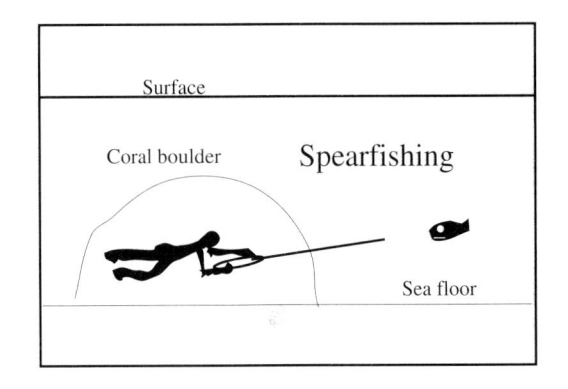

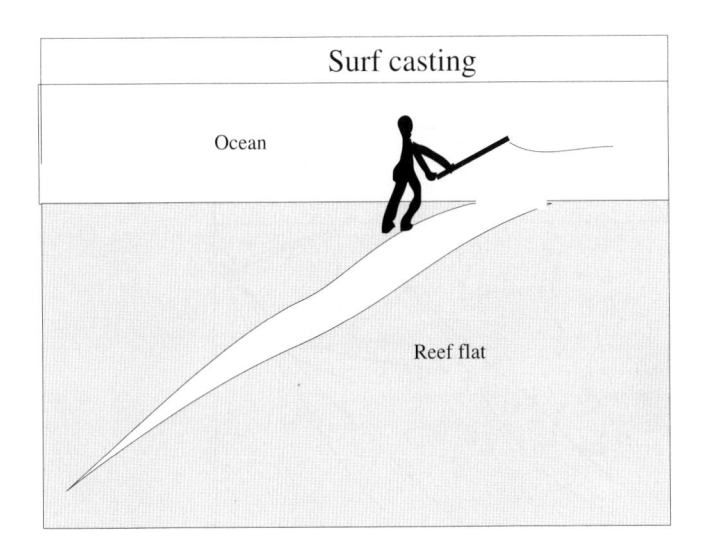

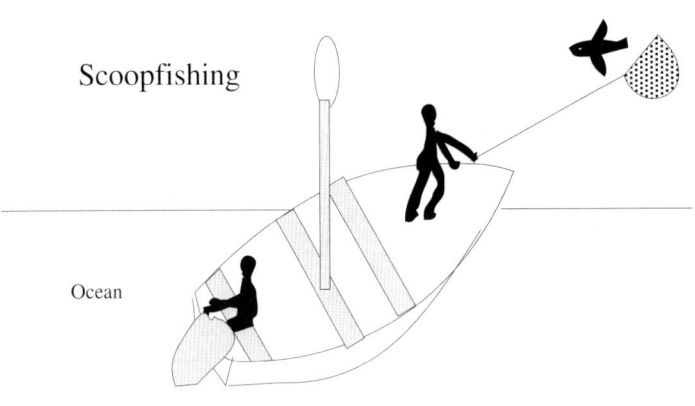

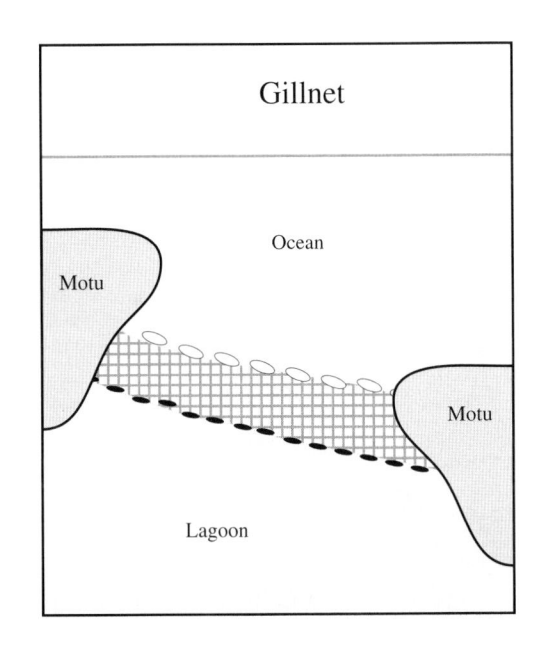

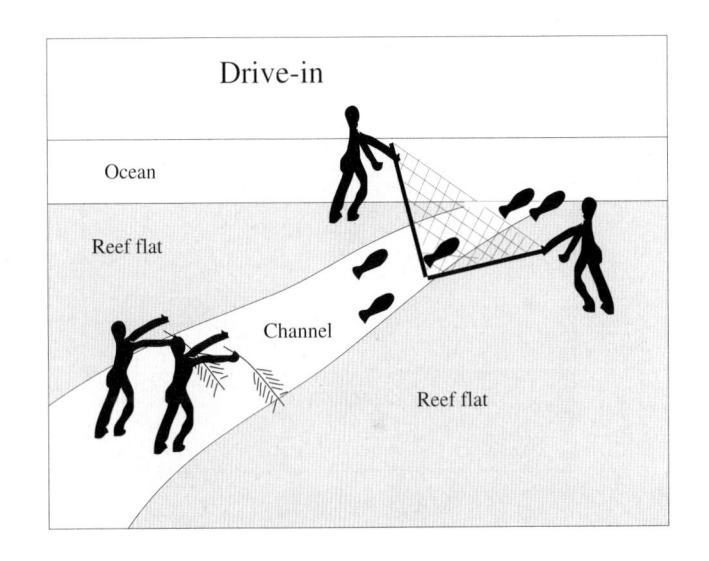

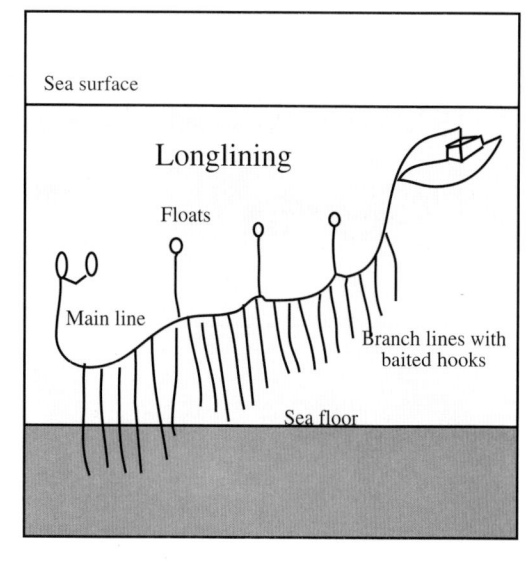

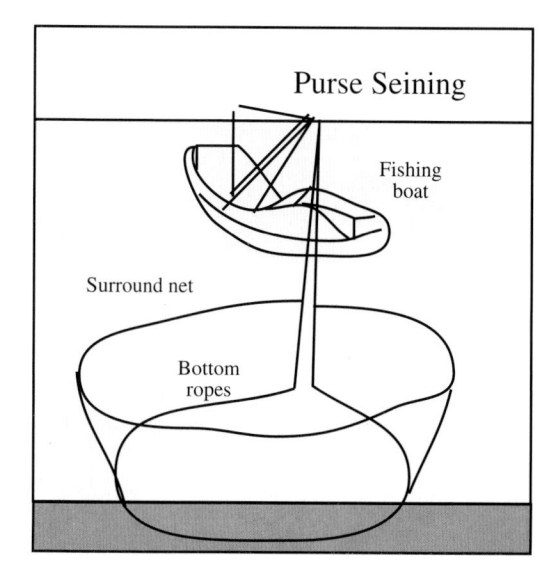

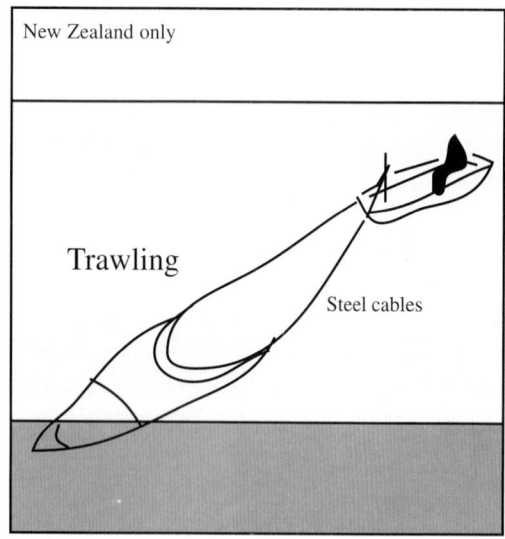

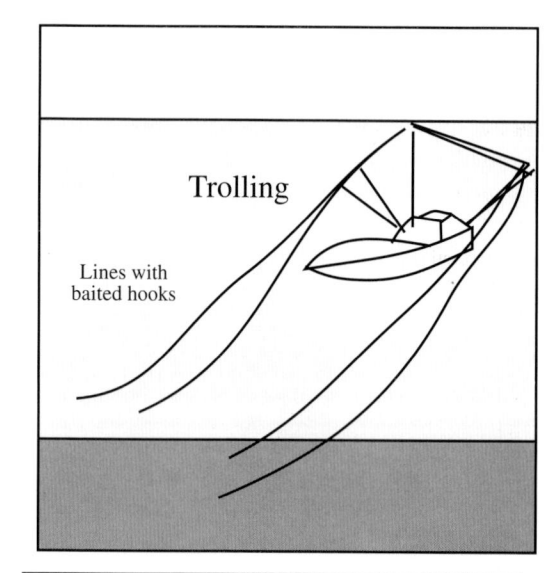

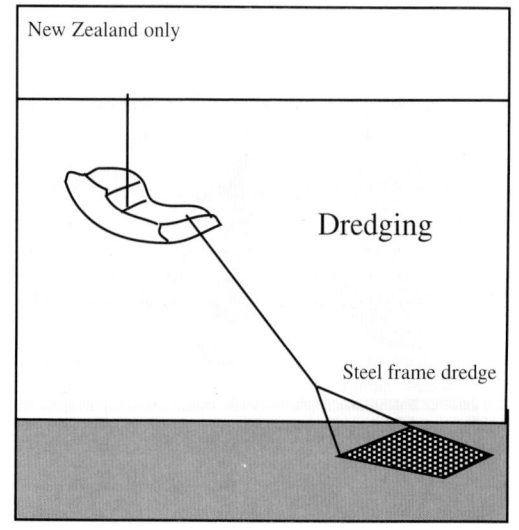

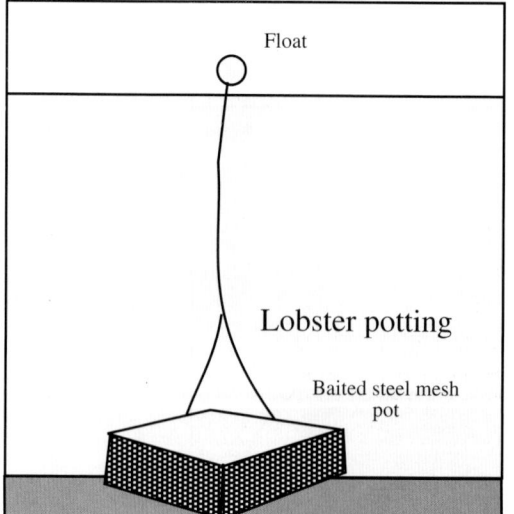

Appendix 30.2  Commercial Fisheries Methods in the Pacific Islands Region (after NZSIC 1998)

# Bibliography

Adams, T. J. H. 1998. Coastal fisheries and marine development issues for small islands. In *A roadmap for the future for fisheries and conservation*, ed. M. J. Williams, 40–50. ICLARM Conference Proceedings 56.

Adams T. J. H., and P. J. Dalzell. In press. Artisanal fishing. In *Proceedings of a workshop on biodiversity issues in the Pacific Islands coastal zone*, ed. L. J. Eldredge and J. Maragos. Honolulu: East-West Center.

Adams, T. J. H., P. J. Dalzell, and R. Farman. 1997. Status of Pacific Island coral reef fisheries. *Proceedings of the 8th International Coral Reef Symposium*.

Belhadjali, K. 1995. Tuvalu country statement. In Manuscript collection of country statements and background papers. SPC/FFA Workshop on the management of South Pacific inshore fisheries, ed. P. J. Dalzell and T. J. H. Adams. ICFMaP Technical Document 11, 55–63. Noumea: South Pacific Commission.

Caddy, J. F., and J. Majkowski. 1996. Tuna and trees: a reflection on a long-term perspective for tuna fishing around floating logs. *Fisheries Research* 25:369–376.

Coyne, T., J. Badcock, and R. Taylor. 1984. *The effect of urbanization and Western diet on the health of Pacific Island populations*. Technical Paper #186. Noumea: South Pacific Commission.

Dalzell, P. J., T. J. H. Adams, and N. V. C. Polunin. 1996. Coastal fisheries in the Pacific Islands. *Oceanography and Marine Biology: An Annual Review* 34:395–531.

Dalzell, P. J., and T. J. H. Adams. 1997. Sustainability and management of reef fisheries in the Pacific Islands. *Proceedings of the 8th International Coral Reef Symposium*, vol. II, 2027-2032.

Food and Agriculture Organization (FAO). 1993. Fish consumption based on food balance sheets. http://www.fao.org/fi%2A/statist/statistf.htm

Food and Agriculture Organization (FAO). 1997. Review of the state of the world fishery resources: marine fisheries. FAO Fisheries Circular No. 920. Rome: United Nations Food and Agriculture Organisation, and http://www.fao.org/waicent/faoinfo/fishery/publ/circular/c920/c920-1.htm

Fiji Fisheries Division. 1978–1994. *Fisheries division annual report* (series). Suva, Fiji: Ministry of Primary Industries/Ministry of Agriculture Fisheries and Forests.

Foale, S. 1997. Ownership and management of traditional trochus fisheries at West Nggela, Solomon Islands. *Proceedings of the 2nd World Fisheries Congress*, 266–272.

Forum Fisheries Agency (FFA). 1996. Forum Fisheries Agency report to the 9th SPC Standing Committee on Tuna and Billfish. Noumea: South Pacific Commission.

Herr, R. ed. 1990. *The Forum Fisheries Agency: achievements, challenges and prospects*. Suva: Institute of Pacific Studies of the University of the South Pacific.

Johannes R. E. 1980. Words of the lagoon: fishing and marine lore in the Palau district of Micronesia. Berkeley and Los Angeles: University of California Press.

Johannes, R. E. 1998. The case for data-less marine resource management: examples from tropical nearshore fisheries. *Trends in Ecology and Evolution* 13:243–246.

Kimball, L. In press. The possibilities of international law for sustainable use of marine and coastal biodiversity. *Proceedings of the IUCN World Conservation Congress Marine and Coastal Workshop, 18–19 October 1996*. Geneva: IUCN.

Lehodey, P., M. Bertignac, J. Hampton, A. Lewis, and J. Picaut. 1997. El Niño Southern Oscillation and tuna in the western Pacific. *Nature* 389:715.

Leis, J. M. 1993. Larval fish assemblages near Indo-Pacific coral reefs. *Bulletin of Marine Science* 53:362–92.

Muller, P. 1993. An overview of living and nonliving marine resources. In *Marine Resources and Development*, ed. G. R. South and G. Rao, 1–34. Suva: University of the South Pacific Library.

New Zealand Seafood Industry (NZSIC) Council and the The New Zealand Fishing Industry Board. 1998. About the New Zealand seafood industry. http://www.seafood.co.nz.

O'Regan, T. 1997. Maori fishing rights and the Quota Management System. In *Developing and sustaining world fisheries resources*, ed. D. A. Hancock, D. C. Smith, A. Grant, and J. P. Beumer, 325–328. Australia: CSIRO.

Petelo, A., S. Matoto, and R. Gillett. 1995. The case for community-based fisheries management in Tonga. *APC/FFA Workshop on the Management of South Pacific Inshore Fisheries*, vol. II, 487–493.

Polunin. N. V. C., and C. M. Roberts, eds. 1996. *Coral reef fisheries*. London: Chapman and Hall.

Pomeroy, R. S., and M. J. Williams. 1994. *Fisheries co-management and small-scale fisheries: a policy brief*. ICLARM Contribution No. 1128. Manila: International Center For Living Aquatic Resources Management.

Rawlinson, N. J. F., D. A. Milton, S. J. M. Blaber, A. Sesewa, and S. P. Sharma. 1995. *A survey of the subsistence and artisanal fisheries in rural areas of Viti Levu, Fiji*. ACIAR Monograph No. 135. Suva: Fiji Fisheries Division, and Canberra, Australia: CSIRO Division of Fisheries.

Rothschild, B. J. 1996. How bountiful are ocean fisheries? *Consequences* 2(1). Saginaw Valley State University http://www.gcrio.org/consequences/winter96

Ruddle, K. 1996. Geography and human ecology of reef fisheries. In *Coral reef fisheries*, ed. N. V. C. Polunin and C. M. Roberts, 137–160. London: Chapman and Hall.

Sale. P. F., ed. 1991. *The ecology of fishes on coral reefs*. San Diego: Academic Press. [Not cited in the text, but a key review of coral reef fish ecological science]

Sherwood, A., and R. Howorth. 1996. *Coasts of Pacific islands*. South Pacific Geosciences Commission Miscellaneous Reports Series No. 222.

Smith S.V. 1978. Coral-reef area and the contributions of reef to processes and resources of the world's oceans. *Nature* 273:225–226

South Pacific Commission (SPC). 1995. *SPC tuna fishery yearbook 1994*. Noumea: South Pacific Commission. http://www.spc.org.nc/ocean-fish/Docs/index.htm#yb

South Pacific Commission (SPC). 1996. *Status of tuna stocks in the western and central Pacific Ocean*. Working Paper 3 presented at the SPC 9th Standing Committee on Tuna and Billfish. Noumea: South Pacific Commission.

World Bank. 1995. *Pacific Island economies: building a resilient economic base for the twenty-first century*. Country Dept III - East Asia and Pacific Region. Washington DC: World Bank Report No. 13803-EAP.

Wright, A., and L. Hill, eds. 1993. *Nearshore marine resources of the South Pacific: information for fisheries development and management*. Suva, Fiji: Institute for Pacific Studies, Honiara, Solomon Islands: Forum Fisheries Agency, Canada: International Center for Ocean Development. [Not cited, but a key review of South Pacific island fishery target resources]

# Chapter 31

# Mining

*Glenn Banks and Frank McShane*

## Introduction

In this chapter we address the exploitation of minerals and petroleum hydrocarbons in the Pacific Islands. The discussion focuses on mining because in terms of investment, economic contribution, areal extent, and social and environmental change it has had far greater impact than oil and gas production. Additionally, we restrict our discussion of mining in New Zealand to contrasts with other areas.

### Digging Deeper: Mining as a Development Dilemma?

Pacific Island states and territories have often found a rich minerals endowment to be a mixed blessing. Papua New Guinea has been disrupted by a separatist uprising associated with the Panguna copper mine on Bougainville (May and Spriggs 1990) and international attention on the disposal of mine wastes (Rosenbaum 1993). Fiji has been troubled by poor labor relations at its Emperor gold mine, dissatisfaction with the amount of revenue from the mine that has gone to government (Emberson-Bain 1994a), and landowner tensions and concern over proposals for future large-scale copper mining (McShane 1993). Nauru has witnessed a protracted battle in the international courts over compensation for environmental damage caused by phosphate mining (Weeramentry 1992). In New Caledonia, mines have been a target for Kanak separatist resistance (Howard 1988), while New Zealand has seen a historically prolonged legal battle by Maori for the recognition of their land and resource rights in the Hauraki gold mining area and on the Tainui tribal lands in the North Island coast coal mining areas (Mahutu 1992). These problems among others warrant a critical appraisal of the mining industry's role in development.

Early inquiries into mining in the region focused on the macroeconomic characteristics of mining development and analysis of the political economy of mining, raising questions about resource ownership and management and in particular the role of the state in minerals development (Henningham and May 1992). The 1990s have seen a growth in much-needed analysis of local-scale social and economic dynamics and an increased emphasis on the environmental practices of mining companies and the issue of sustainability (see Denoon et al. 1995).

The following sections offer some perspectives on these issues. First, there is a summary of the major mineral deposits and a brief review of the history of mining in the region. A discussion of the macroeconomic implications of mining is followed by consideration of the politics of resource ownership and the effects of mining on society and the environment.

Finally, we consider the future of mining: the relevance of corporate responsibility, stewardship, community participation, and sustainable development. We hope that what surfaces clearly is the dilemma created by mining, which is often actively encouraged by host countries, but which may bring many unanticipated conflicts.

### Where Are the Resources?

The islands in the southwest Pacific with rich minerals endowments are part of the Melanesian island arc that marks the meeting of the Indo-Australian and the Pacific tectonic plates. The geology of arc terrains is known to favor minerals formation; accordingly, many of the high volcanic islands are sources of base and precious metals, particularly gold, silver, and copper. The locations of current mine production and exploration are shown on the map (Figure 31.1).

Papua New Guinea has substantial deposits of gold, silver, and copper, which are produced from several "world class" mines (Table 31.1). The Ok Tedi mine for example produced 206,000 tons of copper, 15 tons of gold, and 30 tons of silver in

**TABLE 31.1**

**Comparative Mineral Production Statistics for Selected Countries**

| | 1992 | 1993 | 1994 |
|---|---|---|---|
| **Copper Metal Content** | (000 t) | | |
| Papua New Guinea (Ok Tedi) | 193.4 | 203.9 | 206.4 |
| Australia | 331.5 | 410.7 | 353.4 |
| USA | 1778.8 | 1827.9 | 1808.3 |
| World | 9320.0 | 9490.0 | 9550.0 |
| **Gold Metal Content** | (tons) | | |
| Papua New Guinea | 68.32 | 58.72 | 57.74 |
| New Zealand | 10.53 | 11.16 | 10.12 |
| Fiji (Emperor) | 3.70 | 3.80 | 3.00 |
| South Africa | 609.32 | 615.56 | 571.47 |
| Australia | 233.85 | 236.75 | 249.80 |
| World | 2250.00 | 2235.00 | 2260.00 |
| **Nickel Metal Content** | (000 t) | | |
| New Caledonia | 99.6 | 98.1 | 73.6 |
| Canada | 188.2 | 188.1 | 150.1 |
| Australia | 55.4 | 65.8 | 75.7 |
| World | 900.0 | 550.0 | 509.0 |
| **Coal** | (000 t) | | |
| New Zealand | 2979.7 | 3090.8 | 3033.2 |

Source: Adapted from Roskills Information Services 1995 and Geography Resources Centre 1996.

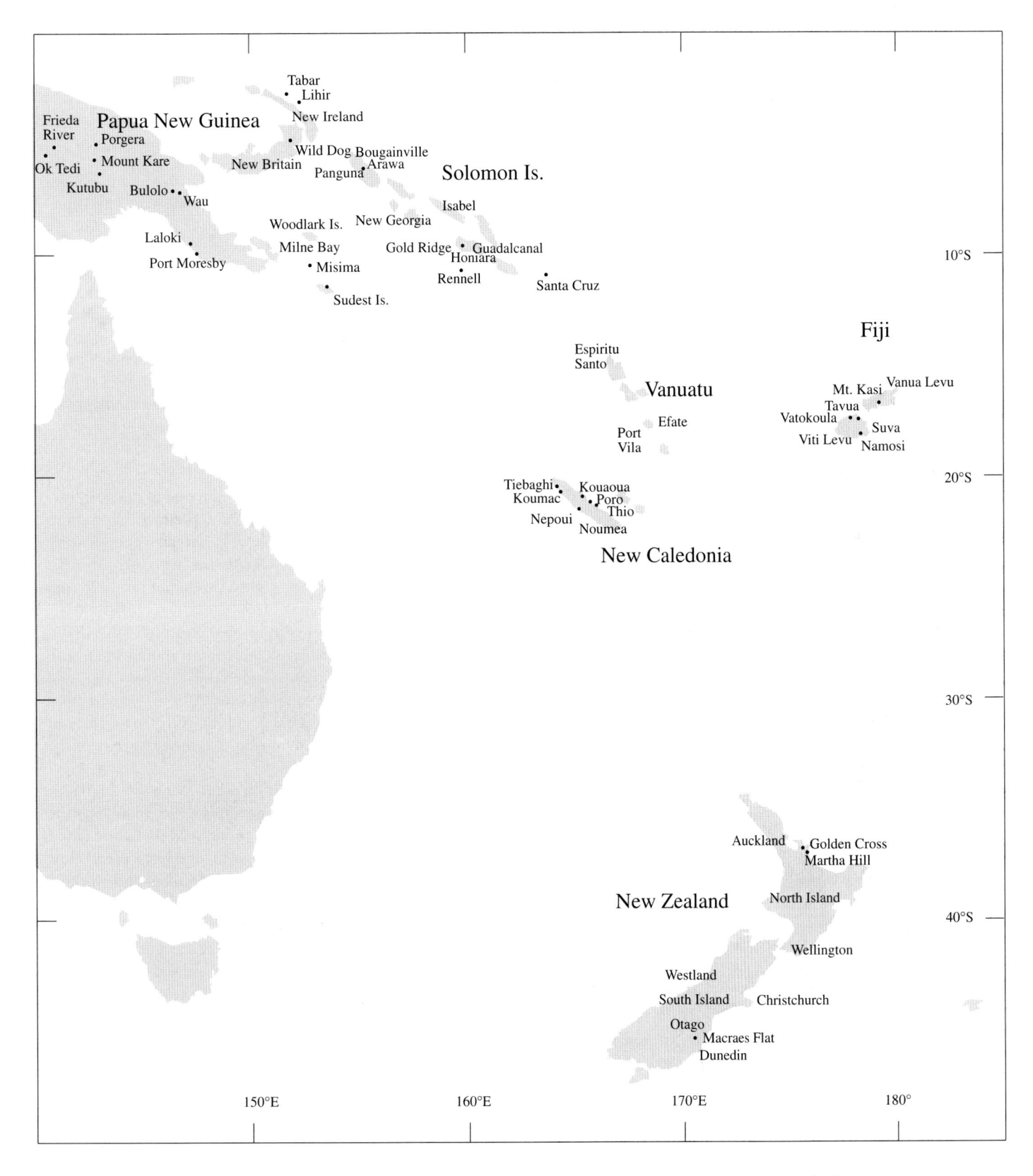

*Figure 31.1.* The location of the major mineral and oil deposits in the southwest Pacific Islands (after Mining Journal 1991).

1994 (Kennedy 1995:104). Porgera is among the highest gold producers in the world, exceeded only by some of the South African giants such as Vaal Reefs (which produces 70 tons of gold).

Production was begun at the Lihir Island gold project in New Britain Province in 1997. The resource is regarded as one of the largest gold deposits in the world, with a projected life of thirty-seven years and an estimated construction cost of US$750 million. New mining leases have been granted for much smaller projects at Tolukuma near Port Moresby and the Wapolu mine in Milne Bay Province. Advanced exploration is continuing at several other projects (Kennedy 1995:105). Oil is produced from the Kutubu Field, while natural gas is produced from the Hides Field. There are plans to develop a gas pipeline from both onshore and offshore gas deposits in Papua New Guinea to supply Queensland.

There are currently three large gold producers in New Zealand: Macraes Flat in Central Otago, and Martha Hill and Golden Cross on the Coromandel Peninsula. These three mines were responsible for 9 of the 12 tons of gold produced in 1995. Alluvial mining is significant in New Zealand, with over 2 tons of alluvial gold produced in 1995, primarily from the west coast of the South Island. Coal mining for export and domestic consumption is a significant industry in New Zealand, with $NZ161 million worth of coal mined in 1994, a third of which was exported. The largest production value from mining in 1995 came from the extraction of 16 million tons of sand and rock for roading, worth $311 million (Geography Resources Centre 1996).

Fiji has produced gold from the Emperor mine at Vatukoula for over sixty years. In 1994 it produced 4 tons of gold and 1.5 tons of silver, and mining is assured for several years (Flint and Nagata 1995). In October 1994 the Fijian government issued the first mining lease since 1968 for a small gold mine at Mount Kasi, which will operate for at least four years (Baker 1995). At the end of 1994 there were twenty-four active prospecting licenses; the largest of these is for the Namosi copper and gold prospect, which has a measured resource of 930 metric tons of low-grade copper and gold (Placer Pacific 1992).

New Caledonia is the world's largest producer of ferronickel (Baker 1995:107). Société Métallurgique le Nickel (SLN) has mines at Nepoui-Kopeto, Kouaoua, Thio, and Étoile du Nord. Canadian-based Inco is developing a mine at Pomalaa East. Inco also owns 55% of a large chromite mine at Tiebaghi. Solomon Islands has one gold mine on Guadalcanal; alluvial deposits are worked at Chovohio. The Gold Ridge area of Guadalcanal is currently being evaluated by an Australian mining company (Baker 1995). Low-grade nickel deposits are reported from other islands (Government of Solomon Islands 1993).

Of the remaining minerals islands, Vanuatu had nine tenements under exploration as of early 1995, and gold deposits are being evaluated by Australian companies on Espiritu Santo and Efate. Nauru produced 640,000 tons of phosphate during 1994. Nauru's deposits are nearing the end of their economic viability, and mining will cease within the next decade. The offshore areas around Papua New Guinea, Vanuatu, Fiji, and Tonga are thought to have some potential as hydrocarbon reservoirs, but they have failed to produce any major finds to date, perhaps because exploration has been limited.

## History of Mineral Extraction in the Pacific

### Prehistory

Quarries in the Highlands of Papua New Guinea have produced stone used for axes for over 5,000 years. The Lapita culture, which spread throughout the Pacific from New Guinea to Samoa over 2,000 years ago, utilized both stone adzes and clay for the distinctive pottery after which the culture was named (Spriggs 1995). Before the introduction of steel by Europeans in the eighteenth and nineteenth centuries, all axes and cutting implements used in the Pacific had blades of stone. Mineral oil from natural seeps was also of symbolic value throughout the Highlands of New Guinea (Ballard 1994). Interisland and interregional trade in axe blades and pottery was commonplace throughout the precontact Pacific.

### Early European Contact to World War II

The lure of gold and other metals was one of the main reasons Europeans ventured into the Pacific. The first European to sight the island of New Guinea was the sixteenth-century Portuguese explorer Alvaro de Soavedrao, who sighted what was probably the north coast of New Guinea in 1528 and named it Isla del Oro (Island of Gold).

Mining in the region began in New Zealand in the 1840s, although the first large-scale rush did not occur until 1861, with a find in Central Otago in the South Island. Between 1866 and 1872 annual gold production was over 20 tons, derived from goldfields through Central Otago and the West Coast. Most of this gold came out through Dunedin, and the prosperity of the cities was built on these rushes.

After a false alarm north of Port Moresby in 1878, Australian miners looking for new prospects following the decline in the Australian goldfields found gold on Sudest Island in Milne Bay in 1888. Over the next ten years prospectors moved through the islands of Milne Bay, finding and working gold on Misima and Woodlark islands. From there the prospectors moved on to the mainland of New Guinea and worked a series of gold fields. Contacts between miners and local people varied markedly: "Local communities evaded [the miners], worked for them, traded with them, fought them, and slept with them" (Nelson 1976:266).

The early stage of exploration in Papua New Guinea ended with the phenomenally rich Edie Creek find of 1926, in the Wau-Bulolo Valley. This find led to the development of what was at the time one of the largest alluvial dredging operations in the world. Every part of the dredges, and every other requirement of the operation—from fuel to food for the staff—was flown in, in what was, until the 1960s, the world's largest airlift operation (Healey 1967).

Gold and copper were mined in New Caledonia in the 1870s, but it was the nickel and chromite mining by European interests from 1880 onward that established the wealth of the colony. By 1920 nickel and chromite made up 47% of the colony's exports, and between 1900 and 1912 New Caledonia produced 25% of the world's supply of chromite (Howard 1988:86). Because both chromite and nickel are used in industrial processes, global economic trends and fluctuating demand for nickel have dramatically affected the economy of New Caledonia.

After 60 years of prospecting, payable gold was discovered in Fiji in 1929, and a series of rapid developments saw it become the territory's second most valuable commodity in the period immediately before World War II. Over 2,000 men were employed, and by 1941 the industry contributed around 10% of the government's revenue through taxes. The 1934 find of gold at Tavua led to the development of three mines, the most significant of which was the Emperor gold mine on Viti Levu (Emberson-Bain 1994a).

Nauru and a number of other small islands in Polynesia were recognized as a source of phosphate around the turn of the century, expanding on earlier guano mining in these islands. Extraction began on Nauru in 1906, following an agreement between the German administrators of the island and an English company, Pacific Phosphate Company (Howard 1988).

The Pacific Islands, then, had a history connected with mineral production that went back to the earliest days of European intrusion into the area. Fiji, Nauru, and New Caledonia all currently have operating mines that were established by European interests prior to World War II.

### Independence and the Colonial Legacy

Mining made a limited contribution to the Pacific in the immediate postwar era. Annual gold production in New Zealand fell to less than 1 ton per year between 1960 and 1980 (Douch and Holden 1994). Although production recovered in New Caledonia and Nauru, and Fiji continued to be a small gold producer (though dogged by poor labor conditions and relations at its mines), the discovery of massive copper and gold deposits on Bougainville in Papua New Guinea in the early 1960s reshaped the role of the Pacific in the world's mineral industry. The Bougainville Copper mine, with a majority shareholding held by CRA of Australia, came into production in 1972 after negotiating an agreement with the Australian Administration in 1968 and in its first year of operation posted the highest profit recorded by a company on the Sydney stock exchange.

In 1974, with independence imminent, leading Papua New Guinea politicians sought and gained a renegotiation of the original Bougainville agreement. Despite fears that Papua New Guinea might seek to nationalize the industry following trends established in Africa and Latin America, this renegotiation instead saw the mine's three-year tax holiday scrapped and a greater share of the value of the resource going to the national government. The renegotiated Bougainville agreement became a model for many developing countries, as it related the government's share of resource rents to mine profitability rather than a high fixed royalty on production. The outcome of this fiscal regime is that lower taxes are levied on marginal projects while Additional Profits Tax (APT), or "windfall" tax, can claim up to 75% of profits above a predetermined rate of return for the mining company. The Papua New Guinea government has also taken a minority shareholding in all the major mines.

Following protracted negotiations, development of Ok Tedi (Figure 31.2) began in 1982, with production starting in 1984 (Jackson 1982). A wave of exploration from the late 1960s found a large number of mineral deposits in Papua New Guinea, and it is these that provide the basis for the current industry in the country and the renewed exploration interest throughout the region.

*Figure 31.2.* Ok Tedi mine, Papua New Guinea (PNG) (photo OTMC).

## Issues in Mineral Extraction

### Mining and the Economy

Table 31.2 uses several common indicators to show the contribution of minerals production to the economies of some Pacific Island countries.

It is important that, in the case of both Fiji and Papua New Guinea, mining is a significant contributor to export earnings but generally contributes much less to GDP. Two outstanding examples, not included in the table, are New Caledonia, where nickel contributed 20% to GDP and 80% to export earnings in 1994 (Baker 1995), and Nauru, where phosphate accounts for virtually all of the island's economic production. While a large minerals endowment is therefore a desirable national resource, in economic terms it poses several management challenges.

In New Zealand, mining is a relatively limited component of the formal economy and is tightly integrated into the country's economic structure, in sharp contrast to mining in the rest of the Pacific. The bulk of the coal mined (73%) is used in manufacturing within New Zealand, particularly in steel making. Likewise, the sand and gravel mined is used internally for maintenance of the roading network. As a result, much of the discussion below does not apply to New Zealand.

Papua New Guinea provides an example of the dilemmas that may stem from strong growth in the minerals sector. In the mid-1980s the government encouraged commercial exploitation of minerals and oil with attractive investment incentives. When a new government took office in 1992, increased minerals revenues were used to introduce tax cuts, and government

### TABLE 31.2

**Mining's Contribution to Some Pacific Island Economies**

| FIJI | 1989 | 1990 | 1991 | 1992 | 1993 | 1994 |
|---|---|---|---|---|---|---|
| Contribution to GDP (%)* | 0.2 | 0.2 | 0.1 | 0.2 | 0.2 | 0.2 |
| Contribution to export earnings (%)* | 13.8 | 12.5 | 8.4 | 10.9 | 11.4 | 11.4 |
| Persons employed** | 1465 | 1402 | - | 1418 | 1890 | - |
| **PAPUA NEW GUINEA** | | | | | | |
| Mining contributions to GDP (%)** | 11.6 | 14.7 | 17.0 | 22.3 | 28.9 | - |
| Contribution to exports earnings (%)+ | 61 | 67 | 72 | 74 | 70 | 67 |
| **NEW ZEALAND** | | | | | | |
| Mining contributions to GDP (%)++ | 1.0 | 1.2 | 1.4 | 1.5 | 1.4 | - |
| Contribution to export earnings (%)++ | - | 3.0 | - | - | - | 2.3 |

Sources: *Reserve Bank of Fiji 1994; **UN 1994; + Bank of Papua New Guinea 1995; ++ New Zealand Yearbook 1996.

spending rose, which increased the budget deficit. With the fiscal deficit at 8% of GDP and domestic public debt at 30% of GDP, the government, facing insolvency, devalued the kina in 1994. Devaluation led to a capital flight and loss of confidence in the economy. At present, exports are declining due to reduced minerals production, while imports are rising to supply the development of new mines that will not generate revenue until 1999, contributing further to the fiscal imbalance (World Bank 1995:424).

Economic management of the minerals sector raises several questions for Pacific Island states and territories. First, how can the maximum share of profits be obtained from mining by local governments without dissuading the foreign corporate investment that the industry requires? Second, what can be done to stabilize minerals revenues that vary with commodity prices on the world market and changes in both the rate of mining and the grade of ore? Third, what alternatives remain when minerals are exhausted? All the policy decisions that arise from these questions are made under conditions of high risk and uncertainty (see Nankani 1980, Daniel 1992, Auty 1993, Auty 1995).

Management of the mining sector is complicated by the tendency of mines to act as "enclaves" in isolation from the local economy (Emerson 1982). Foreign mining corporations are generally obliged to source both specialized technology and skilled labor overseas as these do not exist "in-country." The increase in foreign exchange that accompanies increased exports of minerals may lead to rises in the real exchange rate and a relative decline in the competitiveness of the nonminerals sectors, a situation described as "Dutch Disease" after the economic effects of the North Sea oil boom on the Dutch economy (Auty 1995).

A profitable minerals sector can lead to demands for increased wages, which, in the absence of strong wage restraint policies, bring higher salaries, particularly for those in mining. Politically powerful local elites also place increased pressures on government to satisfy growing consumer demands by increasing foreign imports, creating a trade imbalance and a squeeze on local industry. As consumption increases, wage restraint becomes more difficult, particularly with the entry of highly paid expatriate mine workers. The public sector also grows as new jobs are created, because new abilities to monitor and evaluate the mining industry are required (Auty 1993).

The net effect of mining enclaves is to create a dual economy in which the minerals sector enjoys preferential fiscal arrangements while manufacturing, agricultural, and service sectors decline. The reorientation of the economy toward the minerals sector can create a dependency on minerals exports, characterized by initially rapid growth and spending as the minerals revenues are absorbed and economic collapse when minerals revenues fall (through decreased production or declining commodity prices). The underperformance of developing country economies based on minerals as opposed to those with no mineral endowment has been such a common feature that the term "resource curse" has been applied to the phenomenon (Gelb 1988, Auty 1993, 1995).

Several mechanisms are available to the government for control of minerals projects. First, while the mining codes lay down the statutory conditions for mining practice, these are in reality a starting point for the negotiation of individual project agreements. The minerals agreement reflects the spirit of the mining code, but must also reflect differences in ore bodies, the economic objectives of the government, and changing conditions of national and international trade, among other things. One of the most far-reaching changes to minerals agreements has been the incorporation of renegotiation clauses, which allow contract review after specific periods of time so that new mining and trade conditions can be taken into account.

### The Politics of Resource Ownership

In most parts of the Pacific, prior to the arrival of Europeans, the notion that anyone other than the landowner could possess the rights to resources on or under that land was a foreign one. Ownership of these resources, like other natural resources, was communal and, subject to certain rules, all members of the clan had access to these resources (see Crocombe, this volume).

The arrival of European powers and prospectors introduced new mineral ownership regimes, which vested the ownership of precious mineral resources with the Crown or the state. These new regimes were based on the mineral laws that applied in the home country of the colonial power (in Papua New Guinea's case on the Queensland mining ordinance).

This fundamental difference in notions of rights to resources, and the enforcement by the colonial powers and postcolonial governments of their version, has been, and continues to be, implicated in all the major mineral resource conflict issues in the Pacific. The establishment of the Bougainville mine in the late 1960s saw continued conflicts between the administration and local communities over rights to mineral resources and access to land (Bedford and Mamak 1977). Since independence, there has been a gradual shift in many parts of the Pacific toward local participation in and control over mineral developments. To an extent, this represents the acknowledgment by the governments that the legal regimes relating to minerals do not reflect the realities of ownership in the Pacific context. Development of the Porgera mine (Figure 31.3) in 1989 saw a significant change in this trend when the Papua New Guinea government sat down with the Porgera landowners, the provincial government, and the mine developers to discuss the project.

*Figure 31.3. Porgera mine, PNG (photo GB).*

The outcome of this process was a much greater proportion of the mine's benefits going to the local community, in the form of royalties, equity, and government infrastructure and services. Since then, this trend has intensified. Recent policy changes in Papua New Guinea will see all the royalties from new large mines go to local communities, along with a free 5% shareholding in the development and their integral involvement in development negotiations. Another direction is signaled by developments in North Province of New Caledonia, where locals in 1990 purchased an ailing nickel mine through their new provincial investment company. After five years the mine had increased production ten-fold and accounted for more than half of New Caledonia's nickel output. Profits have been reinvested in new capital and a range of diversifications—agriculture, aquaculture, and a hotel (Keith-Reid 1996:46). Increasingly, these forms of local control amount to a de facto sovereignty over resources, one that is subverting legal categories and definitions and leading to outcomes more in line with traditional notions of resource ownership.

Such developments also reshape the relationship between communities and governments. In Papua New Guinea the legitimacy of the national government is questioned in many rural areas that have seen a decline in health and education services over the last twenty years. As a result, when they are involved in negotiations over a mine development, communities are both eager to see an improvement in these services and reluctant to rely on the rhetoric of government. Recent mine developments have therefore seen communities enter into "contracts" with the government and the mining company for the delivery of health and other services, and while not infallible, these contracts have resulted in improved infrastructure and services for these areas.

Finally, in parts of the Pacific where specific groups have an identity distinct from the broader national culture (as do the Kanaks of New Caledonia, the Bougainvilleans within Papua New Guinea, and the New Zealand Maori), these groups are able to use disputes over resource sovereignty as a focal point for their claims to greater self-determination. In these situations, questions of resource ownership become entangled with the discourses of nationalism and international geopolitics (Howitt et al. 1996:1). In New Zealand, resource ownership questions are entangled with Maori claims for land (Barclay-Kerr 1991). Mineral resource developments in the Pacific have become intensely political for communities. On the one hand, rights to the wealth under their land, which most still believe they hold, are abruptly taken from them by the minerals laws of the country. On the other, they are able to use the mineral development as a strong bargaining chip in securing access to better infrastructure, services, and material wealth. The outcomes of these processes for local communities are not always, however, what they anticipate.

## Social, Cultural and Economic Impacts: Local-Scale Effects

Mining clearly brings changes to traditional economies, demographic structures, polities, and social organization that have far-reaching implications for the cultural integrity of local groups in the locality of a mine (Filer 1990, Connell and Howitt 1991, Davis 1995). For many traditional Pacific societies, land is inalienable, communal, and of great spiritual and cultural importance. Land lies at the heart of the social, cultural, and economic structure; its loss may mean reduced areas for subsistence gardening and a shift from self-sufficiency to dependence on imported foods and a monied economy; economic ruin, particularly for those who work the land under traditional agreements, but are not part of landowning clans eligible for compensation; rural-to-urban migration for those who cannot find alternatives to subsistence agriculture locally; and the breakdown of traditional family structures centered on sharing land and working on it together (Connell and Howitt 1991, Emberson-Bain 1994b).

The most traumatic circumstance of land loss has been expropriation under colonial rule, as happened in Banaba, Bougainville, New Caledonia, and New Zealand. Equally, compensation and royalty payments for land occupation and damage have brought their own dilemmas (Bedford and Mamak 1977, Filer 1990, Gerritsen and MacIntyre 1991, Connell 1992, Banks 1996). Internecine rivalry may lead to community conflict as local elites compete to increase their wealth and power through control of compensation monies and lucrative business spin-offs from a mine. Clan leaders who fail to accumulate and disburse the new forms of wealth may lose respect, power, and influence.

Where mining has come to remote rural areas, the locus of social activity becomes the "mining town" (Color Plate 31A, Figures 31.4-5). Initially, the town comprises housing compounds, local shops, a health center, and perhaps a school. Invariably these settlements attract a migrant population of hopeful people, both from surrounding villages and farther afield looking for access to benefits from the project. The growth of such settlements is hard to avoid even when mine workers are segregated from the surrounding community. Piecemeal dwellings spring up around the core; often poorly serviced, they become centers for prostitution, alcoholism, petty crime, and violence (Hyndman 1994; Emberson-Bain 1994b). Health problems including malnutrition among children may surface. Cross-cultural tension is often high.

*Figure 31.4.* New hospital, Porgera, PNG (photo GB).

*Figure 31.5.* A relocation house, Porgera, PNG (photo GB).

The greatest impact often falls on women. Absentee men working at the mine may mean increased workloads for women denied access to salaried work at the project. Women who do find work at the mine may be eligible only for low-paid work considered unsuitable for men (Emberson-Bain 1994b). Communal activity is replaced with individual rent-seeking activity and the competition for benefits. In the process, women lose the labor and emotional support of the extended family. Alcohol may consume a large part of the family income, and violence toward women is common. Teenage pregnancy and rape are other common symptoms of women's marginalization (Pollock 1996). Few of the other benefits, such as business loans, have been available to women, because men control most avenues of commerce. Lack of access to capital may also impact on educational opportunities.

In discussing the local-scale impacts of mining, three points are worthy of note. First, to balance the picture slightly, these impacts have been recognized by developers, and attempts are made to address them in various ways. The "boomtown" phenomena are ameliorated by "fly-in, fly-out" policies that avoid the establishment of a town at the mine site; community liaison officers are appointed to address community concerns; funds are established for community development; employment preference is often given to local community members (Color Plate 31B). Second, reification of the "traditional village" is misplaced. Traditional societies do not all exist in an absence of social dilemma, political maneuvering, economic inequality, or the marginalization of women. The metamorphoses of traditional structures were not invented by the mining industry; they are part and parcel of village life.

Third, as Emberson-Bain (1994b) points out, community opposition to mining and its impact takes different paths where the mine is the raison d'etre for a settlement in previously uninhabited rural areas and where settlement existed prior to mining. At Vatukoula in Fiji, for example, the focus of attention has not been compensation for land access, but wage ceilings; the hierarchical employment structure, which favors expatriates; appalling living conditions; and the mine's fiscal agreements with the government, which benefit expatriate investors at the expense of local workers (Emberson-Bain 1994a).

Power (1995) states that the Kutubu Oil Project in Papua New Guinea has managed to circumvent many of the traditional problems of conflict and social impact by encouraging landowners to organize themselves so that 1) their lands are successfully registered, 2) they have sound advice for dealing with the corporation, and 3) there are equitable mechanisms for distributing benefits and resolving disputes. Corporations and governments have also sought to channel sustainable benefits, not just cash, to the local level through the use of support grants, business programs, infrastructural development programs, and community infrastructure grants, among others (Stephens 1995). More recently, there has been an increase in the involvement of women in mining projects (Bonnell 1995)(Color Plate 31B). Yet the expertise of mining corporations and their commitment to the "soft skills" has been questioned.

Burton (1995) maintains that despite the rhetoric aimed at addressing social impacts, what materializes is often a piecemeal effort at addressing immediate problems, with little coordinated long-term planning. Disputes at all the Papua New Guinea resource sites during 1995 and 1996 demonstrate that there is at least some stress still in the system.

## Environmental Aspects

A large-scale mine such as the Panguna mine on Bougainville, the Ok Tedi mine, or the proposed Namosi mine on Fiji processes 100,000 tons of ore per day. Of this amount only the 1%–2% copper is extracted, and the rest must be disposed of, along with the similar quantities of waste rock that are shifted to allow access to the ore. Both the waste from the processed ore (known as tailings) and the waste rock must be disposed of, requiring land, river, or ocean dumping sites (Figure 31.6). While large-scale copper and gold deposits rely primarily on mechanical processes to recover ore, gold mining in the region has often utilized chemical processes (involving mercury or cyanide) in the gold recovery process (Hughes and Sullivan 1992).

Pacific Island environments are particularly sensitive to these forms of disruption, although balancing them are a range of factors inherent within these tropical systems that work to reduce these impacts. These include the dynamic nature of the physical systems (with high rainfall, steep relief, and high natural erosion rates—the Ok Tedi catchment, for example experienced a massive landslide in 1989 that added more sediment to the river system over a short period than the mine delivered over several years) and the rapid recovery of many of the environments after disturbance.

The large-scale open-pit mines bring a range of environmental effects. The most obvious and significant impacts are in the immediate mine area. Land is permanently disturbed and lost for open-pit mines (Color Plate 31D). On Bougainville a mountain became a pit over 200 m deep; similar processes are under way at Ok Tedi, Porgera, Freeport, and in New Caledonia. On Nauru almost a century of phosphate mining has consumed two-thirds of the area of the island, turning it into a useless wasteland (Howard 1988, Dupon 1989, Weeramentry 1992). In addition, land is required for the supporting infrastructure—processing mill, workshops, offices, accommodation, township, etc.

Land is also required for waste dumps, some of which are dispersed by natural erosion into river systems. Rock or tailings disposal into river systems can cause flooding and inundation in downstream areas—the Ok Tedi waste covered 100 km$^2$ of riverbank garden and rain forest in the lower Ok Tedi area, 100 km downstream (Burton 1997:39). This damage can in turn generate problems of equity, as these downstream communities rarely receive the same level of attention or compensation as communities located adjacent to the mine operation.

Despite the presence of various heavy metals in most tailings, the most significant impact on the ecology of the affected river systems appears to be physical, related to the higher sediment loads. For example, prior to the mine, the Ok Tedi River carried an average of 30 million tons of sediment annually. The mine trebled this and added 40% to the sediment load carried by the Fly River, into which the Ok Tedi flowed. This rendered the Ok Tedi River biologically dead and affected the biology of the middle Fly River (Rosenbaum 1993). Similar effects have been recorded in New Caledonia (Dupon 1986; Winslow 1993). Ocean disposal of tailings such as occurs at Misima and Lihir in Papua New Guinea appears to be a more environmentally acceptable solution, particularly where the sediment is delivered at depth to steep ocean slopes. The longer-term impacts of this method of disposal in tropical environments is, however, unclear at this stage.

New Zealand has a long history of environmentally destructive mining. Large parts of the Central Otago provide a stark reminder of the long-term damage that can be done by large dredging operations. At the other extreme, the tailings dam at the Golden Cross mine on the Coromandel Peninsula began to move during 1996 and threatened to spill tailings into the downstream environment. This illustrates that in the wrong circumstances not even the best environmental techniques can provide complete protection from the effects of mining.

The environmental protection legislation within most Pacific islands is poor (Hughes and Sullivan 1989). Papua New Guinea's environmental legislation is one of the most comprehensive, yet the capacity of the government to regulate the environmental performance of the mines is limited. The Department of Environment and Conservation, for example, is underresourced and finds it hard to attract and retain quality graduates. Critics also point out that the government in Papua New Guinea has a significant financial stake in the mines through equity holding and taxation receipts, and this conflicts with their role as environmental regulators (Rosenbaum 1993, Hughes and Sullivan 1989).

In this regard, the focus on the planning and regulation of the industry in New Zealand during the 1990s may provide something of a model for other Pacific nations and territories. The remodeling of the planning legislation with the Resource Management Act brought a focus on sustainable management of natural resources and required that developers assess any actual and potential effects on the environment, including the social, economic, and biophysical consequences of the development. Such assessments must also be made by government authorities in relation to policy development.

Increasingly, the transnational mining companies face pressure to provide enhanced environmental management and performance. International court action against BHP by Papua New Guinean landowners at Ok Tedi highlights the growing

*Figure 31.6.* Tailings from Freeport mine, Irian Jaya, Indonesia (photo CB).

sensitivity of communities to environmental issues. Recent court action against Britain, Australia, and New Zealand by Nauru for environmental damage caused during the colonial period shows that polluters may be held responsible for environmental damage that occurred at some time in the past. Equally, the pressure for better environmental practice is increasing on foreign mining companies in their home countries; Australian NGOs have argued for example that a mandatory Code of Conduct should be imposed on Australian miners when operating overseas (Forum: code of conduct: help or hindrance? 1996).

The industry response to this pressure is to promote the notion of "environmental best practice," whereby the most effective waste disposal techniques available are employed, contingent on the culture, priorities, and geography of the country the companies are operating in (Nelson 1996). Critics and cynics believe this simply leaves an excuse for the companies involved to continue to work to lower environmental standards in the developing countries of the Pacific.

## The Future

There is no doubt that mining will be an integral part of the future development path of the region. Exploration is intensifying in Papua New Guinea, Vanuatu, and Solomon Islands. New Caledonia's nickel reserves are anticipated to last well into the later part of next century. The Papua New Guinea oil and gas industry is set for further expansion, with the Pandora field in the Gulf of Papua approved to provide gas to northern Australia. Promising oil seeps have also been located in Bligh Sound, offshore Fiji, and Tonga. The economic potential of the Pacific's mineral-rich deep ocean nodules may be realized in the next century.

Leon Davis, the chief executive of Con Rio-Tinto Australia (CRA), said recently that part of the challenge of mining in the twenty-first century will be "re-capturing the public mandate that we in the mining industry have partially lost" (Davis 1995). This mandate (which one suspects may not have existed among local groups in much of the nonindustrialized world) eroded when it became apparent that sections of the host societies derived few benefits from the mining projects on their doorsteps. Additionally, environmental strategies, particularly for waste disposal, have been questionable, and public confidence in mining has been diluted considerably.

Following the Rio Summit of 1992, the rhetoric of "sustainable" development has been incorporated into the policy statements of most governments and mining companies mindful of their public image. Yet what does sustainability mean in the context of an industry based on extracting minerals at the lowest cost and over a finite time span? Robert Solow (1993:163) states that the term is "an injunction to preserve productive capacity for the indefinite future, [while] society as a whole replaces used up resources with something else." A framework for achieving this goal has been suggested by Auty (1995), who maintains that sustainable minerals-driven development requires pragmatic orthodox economic policies, substitution of alternative wealth-generating assets when the ore is depleted, and incentives to curb environmental degradation. Some of the mechanisms for achieving these objectives are dealt with in brief below.

### Trust Funds

One attempt to address the question of intergenerational equity has been the establishment of a Minerals Resource Stabilization Fund (MRSF), as set up by the government of Papua New Guinea under statute in 1974. Mining revenues are held as part of government reserves by the Bank of Papua New Guinea, and, when required, certain amounts are converted to kina for use in the domestic economy. Unfortunately, in the past, large proportions of the fund have been used by the government for current expenditures, severely reducing the fund's effectiveness (Fairburn 1994). Overseas Trust Funds have fared little better (Fairburn 1994). Nauru's fund has been the subject of several scandals, with huge losses incurred through bad investment, poor advice, and corruption (North 1995).

### Stewardship and Environmental Best Practice

Environmental policy can be exercised through the minerals agreements and the mining code to promote environmental "best practice"; other statutes include pollution abatement and control laws, waste reduction and disposal laws, conservation and recycling laws, and clauses that insist on restoration of disturbed environments or the use of green technologies (for a full discussion see Dias and Begg 1994). Equally, governments may opt for command and control regulations that control emission standards (the amount of pollution discharged), quality standards (the quality of the receiving environment), and process and product standards. Alternatively, economic incentives such as reduced taxes for reduced pollution output can be applied. Liability, environmental litigation, and financial penalties can also be used as economic disincentives to pollution.

### Community Participation

Satisfying community aspirations for involvement in decision making has been the slowest of the "soft skills" to evolve in the mining industry. Labonne (1995:113) remarks that community involvement has to be enforceable through contracts that guarantee information access, economic sustainability, the prioritizing of sustainable technologies, and a range of implementation mechanisms including inspection agreements; external audits of health, safety, and environmental conditions; and enforcement provisions for arbitration, dispute resolution, and penalties.

Several UN charters recognize both the community "right to know," "the power to act," and the "principle of subsidiarity" enunciated in the Agenda 21 of the 1992 Rio Summit, which states that decisions must be made as close as possible to the level they impact (Labonne 1995). Many of these principles have since been included in the Berlin Guidelines on Mining and the Environment (United Nations 1992). Further, agencies such as the UN Fund for Natural Resources Exploration, which provides financial assistance for mining exploration, now give loans contingent on environmental accountability.

Pacific Island governments are in the early stages of both formulating policy and incorporating the concepts into practice. Governments may be unable to implement policy due to a lack of resources. In this case, mining corporations may be asked to assume many of the responsibilities of government in determining "best practice" in environmental performance and monitoring. "Good neighbor" policies involving communication with and accountability to local communities have been the industry's response to its critics' call for sustainability in mining. The result has been increased involvement by mining companies in community affairs; funding of business development cooperatives; setting up of trust funds; and encouragement of community organization.

Mining corporations have to balance the often conflicting objectives of governments and communities for development; the demands of shareholders for low-cost, high-profit minerals production; and the demands of others for minimal environmental and social impact. Achieving the environmental and social standards demanded by stakeholders involves a reassessment of the paradigms that have governed the industry in the past, internalizing many social and environmental costs, which may in turn mean reduced profit. Grassroots awareness of the vulnerability of minerals projects to delays forced by community protest, the potency of international media attention, and the financial costs of ignoring these issues ($500 million in the case of Ok Tedi) have now focused stakeholder attentions on the local dimensions of minerals development. The challenge is to include communities in all stages of planning and development; the dilemma is how this objective can be achieved in a planning processes that is capital driven and rooted in formal Western-knowledge–based ideas of development, which may not be shared by Pacific Islanders.

# Bibliography

Auty, R. 1995. Achieving sustainable minerals driven development. Keynote Speech. In *Mining and mineral resource issues in Asia Pacific: prospects for the 21st century, proceedings, 1–3 November, 1995*, ed. D. Denoon, et al., 3–11. Canberra: Australian National University.

Auty, R. M. 1993. *Sustaining development in minerals economies: the resource curse thesis*. London: Routledge.

Baker, R. 1995. South Pacific Islands. In *Mining Annual Review* 107. London: Mining Journal Publications.

Ballard, C. 1994. The centre cannot hold: trade networks and sacred geography in the Papua New Guinea Highlands. *Archaeology in Oceania* 29:130–148.

Bank of Papua New Guinea. 1995. *Quarterly Economic Bulletin*. March. Port Moresby: Bank of Papua New Guinea.

Banks, G. 1996. Compensation for mining: benefit or time bomb? The Porgera Case. In *Resources, nations and indigenous peoples: case studies from Australasia, Melanesia and Southeast Asia*, ed. R. Howitt, J. Connell, and P. Hirsch, 223–235. Melbourne: Oxford University Press.

Barclay-Kerr, K. 1991. Conflict over Waikato Coal: Maori land rights. In *Mining and indigenous peoples in Australasia*, ed. J. Connell and R. Howitt, 183–219. Sydney: Sydney University Press.

Bedford, R., and A. Mamak. 1977. *Compensating for development: The Bougainville Case*. Christchurch: Bougainville Special Publication No. 2, Department of Geography, University of Canterbury.

Bonnell, S. 1995. Women and mining: from project victims to project beneficiaries. In *Mining and mineral resource issues in Asia Pacific: prospects for the 21st century. proceedings, 1–3 November, 1995*, ed. D. Denoon, et al., 162–166. Canberra: Australian National University.

Burton, J. 1995. What is best practice? social issues and the culture of the corporation in Papua New Guinea. In *Mining and mineral resource issues in Asia Pacific: prospects for the 21st century, proceedings, 1–3 November, 1995*, ed. D. Denoon, et al., 129–134. Canberra: Australian National University.

Burton, J. 1997. Terra nugax and the discovery paradigm. In *The Ok Tedi settlement: issues, outcomes and implications*, ed. G. Banks and C. Ballard, 27–55. Pacific Policy Paper 27. Canberra: National Centre for Development Studies, Australian National University.

Connell, J. 1991. Compensation and conflict: the Bougainville Copper mine, Papua New Guinea. In *Mining and indigenous peoples in Australasia*, ed. J. Connell and R. Howitt, 54–75. Sydney: Sydney University Press.

Connell, J., 1992. "Logic is a capitalist cover-up": compensation and crises in Bougainville, Papua New Guinea. In *Resources, development and politics in the Pacific Islands*, ed. S. Henningham and R. J. May, 30–54. Bathurst, Australia: Crawford House Press.

Connell, J. and R. Howitt. 1991. Mining, dispossession and development. In *Mining and indigenous peoples in Australasia*, ed. J. Connell and R. Howitt, 1–17. Sydney: Sydney University Press.

Daniel, P. 1992. Economic policy in minerals exporting countries: what have we learned? In *Mineral wealth and economic development*, ed. J. E. Tilton, 81–121. John M. Olin Distinguished Lectures in Mineral Economics. Washington, DC: Resources for the Future.

Davis, L. 1995. The new competencies in mining. Speech to the Australian Institute of Company Directors, Melbourne, 3 October.

Denoon, D., C. Ballard, G. Banks, and P. Hancock, eds. 1995. *Mining and mineral resource issues in Asia Pacific: prospects for the 21st century, proceedings, 1–3 November, 1995*. Canberra: Australian National University.

Dias, A. K., and M. Begg. 1994. Environmental policy for sustainable development of natural resources: mechanisms for implementation and enforcement. *Natural Resources Forum* 18(4):275–286.

Douch, C., and D. Holden. 1994. New Zealand goldmining: past, present and future trends. *New Zealand Mining*. April.

Dupon, J. F. 1986. *The effects of mining on the environments of high islands: a case study of nickel mining in New Caledonia*. Noumea: South Pacific Regional Environment Program, Environmental Case Studies No 1.

Dupon, J. F. 1989. *Pacific phosphate islands versus the mining industry: an unequal struggle*. Noumea: South Pacific Regional Environment Program, Environmental Case Studies, No. 4.

Emberson-Bain, A. 1994a. *Labor and gold in Fiji*. Cambridge: Cambridge University Press.

Emberson-Bain, A. 1994b. De-romancing the stones: gender, environment and mining in the Pacific. In *Sustainable development or malignant growth: perspectives of Pacific Island women*, ed. Atu Emberson-Bain, 91–110. Suva: Marama Publications.

Emberson-Bain, A. 1994c. Mining development in the Pacific: Are we sustaining the unsustainable? In *Feminist perspectives on sustainable development*, ed. W. Harcourt, 46–59. London: Zed Books.

Emerson, C. 1982. Mining enclaves and taxation. *World Development* 10(7):561–571.

Fairburn, T. 1994. *Minerals boom in Papua New Guinea: key management issues*. Sydney: Pacific Studies Monograph No. 12. Centre for Pacific Studies, University of New South Wales.

Filer, C. 1990. The Bougainville rebellion, the mining industry and the process of social disintegration in Papua New Guinea. *Canberra Anthropology* 13(1):1–39.

Flint, D. J., and I. Nagata. 1995. Fiji. In *Mining Annual Review*, 106. London: Mining Journal Publications.

Forum: code of conduct: help or hindrance? 1996. *Mining Monitor* 1(1):6–7.

Gelb, A., and Associates. 1988. *Oil windfalls: blessing or curse?* Washington, DC: World Bank Research Publication.

Geography Resources Centre. 1996. *New Zealand mining update no. 6*. Christchurch: Geography Resources Centre.

Gerritsen, R., and M. MacIntyre. 1991. Dilemmas of distribution: the Misima gold mine, Papua New Guinea. In *Mining and indigenous peoples in Australasia*, ed. J. Connell and R. Howitt, 34–53. Sydney: Sydney University Press.

Government of Solomon Islands. 1993. *Solomon Islands national environment management strategy, 1993*. Honiara: Government of Solomon Islands.

Grynberg, R., and J. Nouairi. 1988. *The environmental costs of development in Papua New Guinea: the case of Bougainville Copper*. Suva, Fiji: School of Social and Economic Development, University of the South Pacific.

Healy, A. M. 1967. *Bulolo: a history of the development of the Bulolo region, New Guinea*. Canberra and Port Moresby: New Guinea Research Unit.

Henningham, S., and R. J. May, eds. 1992. *Resources, development and politics in the Pacific Islands*. Bathurst, Australia: Crawford House Press.

Howard, M. 1988. *The impact of the international mining industry on native peoples*. Sydney: Transnational Corporations Research Project, University of Sydney.

Howitt, R., J. Connell, and P. Hirsh. 1996. Resources, nations and indigenous peoples. In *Resources, nations and indigenous peoples: case studies from Australasia, Melanesia and Southeast Asia*, ed. R. Howitt, J. Connell, and P. Hirsch, 1–30. Melbourne: Oxford University Press.

Hughes, P., and M. Sullivan. 1989. Environmental impact assessment in Papua New Guinea: lessons for the wider Pacific region. *Pacific Viewpoint* 30(1):34–55.

Hughes, P., and M. Sullivan. 1992. *The Environmental effects of mining and petroleum production in Papua New Guinea*. Port Moresby: University of Papua New Guinea.

Hyndman, D. 1994. *Ancestral rainforests and the mountains of gold: indigenous peoples and mining in Papua New Guinea.* Boulder: Westview Press.

Jackson, R. 1982. *Ok Tedi: the pot of gold.* Port Moresby: Word Publishing.

Jackson, R. 1993. *Cracked pot or copper-bottomed investment: the development of the Ok Tedi project, 1982–1991, a personal view.* Townsville: Melanesian Studies Centre, James Cook University.

Keith-Reid, R. 1996. The mine that's getting the Kanaks into business. *Islands Business* 22(4):46.

Kennedy, D. M. 1995. Papua New Guinea. In *Mining Annual Review*, 105. London: Mining Journal Publications.

Labonne, B. 1996. Community and minerals resources: from adversarial confrontation to social development through participation, accountability and sustainability. In *Mining and mineral resource issues in Asia Pacific: prospects for the 21st century. proceedings, 1–3 November, 1995*, ed. D. Denoon, et al., 111–116. Canberra: Australian National University.

Mahuta, R. T., 1992. Maaori land and resource issues in New Zealand. In *Resources, development and politics in the Pacific Islands*, ed. S. Henningham and R. J. May, 195–205. Bathurst, Australia: Crawford House Press.

May, R. J., and M. Spriggs, eds. 1990. *The Bougainville crisis.* Bathurst, Australia: Crawford House Press.

McShane, F. 1994. The proposed Namosi Copper Mine (Fiji) in the context of regional mining practice. In *The Margin fades: geographical itineraries in a world of islands*, ed. E. Waddell and P. Nunn, 167–188. Suva: Institute of Pacific Studies, University of the South Pacific.

Mining Journal. 1991. Melanesia showing major minerals deposits. 317(8152):442.

Mining Journal. 1995. *Mining: Annual Review.* London: Mining Journal Books.

Nankani, G. 1980. Developing problems of non-fuel mineral exporting countries. *Finance and Development* 17(1): 6–10.

Nelson, H. 1976. *Black, white and gold: goldmining in Papua New Guinea, 1878–1930.* Canberra: Australian National University.

Nelson, R. 1996. Establishing off-shore environmental performance criteria. In *Mining and mineral resource issues in Asia Pacific: prospects for the 21st century, proceedings, 1–3 November, 1995*, ed. D. Denoon, et al., 185–190. Canberra: Australian National University.

North, D. 1995. Nauru: both swindled and aiding swindlers. *Pacific Islands Monthly* 65 (11):18–20.

Placer Pacific Pty Ltd. 1992. *The current status of the Namosi Project.* Suva: Company Document.

Pollock, N. 1996. Impact of mining on Nauruan women. *Natural Resources Forum.* 20(2):123–134.

Power, T. 1995. Mining and petroleum development under customary land tenure: the Papua New Guinea experience. In *Mining and mineral resource issues in Asia Pacific: prospects for the 21st century, proceedings, 1–3 November, 1995*, ed. D. Denoon, et al., 135–143. Canberra: Australian National University.

Reserve Bank of Fiji. 1994. *Quarterly Review.* Suva: Government Publishers.

Rosenbaum, H. 1993. Ok Tedi: Undermining PNG's future? *Habitat Australia* 21(4): 39–44.

Roskills Information Services. 1995. *Roskills Metals Databook.* London: Roskills.

Solow, R. 1993. An almost practical step towards sustainability. *Resources Policy* 19(3):162–172.

Spriggs, M. 1995. The Lapita culture and Austronesian prehistory in Oceania. In *The Austronesians: historical and contemporary perspectives*, ed. P. Bellwood, J. Fox, and D. Tyron, 112–133. Canberra: Department of Anthropology, RSPAS, Australian National University.

Stephens, A. 1995. Social planning through business and infrastructural development. In *Mining and mineral resource issues in Asia Pacific: prospects for the 21st century, proceedings, 1–3 November, 1995*, ed. D. Denoon, et al., 122–128. Canberra: Australian National University.

United Nations. 1986. *Declaration on the right to development.* General Assembly Resolution 91/128, December 4.

United Nations. 1992. *Mining and the environment: the Berlin Guidelines.* London: Mining Journal Books.

United Nations. 1994. *Statistical yearbook for Asia and the Pacific.* Paris: United Nations Publications E/CN, Ser. A.

Weeramentry, C. 1992. *Nauru: environmental damage under international trusteeship.* Oxford: Oxford University Press.

Winslow, D. 1993. Mining and the environment in New Caledonia: The case of Thio. In *Asia's environmental crisis*, ed. M. Howard, 111–134. Boulder, Colorado: Westview Press.

World Bank. 1996. *Pacific Island economies: building a resilient economic base for the twenty-first century.* Washington, DC: World Bank Country Study, World Bank Publications.

World Bank. 1995. *Trends in developing economies.* Washington, DC: World Bank Publications.

# CHAPTER 32

# Tourism

*Michael Fagence*

## Introduction

International definitions of tourism include forms of travel and activity that extend beyond the hedonistic experience of pleasure seeking. Although there is travel and tourism activity in the Pacific region for the purpose of business and of visiting friends and relatives (VFR), the dominant travel in the Pacific region is for pleasure. Most travelers in the region are from the major Pacific Rim countries (the United States, Canada, Japan, Taiwan, and Australia), or from Europe, with the principal intent to experience the exotic settings of sun, sand, surf, coral reefs, and palm trees, and in some islands, rain forests, waterfalls, mountainous scenery, and volcanoes. In addition to these physical attributes, the region offers the romanticism and mystery of indigenous cultures and the opportunities to indulge in adventurous pursuits such as diving and educational activities probing the archeology, ecology, and history of the region. In sum, the opportunities for various types of pleasure-related activity in the region are "the stuff of which many dreams are made," capable of sustaining a diversity of tourism experiences.

Marketing and promotion strategies have tended to generalize the tourism product, to create almost a stereotype image of South Sea islands that is not reflective of the region's potential (Craig-Smith and Fagence 1994, Hall and Page 1996). Such generalization tends to deny the individuality of the various countries, their heritage and culture, and their unique physical features. New Zealand scarcely fits the tourism model of the South Sea Islands; despite its geographical location and its attractiveness for and performance in tourism, it is more similar to the Pacific Rim than to Pacific Basin countries.

This sameness of projected image, coupled with the concentration of visitor attention on the six "honey pots" in the region (Hawai'i, New Zealand, Guam, Saipan, Fiji, and Tahiti), has the potential for damaging sensitive environments, for distorting the individuality of the distinctive cultures, and for laying the region open to tourism development that is neither distinctive nor authentic. As the region moves unevenly toward a changed tourism profile—from the mass expectation of Tropicana Exotica to the special interests of cultural and ecotourism—new challenges are emerging. Before embarking upon a description and analysis of tourism activity in the Pacific region, it is appropriate to briefly consider some aspects of tourism that give cause for concern.

## Perspectives on Tourism

Tourism development in the Pacific Islands has often been advocated as a policy alternative to assist with economic growth and to accumulate foreign exchange earnings for programs of social, economic, and welfare development expected by the domestic population (Lea 1988). In some circumstances, tourism is advocated as a substitute or companion to previous dependency on subsistence agriculture, commercial agriculture for export, mineral extraction, and fishing. Finney and Watson (1976) refer to this phenomenon as "a new kind of sugar." The adoption of tourism as a support for national economies has been based on the expectation that most states and territories in the Pacific region have the basic ingredients or raw materials for tourism development—Tropicana Exotica. Yet even as some parts of the region were turning to commit themselves to strategies of tourism development (in the 1970s), the Organization for Economic Cooperation and Development (OECD) was cautioning these countries from relying principally on tourism for their economic salvation (Erbes 1973:4, cited in Mill and Morrison 1992:287).

The reason for advocating caution is that tourism is not inevitably good for a country or destination (Britton and Clarke 1987). The fine balance between positive and negative contributions of tourism has to be recognized. Many commentators, some from general viewpoints and others from particular perspectives, have drawn attention to crucial elements in the balance sheet. Mathieson and Wall (1982) have focused on the costs and benefits of tourism activity. Brookfield (1989) has referred to the unreal expectations the visitors from the developed world have of the Pacific. Lutz and Collins (1993) have expressed concern about the impact on the expectant visitor of photographic images and descriptions of the Pacific based on *National Geographic* and travel brochures, as well as the undifferentiated mythology generated by traveler expectations.

Incisive commentaries have been provided in the special editions of the *Cultural Survival Quarterly* (1990). In one commentary the argument referred to the likelihood of both culture and environment becoming commoditized such that they are marketed as "animals in a zoo." Rather less dramatic and more objective assessments have been documented in Smith (1977 and 1989) and, in part, in Smith and Eadington (1992). Douglas (1996) has reviewed some of the anthropological consequences of tourism development in the region. Socioeconomic and political issues have been examined in Brookfield and Ward (1988), Cole and Parry (1986), and Fairbairn et al. (1991). Community development issues have been examined by Wallace and others (1996). Stephen (1993), Helu-Thaman (1993), and Trask (1993) have commented critically and severely on the potential damage to island societies by tourism development. Quarterly commentaries on the current trends in economic and political issues in the region are published by the Economist Intelligence Unit (EIU 1996) and the Pacific Business Economic Council (PBEC 1996).

A balance sheet of the advantages and disadvantages of tourism development across the Pacific region would include both positive and negative contributions (see Table 32.1). Positive contributions of tourism development might include increased levels of business activity, job creation, increased export earnings, targets for off-shore investment, opportunities for development and construction industries, a rationale for infrastructure improvements (including road schemes, water supply, and waste disposal schemes), and selected regional development. Negative contributions of tourism development might include detrimental impact on sensitive environments (through, for example, reef damage and water pollution), irritation to host communities, the disneyfication of indigenous cultures and traditions, competition between projects for priority, congestion at peak destinations, demands on infrastructure services, inappropriate examples of behavior to local communities through the extravagance of visitors, the incorporation of the pathologies of developed countries (such as crime and prostitution), and changes to social structures.

Pacific Island societies do not have full control over their destinies, even in tourism development. The nature, scale, and outcomes of tourism development at destinations in the region will be subject to decisions taken and events occurring outside the region. For example, changes in air traffic routes, schedules, and cost structures, changes in the affluence levels at the points of origin of the visitors, the impacts of changes to world oil prices, the incidence of political struggles in and beyond the region, changes in the strategic significance of the region, and the progressive loosening of war veteran and colonial linkages will have an impact on the region's attractiveness. In addition, competition within the region for market share of visitors may limit the potential for individual countries. Some of the more experienced tourism destinations have begun to adopt niche strategies in ecotourism, adventure tourism, or cultural tourism. In this competitive commercial environment it is likely that the honey pots will retain market dominance in the region because of the strength of their tourism product, their profile as tourism destinations, and their developed infrastructure and organization.

In summary, not all tourism development is necessarily good. Moreover, despite the availability of many of the prerequisites for the Tropicana Exotica experience, not all destinations will become successful tourism destinations. Despite the attractiveness or allure of tourism development as a means of economic development, it is becoming recognized increasingly that there may be detrimental impacts on the environment, the social and cultural fabric and structure, and even the local economy. Thus, a low level of performance need not be detrimental; it might in fact be necessary to protect sensitive environments and cultures. As countries and territories move toward or away from a commitment to tourism development, it is to be hoped that the policy decision and direction are reactions to a well-considered and deliberate strategy.

## The Tourism Product

The visitor market has a particular expectation of the Pacific tourism product. This product is composed of four types of attractions (See Table 32.2).

This range of attractions has led to an exceptional diversity of tourism products, including national parks and forests, historic and cultural sites, conserved beach areas, integrated tourist

---

**TABLE 32.1    Positive and Negative Impacts of Tourism Development**

| Category | Positive | Negative |
|---|---|---|
| Economic | *income to local economy<br>* creation of employment, wealth<br>* improved scale, variety and quality of service levels<br>* additional source of income<br>* attraction for investment | * poor employment spectrum<br>* seasonal unemployment<br>* leakage of profits<br>* increased demand for infrastructure<br>* neglect of other economic opportunities |
| Social, Cultural | * mix of cultures (hosts and guests)<br>* culture revival<br>* rejuvenation of local crafts | * visitors exceed local residents<br>* conflict (hosts and guests)<br>* congestion (at destinations)<br>* visitor behavior<br>* commercialization of culture<br>* crime, prostitution<br>* changes to family structures |
| Environmental | * justification for infrastructure improvement schemes<br>* justification for management of natural areas<br>* renovation, rehabilitation of built environment<br>* finance raised for conservation | * overuse<br>* vandalism, souveniring<br>* threat to flora, fauna<br>* threat to sustainability of habitats, and fauna habits<br>* visual pollution |

### Table 32.2 — The Tourism Product

| | Examples |
|---|---|
| * Physical Attractions | * sun |
| | * (blue) sea, surf |
| | * lagoons, coral reefs |
| | * palm trees, forested slopes |
| | * volcanoes |
| | * myriad islands |
| * Wildlife Attractions | * fauna, including birds, butterflies, lizards, turtles |
| | * whales, sharks, dolphins |
| | * fish |
| * Cultural Attractions | * customs, ceremonies |
| | * art, performing arts and crafts |
| | * buildings (built environment) |
| | * heritage sites and settings |
| | * lifestyle, communities |
| | * Psychological And |
| • Physiological Attractions | * relaxation, comfort, security |
| | * adventure |
| | * learning |

visitation has occurred. The prognosis is that future growth may not achieve recent levels of performance.

The reasons for this different level of performance are not difficult to determine (Craig-Smith and Fagence 1994, ESCAP 1992). One of the ongoing problems for the countries and territories in the region is the degree of geographical dispersal. This problem has a number of dimensions. There are important difficulties of interisland connection and access, particularly for outer islands. Another problem is the image of the Pacific; for many potential visitors the subtleties of difference are not understood, and the region is considered to be almost homogenous. A third major difficulty lies in the development of infrastructure, both of public utilities and services (such as water supply, waste disposal, internal transport links), and of tourism attractions and products. Finally, the increasing discrimination and discernment of the international tourist results in the search for value for money or an unusual tourism experience, so that deficient destinations become abandoned or overlooked.

A definite hierarchy has emerged, with six "honey pots"—Hawai'i, New Zealand, Guam, Saipan (in the Commonwealth of the Northern Mariana Islands—CNMI), Fiji, and Tahiti (in French Polynesia)—dominating the levels of international visitation, accounting for approximately 91% of visitors into the region (Hawai'i accounts for 62.4% of the total level of visitation; see Table 32.3). Two of these destinations—Guam and

resorts, concentrations of entertainment venues, repeated ceremonies and events, and the revival of indigenous crafts and art forms. In summary, the Pacific region affords examples of most types and standards of tourism attractions, facilities, and amenities. However, the product range is in danger of being generalized, commoditized, and rendered almost indistinguishable as market forces come to dominate the tourism planning and development process with an almost indiscriminate repetition of apparently successful tourism products.

Most common is the conventional vacation experience enjoying the facilities and amenities of beach areas, along with the entertainments of cultural centers and museums, bird sanctuaries, animal parks, oceanariums, "wilderness drives," and so on. This is coupled with a hotel- or condominium-based lifestyle in districts of restaurants, night clubs, casinos, shopping malls—i.e. the recreational business district (RBD). Despite the intrinsic differences between the island countries and territories, the ubiquitous Polynesian resort village is becoming the standard. If this were to become general, the emerging interest in the peculiarities of locations would be negated. It would be the newly emerging destinations that would experience the greatest disadvantage from a lessening of interest in the region by international visitors because of the above generalizations.

## Visitor Patterns

Most global assessments of levels of tourism activity in the various regions of the world indicate that the Asia-Pacific region overall has achieved the greatest growth rate in recent years and that this region is expected to outperform other regions in the next decade (EIU 1990). For the Pacific Island countries, however, the recent performance has not been so dynamic, even though a general level of increase in international

### Table 32.3

**Estimated (000's) International Visitation to Pacific Island Countries and Territories 1991-1994**

Sources: ESCAP (forthcoming), country reports to ESCAP meeting (Port Vila, June 1995), DBEDT (Hawai'i), EIU international tourism report No. 2 (1995), TCSP annual report (1995, p.20)

| COUNTRY | 1991 | 1992 | 1993 | 1994 |
|---|---|---|---|---|
| Am. Samoa | 6.8 | 4.7 | 5.0 | 7.3 |
| CNMI | 424.5 | 488.3 | 536.3 | 583.6 |
| Cook Is. | 39.9 | 50.0 | 52.8 | 57.3 |
| FSM | 19.0 | 20.0 | 20.0 | 20.0 |
| Fiji | 259.4 | 278.5 | 287.5 | 318.9 |
| Fr. Polynesia | 120.9 | 123.6 | 147.8 | 166.1 |
| Guam | 737.0 | 877.0 | 784.0 | 1,087.0 |
| Hawai'i | 6,873.9 | 6,513.9 | 6,124.2 | 6,430.3 |
| Kiribati | 3.0 | 3.7 | 4.2 | 3.9 |
| Marshall Is. | 4.0 | 5.7 | 5.1 | 4.9 |
| Nauru | 1.0 | 1.0 | 1.0 | 1.0 |
| New Caledonia | 80.9 | 78.2 | 80.4 | 85.1 |
| New Zealand | 963.5 | 1,055.7 | 1,156.9 | 1,322.6 |
| Niue | 0.9 | 1.7 | 3.4 | 2.8 |
| Palau | 32.7 | 36.1 | 40.5 | 44.1 |
| PNG | 37.4 | 42.8 | 33.5 | 37.7 |
| Samoa | 35.0 | 37.5 | 48.2 | 50.2 |
| Solomon Is. | 11.1 | 12.4 | 11.6 | 11.9 |
| Tokelau | NA | NA | 0.1 | 0.1 |
| Tonga | 22.0 | 23.0 | 25.5 | 28.4 |
| Tuvalu | 0.9 | 0.9 | 0.9 | 1.2 |
| Vanuatu | 39.5 | 42.7 | 43.4 | 42.1 |
| Wallis | 0.1 | 0.1 | 0.1 | 0.1 |
| **TOTAL** | **9,713,400** | **9,697,500** | **9,412,400** | **10,306,600** |

Saipan—benefit from being geographically proximate to the tourism market of Japan and the emerging markets of Taiwan and Korea. Hawai'i has a long association with inbound Japanese tourism and visitors from the mainland United States, while Fiji continues to benefit from linkages with Australia, and Tahiti benefits from the mystique of the French Connection. New Zealand maintains its pattern of attraction to Australia, the United States, Japan, and the UK, with considerable growth emerging from Taiwan and Southeast Asia.

Each of the honey pots has increased its level of visitation by between 30% and 50% in recent years, with CNMI having a fourfold increase in the last decade. Some of the growth for these destinations has been due to their geographical proximity to large markets and to their favored position on international air routes; this is the case, particularly, for Hawai'i. Within the region some of the smaller destinations seek to find their own niche markets so as to exploit their unique selling points. In this connection, some of the small island countries (such as Samoa) are expressing the intention to concentrate their focus on some aspects of ecotourism or cultural tourism, while others (such as Palau) are turning their attention to adventure tourism, principally diving.

Critical events within the region and beyond the region tend to influence the international visitation levels dramatically. For example, internal political disturbances (such as in Fiji and in New Caledonia in the 1980s) tend to discourage visitors. Changes to international air routes and schedules may cause a redirection of visitors to different destinations in the region. In addition, the domestic economic circumstances of the major markets such as Japan, Australia, the United States, and others will influence the level of visitation from those sources. A further factor is competition within the region and around the periphery by emerging tourism destinations in Southeast Asia, East Asia, and Australia (PIDP 1990).

Generalized percentages of visitor growth do not present the "real picture" of international visitation. It is necessary to interpret the percentage gain against the base level of visitation, so that the increase in numbers can be interpreted against a background of real tourism activity. For example, while a growth of 1,000 visitors to American Samoa or the Marshall Islands may be locally significant, the same increase to, for example, Hawai'i, Saipan, Fiji, New Caledonia, or the Cook Islands would be welcome but hardly significant. Some locations may be approaching saturation level, unless environmental and cultural safeguards and protections can be established.

### Trends in Inbound Tourism

There has been a basic growth of visitation levels that approximates to 5% per year; however, this rate of growth has not been consistent in either geographical or temporal terms (see Table 32.3).

Few countries or territories in the region experienced a consistent and progressive change. One of the exceptions was the CNMI, where the total visitation level rose fourfold in the period 1984 to 1994 (from 131,823 to 583,557). Many countries experienced a "hiccup" in the growth rate; such countries included Fiji (with a slight decline in 1987), French Polynesia (with a decline extending through the period of the late 1980s that has been reversed only recently), Papua New Guinea (with a consistently uneven performance), Solomon Islands (which experienced a decline in the period 1988 to 1990), and Vanuatu (which experienced a severe decline in the late 1980s before achieving a significant and uninterrupted growth trend since 1990). The principal destination in the region, Hawai'i experienced continuous growth throughout the 1980s (to a peak of 6.9 million visitors in 1990), followed by three successive years of decline before the upward trend was renewed in 1994. In New Zealand, the growth pattern has been irregular, with growth rates in excess of 10% per annum during the early 1980s, followed by a period of very low growth, with the higher rates returning in the mid 1990s.

In contrast, Palau has recorded almost continuous growth in the 1990s, with visitation levels rising by more than 60% over the most recent five-year period. Similarly, Tonga, at a lower level of visitation, has recorded a steady increase in the levels of international visitation. For the smaller island destinations (such as Kiribati, Nauru, Niue, Tuvalu, and even the Marshall Islands), the levels of international visitation are consistently small.

**Figure 32.1.** Palau Museum (photo LEM).

In quantitative terms, there are six distinguishable groups. The honey pots constitute the first group, with visitation levels amounting to more than 91% of all visitors into the region; the principal destinations are Hawai'i (6.4 million), New Zealand, and Guam (each approximately 1 million). Saipan (600,000) is alone in a second group. Fiji (300,000) and French Polynesia (160,000) constitute the third group in the hierarchy. A fourth group may be distinguished by visitation levels in the range 40,000 to 80,000; this group includes the Cook Islands, New Caledonia, Palau, Papua New Guinea, Vanuatu, and Samoa. With visitation levels in the range from approximately 10,000 to 30,000 is a small fifth group including Solomon Islands and Tonga. The remaining countries and territories in the region do not yet achieve visitation levels of 10,000, and some seldom achieve levels of 1,000 (see Table 32.3).

This pattern is not divisible into Polynesia, Melanesia, and Micronesia, with members of each of the statistical groups present in each of these three regional groups. Among the conclusions that may be drawn are that a) there is a general attractiveness across the region, b) the preference of visitors is for a well-developed tourism destination, and c) the influence of the air transportation routes is strong.

## Visitor Origins

Not all countries in the region are rigorous with tourism data collection. However, a few generalizations are possible. The principal market sources for the destinations within the Pacific region include Japan, the United States, Canada, and Australia. For some destinations, the composition of the visitor markets is changing. Korea and Taiwan are emerging as significant sources for tourists in the westernmost destinations, while some destinations in the southwest are attracting visitors from neighboring Southeast Asian countries. Economic changes and fluctuations in the propensity to travel in source countries have affected the loyalty to some destinations. There are, however, some conspicuous loyalty attachments in such linkages (see Table 32.4)

The sources of visitors into the countries of the region for which the Tourism Council of the South Pacific (TCSP) has a watching brief are reported in Table 32.5 (see also Appendix 32.1). Data provided by TCSP members indicate there have been perceptible shifts in visitor markets. The U.S. market has been declining since the mid-1980s, although a base level seems to have been reached in the early 1990s. Europe is emerging as a significant market, with the market share achieving 24% in 1994. The principal destinations visited by Europeans were (in 1994) Tahiti, Fiji, and New Caledonia, which together hosted 78%. Japan is not yet a significant market for TCSP member countries. However, it is of vital significance to Micronesian entities closest to Japan, such as the CNMI, Guam, and Hawai'i (27.2% of all visitors in 1994). New patterns are emerging, with Japanese visitation to Fiji, New Caledonia, and Tahiti becoming prominent.

In aggregate, TCSP studies have shown that approximately 73% of international visitation to member states and territories is for recreation and pleasure, 10% for business, and 17% for visiting friends and relatives. This generalization includes a number

### Table 32.4

**Loyalty Linkages of Tourist Origins to Principal Destinations** (Source: TCSP and ESCAP)

| Visitor Origins | Principal Destinations |
|---|---|
| * USA | American Samoa, Hawai'i, Palau |
| * Australia | Fiji, New Caledonia, New Zealand, PNG, Solomon Islands, Vanuatu |
| * France and other European countries | French Polynesia (Tahiti), New Caledonia |
| * Japan | Hawai'i, New Caledonia, Saipan (CNMI), Guam, Palau |

**Note:** large VFR (returning residents) traffic Samoa, Tonga, American Samoa, Cook Islands

### Table 32.5

**Sources of Visitors to TCSP Member Countries (1994)**

| To | From | |
|---|---|---|
| TCSP Member Countries | * Australia | 20.9% |
| (For list of TCSP Member countries, see Appendix) | * USA | 14.8% |
| | * Japan | 11.1% |
| | * Other Pacific | 8.9% |
| | * France | 7.7% |
| | * Other Europe | 7.5% |
| | * United Kingdom | 4.3% |
| | * Germany | 4.1% |
| | * Canada | 2.5% |
| | * Others | 3.9% |

Note: New Zealand contributes 14.3% of all visitor movements within the region.

Source: TCSP, ESCAP

of significant variations, with, for example, conventional vacationing accounting for more than 80% in Saipan (actually 97%), Fiji, and the Cook Islands, but only 18% in Samoa and 12% in the Marshall Islands. In contrast, 43% of visitors to the Marshall Islands are recorded as there for business purposes, with Fiji, the Cook Islands, and Palau recording less than 10%. Visits to friends and relatives accounted for only 6% of visits to Fiji and 7% to Vanuatu, whereas to Tonga the record shows 27%, and for Samoa 56%. High levels of VFR visit levels are recorded also for American Samoa and the Cook Islands.

The duration of the visit to a tourism destination has significance for destination economies through commercial accommodation, attractions, services (including internal transport), retailing (including souvenirs), and food. Some of this tourist expenditure will have a direct effect, while other expenditures will filter through the local (and wider) economy indirectly.

Across the region there is a significant variation in the length of the visits. In recent years, the recorded length of an international visit in American Samoa has been 2 days; in the case of Fiji, the average has been around 9 days; in French Polynesia, length of stay has risen from 9.5 days in 1984 to 11 days in 1994. For Vanuatu, the average has been recorded as 9 days, but there are indications that it is falling back toward 7 days. For Hawai'i, westbound visitors (from the United States, Canada) have an average length of stay of 10.5 days, whereas eastbound (Asian and Pacific region visitors) have an average of 6.6 days. In the case of New Zealand, the average for all visitors has been around 19 days, with the long-haul visitors (from Europe) staying for three weeks or more and the short-haul visitors (from Australia, the United States, and Japan) staying approximately two weeks.

The degrees of variation of length of stay are the outcomes of a miscellany of factors including a) general tourism attractiveness, b) special attractiveness for particular interest tourist groups, c) availability of accommodation, services and attractions, d) convenience of air transport connections, and e) whether the destination is the final focus of the trip, a stop en route to another destination, or one stop in a package of a two-center vacation.

## Intraregional Travel

In addition to the conspicuous crossregional tourist movements and the penetration into the region from origin countries around the Rim, there are several distinctive movements within the Pacific region. These movements include stopover and transit travel, destination tourism, the return of expatriates to visit friends and relatives, the travel of officials from island governments and international agencies, the flow of island residents traveling to visit friends and relatives now living "overseas," and short-duration travel for the purposes of shopping and attending conventions and trade meetings, and indigenous people's gatherings.

In Micronesia, only Guam has any significant inbound tourism from elsewhere in the Pacific region. For New Caledonia it is recorded that one-fifth (16,700) of all visitors originated from within the Pacific region, with Vanuatu recording a little more than 30% (13,300) of its visitors from the region. New Caledonia and Fiji have significant cruise ship visitation levels. Hawai'i, New Zealand, and Fiji have significant traffic flows as a result of their regional (air) transport hubs. Fiji records about 10% of its visitors from the Pacific region, whereas less than 6% of visits made to Tahiti are generated from within the region.

Networks established during the colonial period remain important, as do a variety of subsequent networks. For example, New Zealand is a significant source of visitation to the Cook Islands (26.1%, or 14,900) and Samoa (22.7%, or 11,500). Much of this may reflect Polynesian residents of New Zealand and their relatives on vacation to their "home islands." Other networks include Pacific Islanders resident in Hawai'i on vacation with relatives in Guam, American Samoa, and other locations; and Tahitians visiting Hawai'i for both sightseeing and shopping.

*Figure 32.2.* Japanese couple at beach, across Tumon Bay, Guam (photo LEM).

An essential problem in assessing travel patterns within the region is the lack of adequate, consistent, and verifiable data; much of the information is anecdotal or "intelligent guess." The data on intra-regional tourist movements should be interpreted with caution, especially as the visitor numbers may not accurately reflect relative tourism attractiveness and may be derived from data sets that are incomplete (due to problems with existing systems of immigration and passport control).

## Economic Significance of Tourism

There is considerable unevenness in the economic significance of tourism (see e.g. EIU 1995, 1996, ESCAP 1986, Fairbairn 1985, Hawai'i 1996). Among the many reasons for this are differences in the scale of tourism activity; the nature, scope, and quality of the tourism attractions; the longevity and legacy of tourism enterprise; the ease of access to the islands; the range of accommodation in resorts and at major destinations and centers; the commitment of government and the private sector to tourism planning and development; the range and nature of tourism experiences available; the degree of promotion and marketing; the loyalty of the principal visitor markets; the attitudes of indigenous or host communities; and the complications of the land tenure systems.

Some Pacific Island groups are almost guaranteed an international visitor market because of their historical linkages or ease of access, while others have need for strategies to interest international visitors with distinct and novel attractions. Some seem to focus their strategy on meeting the experiential needs of the mass tourism market, while others focus on specialized markets of adventure tourism, ecotourism, and so on. The choice of focus will have an impact on the economic significance of tourism with respect to the number of visitors attracted, the expenditure patterns of the visitors, the level of investment in tourism facilities, and so on.

### Contribution of Tourism to the Economy

It is difficult to determine with much precision the contribution of tourism to the economy of Pacific Island states and territories, not least because of the discrepancies that occur in the published data of different organizations and agencies even within the same government. In particular there are differences in interpreting the contribution of tourism to GDP, to foreign exchange receipts, and to employment.

In some cases, the significance of tourism increases as the industry has matured and new projects have been completed. The regional aggregate performance suggests tourism is 5% of GDP across the region. However, the regional pattern has significant variations; for example, in French Polynesia (Tahiti), New Zealand, Solomon Islands, and Tonga, the contribution of tourism to GDP is approximately 5%; for Fiji, Vanuatu, and Samoa, tourism contributes almost 16%; for Hawai'i the contribution seems to fluctuate around 25%, while for the Cook Islands, the contribution is 37%.

Even this data hides the real contribution of tourism activity. For example, where there is a bigger gross export base, or a specialized export base, the real contribution of tourism is hidden. In the cases of Fiji, Tonga and Tuvalu, tourism contributes more than 50% of the foreign exchange earnings; in the cases of the Cook Islands, French Polynesia, Vanuatu, and Samoa, the earnings from tourism now exceed (or can be expected to in the next five years) the aggregate earnings of all other export sectors. For the small island economies (such as those of Nauru, Niue, and Palau) it may be that tourism receipts will come to dominate the respective economies as the industry expands and other mainstays (such as phosphate export from Nauru) decline.

As with the other economic indicators, data on employment in tourism are inconsistent and incomplete. There are three categories of tourism-related employment—direct, indirect, and induced. The ratio of direct/indirect/induced employment is dependent upon the experience (longevity) of tourism activity in the country, the relative development level of the industry (plant, capital investment, labor skills, attractions), the nature of the tourism activities (mass tourism, budget tourism, special interest tourism), the approach to employment (and entrepreneurship) in tourism by indigenous communities, and the dependence of tourism on support industries (for example, local agricultural production, handicrafts, entertainment). Examples of countries with differentiated tourism employment categories include Fiji (24% of the total labor force, with 6% direct, 6% indirect, and 12% induced) and French Polynesia (14% of the total labor force, with 8.5% direct, 5.5% indirect). Tourism-related employment in Hawai'i has remained relatively stable (at 24–25%) throughout the recent decade.

Some Pacific islands have derived useful performance indicators. For example, Fiji has estimated that approximately US$10,400 of tourism expenditure creates 1 full-time equivalent job. An expenditure of US$1 million creates 96 jobs in tourism, 51 jobs in mining, 52 jobs in agriculture and related industries, and 80 jobs in manufacturing. These potential ratios may be used as the basis for tentative projection elsewhere in the region. Papua New Guinea has noted the special contribution to indirect employment of the agricultural production consumed at resorts, the purchase of handicrafts, and the cultural performances. Tonga expects direct and related tourism employment to increase if the country achieves higher grades of accommodation and attractions.

New Zealand has a different profile. Both inbound and outbound tourism have increased in recent years such that the direct impact of tourism expenditure by international visitors should be cross-referenced to that of the outbound travelers; the net benefit of international tourism to New Zealand may be almost neutral. This profile of visitor movements is more like that of Australia than of the other Pacific Islands.

The general prognosis for future tourism activity in the region is considered by most countries and territories to be positive. Most destinations can anticipate the level of international visitation to increase, new visitor markets (such as Korea, Taiwan and the "tiger economies" of Southeast Asia) to emerge, the multiplier impacts (of tourism visitor and expenditure levels to income generated and jobs created) to remain constant, a diversification (or specialization) of their tourism attractions, increased competition (from each other, from countries around the Pacific Rim, and from Southeast Asia), and problems with delivery of tourists by the international airlines.

## Major Tourism Projects

The growth rate of international visitation has included a number of relative peaks and troughs, so that in recent years the rate has fluctuated from a negative position (1991–1992) through small increases (with political disturbances affecting visitation levels) to an increase of 8% in the period 1993-1994.

The investment and development industries keep a close watch on the growth rates and associated indicators and are persuaded to commence major tourism development projects if the prevailing circumstances offer an acceptable level of financial return. If the region is to continue to grow in tourism capacity, destination states and territories need to appraise carefully their unique role in the regional scheme of tourism attraction. Reviews of tourism activity in the region in 1995 indicate that improvements and additions to the infrastructure, facilities and services, and attractions have been at a very low level (EIU 1996, PBEC 1996).

Only a few indicators are given here of some of the major tourism development projects planned in the region.

*Figure 32.3. Hotel Taharaa, Tahiti (photo LEM).*

### Accommodation Projects

In the first half of the decade of the Nineties there was a lull in development activity. Some countries and territories (such as American Samoa) concentrated on putting in place organizational structures and improving the knowledge base from which tourism plans and strategies can be formulated, rather than on promoting major development projects in tourism. In contrast, the Cook Islands embarked upon a deliberate policy of consolidation and dispersion; there is a moratorium on major development on the main island of Rarotonga, with the focus shifting to developing Aitutaki and to the maintenance of the Polynesian style of small-to-medium–scale resort (up to one hundred units) on the outer islands.

New Caledonia is reviving interest in tourism development

with a number of new small beach resorts. The Solomon Islands is recovering from a period of failures to commence major tourism developments with improvements to hotels in Honiara and Gizo and the Anuha Island resort. In Fiji, a need for major executive hotel development has emerged because the principal world-class resort hotels are often heavily booked. Air Pacific has indicated that it is the shortage of high-class accommodations that is constraining the growth of the Japanese and American markets. There are negotiations with a Fiji national company and Air Pacific to fill the void with a major new resort, and a major hotelier in Fiji is embarking on the construction of a US$1 million convention center.

French Polynesia (Tahiti) is planning to expand and upgrade its hotel and resort development with a projected increase of about 60% in hotel rooms (from 3,040 in 1994 to 5,000 in 2005), and an upgrade to the quality of the *pensions* (budget-style accommodations), with a redirection of some new resort developments to the remote islands and the development of interisland cruise ship and onshore accommodations. For the Marshall Islands there are plans to triple the hotel accommodation capacity (from 158 to 500) with new hotels in Majuro and Mili. One of the problems faced in the Marshall Islands is the quality and efficiency of the infrastructure systems. The Federated States of Micronesia (FSM) are preparing scenarios for two different levels of international visitation, with a target visitor level of 40,000 requiring an additional 600 rooms, and a level of 100,000 requiring an additional 2,300 rooms. There are no definite projects to meet those targets at this time (1996).

Pacific Islands with little tourism traffic (such as Kiribati, Nauru, Niue, and Tuvalu) have no large-scale plans on the drawing board; rather, any intention to increase the capacity of accommodation is directed at upgrading or introducing small-scale resorts (often for the budget traveler). In contrast, the major tourism destinations in the region, such as Saipan and Hawai'i, are seeking both to increase the stock of accommodation and to diversify the range to cater to special requirements of particular visitor groups. In the CNMI, Saipan will continue to dominate the distribution of visitors, but Tinian and Rota will be expected to play more substantial roles in the future. Palau is consolidating its position of attraction for specialist diving activities in the region; this may lead to the need for an increase to accommodation and ancillary facilities in the future.

Papua New Guinea has no new major projects in view. The reasons for this are reported to be the lack of funds in that part of the region, low levels of investor confidence (outside of mining ventures), and the continuing concern about the standards of law and order. Some rural-based guest houses are emerging to provide geographical balance and new opportunities for travelers. Tonga has a multifaceted tourism development strategy for accommodation and resorts that includes the creation of a waterfront tourism precinct at Neiafu and another at Nuku'alofa involving expanding and upgrading the Dateline Hotel, preparing for another international hotel, and reestablishing the wharf and Yellow Pier facilities. Recent developments and upgrading in Vanuatu and Samoa have led to a temporary halt in further major development projects there.

Among the strategies for Hawai'i are the expansion and

**Figure 32.4.** Saipan Continental Hotel, Saipan, CNMI (photo LEM).

upgrading of hotel accommodation in the Waikīkī area and revitalization of Honolulu's waterfront from Kewalo Basin to Ke'ehi Lagoon. Future accommodation projects in New Zealand may continue to be constrained by the national planning legislation and the development approval systems.

### Infrastructure Projects

In addition to the general urban development schemes, of which the waterfront rehabilitation schemes in Tonga are typical, some Pacific Islands have recently embarked upon or are about to embark upon major infrastructure improvement schemes. The Marshall Islands are installing a saltwater sewer system for Majuro, the Federated States of Micronesia (FSM) are undertaking beautification schemes, Nauru has benefited from a desalination plant developed by the phosphate company, and Niue and the CNMI are upgrading and expanding their respective international airports.

In terms of transportation, French Polynesia is determined to improve the accessibility of the remote islands, in part by cruise ship routes. In Fiji, high-speed hydrofoil passenger and ferry cargo services link Lautoka and Savusavu. Regional air services by Air Marshall, Polynesian, Air Nauru, Air Caledonia, Solomon Islands Air, and others have reappraised their routes and their roles in the region. The outcome is likely to be the need for upgraded ground facilities, especially where new hubs emerge to cope with the intersection of air transport routes, for the transshipment of both passengers and cargo. Some airlines are entering into cooperative and code-sharing arrangements. It has been reported that New Zealand may continue to suffer from infrastructure (transport) bottlenecks, despite the upgrading of Auckland airport.

### Attractions

As the profile of the region matures, the tendency to increase attractiveness by the creation and development of new physical attractions and entertainment is being replaced by action to achieve consolidation of the existing range of attractions, perhaps with some upgrading and modernization, or the introduction of new attractions in ecotourism or cultural tourism. Hawai'i's strategy of diversification includes, for example, the development of a state-of-the-art convention center, the installation of the USS *Missouri* at Pearl Harbor, and the development of a new aquarium. In New Zealand, carrying capacity issues continue to influence its nature-based attractions (such as whale-watching) and some of its spectacular sites (such as Milford Sound).

The Pacific region appears to be attractive to tourists more for its natural and cultural resources than for any man-made attractions. Despite a continuing level of attraction and growth in the region, the lack of commitment to major project development may indicate that the region is almost at the capacity threshold for project and attraction development. However, there will be continuing pressure from airlines to increase hotel and resort capacity and to develop appropriate attractions or services for the special-interest visitor. There will also be continuing pressure from governments as tourism becomes an increasingly significant element in the national economic structure.

Two matters of regional significance are becoming the focus of future tourism development strategies; these are the distinctive cultures and ecosystems of the region.

## Cultural Tourism and Ecotourism

The cultural and natural resource base of the Pacific Island countries makes them obvious targets for development as destinations with conspicuous culture and ecotourism opportunities.

### Cultural Tourism

The culture of any society is influenced by a range of social, economic, environmental, political and derived forces. In the case of the Pacific region, territorial isolation and the trans- and inter-Pacific migratory movements of the main ethnic groups have contributed to a wide cultural diversity and have prevented the creation of uniform and even cultural development. The Melanesian, Polynesian, and Micronesian cultural groups have pursued different developmental routes, and it is this diversity that has contributed to the differences that are among the principal attractions for tourism in the region.

A succession of outside influences has not eliminated the fundamental aspects of the traditional cultures. The four elements of cultural distinctiveness that have intrinsic attraction for overseas visitors are the community or social systems, the traditions, customs, and behavior; the artifacts, crafts and art forms; and "the Pacific Way." Recent additions to the prospectus of cultural attractions include the sites, relics, and wrecks of World War II activity, either as observable attractions for special interest groups, or in some cases as the foundation for the adventure diving industry. However, the "demonstration effect" of tourism and other modernizing influences has tended to disturb previously held value and belief systems.

### Ecotourism

Many of the Pacific Island countries are embarking upon programs of ecotourism development (Fagence 1995). This is occurring despite the continuing uncertainty about how the

*Figure 32.5.* Yapese dancers (photo LEM).

commitment to this form of tourism may help to conserve the natural resources tourists wish to see; how to facilitate local community involvement; and how to achieve a return on investment. Examples of the new initiatives in ecotourism, heritage, and cultural tourism include Tonga's major heritage project with the Velata Fortress, Solomon Islands' project to gain World Heritage Listing for two prominent lagoon sites, and Samoa's promotion of pilot ecotourism projects and the restoration of the Robert Louis Stevenson residence.

Ecotourism initiatives are evident in Papua New Guinea, Vanuatu, Fiji, and Samoa. In a more specific manner, Solomon Islands, Kiribati, Vanuatu, Samoa, Papua New Guinea, and Fiji are among the Pacific Island countries that have designated (or that intend to designate) areas of fragile and unspoiled terrain for perpetual conservation. In the case of Hawai'i, government and business have been pursuing ecotourism development opportunities, especially since 1990, through state conferences and specially commissioned studies. Hawai'i is in a unique position in the region, with 30% of endangered flora and fauna in the United States present in the Hawaiian Islands, presenting a diversity of challenges to and opportunities for ecotourism.

The market for the natural and cultural tourism attractions of the Pacific region lies outside the region, particularly in Australia, although markets in North America, Europe, and East Asia are growing in strength. By its nature, ecotourism is usually small scale, which, in economic terms, can be translated into either large volume at the budget end of the market spectrum or low volume at the boutique, exclusive, and expensive end of the spectrum. This is resulting in the packaging of ecotourism experiences across a diverse spectrum of tourist types, cost structures, and time scales. The emergence of special-interest nature-based tourism has created a demand for a new range of experiences for which the potential traveler is willing to pay even high prices. Some of this special-interest market is organized through clubs, associations, and other specialized agencies, and it often results in group travel. The ecotourism product range includes the study of native flora and fauna, the visiting of spectacular sites (such as volcanoes, reefs, lagoons, and forests), and the direct participation in some of the activities associated with interpreting, recording, and collecting.

Ecotourism activity provides opportunities for high levels of involvement by local indigenous communities, not only in ownership and management, but also in employment, including the value-added aspects of the tourism experience, such as interpretation, information, expert commentary, and photographic or filming opportunities. Ecotourism project development is sometimes pursued in projects with joint venture partners, uniting the indigenous communities, the foreign entrepreneur (or aid agency), and the government. The involvement of indigenous communities in ecotourism project development is relatively new in the Pacific region, so the partnership and business arrangements that meet the expectations of those communities, the government agencies, and the foreign investors and tour wholesalers are still the subject of ongoing experimentation.

## Conclusion

Tourism development has been seen as an attractive alternative form of economic development in the Pacific region for more than two decades (Milne 1992, Wilkinson 1987, 1989). From early on, a consistent line of argument has been presented: with the current economic problems facing small island communities, tourism presents one of the more feasible opportunities for improvement. Certainly there is evidence in the region from the honey pots that there have been economic advantages to pursuing this economic strategy; Hawai'i, Guam, and Saipan, in particular, have developed outcomes that others have considered emulating. However, in these three cases, geographic proximity to major markets and air transport connections has been of considerable influence in the success of tourism strategies.

The Pacific region is likely to continue to be an attractive tourism destination because it can still offer exotic, relatively unspoiled tourist destinations, with opportunities for specialist pursuits (in adventure tourism, ecotourism, and cultural tourism), and because it is close to the future major tourist-generating region of East and Southeast Asia. South Korea, Taiwan, Thailand, Malaysia, Singapore, Hong Kong and Indonesia are certainly capable of adding significant increments of international tourists to the conventional generating sources of Japan, the United States and Canada, and Australia.

However, those small island countries that have yet to capture a significant share of the Pacific tourism market need to be aware of the special conditions that set the honey pots apart as major attractions. The honey pots are capable of sustaining their quantitative presence in the region by their own initiative; smaller countries are dependent on the resources of TCSP to assist with marketing the region in the major metropolitan countries (especially North America and Europe). Comforting projections of growth and statements of growth potential for the Asia-Pacific region need to be examined carefully before it is assumed that all destinations will attract their due proportion of incremental growth.

Three situations seem most likely: first, in the Pacific region, the destination pattern is likely to continue to be dominated by the honey pots; second, the pattern of growth in the Asia-Pacific statistical region of the World Tourism Organization (WTO) will continue to be led by East Asian destinations; third, the growth rates in most other destinations in the Pacific Basin are not expected to increase significantly.

Although many Pacific Islands have sought comfort from recent global conferences on sustainable development (Rio de Janeiro in 1992, Barbados in 1994), the very pursuit of the principles of sustainability may, in fact, provide a constraint on the future development of tourism. As the global insistence on sustainability gathers momentum, it may be that island states and territories will not be able to achieve the levels of tourism activity necessary to provide economic sustainability. Some island communities do not wish to embrace the forms of mass tourism that underpin the economic systems of the honey pots. They would rather pursue the ideals of special-interest tourism, where visitor numbers are less, the demands on infrastructure may be less, and the visitors may be more responsible.

In *Pacific Tourism: As Islanders See It* (Rajotte and Crocombe 1980) it is argued that "the superimposition of a highly competitive, profit-based industry serving a high-income, foreign clientele will have a dramatic impact upon every aspect of culture" (p. 7). The question to be asked is whether tourist benefits can be balanced with environmental sustainability and the concerns of indigenous cultures. Inevitable changes in levels of international visitation and changing patterns of preference, product delivery, and accessibility will cause the Pacific region to remain in a state of uncertainty about its future prospects. Whether or not tourism is embraced as a major focus of development, careful management of the natural and cultural resources that are the principal forces of attraction becomes critical.

## Appendix 32.1

The Tourism Council of the South Pacific (TCSP), based in Suva, Fiji, is the "umbrella" organization for overseeing tourism issues in the Pacific region for "member" states and territories (the Cook Islands, Fiji, French Polynesia, Kiribati, New Caledonia, Niue, Papua New Guinea, Solomon Islands, Tonga, Tuvalu, Vanuatu, and Samoa). It is an NGO (nongovernmental organization), with the responsibility to provide planning, marketing and information leadership and service to its members. It is funded under the terms of the Lome Convention (European Union), with additional funding contributions from members.

## Bibliography

Britton, S., and W. Clarke, eds. 1987. *Ambiguous alternative: tourism in small developing countries.* Suva, Fiji: University of the South Pacific.

Brookfield, H. 1989. Global change and the Pacific: problems for the coming half-century. *The Contemporary Pacific* 1:1-18.

Brookfield, M., and R. Ward. 1988. *New directions in the South Pacific:* Canberra: Academy of Social Sciences.

Cole, R., and T. Parry, eds. 1986. *Selected issues in Pacific Island development.* Canberra: National Centre for Development Studies, Australian National University.

Craig-Smith, S., and M. Fagence. 1994. A critique of tourism planning in the Pacific. *Progress in Tourism, Recreation and Hospitality Management* 6:92-110.

*Cultural Survival Quarterly.* 1990. Special editions 14(1 and 2).

Douglas, N. 1996. *They came for savages: 100 years of tourism in Melanesia.* Lismore, NSW: Southern Cross University Press.

EIU. 1990. *Far East and Pacific travel in the 1990s.* London: Economist Intelligence Unit.

EIU. 1995. *International tourism report, No. 2. New Zealand.* London: Economist Intelligence Unit.

EIU. 1996. *Country profiles: Pacific Islands.* London: Economist Intelligence Unit.

ESCAP. 1986. *Development of tourism in Pacific Island countries.* ESCAP Tourism Review 1. New York: United Nations.

ESCAP. 1992. *Sustainable tourism development in Pacific Island Countries.* New York: United Nations.

ESCAP. 1996. *Integrated Tourism Planning in Pacific Island Countries.* ESCAP Tourism Review 17. New York: United Nations.

Fagence, M. 1995. Ecotourism and Pacific Island nations: towards a realistic interpretation. *Cahiers du Tourisme*, Series C, No. 189.

Fairbairn, T. 1985. *Island economics: studies from the South Pacific.* Suva, Fiji: Institute of Pacific Studies, University of the South Pacific.

Fairbairn, T., E. Morrison, R. Baker, and S. Groves. 1991. *The Pacific Islands: politics, economics and international relations.* Honolulu: East-West Center.

Finney, B., and K. Watson. 1976. *A new kind of sugar.* Honolulu: East-West Center.

Hall, M., and S. Page. 1996. *Tourism in the Pacific.* London: International Thomson Business Press.

Hawaii. 1996. The economic impact of tourism in Hawaii. *Hawaii's economy,* 5-8. Honolulu: DBEDT, Hawai'i.

Helu-Thaman, K. 1993. Beyond hula, hotels and handicrafts: a Pacific Islander's perspective of tourism development. *The Contemporary Pacific* 51:104-111.

Lea, J. 1988. *Tourism and development in the Third World.* London: Routledge.

Lutz, C., and J. Collins. 1993. *Reading National Geographic.* Chicago: University of Chicago Press.

Mathieson, A., and G. Wall. 1982. *Tourism: economic, physical and social impacts.* London: Longman.

Mill, R., and A. Morrison. 1992. *The tourism system.* 2nd ed. Englewood Cliffs, NJ.: Prentice Hall.

Milne, S. 1992. Tourism and development in South Pacific microstates. *Annals of Tourism Research* 193:191-212.

PBEC. 1996. *Pacific Business Economic Council statistics 1996.* Tokyo: PBEC.

PIDP. 1990. *Pacific Islands tourism case studies: regional summary.* Honolulu: Pacific Islands Development Program, East-West Center.

Rajotte, F., and R. Crocombe, eds. 1980. *Pacific tourism: as islanders see it.* Suva, Fiji: Institute of Pacific Studies, University of the South Pacific.

Smith, V. 1977/1989. *Hosts and guests: the anthropology of tourism.* 1st and 2nd eds. Philadelphia: University of Pennsylvania Press.

Smith, V., and W. Eadington. 1994. *Tourism alternatives.* Chichester: John Wiley.

Stephen, A. 1993. *Pirating the Pacific: images of trade, travel and tourism.* Haymart, NSW: Powerhouse Publishing.

Trask, H-K. 1993. *From a native daughter: colonialism and sovereignty in Hawai'i.* Monroe, Maine: Common Courage Press.

Wallace, H. ed. 1996. *Developing alternatives.* Melbourne: Victoria University.

Wilkinson, P. 1987. Tourism in small island nations: a fragile dependence. *Leisure Studies* 62:127-146.

Wilkinson, P. 1989. Strategies for tourism in microstates. *Annals of Tourism Research* 16(2):153-177.

# CHAPTER 33

# Communications

*Michael R. Ogden and Suzanna Layton*

> *Of all the technological changes which have been sweeping through the traditional societies of the underdeveloped world . . . the most fundamental and pervasive in their effects on human society have been the changes in communication.*
>
> Max F. Millikan, 1967

Despite the incredible diversity among the Pacific Islands, they all share certain elements in common: the close proximity of the sea, the relatively small and fragmented character of their land area, and the vast distances of open ocean and/or rugged mountainous terrain that have to be spanned to maintain contact within any one island group let alone with other groups or with the rest of the world. Furthermore, most Pacific Island nations gained their political independence prior to the development of modern satellite, fiber optic, or cellular wireless communications technologies. Thus, they also share a common base of antiquated communication infrastructures left over from the waning years of colonialism.

Although there has been a tendency among some social scientists and political leaders to underestimate or even downplay the specific role that telecommunications technology and the media have come to play in economic and social development, the World Telecommunications Advisory Council (WATC) to the International Telecommunications Union (ITU) issued a succinct summary of the importance of the communications sector for regions like the Pacific Islands when it stated that "[t]elecommunications is a fundamental social infrastructure—perhaps the most important infrastructure of the information age. As such, it is an essential public concern and cannot be divorced from basic issues of social equity" (WATC 1993:3).

Therefore, following an introductory review of communications and journalistic theory relevant to the Pacific Islands context, this chapter will trace the pattern of Pacific Island telecommunications and media development, from colonial administration through independence, and explore some of the more recent "critical" telecommunications and media development options now being made available to vastly improve the flow of information and increase Pacific Islander connectivity for domestic, regional, and international communications.

## Currents in Communication Theory

Communication and development began to emerge as a concentrated focus of theoretical attention during post–World War II reconstruction and decolonization—mostly as a result of the rapid diffusion of the mass media into less developed countries. Early pioneers in setting the theoretical agenda of communication and development in what became known as the "Modernization School" were Daniel Lerner (1958), Wilbur Schramm (1964), Everett Rogers (1962), and Fredrick Frey (1973). Through the efforts of these scholars (among others) in the early part of the 1950s and well into the 1960s, the primary goal of economic development was defined as "modernization" (with Western nations as model states), measured primarily by increases in per capita GDP, and facilitated chiefly through the creation of a strong and largely urban industrial base.

This policy perspective assumed that mass media and telecommunications would stimulate economic growth and promote trade (Saunders, Warford, and Wellenius 1983, Karunaratne 1984), improve rural development through the "diffusion of innovation" (Rogers and Shoemaker 1971, Cheah 1986), assist human resource development through "mediated" formal and nonformal education (Schramm 1964; Vusoniwailala 1987), improve the provision of health services (Bouck 1987), encourage regional cooperation and decision-making (Davey 1984), and support indigenous cultural identity (Jussawalla 1986). Therefore, policies were implemented that stressed the acquisition of such capabilities from the outside. It was assumed that these policies would eventually contribute to internal structural adjustments that would in turn result in a reduction of the economic gap that existed between the industrialized countries and the newly independent developing countries. "And so the process spirals upward, with the natural advancement of both telecommunications and the economy as a whole" (ESCAP 1990:5); or so it was hypothesized.

However, the experiences of the late 1960s through the early 1980s brought to light some serious "structural" anomalies in this approach; widespread problems still persisted. Criticism resulting from such failings contributed to the rise of "Dependency" and "World-Systems" theories of "underdevelopment" as critical counterpoint to the modernization model. Some of the main theorists in the "critical approaches" to communication and development include Rogers (1976 and 1978), Schiller (1976), and an increasing number of "Third World" scholars such as Freire (1972), Beltran (1980), and Tehranian (1977 and 1979), among others. By the mid-1970s, such criticism found support in the call for a "new international economic order" (NIEO) with strong support from developing countries in the United Nations, particularly those affiliated with the Non-Aligned Nations Movement. Before the end of the decade, the NIEO gave rise to a corollary demand for a "new world information and communication order" (Sussman and Lent 1991), nurtured within the halls of the United Nations Educational, Scientific, and Cultural Organization (UNESCO).

Even though the focus was on the advocacy of a "balanced" flow of information and a call for the recognition of a universal "human right to communicate" (MacBride 1980), there were also charges that the employment of telecommunications technology under the prescription of the earlier paradigm of development fostered a form of "cultural imperialism" (Galtung 1971, Schiller 1976, 1989). Mass media theorists reacted to these debates by refining cold-war–influenced media models—the "four theories" of the press (Siebert, Peterson and Schramm, 1956)—to reflect the media environments of newly decolonized states, which were constructed as development-oriented or "guided media systems" (Hachten 1981), or as "advancing" media environments (Altschull 1984).

Attention was also focused on the lack of adequate telecommunications in developing countries and the imbalanced distribution of global communication infrastructure. In 1984, the Maitland Commission documented the disparity between the telecommunication "haves" and "have nots," stressing that these "missing links" stymied development in underserviced regions and countries. As a result, the ITU issued the edict that, by the turn of the century, everyone in the world should be within easy walking distance of a telephone (Maitland, et al. 1984).

Concurrently, those within the Pacific Islands who held a world-systems and/or dependency theory perspective (cf. Waqavonovono 1981, Horsefield 1993) argued that communication technologies were merely the tools of capitalist expansion: that the transnational communication corporations blatantly promote the ideology of global capitalism (Schiller 1979 and 1981) and with their immense economic, political and technological resources were rapidly eroding national culture and the authority of national decision-making resulting in increasing cultural, technological, and economic dependency on metropolitan nations (Hamelink 1983, Thomas 1990). Thus, there remains a strong continuity of "formal and informal political, economic, and social linkages from the basis of the contemporary world capitalist economy, including its communication and information infrastructural components" (Sussman and Lent 1991:19) serving to reinforce the core-periphery dependent relationship and the continued underdevelopment of the periphery state. By this perspective, the underlying structures of cultural and information domination (read "imperialism") have, if anything, become even more consolidated.

The communications literature of the 1980s, however, was far less interested in the "dependency critiques" and much more enamored of the "post-industrial" information society, introduced in the writings of Bell (1973) and expanded upon by Toffler (1980), Dizard (1982), Rogers (1986), and Dordick and Wang (1993); many of whom, according to Sussman and Lent, were "inspired by technical breakthroughs in cybernetics and telecommunications technology in the 1970s, [and thus] examined social change through an exaggerated technological determinist view of history" (1991:13). To a certain extent, this criticism is well founded. Nevertheless, these authors suggest that the "economic growth or development process requires the integration of technology, social change, and economic change" as part of the informatization process evident in the emerging global post-industrial society (Dordick and Wang 1993:viii).

Still, it cannot be denied that any set of technologies that holds forth such power and promise must also come with a price:

> Thus, the economic uses of automation translate labor saving into job suppression.... Uneven development on the world scale transforms the impulse for technological innovation into an insurmountable technological gap.... The new media reinforce the tendency toward social isolation.... The most powerful innovative technologies are appropriated and kept secret.... On the edge of liberating its creativity by the means of an unprecedented technological revolution, humankind becomes the slave of its own collective monsters. (Castells 1986:331-332)

The following statement by Majid Tehranian expresses the possibility and the hope that communications development can be sensitive to the above concerns and that communication may indeed become an important and needed constructive factor in remote Pacific Island societies:

> Development *of* communication may be defined as expanding the channel capacity of the communication system. Development *by* communication might mean employing that capacity to provide social services such as tele-education, tele-medicine, tele-libraries, tele-banking, etc., alongside the traditional services. Development *for* communication might be interpreted to mean power-free and dialogic communication between the state and civil society so that public policy decisions are based on communicative rather than instrumental rationality. Thus defined, development communication means increasing levels of economic democracy ... political democracy ... social democracy ... and cultural democracy. (Tehranian 1994:277)

## From Slit Gongs to Satellites

Precontact indigenous communication systems were primarily oral and limited by the proximity and mobility of islander populations. Oratory, chant, storytelling, and gossip were, however, augmented by carved drums (Figure 33.1) or wind instruments. These were used to announce ceremonial activities and regulate daily routine. Likewise, the widespread practice of tattooing (from the Tahitian word *tatau*) transformed human skin itself into a print medium. Western-style "mass"

*Figure 33.1. Slitgong (photo MO).*

media were introduced into these communications micronetworks by European and American missionaries in the early 1800s. The region's first newspapers were created by missionaries primarily as a tool for promoting literacy. Increased European activity in the mid-1800s led colonial administrations into the publishing business to promote the government viewpoint on contentious issues and events. Commercial media likewise appeared with the influx of merchant capital during the 1870s. Often fiercely partisan, these "independent" newspapers represented planter and trader concerns at a time when colonial administrations were struggling to reconcile indigenous and expatriate interests while establishing political legitimacy.

While trying to keep pace with the rest of the world, business enterprises and colonial administrations also introduced "modern" telephone systems, the first of which was installed on Maui in the Kingdom of Hawai'i in 1878—just two years after Alexander Graham Bell introduced his new invention to the world. The Colonial Sugar Refining Company in Fiji built its own private network in 1898; by 1910 Honolulu had nearly 6,000 subscribers, and the first public telephone exchange was opened in Suva that same year.

However, overseas communications was far more problematic. From the arrival of the missionaries until the establishment of regular postal services in the mid-1800s, exchanging letters with home was the only means of staying in touch with the world. Outgoing mail was usually dispatched by arrangement with the captain or crew of European or American sailing vessels visiting the islands and was infrequent at best. Letters were most often sent collect and took months to be delivered, while incoming mail was even less reliable. In 1874, with postal services established in most Pacific Island colonies and the proliferation of steamship routes enhancing international mail services, the Universal Postal Union was formed (eventually claiming as members nearly all the world's nations). The basic treaty, the Universal Postal Convention, regulated the exchange of international mail and has been carefully tended and modified as circumstances warranted, up to the present (Sinclair 1984).

The first reliable electronic communication links across the Pacific were undersea telegraphic cables. The Pacific Cable, completed in 1902, connected Asia and Australia with North America and island-hopped its way across the vast Pacific Ocean, making landfall at only a few geographically strategic colonial centers. The rate for sending a cablegram in the early years was quite high, over $1.00 per word. Thus, outside of important administrative or business communications, the international postal system remained the main mechanism of overseas communications for many years.

In 1957, nearly a century after the first telephones were introduced in the Pacific, the first undersea telephone cable was installed between Hawai'i and the west coast of the United States. However, it was not until the mid-1960s that transoceanic telephone cables (COMPAC in 1963–64, SEACOM in 1967) connected North America with Asia, Australia, and New Zealand. Even in these instances, it was only the islands within the routing path of the undersea cables that were fortunate enough to have land-based relay stations—namely, Hawai'i, Guam, Fiji, and Papua New Guinea.

The real watershed of telecommunications services in the Pacific, however, occurred in the late 1920s with the development of high-frequency radio technology. Indeed, until the Japanese bombing of Pearl Harbor in 1941, a large and growing network of radio communications was expanding hand-in-hand with the newfound strategic and political importance of the Pacific Island territories (Ogden 1986). Furthermore, developments in HF radio-telephony after the war greatly "improved [this] means of communication and most of the Pacific Islands soon had internal radio systems run by their respective administrations" (Robson, 1950:21). HF radio links were soon established throughout the Pacific, initially for wartime purposes, but afterward they were improved and built upon for peaceful activities. As a result, the HF radio medium quickly became the most economical means of maintaining contact with metropolitan governments, colonial offices, and rural village administrations (Davey 1984).

Yet, despite these improvements, few rural villages had access to telephones for even domestic communications, let alone international. Likewise, Pacific islands' reliance on HF radio for international connectivity—once a boon—soon began to limit their traffic and saddled them with old, outmoded networks. Furthermore, the suzerain administrations spent little on infrastructure development in their colonies prior to independence, leaving much of the existing equipment in poor repair. As a result, the nascent governments of the newly independent Pacific Island nations inherited grossly inadequate communication infrastructures in relation to the requirements of modern businesses and government administration.

It was not until 1976 that the International Telecommunications Satellite Organization (INTELSAT)—a global provider of satellite services—changed its long-standing pricing policy, allowing smaller and thus cheaper earth stations[1] access to its satellite network at a reduced rate (Figure 33.2). The telecommunication study's calculations were quickly reexamined and for all but the smallest of island countries, satellite communications became immediately more attractive. Accordingly, SPEC (South Pacific Bureau for Economic Cooperation, now known as the South Pacific Forum Secretariat) immediately initiated the phased introduction of

The Pacific Islands

*Figure 33.2. Satellite earth station (photo MO).*

satellite operations using the INTELSAT Standard B configuration (Ogden 1986). In 1984, Kiribati was the last Pacific Islands country to be provided with a Standard B earth station, while even smaller earth stations (Standard D) brought affordable satellite communications to the smallest of island nations by the early 1990s.

Thus, from the mid-1970s through the early 1990s, Pacific Island governments placed the force of political will behind the construction of international gateways as satellite communications became a part of everyday life in the islands. Today, almost all of the Pacific islands have satellite gateways for international telecommunications (see Table 33.1) and many have embarked upon ambitious modernization plans following a restructuring of their own telecommunications organizations. Some island nations have even entered into joint-venture agreements for the management of their international and domestic communications (see Table 33.2) in an attempt to "leap-frog" their outdated infrastructure into the twenty-first century.

One outcome of this effort has been the interconnection via satellite of isolated outer islands previously reachable only by HF radio links. As the digitization of transmission technology advances and as onboard power for satellites increases, there has been a concomitant decrease in the cost of connection (Ogden 1995). Plans are now under way to make use of new developments in satellite technology to connect even the most remote rural and outer island communities into the domestic, regional, and international communication networks (Ogden 1995). One such effort is the PACT (Pacific Area Cooperative Telecommunications) Network, a regionally focused and operated satellite service (Masterton 1989). Likewise, Papua New Guinea's domestic satellite project is expected to carry a national television service, 2 Mbps restorative digital carriers, and a thin-route telephony service (Ogden and Jussawalla 1994, Gagau and Triebell 1993). Not to be outdone, Tonga has embarked on an ambitious venture to build a regional satellite service on their proposed TongaSat system (Nilson 1991, Nilson and Kite 1992).

Thin-route, repeaterless fiber optic technology is also making inroads as costs come down, spanable distances increase,

## TABLE 33.1

### Intelsat Earth Stations in the Pacific Islands

| Country | Location | Type | Owner | Installation |
|---|---|---|---|---|
| Cook Islands | Rarotonga | Std B | TCI[1] | 1980 |
| Federated States of Micronesia (FSM) | Yap, Chuuk, Pohnpei and Kosrae | Std B | FSMTC[2] | 1983 |
| Fiji | Wailoku | Std A | FINTEL | 1975 (decom. 1987) |
|  | Vatuwaqa | Std A[6] |  | 1987 |
| Kiribati | Tarawa | Std B | Kiribati Telecom | 1983 |
| Marshall Islands | Majuro and Ebeye | Std B | NTA[3] | 1983 |
| Nauru | Yaren District | Std B | Directorate of Telecoms | 1975 |
| Niue | Alofi | Std D[1] | Post & Telecoms | 1989 |
| Papua New Guinea | Port Moresby | Std B | PTC[4] | 1985 |
| Samoa | Afiamalu | Std B | Post & Telecoms | 1980 (decom. 1991) |
|  | Maluafou | Std A[6] |  | 1991 |
| Solomon Islands | Honiara | Std B | STCL[5] | 1975 |
| Tonga | Nuku'alofa | Std B | Cable & Wireless | 1975 |
| Tuvalu | Funafuti | Std D1 | Telecoms Dept. | 1990 |
| Vanuatu | Port Vila | Std B | VANITEL | 1979 |

Source: South Pacific Forum (1991). Regional Telecommunications Report.

Notes:
[1] Telecom Cook Islands Ltd. (TCI), formerly Cook Islands Telecommunications Corp., took over the operation of the international gateway from Cable and Wireless in 1991.
[2] In 1988, the FSM Telecommunications Corp. (FSMTC) purchased each of the four earth stations originally installed and operated by Comsat.
[3] The National Telecommunications Authority (NTA) of the Marshall Islands purchased the two Comsat earth stations in 1987.
[4] Post and Telecommunications Corporation (PTC)
[5] Solomon Telekom Company Ltd. (STCL), joint venture between Cable and Wireless and Solomon Islands government.
[6] New 13 meter Intelsat Standard A earth station antenna.

### Table 33.2 — Organizational Changes in Pacific Islands Telecommunications Administration

| Country | Status 1984 | Status 1994 |
|---|---|---|
| Cook Islands | Government department | Government holding company, joint venture operating company.[1] |
| Federated States of Micronesia (FSM) | Government Statutory Agency | Government owned Corporation |
| Fiji | Government department | Government-owned company |
| Kiribati | Government department | Government holding company, joint venture operating company. |
| Marshall Islands | Government department | 25% government-owned and 75% public-owned authority[2] |
| Nauru | Government department | Government department |
| Niue | Government department | Government department |
| Papua New Guinea | Government corporation | Government corporation |
| Samoa | Government department | Government department |
| Solomon Islands | Government department | Joint venture company[3] |
| Tonga | Government department | Government corporation |
| Tuvalu | Government department | Government department |
| Vanuatu | Government department | Joint venture company[4] |

Notes:

[1] Following the 1991 forced contract termination and acquisition of Cable and Wireless operations by legislative act, Telecom Cook Islands, Ltd. took over domestic and international telecommunications as a 60:40 joint venture between the Cook Islands government and Telecoms New Zealand International.

[2] The Marshall Islands government holds 25% share in the privatized National Telecommunications Authority and retains control over all unsold public shares.

[3] Domestic and international telecommunications is owned and operated by Solomon Telekom Company Ltd., a joint venture between Cable and Wireless and Solomon Islands government.

[4] Telecom Vanuatu Ltd. is the privatized domestic carrier set up as a joint venture between VANITEL, which is in charge of international telecommunications (owned and operated by Cable and Wireless), and the government of Vanuatu.

and bandwidth demands rise. Even wireless communications, with promises of high-quality voice and data services, are making their debut in the Pacific Islands (see Table 33.3), with expectations of rapidly declining costs (Mobile phone service 1994:5, Fiji's New Line 1994:58).

Whereas telephone densities (number of telephones per 100 population) and subscriber waiting lists in the Pacific Islands (see Table 33.4) have greatly improved since the mid-1980s (Jussawalla and Ogden 1989) and are much better than in other developing countries, overall telephone penetration rates remain low "despite detailed telecommunications master plans and extensive aid funding" (Cutler 1994: sec. 2, p. 1). Indeed, only two Pacific Island countries meet or exceed 20% telephone penetration while the average for the entire Pacific Islands region is only 2.1% (ITU 1993, Cutler 1994). Still, the greatest share of telephones remains concentrated in only a few urban areas—widening the access gap—while in most Pacific Island countries the bulk of their populations resident in the rural hinterlands or on isolated outer islands languish without service.

It has been widely recognized that such disparities in access cannot long exist without exacerbating already volatile urban-rural inequalities or placing additional burdens on already overstrained economies. Efforts have been initiated to rectify these disparities (cf., Ogden and Holloway 1988, Forum Secretariat 1991), but there has been little improvement on the 7:1 urban-to-rural telephone ratio. Indeed, no substantial results have yet been reported on rural, thin-route communication initiatives in the Pacific Islands. Obviously, this task has proved more arduous than first assumed since "Pacific Island nations

### Table 33.3 — Pacific Islands Cellular Telephone Networks 1996

| Country | Operators | Subscribers | System | Supplier |
|---|---|---|---|---|
| American Samoa | Office of Com. | 2,500 | AMPS | Motorola |
| Fiji | Vodafone | 2,350 | GMS | Ericsson |
| Guam | Guam Cellular | 14,500 | AMPS | Motorola/NovAtel |
| Marshall Islands | NTA | 400 | AMPS | AT&T |
| Nauru | Telecom Office | 650 | AMPS | Plexsys |
| New Caledonia | PTT | 500 | GMS | Alcatel |
| Papua New Guinea | PTC | 100 | AMPS | Stanilite |
| Solomon Islands | STCL | 250 | AMPS | Stanilite |
| Tonga | TTC | 100 | AMPS | Stanilite |
| Tahiti | Tikiphone | 1,300 | GMS | Alcatel |
| Vanuatu | Telecom | 150 | AMPS | Stanilite |

Notes:
AMPS   Advanced Mobile Phone Service, analog cellular radio.
GMS    Groupe Speciale Mobile, anglicized to mean Global Standard for Mobile Communications; a Pan-European cellular digital system.
Source: Asia-Pacific Mobile Communications Report (1996).

### Table 33.4 Pacific Islands Telephones 1990

| Country | Total Telephones | Total Population | Telephones per 100 Pop. | Telephone Wait List (est.) |
|---|---|---|---|---|
| Cook Islands | 2,540 | 18,552 | 13.7 | 245 |
| Federated States of Micronesia (FSM) | 2,400 | 112,000 | 2.1 | 700 |
| Fiji | 68,532 | 726,000 | 9.4 | 11,500 |
| Kiribati | 1,130 | 68,828 | 1.6 | 133 |
| Marshall Islands | 1,193 | 42,108 | 2.8 | 1,500 |
| Nauru | 1,600 | 9,053 | 17.7 | 160 |
| Niue | 390 | 2,267 | 17.2 | — |
| Papua New Guinea | 73,068 | 3,600,000 | 2.0 | 1,491 |
| Samoa | 4,335 | 181,984 | 2.4 | 2,600 |
| Solomon Islands | 5,976 | 329,000 | 1.8 | 130 |
| Tonga | 3,984 | 95,810 | 4.2 | 680 |
| Tuvalu | 150 | 8,624 | 1.7 | 60 |
| Vanuatu | 6,480 | 159,830 | 4.1 | 88 |

Source: South Pacific Forum (1991). Regional Telecommunications Report.

need to make up for under-investment in telecommunications at a time when most traditional funding sources are under increasing pressure, and other basic needs such as housing, roads, hospitals, and schools continue unabated" (Ogden 1995:22).

## The Mass Media

Increased access to telecommunication services such as telephony in the urban areas during the 1980s also had a marked impact on mass media in the Pacific. The facsimile machine dramatically increased the timely and comprehensive coverage of news and the sharing of news throughout the region. Developments in computer technologies such as desktop publishing and modems further enhanced regional information flow, while making the media industry more economical.

"Modern" mass media dates from the mid-to-late 1970s in the islands, when government focus on localization, training, and education after independence stimulated rapid development in the industry. The combination of journalistic training, aid in the form of equipment grants, and the realization that media take on a more central role in a democracy than in a colony, fueled rapid growth over the next ten years. Newspaper organizations underwent the greatest change during this period, expanding from mainly one- and two-person operations to those resembling community papers in the West. Indigenous ownership more than doubled, indigenous editors began to outnumber their expatriate colleagues (56%), and the number of full-time journalists increased fourfold (Layton 1989). These developments, coupled with advancements in communication technology, resulted in a situation in which, for the first time since the missionary period, Pacific Islanders in the 1980s were setting the news agenda in an institutional fashion.

### Newspapers

Today, twenty-four Pacific nations and territories have at least one locally published newspaper, and eleven have two or more competing papers, along with a variety of specialist periodicals. In addition, six major news magazines are available: *Islands Business, Pacific Islands Monthly,* and *The Review,* published in Fiji; *PNG Business* from Papua New Guinea, *Guam Business News* from Guam, and *Pacific Magazine,* published in Hawai'i.

The biggest newspapers are dailies located in the major English-speaking markets: the *Papua New Guinea Post-Courier* (41,000) (Robie 1995), the *Fiji Times* (31,000), the *Pacific Daily News* on Guam (25,000) (Nygard 1995), and Hawai'i's two major daily newspapers—the *Honolulu Advertiser* (150,000) and the *Honolulu Star-Bulletin* (80,000). Dailies in the French territories are also sizable in regional terms: *La Dépêche de Tahiti* (12,000) and *Les Nouvelles Calédonnienes* (13,000) (Layton 1992). All six dailies are owned by foreign-based media corporations. Gannett Corporation has owned the *Pacific Daily News* on Guam since 1970 and the *Honolulu Advertiser* since 1993.[2] In 1986, Rupert Murdoch's News (South Pacific) Ltd. took over majority shareholding of the *Herald* and *Weekly Times* titles in Papua New Guinea and Fiji (respectively), and Robert Hersant's Groupe Pacifique Presse Communication has owned *Les Nouvelles Calédonnienes, Les Nouvelles de Tahiti,* and *La Dépêche de Tahiti* since the late 1980s.

However, some of the best newspapers in the region are quite small; in 1996, the PINA Media Freedom Award went to the *Cook Islands Press* (circulation 1500). Other microstate newspapers include the government-run *Te Uekera* (1,500) in Kiribati and two small private-sector presses found in Nauru (*Central Star News,* 400) and in Niue (*Niue Star,* 500). Weekly newspapers are also important in the regional media economy; in fact, weekly circulation is nearly twice that of dailies (excluding Hawai'i) and represents one out of three newspaper copies in the region (Layton 1992). Church and nongovernment organizations publish most of the smaller weeklies and monthlies, such as *Ko'e Tohi Fanongonongo* (500) in Tonga and *Mere Save* (500) in Solomon Islands. Though print media primarily serve an urban audience, the *Tok Pisin* language weekly *Wantok* (15,000) has a significant periurban and rural circulation in Papua New Guinea.

## Broadcast Radio

In many places in the Pacific (Hawai'i, Guam, the CNMI, and American Samoa being the notable exceptions) the government is the primary, if not the only, broadcaster. Whereas government radio stations in the Cook Islands, Palau, Papua New Guinea, and Samoa share the market with a single private station, and in the FSM and Tonga with a single religious station, the government broadcaster remains the major source of news and information for its citizens and typically the only station with national coverage. The larger markets in the Pacific support a vibrant and competitive radio broadcasting environment with at least one government or public station and two or more private stations providing a variety of music, entertainment, and news programs. French Polynesia and New Caledonia both have independent radio stations reflecting the views of indigenous nationalists, in addition to the Radio France *d'Outre-mer* network and commercial stations.

Illustrating the important role of radio in the Pacific Islands, a recent study reported that 62% of Palauans and Marshallese surveyed indicated radio was their primary source of information (Ogden 1993). This survey illustrated, more convincingly than previous, "mostly anecdotal reports" that radio "is perhaps the only true mass medium [in the Pacific] because it uses both the local language and English ... and is accessible to anyone who has an AM radio and batteries" (Ogden 1993:19). Economic difficulties in the 1990s, however, have led to the increasing rationalization of government support for the broadcast sector. Stations that previously received government underwriting must now seek commercial advertising and sponsorship to maintain services in an increasingly competitive market and are starting to chafe under continuing government program restrictions.

International and interregional broadcast news and information in English within the Pacific has been primarily received almost exclusively via the British Broadcasting Corporation, Voice of America, Radio Australia, and Radio New Zealand—although the overseas broadcasts from France are important in the French-speaking Pacific. Radio Australia, however, stands out as the most received International Broadcast Service (IBS), primarily because it has the strongest signal targeting the Pacific region and is the only IBS maintaining correspondents in the islands (Ogden and Hailey 1988). Radio Australia's dominant role as the main news and information provider for Pacific Islanders was highlighted in a 1987 survey of Pacific Island radio managers conducted by the East-West Center (Richstad 1987). The response from Pacific broadcasters involved in the study clearly pointed out that news and public affairs programs were then—as they are today—the most listened to and widely rebroadcast service offered by Radio Australia. It should be noted that very few Pacific Islanders possess shortwave radio receivers and therefore rely instead on the rebroadcast of IBS news and information services via local radio stations (Ogden and Hailey 1988). This has raised concerns regarding "single-source" news reporting as well as issues of balanced and fair reporting of Pacific Island issues and events and has remained a sore point between island governments, foreign correspondents, and local journalists.

## Television and Video

In the early 1980s, many Pacific Island nations were facing important policy decisions regarding the establishment of television broadcasting and the adoption of broadcast technologies being offered to them by enterprising foreign interests. Improved satellite as well as terrestrial delivery systems further removed impediments to the establishment of national television services; remoteness from capital cities, rugged terrain, and small, isolated rural populations were no longer proving to be barriers (Stewart, Horsfield and Cook 1993). Early on, the larger urban populations in Papua New Guinea and Fiji represented potentially lucrative markets for Australian and New Zealand entrepreneurs interested in establishing markets in the islands (cf. Royce 1993). It has been speculated that one reason for the incursion of Australia and New Zealand broadcasters into the Pacific Islands is due to the limited size of their own respective domestic markets and the desire to promote exports of their programming (Stewart, Horsfield and Cook 1993). Perhaps also, the perceived advantage of being first to "lock-out" competition in marginally profitable Pacific Islands locales, or the ability to "field test" new technology and marketing approaches in the relatively "low-risk" markets of the Pacific might likewise afford experiences that could translate into competitive advantages in the potentially lucrative Asian markets.

Whatever the case, broadcast television has now become firmly entrenched throughout the urban Pacific. It is interesting to note, however, that until the late 1980s only seven Pacific Island states had television, all of them either territories of France or the United States. Whereas outside the U.S. and French territories television developed far more slowly, the pace substantially quickened in the 1990s. Today, only the microstates of Tuvalu, Kiribati, and Tokelau are without a broadcast television facility of some kind. This has, of course, raised concerns in the Pacific Islands over the percentage of "indigenous" content and the extent to which national governments are able to control television. Indeed, the rapid push for TV service from "outside," along with a perceived lack of government regulatory commitment compounded by insufficient funding and inadequate training, has been blamed for constraining the potential of indigenous television production from the very beginning.

Most television broadcasters in the Pacific are at least partially owned by the government. All, however, are looking toward commercializing operations due to the cost of maintaining broadcast services in an era of government belt-tightening. Programming, the vast bulk of which is imported from the United States, France, New Zealand, and Australia, consumes the largest part of a station's operating budget (outside of personnel). The newer Pacific television stations have had time to reflect on this and have responded by emphasizing the importance of local content appropriate to the social, economic, political, and cultural interests of their countries (Molnar 1993). In fact, many Pacific Island TV stations have stressed their intent to produce local material. However, a UNESCO survey in the early 1990s found local production levels to average only about 5% to 10%—consisting primarily of local news, cultural or official events, and sports (Bentley 1993).

Though the cost of "imported" programming is a significant portion of the broadcast budget, locally made programs can cost up to ten times as much, due primarily to commercial production underwriting of the latter (Figure 33.3). In addition, foreign-made programs often have the highest ratings, particularly in the larger societies, where people are not well known to one another and where the emerging middle class is keen to see how "the other half lives." Still, in an effort to counteract the influx of "culturally insensitive" programming, some Pacific Island governments have held onto the hope that, by introducing local television with programs that appeal to younger people, they can counter the attractiveness of overseas video programs.

*Figure 33.3. Film production crew (photo MO).*

However, prior to the introduction of broadcast television, videotape technology held prominence in the Pacific Islands—some say softening the market for television's eventual arrival. As videotape technology swept into the region in the 1970s, it proved so popular that by the mid-1980s there were reported to be in excess of 60,000 VCRs in Fiji alone. Suva itself has "more than 50 rental shops, with a network which sends tapes to remote villages" (Plange 1993:69). Moreover, "access is multiplied by extended family and communal relations and village social organization" (Plange 1993:69), further extending video's reach. Whereas television reception has primarily been concentrated in the urban and periurban areas, videotape systems spread rapidly throughout the Pacific Islands region. Most of this expansion has been in combination with the expansion of electrification into rural and outer island areas. In the Cook Islands, the introduction of broadcast television actually increased the video market by 33%, because people purchased both television sets and VCRs (Varan 1993). Where television and/or video systems are not present in rural areas, it is more likely due to poor reception or lack of power rather than purely economic reasons (Ogden 1993).

Renewed interest in the social impact of television in developing societies has seen a growing number of ethnographic studies conducted in the Pacific Islands where "natural experiments" of television's introduction are monitored (Varan 1992). Early reports indicate that islanders have attributed to television a number of unwelcome changes to traditional gender, social, and familial roles as well as changes in community structures of interaction, attitudes, and values (Horsfield 1993). Whereas much of the early research provides tantalizing data, the results are still preliminary and by no means conclusive. Still, these studies have raised concerns perhaps best expressed by Ratu Inoke Kubuabola, Fiji's then Minister for Information, Broadcasting, Television, and Telecommunications, during his opening address at the Pacific Regional TV Meeting in 1989, when he stated, "[T]he introduction of television services in the Pacific Islands will be, for most of us, a new industry. A development which I believe may have greater impact on the community than any other single development in our history." The overall extent of this impact has yet to be made fully manifest.

## Regional Media Developments

The development of national media systems was closely followed by the development of professional regional links. The Pacific Islands News Association (PINA), a nongovernmental organization representing the majority of regional media outlets, grew out of the Fiji Press Club in 1972. PINA works to protect media freedom, coordinate training (such as PACJOURN), and foster professional fellowship and cooperation.

The Pacific Islands Broadcasting Association (PIBA), established in 1988, is another important regional consortium representing the region's government radio broadcasters. PIBA also oversees aid-funded efforts such as the PACBROAD training projects and the PACNEWS broadcast news exchange. These were among the first concerted attempts at establishing regional media training: PACBROAD in 1985 for broadcast radio, followed by PACJOURN in 1987 for print journalism, and PACVIDEO in 1989 for video and television. Each project was initiated largely by outside organizations such as UNESCO and the SPC (Molnar 1993).

PACNEWS started in September 1987 through funding from Friedrich Ebert Stiftung, primarily to inform Pacific Islanders of events in the region, to balance overseas coverage of regional events, to provide "development" news, to establish a free and indigenous flow of information, and to more accurately inform an international audience about Pacific life. In its early days, news stories were collected from the member stations by telephone and telex, then redistributed the same way in twice-daily bulletins. The introduction of a facsimile-based exchange in 1989 allowed PACNEWS to market its service externally and to cut costs. In mid-1996, member stations began trials of an email service in a further effort to decrease the significant portion of its budget spent on telecommunication charges.

Many rank-and-file journalists see PINA and PIBA as representing management interests (*PINA Nius* 1989:4). Twenty years ago, most newsroom staffs were small or nonexistent. Today, however, they constitute a sizable professional class, with its own objectives. The Pacific Journalists Association (PJA) was founded in 1989 to improve staff working conditions through trade union development and to "safeguard media freedoms" that neither "governments with their political interests, nor media proprietors with their commercial interests" can be trusted to preserve (*PINA Nius* 1989:4).

Press councils have also been discussed in the region, though with some delicacy, given their lack of popularity with island governments. The PNG Press Council, established in 1975, is the oldest such body; the Fiji Media Council (1994) is the youngest.

## "S/Pacific" Genres[3]

Films made on or about the Pacific Islands tend to be primarily "ethnographic" films that do not, of themselves, constitute a "national cinema," nor do they even display enough unity of purpose to be categorized into a "regional cinema." The most obvious reason for this, of course, is that Pacific film production has, since its inception, remained something that outsiders do—despite the emergence of a small number of islanders working in the field (Douglas 1994). Primarily, this has been due to financial reasons similar to those mentioned earlier for local television production. Furthermore, the long tradition of film production in the Pacific, which began in Hawai'i shortly after the birth of cinema itself with the 1913 productions of two one-reel films (*Hawaiian Love* and *The Shark God*), has tended to be dominated by Western sensibilities of filmmaking and Pacific Island myths.

The first film to be labeled a "documentary,"[4] *Moana: A Romance of the Golden Age* (1925), by Robert Flaherty, used Samoa as its setting. This film has been described as a milestone in Pacific and ethnographic film (Douglas 1994:5). Likewise, Robert Gardner established a name for himself in the Pacific with his first feature length ethnographic film *Dead Birds* (1964), an evocative portrait of the Dani people of the Baliem Valley in Irian Jaya. More recently, and along the same path blazed by Gardner, filmmakers like Dennis O'Rourke (*The Shark Callers of Knotu*, 1982; *Yap: How Did You Know We'd Like TV?* 1982; *Half Life*, 1986; *Cannibal Tours*, 1988) as well as Bob Connolly and Robin Anderson (*First Contact*, 1983; *Joe Leahy's Neighbours*, 1989; *Black Harvest*, 1992) have presented some of the strongest and most sympathetic images of the Pacific Islands in juxtaposition to the "culturally corrosive" effects of Western-introduced cultural trappings (Douglas 1994). It is perhaps telling that, in the "open-ended discourse" presented in the films produced by these independent filmmakers, there has been a blurring of the long-held distinction between documentary and narrative, calling attention to the act of "myth making" most Pacific films engender.

However, far more typical of the film industry has been the use of Pacific Island backdrops and Pacific Islanders as "set dressings" to embellish essentially Western narrative preoccupations. This issue has never really been taken up by the few indigenous filmmakers in the region, nor has any sense of a "Pacific Island genre" emerged to counterbalance the enthusiastically embraced myth of the "exotic" South Seas propagated by Hollywood. Among the difficulties concerning indigenous films is how they might be received by islanders rather than by overseas critics or sympathetic film festival audiences. As Norman Douglas stated in his essay introducing the compendium *Moving Images of the Pacific Islands: A Guide to Films and Videos* (Aoki 1994):

> If in the best possible scenario, a transition from the exotic to the indigenous view is made, and at least as many Islanders as outsiders make films about the Pacific, and a new visual style, a new way of seeing, develops, perhaps a new terminology should also be developed to describe it. Will the films still be narrative or ethnography, or documentary or history, or will they be something else entirely? (Douglas 1994:17)

To this end, a few feature "films"—shot on video—have been produced in Papua New Guinea, among the more notable being *Tukana: Husat i Asua?* (1984), whose screenplay was written by Albert Toro; *Cowboy and Maria in Town* (1992); and *Tinpis Run* (the first "film" directed by Albert Toro). Likewise, the Fiji National Video Centre was at one time a source of locally produced videos prior to its absorption into Fiji's national television service. Perhaps, to paraphrase Maori filmmaker Barry Barclay, director of the internationally acclaimed and almost wholly Maori work *Ngati* (1987): "[We] will get to know what a Pacific Islander film is when islanders get a chance to make more films."

One precedent concerning the "localization" of Western media genres can be seen vividly in island news coverage. The institutional quality of "indigenous" yet "imported" media systems, operating as they do within traditional societies undergoing post-independence social and political stress, has led to conflict with a number of governments since the late 1980s. This conflict, based on a debate about culture, tradition, and "Pacific-style" journalism as distinct from that practiced in the West, touches on all media systems discussed thus far, but is liveliest in the island press. Newspapers in Fiji and Papua New Guinea regularly practice investigative reporting, often to the displeasure of their respective governments. Pacific Island politicians typically argue that such scrutiny is disrespectful of tradition, especially as many officeholders also wear "chiefly hats" (Aiavao 1993). When critical coverage by foreign correspondents is the target, the charge becomes one of cultural insensitivity. The more experienced Pacific journalists reject such criticisms as political expediency.

In addition, though acutely aware that "cultural production is a highly political process" (Keesing 1989:36), Pacific Island journalists have not rejected the cultural norms they grew up with, as "fatal impact" theories of intellectual imperialism would have us believe. Cultural mechanisms are in fact being deliberately appropriated by island journalists, to protect and develop the free flow of information in their societies (Layton 1995). According to Samoan journalist Monica Miller, "It's not what you say, it's how you say it. It's about knowing your culture and knowing what works and what doesn't" (Miller 1993). The resulting difference in style from that of the Western media can be taken by outsiders as evidence of self-censorship. However, a similar process occurs in American, Australian, and New Zealand newsrooms and is called "handling" the story (Layton 1995). Whether reporting, writing, or editing, Pacific journalists are synthesizing a "Pacific-style" journalism out of the two ideologies that shape their identity and give their lives meaning—the traditional conservatism of the Pacific is acknowledged, as is the reality of social change (Layton 1995).

## Islands in an Information Age

For many Pacific Islanders outside of Hawai'i and perhaps Guam, the Internet remains a remote concept. As the rest of the world "logs on" to the Internet at a ferocious pace—over 16 million host computers on the Internet as of January 1997 (see Figure 33.4), a figure growing at a rate of nearly 50% per year—the Pacific Islands are not likely to remain very far behind. At the end of 1996, the best estimate is that there were approximately 45 million people worldwide using the Internet, with roughly 30 million of those in North America, 9 million in Europe, and 6 million in Asia/Pacific (NUA 1997). Such phenomenal growth has captured the interest of Pacific Island governments, businesses, and residents alike, and reports of the

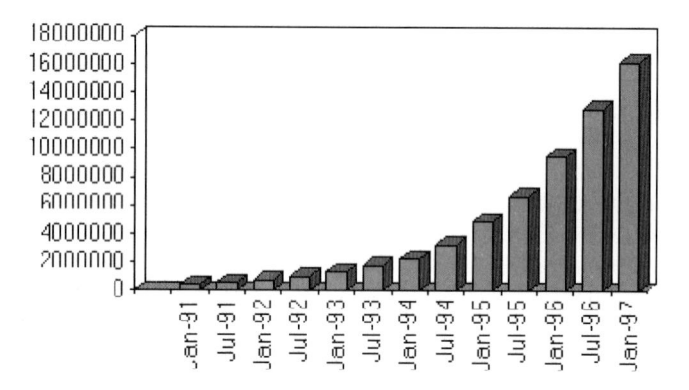

*Figure 33.4.* Global Internet Host Computers (Internet Domain Survey, Host Count Graph, January 1997: http://www.nw.com/zone/WWW/top.html).

Internet's growing usefulness and popularity elsewhere have opened up demand for Internet Service Providers (ISPs) in the Pacific Islands in a big way. However, despite the fact that most Pacific Island countries have primarily digital international and domestic telecommunication infrastructures, telephone densities remain among the lowest in the world (as discussed earlier). Even if one already has a reasonably reliable power supply, a good computer, software and a modem, a telephone line is still needed to connect to the Internet. Therefore, the relatively low telephone densities (see Table 33.4) reported for even the more "modernized" Pacific Island countries represent a substantial entry barrier to accessing the Internet (assuming you can afford the connection fees)—especially if the average wait for a telephone in the capital city is six months to a year, or even longer.

Nevertheless, in early 1996 a consortium consisting of Telecom Fiji Ltd. (formerly Fiji Posts and Telecom Ltd.), Fiji International Telecommunications Ltd. (FINTEL), Telecom New Zealand Ltd., the University of the South Pacific, and the Telecommunications Program of the South Pacific Forum initiated a six-month trial Internet service accessing the University of Waikato's Internet gateway in New Zealand (Sullivan and Morris 1996). FINTEL and Telecom New Zealand provided a 64 Kbps (kilobits per second) circuit for the duration of the trial period, and Telecom Fiji provided the router. Within just a few months of operation, the trial had 143 modem users and 6 leased line users, while traffic reached over 900 Mbps (megabits per second) per month—piquing the interest of other Pacific Island telecommunication service providers studying the feasibility of offering Internet access (Sullivan and Morris 1996).

Internet services have now become an integral part of the communications environment in an increasing number of Pacific Island countries. By November 1996, Fiji had over 400 dial-up modem users and 10 leased line users, with several dozen Web pages online (PIM 1996). The Solomon Islands reported over 80 dial-up users within the same time period, while Vanuatu reported over 50 dial-up users and was experiencing a downturn in fax traffic as customers began using electronic mail (email) for their communication needs (Sullivan and Morris 1996). Likewise, Internet services were initiated in Palau as part of Palau's LightNet 2000 Plan to meet demand for Internet services primarily in the capital city of Koror (Status of PNCC's LightNet 2000 Plan 1997).

The Internet also provided a means for rapid dissemination of information on and about the Pacific Islands. In the early years of the World Wide Web (WWW or Web), academics with interest in the Pacific Islands region began collecting large lists of hypertext[5] data concerning the Pacific Islands. These resources were being amassed through the collective efforts of the World Wide Web Virtual Library's "Pacific Studies" list, and/or collected and categorized on the "Pacific Islands Internet Resources" page (Figure 33.5). Each provided connection to a wealth of information on Pacific islands, including weather, ocean temperatures, business opportunities, tourist information, and "chatty electronic exchanges" where many people swap stories of their Pacific Island homes and/or adventures (North 1996). However, these and other informative Web sites were almost exclusively maintained on host computers

*Figure 33.5.* Pacific Islands Internet Resources Web page.

affiliated with universities in Western metropolitan countries.

First among the Pacific islands to go online was the Government of Western Samoa, with its "Cradle of Polynesia" Web site developed and maintained by a company in the United States. Additional sites, like the Republic of the Marshall Islands Web site, "RMI Online," and The Tourism Council of the South Pacific, also saw advantages to being early adopters, going online in early 1996 with their respective Web sites maintained on host computers in the United States and Australia (Hussein 1996).

In August 1996, the Fiji Visitors Bureau was the first in the Pacific with its own home page (providing information on everything from a simple listing of hotels and the usual tourist information to more adventurous activities "off the beaten track"). Many businesses in the Pacific are also starting to come online, seeing potential benefit in marketing their products to people around the world (PIM 1996). How successful this will be as a mechanism of generating additional trade and investment in the Pacific Islands has yet to be seen, and much will depend upon the success of introducing "electronic commerce" on the Internet in general. However, a possible harbinger of things to come may be the development of offshore interests gaining permission to establish "Internet Casinos" for online gambling in the Pacific Islands, where secrecy laws protect such companies from close scrutiny (Williams 1996).

Nineteen ninety-six was also a year of rapid development for Pacific news sources on the Web, most of them likewise hosted on servers in Australia and the United States. Two daily newspapers in PNG, seven news services, five magazines, and a number of occasional publications joined the first news sites set up in 1995. The "CocoNET Wireless," a Pacific news and information resource site, was established on 5 September 1995 as a clearinghouse for Pacific Islands news. This was followed almost immediately by the Internet issue of the UPNG Journalism student newspaper, *Uni Tavur*, making it the first Pacific periodical on the Web. In October, the first continually published periodicals, *Tahiti-Pacifique Magazine* and the *Tonga Chronicle*, appeared online. These are exceptions to the rule, however, for many of the periodicals that subsequently emerged in 1996 do not publish regularly—their sites exist primarily to generate subscriptions to the hard copy versions and almost all exist on machines outside of the region.

This can be expected to change in the near future. Although island media began experimenting with Internet technologies such as email in the early 1990s, it was not until 1996, when ISPs were established in the Cook Islands, Fiji, Solomon Islands, Vanuatu, and Western Samoa, that media organizations in those countries were afforded reliable access to the Internet. Though few acted quickly to take advantage of the opportunity, the Fiji-based PINA now uses the Web pages of the "CocoNET Wireless" to post "press releases" from its South Pacific Freedom of Information Network, and "hits" from Pacific Island sites are increasing steadily.

Indigenous expertise in Internet publishing is also developing alongside improved Internet infrastructure in the islands. A number of indigenous Web-site managers have discussed the need for an improved Pacific news service on the Web and for a regional news and current affairs Web "zine." The vitality and diversity of migrant Pacific Island communities around the world, as evidenced by the various discussion forums of Taholo Kami (Kava Bowl, Wantok Forum, Bula Forum, Melanesia Forum), Al Aiono (Polynesian Cafe) and Alopi Latukefu (SPIN Forum), ensures that projects such as these will soon come to fruition.

As computer-based communication technologies diffuse throughout the Pacific Islands, some fundamental questions need to be addressed. At issue is the perceived value of such communication technologies and whether or not their "value" matches or exceeds their "cost" (of connection). Among Pacific Island states, issues of equitable and open access to information as well as the more basic issues of computer-based resource awareness and/or relevance as necessary public service priorities are not being adequately discussed. Furthermore, will schools in Pacific Island nations—or other less developed countries for that matter—integrate "computer literacy" into the curriculum to prepare students for jobs in the next millennium? How many Pacific Islanders will be able to afford computers, modems, software, and the online connections without some sort of subsidy? While technology has the potential to promote economic growth, job creation, and other social benefits, without a guiding social contract the information revolution will only aggravate underlying inequalities and may further bifurcate Pacific Island societies as well as widen the gap between developed metropolitan countries and their less developed neighbors.

Likewise, it is important for island governments to remain vigilant in order to ensure that communication and information technologies do not play a corrosive role in island society but, instead, empower Pacific Islanders to preserve their culture. Indeed, these communication technologies offer as many opportunities to erode indigenous language, traditions, and history as they do opportunities to preserve and strengthen them. As Pacific Island nations begin to overhaul existing telecommunication and information systems to meet the demands of the information age, it becomes even more of an imperative that inequalities do not become codified for the next generation.

**Figure 33.6.** *Fiji Visitors Bureau Web page.*

## Notes

[1] INTELSAT earth station standards relevant to the Pacific Islands are as follows:

| INTELSAT Standard | Antenna Size (meters) | Type of Service |
|---|---|---|
| A (old) | 30–32 | voice, data & TV |
| A (present) | 15–18 | voice, data & TV |
| B (old) | aprox. 11 | voice, data & TV |
| B (present) | 10–13 | voice, data & TV |
| D1 | 4.5–6 | Vista |
| D2 | aprox. 11 | Vista |

[2] In 1971 the *Star–Bulletin* and its share of the Hawaii Newspaper Agency were sold to the Gannett Corporation, publishers of *USA Today*. In January 1993, Gannett sold the *Star–Bulletin* to Liberty Newspapers and bought its previous competitor *The Honolulu Advertiser* (Brislin 1996).

[3] The use of the "s/pacific" moniker (first used in Teaiwa 1994) reflects Pacific Islander efforts to counter Western sensibilities about Pacific Islands and garner attention for indigenous efforts at self-representation in the media. Likewise, the term is intended to reflect on the "Pacific-style" journalism debate, calling attention to how islander journalists are localizing Western genres of reporting.

[4] The term "documentary" is said to have been coined by John Grierson in a 1926 *New York Sun* review of Flaherty's *Moana*. Robert Flaherty is perhaps best known for his film *Nanook of the North* (1915).

[5] Hypertext is a term used to describe a nonsequential, random-access arrangement of text-based documents (though images may also be incorporated as well). The World Wide Web, developed in 1991, merges the techniques of networked information and hypertext to make an easy but powerful global information system accessible to anyone with a computer, the right software, and a modem.

## Bibliography

Whereas every attempt has been made to ensure that the Internet resources cited in this chapter are current, such documents are transitory and/or are prone to frequent and capricious URL (Internet address) changes; therefore, the links listed below are not guaranteed to always work.

Aiavao, Ulafala. 1993. News media in Western Samoa and the implication for education and training. In *New views on news*, Journalism Education Association, 173–192. Newcastle, NSW, Australia: Department of Communication and Media Arts, University of New South Wales.

Altschull, H. J. 1984. *Agents of power: the role of news media in human affairs*. New York: Longman.

Aoki, D., ed. 1994. *Moving images of the Pacific Islands: a guide to films and videos* [Occasional Paper 38]. Honolulu, Hawai'i: Center for Pacific Island Studies.

Australian, New Zealand backing for unions, PINA called "bosses" association. 1989. *PINA Nius*. September-October:4.

Bell, D. 1973. *The coming of post-industrial society*. New York: Basic Books.

Beltran, L. R. 1980. Farewell to Aristotle. [mimeo] New York: Unesco.

Bentley, J., speaker. 1993. How local is our TV? Pacific Islands News Association Conference, Suva, Fiji, 10–13 July.

Bouck, G. 1987. Project SHARE: using satellites to improve health and education in remote areas. *Pacific Islands Communication Journal* 15(1):111–113.

Brislin, T. 1996. *Hawaii Journalism History*. http://www2.hawaii.edu/~tbrislin/jourhist.html

Castells, M. 1986. High technology, world development, and structural transformation: the trends and the debate. *Alternatives* 11(3):297–343.

Cheah, C-W. 1986. Telecommunications in the South Pacific: the economic issues. In *Selected issues in Pacific Island development*, ed. R. Cole and T. Parry, 208–225. Canberra: National Centre for Development Studies, Australian National University.

CocoNET Wireless. 1996. http://www.uq.oz.au/jrn/coco.html

Cradle of Polynesia. 1996. http://www.interwebinc.com/samoa/

Cutler, T. 1994. *Telecommunications: the Pacific link*. A Green Paper report for the Pacific Forum on the development of the telecommunications sector in the region. Melbourne: Cutler and Company.

Davey, G. 1984. Telecommunications development in the South Pacific region. In *Transport and communications for Pacific microstates: issues in organization and management*, ed. C. Kissling, 15–24. Suva, Fiji: Institute of Pacific Studies, University of the South Pacific..

Dizard, W., Jr. 1982. *The coming information age: an overview of technology, economics and politics*. New York: Longman.

Dordick, H., and G. Wang. 1993. *The information society: a retrospective view*. Newbury Park, California: Sage.

Douglas, N. 1994. Electric shadows in the South Seas: the Pacific Islands in films—a survey. In *Moving images of the Pacific Islands: a guide to films and videos* [Occasional Paper 38], ed. D. Aoki, 3–19. Honolulu: Center for Pacific Island Studies.

Economic and Social Commission for Asia and the Pacific (ESCAP). 1990. *Study on telecommunication development in the ESCAP region*. New York: United Nations.

Fiji's new line. 1994. *Islands Business Pacific* 20(5):58.

Forum Secretariat (Telecom. Division). 1991. *Regional telecommunications report*. Suva, Fiji: South Pacific Forum Secretariat.

Freire, P. 1972. *Pedagogy of the oppressed* (trans. Myra Bergman Ramos). New York: Herder and Herder.

Frey, F. 1973. Communication and development. In *Handbook of communication*, ed. Ithiel de Sol Pool. Chicago: Rand McNally.

Gagau, S., and E. W. Triebell. 1993. Papua New Guinea: a new satellite telecommunications network. [mimeo] Presented at PTC'93. Honolulu: PTC.

Galtung, J. 1971. A structural theory of imperialism. *Journal of Peace Research* 8(2):81–117.

Hachten, W. 1981. *The world news prism: changing media, changing ideologies*. Ames: Iowa State University.

Hamelink, C. 1983. *Cultural autonomy in global communications: planning national information policy*. New York: Longman.

Horsfield, B. 1993. Pacific Islands television research: a survey of some recent writings. *Pacific Islands Communication Journal* 16(1):143–166.

Hussein, B. 1996. Netting the world. *Pacific Islands Monthly* 66(10):44-45.

International Telecommunications Union (ITU). 1979. Feasibility study for a regional telecommunications network in the South Pacific: summary report of project findings and recommendations. *RAS/74/005, restricted*, unpublished report. Geneva: ITU.

International Telecommunications Union (ITU). 1993. *Asia-Pacific telecommunications indicators*. Geneva: ITU, United Nations.

Jussawalla, M. 1986. Media threat to cultural identity: myth or reality? *The Third Channel* 2(1):380–388.

Jussawalla, M., and M. Ogden. 1989. Pacific Islands: policy options for telecommunications investment. *Telecommunications Policy* 13(1):40–50.

Karunaratne, N. 1984. Telecommunications infrastructure and economic development of the Pacific Island nations. In *Transport and communications for Pacific microstates: issues in organization and management*, ed. C. Kissling, 25–60. Suva, Fiji: Institute of Pacific Studies, University of the South Pacific.

Kava Bowl Forums. 1996. http://www.netstorage.com/kami/wwwboard/kavabowl.html

Keesing, R. 1989. Creating the past: custom and identity in the contemporary Pacific. *The Contemporary Pacific* 1(1–2):19-42.

Kubuabola, Hon. R. I., speaker. 1989. Opening address. *Report of the Pacific Regional TV Meeting* (27 November–1 December 1989), 46-48. Suva, Fiji: Asia-Pacific Broadcast Union and South Pacific Commission.

Layton, S. 1989. The Pacific Island press: diversity, change and continuity. *Australian Journalism Review* 11:125–139.

Layton, S. 1992. *The contemporary Pacific Islands press*. Brisbane: University of Queensland Department of Journalism.

Layton, S. 1995. Introduction. *Pacific Islands Communication Journal* 16(2):1–5.

Lerner, D., and L. Pevsner. 1958. *The passing of traditional society: modernizing the Middle East*. Glencoe, IL: Free Press.

Linking Fiji with the world. 1996. *Pacific Islands Monthly* 66(11):38.

MacBride, S. 1980. *Many voices, one world: communication and society, today and tomorrow*. New York: Unipub.

Maitland, Sir Donald, et al. 1984. *The missing link: report of the Independent Commission for World-wide Telecommunications Development*. [the Maitland Commission Report], Geneva: ITU.

Masterton, R. 1989. Pacific Ocean VISTA system using DAMA technology. In *PTC'89 Proceedings*, ed. L. S. Harms and D. Wedemeyer, 283–290, Honolulu: Pacific Telecommunications Council (PTC).

Miller, M. 1993. Comments made during the Pressure on the media: you, governments and culture session of the *Pacific Islands News Association* conference in Suva, Fiji, 10–13 July.

Mobile phone service opens in Marshall Islands. 1994. *Pacific Report* 7(16):5.

Molnar, H. 1993. Video and television training in the South Pacific: a regional approach. *Pacific Islands Communication Journal* 16(1):125–142.

Nilson, M. 1991. The TongaSat Asia-Pacific regional communications satellite system. In *PTC'91 Proceedings*, ed. D. Wedemeyer and M. Lofstrom, 688–696. Honolulu: PTC.

Nilson, M., and S. Kite. 1992. The TongaSat Asia-Pacific regional satellite communications network. In *PTC'92 Proceedings*, ed. M. Lofstrom and D. Wedemeyer, 431–443. Honolulu: PTC.

North, D. 1996. Internet promises major benefits to the Islands. *Pacific Islands Monthly* 66(9):50–53.

NUA Ltd. 1997. 1996 Internet Review: A NUA Synopsis of the Internet. (31 December 1996) Dublin, Ireland: NUA Ltd. http://www.nua.ie/surveys/1996review.html

Nygard, S. 1995. *Marianas media guide*. Guam: Glimpses of Guam, Inc.

Ogden, M. 1986. *The big push: a critical analysis of telecommunications development in the South Pacific*. M.A. Thesis. Ann Arbor: University Microfilms International (UMI).

Ogden, M. 1993. Foreign influences, local choices: the social impact of television in Micronesia. *Pacific Islands Communication Journal* 16(1):7–27.

Ogden, M. 1995. Pacific Islands, information technology and universal access: it's not just about wires. *Development Bulletin* (Special Issue: Information technology and development) 35(October):19-22.

Ogden, M., and J. Hailey. 1988. International broadcast services to isolated audiences: the role of Radio Australia during the Fiji crisis. *Media Asia* 15(1):22–25, 41.

Ogden, M., and P. L. Holloway. 1988. Old problems meet new technologies: South Pacific regional telecommunications developments. *PTC Quarterly* 8(4):17–19.

Ogden, M., and M. Jussawalla. 1994. Telecommunications and IT in Pacific Islands development. *Asian Journal of Communication* (Special Issue) 4(2):1–32.

Pacific Islands Internet Resources (PIIR). 1997. http://www2.hawaii.edu/~ogden/piir/

Plange, N-K. 1993. Video, TV and Fiji's society: fast-forward into the future or pausing for a closer look. *Pacific Islands Communication Journal* 16(1):63–77.

Richstad, J. 1987. Use of international broadcasts in Pacific Islands radio services: Dependency? Cultural imperialism? Practical necessity? [mimeo.] Honolulu, HI: Institute of Culture and Communication, East-West Center.

RMI Online. 1996. http://www.clark.net/pub/rmiemb/

Robie, D., ed. 1995. *Nius bilong Pasifik*. Port Moresby: University of Papua New Guinea Press.

Robson, R., 1950. *Pacific Island yearbook*. Sydney: Pacific Publications.

Rogers, E. 1962. *Diffusion of innovations*. New York: Free Press.

Rogers, E. 1976. *Communication and development: critical perspectives*. Beverly Hills, California: Sage.

Rogers, E. 1978. The rise and fall of the dominant paradigm. *Journal of Communication* 28 (1):64–69.

Rogers, E. 1986. *Communication technology: the new media in society*. New York: Free Press.

Rogers, E., and F. Shoemaker. 1971. *Communication of innovations*. New York: Free Press.

Royce, P. 1993. TVNZ's Pacific service: a new opportunity for broadcast television. *Pacific Islands Communication Journal* 16(1):101-123.

Saunders, R., J. Warford, and B. Wellenius. 1983. *Telecommunications and economic development*. Baltimore: Johns Hopkins University Press.

Schiller, H. 1976. *Communication and cultural domination*. New York: International Arts and Sciences.

Schiller, H. 1979. Communication accompanies capital flows. Document No. 47, prepared for the International Commission for Communications. Paris: UNESCO.

Schiller, H. 1981. *Who knows: information in the age of the Fortune 500*. Norwood, NJ: Ablex.

Schiller, H. 1989. *Culture, Inc.: The corporate takeover of public expression*. Oxford: Oxford University Press.

Schramm, W. 1964. *Mass media and national development*. Stanford, CA: UNESCO and Stanford University Press.

Senge Kolma, F. 1992. Interview with author. Port Moresby, PNG 27 May.

Siebert, F., T. Peterson, and W. Schramm. 1956. *Four theories of the press*. Urbana: University of Illinois.

Sinclair, J. 1984. *Uniting a nation: the postal and telecommunication services of Papua New Guinea*. Melbourne, Aust.: Oxford University Press.

South Pacific Online. 1996. http://www.infocentre.com/spt/

Status of PNCC's LightNet 2000 Plan. 1997. *Tia Belau* February 22–March 9 (newsletter item).

Stewart, J, B. Horsfield, and P. Cook. 1993. Television and dependency: a case study of policy making in Fiji and Papua New Guinea. *The Contemporary Pacific* 5(2):333–363.

Sullivan, J., and J. E. Morris. 1996. The development of Internet in the South Pacific. *Pacific Telecommunications Profile* 3(2): 455-457.

Sussman, G., and J. Lent, eds. 1991. *Transnational communications: wiring the Third World*. Newbury Park, CA: Sage Publications.

Teaiwa, T. 1994. bikinis and other s/pacific n/oceans. *The Contemporary Pacific*, 6(1):87–109.

Tehranian, M. 1979. Development theory and communication policy: the changing paradigms. In *Progress in communication sciences*, vol. 1, ed. G. J. Hanneman and M. Voigt. Norwood, NJ: Ablex.

Tehranian, M. 1990. *Technologies of power: information machines and democratic prospects*. Norwood, NJ: Ablex.

Tehranian, M. 1994. Communication and development. In *Communication theory today*, ed. D.Crowley and D. Mitchell, 274–306. Stanford, CA: Stanford University Press.

Tehranian, M., F. Hakimzadeh, and M. Vidale, eds. 1977. *Communication policy for national development: a comparative perspective*. London: Routledge.

Thomas, P. 1990. Communication policy and planning in the Pacific. In *Public administration and management in small states: Pacific experiences*, ed. Y. Ghai, 115–133. Suva, Fiji: The Commonwealth Secretariat and the University of the South Pacific.

Toffler, A. 1980. *The third wave*. New York: William Morrow.

Varan, D. 1992. *The costs and benefits of television: applying the emerging paradigms of development communications to the Cook Islands experience*. PhD dissertation. Austin, TX: The University of Texas at Austin.

Varan, D. 1993. Introducing television: seven lessons from the Cook Islands. *Pacific Islands Communication Journal* 16(1):29–61.

Vusoniwailala, L. 1987. Radio in today's Pacific. *Pacific Islands Communication Journal* 15(1), 29–35.

Waqavonovono, M. 1981. Who manipulates Pacific media? influences on newspapers and television. *Pacific Perspective* 10(1):13–36.

Williams, L. 1996. Cooks officials tight-lipped on Internet Casino deal. *Pacific Islands Monthly* 66(9):54.

World Telecommunications Advisory Council (WATC). 1993. *Telecommunications visions of the future: A WATC Perspective*. Geneva: International Telecommunications Union.

World Wide Web Virtual Library. 1996. *Pacific Studies*. http://sunsite.anu.edu.au/spin/wwwvl-pacific/index.html

# Abbreviations

| | |
|---|---|
| ACIAR | Australian Centre for International Agricultural Research |
| ACOA | Australian Council for Overseas Aid |
| ANU | Australian National University |
| APT | additional profits tax |
| ARCS | Achievement Rewards for College Scientists |
| ASAO | Association for Social Anthropology in Oceania |
| BP | before present |
| CBD | central business district |
| CCOP | Committee for Coordination of Joint Prospecting for Mineral |
| CEGET | Centre d'Études de Géographie Tropicale |
| CEP | Centre d'Expérimentation du Pacifique |
| CHEAM | Centre des Hautes Études sur l'Afrique et l'Asie Modernes |
| CNRS | Centre National de la Recherche Scientifique |
| CORAIL | Coordination pour l'Océanie des Recherches sur les Arts, les Idées et les Littératures |
| CPS | Commission du Pacifique Sud |
| CRA | Con Rio-Tinto Australia |
| CRET | Centre de Recherche sur les Espaces Tropicaux |
| CSIRO | Commonwealth Scientific and Industrial Research Organization |
| DAMA | demand assigned multiple access |
| DBEDT | Department of Business and Economic Development |
| DUD | Darrit-Uliga-Delap |
| DYMSET | Dynamique des Milieux et des Sociétés dans les Espaces Tropicauz |
| EAPI | Environment and Policy Institute (currently Program on Environment) |
| EEZ | Exclusive Economic Zone |
| EIU | Economic Intelligence Unit |
| ESCAP | Economic and Social Commission for Asia and the Pacific |
| EWC | East-West Center |
| FADINAP | Fertilizer Advisory, Development and Information Network for Asia and the Pacific |
| FAO | Food and Agriculture Organization |
| FEMM | Forum Economic Minister's Meeting |
| FFA | Forum Fisheries Agency |
| FINTEL | Fiji International Telecommunications, Ltd. |
| FLNKS | Front Libération Nationale Kanak et Socialiste |
| GDP | gross domestic product |
| GNP | gross national product |
| HCNZ | Housing Corporation of New Zealand |
| IAHS | International Association of Hydrological Sciences |
| IASER | Institute of Applied Social and Economic Research |
| IBS | International Broadcast Service |
| IBSRAM | International Board for Soil Research and Management |
| ICLARM | International Center for Living Aquatic Resources Management |
| ICRISAT | International Centre for Research in the Semi-Arid Tropics |
| IHP | International Hydrological Program |
| ILO | International Labor Organization |
| IMF | International Monetary Fund |
| INR | Institute of Natural Resources |
| INTELSAT | International Telecommunications Satellite Organization |
| IPS | Institute of Pacific Studies |
| ISP | Internet service provider |
| IT | information technology |
| ITQ | individual transferable quota |
| ITSEE | Institut Territorial de la Statistique et des Études Économiques |
| ITSTAT | Institut Territorial du Statistiques |
| ITU | International Telecommunications Union |
| IUCN | International Union for Conservation of Nature |
| Ka | thousands of years ago |
| LME | large marine ecosystem |
| LOSC | Law of the Sea Convention |
| Ma | millions of years ago |
| MFNZ | Ministry of Forestry, New Zealand |
| MIRAB | migration, remittances, aid, bureaucracy |
| MRSF | Mineral Resources Stabilisation Fund |
| NAS | National Academy of Science |
| NCDS | National Center for Development Studies |
| NESDIS | National Environmental Satellite, Data and Information Service |
| NGO | nongovernment organization |
| NIEO | new international economic order |
| NMFS | National Marine Fisheries Service |
| NODC | National Oceanographic Data Center |

The Pacific Islands

| | |
|---|---|
| NRC | National Research Council |
| NZSIC | New Zealand Seafood Industry Council |
| OBSNAT | Oceania Benchmark Sites Network for Agrotechnology Transfer |
| OECD | Organization for Economic Cooperation and Development |
| OPM | Organisasi Papua Merdeka (Free Papua Movement) |
| ORSTOM | Office de la Recherche Scientifique et Technique Outre Mer |
| OTMC | Ok Tedi Mining Company |
| PACT | Pacific Area Cooperative Telecommunications |
| PATS | Pohnpei Agriculture and Technology School |
| PBEC | Pacific Business Economic Council |
| PHC | primary health care |
| PIBA | Pacific Islands Broadcasting Association |
| PIDP | Pacific Islands Development Program |
| PIIR | Pacific Islands Internet Resources |
| PIM | Pacific Islands Monthly |
| PINA | Pacific Islands News Association |
| PJA | Pacific Journalists Association |
| PMEL | Pacific Marine Environmental Laboratory |
| PNCC | Palau National Communications Corporation |
| PTC | Pacific Telecommunications Council |
| PUF | Presses Universitaires de France |
| PWRB | Pacific Women's Resource Bureau |
| QMA | quota management area |
| QMS | quota management system |
| RBD | recreational business district |
| RELC | Regional Language Center |
| RSPAS | Research School for Pacific and Asian Studies |
| SHARE | Shared Area Resources Exchange |
| SLN | Société Métallurgique le Nickel |
| SMS | Survey and Marketing Services |
| SNZ | Statistics New Zealand |
| SOPAC | South Pacific Applied Geoscience Commission |
| SPC | Secretariat of the Pacific Community (formerly South Pacific Commission) |
| SPEC | South Pacific Forum Secretariat (formerly South Pacific Bureau for Economic Cooperation) |
| SPIN | South Pacific Information Network |
| SPREP | South Pacific Regional Environmental Program |
| SSED | School of Social and Economic Development |
| TACC | total allowable commercial catch |
| TAO | Tropical Atmosphere Ocean |
| TCSP | Tourism Council for the South Pacific |
| TFR | total fertility rate |
| TNG | Trans New Guinea |
| TVNZ | Television New Zealand |
| UMI | University Microfilms International |
| UNCTAD | United Nations Conference on Trade and Development |
| UNDDSMS | United Nations Department for Development Support and Management Services |
| UNDHA | United Nations Department of Humanitarian Affairs |
| UNE | University of New England |
| UNEP | United Nations Environmental Program |
| UNESCO | United Nations Educational, Scientific, and Cultural Organization |
| UNITECH | University of Technology |
| UPNG | University of Papua New Guinea |
| VFR | visiting friends and relatives |
| VTPS | Viles Tok Ples Skul |
| WATC | World Telecommunications Advisory Council of the International Telecommunications Union |
| WHO | World Health Organization |
| WPRO | Western Pacific Regional Office |
| WTO | World Tourism Organization |

# Island Gazetteer

Note: Abbreviated list. For geographic coordinates of other locations see references:
Bryan, E.H. 1943. *Guide to Pacific Islands*. Honolulu: Fourteenth Naval District Intelligence Office.
Getty Information Institute (GII). 1998. Thesaurus of geographic names. http://www.gii.getty.edu/tgn_browser/index.html
Motteler, L.S. 1986. *Pacific Island names*. Honolulu: Bishop Museum Press.

**Abbreviations used:**

| | |
|---|---|
| Am.Sam. | American Samoa |
| Aus. | Austral Islands |
| Banks | Banks Islands |
| Bis. | Bismarck Archipelago |
| Chuuk | State of Chuuk |
| CI | Cook Islands |
| D'Ent. | D'Entrecasteaux Islands |
| Epac. | East Pacific outliers |
| Fi.out | Fiji Outliers |
| FP | French Polynesia |
| FSM | Federated States of Micronesia |
| Gal. | Galápagos Islands |
| Gam. | Gambier Islands |
| Gil. | Gilbert Islands |
| Ha'ap. | Ha'apai Group |
| Haw. | Hawai'i |
| J.Fer. | Juan Fernandez Islands |
| Kad. | Kadavu Group |
| Kir. | Kiribati |
| Lau | Lau Islands |
| Line | Line Islands |
| Lom. | Lomaiviti Group |
| Lou. | Louisiade Archipelago |
| Loy. | Loyalty Islands |
| Mar. | Northern Mariana Islands |
| Marq. | Marquesas Islands |
| Moala | Moala Group |
| N.Sol. | North Solomon Islands |
| NC.group | New Caledonia Group |
| NC.out. | New Caledonia Outliers |
| NG.group | New Guinea Group |
| NWHI | Northwestern Hawaiian Islands |
| Pal.out. | Palau Outliers |
| Phoe. | Phoenix Islands |
| PNG | Papua New Guinea |
| Pohnpei | State of Pohnpei |
| Ralik | Ralik Chain |
| Ratak | Ratak Chain |
| S.Cruz | Santa Cruz |
| SI | Solomon Islands |
| Soc. | Society Islands |
| Sol.out. | Solomon Island Outliers |
| Sol.Sea | Solomon Sea Islands |
| Tor. | Torres Islands |
| Tuam. | Tuamotu Archipelago |
| USadm. | U.S.–administered Pacific Islands |
| Va.L. | Vanua Levu Group |
| Van. | Vanuatu |
| Vi.L. | Viti Levu Group |
| W&F | Wallis and Futuna |
| Yap | State of Yap |

| Island | Group | Latitude | Longitude |
|---|---|---|---|
| Abaiang | Gil., Kir. | 1°50'N | 173°02'E |
| Abemama | Gil., Kir. | 0°21'N | 173°51'E |
| Agakauitai | Gam., FP | 23°10'S | 136°01'W |
| Agrihan | Mar. | 18°46'N | 145°40'E |
| Aguijan | Mar. | 14°51'N | 145°34'E |
| Ahe | Tuam., FP | 14°30'S | 146°17'W |
| Ahunui | Tuam., FP | 19°40'S | 140°25'W |
| Ailinginae | Ralik, MI | 11°08'N | 166°30'E |
| Ailinglaplap | Ralik, MI | 7°25'N | 168°45'E |
| Ailuk | Ratak, MI | 10°20'N | 169°57'E |
| Aitutaki | CI | 18°52'S | 159°45'W |
| Aiwa | Lau, Fiji | 18°19'S | 178°43'W |
| Akamaru | Gam., FP | 23°11'S | 134°54'W |
| Akiaki | Gam., FP | 18°30'S | 139°14'W |
| Alamagan | Mar. | 17°36'N | 145°50'E |
| Alcester | Sol.Sea, PNG | 9°28'S | 152°28'E |
| Alexander Selkirk | J.Fer. | 33°45'S | 80°45'W |
| Alim | Bis., PNG | 2°55'S | 147°05'E |
| 'Alofi | W&F | 14°19'S | 178°02'W |
| Amanu | Tuam., FP | 17°48'S | 140°45'W |
| Ambitle | Bis., PNG | 4°10'S | 153°35'E |
| Ambrym | Van. | 16°15'S | 168°09'E |
| Anaa | Tuam., FP | 17°25'S | 145°30'W |
| Anatahan | Mar. | 16°21'N | 145°40'E |
| Anatom | Van. | 20°12'S | 169°46'E |
| Aniwa | Van. | 19°17'S | 169°34'E |
| Ant | Pohnpei, FSM | 6°54'N | 157°58'E |
| Anuanuraro | Tuam., FP | 20°28'S | 143°33'W |
| Anuanurunga | Tuam., FP | 20°38'S | 143°19'W |
| Anuta | S.Cruz, SI | 11°35'S | 169°51'E |
| Aoba | Van. | 15°23'S | 167°50'E |
| Apataki | Tuam., FP | 15°25'S | 146°20'W |
| Apolima | Samoa | 13°49'S | 172°07'W |
| Aranuka | Gil., Kir. | 0°10'N | 173°38'E |
| Aratika | Tuam., FP | 15°33'S | 145°30'W |
| Arnavon | SI | 7°24'S | 158°00'E |
| Arno | Ratak, MI | 7°05'N | 171°42'E |
| Arorae | Gil., Kir. | 2°39'S | 176°55'E |
| Art | NC Group, NC | 19°44'S | 163°39'E |
| Arutua | Tuam., FP | 15°10'S | 146°45'W |
| Asuncion | Mar. | 19°40'N | 145°24'E |
| 'Ata | Tonga | 22°20'S | 176°12'W |
| Atafu | Tokelau | 8°32'S | 172°31'W |
| Atiu | CI | 20°02'S | 158°07'W |
| Aua | Bis., PNG | 1°25'S | 143°05'E |
| Aukena | Gam., FP | 23°08S | 134°54'W |
| 'Aunu'u | Am.Sam. | 14°16'S | 170°35'W |
| Aur | Ratak, MI | 8°15'N | 171°05'E |

The Pacific Islands

| Island | Group | Latitude | Longitude | Island | Group | Latitude | Longitude |
| --- | --- | --- | --- | --- | --- | --- | --- |
| Avea | Lau, Fiji | 17°11'S | 178°55'W | Enewetak | Ralik, MI | 11°30'N | 162°15'E |
| Awin | Bis., PNG | 1°40'S | 144°05'E | Eot | Chuuk, FSM | 7°23'N | 151°44'E |
| Babase | Bis., PNG | 4°00'S | 153°40'E | Epi | Van. | 16°44'S | 168°17'E |
| Babeldaob | Palau | 7°30'N | 134°34'E | Erikub | Ratak, MI | 9°08'N | 170°00'E |
| Bacon | Lau, Fiji | 18°01'S | 178°28'W | Erromango | Van. | 18°48'S | 169°05'E |
| Bagaman | Lou., PNG | 11°10'S | 152°40'E | Espa | angoGal. | 1°2'S | 89°40'W |
| Bagbag | NG.group, PNG | 4°50'S | 146°15'E | Espiritu Santo | Van. | 15°20'S | 166°55'E |
| Bakawari | N.Sol., PNG | 6°15'S | 155°35'E | Etal | Chuuk, FSM | 5°35'N | 153°34'E |
| Baker | USadm. | 0°13'N | 176°28'W | 'Eua | Tonga | 21°20'S | 174°57'W |
| Baltra | Gal. | 0°26'S | 90°16'W | Ewose | Van. | 16°57'S | 168°35'E |
| Baluan | Bis., PNG | 2°30'S | 147°15'E | Faaite | Tuam., FP | 16°44'S | 145°15'W |
| Balum | Bis., PNG | 4°00'S | 153°40'E | Fais | Yap, FSM | 9°46'N | 140°31'E |
| Bam | NG.group, PNG | 3°40'S | 144°50'E | Fakahina | Tuam., FP | 15°59'S | 140°07'W |
| Banaba (Ocean) | Gil., Kir. | 0°52'S | 169°55'E | Fakaofo | Tokelau | 9°23'S | 171°15'W |
| Basilaki | Lou., PNG | 10°35'S | 151°00'E | Fakarava | Tuam., FP | 16°15'S | 145°32'W |
| Bat | Bis., PNG | 2°50'S | 146°15'E | Fanapanges | Chuuk, FSM | 7°21'N | 151°40'E |
| Batiki | Lom., Fiji | 17°47'S | 179°08'E | Fangatau | Tuam., FP | 15°49'S | 140°51'W |
| Beautemps-Beaupré | Loy., NC | 20°24'S | 166°10'E | Fangataufa | Tuam., FP | 22°15'S | 138°42'W |
| Bellona | Sol.out., SI | 11°18'S | 159°48'E | Farallon de Medinilla | Mar. | 16°01'N | 146°05'E |
| Beqa | Vi.L., Fiji | 18°24'S | 178°07'E | Farallon de Pajaros | Mar. | 20°32'N | 144°54'E |
| Beru | Gil., Kir. | 1°20'S | 176°00'E | Faraulep | Yap, FSM | 8°36'N | 144°33'E |
| Bikar | Ratak, MI | 12°15'N | 170°05'E | Fatu Hiva | Marq., FP | 10°26'S | 18°38'W |
| Bikini | Ralik, MI | 11°35'N | 165°23'E | Fatu Huku | Marq., FP | 9°27'S | 138°55'W |
| Bipi | Sol.Sea, PNG | 2°05'S | 146°25'E | Fayu | Chuuk, FSM | 8°34'N | 151°22'E |
| Birnie | Phoe., Kir. | 3°35'S | 171°31'W | Fefan | Chuuk, FSM | 7°20'N | 151°51'E |
| Blup Blup | NG.group, PNG | 3°30'S | 144°35'E | Fergusson | D'Ent., PNG | 9°30'S | 150°40'E |
| Boang | Bis., PNG | 3°25'S | 153°15'E | Fernandina | Gal. | 0°25'S | 91°30'W |
| Bokaak (Pokak) | Ratak, MI | 14°35'N | 168°58'E | Flint | Line, Kir. | 11°26'S | 151°48'W |
| Bora-Bora | Soc., FP | 16°30'S | 151°45'W | Floreana | Gal. | 1°20'S | 90°25'W |
| Bougainville | N.Sol., PNG | 6°10'S | 155°10'E | Foa | Ha'ap., Tonga | 19°45'S | 174°17'W |
| Buka | N.Sol., PNG | 5°20'S | 154°38'E | Fonuafo'ou | Ha'ap., Tonga | 20°19'S | 175°25'W |
| Butaritari | Gil., Kir. | 3°05'N | 172°50'E | Fulanga | Lau, Fiji | 19°07'S | 178°35'W |
| Caroline | Line, Kir. | 10°00'S | 150°14'W | Funafuti | Tuvalu | 8°31'S | 179°08'E |
| Choiseul | SI | 7°S | 157°E | Futuna | W&F | 14°16'S | 178°08'W |
| Chuuk (Truk) | Chuuk, FSM | 7°20'N | 151°45'E | Futuna (Erronan) | Van. | 19°32'S | 170°10.5'E |
| Cicia | Lau, Fiji | 17°45'S | 179°20'W | Gaferut | Yap, FSM | 9°14'N | 145°23'E |
| Cikobia | Va.L., Fiji | 15°45'S | 179°56'W | Gagil Tamil | Yap, FSM | 9°32'N | 138°10'E |
| Clipperton | EPac. | 10°18'N | 109°13'W | Garove | Bis., PNG | 4°40'S | 149°30'E |
| Cocos | EPac. | 5°32'N | 87°00'W | Gau | Lom., Fiji | 18°02'S | 179°18'E |
| Crown | NG.group, PNG | 5°10'S | 146°55'E | Gawa | Sol.Sea, PNG | 9°00'S | 151°55'E |
| Culpepper | Gal. | 1°39'N | 92°00'W | Ghizo (Gizo) | SI | 8°04'S | 156°48'E |
| Dobu | D'Ent., PNG | 9°47'S | 150°53'E | Goodenough | D'Ent., PNG | 9°24'S | 150°15'E |
| Dublon | Chuuk, FSM | 7°23'N | 151°52'E | Guadalcanal | SI | 9°40'S | 160°20'E |
| Ducie | Pitcairn | 24°40'S | 124°48'W | Guam | Guam | 13°25'N | 144°45'E |
| Duke of York | Bis., PNG | 4°10'S | 152°25'E | Guguan | Mar. | 17°19'N | 145°51'E |
| Easter (Rapa Nui) | EPac. | 27°06'S | 109°22'W | Ha'ano | Ha'ap., Tonga | 19°40'S | 174°17'W |
| Eauripik | Yap, FSM | 6°41.5'N | 143°3'E | Hao | Tuam., FP | 18°10'S | 140°55'W |
| Ebon | Ralik, MI | 4°38'N | 168°43'E | Haraiki | Tuam., FP | 17°28'S | 143°32'W |
| Efate | Van. | 17°40'S | 168°23'E | Hatutaa | Marq., FP | 7°56'S | 140°34'W |
| Egum | Sol.Sea, PNG | 9°25'S | 152°00'E | Hawai'i | Haw. | 19°40'N | 155°30'W |
| Eiao | Marq., FP | 8°00'S | 140°41'W | Henderson | Pitcairn | 24°22'S | 130°05'W |
| Elato | Yap, FSM | 7°30'N | 146°10'E | Hereheretue | Tuam., FP | 19°53'S | 145°05'W |
| Eloaua | Bis., PNG | 1°40'S | 149°40'E | Hikueru | Tuam., FP | 17°36'S | 142°40'W |
| Emae | Van. | 17°04'S | 168°23'E | Hiti | Tuam., FP | 16°42'S | 144°08'W |
| Emirau | Bis., PNG | 1°40'S | 145°55'E | Hiu | Tor., Van. | 13°09'S | 166°34'E |
| Enderbury | Phoe., Kir. | 3°08'S | 171°05'W | Hiva Oa | Marq., FP | 9°45'S | 139°00'W |

| Island | Group | Latitude | Longitude | Island | Group | Latitude | Longitude |
| --- | --- | --- | --- | --- | --- | --- | --- |
| Howland | USadm. | 0°48'N | 176°38'W | Losap | Chuuk, FSM | 6°52'N | 152°42'E |
| Huahine | Soc., FP | 16°45'S | 151°00'W | Lou | Bis., PNG | 2°25'S | 147°20'E |
| Hunga Tonga | Ha'ap., Tonga | 20°33'S | 175°23'W | Luf | Bis., PNG | 1°35'S | 145°05'E |
| Hunter | NC.out., NC | 22°24'S | 172°94'E | Lukunor | Chuuk, FSM | 5°31'N | 153°46'E |
| Huon | NC Group, NC | 18°03'S | 162°58'E | Maap | Yap, FSM | 9°35'N | 138°11'W |
| Ifalik | Yap, FSM | 7°15'N | 144°27'E | Madau | Sol.Sea, PNG | 9°00'S | 152°25'E |
| Isabela | Gal. | 0°30'S | 91°10'W | Maewo | Van. | 15°10'S | 168°10'E |
| Jabwot | Ralik, MI | 7°45'N | 168°59'E | Mahotani | Marq., FP | 10°S | 138°39'W |
| Jaluit | Ralik, MI | 6°00'N | 169°35'E | Mahur | Bis., PNG | 2°45'S | 152°40'E |
| Jarvis | Line, USadm. | 0°23'S | 160°02'W | Maia | Soc., FP | 17°37'S | 150°37'W |
| Jemo | Ratak, MI | 10°08'N | 169°32'E | Maiana | Gil., Kir. | 1°00'N | 173°01'E |
| Johnston | USadm. | 16°45'N | 169°30'W | Maiao | Soc., FP | 17°37'S | 150°37'W |
| Kadavu | Vi.L., Fiji | 19°01'S | 178°12'E | Majuro | Ratak, MI | 7°07'N | 171°12'E |
| Kaho'olawe | Haw. | 20°33'N | 156°37'W | Makaroa | Gam., FP | 23°13'S | 134°58'W |
| Kaileuna | Sol.Sea, PNG | 8°30'S | 150°55'E | Makatea | Tuam., FP | 15°50'S | 148°13'W |
| Kairiru | NG.group, PNG | 3°20'S | 143°30'E | Makemo | Tuam., FP | 16°35'S | 143°40'W |
| Kamaka | Gam., FP | 23°15'S | 134°57'W | Makin | Gil., Kir. | 3°16'N | 172°58'E |
| Kaniet | Bis., PNG | 0°50'S | 135°30'E | Makogai | Lom., Fiji | 17°27'S | 178°57'E |
| Kanton (Canton) | Phoe., Kir. | 2°50'S | 171°43'W | Malaita | SI | 9°S | 161°E |
| Kao | Ha'ap., Tonga | 19°40'S | 175°02'W | Malakula | Van. | 16°15'S | 167°30'E |
| Kapingamarangi | Pohnpei, FSM | 1°03'N | 154°46'E | Malden | Line, Kir. | 4°03'S | 154°59'W |
| Karkar | NG.group, PNG | 4°40'S | 146°00'E | Malendok | Bis., PNG | 3°30'S | 153°15'E |
| Katiu | Tuam., FP | 16°25'S | 144°20'W | Mali | Bis., PNG | 3°10'S | 152°40'E |
| Kaua'i | Haw. | 22°N | 159°30'W | Maloelap | Ratak, MI | 8°45'N | 171°00'E |
| Kauehi | Tuam., FP | 15°50'S | 145°10'W | Malpelo | EPac. | 4°N | 81°15'W |
| Kaukura | Tuam., FP | 15°40'S | 146°40'W | Malum | N.Sol., PNG | 3°10'S° | 154°25'E |
| Ka'ula | Haw. | 21°39'N | 160°33'W | Manam | NG.group, PNG | 4°05'S | 145°05'E |
| Kili | Ralik, MI | 5°39'N | 169°07'E | Mangaia | CI | 21°55'S | 157°55'W |
| Kiritimati | Line, Kir. | 1°55'N | 157°20'W | Mangareva | Gam., FP | 23°07'S | 134°57'W |
| Kiriwina | Sol.Sea, PNG | 8°40'S | 151°05'E | Manihi | Tuam., FP | 14°26'S | 145°55'W |
| Kitava | Sol.Sea, PNG | 8°36'S | 151°20'E | Manihiki | CI | 10°23'S | 161°01'W |
| Koil | NG.group, PNG | 3°20'S | 144°10'E | Manono | Samoa | 13°50'S | 172°05'W |
| Kolombangara | SI | 8°S | 157°05'E | Manra (Sydney) | Phoe., Kir. | 4°27'S | 171°16'W |
| Koro | Lom., Fiji | 17°16'S | 179°23'E | Manu | Bis., PNG | 1°20'S | 143°35'E |
| Kosrae | Kosrae, FSM | 5°20'N | 162°59'E | Manuae | CI | 19°21'S | 158°56'W |
| Kure | NWHI, Haw. | 28°25'N | 178°25'W | Manuae | Soc., FP | 16°30'S | 154°40'W |
| Kuria | Gil., Kir. | 0°14'N | 173°28'E | Manuhangi | Tuam., FP | 19°11'S | 141°15'W |
| Kwaiawata | Sol.Sea, PNG | 8°55'S | 151°50'E | Manui | Gam., FP | 23°14'S | 134°56'W |
| Kwajalein | Ralik, MI | 9°05'N | 167°20'E | Manus | Bis., PNG | 2°05'S | 147°E |
| Lae | Ralik, MI | 8°56'N | 166°15'E | Marakei | Gil., Kir. | 2°00'N | 173°20'E |
| Lakeba | Lau, Fiji | 18°13'S | 178°43'W | Marchena | Gal. | 0°21'N | 90°30'W |
| Lamotrek | Yap, FSM | 7°30'N | 146°20'E | Maré | Loy., NC | 21°30'S | 168°00'E |
| Lāna'i | Haw. | 20°50'N | 156°55'W | Maria | Tuam., FP | 22°01'S | 136°10'W |
| Late | Vava'u, Tonga | 18°48'S | 174°39'W | Marokau | Tuam., FP | 18°03'S | 142°17'W |
| Lavongai | Bis., PNG | 2°32'S | 150°15'E | Maron | Bis., PNG | 1°35'S | 145°00'E |
| Laysan | NWHI, Haw. | 25°46'N | 171°44'W | Marotiri Nui | Aus., FP | 27°55'S | 143°26'W |
| Lehua | Haw. | 22°01N | 160°06'W | Marutea North | Tuam., FP | 17°00'S | 143°10'W |
| Lib | Ralik, MI | 8°19'N | 167°24'E | Marutea South | Tuam., FP | 21°30'S | 135°30'W |
| Lifou | Loy., NC | 21°00'S | 167°15'E | Masahet | Bis., PNG | 3°00'S | 152°40'E |
| Lifuka | Ha'ap., Tonga | 19°48'S | 174°21'W | Mataiva | Tuam., FP | 14°54'S | 148°40'W |
| Lihir | Bis., PNG | 3°15'S | 152°39'E | Matthew | NC.out., NC | 22°20'S | 171°19'E |
| Likiep | Ratak, MI | 9°55'N | 169°08'E | Matuku | Ha'ap., Tonga | 19°10'S | 179°45'E |
| Liot | Bis., PNG | 1°25'S | 144°30'E | Matureivavao | Tuam., FP | 21°46'S | 136°25'W |
| Lisianski | NWHI, Haw. | 26°04'N | 173°58'W | Maui | Haw. | 20°50'N | 156°25'W |
| Lolobau | Bis., PNG | 4°55'S | 151°10'E | Mauke | CI | 20°09'S | 157°23'W |
| Long | NG.group, PNG | 5°20'S | 147°05'E | Maupihaa | Soc., FP | 16°49'S | 153°57'W |

The Pacific Islands

| Island | Group | Latitude | Longitude | Island | Group | Latitude | Longitude |
|---|---|---|---|---|---|---|---|
| Maupiti | Soc., FP | 16°26'S | 152°15'W | New Georgia | SI | 8°15'S | 157°35'E |
| Mbuke | Bis., PNG | 2°25'S | 146°50'E | New Ireland | Bis., PNG | 3°30'S | 152°E |
| McKean | Phoe., Kir. | 3°36'S | 174°08'W | Ngcheangel | Palau | 8°03'N | 134°43'E |
| Mehetia | Soc., FP | 17°53'S | 148°06'W | Ngeaur | Palau | 6°54'N | 134°09'E |
| Mejit | Ratak, MI | 10°17'N | 170°53'E | Ngemlis | Palau | 7°07'N | 134°15'E |
| Mere Lava | Banks, Van. | 14°26'S | 167°58'E | Ngeruktabel | Palau | 7°15'N | 134°25'E |
| Merig | Banks, Van. | 14°17'S | 167°48'E | Ngetik | Pohnpei, FSM | 5°50'N | 157°15'E |
| Merir | Pal.out., Palau | 4°19'N | 132°19'E | Ngulu | Yap, FSM | 8°27'N | 137°29'E |
| Midway | USadm. | 28°13'N | 177°23'W | Niau | Tuam., FP | 16°10'S | 146°20'W |
| Mili | Ratak, MI | 6°08'N | 171°57'E | Nihiru | Tuam., FP | 16°43'S | 142°50'W |
| Misima | Lou., PNG | 10°40'S | 152°43'E | Nihoa | NWHI, Haw. | 23°03'N | 161°55'W |
| Mitiaro | CI | 19°49'S | 157°43'W | Ni'ihau | Haw. | 21°55'N | 160°10'W |
| Moala | Moala, Fiji | 18°36'S | 179°53'E | Nikumaroro (Gardner) | Phoe., Kir. | 4°40'S | 174°32'W |
| Moce | Lau, Fiji | 18°39'S | 178°31'W | Nikunau | Gil., Kir. | 1°21'S | 176°28'E |
| Moen | Chuuk, FSM | 7°26'N | 151°52'E | Niningo | Bis., PNG | 1°15'S | 144°15'E |
| Mohotani | Marq., FP | 10°S | 138°39'W | Nissan | N.Sol., PNG | 4°30'S | 154°10'E |
| Mole | Bis., PNG | 2°50'S | 146°25'E | Niuafo'ou | Tonga | 15°35'S | 175°38'W |
| Moloka'i | Haw. | 21°08'N | 157°W | Niuatoputapu | Tonga | 15°58'S | 173°48'W |
| Molokini | Haw. | 20°38'N | 156°29'W | Niue | Niue | 19°00'S | 169°50'W |
| Moorea | Soc., FP | 17°30'S | 149°50'W | Niulakita | Tuvalu | 10°45'S | 179°30'E |
| Morane | Tuam., FP | 23°07'S | 137°07'W | Niutao | Tuvalu | 6°06'S | 177°16'E |
| Moruroa | Tuam., FP | 21°50'S | 138°55'W | Nomuka | Ha'ap., Tonga | 20°27'S | 174°46'W |
| Mota | Banks, Van. | 13°49'S | 167°42'E | Nomwin | Chuuk, FSM | 8°31'N | 151°47'E |
| Mota Lava | Banks, Van. | 13°40'S | 167°40'E | Nonouti | Gil., Kir. | 0°40'S | 174°20'E |
| Mota Lava (Valua) | Banks, Van. | 13°40'S | 167°40'E | Normanby | D'Ent., PNG | 10°00'S | 151°00'E |
| Motu Iti | Marq., FP | 16°16'S | 151°49'W | Nuakata | Lou., PNG | 10°15'S | 151°00'E |
| Motu One | Marq., FP | 7°53'S | 140°23'W | Nuguria | N.Sol., PNG | 3°15'S | 154°40'E |
| Motu One | Soc., FP | 15°50'S | 154°30'W | Nui | Tuvalu | 7°16'S | 177°10'E |
| Motutunga | Tuam., FP | 17°05'S | 144°22'W | Nuku Hiva | Marq., FP | 8°52'S | 140°05'W |
| Murilo | Chuuk, FSM | 8°40'N | 152°11'E | Nukufetau | Tuvalu | 8°00'S | 178°29'E |
| Muschu | NG.group, PNG | 3°25'S | 143°30'E | Nukulaelae | Tuvalu | 9°22'S | 179°51'E |
| Mussau | Bis., PNG | 1°25'S | 149°37'E | Nukumanu | N.Sol., PNG | 4°32'S | 159°26'E |
| Muwo | Sol.Sea, PNG | 8°45'S | 151°00'E | Nukunonu | Tokelau | 9°10'S | 171°53'W |
| Muyua (Woodlark) | Sol.Sea, PNG | 9°10'S | 152°45'E | Nukuoro | Pohnpei, FSM | 3°51'N | 154°58'E |
| Mwokil | Pohnpei, FSM | 6°40'N | 159°46'E | Nukutavake | Tuam., FP | 19°16'S | 138°51'W |
| Nairai | Lom., Fiji | 17°49'S | 179°24'E | Nukutipipi | Tuam., FP | 20°42'S | 143°03'W |
| Nama | Chuuk, FSM | 7°00'N | 152°35'E | Nupani | S.Cruz, SI | 10°21'S | 166°17'E |
| Namoluk | Chuuk, FSM | 5°55'N | 153°08'E | O'ahu | Haw. | 21°30'N | 158°W |
| Namonuito | Chuuk, FSM | 8°45'N | 150°05'E | Oeno | Pitcairn | 23°56'S | 130°44'W |
| Namorik | Ralik, MI | 5°35'N | 168°07'E | Ofu | Am.Sam. | 14°11'S | 169°41'W |
| Namu | Ralik, MI | 8°00'N | 168°10'E | Olimarao | Yap, FSM | 7°41'N | 145°52'E |
| Nanumanga | Tuvalu | 6°18'S | 176°21'E | Olosenga | Am.Sam. | 14°11'S | 169°39'W |
| Nanumea | Tuvalu | 5°39'S | 176°08'E | Oneata | Lau, Fiji | 18°24'S° | 178°29'W |
| Napuka | Tuam., FP | 14°09'S | 141°15'W | Ono | Kad., Fiji | 18°54'S | 178°29'W |
| Narage | Bis., PNG | 4°30'S | 149°05'E | Ono-i-lau | Lau, Fiji | 20°40'S | 178°43'W |
| Nasai | Sol.Sea, PNG | 9°10'S | 152°40'E | Onotoa | Gil., Kir. | 1°50'S | 175°33'E |
| Nassau | CI | 11°33'S | 165°25'W | Ontong Java | Sol.out., SI | 5°20'S | 159°30'E |
| Nauna | Bis., PNG | 2°15'S | 148°10'E | Oreor (Koror) | Palau | 7°20'N | 134°30'E |
| Nauru | Nauru | 0°32'S | 166°55'E | Oroluk | Pohnpei, FSM | 7°32'N | 155°18'E |
| Nayau | Lau, Fiji | 17°58'S | 179°03'W | Orona (Hull) | Phoe., Kir. | 4°29'S | 170°43'W |
| New Caledonia | NC Group, NC | 21°28'S | 164°40'E | Ouen | NC Group, NC | 22°26'S | 166°49'E |
| Necker | NWHI, Haw. | 23°35'N | 164°42'W | Ouvéa | Loy., NC | 20°35'S | 166°30'E |
| Nendö | S.Cruz, SI | 10°46'S | 165°55'E | Ovalau | Vi.L., Fiji | 17°41'S | 178°47'E |
| Nengonengo | Tuam., FP | 18°50'S | 141°47'W | Pagan | Mar. | 18°07'N | 145°46'E |
| Neoch | Chuuk, FSM | 7°02'N | 151°55'E | Pak | Bis., PNG | 2°05'S | 147°35'E |
| New Britain | Bis., PNG | 4°10'S | 6°20'E | Pakin | Pohnpei, FSM | 7°03'N | 157°48'E |

| Island | Group | Latitude | Longitude | Island | Group | Latitude | Longitude |
|---|---|---|---|---|---|---|---|
| Palmerston | CI | 18°04'S | 163°10'W | Rurutu | Aus., FP | 22°26'S | 151°20'W |
| Palmyra | Line, USadm. | 5°52'N | 162°06'W | Sae | Bis., PNG | 0°40'S | 145°15'E |
| Panaeati | Lou., PNG | 10°40'S | 152°20'E | Saipan | Mar. | 15°10'N | 145°45'E |
| Panatinane | Lou., PNG | 11°15'S | 153°10'E | Sakar | NG.group, PNG | 5°25'S | 148°05'E |
| Panawina | Lou., PNG | 11°10'S | 153°00'E | Sala-y-Gomez | EPac. | 26°28'S | 105°28'W |
| Paraoa | Tuam., FP | 19°09'S | 140°43'W | Samarai | Lou., PNG | 10°35'S | 150°35'E |
| Peleliu (Beliliou) | Palau | 7°00'N | 134°15'E | San Ambrosio | EPac. | 26°21'S | 79°52'W |
| Pelelun | Bis., PNG | 1°05'S | 144°25'E | San Cristobal | Gal. | 0°50'S | 89°30'W |
| Penrhyn | CI | 9°00'S | 158°03'W | San Cristobal | SI | 10°35'S | 161°45'E |
| Pentecost | Van. | 15°45'S | 168°12'E | San Felix | EPac. | 26°17'S | 80°05'W |
| Pikelot | Yap, FSM | 8°05'N | 147°38'E | Sanaroa | D'Ent., PNG | 9°40'S | 151°00'E |
| Pinaki | Tuam., FP | 19°22'S | 138°42'W | Sandy | NC.out., NC | 19°10'S | 159°57'E |
| Pines | NC Group, NC | 22°39'S | 167°28'E | Santa Cruz | Gal. | 0°35'S | 90°25'W |
| Pingelap | Pohnpei, FSM | 6°13'N | 160°46'E | Santa Fe | Gal. | 0°50'S | 90°04'W |
| Pinipel | N.Sol., PNG | 4°25'S | 154°05'E | Santa Isabel | SI | 8°S | 159°E |
| Pinta | Gal. | 0°35'N | 90°45'W | Santa Maria (Gaua) | Banks, Van. | 14°20'S | 167°28'E |
| Pitcairn | Pitcairn | 25°04'S | 130°05'W | Santiago | Gal. | 0°15'S | 90°45'W |
| Pohnpei | Pohnpei, FSM | 6°52'N | 158°14'E | Sariba | Lou., PNG | 10°35'S | 140°40'E |
| Pott | NC Group, NC | 19°35'S | 163°36'E | Sarigan | Mar. | 16°42'N | 145°47'E |
| Pukapuka | CI | 10°55'S | 165°50'W | Satawal | Yap, FSM | 7°21'N | 147°02'E |
| Pukapuka | Tuam., FP | 14°56'S | 138°45'W | Satawan | Chuuk, FSM | 5°23'N | 153°35'E |
| Pukarua | Tuam., FP | 18°20'S | 137°02'W | Savai'i | Samoa | 13°40'S | 172°30'W |
| Pulap | Chuuk, FSM | 7°35'N | 149°25'E | Savo | SI | 9°08'S | 159°48'E |
| Pulo Anna | Pal.out., Palau | 4°40'N | 131°58'E | Shortland | SI | 7°03'S | 155°48'E |
| Pulusuk | Chuuk, FSM | 6°41'N | 149°19'E | Sideia | Lou., PNG | 10°35'S | 150°50'E |
| Puluwat | Chuuk, FSM | 7°21'N | 149°11'E | Siis | Chuuk, FSM | 7°18'N | 1551°49'E |
| Qamea | Va.L., Fiji | 16°45'S | 179°46'W | Sikaiana | Sol.out., SI | 8°22'S | 162°40'W |
| Rabi | Va.L., Fiji | 16°31'S° | 179°59'W | Simberi | Bis., PNG | 2°35'S | 152°E |
| Raiatea | Soc., FP | 16°50'S | 151°25'W | Sonsorol | Pal.out., Palau | 5°20'N | 132°13'E |
| Raivavae | Aus., FP | 23°52'S | 147°40'W | Sorol | Yap, FSM | 8°08'N | 140°23'E |
| Rakahanga | CI | 10°02'S | 161°06'W | Starbuck | Line, Kir. | 5°37'S | 153°53'W |
| Rambutyo | Bis., PNG | 2°20'S | 147°50'E | Sudest (Tagula) | Lou., PNG | 11°30'S | 153°30'E |
| Rangiroa | Tuam., FP | 15°05'S | 147°40W | Sumasuma | Bis., PNG | 1°30'S | 144°05'E |
| Ranongga | SI | 8°05'S | 156°35'E | Surprise | NC Group, NC | 18°29'S | 163°07'E |
| Rapa | Aus., FP | 27°36'S | 144°18'W | Suwarrow | CI | 13°15'S | 163°05'W |
| Raraka | Tuam., FP | 16°10'S | 144°50'W | Swains | Am.Sam. | 11°03'S | 171°05'W |
| Raroia | Tuam., FP | 16°05'S | 142°23'W | Tabar | Bis., PNG | 2°55'S | 152°E |
| Rarotonga | CI | 21°14'S | 159°46'W | Tabiteuea | Gil., Kir. | 1°25'S | 174°50'E |
| Rat | Bis., PNG | 2°55'S | 146°20'E | Tabuaeran (Fanning) | Line, Kir. | 3°54'N | 159°23'W |
| Ravahere | Tuam., FP | 18°13'S | 142°10'W | Taenga | Tuam., FP | 16°19'S | 143°06'W |
| Rawaki (Phoenix) | Phoe., Kir. | 3°43'S | 170°43'W | Tafahi | Tonga | 15°51'S | 173°44'W |
| Reao | Tuam., FP | 18°30'S | 136°20'W | Tahaa | Soc., FP | 16°38'S | 151°28'W |
| Reitoru | Tuam., FP | 17°48'S | 143°06'W | Tahanea | Tuam., FP | 16°56'S | 144°47'W |
| Rekareka | Tuam., FP | 16°49'S | 141°55'W | Tahiti | Soc., FP | 17°38'S | 149°25'W |
| Rendova | SI | 8°34'S | 157°20'E | Tahuata | Marq., FP | 9°55'S | 139°05'W |
| Rennell | Sol.out., SI | 11°32'S | 160°10'E | Taiaro | Tuam., FP | 15°44'S | 144°37'W |
| Rimatara | Aus., FP | 22°38'S | 152°45'W | Taiof | N.Sol., PNG | 5°35'S | 154°40'E |
| Robinson Crusoe | J.Fer. | 33°38'S | 78°50'W | Taka | Ratak, MI | 11°08'N | 168°38'E |
| Romonum | Chuuk, FSM | 7°25'N | 151°40'E | Takapoto | Tuam., FP | 14°36'S | 145°12'W |
| Rongelap | Ralik, MI | 11°20'N | 166°50'E | Takaroa | Tuam., FP | 14°27'S | 144°55'W |
| Rongrik | Ralik, MI | 11°20'N | 167°27'E | Takume | Tuam., FP | 15°45'S | 142°10'W |
| Rose | Am.Sam. | 14°33'S | 168°09'W | Takuu | N.Sol., PNG | 4°50'S | 157°05'E |
| Rossel | Lou., PNG | 11°22'S | 154°10'E | Tamana | Gil., Kir. | 2°32'S | 175°58'E |
| Rota | Mar. | 14°09'N | 145°12'E | Tanna | Van. | 19°30'S | 169°20'E |
| Rotuma | Fi.out., Fiji | 12°30'S | 175°52'E | Taravai | Gam., FP | 23°09'S | 136°01'W |
| Rumung | Yap, FSM | 9°37'N | 138°10'E | Tarawa | Gil., Kir. | 1°30'N | 173°00'E |

| Island | Group | Latitude | Longitude | Island | Group | Latitude | Longitude |
|---|---|---|---|---|---|---|---|
| Tarawai | NG.group, PNG | 3°15'S | 143°20'E | Ureparapara | Banks, Van. | 13°31'S | 167°20'E |
| Tatakoto | Tuam., FP | 17°20'S | 138°22'W | Utrik | Ratak, MI | 11°15'N | 169°48'E |
| Tatau | Bis., PNG | 2°0'S | 151°55'E | Utupua | S.Cruz, SI | 11°19'S | 166°33'E |
| Ta'u | Am.Sam. | 14°14'S | 169°28'W | 'Uvea (Wallis) | W&F | 13°18'S | 176°10'W |
| Tauere | Tuam., FP | 17°22'S | 141°28'W | Vahanga | Tuam., FP | 21°20'S | 136°39'W |
| Taveuni | Va.L., Fiji | 16°50'S | 179°58'W | Vahitahi | Tuam., FP | 18°44'S | 138°52'W |
| Tefa | Bis., PNG | 3°35'S | 153°10'E | Vairaatea | Tuam., FP | 19°18'S | 139°19'W |
| Tegua | Tor., Van. | 13°14'S | 166°36'E | Vaitupu | Tuvalu | 7°28'S | 178°41'E |
| Tekokota | Tuam., FP | 17°19'S | 142°37'W | Vakuta | Sol.Sea, PNG | 8°50'S | 151°10'E |
| Tematangi | Tuam., FP | 21°40'S | 140°40'W | Vanavana | Tuam., FP | 20°37'S | 139°08'W |
| Temoe | Gam., FP | 23°20'S | 134°30'W | Vangunu | SI | 8°40'S | 158°00'E |
| Tenararo | Tuam., FP | 21°19'S | 136°46'W | Vanikolo | S.Cruz, SI | 11°40'S | 166°54'E |
| Tenarunga | Tuam., FP | 21°19'S | 136°33'W | Vanua Balavu | Lau, Fiji | 17°15'S | 178°59'W |
| Tench | Bis., PNG | 1°40'S | 150°40'E | Vanua Lava | Banks, Van. | 13°48'S | 167°26'E |
| Tepoto North | Tuam., FP | 14°05'S | 141°24'W | Vanua Levu | Va.L., Fiji | 16°09'S | 179°57'E |
| Tepoto South | Tuam., FP | 16°48'S | 144°17'W | Vatoa | Lau, Fiji | 19°50'S | 178°13'W |
| Teraina (Washington) | Line, Kir. | 4°43'N | 160°26'W | Vatulele | Vi.L., Fiji | 18°33'S | 177°38'E |
| Tetepare | SI | 8°44'S | 157°33'E | Vava'u | Vava'u, Tonga | 18°35'S | 174°00'W |
| Tetiaroa | Soc., FP | 17°05'S | 149°32'W | Vella Lavella | SI | 7°45'S | 156°40'E |
| Tikehau | Tuam., FP | 15°00'S | 148°10'W | Viti Levu | Vi.L., Fiji | 17°50'S | 178°00'E |
| Tikei | Tuam., FP | 14°54'S | 144°32'W | Vokeo | NG.group, PNG | 3°15'S | 144°05'E |
| Tikopia | S.Cruz, SI | 12°18'S | 168°49'E | Vonavona | SI | 8°15'S | 157°15'E |
| Tinian | Mar. | 15°00'N | 145°38'E | Vostok | Line, Kir. | 10°06'S | 152°23'W |
| Toau | Tuam., FP | 15°52'S | 146°W | Wake | USadm. | 19°17'N | 166°35'E |
| Tobi | Pal.out., Palau | 3°00'N | 131°10.5'E | Walis | NG.group, PNG | 3°15'S | 143°20'E |
| Tofua | Ha'ap., Tonga | 19°43'S | 175°03'W | Walpole | NC.out., NC | 22°38'S | 168°56'E |
| Toga | Tor., Van. | 13°26'S | 166°41'E | Wamea | D'Ent., PNG | 9°15'S | 150°55'E |
| Toku | Tonga | 18°09'S | 174°09'W | Watom | Bis., PNG | 4°10'S | 152°05'E |
| Tol | Chuuk, FSM | 7°21'N | 151°38'E | Wawiwa | D'Ent., PNG | 9°20'S | 150°45'E |
| Tolokiwa | NG.group, PNG | 5°20'S | 147°35'E | Wenman | Gal. | 1°23'N | 91°49'W |
| Tongariki | Van. | 17°00'S | 168°38'E | West Fayu | Yap, FSM | 8°05'N | 146°44'E |
| Tongatapu | Tonga | 21°10'S | 175°10'W | Woleai | Yap, FSM | 7°21'N | 143°53'E |
| Tongoa | Van. | 16°54'S | 168°34'E | Wotho | Ralik, MI | 10°07'N | 165°58'E |
| Totoya | Moala, Fiji | 18°57'S | 179°51'W | Wotje | Ratak, MI | 9°28'N | 170°00'E |
| Tower | Gal. | 0°20'N | 89°57'W | Wuvulu | Bis., PNG | 1°45'S | 142°45'E |
| Tuanake | Tuam., FP | 16°40'S | 144°14'W | Yap | Yap, FSM | 9°31'N | 138°08'E |
| Tubuai | Aus., FP | 23°23'S | 149°26'W | Yeina | Lou., PNG | 11°20'S | 153°25'E |
| Tulun (Kilinilau) | N.Sol., PNG | 4°44'S | 155°24'E | | | | |
| Tupai | Soc., FP | 16°16'S | 151°49'W | | | | |
| Tureia | Tuam., FP | 20°46'S | 138°31'W | | | | |
| Tutuila | Am.Sam. | 14°18'S | 170°42'W | | | | |
| Tuvana-i-Colo | Lau, Fiji | 21°02'S | 178°50'W | | | | |
| Tuvana-i-Ra | Lau, Fiji | 21°00'S | 178°44'W | | | | |
| Ua Huka | Marq., FP | 8°54'S | 139°32'W | | | | |
| Ua Pou | Marq., FP | 9°24'S | 140°03'W | | | | |
| Udot | Chuuk, FSM | 7°23'N | 151°43'E | | | | |
| Ujae | Ralik, MI | 9°04'N | 165°38'E | | | | |
| Ujelang | Ralik, MI | 9°50'N | 160°55'E | | | | |
| Uki Ni Masi (Ugi) | SI | 10°15'S | 161°44'E | | | | |
| Ulithi | Yap, FSM | 9°56'N | 139°40'E | | | | |
| Ulu | Bis., PNG | 4°15'S | 152°25'E | | | | |
| Uman | Chuuk, FSM | 7°18'N | 151°53'E | | | | |
| Umboi | NG.group, PNG | 5°29'S | 147°48'E | | | | |
| Unea | Bis., PNG | 4°55'S | 149°10'E | | | | |
| Uoleva | Ha'ap., Tonga | 19°51'S | 174°25'W | | | | |
| 'Upolu | Samoa | 13°55'S | 171°45'W | | | | |

# Climate

CHAPTER 1

*Plate 1A.* Fair-weather cumulus with flattened tops indicating the presence of a subsidence inversion (photo APS).

*Plate 1B.* Mature thunderstorm cell with well-defined anvil cloud (photo APS).

Right:

*Plate 1C.* Sequential development of a tropical island thunderstorm from small cumulus to cumulonimbus cloud forms (photo AO).

# CHAPTER 2
# Oceanography

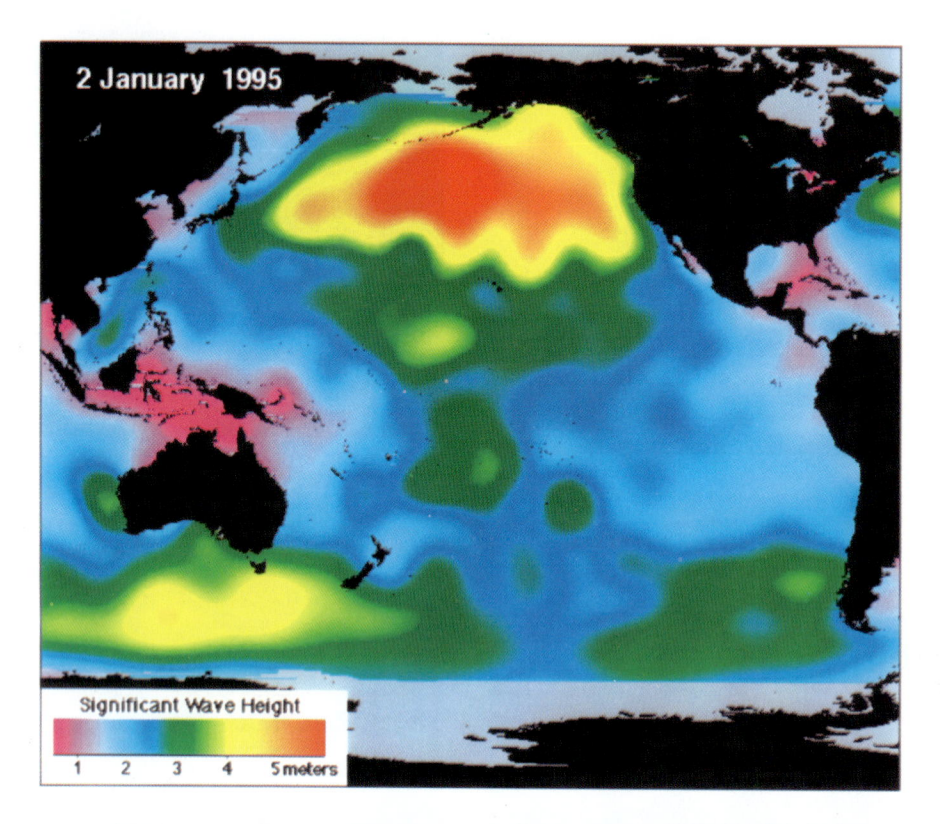

*Plate 2A.* Significant wave height in meters for two 10-day periods typifying northern winter and northern summer conditions: January 1995 (top) and July 1995 (bottom). The figures are modified from online gif images from the Topex/Poseidon satellite altimeter measurements and are based on observations collected over a 10-day period. Courtesy Jet Propulsion Laboratory. Copyright (c) California Institute of Technology, Pasadena, CA. All rights reserved.

## K₁ AMPLITUDE (cm)

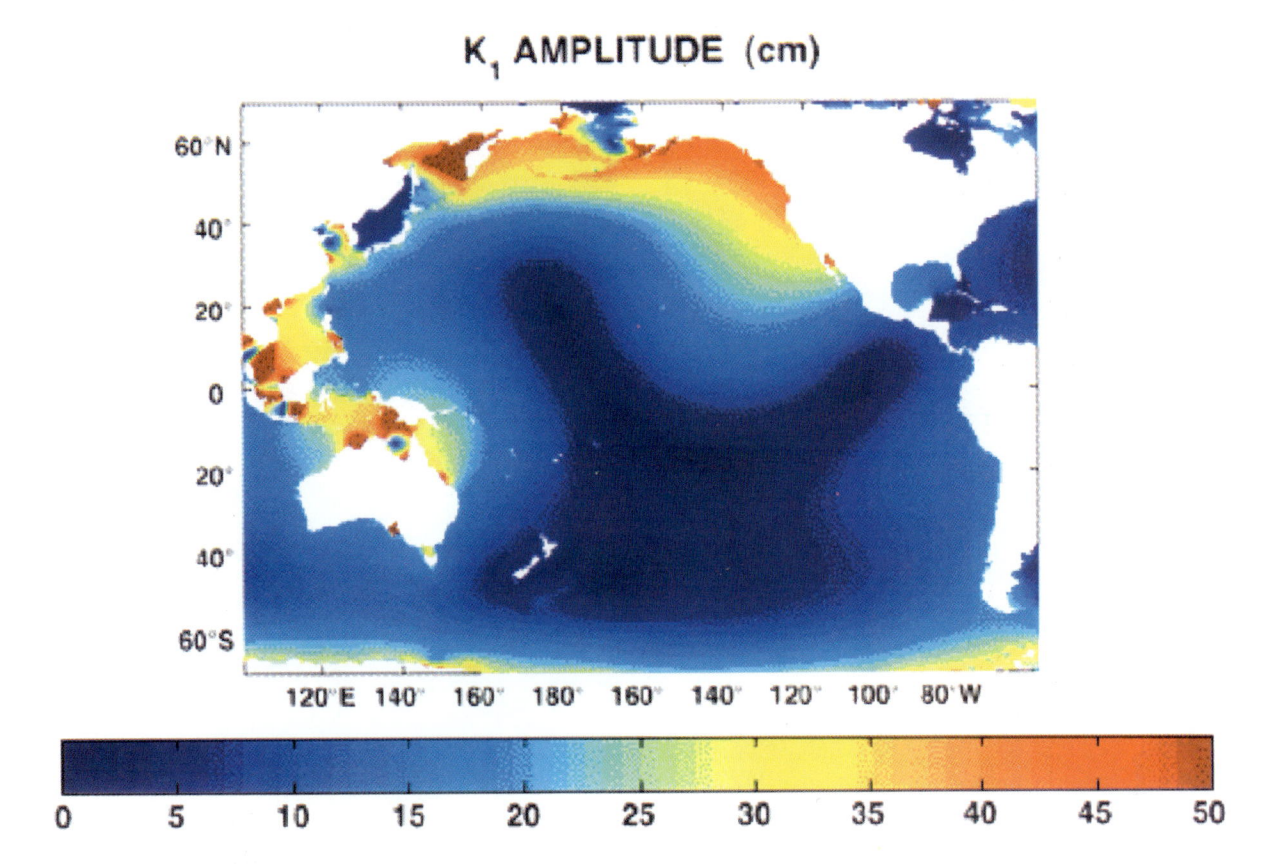

**Plate 2B.** Tidal amplitude (in cm).

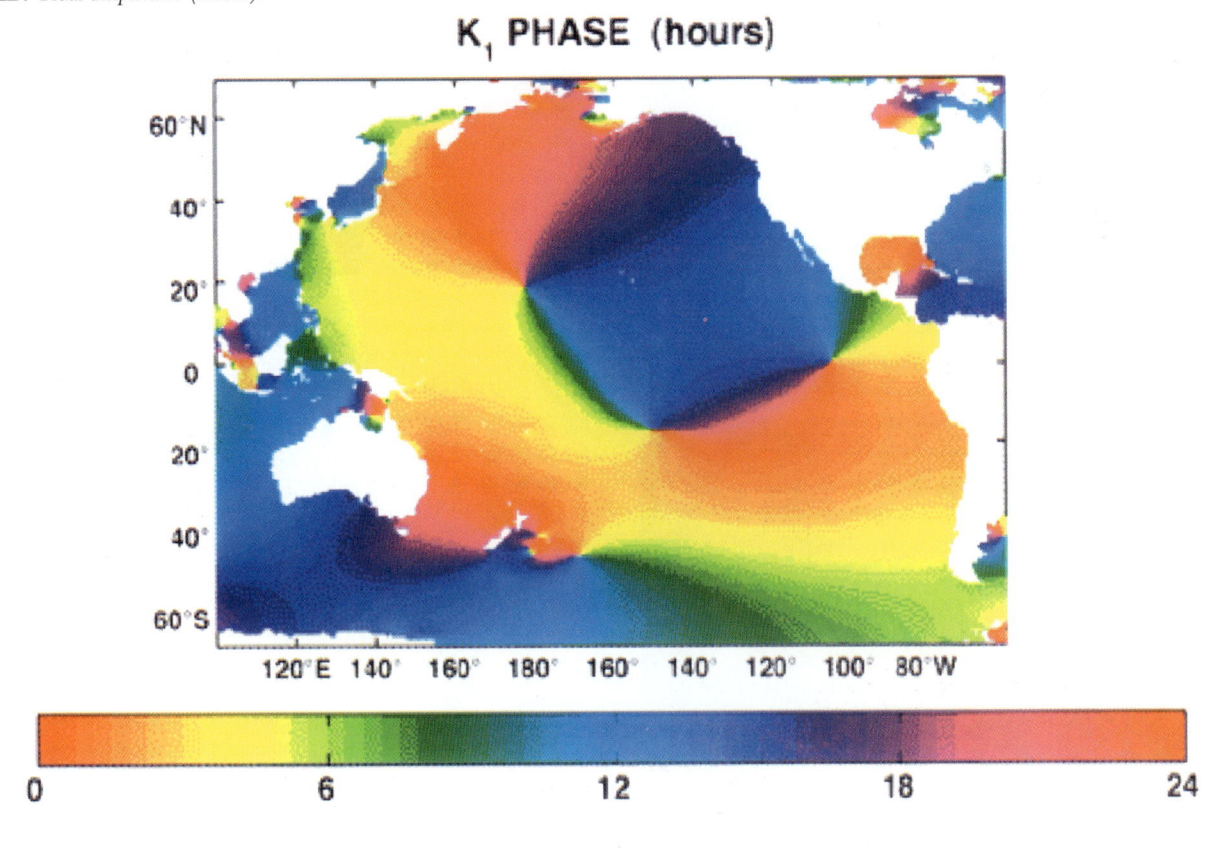

## K₁ PHASE (hours)

**Plate 2C.** Phase of the main diurnal tide (referred to as the K1 tide); the contours show the time of high water associated with this tidal component. In most of the North Pacific the k1 tide progresses in a counterclockwise direction around the amphidrome found at (15N, 175E). In the South Pacific, the tide progresses in a clockwise direction around the amphidromes.

# CHAPTER 3

# Geology

*Plate 3A.* An active lava flow in Hawai'i. The lava cools to form the black, fine-grained rock basalt. This lava texture is pāhoehoe (photo GJF).

*Plate 3B.* A young, uneroded shield volcano: Mauna Loa, Hawai'i. The rounded form is deceptive; Mauna Loa is Earth's largest volcano (photo SR).

*Plate 3C.* A steep-sided volcano in eruption: Yasur Volcano, Tanna Island, Vanuatu (photo JW).

*Plate 3D.* Deposit from the catastrophic 15th-century eruption of Kuwae, Vanuatu. The eruption separated the islands of Tongoa and Epi. The lava blocks at the base of the cliff are andesite. The layers above the blocks are ash falls. As the eruption continued the lavas became more silica rich, eventually producing the rock dacite, which is intermediate in silica content between andesite and rhyolite. Most of the ash in the photograph is dacite (photo JW).

# Geomorphology

CHAPTER 4

*Plate 4A.* Windward Viti Levu (photo WA).

*Plate 4B.* Leeward Viti Levu (photo WA).

*Plate 4C.* Residual volcanic ridge on the west side of Vatia Bay, Tutuila Island, American Samoa. Like many valleys on the island, Vatia Bay is probably a drowned amphitheater-headed valley (photo PDN).

*Plate 4D.* Emerged reef in the Eastern Tuamotus, French Polynesia, possibly an indication of a former sea level high (photo MR).

*Plate 4E.* Deforested polygonal karst in Oligocene limestones, Waitomo, New Zealand. Residual rainforest is visible in the doline in the foreground (photo PW).

# Chapter 5

# Soils

*Plate 5A.* Etemuli series, 'Upolu, Samoa, a typical Pacific Island Inceptisol.

*Plate 5B.* A typical Pacific Island Mollisol from Vaivai, western Viti Levu, Fiji.

*5G* Tanaea series, Tarawa, Kiribati, a typical Pacific Island Entisol

Rarotonga

Volcanic center
Rolling hills
Fan
Swamp
Plain
Beach ridge

- Inceptisols
- Inceptisols/Entisols
- Entisols/Mollisols

*Plate 5C.* Akina series, Guam, a typical Pacific Island Alfisol.

*Plate 5D.* Barakoma series, Vella Levella, Solomon Islands, a typical Pacific Island Ultisol.

Mangaia

Volcanic center
Makatea limestone
Alluvial deposits and swamps
Coastal margin

- Ultisols/Inceptisols
- Inceptisols/Entisols
- Oxisols
- Entisols/Mollisols

*Plate 5E.* Seaqaqa series, Vanua Levu, Fiji, a typical Pacific Island Oxisol.

*Plate 5F.* A typical Pacific Island Andisol from Surukavian, Pentecost, Vanuatu.

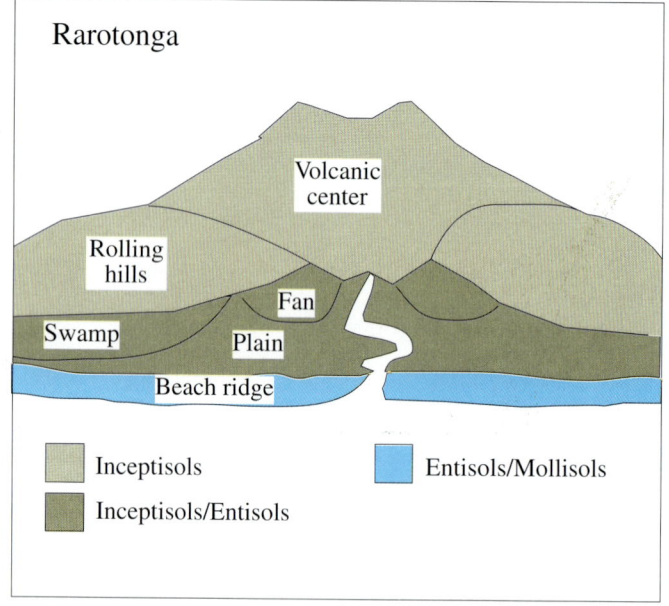

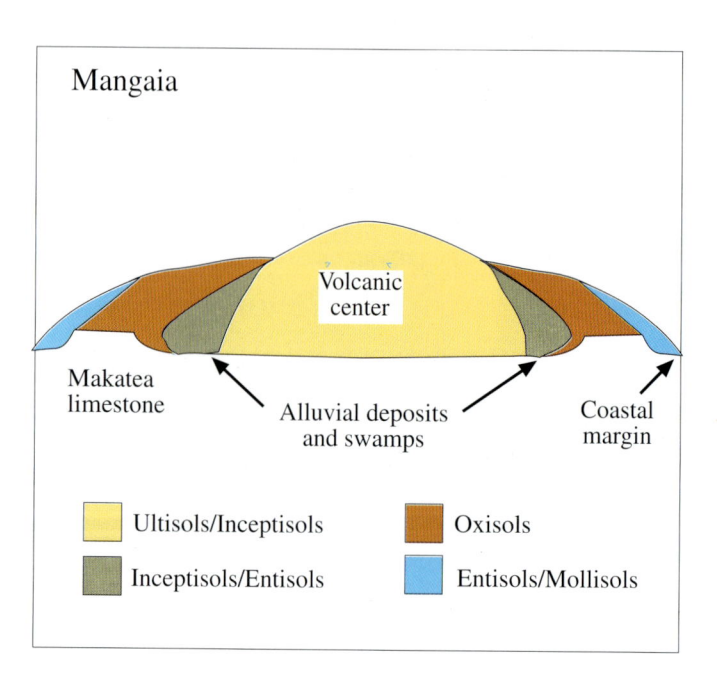

*Plate 5H.* Soils of Rarotonga and Mangaia, Cook Islands (after New Zealand Soil Survey 1979).

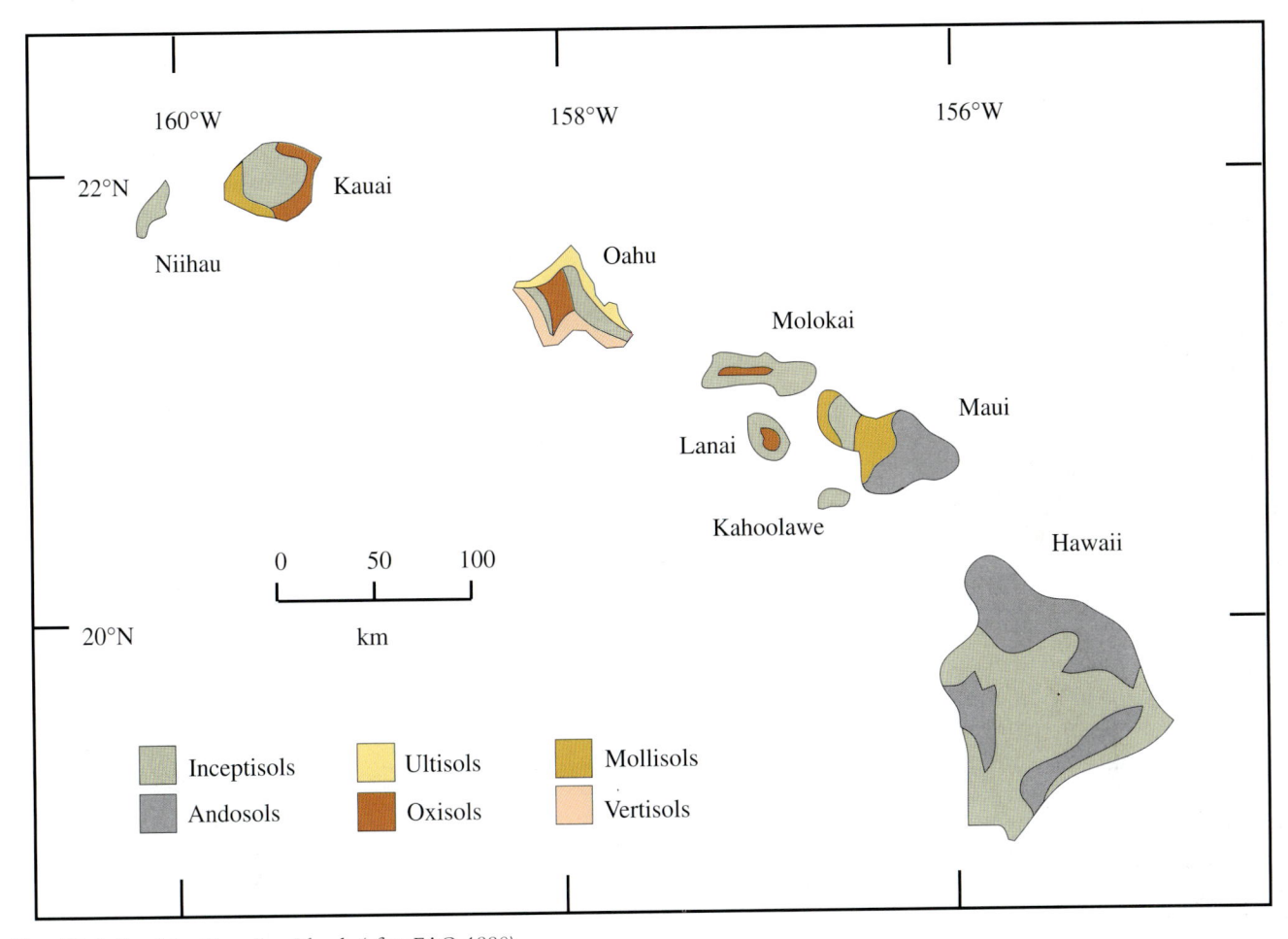

**Plate 5I.** Soils of the Hawaiian Islands (after FAO 1990).

## CHAPTER 6

# Water

**Plate 6A.** Water catchment, Tokelau. Such cisterns form the primary source of drinking water (photo MR).

**Plate 6B.** Shallow well, Tuamotu Archipelago. Such wells are used today for cooking, laundry, and showering (photo MR).

**Plate 6C.** Outhouses overhanging lagoon, Tokelau (photo MR).

CHAPTER 7

# Biogeography

**Plates 7A–B.** Endemic Hawaiian land shells. 7A. Achatinella from Oʻahu. 7B. Carelia in the endemic family Amastridae from Kauaʻi (photos EAK).

**Plate 7C.** The giant clam Tridacna, which is in the Marshall and Society islands but not in Hawaiʻi (photo EAK).

**Plates 7D–F.** Species in the endemic Hawaiian silversword alliance. **Clockwise from left**: 7D. Dubautia in Haleakalā, Maui. 7E. the Hawaiʻi silversword on Mauna Kea. 7F. Wilkesia on Kauaʻi (photos EAK).

# Terrestrial Ecosystems

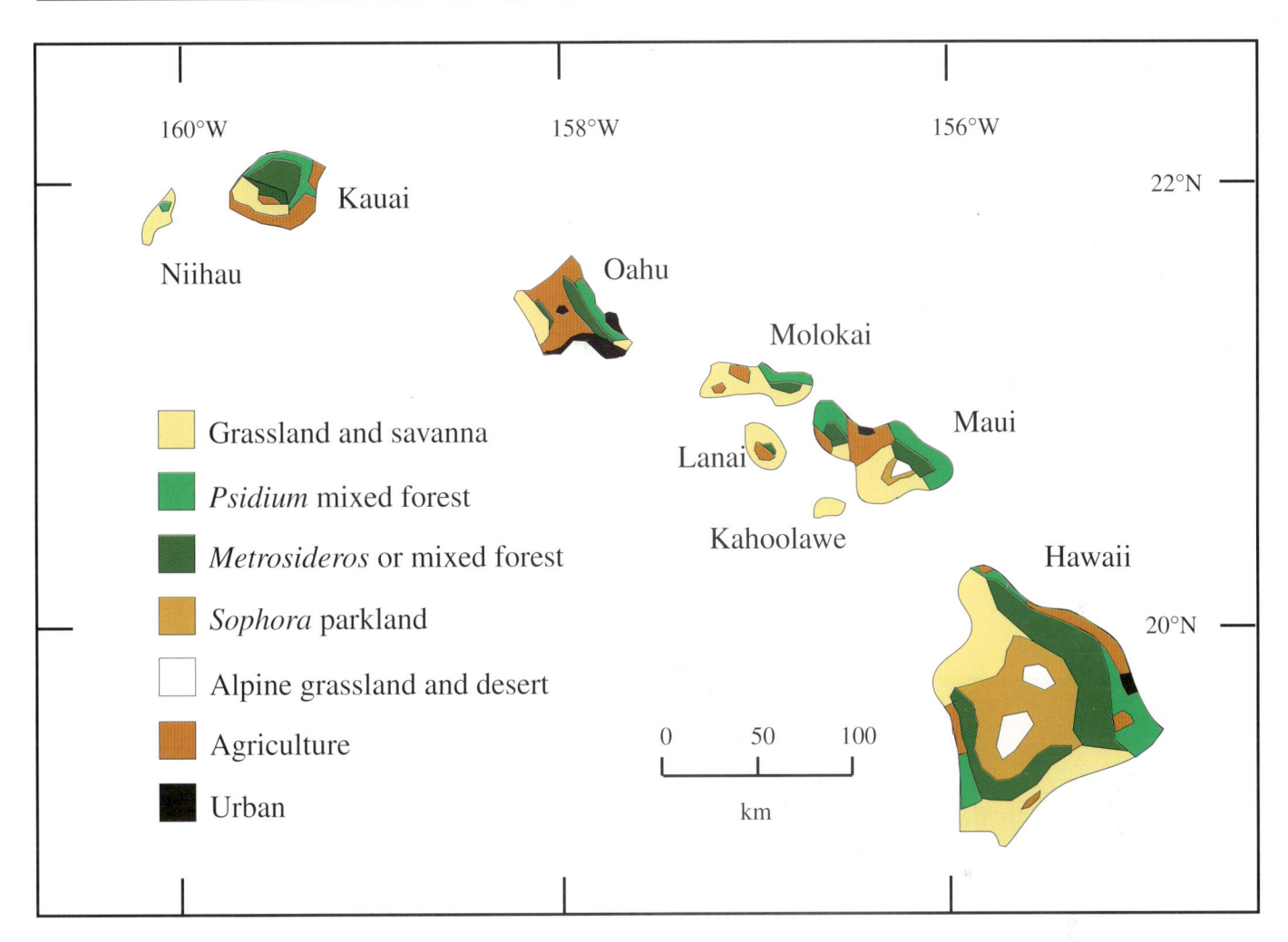

CHAPTER 8

Legend:
- Grassland and savanna
- *Psidium* mixed forest
- *Metrosideros* or mixed forest
- *Sophora* parkland
- Alpine grassland and desert
- Agriculture
- Urban

*Plate 8A.* Major terrestrial ecosystems in the Hawaiian Islands.

*Plate 8B.* Strand forest on the inner lagoon of Mwoakilloa Atoll. A *Pemphis acidula* tree about 6 m high is prominent in the center of the photo (photo HIM).

*Plate 8C.* Mixed broadleaf lower and *Araucaria* lower montane forest at Bulolo, Papua New Guinea. *Araucaria cunninghami* and *A. klinkii* tower over the forest. Both species form the basis of the logging industry in this area (photo HIM).

# CHAPTER 8

# Terrestrial Ecosystems (continued)

*Plate 8D.* Dry grassland at Hilina Pali, Hawai'i Island, in the rain shadow of the high mountain Mauna Loa. It was formerly overgrazed by feral goats. Recent lava substrate is visible in the background (photo HIM).

*Plate 8E.* Sophora tree in mountain parkland at 2,000 m. elevation in Mauna Kea, Hawai'i (photo MR)

*Plate 8F.* Undergrowth of a temperate forest, between Milford Sound and Dunedin, South Island, New Zealand (photo HIM).

*Plate 8G.* New vegetation in lava flow in Kīlauea, Hawai'i (photo MR).

# Aquatic Ecosystems

CHAPTER 9

*Plate 9A.* The Ngermeskang River, Palau.

*Plate 9B.* Mangrove ecosystem, Micronesia.

*Plate 9C.* Seagrass meadow, Micronesia.

*Plate 9D.* Coral reef, Palau.

*Plate 9E.* Sea cliffs, New Zealand.

*Plate 9F.* Pelagic jellyfish.

(Photos SN/UOGML)

# CHAPTER 10

# The Precontact Period

*Plate 10A.* Remains of marae (precontact temple platform) on Pukarua, Tuamotus (photo MR).

*Plate 10B.* Shell middens in the lagoon at Vairaatea, Tuamotus (photo MR).

*Plate 10C.* Petroglyphs at Kīlauea, Hawai'i (photo MR).

*Plate 10D.* Remains of Nan Madol, Pohnpei (photo LEM)

*Plate 10E.* Latte post and capstone, Tinian, Northern Marianas (photo LEM).

# Social Relations

**CHAPTER 16**

*Plate 16A.* Two boys, whose circumcision wounds have healed, rejoin their father and mother in a celebratory feast after a period of ritual seclusion.

*Plate 16B.* A circumcised boy and his father along with a decorated kava plant they will present to the boy's mother's brother.

*Plate 16C.* Taro and cow given by a man's family to the family of his future wife.

*Plate 16D.* Preparation of the earth oven.

*Plate 16E.* Pile of goods (food, mats, baskets, cloth, blankets, kava) exchanged between families after a marriage.

*Plate 16F.* People mourn as they bury a family member.

(Photos LL)

## Chapter 18

# Law

**Plate 18A.** Traditional Haus Tambaran (ceremonial house). Conflict management meetings often take place in front of these houses.

**Plates 18B–E.** Onlookers and speakers during the process of conflict management.

**Plate 18F.** Food division accompanying a conflict resolution ceremony.

(Photos RS)

# Religion

CHAPTER 19

*Plate 19A.* Pacific Islanders commonly celebrate life passages—birth, adolescence, marriage, and death—with elaborate rites of passage. In such rituals, the social transition of a person between life stages is often physically marked upon their bodies in various types of decorations. In this picture, two Maisin girls in Papua New Guinea have emerged highly decorated after a month of isolation during which their faces were tatooed. They are now ready for marriage (photo JB).

*Plate 19B.* Preparation of carving for traditional ceremony, Sepik region, Papua New Guinea (photo RS).

*Plate 19C.* The old and the new in Pacific religion. Maisin men, in sacred decorations passed from the ancestors, await communion in an Anglican church service (photo JB).

*Plate 19D.* Tunui, lay leader of Catholic Church, Vairaatea, Tuamotus (photo MR).

# Chapter 20

# Art

*Plate 20A.* Woman dressed for funeral, Nukualofa, Tonga, 1995 (photo WA).

*Plate 20B.* Men from Poro, Santa Isabel, Solomon Islands, at the Independence Day Festival in Honiara, July 1996 (photo DW).

*Plate 20C.* Tuaman (leader) of malangan wearing kapkap accompanied by two malangan dancers, Kaviang, New Ireland, September 1993 (photo DCY).

*Plate 20D.* Prow of war canoe, New Georgia Island, Solomon Islands. Solomon Islands National Museum, Honiara (photo DW).

*Plate 20E.* Initiated men presenting shell currency to Dukduk, Tubuan, and Maus masks. Kabilomo, Duke of York Islands, September 1993 (photo DCY).

*Plate 20F.* Men's nighttime fire dance (kavat and other masks). Baining, Gaulim, New Britain (photo FBM).

# CHAPTER 22 Mobility

*Plate 22A.* Cook Island woman (left), employed as a schoolteacher in New Zealand, on holiday in Atiu with sister.

*Plate 22B.* Tuamotuan emigrant pioneer, Lā'ie, Hawai'i (now deceased).

*Plate 22C.* Return migrant to Takaroa (seated), after several generations off-island.

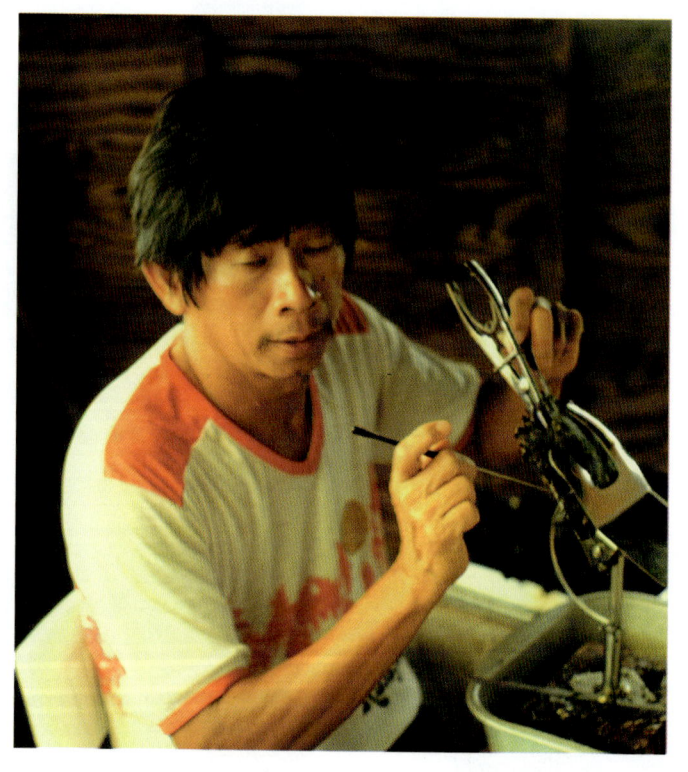

*Plate 22D.* Tahitian-Chinese pearl farmer on Takaroa, Tuamotus.

(Photos MR)

# Urbanization

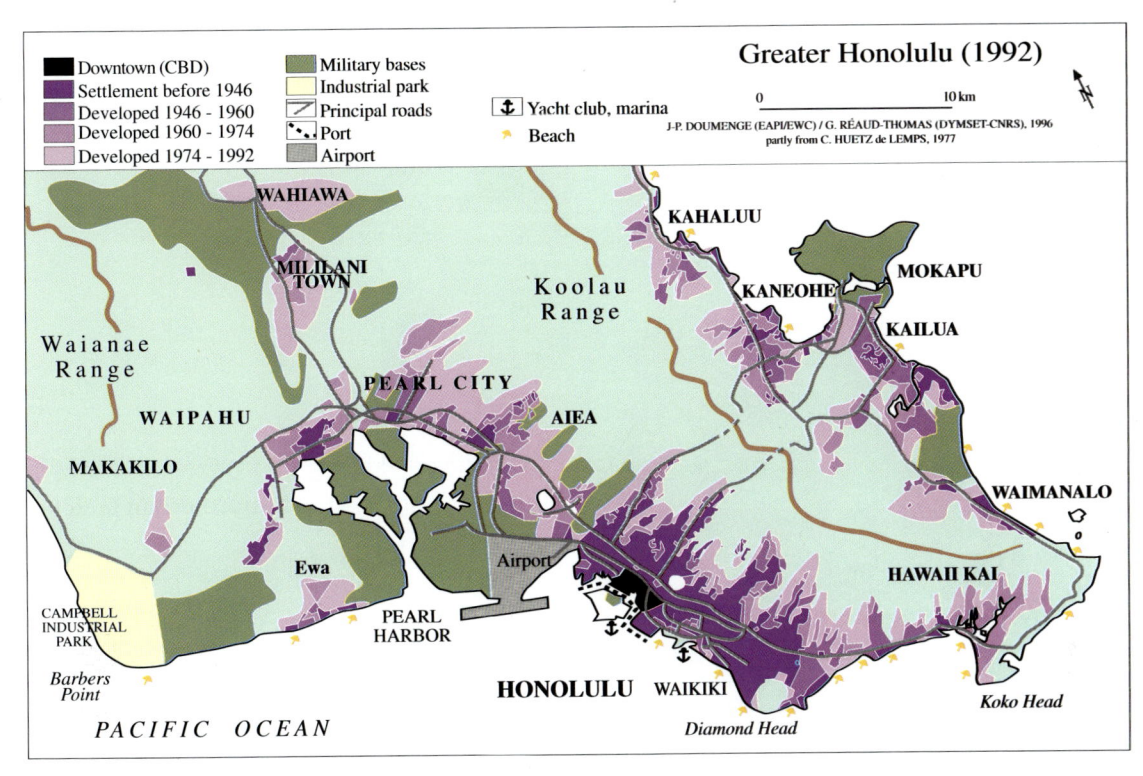

**CHAPTER 26**

**Plate 26A.** Greater Honolulu (1992).

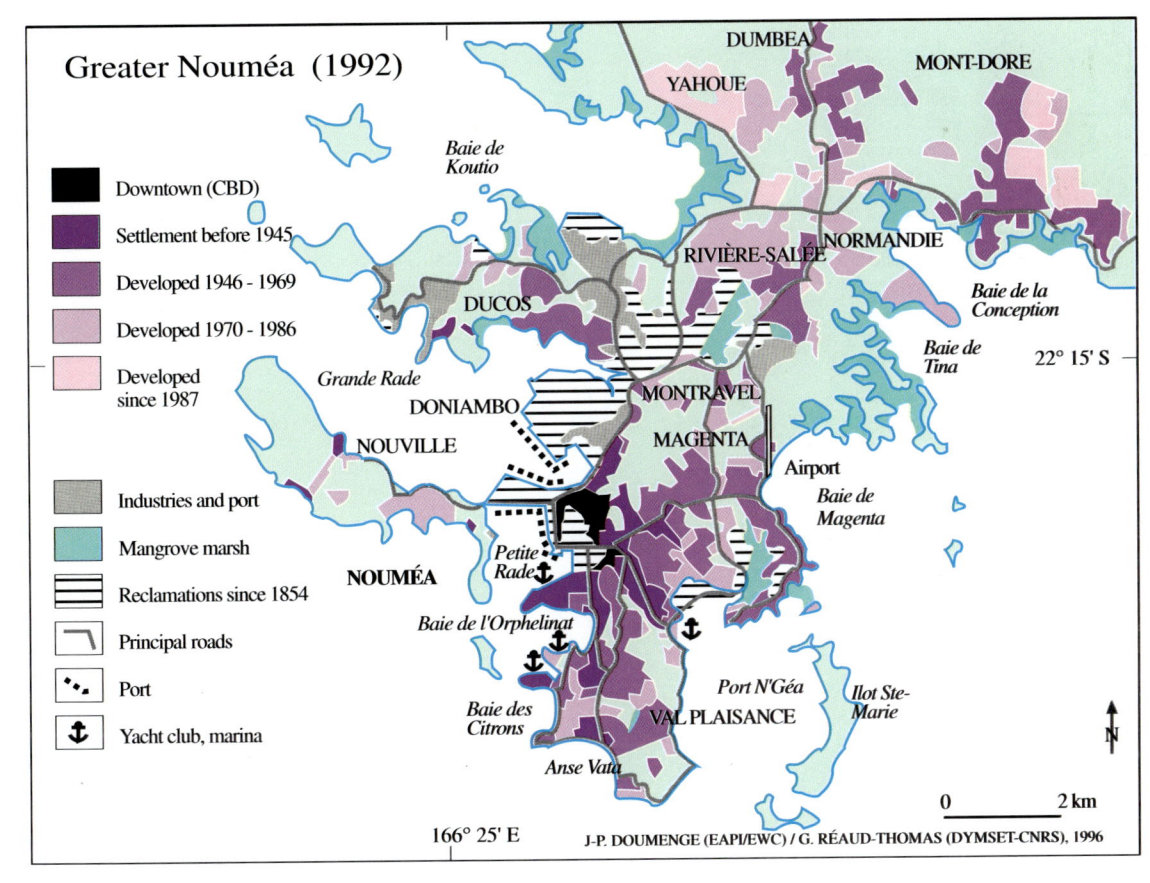

**Plate 26B.** Greater Nouméa (1992).

# CHAPTER 26
# Urbanization (continued)

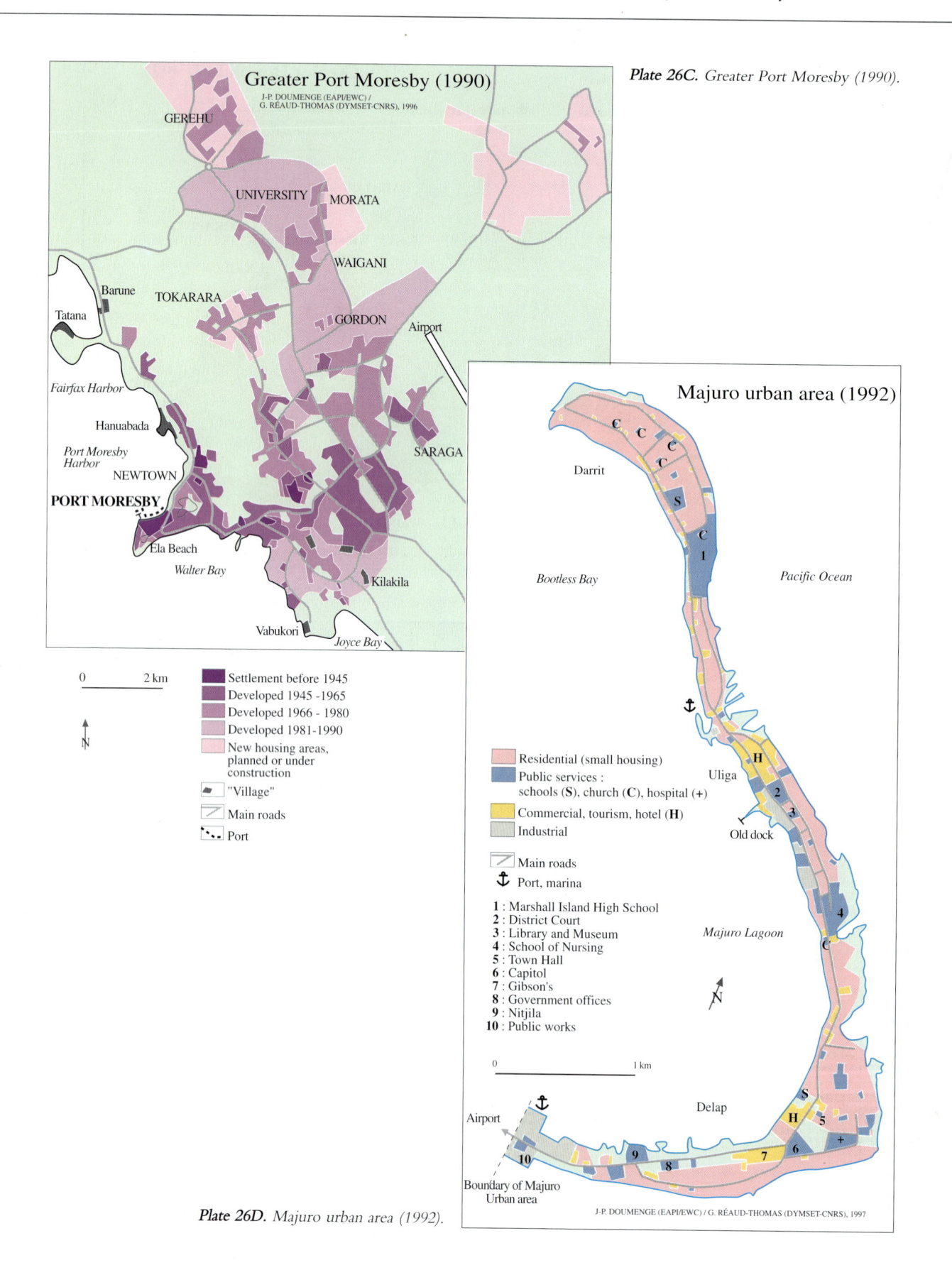

*Plate 26C.* Greater Port Moresby (1990).

*Plate 26D.* Majuro urban area (1992).

# Agriculture and Forestry

CHAPTER 29

*Plate 29A.* A recently slashed swidden in the lower montane forest, Western Highlands, Papua New Guinea. The litter will be burned and the site planted with a wide range of food species and varieties. Older gardens with bananas and secondary vegetation, in the foreground, complete the swidden cycle (photo HM).

*Plate 29B.* Giant swamp taro (Cyrtosperma chamissonis) cultivation on Mwoakilloa (Mokil) Atoll, Federated States of Micronesia. Freshwater depressions are excavated and filled with organic matter to form the soil. The intensity of taro cultivation throughout Micronesia is less today than before because of outmigration, remittances, and the greater availability of trade stores (photo HM).

*Plate 29C.* Cultivation of taro and other species in makatea swamps on Atiu, Cook Islands (photo MR).

*Plate 29D.* Preparing land for paddy rice cultivation with a bullock-drawn plow at Navua, Viti Levu, Fiji. Rice is mainly cultivated by ethnic Indian citizens in Fiji for subsistence on small plots. There are larger rice-growing projects sponsored by the government where modern machinery is used (photo HM).

# CHAPTER 29 Agriculture and Forestry (continued)

**Plate 29E.** Commercial vegetable agriculture on the alluvial plain of the Rewa River, Viti Levu Fiji. Small farms produce a significant amount of subtropical and tropical vegetables for the nearby urban markets of Suva and Nausori (photo HM).

**Plate 29F.** Coconut plantation on Guadalcanal, Solomon Islands, with cocoa (Theobroma cacao) seedlings beneath a shade of old coconut fronds. The multiple use of coconut plantations for more than one agricultural crop increases the productivity of the lands and helps to mitigate coconut price fluctuations (photo HM).

# Ocean Resources

CHAPTER 30

*Plate 30A.* Makatea beach and fringing reef on Atiu, Cook Islands (photo MR).

*Plate 30B.* Polefishing (photo MR).

*Plate 30C.* Drop net fishing (photo SPC).

*Plate 30D.* Outrigger canoe (photo SPC).

*Plate 30E.* Motorized fishing boat (photo SPC).

## Chapter 31

# Mining

**Plate 31A.** Mining town, Porgera, PNG (photo GB).

**Plate 31B.** Company meeting with community, Porgera, PNG (photo GB).

**Plate 31C.** Women's association meeting, Porgera, PNG (photo GB).

**Plate 31D.** Open pit, Freeport Mine, Irian Jaya (photo FMC).

# SECTIONAL MAPS

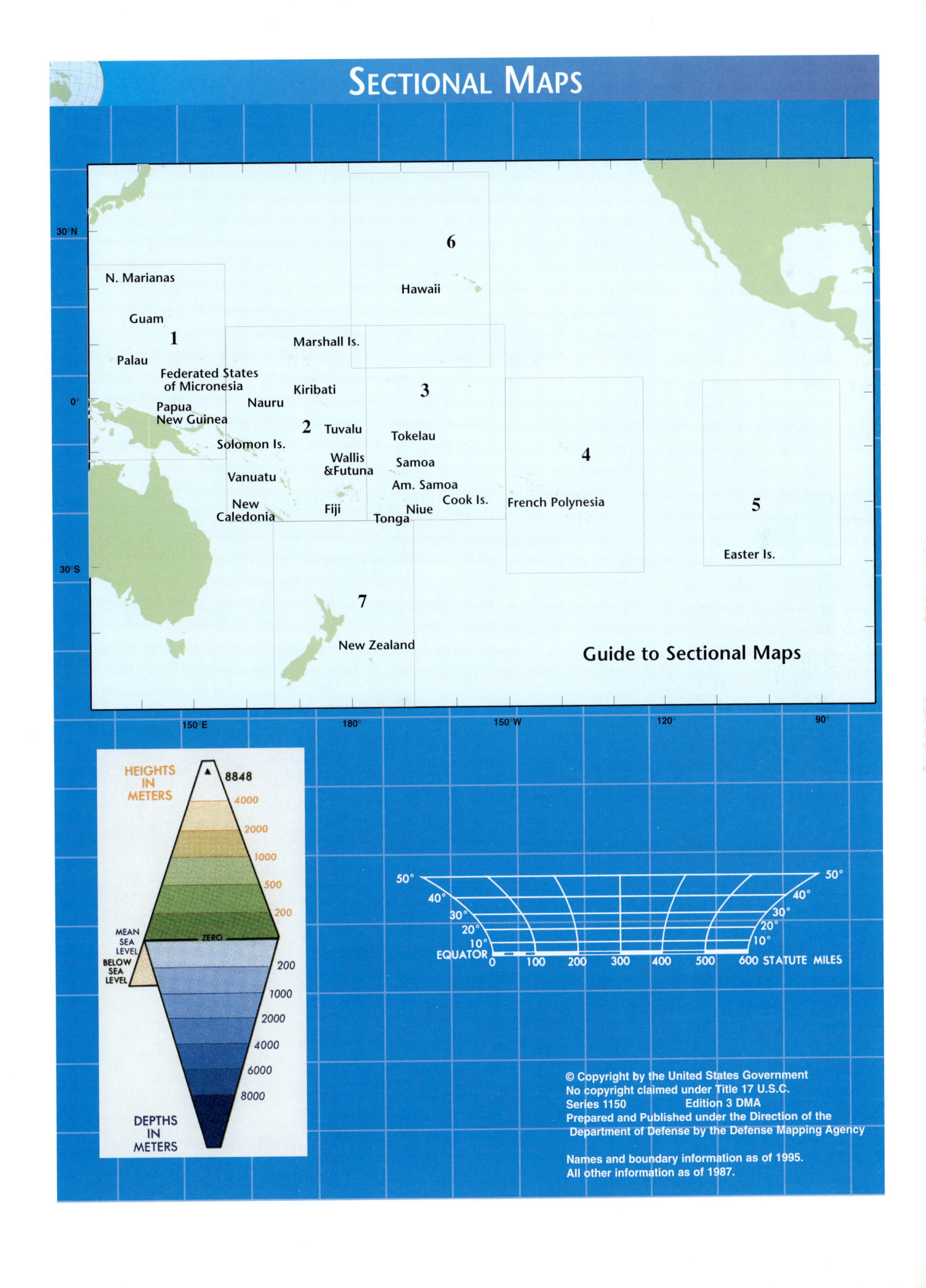

## Guide to Sectional Maps

**1:** N. Marianas, Guam, Palau, Federated States of Micronesia, Papua New Guinea, Solomon Is., Vanuatu, New Caledonia

**2:** Marshall Is., Kiribati, Nauru, Tuvalu, Wallis & Futuna, Fiji

**3:** Tokelau, Samoa, Am. Samoa, Niue, Tonga, Cook Is.

**4:** French Polynesia

**5:** Easter Is.

**6:** Hawaii

**7:** New Zealand

HEIGHTS IN METERS: 8848, 4000, 2000, 1000, 500, 200, MEAN SEA LEVEL ZERO
BELOW SEA LEVEL
DEPTHS IN METERS: 200, 1000, 2000, 4000, 6000, 8000

© Copyright by the United States Government
No copyright claimed under Title 17 U.S.C.
Series 1150     Edition 3 DMA
Prepared and Published under the Direction of the
Department of Defense by the Defense Mapping Agency

Names and boundary information as of 1995.
All other information as of 1987.

# Map 1

# West Pacific

# East Melanesia and Micronesia

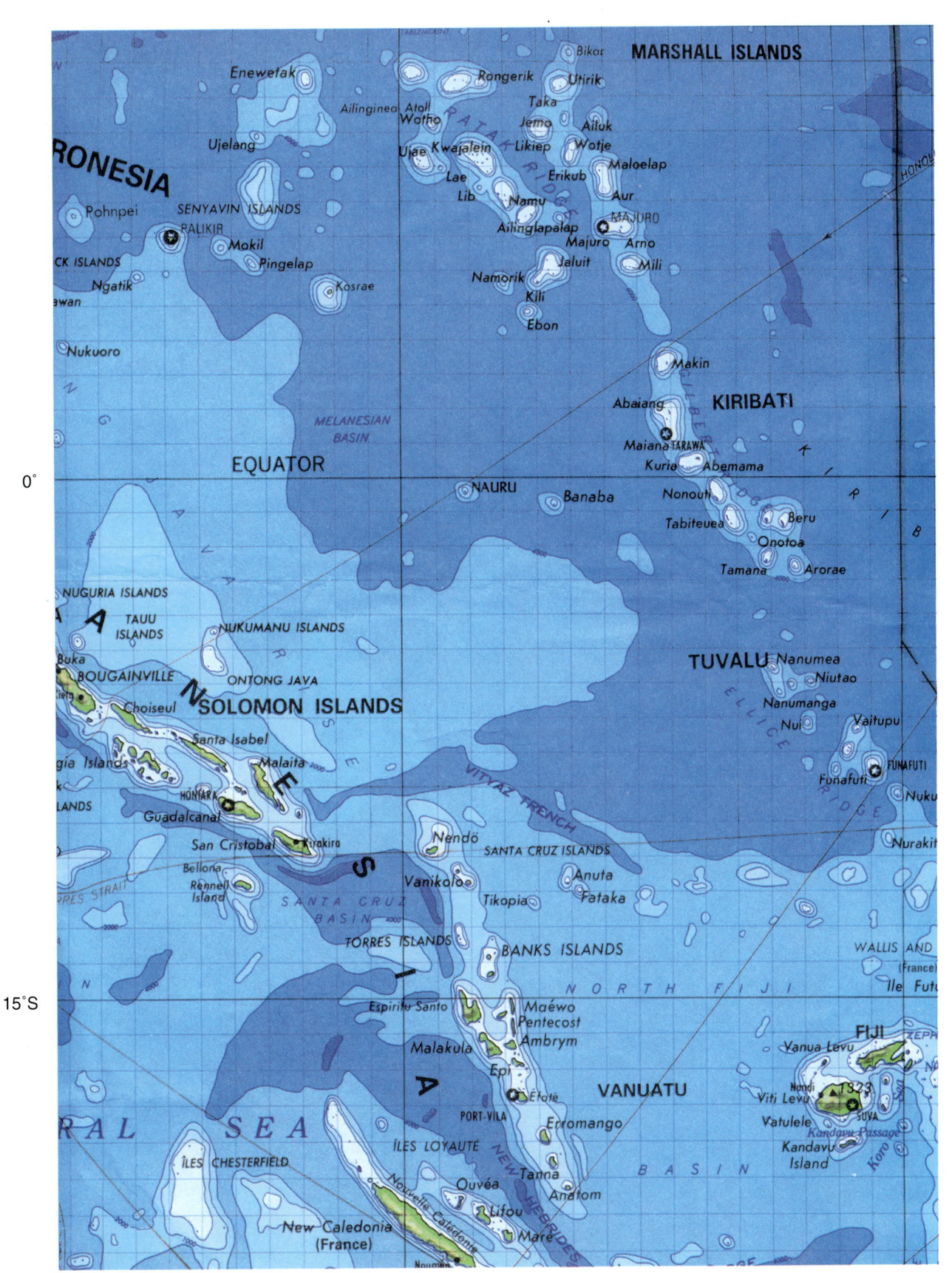

MAP 2

# Map 3

# Central Pacific

# East Polynesia

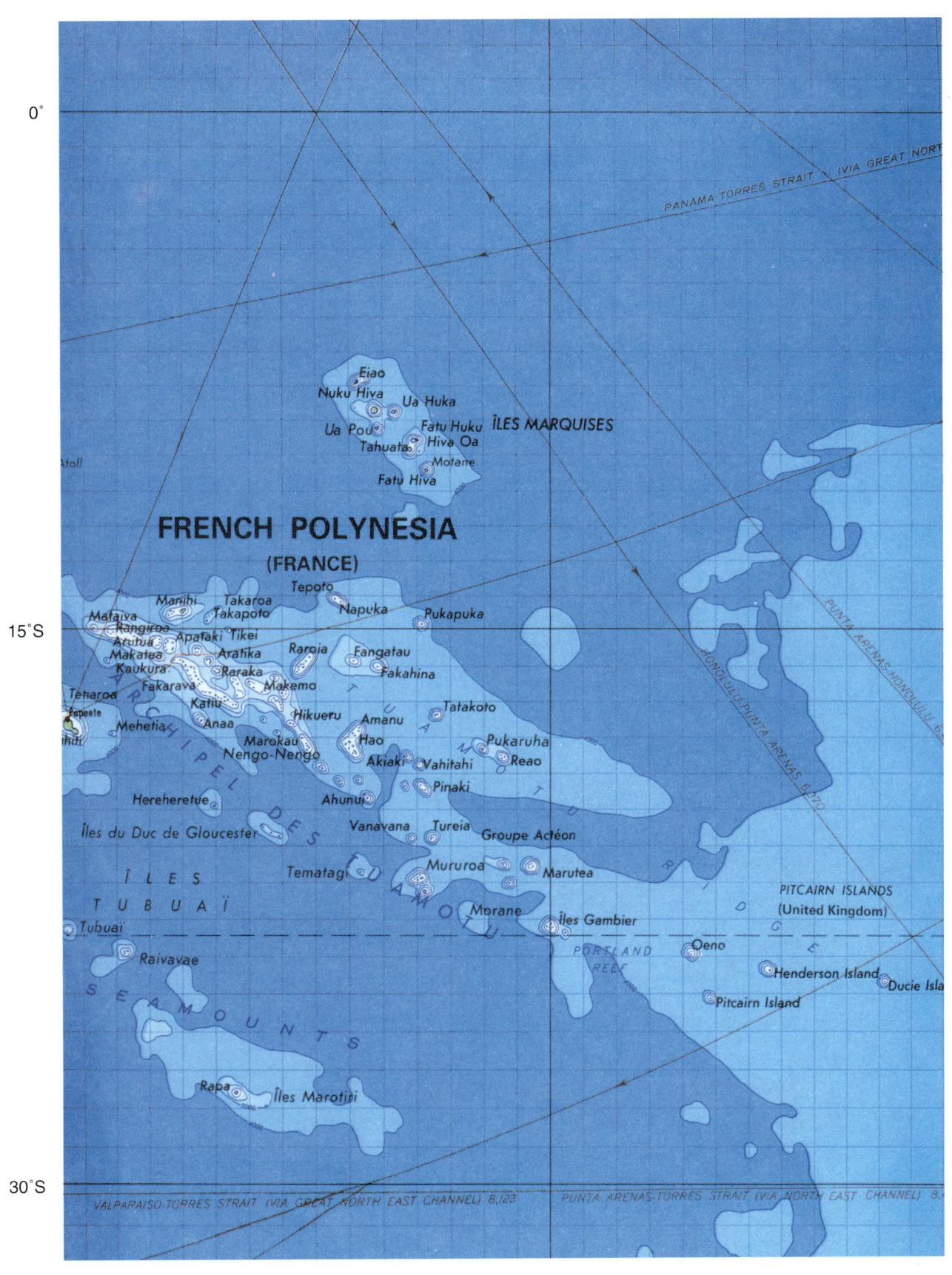

MAP 4

# East Pacific

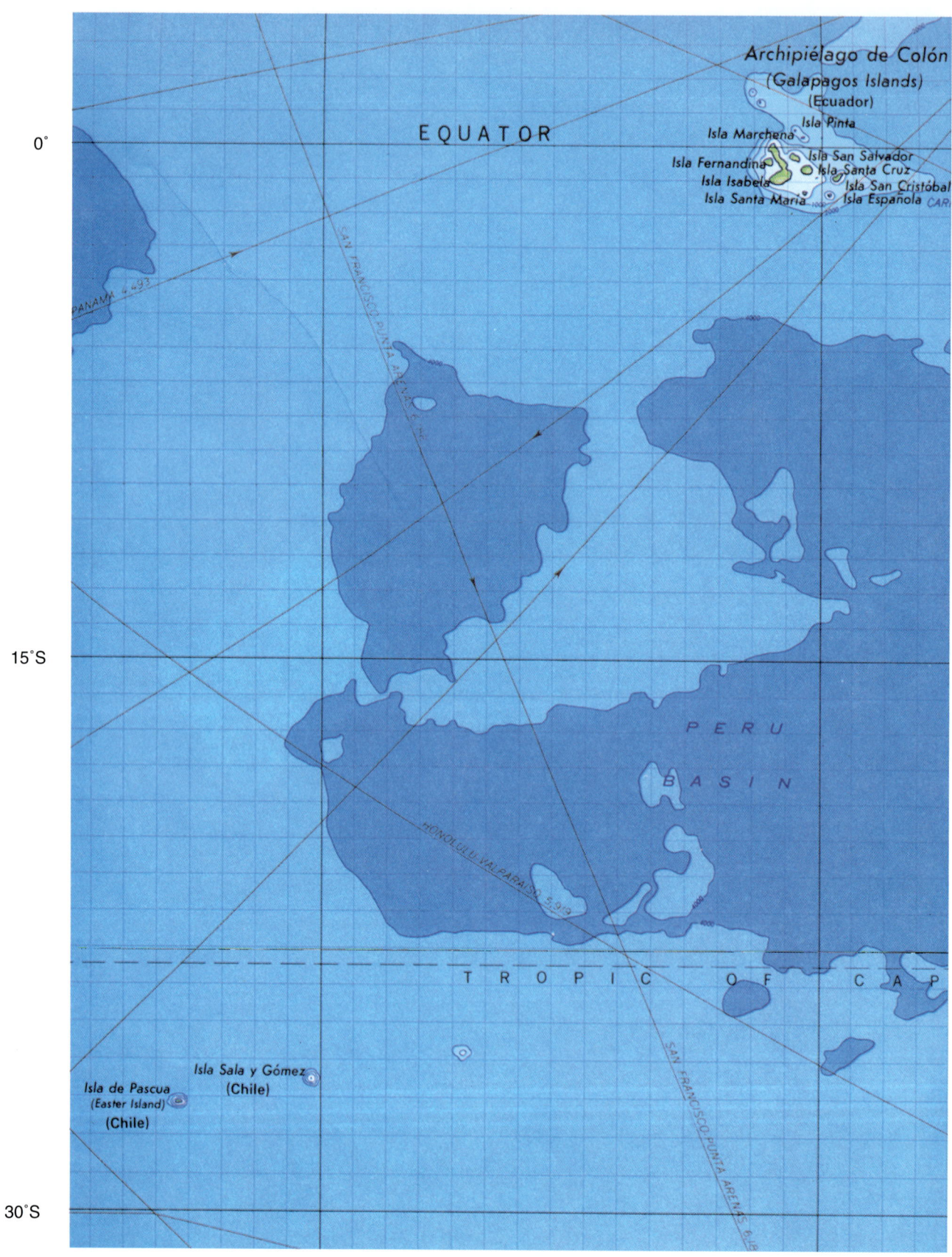

MAP 5

0°  EQUATOR

Archipiélago de Colón
(Galapagos Islands)
(Ecuador)
Isla Pinta
Isla Marchena
Isla Fernandina  Isla San Salvador
Isla Santa Cruz
Isla Isabela  Isla San Cristóbal
Isla Santa María  Isla Española

15°S

PERU BASIN

TROPIC OF CAP

Isla Sala y Gómez
(Chile)
Isla de Pascua
(Easter Island)
(Chile)

30°S

105°W          90°W

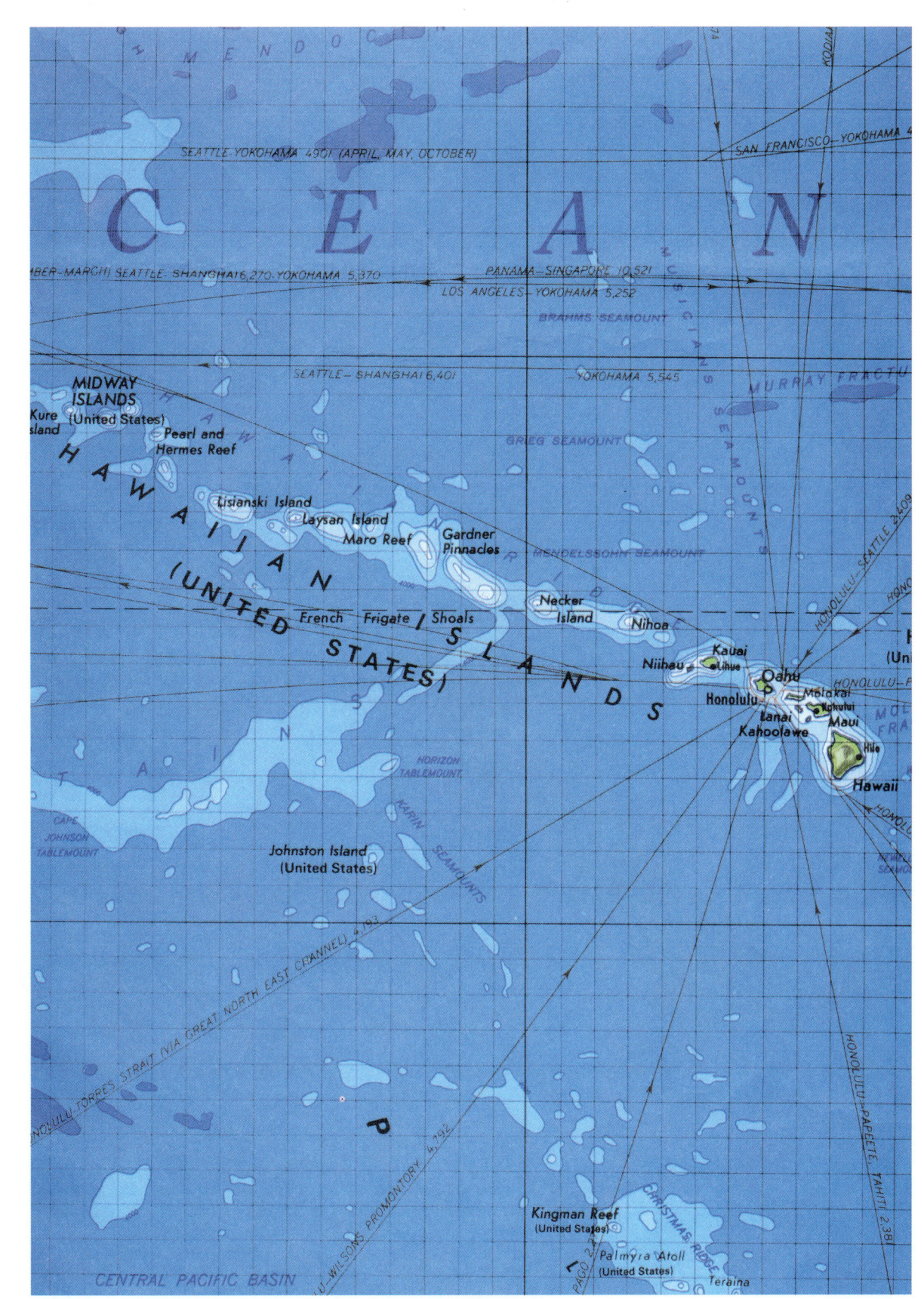

# Hawai'i

MAP 6

MAP 7

# New Zealand

# Contributors

**Tim Adams** is Director of Marine Resources at the Secretariat of the Pacific Community (SPC, formerly the South Pacific Commission), headquartered in Nouméa, New Caledonia. He began his fisheries career in 1984 working for the Fiji Fisheries Division along with Esaroma Ledua on a massive field survey of the remaining giant clam populations in Fiji. The results of this survey led to a ban on clam exports and a government clam–culture-and-rehabilitation effort.

**Dennis A. Ahlburg** is Professor of Human Resources and Industrial Relations, Industrial Relations Center, Carlson School of Management, University of Minnesota. He has held visiting appointments at the Australian National University, the Program on Population at the East-West Center, and the Centre for Population Studies at the London School of Hygiene and Tropical Medicine. He has published widely on various economic and demographic aspects of the Pacific Islands, including the impact of population growth on economic development, determinants and consequences of migration and remittance flows, poverty, job creation, and the economic and demographic impact of HIV/AIDS.

**Glenn Banks** is Lecturer, School of Geography and Oceanography, University College, University of New South Wales. He completed his Ph.D. at the Australian National University (1997) with thesis work entitled "Mountain of Desire: Mining Company and Local Community at the Porgera Gold Mine, Papua New Guinea." Dr. Banks is co-editor of *The Ok Tedi Settlement: Issues, Outcomes and Implications* (NCDS, ANU, 1997). His research interests include large-scale mining in Melanesia, globalization processes in the periphery, and development in the Asia-Pacific region.

**John Barker**, Associate Professor of Anthropology at the University of British Columbia, writes on the religions, politics, and history of indigenous societies in Papua New Guinea and Canada. He edited the widely read *Christianity in Oceania: Ethnographic Perspectives* (University Press of America, 1990) and is currently preparing a book on the religious history of the Maisin people of Papua New Guinea.

**Geoffrey Bertram** is Senior Lecturer in the School of Economics and Finance, Victoria University of Wellington, New Zealand. He holds a B.A. Honours degree in Geography from Victoria University, an M.Phil. in Latin American Studies from Oxford University, and a D.Phil. in Economics from Oxford. He has published extensively on development issues in Peru and the Pacific Islands. His other research areas include economics of climate change, energy economics, and regulation of natural monopolies.

**David A. Chappell** is Associate Professor of Pacific Islands History at the University of Hawai'i at Mānoa. He has published articles in scholarly journals, such as the *Journal of Pacific History*, *The Contemporary Pacific*, and *Pacific Studies*, as well as in the *Samoan News*, *Pacific Islands Monthly*, and *Islands Business*. In 1997, he published *Double Ghosts: Oceanian Voyagers on Euroamerican Ships* (M. E. Sharpe, 1997). He is on the executive committee of the Pacific History Association, presenting papers at its conferences in New Zealand, Kiribati, and the Solomon Islands and co-editing its newsletter. He has also taught history courses in the Marshall Islands and American Samoa and is book review editor of the *Journal of World History*.

**William C. Clarke** began research in the Pacific in 1964, when he carried out an ecological study of a remote community in Papua New Guinea, work that was published in 1971 (*Place and People: An Ecology of a New Guinean Community*, Australian National University). He has since continued research on traditional agriculture, arboriculture, and conservation issues in the Pacific, while based at the Australian National University, the University of Papua New Guinea, and, most recently, the University of the South Pacific.

**Camilla Cockerton** is Lecturer in Geography at the University of Canterbury, Christchurch, New Zealand. She teaches Pacific and feminist geography and is a co-organizer of the Doing Feminist Scholarship seminar series at the university. Her research interests include migration, development, gender, and historical geography. She has recently completed a project on a medical officer in 1920s Fiji who contributed to miscegenation and immigration debates in New Zealand.

**John Connell** is Associate Professor at the University of Sydney. He worked from 1974–1976 in Bougainville on issues of rural development, and in Nouméa from 1981–1983 as coordinator of the joint SPC/ILO project on Migration, Employment, and Development in the South Pacific. He has written more than a dozen books, mainly on the Pacific, including two on New Caledonia, and several on Pacific urbanization with John Lea. Most recently he published *Papua New Guinea: The Struggle for Development* (Routledge, 1997) and with Robert Aldrich *The Last Colonies* (Cambridge University Press, 1998)

**Ron Crocombe** is Professor Emeritus of the University of the South Pacific, where he was Professor of Pacific Studies from 1969 to 1989. In 1976, he founded the university's Institute of Pacific Studies and was director through 1985. Dr. Crocombe was Director of the New Guinea Research Unit of the Australian National University from 1965 to 1969. He has authored or co-authored and edited forty books, seventeen of them dealing with land tenure and/or rural development in the Pacific. Others deal with social and cultural policy, higher education, politics, and international relations in the Pacific region. He now consults from his home in Rarotonga, Cook Islands.

**Paul Dalzell** is Fishery Biologist with the Western Pacific Regional Fishery Management Council in Honolulu. He has spent most of his professional life as a fishery biologist in the South Pacific and Southeast Asia. He is a graduate of the University of Newcastle upon Tyne (UK), where he also obtained his masters degree. Mr. Dalzell has worked on a variety of tropical fisheries, including those for tunas, small pelagic fishes, coral reef fishes, and reef invertebrates. He has authored numerous papers and articles on the biology, stock assessment, and socioeconomic aspects of Southeast Asian and Pacific Islands fisheries.

**Derrick Depledge** is a consulting hydrogeologist and engineering geologist, with an M.Sc. from Imperial College in London. He has been working in the Pacific since 1989 on various major water and sanitation projects in the Solomon Islands, Vanuatu, Fiji, and Kiribati and has visited many of the other island nations in both the South and North Pacific. His publications include subjects as varied as the water resources of urban areas in Vanuatu, sanitation for small islands, and geothermal resources of the South Pacific. He delivered a keynote paper on the water resources of the Pacific at an Asian Development Bank workshop.

**Jean-Pierre Doumenge** has been working for the National Center for Scientific Research (France) since 1972. Now Director of Research, he has participated for many years in programs on island development in the Pacific as well as on health at the global scale. During 1992, he was a Visiting Fellow at the Environment and Policy Institute, East-West Center, Honolulu, in a program on urbanization in the Pacific Islands. Following this he was in charge of France's 28th district for public education (French Antilles and French Guiana). Since 1996, he has managed the Center for High Studies on Modern Africa and Asia (CHEAM), in Paris. He will edit a book on the French Overseas Islands during 1999.

**Michael Fagence** is engaged in teaching and research at the University of Queensland (Australia). He is Coordinator of a CRC subprogram in tourism planning and has been Dean of the Faculty of Architecture and Planning. His recent research in tourism planning in Pacific Island microstates has been supported by a number of grants from UN-ESCAP, from which have come reports including *Guidelines on Integrated Tourism Planning in Pacific Island Countries* (UN, 1996). Recent papers on sustainable tourism development and Pacific Island countries have been published in *Tourism Management, Sustainable Development, Third World Planning Review,* and *Journal of Tourism Studies.*

**Sitaleki A. Finau** is currently Senior Lecturer in Pacific Health at the Department of Maori and Pacific Health, the University of Auckland Medical School. He also works at Primary Care Clinics for Pacific Peoples in Auckland. Dr. Finau has over twenty years of experience in clinical practice and public health, encompassing academic, research, policy, and prevention programs in Fiji, Tonga, Micronesia, New Caledonia, New Zealand, and remote aboriginal communities in central Australia. His involvement includes appointments at the South Pacific Commission and the University of the South Pacific. He is editor of *Pacific Health Dialog* and has published more than one hundred professional papers.

**Gerard J. Fryer** is Associate Geophysicist at Hawai'i Institute of Geophysics and Planetology at the University of Hawai'i-Mānoa. He teaches introductory geology, studies local tsunamis in the Hawaiian Islands, and is one of two tsunami hazard advisors to the City and County of Honolulu. He is currently writing a book on tsunamis.

**Patricia Fryer** is Planetary Scientist (Senior Researcher) at Hawai'i Institute of Geophysics and Planetology at the University of Hawai'i-Mānoa. Her expertise is in convergent plate margin processes. Her work includes twenty-seven marine geology research cruises; fieldwork on land in Papua New Guinea, the Mariana island arc system, and central California; three books edited and sixty refereed publications.

**RDK Herman** received his Ph.D. from the University of Hawai'i in 1995. He has published several articles on colonialism and modernization in the Hawaiian Islands, and his book "Kālai'āina—Carving the Land: Geography, Desire and Possession in the Hawaiian Islands" is under review with the University of Wisconsin Press. Having taught at several universities in the United States, Japan, and Australia, he now resides in Washington D.C. and works at the Smithsonian's National Museum of the American Indian. Current research focuses on sustainable development.

**E. Alison Kay** is Professor of Zoology Emeritus at the University of Hawai'i. She has degrees from Mills College and Cambridge University, and a Ph.D. from the University of Hawai'i. She is author of *Hawaiian Marine Shells* and *Shells of Hawaii* (with Olive Schoenberg Dole) and editor of *A Natural History of the Hawaiian Islands: Selected Readings.* Her recent articles include papers on the Cypraeidae of the Indo-Pacific, Cenozoic phylogeny and biogeography, Darwin's biogeography and the oceanic islands of the central Pacific, and biogeography of the Pacific. Dr. Kay is Associate Editor of the *Hawaiian Journal of History* and Fellow of the American Association for the Advancement of Science and of the Linnean Society of London. She was named Scientist of the Year by ARCS Hawai'i in 1998.

**Suzanna Layton** teaches journalism in the School of Film, Media and Cultural Studies at Griffith University in Australia. Her research interests include Pacific Islands media, international and comparative journalism, and new communication technologies. She has masters degrees in Communication and Pacific Islands Studies from the University of Hawai'i and a doctorate in Journalism from the University of Queensland.

**John P. Lea** is Associate Professor in the Department of Architecture, Planning and Allied Arts at the University of Sydney, Australia. He has undertaken research in Africa, Asia, and the Pacific and in recent years has been regional planning adviser to the Central Planning Department of the Kingdom of Tonga and to the Regional Council of the Torres Strait. Among his publications are *Housing in Third World Countries* (Macmillan, 1979); *Cities in Conflict* (World Bank, 1985); *Yellowcake and Crocodiles* (Allen and Unwin, 1986); *Tourism and Development in the Third World*; and, with John Connell, three studies of urbanization in the Pacific: *Planning the Future: Melanesian Cities in 2010* (NCDS, 1993), *Urbanisation in Polynesia* (NCDS, 1995), and *Island Towns: Managing Urbanization in Micronesia* (Center for Pacific Island Studies, 1998).

**Esaroma Ledua** is Principal Fisheries Officer, Ministry of Agriculture, Fisheries, and Forests, Suva, Fiji. He began his fisheries career in 1984 working along with Tim Adams for the Fiji Fisheries Division on a survey of giant clam populations in Fiji, and rose rapidly through the ranks in government service. He has published several articles on coastal fisheries in the Pacific Islands.

**Lamont Lindstrom** is Professor of Anthropology at the University of Tulsa. He has published a number of studies of Pacific cultures, including *Knowledge and Power in a South Pacific Society* (Smithsonian Institution Press, 1990) and *Cargo Cult: Strange Stories of Desire From Melanesia and Beyond* (University of Hawai'i Press, 1993). He has also edited several volumes of Pacific scholarship with Geoffrey M. White, most recently *Chiefs Today: Traditional Pacific Leadership and the Postcolonial State* (Stanford University Press, 1998).

**Claude Frederick (Rick) Lumpkin** is currently completing his Ph.D. in Oceanography at the University of Hawai'i, where he is studying eddies and currents in the Hawaiian Islands region. His M.S. thesis involved a study of island-trapped waves in Hawai'i. As an undergraduate, he attended North Carolina State University, where he studied physics and mathematics.

**Harley I. Manner** is Professor of Geography and Chair of the Division of Social/Behavioral Sciences and Social Work at the University of Guam. He received his degrees in Geography from the University of Hawai'i at Mānoa and has taught at Bucknell University, Yale, and the University of the South Pacific in Suva, Fiji. Dr. Manner has conducted fieldwork in Fiji, Guam, the Federated States of Micronesia, Nauru, Palau, Papua New Guinea, and many other Pacific islands. His research specializations include traditional subsistence systems, ethnobotany, and tropical ecology.

**Selina Tusitala Marsh** is of Samoan, Tuvaluan, and New Zealand descent. She is currently completing a doctorate at the University of Auckland on Pacific Islands women poets. She has completed research in Hawai'i and Samoa with the aid of a Fulbright award and an East-West Center fellowship. She is the Pacific Islands Student support person for the English Department at Auckland, is a founding member of a Pacific Women's creative writing group, and has shared her research at conferences in Kuala Lumpur, Hawai'i, and San Francisco.

**Glenda Mather** teaches in Women's Studies/Social Inquiry at the University of Adelaide and Screen Studies at Flinders University of South Australia. She was born in Aotearoa/New Zealand, resident in Australia since 1979. Her Ph.D. was conferred by the Politics Department, University of Adelaide. Her thesis, entitled "A Politics of Culture and Identity: Education and Development in Oceania," focused on Vanuatu/Australian politics. She is currently working on identity politics and regional relationships between Australia, Aotearoa/New Zealand, and Oceania.

**Hamish A. McGowan** is a Lecturer in Environmental Science and Physical Geography at the Institute of Geography, Victoria University of Wellington, New Zealand. He received his Ph.D. in 1995 from the University of Canterbury, where he studied dust storm genesis in the central Southern Alps of New Zealand. His research interests, on which he has published widely, center on atmospheric processes in complex terrain and cold climate aeolian geomorphology.

**Frank McShane** is a Ph.D. candidate in the Department of Geography at McGill University, researching community issues relating to minerals development in Fiji. Prior to working at McGill, he was a lecturer at the University of the South Pacific teaching natural resource management–related courses. He has published several book chapters on community and sustainable development policy in the minerals industry and has written articles for some of the leading Canadian agencies interested in this field. In February 1999, he joins the School of Commerce and Administration's Tourism Unit at Victoria University in Wellington to begin teaching and researching resource management and conflict issues in the Pacific.

**R. John Morrison** is BHP Professor of Environmental Science and Director of the Environment Research Institute at the University of Wollongong, where he has worked since the end of 1992. Originally trained as a chemist, he has spent much of his working life in developing countries (two years in East Africa, almost twenty in the Pacific Islands), where he applied his scientific expertise to addressing environmental issues, particularly land and water management. He has also been Professor of Chemistry at the University of the South Pacific (1985–1992), Director of that university's Institute of Natural Resources (1982–1986), and Scientific Coordinator of the SPREP POL project, Assessment and Control of Pollution in Coastal and Open Ocean Areas in the South Pacific (1988–1992). He has published over eighty papers in refereed journals, over twenty book chapters, and over twenty major technical reports on soil genesis and management, marine pollution, water quality, hazardous chemicals management, and environmental impact assessment.

**Dieter Mueller-Dombois** is Emeritus Professor in the Botany Department, University of Hawai'i. He wrote *Aims and Methods of Vegetation Ecology* (Wiley & Sons, 1974) with Prof. Ellenberg, a first synthesis of European and Anglo-American approaches to vegetation science. In the 1970s, he was the scientific coordinator of the Hawai'i contribution to the International Biological Program (IBP). This collaborative research effort culminated in the book *Island Ecosystems* (Hutchinson Ross Publications, IBP Synthesis Series 15, 1981). His latest effort is a book with F. R. Fosberg, *Vegetation of the Tropical Pacific Islands* (Springer Ecological Studies 132, 1998).

**Stephen G. Nelson** is a Senior Research Scientist at the Environmental Research Laboratory of the University of Arizona, in Tucson, where he is working in the areas of aquatic ecology and aquaculture. He received a Ph.D. in Ecology from the University of California-Davis in 1976, and from 1977 until 1997 he was a member of the faculty of the University of Guam Marine Laboratory, including two, three-year stints as Director of the laboratory.

**Patrick D. Nunn** is Head of the Geography Department and Professor of Oceanic Geoscience at the University of the South Pacific, an international university serving twelve Pacific Island nations, based at its main teaching campus in Suva, Fiji. He is also Adjunct Senior Fellow in the Research School of Pacific and Asian Studies at the Australian National University. He has carried out research in many Pacific Island countries and in 1994 published *Oceanic Islands* (Blackwell), a book that recounts the physical development of islands. In 1998 his monograph *Pacific Island Landscapes* (Institute of Pacific Studies, the University of the South Pacific) appeared, and in 1999, his book *Environmental Change in the Pacific Basin* (Wiley) is due for release.

**Michael R. Ogden** is Assistant Professor in the Department of Communication at the University of Hawai'i at Mānoa. Dr. Ogden has over fifteen years of research and consulting experience in the Pacific Islands, focusing on issues of communication policy, technology impact, and sustainable development. He has previously been affiliated with the University of the South Pacific, the East-West Center, and the University of Hawai'i Center for Pacific Island Studies. He has published many journal articles and book chapters dealing with the challenges of development in Pacific Island microstates and the impact of information and communication technologies.

**Andrew Pawley** is Professor of Linguistics, Research School of Pacific and Asian Studies, Australian National University. He has done linguistic fieldwork in Papua New Guinea, Fiji, and Samoa and has published extensively on the languages and culture history of the Pacific Islands.

**Nancy J. Pollock** is Professor of Anthropology at Victoria University, Wellington. She has worked in the Marshall Islands, Fiji, Wallis and Futuna, Tonga, Samoa, Cook Islands, French Polynesia, and New Caledonia. The focus of her work over twenty-five years has been on food and health issues, as can be seen in *These Roots Remain* (IPS, 1992), *Social Aspects of Obesity* (Gordon and Breach, 1995), and *The Power of Kava* (RSPS, ANU, 1995).

**Jean-Louis Rallu** has been a Demographer at INED (National Institute for Population Studies) since 1977. He worked for ORSTOM (Institute for Development and Cooperation) at the University of the South Pacific in Suva, Fiji, from 1992–1994. His interests are in fertility analysis in developed and developing countries, population and migration in Asia and Pacific, and historical demography of the South Pacific. He published *Les Populations Océaniennes aux 19e et 20e Siècles* (INED, 1990) and *Population, Migration et Développement dans le Pacifique Sud* (UNESCO-MOST, 1997).

**Moshe Rapaport** is Lecturer in Geography at the University of Hawai'i-Mānoa and Kapi'olani Community College, Honolulu. His doctoral dissertation concerned socioeconomic aspects of pearl farming in the Tuamotu Archipelago, based on research in Takaroa Atoll (1990–1991). He has also conducted fieldwork in Tokelau and Hawai'i. His research has appeared in *Atoll Research Bulletin, Ocean Yearbook, Journal of Pacific History*, and other publications. Prior to his academic career, he was employed in rural development projects in Israel (1974–1978) and Kenya (1978–1980).

**Richard Scaglion** is Professor of Anthropology at the University of Pittsburgh. His primary interests are Melanesia, comparative Austronesia, and the anthropology of law. Dr. Scaglion has conducted long-term field research with the Abelam people, beginning in 1974. He is the former Director of Customary Law Development for the Law Reform Commission of Papua New Guinea and has been a Visiting Fellow at the Australian National University, the University of Hawai'i, and the East-West Center. He is editor of *Homicide Compensation in Papua New Guinea* and *Customary Law in Papua New Guinea* and author or editor of numerous books and articles about Pacific cultures.

**Andrew P. Sturman** is Associate Professor in Geography at the University of Canterbury, New Zealand. He has extensive teaching and research interests at the university level in weather and climate, particularly in New Zealand, Australia, and the southwest Pacific. His systematic interests include synoptic, mesoscale, and local weather and climate, as well as applications to environmental issues such as air pollution. He has recently received two major national funding awards (Marsden Fund and Public Good Science Fund) in New Zealand and is the leader of an atmospheric research group at the University of Canterbury. Publications include *The Weather and Climate of Australia and New Zealand* (Oxford University Press, 1996), as well as more than sixty national and international publications.

**Lynne D. Talley** is Professor at the Scripps Institution of Oceanography, University of California-San Diego. She was Presidential Young Investigator (1987). She has published extensively regarding large-scale ocean circulation, water properties, heat transport, and ocean variability.

**Randolph R. Thaman** is Professor of Pacific Islands Biogeography at the University of the South Pacific, Suva, Fiji, where he has taught for twenty-five years. He is co-author with William C. Clarke of *Pacific Islands Agroforestry: Systems for Sustainability* and has authored numerous other works on Pacific Islands biogeography, sustainable development, food systems, and community-based biodiversity conservation.

**Frank R. Thomas** is a Ph.D. candidate in Anthropology at the University of Hawai'i-Mānoa. His research interests include archaeology and cultural ecology on coral atolls, marine tenure, and traditional conservation methods. His dissertation, nearing completion, focuses on exploitation and ecology of marine molluscs in Kiribati.

**Deborah Waite** is Professor of Pacific Art History, Department of Art, University of Hawai'i, and was formerly curator of Ethnology at the Newark Museum, Newark, New Jersey. Her published books *include Art of the Solomon Islands* (Barbier Mueller Collection, 1983) and *The Julius L. Brenchley Collection of Artifacts from the Solomon Islands in the British Museum and The Maidstone Museum, Maidstone Kent* (British Museum Press, 1987). She has published numerous articles in scholarly journals and is currently working on a book, "Shields from the Solomon Islands in Changing Social Contexts."

**Terence Wesley-Smith** is Associate Professor and Graduate Chair in the Center for Pacific Island Studies at the University of Hawai'i-Mānoa. He writes and teaches about contemporary issues in Oceania, with a particular interest in mining, development, and the war in Bougainville. He is Associate Editor of *The Contemporary Pacific: A Journal of Island Affairs* and recently directed a collaborative research and instructional project funded by the Ford Foundation called Moving Cultures: Remaking Asia-Pacific Studies. The project explored new ways of doing "area studies" and focused on transnational flows of capital, labor, and tourists from Asia into the Republic of Palau.

# Subject Index

## A

Adoption (child), 199; and land rights, 208
Age structures. *See* Demography
Aging, 267, 286–287
Agriculture: commercial, 358–361; crop disease, 359; crop yields, 362; dynamics of, 357–358; and logging, 361–362; origins of, 353–354; precontact, 124, 125; production systems, 354; and sustainability, 362–363; traditional, 354–357; women's roles in, 306–307
Aid (economic): statistics, 340–342, 367; theoretical aspects of, 344
Air traffic, 215, 401
Alcohol consumption: and domestic violence, 203, 290; and road accidents, 309.
Algae, 80, 109, 112. *See also* Kelp; Plankton
Algal ridges, 45
Altitudinal zonation (biota), 100, 104
Amphitheater-headed valleys, 47–48
Andesite line, 37
Animal husbandry, 358, 361. *See also* Ranching
Annexations, 138
Anticyclones, 6
Aquifers, 67
Arboriculture, 355
Armor, 250
Art: body painting, 248; ceramics, 246; clothing, 248–249; contemporary, 254; featherwork, 247; fiber arts, 247; ornaments, 248–249; prehistoric, 246–247; and ritual, 251–253; scarification, 248, stonework, 246, 247; tattoos, 248, 251, 254; weapons, 250–251; woodcarving, 247
Artists, 247
Asians: as first colonists, 121–122; in fisheries, 370–374; Japanese colonialism, 138; land rights of, 216; languages, 186; in logging, 361; as migrant laborers, 316–317; as minorities, 140, 163, 204; in tourism, 398; in war, 139
Assimilation, 159. *See also* Ethnicity; Identity; Localism
Atmospheric circulation, 3–6
Atolls: agriculture on, 356; biota of, 79, 94–95; geomorphology of, 49–50; and island life cycle, 35; urbanization on, 318, 323–324, 330
Austronesians, 146–147, 190, 221–222
Authority (political), 221–222

## B

Beachcombers, 135
Bêche-de-mer, 372–373
Benthos, 114–115
Big-men, 146, 222, 227. See also Chiefs; Great-men
Biodiversity. *See* Biogeography
Biogeography: and adaptive shifts, 83; of atolls and *makatea*, 79; distribution patterns, 82; diversity in, 77–80; and endemism, 79; and extinctions, 86–88; human impact on, 87–88; indigenous taxonomy, 187–188; marine, 80; of high islands, 77–79; mapping of, 80–81; source areas, 85–86; and speciation, 83–85; theory of, 86; and vicariance, 85. *See also* Ecosystems
Birth: and kinship, 199; as metaphor, 167, 169; rituals, 238, 283. *See also* Fertility

Blackbirding, 137
Body art, 248–250
Bogs, 98
Boomtowns, 388

## C

Cancer, 286
Canoes. *See* Seafaring
Capital flows, 340–344, 349
Capitalism, 134, 144, 157, 204
Cardiovascular disease, 285
Cargo cults, 241–242
Carrying capacity (demographic), 127
Cash cropping, 354
Causeways, 323
Caves, 51, 181
Ceramics, 122–123, 246, 247
Chiefdoms, 127, 146, 147–148
Chiefly rights, 208, 218
Chiefs: postcontact, 135, 227, 237; precontact, 128–129, 146
Ciguatera, 290
Circumcision, 200. *See also* Initiation rites
Civilization, concept of, 159
Class. *See* Hierarchy
Climate: atmospheric circulation, global, 3–6; change and variability, 14–16, 113; graphs, 12–13; regional patterns, 11–14; weather systems, 6–11
Clothing, 248, 249–250
Cloud cover, 14
Cloud forest, 97
Coal, 382
Coevolution, 87–88
Colonialism: gender aspects of, 306; and governments, 147–149; and mineral rights, 386; narratives of, 170; and racism, 159–161; resistance to, 137–139; and towns, 317. *See also* Decolonization
Colonization (by islanders): Holocene, 122–123, 189–191; Pleistocene, 121–122, 189
Colonization (by natural biota), 82–83
Commercial balance, 339–340
Commoditization, 394
Commodity prices, 359, 373, 386
Communications (mass): historical aspects, 406–410; Internet, 414–415; mass media, 410–415; and mobility, 270–281; positive and negative aspects of, 405–406; regional linkages, 412–413; theory of, 405–406
Community participation, 291, 386, 390
Compact of Free Association, 141
Company contracts, 386
Conquest rights, 209
Conservation: contemporary need for, 105–106, 117; government policies toward, 389; precontact attitudes toward, 53
Continental islands, 40–41
Continental shelves and slopes, 114–115, 367
Convection: atmospheric, 3; and mantle, 34, 39
Convention centers, 401
Copper, 382, 385
Copra, 359
Coral reefs: distribution of, 45, 113, 367–368; as ecosystems 112–113; fossils in, 86; and island aging, 35–36; and uplift, 45, 48. *See also* Atolls; Limestone; *Makatea* islands

Cosmologies, 167, 176, 238
Coups, 144
Courts, 210, 225–226
Creation chants, 167
Crime, 202, 387
Cultural misunderstandings, 212
Cultural relativism, 235–236
Currency (monetary), 201, 349
Currents, 20–21, 24–30
Cyclones, tropical, 7–8, 15, 52–53

# D

Dams, 110
Dance, 200, 234, 239
Death: rituals, 238, 239. See also Mortality
Decentralization, urban, 334
Decolonization, 139–141, 149–150, 169–170. See also Nationalism
Deforestation, 45–46, 124
Deification, 162
Democracy, 150–152
Demographic transition, 258, 278
Demography: age structures, 264; boom growth, 258; contemporary, 260–265; depopulation, 258; and development, 265–267; forecasts, 267; historical background, 258; indicators, 260–261; postwar period, 258–260. See also Demographic transition; Epidemiological transition; Ethnicity; Fertility; Migration; Mobility; Mortality
Denationalization, 151
Dependency ratios, 265
Dependency theory, 134, 278, 405
Depopulation, 134, 284
Depressions (atmospheric), 8
Depth zonation (marine biota), 115
Descent (familial), 198–199, 223–224
Development. See Economic development; Environmental impact; Infrastructure
Diabetes, 285
Diet, 283, 286, 287–288. See also Foods
Disease. See Morbidity
Dispersal (biota), 82
Dispossession. See Land alienation
Dispute resolution, 202, 222–224, 225–226
Dissection, landform, 44, 47
Doomsday scenarios, 144–145
Driftnetting, 371–372
Drought: in eastern Pacific, 6, 12–13; El Niño–related, 15; and global warming, 16
Dryfield agriculture, 356–357
Drylands, 98
Dual economy, 386
"Dutch disease," 386

# E

Earthquakes: and lithospheric uplift, 52; on midplate islands, 35; on plate boundaries, 48; and plate tectonics, 34; and tsunamis, 21
East Pacific barrier, 85
Economic development: and agriculture, 362–363; and art, 254; assessment of, 265; and communications, 405–406; and fisheries, 366–367; indicators of, 298; and mining, 390–391; theory of, 343–347; and tourism, 403; in towns, 329–330
Economy: balance of payments, 340–343; currency, 349; development theories, 343–346; dual, 349–350; indicators of, 338, 340, 341; MIRAB, 344–346; macroeconomics, 348–349; and migration, 347–348; and modernization, 344, 349–350; output, 337–339; and political status, 338; regional integration, 339; success stories, 346–347. See also Aid; Economic Development; Remittances; Trade; Trust funds
Ecosystems: classification of, 105, 117; concept of, 93; continental shelf and slope, 114–115; controls on, 105; coral reef, 112–113; deep sea, 116–117; dryland, 98; fauna in, 104–105; freshwater, 109–110; high-altitude, 100; high-latitude, 100–101; indigenous knowledge of, 186–187; kelp, 113–114; lowland rain forest, 96–97; mangrove, 95, 110–111; montane forest, 97–98; pelagic, 115–116; profile diagrams of, 94, 97; savanna, 99–100; seagrass meadow, 111–112; secondary, 98–99; strand, 94; ultramafic maquis, 101–102; volcanic, 102–103; wetland, 95–96. See also Biogeography
Eddies, 27, 30
Education: under colonial rule, 297–298; comparative data, 301–302; curriculum options in, 300; distance, 298; gender aspects of, 308–309; and languages, 299–300; local adaptations in, 300; local knowledge in, 300; missionaries, role in, 296–297; traditional, 240, 296
Egalitarianism, 227
Ekman transport, 27–29
El Niño–Southern Oscillation (ENSO), 14–15, 30–31, 66
Embayment, 45
"Emotional truths," 166
Employment. See Labor
Endemism, 79. See also Biogeography
Energy balance, atmospheric, 3
Energy production, raw materials for: See Geothermal energy; Hydroelectric power; Oil
Environmental impact: on aquatic ecosystems, 110, 111, 113, 114, 115; on biota, 87–88; on landforms, 52–53; on soil, 59; on terrestrial ecosystems, 105–106, 129–130. See also Exotic introductions (biota); Pollution
Environmental knowledge, traditional, 186–189
Epidemics, 258. See also Mortality
Epidemiological transition, 261–262, 282, 285
Equivalence (societal), 203
Erosion: and agriculture, 362–363; and island dissection, 44–45; and island life cycle, 35; and mining, 389; rates of, 51–52; and sediment flows, 62–63
Ethnicity: demographic percentages of, 264–265; perspectives on, 162–163, 204–205; politics of, 150–151; and tenure, 216
"Ethnographic history," 134
Evapotranspiration, 3, 66, 67
Exchange rate, 348–349
Exchange. See Trade
Exclusive Economic Zone (EEZ), 214, 367, 369–370
Exile, precontact, 272
Exotic introductions (biota): ecosystem disruption, 87–88, 98, 101; as habitat for native species, 104; precontact, 124; recovery in maquis, 102; and species turnover, 88; in streams, 110. See also Extinctions
Exoticism (cultural), 159, 161
Explorers, 134–135, 157–158
Exports: agricultural, decline in production of, 360; economic role of, 344, fish and trochus shell, 370–373; minerals, 382–384

Extended families, 198. *See also* Kinship
Extinctions, 86–88, 104–105

## F

Fallow periods, 98–99, 358
Family planning, 258
"Fatal impact," 134, 413
Feminism, 305
Feminization, 161
Fertility, human, 258, 260–261, 278
Films and videos, 413–414; Maori, 174-175
Fire: and erosion, 129; and grasslands, 59, 100; plant adaptations after, 99; and settlement dating, 53
Fiscal policy, 348–349
Fisheries: coastal, 372–376; deepwater, 376–377; environmental aspects of, 367–369; fishponds, 125; gear restrictions in, 376; historical aspects of, 369–370; management of, 375–376; methods, commercial, 380; methods, subsistence, 378; and moratoria, 369, 376; oceanic, 370–372; overexploitation of, 369; precontact, 125; production statistics for, 367, 371, 372, 373, 374, 377; protected areas in, 376; size limits of, 376; socioeconomic aspects of, 366–367; and subsistence, 366; trends in, 370, 372, 373
Flooding, 7
Fog drip, 97
Fono, 226
Foods: fish consumption, 366; and nutrition, 287–289; places of origin, 122–123; Proto-Oceanic food terminology, 191; in ritual, 239, 353. *See also* Nutrition
Forestry, 361–362
Fortifications, military, 127–128, 129
Fossils, 86–87
Free association, 149
Freshwater lens, 67

## G

Gender. *See* Women
Geology: continental islands, 40–41; island arcs, 37–38, 48; linear island chains, 34–37, 47–48; marginal seas and backarc basins, 38–39; plate tectonics, 34, seafloor spreading, 37
Geomorphology. *See* Landforms
Geostrategic footprints, 344
Geostrophic transport, 28–29
Geothermal energy, 168
Geothermal water, 68
Ghosts, 238. *See also* Spiritual beings
Glaciation, 36, 43, 45, 48, 86
Global warming, 16, 113, 285. *See also* Sea-level changes
Gold, 382, 384, 385
Gondwana, 39, 40; relicts (biota) of, 101, 102, 104–105
Governments. *See* Nationalism, Politics, States
Grasslands, 59, 99–100
Great-men, 146, 148
Gross domestic product (GDP), 337–340
Gross national expenditure (GNE), 343
Groundwater, 67–68
Guerilla movements , 150
Guyots, 36, 44
Gyres, subtropical, 24, 27

## H

Hazards, environmental. *See* Cyclones, tropical; Drought; Earthquakes; Flooding; Sea-level changes; Storms; Tornadoes; Tsunamis; Volcanoes; Wind
Health: concept of, 282–283; and diseases of modernization, 285–286; and medicine, 282; historical overview of, 283–284; indicators of, 287–288; and infectious disease, 283–285; maternal-child, 286–287; mental, 286; and primary care, 291; services, 266; and social disparities, 290; and suicide, 290; and traditional healing, 283–284; and women, 289
Heat flux, ocean, 29–30
*Heiau*, 129, 253. *See also* Temples
Hierarchy (sociopolitical): and class, 204; and colonialism, 147–149; contemporary, 203, 204; and law, 221–225; precontact, 128–129, 145–147.
Historiography, 134
History, postcontact: beachcombers, 135–136; colonialism, 137–138; decolonization, 139–141; explorers, 134–135; missionaries, 135–136; resistance to colonialism, 138–139; traders, 136–137
History, precontact: communications, 406; demography, 127; exchange, 125–127; environmental impact, 129–130; intensification of production, 125; settlement, 121–124; sociopolitical evolution, 128–129; subsistence, 124–125; warfare, 127–128
Hot spots, 34–35
Houseyard gardens, 357
Housing: and homelessness, 331–332; precontact, 190; and ritual, 253; squatter settlements, 331; gender aspects of, 200; in towns, 316, 317
Humidity, 66
Humification, 59, 60
Hurricanes. *See* Cyclones, tropical
Hydroelectric power, 71
Hydrothermal vents, 37, 39, 116

## I

Identity: and colonialism, 168–170; multicultural, 174; oppositional, 162–164; personal, 195–198. *See also* Race; Representation
*Ifoga*, 202
Income disparities, 310
Indigenous peoples: rights of, 386; spirit of, 167
Individualism, 195, 196, 224
Infiltration capacity, 62
Infrastructure: communications, 406–410, 414–415; and flooding, 46; housing, 331–332; tourist accommodations, 400–401; and towns, 319; water and sanitation, 69–70, 71–73. *See also* Air traffic; Energy; Transportation
Inheritance rights, 209
Initiation rites, 239, 240, 248, 271
Integration (political), 149
Intensification of production, agricultural, 125, 358
International law of the sea convention (LOSC), 214, 369–370
Internet, 414–415
Intertropical convergence zone (ITCZ), 4
Irrigation, 110, 355–356
Island arcs, 37–38, 48
Islands: classification of, 33–41, 47–50, 76–77

## K

Karst, 45, 48–49, 68, 103
*Kauna*, 168–169
Kava, 199–201, 248, 290
Kelp, 113–114
Kinship, 198–199. *See also* Marriage
*Kīpuka*, 102
Knowledge, traditional: art, 247; aesthetics, 167; agriculture, 125, 354–357; conservation, 53, 362, 375–376; education, 296; environment, 186–189; ethnicity, 162–163; fisheries, 374–375; genealogy and tenure, 208–209; health, 283–284; law, 221–224; leadership, 145–147; oral traditions, 166–167; personhood, 196–198; seafaring, 190, 270; spirituality, 239–240
Köppen map, 11

## L

Labor: demographics of, 265; historical aspects of, 137, 160, 272–274, 316–317; market, 349; and migration, 137, 141, 273, 274, 347–348; and mining, 387–388; and tourism, 400; and towns, 328–329; and women, 306–308
Lagoon rights, 209
Lakes, 67, 109
Land, concept of, 167–169, 199, 353. *See also* Tenure
Land alienation: and contemporary tenure, 212–213; history of, 137; in literature, 168; and mining, 387; and resettlement, 274–276
Land reclamation, 46
Landforms: development of, 43–47; erosion of, 44–45, 51–52; human impact on, 52–53; varieties of, 47–51
Landscapes, metaphorical, 167–168
Language families, 181–186
Language nests (*kohanga reo*), 299
Languages: Asian, 186; Austronesian, 182–184, 189–191; diversity of, 185; and environmental knowledge, 186–189; European, 186; hybrid, 186; non-Austronesian, 184–185, 189
Lapita, 122–123, 246
Latitudinal zonation (biota), 100–101, 113
Lava, 34, 35, 36
Law: and authority, 221–222; and conflict management, 225–226; contemporary, 224–227; customary systems, compared, 230–232; and legal centralism, 228; legal interactionism, 228; and legal pluralism, 221; local, 227–229; and succession, 223–224; traditional, 221–224
Leadership, 227, 239–240. *See also* Big-men; Chiefs; Hierarchy
Life expectancy, 261–262
Limestone: ecological significance of, 113; islands, 49; forests, 103; soils, 61. *See also* Karst
Linear island chains, 34–37, 47–48
Literacy, 298
Literature: colonial transformations of: 168–169; and decolonization, 169–170; integrationist, 173–175; metaphorical landscaping in, 167–168; multicultural, 175–176; and orature, 166–167; postcolonial, 171–176; reactionary, 172; stereotypes in, 170–171
Loans, 359
Localism, 205
Logging, 361–362
Longlining, 371, 380

## M

Macroeconomics, 348–349
Magic, 237–238
Magma, 34–35, 37
Magmatic intrusion, 40
*Makatea* islands, 50–51, 79, 103
*Malangan* images, 252
Malaria, 285
Malthusianism, 344
*Mana*: concept of, 237
Mangroves, 95, 110–111
Manicheanism, 168–169, 176
*Marae*, 239, 252. *See also* Temples
Marginal Polynesia, 123
Marginal seas, 38–39
Marketing, 307, 329, 394. *See also* Economy; Trade
Marriage: and domestic abuse, 203; as exchange, 201–202; intermarriage, 316; and kinship, 198; in oral tradition, 271; polygyny, 198; rituals, 238; and tenure, 208. *See also* Kinship; Women
Marshes, 95–96
Masks, 252–253
Mass media. *See* Communications
Mass wasting, 44
*Massenerhebung's* effect, 97
Matignon Accords, 141, 144
*Mbis* poles, 251
Media, mass. *See* Communications
Medicine. *See* Health
Men's houses (*bai*), 253
Menstruation, 200
Mercenaries, 151
Midocean ridges, 34
Migration: and economy, 344, 347–348; and identity, 162–163, 174; illegal, 279; immigrant needs for, 212; impact of, 279; indicators of, 259, 276; internal, 277; international, 262–264, 277; motives for, 263; policies of, 263–264; return, 279; and tenure, 210; theories of, 277–278. *See also* Mobility
Military intimidation, 137, 138
Mining: and culture, 387–388; and economy, 385–386; and environment, 46, 388–390; and gender, 388; "Dutch disease," 386; in historical perspective, 384–385; and land rights, 215, 386, 387; locations, 382–385; political aspects of, 386–387; production statistics for, 382; resource exhaustion from, 386; towns, 316, 317; trends, 386
Minorities, 140–141, 150, 267
MIRAB, 141, 280, 344–346
Missionaries, 134–135, 136, 159, 240–241, 243, 306. *See also* Religion
Mobility: circulation, 272–274, 317, 327; contemporary, 276–280; postcontact, 272–273; precontact, 270–282; settlement and displacement, 274–275; varieties of, 272–273. *See also* Migration
Modernization theory, 344, 405
Money supply, 349
Money. *See* Currency
Monsoons, 4–6, 48
Morbidity: postcontact, 284–286; precontact, 283. *See also* Health
Mortality: postcontact, 261–262, 284–287; precontact, 258. *See also* Health
*Motus*, 49
Movies. *See* Films and videos
Multiphasic demographic response theory, 278
Multiple ownership, 209, 211

# N

Name-sets, 199
Nation-building, 140, 141, 150–152
Nationalism, 141, 150–152, 163. See also Decolonization
Natural increase, 262
Naval bases, 315
Near/Remote Oceania, 121–123
Neo-colonial syndrome, 170
Neogene: defined, 44
Neotraditional economy, 349
Newspapers, 407–410
Niche products, 359
Nickel, 382, 384–385
Non-Austronesians (Papuans), 146–147, 221–222, 238
Nuclear testing: and displacement, 275–276; health consequences of, 290; history of, 140–141; women's protests against, 308
Nutrient cycling: in aquatic ecosystems, 109–117; in rain forests, 97
Nutrition, 283, 287–289, 292

# O

Occupational mobility, 267
Oceanic language subgroups, 182, 183
Oceanography, 19–32; currents, 24–30; salinity, 23–24; tides, 20–21; temperature, 22–23; tsunamis, 21–22; waves, 19–20
Oil, 378, 385
Open-sea rights, 209
Oral traditions: in education, 296; as literary canon, 167–168; and memory, 208; and scientific approaches, 121; and voyaging, 270–272
Oration, 200
Orature, 166–167
Ore formation, 37, 38, 39
Ornaments (body), 248–249
Orographic effects, 9

# P

Pacific paradox, 144
Pacification, 202, 210
Paleodemography, 127
Pandanus language, 189
Papuan languages, 184–185
Papuans, 146–147
Pearl farming, 214, 279, 373
Pedogenesis, 57–60
Pelagic ecosystems, 115–116
Pele, 168, 271
Personal boundaries, 196–198
Personhood, 196–198. See also Kinship; Marriage; Violence; Women
Petroglyphs, 246
Phosphate, 43, 377–378
Photic zone, 115
Pidgins, 186, 300
Pigs, 98, 201
Pilgrimages: precontact, 272
Plankton, 115–116
Plantations: and emergence of towns, 315; as labor sources, 137; and laborers, 137, 160; obstacles to, 350; as production system, 354

Plate boundaries, 34
Plate tectonics, 34, 41
Political boundaries: colonial period, 147
Political status: comparison of island groups, 142
Politics: colonial state, 147–149; during decolonization, 149–150; doomsday scenarios, 144–145; forecasts, 152–153; gender aspects of, 308; precontact power relations, 145–147; role of the state in, 145; state and nation building, 150–152
Pollen record, 45, 86
Pollution: of aquatic ecosystems, 110, 111, 114, 115; mining-related, 388–390; and urbanization, 323; of water, 68–70
Polymetallic crusts and nodules, 378
Polynesian Triangle, 123
Population. See Demography
Postal services, 407
Pottery. See Ceramics; Lapita
Poverty, 267, 329
"Power encounters," 241
Precipitation, 11, 13, 31, 66
Prehistory. See History, precontact
Pressure: atmospheric, 3–4, 5, 6–7; ocean, 28
Priestly specialization, 240
Primary productivity, 111, 112, 115
Primitivism, 160
Primogeniture, 223–224
Privacy: islander attitudes toward, 197
Private sector, 204, 344, 349
Proletarianization, 204, 349
Prophetic movements, 241
Proto-states, 147
Public domain, 213
Public service: contemporary contraction of, 328, 339; dependence on aid, 345; and urbanization, 326–327
Purchasing power, 348–349
Purse-seining, 369

# Q

Quarries, 377, 384

# R

Race, 157, 159–161. See also Ethnicity; Representation
Radio, 407, 411
Rain forests: lowland, 96–97; montane, 97–98
Rain shadow, 10
Rainfall, 66. See also Precipitation
Ranching, 46, 70, 274–275, 361
Rangatiratanga, 226, 300
Reefs. See Coral reefs
Refugee rights, 208
Regionalism: "Oceania," notion of, 142; pan-Pacific identity, 174; transnational networks, 280, 347–348
Relatedness. See Kinship
Religion: and activism, 243; cargo cults, 242; cosmologies of, 238; and cultural relativism, 235; and life cycle, 238–239; and magic and sorcery, 235; and nationalism, 243; postcontact, 240–242; power and knowledge in, 239–240; prophetic movements, 241; rituals of, 238–239; and spirits, 237; traditional, 237–240; traditionalism in, 242. See also Missionaries

Remittances: comparative data, 341; and savings, 264; and sustainability, 280; theory of, 344
Representation: by islanders, 139, 162–164, 172–173, 241–242, 279, 330; of Asian minorities, 163; by Westerners, 134, 139, 142, 157–162, 170–171, 235–236, 283. See also Identity; Race
Resource competition, 127
Resource management, 367, 386
Ridges, high-pressure. See Pressure: atmospheric
Ridges, sea-floor, 27
Rift zones, 35
Riots, 144
Rituals: and art, 251–253; contemporary fusions of, 234; and education, 296; and life cycle, 238, 248; traditional, 238–239
Rivers, 66–67, 109–110
Rock art, 246
Rock types, 37, 38, 40
Roles, social, 195–196
Runoff, 62, 66

## S

Sago, 96
Sahulland (Sahul), 121
Saline intrusion, 68, 72
Salinity, ocean, 23–24
Salt water: uses, 72
Sanitation: comparative data, 287; systems, design of, 69–70;
Satellites: telecommunications, 407; weather, 19–20
Savannas. See Grasslands
Scarification, 248
Scholarships, overseas, 299
Science, indigenous, 300
Sea breezes, 9
Sea-floor spreading, 37
Sea-level changes: and extinctions, 86; and geomorphology, 36, 45–46; effect of greenhouse gases on, 16; and human colonization, 121–122; Huon reef record of, 43
Seafaring, 122–124, 270–271; Proto Oceanic terminology, 191
Seafood: consumption of, 366
Seagrass, 111–112
Seamounts, 35
Seasonal terms: indigenous concepts of, 188
Secessionism, 144, 151, 152
Secondary ecosystems, 98–99
Sediment flows: comparative measurements, 48, 62–63; impact on wetlands, 68–69, 109–110; and mangroves, 111
Self-alienation, 170
Self-denigration, 162
Senescence (forest dieback), 102
Settlement. See Colonialism; Colonization
Settler colonies, 148, 150, 346–347
Sexuality: as form of commerce, 135; and family roles, 198; and "promiscuity," 158; and sexual maturity, 238; symbolism of, 200–201. See also Women
Shantytowns. See Squatter settlements
Shields, 250
Shifting cultivation, 125, 354–355
Shrimp farms, 111
Sibling ties, 198
Slave raids, 275
Slavery, precontact, 203
Smoking, 289

Snowfall, 11
Sociopolitical evolution, 128–129
Soil: chemistry, 57, 60–61; degradation, 362; erosion, 61–63, 68, 362; hydrology, 58; management, 60–61; moisture, 57; nutrients, 63; parent material, 57–58; profiles, 57; radioactivity, 58; and relief, 58; texture, 57; types, 56–57; use, 60–61; and vegetation, 59
Sorcery, 240. See also Magic
South Pacific Convergence Zone (SPCZ), 4
Southern Oscillation Index (SOI), 14
Sovereignty. See Nationalism
Speciation: allopatric, 83; on land, 83; in sea, 84–85
Spiritual beings, 237, 238, 239
Squatter settlements, 317, 331–332
States: colonial, 147–149; contemporary, 150–152
Status marking, 249
Status rivalry, 127–129
Stereotypes: in literature, 170–171
Stonework, 246, 247
Storms, 10, 19
Story boards, 253
Storytelling, 170
Strand, 94
Stratification, social, 128–129, 145–147. See also Hierarchy
Streams, 44, 66–67, 109–110
Subduction, 34, 37–38
Submarine terraces, 36
Subsidence, lithosphere, 36, 44
Subsistence: agricultural, 354; and neotraditional village economy, 349; strategies, 124–125
Succession (ecological), 95–96, 98–99, 102, 106
Sugar, 216, 354, 361
Suicide, 203, 290
Sundaland (Sunda), 121
Surface water, 66–67
Sustainability: and agriculture, 362–363; and fisheries, 369–370, 377; and economy, 280. See also Conservation
Swamps, 50–51, 96
Sweet potato, 123.
Symbiosis, 112

## T

*Tabu*, 237
Tapa, 249
Taro, 96, 125, 214–215
Tattoos, 239, 247, 248, 251, 254
Taukei movement, 151
Tax base, 349
Taxonomy, indigenous concepts of, 187–188
Technology, indigenous, 300
Teen pregnancy, 309
Telecommunications. See Communications
Telegraphic cables, 407
Telephone systems, 407
Television, 411–412
Temperature, atmospheric: 11, 43; inversions, 6, 100; ocean, 22–23
Temples, 240, 253, 272
Tenure: and absenteeism, 211, 217; and air space, 215; and chiefly rights, 218; concepts of, 167; codification of, 210; contemporary, 209–210; marine, 213–214; and mineral rights, 215; and minorities, 218; and registration, 211–212; solutions, 218; traditional precedents for, 208–209, 387; water, 214–215; women, 215. See also Land, concept of; Land alienation

*Terra nullius* doctrine, 160
Terracing, 358
Thermocline, 23
Tides, 20–21
Titles (chiefly), 150, 204; and descent, 223–224
Tornadoes, 10
Tourism: and art, 254; attractions, 395–396; comparative data, 396; cultural, 402; destinations, 394, 396–398; and duration of stay, 398–399; economic significance of, 399–400; ecotourism, 402–403; and employment, 400; and infrastructure, 401; interisland, 399; positive and negative aspects of, 394–395; projects, 400–402; visitor origins, 398–399
Towns: case studies, 320–324; comparative data, 318, 319; contemporary, 317–320; demography of, 316–317, 319, 326–328; and epidemics, 333; gender aspects of, 307–308; hierarchies of, 319, 322; historical emergence of, 315–317; homelessness in, 331–332; housing in, 319, 324; industries in, 328; migration to, 278; minorities in, 316–317; planning of, 329–331; pollution in, 323; safety of, 333; social divisions in, 332–333; social organization of, 327; social stresses in, 324; and tenure, 318–319, 330; violence in, 332; water supply for, 324
Trade: balance of, 386; deficits, 339–340; postcontact, 134, 135, 136, 137, 139–141, 339–340; precontact, 125–127
Trans–New Guinea languages, 184–185, 189
Transnational corporation of kin, 142, 277–278, 348
Transportation: economic costs of, 344; galleon trade, 328; and precontact interaction spheres, 125–127; and tourism, 396, 401
Trawling, 367, 370, 376
Treaty of Waitangi, 137, 176, 226
Trenches, geologic, 37
Trophic relationships, 113
Troughs, low-pressure. *See* Pressure, atmospheric
Troughs, sea-floor, 39–40
Trust funds, 390
Trust territory, 139
Tsunamis, 21–22, 52
Tuna, 368–369, 370–372
Typhoons. See Cyclones, tropical

## U

Ultramafic maquis, 101–102
Universities, 297
Uplift, lithospheric, 36, 40, 45, 52
Upthrusting, ocean floor, 38
Upwelling and downwelling, 23, 24, 28, 30, 115
Urbanization. *See* Towns

## V

Vicariance: of biota, 85
Violence: by Europeans, 134, 135; by islanders, 144, 202–203; against women, 309. *See also* Warfare
Volcanoes: ash from, 35, 36, 38; atmospheric effects of, 16; ecosystems, 102–103; as hazard, 16, 41; as metaphor, 167–168; shield, 35; and soils, 56, 58; stratovolcanoes, 38, 44

## W

Wages, 386
Waitangi Tribunal, 141, 227
Walker circulation, 4
Wallace–Huxley Line, 121
Wantok groups, 322
Warfare: and art, 250–251; in colonial period, 135, 136, 137–139; evidence of, 127–128; and land rights, 209; reasons for, 128, 202, 209; theories of, 127–128. *See also* Military intimidation; Violence
Water: access statistics, 287; allocation of, 73; catchment of, 66–67, 71; and disease, 69; importation of, 72; impoundment of, 72; metering of, 72; policy, 72–73; pollution of, 68–70; purification of, 69–70; quality of, 68–70, 287; sources of, 66–68; table, 67; rights to, 209; use of, 70–72. *See also* Precipitation; Sanitation
Watersheds, 214
Waves, 19–20
Weapons, 250–251
Weather, local, 8–11; synoptic-scale, 6–8. *See also* Cyclones, tropical; Precipitation; Storms
Weathering, 57, 59, 60; on Viti Levu, 44
Wells, water, 67, 70, 72
Wetlands, 95–96
Whaling, 136
Winds: anabatic and katabatic, 8; coastal, 9; global, 3; as hazard, 7; trades, 6; westerlies, 8
Windward/leeward division: ecological significance, 98, 101; erosion differences, 44; orographic effect, 9–10
Women: activism of, 310; in agriculture, 306–307; and colonialism, 306; and development, 310; as domestic laborers, 306; and domestic violence, 309; economic contributions of, 306–308; and education, 308–309; and feminism, 305; in fisheries, 366; and health, 289; and mining, 388; in politics, 308–309; and suffrage, 150. *See also* Marriage
Woodcarving, 247
World systems theory, 134, 405
World War I, 138
World War II, 139, 317

# Place-Name Index

Notes:
1. Principal island groups (e.g. Fiji, and to a lesser extent even Tuvalu and Nauru) are mentioned so frequently in the text that exhaustive listing is not feasible.
2. Tabular comparisons for principal island groups (demography, education, etc.) are referenced as subentries under the Subject Index.
3. Considerable variation exists with regard to nomenclature, spelling, and diacritics. The names listed below should not be regarded as the single "correct" version
4. This list is limited to locations within the Pacific Islands region.

Abbreviations of island groups:
- CI — Cook Islands
- FP — French Polynesia
- HI — Hawai'i
- IJ — Irian Jaya
- MI — Marshall Islands
- NC — New Caledonia
- NWHI — Northwestern Hawaiian Islands
- NZ — New Zealand
- SI — Solomon Islands

## A

Admiralty Islands, PNG, 122, 182
Agana, Guam, 135, 334
Agats Village, PNG, 254
Aitutaki, CI, 70
Alafua, Samoa, 302
Alpine Fault, NZ, 34, 40
Amanamkai Village, PNG, 254
Ambae, Vanuatu, 228
Ambitle, PNG, 122, 126
American Samoa, 87, 141, 142
Anaa, Tumotus, 52, 87
Antahan, Marianas, 44
'Apia, Samoa, 69, 265, 315, 318, 319
Arawa, Bougainville, 383
Arno, MI, 113
Atiu, CI, diet, 288; *makatea* swamps, 51; women, 307
Auckland, NZ: demography, 318, 319; harbor, 332; immigrants, 279; urbanization, 315, 317; volcanic hazards, 41; water treatment, 69; weather, 9, 13
Austral Islands, FP, 21
Avarua, CI, 318, 319

## B

Ba, Fiji, 322
Bairiki, Tarawa, 319
Baliem Valley, PNG, 124
Balof, PNG, 122, 126
Banaba, Kiribati, 138, 163, 174, 323
Bau, Fiji, 182
Bellona, SI, 122
Betio, Tarawa, 323
Bikini, MI, 87, 140, 276
Bird's Head, Irian Jaya, 183, 185
Bismarck Archipelago, PNG: Austronesian origins, 146; images and masks, 252; languages, 182, 189; Lapita sites, 122-123; obsidian trade, 125-126; plate subduction 37; Pleistocene sites, 122; species introductions, 124
Bismarck Range, PNG, 186, 189
Bonriki, Tarawa, 67
Bougainville, PNG: changing mobility patterns, 262; landowner rights, 215; languages, 182, 185; mercenaries, 152; mining, 385; ore formation, 38; secessionism, 140, 144, 151
Buang Merabang, PNG, 122
Buka, PNG, 122
Bulolo, PNG, 383, 384

## C

Campbell Plateau, 40
Canton (Kanton), Phoenix Is., 12, 13, 95
Caroline Islands (FSM), 123, 137
Cenderawashih, PNG, 185
Central Province, PNG, 183
Chatham Islands, 124
Chatham Rise, 30
Choiseul, SI, 58
Christchurch, NZ, 71, 316, 318
Chuuk (Truk): alcoholism, 290; domestic violence, 203; Pulapese in, 163; relocation of Nauruans, 139
Colonia, Yap, 296
Cook Islands: archaeological "gap," 123; biota, 78; climate, 11; decolonization, 141, 142, 149; deforestation, 362; education, 299; multiphasic demographic response, 278; personality, 286; soil types, 57; tourism, 400
Cook Straits, NZ, 30
Coral Sea, 26, 39
Coromandel Peninsula, NZ, 384, 389

## D

Darrit-Uliga-Delap, Majuro, 319, 323, 330
Diamond Head, O'ahu, 36
Ducie, Pitcairn, 79
Dunedin, NZ, 12, 13, 315, 316, 384

## E

East Pacific Rise, 34, 37
Easter Island: agriculture, 356; arid landforms, 43; colonialism, 138, 141, 142; colonization, 123; effect of fire, 87; environmental change, 45; environmental impact, 129; and midocean ridge, 37; precontact exchange, 126; social stratification, 146
Eauripik, FSM, 272
Ebeye, Marshall Islands: population density, 330; water supply, 72
Ebeye, MI, 70, 72, 318
Ebon, MI, 318
Efate, Vanuatu, 384
Elato, FSM, 272
Elouae, PNG, 122
Emperor Seamounts: fossil reefs, 84, 86; subsidence, 44
Enewetak, MI: geological subsidence, 52; biota, 79, 84, 87
Erromanga, Vanuatu, 249
Erueti, Vanuatu, 122
Espiritu Santo, Vanuatu, 140, 151, 384
Etoile du Nord, NC, 384
'Eua, Tonga: lizard fossils, 87; uplifting, 37; water sources, 67

## F

Fais, FSM, 103, 272
Fakaofo, Tokelau: Council of Elders, 148; economy, 349-350; education, 298; health care, 291; patch reef, 368; rubble rampart, 53
Fanning, Line Islands, 80

438     The Pacific Islands

Faraulep, FSM, 272
Federated States of Micronesia, 141, 142, 149, 153. *See also* Chuuk (Truk); Kosrae; Pohnpei; Satawan; Yap
Fiji: agriculture, 358, 359; British contact, 138; clam extinctions, 369; colonialism, 137, 160; coups, 140, 144, 150-151; decolonization, 140, 150-151; economic development, 216, 265; Great Council of Chiefs, 138; ethnic tensions, 140-141, 204, 265; exports, 342; grasslands, 100; hospitals, 291; language, 182, 186; Lapita expansion, 123; mineral resources, 384; postcontact trade, 136; precontact exchange, 125, 126; soil erosion, 61-62; soil types, 58; tobacco use, 289; tourism, 161, 400; University of the South Pacific, 172; urbanization, 322, 327; warfare, 127; water supply, 71, 72
Fly River, PNG, 48, 67, 110
Fongafale, Tuvalu, 318
Fonuafo'ou, Tonga, 44
Freeport, IJ, 389
French Frigate Shoals, NWHI, 79, 113
French Polynesia: colonialism, 137, 147, 149; urbanization, 321-322
Frieda River, PNG, 383
Funafuti, Tuvalu: demography, 318; education, 302; environmental stress, 266; soils, 58; water distillation, 72
Futuna (E), 122

## G

Gafelut, FSM, 272
Galápagos Islands: adaptive radiation, 83; biodiversity, 82; endemic species, 78-79; extinctions, 88
Gilbert Islands, Kiribati, 137, 146
Gold Ridge, Guadalcanal, 383
Goroka, PNG, 297, 322
Guadalcanal, SI: geologic uplift, 52, 59; languages, 183; soils, 58, 60; World War II, 139
Guam: agriculture, 359; climate, 13; colonialism, 147, 149; forest, limestone, 103; forest, secondary, 99; grasslands, 99; indigenous minority, 140; Spanish contact, 134-135; suburban development, 328; tourism, 334; traffic jams, 324; tree snakes, 87; tropical cyclones, 6, 7; uplift, 37; water supply, 70
Gulf of Papua, 241, 390
Gulf Province, PNG, 327

## H

Ha'apai, Tonga, 122
Haleakalā, Maui, 100
Hale'iwa, O'ahu, 21
Hangan, PNG, 126
Hanuabada, Port Moresby, 327
Hauraki, NZ, 382
Hawai'i: acid rain, 68; adaptive radiation, 82-83; agricultural intensification, 125; agriculture, 361; art, 247; bogs, 98; chiefly insignia, 249; demography, 267-268; domestic violence, 309; drylands, 98; early contact period, 135, 136; eddies, 27; endemism, 79, 80; geothermal energy, 168; homelessness, 332; Kona storms, 8; land tenure, 212, 274-275; landslides, 35, 47-48; moat phenomenon, 36; orographic effect, 10; pollen record, 86; Pidgin, 186; race relations, 160, 161, 163; reception of Cook, 162; revolution, 138, 160; shoreline recession, 51; soil types, 56, 57; sovereignty movement, 140-141, 168; species dispersal, 82; species introductions, 87; tidal currents, 20-21; tsunamis, 21, 22, 52; unification, 135; urbanization, 320-321; water supply, 67, 70, 72, 73; weapons, 251
Hawai'i (Island): altitudinal zonation, 100; ecological succession, 102-103; geological subsidence, 52; local weather, 8, 9, 10; precontact agriculture, 125; towns, 320

Henderson Island, Pitcairn, 79, 103, 126
Hikurangi Trench, 40
Hilo, HI, 13, 21
Hiva Oa, Marquesas, 21
Hokitika, NZ, 12
Honiara, SI, 69, 72, 254, 318, 319
Honolulu, HI: climate, 13; demography, 318, 319; housing, 324, 328; urbanization, 315, 317
Huon Peninsula, Papua New Guinea, 43, 52, 122

## I

Ifalik (Ifaluk), FSM, 197, 238, 272
Indo-West Pacific, 81
Irian Jaya, 150, 181, 182; Free Papua Movement, 150; Freeport mine, 389

## J

Jaluit, MI, 323
Jimi Valley, PNG, 186
Johnston Island, 84
Juan Fernandez Islands, 83

## K

Kaho'olawe, HI, 141
Kaironk Valley, PNG, 186, 187
Kāne'ohe Bay, HI, 73
Kapingamarangi, FSM, 79, 162
Kapolei, O'ahu, 321
Kaua'i, HI, 51, 83, 85, 271, 320
Kayangel, Palau, 80
Kermadec Islands, 41, 97, 124
Kermadec Trench, 40
Kīlauea, HI, 102
Kili, MI, 276
Kilu, PNG, 122, 124
Kiribati: archaeological gap, 123; blackbirding, 137; decolonization, 140, 149; economy, 341; land sales, 211-212; offshore assets, 342-343; rainfall seasonality, 12, 43; sanitation, 69-70; urbanization, 323; warfare, 128; weapons, 250; wells, 71
Kiritimati, Kiribati, 213, 69, 70
Ko'olau Range, O'ahu, 35
Kolombangara, SI, 97
Kolonia, Pohnpei, 318, 319
Kona, HI, 320
Koronovia, Fiji, 58
Koror, Palau, 13, 318, 319
Kororareka, NZ, 315
Kosipe, PNG, 122, 124
Kosrae, FSM, 70, 96
Kuk, PNG, 58
Kutubu, PNG, 388
Kwajalein, MI, 140, 276, 318

## L

Labasa, Fiji, 322
Lae, PNG, 318, 322, 327
Lahaina, Maui, 320
Lake Karapiro, NZ, 71
Lakeba, Fiji, 100
Laloki, PNG, 383
Lamotrek, FSM, 272
Lāna'i, HI, 52
Langa Langa Lagoon, SI, 46
Lapita, NC, 122

Lau Basin, 378
Lau Islands, Fiji, 44
Laysan, NWHI, 79, 84
Levuka, Fiji, 315, 322
Lifou, NC, 321
Lifuka, Tonga, 130
Lihir, PNG, 383, 384
Līhu'e, Kaua'i, 320
Line Islands, 86
Lord Howe Rise, 40
Losap, FSM, 95
Lou Island, PNG, 123, 125, 126
Loyalty Islands, NC, 36, 103

# M

Macrae's Flat, NZ, 383
Madang Province, PNG, 183, 186, 189
Madang, PNG, 322
Maiana, Kiribati, 214
Majuro, Marshall Islands: climate, 13; education, 301; demography, 318, 319; urbanization, 323; water 70, 71
Mākaha Valley, O'ahu, 129
Makatea, Tuamotus, 49, 103, 259
Makemo, Tuamotus 271
Malaita, SI, 37, 138-139, 183, 242, 355; artificial islands, 46; Maasina Rule, 139; shifting cultivation, 355
Malakula, Vanuatu, 52, 262
Malo, Vanuatu, 122
Mangaia, CI: bird fossils, 87; environmental impact, 129; pollen record, 86; precontact exchange, 126
Mangareva, FP, 126
Manu'a, American Samoa, 123
Manus Basin, 378
Manus, PNG, 122, 214, 238, 246
Maré, NC, 52, 321
Marginal Polynesia, 123
Mariana Islands: arc volcanism, 37; backarc basins, 39-40; climate, 6; colonialism, 137; decolonization, 141, 142, 149; European contact, 134, 135; first settlement, 123
Mariana Trough, 40
Markham River, PNG, 99
Marovo Lagoon, SI, 254
Marquesas, FP: biodiversity, 78; ceramics, 246; depopulation, 258, 284; ornaments, 249; weapons, 251
Marshall Islands: aid, 153; annexation, 137; decolonization, 141, 142, 149; diet, 288; limestone soils, 59; mangroves, 95; nuclear testing, 140, 275-276; urbanization, 323-324
Matainasau, Viti Levu, 46
Matenkupkup, PNG, 122
Maui, HI: cloud forests, 98; land tenure, 212; *Metrosideros* dieback, 103; ocean currents, 27; pollen record, 86; precontact agriculture, 125; urbanization, 320
Mauke, CI: fossil reefs, 85; *makatea* formation, 50
Mauna Loa, HI, 100
Mekeo, PNG, 238
Midway Atoll, NWHI, 86
Mililani, O'ahu, 321
Milne Bay Province, PNG, 183, 384
Misima, PNG, 383, 384
Misisil, PNG, 122
Mitiaro, CI, 66
Moen, Chuuk, 163, 318
Mokil, FSM, 95

Moloka'i, HI, 98
Moorea, Tahiti, 87, 321
Mopir Island, PNG, 122
Morobe Province, PNG, 183
Mortlock Islands. *See* Satawan
Moruroa (Mururoa), FP, 52, 290
Mount Egmont (Taranaki), NZ, 41
Mount Hagen, PNG, 322
Mount Kare, PNG, 383
Mount Kasi, Fiji, 383-384
Mount Nanalaud, Pohnpei, 95
Mulifenua, Samoa, 122
Mussau Island, PNG, 126, 182

# N

Nadi, Fiji, 62, 265, 322
Namonuito, FSM, 272
Namosi, Fiji, 388
Nan Madol, Pohnpei, 315
Nanngu, SI, 122
Napuka, Tuamotus, 271
Natunuku, Fiji, 122, 123
Nauru: colonialism, 148; diet, 142; ecological succession, 106; economy, 217; labor migration, 141; mining, 138, 385; phosphate soils, 57, 59; wartime relocation, 139;
Nausori, Fiji, 13
Nenumbo, SI, 122
Nepoui, NC, 383-384
New Britain, PNG: archaeology, 122, 124, 125; art 247; language, 182, 183; ore formation, 37
New Caledonia: annexation, 137; ethnic diversity, 163; fauna, 105; grasslands, 99; independence movement, 150; indigenous reserves, 137, 212, 274; Kanaks, 150; languages, 182, 186; Lapita site, 122; Matignon Accords, 141; migration, 317; nickel mining, 384-385, 387; ore formation, 38; postcontact trade, 136; shoreline progradation, 46; ultramafic maquis, 101-102; urbanization, 321-322
New Georgia, SI, 250
New Guinea Highlands: accommodating return migrants, 279; class formation, 204; customary law, 222-223; deforestation, 124; early agriculture, 122; personhood, 197; Pleistocene sites, 122; recency of contact, 147; sweet potato cultivation, 208; traditional mobility patterns, 272; warfare, 50
New Ireland, PNG: archaeology, 122, 124, 125; languages, 182, 185; *malangan* figures, 252
New Zealand: agriculture, 361; biodiversity, 78; chiefly insignia, 249-250; colonization, 123-124; demography, 258, 267-268, 277; economy, 346-347; ecosystem diversity, 100-101; endemism, 79; ethnic relations, 204; European settlement, 274; fauna, 104; fisheries, 115, 376-377; forestry, 362; frontal precipitation, 6-7; geologic history, 40-41; homelessness, 331-332; kelp beds, 113-114; landforms, 45; language nests, 299; mangroves, 95; migration policy, 263, 279; mining, 384, 385, 389; moa extinctions, 130; oceanography, 30; orographic effect, 9-10; Pacific territories, 149, 259; pollution, 68; shoreline progradation, 51; snowfall, 11; soil types, 56, 57; stream life, 110; tourism, 400; towns, 316; Treaty of Waitangi, 137, 236; voyaging traditions, 270-271; Waitangi Tribunal, 237; water needs, 70-71; weathering, 44
Ngulu, FSM, 272
Niua Group, Tonga, 37
Niuatoputapu, Tonga, 122, 123
Niue: absenteeism, 217; decolonization, 141, 149; emigration, 174, 217; fossil reefs, 85; phosphate soils, 57; natural radioactivity, 58;

uplift, 36; water supply, 67
Niutao, Tuvalu, 49
Nombe, PNG, 122
Norfolk Island: biota, 97, 124; political status, 142
North Island, NZ: geologic uplift, 52; kelp communities, 114; mangroves, 110; mining, 382; prehistory, 127; Treaty of Waitangi, 226
Northern Marianas, 328. See also Mariana Islands
Northwest Hawaiian Islands, 79
Nouméa, NC: climate, 13; water use, 70; migrant labor, 263; urbanization, 315, 316, 319, 321-322; sports, 324
Nuku Hiva, Marquesas, 44
Nuku'alofa, Tonga, 318, 319, 330
Nukulaelae, Tuvalu, 227

## O

O'ahu, Hawai'i: cloud forests, 98; extinct snails, 86; fossil reefs, 85; land, reclaimed, 46; leeward scrub, 98; 125, 315; swell, winter, 20; social stratification, 129; tidal currents, 20; water politics, 73
Oeno, Pitcairn, 79, 84
Ok Ningi, PNG, 51
Ok Tedi, PNG: mining, 382-383, 388, 389; sediment flows, 48
Olimarao, FSM, 272
Ontong Java, SI, 52, 53
Oro Province, PNG, 237
Otago, NZ, 384
Ouvéa, New Caledonia, 321
Ovalau, Fiji, 322

## P

Pago Pago, American Samoa: agriculture, 359; annexation, 138; demography, 318; early town, 315; fish canneries, 317
Palau (Belau): alcoholism, 309; *bai* (men's houses), 253; decolonization, 141, 142, 149; language, 182; precontact exchange, 126; settlement, 123; story boards, 253; trochus exports, 373
Pali (cliffs), O'ahu, 47
Pamwak, PNG, 122, 124
Panakiwuk, PNG, 122
Panguna, Bougainville, 144, 151, 388
Papeete, Tahiti: downtown, 330; early town, 315; poverty, 329; urbanization, contemporary, 321-322
Papua New Guinea: altitudinal zonation, 100; artists, 247; belief in spirits, 237, 238; biodiversity, 78; cargo cults, 139, 241-242; climate change, 45; currents, 26; decolonization, 150; discursive strategies, 227-228; dispute resolution, 224; domestic violence, 309; education, 267, 298-299, 309; employment, 327; environmental knowledge, indigenous, 186-189; erosion, 46, 48, 51; ethnic relations, 162, 204-205; fauna, 104; in film, 413; grasslands, 59; health, 285, 292; infant mortality, 69; initiation ceremonies, 248; irrigation and drainage, 355; karst, 48-49; kin groups, continuing relevance of, 332; logging, 361-362; mangroves, 95; *mbis* poles, 251; mining, 382-384, 387, 388; mining towns, 328; Papuan languages, 184-185, 189; political instability, 140, 152; rain forests, 97; ritual, 238, 239; rivers, 66-67, 99; security concerns, 144, 324, 333; sediment yields, 63; sex ratios, 328; shantytowns, 331; sorcery, 238; swamps, 96; Tok Pisin, 186; tourist art, 254; trading networks, precontact, 271; urbanization, 266, 322-323; village courts, 225; warfare, 250; weather, local, 9, 10; writing workshops, 172
Pearl Harbor, HI, 139, 321
Pikelot, FSM, 272
Pines, Isle of, 103
Pinzon, Galápagos, 45

Pio, SI, 103
Pitcairn Island, 126, 141, 142
Pohnpei, FSM: chiefly succession, rules of, 223-224; cloud forest, 98; education, contemporary, 297; education, traditional, 296; ethnic identity, 162; mangroves, inland, 95; resistance to colonialism, 138; social stratification, 146; Sokehs rebellion, 138; water policy, 72
Pokak (Bokaak), MI, 79
Pomalaa East, NC, 384
Porgera, PNG, 387, 388
Port Moresby, PNG: Catholic cathedral, 243; Chinese merchants, 163; climate, 13; demography, 318, 319; epidemics, 69; houseyard gardens, 357; land tenure, 330; migrants, 327; mining, 384; transportation, 332; urbanization, 322
Port Vila, Vanuatu, 72: demography, 318, 319; education, 297; rioting, 144; septic tanks, 73
Pukapuka, CI, 146, 270
Pulap, FSM, 163, 272
Pulusuk, FSM, 272
Puluwat, FSM, 113, 182, 272
Purari River, PNG, 48, 67, 110

## R

Rabaul, PNG, 139
Rabi, Fiji, 163
Raiatea, French Polynesia, 272
Ramu River, PNG, 99, 186
Rapa Nui. *See* Easter Island
Rapa, FP, 80, 124, 127, 128, 222
Rarotonga, CI: arborescence, 79; distance education, 299; lithospheric loading, 45; soils, 57, 58; urbanization, 278; voyaging traditions, 270; water, 70, 71
Reef Islands, SI, 125
Rennell, SI, 122, 383
Rock Islands, Palau, 103
Rongelap, MI, 276
Rota, Marianas, 87, 290
Rotorua, NZ, 72
Rotuma, Fiji, 162, 358

## S

Saipan, CNMI, 141, 263, 318, 319
Samoa: colonialism, 137, 138; colonization, 123; crop disease, 360; decolonization, 149, 150; deforestation, 362; dietary concept, 283; Land and Titles Court, 225-226; land tenure, 211; mangroves, 95; Mau movement, 138; migration, 263-264; missionaries, indigenous, 136; missionary views, 160; personhood, 196-197; remittances, 342-343; transforming identities, 174;
San Cristobal, SI, 121, 183
Santa Cruz, Galápagos, 101
Santa Cruz, SI, 57, 122, 123, 125, 185
Santa Isabel, SI, 251
Santo. *See* Espiritu Santo
Satawan, FSM, 246, 252, 253
Savai'i, Samoa, 10, 57
Schrader Ranges, PNG, 181, 186, 189
Sepik River, PNG, 67, 99, 110, 183, 248
Sepik-Ramu Basin, PNG, 185
Sigatoka, Fiji, 122, 322, 359
Simbai Valley, PNG, 186
Snake River, PNG, 99
Society Islands, 123, 137, 146, 77, 249
Solomon Islands: colonialism, 138-139; decolonization, 151-152;

The Pacific Islands

441

disintegrative political tendencies, 151; fertility, 262; fisheries, 375; languages, 186; logging, 361-362; missionization, 241; prehistory, 121, 134; rituals, 251; uplifted reefs, 48; war canoes, 250
Sorol, FSM, 272
South Island, NZ, 44, 226, 384
Southern Alps, NZ, 9-10, 41, 44
Star Mountains, IJ, 11
Stewart Island, NZ, 226
Sudest Island, PNG, 383, 384
Suva, Fiji: demography, 318, 319; downtown, 266; education, 301; hospital, 291; in literature, 174; urbanization, 322-323; women activists, 309

## T

Tabar, New Ireland, 383
Tabubil, PNG, 328
Tahauku Bay, Hiva Oa, 21
Tahiti, FP: biotic endemism, 83; climate, 13; colonialism, 137; demographic decline, 258; early contact period, 135-136; embayment, 45-46; tourism, 400, 401; Western understandings of, 135, 158, 236
Takapoto, Tuamotus, 308
Takaroa, Tuamotus, 214, 279, 308, 311
Talafofo, Guam, 96, 359
Talasea, New Britain, 122, 125, 126
Talekosovi, Viti Levu, 47
Tanna, Vanuatu: ceremonies, 201-202; custom villages, 148; gender relations, 199-201; kava, 200; missionaries, 138; name-sets, 199; secessionism, 140
Taongi, MI, 113
Taravao, Tahiti, 321
Tarawa, Kiribati: climate, 13, 43; environmental stress, 266, 333; octopus exports, 214; soil moisture, 61; urbanization, 318, 323; water supply, 67, 70
Tasman Bay, South Island, 30
Tasman Sea, 38
Tauranga Harbor, NZ, 51
Tautira, Tahiti, 321
Taveuni, Fiji, 57, 58, 59
Tavua, Fiji, 385
Telefomin, PNG, 124
Thio, NC, 384
Tiebaghi, NC, 384
Tikopia, SI, 37, 123, 237, 246
To'aga, American Samoa, 87, 122
Tokelau: Council of Elders, 148; dual economy, 349-350; education, 298; health, 287, 291; migrant health, 285; reefs, 368
Tonga: democracy movement, 150; land reforms, 210; markets, 329; migration, 263-264; missionization, 136; monarchy, 147, 262; relations with Britain, 138; tapa production, 307
Tongatapu, Tonga: palace, 147; prehistory, 122, 126; uplift, 36, 45; volcanic ash soils, 58
Trobriand Islands, PNG, 239
Truk. See Chuuk
Tuamotu Archipelago, FP: demographic boom, 279; pearl farming, 214, 307; pearl oysters, 87, 136; smoking, 289; tours, administrative, 153; women, 308
Tumon Bay, Guam, 399
Tutuila, American Samoa, 126
Tuvalu: cays and *motus*, 49; changing mobility patterns, 273-274; decolonization, 149; soils, 60

## U

Ujelang, MI, 234, 276
Ulithi, FSM, 80, 272, 356
'Upolu, Samoa: climate, 10; coastal erosion, 51; 355; land tenure, 211
Utrik (Utirik), MI, 276
Uturoa, FP, 321

## V

Vairaatea, Tuamotus, 50, 306, 311
Vanua Levu, Fiji, 58, 100, 316
Vanuatu: age structures, 264; condominium, 137; decolonization, 140; karst, 45; land returns, 213; languages, 182; logging, 361-362; migrant labor, 137; mobility in transition, 272; nation-building, 151; political upheavals, 151; sandalwood trade, 136; settlement, 122; volcanic metaphors, 167; volcanic succession, 38-39; women's meetings, 266
Vatcha, NC, 122
Vatu Vara, Fiji, 59
Vatukoula, Fiji, 384, 388
Vatulele, Fiji, 52
Vava'u, Tonga, 45, 122
Viti Levu, Fiji: early towns, 316; erosion, 44, 51-52; flooding, 46; irrigation, 70; rain forest, 96; soil, 60; *talasiqa* savannas, 100; water supply, 70
Vitiaz Strait, 271

## W

Wahiawā, O'ahu, 321
Waikīkī, Honolulu, 46, 319, 321
Wailuku, Maui, 320
Waimea, O'ahu, 51, 320
Wairarapa, NZ, 46
Wake Island, 79
Wallace-Huxley Line, 123
Wallis ('Uvea), 284
Wallis and Futuna, 137, 141, 142, 263
Wapolu, PNG, 384
Watom Island, PNG, 126
Wau, PNG, 139, 384
Wellington, NZ, 70, 279, 315, 318
West Fayu, FSM, 272
West Sepik Province, PNG, 185
Wewak, PNG, 322
Willaumez Peninsula, PNG, 183
Witu (Vitu) Islands, PNG, 37
Woleai, FSM, 95, 272
Woodlark Is. (Muyua), PNG, 384

## Y

Yambon, PNG, 122
Yanuca, Fiji, 122, 282
Yap: agriculture, 355, 356; chief's meeting place, 146; dance, 402; dryfield horticulture, 356; education, traditional, 296; trade, precontact, 126, 271
Yapen Island, PNG, 185